CIVIL AIRCRAFT MARKINGS 2026

CIVIL AIRCRAFT MARKINGS 2026

Allan S Wright

Crécy Publishing Ltd

This 77th edition published by Crécy Publishing Ltd 2026

ISBN 9781800353572

Print and Bound in Türkiye by Özlem Print

Printed using sustainable paper materials.

Crécy Publishing Ltd
1a Ringway Trading Est
Shadowmoss Rd
Manchester
M22 5LH
Tel +44 (0)161 499 0024
www.crecy.co.uk

Front cover:
Boeing 777-200F G-ONEG of One Air,
pictured here at Birmingham Airport,
UK, in September 2025. *Stuart
Lawson/Air Team Images*

Back cover:
Top: G-BECU CASA 1.131E Jungmann
2000. *Peter R. March*
Middle: G-RNJW Robinson R66.
Peter R. March
Bottom: G-TUIO Boeing 787-9 of TUI
Airways. *Allan S. Wright*

CONTENTS

The familiar 'G' prefixed four-letter registration system was adopted in 1919 after a short-lived spell with serial numbers commencing at K-100. Until July 1928 the UK allocations were issued in the G-Exxx range but, as a result of further international agreements, this series ended at G-EBZZ, the replacement being G-Axxx. From this point registrations were issued in a reasonably orderly manner through to G-AZZZ, the position reached in July 1972. There were, however, two exceptions. In order to prevent possible confusion with signal codes, the G-AQxx sequence was omitted, while G-AUxx was reserved for Australian use originally. In recent years however, individual requests for a mark in the latter range have been granted by the Authorities. Although the next logical sequence was started at G-Bxxx, it was not long before the strictly applied rules relating to aircraft registration began to be relaxed. Permission was readily given for personalised marks to be issued, incorporating virtually any four-letter combination, while re-registration also became a common feature – a practice almost unheard of in the past. In this book, where this has taken place at some time, all previous UK identities carried appear in parenthesis after the operator's/owner's name. For example, during its career Cherokee Six G-PECK has also carried the identities G-AYWK, G-LADA, G-MCAR and G-ETAV.

Some aircraft have also been allowed to wear military markings without displaying their civil identity. In this case the serial number actually carried is shown in parenthesis after the type's name. For example Auster 6A G-ARRX flies in military colours as VF512, its genuine previous identity. As an aid to the identification of such machines, a conversion list is provided.

Various factors caused an acceleration in the number of registrations allocated by the Civil Aviation Authority in the early 1980s. The first surge followed the discovery that it was possible to register plastic bags, and other items even less likely to fly, on payment of the standard fee. This erosion of the main register was checked in early 1982 by the issue of a special sequence for such devices commencing with G-FYAA. Powered hang-gliders provided the second glut of allocations as a result of the decision that these types should be officially registered. Although a few of the early examples penetrated the current in-sequence register, in due course all new applicants were given marks in special ranges, this time G-MBxx, G-MGxx, G-MJxx, G-MMxx, G-MNxx, G-MTxx, G-MVxx, G-MWxx, G-MYxx and G-MZxx. It took some time before all microlights displayed an official mark but gradually the registration was carried, the size and position depending on the dimensions of the component to which it was applied.

There was news of a further change in mid-1998 when the CAA announced that with immediate effect microlights would be issued with registrations in the normal sequence alongside aircraft in other classes. In addition, it meant that owners could also apply for a personalised identity upon payment of the then current fee of £170 from April 1999, a low price for those wishing to display their status symbol. These various changes played their part in exhausting the G-Bxxx range after some 26 years, with G-BZxx coming into use before the end of 1999. As this batch approached completion the next series to be used began at G-CBxx instead of the anticipated G-CAxx. The reason for this step was to avoid the re-use of marks issued in Canada during the 1920s, although a few have appeared as personalised UK registrations. Another large increase in the number of aircraft registered resulted from the EU-inspired changes in glider registration. After many years of self-regulation by the British Gliding Association, since 2008 gliders have received registrations in the main aircraft register. It was a fairly lengthy process phasing in the registration of the then existing glider fleet but this came to an end by the beginning of 2012.

September 2007 saw the issue of the 50,000th UK aircraft registration with G-MITC being allocated to a Robinson R44 Raven. The total number of aircraft on the Register for many years rose year on year. From a figure of just under 10,000 at the beginning of 1985 this grew to around 21,000 at one point. Over the past few years numbers have fallen back slightly and now stands below 19,000. Each year there are changes made to about 35% of the total, whether by new allocations, cancellations, changes of ownership or changes of type.

The Isle of Man launched its own aircraft register in May 2007 aimed mainly at corporate business jets and helicopters with the first aircraft to be allocated being Cessna 525B M-ELON. This was followed by the Channel Islands Aircraft Registry which was launched by the States of Guernsey on 9 December 2013 and the Jersey Aircraft Regstry in November 2015. The Jersey Register (ZJ) was closed down in 2022. The M- (Isle of Man) and 2- (Guernsey) registers can be found after the British Civil Aircraft Registrations section of this book. Also included are some non-airworthy and preserved aircraft which are shown with a star (★) after the type.

Included in this book are details of those overseas airliners most likely to be seen at UK airports on scheduled or charter passenger or cargo flights. It is always difficult knowing what to include as at the time of writing the airlines' summer programmes have not been finalised. It is even harder at present to predict which companies will operate to the UK and with what equipment. The ban imposed upon Pakistan International Airlines in 2020 was lifted in 2025 and therefore the airline makes a return in the listings this year. Dedicated cargo aircraft movements, particularly from China, continued to grow over the past year and helped to boost the number of movements at several UK airports. Among the other new entries this year are the Boeing 787s of Alaska Airlines which should be come a regular sight at Heathrow this year after the launch of a Seattle service and brand new Airbus A.321XLRs of Air Canada and American Airlines are also scheduled to operate into the UK this year. As in previous editions, the full fleets of the big European 'national' or 'Legacy' carriers such as Air France, KLM, Lufthansa, SAS and others are listed notwithstanding that it is unlikely that many of their long haul aircraft will visit the UK in any given year. Both of the major airliner manufacturers, Boeing and Airbus, enjoyed a significant upturn in orders and deliveries in 2025 with both recording their best numbers since 2019. Boeing was able to deliver 600 new aircraft during the year comprised of 447 Boeing 737MAX, 30 767, 35 777 and 88 787 and orders for 1,173 new aircraft were received. Meanwhile Airbus delivered 793 aircraft which figure was made up as to 93 A.220, 607 A.320/321, 36 A.330 and 57 A.350 and, like Boeing, the company secured over a thousand new orders during the year.

The International Civil Aviation Organisation (ICAO) three-letter codes used by airlines to prefix flight numbers are included for those carriers most likely to appear in the UK. Radio frequencies for the many UK airfields and airports are also listed. Included in this edition is a list of those airliners which have been cancelled from the UK register over the past year with details of their subsequent fate.

A book of this nature is already out of date before it is published as changes to aircraft registers and airline fleets take place on a daily basis. The 2026 edition includes new allocations to the UK Register up to early February 2026.

ASW

ACKNOWLEDGEMENTS: Once again thanks are extended to the Registration Department of the Civil Aviation Authority for its assistance and allowing access to its files. Thanks are also given to all those who have contributed items for possible use in this edition.

A2-	Botswana		JA-	Japan
A3-	Tonga		JU-	Mongolia
A4O-	Oman		JY-	Jordan
A5-	Bhutan		LN-	Norway
A6-	United Arab Emirates		LV-	Argentina
A7-	Qatar		LX-	Luxembourg
A8-	Liberia		LY-	Lithuania
A9C-	Bahrain		LZ-	Bulgaria
AP-	Pakistan		M-	Isle of Man
B-	China/Taiwan/Hong Kong/Macao		N-	United States of America
C-	Canada		OB-	Peru
C2-	Nauru		OD-	Lebanon
C3-	Andorra		OE-	Austria
C5-	Gambia		OH-	Finland
C6-	Bahamas		OK-	Czechia
C9-	Mozambique		OM-	Slovakia
CC-	Chile		OO-	Belgium
CN-	Morocco		OY-	Denmark/Faroe Islands/Greenland
CP-	Bolivia		P-	North Korea
CS-	Portugal		P2-	Papua New Guinea
CU-	Cuba		P4-	Aruba
CX-	Uruguay		PH-	Netherlands
D-	Germany		PJ-	Netherlands Antilles
D2-	Angola		PK-	Indonesia
D4-	Cape Verde Islands		PP-	Brazil
D6-	Comores Islands		PR-	Brazil
DQ-	Fiji		PT-	Brazil
E3-	Eritrea		PU-	Brazil
E5-	Cook Islands		PZ-	Surinam
E7-	Bosnia and Herzegovina		RA-	Russia
EC-	Spain		RDPL-	Laos
EI-	Republic of Ireland		RP-	Philippines
EJ-	Republic of Ireland		S2-	Bangladesh
EK-	Armenia		S5-	Slovenia
EP-	Iran		S7-	Seychelles
ER-	Moldova		S9-	São Tomé
ES-	Estonia		SE-	Sweden
ET-	Ethiopia		SP-	Poland
EW-	Belarus		ST-	Sudan
EX-	Kyrgyzstan		SU-	Egypt
EY-	Tajikistan		SX-	Greece
EZ-	Turkmenistan		T2-	Tuvalu
F-	France, inc Colonies and		T3-	Kiribati
	Protectorates		T7-	San Marino
G-	United Kingdom		T8-	Palau
H4-	Solomon Islands		T9-	Bosnia and Herzegovina
HA-	Hungary		TC	Turkey
HB-	Switzerland and Liechtenstein		TF-	Iceland
HC-	Ecuador		TG-	Guatemala
HH-	Haiti		TI-	Costa Rica
HI-	Dominican Republic		TJ-	Cameroon
HK-	Colombia		TL-	Central African Republic
HL-	South Korea		TN-	Republic of Congo
HP-	Panama		TR-	Gabon
HR-	Honduras		TS-	Tunisia
HS-	Thailand		TT-	Tchad
HZ-	Saudi Arabia		TU-	Ivory Coast
I-	Italy		TY-	Benin
J2-	Djibouti		TZ-	Mali
J3-	Grenada		UK-	Uzbekistan
J5-	Guinea Bissau		UP-	Kazakhstan
J6-	St. Lucia		UR-	Ukraine
J7-	Dominica		V2-	Antigua
J8-	St. Vincent		V3-	Belize

V4	St. Kitts & Nevis		3A-	Monaco
V5-	Namibia		3B-	Mauritius
V6-	Micronesia		3C-	Equatorial Guinea
V7-	Marshall Islands		3DC-	Eswatini
V8-	Brunei		3X-	Guinea
VH-	Australia		4K-	Azerbaijan
VN-	Vietnam		4L-	Georgia
VP-A	Anguilla		4O-	Montenegro
VP-B	Bermuda		4R-	Sri Lanka
VP-C	Cayman Islands		4W	East Timor
VP-F	Falkland Islands		4X-	Israel
VP-G	Gibraltar		5A-	Libya
VP-L	British Virgin Islands		5B-	Cyprus
VP-M	Montserrat		5H-	Tanzania
VQ-B	Bermuda		5N-	Nigeria
VQ-C	Cayman Islands		5R-	Madagascar
VQ-H	Saint Helena/Ascension		5T-	Mauritania
VQ-T	Turks & Caicos Islands		5U-	Niger
VT-	India		5V-	Togo
XA-	Mexico		5W-	Western Samoa
XB-	Mexico		5X-	Uganda
XC-	Mexico		5Y-	Kenya
XT-	Burkina Faso		6O-	Somalia
XU-	Cambodia		6V-	Senegal
XW-	Laos		6Y-	Jamaica
XY/XZ-	Myanmar		7O-	Yemen
YA-	Afghanistan		7P-	Lesotho
YI-	Iraq		7Q-	Malawi
YJ-	Vanuatu		7T-	Algeria
YK-	Syria		8P-	Barbados
YL-	Latvia		8Q-	Maldives
YN-	Nicaragua		8R-	Guyana
YR-	Romania		9A-	Croatia
YS-	El Salvador		9G-	Ghana
YU-	Serbia		9H-	Malta
YV-	Venezuela		9J-	Zambia
Z-	Zimbabwe		9K-	Kuwait
Z3-	Macedonia		9L-	Sierra Leone
Z6-	Kosovo		9M-	Malaysia
ZA-	Albania		9N-	Nepal
ZJ-	Jersey		9Q-	DR Congo
ZK-	New Zealand		9U-	Burundi
ZP-	Paraguay		9V-	Singapore
ZS-	South Africa		9XR-	Rwanda
2-	Guernsey		9Y-	Trinidad and Tobago

TC-MKG Boeing 737-MAX8 of Corendon Airlines. Peter R. March

Reg	Type	Owner or Operator	Notes
G-AAAH	DH.60G Moth (replica) (BAPC 168) ★	Yorkshire Air Museum/Elvington	
G-AAAH	DH.60G Gipsy Moth ★	Science Museum/South Kensington	
G-AACA	Avro 504K (BAPC 177) ★	Brooklands Museum of Aviation/Weybridge	
G-AACN	HP.39 Gugnunc★	Science Museum/South Kensington	
G-AADR	DH.60GM Gipsy Moth	E. V. Moffatt	
G-AAEG	DH.60G Gipsy Moth	I. B. Grace	
G-AAHI	DH.60G Gipsy Moth	Nigel John Western Reid Discretionary Settlement 2008	
G-AAHY	DH.60M Moth	D. J. Elliott	
G-AAIN	Parnall Elf II	The Shuttleworth Collection/Old Warden	
G-AAJT	DH.60G Gipsy Moth	M. R. Paul	
G-AALY	DH.60G Gipsy Moth	K. M. Fresson	
G-AAMX	DH.60M Gipsy Moth	S. J. Beaty	
G-AANG	Blériot XI	The Shuttleworth Collection/Old Warden	
G-AANH	Deperdussin Monoplane	The Shuttleworth Collection/Old Warden	
G-AANI	Blackburn Monoplane	The Shuttleworth Collection/Old Warden	
G-AANJ	L.V.G. C VI (7198/18)	Aerospace Museum/Cosford	
G-AANL	DH.60M Moth	M. D. Souch	
G-AANO	DH.60GMW Gipsy Moth	K. F. Crumplin	
G-AAOK	Curtiss Wright Travel Air 12Q	J. P. Taylor	
G-AAPZ	Desoutter I (mod.)	The Shuttleworth Collection	
G-AATC	DH.80A Puss Moth	M. D. Souch	
G-AAUP	Klemm L.25-1A	Oldstead Aero LLP	
G-AAVJ	DH.60G Gipsy Moth	G. Cormack	
G-AAWO	DH.60G Gipsy Moth	Iain Charles Reid Discretionary Settlement 2009	
G-AAXG	DH 60M Moth	S. H. Kidston	
G-AAXK	Klemm L.25-1A ★	C. C. Russell-Vick (stored)	
G-AAYT	DH.60G Gipsy Moth	P. Groves	
G-AAYX	Southern Martlet	The Shuttleworth Collection	
G-AAZG	DH.60G Gipsy Moth	C. A. Hawkins	
G-AAZP	DH.80A Puss Moth	R. P. Williams	
G-ABAA	Avro 504K ★	Manchester Museum of Science & Industry	
G-ABAG	DH.60G Gipsy Moth	A. Wood	
G-ABBB	B.105A Bulldog IIA (K2227) ★	RAF Museum/Hendon	
G-ABDA	DH.60G Gipsy Moth	T. A. Bechtolsheimer	
G-ABDW	DH.80A Puss Moth (VH-UQB) ★	Museum of Flight/East Fortune	
G-ABDX	DH.60G Gipsy Moth	M. D. Souch	
G-ABEV	DH.60G Gipsy Moth	S. L. G. Darch	
G-ABHE	Aeronca C.2	N. S. Chittenden	
G-ABIH	DH.80A Puss Moth	M. D. Souch	
G-ABJJ	DH.60G Gipsy Moth	B. R. Cox	
G-ABLM	Cierva C.24 ★	De Havilland Heritage Museum/London Colney	
G-ABLS	DH.80A Puss Moth	T. W. Harris	
G-ABMR	Hawker Hart 2 (J9941) ★	RAF Museum/Hendon	
G-ABNT	Civilian C.A.C.1 Coupe	Shipping & Airlines Ltd	
G-ABNX	Redwing 2	M. D. Souch	
G-ABOI	Wheeler Slymph ★	Midland Air Museum/Coventry	
G-ABOX	Sopwith Pup (N5195)	C. M. D. & M. F. St. Cyrien	
G-ABSD	DH.60G Gipsy Moth	M. E. Vaisey	
G-ABTC	Comper CLA.7 Swift	C. D. Cheese & T. M. Jones	
G-ABUL†	DH.82A Tiger Moth ★	F.A.A. Museum/Yeovilton (G-AOXG)	
G-ABUS	Comper CLA.7 Swift	R. C. F. Bailey	
G-ABVE	Arrow Active 2	B. R. Cox	
G-ABWD	DH.83 Fox Moth	M. D. Souch	
G-ABWP	Spartan Arrow	L. A. French	
G-ABXL	Granger Archaeopteryx ★	J. R. Granger	
G-ABYA	DH.60G Gipsy Moth	M. J. Luck	
G-ABZB	DH.60G-III Moth Major	G. M. Turner	
G-ABZE	DH.60G Gipsy Moth	J. Cresswell	
G-ACBH	Blackburn B.2 ★	South Yorkshire Aircraft Museum/Doncaster	
G-ACCB	DH.83 Fox Moth	E. A. Gautrey	
G-ACDA	DH.82A Tiger Moth	J. Turnbull	
G-ACDC	DH.82A Tiger Moth	Tiger Club Ltd	
G-ACDI	DH.82A Tiger Moth	D. J. Wood	
G-ACDJ	DH.82A Tiger Moth	R. H. & J. A. Cooper	
G-ACET	DH.84 Dragon	G. Cormack	
G-ACGL	Comper Swift ★	RAF Museum/Cosford	
G-ACGS	DH.85 Leopard Moth	M. J. Miller (G-APKH)	

BRITISH CIVIL AIRCRAFT MARKINGS

Notes	Reg	Type	Owner or Operator
	G-ACGT	Avro 594 Avian IIIA	B. R. Cox
	G-ACGZ	DH.60G-III Moth Major	N. H. Lemon
	G-ACIT	DH.84 Dragon ★	Science Museum/Wroughton
	G-ACLL	DH.85 Leopard Moth	V. M & D. C. M. Stiles
	G-ACMA	DH.85 Leopard Moth	C. A. Hawkins
	G-ACMD	DH.82A Tiger Moth	M. J. Bonnick
	G-ACMN	DH.85 Leopard Moth	D. E. Starkey
	G-ACNS	DH.60G-III Moth Major	M. D. Souch
	G-ACOJ	DH.85 Leopard Moth	Norman Aeroplane Trust
	G-ACOL	DH.85 Leopard Moth	J. Cresswell
	G-ACSP	DH.88 Comet ★	T. M., M. L., D. A. & P. M. Jones
	G-ACSS	DH.88 Comet ★	The Shuttleworth Collection *Grosvenor House*/Old Warden
	G-ACSS†	DH.88 Comet (replica) ★	G. Gayward (BAPC216)
	G-ACSS†	DH.88 Comet (replica) ★	The Comet Hotel Hatfield (BAPC257)
	G-ACTF	Comper CLA.7 Swift ★	The Shuttleworth Collection/Old Warden
	G-ACUS	DH.85 Leopard Moth	R. A. & V. A. Gammons
	G-ACUU	Cierva C.30A (HM580) ★	Imperial War Museum/Duxford
	G-ACUX	S.16 Scion (VH-UUP) ★	Ulster Folk & Transport Museum
	G-ACVA	Kay Gyroplane ★	National Museum of Scotland/Edinburgh
	G-ACWM	Cierva C.30A (AP506) ★	The Helicopter Museum/Weston-super-Mare
	G-ACWP	Cierva C.30A (AP507) ★	Science Museum/South Kensington
	G-ACXB	DH.60G-III Moth Major	D. F. Hodgkinson
	G-ACXE	B.K. L-25C Swallow	J. F. Copeman
	G-ACYK	Spartan Cruiser III ★	Museum of Flight (front fuselage)/East Fortune
	G-ACYZ	Miles M.2H Hawk Major	M. R. Paul
	G-ADAH	DH.89A Dragon Rapide ★	The Aeroplane Collection/Hooton Park
	G-ADEV	Avro 504K (E3273)	The Shuttleworth Collection/Old Warden (G-ACNB)
	G-ADGP	M.2L Hawk Speed Six	The Richard Ormonde Shuttleworth Remembrance Trust
	G-ADGT	DH.82A Tiger Moth (BB697)	The London Aerobatic Company Ltd
	G-ADGV	DH.82A Tiger Moth	M. van Dijk & M. R. Van der Straaten (G-BACW)
	G-ADHD	DH.60G-III Moth Major	M. E. Vaisey
	G-ADIA	DH.82A Tiger Moth	S. J. Beaty
	G-ADJJ	DH.82A Tiger Moth	G. P. Halley
	G-ADKC	DH.87B Hornet Moth	C. G. & S. Winch
	G-ADKK	DH.87B Hornet Moth	S. W. Barratt & A. J. Herbert
	G-ADKL	DH.87B Hornet Moth	J. S. & P. R. Johnson
	G-ADKM	DH.87B Hornet Moth	J. M. O. Miller
	G-ADLY	DH.87B Hornet Moth	Treetops Aircraft LLP
	G-ADMF	BA L.25C Swallow II	D. A. Edwards
	G-ADMT	DH.87B Hornet Moth	J. A. Jennings
	G-ADMW	M.2H Hawk Major (DG590) ★	Montrose Air Station Heritage Centre
	G-ADND	DH.87B Hornet Moth (W9385)	D. M. & S. M. Weston
	G-ADNE	DH.87B Hornet Moth	G-ADNE Group
	G-ADNL	M.5 Sparrowhawk	M. D. Souch
	G-ADNZ	DH.82A Tiger Moth (DE673)	D. C. Wall
	G-ADOT	DH.87B Hornet Moth ★	De Havilland Heritage Museum/London Colney
	G-ADPC	DH.82A Tiger Moth	P. D. & S. E. Ford
	G-ADPJ	B.A.C. Drone ★	M. J. Aubrey
	G-ADPS	B.A. Swallow 2	J. T. Milson
	G-ADRA	Pietenpol Air Camper	A. J. Mason
	G-ADRR	Aeronca C.3	R. A. Fleming
	G-ADRX†	Mignet HM.14 (replica) ★	Solway Aviation Museum/Carlisle (BAPC231)
	G-ADRY†	Mignet HM.14 (replica) (BAPC29) ★	Brooklands Museum of Aviation/Weybridge
	G-ADUR	DJ.87B Hornet Moth	C. J. & P. R. Harvey
	G-ADVU†	Mignet HM.14 (replica) ★	North East Aircraft Museum/Usworth (BAPC211)
	G-ADWJ	DH.82A Tiger Moth (BB803)	K. F. Crumplin
	G-ADWO	DH.82A Tiger Moth (BB807) ★	Solent Sky, Southampton
	G-ADXS	Mignet HM.14 ★	The Real Aeroplane Company/Breighton
	G-ADYO+	Mignet HM.14 ★	The Aeroplane Collection/Hooton Park (BAPC12)
	G-ADYS	Aeronca C.3	E. P. & P. A. Gliddon
	G-ADYV†	Mignet HM.14 (replica) ★	Lakeland Motor Museum/Ulverston (BAPC243)
	G-ADZW†	Mignet HM.14 (replica) ★	Solent Sky/Southampton (BAPC253)
	G-AEBB	Mignet HM.14 8	The Shuttleworth Collection/Old Warden

Reg	Type	Owner or Operator	Notes
G-AEBJ	Blackburn B-2	Richard Shuttleworth Trustees	
G-AEDB	B.A.C. Drone 2	M. J. & S. Honeychurch	
G-AEDU	DH.90 Dragonfly	GAEDU Ltd	
G-AEEG	M.3A Falcon Skysport	Shipping & Airlines Ltd	
G-AEEH	Mignet HM.14 ★	RAF Museum/Cosford	
G-AEFG	Mignet HM.14 (BAPC75) ★	N. H. Ponsford/Breighton	
G-AEFT	Aeronca C.3	N. S. Chittenden	
G-AEGV	Mignet HM.14 ★	Midland Air Museum/Coventry	
G-AEHM	Mignet HM.14 ★	Science Museum/Wroughton	
G-AEJZ	Mignet HM.14 (BAPC120) ★	South Yorkshire Aircraft Museum	
G-AEKR	Mignet HM.14 (BAPC121) ★	Doncaster Museum & Art Gallery	
G-AEKV	Kronfeld Drone ★	Brooklands Museum of Aviation/Weybridge	
G-AEKW	M.12 Mohawk ★	RAF Museum	
G-AELO	DH.87B Hornet Moth	M. J. Miller	
G-AENP	Hawker Hind (K5533) (BAPC78)	The Shuttleworth Collection	
G-AEOA	DH.80A Puss Moth	A. Wood	
G-AEOF†	Mignet HM.14 (BAPC22) ★	Aviodrome/Lelystad, Netherlands	
G-AEOF	Rearwin 8500	Natton Garage	
G-AEPH	Bristol F.2B (B1162/F)	The Shuttleworth Collection	
G-AERV	M.11A Whitney Straight	P. W. Bishop	
G-AESB	Aeronca C.3	J. Cresswell	
G-AESE	DH.87B Hornet Moth	B. R. Cox	
G-AESZ	Chilton D.W.1	R. A. Fleming	
G-AETA	Caudron G.3 (3066) ★	RAF Museum/Hendon	
G-AETG	Aeronca 100	J. Teagle and Partners	
G-AEUJ	M.11A Whitney Straight	R. E. Mitchell	
G-AEVS	Aeronca 100	R. A. Fleming	
G-AEXF	P.6 Mew Gull	Richard Shuttleworth Trustees	
G-AEXT	Dart Kitten II	R. A. Fleming	
G-AEXZ	Piper J-2 Cub	M. J. Honeychurch	
G-AEZF	S.16 Scion 2 ★	Medway Aircraft Preservation Society/Rochester	
G-AEZJ	P.10 Vega Gull	Comanche Warbirds Ltd	
G-AEZX	Bucker Bu.133C Jungmeister	Westh Flyg AB/Sweden (G-PTDP)	
G-AFAP†	CASA C.352L ★	RAF Museum/Cosford	
G-AFBS	M.14A Hawk Trainer 3 ★	Imperial War Museum/Duxford (G-AKKU)	
G-AFCL	B. A. Swallow 2	D. & J. Cresswell	
G-AFDO	Piper J-3C-65 Cub	N. S. Lomax	
G-AFDX	Hanriot HD.1 (HD-75) ★	RAF Museum/Hendon	
G-AFEL	Monocoupe 90A	M. Rieser	
G-AFFD	Percival Type Q Six (X9407)	The London Aerobatic Company Ltd	
G-AFFH	Piper J-2 Cub	M. J. Honeychurch	
G-AFFI†	Mignet HM.14 (replica) (BAPC76) ★	Yorkshire Air Museum/Elvington	
G-AFGD	B. A. Swallow 2	South Wales Swallow Group	
G-AFGE	B. A. Swallow 2	A. A. M. & C. W. N. Huke	
G-AFGH	Chilton D.W.1.	M. L. & G. L. Joseph	
G-AFGM	Piper J-4A Cub Coupé	T. W. Watson	
G-AFGZ	DH.82A Tiger Moth	M. R. Paul (G-AMHI)	
G-AFHA	Mosscraft MA.1.	K. Miller	
G-AFIN	Chrislea LC.1 Airguard (BAPC203) ★	Skyblue Aero Simulation Ltd	
G-AFIU	Parker CA-4 Parasol ★	The Aeroplane Collection/Hooton Park	
G-AFJA	Taylor-Watkinson Dingbat	M. Young	
G-AFJB	Foster-Wikner G.M.1. Wicko	J. Dible	
G-AFJR	Tipsy Trainer 1 ★	Royal Museum of the Armed Forces and Military History/Brussels	
G-AFJU	M.17 Monarch	Museum of Flight/East Fortune	
G-AFJV	Mosscraft MA.2	K. Miller	
G-AFNI	DH.94 Moth Minor	J. Jennings	
G-AFOB	DH.94 Moth Minor	K. Cantwell	
G-AFOJ	DH.94 Moth Minor	J. H. D. Newman	
G-AFPN	DH.94 Moth Minor	S. L. Childs	
G-AFRV	Tipsy Trainer 1★	Royal Museum of the Armed Forces and Military History/Brussels	
G-AFRZ	M.17 Monarch	R. E. Mitchell/Sleap (G-AIDE)	
G-AFSC	Tipsy Trainer 1	D. M. Forshaw	
G-AFSV	Chilton D.W.1A	R. A. Fleming	
G-AFTA	Hawker Tomtit (K1786)	The Shuttleworth Collection	
G-AFTL	Lockheed 12A Electra Junior	Fighter Aviation Engineering Ltd	
G-AFTN	Taylorcraft Plus C2 ★	Leicestershire County Council Museums/Snibston	
G-AFUP	Luscombe 8A Silvaire	W. R. Sturgess	

Notes	Reg	Type	Owner or Operator
	G-AFWH	Piper J-4A Cub Coupé	C. W. Stearn & R. D. W. Norton
	G-AFWI	DH.82A Tiger Moth	M. Sheppard & P. R. Johnson
	G-AFWN	Auster J/1 Autocrat ★	Danmarks Flymuseum/Stauning
	G-AFWT	Tipsy Trainer 1	P. J. Wood
	G-AFYD	Luscombe 8F Silvaire	C. A. Roberts
	G-AFYO	Stinson H.W.75	M. Lodge
	G-AFZA	Piper J-4A Cub Coupe	R. A. Benson
	G-AFZE	Heath Parasol	C. J. Essex
	G-AFZK	Luscombe 8A Silvaire	M. G. Byrnes
	G-AFZL	Porterfield CP.50	Skinny Bird Flyers
	G-AGBN	GAL.42 Cygnet 2 ★	Museum of Flight/East Fortune
	G-AGEG	DH.82A Tiger Moth	The London Aerobatic Company Ltd
	G-AGHY	DH.82A Tiger Moth	P. Groves
	G-AGIV	Piper J-3C-65 Cub	R. P. Marks
	G-AGJG	DH.89A Dragon Rapide	M. J. & D. J. T. Miller
	G-AGLK	Auster 5D	M. A. Farrelly & D. K. Chambers
	G-AGMI	Luscombe 8A Silvaire	Oscar Flying Group
	G-AGNV	Avro 685 York 1 (TS798) ★	Aerospace Museum/Cosford
	G-AGOS	R.S.4 Desford Trainer (VZ728) ★	Newark Air Museum
	G-AGOY	Miles M.48 Messenger 3	S. A. Blanchard
	G-AGPG	Avro 19 Srs 2 ★	The Aeroplane Collection/Hooton Park
	G-AGPK	DH.82A Tiger Moth (PG657)	Cirrus Aviation L;td
	G-AGRU	Vickers Viking 1A ★	Brooklands Museum of Aviation/Weybridge
	G-AGRW	Vickers Viking 1A ★	The Blackbushe Heritage Trust/Blackbushe§
	G-AGSH	DH.89A Dragon Rapide 6	P. H. Meeson
	G-AGTM	DH.89A Dragon Rapide 6	B. R. Cox & D. E. Starkey
	G-AGTO	Auster 5 J/1 Autocrat	M. J. Barnett & D. J. T. Miller
	G-AGVG	Auster 5 J/1 Autocrat (modified)	S. J. Benest
	G-AGXN	Auster J/1N Alpha	Gentleman's Aerial Touring Carriage Group
	G-AGXU	Auster J/1N Alpha	E. R. O'Hara
	G-AGXV	Auster J/1 Autocrat	M. J. Barnett
	G-AGYH	Auster J/1N Alpha	I. M. Staves
	G-AGYU	DH.82A Tiger Moth (DE208)	D. & S. A. Firth
	G-AGZZ	DH.82A Tiger Moth	C. R. Davies
	G-AHAA	Miles M.28 Mercury 6	S. A. Blanchard
	G-AHAG	DH.89A Rapide	Scillonia Airways Ltd
	G-AHAL	Auster J/1N Alpha	K. Harness
	G-AHAM	Auster J/1 Autocrat	Interna Engineering BV/Belgium
	G-AHAN	DH.82A Tiger Moth	G-AHAN Flying Group
	G-AHAO	Auster 5 J/1 Autocrat	R. Callaway-Lewis
	G-AHAP	Auster J/1 Autocrat	W. D. Hill
	G-AHAT	Auster J/1N Alpha ★	Dumfries & Galloway Aviation Museum
	G-AHAU	Auster 5 J/1 Autocrat	Andreas Auster Group
	G-AHBL	DH.87B Hornet Moth	Shipping and Airlines Ltd
	G-AHBM	DH.87B Hornet Moth	P. A. & E. P. Gliddon
	G-AHCL	Auster J/1N Alpha (modified)	N. Musgrave
	G-AHCR	Gould-Taylorcraft Plus D Special (LB352)	M. J. Laundy
	G-AHEC	Luscombe 8A Silvaire	J. M. Kimberley
	G-AHED	DH.89A Dragon Rapide (RL962) ★	RAF Museum Storage & Restoration Centre/RAF Stafford
	G-AHGW	Taylorcraft Plus D (LB375)	K. Kouba
	G-AHGZ	Taylorcraft Plus D (LB367)	A. D. Pearce
	G-AHHH	Auster J/1 Autocrat	R. Greatrex
	G-AHHT	Auster J/1N Alpha	South Downs Auster Group
	G-AHHY	Taylorcraft Plus D (LB369)	M. G. Maddams
	G-AHIP	Piper J-3C-65 Cub (479712:8-R)	A. D. Pearce
	G-AHIZ	DH.82A Tiger Moth	C.F.G. Flying Ltd
	G-AHKX	Avro 19 Srs 2 (TX176)	Richard Shuttleworth Trustees
	G-AHKY	Miles M.18 Series 2 ★	Museum of Flight/East Fortune
	G-AHLK	Auster 3 (NJ889)	J. H. Powell-Tuck
	G-AHLT	DH.82A Tiger Moth	M. P. Waring
	G-AHMN	DH.82A Tiger Moth	A. D. Barton
	G-AHOO	DH.82A Tiger Moth	J. T. Milsom
	G-AHPZ	DH.82A Tiger Moth	N. J. Wareing
	G-AHRI	DH.104 Dove 1 ★	Newark Air Museum/Newark
	G-AHSA	Avro 621 Tutor (K3241)	The Shuttleworth Collection
	G-AHSP	Auster J/1 Autocrat	R. M. Weeks
	G-AHSS	Auster J/1N Alpha	C. S. Randall
	G-AHST	Auster J/1N Alpha	A. C. Frost

Reg	Type	Owner or Operator	Notes
G-AHTE	P.44 Proctor V	D. K. Tregilgas	
G-AHTW	A.S.40 Oxford (V3388) ★	Skyfame Collection/Duxford	
G-AHUF	DH.Tiger Moth (T7997)	Eaglescott Tiger Moth Group	
G-AHUG	Taylorcraft Plus D	Taildraggers Ltd	
G-AHUI	M.38 Messenger 2A ★	The Aeroplane Collection/Hooton Park	
G-AHUJ	M.14A Hawk Trainer 3 (R1914)	F. Baldanza	
G-AHUN	Globe GC-1B Swift	R. J. Hamlett	
G-AHUV	DH.82A Tiger Moth	A. D. Gordon	
G-AHVU	DH.82A Tiger Moth	Vintage Aircraft Factory Ltd	
G-AHVV	DH.82A Tiger Moth	M. Arter	
G-AHXE	Taylorcraft Plus D (LB312)	Historic Aircraft Flight Trust	
G-AIBE	Fulmar II (N1854) ★	F.A.A. Museum/Yeovilton	
G-AIBH	Auster J/1N Alpha	M. J. Bonnick	
G-AIBR	Auster J/1 Autocrat	M. P. Davies	
G-AIBW	Auster J/1N Alpha	C. R. Sunter	
G-AIBX	Auster J/1 Autocrat	D. Perry	
G-AIBY	Auster J/1 Autocrat	D. Morris	
G-AICX	Luscombe 8A Silvaire	J. P. Coyne-Downhill	
G-AIDL	DH.89A Dragon Rapide 6 (TX310)	Avalon Ventures Ltd	
G-AIDN	VS.502 Spitfire T.VII (MT818:WZ-JJ)	Warbird Experiences Ltd	
G-AIDS	DH.82A Tiger Moth	N. A. A. Pogmore	
G-AIEK	M.38 Messenger 2A (RG333)	M. Hales	
G-AIFZ	Auster J/1N Alpha	M. D. Ansley	
G-AIGD	Auster V J/1 Autocrat	R. M. D. Saw	
G-AIGF	Auster J/1N Alpha	D. W. Mathie	
G-AIGP	Auster V J/1 Autocrat ★	The Aeroplane Collection/Hooton Park Hangers	
G-AIGT	Auster J/1N Alpha	M. J. Miller & G. Langlery	
G-AIIH	Piper J-3C-65 Cub (44-79649/69-K)	Wildcat WP Ltd	
G-AIJM	Auster J/4	N. Huxtable	
G-AIJS	Auster J/4	R. J. Lane	
G-AIJT	Auster J/4 Srs 100	Aberdeen Auster Flying Group	
G-AIKE	Auster 5 (NJ728)	J. D. C. Pritchard	
G-AIPR	Auster J/4	N. Mills	
G-AIPV	Auster J/1 Autocrat	S. P. Miller	
G-AIRC	Auster J/1 Autocrat	K. & C. Jones & C. Morris	
G-AIRK	DH.82A Tiger Moth	J. S. & P. R. Johnson	
G-AISA	Tipsy B Srs 1	J. Pollard	
G-AISS	Piper J-3C-65 Cub	K. W. Wood & F. Watson	
G-AIST	VS.300 Spitfire 1A (P7308/XR-D)	Spitfire The One Ltd	
G-AISX	Piper J-3C-65 Cub (330372)	Cubfly	
G-AITB	A.S.10 Oxford (MP425) ★	RAF Museum/Hendon	
G-AIUA	M.14A Hawk Trainer 3 (T9768)	D. S. Hunt	
G-AIUL	DH.89A Dragon Rapide 6	I. Jones	
G-AIXA	Taylorcraft Plus D (LB264) ★	RAF Museum/Hendon	
G-AIXJ	DH.82A Tiger Moth	D. C. D. Green	
G-AIYR	DH.89A Dragon Rapide (HG691)	Cirrus Aviation Ltd	
G-AIYS	DH.85 Leopard Moth	M. R. Paul	
G-AIZE	Fairchild F.24W Argus 2 (FS628) ★	RAF Museum/Cosford	
G-AIZG	VS.236 Walrus 1 (L2301) ★	F.A.A. Museum/Yeovilton	
G-AIZU	Auster J/1 Autocrat	C. J. & J. G. B. Morley	
G-AJAD	Piper J-3C-65 Cub	C. R. Shipley	
G-AJAJ	Auster J/1N Alpha	N. K. Geddes	
G-AJAM	Auster J/2 Arrow	T. Jarvis	
G-AJAP	Luscombe 8A Silvaire	M. Flint	
G-AJAS	Auster J/1N Alpha	S. D. Palfrey	
G-AJCP	D.31 Turbulent	B. R. Pearson	
G-AJDW	Auster J/1 Autocrat	D. R. Hunt	
G-AJEB	Auster J/1N Alpha ★		
G-AJEE	Auster J/1 Autocrat	A. C. Whitehead	
G-AJEH	Auster J/1N Alpha	T. J. Harrison	
G-AJEI	Auster J/1N Alpha	G. J. Siddall	
G-AJEM	Auster J/1 Autocrat	A. L. Aish	
G-AJER	Auster J/5A Adventurer	J. Wesson	
G-AJES	Piper J-3C-65 Cub (330485:C-44)	D. E. Jarvis	
G-AJGJ	Auster 5 (RT486) ★	RAF Manston History Museum	
G-AJIH	Auster J/1 Autocrat (TJ518)	S. Alexander	
G-AJIS	Auster J/1N Alpha	J. J. Hill	
G-AJIT	Auster J/1 Kingsland Autocrat	S. J. Farrant	
G-AJIU	Auster J/1 Autocrat	J. S. Allison	

Notes	Reg	Type	Owner or Operator
	G-AJIW	Auster J/1N Alpha	R. J. Guess
	G-AJIX	Auster J/1 Autocrat	S. G. Rule
	G-AJJP	Fairey Jet Gyrodyne (XJ389) ★	Museum of Berkshire Aviation/Woodley
	G-AJJS	Cessna 120	G. A. Robson
	G-AJJU	Luscombe 8E Silvaire	M. F. A. Hudson
	G-AJKB	Luscombe 8E Silvaire	T. Carter
	G-AJOA	DH.82A Tiger Moth	K. A. Nutley
	G-AJOC	M.38 Messenger 2A ★	Ulster Folk & Transport Museum
	G-AJOE	M.38 Messenger 2A	P. W. Bishop
	G-AJOV†	Westland WS-51 Dragonfly ★	RAF Museum/Cosford
	G-AJOZ	Fairchild F.24W Argus 2 (FK338) ★	Yorkshire Air Museum/Elvington
	G-AJPI	Fairchild F.24R-41a Argus 3 (314887)	R. Sijben/Netherlands
	G-AJRB	Auster J/1 Autocrat	Northumbrian Vintage Aircraft Group
	G-AJRH	Auster J/1N Alpha ★	Charnwood Museum/Loughborough
	G-AJRS	M.14A Hawk Trainer 3 (P6382:C)	The Shuttleworth Collection
	G-AJSN	Fairchild 24W-41A Argus (HB612) ★	Ulster Aviation Society/Long Kesh
	G-AJTW	DH.82A Tiger Moth (N6965:FL-J)	J. A. Barker
	G-AJUE	Auster J/1 Autocrat	V. R. Goddard
	G-AJVE	DH.82A Tiger Moth	R. A. Gammons
	G-AJVH	Faireyu Swordfish II (LS326)	Fly Navy Heritage Trust Ltd
	G-AJWB	M.38 Messenger 2A	P. W. Bishop
	G-AJXC	Auster 5 (TJ343)	R. D. Helliar-Symonds, K. A. & S. E. W. Williams
	G-AJXV	Auster 4 (NJ695)	M. D. Roberts
	G-AJXY	Auster 4	X-Ray Yankee Group
	G-AJYB	Auster J/1N Alpha	P. J. Shotbolt
	G-AKAT	M.14A Hawk Trainer 3 (T9738)	R. A. Fleming
	G-AKBO	M.38 Messenger 2A	N. P. Lee
	G-AKDK	M.65 Gemeni 1A ★	The Aeroplane Collection/Hootton Park
	G-AKDN	DHC.1A-1 Chipmunk	K. A. Large & J. Morley
	G-AKDW	DH.89A Dragon Rapide ★	De Havilland Heritage Museum/London Colney
	G-AKEL	M.65 Gemini 1A ★	Ulster Folk & Transport Museum
	G-AKEN	M.65 GemIni 1A ★	The Aeroplane Collection/Hooton Park
	G-AKEX	Percival Proctor III	M. Biddulph (G-AKIU)
	G-AKGE	M.65 Gemini 3C ★	Ulster Folk & Transport Museum
	G-AKHP	M.65 Gemini 1A	S. A. Blanchard
	G-AKHU	M.65 Gemini 1A ★	The Aeroplane Collection/Hooton Park
	G-AKIB	Piper J-3C-90 Cub (480015:M-44)	C. R. J. Walker & E. Carter
	G-AKIF	DH.89A Dragon Rapide	Avalon Ventures Ltd
	G-AKIN	M.38 Messenger 2A	A. R. Hardwick
	G-AKIU	P.44 Proctor V	G. G. L. James
	G-AKKB	M.65 Gemini 1A	S. Woodgate & R. A. Pike
	G-AKKH	M.65 Gemini 1A	P. J. Hebdon
	G-AKKR	M.14A Magister (T9707) ★	Museum of Army Flying/Middle Wallop
	G-AKKY	M.14A Hawk Trainer 3 (L6906) ★ (BAPC44)	Museum of Berkshire Aviation/Woodley
	G-AKLW	Short SA.6 Sealand 1 ★	Ulster Folk & Transport Museum
	G-AKNV	DH.89A Rapide	Royal Museum of the Armed Forces and Military History/Brussels
	G-AKOW	Auster 5 (TJ569) ★	Museum of Army Flying/Middle Wallop
	G-AKPF	M.14A Hawk Trainer 3 (N3788)	D. S. Bramwell
	G-AKPI	Auster 5 (NJ703)	M. D. Grinstead
	G-AKRP	DH.89A Dragon Rapide 4	Eaglescott Dominie Group
	G-AKSY	Auster 5 (TJ534)	M. H. Schoonderbeek
	G-AKSZ	Auster 5D (modified)	M. A. Farrelly & D. K. Chambers
	G-AKTH	Piper J-3C-65 Cub	G. W. S. Turner
	G-AKTK	Aeronca 11BC Chief	A. C. Batchelar
	G-AKTP	PA-17 Vagabond	I. D. Worthington
	G-AKTR	Aeronca 7AC Champion	E. Gordon
	G-AKTS	Cessna 120	K. W. Wood
	G-AKTT	Luscombe 8A Silvaire	S. J. Charters
	G-AKUE	DH.82A Tiger Moth	D. F. Hodgkinson
	G-AKUF	Luscombe 8E Silvaire	P. B. Davey
	G-AKUH	Luscombe 8E Silvaire	A. H. Ager (G-GIST)
	G-AKUJ	Luscombe 8E Silvaire	P. R. Bentley
	G-AKUK	Luscombe 8A Silvaire	O. R. Watts
	G-AKUL	Luscombe 8A Silvaire	G. E. Clegg
	G-AKUM	Luscombe 8F Silvaire	D. A. Young
	G-AKUN	Piper J-3C-65 Cub	W. R. Savin
	G-AKUO	Aeronca 11AC Chief	C. V. Dadswell & A. G. Collicot

Reg	Type	Owner or Operator	Notes
G-AKUP	Luscombe 8E Silvaire	D. A. Young	
G-AKUW	Chrislea CH.3 Super Ace 2	R. J. S. G. Clark	
G-AKVF	Chrislea CH.3 Super Ace 2	T. W. J. Carnall	
G-AKVM	Cessna 120	P. A. Espin	
G-AKVN	Aeronca 11BC Chief	T. R. Villa	
G-AKVO	Taylorcraft BC-12D	G. Taylor	
G-AKVR	Chrislea CH.3 Skyjeep 4	R. B. Webber	
G-AKVZ	M.38 Messenger 4B	Shipping & Airlines Ltd	
G-AKWS	Auster 5A-160 (RT610)	M. C. Hayes, P. L. Poole & K. M. Powell	
G-AKWT	Auster 5 ★	C. Baker	
G-AKXP	Auster 5 (NJ633)	M. J. Nicholson	
G-AKXS	DH.82A Tiger Moth	J. & G. J. Eagles	
G-AKZN	P.34A Proctor 3 (Z7197) ★	RAF Museum/Hendon	
G-ALAH	Miles M.38 Messenger 4A ★	The Aeroplane Collection/Hooton Park	
G-ALAR	Miles M.38 Messenger 4A ★	The Aeroplane Collection/Hooton Park	
G-ALAX	DH.89A Dragon Rapide ★	Durney Aeronautical Collection/Andover	
G-ALBD	DH.82A Tiger Moth	K. Redfearn	
G-ALBJ	Auster 5 (TW501)	B. M. Vigor	
G-ALBK	Auster 5	J. S. Allison	
G-ALBN	Bristol 173 (XF785) ★	RAF Museum Storage & Restoration Centre/Cardington	
G-ALCK	P.34A Proctor 3 (LZ766) ★	Imperial War Museum/Duxford	
G-ALCU	DH.104 Dove 2 (G-ALVD) ★	Midland Air Museum/Coventry	
G-ALDG	HP.81 Hermes 4 ★	Imperial War Museum/Duxford	
G-ALEH	PA-17 Vagabond	A. J. Coker	
G-ALFA	Auster 5	A. E. Jones	
G-ALFU	DH.104 Dove 6 ★	Imperial War Museum/Duxford	
G-ALGA	PA-15 Vagabond	G. W., H.K., T.W. & W. S. Gilbert	
G-ALIJ	PA-17 Vagabond	D. J. Jack	
G-ALIW	DH.82A Tiger Moth	E. H. W. Moore	
G-ALJL	DH.82A Tiger Moth	T. A. Kinnaird	
G-ALJR	Abbott-Baynes Scud III	The Gliding Heritage Centre	
G-ALLF	Slingsby T.30A Prefect (ARK)	The Gliding Heritage Centre	
G-ALMA	Piper J3C-65 Cub	M. J. Butler (G-BBXS)	
G-ALNA	DH.82A Tiger Moth (EM973)	S. E. Ford	
G-ALND	DH.82A Tiger Moth	K. J. Fraser	
G-ALPU+	Slingsby T.8 Cadet ★	Hooton Park Trust/Hooton Park	
G-ALSP	Bristol 171 Sycamore (WV783) ★	RAF Museum/Hendon	
G-ALSS	Bristol 171 Sycamore (WA576) ★	Dumfries & Galloway Aviation Museum	
G-ALST	Bristol 171 Sycamore (WA577) ★	North East Aircraft Museum/Usworth	
G-ALSW	Bristol 171 Sycamore (WT933) ★	Newark Air Museum	
G-ALSX	Bristol 171 Sycamore (G-48-1) ★	The Helicopter Museum/Weston-super-Mare	
G-ALTO	Cessna 140	T. M. Jones & ptnrs	
G-ALUC	DH.82A Tiger Moth	P. D.& S. E. Ford	
G-ALWB	DHC.1 Chipmunk 22A	D. M. Neville	
G-ALWF	V.701 Viscount ★	Imperial War Museum/Duxford	
G-ALWS	DH.82A Tiger Moth (N9328)	J. G. Norris	
G-ALWW	DH.82A Tiger Moth	D. E. Findon	
G-ALXT	DH.89A Dragon Rapide ★	Science Museum/Wroughton	
G-ALXZ	Auster 5-150 (NJ689)	P. J. Tyler	
G-ALYB	Auster 5 (RT520) ★	South Yorkshire Aviation Museum/Doncaster	
G-ALYW	DH.106 Comet 1 ★	RAF Exhibition Flight (fuselage converted to 'Nimrod')	
G-ALZE	BN-1F ★	Solent Sky Museum/Southampton	
G-ALZO	A.S.57 Ambassador ★	Imperial War Museum/Duxford	
G-AMAW	Luton LA-4 Minor	The Real Aeroplane Company/Breighton	
G-AMBB	DH.82A Tiger Moth	J. Eagles	
G-AMCK	DH.82A Tiger Moth	M. R. Masters	
G-AMCM	DH.82A Tiger Moth	A. K. & K. J. O'Brien	
G-AMDA	Avro 652A Anson 1 (N4877:MK-V) ★	Imperial War Museum/Duxford	
G-AMEN	PA-18 Super Cub 95	The G-AMEN Flying Group	
G-AMHF	DH.82A Tiger Moth	A. J. West	
G-AMHJ	Douglas C-47A Dakota 6 (KG651) ★	Assault Glider Association/Shawbury	
G-AMIV	DH.82A Tiger Moth (R5246)	RAF Station Czechoslovakia SRO	
G-AMJM	Auster 5	J. R. Davison	
G-AMKU	Auster J/1B Aiglet	P. G. Lipman	
G-AMLZ	P.50 Prince 6E ★	Speke Aerodrome Heritage Group	
G-AMMS	Auster J/5K Aiglet Trainer	G. P. J. Rowden	
G-AMNN	DH.82A Tiger Moth	I. J. Perry	

Notes	Reg	Type	Owner or Operator
	G-AMOG	V.701 Viscount ★	Museum of Flight/East Fortune
	G-AMPG	PA-12 Super Cruiser	D. J. Harrison
	G-AMPI	SNCAN Stampe SV.4C	Ardmore Aviation Services Ltd
	G-AMPO	Douglas C-47B (FZ626/YS-DH) ★	(gate guardian)/RAF Lyneham
	G-AMRF	Auster J/5F Aiglet Trainer	D. A. Hill
	G-AMRK	G.37 Gladiator I (K7985)	The Shuttleworth Collection
	G-AMSG	SIPA 903	S. W. Markham
	G-AMSN	Douglas C-47B ★	Aceball Aviation/Redhill
	G-AMTA	Auster J/5F Aiglet Trainer	J. D. Manson
	G-AMTF	DH.82A Tiger Moth (T7842)	H. A. D. Monro
	G-AMTK	DH.82A Tiger Moth	S. W. McKay & M. E. Vaisey
	G-AMTM	Auster J/1 Autocrat	R. J. Stobo (G-AJUJ)
	G-AMTV	DH.82A Tiger Moth	J. H. Scurr
	G-AMUF	DHC.1 Chipmunk 21	C. L. S. von Altishofen
	G-AMUI	Auster J/5F Aiglet Trainer	D. J. Colclough
	G-AMVD	Auster 5 (TJ565)	M.Hammond
	G-AMVP	Tipsy Junior	R. A. Fleming
	G-AMVS	DH.82A Tiger Moth	D. Shew
	G-AMYD	Auster J/5L Aiglet Trainer	D. J. Houghton
	G-AMYJ	Douglas C-47B (KN353) ★	Yorkshire Air Museum/Elvington
	G-ANAF	Douglas C-47B (KP220)	Aero Legends Leasing Ltd
	G-ANAP	DH.104 Dove 6 ★	Brunel Technical College/Lulsgate
	G-ANBY	DH.82A Tiger Moth ★ (EM840)	The Aeroplane Collection/Hooton Park
	G-ANBZ	DH.82A Tiger Moth	M. D. Souch
	G-ANCF	B.175 Britannia 308 ★	Bristol Aero Collection (stored)/Kemble
	G-ANCS	DH.82A Tiger Moth	C. E. Edwards & E. A. Higgins
	G-ANDE	DH.82A Tiger Moth (EM726)	Aero Legends Leasing Ltd
	G-ANDM	DH.82A Tiger Moth	N. J. Stagg
	G-ANDP	DH.82A Tiger Moth	R. A. Pike
	G-ANEH	DH.82A Tiger Moth (N6797)	G. J. Wells
	G-ANEL	DH.82A Tiger Moth	E. R. Boshoff
	G-ANEM	DH.82A Tiger Moth	T. W. J. Dann
	G-ANEN	DH.82A Tiger Moth	G-ANEN Group
	G-ANEW	DH.82A Tiger Moth (NM138)	K. F. Crumplin
	G-ANEZ	DH.82A Tiger Moth	D. A. Burns
	G-ANFH	Westland WS-55 Whirlwind ★	The Helicopter Museum/Weston-super-Mare
	G-ANFI	DH.82A Tiger Moth (DE623)	G. P. Graham
	G-ANFL	DH.82A Tiger Moth	Felthorpe Tiger Group Ltd
	G-ANFM	DH.82A Tiger Moth	Reading Flying Group
	G-ANFP	DH.82A Tiger Moth (N9503)	R. Santus
	G-ANFV	DH.82A Tiger Moth	Avalon Ventures Ltd
	G-ANHI	DH.82A Tiger Moth	A. D. Barton
	G-ANHK	DH.82A Tiger Moth (N9372)	A. S. Rawson
	G-ANHR	Auster 5	H. L. Swallow
	G-ANHS	Auster 4 (MT197)	C. E. Tyers
	G-ANHX	Auster 5D (TW519)	T. Taylor
	G-ANIE	Auster 5 (TW467)	R. T. Ingram
	G-ANIJ	Auster 5D (TJ672)	G. M. Rundle
	G-ANIS	Auster 5	J. Clarke-Cockburn
	G-ANJA	DH.82A Tiger Moth (N9389)	A. D. Hodgkinson
	G-ANJD	DH.82A Tiger Moth	A. J. Gillson
	G-ANJI	DH.82A Tiger Moth (T6830)	A. Watt
	G-ANJK	DH.82A Tiger Moth	P. H. C. Hall & S. P. Evans
	G-ANJV	Westland Whirlwind Series 3 ★	The Helicopter Museum/Weston-super-Mare
	G-ANKK	DH.82A Tiger Moth	Fly Tiger Moth Ltd
	G-ANKT	DH.82A Tiger Moth (K2585)	The Shuttleworth Collection
	G-ANKV	DH.82A Tiger Moth (C8500/16)	J. A. Cooper
	G-ANKZ	DH.82A Tiger Moth (N6466)	P. Groves
	G-ANLD	DH.82A Tiger Moth	M. Groves
	G-ANLS	DH.82A Tiger Moth	P. A. Gliddon
	G-ANLW	Westland WS-51/2 Widgeon	Lift West (Helicopters) Ltd
	G-ANMO	DH.82A Tiger Moth (K4259:71)	Aero Legends Leasing Ltd
	G-ANMY	DH.82A Tiger Moth (DE470)	C. S. Gowers
	G-ANNG	DH.82A Tiger Moth	Parachuting Aircraft Ltd
	G-ANNI	DH.82A Tiger Moth (T6953)	C. E. Ponsford & ptnrs
	G-ANNK	DH.82A Tiger Moth (T7290)	J. Y. Kaye
	G-ANNN	DH.82A Tiger Moth ★	Thorpe Park Visitor Centre/Tattershall Thorpe
	G-ANOA	Hiller UH-12A ★	Redhill Technical College
	G-ANOD	DH.82A Tiger Moth	M. D. Souch
	G-ANOH	DH.82A Tiger Moth	H. van den Brink

Reg	Type	Owner or Operator	Notes
G-ANOK	SAAB S.91C Safir	N. C. Stone	
G-ANOM	DH.82A Tiger Moth	W. J. Pitts	
G-ANON	DH.82A Tiger Moth (T7909)	Tiger Moth Experience Ltd	
G-ANOO	DH.82A Tiger Moth	R. K. Packman	
G-ANOV	DH.104 Dove 6 ★	Museum of Flight/East Fortune	
G-ANPE	DH.82A Tiger Moth	T. K. Butcher (G-IESH)	
G-ANPK	DH.82A Tiger Moth	A. D. Hodgkinson	
G-ANPP	P.34A Proctor 3	C. P. A. & J. Jeffrey	
G-ANRF	DH.82A Tiger Moth	C. D. Cyster	
G-ANRM	DH.82A Tiger Moth (DF112)	Avalon Ventures Ltd	
G-ANRN	DH.82A Tiger Moth	J. J. V. Elwes	
G-ANRP	Auster 5 (TW439)	C. L. Petty	
G-ANRX	DH.82A Tiger Moth ★	De Havilland Heritage Museum/London Colney	
G-ANSM	DH.82A Tiger Moth	Douglas Aviation	
G-ANTE	DH.82A Tiger Moth	Thomas Castle Aviation Heritage Ltd	
G-ANTK	Avro 685 York ★	Imperial War Museum/Duxford	
G-ANUO	DH.114 Heron 2D (G-AOXL) ★	Westmead Business Group/Croydon Airport	
G-ANUW	DH.104 Dove 6 ★	Aeropark/East Midlands	
G-ANVY	Proctor 4 ★ (RM169)	The Aeroplane Collection/Hooton Park	
G-ANWB	DHC-1 Chipmunk 21	J. & A. Zemlik	
G-ANXB	DH.114 Heron 1B ★	Newark Air Museum/Newark	
G-ANXC	Auster J/5R Alpine	H. A. Jones	
G-ANXR	P.31C Proctor 4 (RM221)	N. H. T. Cottrell	
G-ANZT	Thruxton Jackaroo	D. J. Neville & P. A. Dear	
G-ANZU	DH.82A Tiger Moth	M. I. Lodge	
G-ANZZ	DH.82A Tiger Moth (DE974)	Avalon Ventures Ltd	
G-AOAA	DH.82A Tiger Moth	R. C. P. Brookhouse	
G-AOBG	Somers-Kendall SK.1	P. W. Bishop	
G-AOBH	DH.82A Tiger Moth (NL750)	P. Nutley	
G-AOBJ	DH.82A Tiger Moth	A. D. Hodgkinson	
G-AOBU	P.84 Jet Provost T.1 (XD693)	T. J. Manna	
G-AOBX	DH.82A Tiger Moth	David Ross Flying Group	
G-AOCP	Auster 5 ★	C. J. Baker (stored)	
G-AOCR	Auster 5D (NJ673)	D. A. Hill	
G-AOCU	Auster 5	S. J. Ball	
G-AODA	Westland S-55 Srs 3 ★	The Helicopter Museum/Weston-super-Mare	
G-AODR	DH.82A Tiger Moth	G-AODR Group (G-ISIS)	
G-AODT	DH.82A Tiger Moth	R. A. Harrowven	
G-AOEH	Aeronca 7AC Champion	A. Gregori	
G-AOEI	DH.82A Tiger Moth	C.F.G. Flying Ltd	
G-AOEL	DH.82A Tiger Moth ★	National Museum of Scotland/Edinburgh	
G-AOES	DH.82A Tiger Moth	P. D. & S. E. Ford	
G-AOET	DH.82A Tiger Moth	P. H. Meeson	
G-AOEX	Thruxton Jackaroo	J. A. Christian	
G-AOFE	DHC.1 Chipmunk 22A (WB702)	W. J. Quinn	
G-AOFS	Auster J/5L Aiglet Trainer	P. N. A. Whitehead	
G-AOGA	M.75 Aries ★	Irish Aviation Museum (stored)	
G-AOGI	DH.82A Tiger Moth	A. E. Taylor	
G-AOGR	DH.82A Tiger Moth (XL714)	R. J. S. G. Clark	
G-AOGV	Auster J/5R Alpine	R. E. Heading	
G-AOHY	DH.82A Tiger Moth (N6537)	S. W. Turley	
G-AOHZ	Auster J/5P Autocar	R. W. Eaton	
G-AOIM	DH.82A Tiger Moth (T7109)	D. A. Burns	
G-AOIR	Thruxton Jackaroo	Aero Legends Leasing Ltd	
G-AOIS	DH.82A Tiger Moth (R5172)	The London Aerobatic Company Ltd	
G-AOJH	DH.83C Fox Moth	Connect Properties Ltd	
G-AOJJ	DH.82A Tiger Moth (DF128)	JJ Flying Group	
G-AOJK	DH.82A Tiger Moth	P. L. Green	
G-AOJT	DH.106 Comet 1 (F-BGNX) ★	De Havilland Heritage Museum (fuselage only)	
G-AOKH	P.40 Prentice 1	J. F. Moore	
G-AOKL	P.40 Prentice 1 (VS610)	N. J. Butler	
G-AOKO	P.40 Prentice 1 ★	Aero Venture	
G-AOKZ	P.40 Prentice 1 (VS623) ★	Midland Air Museum/Coventry	
G-AOLK	P.40 Prentice 1 ★	RAF Museum	
G-AOLU	P.40 Prentice 1	N. J. Butler	
G-AORG	DH.114 Heron 2	Jersey Airlines Ltd	
G-AORW	DHC.1 Chipmunk 22A	S. Maric	
G-AOSK	DHC.1 Chipmunk 22 (WB726)	P. McMillan	
G-AOSY	DHC.1 Chipmunk 22 (WB585:M)	AOSY Group	
G-AOTD	DHC.1 Chipmunk 22 (WB588)	S. Piech	

Notes	Reg	Type	Owner or Operator
	G-AOTF	DHC.1 Chipmunk 23 (Lycoming)	Buckminster Gliding Club Ltd
	G-AOTI	DH.114 Heron 2D ★	De Havilland Heritage Museum/London Colney
	G-AOTK	D.53 Turbi	J. S. & P. R. Johnson
	G-AOTR	DHC.1 Chipmunk 22	S. J. Sykes
	G-AOTY	DHC.1 Chipmunk 22A (WG472)	Retro Track & Air (UK) Ltd
	G-AOUJ	Fairey Ultra-Light ★	IHM/Weston-super-Mare
	G-AOUO	DHC.1 Chipmunk 22 ★	The Aeroplane Collection/Hooton Park
	G-AOUP	DHC.1 Chipmunk 22	A. R. Harding
	G-AOUR	DH.82A Tiger Moth ★	Ulster Folk & Transport Museum
	G-AOVF	B.175 Britannia 312F (XM497) ★	RAF Museum/Cosford
	G-AOVT	B.175 Britannia 312F ★	Imperial War Museum/Duxford
	G-AOVW	Auster 5	C. W. Tattershall
	G-AOXL	DHC.114 Heron 2D ★	Croydon Airport Visitor Centre
	G-AOXN	DH.82A Tiger Moth	S. L. G. Darch
	G-AOZE	Westland Widgeon 2 ★	The Helicopter Museum/Weston-super-Mare
	G-AOZH	DH.82A Tiger Moth (K2572)	The Frensham Tiger Company Ltd
	G-AOZL	Auster J/5Q Alpine	R. M. Weeks
	G-AOZP	DHC.1 Chipmunk 22	S. J. Davies
	G-APAF	Auster 5 (TW511)	C. S. Randall (G-CMAL)
	G-APAH	Auster 5	T. J. Goodwin
	G-APAJ	Thruxton Jackaroo	A. J. Perry
	G-APAL	DH.82A Tiger Moth (N6847)	P. J. Shotbolt
	G-APAM	DH.82A Tiger Moth	R. P. Williams
	G-APAO	DH.82A Tiger Moth (R4922)	H. J. Maguire
	G-APAP	DH.82A Tiger Moth (R5136)	S. E. Ford
	G-APAS	DH.106 Comet 1XB ★	RAF Museum/Cosford
	G-APBE	Auster 5	J. G. Langley & S. C. Cooper
	G-APBI	DH.82A Tiger Moth	C. J. Zeal
	G-APBO	D.53 Turbi	R. C. Hibberd
	G-APBW	Auster 5	N. Huxtable
	G-APCB	Auster J/5Q Alpine	A. A. Beswick
	G-APDB	DH.106 Comet 4 ★	Imperial War Museum/Duxford
	G-APEP	V.953C Merchantman ★	Brooklands Museum of Aviation/Weybridge
	G-APFA	D.54 Turbi	B. L. Procter, M. B. Blackmore & D. Silsbury
	G-APFJ	Boeing 707-436 ★	Museum of Flight/East Fortune
	G-APFU	DH.82A Tiger Moth	C. L. Griffiths
	G-APFV	PA-23-160 Apache	J. L. Thorogood (G-MOLY)
	G-APHV	Avro 19 Srs 2 (VM360) ★	Museum of Flight/East Fortune
	G-APIE	Tipsy Belfair B	D. Beale
	G-APIK	Auster J/1N Alpha	A. Bell
	G-APIM	V.806 Viscount ★	Brooklands Museum of Aviation/Weybridge
	G-APIT	P.40 Prentice 1 (VR192) ★	WWII Aircraft Preservation Society/Lasham
	G-APIY	P.40 Prentice 1 (VR249) ★	Newark Air Museum
	G-APIZ	D.31 Turbulent	Ranfurly Flying Group
	G-APJB	P.40 Prentice 1 (VR259)	Aero Legends Leasing Ltd
	G-APJJ	Fairey Ultra-light ★	Midland Air Museum/Coventry
	G-APJZ	Auster J/1N Alpha	H. A. Jones
	G-APLG	Auster J/5L Aiglet Trainer ★	Solway Aviation Museum/Carlisle
	G-APLK	Miles M.100 Student ★	Museum of Berkshire Aviation/Woodley
	G-APLO	DHC.1 Chipmunk 22A (WD379)	P. M. Luijken/Netherlands
	G-APLU	DH.82A Tiger Moth	M. E. Vaisey
	G-APMH	Auster J/1U Workmaster	M. R. P. Thorogood
	G-APMX	DH.82A Tiger Moth	Tiger Air Group
	G-APMY	PA-23-160 Apache ★	South Yorkshire Aircraft Museum/Doncaster
	G-APNJ	Cessna 310 ★	Newark Air Museum/Newark
	G-APNT	Currie Wot	S. Slater
	G-APNZ	D.31 Turbulent	Turbulent G-APNZ Preservation Society
	G-APOI	Westland Skeeter 8 ★	Solent Sky Museum/Southampton
	G-APPA	DHC.1 Chipmunk 22	H G Flight Training
	G-APPL	P.40 Prentice 1	A. J. Palmer
	G-APPM	DHC.1 Chipmunk 22 (WB711)	E. H. W. Moore
	G-APRL	AW.650 Argosy 101 ★	Midland Air Museum/Coventry
	G-APRO	Auster 6A	A. F. & H. Wankowski
	G-APRT	Taylor JT.1 Monoplane ★	Newark Air Museum/Newark
	G-APSA	Douglas DC-6A ★	South Wales Aviation Museum
	G-APSR	Auster J/1U Workmaster	W. Mellaerts/Belgium
	G-APTR	Auster J/1N Alpha	C. R. Shipley
	G-APTU	Auster 5	G-APTU Flying Group
	G-APTW	Westland WS-51/2 Widgeon ★	North East Land Sea and Air Museum/Sunderland
	G-APTZ	D.31 Turbulent	R. A. H. Vary

Reg	Type	Owner or Operator	Notes
G-APUD	Bensen B.7M (modified) ★	The Aeroplane Collection/Hooton Park	
G-APUE	L.40 Meta Sokol	I. Tvrdik	
G-APUG	Luton LA-5 Minor ★	Norfolk and Suffolk Aviation Museum/Flixton	
G-APUP	Sopwith Pup (replica) (N5182) ★	RAF Museum/Hendon	
G-APUW	Auster J/5V-160 Autocar	E. S. E. & P. B. Hibbard	
G-APUY	D.31 Turbulent	A. Parnell	
G-APVG	Auster J/5L Aiglet Trainer	R. E. Tyers	
G-APVN	D.31 Turbulent	R. Sherwin	
G-APVS	Cessna 170B	B. D. Murphy	
G-APVT	DH.82A Tiger Moth	M. C. Boddington	
G-APVU	L.40 Meta Sokol	S. E. & M. J. Aherne	
G-APVV	Mooney M.20A ★	Newark Air Museum/Newark	
G-APVZ	D.31 Turbulent	The Tiger Club (1990) Ltd	
G-APWA	HPR.7 Herald 101 ★	Museum of Berkshire Aviation/Woodley	
G-APWJ	HPR.7 Herald 201 ★	Morayvia Sci-Tech Experience Project/Kinloss	
G-APWN	Westland WS-55 Whirlwind 3 ★	Midland Air Museum/Coventry	
G-APWY	Piaggio P.166 ★	Science Museum/Wroughton	
G-APXJ	PA-24-250 Comanche	T. Wildsmith	
G-APXR	PA-22-160 Tri-Pacer	A. & K. A. Troughton	
G-APXT	PA-22-150 Tri-Pacer (modified)	A. D. A. Smith	
G-APXU	PA-22-125 Tri-Pacer (modified)	L. Mariscotti	
G-APXW	EP.9 Prospector (XM819) ★	Museum of Army Flying/Middle Wallop	
G-APXX	DHA.3 Drover 2 (VH-FDT) ★	WWII Aircraft Preservation Society/Lasham	
G-APYB	Tipsy T.66 Nipper 3	B. O. Smith	
G-APYD	DH.106 Comet 4B ★	Science Museum/Wroughton	
G-APYG	DHC.1 Chipmunk 22	J. M. Doyle	
G-APYT	Champion 7FC Tri-Traveller	N. F. O'Neill	
G-APZJ	PA-18-150 Super Cub	S. G. Jones	
G-APZL	PA-22-160 Tri-Pacer	B. Robins	
G-ARAD	Luton LA-5 Major ★	North East Land Sea and Air Museum/Sunderland	
G-ARAM	PA-18-150 Super Cub	A. Richards	
G-ARAN	PA-18-150 Super Cub	G-ARAN Group	
G-ARAP	Champion 7EC	J. McCullough	
G-ARAS	Champion 7FC Tri-Traveller	G. J. Taylor	
G-ARAW	Cessna 182C	Sky Banner Ltd	
G-ARAX	PA-22-150 Tri-Pacer	C. W. Carnall	
G-ARAZ	DH.82A Tiger Moth (R4959:59)	Avalon Adventures Ltd	
G-ARBE	DH.104 Dove 8 ★	East Midlands Aeropark	
G-ARBG	Tipsy T.66 Nipper 2	D. Shrimpton	
G-ARBM	Auster V J1B Aiglet	A. D. Hodgkinson	
G-ARBS	PA-22-160 Tri-Pacer (tailwheel)	S. D. Rowell	
G-ARBZ	D.31 Turbulent	G-ARBZ Group	
G-ARCF	PA-22-150 Tri-Pacer	T. A. Hodges	
G-ARCS	Auster D6/180	L. I. Bailey	
G-ARCV	Cessna 175A	J. R. Campbell	
G-ARCW	PA-23-160 Apache	F. W. Ellis	
G-ARCX	A.W. Meteor 14 ★	Museum of Flight/East Fortune	
G-ARDB	PA-24-250 Comanche	D. Silenskyte	
G-ARDD	CP.301C1 Emeraude	B. L. R. J. Keeping & R. N. R. Bellamy	
G-ARDE	DH.104 Dove 6 ★	T. E. Evans	
G-ARDJ	Auster D.6/180	P. N. A. Whitehead	
G-ARDO	Jodel D.112	W. R. & J. P. K. Prescott	
G-ARDS	PA-22-150 Caribbean	W. S. Gilbert	
G-ARDY	Tipsy T.66 Nipper 2	J. K. Davies	
G-ARDZ	Jodel D.140A	G-ARDZ Flying Group	
G-AREA	DH.104 Dove 8 ★	De Havilland Heritage Museum/London Colney	
G-AREH	DH.82A Tiger Moth	A. J. Hastings & A. Mustard	
G-AREI	Auster 3 (MT438)	C. J. Salter	
G-AREL	PA-22-150 Caribbean	The Caribbean Flying Club	
G-AREO	PA-18-150 Super Cub	E. P. Parkin	
G-ARET	PA-22-160 Tri-Pacer	W. S. Gilbert	
G-AREX	Aeronca 15AC Sedan	R. J. M. Turnbull	
G-AREZ	D.31 Turbulent	C. M. Bracewell	
G-ARFD	PA-22-160 Tri-Pacer	T. J. Alderdice	
G-ARFO	Cessna 150A	P. M. Fawley	
G-ARFT	Jodel DR.1050	A. G. & J. C. Shaw	
G-ARFV	Tipsy T.66 Nipper 2	J. J. Austin	
G-ARGB	Auster 6A ★	The Aeroplane Collection/Hooton Park	
G-ARGO	PA-22-108 Colt	I. J. Perry	

Notes	Reg	Type	Owner or Operator
	G-ARGV	PA-18-180 Super Cub	Wolds Gliding Club Ltd
	G-ARGZ	D.31 Turbulent	The Tiger Club (1990) Ltd
	G-ARHB	Forney F-1A Aircoupe	K. W. South
	G-ARHC	Forney F-1A Aircoupe	E. G. Girardey
	G-ARHL	PA-23-250 Aztec	C. J. Freeman
	G-ARHM	Auster 6A (VF557:H)	R. C. P. Brookhouse
	G-ARHR	PA-22-150 Caribbean	A. R. Wyatt
	G-ARHX	DH.104 Dove 8 ★	South Yorkshire Aircraft Museum/Doncaster
	G-ARHZ	D.62 Condor	B. R. Hunter
	G-ARIF	Ord-Hume O-H.7 Minor Coupé ★	M. J. Aubrey
	G-ARIK	PA-22-150 Caribbean	A. Taylor
	G-ARIL	PA-22-150 Caribbean	S. Eustathiou
	G-ARIM	D.31 Turbulent	S. R. P. Harper
	G-ARJS	PA-23-160G Apache	Bencray Ltd
	G-ARJT	PA-23-160G Apache	Peace Guest House Ltd
	G-ARJU	PA-23-160G Apache	I. C. Marshall
	G-ARKG	Auster J/5G Autocar (A11-301/931)	J. M. Fulton & P. D. G. Grist
	G-ARKJ	Beech N35 Bonanza	G. D. E. Macdonald
	G-ARKK	PA-22-108 Colt	R. D. Welfare
	G-ARKM	PA-22-108 Colt	G. D. Williamson
	G-ARKP	PA-22-108 Colt	G. Williamson
	G-ARKS	PA-22-108 Colt	Pure Aviation Support Services Ltd
	G-ARLG	Auster D.4/108	A. P. Barber
	G-ARLK	PA-24-250 Comanche	R. P. Jackson
	G-ARLR	Beagle A.61 Terrier 2	M. Palfreman
	G-ARLU	Cessna 172B ★	Instructional airframe/Irish Air Corps Museum/Baldonnel
	G-ARLZ	D.31A Turbulent	B. W. Faulkner
	G-ARMC	DHC.1 Chipmunk 22 (WB703)	DHC-1 Ltd
	G-ARMF	DHC.1 Chipmunk 22A (WG322:H)	M. Harvey
	G-ARMG	DHC.1 Chipmunk 22A (WK558:DH)	PGM Partners
	G-ARMN	Cessna 175B	B. C. Faulkner
	G-ARMO	Cessna 172B	R. D. Leigh
	G-ARMR	Cessna 172B	C. N. Kriel
	G-ARMZ	D.31 Turbulent	The Tiger Club (1990) Ltd
	G-ARNE	PA-22-108 Colt	G-ARNE Group
	G-ARNG	PA-22-108 Colt	D. Lamb
	G-ARNJ	PA-22-108 Colt	R. A. Keech
	G-ARNK	PA-22-108 Colt	S. Armstrong & D. A. Gathercole
	G-ARNO	Beagle A.61 Terrier 1 (VX113)	J. L. Sparks
	G-ARNP	Beagle A.109 Airedale	S. W. & M. Isbister
	G-ARNY	Jodel D.117	P. W. Armstrong
	G-AROA	Cessna 172B	VuJV24 Ltd
	G-AROW	Jodel D.140B	J. P. M. & P. M. White
	G-AROY	Boeing Stearman A75N.1	J. S. Mann
	G-ARPH	HS.121 Trident 1C ★	National Museum of Flight/East Fortune (cockpit only)
	G-ARPO	HS.121 Trident 1C ★	North East Land Sea and Air Museum/Sunderland
	G-ARPP	HS.121 Trident 1C ★	Solway Aviation Museum/Carlisle (cockpit only)
	G-ARRD	Jodel DR.1050	R. J. Arnold
	G-ARRE	Jodel DR.1050	R. Weininger
	G-ARRI	Cessna 175B	R. J. Bentley
	G-ARRK	Taylorcraft Plus D (LB286)	D. J. Baker (G-AHUM)
	G-ARRL	Auster J/1N Alpha	G-ARRL Group LLP
	G-ARRM	Beagle B.206-X ★	Aeropark/East Midlands
	G-ARRS	CP.301A Emeraude	J. F. Sully
	G-ARRX	Auster 6A (VF512)	W. R. Pickett
	G-ARRY	Jodel D.140B	C. Thomas
	G-ARRZ	D.31 Turbulent	T. A. Stambach
	G-ARSG	Roe Triplane Type IV (replica)	The Shuttleworth Collection/Old Warden
	G-ARTH	PA-12 Super Cruiser	G. R. Trotter
	G-ARTJ	Bensen B.8M ★	Museum of Flight/East Fortune
	G-ARTL	DH.82A Tiger Moth (T7281)	J. J. Hill
	G-ARTM	Beagle A.61 Terrier I	R. G. Callaway-Lewis
	G-ARTT	MS.880B Rallye Club	R. N. Scott
	G-ARUG	Auster J/5G Autocar	D. P. H. Hulme
	G-ARUI	Beagle A.61 Terrier	T. W. J. Dann
	G-ARUL	LeVier Cosmic Wind	P. G. Kynsey
	G-ARUY	Auster J/1N Alpha	D. K. Tregilgas
	G-ARVM	V.1101 VC10 ★	Brooklands Museum of Aviation/Weybridge

Reg	Type	Owner or Operator	Notes
G-ARVN	Servotec Grasshopper ★	The Helicopter Museum/Weston-super-Mare	
G-ARVO	PA-18-95 Super Cub	M. P. & S. T. Barnard	
G-ARVU	PA-28-160 Cherokee	Vu JV43 Ltd	
G-ARVV	PA-28-160 Cherokee	Karusha Ltd	
G-ARVZ	D.62B Condor	A. A. M. Huke	
G-ARWB	DHC.1 Chipmunk 22 (WK611)	Thruxton Chipmunk Flying Club	
G-ARWR	Cessna 172C	Devanha Flying Group	
G-ARWS	Cessna 175C	M. D. Fage	
G-ARXD	Beagle A.109 Airedale	D. Howden	
G-ARXG	PA-24-250 Comanche	J. M. Drew-Williams	
G-ARXH	Bell 47G	T. B. Searle	
G-ARXP	Luton LA-4 Minor	R. M. Weeks	
G-ARXT	Jodel DR.1050	CJM Flying Group	
G-ARXU	Auster 6A (VF526)	S. D. & S. P. Allen	
G-ARYB	HS.125 Srs 1 ★	Midland Air Museum/Coventry	
G-ARYC	HS.125 Srs 1 ★	De Havilland Heritage Museum/London Colney	
G-ARYD	Auster AOP.6 (WJ358) ★	Museum of Army Flying/Middle Wallop	
G-ARYK	Cessna 172C	Garys Flying Group	
G-ARYR	PA-28-180 Cherokee	T. W. Gilbert	
G-ARYS	Cessna 172C	Garys Flying Group	
G-ARYZ	Beagle A.109 Airedale ★	South Yorkshire Aircraft Museum/Doncaster	
G-ARZW	Currie Wot	B. R. Pearson	
G-ASAA	Luton LA-4 Minor	M. J. Aubrey (stored)	
G-ASAI	Beagle A.109 Airedale	K. R. Howden	
G-ASAJ	Beagle A.61 Terrier 2 (WE569)	C. R. Shipley	
G-ASAL	SA Bulldog Srs 120/124	Pioneer Flying Co Ltd	
G-ASAT	MS.880B Rallye Club ★	City of Norwich Aviation Museum/Norwich	
G-ASAX	Beagle A.61 Terrier 2	A. D. Hodgkinson	
G-ASBA	Phoenix Currie Wot	K. Higbee	
G-ASBH	Beagle A.109 Airedale	D. T. Smollett	
G-ASCC	Beagle E3 Mk 11 (XP254)	R. J. Ellingworth, N. M. Goodacre & N. A. Whatling	
G-ASCD	Beagle A.61 Terrier 2 (VW993) ★	The Aeroplane Collection/Hooton Park	
G-ASCH	Beagle A.61 Terrier 2	D. S. Wilkinson	
G-ASCM	Isaacs Fury II (K2050)	P. J. Shenton	
G-ASCT	Bensen B.7M ★	The Helicopter Museum/Weston-super-Mare	
G-ASCZ	CP.301A Emeraude	J. J. Hill	
G-ASDF	Edwards Gyrocopter ★	M. J. Aubrey	
G-ASDK	Beagle A.61 Terrier 2	J. Swallow (G-ARLM)	
G-ASEA	Luton LA-4A Minor	M. W. Collington	
G-ASEB	Luton LA-4A Minor	S. R. P. Harper	
G-ASEJ	PA-28-180 Cherokee B	Perranporth Pilots Group	
G-ASEO	PA-24-250 Comanche	M. E. Scott	
G-ASEP	PA-23-235 Apache	J. R. Upex	
G-ASEU	D.62A Condor	R. A. S. Sutherland	
G-ASFL	PA-28-180 Cherokee	G-ASFL Group	
G-ASFR	Bölkow Bö.208A1 Junior	S. T. Dauncey	
G-ASFX	D.31 Turbulent	E. F. Clapham & T. A. Wilcox	
G-ASGC	V.1151 Super VC-10 ★	Imperial War Museum/Duxford	
G-ASHD	Brantly B.2A ★	The Helicopter Museum/Weston-super-Mare	
G-ASHS	SNCAN Stampe SV.4C	J. W. Beaty	
G-ASHT	D.31 Turbulent	C. W. N. Huke	
G-ASHU	PA-15 Vagabond (modified)	V. R. Dennay	
G-ASHX	PA-28-180 Cherokee	Powertheme Ltd	
G-ASII	PA-28-180 Cherokee	T. N. & T. R. Hart & R. W. S. Matthews	
G-ASIJ	PA-28-180 Cherokee	Vu JV43 Ltd	
G-ASIL	PA-28-180 Cherokee	R. Pink	
G-ASIS	Jodel D.112	W. R. & J. P. K. Prescott	
G-ASIT	Cessna 180	A. P. Rouse	
G-ASIY	PA-25-235 Pawnee	Kent Gliding Club Ltd	
G-ASJV	VS.361 Spitfire IX (MH434/PK-K)	Merlin Aviation Ltd	
G-ASJZ	Jodel D.117A	E. L. Watts	
G-ASKC	DH.98 Mosquito 35 (TA719) ★	Skyfame Collection/Duxford	
G-ASKK	HPR.7 Herald 211 ★	City of Norwich Aviation Museum/Norwich	
G-ASKL	Jodel D.150	A. T. D. Robertson	
G-ASKP	DH.82A Tiger Moth	Tiger Club (1990) Ltd	
G-ASKT	PA-28-180 Cherokee	T. A & D. W. Herbert	
G-ASMA	PA-30 Twin Comanche 160 C/R	K. Cooper	
G-ASME	Bensen B8M	J. W. Cope	
G-ASMJ	Cessna F.172E	N. Hempel	
G-ASML	Luton LA-4A Minor	O. D. Lewis	

Notes	Reg	Type	Owner or Operator
	G-ASMM	D.31 Tubulent	K. J. Butler
	G-ASMS	Cessna 150A	C. P. Davies
	G-ASMT	Fairtravel Linnet 2	J. J. Hill
	G-ASMV	CP.1310-C3 Super Emeraude	D. G. Hammersley
	G-ASMW	Cessna 150D	Skydive St. Andrews Ltd
	G-ASMY	PA-23-160 Apache ★	R. D. Forster
	G-ASMZ	Beagle A.61 Terrier 2 (VF516)	Chipmunk WD292 Ltd
	G-ASNC	Beagle D.5/180 Husky	Peterborough & Spalding Gliding Club Ltd
	G-ASNK	Cessna 205	Justgold Ltd
	G-ASNW	Cessna F.172E	G-ASNW Group
	G-ASNY	Campbell-Bensen B.8M gyroplane ★	Newark Air Museum/Newark
	G-ASOH	Beech 95-B55A Baron	A. A. Mattacks
	G-ASOI	Beagle A.61 Terrier 2 (WJ404)	G.D.B. Delmege
	G-ASOK	Cessna F.172E	R. A. Evans
	G-ASOL	Bell 47D ★	North East Land Sea and Air Museum/Sunderland
	G-ASOM	Beagle A.61 Terrier 2	GASOM.org (G-JETS)
	G-ASPF	Jodel D.120	Devon D120 Group
	G-ASPP	Bristol Boxkite (replica)	The Shuttleworth Collection/Old Warden
	G-ASPS	Piper J-3C-90 Cub	Delta Juliett Bravo Ltd
	G-ASPV	DH.82A Tiger Moth (T7794)	Oldstead Aero LLP
	G-ASRC	D.62C Condor	D. Bowman & B. Smee
	G-ASRF	Gowland Jenny Wren ★	Norfolk and Suffolk Aviation Museum/Flixton
	G-ASRK	Beagle A.109 Airedale	M. Wilson
	G-ASRO	PA-30-160 Twin Comanche	Five Star Flying Group
	G-ASRT	Jodel 150	P. Turton
	G-ASRW	PA-28-180 Cherokee	R. M. Davies
	G-ASSM	HS.125 Srs 1/522 ★	Science Museum/South Kensington
	G-ASSP	PA-30-160 Twin Comanche	L. R. Colman
	G-ASSS	Cessna 172E	P. R. & A. P. March t/a Triple Sierra Flying Group
	G-ASSV	Kensinger KF	C. I. Jefferson
	G-ASSY	D.31 Turbulent	D. E. Hall
	G-ASTG	Nord 1002 Pingouin II (BG + KM)	R. J. Fray
	G-ASTI	Auster 6A	J. A. Rayment & D. S. McKay
	G-ASTL	Fairey Firefly I (Z2033) ★	F.A. A. Museum/Yeovilton
	G-ASTP	Hiller UH-12C ★	The Helicopter Museum/Weston-super-Mare
	G-ASUB	Mooney M.20E Super 21	S. C. Coulbeck
	G-ASUD	PA-28-180 Cherokee	G-ASUD Group
	G-ASUE	Cessna 150D	D. Huckle
	G-ASUG	Beech E18S ★	Museum of Flight/East Fortune
	G-ASUP	Cessna F.172E	A. M. Moore
	G-ASUS	Jurca MJ.2B Tempete	D. J. Millin & R. E. Hughes
	G-ASVG	CP.301B Emeraude	C. M. Knight
	G-ASVM	Cessna F.172E	M. Tobutt
	G-ASVO	HPR.7 Herald 214 ★	Morayvia Sci-Tech Experience Project/Kinloss (cockpit section)
	G-ASVZ	PA-28-140 Cherokee	Scillonian Marine Consultants Ltd
	G-ASWE	Bolkow Bo.208A2 Junior	Bolkow Group (G-CLEM)
	G-ASWJ	Beagle 206 Srs 1 (8449M) ★	Midland Air Museum/Coventry
	G-ASWX	PA-28-180 Cherokee	Gasworks Flying Group Ltd
	G-ASXD	Brantly B.2B	G-ASXD Group
	G-ASXS	Jodel DR.1050	C. P. Wilkinson
	G-ASXU	Jodel D.120A	P. B. Davey
	G-ASXX	Avro 683 Lancaster 7 (NX611) ★	Panton Family Trust/East Kirkby
	G-ASYD	BAC One-Eleven 475 ★	Brooklands Museum of Aviation/Weybridge
	G-ASYG	Beagle A.61 Terrier 2 (VX927)	I. R. Caesar
	G-ASYP	Cessna 150E	Henlow Flying Group
	G-ASZD	Bölkow Bö.208A2 Junior	S. L. Wilkes
	G-ASZR	Fairtravel Linnet 2	R. Hodgson
	G-ASZU	Cessna 150E	North East Aviation Training Ltd
	G-ASZV	Tipsy T.66 Nipper 2	A. M. E. Vervaeke/Belgium
	G-ASZX	Beagle A.61 Terrier 1 (WJ368)	C. J. Beazley
	G-ATAS	PA-28-180 Cherokee	M. Khoshkhou
	G-ATBG	Nord 1002 (NJ+C11)	Ardmore Aviation Service
	G-ATBH	Aero 145	P. D. Aberbach
	G-ATBL	DH.60G Moth	Comanche Warbirds Ltd
	G-ATBP	Fournier RF-3	D. McNicholl
	G-ATBS	D.31 Turbulent	C. J. L. Wolf
	G-ATBU	Beagle A.61 Terrier 2	T. Jarvis

Reg	Type	Owner or Operator	Notes
G-ATBX	PA-20-135 Pacer	G. D. & P. M. Thomson	
G-ATBZ	Westland WS-58 Wessex 60 ★	The Helicopter Museum/Weston-super-Mare	
G-ATCC	Beagle A.109 Airedale	North East Flight Training Ltd	
G-ATCD	Beagle D.5/180 Husky	M. Stewart	
G-ATCJ	Luton LA-4A Minor	A. R. Hutton	
G-ATCN	Luton LA-4A Minor	The Real Aeroplane Co.Ltd	
G-ATDA	PA-28-160 Cherokee	Henstridge Airfield Ltd	
G-ATDN	Beagle A.61 Terrier 2 (TW641)	A. J. Palmer	
G-ATDO	Bölkow Bö.208C1 Junior	P. Thompson	
G-ATEF	Cessna 150E	Swans Aviation	
G-ATEM	PA-28-180 Cherokee	G. D. Wyles	
G-ATEP	EAA Biplane ★	E. L. Martin (red)/Guernsey	
G-ATEV	Jodel DR.1050	J. C. Carter & J. L. Altrip	
G-ATEX	Victor Airtourer 100	S. Turner	
G-ATEZ	PA-28-140 Cherokee	EFI Aviation Ltd	
G-ATFD	Jodel DR.1050	K. D. Hills	
G-ATFG	Brantly B.2B ★	The Helicopter Museum/Weston-super-Mare	
G-ATFY	Cessna F.172G	J. M. Vinall	
G-ATGN	Thorn Coal Gas Balloon	British Balloon Museum/Newbury	
G-ATGP	Jodel DR.1050	Madley Flying Group	
G-ATGY	Gardan GY-80 Horizon	D. H. Mackay	
G-ATHD	DHC.1 Chipmunk 22	O. L. Cubitt	
G-ATHK	Aeronca 7AC Champion	T. C. Barron	
G-ATHR	PA-28-180 Cherokee	Azure Flight Training Centre	
G-ATHT	Victa Airtourer 115	Cotswold Flying Group	
G-ATHU	Beagle A.61 Terrier 1	J. A. L. Irwin	
G-ATHV	Cessna 150F	Air Navgation & Trading Co.Ltd	
G-ATHZ	Cessna 150F	R. D. Forster	
G-ATIC	Jodel DR.1050	T. A. Major	
G-ATIN	Jodel D.117	C. E. C. & C. M. Hives	
G-ATIR	AIA Stampe SV.4C	A. Trueman	
G-ATIS	PA-28-160 Cherokee	S. W. Hannigan	
G-ATIZ	Jodel D.117	A. R. Hardwick	
G-ATJA	Jodel DR.1050	S. L. Childs	
G-ATJC	Victa Airtourer 100	Aviation West Ltd	
G-ATJG	PA-28-140 Cherokee	D. & J. Albon	
G-ATJL	PA-24-260 Comanche	R. M. Lawson	
G-ATJN	Jodel D.119	Real Hart Flying Group	
G-ATJV	PA-32-260 Cherokee Six	Wingglider Ltd	
G-ATKH	Luton LA-4A Minor	H. E. Jenner	
G-ATKI	Piper J-3C-65 Cub	M. B. Blackmore	
G-ATKT	Cessna F.172G	S. J. Wearing	
G-ATKX	Jodel D.140C	Kilo Xray Syndicate	
G-ATLA	Cessna 182J Skylane	G. R. Read	
G-ATLB	Jodel DR.1050/M1	Le Syndicate du Petit Oiseau	
G-ATLM	Cessna F.172G	M. Thomson	
G-ATLP	Bensen B.8M	R. F. G. Moyle	
G-ATLT	Cessna U.206A	Skydive Jersey Ltd	
G-ATLV	Jodel D.120	C. V. Conidaris	
G-ATMC	Cessna F.150F	M. Biddulph	
G-ATMH	Beagle D.5/180 Husky	R. E. Tyers	
G-ATNF	Cessna F.150F	T. E. C. Cushing	
G-ATNV	PA-24-260 Comanche	K. Powell	
G-ATOH	D.62B Condor	Three Spires Flying Group	
G-ATOI	PA-28-140 Cherokee	N. & E. J. Padgham	
G-ATOK	PA-28-140 Cherokee	P. Moggridge	
G-ATON	PA-28-140 Cherokee	Sterling Flying Syndicate	
G-ATOO	PA-28-140 Cherokee	Caralair Aviation	
G-ATOP	PA-28-140 Cherokee	P. R. Coombs	
G-ATOR	PA-28-140 Cherokee	S. J. McBride	
G-ATOT	PA-28-180 Cherokee	Vu JV24 Ltd	
G-ATOY	PA-24-260 Comanche ★	Museum of Flight/East Fortune	
G-ATPT	Cessna 182J Skylane	C. Beer t/a Papa Tango Group	
G-ATPV	JB.01 Minicab	S. A. Mayo	
G-ATRG	PA-18-150 Super Cub	Dorset Gliding Club Ltd	
G-ATRK	Cessna F.150F	Falcon Aviation Ltd	
G-ATRL	Cessna F.150F	A. A. W. Stevens	
G-ATRM	Cessna F.150F	North East Aviation Training Ltd	
G-ATRW	PA-32-260 Cherokee Six	H. James	
G-ATRX	PA-32-260 Cherokee Six	S. P. Vincent	
G-ATSI	Bölkow Bö.208C1 Junior	A. N. Schutte	

Notes	Reg	Type	Owner or Operator
	G-ATSL	Cessna F.172G	Cloneygate Flying Group
	G-ATSR	Beech M.35 Bonanza	V. S. E. Norman
	G-ATSZ	PA-30 Twin Comanche 160B	Sierra Zulu Aviation Ltd
	G-ATTB	Wallis WA-116-1 (XR944)	Aerial Media Ltd
	G-ATTI	PA-28-140 Cherokee	A. I. Wilson
	G-ATTN	Piccard HA Balloon ★	Science Museum/South Kensington
	G-ATTR	Bölkow Bö.208C1 Junior	S. Luck
	G-ATTV	PA-28-140 Cherokee	M. Khoshkhou
	G-ATTX	PA-28-180 Cherokee	Brinkley Aircraft Services Ltd
	G-ATUG	D.62B Condor	S. K. Teasdale
	G-ATUH	Tipsy T.66 Nipper 1	H. Abraham
	G-ATUI	Bölkow Bö.208C1 Junior	G. J. Ball
	G-ATVF	DHC.1 Chipmunk 22 (WD327)	ATVF Syndicate
	G-ATVK	PA-28-140 Cherokee	J. Turner
	G-ATVO	PA-28-140 Cherokee	Perryair Ltd
	G-ATVP	Vickers FB.5 Gunbus replica (2345) ★	RAF Museum/Hendon
	G-ATVW	D.62B Condor	J. L. Gerretsen
	G-ATVX	Bölkow Bö.208C1 Junior	Cawdor Flying Group
	G-ATWA	Jodel DR.1050	One Twenty Group
	G-ATWB	Jodel D.117	Andrewsfield Whisky Bravo Group
	G-ATWJ	Cessna F.172F	J. P. A. Freeman
	G-ATXA	PA-22-150 Tri-Pacer	I. C. Mills
	G-ATXD	PA-30-160B Twin Comanche	L. R. Colman
	G-ATXN	Mitchell-Proctor Kittiwake 1	R. G. Day
	G-ATXO	SIPA 903	D. F. Hurn
	G-ATXX	McCandless M.4 gyroplane ★	Ulster Folk & Transport Museum
	G-ATXZ	Bölkow Bö.208C1 Junior	M. J. Beardmore
	G-ATYM	Cessna F.150G	Islander Aircraft Ltd
	G-ATYN	Cessna F.150G	J. S. Grant
	G-ATYS	PA-28-180 Cherokee	Cherokee Challenge Syndicate
	G-ATZM	Piper J-3C-90 Cub	N. D. Marshall
	G-ATZS	Wassmer Wa.41 Super Baladou IV	I. R. Siddell
	G-AVAA	Cessna F.150G ★	South Yorkshire Aircraft Museum/Doncaster
	G-AVAW	D.62B Condor	Condor Aircraft Group
	G-AVBG	PA-28-180 Cherokee	R. J. Fergusson
	G-AVBH	PA-28-180 Cherokee	Tenterfield (Holdings) Ltd
	G-AVBR	PA-28-180 Cherokee	G. Cormack
	G-AVBS	PA-28-180 Cherokee	D. T. Pangbourne
	G-AVCM	PA-24-260 Comanche	R. F. Smith
	G-AVCN	BN-26A-8 Islander ★	Wight Military and Heritage Museum/Isle of Wight
	G-AVCV	Cessna 182J	P. W. Moorcroft
	G-AVDA	Cessna 182K Skylane	Rubric Aviation Ltd
	G-AVDF	Beagle B.121 Pup 1	D. I. Collings
	G-AVDR	Beech 65-B80 Queen Air ★	City of Bristol College Advanced Engineering Centre/Bristol
	G-AVDT	Aeronca 7AC Champion	D. & N. Cheney
	G-AVDV	PA-22-150 Tri-Pacer	L. Beardmore & R. W. Taberner
	G-AVEF	Jodel 150	N. G. Port
	G-AVEH	SIAI-Marchetti S.205	S. W. Brown
	G-AVEM	Cessna F.150G	N. J. A. Rutherford
	G-AVEN	Cessna F.150G	D. Nutt
	G-AVEO	Cessna F.150G	D. N. Sluman (G-DENA)
	G-AVER	Cessna F.150G	LAC Flying School
	G-AVEU	Wassmer Wa.41 Baladou IV	The Baladou Flying Group
	G-AVEX	D.62B Condor	Prestwick Tailwheel Group
	G-AVEY	Currie Super Wot	F. R. Donaldson
	G-AVFB	HS.121 Trident 2E ★	Imperial War Museum/Duxford
	G-AVFE	HS.121 Trident 2E ★	Belfast Airport Authority
	G-AVFH	HS.121 Trident 2E ★	De Havilland Heritage Museum /London Colney (fuselage only)
	G-AVFM	HS.121 Trident 2E ★	South Wales Aviation Museum/St. Athan
	G-AVFR	PA-28-140 Cherokee	M. Khalid
	G-AVFX	PA-28-140 Cherokee	J. Allan
	G-AVFZ	PA-28-140 Cherokee	G-AVFZ Flying Group
	G-AVGA	PA-24-260 Comanche	G. McD. Moir
	G-AVGC	PA-28-140 Cherokee	L. McIlwain
	G-AVGE	PA-28-140 Cherokee	I. Denham-Brown
	G-AVGJ	Jodel DR.1050	I. B. Melville
	G-AVGZ	Jodel DR.1050	A. F. & S. Williams
	G-AVHH	Cessna F.172	Alpha Victor Ltd

Reg	Type	Owner or Operator	Notes
G-AVHL	Jodel DR.105A	Seething Jodel Group	
G-AVHM	Cessna F.150G	R. D. Forster	
G-AVHY	Fournier RF.4D	I. G. K. Mitchell	
G-AVIB	Cessna F.150G	K. W. Wood	
G-AVIL	Alon A.2 Aircoupe (VX147)	Lawrence Hawthorne Group	
G-AVIN	MS.880B Rallye Club	R. A. C. Stephens	
G-AVIP	Brantly B.2B	Eaglescott Brantly Group	
G-AVIS	Cessna F.172	J. P. A. Freeman	
G-AVIT	Cessna F.150G	J. W. Summers	
G-AVJF	Cessna F.172H	Poyston Aviation	
G-AVJJ	PA-30-160B Twin Comanche	P. M. Jones	
G-AVJK	Jodel DR.1050/M1	Juliet Kilo Syndicate	
G-AVJO	Fokker E.III (replica) (422/15)	Flying Aces Movie Aircraft Collection	
G-AVKB	Brochet MB.50 Pipistrelle	R. E. Garforth	
G-AVKD	Fournier RF-4D	Lasham RF4 Group	
G-AVKE	Gadfly HDW.1 ★	The Helicopter Museum/Weston-super-Mare	
G-AVKI	Slingsby T.66 Nipper 3	T. C. R. Trudgill	
G-AVKK	Slingsby T.66 Nipper 3	C. F. O'Neill	
G-AVKP	Beagle A.109 Airedale	R. Callaway-Lewis	
G-AVKR	Bölkow Bö.208C1 Junior	J. E. Chorley	
G-AVLB	PA-28-140 Cherokee	M. Wilson	
G-AVLC	PA-28-140 Cherokee	R. G. Allgood	
G-AVLE	PA-28-140 Cherokee	M. Hill	
G-AVLF	PA-28-140 Cherokee	Woodbine Group	
G-AVLG	PA-28-140 Cherokee	Lima Golf Group	
G-AVLI	PA-28-140 Cherokee	Lima India Aviation Group	
G-AVLJ	PA-28-140 Cherokee	D. B. Le Peurian	
G-AVLM	Beagle B.121 Pup 3	T. M. & D. A. Jones	
G-AVLN	Beagle B.121 Pup 2	Dogs Flying Group	
G-AVLT	PA-28-140 Cherokee	J. L. Sparks (G-KELC)	
G-AVLW	Fournier RF-4D	J. C. A. C. da Silva	
G-AVLY	Jodel D.120A	S. M. S. Smith	
G-AVMA	Gardan GY-80-180 Horizon	Z. R. Hildick	
G-AVMB	D.62B Condor	J. A. P. Vallance	
G-AVMD	Cessna 150G	LAC Flying School	
G-AVMF	Cessna F. 150G	J. F. Marsh	
G-AVMJ	BAC One-Eleven 510ED ★	Tresham College/Kettering (cabin trainer)	
G-AVMO	BAC One-Eleven 510ED ★	National Museum of Flight/East Fortune	
G-AVMU	BAC One-Eleven 510ED ★	Imperial War Museum/Duxford	
G-AVMZ	BAC One-Eleven 510ED ★	Shannon Aviation Museum/Shannon (forward fuselage)	
G-AVNC	Cessna F.150G	J. Turner	
G-AVNE	Westland WS-58 Wessex Mk 60 Srs 1 ★	The Helicopter Museum/Weston-super-Mare	
G-AVNN	PA-28-180 Cherokee	West Yorkshire Aviation	
G-AVNO	PA-28-180 Cherokee	November Oscar Flying Group	
G-AVNS	PA-28-180 Cherokee	Fly (Fu Lai) Aviation Ltd	
G-AVNU	PA-28-180 Cherokee	C. E. Feltwell	
G-AVNW	PA-28-180 Cherokee	R. Loveday	
G-AVNY	Fournier RF-4D	J. B. Giddins (G-IVEL)	
G-AVNZ	Fournier RF-4D	C. D. Pidler	
G-AVOA	Jodel DR.1050	G. Slater	
G-AVOD	Beagle D.5/180 Husky	T. E. Reeder	
G-AVOH	D.62B Condor	The Condor Group	
G-AVOM	CEA Jodel DR.221	W. G. Nutt	
G-AVOO	PA-18-150 Super Cub	Dublin Gliding Club Ltd	
G-AVOU	Slingsby T.56 S.E.5 Replica (C8846/M)	Sywell SE5 Group	
G-AVOZ	PA-28-180 Cherokee	Oscar Zulu Flying Group	
G-AVPC	D.31 Turbulent ★	Museum of Flight/East Fortune	
G-AVPD	Jodel D.9 Bébé ★	S. W. McKay (stored)	
G-AVPI	Cessna F.172H	D. R. Larder	
G-AVPJ	DH.82A Tiger Moth	C. C. Silk	
G-AVPM	Jodel D.117	L. B. Clark	
G-AVPN	HPR.7 Herald 213 ★	Yorkshire Air Museum/Elvington	
G-AVPO	Hindustan HAL-26 Pushpak	Bumble Bee Group	
G-AVPY	PA-25-235C Pawnee	Wolds Gliding Club Ltd	
G-AVRS	Gardan GY-80 Horizon 180	N. M. Robbins	
G-AVRW	Gardan GY-20 Minicab	Kestrel Flying Group	
G-AVRZ	PA-28-180 Cherokee	RZ Group	
G-AVSA	PA-28-180 Cherokee	Easter Flying Group	
G-AVSB	PA-28-180 Cherokee	G. Cormack	
G-AVSD	PA-28-180 Cherokee	VU JV40 Ltd	

Notes	Reg	Type	Owner or Operator
	G-AVSE	PA-28-180 Cherokee	F. Glendon/Ireland
	G-AVSF	PA-28-180 Cherokee	The Monday Club - Blackbushe
	G-AVSI	PA-28-140 Cherokee	G-AVSI Flying Group
	G-AVSP	PA-28-180 Cherokee	G-AVSP Syndicate
	G-AVSR	Beagle D.5/180 Husky	S. D. J. Holwill
	G-AVTC	Slingsby Nipper T.66 RA.45 Srs 3	J. Crawford
	G-AVTP	Cessna F.172H	West London Accounting Ltd
	G-AVTT	Ercoupe 415D ★	South Yorkshire Aircraft Museum/Doncaster
	G-AVUG	Cessna F.150H	Skyways Flying Group
	G-AVUH	Cessna F.150H	A. G. McLaren
	G-AVUO	Luton LA4 Minor	M. W. Collington
	G-AVUS	PA-28-140 Cherokee	AP Asset Holdings Ltd
	G-AVUT	PA-28-140 Cherokee	Bencray Ltd
	G-AVVC	Cessna F.172H	Aereohire Ltd
	G-AVVO	Avro 652A Anson 19 (VL348) ★	Newark Air Museum
	G-AVWA	PA-28-140 Cherokee	Ovin Ltd
	G-AVWD	PA-28-140 Cherokee	R. L. Northover
	G-AVWI	PA-28-140 Cherokee	L. M. Veitch
	G-AVWL	PA-28-140 Cherokee	D. H. Kirkwood
	G-AVWM	PA-28-140 Cherokee	G-AVWM Group
	G-AVWO	PA-28R-180 Cherokee Arrow	D. N. Dunphy
	G-AVWR	PA-28R-180 Cherokee Arrow	V. S. Hussain
	G-AVWT	PA-28R-180 Cherokee Arrow	A. C. Brett
	G-AVWU	PA-28R-180 Cherokee Arrow	M. Ali & S. Din
	G-AVWV	PA-28R-180 Cherokee Arrow	R. V. Thornton
	G-AVWY	Fournier RF-4D	S. A. Blanchard
	G-AVXA	PA-25 Pawnee 235	S. Wales Gliding Club Ltd
	G-AVXD	Slingsby T.66 Nipper 3	P. Archer
	G-AVXF	PA-28R-180 Cherokee Arrow	G-AVXF Group
	G-AVXW	D.62B Condor	C. W. A. Holliday
	G-AVXY	Auster AOP.9	G. J. Siddall
	G-AVYK	Beagle A.61 Terrier 3	R. Burgun
	G-AVYL	PA-28-180 Cherokee	Cotswold Aero Maintenance Ltd
	G-AVYM	PA-28-180 Cherokee	R. A. Danby
	G-AVYS	PA-28R-180 Cherokee Arrow	Kerber Charlesworth Ltd
	G-AVYT	PA-28R-180 Cherokee Arrow	M. Bonsall
	G-AVZB	Aero Z-37 Cmelak ★	Science Museum/Wroughton
	G-AVZP	Beagle B.121 Pup 1	T. A. White
	G-AVZW	EAA Biplane Model P	R. K. Galbally
	G-AWAC	Gardan GY-80 Horizon 180	P. B. Hodgson
	G-AWAJ	Beech 95-D55 Baron	B. F. Whitworth
	G-AWAU	Vickers FB.27A Vimy (replica) (F8614) ★	RAF Museum/Hendon
	G-AWAW	Cessna F.150F ★	Science Museum/South Kensington
	G-AWAX	Cessna 150D	Gee Bee Flying Ltd
	G-AWAZ	PA-28R-180 Cherokee Arrow	General Aero Services Ltd
	G-AWBB	PA-28R-180 Cherokee Arrow	J. G. S. Dowie-Young
	G-AWBC	PA-28R-180 Cherokee Arrow	Anglo Property Services Ltd
	G-AWBG	PA-28-140 Cherokee	G-AWBG140 Group
	G-AWBM	D.31 Turbulent	J. J. B. Leasor
	G-AWBN	PA-30 Twin Comanche B	D. P. Esterson
	G-AWBU	Morane-Saulnier N (replica) (MS824)	Flying Aces Movie Aircraft Collection
	G-AWBX	Cessna F.150H	J. D. C. Lea
	G-AWCM	Cessna F.150H	R. Garbett
	G-AWCN	Cessna FR.172E	S. Coates
	G-AWCP	Cessna F.150H (tailwheel)	G. G. Povey
	G-AWDA	Slingsby T.66 Nipper 3	H. Abraham
	G-AWDO	D.31 Turbulent	R. N. Crosland
	G-AWDU	Brantly B.2B	N. J. M. Freeman
	G-AWEA	Beagle B.121 Pup Srs.1	T. S. Walker
	G-AWEI	D.62B Condor	C. M. Hall & M. J. Davis
	G-AWEK	Fournier RF-4D	M. P. J. Hill
	G-AWEL	Fournier RF-4D	Hallam Aviation Services Ltd
	G-AWEP	Barritault JB-01 Minicab	R. K. Thomas
	G-AWES	Cessna 150H	R. J. Willis
	G-AWEV	PA-28-140 Cherokee	Skysure Aviation Ltd
	G-AWEX	PA-28-140 Cherokee	CBM Associates Consulting Ltd
	G-AWFB	PA-28R-180 Cherokee Arrow	Sparrows SW
	G-AWFC	PA-28R-180 Cherokee Arrow	SAF Prestwick Ltd
	G-AWFD	PA-28R-180 Cherokee Arrow	C. G. Sims
	G-AWFF	Cessna F.150H	C. S. Ray

Reg	Type	Owner or Operator	Notes
G-AWFJ	PA-28R-180 Cherokee Arrow	Stars Fly Ltd	
G-AWFN	D.62B Condor	C. C. Bland	
G-AWFO	D.62B Condor	T. A. Major	
G-AWFP	D.62B Condor	S. J. Westley	
G-AWFT	Jodel D.9 Bébé	W. H. Cole	
G-AWFZ	Beech A23 Musketeer	H. J. King	
G-AWGB	Supermarine Spitfire T.IX (A58-606/ZP-W)	Warbird Experiences Ltd	
G-AWGK	Cessna F.150H	G. E. Allen	
G-AWGM	Mitchell Kittiwake II	P. J. Tanulak	
G-AWGN	Fournier RF-4D	R. J. Grimstead	
G-AWGZ	Taylor JT.1 Monoplane	A. D. Szymanski	
G-AWHC	Hispano HA.1112 M4L (11)	Air Leasing Ltd	
G-AWHH	Hispano HA.1112 M1L (9)	Warbird Experiences Ltd	
G-AWHK	Hispano HA.1112 M1L (10)	Fly to Inspire Ltd (G-BWUE)	
G-AWHX	Rollason Beta B.2	T. Jarvis	
G-AWII	VS.349 Spitfire VC (AR501:DU-E)	The Shuttleworth Collection	
G-AWIV	Airmark TSR.3	J. A. Wardlow	
G-AWIW	SNCAN Stampe SV.4B	R. E. Mitchell	
G-AWJE	Slingsby T.66 Nipper 3	R. H. Cooper	
G-AWJV	DH.98 Mosquito TT Mk 35 (TA634) ★	De Havilland Heritage Museum/London Colney	
G-AWJX	Zlin Z.526 Trener Master	M. Baer	
G-AWKD	PA-17 Vagabond	Kilo Delta Flying Group	
G-AWKO	Beagle B.121 Pup 1	Osprey Group	
G-AWKP	Jodel DR.253	G-AWKP Group	
G-AWKX	Beech A65 Queen Air ★	(Instructional airframe)/Shoreham	
G-AWLF	Cessna F.172H	C. Robb	
G-AWLG	SIPA 903	S. W. Markham	
G-AWLO	Boeing Stearman E75	N. D. Pickard	
G-AWLP	Mooney M.20F	I. C. Lomax	
G-AWLS	Slingsby T.66 Nipper 3	T. E. Moore	
G-AWLX	Auster 5 J/2 Arrow	A. E..Taylor	
G-AWLZ	Fournier RF-4D	Nympsfield RF-4 Group	
G-AWMF	PA-18-150 Super Cub (modified)	AWMF Syndicate	
G-AWMR	D.31 Turbulent	B. E. Holz	
G-AWMT	Cessna F.150H	M. Paisley	
G-AWNT	BN-2A Islander	Pixair Survey SAS	
G-AWOH	PA-17 Vagabond	A. Lovejoy & K. Downes	
G-AWOT	Cessna F.150H	North East Aviation Training Ltd	
G-AWOU	Cessna 170B	S. Billington	
G-AWOX	Westland WS-58 Wessex 60 (150225) ★	Deltaforce Paintball South Bristol	
G-AWPH	P.56 Provost T.1	J. A. D. Bradshaw	
G-AWPJ	Cessna F.150H	R. W. Marchant & M. A. Maxted	
G-AWPN	Shield Xyla	J. P. Gilbert	
G-AWPU	Cessna F.150J	Westair Flying Services Ltd	
G-AWPW	PA-12 Super Cruiser	C. R. Shipley	
G-AWPZ	Andreasson BA-4B	J. M. Vening	
G-AWRP	Cierva Rotorcraft ★	The Helicopter Museum/Weston-super-Mare	
G-AWRS	Avro 19 Srs. 2 ★	North East Land Sea and Air Museum/Sunderland	
G-AWRY	P.56 Provost T.1 (XF836)	G. Priestley	
G-AWSA	Avro 652A Anson 19 (VL349) ★	Norfolk & Suffolk Aviation Museum/Flixton	
G-AWSH	Zlin Z.526 Trener Master	P. A. Colman	
G-AWSL	PA-28-180D Cherokee	A. H. & A. H. Brown	
G-AWSM	PA-28-235 Cherokee	N. A. R. Wright	
G-AWSN	D.62B Condor	C. J. Fox	
G-AWSP	D.62B Condor	M. C. Burlock	
G-AWSS	D.62A Condor	N. J. Butler	
G-AWST	D.62B Condor	Bluebird Aviation Services Ltd	
G-AWSV	Skeeter 12 (XM553) ★	Yorkshire Air Museum/Elvington	
G-AWSW	Beagle D.5/180 Husky (XW635)	Windmill Aviation	
G-AWTP	Schleicher Ka 6E	R. A. Youngs	
G-AWTV	Beech 19A Musketeer Sport	H. J. King	
G-AWTX	Cessna F.150J	R. D. Forster	
G-AWUB	Gardan GY-201 Minicab	R. A. Hand	
G-AWUE	Jodel DR.1050	K. W. Wood & F. M. Watson	
G-AWUJ	Cessna F.150H	North East Aviation Training Ltd	
G-AWUL	Cessna F.150H	A. J. Baron	
G-AWUN	Cessna F.150H	S. Nadeem & W. Ali	
G-AWUT	Cessna F.150J	Aerospace Resources Ltd	
G-AWUU	Cessna F.150J	D. P. Jones	
G-AWUZ	Cessna F.172H	Five Percent Flying Group	
G-AWVA	Cessna F.172H	Barton Air Ltd	

Notes	Reg	Type	Owner or Operator
	G-AWVC	Beagle B.121 Pup 1	Beagle Victor Charlie Group
	G-AWVE	Jodel DR.1050/M1	J. Owen
	G-AWVG	AESL Airtourer T.2	C. J. Schofield
	G-AWVN	Aeronca 7AC Champion	R. C. Hibberd
	G-AWVV	Schleicher ASK14	A. C. Jarvis
	G-AWVZ	Jodel D.112	D. C. Stokes
	G-AWWE	Beagle B.121 Pup 2	Pup Flyers
	G-AWWI	Jodel D.117	W. J. Ingham
	G-AWWN	Jodel DR.1050	S. Billington
	G-AWWO	Jodel DR.1050	W. G. Brooks
	G-AWWP	Aerosport Woody Pusher III	M. S. Bird & R. D. Bird
	G-AWWU	Cessna FR.172F	V. A. Aldea
	G-AWXS	PA-28 Cherokee 180D	J. E. Rowley
	G-AWXY	MS.885 Super Rallye	K. Henderson
	G-AWXZ	SNCAN Stampe SV.4C	Bianchi Aviation Film Services Ltd
	G-AWYI	BE.2c replica (687)	M. C. Boddington
	G-AWYJ	Beagle B.121 Pup 2	H. C. Taylor
	G-AWYL	Jodel DR.253B	T. C. Van Lonkhuyzen
	G-AWYO	Beagle B.121 Pup 1	B. R. C. Wild
	G-AWYY	Slingsby T.57 Camel replica (B6401) ★	F.A.A. Museum/Yeovilton
	G-AWZI	HS.121 Trident 3B ★	FAST Museum Farnborough (nose only)
	G-AWZJ	HS.121 Trident 3B ★	Dumfries & Galloway Museum
	G-AWZK	HS.121 Trident 3B ★	Runway Visitor Park/Manchester
	G-AWZM	HS.121 Trident 3B ★	Science Museum/Wroughton
	G-AWZP	HS.121 Trident 3B ★	de Havilland Museum/London Colney (nose only)
	G-AWZS	HS.121 Trident 3B ★	International Fire Training Centre/Teesside
	G-AWZU	HS.121 Trident 3B ★	Jet Age Museum/Gloucestershire (forward fuselage only)
	G-AXAB	PA-28-140 Cherokee	Bencray Ltd
	G-AXAN	DH.82A Tiger Moth (EM720)	A. J. Harrison
	G-AXAT	Jodel D.117A	G-AXAT Group
	G-AXBF	Beagle Auster D5 series 180 Husky	J. Smith
	G-AXBJ	Cessna F.172H	J. Allan
	G-AXBW	DH.82A Tiger Moth	Eptonair Aviation Services
	G-AXBZ	DH.82A Tiger Moth	W. J. de Jong Cleyndert
	G-AXCA	PA-28R-200 Cherokee Arrow	The Charlie Alpha Group
	G-AXCG	Jodel D.117	D. J. Millin
	G-AXCY	Jodel D.117A	R. S. Marom
	G-AXCZ	SNCAN Stampe SV-4C	D. De Ruiter
	G-AXDI	Cessna F.172H	M. F. & J. R. Leusby
	G-AXDK	Jodel DR.315	A. P. Aspinall
	G-AXDN	BAC-Sud Concorde 01 ★	Imperial War Museum/Duxford
	G-AXDV	Beagle B.121 Pup 1	S. R. Hopkins
	G-AXDZ	Cassutt Racer IIIM	A. Chadwick
	G-AXED	PA-25-235 Pawnee	The Borders (Milfield) Gliding Club Ltd
	G-AXEH	B.125 Bulldog 1 ★	Museum of Flight/East Fortune
	G-AXEI	Ward Gnome ★	Real Aeroplane Company/Breighton
	G-AXEO	Scheibe SF.25B Falke	P. F. Moffatt
	G-AXEV	Beagle B.121 Pup 2	D. S. Russell & D. G. Benson
	G-AXFG	Cessna 337D	County Garage (Cheltenham) Ltd
	G-AXFM	Servotec Grasshopper III ★	The Helicopter Museum/Weston-super-Mare
	G-AXFN	Jodel D.119	D. W. Garbe
	G-AXGE	MS.880B Rallye Club	R. E. Dagless
	G-AXGG	Cessna F.150J	A. J. Simpson
	G-AXGP	Piper J-3C-90 Cub (3681)	A. P. Acres
	G-AXGR	Phoenix Luton LA-4A Minor	C. M. Bracewell
	G-AXGS	D.62B Condor	SAS Flying Group
	G-AXGZ	D.62B Condor	G. E. Horder
	G-AXHP	Piper J-3C-65 Cub (480636:A-58)	Witham (Specialist) Vehicles Ltd
	G-AXHR	Piper J-3C-65 Cub (329601:D-44)	D. J. Dash
	G-AXHV	Jodel D.117A	Derwent Flying Group
	G-AXIA	Beagle B.121 Pup 1	C. K. Parsons
	G-AXIE	Beagle B.121 Pup 2	M. Cowan
	G-AXIG	Scottish Aviation B.125 Bulldog 104 ★	National Museum of Scotland/Edinburgh
	G-AXIO	PA-28-140 Cherokee	R. Wallace
	G-AXJB	Omega 84 balloon	Southern Balloon Group
	G-AXJH	Beagle B.121 Pup 2	The Henry Flying Group
	G-AXJI	Beagle B.121 Pup 2	High Flight Training Solutions Ltd
	G-AXJJ	Beagle B.121 Pup 2	M. L. Jones & ptnrs
	G-AXJO	Beagle B.121 Pup 2	M. P. & V. A. Whitley

Reg	Type	Owner or Operator	Notes
G-AXJV	PA-28-140 Cherokee	KMS Aviation Services Ltd	
G-AXJX	PA-28-140 Cherokee	T. W. Gilbert	
G-AXKH	Luton LA-4A Minor	M. W. Collington	
G-AXKJ	Jodel D.9	K. D. Boyle	
G-AXKO	Westland-Bell 47G-4A	M. Gallagher	
G-AXKS	Westland Bell 47G-4A ★	Museum of Army Flying/Middle Wallop	
G-AXKX	Westland Bell 47G-4A	R. A. Dale	
G-AXLI	Slingsby T.66 Nipper 3	P. R. Howson	
G-AXLJ	Slingsby T.66 Nipper 3	P. B. Davey	
G-AXLS	Jodel DR.105A	Axle Flying Club	
G-AXLZ	PA-18-95 Super Cub	Perryair Ltd	
G-AXMA	PA-24-180 Comanche	P. Holding	
G-AXMD	Omega O-56 balloon ★	British Balloon Museum/Newbury	
G-AXMT	Bucker Bu.133 Jungmeister	A. J. E. Smith & R. A. Fleming	
G-AXMW	Beagle B.121 Pup 1	J. J. Griessel	
G-AXMX	Beagle B.121 Pup 2	Bob The Beagle Group	
G-AXNJ	Jodel D.120	D. C. Lewis	
G-AXNN	Beagle B.121 Pup 2	November November Flying Group	
G-AXNP	Beagle B.121 Pup 2	J. W. Ellis & R. J. Hemmings	
G-AXNR	Beagle B.121 Pup 2	G-AXNR Group	
G-AXNS	Beagle B.121 Pup 2	Derwent Aero Group	
G-AXNW	SNCAN Stampe SV.4C	D. H. Grace	
G-AXNZ	Pitts S.1C Special	November Zulu Group	
G-AXOG	PA-E23-250D Aztec	G. H. Nolan	
G-AXOH	MS.894 Rallye Minerva	L. C. Clark	
G-AXOJ	Beagle B.121 Pup 2	Pup Flying Group	
G-AXOM	Penn-Smith Gyroplane ★	Stondon Motor Museum/Lower Stondon	
G-AXOR	PA-28-180D Cherokee	Oscar Romeo Aviation Ltd	
G-AXOT	MS.893 Rallye Commodore 180	R. Bone	
G-AXPA	Beagle B.121 Pup 1	C. B. Copsey	
G-AXPC	Beagle B.121 Pup 2	T. A. White	
G-AXPF	Cessna F.150K	T. W. Gilbert	
G-AXPG	Mignet HM.293	W. H. Cole (stored)	
G-AXPN	Beagle B.121 Pup 2	G. N. E. Waring	
G-AXPZ	Campbell Cricket	W. R. Partridge	
G-AXRC	Campbell Cricket	L. R. Morris	
G-AXRP	SNCAN Stampe SV-4C	C. C. & C. D. Manning (G-BLOL)	
G-AXRR	Auster AOP.9 (XR241)	C. J. Salter	
G-AXSC	Beagle B.121 Pup 1	M. P. Whitley	
G-AXSG	PA-28-180 Cherokee	Perranporth Flying Club Ltd	
G-AXSM	Jodel DR.1051	T. R. G. & M. S. Barnby	
G-AXSW	Cessna FA.150K	R. J. Whyham	
G-AXSZ	PA-28-140B Cherokee	White Wings Flying Group	
G-AXTA	PA-28-140B Cherokee	G-AXTA Aircraft Group	
G-AXTC	PA-28-140B Cherokee	G-AXTC Group	
G-AXTJ	PA-28-140B Cherokee	S. J. Jones	
G-AXTL	PA-28-140B Cherokee	Ocean Heights Aviation Training Centre Ltd	
G-AXTO	PA-24-260 Comanche	D. L. Edwards	
G-AXTX	Jodel D.112	C. Sawford	
G-AXUA	Beagle B.121 Pup 1	P. Wood	
G-AXUC	PA-12 Super Cruiser	Weald Air Services Ltd	
G-AXUJ	Auster J/1 Autocrat	S. Seale-Finch (G-OSTA)	
G-AXUK	Jodel DR.1050	Downland Flying Group	
G-AXWA	Auster AOP.9 (XN437)	C. M. Edwards	
G-AXWT	Jodel D.11	C. S. Jackson	
G-AXWV	Jodel DR.253	R. Friedlander & D. C. Ray	
G-AXWZ	PA-28R-200 Cherokee Arrow	Whisky Zulu Group	
G-AXXV	DH.82A Tiger Moth (DE992)	D. A. & S. J. Hardie	
G-AXXW	Jodel D.117	R. K. G. Delve	
G-AXYK	Taylor JT.1 Monoplane	D. E. Findoin	
G-AXYU	Jodel D.9 Bébé	P. Turton	
G-AXZH	Glasflugel H201B Standard Libelle	M. C. Gregorie	
G-AXZM	Slingsby T.66 Nipper 3	T. C. Caldecourt	
G-AXZO	Cessna 180	M. D. Pryce & D. A. Hunt	
G-AXZP	PA-E23-250 Aztec	R. A. Doherty	
G-AXZT	Jodel D.117	P. Guest	
G-AXZU	Cessna 182N	R. C. Weininger	
G-AYAB	PA-28-180 Cherokee E	C. Hawkins & J. P. Bate	
G-AYAJ	Cameron O-84 balloon	E. T. Hall	
G-AYAL	Omega 56 balloon ★	British Balloon Museum/Newbury	

Notes	Reg	Type	Owner or Operator
	G-AYAN	Slingsby Motor Cadet III	G. Smith
	G-AYAR	PA-28-180 Cherokee E	A. M. S. Sher
	G-AYAT	PA-28-180 Cherokee E	G-AYAT Flying Group
	G-AYAW	PA-28-180 Cherokee E	North East Flyers Group
	G-AYBP	Jodel D.112	G. B. Wilson
	G-AYBR	Jodel D.112	M. H. Simms
	G-AYCC	Campbell Cricket	J. G. Pumford
	G-AYCE	Scintex CP.301-C1 Emeraude	P. J. Tyler
	G-AYCG	SNCAN Stampe SV.4C	A. Page
	G-AYCK	AIA Stampe SV.4C	A. A. M. & C. W. M. Huke (G-BUNT)
	G-AYCN	Piper J-3C-65 Cub	M. Collenette
	G-AYCP	Jodel D.112	J. D. Bradley
	G-AYDI	DH.82A Tiger Moth	E. G. & G. R. Woods
	G-AYDR	SNCAN Stampe SV.4C	D. J. Ashley
	G-AYDV	Coates Swalesong SA11	The Real Aeroplane Co.Ltd
	G-AYDW	Beagle A.61 Terrier 2	A. S. Topen
	G-AYDX	Beagle A.61 Terrier 2	T. S. Lee
	G-AYDY	Luton LA-4A Minor	J. Dible/Ireland
	G-AYDZ	Jodel DR.200	M. R. Masters
	G-AYEB	Jodel D.112	D. W. Finlay
	G-AYEF	PA-28-180 Cherokee E	Pegasus Flying Group
	G-AYEG	Falconar F-9	J. P. Taylor
	G-AYEH	Jodel DR.1050	T. J. N. H. Palmer
	G-AYEJ	Jodel DR.1050	The Bluebird Flying Group
	G-AYEN	Piper J-3C-65 Cub	G-AYEN Group
	G-AYET	MS.892A Rallye Commodore 150	A. T. R. Bingley
	G-AYEW	Jodel DR.1051	J. R. Hope
	G-AYFC	D.62B Condor	C. S. Whitwell
	G-AYFD	D.62B Condor	B. G. Manning
	G-AYFE	D.62C Condor	M. Soulsby
	G-AYFF	D.62B Condor	H. Stuart
	G-AYFJ	MS.880B Rallye Club	Rallye FJ Group
	G-AYFV	Crosby BA-4B	N. J. W. Reid
	G-AYGA	Jodel D.117	J. W. Bowes
	G-AYGC	Cessna F.150K	Alpha Aviation Group
	G-AYGD	Jodel DR.1051	J. P. Liber
	G-AYGE	SNCAN Stampe SV.4C	B. R. Perkins
	G-AYGG	Jodel D.120	J. M. Dean
	G-AYGX	Cessna FR.172G	AW Aviation Consultancy Services Ltd
	G-AYHA	AA-1 Yankee	J. R. Batey
	G-AYHX	Jodel D.117A	L. E. Cowling
	G-AYIA	Hughes 369HS	G. D. E. Bilton/Sywell
	G-AYII	PA-28R-200 Cherokee Arrow	N. P. Wilson
	G-AYIJ	SNCAN Stampe SV.4B	G-AYIJ Syndicate
	G-AYJA	Jodel DR.1050	D. M. Blair
	G-AYJB	SNCAN Stampe SV.4C	F. J. M. & J. P. Esson
	G-AYJD	Alpavia-Fournier RF-3	R. T. C. Connors
	G-AYJP	PA-28-140C Cherokee	T. W. Gilbert
	G-AYJR	PA-28-140C Cherokee	T. W. Gilbert
	G-AYJY	Isaacs Fury II (K2065)	M. J. H. White & D. J. Fry
	G-AYKD	Jodel DR.1050	A. James
	G-AYKJ	Jodel D.117A	R. J. Hughes
	G-AYKK	Jodel D.117	J. M. Whitham
	G-AYKT	Jodel D.117	AYKT Flying Group
	G-AYKW	PA-28-140C Cherokee	Kilo Whiskey Group
	G-AYKZ	SAI KZ-8	R. E. Mitchell
	G-AYLA	Glos-Airtourer 115	C. P. L. Jenkins
	G-AYLC	Jodel DR.1051	D. J. M. White
	G-AYLF	Jodel DR.1051	S. C. Smith & M. C. Lawton
	G-AYLL	Jodel DR.1050	G. Bell
	G-AYME	Fournier RF-5	Mike Echo Group
	G-AYMK	PA-28-140C Cherokee	R. Quinn & B. Hutchinson
	G-AYMO	PA-23-250 Aztec ★	City of Norwich Aviation Museum/Norwich
	G-AYMP	Currie Wot	R. C. Hibberd
	G-AYMU	Jodel D.112	C. Evans
	G-AYMV	Western 20 balloon	R. G. Turnbull
	G-AYNF	PA-28-140C Cherokee	BW Aviation Ltd
	G-AYNJ	PA-28-140C Cherokee	J. F. L. R. Whitehead
	G-AYNN	Cessna 185B	Bencray Ltd
	G-AYNP	Westland WS-55 Whirlwind Srs 3 ★	IHM/Weston-super-Mare
	G-AYOW	Cessna 182N	N. Hedley

Reg	Type	Owner or Operator	Notes
G-AYOZ	Cessna FA.150L	P. J. Worrall	
G-AYPE	MBB Bö.209 Monsun	B. K. Ranger	
G-AYPG	Cessna F.177RG	Warwickshire Aviation Ltd	
G-AYPH	Cessna F.177RG	M. L. & T. M. Jones	
G-AYPJ	PA-28-180 Cherokee	Glasgow Flying Club Ltd	
G-AYPM	PA-18-95 Super Cub (115373)	R. C. Piper	
G-AYPO	PA-18-95 Super Cub	A. W. Knowles	
G-AYPS	PA-18-95 Super Cub	D. Racionzer & P. Wayman	
G-AYPU	PA-28R-200 Cherokee Arrow	Monalto Investments Ltd	
G-AYPV	PA-28-140D Cherokee	Ashley Gardner Flying Club Ltd	
G-AYPZ	Campbell Cricket	A. Melody	
G-AYRC	Campbell Cricket	R. H. Braithwaite	
G-AYRG	Cessna F.172K	A. J. Brophy	
G-AYRI	PA-28R-200 Cherokee Arrow	J. C. Houdret	
G-AYRJ	Le Vier Cosmic Wind	Ultimate Warbird Flights Ltd (G-NZOC)	
G-AYRL	Sportavia-Putzer SFS31 Milan	A.Hoskins & K. M. Fresson	
G-AYRM	PA-28-140D Cherokee	Juliet Tango Group	
G-AYRO	Cessna FA.150L Aerobat	Plane Rentals Ltd	
G-AYRS	Jodel D.120A	O. D. Lewis	
G-AYRT	Cessna F.172K	G-AYRT Group	
G-AYSB	PA-30-160C Twin Comanche	Charles Lock (1963) Ltd	
G-AYSH	Taylor JT.1 Monoplane	C. J. Lodge	
G-AYSK	Luton LA-4A Minor	M. W. Collington	
G-AYSY	Cessna F.177RG	T. Ong	
G-AYTA	SOCATA MS.880B Rallye Club ★	Fishburn Historic Aviation Centre/Fishburn	
G-AYTR	CP.301A Emeraude	M. A. Smith	
G-AYTT	Phoenix PM-3 Duet	Devon Duet AYTT Group	
G-AYTV	Jurca Tempete	C. W. Kirk	
G-AYUB	CEA DR.253B	R. G. Ferguson	
G-AYUJ	Evans VP-1	T. N. Howard	
G-AYUN	Slingsby T.61A Falke	B. L. Pompilis	
G-AYUR	Slingsby T.61A Falke	C. O'Mahoney	
G-AYUS	Taylor JT.1 Monoplane	J. G. W. Newton	
G-AYUT	Jodel DR.1050	M. W. Olliver	
G-AYUV	Cessna F.172H	Justgold Ltd	
G-AYVP	Woody Pusher	J. R. Wraight	
G-AYWD	Cessna 182N	P. G. Slinger	
G-AYWH	Jodel D.117A	D. Kynaston	
G-AYWM	Glos-Airtourer Super 150	Star Flying Group	
G-AYWT	AIA Stampe SV.4C	A. J. Rice	
G-AYXP	Jodel D.117A	G. N. Davies	
G-AYXT	WS-55 Whirlwind Srs 2 (XK940:911) ★	IHM/Weston-super-Mare	
G-AYYO	Jodel DR.1050/M1	Bustard Jodel Group	
G-AYYT	Jodel DR.1050/M1	A. L. Moore	
G-AYYU	Beech C23 Musketeer	M. R. Harness	
G-AYZH	Taylor JT.2 Titch	T. Jarvis	
G-AYZI	SNCAN Stampe SV.4C	R. J. Anderson	
G-AYZJ	Westland WS-55 Whirlwind HAS.7 ★	Newark Air Museum (XM685)	
G-AYZK	Jodel DR.1050/M1	G. J. McDill	
G-AYZS	Druine D.62B Condor	M. C. Burlock	
G-AYZW	Slingsby T.61A Falke	The Gliding Heritage Centre	
G-AZAB	PA-30-160B Twin Comanche	D. T. Cairns	
G-AZAJ	PA-28R-200B Cherokee Arrow	P. Woulfe	
G-AZAU	Servotec Grasshopper III ★	The Helicopter Museum/Weston-super-Mare	
G-AZAZ	Bensen B.8M ★	F.A.A. Museum/Yeovilton	
G-AZBI	Jodel 150	R. J. Wald	
G-AZBL	Jodel D9 Bebe	V. D. Long	
G-AZBN	Noorduyn AT-16 Harvard IIB (FT391)	G. C. Cawley	
G-AZBU	Auster AOP.9 (XR246)	Auster Nine Group	
G-AZCB	SNCAN Stampe SV.4C	M. Coward	
G-AZCE	Pitts S-1C Special	D. J.Taudevin	
G-AZCK	Beagle B.121 Pup 2	P. Crone	
G-AZCL	Beagle B.121 Pup 2	Flew LLP & J. M. Henry	
G-AZCN	Beagle B.121 Pup 2	Snoopy Flying Group	
G-AZCT	Beagle B.121 Pup 1	J. E. Rowley	
G-AZCU	Beagle B.121 Pup 1	D. W. Locke	
G-AZCV	Beagle B.121 Pup 2	N. R. W. Long	
G-AZDD	MBB Bö.209 Monsun 150FF	Double Delta Flying Group	
G-AZDE	PA-28R-200B Cherokee Arrow	Insight Aviation Group Ltd	
G-AZDG	Beagle B.121 Pup 2	P. J. Beeson	

Notes	Reg	Type	Owner or Operator
	G-AZDJ	PA-32-300Cherokee Six	P. J. Dalton, C. J. Mace & M. Bandari
	G-AZDK	Beech 95-B55 Baron	T. W. Harris (G-SWEE)
	G-AZDY	DH.82A Tiger Moth	J. B. Mills
	G-AZEF	Jodel D.120	Boscombe EF Paris Nice
	G-AZEG	PA-28-140D Cherokee	M. Drijfhout & P. C. Baker
	G-AZEU	Beagle B.121 Pup 2	G. M. Moir
	G-AZEV	Beagle B.121 Pup 2	A. P. Amor
	G-AZEW	Beagle B.121 Pup 2	Fluoro-Tech Ltd
	G-AZEY	Beagle B.121 Pup 2	A. H. Cameron
	G-AZFA	Beagle B.121 Pup 2	K. J. Amies
	G-AZFC	PA-28-140D Cherokee	WLS Flying Group
	G-AZFI	PA-28R-200B Cherokee Arrow	G-AZFI Ltd
	G-AZFM	PA-28R-200B Cherokee Arrow	Tashimyah Ltd
	G-AZGA	Jodel D.120	P. Turton & N. J. Owen
	G-AZGC	SNCAN Stampe SV.4C	D. J. Ashley
	G-AZGE	SNCAN Stampe SV.4C	D. Capon & M. Flint
	G-AZGF	Beagle B.121 Pup 2	B. R. Irons & D. R. Budden
	G-AZGL	MS.894A Rallye Minerva	A. L. Hall-Carpenter
	G-AZGY	CP.301B Emeraude	R. H. Braithwaite
	G-AZGZ	DH.82A Tiger Moth (NM181)	A. R. Hardwick
	G-AZHC	Jodel D.112	Aerodel Flying Group
	G-AZHD	Slingsby T.61A Falke	J. Pool
	G-AZHH	SA 102.5 Cavalier	M. W. Place
	G-AZHU	Luton LA-4A Minor	J. C. Gates
	G-AZHX	SA Bulldog Srs 100/101	K. J. Fraser (G-DOGE)
	G-AZIB	ST-10 Diplomate	W. B. Bateson
	G-AZII	Jodel D.117A	D. H. G. Cotter
	G-AZIJ	Jodel DR.360	T. E. Dighton
	G-AZIL	Slingsby T.61A Falke★	The Dumfries & Galloway Aviation Museum
	G-AZJC	Fournier RF-5	Seighford RF5 Group
	G-AZJE	Ord-Hume JB-01 Minicab	J. Evans
	G-AZJN	Robin DR.300/140	B. J. Atkins
	G-AZJV	Cessna F.172L	British Parachute Schools Ltd
	G-AZKR	PA-24 Comanche	A. Lawson
	G-AZKW	Cessna F.172L	D. N. Emery
	G-AZKZ	Cessna F.172L	R. D. Forseter
	G-AZLE	Boeing N2S-5 Kaydet (1102:102)	DH Heritage Flights Ltd
	G-AZLF	Jodel D.120	D. C. O'Dwyer
	G-AZLN	PA-28-180 Cherokee F	P. G. Fowler
	G-AZLV	Cessna 172K	Devon & Somerset Flight Training Ltd
	G-AZLY	Cessna F.150L	British Parachute Schools Ltd
	G-AZMC	Slingsby T.61A Falke	P. J. R. White
	G-AZMD	Slingsby T.61C Falke	Delta Juliett Bravo Ltd
	G-AZMJ	AA-5 Traveler	W. R. Partridge
	G-AZMZ	MS.893A Rallye Commodore 150	R. E. Lee
	G-AZNK	SNCAN Stampe SV.4A	I. Noakes
	G-AZNL	PA-28R-200 Cherokee Arrow II	B. P. Liversidge
	G-AZNO	Cessna 182P	Dolphin ICT Ltd
	G-AZNT	Cameron O-84 balloon	P. Glydon
	G-AZOA	MBB Bö.209 Monsun 150FF	M. W. Hurst
	G-AZOE	Glos-Airtourer 115	Robin Flying Club Ltd
	G-AZOF	Glos-Airtourer Super 150	607 Group
	G-AZOG	PA-28R-200D Cherokee Arrow	S. J. Lowe
	G-AZOL	PA-34-200 Seneca II	Stapleford Flying Club Ltd
	G-AZOS	Jurca MJ.5-H1 Sirocco	P. J. Tanulak
	G-AZOU	Jodel DR.1050	Horsham Flying Group
	G-AZOZ	Cessna FRA.150L	WF Aviation
	G-AZPA	PA-25-235 Pawnee	The Borders (Milfield) Gliding Club Ltd
	G-AZPC	Slingsby T.61C Falke	D. Heslop & J. R. Kimberley
	G-AZPF	Fournier RF-5	E. C. Mort
	G-AZPH	Craft-Pitts S-1S Special ★	Science Museum/South Kensington
	G-AZPX	Western O-31 balloon	Zebedee Balloon Service Ltd
	G-AZRA	MBB Bö.209 Monsun 150FF	Alpha Flying Ltd
	G-AZRH	PA-28-140 Cherokee D	Fly With Me Aviation Ltd
	G-AZRI	Payne Free Balloon	C. A. Butter & J. J. T. Cooke
	G-AZRK	Fournier RF-5	J. F. Rogers
	G-AZRL	PA-18-95 Super Cub	Foxy Air-Service Ltd
	G-AZRM	Fournier RF-5	Romeo Mike Group
	G-AZRN	Cameron O-84 balloon	C. J. Desmet/Belgium
	G-AZRS	PA-22-150 Tri-Pacer	R. H. Hulls
	G-AZRZ	Cessna U.206F	Cornish Parachute Club Ltd

Reg	Type	Owner or Operator	Notes
G-AZSA	Stampe et Renard SV.4B	M. R. Dolman	
G-AZSC	Noorduyn AT-16 Harvard IIB (43:SC)	Goodwood Road Racing Co Ltd	
G-AZSD	Slingsby T.29B	R. O. Johnson	
G-AZSF	PA-28R-200 Cherokee Arrow II	Aeros Leasing Ltd	
G-AZTA	MBB Bö.209 Monsun 150FF	D. J. Hampson	
G-AZTF	Cessna F.177RG	P. A. Spurrs	
G-AZTM	AESL Airtourer 115	Victa Restoration Group	
G-AZTR	SNCAN Stampe SV-4C	G. W. Lynch	
G-AZTS	Cessna F.172L	MPS Aviation Ltd	
G-AZTV	Stolp SA.500 Starlet	F. R. Donaldson	
G-AZUM	Cessna F.172L	Fowlmere Flyers	
G-AZUY	Cessna E.310L	W. B. Bateson	
G-AZUZ	Cessna FRA.150L	J. T. Bonsall	
G-AZVB	MBB Bö.209 Monsun 150FF	R. K. Galbally & E. W. Russell	
G-AZVL	Jodel D.119	T. E. Brooke	
G-AZWB	PA-28-140 Cherokee	G-AZWB Flying Group	
G-AZWS	PA-28R-180 Cherokee Arrow	K. M. Turner	
G-AZWT	Westland Lysander IIIA (V9367)	The Shuttleworth Collection	
G-AZWY	PA-24-260 Comanche	H. M. Donnan	
G-AZXD	Cessna F.172L	A. M. Dinnie	
G-AZYB	Bell 47H-1 ★	The Helicopter Museum/Weston-super-Mare	
G-AZYD	MS.893A Rallye Commodore	Staffordshire Gliding Club Ltd	
G-AZYF	PA-28-180 Cherokee D	Meddyg Care Group Holdings Ltd	
G-AZYS	CP.301C-1 Emeraude	C. G. Ferguson & D. Drew	
G-AZYU	PA-23-250 Aztec	M. E. & M. H. Cromati	
G-AZYY	Slingsby T.61A Falke	T. A. Smith	
G-AZYZ	Wassmer Wa.51A Pacific	W. A. Stewart	
G-AZZR	Cessna F.150L	G-AZZR Group Ltd	
G-AZZV	Cessna F.172L	S. Heale	
G-AZZZ	DH.82A Tiger Moth	S. W. McKay	
G-BAAD	Evans Super VP-1	Klyne Training Ltd	
G-BAAF	Manning-Flanders MF1 (replica)	Aviation Film Services Ltd	
G-BAAW	Jodel D.119	Alpha Whiskey Flying Group	
G-BABC	Cessna F.150L	P. Tribble	
G-BABD	Cessna FRA.150L (modified)	G. G. Chandler	
G-BABE	Taylor JT.2 Titch	Acroflight Ltd	
G-BABG	PA-28-180 Cherokee	R. Nightingale	
G-BABY	Taylor JT.2 Titch ★	Norfolk and Suffolk Aviation Museum/Flixton	
G-BACB	PA-34-200 Seneca II	Milbrooke Motors Ltd	
G-BACE	Fournier RF-5	G-BACE Fournier Group	
G-BACJ	Jodel D.120	M. H. Smith	
G-BACN	Cessna FRA.150L	AT Aviation Sales Ltd	
G-BADC	Rollason Beta B.2A	T. D. Bridge	
G-BADH	Slingsby T.61A Falke	D. C. Gell	
G-BADM	D.62B Condor	Delta Mike Group	
G-BADW	Pitts S-2A Special	R. E. Mitchell	
G-BADZ	Aerotek Pitts S-2A Special	M. J. M. Edwards	
G-BAEM	Robin DR.400/125	Vision Aerospace Ltd	
G-BAEN	Robin DR.400/180	C. R. Brown	
G-BAEP	Cessna FRA.150L (modified)	Peterborough Flying School Ltd	
G-BAER	Cosmic Wind	A. G. Truman	
G-BAET	Piper J-3C-65 Cub (330314)	C. J. Rees	
G-BAEZ	Cessna FRA.150L	Donair Flying Club Ltd	
G-BAFA	AA-5 Traveler	C. F. Mackley	
G-BAFG	DH.82A Tiger Moth	Tiger Moth Experience Ltd	
G-BAFL	Cessna 182P	R. B. Hopkinson & A. S. Pike	
G-BAFT	PA-18-150 Super Cub	R. A. Stephens	
G-BAFU	PA-28-140 Cherokee	C. E. Taylor	
G-BAFV	PA-18-95 Super Cub	T. F. & S. J. Thorpe	
G-BAFW	PA-28-140 Cherokee	A. J. Peters	
G-BAFX	Robin DR.400/140	R. J. Garrett	
G-BAGC	Robin DR.400/140	S. Marriott	
G-BAGF	Jodel D.92 Bébé	J. Hoskins	
G-BAGG	PA-32-300 Cherokee Six E	Aero Rentals Ltd	
G-BAGJ	Westland SA.341G Gazelle ★	North East Land Sea and Air Museum/Sunderland	
G-BAGR	Robin DR.400/140	Global Sustainability Matters Ltd	
G-BAGX	PA-28-140 Cherokee	KMS Aviation Services Ltd	
G-BAHF	PA-28-140 Cherokee	Warwickshire Leasing Ltd	
G-BAHJ	PA-24-250 Comanche	Skylease Ltd	
G-BAHL	Robin DR.400/160	J. B. McVeighty	

BRITISH CIVIL AIRCRAFT MARKINGS

Notes	Reg	Type	Owner or Operator
	G-BAHP	Volmer VJ.22 Sportsman	G. K. Holloway
	G-BAHS	PA-28R-200 Cherokee Arrow II	L. Cobley
	G-BAHX	Cessna 182P	M. D. J. Moore
	G-BAIG	PA-34-200-2 Seneca	Mid-Anglia School of Flying
	G-BAIH	PA-28R-200 Cherokee Arrow II	M. G. West
	G-BAIK	Cessna F.150L	D. A. & T. M. Jones
	G-BAIS	Cessna F.177RG	Cardinal Flying Group G-BAIS
	G-BAIW	Cessna F.172M	Jindalee Ltd
	G-BAIZ	Slingsby T.61A Falke	Falke Syndicate
	G-BAJB	Cessna F.177RG	J. D. Loveridge
	G-BAJN	AA-5 Traveler	M. D. Wild
	G-BAJO	AA-5 Traveler	Montgomery Aviation Ltd
	G-BAJR	PA-28-180 Cherokee	A. C. Sturgeon
	G-BAJZ	Robin DR.400/125	Prestwick Flying Club Ltd
	G-BAKJ	PA-30-160B Twin Comanche	E. R. & P. M. Jones
	G-BAKM	Robin DR.400/140	Bustard Flying Club Ltd
	G-BAKN	SNCAN Stampe SV.4C	A. J. L. Eves & T. O. Dews
	G-BAKR	Jodel D.117	J & F Aircraft
	G-BAKW	Beagle B.121 Pup 2	Cunning Stunts Flying Group
	G-BALD	Cameron O-84 balloon	C. A. Gould
	G-BALF	Robin DR.400/140	G. & D. A. Wasey
	G-BALG	Robin DR.400/180	S. G. Jones
	G-BALH	Robin DR.400/140B	SARL HM MAT Import/France
	G-BALJ	Robin DR.400/180	G-BALJ Group
	G-BALN	Cessna T.310Q	O'Brien Properties Ltd
	G-BALS	Tipsy Nipper T.66 Srs.3	N. C. Spooner
	G-BAMB	Slingsby T.61C Falke	H. J. Bradley
	G-BAMC	Cessna F.150L	G-BAMC Owners Group
	G-BAML	Bell 206B Jet Ranger II ★	Aero Venture
	G-BAMR	PA-16 Clipper	R. H. Royce
	G-BAMU	Robin DR.400/160	Alternative Flying Group
	G-BAMV	Robin DR.400/180	K. Jones
	G-BAMY	PA-28R-200 Cherokee Arrow II	Flying Pig UK Ltd
	G-BANA	Robin DR.221	Hampshire Flying Group
	G-BANB	Robin DR.400/180	M. Ingvardsen
	G-BANC	Gardan GY-201 Minicab	C. R. Shipley
	G-BANF	Luton LA-4A Minor	N. F. O'Neill
	G-BANU	Wassmer Jodel D.120	C. H. Kilner
	G-BANV	Phoenix Currie Wot	A. A. M. & C. W. N. Huke
	G-BANW	CP.1330 Super Emeraude	A. Berry
	G-BANX	Cessna F.172M	Oakfleet 2000 Ltd
	G-BAOM	MS.880B Rallye Club	P. J. D. Feehan
	G-BAPB	DHC.1 Chipmunk 22 (WB549:7)	M. T. Ivarsson
	G-BAPI	Cessna FRA.150L	M. Bonsall
	G-BAPL	PA-23-250E Turbo Aztec	Donington Aviation Ltd
	G-BAPR	Jodel D.11	D. J. Bobka
	G-BAPS	Campbell Cougar ★	The Helicopter Museum/Weston-super-Mare
	G-BAPV	Robin DR.400/160	J. D. & M. Millne
	G-BAPW	PA-28R-180 Cherokee Arrow	M. Meddle
	G-BAPX	Robin DR.400/160	White Rose Aviators
	G-BARC	Cessna FR.172J	Severn Valley Aviation Group
	G-BARF	Jodel D.112 Club	R. N. Jones
	G-BARH	Beech C.23 Sundowner	A. Ballan
	G-BARN	Taylor JT.2 Titch	R. G. W. Newton
	G-BARS	DHC.1 Chipmunk 22 (1377)	J. Beattie & R. M. Scarre
	G-BARZ	Scheibe SF.28A Tandem Falke	Wiltshire Ventures Group
	G-BASH	AA-5 Traveler	S. P. Adshead
	G-BASJ	PA-28-180 Cherokee	Bristol Aero Club
	G-BASN	Beech C.23 Sundowner	Beech G-BASN Group Syndicate
	G-BASO	Lake LA-4 Amphibian	Uulster Seaplane Association Ltd
	G-BASP	Beagle B.121 Pup 1	M. P. Whitley & J. M. Hunter
	G-BATV	PA-28-180D Cherokee	Scoreby Flying Group
	G-BAUC	PA-25-235 Pawnee	The South Wales Gliding Club Ltd
	G-BAUH	Jodel D.112	T. I. Bale
	G-BAVB	Cessna F.172M	D. G. Smith
	G-BAVH	DHC.1 Chipmunk 22	G-BAVH Syndicate
	G-BAVL	PA-23-250E Aztec	S. P. & A. V. Chillott
	G-BAVO	Boeing Stearman N2S (26)	RM Classic Aviation Ltd
	G-BAWG	PA-28R Cherokee Arrow 200-II	Solent Air Ltd
	G-BAXS	Bell 47G-5	M. R. J. Pearson
	G-BAXU	Cessna F.150L	Peterborough Flying School Ltd

Reg	Type	Owner or Operator	Notes
G-BAXV	Cessna F.150L	S. P. Edghill	
G-BAXY	Cessna F.172M	Peterborough Flying School Ltd	
G-BAYL	SNCAN Nord 1101 Norecrin ★	(stored)/Chirk	
G-BAYO	Cessna 150L	Poyston Aviation	
G-BAYP	Cessna 150L	Aviolease Ltd	
G-BAYR	Robin HR.100/210	D. G. Doyle	
G-BAYZ	Champion 7GCBC Citabria	M. Colson	
G-BAZC	Robin DR.400/160	S. G. Jones	
G-BAZM	Jodel D.11	A. R. Morris	
G-BAZS	Cessna F.150L	Aerohire Ltd	
G-BBAW	Robin HR.100/210	F. A. Purvis	
G-BBAX	Robin DR.400/140	P. H. Garbutt	
G-BBAY	Robin DR.400/140	Just Plane Trading Ltd	
G-BBBB	Taylor JT.1 Monoplane	M. C. Arnold	
G-BBBC	Cessna F.150L	S. Collins & C. A. Widdowson	
G-BBBI	AA-5 Traveler	R. Madden	
G-BBBN	PA-28-180 Cherokee	Estuary Aviation Ltd	
G-BBBO	SIPA 903	A. Rayner	
G-BBBW	FRED Srs 2	M. Palfreman	
G-BBBY	PA-28-140 Cherokee	Davidson Aviation Ltd	
G-BBCH	Robin DR.400/2+2	S. H. Williams	
G-BBCN	Robin HR.100/210	S. J. Nash	
G-BBCS	Robin DR.400/140	M. J. Medland	
G-BBCY	Luton LA-4A Minor	A. W. McBlain	
G-BBDC	PA-28-140 Cherokee	Vu JV20 Ltd	
G-BBDE	PA-28R-200 Cherokee Arrow	Solanki Capital Ltd	
G-BBDG	BAC-Aérospatiale Concorde 100 ★	Brooklands Museum of Aviation/Weybridge	
G-BBDH	Cessna F.172M	J. D. Woodward	
G-BBDL	AA-5 Traveler	M. Kadir	
G-BBDM	AA-5 Traveler	C. M. James	
G-BBDP	Robin DR.400-160	Robin Flyers Ltd	
G-BBDT	Cessna 150H	Sherburn Aero Club Ltd	
G-BBDV	SIPA S.903	C. M. Knight	
G-BBEA	Luton LA-4 Minor	N. G. Sowden	
G-BBEB	PA-28R-200 Cherokee Arrow II	March Flying Group	
G-BBED	MS.894A Rallye Minerva ★	Aeropark/East Midlands	
G-BBEN	Bellanca 7GCBC Citabria	M. A. Flanigan	
G-BBEO	Cessna FRA.150L	Dukeries Aviation (G-PNIX)	
G-BBFD	PA-28R-200 Cherokee Arrow II	G-BBFD Flying Group	
G-BBFL	Gardan GY-201 Minicab	K. A. Hyam	
G-BBFV	PA-32-260 Cherokee Six	A. M. W. Driskell	
G-BBGI	Fuji FA.200-160	R. G. Fielding	
G-BBHJ	Piper J-3C-65 Cub	Wellcross Flying Group	
G-BBHK	Noorduyn AT-16 Harvard IIB (FH153)	M. Kubrak	
G-BBHY	PA-28-180 Cherokee	G. K. Clarkson	
G-BBIF	PA-23-250E Aztec	Marshall of Cambridge Aerospace Ltd	
G-BBIL	PA-28-140 Cherokee	Saxondale Group	
G-BBIO	Robin HR.100/210	R. P. Caley	
G-BBIX	PA-28-140 Cherokee	R. D. Hale	
G-BBJI	Isaacs Spitfire	M. J. Bond	
G-BBJU	Robin DR.400/140	P. F. Moderate	
G-BBJX	Cessna F.150L	Aviolease Ltd	
G-BBJY	Cessna F.172M	D. G. Wright	
G-BBJZ	Cessna F.172M	Aerographics GIS Ltd	
G-BBKA	Cessna F.150L	Aviolease Ltd	
G-BBKB	Cessna F.150L	Aviolease Ltd	
G-BBKG	Cessna FR.172J	R. Wright	
G-BBKI	Cessna F.172M	R. Hunt & R. B. Hunter	
G-BBKL	CP.301A Emeraude	K. R. Nestor	
G-BBKX	PA-28-180 Cherokee	DRA Flying Club Ltd	
G-BBKY	Cessna F.150L	F. W. Astbury	
G-BBKZ	Cessna 172M	KZ Flying Group	
G-BBLH	Piper J-3C-65 Cub (31145:G-26)	Shipping & Airlines Ltd	
G-BBLM	SOCATA Rallye 100S ★	Aeropark/East Midlands	
G-BBLS	AA-5 Traveler	Bubbles Flying Group	
G-BBLU	PA-34-200 Seneca II	R. H. R. Rue	
G-BBMB	Robin DR.400/180	R. A. Doorgakant & V. J. Pellatt	
G-BBMH	EAA. Sports Biplane Model P.1	G-BBMH Flying Group	
G-BBMN	DHC.1 Chipmunk 22	S. Baker	
G-BBMO	DHC.1 Chipmunk 22 (WK514)	Mike Oscar Group	

Notes	Reg	Type	Owner or Operator
	G-BBMR	DHC.1 Chipmunk 22 (WB763:14)	Lockon Aviation Services Ltd
	G-BBMT	DHC.1 Chipmunk 22	MT Group
	G-BBMV	DHC.1 Chipmunk 22 (WG348)	Angels 13 Ltd
	G-BBMW	DHC.1 Chipmunk 22 (WK628)	G. Fielder & A. Wilson
	G-BBMZ	DHC.1 Chipmunk 22	G-BBMZ Chipmunk Syndicate
	G-BBNA	DHC.1 Chipmunk 22 (Lycoming)	Husbands Bosworth Gliding Club Ltd
	G-BBNC	DHC.1 Chipmunk T.10 (WP790) ★	De Havilland Heritage Museum/London Colney
	G-BBND	DHC.1 Chipmunk 22 (WD286)	Bernoulli Syndicate
	G-BBNI	PA-34-200 Seneca II	D. H. G. Penney
	G-BBNT	PA-31-350 Navajo Chieftain	Gulfjet Aviation Ltd
	G-BBOA	Cessna F.172M	Avalon Ventures Ltd
	G-BBOH	Pitts S-1S Special	P. H. Meeson
	G-BBOL	PA-18-150 Super Cub	N. Moore
	G-BBOR	Bell 206B JetRanger 2	G. D. B. Budworth
	G-BBPP	PA-28-180 Cherokee	Starlift Aviations Ltd (G-WACP)
	G-BBPS	Jodel D.117	V. F. Flett
	G-BBRA	PA-23 Aztec 250D	Sulafat OU/Estonia
	G-BBRB	DH.82A Tiger Moth	R. Barham
	G-BBRC	Fuji FA.200-180	BBRC Ltd
	G-BBRI	Bell 47G-5A	Alan Mann Aviation Group Ltd
	G-BBRN	Procter Kittiwake 1 (XW784/VL)	D. G. Jones
	G-BBRZ	AA-5 Traveler	M. A. & R. Wilson
	G-BBSS	DHC.1A Chipmunk 22	Husbands Bosworth Gliding Club Ltd
	G-BBTB	Cessna FRA.150L	A. D. Taylor
	G-BBTG	Cessna F.172M	M. Walton
	G-BBTK	Cessna FRA.150L	Cleveland Flying School Ltd
	G-BBTY	Beech C23 Sundowner	M. Porter
	G-BBUJ	Cessna 421B	Aero VIP Companhia de Transportes & Servicios Aereos SA/Portugal
	G-BBUT	Western O-65 balloon	R. G. Turnbull
	G-BBUU	Piper J-3C-65 Cub	C. Stokes
	G-BBVF	SA Twin Pioneer Srs 3 ★	Museum of Flight/East Fortune
	G-BBVO	Isaacs Fury II (K5682)	S. Vince
	G-BBXB	Cessna FRA.150L	D. C. Somerville
	G-BBXK	PA-34-200 Seneca	J. D. Moon (G-FBPL)
	G-BBXW	PA-28-151 Cherokee Warrior	Bristol Aero Club
	G-BBXY	Bellanca 7GCBC Citabria	S. A. Windus
	G-BBYB	PA-18-95 Super Cub	Perryair Ltd
	G-BBYH	Cessna 182P	Ramco (UK) Ltd
	G-BBYM	HP.137 Jetstream 200 ★	Aerospace Museum/Cosford (G-AYWR)
	G-BBYP	PA-28-140 Cherokee	Emsworth Heating Ltd
	G-BBYU	Cameron O-56 balloon ★	British Balloon Museum
	G-BBZH	PA-28R-200 Cherokee Arrow II	S. I. Tugwell
	G-BBZN	Fuji FA.200-180	D. Kynaston
	G-BBZV	PA-28R-200 Cherokee Arrow II	P. B. Mellor
	G-BCAH	DHC.1 Chipmunk 22 (WG316)	P. M. Shelton & J. R. C. Spooner
	G-BCAP	Cameron O-56 balloon ★	Balloon Preservation Group/Lancing
	G-BCAR	Thunder Ax7-77 balloon ★	British Balloon Museum/Newbury
	G-BCAZ	PA-12 Super Cruiser	J. Forshaw
	G-BCBH	Fairchild 24R-46A Argus III (HB737)	H. Mackintosh
	G-BCBJ	PA-25-235 Pawnee	Deeside Gliding Club (Aberdeenshire) Ltd
	G-BCBL	Fairchild 24R-46A Argus III (HB751)	R. A. Fleming
	G-BCBR	AJEP/Wittman W.8 Tailwind	D. P. Jones
	G-BCBX	Cessna F.150L	Fly With Me Aviation Ltd
	G-BCCE	PA-23-250E Aztec	Golf Charlie Echo Ltd
	G-BCCF	PA-28-180 Cherokee	Charlie Foxtrot Aviation
	G-BCCK	AA-5 Traveler	J. B. Mills
	G-BCCR	CP.301A Emeraude (modified)	I. Taberer
	G-BCCX	DHC.1 Chipmunk 22 (Lycoming)	Charlie X-Ray Syndicate Ltd
	G-BCCY	Robin HR.200/100	Fly With Me Aviation Ltd
	G-BCDN	F.27 Friendship Mk 200 ★	City of Norwich Aviation Museum/Norwich
	G-BCDY	Cessna FRA.150L	M. Bonsall
	G-BCEE	AA-5 Traveler	D. Joy
	G-BCEP	AA-5 Traveler	S. P. Adshead
	G-BCER	Gardan GY-201 Minicab	M. J. Sharp
	G-BCEU	Cameron O-42 balloon	P. Glydon
	G-BCEY	DHC.1 Chipmunk 22 (WG465)	The Roger Mills Flying Group
	G-BCFO	PA-18-150 Super Cub	D. J. Ashley (G-MUDI)
	G-BCFR	Cessna FRA.150L	Foxtrot Romeo Group
	G-BCFW	SAAB 91D Safir	R. Callaway-Lewis

Reg	Type	Owner or Operator	Notes
G-BCGB	Bensen B.8	A. Melody	
G-BCGC	DHC.1 Chipmunk 22 (WP903)	Henlow Chipmunk Group	
G-BCGH	SNCAN NC.854S	J. A. S. Everett	
G-BCGI	PA-28-140 Cherokee	D. H. G. Penny	
G-BCGJ	PA-28-140 Cherokee	LS Airmotive Ltd	
G-BCGM	Jodel D.120	P. Armstrong	
G-BCGN	PA-28-140 Cherokee	C. F. Hessey	
G-BCGS	PA-28R-200 Cherokee Arrow	Academy Aviation Ltd	
G-BCGW	Jodel D.11	G. H. Chittenden	
G-BCHL	DHC.1 Chipmunk 22A (WP788)	Shropshire Soaring Ltd	
G-BCHP	CP.1310-C3 Super Emeraude	Emeraude Flying Group (G-JOSI)	
G-BCHT	Schleicher ASK.16	P. T. Claiden	
G-BCIH	DHC.1 Chipmunk 22 (WD363)	J. F. Hogan	
G-BCIR	PA-28-151 Cherokee Warrior	Aerobility	
G-BCJM	PA-28-140 Cherokee	A. M. S. Sher	
G-BCJO	PA-28R-200 Cherokee Arrow	G-BCJO Group	
G-BCJP	PA-28 -140 Cherokee	S. Turton	
G-BCKN	DHC.1A Chipmunk 22 (Lycoming) (WP811)	M. D. Cowburn	
G-BCKS	Fuji FA.200-180AO	G. J. Ward	
G-BCKT	Fuji FA.200-180	A. G. Dobson	
G-BCKV	Cessna FRA.150L	M. Bonsall	
G-BCLI	AA-5 Traveler	A. Vaicvenas	
G-BCLS	Cessna 170B	M. J. Whiteman-Haywood	
G-BCLU	Jodel D.117	D. H. G. Cotter	
G-BCMD	PA-18-95 Super Cub	P. Stephenson	
G-BCMJ	Squarecraft Cavalier SA.102-5	N. F. Andrews	
G-BCMT	Isaacs Fury II	C. M. Barnes	
G-BCNC	Gardan GY-201 Minicab	J. R. Wraight	
G-BCNP	Cameron O-77 balloon	P. Spellward	
G-BCNX	Piper J-3C-65 Cub (540)	C. M. L. Edwards	
G-BCOB	Piper J-3C-65 Cub (329405:A-23)	C. Marklew-Brown	
G-BCOI	DHC.1 Chipmunk 22 (WP870:12)	A. A. C. Carter	
G-BCOM	Piper J-3C-65 Cub	BCOM Flying Group	
G-BCOO	DHC.1 Chipmunk 22	Double Oscar Chipmunk Group	
G-BCOU	DHC.1 Chipmunk 22 (WK522)	Loweth Flying Group	
G-BCOW	Hawker Sea Fury T.20 (VX281)	The Fighter Collection Ltd (G-RNHF)	
G-BCOY	DHC.1 Chipmunk 22	T. W. Treadaway	
G-BCPD	Gardan GY-201 Minicab	P. R. Cozens	
G-BCPG	PA-28R-200 Cherokee Arrow II	W. Ali & Denderah SA	
G-BCPH	Piper J-3C-65 Cub (329934:B-72)	G. Earl	
G-BCPJ	Piper J-3C-65 Cub	J. C. Tempest	
G-BCPN	AA-5 Traveler	C. M. Davis & C. Scott	
G-BCPU	DHC.1 Chipmunk 22 (WP973)	G-BCPU Group	
G-BCRB	Cessna F.172M	Wingstask 1995Ltd	
G-BCRE	Cameron O-77 balloon ★	Balloon Preservation Group/Lancing	
G-BCRL	PA-28-151 Cherokee Warrior	Praeluceo Property Ltd	
G-BCRR	AA-5B Tiger	S. Waite	
G-BCRX	DHC.1 Chipmunk 22 (WD292)	Chipmunk WD292 Ltd	
G-BCSA	DHC.1 Chipmunk 22 (Lycoming)	Edgehill Gliding Centre Ltd	
G-BCSL	DHC.1 Chipmunk 22	I. L. Smith	
G-BCTF	PA-28-151 Cherokee Warrior	I. J. Hiatt	
G-BCTI	Schleicher ASK 16	Tango India Syndicate	
G-BCTK	Cessna FR.172J	M. G. E. Morton	
G-BCUB	Piper J-3C-65 Cub	S. L. Goldspink	
G-BCUH	Cessna F.150M	W. Ali & Denderah SA	
G-BCUJ	Cessna F.150M	C. G. Dodds	
G-BCUL	SOCATA Rallye 100ST	C. A. Ussher & Fountain Estates Ltd	
G-BCUO	SA Bulldog Srs 120/122	Cranfield University	
G-BCUS	SA Bulldog Srs 120/122	Falcon Group	
G-BCUV	SA Bulldog Srs 120/122 (XX704)	Flew LLP	
G-BCUW	Cessna F.177RG	S. J. Westley	
G-BCUY	Cessna FRA.150M	Dunmall Construction Ltd	
G-BCVB	PA-17 Vagabond	A. T. Nowak	
G-BCVE	Evans VP-2	D. Masterson & D. B. Winstanley	
G-BCVF	Practavia Pilot Sprite	A. C. Barber	
G-BCVG	Cessna FRA.150L	N. A. Baxter	
G-BCVJ	Cessna F.172M	Rothland Ltd	
G-BCVY	PA-34-200T Seneca II	Topex Ltd	
G-BCWB	Cessna 182P	V. Phillips	
G-BCWH	Practavia Pilot Sprite	J. C. Farquhar	
G-BCWK	Alpavia Fournier RF-3	P. Andrews	

Notes	Reg	Type	Owner or Operator
	G-BCXE	Robin DR.400/2+2	Weald Air Services Ltd
	G-BCXJ	Piper L-4J Cub (480752:E-39)	N. S. Lomax
	G-BCXN	DHC.1 Chipmunk 22 (WP800)	J. A. Moolenschot
	G-BCYH	DAW Privateer Mk. 3	G-BCYH Group
	G-BCYK	Avro CF.100 Mk 4 Canuck (18393) ★	Imperial War Museum/Duxford
	G-BCYM	DHC.1 Chipmunk 22 (WK577)	C. H. M. Brown
	G-BCYR	Cessna F.172M	D. N. Sluman
	G-BDAD	Taylor JT.1 Monoplane	B. M. Dews
	G-BDAG	Taylor JT.1 Monoplane	G. T. Bayliss & B. M. Buglass
	G-BDAH	Evans VP-1	M. W. Roberts
	G-BDAI	Cessna FRA.150M	D. J. M. Randall
	G-BDAK	Rockwell Commander 112	M. C. Wilson
	G-BDAM	RT-16 Harvard IIB (FE992:ER-992)	T. W. Harris
	G-BDAO	SIPA S.91	S. J. Weiss
	G-BDAP	AJEP Tailwind	D. G. Kelly
	G-BDAR	Evans VP-1	A. J. Gillson & P. W. Cooper
	G-BDAY	Thunder Ax5-42S1 balloon	J. F. Till
	G-BDBD	Wittman W.8 Tailwind	I. N. Scott
	G-BDBI	Cameron O-77 balloon	C. Jones
	G-BDBS	Short SD3-30 ★	Ulster Aviation Society/Long Kesh
	G-BDBV	Jodel D.11A	Seething Jodel Group
	G-BDBZ	Westland WS-55 Whirlwind (XJ398) ★	Yorkshire Helicopter Preservation Group/Doncaster
	G-BDCD	Piper J-3C-85 Cub (480133:B-44)	Cubby Cub Group
	G-BDCI	CP.301A Emeraude	M. T. Slater
	G-BDDF	Jodel D.120	J. V. Thompson
	G-BDDG	Jodel D.112	J. Pool & D. G. Palmer
	G-BDDS	PA-25-235 Pawnee	Black Mountains Gliding Club
	G-BDDX	Whittaker MW2B Excalibur ★	Cornwall Aero Park/Helston
	G-BDEH	Jodel D.120A	N. J. Cronin
	G-BDEI	Jodel D.9 Bébé	The Noddy Group
	G-BDEY	Piper J-3C-65 Cub	A. V. Williams
	G-BDFB	Currie Wot	J. Jennings
	G-BDFH	Auster AOP.9 (XR240)	J. K. Houlgrave
	G-BDFR	Fuji FA.200-160	C. B. Mellor
	G-BDFU	Dragonfly MPA Mk 1 ★	Museum of Flight/East Fortune
	G-BDFX	Taylorcraft Auster 5	A. D. Pearce
	G-BDFY	AA-5 Traveler	Grumman Group
	G-BDGB	Gardan GY-20 Minicab	K. M. Charlton
	G-BDGM	PA-28-151 Cherokee Warrior	W. Ali & Denderah SA
	G-BDGY	PA-28-140 Cherokee	J. Eagles
	G-BDHJ	Pazmany PL-1	R. Loveday
	G-BDHK	J-3C-65 Cub (329417)	S. Pritchard
	G-BDIE	Rockwell Commander 112	J. McAleer & R. J. Adams
	G-BDIG	Cessna 182P	J. A. Lee
	G-BDIX	DH.106 Comet 4C ★	Museum of Flight/East Fortune
	G-BDJD	Jodel D.112	The Real Aeroplane Company Ltd
	G-BDJG	Luton LA-4A Minor	Luton Minor Group
	G-BDJP	Piper J-3C-90 Cub	L. J. Gilbert
	G-BDKC	Cessna A185F	Lude & Invergarry Farm Partnership
	G-BDKH	CP.301A Emeraude	R. K. Griggs
	G-BDKM	SIPA 903	S. W. Markham
	G-BDKW	Rockwell Commander 112A	D. I. King
	G-BDLO	AA-5A Cheetah	J. M. Emmett
	G-BDLT	Rockwell Commander 112	I. Parkinson
	G-BDLY	K & S SA.102.5 Cavalier	P. R. Stevens
	G-BDMS	Piper J-3C-65 Cub (FR886)	A. J. Blackford
	G-BDMW	Jodel DR.100A	Mike Whiskey Group
	G-BDNG	Taylor JT.1 Monoplane	C. E. A. J. Pearce
	G-BDNI	Westland Sea King Mk.48 (RS02)	Lift West (Helicopters) Ltd
	G-BDNK	Westland Sea King Mk.48 (RS04)	Lift West (Helicopters) Ltd
	G-BDNR	Cessna FRA.150M	M. Bonsall
	G-BDNT	Jodel D.92 Bébé	R. J. Stobo
	G-BDNU	Cessna F.172M	Greenbaum Training & Consultancy Ltd
	G-BDNW	AA-1B Trainer	N. A. Baxter
	G-BDNX	AA-1B Trainer	Eshott Grumman Group
	G-BDOD	Cessna F.150M	Community Air Support Service (SCIO)
	G-BDOG	SA Bulldog Srs 200	D. C. Bonsall
	G-BDOL	Piper J-3C-65 Cub (454630)	L. R. Balthazor
	G-BDPA	PA-28-151 Cherokee Warrior	AN Associates

Reg	Type	Owner or Operator	Notes
G-BDRD	Cessna FRA.150M	CBM Associates Consulting Ltd	
G-BDSB	PA-28-181 Cherokee Archer II	Testair Ltd	
G-BDSF	Cameron O-56 balloon	D. M. Wade	
G-BDSH	PA-28-140 Cherokee (modified)	The Wright Brothers Flying Group	
G-BDSM	Slingsby T.31B Cadet III	F. C. J. Wevers/Netherlands	
G-BDTB	Evans VP-1	J. M. Graves	
G-BDTL	Evans VP-1 series 2	S. A. Daniels	
G-BDTU	Omega III gas balloon	R. G. Turnbull	
G-BDTX	Cessna F.150M	Virage Aviation LLP	
G-BDUL	Evans VP-1 Srs.2	O. Craggs	
G-BDUO	Cessna F.150M	Z. S. Khan	
G-BDUY	Robin DR.400/140B	I. A. Anderson	
G-BDUZ	Cameron V-56 balloon	Zebedee Balloon Service	
G-BDVA	PA-17 Vagabond	M. G. Britten	
G-BDVB	PA-15 (PA-17) Vagabond	B. P. Gardner	
G-BDVC	PA-17 Vagabond	C. R. & R. J. Whitcombe	
G-BDWE	Flaglor Scooter	D. P. Murphy	
G-BDWJ	SE-5A (replica) (F8010:Z)	D. W. Linney	
G-BDWM	Mustang scale replica (414673:LH-I))	D. V. Griffith	
G-BDXX	SNCAN NC.858S	K. M. Davis	
G-BDYG	P.56 Provost T.1 (WV493) ★	Museum of Flight/East Fortune	
G-BDZA	Scheibe SF.25E Super Falke	Hereward Flying Group	
G-BDZD	Cessna F.172M	M. Watkinson	
G-BDZG	Slingsby T.59H Kestrel	M. Williamson	
G-BEAB	Jodel DR.1051	R. C. Hibberd & P. J. Fell	
G-BEAC	PA-28-140 Cherokee	Aircraft Leasing UK Ltd	
G-BEAD	WG.13 Lynx ★	Instructional airframe/Middle Wallop	
G-BEAH	Auster J/2 Arrow	Bedwell Hey Flying Group	
G-BEBC	Westland WS-55 Whirlwind 3 (XP355) ★	Norwich Aviation Museum	
G-BEBN	Cessna 177B	S. K. Gheyi	
G-BEBS	Andreasson BA-4B	T. D. Wood	
G-BEBT	Andreasson BA-4B	T. D. Wood (G-JEDS)	
G-BEBZ	PA-28-151 Cherokee Warrior	P. E. Taylor	
G-BECB	SOCATA Rallye 100ST	J. C. H. Tonkin	
G-BECK	Cameron V-56 balloon	N. H. & A. M. Ponsford	
G-BECN	Piper J-3C-65 Cub (480480:E-44)	CN Cub Group	
G-BECU	CASA 1.131E Jungmann 2000	R. J. Watts	
G-BECW	CASA 1.131E Jungmann 2000 (A-10)	C. Butler	
G-BECZ	CAARP CAP-10B	The London Aerobatic Company Ltd	
G-BEDA	CASA 1-131E Jungmann Srs.2000	T. Callier	
G-BEDB	Nord 1203 Norecrin ★	B. F. G. Lister (stored)/Chirk	
G-BEDF	Boeing B-17G-105-VE (124485:DF-A)	B-17 Preservation Ltd	
G-BEDG	Rockwell Commander 112	G-BEDG Group	
G-BEDJ	Piper J-3C-65 Cub (44-80504)	B. J. Portus	
G-BEDV	V.668 Varsity T.1 (WJ945) ★	Cornwall Aviation Heritage Centre/Newquay	
G-BEEE	Thunder Ax6-56A balloon ★	British Balloon Museum/Newbury	
G-BEER	Isaacs Fury II (K2075)	C. E. Styles	
G-BEFA	PA-28-151 Cherokee Warrior	M. Lawrynowicz	
G-BEGG	Scheibe SF.25E Super Falke	G-BEGG Motorfalke	
G-BEHH	PA-32R-300 Cherokee Lance	K. Swallow	
G-BEHU	PA-34-200T Seneca II	Heli Air Ltd	
G-BEHV	Cessna F.172N	Leading Edge Flight Training Ltd	
G-BEIF	Cameron O-65 balloon	C. Vening	
G-BEIG	Cessna F.150M	R. D. Forster	
G-BEII	PA-25-235D Pawnee	Burn Gliding Club Ltd	
G-BEIS	Evans VP-1	D. L. Haines	
G-BEJD	Avro 748 Series 1 ★	Speke Aerodrome Heritage Group	
G-BEJK	Cameron S-31 balloon	Rango Balloon and Kite Company	
G-BEKN	Cessna FRA.150M	Peterborough Flying School Ltd	
G-BEKO	Cessna F.182Q	G. J. & F. J. Leese	
G-BELF	BN-2A-26 Islander ★	Museum of Flight/East Fortune	
G-BELT	Cessna F.150J	W. B. Bateson (G-AWUV)	
G-BEMB	Cessna F.172M	I. R. Bennett	
G-BEMW	PA-28-181 Cherokee Archer II	Touch & Go Ltd	
G-BEMY	Cessna FRA.150M	J. R. Power	
G-BEND	Cameron V-56 balloon	Dante Balloon Group	
G-BENJ	Rockwell Commander 112B	BENJ Flying Group	
G-BEOE	Cessna FRA.150M	W. J. Henderson	
G-BEOH	PA-28R-201T Turbo Cherokee Arrow III	Gloucestershire Flying Club	
G-BEOI	PA-18-150 Super Cub	A. E. Leoning	

Notes	Reg	Type	Owner or Operator
	G-BEOX	Lockheed 414 Hudson IV (A16-199) ★	RAF Museum/Hendon
	G-BEOY	Cessna FRA.150L	G. A. P. Walker
	G-BEOZ	A.W.650 Argosy 101 ★	Aeropark/East Midlands
	G-BEPV	Fokker S.11-1 Instructor (174)	S. W. & M. Isbister & C. Tyers
	G-BEPY	Rockwell Commander 112B	T. L. Rippon
	G-BERI	Rockwell Commander 114	G-BERI Group
	G-BERN	Saffrey S-330 balloon	B. Martin
	G-BERT	Cameron V-56 balloon	E. C. Barker
	G-BERY	AA-1B Trainer	Glasgow Prestwick Flight Centre
	G-BETD	Robin HR.200/100	M. P. Holdstock
	G-BETE	Rollason B.2A Beta	T. M. Jones
	G-BETF	Cameron 'Champion' SS balloon ★	British Balloon Museum/Newbury
	G-BEUA	PA-18-150 Super Cub	London Gliding Club (Pty) Ltd
	G-BEUD	Robin HR.100/285R	A. J. Verlander
	G-BEUI	Piper J-3C-65 Cub (479878)	C. F. Dukes
	G-BEUP	Robin DR.400/180	C. A. Woehrel
	G-BEUU	PA-18-95 Super Cub	J. W. Wolfe
	G-BEUX	Cessna F.172N	Aerohire Ltd
	G-BEVB	SOCATA Rallye 150ST	A. C. Stamp
	G-BEVC	SOCATA Rallye 150ST	M. Jennings & A. Foster
	G-BEVG	PA-34-200T Seneca II	AWA Aeronautical Web Academy LDA
	G-BEVO	Sportavia-Pützer RF-5	RF Syndicate
	G-BEVP	Evans VP-2	G. Moscrop & R. C. Crowley
	G-BEVS	Taylor JT.1 Monoplane	N. D. Hunter
	G-BEVT	BN-2A Mk III-2 Trislander ★	Imperial War Museum/Duxford
	G-BEWN	DH.82A Tiger Moth	H. D. Labouchere
	G-BEWR	Cessna F.172N	Bliss Aviation Ltd
	G-BEWX	PA-28R-201 Cherokee Arrow III	Three Greens Arrow Group
	G-BEXN	AA-1C Lynx	Fly With Me Aviation Ltd
	G-BEXW	PA-28-181 Cherokee Archer II	AT Aviation Sales Ltd
	G-BEYB	Fairey Flycatcher (replica) (S1287) ★	F.A.A. Museum/Yeovilton
	G-BEYF	HPR.7 Herald 401 ★ (nose section)	Bournemouth Aviation Museum/Bournemouth
	G-BEYL	PA-28-180 Cherokee	Yankee Lima Group
	G-BEYT	PA-28-140 Cherokee	J. N. Plange
	G-BEYV	Cessna T.210M	P. Middleton
	G-BEYZ	Jodel DR.1051/M1	W. H. Bliss
	G-BEZC	AA-5 Traveler	Easter Flying Group
	G-BEZE	Rutan Vari-Eze	S. K. Cockburn
	G-BEZF	AA-5 Traveler	Phoenix Flying Group
	G-BEZG	AA-5 Traveler	G-BEZG Flying Group
	G-BEZI	AA-5 Traveler	J. R. & L. J. Campbell
	G-BEZK	Cessna F.172H	J. P. Nugent
	G-BEZL	PA-31-310 Turbo Navajo C	2 Excel Aviation Ltd
	G-BEZO	Cessna F.172M	Staverton Flying School @ Skypark Ltd
	G-BEZP	PA-32-300 Cherokee Six	T. P. McCormack & J. K. Zealley
	G-BEZV	Cessna F.172M	Alexander Air Ltd
	G-BEZY	Rutan Vari-Eze	J. P. Kynaston
	G-BFAF	Aeronca 7BCM Champion (47-797:A-797)	D. A. Crompton
	G-BFAP	SIAI-Marchetti S.205-20R	N. C. du Piesanie
	G-BFAS	Evans VP-1	A. I. Sutherland
	G-BFAW	DHC.1 Chipmunk 22 (WP848)	M. L. J. Goff
	G-BFAX	DHC.1 Chipmunk 22 (WG422)	R. Harrison
	G-BFBE	Robin HR.200/100	A. C. Pearson
	G-BFBM	Saffery S.330 balloon	B. Martin
	G-BFBR	PA-28-161 Cherokee Warrior II	Phoenix Aviation
	G-BFBY	Piper J-3C-65 Cub (329707:S-44)	M. Shaw
	G-BFCZ	Sopwith Camel F.1 Replica (B7270) ★	Brooklands Museum of Aviation/Weybridge
	G-BFDC	DHC.1 Chipmunk 22 (WG475)	N. F. O'Neill
	G-BFDE	Sopwith Tabloid (replica) (168) ★	RAF Museum/Hendon
	G-BFDI	PA-28-181 Cherokee Archer II	Truman Aviation Ltd
	G-BFDK	PA-28-161 Cherokee Warrior II	L. J. Gilbert
	G-BFDL	Piper J-3C-65 Cub (454537:J-04)	B. A. Nicholson
	G-BFDO	PA-28R-201T Turbo Cherokee Arrow III	B. Simon
	G-BFEB	Jodel 150	G-BFEB Syndicate
	G-BFEF	Agusta-Bell 47G-3B1	I. F. Vaughan
	G-BFEH	Jodel D.117A	D. J. Lockett
	G-BFEK	Cessna F.152	Staverton Flying School @ Skypark Ltd
	G-BFEV	PA-25-235 Pawnee	Yorkshire Gliding Club (Proprietary) Ltd
	G-BFFE	Cessna F.152-II	A. J. Hastings
	G-BFFP	PA-18-150 Super Cub (modified)	G-BFFP Group

Reg	Type	Owner or Operator	Notes
G-BFFW	Cessna F.152	Stapleford Flying Club Ltd	
G-BFGD	Cessna F.172N-II	Wannabe Flyers	
G-BFGG	Cessna FRA.150M	G. Oliver	
G-BFGH	Cessna F.337G	S. Findlay	
G-BFGK	Jodel D.117	A. D. Eastwood	
G-BFGL	Cessna FA.152	Sherburn Aero Club Ltd	
G-BFGS	MS.893E Rallye 180GT	Chiltern Flyers Ltd	
G-BFGZ	Cessna FRA.150M	India Victor Flying Group	
G-BFHH	DH.82A Tiger Moth	T. J. Harrison	
G-BFHI	Piper J-3C-65 Cub	J. Glass & A. J. Richardson	
G-BFHP	Champion 7GCAA Citabria	M. Walker & M. R. Keen	
G-BFHR	Jodel DR.220/2+2	D. E. Seagrave	
G-BFHU	Cessna F.152-II	M. Bonsall	
G-BFHX	Evans VP-1	D. A. Milstead	
G-BFID	Taylor JT.2 Titch Mk III	M. V. Brown	
G-BFIN	AA-5A Cheetah	Aircraft Engineers Ltd	
G-BFIP	Wallbro Monoplane 1909 (replica) ★	Norfolk & Suffolk Aviation Museum/Flixton	
G-BFIT	Thunder Ax6-56Z balloon	J. A. G. Tyson	
G-BFIU	Cessna FR.172K XP	A. C. Saunders	
G-BFIV	Cessna F.177RG	C. Fisher & M. L. Miller	
G-BFIX	Thunder Ax7-77A balloon	S. J. Owen	
G-BFJR	Cessna F.337G	Centreline Aviation Ltd	
G-BFJZ	Robin DR.400/140B	Weald Air Services Ltd	
G-BFKB	Cessna F.172N	S. A. Jordan	
G-BFLU	Cessna F.152	Brinkley Aviation Ltd	
G-BFLX	AA-5A Cheetah	A. M. Verdon	
G-BFMF	Cassutt Racer IIIM	T. Jarvis	
G-BFMG	PA-28-161 Cherokee Warrior II	Andrewsfield Aviation Ltd	
G-BFMH	Cessna 177B	L. S. Walker	
G-BFMK	Cessna FA.152	The Leicestershire Aero Club Ltd	
G-BFMR	PA-20-125 Pacer	Weald Air Services Ltd	
G-BFMX	Cessna F.172N	M. Rowe	
G-BFNG	Jodel D.112	NG Group	
G-BFNI	PA-28-161 Cherokee Warrior II	Air Training Club Aviation Ltd	
G-BFNK	PA-28-161 Cherokee Warrior II	Parachuting Aircraft Ltd	
G-BFNM	Globe GC-1B Swift	M. J. Butler	
G-BFOE	Cessna F.152	Redhill Air Services Ltd	
G-BFOJ	AA-1 Yankee	Fly With Me Aviation Ltd	
G-BFOU	Taylor JT.1 Monoplane	G. Bee	
G-BFPA	Scheibe SF.25B Falke	W. J. Grieve	
G-BFPH	Cessna F.172K	Linc-Air Flying Group	
G-BFPP	Bell 47J-2 Ranger	M. R. Masters	
G-BFPR	PA-25-235 Pawnee	Peterborough & Spalding Gliding Club Ltd	
G-BFPZ	Cessna F.177RG	G. E. Thompson	
G-BFRR	Cessna FRA.150M	Romeo Romeo Flying Group	
G-BFRS	Cessna F.172N	Aerocomm Ltd	
G-BFRV	Cessna FA.152	Ovin Ltd	
G-BFSA	Cessna F.182Q	Delta Lima Flying Group	
G-BFSC	PA-25-235 Pawnee	Essex Gliding Club Ltd	
G-BFSD	PA-25-235 Pawnee	Deeside Gliding Club (Aberdeenshire) Ltd	
G-BFSS	Cessna FR.172G	Albedale Farms Ltd	
G-BFSY	PA-28-181 Cherokee Archer II	Downland Aviation	
G-BFSZ	PA-28-161 Cherokee Warrior II	R. J. Whyham (G-KBPI)	
G-BFTC	PA-28R-201T Turbo Cherokee Arrow III	Top Cat Flying Group	
G-BFTF	AA-5B Tiger	F. C. Burrow Ltd	
G-BFTG	AA-5B Tiger	G. R. Montgomery	
G-BFTH	Cessna F.172N	W. Ali & D. O. Kleszcz	
G-BFTZ	MS.880B Rallye Club ★	Newark Air Museum/Newark	
G-BFUB	PA-32RT-300 Lance II	J. Lowndes	
G-BFUD	Scheibe SF.25E Super Falke	C. Le Brocq & N. A. C. E. Barnes	
G-BFVH	DH.2 (replica) (5964)	S. W. Turley	
G-BFVS	AA-5B Tiger	G. M. Diamond	
G-BFVU	Cessna 150L	A. N. Mole	
G-BFWB	PA-28-161 Cherokee Warrior II	Mid-Anglia School of Flying	
G-BFWD	Currie Wot (A8936)	J. W. Wolfe	
G-BFXF	Andreasson BA.4B	P. N. Birch	
G-BFXG	D.31 Turbulent	XG Group	
G-BFXK	PA-28-140 Cherokee	S. Fotheringham & P. V. Newman	
G-BFXL	Albatros D.5a replica (D5397/17) ★	F.A.A. Museum/Yeovilton	
G-BFXR	Jodel D.112	R. G. Marshall	
G-BFXW	AA-5B Tiger	Xray Whiskey Group	

Notes	Reg	Type	Owner or Operator
	G-BFXX	AA-5B Tiger	W. R. Gibson
	G-BFYA	MBB Bö.105DB	Wessex Aviation Ltd
	G-BFYI	Westland-Bell 47G-3B1	K. P. Mayes
	G-BFYK	Cameron V-77 balloon	L. E. Jones
	G-BFYL	Evans VP-2	F. C. Handy
	G-BFYO	SPAD XIII (replica) (4513:1) ★	American Air Museum/Duxford
	G-BFYW	Slingsby T.65 Vega 17L	D. A. Blunden
	G-BFZB	Piper J-3C-85 Cub (480723:E5-J)	M. S. Pettit
	G-BFZD	Cessna FR.182RG	R. Everitt
	G-BFZM	Rockwell Commander 112TC	J. A. Hart & R. J. Lamplough
	G-BGAA	Cessna 152 II	PJC Leasing Ltd
	G-BGAB	Cessna F.152 II	Touchdown Engineering Ltd
	G-BGAE	Cessna F.152 II	Aerolease Ltd
	G-BGAJ	Cessna F.182Q II	J. S. Thrush
	G-BGAZ	Cameron V-77 balloon	C. J. Madigan & D. H. McGibbon
	G-BGBE	Jodel DR.1050	J. A. & B. Mawby
	G-BGBF	Druine D.31 Turbulent	T. A. Stambach
	G-BGBG	PA-28-181 Cherokee Archer II	North East Flight Academy Ltd
	G-BGBI	Cessna F.150L	Aviolease Ltd
	G-BGBK	PA-38-112 Tomahawk	British Aviation Academy Ltd
	G-BGBV	Slingsby T65 Vega 17L	J. P. W. Roche-Kelly
	G-BGBW	PA-38-112 Tomahawk	D. H. G. Penney
	G-BGCB	Slingsby T.65 Vega 17L	UWE Students' Union, University of the West of England Gliding Club
	G-BGCO	PA-44-180 Seminole	Merseyflight Ltd
	G-BGCU	Slingsby T.65A Vega	P. Hadfield
	G-BGCY	Taylor JT.1 Monoplane	S. W. Barnett
	G-BGEF	Jodel D.112	G. G. Johnson
	G-BGEI	Baby Great Lakes	G. D. Thomas
	G-BGES	Phoenix Currie Super Wot	ZE Shadow Team Ltd
	G-BGFX	Cessna F.152	Redhill Air Services Ltd
	G-BGGA	Bellanca 7GCBC Citabria	R. N. R. Bellamy
	G-BGGB	Bellanca 7GCBC Citabria	G. Williamson
	G-BGGC	Bellanca 7GCBC Citabria	P. E. McShane
	G-BGGD	Bellanca 8GCBC Scout	Bidford Gliding & Flying Club Ltd
	G-BGGE	PA-38-112 Tomahawk	Cutting Edge London Ltd
	G-BGGI	PA-38-112 Tomahawk	British Aviation Academy Ltd
	G-BGGO	Cessna F.152	East Midlands Flying School Ltd
	G-BGGP	Cessna F.152	East Midlands Flying School Ltd
	G-BGHF	Westland WG.30 ★	The Helicopter Museum/Weston-super-Mare
	G-BGHJ	Cessna F.172N	Air Plane Ltd
	G-BGHM	Robin R.1180T	P. Price
	G-BGHT	Falconar F-12	C. R. Coates
	G-BGHU	NA T-6G Texan (115042:TA-042)	Aero Legends Leasing Ltd
	G-BGHY	Taylor JT.1 Monoplane	B. F. Bridges
	G-BGIB	Cessna 152 II	Redhill Air Services Ltd
	G-BGIG	PA-38-112 Tomahawk	Leading Edge Flight Training Ltd
	G-BGIU	Cessna F.172H	S. J. Burke
	G-BGIY	Cessna F.172N	Leading Edge Flight Training Ltd
	G-BGKS	PA-28-161 Cherokee Warrior II	LAC Flying School
	G-BGKT	Auster AOP.9 (XN441)	Kilo Tango Group
	G-BGKU	PA-28R-201 Cherokee Arrow III	Tor Financial Consulting Ltd
	G-BGKV	PA-28R-201 Cherokee Arrow III	R. O. Wells
	G-BGKY	PA-38-112 Tomahawk	APB Leasing Ltd
	G-BGLA	PA-38-112 Tomahawk	E. J. Partridge
	G-BGLB	Bede BD-5B ★	Science Museum/Wroughton
	G-BGLF	Evans VP-1 Srs 2	B. A. Schlussler
	G-BGLG	Cessna 152	Cloud Global Ltd
	G-BGLO	Cessna F.172N	Academy Aviation Ltd
	G-BGLZ	Stits SA-3A Playboy	R. Kane
	G-BGME	SIPA 903	C. M. Knight (G-BCML)
	G-BGMJ	Gardan GY-201 Minicab	G-BGMJ Group
	G-BGMP	Cessna F.172G	Davidson Training Solutions Ltd
	G-BGMR	Gardan GY-20 Minicab	M. P. M. Clements
	G-BGMS	Taylor JT.2 Titch	M. A. J. Spice
	G-BGMT	SOCATA Rallye 235E	C. G. Wheeler & M. Faulkner
	G-BGND	Cessna F.172N	A J Freeman Aircraft Management Ltd
	G-BGNT	Cessna F.152	Aerolease Ltd
	G-BGNV	GA-7 Cougar	Grade Digital Ltd
	G-BGOG	PA-28-161 Cherokee Warrior II	W. D. Moore & F. J. Morris

Reg	Type	Owner or Operator	Notes
G-BGOL	PA-28R-201T Turbo Cherokee Arrow III	L. C. Brown-Ahern	
G-BGOR	AT-6D Harvard III (133908)	M. & W. M. Wilkins	
G-BGPB	CCF T-6J Texan (1747)	Aircraft Spares & Materials Ltd	
G-BGPD	Piper J-3C-65 Cub (479744:M-49)	P. R. Whiteman	
G-BGPH	AA-5B Tiger	S. J. Gidley	
G-BGPI	Plumb BGP-1	B. G. Plumb	
G-BGPJ	PA-28-161 Cherokee Warrior II	W. Lancs Warrior Co Ltd	
G-BGPN	PA-18-150 Super Cub	A. R. Darke	
G-BGRI	Jodel DR.1051	A. P. Woods	
G-BGRO	Cessna F.172M	C. M. Brittlebank	
G-BGRR	PA-38-112 Tomahawk	M. Porter	
G-BGSJ	Piper J-3C-65 Cub (236657)	P. J. Chriswick & A. Cserhalmi	
G-BGTC	Auster AOP.9 (XP282)	J. R. Davison	
G-BGTF	PA-44-180 Seminole	N. A. Baxter (G-OPTC)	
G-BGTI	Piper J-3C-65 Cub	A. P. Broad	
G-BGUB	PA-32-300E Cherokee Six	D. P. & E. A. Morris	
G-BGVE	CP.1310-C3 Super Emeraude	R. Whitwell	
G-BGVH	Beech 76 Duchess	Cerbydau Cenarth Cyf	
G-BGVS	Cessna F.172M	Egoli Enterprises Ltd	
G-BGVV	AA-5A Cheetah	A. D. Long	
G-BGVY	AA-5B Tiger	G-BGVY Ownership	
G-BGVZ	PA-28-181 Cherokee Archer II	Skysure Aviation Ltd	
G-BGWC	Robin DR.400/180	SARL HM MAT Import	
G-BGWM	PA-28-181 Cherokee Archer II	Thames Valley Flying Club Ltd	
G-BGWO	Jodel D.112	S. A. Crossland	
G-BGWZ	Eclipse Super Eagle ★	F.A.A. Museum/Yeovilton	
G-BGXA	Piper J-3C-65 Cub (329471:F-44)	P. King	
G-BGXC	SOCATA TB10 Tobago	M. H. Cundey & S. H. Harley	
G-BGXD	SOCATA TB10 Tobago	Whitewest Ltd	
G-BGXO	PA-38-112 Tomahawk	Goodwood Terrena Ltd	
G-BGXR	Robin HR.200/100	J. W. Cross	
G-BGXS	PA-28-236 Dakota	G-BGXS Group	
G-BGXT	SOCATA TB10 Tobago	P. F. Rothwell	
G-BGYH	PA-28-161 Cherokee Warrior II	Bournemouth Flight Training	
G-BGYN	PA-18-150 Super Cub	W. J. Dunford	
G-BHAA	Cessna 152 II	Herefordshire Aero Club Ltd	
G-BHAD	Cessna A.152	Touchdown Engineering Ltd	
G-BHAI	Cessna F.152	London Flight Experience Ltd	
G-BHAJ	Robin DR.400/160	Rowantask Ltd	
G-BHAR	Westland Bell 47G-3B1	W. K. MacGillivray	
G-BHAV	Cessna F.152	T. M. & M. L. Jones	
G-BHBA	Campbell Cricket	C. R. Anderson	
G-BHBB	Colt 77C balloon	R. H. A. Hall	
G-BHBE	Westland-Bell 47G-3B1 (Solov)	T. R. Smith (Agricultural Machinery) Ltd	
G-BHBT	Marquart MA.5 Charger	Bravo Tango Group	
G-BHCC	Cessna 172M	Staverton Flying School @ Skypark	
G-BHCE	Jodel D.112	Charles Echo Group	
G-BHCM	Cessna F.172H	J. Scurr	
G-BHCP	Cessna F.152	Synergy Flight Centres Ltd	
G-BHCZ	PA-38-112 Tomahawk	A. J. Powell	
G-BHDD	V.668 Varsity T.1 (WL626:P) ★	Aeropark/East Midlands	
G-BHDE	SOCATA TB10 Tobago	J. C. Parker	
G-BHDK	Boeing B-29A-BN (461748:Y) ★	Imperial War Museum/Duxford	
G-BHDM	Cessna F.152 II	A. D. R. Northeast	
G-BHDP	Cessna F.182Q II	M. S. Vonk	
G-BHDS	Cessna F.152 II	P. M. M. dos Santos Francisco	
G-BHDV	Cameron V-77 balloon	P. Glydon	
G-BHDX	Cessna F.172N	D. M. Hobson	
G-BHDZ	Cessna F.172N	H. Mackintosh	
G-BHEG	Jodel 150	M. J. Wood	
G-BHEK	CP.1315-C3 Super Emeraude	D. B. Winstanley	
G-BHEL	Jodel D.117	G-BHEL Jodel Flying Group	
G-BHEN	Cessna FA.152	Leicestershire Aero Club Ltd	
G-BHEU	Thunder Ax7-65 balloon	L. J. Wigfield	
G-BHEV	PA-28R-200 Cherokee Arrow	Seven-Up Group	
G-BHFC	Cessna F.152	Enstone Ventures Ltd	
G-BHFE	PA-44-180 Seminole	Transport Command Ltd	
G-BHFG	SNCAN Stampe SV.4C	G. W. Lynch	
G-BHFI	Cessna F.152	Westair Flying Services Ltd	
G-BHFJ	PA-28RT-201T Turbo Cherokee Arrow IV	S. A. Cook & D. R. Northeast	

Notes	Reg	Type	Owner or Operator
	G-BHFK	PA-28-151 Cherokee Warrior	G-BHFK Flying Group
	G-BHGC	PA-18-150 Super Cub	C. R. Dacey
	G-BHGF	Cameron V-56 balloon	P. Smallward
	G-BHGJ	Jodel D.120	M. Devlin
	G-BHGO	PA-32-260 Cherokee Six	G-BHGO Group
	G-BHGY	PA-28R-200 Cherokee Arrow	Aeros Leasing Ltd
	G-BHHE	Jodel DR.1051/M1	M. Hales
	G-BHHG	Cessna F.152 II	Academy Aviation Ltd
	G-BHHH	Thunder Ax7-65 balloon	J. M. J. Roberts
	G-BHHK	Cameron N-77 balloon ★	British Balloon Museum
	G-BHHN	Cameron V-77 balloon	Itchen Valley Balloon Group
	G-BHIB	Cessna F.182Q	M. S. Williams
	G-BHIJ	Eiri PIK-20E-1 (898)	P. J. Shout & I. P. Freestone
	G-BHIR	PA-28R-200 Cherokee Arrow	Factorcore Ltd
	G-BHIS	Thunder Ax7-65 balloon	Hedgehoppers Balloon Group
	G-BHIY	Cessna F.150K	N. J. Butler
	G-BHJF	SOCATA TB10 Tobago	S. Yazydzhi & O. Maksmymov
	G-BHJK	Maule M5-235C Lunar Rocket	M. K. H. Bell
	G-BHJN	Fournier RF-4D	RF-4 Group
	G-BHJO	PA-28-161 Cherokee Warrior II	S C Airlease Ltd
	G-BHJS	Partenavia P.68B	Flew LLP
	G-BHJU	Robin DR.400/2+2	R. W. Hinton
	G-BHKE	Bensen B.8MS	A. R. Hawes
	G-BHKR	Colt 12A balloon ★	British Balloon Museum/Newbury
	G-BHKT	Jodel D.112	G. Dawes
	G-BHLE	Robin DR.400/180	A. V. Harmer
	G-BHLH	Robin DR.400/180	G-BHLH Group
	G-BHLJ	Saffery-Rigg S.200 balloon	I. A. Rigg
	G-BHLU	Alpavia Fournier RF-3	J. D. C. Henslow & C. B. Jones
	G-BHLW	Cessna 120	Moray Flying Group
	G-BHLX	AA-5B Tiger	Advanced Alloy Services Ltd
	G-BHMA	SIPA 903	H. J. Taggart
	G-BHMJ	Avenger T.200-2112 balloon	R. Light *Lord Anthony 1*
	G-BHMK	Avenger T.200-2112 balloon	P. Kinder *Lord Anthony 2*
	G-BHMT	Evans VP-1	D. W. Curtis
	G-BHMY	F.27 Friendship Mk.200 ★	City of Norwich Aviation Museum/Norwich
	G-BHNC	Cameron O-65 balloon	D. & C. Bareford
	G-BHNK	Jodel D.120A	D. J. Marchand
	G-BHNP	Eiri PIK-20E-1	D. A. Sutton
	G-BHNV	Westland-Bell 47G-3B1	S. W. Hutchinson
	G-BHNX	Jodel D.117	C. P. Davey
	G-BHOA	Robin DR.400/160	A. J. Rumsey
	G-BHOL	Jodel DR.1050	K. D. Doyle
	G-BHOM	PA-18-95 Super Cub	D. R. & R. M. Lee
	G-BHOR	PA-28-161 Cherokee Warrior II	Oscar Romeo Flying Group
	G-BHOT	Cameron V-65 balloon	Dante Balloon Group
	G-BHOZ	SOCATA TB9 Tampico	A. W. Hill
	G-BHPK	Piper J-3C-65 Cub (238410:A-44)	L-4 Group
	G-BHPL	CASA 1.131E Jungmann 1000 (DG+BE)	A. Burroughes
	G-BHPS	Jodel D.120A	BHPS Group
	G-BHPZ	Cessna 172N	T. M. O'Brien & J. Brown
	G-BHRC	PA-28-161 Cherokee Warrior II	Sherwood Flying Club Ltd
	G-BHRH	Cessna FA.150K	Merlin Flying Club Ltd
	G-BHRK	Colt Saucepan 56 SS balloon	D. P. Busby
	G-BHRO	Rockwell Commander 112	Skyblue Aero Services Ltd
	G-BHRR	CP.301A Emeraude	B. Mills
	G-BHSB	Cessna 172N	J. W. Cope & M. P. Wimsey
	G-BHSD	Scheibe SF.25E Super Falke	K. E. Ballington
	G-BHSL	CASA 1-131E Jungmann	A. F. Kutz
	G-BHSY	Jodel DR.1050	S. J. Westley
	G-BHTA	PA-28-236 Dakota	Dakota Ltd
	G-BHTG	Thunder Ax6-56 Bolt balloon	The British Balloon Museum & Library Ltd
	G-BHUB	Douglas C-47A (315509:W7-S) ★	Imperial War Museum/Duxford
	G-BHUG	Cessna 172N	A. Humphreys & R. Wainwright
	G-BHUI	Cessna 152	South Warwickshire School of Flying Ltd
	G-BHUM	DH.82A Tiger Moth	S. G. Towers
	G-BHVB	PA-28-161 Cherokee Warrior II	Falcon Flying Services
	G-BHVF	Jodel 150A	C. G. Winch
	G-BHVP	Cessna 182Q	The G-BHVP Flying Group
	G-BHVR	Cessna 172N	Aviolease Ltd
	G-BHVV	Piper J-3C-65 Cub (42-38384)	T. Kattinger

Reg	Type	Owner or Operator	Notes
G-BHWA	Cessna F.152	M. Bonsall	
G-BHWY	PA-28R-200 Cherokee Arrow II	Kilo Foxtrot Flying Group	
G-BHWZ	PA-28-181 Archer II	M. A. Abbott	
G-BHXA	SA Bulldog Srs 120/1210	Air Plan Flight Equipment Ltd	
G-BHXB	SA Bulldog Srs 120/1210	XB Group (G-JWCM)	
G-BHXD	Jodel D.120	D. J. Hatton	
G-BHXS	Jodel D.120	Plymouth Jodel Group	
G-BHXY	Piper J-3C-65 Cub (44-79609:44-S)	F. W. Rogers	
G-BHYC	Cessna 172RG II	P. W. Spires	
G-BHYI	SNCAN Stampe SV.4A	D. Hicklin	
G-BHYP	Cessna F.172M	Avior Ltd	
G-BHYR	Cessna F.172M	G-BHYR Group	
G-BHZE	PA-28-181 Cherokee Archer II	Brinkley Aviation Ltd	
G-BHZH	Cessna F.152	Fly NQY Pilot Training	
G-BHZK	AA-5B Tiger	S. Meznaric	
G-BHZR	SA Bulldog Srs 120/1210	Archdog Group	
G-BHZT	SA Bulldog Srs 120/1210	D. M. Curties	
G-BHZU	Piper J-3C-65 Cub (3914)	P. F. Durnford	
G-BHZV	Jodel D.120A	G-BHZV Group	
G-BIAH	Jodel D.112	K. J. Steele	
G-BIAI	WMB.2 Windtracker balloon	I. Chadwick	
G-BIAP	PA-16 Clipper	G-BIAP Flying Group	
G-BIAR	Rigg Skyliner II balloon	I. A. Rigg	
G-BIAU	Sopwith Pup (replica) (N6452) ★	F.A.A. Museum/Yeovilton	
G-BIAX	Taylor JT.2 Titch	R. D. Ward	
G-BIBA	SOCATA TB9 Tampico	TB Aviation Ltd	
G-BIBO	Cameron V-65 balloon	D. M. Hoddinott	
G-BIBS	Cameron P-20 balloon	Cameron Balloons Ltd	
G-BIBT	AA-5B Tiger	J. M. Wood	
G-BIBX	WMB.2 Windtracker balloon	I. A. Rigg	
G-BICD	Auster 5 (MT166)	M. Parsons	
G-BICE	NA AT-6C Harvard IIA (41-33275:CE)	C. M. L. Edwards	
G-BICG	Cessna F.152 II	W. Ali & Denderah SA	
G-BICM	Colt 56A balloon	M. R. Stokoe	
G-BICP	Robin DR.360	B. McVeighty	
G-BICU	Cameron V-56 balloon	S. D. Bather	
G-BICW	PA-28-161 Cherokee Warrior II	Blueplane Ltd	
G-BIDD	Evans VP-1	J. Hodgkinson	
G-BIDG	Jodel 150A	D. H. Greenwood	
G-BIDH	Cessna 152 II	Hull Aero Club Ltd (G-DONA)	
G-BIDI	PA-28R-201 Cherokee Arrow III	S. Jameson	
G-BIDJ	PA-18A-150 Super Cub	T. Cont	
G-BIDK	PA-18-150 Super Cub	S. W. Abbott	
G-BIDO	CP.301A Emeraude	A. R. Plumb	
G-BIDV	Colt 14A balloon ★	British Balloon Museum/Newbury	
G-BIDW	Sopwith 1½ Strutter (replica) (A8226) ★	RAF Museum/Cosford	
G-BIDX	Jodel D.112	P. Turton	
G-BIEN	Jodel D.120A	A. R. Hill	
G-BIEO	Jodel D.112	R. S. & S. C. Solley	
G-BIES	Maule M5-235C Lunar Rocket	William Proctor Ltd	
G-BIET	Cameron O-77 balloon	G. M. Westley	
G-BIEY	PA-28-151 Cherokee Warrior	M. J. Isaac	
G-BIFB	PA-28-150 Cherokee C	D. H. G. Penney	
G-BIFO	Evans VP-1 Series 2	E. L. E. Webley	
G-BIFP	Colt 56A balloon	C. J. Freeman	
G-BIFY	Cessna F.150L	Biffy Flying Group	
G-BIGB	Bell 212	Heli-Lift Services	
G-BIGJ	Cessna F.172M	Cirrus Aviation Ltd	
G-BIGK	Taylorcraft BC12D	M. J. Kirk	
G-BIGL	Cameron O-65 balloon	E. P. Smith	
G-BIGP	Bensen B.8M ★	The Helicopter Museum/Weston-super-Mare	
G-BIGR	Avenger T.200-2112 balloon	R. Light	
G-BIHF	SE-5A (replica) (F943)	C. J. Zeal	
G-BIHI	Cessna 172M	D. H. G. Penney	
G-BIHO	DHC.6 Twin Otter 310	Isles of Scilly Skybus Ltd	
G-BIHT	PA-17 Vagabond	N. F. Andrews	
G-BIHU	Saffrey S.200 balloon	B. L. King	
G-BIIA	Fournier RF-3	P. King	
G-BIID	PA-18-95 Super Cub 95	D. A. Lacey	
G-BIIF	Fournier RF-4D	K. M. Fresson (G-BVET)	

Notes	Reg	Type	Owner or Operator
	G-BIIK	MS.883 Rallye 115	T. P. Luft
	G-BIIO	BN-2T Islander	Draken
	G-BIIT	PA-28-161 Cherokee Warrior II	Henshaw Aviation Ltd
	G-BIIZ	Great Lakes 2T-1A Sport Trainer	D. D. Holtom
	G-BIJB	PA-18-150 Super Cub	G. T. Bowes
	G-BIJD	Bölkow Bö.208C Junior	A. J. Rex & T. E. Mallorie
	G-BIJE	Piper J-3C-65 Cub	R. L. Hayward & A. G. Scott
	G-BIJU	CP-301A Emeraude	Eastern Taildraggers Flying Group (G-BHTX)
	G-BIJV	Cessna F.152 II	Falcon Flying Services
	G-BIJW	Cessna F.152 II	Academy Aviation Ltd
	G-BIJX	Cessna F.152 II	Falcon Flying Services
	G-BIKE	PA-28R-200 Cherokee Arrow	R. Taylor
	G-BILB	WMB.2 Windtracker balloon	B. L. King
	G-BILE	Scruggs BL.2B balloon	P. D. Ridout
	G-BILG	Scruggs BL.2B balloon	P. D. Ridout
	G-BILH	Slingsby T.65C Vega	P. Woodcock
	G-BILI	Piper J-3C-65 Cub (454467:J-44)	P. McDermott
	G-BILR	Cessna 152 II	APB Leasing Ltd
	G-BILS	Cessna 152 II	Mona Flying Club
	G-BILU	Cessna 172RG	Full Sutton Flying Centre Ltd
	G-BIMK	Tiger T.200 Srs 1 balloon	M. K. Baron
	G-BIMM	PA-18-150 Super Cub	Avalon Ventures Ltd
	G-BIMN	Steen Skybolt	R. J. Thomas
	G-BIMT	Cessna FA.152	Staverton Flying School @ Skypark Ltd
	G-BIMX	Rutan Vari-Eze	G. A. Hoodless
	G-BIMZ	Beech 76 Duchess	Aviation South West Ltd
	G-BINL	Scruggs BL.2B balloon	P. D. Ridout
	G-BINM	Scruggs BL.2B balloon	P. D. Ridout
	G-BINR	Unicorn UE.1A balloon	Unicorn Group
	G-BINS	Unicorn UE.2A balloon	Unicorn Group
	G-BINT	Unicorn UE.1A balloon	D. E. Bint
	G-BINX	Scruggs BL.2B balloon	P. D. Ridout
	G-BINY	Oriental balloon	J. L. Morton
	G-BIOA	Hughes 369D	AH Helicopter Services Ltd
	G-BIOB	Cessna F.172P	High Level Photography Ltd
	G-BIOI	Jodel DR.1051/M	A. A. Alderdice
	G-BIOM	Cessna F.152	J. B. P. E. Fernandes
	G-BION	Cameron V-77 balloon	Zebedee Balloon Service Ltd
	G-BIOU	Jodel D.117A	P. B. Davey
	G-BIPH	Scruggs BL.2B balloon	C. M. Dewsnap
	G-BIPN	Fournier RF-3	C. J. Riley
	G-BIPT	Jodel D.112	C. R. Davies
	G-BIPV	AA-5B Tiger	Fly With Me Aviation Ltd
	G-BIPW	Avenger T.200-2112 balloon	B. L. King
	G-BIRD	Pitts S-1D Special	N. E. Smith
	G-BIRI	CASA 1.131E Jungmann 1000	D. Watt
	G-BIRL	Avenger T.200-2112 balloon	R. Light
	G-BIRP	Arena Mk 17 Skyship balloon	A. S. Viel
	G-BIRT	Robin R.1180TD	W. D'A. Hall
	G-BIRW	MS.505 Criquet (F+IS)	Aircraft Restoration Company
	G-BISG	FRED Srs 3	N. S. Chittenden
	G-BISH	Cameron V-65 balloon	P. J. Bish
	G-BISL	Scruggs BL.2B balloon	P. D. Ridout
	G-BISM	Scruggs BL.2B balloon	P. D. Ridout
	G-BISS	Scruggs BL.2C balloon	P. D. Ridout
	G-BIST	Scruggs BL.2C balloon	P. D. Ridout
	G-BISX	Colt 56A balloon	C. D. Steel
	G-BITA	PA-18-150 Super Cub	P. T. Shaw
	G-BITE	SOCATA TB10 Tobago	C. Burton
	G-BITF	Cessna F.152 II	G-BITF Owners
	G-BITH	Cessna F.152 II	Cherokee Aviation Ltd (G-TFSA)
	G-BITO	Jodel D.112D	A. Dunbar
	G-BITY	FD.31T balloon	A. J. Bell
	G-BIUP	SNCAN NC.854S	S. A. Richardson
	G-BIUY	PA-28-181 Cherokee Archer II	Redhill Air Services Ltd
	G-BIVA	Robin R.2112	Victor Alpha Group
	G-BIVB	Jodel D.112	D. Neave
	G-BIVC	Jodel D.112	T. D. Wood
	G-BIVF	CP.301C-3 Emeraude	C. R. Hoveman
	G-BIWB	Scruggs RS.5000 balloon	P. D. Ridout
	G-BIWC	Scruggs RS.5000 balloon	P. D. Ridout

Reg	Type	Owner or Operator	Notes
G-BIWF	Warren balloon	P. D. Ridout	
G-BIWG	Zelenski Mk 2 balloon	P. D. Ridout	
G-BIWJ	Unicorn UE.1A balloon	B. L. King	
G-BIWN	Jodel D.112	J. Steele	
G-BIWR	Mooney M.20F	M. Broady	
G-BIWY	Westland WG.30 ★	Instructional airframe/Yeovil	
G-BIXA	SOCATA TB9 Tampico	P. Jones	
G-BIXL	P-51D Mustang (472216:HO-M)	Anpartsselskabet AF 19.9.2006 APS/Denmark	
G-BIXN	Boeing Stearman A75N1 (FJ777)	V. S. E. Norman	
G-BIXW	Colt 56B balloon	N. A. P. Bates	
G-BIXX	Pearson Srs 2 balloon	D. Pearson	
G-BIXZ	Grob G-109	Buckminster Gliding Club Ltd	
G-BIYI	Cameron V-65 balloon	Sarnia Balloon Group	
G-BIYK	Isaacs Fury II	J. C. J. Elliott	
G-BIYR	PA-18-150 Super Cub (R-151)	Delta Foxtrot Flying Group	
G-BIYW	Jodel D.112	R. C. Hibberd	
G-BIYX	PA-28-140 Cherokee	W. B. Bateson	
G-BIYY	PA-18-95 Super Cub	D. R. Puleston	
G-BIZF	Cessna F.172P	C. Papworth	
G-BIZG	Cessna F.152	Joe Bill Aviation Ltd	
G-BIZK	Nord 3202 (78)	A. I. Milne	
G-BIZM	Nord 3202	Global Aviation Ltd	
G-BIZO	PA-28R-200 Cherokee Arrow	Bristol Flying Club Ltd	
G-BIZW	Champion 7GCBC Citabria	D. Williams	
G-BIZY	Jodel D.112	S. J. Southan	
G-BJAD	FRED Srs 2 ★	Newark Air Museum/Newark	
G-BJAE	Lavadoux Starck AS.80	D. J. & S. A. E. Phillips/Coventry	
G-BJAF	Piper J-3C-65 Cub	V. R. Goddard	
G-BJAG	PA-28-181 Cherokee Archer II	Invicta Aero Club Ltd	
G-BJAJ	AA-5B Tiger	Grade Digital Ltd	
G-BJAL	CASA 1.131E Jungmann 1000	G-BJAL Group	
G-BJAP	DH.82A Tiger Moth (K2587)	T. J. Orchard	
G-BJAS	Rango NA.9 balloon	A. Lindsay	
G-BJBK	PA-18-95 Super Cub	M. S. Bird	
G-BJBM	Monnett Sonerai I	M. F. A. Hudson	
G-BJBO	Jodel DR.250/160	G-BJBO Flying Group	
G-BJBW	PA-28-161 Cherokee Warrior II	152 Group	
G-BJCA	PA-28-161 Cherokee Warrior II	Falcon Flying Services Ltd	
G-BJCI	PA-18-150 Super Cub 150 (modified)	The Borders (Milfield) Gliding Club Ltd	
G-BJCW	PA-32R-301 Saratoga SP	Golf Charlie Whisky Ltd	
G-BJDE	Cessna F.172M	M. Rowntree & S. Bridgeman	
G-BJDJ	HS.125 Srs 700B	TAG Farnborough Engineering Ltd (G-RCDI)	
G-BJDK	European E.14 balloon	Aeroprint Tours	
G-BJDW	Cessna F.172M	Above & Beyond School of Flying Ltd	
G-BJEC	BN-2T Turbine Islander	Draken (G-SELX)	
G-BJED	BN-2T Turbine Islander	Draken (G-MAFF)	
G-BJEI	PA-18-95 Super Cub	A. N. MacMillen	
G-BJEJ	BN-2T Turbine Islander	Islander Aircraft Ltd	
G-BJEL	SNCAN NC.854	C. A. James	
G-BJEV	Aeronca 11AC Chief (897)	D. J. Howell	
G-BJEX	Bölkow Bö.208C Junior	G. D. H. Crawford	
G-BJFC	European E.8 balloon	P. D. Ridout	
G-BJFE	PA-18-95 Super Cub	J. Allistone	
G-BJFM	Jodel D.120	J. V. George	
G-BJGE	Thunder Ax3 Mini Sky Chariot balloon	D. J. Stagg	
G-BJGM	Unicorn UE.1A balloon	D. Eaves & P. D. Ridout	
G-BJGY	Cessna F.172P	K. & S. Martin	
G-BJHB	Mooney M.20J	Zitair Flying Club Ltd	
G-BJHK	EAA Acro Sport	M. R. Holden	
G-BJHV	Voisin Replica ★	Brooklands Museum of Aviation/Weybridge	
G-BJIA	Allport balloon	D. J. Allport	
G-BJIC	Dodo 1A balloon	P. D. Ridout	
G-BJID	Osprey 1B balloon	P. D. Ridout	
G-BJIG	Slingsby T.67A	A. D. Hodgkinson	
G-BJIV	PA-18-150 Super Cub	Cubiv Ltd	
G-BJLC	Monnett Sonerai IIL	P. O. Yeo	
G-BJLX	Cremer balloon	P. W. May	
G-BJLY	Cremer balloon	P. Cannon	
G-BJML	Cessna 120	R. A. Smith	
G-BJMR	Cessna 310R	M. D. S. Williams	

Notes	Reg	Type	Owner or Operator
	G-BJMW	Thunder Ax8-105 balloon	G. M. Westley
	G-BJMX	Jarre JR.3 balloon	P. D. Ridout
	G-BJMZ	European EA.8A balloon	P. D. Ridout
	G-BJNA	Arena Mk 117P balloon	P. D. Ridout
	G-BJNG	Slingsby T.67AM	D. F. Hodgkinson
	G-BJOB	Jodel D.140C	R. P. Beck
	G-BJOE	Jodel D.120A	R. N. L. Howarth
	G-BJOH	Britten-Norman BN-2T Islander	Draken (G-SRAY/G-OPBN)
	G-BJOT	Jodel D.117	Cark Flying Group
	G-BJRA	Osprey Mk 4B balloon	E. Osborn
	G-BJRG	Osprey Mk 4B balloon	A. E. de Gruchy
	G-BJRH	Rango NA.36 balloon	N. H. Ponsford
	G-BJRP	Cremer balloon	M. D. Williams
	G-BJRR	Cremer balloon	M. D. Williams
	G-BJRV	Cremer balloon	M. D. Williams
	G-BJSS	Allport balloon	D. J. Allport
	G-BJST	CCF T-6J Harvard IV (AJ841)	G-BJST Group
	G-BJSV	PA-28-161 Cherokee Warrior II	Flevo Aviation BV/Netherlands
	G-BJSZ	Piper J-3C-65 Cub	G. W., H. K., T. W. & W. S. Gilbert
	G-BJTP	PA-18-95 Super Cub (MM51-15302:EI-51)	G. J. Molloy
	G-BJTY	Osprey Mk 4B balloon	A. E. de Gruchy
	G-BJUB	BVS Special 01 balloon	P. G. Wild
	G-BJUD	Robin DR.400/180R	Lasham Gliding Society Ltd
	G-BJUS	PA-38-112 Tomahawk	Abbotsinch Aviation Ltd
	G-BJUV	Cameron V-20 balloon	P. Spellward
	G-BJVH	Cessna F.182Q	S. Rigg
	G-BJVJ	Cessna F.152 II	P. Tribble
	G-BJVK	Grob G-109	J. M. & J. R. Kimberley
	G-BJVM	Cessna 172N	R. D. Forster
	G-BJVS	CP.1310-C3 Super Emeraude	D. Barrow
	G-BJVU	Thunder Ax6-56 Bolt balloon	N. R. Beckwith
	G-BJWT	Wittman W.10 Tailwind	R. F. Lea
	G-BJWV	Colt 17A balloon	B. T. Lewis
	G-BJWW	Cessna F.172N	P. J. Westoby
	G-BJWX	PA-18-95 Super Cub	R. A. G. Lucas
	G-BJWY	S-55 Whirlwind HAR.21(WV198) ★	Solway Aviation Museum/Carlisle
	G-BJWZ	PA-18-95 Super Cub	G-BJWZ Syndicate
	G-BJXA	Slingsby T.67A	L. Clare (G-GFAA)
	G-BJXB	Slingsby T.67A	D. Pegley
	G-BJXK	Fournier RF-5	RF5 Syndicate
	G-BJXR	Auster AOP.9 (XR267)	I. Churm & J. Hanson
	G-BJXX	PA-23-250 Aztec	V. Bojovic
	G-BJXZ	Cessna 172N	T. M. Jones
	G-BJYD	Cessna F.152 II	M. J. Hillier
	G-BJYK	Jodel D.120A	P. W. Armstrong
	G-BJYT	PBN BN-2T Islander	Draken
	G-BJZB	Evans VP-2	J. L. & M. P. Loweth
	G-BJZN	Slingsby T.67A	ZN Group
	G-BJZR	Colt 42A balloon	Selfish Balloon Group
	G-BKAM	Slingsby T.67M Firefly160	R. C. B. Brookhouse
	G-BKAO	Jodel D.112	P. A. Harris
	G-BKAY	Rockwell Commander 114	D. L. Bunning
	G-BKAZ	Cessna 152	Cloud Global Ltd
	G-BKBK	SNCAN Stampe SV-4A	G. P. J. M. Valvekens
	G-BKBP	Bellanca 7GCBC Scout	M. G. & J. R. Jefferies
	G-BKBV	SOCATA TB10 Tobago	G-BKBV Group
	G-BKBW	SOCATA TB10 Tobago	Merlin Aviation
	G-BKCC	PA-28-180 Cherokee	DR Flying Club Ltd
	G-BKCE	Cessna F.172P II	The Leicestershire Aero Club Ltd
	G-BKCI	Brügger MB.2 Colibri	S. I. Hatherall
	G-BKCJ	Oldfield Baby Lakes	B. L. R. J. Keeping
	G-BKCN	Phoenix Currie Wot	N. A. A. Pogmore
	G-BKCV	EAA Acro Sport II	S. E. Barker
	G-BKCW	Jodel D.120	T. A. S. Rayner (G-BMYF)
	G-BKCX	Mudry/CAARP CAP-10B	G. N. Davies
	G-BKCZ	Jodel D.120A	L. J. Rook
	G-BKDH	Robin DR.400/120	Marine & Aviation Ltd
	G-BKDJ	Robin DR.400/120	S. Pritchard & I. C. Colwell
	G-BKDP	FRED Srs 3	M. Whittaker
	G-BKDR	Pitts S-1S Special	L. E. Wilson

Reg	Type	Owner or Operator	Notes
G-BKDT	SE-5A (replica) (F943) ★	Yorkshire Air Museum/Elvington	
G-AKDW	DH.89A Dragon Rapide ★	De Havilland Heritage Museum/London Colney	
G-BKDX	Jodel DR.1050	D. G. T. & R. J. Ward	
G-BKER	SE-5A (replica) (F5447:N)	N. K. Geddes	
G-BKET	PA-18-95 Super Cub	N. J. F. Campbell	
G-BKEV	Cessna F.172M	Derby Arrows	
G-BKEW	Bell 206B JetRanger 3	R. Toghill & C. Bendall	
G-BKFC	Cessna F.152 II	The Leicestershire Aero Club Ltd	
G-BKFG	Thunder Ax3 Maxi Sky Chariot balloon	S. G. Whatley	
G-BKFK	Isaacs Fury II	R. S. & S. C. Solley	
G-BKFR	CP.301C Emeraude	The Devonshire Flying Group	
G-BKFW	P.56 Provost T.1 (XF597)	P. Wood	
G-BKGA	MS.892E Rallye 150GT	M. O. Biddulph	
G-BKGB	Jodel D.120	B. A. Ridgway	
G-BKGC	Maule M.6-235	K. V. Marks	
G-BKGD	Westland WG.30 Srs.100 ★	IHM/Weston-super-Mare	
G-BKGM	Beech D.18S	A. M. Holman-West	
G-BKGW	Cessna F.152-II	Leicestershire Aero Club Ltd	
G-BKHW	Stoddard-Hamilton Glasair IIRG	D. W. Rees	
G-BKHY	Taylor JT.1 Monoplane	B. C. J. O'Neill	
G-BKHZ	Cessna F.172P	L. R. Leader	
G-BKIC	Cameron V-77 balloon	C. A. Butler	
G-BKII	Cessna F.172M	Sealand Aerial Photography Ltd	
G-BKIJ	Cessna F.172M	Cirrus Aviation Ltd	
G-BKIK	Cameron DG-19 airship ★	Balloon Preservation Group/Lancing	
G-BKIS	SOCATA TB10 Tobago	D. Hoare	
G-BKIT	SOCATA TB9 Tampico	R. K. Wright	
G-BKIU	Colt 17A Cloudhopper balloon	S. R. J. Pooley	
G-BKIY	Thunder Ax3 balloon ★	Balloon Preservation Group/Lancing	
G-BKJB	PA-18-135 Super Cub	K. E. Burnham	
G-BKJM	BN-2B-21 Islander	Britten-Norman Aerospace Ltd	
G-BKJS	Jodel D.120A	T. A. Odlin	
G-BKKN	Cessna 182R	G. Farrar	
G-BKKO	Cessna 182R	M. A. Smith	
G-BKKP	Cessna 182R	D. Jaffa	
G-BKLO	Cessna F.172M	Easy Aircraft Rental Ltd	
G-BKMA	Mooney M.20J Srs 201	Foxtrot Whisky Aviation	
G-BKMB	Mooney M.20J Srs 201	G-BKMB Flying Group	
G-BKMG	Handley Page O/400 (replica)	The Paralyser Group	
G-BKMT	PA-32R-301 Saratoga SP	P. Ashworth	
G-BKNO	Monnett Sonerai IIL	S. Hardy	
G-BKNZ	CP.301A Emeraude	A. K. Halvorsen	
G-BKOA	SOCATA MS.893E Rallye 180GT	M. Jarrett	
G-BKOB	Z.326 Trener Master	A. L. Rae	
G-BKOK	BN-2B-26 Islander	Cormack Islander Aircraft	
G-BKOT	Wassmer WA.81 Piranha	D. J. Griffiths	
G-BKOU	P.84 Jet Provost T.3 (XN637)	G-BKOU/2 Ltd	
G-BKPA	Hoffmann H-36 Dimona	R. C. Bettany	
G-BKPB	Aerosport Scamp	J. M. Brightwell	
G-BKPC	Cessna A.185F	C. Taylor & P. C. Hambilton	
G-BKPD	Viking Dragonfly	E. P. Browne & G. J. Sargent	
G-BKPG	Luscombe Rattler ★	Newark Air Museum/Newark	
G-BKPS	AA-5B Tiger	A. E. T. Clarke	
G-BKPX	Jodel D.120A	HPP Aviation	
G-BKPY	SAAB 91B/2 Safir (56321:U-AB) ★	Newark Air Museum	
G-BKPZ	Pitts S-1T Special	CK Aviation Services Ltd	
G-BKRA	NA T-6G Texan (51-15227)	First Air Ltd	
G-BKRF	PA-18-95 Super Cub	T. F. F. van Erck	
G-BKRH	Brügger MB.2 Colibri	G-BKRH Group	
G-BKRK	SNCAN Stampe SV.4C	Strathgadie Stampe Group	
G-BKRL	Chichester-Miles Leopard ★	Bournemouth Aviation Museum	
G-BKRN	Beechcraft D.18S (43-35943)	M. E. V. Wakefield	
G-BKRU	Crossley Racer	S. Alexander	
G-BKSC	Saro Skeeter AOP.12 (XN351) ★	Morayvia Sci-Tech Experience Project/Kinloss	
G-BKSE	QAC Quickie Q.1	C. R. Hopkins	
G-BKSK	QAC Quickie Tri-Q 200	T. S. Marlow	
G-BKST	Rutan Vari-Eze	R. Towle	
G-BKTA	PA-18-95 Super Cub	M. J. Dyson	
G-BKTH	CCF Hawker Sea Hurricane IB (Z7015)	The Shuttleworth Collection	
G-BKTM	PZL SZD-45A Ogar	Hinton Ogar Group	
G-BKUE	SOCATA TB9 Tampico	Fife TB9ers	

Notes	Reg	Type	Owner or Operator
	G-BKUI	D.31 Turbulent	R. A. H. Vary
	G-BKUR	CP.301A Emeraude	T. Harvey
	G-BKVG	Scheibe SF.25E Super Falke	G-BKVG Ltd
	G-BKVK	Auster AOP.9 (WZ662)	J. K. Houlgrave
	G-BKVL	Robin DR.400/160	Off Group Ltd
	G-BKVM	PA-18-150 Super Cub (115684)	M. C. Curtis
	G-BKVP	Pitts S-1D Special	C. M. Evans & J. W. Blaylock
	G-BKWD	Taylor JT.2 Titch	J. F. Sully
	G-BKXA	Robin R.2100	M. Wilson
	G-BKXF	PA-28R-200 Cherokee Arrow	Just Plane Trading Ltd
	G-BKXJ	Rutan VariEze	J. P. Kynaston (G-TIMB)
	G-BKXM	Colt 17A balloon	R. G. Turnbull
	G-BKXO	Rutan LongEz	Inverness Long-Ez
	G-BKXR	D.31A Turbulent	G-BKXR Turbulent Group
	G-BKZM	Isaacs Fury	L. C. Wells
	G-BKZT	FRED Srs 2	U. Chakravorty
	G-BLAC	Cessna FA.152	W. Ali
	G-BLAF	Stolp SA.900 V-Star	Stolp V Star Group
	G-BLAG	Pitts S-1D Special	M. J. S. Wright (G-IIIP)
	G-BLAI	Monnett Sonerai 2L	M. J. Rowland
	G-BLAM	Jodel DR.360	J. S. Dalton
	G-BLCH	Colt 65D balloon	R. S. Breakwell
	G-BLCI	EAA Acro Sport	M. R. Holden
	G-BLCT	Jodel DR.220 2+2	F. N. P. Maurin
	G-BLCU	Scheibe SF.25B Falke	J. Pool
	G-BLCY	Thunder Ax7-65Z balloon	M. A. Stelling
	G-BLDB	Taylor JT.1 Monoplane	J. R. Davidson & J. A. Wardlow
	G-BLDN	Rand-Robinson KR-2	P. R. Diffey
	G-BLDV	BN-2B-26 Islander	Loganair Ltd
	G-BLES	Stolp SA.750 Acroduster Too	I. Annett
	G-BLFI	PA-28-181 Cherokee Archer II	Fly Elstree Ltd
	G-BLGH	Robin DR.300/180R	Booker Gliding Club Ltd
	G-BLGV	Bell 206B JetRanger 3	Heliflight (UK) Ltd
	G-BLHH	Jodel DR.315	M. V. Male & D. P. Murphy
	G-BLHJ	Cessna F.172P	Enstone Ventures Ltd
	G-BLHM	PA-18-95 Super Cub	J. G. Jones
	G-BLHR	GA-7 Cougar	H. Mackintosh & R. Ellingworth
	G-BLHS	Bellanca 7ECA Citabria	G. D. Williamson
	G-BLHW	Varga 2150A Kachina	M. J. Pamphilon
	G-BLID	DH.112 Venom FB.50 (J-1605) ★	P. G. Vallance Ltd
	G-BLIT	Thorp T-18 CW	R. M. Weeks
	G-BLIW	P.56 Provost T.51 (WV514)	A. D. M. & K. B. Edie
	G-BLIX	Saro Skeeter Mk 12 (XL809)	K. M. Scholes
	G-BLJO	Cessna F.152	Redhill Air Services Ltd
	G-BLKA	DH.112 Venom FB.54 (J-1790) ★	Fishburn Historic Aviation Centre
	G-BLKM	Jodel DR.1051	Kilomike Flying Group
	G-BLLA	Bensen B.8M	K. T. Donaghey
	G-BLLB	Bensen B.8M	D. H. Moss
	G-BLLH	Jodel DR.220A 2+2	A. D. Millington
	G-BLLO	PA-18-95 Super Cub	M. F. Watts
	G-BLLP	Slingsby T.67B	Air Navigation and Trading Co Ltd
	G-BLLR	Slingsby T.67B	R. L. Brinklow
	G-BLLS	Slingsby T.67B	T. Lawrence
	G-BLLW	Colt 56B balloon	C. J. Dunkley
	G-BLLZ	Rutan LongEz	R. S. Stoddart-Stones
	G-BLMA	Zlin 326 Trener Master	G. P. Northcott
	G-BLMC	Avro 698 Vulcan B.2A ★	Aeropark/East Midlands
	G-BLMG	Grob G.109B	G-BLMG Group
	G-BLMN	Rutan LongEz	K. W. Taylor
	G-BLMP	PA-17 Vagabond	C. W. Thirtle
	G-BLMR	PA-18-150 Super Cub	M. Vickers
	G-BLMT	PA-18-135 Super Cub	W. S. Gilbert
	G-BLMW	T.66 Nipper 3	S. L. Millar
	G-BLNE	BN-2T Islander	Britten-Norman Aerospace Ltd
	G-BLNI	BN-2B-26 Islander	Hebridean Air Services Ltd
	G-BLNO	FRED Srs 3	L. W. Smith
	G-BLNT	BN-2T Islander	Draken
	G-BLNU	BN-2T Islander	Draken
	G-BLNV	BN-2T Islander	Britten-Norman Aerospace Ltd
	G-BLNY	BN-2T Islander	Draken Europe

Reg	Type	Owner or Operator	Notes
G-BLOT	Colt Ax6-56B balloon	M. A. Stelling	
G-BLPB	Turner TSW Hot Two Wot	Papa Bravo Group	
G-BLPE	PA-18-95 Super Cub	A. A. Haig-Thomas	
G-BLPF	Cessna FR.172G	S. Culpin	
G-BLPG	Auster J/1N Alpha (16693:693)	E. Haxe (G-AIZH)	
G-BLPP	Cameron V-77 balloon	A. C. Davies	
G-BLRC	PA-18-135 Super Cub	Supercub Group	
G-BLRF	Slingsby T.67C	R. C. Nicholls	
G-BLRL	CP.301C-1 Emeraude	A. M. Smith	
G-BLSD	DH.112 Venom FB.54 (J-1758) ★	R. Lamplough/North Weald	
G-BLSX	Cameron O-105 balloon	B. J. Petteford	
G-BLTC	D.31A Turbulent	S. J. Butler	
G-BLTM	Robin HR.200/100	Troughton Engineering Aircraft Maintenance Ltd	
G-BLTN	Thunder Ax7-65 balloon	V. Michel	
G-BLTR	Scheibe SF.25B Falke	V. Mallon/Germany	
G-BLTS	Rutan LongEz	R. W. Cutler	
G-BLTV	Slingsby T.67B	R. L. Brinklow	
G-BLTW	Slingsby T.67B	Cheshire Air Training Services Ltd	
G-BLTY	Westland WG.30 Srs 160	D. Brem-Wilson	
G-BLUE	Colt 77A balloon	D. P. Busby	
G-BLUV	Grob G.109B	109 Flying Group	
G-BLUX	Slingsby T.67M Firefly 200	R. L. Brinklow	
G-BLUZ	DH.82B Queen Bee (LF858)	The Bee Keepers Group	
G-BLVA	Airtour AH-31 balloon	D. L. Peltan & S. Church	
G-BLVB	Airtour AH-56 balloon	Z. Daly	
G-BLVI	Slingsby T.67M Firefly Mk II	Chris Wade Aviation Ltd	
G-BLVK	CAARP CAP-10B	R. W. H. Cole	
G-BLVL	PA-28-161 Cherokee Warrior II	Henshaw Aviation Ltd	
G-BLVW	Cessna F.172H	S. P. Miller	
G-BLWD	PA-34-200T Seneca 2	Bencray Ltd	
G-BLWH	Fournier RF-6B-100	Gloucester Aero Group	
G-BLWM	Bristol M.1C (replica) (C4994) ★	RAF Museum/Cosford	
G-BLWP	PA-38-112 Tomahawk	APB Leasing Ltd	
G-BLWT	Evans VP-1 Series 2	G. R. Howitt	
G-BLWY	Robin R.2160D	Brix Aviation Ltd	
G-BLXG	Colt 21A balloon	D. P. Busby	
G-BLXH	Fournier RF-3	G-BLXH Group	
G-BLXI	CP.1310-C3 Super Emeraude	W. D. Garlick	
G-BLXO	Jodel 150	P. P. Chapman	
G-BLXT	Eberhardt S.E.5E (22-296)	Flying A Services Ltd	
G-BLZA	Scheibe SF.25B Falke	Zulu Alpha Syndicate	
G-BLZH	Cessna F.152 II	P. A. Gomez	
G-BLZP	Cessna F.152	East Midlands Flying School Ltd	
G-BMAD	Cameron V-77 balloon	M. A. Stelling	
G-BMAO	Taylor JT.1 Monoplane	B. B. Gilmore	
G-BMAX	FRED Srs 2	J. P. Gilbert	
G-BMBB	Cessna F.150L	Praeluceo Property Ltd	
G-BMBJ	Schempp-Hirth Janus CM	BJ Flying Group	
G-BMCC	Thunder Ax7-77 balloon	D. P. Busby	
G-BMCD	Cameron V-65 balloon	R. Lillyman	
G-BMCG	Grob G.109B	J. C. M. Docherty	
G-BMCI	Cessna F.172H	A. B. Davis	
G-BMCN	Cessna F.152	Skytrek Air Services	
G-BMCV	Cessna F.152	M. Bonsall	
G-BMDB	Replica SE-5A (F235:B)	M. V. Brown	
G-BMDE	Pietenpol AirCamper	P. B. Childs	
G-BMDJ	Price Ax7-77S balloon	R. A. Benham	
G-BMDP	Partenavia P.64B Oscar 200	J. L. Sparks	
G-BMDS	Jodel D.120	D. F. & J. V. McGarvey	
G-BMEA	PA-18-95 Super Cub	M. J. Butler	
G-BMEH	Jodel 150 Special Super Mascaret	R. J. & C. J. Lewis	
G-BMET	Taylor JT.1 Monoplane	R. C. Chandler	
G-BMEU	Isaacs Fury II	I. G. Harrison	
G-BMEX	Cessna A.150K	J. Menzies	
G-BMFD	PA-23-250 Aztec	WGS Aviation Ltd (G-BGYY)	
G-BMFN	QAC Quickie Tri-Q 200	R. F. Thomson	
G-BMFP	PA-28-161 Warrior II	Aerobility	
G-BMFY	Grob G.109B	P. J. Shearer	
G-BMGB	PA-28R-200 Cherokee Arrow	R. A. Pugh & G. A. Wright	
G-BMGC	Fairey Swordfish TSR Mk.I (W5856)	Fly Navy Heritage Trust Ltd	

Notes	Reg	Type	Owner or Operator
	G-BMGR	Grob G.109B	G-BMGR Group
	G-BMHL	Wittman W.8 Tailwind	J. C. Wood
	G-BMHS	Cessna F.172M	G. Campbell
	G-BMHT	PA-28RT-201T Turbo Cherokee Arrow	G-BMHT Flying Group
	G-BMID	Jodel D.120	G-BMID Flying Group
	G-BMIG	Cessna 172N	Fly With Me Aviation Ltd
	G-BMIM	Rutan LongEz	V. E. Jones
	G-BMIO	Stoddard-Hamilton Glasair RG	D. G. Curran
	G-BMIP	Jodel D.112	F. J. E. Brownsill
	G-BMIR	Westland Wasp HAS.1 (XT788) ★	private/Storwood
	G-BMIV	PA-28R-201T Turbo Cherokee Arrow III	The Flying Reporter Group
	G-BMIW	PA-28-181 Archer II	Oldbus Ltd
	G-BMIX	SOCATA TB20 Trinidad	Cloneygate Flying Group
	G-BMIZ	Robinson R22 Beta	Dragonfly Aviation
	G-BMJA	PA-32R-301 Saratoga SP	J. Cottrell
	G-BMJB	Cessna 152	Endrick Aviation LLP
	G-BMJD	Cessna 152 II	Donair Flying Club Ltd
	G-BMJJ	Cameron Watch 75 SS balloon	D. P. Busby
	G-BMJL	Rockwell Commander 114	D. J. & S. M. Hawkins
	G-BMJM	Evans VP-1 Series 2	G-BMJM Group
	G-BMJN	Cameron O-65 balloon	P. M. Traviss
	G-BMJY	Yakovlev C18M (07)	W. A. E. Moore
	G-BMKB	PA-18-135 Super Cub	D. J. & S. N. Taplin
	G-BMKC	Piper J-3C-65 Cub (329854:R-44)	P. R. Monk
	G-BMKF	Jodel DR.221	L. J. Gilbert
	G-BMKJ	Cameron V-77 balloon	Zebedee Balloon Service Ltd
	G-BMKK	PA-28R-200 Cherokee Arrow II	P. M. Murray
	G-BMKR	PA-28-161 Cherokee Warrior II	Joe Bill Aviation Ltd (G-BGKR)
	G-BMKV	Thunder Ax7-77 balloon	R. S. Frankham
	G-BMLK	Grob G.109B	Brams Syndicate
	G-BMLL	Grob G.109B	G-BMLL Flying Group
	G-BMLS	PA-28R-201 Cherokee Arrow III	R. N. Mayle
	G-BMLT	Pietenpol Air Camper	W. E. R. Jenkins
	G-BMLX	Cessna F.150L	J. P. A. Freeman
	G-BMMF	FRED Srs 2	R. C. Thomas
	G-BMMI	Pazmany PL.4A	P. I. Morgans
	G-BMMK	Cessna 182P	Lambley Flying Group
	G-BMMP	Grob G.109B	G-BMMP Ltd
	G-BMOE	PA-28R-200 Cherokee Arrow	S. C. Airlease Ltd
	G-BMOF	Cessna U206G	British Parachute Schools Ltd
	G-BMOH	Cameron N-77 balloon	I. M. Taylor
	G-BMOK	ARV Super 2	R. E. Griffiths
	G-BMOL	PA-23-250 Aztec	LDL Enterprises (G-BBSR)
	G-BMPC	PA-28-181 Cherokee Archer II	C. J. & R. J. Barnes
	G-BMPL	Optica Industries OA.7 Optica	J. K. Edgley
	G-BMPR	PA-28R-201 Cherokee Arrow III	Sterling Aviation
	G-BMPY	DH.82A Tiger Moth	C. H. M. Brown
	G-BMRA	Boeing 757-236F	DHL Air (UK) Ltd
	G-BMRB	Boeing 757-236F	DHL Air (UK) Ltd
	G-BMRD	Boeing 757-236F	DHL Air (UK) Ltd
	G-BMRI	Boeing 757-236F	DHL Air (UK) Ltd
	G-BMRJ	Boeing 757-236F	DHL Air (UK) Ltd
	G-BMSA	Stinson HW-75 Voyager	P. Fraser-Bennison (G-MIRM/G-BCUM)
	G-BMSB	VS.509 Spitfire IX (MJ627:9G-Q)	Warbird Experiences Ltd (G-ASOZ)
	G-BMSD	PA-28-181 Cherokee Archer II	M. Khoshkhou
	G-BMSE	Valentin Taifun 17E	D. O'Donnell
	G-BMSI	Cameron N-105 balloon	A. O. H. Harvey
	G-BMSL	Clutton FRED Series 3	Middlezoy FRED Group
	G-BMTB	Cessna 152 II	Stapleford Flying Club Ltd
	G-BMTJ	Cessna 152 II	The Pilot Centre Ltd
	G-BMTU	Pitts S-1E Special	N. A. A. Pogmore
	G-BMTX	Cameron V-77 balloon	J. A. Langley
	G-BMUG	Rutan LongEz	W. S. Allen
	G-BMUJ	Colt Drachenfisch balloon	Virgin Airship & Balloon Co Ltd
	G-BMUO	Cessna A.152	Redhill Air Services Ltd
	G-BMUT	PA-34-200T Seneca II	M. Iqbal
	G-BMUZ	PA-28-161 Cherokee Warrior II	Redhill Air Services Ltd
	G-BMVB	Cessna F.152	A. J. Gomes
	G-BMWF	ARV1 Super 2	D. L. Aspinall
	G-BMWR	Rockwell Commander 112	T. A. Stoate
	G-BMWU	Cameron N-42 balloon	I. Chadwick

Reg	Type	Owner or Operator	Notes
G-BMXC	Cessna 152 II	MK Aero Support Ltd	
G-BMYG	Cessna FA.152	Brinkley Aviation Ltd	
G-BMYI	AA-5 Traveler	Community Air Support Service (SCIO)	
G-BMYU	Jodel D.120	L. J. Rook	
G-BMZF	WSK-Mielec LiM-2 (MiG-15*bis*) (01420) ★	F.A.A. Museum/Yeovilton	
G-BMZN	Everett gyroplane	J. W. Cope	
G-BMZP	Everett gyroplane	P. A. Gardner	
G-BMZS	Everett gyroplane	R. F. G. Moyle	
G-BMZW	Bensen B.8MR	P. D. Widdicombe	
G-BMZX	Wolf W-11 Boredom Fighter	N. Wright	
G-BNAI	Wolf W-II Boredom Fighter (146-11083)	J. A. B. Nutall	
G-BNAJ	Cessna 152 II	Arion Aviation Ltd	
G-BNAN	Cameron V-65 balloon	Rango Balloon and Kite Company	
G-BNAW	Cameron V-65 balloon	A. Walker	
G-BNBU	Bensen B.8MV	B. A. Lyford	
G-BNCB	Cameron V-77 balloon	E. K. Read	
G-BNCM	Cameron N-77 balloon	C. A. Stone	
G-BNCR	PA-28-161 Cherokee Warrior II	Airways Aero Associations Ltd	
G-BNCS	Cessna 180	C. Elwell Transport Ltd	
G-BNCX	Hawker Hunter T.7 (XL621) ★	Aviation Filming Ltd/Dunsfold	
G-BNDP	Brügger MB.2 Colibri	D. M. Casey	
G-BNDT	Brügger MB.2 Colibri	G. D. Gunby & P. Coman	
G-BNEE	PA-28R-201 Cherokee Arrow III	Britannic Management Aviation	
G-BNEL	PA-28-161 Cherokee Warrior II	N. McGowan & N. K. Miller	
G-BNEO	Cameron V-77 balloon	J. G. O'Connell	
G-BNFP	Cameron O-84 balloon	M. Clarke	
G-BNFR	Cessna 152 II	A. Jahanfar	
G-BNFV	Robin DR.400/120	J. P. A. Freeman	
G-BNGE	Auster AOP.6 (TW536)	K. A. Hale	
G-BNGJ	Cameron N-77 balloon	S. W. K. Smeeton	
G-BNGT	PA-28-181 Cherokee Archer II	W. Ali & Denderah SA	
G-BNGV	ARV Super 2	N. A. Onions	
G-BNGW	ARV Super 2	Southern Gas Turbines Ltd	
G-BNGY	ARV Super 2	P. R. D. Morris (G-BMWL)	
G-BNHB	ARV Super 2	N. A. Onions	
G-BNHJ	Cessna 152 II	The Pilot Centre Ltd	
G-BNHK	Cessna 152 II	Wayfarers Flying Group	
G-BNHL	Colt beer glass SS balloon	M. R. Stokoe	
G-BNHN	Colt Ariel Bottle SS balloon ★	British Balloon Museum	
G-BNHT	Fournier RF-3	G-BNHT Group	
G-BNID	Cessna 152 II	MK Aero Support Ltd	
G-BNIK	Robin HR.200/120	Ledbury Flying Group	
G-BNIO	Luscombe 8A Silvaire	M. Richardson & R. C. Dyer	
G-BNIP	Luscombe 8A Silvaire	J. P. Coyne-Downhill	
G-BNIV	Cessna 152 II	Acros Leasing Ltd	
G-BNJB	Cessna 152 II	Aerolease Ltd	
G-BNJH	Cessna 152 II	ACS Aviation Ltd	
G-BNJL	Bensen B8MR	A. J. Lloyd	
G-BNJT	PA-28-161 Cherokee Warrior II	Hawarden Flying Group	
G-BNJX	Cameron N-90 balloon	Mars UK Ltd	
G-BNKC	Cessna 152 II	Herefordshire Aero Club Ltd	
G-BNKD	Cessna 172N	R. Nightingale	
G-BNKE	Cessna 172N	Kilo Echo Flying Group	
G-BNKI	Cessna 152 II	RAF Halton Aeroplane Club Ltd	
G-BNKP	Cessna 152 II	Avalon Ventures Ltd	
G-BNKR	Cessna 152 II	APB Leasing Ltd	
G-BNKS	Cessna 152 II	APB Leasing Ltd	
G-BNKT	Cameron O-77 balloon	A. A. Brown	
G-BNKV	Cessna 152 II	North Weald Flight Training Ltd	
G-BNLY	Boeing 747-436 ★	preserved/Dunsfold	
G-BNMB	PA-28-151 Warrior	Vision Aerospace Ltd	
G-BNMD	Cessna 152 II	T. M. Jones	
G-BNME	Cessna 152 II	M. Bonsall	
G-BNMF	Cessna 152 II	Redhill Air Services Ltd	
G-BNMH	Pietenpol Air Camper	N. M. Hitchman	
G-BNMI	Colt Flying Fantasy SS balloon	Air 2 Air Ltd	
G-BNNE	Cameron N-77 balloon	R. D. Allen, L. P. Hooper & M. J. Streat	
G-BNNO	PA-28-161 Cherokee Warrior II	Tor Financial Consulting Ltd	
G-BNNT	PA-28-151 Cherokee Warrior	L. J. Gilbert	
G-BNNX	PA-28R-201T Turbo Cherokee Arrow III	Professional Flying Ltd	

Notes	Reg	Type	Owner or Operator
	G-BNNY	PA-28-161 Cherokee Warrior II	Falcon Flying Services
	G-BNNZ	PA-28-161 Cherokee Warrior II	Falcon Flying Services Ltd
	G-BNOB	Wittman W.8 Tailwind	D. G. Hammersley
	G-BNOF	PA-28-161 Cherokee Warrior II	A. Soojeri
	G-BNOH	PA-28-161 Cherokee Warrior II	Sherburn Aero Club Ltd
	G-BNOJ	PA-28-161 Cherokee Warrior II	BAe (Warton) Flying Club
	G-BNOM	PA-28-161 Cherokee Warrior II	Gamston Flying School Ltd
	G-BNON	PA-28-161 Cherokee Warrior II	CG Aviation Ltd
	G-BNOP	PA-28-161 Cherokee Warrior II	BAe (Warton) Flying Club
	G-BNPE	Cameron N-77 balloon	R. N. Simpkins
	G-BNPF	Slingsby T.31M	R. O. Johnson
	G-BNPM	PA-38-112 Tomahawk	Grade Digital Ltd
	G-BNPO	PA-28-181 Cherokee Archer II	A. Sweeney
	G-BNPV	Bowers Fly-Baby 1B (1801/18)	A. Berry
	G-BNRA	SOCATA TB10 Tobago	Double D Airgroup
	G-BNRG	PA-28-161 Cherokee Warrior II	T. W. Gilbert
	G-BNRL	Cessna 152 II	Andrewsfield Aviation Ltd
	G-BNRP	PA-28-181 Cherokee Archer II	Concorde Analytics Ltd
	G-BNRW	Colt 69A balloon	J. F. Till
	G-BNSG	PA-28R-201 Cherokee Arrow III	G-BNSG Group
	G-BNSM	Cessna 152 II	T. W. Gilbert
	G-BNSN	Cessna 152 II	The Pilot Centre Ltd
	G-BNSR	Slingsby T.67M Firefly Mk II	Slingsby SR Group
	G-BNST	Cessna 172N	J. Revill
	G-BNSZ	PA-28-161 Cherokee Warrior II	O. H. Hogan
	G-BNTP	Cessna 172N	Westnet Ltd
	G-BNUL	Cessna 152 II	A. D. R. Northeast
	G-BNUT	Cessna 152 Turbo	Stapleford Flying Club Ltd
	G-BNUY	PA-38-112 Tomahawk II	D. C. Storey
	G-BNVB	AA-5A Cheetah	M. E. Hicks
	G-BNVE	PA-28-181 Cherokee Archer II	Warwickshire Leasing Ltd
	G-BNVT	PA-28R-201T Turbo Cherokee Arrow III	W. Ali & Denderah SA
	G-BNXE	PA-28-161 Cherokee Warrior II	Aviation South West Ltd
	G-BNXL	Glaser-Dirks DG.400	J. Mjels
	G-BNXM	PA-18 Super Cub 95 (26359)	K. A. A. McDonald & N. G. Rhind
	G-BNXU	PA-28-161 Cherokee Warrior II	Friendly Warrior Group
	G-BNXV	PA-38-112 Tomahawk	W. B. Bateson
	G-BNYD	Bell 206B JetRanger 3	Halchar Ltd
	G-BNYL	Cessna 152 II	V. J. Freeman
	G-BNYM	Cessna 172N	Kestrel Syndicate
	G-BNYP	PA-28-181 Cherokee Archer II	Brinkley Aviation Ltd
	G-BNYZ	SNCAN Stampe SV.4E	Bianchi Film Aviation Services Ltd
	G-BNZB	PA-28-161 Cherokee Warrior II	Falcon Flying Services Ltd
	G-BNZC	DHC.1 Chipmunk 22 (671)	The Shuttleworth Collection
	G-BNZK	Thunder Ax7-77 balloon	T. D. Marsden
	G-BNZL	Rotorway Scorpion 133	J. R. Wraight
	G-BNZM	Cessna T.210N	A J Freeman Aircraft Management Ltd
	G-BNZN	Cameron N-56 balloon	P. Lesser
	G-BNZO	Rotorway Executive	J. S. David
	G-BNZZ	PA-28-161 Cherokee Warrior II	Sherburn Aero Club Ltd
	G-BOAA	BAC-Aérospatiale Concorde 102 ★	Museum Of Flight East Fortune (G-N94AA)
	G-BOAB	BAC-Aérospatiale Concorde 102 ★	Preserved at Heathrow (G-N94AB)
	G-BOAC	BAC-Aérospatiale Concorde 102 ★	Runway Visitor Park/Manchester International (G-N81AC)
	G-BOAF	BAC-Aérospatiale Concorde 102 ★	Bristol Aero Collection/Filton (G-N94AF)
	G-BOAH	PA-28-161 Cherokee Warrior II	CG Aviation Ltd
	G-BOAI	Cessna 152 II	Aviation Spirit Ltd
	G-BOAL	Cameron V-65 balloon	N. H. & A. M. Ponsford
	G-BOAU	Cameron V-77 balloon	G. T. Barstow
	G-BOBA	PA-28R-201 Cherokee Arrow III	Three Greens Flying Group
	G-BOBR	Cameron N-77 balloon	I. R. F. Worsman
	G-BOBT	Stolp SA.300 Starduster Too	I. C. Storrie
	G-BOBV	Cessna F.150M	M. L. Brown & P. L. Hill
	G-BOBY	Monnett Sonerai II	R. F. Hallam
	G-BOCI	Cessna 140A	D. J. Palmer
	G-BOCK	Sopwith Triplane (replica) (N6290)	The Shuttleworth Collection
	G-BOCL	Slingsby T.67C	Richard Brinklow Aviation Ltd
	G-BOCU	PA-34-220T Seneca III	Advanced Aircraft Leasing (Teesside) Ltd
	G-BODB	PA-28-161 Cherokee Warrior II	Sherburn Aero Club Ltd
	G-BODD	PA-28-161 Cherokee Warrior II	CG Aviation Ltd

Reg	Type	Owner or Operator	Notes
G-BODE	PA-28-161 Cherokee Warrior II	Sherburn Aero Club Ltd	
G-BODI	Glasair III Model SH-3R	A. P. Durston	
G-BODO	Cessna 152	P. G. Fowler	
G-BODR	PA-28-161 Cherokee Warrior II	Napkin Group Ltd	
G-BODS	PA-38-112 Tomahawk	T. W. Gilbert	
G-BODT	Jodel D.18	G-BODT Flying Group	
G-BODU	Scheibe SF.25C Falke	Hertfordshire County Scout Council	
G-BODW	Bell 206B Jet Ranger II ★	The Helicopter Museum/Weston-super-Mare	
G-BODY	Cessna 310R	Modern Air (UK) Ltd	
G-BODZ	Robinson R22 Beta	Langley Aviation Ltd	
G-BOEE	PA-28-181 Cherokee Archer II	J. C. & G. M. Brinkley	
G-BOEH	Jodel DR.340	B. W. Griffiths	
G-BOEK	Cameron V-77 balloon	L. J. Whitelock & T. J. Gouder	
G-BOEM	Pitts S-2A	M. Murphy	
G-BOER	PA-28-161 Cherokee Warrior II	E. L. Fox	
G-BOET	PA-28RT-201 Cherokee Arrow IV	B. C. Chambers (G-IBEC)	
G-BOFC	Beech 76 Duchess	Odhams Air Services Ltd	
G-BOFW	Cessna A.150M	Golf Fox Whisky Group	
G-BOFY	PA-28-140 Cherokee	Cherokee Aviation Ltd	
G-BOGI	Robin DR.400/180	J. R. Althorp	
G-BOGM	PA-28RT-201T Turbo Cherokee Arrow IV	G-BOGM Aircraft Group	
G-BOHA	PA-28-161 Cherokee Warrior II	Phoenix Aviation	
G-BOHD	Colt 77A balloon	D. B. Court	
G-BOHI	Cessna 152 II	Academy Aviation Ltd	
G-BOHJ	Cessna 152 II	Brinkley Aviation Ltd	
G-BOHM	PA-28-180 Cherokee	R. A. Scott	
G-BOHO	PA-28-161 Cherokee Warrior II	Egressus Flying Group	
G-BOHR	PA-28-151 Cherokee Warrior	North Eat Flight Academy Ltd	
G-BOHV	Wittman W.8 Tailwind	D. M. Casey	
G-BOHW	Van's RV-4	E. C. Murgatroyd	
G-BOIB	Wittman W.10 Tailwind	C. R. Nash	
G-BOIC	PA-28R-201T Turbo Cherokee Arrow III	S. P. Donoghue	
G-BOID	Bellanca 7ECA Citabria	D. Mallinson & R. G. Marshall	
G-BOIG	PA-28-161 Cherokee Warrior II	GFT Warrior Group	
G-BOIJ	Thunder Ax7-77 balloon	A. Marshall	
G-BOIL	Cessna 172N	Upperstack Ltd	
G-BOIO	Cessna 152	Enstone Ventures Ltd	
G-BOIR	Cessna 152	APB Leasing Ltd	
G-BOIT	SOCATA TB-10 Tobago	Hessle Dock Company Ltd	
G-BOIV	Cessna 150M	F. & M. Pilkington	
G-BOIX	Cessna 172N	J. W. N. Sharpe	
G-BOIY	Cessna 172N	Fly Llanbedr Ltd	
G-BOJB	Cameron V-77 balloon	T. Taylor	
G-BOJI	PA-28RT-201 Cherokee Arrow IV	Arrow Two Group	
G-BOJM	PA-28-181 Cherokee Archer II	R. P. Emms	
G-BOJS	Cessna 172P	Paul's Planes Ltd	
G-BOJW	PA-28-161 Cherokee Warrior II	Phoenix Aviation	
G-BOJZ	PA-28-161 Cherokee Warrior II	Praeluceo Property Ltd	
G-BOKA	PA-28-201T Turbo Dakota	CBG Aviation Ltd	
G-BOKH	Whittaker MW7	I. Pearson	
G-BOKW	Bolkow Bo.208C Junior	N. A. D. Gribble & J. C. Brown	
G-BOKX	PA-28-161 Cherokee Warrior II	Turweston Flying Club Ltd	
G-BOKY	Cessna 152 II	D. F. F. & J. E. Poore	
G-BOLB	Taylorcraft BC-12-65	C. E. Tudor	
G-BOLC	Fournier RF-6B-100	Devon & Somerset RF Group	
G-BOLD	PA-38-112 Tomahawk	G-BOLD Group	
G-BOLE	PA-38-112 Tomahawk	Merseyflight Ltd	
G-BOLG	Bellanca 7KCAB Citabria	B. R. Pearson	
G-BOLI	Cessna 172P	Boli Flying Club	
G-BOLL	Lake LA-4 Skimmer	M. C. Holmes	
G-BOLO	Bell 206B JetRanger	Time Line International Ltd	
G-BOLR	Colt 21A balloon	C. J. Sanger-Davies	
G-BOLS	FRED Srs 2	I. F. Vaughan	
G-BOLT	Rockwell Commander 114	R. Vella & M. Farrugia	
G-BOLU	Robin R.3000/120	P. J. R. White & J. M. Smith	
G-BOLV	Cessna 152 II	A. J. Gomes	
G-BOLW	Cessna 152 II	G-BOLW Flying Group	
G-BOLY	Cessna 172N	Lima Yankee Flying Group	
G-BOMB	Cassutt Racer IIIM	Air Race CC Ltd	
G-BOMO	PA-38-112 Tomahawk II	APB Leasing Ltd	
G-BOMP	PA-28-181 Cherokee Archer II	A. Flinn	

Notes	Reg	Type	Owner or Operator
	G-BOMS	Cessna 172N	Penchant Ltd
	G-BOMU	PA-28-181 Cherokee Archer II	R. J. Houghton
	G-BOMY	PA-28-161 Cherokee Warrior II	The Sherwood Flying Club Ltd
	G-BOMZ	PA-38-112 Tomahawk	G-BOMZ Aviation
	G-BONC	PA-28RT-201 Cherokee Arrow IV	SC Airlease Ltd
	G-BONO	Cessna 172N	R. E. Rayner
	G-BONP	CFM Streak Shadow	G. J. Chater
	G-BONR	Cessna 172N	D. I. Craikl
	G-BONS	Cessna 172N	Robhurst Aviation Ltd
	G-BONT	Slingsby T.67M Firefly II	Vigilant Aviation Ltd (G-UCRM)
	G-BONU	Slingsby T.67B	R. L. Brinklow
	G-BONW	Cessna 152 II	LAC Flying School
	G-BONY	Denney Kitfox	E. C. R. Holland
	G-BOOB	Cameron N-65 balloon	D. R. Firkins
	G-BOOC	PA-18-150 Super Cub	S. A. C. Whitcombe
	G-BOOD	Slingsby T.31M Motor Tutor	D. G. Bilcliffe
	G-BOOF	PA-28-181 Cherokee Archer II	Winglets Ltd
	G-BOOH	Jodel D.112	G. Taylor
	G-BOOL	Cessna 172N	Gala Motors Ltd
	G-BOOX	Rutan LongEz	I. R. Wilde
	G-BOPA	PA-28-181 Cherokee Archer II	Flyco Ltd
	G-BOPC	PA-28-161 Cherokee Warrior II	Aeros Leasing Ltd
	G-BOPD	Bede BD-4	S. T. Dauncey
	G-BOPH	Cessna TR.182RG	J. M. Mitchell
	G-BOPO	Brooklands OA.7 Optica	J. K. Edgley
	G-BOPR	Brooklands OA.7 Optica	Aeroelvira Ltd
	G-BOPU	Grob G.115	Community Air Support Service (SCIO)
	G-BORB	Cameron V-77 balloon	B. M. O'Brien
	G-BORE	Colt 77A balloon	C. J. Medcalf
	G-BORG	Campbell Cricket	R. L. Gilmore
	G-BORK	PA-28-161 Cherokee Warrior II	Turweston Flying Club Ltd (G-IIIC)
	G-BORL	PA-28-161 Cherokee Warrior II	Westair Flying Services Ltd
	G-BORN	Cameron N-77 balloon	I. Chadwick
	G-BORW	Cessna 172P	Briter Aviation Ltd
	G-BORY	Cessna 150L	D. H. G. Penney
	G-BOSE	PA-28-181 Cherokee Archer II	G-BOSE Group
	G-BOSM	Jodel DR.253B	A. G. Stevens
	G-BOSN	AS.355F1 Ecureuill II	Helicopter & Pilot Services Ltd
	G-BOSO	Cessna A.152	Redhill Air Services Ltd
	G-BOTD	Cameron O-105 balloon	J. Taylor
	G-BOTF	PA-28-151 Cherokee Warrior	G-BOTF Group
	G-BOTG	Cessna 152 II	Donington Aviation Ltd
	G-BOTH	Cessna 182Q	Viscount Cobham
	G-BOTI	PA-28-151 Cherokee Warrior	Falcon Flying Services
	G-BOTN	PA-28-161 Cherokee Warrior II	Henshaw Aviation Ltd (G-FTAG)
	G-BOTO	Bellanca 7ECA Citabria	Tango Oscar Group
	G-BOTU	Piper J-3C-65 Cub	T. L. Giles
	G-BOTV	PA-32RT-300 Lance II	High Aviation Ltd
	G-BOTW	Cameron V-77 balloon	M. R. Jeynes
	G-BOUE	Cessna 172N	Swift Group
	G-BOUK	PA-34-200T Seneca II	C. J. & R. J. Barnes
	G-BOUM	PA-34-200T Seneca II	Work Zone LDA
	G-BOUV	Bensen B.8MR	L. R. Phillips
	G-BOVB	PA-15 Vagabond	J. R. Kimberley
	G-BOVK	PA-28-161 Cherokee Warrior II	Henshaw Aviation Ltd
	G-BOVU	Stoddard-Hamilton Glasair III	E. Andersen
	G-BOWM	Cameron V-56 balloon	R. S. Breakwell
	G-BOWN	PA-12 Super Cruiser	T. L. Giles
	G-BOWO	Cessna R.182	P. E. Crees (G-BOTR)
	G-BOWP	Jodel D.120A	T. E. Cummins
	G-BOWV	Cameron V-65 balloon	R. A. Harris
	G-BOWY	PA-28RT-201T Turbo Cherokee Arrow IV	Blueplane Ltd
	G-BOWZ	Bensen B80V	J. Cropper
	G-BOXA	PA-28-161 Cherokee Warrior II	Westwings International Ltd
	G-BOXC	PA-28-161 Cherokee Warrior II	Falcon Flying Services
	G-BOXG	Cameron O-77 balloon	Aociazione Sportiva Dilettantistica Experience/Italy
	G-BOXH	Pitts S-1S Special	S. A. Wilson
	G-BOXJ	Piper J-3C-65 Cub (479897)	A. Bendkowski
	G-BOXT	Hughes 269C	Goldenfly Ltd
	G-BOYB	Cessna A.152	Advanced Avionics

Reg	Type	Owner or Operator	Notes
G-BOYC	Robinson R22 Beta	Yorkshire Helicopters	
G-BOYF	Sikorsky S-76B	Von Essen Aviation Ltd	
G-BOYH	PA-28-151 Cherokee Warrior	R. Nightingale	
G-BOYI	PA-28-161 Cherokee Warrior II	Henshaw Aviation Ltd	
G-BOYL	Cessna 152 II	Redhill Air Services Ltd	
G-BOYO	Cameron V-20 balloon	T. Ward	
G-BOYV	PA-28R-201T Turbo Cherokee Arrow III	P. Lodge	
G-BOYX	Robinson R22 Beta	R. Towle	
G-BOZI	PA-28-161 Cherokee Warrior II	Aerolease Ltd	
G-BOZO	AA-5B Tiger	Griffin Flight Ltd	
G-BOZV	CEA DR.340 Major	A. C. Sayers	
G-BOZY	Cameron RTW-120 balloon	Magical Adventures Ltd	
G-BPAA	Acro Advanced	B. O. & F. A. Smith	
G-BPAB	Cessna 150M	G. D. Williamson	
G-BPAF	PA-28-161 Cherokee Warrior II	T. W. Gilbert	
G-BPAJ	DH.82A Tiger Moth	J. M. Hodgson & J. D. Smith (G-AOIX)	
G-BPAL	DHC.1 Chipmunk 22 (WG350)	K. F. & P. Tomsett (G-BCYE)	
G-BPAW	Cessna 150M	G-BPAW Group	
G-BPAY	PA-28-181 Cherokee Archer II	White Waltham Airfield Ltd	
G-BPBJ	Cessna 152 II	Brinkley Aviation Ltd	
G-BPBK	Cessna 152 II	APB Leasing Ltd	
G-BPBM	PA-28-161 Cherokee Warrior II	Redhill Air Services Ltd	
G-BPBO	PA-28RT-201T Turbo Cherokee Arrow IV	G. N. Broom & T. R. Lister	
G-BPBP	Brügger MB.2 Colibri	D. A. Preston	
G-BPCA	BN-2B-26 Islander	Loganair Ltd (G-BLNX)	
G-BPCF	Piper J-3C-65 Cub	Taildraggers Ltd	
G-BPCI	Cessna R.172K	Shacklewell Cessna XP	
G-BPCK	PA-28-161 Cherokee Warrior II	Social Infrastructure Ltd	
G-BPCL	SA Bulldog Srs 120/128 (HKG-6)	Isohigh Ltd	
G-BPCR	Mooney M.20K	Falcon Flying Services Ltd	
G-BPCX	PA-28-236 Dakota	Blue Yonder Aviation Ltd	
G-BPDE	Colt 56A balloon	J. E. Weidema/Netherlands	
G-BPDJ	Christena Mini Coupe	R. B. McCornish	
G-BPDM	CASA 1.131E Jungmann 2000(781-32)	J. D. Haslam	
G-BPDV	Pitts S-1S Special	G-BPDV Syndicate	
G-BPEM	Cessna 150K	B. N. Johnston	
G-BPEO	Cessna 152 II	W. Ali & D. Kleszcz	
G-BPES	PA-38-112 Tomahawk II	Zola Aviation Services	
G-BPFD	Jodel D.112	M. & S. Mills	
G-BPFH	PA-28-161 Cherokee Warrior II	CG Aviation Ltd	
G-BPFI	PA-28-181 Cherokee Archer II	Sarah Wass Consulting Ltd	
G-BPFL	Davis DA-2	P. E. Barker	
G-BPFM	Aeronca 7AC Champion	C. A. Roberts	
G-BPGD	Cameron V-65 balloon	A. Dunnington	
G-BPGE	Cessna U.206C	Scottish Parachute Club	
G-BPGU	PA-28-181 Cherokee Archer II	G. Underwood	
G-BPGZ	Cessna 150G	J. B. Scott	
G-BPHG	Robin DR.400/180	R. J. S. Knight	
G-BPHH	Cameron V-77 balloon	C. D. Aindow	
G-BPHI	PA-38-112 Tomahawk	Flying Fox Aviation	
G-BPHP	Taylorcraft BC-12-65	J. M. Brightwell	
G-BPHR	DH.82A Tiger Moth (A17-48)	A1748 Group	
G-BPHU	Thunder Ax7-77 balloon	R. P. Waite	
G-BPHW	Cessna 140	M. C. Boddington	
G-BPHZ	MS.500 Criquet (DM+BK)	Aero Vintage Ltd	
G-BPIF	Bensen-Parsons 2-place gyroplane	B. J. L. P. & W. J. A. L. de Saar	
G-BPII	Denney Kitfox	A. R. Newman	
G-BPIR	Scheibe SF.25E Super Falke	A. P. Askwith	
G-BPIU	PA-28-161 Cherokee Warrior II	Golf India Uniform Group	
G-BPIV	B.149 Bolingbroke Mk IVT (L6739)	Blenheim (Duxford) Ltd	
G-BPIZ	AA-5B Tiger	D. A. Horsley	
G-BPJG	PA-18-150 Super Cub	N. P. Shields	
G-BPJP	Slingsby T31 Motor Cadet III	R. E. Arnold	
G-BPJS	PA-28-161 Cadet	Redhill Air Services Ltd	
G-BPJZ	Cameron O-160 balloon	M. L. Gabb	
G-BPKF	Grob G.115	M. N. Duncan	
G-BPKK	Denney Kitfox Mk 1	A. M. Burns	
G-BPKM	PA-28-161 Cherokee Warrior II	Alexander Air Ltd	
G-BPKT	Piper J.5A Cub Cruiser (5-624KT)	A. J. Greenslade	
G-BPLM	AIA Stampe SV.4C	R. Harrison	

Notes	Reg	Type	Owner or Operator
	G-BPME	Cessna 152 II	Free-Air Ltd
	G-BPMF	PA-28-151 Cherokee Warrior	Mike Foxtrot Group
	G-BPML	Cessna 172M	N. A. Bilton
	G-BPMM	Champion 7ECA Citabria	J. P. R. & R. J. Logan
	G-BPNI	Robinson R22 Beta	G. J. Collins
	G-BPNO	Zlin Z.326 Trener Master	E. Bunnage-Flavell
	G-BPOA	Gloster Meteor T.7 ★	Pima Air and Space Museum/Tucson,USA
	G-BPOB	Sopwith Camel F.1 (replica) (N6377)	Flying Aces Movie Aircraft Collection
	G-BPOM	PA-28-161 Cherokee Warrior II	POM Flying Group
	G-BPOS	Cessna 150M	Hull Aero Club Ltd
	G-BPOT	PA-28-181 Cherokee Archer II	P. S. Simpson
	G-BPOU	Luscombe 8A Silvaire	J. L. Grayer
	G-BPPE	PA-38-112 Tomahawk	First Air Ltd
	G-BPPF	PA-38-112 Tomahawk	Bristol Strut Flying Group
	G-BPPJ	Cameron A-180 balloon	D. J. Farrar
	G-BPPK	PA-28-151 Cherokee Warrior	Aviation South West Ltd
	G-BPPO	Luscombe 8A Silvaire	P. Dyer
	G-BPPP	Cameron V-77 balloon	Sarnia Balloon Group
	G-BPPZ	Taylorcraft BC-12D	G. C. Smith
	G-BPRC	Cameron 77 Elephant SS balloon	A. Schneider/Germany
	G-BPRD	Pitts S-1C Special	R. J. Hodder
	G-BPRI	AS.355F1 Twin Squirrel	Excel Charter Ltd (G-TVPA)
	G-BPRJ	AS.355F1 Twin Squirrel	PDG Helicopters and PDG Aviation Services
	G-BPRL	AS.355F1 Twin Squirrel	Excel Charter Ltd
	G-BPRM	Cessna F.172L	BJ Aviation Ltd (G-AZKG)
	G-BPRX	Aeronca 11AC Chief	J. E. S. Turner
	G-BPRY	PA-28-161 Cherokee Warrior II	Henshaw Aviation Ltd
	G-BPSR	Cameron V-77 balloon	K. J. A. Maxwell
	G-BPTA	Stinson 108-2	T. W. Watson
	G-BPTD	Cameron V-77 balloon	J. Lippett
	G-BPTE	PA-28-181 Cherokee Archer II	A. J. Gomes
	G-BPTG	Rockwell Commander 112TC	R. S. Wear
	G-BPTI	SOCATA TB20 Trinidad	Blueplane Ltd
	G-BPTL	Cessna 172N	Woodland Plant
	G-BPTS	CASA 1.131E Jungmann 1000 (E3B-153:781-75)	E. P. Parkin
	G-BPTV	Bensen B.8	C. Munro
	G-BPUA	EAA Sport Biplane	A. S. King
	G-BPUB	Cameron V-31 balloon	M. T. Evans
	G-BPUL	PA-18-150 Super Cub	The Vintage Tug Group
	G-BPUM	Cessna R.182RG	R. C. Chapman
	G-BPUR	Piper J-3L-65 Cub (379994 52/J)	L. C. Griffiths
	G-BPUU	Cessna 140	D. R. Speight
	G-BPVA	Cessna 172F	South Lancashire Flyers Group
	G-BPVE	Bleriot IX (replica) (1)	Bianchi Aviation Film Services Ltd
	G-BPVH	Cub Aircraft J-3C-65 Prospector	D. E. Cooper-Maguire
	G-BPVI	PA-32R-301 Saratoga SP	M. T. Coppen
	G-BPVK	Varga 2150A Kachina	D. G. Hart
	G-BPVN	PA-32R-301T Turbo Saratoga SP	O. Green
	G-BPVW	CASA 1.131E Jungmann 2000	C. & J-W. Labeij/Netherlands
	G-BPVZ	Luscombe 8E Silvaire	M. D. Livermore
	G-BPWD	Cessna 120	C. G. Applegarth
	G-BPWE	PA-28-161 Cherokee Warrior II	Warrior BPWE Ltd
	G-BPWG	Cessna 150M	GB Pilots Wilsford Group
	G-BPWK	Sportavia-Putzer RF-5B	K. J. Burns
	G-BPWM	Cessna 150L	P. D. Button
	G-BPWN	Cessna 150L	Cherokee Aviation Ltd
	G-BPWR	Cessna R.172K	Poyston Aviation
	G-BPWS	Cessna 172P	Chartstone Ltd
	G-BPXE	Enstrom 280C Shark	A. Healy
	G-BPXF	Cameron V-65 balloon	C. A. Gould
	G-BPXJ	PA-28RT-201T Turbo Cherokee Arrow IV	Stapleoffice Ltd
	G-BPXY	Aeronca 11AC Chief	J. H. Tetley
	G-BPYJ	Wittman W.8 Tailwind	J. P. & Y. Mills
	G-BPYK	Thunder Ax7-77 balloon	P. Spellward
	G-BPYL	Hughes 369D	Morcorp (BVI) Ltd
	G-BPYN	Piper J-3C-65 Cub	The Aquila Group
	G-BPYR	PA-31-310 Turbo Navajo	Excel Aviation Ltd
	G-BPYT	Cameron V-77 balloon	M. H. Redman
	G-BPYY	Cameron A-180 balloon	G. D. Fitzpatrick
	G-BPZB	Cessna 120	D. N. Tallent

Reg	Type	Owner or Operator	Notes
G-BPZD	SNCAN NC.858S	M. S. Barnby	
G-BPZY	Pitts S-1C Special	J. S. Mitchell	
G-BRAA	Pitts S-1C Special	A. Stiff	
G-BRAK	Cessna 172N	W. Ali	
G-BRAM	Mikoyan MiG-21PF (503) ★	RAF Museum/Cosford	
G-BRAP	Thermal Aircraft 104 balloon	J. Yarrow	
G-BRAR	Aeronca 7AC Champion	A. W. Crutcher	
G-BRBA	PA-28-161 Cherokee Warrior II	Fly Llanbedr Ltd	
G-BRBC	NA T-6G Texan	A. P. Murphy	
G-BRBD	PA-28-151 Cherokee Warrior	Social Infrastructure Ltd	
G-BRBE	PA-28-161 Cherokee Warrior II	Jesterhoudt Holding BV/Netherlands	
G-BRBG	PA-28-180 Cherokee	S. D. J. Hagen	
G-BRBI	Cessna 172N	Skyhawk Flying Group	
G-BRBK	Robin DR.400/180	S. M. Allfrey	
G-BRBL	Robin DR.400/180	U. A. Schliessler & R. J. Kelly	
G-BRBM	Robin DR.400/180	R. W. H. Cole	
G-BRBN	Pitts S-1S Special	G-BRBN Flying Group	
G-BRBP	Cessna 152	The Pilot Centre Ltd	
G-BRBV	Piper J-4A Cub Coupe	P. Clarke	
G-BRBW	PA-28-140 Cherokee	Air Navigation and Trading Co Ltd	
G-BRBX	PA-28-181 Cherokee Archer II	Trent 199 Flying Group	
G-BRCD	Cessna A.152	Cristal Air Ltd	
G-BRCE	Pitts S-1C Special	M. P. & S. T. Barnard	
G-BRCJ	Cameron H-20 balloon	P. A. Sweatman	
G-BRCT	Denney Kitfox Mk 2	J. Shrosbree	
G-BRCV	Aeronca 7AC Champion	D. A. Vermeulen	
G-BRCW	Aeronca 11AC Chief	J. L. Gerretsen	
G-BRDD	Avions Mudry CAP-10B	Hercules Propellers Ltd	
G-BRDF	PA-28-161 Cherokee Warrior II	White Waltham Airfield Ltd	
G-BRDG	PA-28-161 Cherokee Warrior II	Falcon Flying Services	
G-BRDJ	Luscombe 8A Silvaire	G-BRDJ Group	
G-BRDM	PA-28-161 Cherokee Warrior II	White Waltham Airfield Ltd	
G-BRDO	Cessna 177B	Cardinal Aviation	
G-BRDV	Viking Wood Products Spitfire Prototype replica (K5054) ★	Solent Sky, Southampton	
G-BREA	Bensen B.8MR	D. J. Martin	
G-BREB	Piper J-3C-65 Cub	S. Turner	
G-BREL	Cameron O-77 balloon	R. A. Patey	
G-BRER	Aeronca 7AC Champion	G-BRER Group	
G-BREU	Montgomerie-Bensen B.8MR	J. S. Firth	
G-BREX	Cameron O-84 balloon	R. T. Gourley	
G-BREY	Taylorcraft BC-12D	H. R. D. Fulford	
G-BREZ	Cessna 172M	R. W. Marchant	
G-BRFB	Rutan LongEz	G. T. Bowker	
G-BRFC	Percival P.57 Sea Prince T.Mk.1 (WP321) ★	South Wales Aviation Museum/St.Athan	
G-BRFF	Colt 90A balloon	Amber Valley Aviation	
G-BRFJ	Aeronca 11AC Chief	J. M. Mooney	
G-BRFM	PA-28-161 Cherokee Warrior II	Trent Aviation	
G-BRFW	Montgomerie-Bensen B.8 2-seat	A. J. Barker	
G-BRFX	Pazmany PL.4A	S. L. Wilkes	
G-BRGD	Cameron O-84 balloon	P. A. Davies	
G-BRGE	Cameron N-90 balloon	Oakfield Farm Products Ltd	
G-BRGF	Luscombe 8E Silvaire	M. D. Livermore	
G-BRGI	PA-28-180 Cherokee	R. A. Buckfield	
G-BRGT	PA-32-260 Cherokee Six	A. A. Mattacks & T. J. W. Hood	
G-BRGW	Gardan GY-201 Minicab	R. G. White	
G-BRHA	PA-32RT-300 Lance II	Lance G-BRHA Group	
G-BRHP	Aeronca O-58B Grasshopper (31923)	P. D. & S. E. Ford	
G-BRHR	PA-38-112 Tomahawk	D. G. Price	
G-BRHX	Luscombe 8E Silvaire	N. F. Hemming	
G-BRHY	Luscombe 8E Silvaire	R. A. Keech	
G-BRIH	Taylorcraft BC-12D	M. J. Medland	
G-BRIK	T.66 Nipper 3	M. G. Read	
G-BRIL	Piper J-5A Cub Cruiser	D. J. Bone	
G-BRIV	SOCATA TB9 Tampico Club	Lincoln Aero Cluib Ltd	
G-BRIY	Taylorcraft DF-65 (42-58678:IY)	S. R. Potts	
G-BRJA	Luscombe 8A Silvaire	R. B. McKenzie	
G-BRJC	Cessna 120	A. J. Cummings	
G-BRJK	Luscombe 8A Silvaire	M. Richardson & R. C. Dyer	
G-BRJL	PA-15 Vagabond	A. R. Williams	

Notes	Reg	Type	Owner or Operator
	G-BRJV	PA-28-161 Cadet	Redhill Air Services Ltd
	G-BRJX	Rand-Robinson KR-2	B. L. R. J. Keeping
	G-BRKC	Auster J/1 Autocrat	Austerix Ltd
	G-BRKH	PA-28-236 Dakota	T. A. White
	G-BRKL	Cameron H-34 balloon	M. H. Read
	G-BRKY	Viking Dragonfly Mk II	Polar Bear Services Ltd
	G-BRLB	Air Command 532 Elite	F. G. Shepherd
	G-BRLF	Campbell Cricket (replica)	J. L. G. McLane
	G-BRLG	PA-28RT-201T Turbo Cherokee Arrow IV	N. R. Quirk
	G-BRLI	Piper J-5A Cub Cruiser	D. J. M. Eardley
	G-BRLL	Cameron A-105 balloon	P. A. Sweatman
	G-BRLO	PA-38-112 Tomahawk	E. J. Partridge
	G-BRLP	PA-38-112 Tomahawk	Highland Aviation Training Ltd
	G-BRLR	Cessna 150G	Aviolease Ltd
	G-BRMA	WS-51 Dragonfly HR.5 (WG719) ★	IHM/Weston-super-Mare
	G-BRMB	Bristol192 Belvedere HC.1 ★	IHM/Weston-super-Mare
	G-BRME	PA-28-181 Cherokee Archer II	M. E. & M. W. Lowdell
	G-BRMI	Cameron V-65 balloon	M. A. Stelling
	G-BRMT	Cameron V-31 balloon	B. Reed
	G-BRMU	Cameron V-77 balloon	P. Spellward
	G-BRNC	Cessna 150M	Aviolease Ltd
	G-BRND	Cessna 152 II	T. M. & M. L. Jones
	G-BRNK	Cessna 152 II	M. Bonsall
	G-BRNM	Chichester-M iles Leopard ★	Midland Air Museum/Coventry
	G-BRNT	Robin DR.400/180	C. E. Ponsford & ptnrs
	G-BRNU	Robin DR.400/180	Bruno Aviation Syndicate
	G-BRNW	Cameron V-77 balloon	N. Robertson & G. Smith
	G-BRNX	PA-22-150 Tri-Pacer	S. N. Askey
	G-BROE	Cameron N-65 balloon	A. I. Attwood
	G-BROG	Cameron V-65 balloon	R. Kunert
	G-BROJ	Colt 31A balloon	N. J. Langley
	G-BROO	Luscombe 8E Silvaire	C. & M. Chambers
	G-BROP	Van's RV-4	M. W. Bodger (G-NADZ)
	G-BROR	Piper J-3C-65 Cub (329594)	White Hart Flying Group
	G-BROX	Robinson R22 Beta	D. H. Baker
	G-BROY	Cameron V-77 balloon	R. Rebosio
	G-BROZ	PA-18-150 Super Cub	P. G. Kynsey
	G-BRPC	BN-2T Islander	Draken
	G-BRPE	Cessna 120	C. G. Applegarth
	G-BRPF	Cessna 120	M. A. Potter
	G-BRPG	Cessna 120	I. C. Lomax
	G-BRPH	Cessna 120	GBRPH Syndicate
	G-BRPK	PA-28-140 Cherokee	G-BRPK Group
	G-BRPM	T.66 Nipper 3	N. C. Spooner
	G-BRPP	Brookland Hornet (modified)	B. J. L. P. & W. J. A. L. de Saar
	G-BRPR	Aeronca O-58B Grasshopper (31952)	S. Godfrey
	G-BRPT	Rans S.10 Sakota	J. A. Harris
	G-BRPV	Cessna 152	Tatenhill Aviation Ltd
	G-BRPX	Taylorcraft BC-12D	G-BRPX Group
	G-BRPY	PA-15 Vagabond	C. S. Whitwell
	G-BRPZ	Luscombe 8A Silvaire	C. A. Flint
	G-BRRA	VS.361 Spitfire LF.IX (MK912:SH-L)	Lilham Aviation Ltd
	G-BRRF	Cameron O-77 balloon	K. P. & G. J. Storey
	G-BRRK	Cessna 182Q	Werewolf Aviation Ltd
	G-BRRP	Pitts S-1S Special	T. Q. Short (G-WAZZ)
	G-BRRR	Cameron V-77 balloon	K. P. & G. J. Storey
	G-BRRU	Colt 90A balloon	N. J. Bettin
	G-BRSF	VS.361 Spitfire HF.9c (RR232)	M. B. Phillips
	G-BRSL	Cameron N-56 balloon	S. Budd
	G-BRSV	Pilatus B-N BN-2T Islander	Islander Aircraft Ltd
	G-BRSW	Luscombe 8A Silvaire	M. F. Lynn & S. G. Messenger
	G-BRSX	PA-15 Vagabond	Sierra Xray Group
	G-BRTD	Cessna 152 II	152 Group
	G-BRTJ	Cessna 150F	J. A. Clegg & K. I. Bater
	G-BRTP	Cessna 152 II	R. Lee
	G-BRTW	Glaser-Dirks DG.400	I. J. Carruthers
	G-BRTX	PA-28-151 Cherokee Warrior	W. Ali & Denderah SA
	G-BRUB	PA-28-161 Cherokee Warrior II	Flytrek Ltd
	G-BRUD	PA-28-181 Cherokee Archer II	Falcon Flying Services
	G-BRUG	Luscombe 8E Silvaire	N. W. Barratt
	G-BRUM	Cessna A.152	A. J. Gomes

Reg	Type	Owner or Operator	Notes
G-BRUN	Cessna 120	J. M. Keane (G-BRDH)	
G-BRUO	Taylor JT.1 Monoplane	T. P. Eglinton	
G-BRUV	Cameron V-77 balloon	T. W. & R. F. Benbrook	
G-BRUX	PA-44-180 Seminole	M. Ali	
G-BRVE	Beech D.17S	E. P. Parkin	
G-BRVF	Colt 77A balloon	J. Adkins	
G-BRVG	NA SNJ-7 Texan	Quattro Plant Ltd	
G-BRVH	Smyth Model S Sidewinder	B. D. Deleporte	
G-BRVI	Robinson R22 Beta	York Helicopters	
G-BRVJ	Slingsby T.31 Motor Cadet III	B. Outhwaite	
G-BRVL	Pitts S-1C Special	S. D. Blakey	
G-BRVO	Aerospatiale AS.350B Ecureuil	Helicopter Times Ltd	
G-BRWA	Aeronca 7AC Champion	P. T. Price	
G-BRWB	NA T-6G Texan (526)	R. Clifford	
G-BRWR	Aeronca 11AC Chief	A. W. Crutcher	
G-BRWT	Scheibe SF.25C Falke	Booker Gliding Club Ltd	
G-BRWU	Luton LA-4A Minor	C. M. Bracewell	
G-BRWV	Brügger MB.2 Colibri	N. M. Robbins	
G-BRXD	PA-28-181 Cherokee Archer II	Xraydelta Ltd	
G-BRXE	Taylorcraft BC-12D	B. T. Morgan & W. J. Durrad	
G-BRXF	Aeronca 11AC Chief	Aeronca Flying Group	
G-BRXG	Aeronca 7AC Champion	X-Ray Golf Flying Group	
G-BRXH	Cessna 120	BRXH Group	
G-BRXL	Aeronca 11AC Chief (42-78044)	P. L. Green	
G-BRXS	Howard Special T Minus	F. A. Bakir	
G-BRXY	Pietenpol Air Camper	G. Chisnall	
G-BRZA	Cameron O-77 balloon	O. B. Bereczki	
G-BRZB	Cameron A-105 balloon	Headland Services Ltd	
G-BRZD	HAPI Cygnet SF-2A	J. B. Campbell	
G-BRZK	Stinson 108-2 Voyager	R. Farrer	
G-BRZL	Pitts S-1D Special	T. R. G. Barnby	
G-BRZS	Cessna 172P	YP Flying Group	
G-BRZW	Rans S.10 Sakota	D. L. Davies	
G-BRZX	Pitts S-1S Special	Zulu Xray Group	
G-BSAH	BN-2T Turbine Islander	Draken	
G-BSAI	Stoddard-Hamilton Glasair III	W. K. McCleod & S. Eardley	
G-BSAJ	CASA 1.131E Jungmann 2000	P. G. Kynsey	
G-BSAW	PA-28-161 Cherokee Warrior II	Whiskey Flying Group	
G-BSAX	J-3C-65 Cub	A. J. L. Eves (G-OLEZ)	
G-BSBA	PA-28-161 Cherokee Warrior II	Falcon Flying Services Ltd	
G-BSBT	Piper J-3C-65 Cub	A. R. Elliott	
G-BSBV	Rans S.10 Sakota	S. Bain	
G-BSCG	Denney Kitfox Mk 2	D. J. Couzens	
G-BSCI	Colt 77A balloon	S. C. Kinsey	
G-BSCK	Cameron H-24 balloon	J. D. Shapland	
G-BSCM	Denney Kitfox Mk 2	H. D. Colliver (G-MSCM)	
G-BSCN	SOCATA TB20 Trinidad	Zimnet Aviation Ltd	
G-BSCO	Thunder Ax7-77 balloon	F. J. Whalley	
G-BSCP	Cessna 152 II	Synergy Flight Centres Ltd	
G-BSCS	PA-28-181 Cherokee Archer II	A. C. Renouf	
G-BSCV	PA-28-161 Cherokee Warrior II	Southwood Flying Group	
G-BSCW	Taylorcraft BC-65	G. Johnson	
G-BSCY	PA-28-151 Cherokee Warrior	M. C. Plomer-Roberts	
G-BSCZ	Cessna 152 II	T. W. Gilbert	
G-BSDA	Taylorcraft BC-12D	A. D. Pearce	
G-BSDD	Denney Kitfox Mk 2	C. Morris	
G-BSDH	Robin DR.400/180	G-BSDH Group	
G-BSDO	Cessna 152 II	Cloud Global Ltd	
G-BSDP	Cessna 152 II	Paul's Planes Ltd	
G-BSDW	Cessna 182P	R. Forman & G. Slater	
G-BSDX	Cameron V-77 balloon	G. P. & S. J. Allen	
G-BSDZ	Enstrom 280FX	One Parking Solution Ltd	
G-BSEA	Thunder Ax7-77 balloon	B. T. Lewis	
G-BSED	PA-22-160 Tri-Pacer (modified)	P. G. Whitehead	
G-BSEF	PA-28-180 Cherokee	I. D. Wakeling	
G-BSEH	Cameron V-77 balloon	R. M. Rebosio	
G-BSEJ	Cessna 150M	G. Mappledorham	
G-BSEL	Slingsby T.61G Super Falke	D. G. Holley	
G-BSER	PA-28-160 Cherokee	Yorkair Ltd	
G-BSEU	PA-28-181 Cherokee Archer II	Herefordshire Aero Club Ltd	

Notes	Reg	Type	Owner or Operator
	G-BSEV	Cameron O-77 balloon	L. J. Whitelock
	G-BSEX	Cameron A-180 balloon	Heart of England Balloons
	G-BSEY	Beech A36 Bonanza	E. S-M. Ramsay
	G-BSFA	Aero Designs Pulsar	P. F. Lorriman
	G-BSFD	Piper J-3C-65 Cub (16037)	P. E. S. Latham
	G-BSFE	PA-38-112 Tomahawk II	Leading Edge Flight Training Ltd
	G-BSFF	Robin DR.400/180R	Lasham Gliding Society Ltd
	G-BSFP	Cessna 152T	The Pilot Centre Ltd
	G-BSFR	Cessna 152 II	Galair Ltd
	G-BSFV	Woods Woody Pusher	C. Marti
	G-BSFW	PA-15 Vagabond	G. R. French
	G-BSGB	Gaertner Ax4 Skyranger balloon	D. P. Busby
	G-BSGF	Robinson R22 Beta	Swift Helicopter Services Ltd
	G-BSGG	Denney Kitfox Mk 2	N. Allen
	G-BSGJ	Monnett Sonerai 2	J. L. Loweth
	G-BSGS	Rans S.10 Sakota	S. McGirr
	G-BSHA	PA-34-200T Seneca II	Justgold Ltd
	G-BSHC	Colt 69A balloon	Magical Adventures Ltd
	G-BSHH	Luscombe 8E Silvaire	M. Craft & P. R. Bush
	G-BSHO	Cameron V-77 balloon	D. J. Duckworth & J. C. Stewart
	G-BSHR	Cessna F.172N	Deep Cleavage Ltd (G-BFGE)
	G-BSIC	Cameron V-77 balloon	M. P. Pritchard
	G-BSIF	Denney Kitfox Mk 2	S. M. Dougan
	G-BSIG	Colt 21A Cloudhopper balloon	G. Gray
	G-BSIJ	Cameron V-77 balloon	G. B. Davies
	G-BSIO	Cameron 80 Shed SS balloon	R. E. Jones
	G-BSIY	Schleicher ASK.14	D. & M. Shrimpton
	G-BSJX	PA-28-161 Cherokee Warrior II	Andrewsfield Aviation Ltd
	G-BSKA	Cessna 150M	Aviolease Ltd
	G-BSKG	Maule MX-7-180	A. J. Lewis
	G-BSKW	PA-28-181 Cherokee Archer II	R. J. Whyham
	G-BSLA	Robin DR.400/180	A. B. McCoig
	G-BSLH	CASA 1.131E Jungmann 2000	M. A. Warden
	G-BSLK	PA-28-161 Cherokee Warrior II	T. W. Gilbert
	G-BSLM	PA-28-160 Cherokee	Fly (Fu Lai) Aviation Ltd
	G-BSLT	PA-28-161 Cherokee Warrior II	CG Aviation Ltd
	G-BSLU	PA-28-140 Cherokee	Ovin Ltd
	G-BSLV	Enstrom 280FX	J. P. C. Alunni
	G-BSLW	Bellanca 7ECA Citabria	Invicta Aero Group
	G-BSLX	WAR Focke-Wulf Fw 190 (replica) (4+)	S. Freeman
	G-BSME	Bölkow Bö.208C1 Junior	J. A. Webb
	G-BSMM	Colt 31A balloon	P. Spellward
	G-BSMN	CFM Streak Shadow	D. R. C. Pugh
	G-BSMT	Rans S-10 Sakota	T. D. Wood
	G-BSMV	PA-17 Vagabond	H. E. Cummings
	G-BSNE	Luscombe 8E Silvaire	O. R. Watts
	G-BSNF	Piper J-3C-65 Cub	D. A. Hammant
	G-BSNT	Luscombe 8A Silvaire	S. M. Owen
	G-BSNX	PA-28-181 Cherokee Archer II	Redhill Air Services Ltd
	G-BSOE	Luscombe 8A Silvaire	R. G. Downhill
	G-BSOF	Colt 25A balloon	L. P. Hooper
	G-BSOG	Cessna 172M	Gloster Aero Group
	G-BSOK	PA-28-161 Cherokee Warrior II	G. E. Fox
	G-BSOM	Glaser-Dirks DG.400	P. G. Noonan
	G-BSON	Green S.25 balloon	J. J. Green
	G-BSOO	Cessna 172F	The Oscar Oscar Group
	G-BSOR	CFM Streak Shadow Srs SA	A. Parr
	G-BSOU	PA-38-112 Tomahawk II	Leading Edge Flight Training Ltd
	G-BSOX	Luscombe 8AE Silvaire	R. Dauncey
	G-BSPA	QAC Quickie Q.2	G. V. McKirdy & B. K. Glover
	G-BSPC	Jodel D.140C	B. E. Cotton
	G-BSPE	Cessna F.172P	G. E. Fox
	G-BSPK	Cessna 195A	A. G. & D. L. Bompas
	G-BSPL	CFM Streak Shadow Srs SA	G. L. Turner
	G-BSPN	PA-28R-201T Turbo Cherokee Arrow III	K. Woodcock
	G-BSRH	Pitts S-1C Special	A. C. Richards
	G-BSRK	ARV Super 2	K. L. M. Ikelle
	G-BSRL	Campbell Cricket replica	M. Brudnicki
	G-BSRP	Rotorway Executive	P. J. Chandler
	G-BSRX	CFM Streak Shadow	J. D. Winder
	G-BSSA	Luscombe 8E Silvaire	Luscombe Flying Group

Reg	Type	Owner or Operator	Notes
G-BSSB	Cessna 150L	Poyston Aviation	
G-BSSC	PA-28-161 Cherokee Warrior II	Tor Financial Consulting Ltd	
G-BSSF	Denney Kitfox Mk 2	I. J. Webb	
G-BSSK	QAC Quickie Q.2	R. Greatrex	
G-BSSP	Robin DR.400/180R	Soaring (Oxford) Ltd	
G-BSST	BAC-Sud Concorde 002 ★	F.A.A. Museum/Yeovilton	
G-BSSV	CFM Streak Shadow	C. G. Chambers	
G-BSSY	Polikarpov Po-2 (28)	Richard Shuttleworth Trustees	
G-BSTC	Aeronca 11AC Chief	J. Armstrong & D. Lamb	
G-BSTI	Piper J-3C-65 Cub	S. P. Reeve	
G-BSTK	Thunder Ax8-90 balloon	M. Williams	
G-BSTL	Rand-Robinson KR-2	C. S. Hales & N. Brauns	
G-BSTM	Cessna 172L	G-BSTM Group	
G-BSTO	Cessna 152 II	M. A. Stott	
G-BSTP	Cessna 152 II	J. Elankeeran & J. B. P. E. Fernandes	
G-BSTR	AA-5 Traveler	J. C. M. Alty	
G-BSTT	Rans S-6 Coyote II	D. G. Palmer	
G-BSTX	Luscombe 8A Silvaire	J. D. Drury	
G-BSTZ	PA-28-140 Cherokee	Air Navigation & Trading Co Ltd	
G-BSUA	Rans S.6 Coyote II	A. J. Todd	
G-BSUD	Luscombe 8A Silvaire	Luscombe Quartet	
G-BSUK	Colt 77A balloon	T. Knight	
G-BSUX	Carlson Sparrow II	K. Redfearn	
G-BSVB	PA-28-181 Cherokee Archer II	Veebee Aviation Ltd	
G-BSVE	Binder CP.301S Smaragd	A. C. Oliver	
G-BSVG	PA-28-161 Cherokee Warrior II	Airways Aero Associations Ltd	
G-BSVH	Piper J-3C-65 Cub	G. J. Digby	
G-BSVK	Denney Kitfox Model 2	D. C. Marsh	
G-BSVM	PA-28-161 Cherokee Warrior II	EFG Flying Services	
G-BSVN	Thorp T-18	M. D. Moaby	
G-BSVP	PA-23-250 Aztec	S. G. Spier	
G-BSVR	Schweizer 269C	A & W Demolition (Bracknell)	
G-BSVS	Robin DR.400/100	A. G. Bell & M. P. Boulton	
G-BSWB	Rans S.10 Sakota	F. A. Hewitt	
G-BSWC	Boeing Stearman E75 (112)	D. A. Jack	
G-BSWG	PA-17 Vagabond	J. P. Taylor	
G-BSWH	Cessna 152 II	Airspeed Aviation Ltd	
G-BSWL	Slingsby T.61F Venture T.2	Trent Valley Venture Group	
G-BSWM	Slingsby T.61F Venture T.2	Venture Gliding Group	
G-BSWR	BN-2T-26 Turbine Islander	Police Service of Northern Ireland	
G-BSXA	PA-28-161 Cherokee Warrior II	Falcon Flying Services	
G-BSXB	PA-28-161 Cherokee Warrior II	A. J. Gomes	
G-BSXC	PA-28-161 Cherokee Warrior II	G-BSXC LLP	
G-BSXD	Soko P-2 Kraguj (30146)	S. M. Robertson	
G-BSXI	Mooney M.20E	D. H. G. Penney	
G-BSXT	Piper J-5A Cub Cruiser (42-5772)	J. R. Hodgson	
G-BSYA	Jodel D.18	R. W. Rose & J. T. Houghton	
G-BSYF	Luscombe 8A Silvaire	M. Flint	
G-BSYG	PA-12 Super Cruiser	Fat Cub Group	
G-BSYH	Luscombe 8A Silvaire	N. R. Osborne	
G-BSYJ	Cameron N-77 balloon	Chubb Fire Ltd	
G-BSYO	Piper J-3C-90 Cub	A. Coigny (G-BSMI/G-BRHF)	
G-BSYU	Robin DR.400/180	R. L. H. Walker	
G-BSYV	Cessna 150M	Aviolease Ltd	
G-BSYY	PA-28-161 Cherokee Warrior II	White Waltham Airfield Ltd	
G-BSYZ	PA-28-161 Cherokee Warrior II	N. J. Butler	
G-BSZB	Stolp SA.300 Starduster Too	P. J. B. Lewis	
G-BSZF	Jodel DR.250/160	Cole Aviation Ltd	
G-BSZJ	PA-28-181 Cherokee Archer II	M. L. A. Pudney & R. D. Fuller	
G-BSZM	Montgomerie-Bensen B.8MR	S. H. Broszek	
G-BSZO	Cessna 152	A. Jahanfar	
G-BSZT	PA-28-161 Cherokee Warrior II	Golf Charlie Echo Ltd	
G-BSZV	Cessna 150F	Bnett Aviation Ltd	
G-BSZW	Cessna 152	T. W. Gilbert	
G-BTAK	EAA Acrosport II	S. R. Green	
G-BTAL	Cessna F.152 II	Herefordshire Aero Club Ltd	
G-BTAM	PA-28-181 Cherokee Archer II	Sondica Group Inc	
G-BTAW	PA-28-161 Cherokee Warrior II	Piper Flying Group	
G-BTAZ	Evans VP-2 ★	City of Norwich Aviation Museum/Norwich	
G-BTBC	PA-28-161 Cherokee Warrior II	W. Ali & Denderah SA	

Notes	Reg	Type	Owner or Operator
	G-BTBG	Denney Kitfox Mk 2	A. S. Cadney
	G-BTBH	Ryan ST3KR (854)	R. C. Piper
	G-BTBJ	Cessna 190	P. W. Moorcroft
	G-BTBL	Montgomerie-Bensen B.8MR	A. R. Hawes
	G-BTBU	PA-18-150 Super Cub	D. E. Starkey
	G-BTBY	PA-17 Vagabond	C. J. Mace
	G-BTCE	Cessna 152	J. R. George
	G-BTCH	Luscombe 8E Silvaire Deluxe	M. W. Orr
	G-BTCI	PA-17 Vagabond	T. R. Whittome
	G-BTCJ	Luscombe 8E Silvaire	D. Snook
	G-BTCZ	Cameron Chateau 84 balloon	Balleroy Developpement SAS/France
	G-BTDA	Slingsby T.61G Falke (XZ550)	G-BTDA Group
	G-BTDC	Denney Kitfox Mk 2	R. Palmer
	G-BTDD	CFM Streak Shadow	R. J. Creasey
	G-BTDE	Cessna C-165 Airmaster	N. Saberi
	G-BTDF	Luscombe 8A Silvaire	Lusc Flying Group
	G-BTDN	Denney Kitfox Mk 2	D. Rudd
	G-BTDT	CASA 1.131E Jungmann 2000	T. J. Alderdice
	G-BTDV	PA-28-161 Cherokee Warrior II	Falcon Flying Services Ltd
	G-BTDW	Cessna 152 II	Falcon Flying Services Ltd
	G-BTDY	PA.18-150 Super Cub	N. J. Butler
	G-BTDZ	CASA 1.131E Jungmann 2000	R. J. & M. Pickin
	G-BTES	Cessna 150H	E. M. Burton
	G-BTET	Piper J-3C-65 Cub	P. G. Fowler
	G-BTEW	Cessna 120	J. H. Milne
	G-BTFC	Cessna F.152 II	O. G. Haynes & W. Ali
	G-BTFE	Bensen-Parsons 2-seat gyroplane	A. Corleanca
	G-BTFG	Boeing Stearman A75N1 (441)	R. Everitt
	G-BTFJ	PA-15 Vagabond	R. Ellingworth & N. A. Preston
	G-BTFL	Aeronca 11AC Chief	BTFL Group
	G-BTFO	PA-28-161 Cherokee Warrior II	Flyfar Ltd
	G-BTFP	PA-38-112 Tomahawk	M. Lee
	G-BTFT	Beech 58 Baron	Fastwing Air Charter Ltd
	G-BTFU	Cameron N-90 balloon	J. J. Rudoni & A. C. K. Rawson
	G-BTGD	Rand-Robinson KR-2 (modified)	N. W. Cawley
	G-BTGI	Rearwin 175 Skyranger	J. M. Fforde
	G-BTGJ	Smith DSA-1 Miniplane	A. M. Smith
	G-BTGL	Light Aero Avid Flyer	J. S. Clair-Quentin
	G-BTGM	Aeronca 7AC Champion	Heligan Champ Group
	G-BTGO	PA-28-140 Cherokee	LS Airmotive Ltd
	G-BTGR	Cessna 152 II	A. J. Gomes
	G-BTGS	Stolp SA.300 Starduster Too	G. N. Elliott & ptnrs (G-AYMA)
	G-BTGT	CFM Streak Shadow	I. Heunis (G-MWPY)
	G-BTGW	Cessna 152 II	Stapleford Flying Club Ltd
	G-BTGY	PA-28-161 Cherokee Warrior II	Stapleford Flying Club Ltd
	G-BTGZ	PA-28-181 Cherokee Archer II	Blue Peak Enterprises Ltd
	G-BTHE	Cessna 150L	UK Flying Clubs Ltd
	G-BTHF	Cameron V-90 balloon	N. J. & S. J. Langley
	G-BTHK	Thunder Ax7-77 balloon	M. S.Trend
	G-BTHP	Thorp T.211	M. Gardner
	G-BTHX	Colt 105A balloon	I. J. Wadey
	G-BTHY	Bell 206B JetRanger 3	P. J. Hollywood
	G-BTID	PA-28-161 Cherokee Warrior II	Falcon Flying Services Ltd
	G-BTIE	SOCATA TB10 Tobago	D. J. & S. N. Taplin
	G-BTIF	Denney Kitfox Mk 3	D. S. Lally
	G-BTIG	Montgomerie-Bensen B.8MR	E. Mangles
	G-BTII	AA-5B Tiger	G-BTII Group
	G-BTIJ	Luscombe 8E Silvaire	S. J. Hornsby
	G-BTIL	PA-38-112 Tomahawk	B. J. Pearson
	G-BTIM	PA-28-161 Cadet	White Waltham Airfield Ltd
	G-BTIV	PA-28-161 Cherokee Warrior II	Warrior Group
	G-BTJA	Luscombe 8E Silvaire	N. C. Wildey
	G-BTJB	Luscombe 8E Silvaire	M. Loxton
	G-BTJC	Luscombe 8F Silvaire	M. Colson
	G-BTJD	Thunder Ax8-90 S2 balloon	L. J. Whitelock
	G-BTJS	Montgomerie-Bensen B.8MR	B. F. Pearson
	G-BTJX	Rans S.10 Sakota	J. A. Harris
	G-BTKA	Piper J-5A Cub Cruiser	J. M. Cockings
	G-BTKB	Renegade Spirit 912	P. J. Calvert
	G-BTKD	Denney Kitfox Mk 4	S. F. Beardsell
	G-BTKP	CFM Streak Shadow	M. J. Mawle & P. F. Morgan

Reg	Type	Owner or Operator	Notes
G-BTKT	PA-28-161 Cherokee Warrior II	Falcon Flying Services Ltd	
G-BTKV	PA-22-160 Tri-Pacer	R. A. Moore	
G-BTKW	Cameron O-105 balloon	L. J. Whitelock	
G-BTKX	PA-28-181 Cherokee Archer II	D. J. Perkins	
G-BTLB	Wassmer Wa.52 Europa	Hampshire Flying Group	
G-BTLG	PA-28R-200 Cherokee Arrow	Saeed Aviation Ltd	
G-BTLL	Pilatus P.3-03 (A-806)	R. E. Dagless	
G-BTLP	AA-1C Lynx	Partlease Ltd	
G-BTLY	BN-2B-26 Islander	D. Brem-Wilson	
G-BTMA	Cessna 172N	R. F. Wondrak	
G-BTMK	Cessna R.172K XPII	K. E. Halford	
G-BTML	Cameron Rupert Bear 90 balloon	S. C. Kinsey	
G-BTMO	Colt 69A balloon	Cameron Balloons Ltd	
G-BTMP	Campbell Cricket replica	N. D. Dykes	
G-BTMR	Cessna 172M	Hull Aero Club Ltd	
G-BTMV	Everett Srs 2 gyroplane	L. Armes	
G-BTNH	PA-28-161 Cherokee Warrior II	Falcon Flying Services Ltd (G-DENH)	
G-BTNO	Aeronca 7AC Champion	J. M. Farquhar	
G-BTNT	PA-28-151 Cherokee Warrior	Cherokee Aviation Ltd	
G-BTNV	PA-28-161 Cherokee Warrior II	A. J. & A. M. Twemlow	
G-BTNW	Rans S.6-ESA Coyote II	B. J. Jeffery	
G-BTOG	DH.82A Tiger Moth (DE745)	TOG Group	
G-BTOI	Cameron N-77 balloon	Zebedee Balloon Service Ltd	
G-BTOL	Denney Kitfox Mk 3	P. J. Gibbs	
G-BTON	PA-28-140 Cherokee	Fly With Me Aviation Ltd	
G-BTOP	Cameron V-77 balloon	J. J. Winter	
G-BTOT	PA-15 Vagabond	B. J. Robe	
G-BTOW	SOCATA Rallye 180GT	M. Jarrett	
G-BTOZ	Thunder Ax9-120 S2 balloon	H. G. Davies	
G-BTRC	Avid Speed Wing	H. Bishop	
G-BTRF	Aero Designs Pulsar	G. Smith	
G-BTRI	Aeronca 11CC Super Chief	Golf Romeo India Aviation	
G-BTRK	PA-28-161 Cherokee Warrior II	Stapleford Flying Club Ltd	
G-BTRL	Cameron N-105 balloon	J. Lippett	
G-BTRR	Thunder Ax7-77 balloon	P. J. Wentworth	
G-BTRS	PA-28-161 Cherokee Warrior II	Airwise Flying Group	
G-BTRT	PA-28R-200 Cherokee Arrow	P. J. Alexander, J. Durrell & I. J. Black	
G-BTRU	Robin DR.400/180	R. H. Mackay	
G-BTRW	Slingsby T.61F Venture T.2	P. Asbridge	
G-BTRY	PA-28-161 Cherokee Warrior II	C. S. Jennings	
G-BTRZ	Jodel D.18	A. P. Aspinall	
G-BTSC	Evans VP-2	I. Pearson	
G-BTSJ	PA-28-161 Cherokee Warrior II	Coastal Air (SW) Ltd	
G-BTSP	Piper J-3C-65 Cub	C. M. Brittlebank	
G-BTSR	Aeronca 11AC Chief	J. M. Miller	
G-BTSV	Denney Kitfox Mk 3	Fox Flyers	
G-BTSW	Colt AS-105 GD balloon	K-L C. M. Busemeyer	
G-BTSY	EE Lightning F.6 (XR724) ★	Lightning Association/Binbrook	
G-BTSZ	Cessna 177A	D. Kiminiene	
G-BTTR	Aerotek Pitts S-2A Special	Collett Aviation Services Ltd	
G-BTTY	Denney Kitfox Mk 2	L. W. Whittington	
G-BTTZ	Slingsby T.61F Venture T.2	T61F Group	
G-BTUA	Slingsby T.61F Venture T.2	R. T. C. Connors	
G-BTUB	Yakovlev C.11	B. R. Cox	
G-BTUC	EMB-312 Tucano ★	Ulster Aviation Society/Long Kesh	
G-BTUG	SOCATA Rallye 180T	J. J. Mion	
G-BTUK	Aerotek Pitts S-2A Special	Ultimate Aerobatics	
G-BTUM	Piper J-3C-65 Cub	G-BTUM Syndicate	
G-BTUR	PA-18-95 Super Cub (modified)	C. G. Applegarth	
G-BTUS	Whittaker MW7 ★	South Wales Aviation Museum/St. Athan	
G-BTUW	PA-28-151 Cherokee Warrior	T. S. Kemp	
G-BTUZ	American General AG-5B Tiger	Meadowland Aviation Ltd	
G-BTVC	Denney Kitfox Mk 2	P. T. Catanach	
G-BTVX	Cessna 152 II	M. Bonsall	
G-BTWB	Denney Kitfox Mk 3	C. J. Scott (G-BTTM)	
G-BTWC	Slingsby T.61F Venture T.2 (ZA656)	621 Venture Syndicate	
G-BTWD	Slingsby T.61F Venture T.2	York Gliding Centre	
G-BTWE	Slingsby T.61F Venture T.2	Aston Down G-BTWE Syndicate	
G-BTWI	EAA Acro Sport I	J. O'Connell	
G-BTWL	WAG-Aero Acro Sport Trainer	F. E. Tofield	
G-BTWY	Aero Designs Pulsar	R. Bishop	

Notes	Reg	Type	Owner or Operator
	G-BTXD	Rans S.6-ESA Coyote II	A. I. Sutherland
	G-BTXF	Cameron V-90 balloon	G. Thompson
	G-BTXH	Colt A5-56 Airship	H. Moine
	G-BTXI	Noorduyn AT-16 Harvard IIB (FE695)	R. W. Tyrell
	G-BTXK	Thunder Ax7-65 balloon	A. F. Selby
	G-BTXM	Colt 21A Cloudhopper balloon	I. M. Taylor
	G-BTXZ	Zenair CH.250	T. B. R. Laidler
	G-BTYI	PA-28-181 Cherokee Archer II	S. W. Hedges
	G-BTYX	Cessna 140 ★	South Yorkshire Aircraft Museum/Doncaster
	G-BTYY	Curtiss Robertson C-2 Robin	R. W. Hatton
	G-BTZA	Beech F33A Bonanza	H. Mendelssohn & C. S. Wright
	G-BTZB	Yakovlev Yak-50 (10 yellow)	Airborne Services Ltd
	G-BTZD	Yakovlev Yak-1 (1342)	Historic Aircraft Collection Ltd
	G-BTZP	SOCATA TB9 Tampico	M. W. Orr
	G-BTZS	Colt 77A balloon	P. T. R. Ollivere
	G-BTZU	Cameron C-60 balloon	D. R. & M. J. King
	G-BTZX	Piper J-3C-65 Cub	ZX Cub Group
	G-BTZY	Colt 56A balloon	M. H. Read
	G-BTZZ	CFM Streak Shadow	B. P. Cater
	G-BUAB	Aeronca 11AC Chief	C. Conidaris
	G-BUAG	Jodel D.18	A. M. Crosby
	G-BUAI	Everett Srs 3 gyroplane	D. Stevenson
	G-BUAO	Luscombe 8E Silvaire	C. R. Carroll
	G-BUAR	Westland Seafire Mk.III (PP972:II-5)	Flying A Services Ltd
	G-BUBL	Thunder Ax8-105 balloon ★	British Balloon Museum/Newbury
	G-BUBN	BN-2B-26 Islander	Isles of Scilly Skybus Ltd
	G-BUBT	Stoddard-Hamilton Glasair II-SRG	Signs Plus Ltd
	G-BUCA	Cessna A.150K	R. J. Whyham
	G-BUCC	CASA 1.131E Jungmann 2000 (BU+CC)	R. N. Crosland (G-BUEM)
	G-BUCH	Stinson V-77 Reliant	Sopwith Court Ltd
	G-BUCK	CASA 1.131E Jungmann 1000 (BU+CK)	T. W. Gilbert
	G-BUCM	Hawker Sea Fury FB.11 (VX653)	Patina Ltd
	G-BUCO	Pietenpol Air Camper	A. James
	G-BUCT	Cessna 150L	Air Navigation & Trading Co.Ltd
	G-BUDA	Slingsby T.61F Venture T.2	The Northumbria Gliding Club Ltd
	G-BUDE	PA-22-135 Tri-Pacer (tailwheel)	N. J. Szkiler
	G-BUDI	Aero Designs Pulsar	R. M. Alleyne
	G-BUDL	Auster 3 (NX534)	L. R. Leek
	G-BUDN	Cameron 90 Shoe SS balloon	Magical Adventures Ltd
	G-BUDO	PZL-110 Koliber 150	A. S. Vine
	G-BUDR	Denney Kitfox Mk 3	S. M. L. Fernandes
	G-BUDT	Slingsby T.61F Venture T.2 (XZ563)	G-BUDT Group
	G-BUEC	Van's RV-6	I. N. Scott
	G-BUEF	Cessna 152 II	British Aviation Academy Ltd
	G-BUEG	Cessna 152 II	P. Rudd
	G-BUEI	Thunder Ax8-105 balloon	J. London
	G-BUEK	Slingsby T.61F Venture T.2	G-BUEK Group
	G-BUEN	VPM M-14 Scout	C. R. Gordon
	G-BUEP	Maule MX-7-180	N. J. B. Bennett
	G-BUEW	Rans S-6 Coyote II	C. Cheeseman (G-MWYE)
	G-BUFG	Slingsby T.61F Venture T.2	G. W. Withers
	G-BUFH	PA-28-161 Cherokee Warrior II	Bliss Aviation Ltd
	G-BUFR	Slingsby T.61F Venture T.2	Oxfordshire Sportflying Ltd
	G-BUFY	PA-28-161 Cherokee Warrior II	Bickertons Aerodromes Ltd
	G-BUGJ	Robin DR.400/180	W. E. R. Jenkins
	G-BUGL	Slingsby T.61F Venture T.2	S. L. Hoy
	G-BUGP	Cameron V-77 balloon	R. Churcher
	G-BUGS	Cameron V-77 balloon	T. J. Orchard
	G-BUGV	Slingsby T.61F Venture T.2	GBUGV Flying Group
	G-BUGW	Slingsby T.61F Venture T.2	BR Aviation Ltd
	G-BUGY	Cameron V-90 balloon	Dante Balloon Group
	G-BUGZ	Slingsby T.61F Venture T.2	R. W. Spiller
	G-BUHA	Slingsby T.61F Venture T.2 (ZA634:C)	Saltby Flying Group
	G-BUHM	Cameron V-77 balloon	P. T. Lickorish
	G-BUHO	Cessna 140	Adastral Flying Displays Ltd
	G-BUHR	Slingsby T.61F Venture T.2	M. R. Fox
	G-BUHS	Stoddard-Hamilton Glasair SH TD-1	T. F. Horrocks
	G-BUHZ	Cessna 120	The Cessna 140 Group
	G-BUIF	PA-28-161 Cherokee Warrior II	Redhill Air Services Ltd
	G-BUIG	Campbell Cricket (replica)	R. H. Braithwaite

Reg	Type	Owner or Operator	Notes
G-BUIH	Slingsby T.61F Venture T.2	The Falcon Gliding Group	
G-BUIJ	PA-28-161 Cherokee Warrior II	D. J. Taplin	
G-BUIK	PA-28-161 Cherokee Warrior II	E. J. Lamb	
G-BUIL	CFM Streak Shadow	Shadow Builder Group	
G-BUIP	Denney Kitfox Mk 2	S. A. Wilson	
G-BUJA	Slingsby T.61F Venture T.2	Wolds Gliding Club Ltd	
G-BUJB	Slingsby T.61F Venture T.2	Falke Syndicate	
G-BUJE	Cessna 177B	FG93 Group	
G-BUJH	Colt 77B balloon	B. Fisher	
G-BUJI	Slingsby T.61F Venture T.2	The Burn Gliding Club Ltd	
G-BUJM	Cessna 120	K. G. Grayson	
G-BUJN	Cessna 172N	Warwickshire Leasing Ltd	
G-BUJO	PA-28-161 Cherokee Warrior II	Falcon Flying Services	
G-BUJP	PA-28-161 Cherokee Warrior II	Phoenix Aviation	
G-BUJV	Light Aero Avid Speedwing Mk 4	C. Thomas	
G-BUJZ	Rotorway Executive 90	Southern Helkicopters Ltd	
G-BUKB	Rans S.10 Sakota	M. K. Blatch	
G-BUKF	Denney Kitfox Mk 4	Kilo Foxtrot Group	
G-BUKH	D.31 Turbulent	G. Haye	
G-BUKI	Thunder Ax7-77 balloon	Virgin Balloon Flights	
G-BUKK	Bücker Bü 133C Jungmeister (U-80)	N. Barnard	
G-BUKO	Cessna 120	C. J. Varley	
G-BUKP	Denney Kitfox Mk 2	K. C. Smith	
G-BUKR	MS.880B Rallye Club 100T	G-BUKR Flying Group	
G-BUKU	Luscombe 8E Silvaire Deluxe	Silvaire Flying Group	
G-BUKZ	Evans VP-2	P. R. Farnell	
G-BULC	Light Aero Avid Flyer Mk 4	Lima Charlie Group	
G-BULG	Van's RV-4	V. D. Long	
G-BULJ	CFM Streak Shadow	D. R. Stansfield	
G-BULL	SA Bulldog Srs 120/128 (HKG-5)	Bulldog Aeros Ltd	
G-BULO	Luscombe 8A Silvaire	C. Hutchinson & K. B. Hughes	
G-BULR	PA-28-140 Cherokee B	D. H. G. Penny	
G-BULY	Light Aero Avid Flyer	C. Coleman	
G-BULZ	Denney Kitfox Mk 2	T. G. F. Trenchard	
G-BUMP	PA-28-181 Cherokee Archer II	G-MC Aviation	
G-BUNA	SNCAN Stampe SV-4C	J. P. O'Donnell	
G-BUNB	Slingsby T.61F Venture T.2	T61F Syndicate	
G-BUNC	PZL-104 Wilga 35	R. F. Goodman	
G-BUNG	Cameron N-77 balloon	A. Kaye	
G-BUNO	Lancair 320	J. Softley	
G-BUOA	Whittaker MW6-S Fatboy Flyer	H. N. Graham	
G-BUOB	CFM Streak Shadow	J. M. Hunter	
G-BUOD	SE-5A (replica) (B595:W)	M. D. Waldron/Belgium	
G-BUOF	D.62B Condor	Deadwood Flying Group	
G-BUOL	Denney Kitfox Mk 3	I. Handzyuk	
G-BUOS	Supermarine 394 Spitfire FR.XVIIIe	Fly to Inspire Ltd	
G-BUOW	Aero Designs Pulsar XP	T. J. Hartwell	
G-BUPA	Rutan LongEz	N. G. Henry	
G-BUPF	Bensen B.8MR	D. J. Farrar	
G-BUPH	Colt 25A balloon	M. E. White	
G-BUPM	VPM M-16 Tandem Trainer	A. Kitson	
G-BUPP	Cameron V-42 balloon	C. L. Schoeman	
G-BUPU	Thunder Ax7-77 balloon	R. C. Darkworth & D. G. Maguire/USA	
G-BUPV	Great Lakes 2T-1A	R. J. Fray	
G-BUPW	Denney Kitfox Mk 3	J. Metcalfe	
G-BURI	Enstrom F-28C	D. W. C. Holmes	
G-BURL	Colt 105A balloon	J. E. Rose	
G-BURP	Rotorway Executive 90	D. H. Baker	
G-BURR	Auster AOP.9 (WZ706)	N. A. Whatling	
G-BURZ	Hawker Nimrod II (K3661:562)	Historic Aircraft Collection Ltd	
G-BUSN	Rotorway Executive 90	D. & J. Parke	
G-BUSR	Aero Designs Pulsar	S. S. Bateman & R. A. Watts	
G-BUSS	Cameron 90 Bus SS balloon	Magical Adventures Ltd	
G-BUSV	Colt 105A balloon	H. C. J. Williams	
G-BUSW	Rockwell Commander 114	M. J. P. Lynch	
G-BUTB	CFM Streak Shadow	H. O. Maclean	
G-BUTD	Van's RV-6	Watchford RV-6 Group	
G-BUTF	Aeronca 11AC Chief	A. W. Crutcher	
G-BUTH	CEA DR.220 2+2	Phoenix Flying Group	
G-BUTM	Rans S.6-116 Coyote II	Coyote Flying Group	
G-BUTT	Cessna FA150K	Fis Ato Europe SL/Spain (G-AXSJ)	

Notes	Reg	Type	Owner or Operator
	G-BUTX	CASA 1.133C Jungmeister (ES.1-4)	S. R. Stead
	G-BUTZ	PA-28-180 Cherokee C	H. L. Carter (G-DARL)
	G-BUUA	Slingsby T.67M Firefly Mk II	Heartland Aviation Ltd
	G-BUUE	Slingsby T.67M Firefly Mk II	J. R. Bratty
	G-BUUF	Slingsby T.67M Firefly Mk II	Nautx Ltd
	G-BUUG	Slingsby T.67M Firefly Mk II	High Flight Training Solutions Ltd
	G-BUUI	Slingsby T.67M Firefly Mk II	Bustard Flying Club Ltd
	G-BUUJ	Slingsby T.67M Firefly Mk II	Skyboard Aerobatics Ltd
	G-BUUK	Slingsby T.67M Firefly Mk II	Avalanche Aviation Ltd
	G-BUUL	SlingsbyT.67M Firefly Mk II	R. R. K. Mayall
	G-BUUT	Interavia 70TA	M. A. Stelling
	G-BUUU	Cameron Bottle SS balloon ★	British Balloon Museum/Newbury
	G-BUUX	PA-28-180 Cherokee D	Aero Group 78
	G-BUVA	PA-22-135 Tri-Pacer	Oaksey VA Group
	G-BUVB	Colt 77A balloon	G. Everett
	G-BUVM	CEA DR.250/160	T. W. Gilbert
	G-BUVO	Cessna F.182P	Romeo Mike Flying Group (G-WTFA)
	G-BUVR	Christen A.1 Husky	S. P. H. Thomas
	G-BUVT	Colt 77A balloon	B. J. Sanger-Davies
	G-BUVW	Cameron N-90 balloon	L. J. Whitelock
	G-BUVX	CFM Streak Shadow	J. B. Campbell
	G-BUWE	SE-5A (replica) (C9533:M)	A. J. L. Eves
	G-BUWH	Parsons 2-seat gyroplane	R. V. Brunskill
	G-BUWI	Lindstrand LBL-77A balloon	G. A. Chadwick
	G-BUWR	CFM Streak Shadow	T. Harvey
	G-BUWT	Rand-Robinson KR-2	G. Bailey-Woods
	G-BUWU	Cameron V-77 balloon	D. L. Peltan & O. N. James
	G-BUXC	CFM Streak Shadow SA-M	L. F. Tanner
	G-BUXI	Steen Skybolt	Leipzig Aviators Group
	G-BUXL	Taylor JT.1 Monoplane	P. J. Hebdon
	G-BUXW	Thunder Ax8-90 S2 balloon	N. T. Parry
	G-BUXX	PA-17 Vagabond	M. Flint
	G-BUXY	PA-25-235 Pawnee	The Vale of the White Horse Gliding Centre Ltd
	G-BUYB	Aero Designs Pulsar	A. R. Thorpe
	G-BUYE	Aeronca 7AC Champion	A. A. Gillon
	G-BUYF	Falcon XP	M. J. Hadland
	G-BUYK	Denney Kitfox Mk 4	M. S. Shelton
	G-BUYL	RAF 2000GT gyroplane	M. H. J. Goldring
	G-BUYS	Robin DR.400/180	G-BUYS Flying Group
	G-BUYU	Bowers Fly-Baby 1A (1803/18)	R. C. Piper
	G-BUYY	PA-28-180 Cherokee B	G-BUYY Group
	G-BUZA	Denney Kitfox Mk 3	S. D. Grove
	G-BUZB	Aero Designs Pulsar XP	S. M. Macintyre
	G-BUZG	Zenair CH.601HD	L. J. Cole
	G-BUZK	Cameron V-77 balloon	Zebedee Balloon Service Ltd
	G-BUZL	VPM M.16 Tandem Trainer	P. M. Harrison & M. P. Wimsey
	G-BUZM	Light Aero Avid Flyer Mk 3	C. A. Husain
	G-BUZO	Pietenpol Air Camper	D. A. Jones
	G-BUZZ	Agusta-Bell 206B JetRanger 2	Skypark (UK) Ltd
	G-BVAB	Zenair CH.601HDS	B. N. Rides
	G-BVAC	Zenair CH.601HD	A. J. W. Sturgess
	G-BVAF	Piper J-3C-65 Cub	G-BVAF Group
	G-BVAH	Denney Kitfox Mk.3	R. Jaggi
	G-BVAM	Evans VP-1 Series 2	S. F. Dreyer
	G-BVAW	Staaken Z-1 Flitzer	L. R. Williams
	G-BVBF	PA-28-151 Cherokee Warrior	R. K. Spence
	G-BVBJ	Colt Flying Coffee Jar SS balloon	The British Balloon Museum & Library Ltd
	G-BVBK	Colt Flying Coffee Jar SS balloon	M. T. Joyce
	G-BVBU	Cameron V-77 balloon	J. Ricards
	G-BVCA	Cameron N-105 balloon	J. D. Phillips
	G-BVCG	Van's RV-6	A. W. Shellis
	G-BVCL	Rans S.6-116 Coyote II	A. M. Colman
	G-BVCN	Colt 56A balloon	G. A. & I. Chadwick & S. Richards
	G-BVCP	Piper CP.1 Metisse	B. M. Diggins
	G-BVCS	Aeronca 7BCM Champion	C. A. Roberts
	G-BVCT	Denney Kitfox Mk 4	A. F. Reid
	G-BVCY	Cameron H-24 balloon	A. C. K. Rawson & J. J. Rudoni
	G-BVDB	Thunder Ax7-77 balloon	A. Marshall (G-ORDY)
	G-BVDC	Van's RV-3	R. S. Hatwell
	G-BVDF	Cameron Doll 105 SS balloon	M. T. Joyce

Reg	Type	Owner or Operator	Notes
G-BVDG	VPM M-15	R. F. G. Moyle	
G-BVDI	Van's RV-4	J. G. Gorman & H. Tallini	
G-BVDP	Sequoia F.8L Falco	D. G. Hart & D. Marshall	
G-BVDT	CFM Streak Shadow	R. Holt	
G-BVDW	Thunder Ax8-90 balloon	S. C. Vora	
G-BVDY	Cameron 60 Concept balloon	P. Baker/Ireland	
G-BVDZ	Taylorcraft BC-12D	A. Sharp	
G-BVEH	Jodel D.112	M. L. Copland	
G-BVEN	Cameron 80 Concept balloon	B. J. & M. A. Alford	
G-BVEP	Luscombe 8A Master	R. Pink	
G-BVER	DHC.2 Beaver 1 (XV268) ★	Seaflite Ltd (G-BTDM)/Cumbernauld	
G-BVEV	PA-34-200 Seneca	M. Ali	
G-BVEY	Denney Kitfox Mk 4-1200	J. H. H. Turner	
G-BVEZ	P.84 Jet Provost T.3A (XM479)	Newcastle Jet Provost Group	
G-BVFB	Cameron N-31 balloon	M. A. Rate	
G-BVFF	Cameron V-77 balloon	J. Ricards	
G-BVFM	Rans S.6-116 Coyote II	J. Fleming	
G-BVFO	Light Aero Avid Speedwing	C. A. Husain	
G-BVFR	CFM Streak Shadow	S. N. Waite	
G-BVFS	Slingsby T.31M	S. R. Williams	
G-BVFZ	Maule M5-180C Lunar Rocket	S. & S. V. Butzkies-Schiemann	
G-BVGA	Bell 206B JetRanger 3	R. P. Coplestone	
G-BVGE	WS-55 Whirlwind HAR.10 (XJ729)	A. D. Whitehouse	
G-BVGH	Hawker Hunter T.7 (XL573) ★	South Wales Aviation Museum/St. Athan	
G-BVGI	Pereira Osprey II	C. P. Dawes	
G-BVGK	Lindstrand LBL Newspaper SS balloon	H. Holmqvist	
G-BVGO	Denney Kitfox Mk 4-1200	P. Madden	
G-BVGP	Bücker Bü 133 Jungmeister (U-95)	T. A. Bechtolsheimer	
G-BVGT	Crofton Auster J/1	V. R. Leggott	
G-BVGW	Luscombe 8A Silvaire	S. M. Owen	
G-BVGY	Luscombe 8E Silvaire	M. R. Skeer	
G-BVGZ	Fokker Dr.1 (replica) (152/17)	R. A. Fleming	
G-BVHC	Grob G.115D-2 Heron	British Aviation Academy Ltd	
G-BVHD	Grob G.115D-2 Heron	J. A. Woodcock	
G-BVHE	Grob G.115D-2 Heron	G-BVHE Grob Group	
G-BVHI	Rans S.10 Sakota	S. H. Leahy	
G-BVHK	Cameron V-77 balloon	C. M. Duggan & M. J. Axtell	
G-BVHL	Nicollier HN.700 Menestrel II	G. W. Lynch	
G-BVHR	Cameron V-90 balloon	G. P. Walton	
G-BVHS	Murphy Rebel	S. T. Raby	
G-BVHT	Avid Speed Wing Mk.4	K. Redfearn	
G-BVHV	Cameron N-105 balloon	K. J. Parsons	
G-BVIE	PA-18-95 Super Cub (modified)	J. C. Best (G-CLIK/G-BLMB)	
G-BVIK	Maule MXT-7-180 Star Rocket	N. C. Morland	
G-BVIS	Brügger MB.2 Colibri	P. A. Dickens	
G-BVIV	Light Aero Avid Speedwing	S. Styles	
G-BVIW	PA-18-150 Super Cub	I. H. Logan	
G-BVIZ	Europa	M. Dovey	
G-BVJK	Glaser-Dirks DG.800A	S. R. Watson	
G-BVJT	Cessna F.406	RVL Aviation Ltd	
G-BVJX	Marquart MA.5 Charger	Lancashire Barnstormers Group	
G-BVKK	Slingsby T.61F Venture T.2	Buckminster Gliding Club Ltd	
G-BVKM	Rutan Vari-Eze	J. P. G. Lindquist/Switzerland	
G-BVKU	Slingsby T.61F Venture T.2	G-BVKU Syndicate	
G-BVKV	Cameron N-90 balloon	I. R. Jones	
G-BVLA	Lancair 320	K. W. Scrivens	
G-BVLD	Campbell Cricket (replica)	S. J. Smith	
G-BVLF	CFM Starstreak Shadow SS-D	J. C. Pratelli	
G-BVLN	Aero Designs Pulsar XP	D. A. Campbell	
G-BVLR	Van's RV-4	RV4 Group	
G-BVLT	Bellanca 7GCBC Citabria	Slade Associates	
G-BVLU	D.31 Turbulent	Air Caernarfon Ltd	
G-BVLV	Europa	P. R. Dalton	
G-BVND	BN-2B-20 Islander	Caledonian Aircraft Spares Ltd	
G-BVNG	DH.60G-III Moth Major	P. & G. Groves	
G-BVNI	Taylor JT-2 Titch	P. M. Jones	
G-BVNU	FLS Aerospace Sprint Club	D. R. & M. R. Davis	
G-BVNY	Rans S.7 Courier	S. Hazleden	
G-BVOH	Campbell Cricket (replica)	A. M. Eckersley	
G-BVOI	Rans S.6-116 Coyote II	S. J. Taft	
G-BVOP	Cameron N-90 balloon	M. A. Stelling	

Notes	Reg	Type	Owner or Operator
	G-BVOR	CFM Streak Shadow	J. M. Chandler
	G-BVOS	Europa	R. M. Peach
	G-BVOY	Rotorway Executive 90	C. O'Neill
	G-BVOZ	Colt 56A balloon	G. G. Scaife
	G-BVPA	Thunder Ax8-105 S2 balloon	B. J. B. Smith
	G-BVPD	CASA 1-131E Jungmann Series 2000	M. L. Blaze
	G-BVPM	Evans VP-2 Coupé ★	South Wales Aviation Museum/St. Athan
	G-BVPS	Jodel D.112	I. P. Reader
	G-BVPV	Lindstrand LBL-77B balloon	I. W. Robertshaw
	G-BVPX	Bensen B.8 (modified) Tyro Gyro	A. W. Harvey
	G-BVPY	CFM Streak Shadow	P. D. Curtis
	G-BVRA	Europa	J. C. Gazzard
	G-BVRV	Van's RV-4	A. Troughton
	G-BVRZ	PA-18-95 Super Cub	R. W. Davison
	G-BVSB	TEAM mini-MAX	D. G. Palmer
	G-BVSF	Aero Designs Pulsar	R. J. Freestone
	G-BVSK	BN-2T Turbine Islander	Draken
	G-BVSM	RAF2000	M. P. Wiseman
	G-BVSP	P.84 Jet Provost T.3A	Weald Aviation Services Ltd
	G-BVSS	Jodel D.150	N. Steele
	G-BVST	Jodel D.150	R. J. Brown
	G-BVSX	TEAM mini-MAX 91	R. S. Acreman
	G-BVSZ	Pitts S-1E (S) Special	H. J. Morton
	G-BVTC	P.84 Jet Provost T.5A (XW333)	Global Aviation Ltd
	G-BVTL	Colt 31A balloon	A. Lindsay
	G-BVTM	Cessna F.152 II	RAF Halton Aeroplane Club (G-WACS)
	G-BVTW	Aero Designs Pulsar	C. N. Hannan
	G-BVTX	DHC.1 Chipmunk 22A (WP809)	TX Flying Group
	G-BVUA	Cameron O-105 balloon	R. P. Waite
	G-BVUH	Thunder AX7-65B balloon	H. J. M. Lacoste
	G-BVUK	Cameron V-77 balloon	H. G. Griffiths & W. A. Steel
	G-BVUM	Rans S.6-116 Coyote II	M. A. Abbott
	G-BVUN	Van's RV-4	M. S. Pettit
	G-BVUT	Evans VP-1 Srs. 2	M. J. Barnett
	G-BVUV	Europa	R. J. Mills
	G-BVUZ	Cessna 120	A. Fairfield
	G-BVVB	Carlson Sparrow II	D. Patterson
	G-BVVE	Jodel D.112	M. Balls
	G-BVVG	Nanchang CJ-6A (68)	P. C. Woolley
	G-BVVH	Europa	M. Giudici
	G-BVVI	Hawker Audax I (K5600)	Aero Vintage Ltd
	G-BVVK	DHC.6 Twin Otter 310	Loganair Ltd
	G-BVVL	EAA Acro Sport II	G-BVVL Syndicate
	G-BVVM	Zenair CH.601HD	T. H. Jones
	G-BVVN	Brügger MB.2 Colibri	M. A. Wood
	G-BVVO	Yakovlev Yak-50	R. Greatrex
	G-BVVP	Europa	A. Fletcher
	G-BVVS	Van's RV-4	E. G. & N. S. C. English
	G-BVVU	Lindstrand LBL Four SS balloon	Magical Adventures Ltd/USA
	G-BVVW	Yakovlev Yak-52	M. Blackman
	G-BVVZ	Corby CJ-1 Starlet	P. V. Flack
	G-BVWB	Thunder Ax8-90 S2 balloon	G. B. Davies
	G-BVWI	Cameron light bulb SS balloon	M. T. Joyce & C. L. Hayden
	G-BVWL	Air & Space 18A Gyroplane ★	The Helicopter Museum/Weston-super-Mare
	G-BVWM	Europa	A. Head
	G-BVWZ	PA-32-301 Saratoga	Ambar Kelly Ltd
	G-BVXC	EE Canberra B.6 (WT333) ★	Classic Aviation Projects Ltd/Bruntingthorpe
	G-BVXD	Cameron O-84 balloon	C. J. Dunkley
	G-BVXK	Yakovlev Yak-52 (26 grey)	A. R. Dent
	G-BVXY	BN-2B-20 Islander	Islander Aircraft Ltd
	G-BVYG	CEA DR.300/180	J. R. Edyvean
	G-BVYM	CEA DR.300/180	London Gliding Club (Pty) Ltd
	G-BVYP	PA-25-235 Pawnee	Bidford Gliding & Flying Club Ltd
	G-BVYX	Light Aero Avid Speedwing Mk 4	A. J. L. Eves
	G-BVYY	Pietenpol Air Camper	M. B. North
	G-BVZJ	Rand-Robinson KR-2	G. M. Rundle
	G-BVZN	Cameron C-80 balloon	S. J. Clarke
	G-BVZO	Rans S.6-116 Coyote II	P. J. Brion
	G-BVZR	Zenair CH.601HD	R. A. Perkins
	G-BVZT	Lindstrand LBL-90A balloon	J. Edwards
	G-BVZY	Mooney M.20R Ovation	DK Mecatronic-Engineering Innovation Ltd

Reg	Type	Owner or Operator	Notes
G-BVZZ	DHC.1 Chipmunk 22 (WP795)	Portsmouth Naval Gliding Centre	
G-BWAB	Jodel D.14	J. D. A. Burgess	
G-BWAC	Waco YKS-7	D. N. Peters	
G-BWAD	RAF 2000GT gyroplane	B. J. Payne	
G-BWAF	Hawker Hunter F.6A (XG160:U) ★	Bournemouth Aviation Museum/Bournemouth	
G-BWAH	Montgomerie-Bensen B.8MR	S. H. Broszek	
G-BWAI	CFM Streak Shadow	G. A. McCarthy	
G-BWAN	Cameron N-77 balloon	I. Chadwick	
G-BWAP	FRED Srs 3	G. A. Shepherd	
G-BWAR	Denney Kitfox Mk 3	J. Moss	
G-BWAT	Pietenpol Air Camper	P. W. Aitchison	
G-BWAW	Lindstrand LBL-77A balloon	D. Bareford	
G-BWBI	Taylorcraft F-22A	Kernow Flying Group Ltd	
G-BWBO	Lindstrand LBL-77A balloon	T. J. Orchard	
G-BWBZ	ARV-1 Super 2	M. P. Holdstock	
G-BWCA	CFM Streak Shadow	D. A. Crosbie	
G-BWCK	Everett Srs 2 gyroplane	N. M. Gent	
G-BWCS	BAC 145 Jet Provost T.5	Peace Guest House Ltd	
G-BWCT	Tipsy T.66 Nipper 1	K. G. G. Howe	
G-BWCY	Murphy Rebel	A. J. Glading	
G-BWDH	Cameron N-105 balloon	M. W. Shepherd	
G-BWDP	Europa	S. Attubato	
G-BWDS	P.84 Jet Provost T.3A (XM424)	M. L. B. Hooton & M. Winterburn	
G-BWDV	Schweizer 269C	Cirrus UK Training Ltd & JBS-Helicopters Ltd	
G-BWDX	Europa	C. J. Sweenie	
G-BWEB	P.84 Jet Provost T.5A (XW422:3)	Flight Test Support	
G-BWEE	Cameron V-42 balloon	N. C. A. Edmunds	
G-BWEF	SNCAN Stampe SV.4C	Acebell G-BWEF Syndicate (G-BOVL)	
G-BWEG	Europa	J. W. Kelly	
G-BWEM	VS.358 Seafire L.IIIC (RX168)	Fly to Inspire Ltd	
G-BWEN	Macair Merlin GT	D. A. Hill	
G-BWEW	Cameron N-105 balloon	Unipart Balloon Club	
G-BWEY	Bensen B.8	F. G. Shepherd	
G-BWEZ	Piper J-3C-65 Cub (436021)	J. G. McTaggart	
G-BWFG	Robin HR.200/120B	T. J. Lowe	
G-BWFH	Europa	D. J. Shipley	
G-BWFJ	Evans VP-1	G. Robson	
G-BWFM	Yakovlev Yak-50	Fox Mike Group	
G-BWFN	Hapi Cygnet SF-2A	I. P. Manley	
G-BWFO	Colomban MC.15 Cri-Cri	K. D. & C. S. Rhodes	
G-BWFX	Europa	T. P. R. Pickford	
G-BWFZ	Murphy Rebel	M. R. Hudson (G-SAVS)	
G-BWGF	P.84 Jet Provost T.5A (XW325)	G-JPVA Ltd	
G-BWGJ	Chilton DW.1A	T. J. Harrison	
G-BWGO	Slingsby T.67M Firefly 200	R. Gray	
G-BWHA	Hawker Hurricane IIB	T. J. A. Daley	
G-BWHD	Lindstrand LBL-31A balloon	M. R. Noyce & R. P. E. Phillips	
G-BWHI	DHC.1 Chipmunk 22A (WK624)	E. H. N. M. Clare	
G-BWHK	Rans S.6-116 Coyote II	D. C. Stokes	
G-BWHP	CASA 1.131E Jungmann (S4+A07)	J. F. Hopkins	
G-BWHS	RAF 2000 gyroplane	V. G. Freke	
G-BWHU	Westland Scout AH.1 (XR506)	Davillion Design & Build Ltd	
G-BWIP	Cameron N-90 balloon	O. J. Evans	
G-BWIV	Europa	T. G. Ledbury	
G-BWIX	Sky 120-24 balloon	J. M. Percival	
G-BWIZ	QAC Quickie Tri-Q 200	M. C. Davies	
G-BWJH	Europa	D. Cripps	
G-BWJM	Bristol M.1C (replica) (C4918)	The Shuttleworth Collection	
G-BWKT	Stephens Akro Laser	P. J. Kaplan	
G-BWKW	Thunder Ax8-90 balloon	A. Dunnington	
G-BWKZ	Lindstrand LBL-77A balloon	J. H. Dobson	
G-BWLD	Cameron O-120 balloon	D. Pedri/Italy	
G-BWLJ	Taylorcraft DCO-65 (42-35870/129)	B. J. Robe	
G-BWLL	Murphy Rebel	A. F. Ratcliffe	
G-BWLM	Sky 65-24 balloon	W. J. Brogan	
G-BWLW	Avid Speed Wing Mk.4	F. E. Tofield (G-XXRG)	
G-BWLY	Rotorway Executive 90	P. W. & I. P. Bewley	
G-BWMB	Jodel D.119	C. Hughes	
G-BWMC	Cessna 182P	Aeroplane Views	
G-BWMH	Lindstrand LBL-77B balloon	W. C. Wood	

Notes	Reg	Type	Owner or Operator
	G-BWMI	PA-28RT-201T Turbo Cherokee Arrow IV	R. W. Pascoe
	G-BWMJ	Nieuport 17/2B (replica) (N1977:8)	J. P. Gilbert
	G-BWMK	DH.82A Tiger Moth (T8191)	K. F. Crumplin
	G-BWMN	Rans S.7 Courier	A. R. Newman
	G-BWMO	Oldfield Baby Lakes	G. Frederick (G-CIII)
	G-BWMU	Cameron 105 Monster Truck SS balloon	Magical Adventures Ltd/Canada
	G-BWMX	DHC.1 Chipmunk 22 (WG407:67)	407th Flying Group
	G-BWMY	Cameron Bradford & Bingley SS balloon	Magical Adventures Ltd/USA
	G-BWNB	Cessna 152 II	South Warwickshire School of Flying Ltd
	G-BWNC	Cessna 152 II	South Warwickshire School of Flying Ltd
	G-BWND	Cessna 152 II	South Warwickshire School of Flying Ltd
	G-BWNI	PA-24-180 Comanche	B. V. & J. B. Haslam
	G-BWNJ	Hughes 269C	Scott Aviation (Berkshire) Ltd
	G-BWNK	D,H,C,1 Chipmunk 22 (WD390)	WD390 Group
	G-BWNM	PA-28R-180 Cherokee Arrow	Helix AV Ltd
	G-BWNO	Cameron O-90 balloon	T. Knight
	G-BWNU	PA-38-112 Tomahawk	Kemble Aero Club Ltd
	G-BWNY	Aeromot AMT-200 Super Ximango	C. M. Davey, T. E. Moyes, J. C. Ferguson & L. J. Kearney
	G-BWOH	PA-28-161 Cadet	Redhill Air Services Ltd
	G-BWOK	Lindstrand LBL-105G balloon	C. J. Sanger-Davies
	G-BWOR	PA-18-135 Super Cub	S. S. & R. D. Houston
	G-BWOT	P.84 Jet Provost T.3A (XN459)	G-BKOU/2 Ltd
	G-BWOV	Enstrom F-28A	Shark Helicopters Ltd
	G-BWPH	PA-28-181 Cherokee Archer II	Papa Hotel Group
	G-BWPJ	Steen Skybolt	A. J. Hurran
	G-BWPO	BN-2T-4S Islander	Britten-Norman Aerospace Ltd
	G-BWPP	Sky 105-24 balloon	Sarnia Balloon Group
	G-BWPR	BN-2T-4S Islander	Britten-Norman Aerospace Ltd
	G-BWPS	CFM Streak Shadow SA	P. J. Mogg
	G-BWPV	BN-2T-4S Islander	Britten-Norman Aerospace Ltd
	G-BWPX	BN-2T-4S Islander	Britten-Norman Aerospace Ltd
	G-BWRA	Sopwith LC-1T Triplane (replica) (N500)	P. Anderson (G-PENY)
	G-BWRO	Europa	R. A. Darley
	G-BWRR	Cessna 182Q	A. & R. Reid
	G-BWRS	SNCAN Stampe SV.4C	G. P. J. M. Valvekens/Belgium
	G-BWSB	Lindstrand LBL-105A balloon	R. Calvert-Fisher
	G-BWSD	Campbell Cricket	R. F. G. Moyle
	G-BWSG	P.84 Jet Provost T.5 (XW324/K)	Viper Classic Aircraft Ltd
	G-BWSH	P.84 Jet Provost T.3A	Global Aviation Ltd
	G-BWSI	Squarecraft Cavalier SA.102-5	M. W. Place
	G-BWSJ	Denney Kitfox Mk 3	A. J. Calvert
	G-BWSL	Sky 77-24 balloon	E. P. Braund-Smith
	G-BWSN	Denney Kitfox Mk 3	R. J. Mitchell
	G-BWSU	Cameron N-105 balloon	A. M. Marten
	G-BWSV	Yakovlev Yak-52 (43)	M. W. Fitch
	G-BWTE	Cameron O-140 balloon	T. G. Church
	G-BWTG	DHC.1 Chipmunk 22 (WB671:910)	R. G. T. de Man/Netherlands
	G-BWTJ	Cameron V-77 balloon	C. M. Montgomery
	G-BWTO	DHC.1 Chipmunk 22 (WP984)	Skycraft Services Ltd
	G-BWTW	Mooney M.20C	Foto Plus Ltd
	G-BWUH	PA-28-181 Cherokee Archer III	Phoenix Aviation
	G-BWUJ	Rotorway Executive 162F	Southern Helicopters Ltd
	G-BWUN	DHC.1 Chipmunk 22 (WD310)	E. H. W. Moore
	G-BWUP	Europa	E. A Yates
	G-BWUS	Sky 65-24 balloon	N. A. P. Bates
	G-BWUT	DHC.1 Chipmunk 22 (WZ879)	A. J. Herbert
	G-BWUU	Cameron N-90 balloon	M. J. Axtell
	G-BWVF	Pietenpol Air Camper	N. Clark
	G-BWVR	Yakovlev Yak-52 (52 yellow)	I. Parkinson
	G-BWVS	Europa	D. R. Bishop
	G-BWVT	DHA.82A Tiger Moth	N. L. MacKaness
	G-BWVU	Cameron O-90 balloon	J. J. Holmes
	G-BWVY	DHC.1 Chipmunk 22 (WP896)	N. Gardner
	G-BWWA	Ultravia Pelican Club GS	J. S. Aplin
	G-BWWB	Europa	G. C. Rogers
	G-BWWK	Hawker Nimrod I (S1581)	Patina Ltd
	G-BWWL	Colt Flying Egg SS balloon	Magical Adventures Ltd/USA
	G-BWWN	Isaacs Fury II (K8303:D)	J. S. Marten-Hale
	G-BWWU	PA-22-150 Caribbean	M. van Goor
	G-BWWX	Yakovlev Yak-50	D. P. McCoy

Reg	Type	Owner or Operator	Notes
G-BWWY	Lindstrand LBL-105A balloon	T. S. Davis	
G-BWXA	Slingsby T.67M 260 Firefly	Power Aerobatics Ltd	
G-BWXB	Slingsby T.67M 260 Firefly	Power Aerobatics Ltd	
G-BWXJ	Slingsby T.67M 260 Firefly	Bulldog Aviation Ltd	
G-BWXS	Slingsby T.67M 260 Firefly	Power Aerobatics Ltd	
G-BWXT	Slingsby T.67M 260 Firefly	Cranfield University	
G-BWYB	PA-28-160 Cherokee	A. J. Peters	
G-BWYD	Europa	D. L. Morris	
G-BWYO	Sequoia F.8L Falco	S. G. Roux	
G-BWZA	Europa	M. Bond	
G-BWZY	Hughes 269A	P. A. Harvie (G-FSDT)	
G-BXAB	PA-28-161 Cherokee Warrior II	LAC Flying School (G-BTGK)	
G-BXAC	RAF 2000 GTX-SE gyroplane	R. Jaggi	
G-BXAF	Pitts S-1D Special	N. J. Watson	
G-BXAK	Yakovlev Yak-52	A. M. Holman-West	
G-BXAN	Scheibe SF-25C Falke	C. Falke Syndicate	
G-BXAO	Avtech Jabiru SK	P. J. Thompson	
G-BXAX	Cameron N-77 balloon ★	Balloon Preservation Group	
G-BXAY	Bell 206B JetRanger 3	Rumwood Green Farm Ltd	
G-BXBB	PA-20-150 Pacer	M. E. R. Coghlan	
G-BXBK	Avions Mudry CAP-10B	S. Skipworth	
G-BXBZ	PZL-104 Wilga 80	J. H. Sandham Aviation	
G-BXCA	Hapi Cygnet SF-2A	W. N. I. Gordon	
G-BXCC	PA-28-201T Turbo Dakota	Greer Aviation Ltd	
G-BXCG	Jodel 250 replica	R. Marsden & G. C. Clark	
G-BXCO	Colt 120A balloon	J. R. Lawson	
G-BXCU	Rans S.6-116 Coyote II	T. C. Garner	
G-BXCV	DHC.1 Chipmunk 22 (WP929)	Fly to Inspire Ltd	
G-BXCW	Denney Kitfox Mk 3	D. R. Piercy	
G-BXDB	Cessna U.206F	D. A. Howard (G-BMNZ)	
G-BXDE	RAF 2000GTX-SE gyroplane	V. G. Freke	
G-BXDG	DHC.1 Chipmunk 22 (WK630)	Felthorpe Flying Group	
G-BXDH	DHC.1 Chipmunk 22 (WD331)	The Farnborough Chipmunk Company Ltd	
G-BXDI	DHC.1 Chipmunk 22 (WD373)	S. J. L. Jones	
G-BXDN	DHC.1 Chipmunk 22 (WK609)	W. D. Lowe, G. James & L. A. Edwards	
G-BXDO	Rutan Cozy	Cozy Group	
G-BXDR	Lindstrand LBL-77A balloon	R. J. & W. Ng-Zeederberg	
G-BXDS	Bell 206B JetRanger III	Aerospeed Limited (G-TAMF/G-OVBJ)	
G-BXDU	Aero Designs Pulsar	C. Dray	
G-BXDY	Europa	S. Attubato & D. G. Watts	
G-BXDZ	Lindstrand LBL-105A balloon	D. J. & A. D. Sutcliffe	
G-BXEA	RAF 2000 GTX-SE	A. G. W. Davis	
G-BXEC	DHC.1 Chipmunk 22 (WK633)	A. J. Robinson & M. J. Miller	
G-BXEF	Europa	C. Busuttil-Reynard	
G-BXEJ	VPM M-16 Tandem Trainer	J. D. Winder	
G-BXEX	PA-28-181 Cherokee Archer II	Nottingham Archer Aviators	
G-BXEZ	Cessna 182P	Forhawk Ltd	
G-BXFB	Pitts S-1 Special	J. F. Dowe	
G-BXFC	Jodel D.18	M. Godbold	
G-BXFE	Avions Mudry CAP 10B	Avion Aerobatic	
G-BXFG	Europa	A. Rawicz-Szczerbo	
G-BXFK	CFM Streak Shadow	C. R. Buckle	
G-BXFN	Colt 77A balloon	M. C. Mawson	
G-BXGA	AS.350B2 Ecureuil	PDG Helicopters and PDG Aviation Services	
G-BXGG	Europa	H. D. Gurney	
G-BXGL	DHC.1 Chipmunk 22	S. R. Tilling	
G-BXGM	DHC.1 Chipmunk 22 (WP928:D)	Skyblue Aero Services Ltd	
G-BXGO	DHC.1 Chipmunk 22 (WB654:U)	B. C. Griffiths & A. J. Gurr	
G-BXGP	DHC.1 Chipmunk 22 (WZ882)	C. A. Hawkins	
G-BXGS	RAF 2000 gyroplane	D. W. Howell	
G-BXGT	I.I.I. Sky Arrow 650T	S. S. & T. C. Caldecourt	
G-BXGV	Cessna 172R	G-BXGV Skyhawk Group	
G-BXGX	DHC.1 Chipmunk 22 (WK586:V)	N. Westwood & I. J. Flitcroft	
G-BXGY	Cameron V-65 balloon	Dante Balloon Group	
G-BXGZ	Stemme S.10V	C. T. & S. D. F. Nebel	
G-BXHA	DHC.1 Chipmunk 22 (WP925:C)	Shipping & Airlines Ltd (G-HVII)	
G-BXHF	DHC.1 Chipmunk 22 (WP930:J)	Hotfox Syndicate	
G-BXHJ	Hapi Cygnet SF-2A	V. M. Smith	
G-BXHL	Sky 77-24 balloon ★	Bristol Balloon Collectors	
G-BXHO	Lindstrand Telewest Sphere SS balloon	Magical Adventures Ltd	

Notes	Reg	Type	Owner or Operator
	G-BXHR	Stemme S.10V	D. J. Pilkington
	G-BXHT	Bushby-Long Midget Mustang	S. A. Smith
	G-BXHU	Campbell Cricket Mk 6	K. Winder
	G-BXHY	Europa	A. L. Thorne
	G-BXIA	DHC.1 Chipmunk 22 (WB615)	WB615 Group
	G-BXIE	Colt 77B balloon	I. R. Warrington
	G-BXIF	PA-28-161 Cherokee Warrior II	Piper Flight Ltd
	G-BXIG	Zenair CH.701 STOL	C. Buttery
	G-BXIH	Sky 200-24 balloon	Kent Ballooning
	G-BXII	Europa	D. A. McFadyean
	G-BXIJ	Europa	P. N. Birch
	G-BXIM	DHC.1 Chipmunk 22 (WK512)	A. B. Ashcroft & P. R. Joshua
	G-BXIT	Zebedee V-31 balloon	Zebedee Balloon Service Ltd
	G-BXIW	Sky 105-24 balloon	A. G. A. Barclay-Faulkner
	G-BXIX	VPM M-16 Tandem Trainer	P. P. Willmott
	G-BXIY	Blake Bluetit (BAPC37) ★	M. J. Aubrey
	G-BXJB	Yakovlev Yak-52	N. C. Lewton
	G-BXJD	PA-28-180C Cherokee	S. Atherton
	G-BXJH	Cameron N-42 balloon	D. M. Hoddinott
	G-BXJI	Tri Kis	D. J. Shipley
	G-BXJO	Cameron O-90 balloon	Dragon Balloon Co Ltd
	G-BXJT	Sky 90-24 balloon	J. G. O'Connell
	G-BXJY	Van's RV-6	J. P. Kynaston
	G-BXJZ	Cameron C-60 balloon	N. J. & S. J. Bettin
	G-BXKF	Hawker Hunter T.7(XL577/V)	R. F. Harvey
	G-BXKL	Bell 206B JetRanger 3	B. H. Austen
	G-BXKU	Colt AS-120 Mk II airship	D. C. Chipping/Portugal
	G-BXKW	Slingsby T.67M Firefly 200 (HKG-13)	J-F Jansen
	G-BXKX	Auster V	A. Hoskins
	G-BXLF	Lindstrand LBL-90A balloon	O. W. T. Surridge
	G-BXLG	Cameron C-80 balloon	S. M. Anthony
	G-BXLK	Europa	A. Daujotis
	G-BXLN	Fournier RF-4D	P. W. Cooper
	G-BXLO	P.84 Jet Provost T.4 (XR673/L)	Flying Adventures Ltd
	G-BXLS	PZL-110 Koliber 160A	P. R. Powell
	G-BXLT	SOCATA TB200 Tobago XL	C., G. & J. Fisher & D. Fitton
	G-BXLW	Enstrom F.28F	N. R. H. Briggs
	G-BXLY	PA-28-151 Cherokee Warrior	Aviation South West Ltd (G-WATZ)
	G-BXMX	Currie Wot	D. P. Murphy
	G-BXMY	Hughes 269C	K. & M. Pinfold
	G-BXNC	Europa	J. K. Cantwell
	G-BXND	Cameron Thomas-110 balloon	L. J. Whitelock
	G-BXNN	DHC.1 Chipmunk 22 (WP983:B)	E. N. Skinner
	G-BXOI	Cessna 172R	Aeroscene Aviation LLP
	G-BXOJ	PA-28-161 Cherokee Warrior III	CG Aviation Ltd
	G-BXOX	AA-5A Cheetah	R. L. Carter & P. J. Large
	G-BXOY	QAC Quickie Q.235	C. C. Clapham
	G-BXOZ	PA-28-181 Cherokee Archer II	Spritetone Ltd
	G-BXPC	Diamond Katana DA20-A1	D. J. & S. N. Taplin
	G-BXPD	Diamond Katana DA20-A1	D. J. & S. N. Taplin
	G-BXPI	Van's RV-4	B. M. Diggins
	G-BXPT	Ultramagic H-77 balloon	P. Spellward
	G-BXRA	Avions Mudry CAP-10B	Cole Aviation Ltd
	G-BXRB	Avions Mudry CAP-10B	I. Watts
	G-BXRF	CP.1310-C3 Super Emeraude	P. J. B. Lewis
	G-BXRT	Robin DR.400-180	Bon Bois Ltd
	G-BXRV	Van's RV-4	Cleeve Flying Grouip
	G-BXRZ	Rans S.6-116 Coyote II	R. Jaggi
	G-BXSD	Cessna 172R	Warwickshire Leasing Ltd
	G-BXSE	Cessna 172R	M. Khoshkhou
	G-BXSG	Robinson R22 Beta II	Swift Helicopter Services Ltd
	G-BXSH	Glaser-Dirks DG.800B	D. Crimmins
	G-BXSI	Avtech Jabiru SK	P. F. Gandy
	G-BXSP	Grob G.109B	Deeside Grob Group
	G-BXST	PA-25-235 Pawnee	Staffordshire Gliding Club Ltd
	G-BXTF	Cameron N-105 balloon	C. J. Dunkley
	G-BXTG	Cameron N-42 balloon	P. M. Watkins & S. M. M. Carden
	G-BXTI	Pitts S-1S Special	A. Schmer
	G-BXTO	Hindustan HAL-6 Pushpak	P. Q. Benn
	G-BXTS	Diamond DA20-A1 Katana	Eagle Flight Training Ltd
	G-BXTW	PA-28-181 Cherokee Archer III	Davison Plant Hire

Reg	Type	Owner or Operator	Notes
G-BXUA	Campbell Cricket Mk.5	A. W. Harvey	
G-BXUC	Robinson R22 Beta	Swift Helicopter Services Ltd	
G-BXUF	Agusta-Bell 206B JetRanger 3	SJ Contracting Services Ltd	
G-BXUG	Lindstrand Baby Bel SS balloon	G. C. N. van der Pluijm/Netherlands	
G-BXUH	Lindstrand LBL-31A balloon	R. A. Lovell	
G-BXUI	Glaser-Dirks DG.800B	Top TA Syndicate	
G-BXUU	Cameron V-65 balloon	M. & S. Mitchell	
G-BXUW	Cameron Colt 90A balloon	M. Sampson	
G-BXUX	Cherry BX-2	A. R. Boxall & T. J. Searle	
G-BXVG	Sky 77-24 balloon	M. Wolf	
G-BXVO	Van's RV-6A	P. I. Lewis	
G-BXVP	Sky 31-24 balloon	P. A. Bonner	
G-BXVR	Sky 90-24 balloon	P. Hegarty	
G-BXVS	Brügger MB.2 Colibri	G. T. Snoddon	
G-BXVU	PA-28-161 Cherokee Warrior II	T. W. Gilbert	
G-BXVY	Cessna 152	Stapleford Flying Club Ltd	
G-BXVZ	PZL TS-11 Iskra ★	RAF Manston History Museum/Manston	
G-BXWB	Robin HR.100/200B	A. M. Leahy	
G-BXWG	Sky 120-24 balloon	A. R. Rich	
G-BXWH	Denney Kitfox Mk.4-1200	R. W. Pascoe	
G-BXWK	Rans S.6-ESA Coyote II	R. D. Shaw	
G-BXWO	PA-28-181 Cherokee Archer II	A. J. Gomes	
G-BXWP	PA-32-300 Cherokee Six	Fortytwo Marketing Ltd	
G-BXWR	CFM Streak Shadow	J. C. Pratelli (G-MZMI)	
G-BXWT	Van's RV-6	R. C. Owen	
G-BXWU	FLS Aerospace Sprint 160	J. K. Edgley	
G-BXWV	FLS Aerospace Sprint 160	CFS Aeroproducts Ltd	
G-BXWX	Sky 25-16 balloon	C. O'N. Davis	
G-BXXG	Cameron N-105 balloon	R. N. Simpkins	
G-BXXH	Hatz CB-1	R. D. Shingler	
G-BXXI	Grob G.109B	Malcolm Martin Flying Group	
G-BXXJ	Colt Flying Yacht SS balloon	Magical Adventures Ltd/USA	
G-BXXL	Cameron N-105 balloon	C. J. Dunkley	
G-BXXO	Lindstrand LBL-90B balloon	G. P. Walton	
G-BXXP	Sky 77-24 balloon	T. R. Wood	
G-BXXR	Lovegrove BGL Four-Runner ★	Science Museum/Wroughton	
G-BXXT	Beech 76 Duchess	Air Navigation & Trading Co.Ltd	
G-BXXU	Colt 31A balloon	P. Gunning-Stevenson	
G-BXXZ	CFM Starstreak Shadow SA-II	G. E. Arnott	
G-BXYE	CP.301-C1 Emeraude	K. A. Jones	
G-BXYI	Cameron H-34 balloon	D. J. Groombridge	
G-BXYJ	Jodel DR.1050	G-BXYJ Group	
G-BXYM	PA-28-235 Cherokee	I. K. Burnett	
G-BXYO	PA-28RT-201 Cherokee Arrow IV	M. Rowlingson	
G-BXYP	PA-28RT-201 Cherokee Arrow IV	G. W. Eves	
G-BXYT	PA-28RT-201 Cherokee Arrow IV	A. M. S. Sher	
G-BXZA	PA-38-112 Tomahawk	J. J. Griessel	
G-BXZB	Nanchang CJ-6A (CT180)	G-BXZB Group	
G-BXZF	Lindstrand LBL-90A balloon	S. McGuigan	
G-BXZI	Lindstrand LBL-90A balloon	O. G. V. Stallwood	
G-BXZO	Pietenpol Air Camper	S. A. Linklater	
G-BXZU	Micro Aviation Bantam B.22-S	M. E. Whapham & R. W. Hollamby	
G-BXZV	CFM Streak Shadow	J. N. Bailey	
G-BXZY	CFM Streak Shadow Srs DD	G. L. Turner	
G-BYAV	Taylor JT.1 Monoplane	A. F. S. & T. C. Caldecourt	
G-BYAY	Boeing 757-204ER	TUI Airways Ltd	
G-BYAZ	CFM Streak Shadow	A. G. Wright	
G-BYBD	Cessna F.172H	RAF Akrotiri Flying Club (G-OBHX/G-AWMU)	
G-BYBF	Robin R.2160i	D. J. R. Lloyd-Evans	
G-BYBI	Bell 206B JetRanger 3	Adventure 001 Ltd	
G-BYBK	Murphy Rebel	B. Inker	
G-BYBL	Gardan GY-80 Horizon 160D	Bluewing Flying Group	
G-BYBM	Avtech Jabiru SK	D. O'Keefe & K. Davies	
G-BYBP	Cessna A.185F	G. Lloyd & R. F. M. Jones	
G-BYBS	Sky 80-16 balloon	Musson + Retallick	
G-BYBU	Renegade Spirit UK	M. E. Gilman	
G-BYBV	Mainair Rapier	M. W. Robson	
G-BYBY	Thorp T.18C Tiger	P. G. Mair	
G-BYBZ	Jabiru SK	P. J. Whitehouse	
G-BYCA	PA-28-140 Cherokee D	Fourteen Days Company LLC	

Notes	Reg	Type	Owner or Operator
	G-BYCD	Cessna 140	Airventure Ltd
	G-BYCJ	CFM Shadow Srs DD	P. W. Dunn, C. A. S. Powell & A. R. Vincent
	G-BYCL	Raj Hamsa X'Air Jabiru(3)	A. M. Morris
	G-BYCN	Rans S.6-ES Coyote II	T. J. Croskery
	G-BYCS	Jodel DR.1051	G. A. Stops
	G-BYCT	Aero L-29A Delfin	G-BKOU/2 Ltd
	G-BYCW	Mainair Blade 912	P. C. Watson
	G-BYCX	Westland Wasp HAS.1 (92)	Military Vehicle Solutions Ltd
	G-BYCY	Sky Arrow 650T	E. I. Rowlands-Jones
	G-BYCZ	Avtech Jabiru SK	T. Herbert
	G-BYDB	Grob G.115B	A. R. Willis
	G-BYDK	SNCAN Stampe SV.4C	Bianchi Aviation Film Services Ltd
	G-BYDV	Van's RV-6	P. R. Sears
	G-BYDZ	Pegasus Quantum 15-912	J. A. Ryder
	G-BYEA	Cessna 172P	M. Thambiah
	G-BYEC	Glaser-Dirks DG.800B	S. H. C. Harding
	G-BYEE	Mooney M.20K	Like Feather Ltd
	G-BYEH	CEA Jodel DR.250	J. D. Bally
	G-BYEJ	Scheibe SF-28A Tandem Falke	D. Shrimpton
	G-BYEK	Stoddard Hamilton Glastar	J. Soper
	G-BYEL	Van's RV-6	D. Millar
	G-BYEM	Cessna R.182 RG	Bickertons Aerodromes Ltd
	G-BYEO	Zenair CH.601HDS	C. S. Doggett
	G-BYER	Cameron C-80 balloon	J. M. Langley
	G-BYFA	Cessna F.152 II	Redhill Air Services Ltd (G-WACA)
	G-BYFF	Pegasus Quantum 15-912	T. A. Willcox
	G-BYFI	CFM Starstreak Shadow SA	J. A. Cook
	G-BYFK	Cameron Printer 105 SS balloon	Mobberley Balloon Collection
	G-BYFL	Diamond HK.36 TTS	Seahawk Gliding Club
	G-BYFR	PA-32R-301 Saratoga II HP	Pump & Plant Services Ltd
	G-BYFT	Pietenpol Air Camper	G. Everett
	G-BYFY	Avions Mudry CAP-10B	R. N. Crosland
	G-BYGC	Boeing 747-436 ★	preserved
	G-BYHE	Robinson R22 Beta	R. J. Everett
	G-BYHH	PA-28-161 Cherokee Warrior III	Stapleford Flying Club Ltd
	G-BYHI	PA-28-161 Cherokee Warrior II	T. W. & W. S. Gilbert
	G-BYHJ	PA-28R-201 Cherokee Arrow	White Waltham Airfield Ltd
	G-BYHK	PA-28-181 Cherokee Archer III	J. W. Trenell
	G-BYHL	DHC.1 Chipmunk 22 (WG308)	I. D. Higgins
	G-BYHO	Mainair Blade 912	M. J. Crocker
	G-BYHP	CEA DR.253B	G-BYHP Group
	G-BYHR	Pegasus Quantum 15-912	I. D. Chantler
	G-BYHS	Mainair Blade 912	J. Flynn
	G-BYHT	Robin DR.400/180R	Deeside Robin Group
	G-BYHU	Cameron N-105 balloon	R. S. & M. J. C. Waycott & V. A. Colbourne
	G-BYHY	Cameron V-77 balloon	P. Spellward
	G-BYIA	Avtech Jabiru SK	M. D. Doyle
	G-BYID	Rans S.6-ES Coyote II	R. M. Watson
	G-BYIE	Robinson R22 Beta II	JZP Ltd
	G-BYIJ	CASA 1.131E Jungmann 2000	R. N. Crosland
	G-BYIN	RAF 2000 gyroplane	C. J. Watkinson
	G-BYIP	Aerotek Pitts S-2A Special	D. P. Heather-Hayes
	G-BYIS	Pegasus Quantum 15-912	M. E. Sanders
	G-BYIV	Cameron PM-80 balloon	A. Schneider/Germany
	G-BYJA	RAF 2000 GTX-SE	C. R. W. Lyne
	G-BYJD	Avtech Jabiru UL	C. R. Coates
	G-BYJE	TEAM Mini-MAX 91	S. Meester
	G-BYJF	Thorpe T.211	M. J. Newton
	G-BYJH	Grob G.109B	GJH Group
	G-BYJI	Europa	M. Gibson (G-ODTI)
	G-BYJK	Pegasus Quantum 15-912	S. J. Wilson
	G-BYJL	Aero Designs Pulsar	A. Young
	G-BYJO	Rans S.6-ES Coyote II	K. Garnett
	G-BYJP	Aerotek Pitts S-1S Special	Eaglescott Pitts Group
	G-BYJR	Lindstrand LBL-77B balloon	B. M. Reed
	G-BYJS	SOCATA TB20 Trinidad	T. Crampin
	G-BYJT	Zenair CH.601HD	C. C. Beardmore
	G-BYJW	Cameron Sphere 105 balloon	Balleroy Developpement SAS/France
	G-BYKA	Lindstrand LBL-69A balloon	B. Meeson
	G-BYKB	Rockwell Commander 114	D. L. Macdonald
	G-BYKD	Mainair Blade 912	D. C. Boyle

Reg	Type	Owner or Operator	Notes
G-BYKG	Pietenpol Air Camper	K. D. Doyle	
G-BYKL	PA-28-181 Cherokee Archer II	Transport Command Ltd	
G-BYKP	PA-28R-201T Turbo Cherokee Arrow IV	G. A. Ponsford	
G-BYKT	Pegasus Quantum 15-912	Over Farm Microlight Quantum Group	
G-BYKU	BFC Challenger II	J. P. Comerford	
G-BYKX	Cameron N-90 balloon	D. J. Sayer	
G-BYLB	D. H. 82A Tiger Moth	H. E. Snowling	
G-BYLC	Pegasus Quantum 15-912	R. J. Coppin	
G-BYLD	Pietenpol Air Camper	S. Bryan	
G-BYLF	Zenair CH.601HDS Zodiac	S. Plater	
G-BYLI	Nova Vertex 22 hang glider	M. Hay	
G-BYLO	T.66 Nipper Srs 1	M. J. A. Trudgill	
G-BYLP	Rand-Robinson KR-2	C. S. Hales	
G-BYLS	Bede BD-4	P. J. Greenrod	
G-BYLT	Raj Hamsa X'Air 582(1)	S. A. Taylor	
G-BYLW	Lindstrand LBL-77A balloon	Associazione Gran Premio Italiano	
G-BYLZ	Rutan Cozy	W. S. Allen	
G-BYMD	PA-38-112 Tomahawk II	B. R. B. & C. W. B. Thompson	
G-BYMF	Pegasus Quantum 15-912	G. R. Stockdale	
G-BYMI	Pegasus Quantum 15	R. Annison	
G-BYMJ	Cessna 152	PJC (Leasing) Ltd	
G-BYMN	Rans S.6-ESA Coyote II	R. J. P. Herivel	
G-BYMR	Raj Hamsa X'Air R100(3)	W. Drury	
G-BYMW	Boland 52-12 balloon	C. Jones	
G-BYNA	Cessna F.172H	D. M. White (G-AWTH)	
G-BYND	Pegasus Quantum 15	W. J. Upton	
G-BYNK	Robin HR.200/160	R. N. R. Bellamy & C. R. S. Payne	
G-BYNN	Cameron V-90 balloon	Cloud Nine Balloon Group	
G-BYNP	Rans S.6-ES Coyote II	C. J. Lines	
G-BYNS	Avtech Jabiru SK	D. K. Lawry	
G-BYNU	Cameron Thunder Ax7-77 balloon	B. J. Bradley	
G-BYNW	Cameron H-34 balloon	S. R. Skinner	
G-BYNX	Cameron RX-105 balloon	M. T. Joyce & L. J. Whitelock	
G-BYOB	Slingsby T.67M Firefly 260	Stapleford Flying Club Ltd	
G-BYOD	Slingsby T.67C	D. I. Stanbridge	
G-BYOG	Pegasus Quantum 15-912	H. M. Roberts	
G-BYOH	Raj Hamsa X'Air 582 (5)	G. Lafferty	
G-BYOI	Sky 80-16 balloon	S. N. Whitehead	
G-BYOJ	Raj Hamsa X'Air 582 (1)	S. M. Oxbrow	
G-BYOO	CFM Streak Shadow	C. R. Dunford	
G-BYOR	Raj Hamsa X'Air 582(7)	L. E. Evans	
G-BYOS	Mainair Blade 912	C. Rider	
G-BYOT	Rans S.6-ES Coyote II	C. A. Purvis	
G-BYOV	Pegasus Quantum 15-912	M. Howland	
G-BYOW	Mainair Blade	P. Szymanski & P. Cadek	
G-BYOZ	Mainair Rapier	G. P. Hodgson	
G-BYPB	Pegasus Quantum 15-912	D. J. Swinden	
G-BYPF	Thruster T.600N	A. J. Fell	
G-BYPH	Thruster T.600N	D. M. Canham	
G-BYPJ	Pegasus Quantum 15-912	L. D. W. M. Adams	
G-BYPM	Europa XS	North East Mechanical Ltd	
G-BYPN	MS.880B Rallye Club	Wilco Aviation Ltd	
G-BYPR	Zenair CH.601HD Zodiac	N. Surman	
G-BYPU	PA-32R-301 Saratoga SP	GOBOB Flying Group	
G-BYPZ	Rans S.6-116 Super 6	R. A. Blackbourne	
G-BYRC	Westland WS-58 Wessex HC.2 (XT671)	D. Brem-Wilson	
G-BYRG	Rans S.6-ES Coyote II	S. J. Macmillan	
G-BYRJ	Pegasus Quantum 15-912	R. A. Kubon	
G-BYRK	Cameron V-42 balloon	R. Kunert	
G-BYRO	Mainair Blade	T. W. Thiele	
G-BYRR	Mainair Blade 912	S. J. N. Brown	
G-BYRU	Pegasus Quantum 15-912	A. M. Tutcher	
G-BYRV	Raj Hamsa X'Air 582 (1)	A. D. Russell	
G-BYSF	Avtech Jabiru UL	Jabber 430	
G-BYSI	WSK-PZL Koliber 160A	J. & D. F. Evans	
G-BYSJ	DHC.1 Chipmunk 22 (WB569:R)	Specialist Procurement Services Ltd	
G-BYSP	PA-28-181 Cherokee Archer II	North Weald Flight Training Ltd	
G-BYSX	Pegasus Quantum 15-912	A. A. Bolton	
G-BYSY	Raj Hamsa X'Air 582 (1)	A. Cochrane	
G-BYTB	SOCATA TB20 Trinidad	Watchman Aircraft Ltd	
G-BYTC	Pegasus Quantum 15-912	J. C. & J. E. Munro-Hunt	

Notes	Reg	Type	Owner or Operator
	G-BYTI	PA-24-250 Comanche	G. J. Keating
	G-BYTJ	Cameron C-80 balloon	J. D. Smallridge
	G-BYTK	Avtech Jabiru UL	G. R. Phillips
	G-BYTL	Mainair Blade 912	G. Meekin
	G-BYTN	DH.82A Tiger Moth (N6720:VX)	G. A. Rossington
	G-BYTR	Raj Hamsa X'Air 582 (5)	L. A. Dotchin
	G-BYTS	Montgomerie-Bensen B.8MR gyroplane	B. F. Pearson
	G-BYTV	Avtech Jabiru UL-450	F. McDonagh
	G-BYTW	Cameron O-90 balloon	D. R. King
	G-BYTX	MW6-S Fat Boy Flyer	J. K. Ewing
	G-BYTZ	Raj Hamsa X'Air 582 (1)	J. R. Kinder
	G-BYUB	Grob G.115E Tutor	Babcock Aerospace Ltd
	G-BYUC	Grob G.115E Tutor	Babcock Aerospace Ltd
	G-BYUD	Grob G.115E Tutor	Babcock Aerospace Ltd
	G-BYUE	Grob G.115E Tutor	Babcock Aerospace Ltd
	G-BYUF	Grob G.115E Tutor	Babcock Aerospace Ltd
	G-BYUH	Grob G.115E Tutor	Babcock Aerospace Ltd
	G-BYUI	Grob G.115E Tutor	Babcock Aerospace Ltd
	G-BYUJ	Grob G.115E Tutor	Babcock Aerospace Ltd
	G-BYUK	Grob G.115E Tutor	Babcock Aerospace Ltd
	G-BYUL	Grob G.115E Tutor	Babcock Aerospace Ltd
	G-BYUM	Grob G.115E Tutor	Babcock Aerospace Ltd
	G-BYUN	Grob G.115E Tutor	Babcock Aerospace Ltd
	G-BYUO	Grob G.115E Tutor	Babcock Aerospace Ltd
	G-BYUR	Grob G.115E Tutor	Babcock Aerospace Ltd
	G-BYUS	Grob G.115E Tutor	Babcock Aerospace Ltd
	G-BYUU	Grob G.115E Tutor	Babcock Aerospace Ltd
	G-BYUV	Grob G.115E Tutor	Babcock Aerospace Ltd
	G-BYUW	Grob G.115E Tutor	Babcock Aerospace Ltd
	G-BYUX	Grob G.115E Tutor	Babcock Aerospace Ltd
	G-BYUY	Grob.G.115E Tutor	Babcock Aerospace Ltd
	G-BYUZ	Grob G.115E Tutor	Babcock Aerospace Ltd
	G-BYVA	Grob G.115E Tutor	Babcock Aerospace Ltd
	G-BYVB	Grob G.115E Tutor	Babcock Aerospace Ltd
	G-BYVC	Grob G.115E Tutor	Babcock Aerospace Ltd
	G-BYVD	Grob G.115E Tutor	Babcock Aerospace Ltd
	G-BYVE	Grob G.115E Tutor	Babcock Aerospace Ltd
	G-BYVF	Grob G.115E Tutor	Babcock Aerospace Ltd
	G-BYVG	Grob G.115E Tutor	Babcock Aerospace Ltd
	G-BYVH	Grob G.115E Tutor	Babcock Aerospace Ltd
	G-BYVI	Grob G.115E Tutor	Babcock Aerospace Ltd
	G-BYVK	Grob G.115E Tutor	Babcock Aerospace Ltd
	G-BYVL	Grob G.115E Tutor	Babcock Aerospace Ltd
	G-BYVM	Grob G.115E Tutor	Babcock Aerospace Ltd
	G-BYVO	Grob G.115E Tutor	Babcock Aerospace Ltd
	G-BYVP	Grob G.115E Tutor	Babcock Aerospace Ltd
	G-BYVR	Grob G.115E Tutor	Babcock Aerospace Ltd
	G-BYVU	Grob G.115E Tutor	Babcock Aerospace Ltd
	G-BYVW	Grob G.115E Tutor	Babcock Aerospace Ltd
	G-BYVY	Grob G.115E Tutor	Babcock Aerospace Ltd
	G-BYVZ	Grob G.115E Tutor	Babcock Aerospace Ltd
	G-BYWA	Grob G.115E Tutor	Babcock Aerospace Ltd
	G-BYWB	Grob G.115E Tutor	Babcock Aerospace Ltd
	G-BYWD	Grob G.115E Tutor	Babcock Aerospace Ltd
	G-BYWF	Grob G.115E Tutor	Babcock Aerospace Ltd
	G-BYWG	Grob G.115E Tutor	Babcock Aerospace Ltd
	G-BYWH	Grob G.115E Tutor	Babcock Aerospace Ltd
	G-BYWI	Grob G.115E Tutor	Babcock Aerospace Ltd
	G-BYWK	Grob G.115E Tutor	Babcock Aerospace Ltd
	G-BYWL	Grob G.115E Tutor	Babcock Aerospace Ltd
	G-BYWM	Grob G.115E Tutor	Babcock Aerospace Ltd
	G-BYWO	Grob G.115E Tutor	Babcock Aerospace Ltd
	G-BYWR	Grob G.115E Tutor	Babcock Aerospace Ltd
	G-BYWS	Grob G.115E Tutor	Babcock Aerospace Ltd
	G-BYWU	Grob G.115E Tutor	Babcock Aerospace Ltd
	G-BYWV	Grob G.115E Tutor	Babcock Aerospace Ltd
	G-BYWW	Grob G.115E Tutor	Babcock Aerospace Ltd
	G-BYWX	Grob G.115E Tutor	Babcock Aerospace Ltd
	G-BYWY	Grob G.115E Tutor	Babcock Aerospace Ltd
	G-BYWZ	Grob G.115E Tutor	Babcock Aerospace Ltd
	G-BYXA	Grob G.115E Tutor	Babcock Aerospace Ltd

Reg	Type	Owner or Operator	Notes
G-BYXC	Grob G.115E Tutor	Babcock Aerospace Ltd	
G-BYXD	Grob G.115E Tutor	Babcock Aerospace Ltd	
G-BYXE	Grob G.115E Tutor	Babcock Aerospace Ltd	
G-BYXF	Grob G.115E Tutor	Babcock Aerospace Ltd	
G-BYXG	Grob G.115E Tutor	Babcock Aerospace Ltd	
G-BYXH	Grob G.115E Tutor	Babcock Aerospace Ltd	
G-BYXI	Grob G.115E Tutor	Babcock Aerospace Ltd	
G-BYXJ	Grob G.115E Tutor	Babcock Aerospace Ltd	
G-BYXK	Grob G.115E Tutor	Babcock Aerospace Ltd	
G-BYXL	Grob G.115E Tutor	Babcock Aerospace Ltd	
G-BYXM	Grob G.115E Tutor	Babcock Aerospace Ltd	
G-BYXO	Grob G.115E Tutor	Babcock Aerospace Ltd	
G-BYXP	Grob G.115E Tutor	Babcock Aerospace Ltd	
G-BYXS	Grob G.115E Tutor	Babcock Aerospace Ltd	
G-BYXT	Grob G.115E Tutor	Babcock Aerospace Ltd	
G-BYXW	Medway Eclipser	G. A. Hazell	
G-BYXX	Grob G.115E Tutor	Babcock Aerospace Ltd	
G-BYXZ	Grob G.115E Tutor	Babcock Aerospace Ltd	
G-BYYA	Grob G.115E Tutor	Babcock Aerospace Ltd	
G-BYYB	Grob G.115E Tutor	Babcock Aerospace Ltd	
G-BYYC	Hapi Cygnet SF-2A	G. H. Smith	
G-BYYE	Lindstrand LBL-77A balloon	K. R. Karlstrom	
G-BYYG	Slingsby T.67C	Royal Air Force Sport Aircraft	
G-BYYJ	Lindstrand LBL-25A balloon	A. B. Court	
G-BYYL	Jabiru SPL-450	Aztec Holdings (UK) Ltd	
G-BYYN	Pegasus Quantum 15-912	R. J. Bullock	
G-BYYO	PA-28R -201 Cherokee Arrow III	Stapleford Flying Club Ltd	
G-BYYP	Pegasus Quantum 15	D. A. Linsey	
G-BYYT	Jabiru UL-450	D. G. King	
G-BYYX	TEAM mini-MAX 91	S. S. Aujla	
G-BYYY	Pegasus Quantum 15-912	Quantum 1 Group	
G-BYZA	AS.355F2 Twin Squirrel	PDG Helicopters and PDG Aviation Services	
G-BYZB	Mainair Blade	A. M. Thornley	
G-BYZF	Raj Hamsa X'Air 582 (1)	R. P. Davies	
G-BYZR	I.I.I. Sky Arrow 650TC	G-BYZR Flying Group	
G-BYZS	Jabiru UL-450	R. J. Almey	
G-BYZT	Nova Vertex 26	M. Hay	
G-BYZU	Pegasus Quantum 15	J. L. Ashby	
G-BYZV	Sky 90-24 balloon	M. A. Stelling	
G-BYZW	Raj Hamsa X'Air 582 (2)	M. Atkinson & G. L. Risley	
G-BYZY	Pietenpol Aircamper	D. M. Hanchett	
G-BZAE	Cessna 152	Tatenhill Aviation Ltd	
G-BZAG	Lindstrand LBL-105A balloon	S. S. Sekhon	
G-BZAH	Cessna 208B Grand Caravan	Army Parachute Aircraft Company Ltd	
G-BZAP	Jabiru UL-450	I. J. Grindley & D. R. Griffiths	
G-BZAR	Denney Kitfox 4-1200 Speedster	J. M. Chapman (G-LEZJ)	
G-BZAS	Isaacs Fury II (K5673)	S. L. Childs	
G-BZBC	Rans S.6-ES Coyote II	A. J. Baldwin	
G-BZBF	Cessna 172M	Aviolease Ltd	
G-BZBH	Thunder Ax6-65 balloon	P. J. Hebdon & A. C. Fraser	
G-BZBJ	Lindstrand LBL-77A balloon	P. T. R. Ollivere	
G-BZBO	Stoddard-Hamilton Glasair III	C. R. P. Hamlett	
G-BZBS	PA-28-161 Cherokee Warrior III	White Waltham Airfield Ltd	
G-BZBT	Cameron H-34 Hopper balloon	P. Lesser	
G-BZBW	Rotorway Executive 162F	G-BZBW Group	
G-BZBX	Rans S.6-ES Coyote II	M. T. Butler	
G-BZBZ	Jodel D.9	D. C. Unwin	
G-BZDA	PA-28-161 Cherokee Warrior III	White Waltham Airfield Ltd	
G-BZDC	Mainair Blade	E. J. Wells & P. J. Smith	
G-BZDD	Mainair Blade 912	C. Lambropoulos	
G-BZDE	Lindstrand LBL-210A balloon	D. J. Stagg	
G-BZDF	CFM Streak Shadow SA	A. D. Parsons	
G-BZDH	PA-28R-200 Cherokee Arrow II	R. P. Pearson & A. M. Mumford	
G-BZDP	SA Bulldog Srs 120/121 (XX551:E)	R. M. Raikes	
G-BZDR	Tri Kis	W. F. Pocock & W. H. C. Reid	
G-BZDS	Pegasus Quantum 15-912	Hadair Flight Training Ltd	
G-BZDT	Maule MXT-7-180	Strongcrew Ltd	
G-BZDV	Westland Gazelle HT.2	G. R. Harrison	
G-BZEA	Cessna A.152	Davidson Aviation Ltd	
G-BZEB	Cessna 152	Davidson Aviation Ltd	

Notes	Reg	Type	Owner or Operator
	G-BZEC	Cessna 152	Redhill Air Services Ltd
	G-BZED	Pegasus Quantum 15-912	D. Crozier
	G-BZEG	Mainair Blade 912	I. Stanulet
	G-BZEN	Avtech Jabiru UL-450	B. R. Whitehead
	G-BZEP	SA Bulldog Srs 120/121 (XX561:7)	R. C. Skinner
	G-BZER	Raj Hamsa X'Air 582(2)	H. Lloyd-Hughes
	G-BZEW	Rans S.6-ES Coyote II	N. P. Gayton
	G-BZEY	Cameron N-90 balloon	G. L. Forde
	G-BZEZ	CFM Streak Shadow	M. J. Downes
	G-BZFB	Robin R.2112A	O. Bryan
	G-BZFD	Cameron N-90 balloon	C. D. & E. Gingell
	G-BZFG	Sky 105 balloon	Virgin Airship & Balloon Co Ltd
	G-BZFH	Pegasus Quantum 15-912	G. R. Ambrose
	G-BZFI	Avtech Jabiru UL	B. S. Lapthorn
	G-BZFN	SA Bulldog Srs 120/121 (XX667:16)	Risk Logical Ltd
	G-BZFS	Mainair Blade 912	Snowdonia Flyers Group
	G-BZFT	Murphy Rebel	A. S. D. Lyons
	G-BZGA	DHC.1 Chipmunk 22 (WK585)	J. Bishop
	G-BZGB	DHC.1 Chipmunk 22 (WZ872)	A. & J. Zemlik
	G-BZGF	Rans S.6-ES Coyote II	C. A. Purvis
	G-BZGJ	Thunder Ax10-180 S2 balloon	Spirit Operations Ltd
	G-BZGL	NA OV-10B Bronco	Liberty Aviation Ltd
	G-BZGT	Avtech Jabiru SPL-450	C. M. Bellas
	G-BZGV	Lindstrand LBL-77A balloon	J. H. Dryden
	G-BZGW	Mainair Blade	M. Liptrot
	G-BZGY	Dyn'Aéro CR.100	B. Appleby
	G-BZGZ	Pegasus Quantum 15-912	D. W. Beech
	G-BZHE	Cessna 152	Andrewsfield Aviation Ltd
	G-BZHF	Cessna 152	Modi Aviation Ltd
	G-BZHG	Tecnam P92 Echo	R. W. F. Boarder
	G-BZHJ	Raj Hamsa X'Air 582 (7)	T. R. Allebone
	G-BZHL	Noorduyn AT-16 Harvard IIB	S. Swallow
	G-BZHN	Pegasus Quantum 15-912	A. M. Sirant
	G-BZHO	Pegasus Quantum 15	BZHO Group
	G-BZHR	Avtech Jabiru UL-450	N. Morrison
	G-BZHT	PA-18A-150 Super Cub	D. Bennett
	G-BZHU	Wag-Aero Sport Trainer	Teddy Boys Flying Group
	G-BZHV	PA-28-181 Cherokee Archer III	R. M. & T. A. Limb
	G-BZHY	Mainair Blade 912	M. J. Booth
	G-BZIC	Lindstrand LBL Sun SS balloon	H. Holmqvist/Sweden
	G-BZID	Montgomerie-Bensen B.8MR	A. Gault
	G-BZIG	Thruster T.600N	R. NG-Zeederberg & P. R. Butler
	G-BZIH	Lindstrand LBL-31A balloon	H. & L. D. Vaughan
	G-BZII	Extra EA.300/1	G-BZII Syndicate
	G-BZIJ	Robin DR.400/500	Rob Airways Ltd
	G-BZIM	Pegasus Quantum 15-912	M. J. Stalker
	G-BZIO	PA-28-161 Cherokee Warrior III	White Waltham Airfield Ltd
	G-BZIP	Montgomerie-Bensen B.8MR	J. W. Cope
	G-BZIT	Beech 95-B55 Baron	J. F. Busby
	G-BZIV	Avtech Jabiru UL-450	A. Parr
	G-BZIW	Pegasus Quantum 15-912	J. M. Hodgson
	G-BZIY	Raj Hamsa X'Air 582 (2)	A. M. Morris
	G-BZIZ	Ultramagic H-31 balloon	C. J. Davies
	G-BZJA	Cameron Fire-90 balloon	Chubb Fire and Security Ltd
	G-BZJC	Thruster T.600N	D. P. Chappell
	G-BZJD	Thruster T.600T	R. J. Humphries
	G-BZJH	Cameron Z-90 balloon	Egroup SRL/Italy
	G-BZJI	Nova X-Large 37 paraplane	M. Hay
	G-BZJM	VPM M-16 Tandem Trainer	A. Phillips & J. K. Padden
	G-BZJO	Pegasus Quantum 15	D. Minnock
	G-BZJR	Montgomerie-Bensen B.8MR	M. H. Hillier (G-IPFM)
	G-BZJV	CASA 1-131E Jungmann 1000 (NM+AA)	R. A. Cumming
	G-BZJW	Cessna 150F	P. Ligertwood
	G-BZJZ	Pegasus Quantum 15	S. Baker
	G-BZKC	Raj Hamsa X'Air Jabiru (3)	G. A. Hazell
	G-BZKD	Stolp Starduster Too	P. & C. Edmunds
	G-BZKF	Rans S.6-ES Coyote II	S. Cartwright
	G-BZKL	PA-28R-201 Cherokee Arrow III	M. A. & M. H. Cromati
	G-BZKO	Rans S-6-ES Coyote II	W. J. I. Robb
	G-BZKU	Cameron Z-105 balloon	N. A. Fishlock
	G-BZKV	Cameron Sky 90-24 balloon	D. P. Busby

Reg	Type	Owner or Operator	Notes
G-BZKW	Ultramagic M-77 balloon	Slowfly Montgolfiere SNC/Italy	
G-BZLC	WSK-PZL Koliber 160A	A. C. Stamp	
G-BZLE	Rans S.6-ES Coyote II	D. I. Lee	
G-BZLF	CFM Shadow Srs CD	D. W. Stacey	
G-BZLG	Robin HR.200/120B	D. Dunn	
G-BZLK	Slingsby T.31M Motor Tutor	G. Smith	
G-BZLL	Pegasus Quantum 15-912	P. F. Willey	
G-BZLP	Robinson R44	Polar Helicopters Ltd	
G-BZLS	Cameron Sky 77-24 balloon	D. W. Young	
G-BZLU	Lindstrand LBL-90A balloon	A. E. Lusty	
G-BZLV	Avtech Jabiru UL-450	M. Cheetham	
G-BZLX	Pegasus Quantum 15-912	N. W. Barnett	
G-BZLY	Grob G.109B	G-BZLY Group	
G-BZLZ	Pegasus Quantum 15-912	H. Beckett	
G-BZMB	PA-28R-201 Cherokee Arrow III	Thurrock Arrow Group	
G-BZMC	Avtech Jabiru UL	S. Farnworth	
G-BZME	SA Bulldog Srs 120/121 (XX698:9)	XX698 Bulldog Group	
G-BZMF	Rutan LongEz	M. Skene	
G-BZMH	SA Bulldog Srs 120/121 (XX692:A)	M. E. J. Hingley	
G-BZMJ	Rans S-6-ES Coyote II	R. J. G. Clark	
G-BZML	SA Bulldog Srs 120/121 (XX693:07)	I. D. Anderson	
G-BZMM	Robin DR.400/180R	Cairngorm Gliding Club	
G-BZMS	Mainair Blade	S. Elmazouri	
G-BZMY	SPP Yakovlev Yak C-11 (I)	A. M. Holman-West	
G-BZNA	Lindstrand LBL-90A balloon	M. A. Stelling & A. J. Kinsella	
G-BZNH	Rans S-6-ES Coyote II	B. A. Coombe	
G-BZNI	Bell 206B Jet Ranger II	Leasing UK Ltd (G-ODIG/G-NEEP)	
G-BZNJ	Rans S-6-ES Coyote II	R. A. McKee	
G-BZNK	Morane Saulnier MS.315-D2 (354)	R. H. Cooper & S. Swallow	
G-BZNM	Pegasus Quantum 15	G. J. P. Skinner	
G-BZNP	Thruster T.600N	P. D. Twissell	
G-BZNV	Lindstrand LBL-31A balloon	G. R. Down	
G-BZNW	Isaacs Fury II (K2048)	P. King	
G-BZNY	Europa XS	T. J. Poulter	
G-BZOB	Slepcev Storch (6G-ED)	A. Bendkowski	
G-BZOE	Pegasus Quantum 15	B. Dale	
G-BZOF	Montgomerie-Bensen B.8MR gyroplane	S. J. M. Ledingham	
G-BZOI	Nicollier HN.700 Menestrel II	R. P. Hipson, R. P. Hogg, A. D. Smyth & R. Nelson	
G-BZOL	Robin R.3000/140	M. C. R. Willis	
G-BZOM	Rotorway Executive 162F	I. C. Bedford (G-RALF)	
G-BZON	SA Bulldog Srs 120/121 (XX528:D)	D. J. Critchley	
G-BZOO	Pegasus Quantum 15-912	D. W. Guest	
G-BZOR	TEAM mini-MAX 91	A. W. Gunn	
G-BZOU	Pegasus Quantum 15-912	M. A. Bradford	
G-BZOW	Whittaker MW7	G. W. Peacock	
G-BZOX	Cameron Colt 90B balloon	D. J. Head	
G-BZOZ	Van's RV-6	A. C. Beech	
G-BZPA	Mainair Blade 912S	W. McDowell	
G-BZPD	Cameron V-65 balloon	P. Spellward	
G-BZPF	Scheibe SF-24B Motorspatz	D. & M. Shrimpton	
G-BZPG	Beech C24R Sierra 200	Beech Fenland Flying (BFF) Club	
G-BZPH	Van's RV-4	G-BZPH RV-4 Group	
G-BZPI	SOCATA TB20 Trinidad	Transair (UK) Ltd	
G-BZPN	Mainair Blade 912S	J. Kilpatrick	
G-BZPW	Cameron V-77 balloon	R. G. Griffin	
G-BZPX	Ultramagic S-105 balloon	Scotair Balloons	
G-BZPY	Ultramagic H-31 balloon	Scotair Balloons	
G-BZPZ	Mainair Blade	R. J. Burke	
G-BZRF	Percival P.56 Provost T.Mk.1	P. B. Childs	
G-BZRJ	Pegasus Quantum 15-912	D. A. Hutchinson	
G-BZRO	PA-30 Twin Comanche C	Praeluceo Property Ltd	
G-BZRP	Pegasus Quantum 15-912	M. F. Sheerman-Chase	
G-BZRR	Pegasus Quantum 15-912	C. M. Boswell	
G-BZRS	Eurocopter EC 135T2	Babcock Mission Critical Services Onshore Ltd	
G-BZRV	Van's RV-6	N. M. Hitchman	
G-BZRW	Mainair Blade 912S	Ulster Flying Club (1961) Ltd	
G-BZRY	Rans S.6-ES Coyote II	S. P. H. Calvert	
G-BZSB	Pitts S-1S Special	A. J. Harris	
G-BZSC	Sopwith Camel F.1 (replica) (D1851)	The Shuttleworth Collection	
G-BZSE	Hawker Hunter T.8B (WV322:VL)	Twyford Aviation Services (UK) Ltd	
G-BZSG	Pegasus Quantum 15-912	A. J. Harris	

Notes	Reg	Type	Owner or Operator
	G-BZSI	Pegasus Quantum 15	T. C. Hemsley
	G-BZSM	Pegasus Quantum 15	P. Mansfield
	G-BZSP	Stemme S.10	A. Flewelling & L. Bleaken
	G-BZSS	Pegasus Quantum 15-912	W. O. Miller
	G-BZST	Jabiru SPL-450	M. D. Tulloch
	G-BZSX	Pegasus Quantum 15-912	G. Reid
	G-BZSZ	Jabiru UL-450	R. J. Almey
	G-BZTA	Robinson R44	Jarretts Motors Ltd
	G-BZTC	TEAM mini-MAX 91	G. G. Clayton
	G-BZTD	Thruster T.600T 450 JAB	S. A. Harvey
	G-BZTH	Europa	D. J. Shipley
	G-BZTK	Cameron V-90 balloon	E. Appollodorus
	G-BZTN	Europa XS	P. R. Norwood
	G-BZTS	Cameron 90 Bertie Bassett SS balloon	Trebor Bassett Ltd
	G-BZTV	Mainair Blade 912S	R. D. McManus
	G-BZTW	Hunt Wing Avon 582 (1)	T. S. Walker
	G-BZTX	Mainair Blade 912	K. A. Ingham
	G-BZTY	Avtech Jabiru UL	R. P. Lewis
	G-BZUB	Mainair Blade	J. Campbell
	G-BZUD	Lindstrand LBL-105A balloon	D. Venegoni/Italy
	G-BZUE	Pagasus Quantum 15-912	S. J. Ward
	G-BZUF	Mainair Rapier	B. Craig
	G-BZUG	RL.7A XP Sherwood Ranger	J. G. Boxall
	G-BZUH	Rans S.6-ES Coyote II	R. A. Darley
	G-BZUI	Pegasus Quantum 15-912	C. Garton
	G-BZUL	Avtech Jabiru UL	J. G. Campbell
	G-BZUP	Raj Hamsa X'Air Jabiru(3)	M. T. Sheelan
	G-BZUU	Cameron C-90 balloon	D. C. Ball
	G-BZUV	Cameron H-24 balloon	M. J. Axtell
	G-BZUX	Pegasus Quantum 15	C. Gorvett
	G-BZUY	Van's RV-6	D. J. Butt
	G-BZUZ	Hunt Avon-Blade R.100 (1)	T. J. Wiltshire
	G-BZVA	Zenair CH.701UL	W. K. MacGillivray
	G-BZVB	Cessna FR.172H	Victor Bravo Group Ltd (G-BLMX)
	G-BZVI	Nova Vertex 24 hang glider	M. Hay
	G-BZVJ	Pegasus Quantum 15	R. Blackhall
	G-BZVK	Raj Hamsa X'Air 582 (2)	R. J. Hamilton
	G-BZVM	Rans S.6-ES Coyote II	M. P. Booth
	G-BZVN	Van's RV-6	Syndicate RV6 G-BZVN
	G-BZVR	Raj Hamsa X'Air 582 (4)	R. F. E. Berry
	G-BZVT	I.I.I. Sky Arrow 650T	E. J. Hadley
	G-BZVV	Pegasus Quantum 15-912	S. Smith & J. Giladjian
	G-BZWB	Mainair Blade 912	J. Januszczyk
	G-BZWC	Raj Hamsa X'Air Falcon 912 (1)	J. Webb
	G-BZWJ	CFM Streak Shadow	T. A. Morgan
	G-BZWK	Avtech Jabiru SK	J. M. Angiolini
	G-BZWM	Pegasus XL-Q	D. T. Evans
	G-BZWN	Van's RV-8	A. J. Symms
	G-BZWR	Mainair Rapier	M. A. Steele
	G-BZWS	Pegasus Quantum 15-912	G-BZWS Syndicate
	G-BZWT	Technam P.92-EM Echo	R. F. Cooper
	G-BZWU	Pegasus Quantum 15-912	M. D. Evans
	G-BZWV	Steen Skybolt	D. E. Blaxland, P. D. Baisden & J. P. Gilbert
	G-BZWZ	Van's RV-6	Bizzywizzy Group
	G-BZXB	Van's RV-6	R. A. Pritchard & G. W. Cunningham
	G-BZXI	Nova Philou 26 hang glider	M. Hay
	G-BZXM	Mainair Blade 912	S. Dolan
	G-BZXN	Avtech Jabiru SPL-450	Dash Aviation Europe Ltd
	G-BZXP	Kiss 400-582 (1)	A. Fairbrother
	G-BZXR	Cameron N-90 balloon	M. P. Pritchard
	G-BZXS	SA Bulldog Srs 120/121 (XX631:W)	G. N. E. Waring
	G-BZXT	Mainair Blade 912	J. D. Sings & S. C. Stinchcombe
	G-BZXV	Pegasus Quantum 15-912	J. L. Smith
	G-BZXW	VPM M-16 Tandem Trainer	P. J. Troy-Davies (G-NANA)
	G-BZXX	Pegasus Quantum 15-912	D. Ostle
	G-BZXY	Robinson R44	Flight Checks Ltd
	G-BZXZ	SA Bulldog Srs 120/121 (XX629:V)	H. Zhuang
	G-BZYA	Rans S.6-ES Coyote II	M. D. Rose
	G-BZYD	Westland Gazelle AH.1 (XZ329)	C. D. Meek
	G-BZYG	Glaser-Dirks DG.500MB	R. C. Bromwich
	G-BZYI	Nova Phocus 123 hang glider	M. Hay

Reg	Type	Owner or Operator	Notes
G-BZYN	Pegasus Quantum 15-912	J. Cannon	
G-BZYR	Cameron N-31 balloon	C. J. Sanger-Davies	
G-BZYS	Micro Aviation B.22 Bantam	R. W. Hollamby	
G-BZYX	Raj Hamsa X'Air 700 (1A)	S. Carter	
G-BZYY	Cameron N-90 balloon	M. E. Mason	
G-CAHA	PA-34-200T Seneca II	Highland Aviation Training Ltd	
G-CALL	PA-23 Aztec 250F	J. D. Moon	
G-CAMM	Hawker Cygnet (replica)	Richard Shuttleworth Trustees	
G-CAMR	BFC Challenger II	P. R. A. Walker	
G-CAPI	Mudry/CAARP CAP-10B	A. V. Harmer (G-BEXR)	
G-CAPX	Avions Mudry CAP-10B	J. P. O' Donnell	
G-CBAD	Mainair Blade 912	G. Mowll	
G-CBAF	Lancair 320	L. H. & M. van Cleeff	
G-CBAJ	DHC.1 Chipmunk 22	M. Harvey	
G-CBAK	Robinson R44	Robert Howell Construction Service	
G-CBAL	PA-28-161 Cherokee Warrior II	CBAL Flying Group	
G-CBAN	SA Bulldog Srs 120/121 (XX668:1)	Bulldog XX668 Flying Group	
G-CBAP	Zenair CH.601ULA	G. D. Summers	
G-CBAR	Stoddard-Hamilton Glastar	Fishburn Flyers	
G-CBAS	Rans S.6-ESA Coyote II	M. W. Luke	
G-CBAT	Cameron Z-90 balloon	D. Baker	
G-CBAU	Rand-Robinson KR-2	C. B. Copsey	
G-CBAW	Cameron A-300 balloon	Bailey Balloons Ltd	
G-CBAX	Tecnam P92-EA Echo	K. W. Eskins	
G-CBAZ	Rans S.6-ES Coyote II	S. J. Heighway	
G-CBBB	Pegasus Quantum 15-912	F. A. Dimmock	
G-CBBC	SA Bulldog Srs 120/121 (XX515:4)	Bulldog Support Ltd	
G-CBBG	Mainair Blade	B. Donnan	
G-CBBH	Raj Hamsa X'Air 582 (11)	K. Young & L. C. Owen	
G-CBBK	Robinson R22	R. J. Everett	
G-CBBL	SA Bulldog Srs 120/121 (XX550:Z)	A. Cunningham	
G-CBBM	Savannah VG Jabiru (1)	J. L. Ellingworth	
G-CBBN	Pegasus Quantum 15-912	G-CBBN Flying Group	
G-CBBO	Whittaker MW5D Sorcerer	B. Outhwaite & M. Cottle	
G-CBBP	Pegasus Quantum 15-912	A. C. Richards	
G-CBBS	SA Bulldog Srs 120/121 (XX694:E)	D. R. Keene	
G-CBBT	SA Bulldog Srs 120/121 (XX695:3)	K. A. Johnston	
G-CBBW	SA Bulldog Srs 120/121 (XX619:T)	S. E. Robottom-Scott	
G-CBCB	SA Bulldog Srs 120/121 (XX537:C)	M. W. Minary & M. R. Bromiley	
G-CBCD	Pegasus Quantum 15	I. A. Lumley	
G-CBCF	Pegasus Quantum 15-912	P. A. Bromley	
G-CBCI	Raj Hamsa X'Air 582 (2)	J. M. Rolfe	
C CBCL	Stoddard Hamilton Glastar	A. P. Barrow	
G-CBCM	Raj Hamsa X'Air Jabiru(3)	P. J. Hellyer	
G-CBCP	Van's RV-6A	G-CBCP Group	
G-CBCR	SA Bulldog Srs 120/121 (XX702:P)	J. E. Rowley	
G-CBCZ	CFM Streak Shadow SLA	J. O'Malley-Kane	
G-CBDC	Thruster T.600N 450-JAB	I. W. Walsh	
G-CBDG	Zenair CH.601HD	R. E. Lasnier	
G-CBDH	Flight Design CT2K	S. J. Goate	
G-CBDI	Denney Kitfox Mk.2	M. Barbour & G. Wilson	
G-CBDK	SA Bulldog Srs 120/121 (XX611:7)	G. N. E. & L. Waring	
G-CBDL	Mainair Blade	T. R. Villa	
G-CBDM	Tecnam P92-EM Echo	J. J. Cozens	
G-CBDN	Mainair Blade	A. J. Phillips	
G-CBDO	Raj Hamsa X'Air 582(1)	J. Hennessy	
G-CBDP	Mainair Blade 912	M. Atkinson	
G-CBDU	Quad City Challenger II	E. J. Brooks	
G-CBDV	Raj Hamsa X'Air 582	U. J. Anderson	
G-CBDX	Pegasus Quantum 15	P. Sinkler	
G-CBDZ	Pegasus Quantum 15-912	P. Smith	
G-CBEB	Kiss 400-582 (1)	E. McCallum	
G-CBEC	Cameron Z-105 balloon	John Aimo Balloons SAS/Italy	
G-CBEE	PA-28R-200 Cherokee Arrow	D. S. A. Halstead, D. K. Matthews & A. J. McCallister	
G-CBEF	SA Bulldog Srs 120/121 (XX621:H)	A. L. Butcher & F. W. Sandwell	
G-CBEH	SA Bulldog Srs 120/121 (XX521:H)	J. E. Lewis	
G-CBEI	PA-22 Colt 108	L. W. Armitage & C. Rudy	
G-CBEJ	Colt 120A balloon	Airxcite Ltd	

Notes	Reg	Type	Owner or Operator
	G-CBEK	SA Bulldog Srs 120/121 (XX700:17)	J. T. Crump
	G-CBEL	Hawker Fury F.Mk.11 (SR661)	Fighter Aviation Engineering Ltd
	G-CBEM	Mainair Blade	K. W. Bodley
	G-CBES	Europa XS	D. J. Shipley
	G-CBEU	Pegasus Quantum 15-912	I. Flack
	G-CBEV	Pegasus Quantum 15-912	A. W. G. Ambler
	G-CBEW	Flight Design CT2K	S. A. Harvey & D. R. Crump
	G-CBEX	Flight Design CT2K	K. J. Gosling
	G-CBEY	Cameron C-80 balloon	G. C. Dare
	G-CBEZ	Robin DR.400/180	J. D. L. Richardson
	G-CBFA	Diamond DA40 Star	Lyrastar Ltd
	G-CBFE	Raj Hamsa X'Air V.2 (1)	W. H. Ahmed
	G-CBFJ	Robinson R44	R. R. Orr
	G-CBFK	Murphy Rebel	P. J. Gibbs
	G-CBFP	SA Bulldog Srs 120/121 (XX636:Y)	Shacklewell Bulldog Group
	G-CBFU	SA Bulldog Srs 120/121 (XX628:9)	J. R. & S. J. Huggins
	G-CBFW	Bensen B.8	A. J. Thomas
	G-CBFX	Rans S.6-ES Coyote II	W. R. Furness
	G-CBGD	Zenair CH.701UL	I. S. Walsh
	G-CBGE	Tecnam P92-EM Echo	N. Sadler
	G-CBGH	Teverson Bisport	Phoenix Flyers
	G-CBGJ	Aeroprakt A.22 Foxbat	E. Smyth & T. G. Fitzpatrick
	G-CBGL	MH.1521M Broussard	Aero Legends Leasing Ltd
	G-CBGO	Murphy Maverick 430	K. J. Miies & R. Withall
	G-CBGP	Ikarus C.42 FB UK	C. F. Welby
	G-CBGU	Thruster T.600N 450-JAB	B. R. Cardosi
	G-CBGV	Thruster T.600N 450	West Flight Aviators
	G-CBGW	Thruster T.600N 450-JAB	K. D. Smith
	G-CBGX	SA Bulldog Srs 120/121 (XX622:B)	Bulldog GX Group
	G-CBHA	SOCATA TB10 Tobago	Oscar Romeo Aviation Ltd
	G-CBHG	Mainair Blade 912S	C. R. Buckle
	G-CBHI	Europa XS	Alpha Syndicate
	G-CBHJ	Mainair Blade 912	A. W. Leadley
	G-CBHN	Pegasus Quantum 15-912	P. Hunt
	G-CBHO	Gloster Gladiator II (N5719)	Retro Track & Air (UK) Ltd
	G-CBHR	Lazer Z200	P. O'Connor
	G-CBHU	RL.5A Sherwood Ranger	D. J. Seymour
	G-CBHW	Cameron Z-105 balloon	Bristol Chamber of Commerce, Industry & Shipping
	G-CBHX	Cameron V-77 balloon	A. Hook
	G-CBHY	Pegasus Quantum 15-912	D. W. Allen
	G-CBHZ	RAF 2000 GTX-SE gyroplane	M. P. Donnelly
	G-CBIB	Flight Design CT2K	P. K. Rogers & F. C. Weber
	G-CBIC	Raj Hamsa X'Air V2 (2)	R. J. Ripley
	G-CBID	SA Bulldog Srs 120/121(XX549:6)	The Red Dog Group
	G-CBIE	Flight Design CT2K	S. Willis
	G-CBII	Raj Hamsa X'Air 582(8)	J. L. Pozniak
	G-CBIL	Cessna 182K	E. Bannister (G-BFZZ)
	G-CBIM	Lindstrand LBL-90A balloon	R. K. Parsons
	G-CBIN	TEAM mini-MAX 91	A. R. Mikolaczyk
	G-CBIP	Thruster T.600N 450-JAB	G. Crossan
	G-CBIS	Raj Hamsa X'Air 582 (2)	P. T. W. T. Derges
	G-CBIT	RAF 2000 GTX-SE gyroplane ★	The Helicopter Museum/Weston-Super-Mare
	G-CBIV	Skyranger 912 (1)	R. H. Dennis
	G-CBIX	Zenair CH.601UL	M. van der Horn
	G-CBIY	Aerotechnik EV-97 Eurostar	W. R. Grantham & B. J. Sheppard
	G-CBJD	Stoddard-Hamilton Glastar	P. A. Colman
	G-CBJE	RAF 2000 GTX-SE gyroplane	V. G. Freke
	G-CBJG	DHC.1 Chipmunk 20 (1373)	C. J. Rees
	G-CBJH	Aeroprakt A.22 Foxbat	J. R. Hunt
	G-CBJL	Kiss 400-582 (1)	R. E. Morris
	G-CBJM	Avtech Jabiru SP-470	J. M. P. Elliott
	G-CBJN	RAF 2000 GTX-SE	B. Agyemang
	G-CBJO	Pegasus Quantum 15-912	A. E. Kemp
	G-CBJP	Zenair CH.601UL	T. J. Heaton
	G-CBJR	Aerotechnik EV-97A Eurostar	Madley Flying Group
	G-CBJS	Cameron C-60 balloon	N. Ivison
	G-CBJW	Ikarus C.42 Cyclone FB UK	E. Foster & J. H. Peet
	G-CBJX	Raj Hamsa X'Air Falcon J22	R. D. Bateman
	G-CBJY	Jabiru UL-450	O. N. Fooks
	G-CBJZ	Westland Gazelle HT.3	K. G. Theurer/Germany

Reg	Type	Owner or Operator	Notes
G-CBKA	Westland Gazelle HT.3	G. P. Hinkley	
G-CBKB	Bücker Bü 181C Bestmann	S. P. Watts	
G-CBKD	Westland Gazelle HT.2	S. J. L. Fish	
G-CBKF	Easy Raider J2.2 (2)	N. Chachlakis	
G-CBKG	Thruster T.600N 450 JAB	K. W. Millar	
G-CBKK	Ultramagic S-130 balloon	Hayrick Ltd	
G-CBKL	Raj Hamsa X'Air Jabiru(2)	P. A. Wilman	
G-CBKM	Mainair Blade 912	T. E. Robinson	
G-CBKN	Mainair Blade 912	G. C. Hobson	
G-CBKO	Mainair Blade 912S	S. J. Taft	
G-CBKR	PA-28-161 Warrior III	Yeovil Auto Tuning	
G-CBKU	Ikarus C.42 Cyclone FB UK	C. Blackburn	
G-CBKW	Pegasus Quantum 15-912	A. Sharma	
G-CBKY	Avtech Jabiru SP-470	I. A.Lavey	
G-CBLA	Aero Designs Pulsar XP	A. Yoosefinejad	
G-CBLB	Technam P.92-EM Echo	R. Lewis-Evans	
G-CBLD	Mainair Blade 912S	N. E. King	
G-CBLF	Raj Hamsa X'Air 582(11)	L. J. Nelson	
G-CBLK	Hawker Hind (L7181)	Aero Vintage Ltd	
G-CBLL	Pegasus Quantum 15-912	P. D. Alford	
G-CBLM	Mainair Blade 912	A. S. Saunders	
G-CBLN	Cameron Z-31 balloon	J. T. Stevens	
G-CBLO	Lindstrand LBL-42A balloon	D. G. Such	
G-CBLP	Raj Hamsa X'Air Falcon	A. C. Parsons	
G-CBLS	Fiat CR.42 (MM6976:16-85)	Fighter Collection Ltd	
G-CBLT	Mainair Blade 912	C. M. Dale	
G-CBLW	Raj Hamsa X'Air Falcon 582(3)	R. G. Halliwell	
G-CBLY	Grob G.109B	G-CBLY Syndicate	
G-CBLZ	Rutan LongEz	Agent CEL, SLU	
G-CBMB	Cyclone Ax2000	N. Farnden	
G-CBME	Cessna F.172M	Skytrax Aviation Ltd	
G-CBML	DHC.6 Twin Otter 310	Isles of Scilly Skybus Ltd	
G-CBMO	PA-28-180 Cherokee	M. Crane	
G-CBMP	Cessna R.182	Orman (Carrolls Farm) Ltd	
G-CBMR	Medway Eclipser	D. S. Blofeld	
G-CBMT	Robin DR.400/180	R. J. Williamson	
G-CBMV	Pegasus Quantum 15	K. J. Webb	
G-CBMZ	Aerotechnik EV-97 Eurostar	K. G. Smith	
G-CBNC	Mainair Blade 912	K. L. Smith	
G-CBNF	Rans S.7 Courier	I. M. Ross	
G-CBNI	Lindstrand LBL-180A balloon	M. B. Siddiqui	
G-CBNJ	Raj Hamsa X'Air 582 (11)	H. G. Budd	
G-CBNL	Dyn'Aéro MCR-01 Club	D. H. Wilson	
G-CBNO	CFM Streak Shadow	P. J. Porter	
G-CBNT	Pegasus Quantum 15-912	W. P. Seward	
G-CBNV	Rans S6-ES Coyote II	C. D. Ward	
G-CBNW	Cameron N-105 balloon	J. W. Dolman	
G-CBNX	Mongomerie-Bensen B.8MR	S. H. Broszek	
G-CBNZ	TEAM hi-MAX 1700R	J. D. Reynolds & C. A. Mason	
G-CBOF	Europa XS	P. R. Tunney	
G-CBOG	Mainair Blade 912S	OG Group	
G-CBOM	Mainair Blade 912	J. Howarth	
G-CBOP	Avtech Jabiru UL-450	D. D. Petrov	
G-CBOR	Cessna F.172N	R. P. Rochester	
G-CBOS	Rans S.6-ES Coyote II	J. T. Athulathmudali	
G-CBOW	Cameron Z-120 balloon	G. C. Dare	
G-CBOY	Pegasus Quantum 15-912	A. P. Laws	
G-CBOZ	IDA Bacau Yakovlev Yak-52	G. G. L. James	
G-CBPC	Sportavia-Putzer RF-5B	I. K. G. Mitchell	
G-CBPD	Ikarus C.42 Cyclone FB UK	Waxwing Group	
G-CBPE	SOCATA TB10 Tobago	D. P. McDermott	
G-CBPI	PA-28R-201 Arrow III	D. Crozier	
G-CBPM	Yakovlev Yak-50	P. W. Ansell	
G-CBPR	Avtech Jabiru UL-450	N. R. Andrew	
G-CBPV	Zenair CH.601UL	C. J. Meadows	
G-CBPW	Lindstrand LBL-105A balloon	P. Donkin	
G-CBRB	Ultramagic S-105 balloon	P. C. Bailey	
G-CBRC	Jodel D.18	A. H. Sheikh	
G-CBRD	Jodel D.18	J. D. Haslam	
G-CBRE	Mainair Blade 912	M. D. Vearncombe	
G-CBRF	Ikarus C42 FB100 VLA	M. J. Donnelly	

Notes	Reg	Type	Owner or Operator
	G-CBRK	Ultramagic M-77 balloon	A. G. Aldous
	G-CBRM	Mainair Blade	M. H. Levy
	G-CBRR	Aerotechnik EV-97A Eurostar	M. S. Turner & A. W. Parker
	G-CBRV	Cameron C-90 balloon	Turner Balloons Ltd
	G-CBRX	Zenair CH.601UL Zodiac	A. L. & S. Roberts
	G-CBSF	Westland Gazelle HT.2	Falcon Aviation Ltd
	G-CBSI	Westland Gazelle HT.3 (XZ934:U)	P. S. Unwin
	G-CBSK	Westland Gazelle HT.3 (ZB627:A)	Falcon Flying Group
	G-CBSO	PA-28-181 Cherokee Archer II	Archer One Ltd
	G-CBSU	Avtech Jabiru UL	K. R. Crawley
	G-CBSV	Montgomerie-Bensen B8MR	R. S. Sanby
	G-CBSZ	Mainair Blade 912S	M. R. Mosley
	G-CBTB	I.I.I. Sky Arrow 650TS	C. J. Green
	G-CBTD	Pegasus Quantum 15-912	D. Baillie
	G-CBTE	Mainair Blade 912	C. R. Buckle
	G-CBTN	PA-31 Navajo C	M. E. Gradwell
	G-CBTO	Rans S.6-ES Coyote II	A. J. Gibson
	G-CBTS	Gloster Gamecock (replica)	Retro Track & Air (UK) Ltd
	G-CBTT	PA-28-181 Cherokee Archer II	Sonic Enterprises Ltd (G-BFMM)
	G-CBTW	Mainair Blade 912	H. R. Davis
	G-CBTX	Denney Kitfox Mk.2	G. I. Doake
	G-CBUC	Raj Hamsa X'Air 582 (5)	G-CBUC Group
	G-CBUD	Pegasus Quantum 15-912	G. N. S. Farrant
	G-CBUF	Flight Design CT2K	D. B. Bluff
	G-CBUG	Technam P.92-EM Echo	S. R. A. Brierley & K. D. Mitchell
	G-CBUI	Westland Wasp HAS.1 (XT420:606)	Fly Navy Heritage Trust Ltd
	G-CBUJ	Raj Hamsa X'Air 582 (10)	R. J. Lewis
	G-CBUK	Van's RV-6A	P. G. Greenslade
	G-CBUN	Barker Charade	T. M. Jones
	G-CBUO	Cameron O-90 balloon	G. B. Davies
	G-CBUP	VPM M-16 Tandem Trainer	J. S. Firth
	G-CBUS	Pegasus Quantum 15	G. Hitchcox
	G-CBUU	Pegasus Quantum 15-912	S. Gaskell & D. S. Walsh
	G-CBUX	Cyclone AX2000	J. R. Huggett
	G-CBUY	Rans S.6-ES Coyote II	Phoenix Aviation
	G-CBVC	Raj Hamsa X'Air 582 (6)	J. P. Ribi
	G-CBVD	Cameron C-60 balloon	J-P. Luttrell
	G-CBVF	Murphy Maverick 430	D. S. Evans
	G-CBVH	Lindstrand LBL-120A balloon	P. M. Forster
	G-CBVM	Aerotechnik EV-97 Eurostar	M. Sharpe
	G-CBVN	Pegasus Quik	A. C. Hardiman
	G-CBVR	Skyranger 912 (2)	S. H. Lunney
	G-CBVS	Skyranger 912 (1)	S. C. Cornock
	G-CBVU	PA-28R-200 Cherokee Arrow	N. F. Ball
	G-CBVX	Cessna 182P	N. Robinson
	G-CBVY	Ikarus C.42 Cyclone FB UK	Grandpa's Flying Group
	G-CBVZ	Flight Design CT2K	C. J. Meadows
	G-CBWD	PA-28-161 Cherokee Warrior III	D. M. Wright
	G-CBWE	Aerotechnik EV-97 Eurostar	J. & C. W. Hood
	G-CBWG	Aerotechnik EV-97 Eurostar	W. J. Upton
	G-CBWJ	Thruster T. 600N 450	J. W. Kelsey
	G-CBWN	Campbell Cricket Mk.6	R. S. Sanby
	G-CBWO	Rotorway Executive 162F	JJ Mac Ltd
	G-CBWS	Whittaker MW6 Merlin	K. R. Emery
	G-CBWW	Skyranger Swift 912 (1)	H. M. Roberts
	G-CBWY	Raj Hamsa X'Air 582 (6)	J. C. Rose
	G-CBWZ	Robinson R22 Beta	J. Fleming
	G-CBXB	Lindstrand LBL-150A balloon	M. A. Webb
	G-CBXC	Ikarus C.42 Cyclone FB UK	M. & P. L. Eardley
	G-CBXE	Easy Raider J2.2 (3)	J. W. Reece
	G-CBXF	Easy Raider J2.2 (2)	S. F. Beardsell
	G-CBXG	Thruster T.600N 450	D. R. Harper
	G-CBXR	Raj Hamsa X-Air Falcon 582 (1)	J. F. Heath
	G-CBXS	Skyranger 912 (1)	The Ince Skyranger Group
	G-CBXU	TEAM miniMAX 91A	Minimax Group
	G-CBYB	Rotorway Executive 162F	Clark Contracting
	G-CBYD	Rans S.6-ES Coyote II	I. R. M. Scott
	G-CBYF	Mainair Blade	R. W. Douglas
	G-CBYH	Aeroprakt A.22 Foxbat	M. J. Barrett
	G-CBYI	Pegasus Quantum 15-503	The G-BCYI Group
	G-CBYM	Mainair Blade	D. Reid

Reg	Type	Owner or Operator	Notes
G-CBYN	Europa XS	G. M. Tagg	
G-CBYO	Pegasus Quik	G-CBYO Syndicate	
G-CBYP	Whittaker MW6-S Fat Boy Flyer	W. G. Reynolds	
G-CBYS	Lindstrand LBL-21 balloon France	B. M. Reed/France	
G-CBYT	Thruster T.600N 450	M. A. Curtis	
G-CBYU	PA-28-161 Cherokee Warrior II	Stapleford Flying Club Ltd	
G-CBYV	Pegasus Quantum 15-912	S. J. Ward	
G-CBYW	Hatz CB-1	T. A. Hinton	
G-CBZA	Mainair Blade	M. Lowe	
G-CBZD	Mainair Blade	G. P. J. Davies	
G-CBZE	Robinson R44	Cenegex Aviation Ltd	
G-CBZH	Pegasus Quik	Team CBZH	
G-CBZJ	Lindstrand LBL-25A balloon	Pegasus Ballooning	
G-CBZM	Avtech Jabiru UL-450	M. J. Jackson	
G-CBZN	Rans S.6-ES Coyote II	K. Stevens	
G-CBZP	Hawker Fury 1 (K5674)	Historic Aircraft Collection	
G-CBZR	PA-28R-201 Arrow III	T. W. Gilbert	
G-CBZT	Pegasus Quik	R. G. Fullerton & T. J. Feeney	
G-CBZW	Zenair CH.701 STOL	S. Richens	
G-CBZX	Dyn' Aero MCR-01 ULC	A. C. N. Freeman	
G-CBZZ	Cameron Z-275 balloon	A. C. K. Rawson & J. J. Rudoni	
G-CCAB	Mainair Blade	P. Dean	
G-CCAC	Aerotechnik EV-97 Eurostar	C. Long	
G-CCAD	Mainair Pegasus Quik	M. Richardson	
G-CCAE	Avtech Jabiru UL-450	S. Coulton	
G-CCAF	Skyranger 912 (1)	G. Everett & D. N. Smith	
G-CCAG	Mainair Blade 912	A. Robinson	
G-CCAK	Zenair CN.601HD	M. T. Butler	
G-CCAL	Technam P.92-EA Echo	K. Flook	
G-CCAP	Robinson R22 Beta II	D. W. Baker	
G-CCAS	Pegasus Quik	Caunton Alpha Syndicate	
G-CCAT	AA-5A Cheetah	Rate 1 Aero Ltd (G-OAJH/G-KILT/G-BJFA)	
G-CCAV	PA-28-181 Cherokee Archer II	Alpha Victor Group	
G-CCAW	Mainair Blade 912	I. G. Molesworth	
G-CCAZ	Mainair Pegasus Quik	D. A. Appleby	
G-CCBA	Skyranger R.100	M. A. Cox	
G-CCBB	Cameron N-90 balloon	D. M. Turley & L. M. Franks	
G-CCBG	Skyranger Swift 912(1)	K. Wileman	
G-CCBH	PA-28-236 Cherokee	B. P. Bradley-Winzer	
G-CCBJ	Skyranger 912S (1)	R. E. Williams	
G-CCBK	Aerotechnik EV-97 Eurostar	Starship Flying Group	
G-CCBM	Aerotechnik EV-97 Eurostar	J. S. Baldwin & B. Hunter	
G-CCBN	Scale Replica SE-5a (80105/19)	S. P. Rollason	
G-CCBR	Jodel D.120	A. & S. Dunne	
G-CCBT	Cameron Z-90 balloon	I. J. Sharpe	
G-CCBW	Sherwood Ranger	A. L. Virgoe	
G-CCBX	Raj Hamsa X'Air 133 (2)	S. Hunt	
G-CCBZ	Aero Designs Pulsar	J. M. Keane	
G-CCCA	VS.509 Spitfire Tr.IX (PV202)	Spitfire Productions PV202 Ltd (G-TRIX)	
G-CCCB	Thruster T.600N 450	J. Hartland	
G-CCCD	Mainair Pegasus Quantum 15	I. J. Gornall	
G-CCCE	Aeroprakt A 22 Foxbat	P. Sykoo	
G-CCCF	Thruster T.600N 450	Charlie Foxtrot Group	
G-CCCG	Mainair Pegasus Quik	J. W. Sandars	
G-CCCH	Thruster T600N 450	G. Scullion	
G-CCCJ	Nicollier HN.700 Menestrel II	M. P. Wakem	
G-CCCK	Skyranger 912 (2)	J. McKeown	
G-CCCM	Skyranger 912 (2)	Connel Gliding Group	
G-CCCO	Aerotechnik EV-97A Eurostar	D. R. G. Whitelaw	
G-CCCR	Sky Ranger 912(2)	M. Norman	
G-CCCT	Ikarus C42 FB UK	M. M. Donnelly	
G-CCCV	Raj Hamsa X'Air Falcon 133 (1)	G. J. Boyer	
G-CCCW	Pereira Osprey 2	D. J. Southward	
G-CCCY	Skyranger 912 (2)	A. Watson	
G-CCDB	Mainair Pegasus Quik	M. J. Sunter	
G-CCDD	Mainair Pegasus Quik	G. Clark	
G-CCDF	Mainair Pegasus Quik	R. P. McGann	
G-CCDG	Skyranger 912 (1)	Freebird Group	
G-CCDH	Skyranger 912 (2)	C. F. Rogers	
G-CCDJ	Raj Hamsa X'Air Falcon 582 (2)	A. L. Lyons	

BRITISH CIVIL AIRCRAFT MARKINGS

Notes	Reg	Type	Owner or Operator
	G-CCDO	Mainair Pegasus Quik	S. T. Welsh
	G-CCDP	Raj Hamsa X'Air R.100 (3)	F. C. MacDonald
	G-CCDS	Nicollier HN.700 Menestrel II	J. J. Mason
	G-CCDU	Tecnam P92-EM Echo	G. S. Jefferies
	G-CCDX	Aerotechnik EV-97 Eurostar	G-CCDX Syndicate
	G-CCDY	Skyranger 912 (2)	J. P. & P. A. Cooke
	G-CCDZ	Pegasus Quantum 15-912	M. J. Hilton
	G-CCEA	Mainair Pegasus Quik	G. D. Ritchie
	G-CCEB	Thruster T600N 450	D. S. P. Mantle
	G-CCED	Zenair CH.601UL Zodiac	S. J. Smith
	G-CCEF	Europa	C. P. Garner
	G-CCEH	Skyranger 912(2)	A. C. M. Fleming
	G-CCEJ	Aerotechnik EV-97 Eurostar	P. J. Watson
	G-CCEK	Kiss 400-582 (1)	B. D. Walker
	G-CCEL	Avtech Jabiru UL	F. McMullan
	G-CCEM	Aerotechnik EV-97 Eurostar	R. Wilkinson
	G-CCEN	Cameron Z-120 balloon	T. Hook
	G-CCES	Raj Hamsa X'Air 3203(1)	G. V. McCloskey
	G-CCET	Nova Vertex 28 hang glider	M. Hay
	G-CCEU	RAF 2000 GTX-SE gyroplane	R. Jaggi
	G-CCEW	Mainair Pegasus Quik	A. B. Mackinnon
	G-CCEY	Raj Hamsa X'582 (11)	B. A. Skelding
	G-CCEZ	Easy Raider J2.2	A. W. Gunn
	G-CCFC	Robinson R44 II	Cenegex Ltd
	G-CCFE	Tipsy Nipper T.66 Srs 2	N. S. Dell
	G-CCFG	Dyn'Aéro MCR-01 Club	P. H. Milward
	G-CCFI	PA-32 -260 Cherokee Six	P. Knappertsbusch
	G-CCFK	Europa	P. T. Stephenson
	G-CCFL	Mainair Pegasus Quik	N. Turner
	G-CCFS	Diamond DA40D Star	A. Tullie
	G-CCFV	Lindstrand LBL-77A balloon	Lindstrand Media Ltd
	G-CCFW	WAR Focke-Wulf Fw.190 (9)	A. S. King
	G-CCFX	EAA Acrosport 2	G. Cameron
	G-CCFY	Rotorway Executive 162F	T. E. Twyman
	G-CCFZ	Ikarus C.42 FB UK	H. R. Davis
	G-CCGA	Medway EclipseR	N. Brigginshaw
	G-CCGB	TEAM mini-MAX	A. D, Pentland
	G-CCGH	Supermarine Aircraft Spitfire Mk.26 (AB196)	Cokebusters Ltd
	G-CCGK	Mainair Blade	A. J. Mason
	G-CCGO	Medway EclipseR	D. A. Coupland
	G-CCGW	Europa	A. R. Christie
	G-CCHH	Pegasus Quik	The Quik Group
	G-CCHI	Mainair Pegasus Quik	M. R. Starling
	G-CCHL	PA-28-181 Cherokee Archer III	Archer Three Ltd
	G-CCHM	Kiss 450-582(1)	M. J. Jessup
	G-CCHN	Corby CJ.1 Starlet	M. J. Sharp
	G-CCHP	Cameron Z-31 balloon	M. H. Redman
	G-CCHR	Easy Raider 583 (1)	S. Wilkes
	G-CCHT	Cessna 152	A. J. Gomes
	G-CCHV	Mainair Rapier	B. J. Wesley
	G-CCHX	Scheibe SF.25C Falke	Lasham Gliding Society Ltd
	G-CCID	Jabiru Aircraft Jabiru J430	D. M. Dordoy
	G-CCIF	Mainair Blade	A. R. Vincent & P. W. Dunn
	G-CCII	ICP MXP-740 Savannah VG Jabiru	D. Dance
	G-CCIJ	PA-28R-180 Cherokee Arrow	J. M. Perfettini
	G-CCIK	Skyranger 912 (2)	M. D. Kirby
	G-CCIR	Van's RV-8	G-CCIR Group
	G-CCIT	Zenair CH.701UL	R. K. Thomas
	G-CCIW	Raj Hamsa X'Air 582 (2)	T. Garnham
	G-CCIY	Skyranger 912 (2)	A. M. Donkin
	G-CCJA	Skyranger 912 (2)	G-CCJA Syndicate
	G-CCJD	Pegasus Quantum 15	P. Clark
	G-CCJH	Lindstrand LBL-90A balloon	L. J. Whitelock
	G-CCJI	Van's RV-6	The Doghouse Group
	G-CCJJ	Medway Pirana	J. K. Sargent
	G-CCJK	Aerostar Yakovlev Yak-52	G-CCJK Group
	G-CCJL	Supermarine Spitfire XXVI (PV303)	P. A. Harvie
	G-CCJM	Mainair Pegasus Quik	S. R. Smyth
	G-CCJN	Rans S.6ES Coyote II	W. A. Ritchie
	G-CCJO	ICP-740 Savannah Jabiru 4	M. Taylor
	G-CCJT	Skyranger 912 (2)	Juliet Tango Group

Reg	Type	Owner or Operator	Notes
G-CCJU	ICP MXP-740 Savannah VG	M. D. Gregory	
G-CCJV	Aeroprakt A.22 Foxbat	J. Keats	
G-CCJW	Skyranger 912 (2)	J. R. Walter	
G-CCJX	Europa XS	Pilot in Command Ltd	
G-CCKF	Skyranger 912 (1)	M. Johnson	
G-CCKG	Skyranger 912 (2)	S. Warburton	
G-CCKJ	Raj Hamsa X'Air 133 (3)	A. Robinson	
G-CCKL	Aerotechnik EV-97A Eurostar	G-CCKL Group	
G-CCKN	Nicollier HN.700 Menestrel II	C. R. Partington	
G-CCKO	Mainair Pegasus Quik	K. Walker	
G-CCKR	Pietenpol Air Camper	N. L. Parker & E. S. E. Hibbard	
G-CCKT	Hapi Cygnet SF-2	P. W. Abraham	
G-CCKV	Isaacs Fury II (K7271)	Middlezoy Fury Group	
G-CCKZ	Customcraft A-25 balloon	P. A. George	
G-CCLF	Skyranger 912 (2)	S. Uzochukwu	
G-CCLG	Lindstrand LBL-105A balloon	M. A. Derbyshire	
G-CCLH	Rans S.6-ES Coyote II	N. W. Collins	
G-CCLJ	PA-28-140 Cherokee Cruiser	A. M. George	
G-CCLM	Mainair Pegasus Quik	G. Cole	
G-CCLO	Ultramagic H-77 balloon-	S. J. M. Hornsby	
G-CCLP	ICP MXP-740 Savannah	B. J. Fallows	
G-CCLR	Schleicher Ash 26E	A. J. Darby & M. S. Biggs	
G-CCLS	Comco Ikarus C.42 FB UK	B. D. Wykes	
G-CCLT	Powerchute Kestrel ★	Newark Air Museum/Newark	
G-CCLU	Skyranger Swift 912(1)	Clwb Aero CCLU	
G-CCLX	Mainair Pegasus Quik	R. V. Cannell	
G-CCMC	Jabiru UL 450	F. C. MacDonald	
G-CCMD	Mainair Pegasus Quik	J. T. McCormack	
G-CCME	Mainair Pegasus Quik	S. A. Harvey	
G-CCMH	M.2H Hawk Major	M. C. Ochoa	
G-CCMJ	Easy Raider J2.2 (1)	G. F. Clews	
G-CCMK	Raj Hamsa X'Air Falcon	M. J. J. Clutterbuck	
G-CCML	Mainair Pegasus Quik	G-CCML Syndicate	
G-CCMM	Dyn'Aéro MCR-01 ULC Banbi	C. P. Anstey	
G-CCMN	Cameron C-90 balloon	C. Butler	
G-CCMO	Aerotechnik EV-97A Eurostar	M. P. Henderson	
G-CCMP	Aerotechnik EV-97A Eurostar	H. J. Webber	
G-CCMR	Robinson R22 Beta	Sloane Charter	
G-CCMT	Thruster T.600N 450	M. J. Carlos	
G-CCMW	CFM Shadow Srs.DD	K. H. Creed	
G-CCMZ	Best Off Skyranger 912 (2)	D. D. Appleford	
G-CCND	Van's RV-9A	P. Webb	
G-CCNE	Mainair Pegasus Quantum 15	G. D. Barker	
G-CCNF	Raj Hamsa X'Air Falcon 912(2)	G-CCNF Group	
G-CCNG	Flight Design CT2K	C. McCallum	
G-CCNH	Rans S.6ES Coyote II	R. S. Noremberg	
G-CCNJ	Skyranger 912 (1)	K. Garnett	
G-CCNL	Raj Hamsa X'Air Falcon 133(1)	A. F. Walters	
G-CCNM	Mainair Pegasus Quik	P. A. Lee	
G-CCNP	Flight Design CT2K	D. L. Goode	
G-CCNR	Skyranger 912 (2)	P. Horsley	
G-CCNS	Skyranger 912 (2)	P. V. Griffiths	
G-CCNT	Ikarus C.42 FB80	November Tango Group	
G-CCNW	Mainair Pegasus Quantum Lite	M. J. Hyde	
G-CCNX	CAB CAP-10B	Arc Input Ltd	
G-CCOB	Aero C.104 Jungmann	C. M. Tomkins	
G-CCOC	Mainair Pegasus Quantum 15	E. R. Termini	
G-CCOF	Rans S.6-ESA Coyote II	C. R. Cawley	
G-CCOG	Mainair Pegasus Quik	P. J. Kirkpatrick	
G-CCOH	Raj Hamsa X'Air Falcon Jabiru(3)	D. M. Wilson	
G-CCOM	Westland Lysander IIIA (V9312)	Lysander V9312 Ltd	
G-CCOP	Ultramagic M-105 balloon	M. E. J. Whitewood	
G-CCOR	Sequoia F.8L Falco	D. J. Thoma	
G-CCOU	Mainair Pegasus Quik	D. E. J. McVicker	
G-CCOV	Europa XS	B. C. Barton	
G-CCOW	Mainair Pegasus Quik	S. J. Gibson	
G-CCOY	NA AT-6D Harvard II	Classic Flying Machine Collection Ltd	
G-CCOZ	Monnett Sonerai II	W. H. Cole	
G-CCPD	Campbell Cricket Mk.4	Tomas UK Trust	
G-CCPE	Steen Skybolt	C. Moore	
G-CCPF	Skyranger 912 (2)	S. M. Bayne	

Notes	Reg	Type	Owner or Operator
	G-CCPG	Mainair Pegasus Quik	A.W. Lowrie
	G-CCPH	Cosmik EV-97 TeamEurostar UK	A. H. Woolley
	G-CCPJ	Cosmik EV-97 TeamEurostar UK	J. S. Webb
	G-CCPL	Skyranger 912 (2)	B. Drinkwater
	G-CCPM	Mainair Blade 912	P. S. Davies
	G-CCPN	Dyn'Aéro MCR-01 Club	J. C. Thompson
	G-CCPP	Cameron 70 Concept balloon	Sarnia Balloon Group
	G-CCPS	Ikarus C.42 FB100 VLA	M. J. Harrison
	G-CCPT	Cameron Z-90 balloon	A. Hall
	G-CCPV	Jabiru J400	J. R. Lawrence
	G-CCRF	Mainair Pegasus Quantum 15	C. J. Middleton
	G-CCRG	Ultramagic M-77 balloon	T. B. Davis
	G-CCRI	Raj Hamsa X'Air 582 (5)	D. K. Beaumont
	G-CCRJ	Europa	F. M. Ward
	G-CCRK	Luscombe 8A Silvaire	J. R. Kimberley
	G-CCRN	Thruster T.600N 450	S. Maddock & B. J. Clews
	G-CCRP	Thruster T.600N 450	W. B. Breakell (G-ULLY)
	G-CCRV	Skyranger 912 (1)	D. Matthews
	G-CCRW	Mainair Pegasus Quik	M. L. Cade
	G-CCRX	Jabiru UL-450	M. Everest
	G-CCSD	Mainair Pegasus Quik	A. D. Dias
	G-CCSF	Mainair Pegasus Quik	D. Seiler
	G-CCSH	Mainair Pegasus Quik	R. C. Moore
	G-CCSL	Mainair Pegasus Quik	A. J. Harper
	G-CCSP	Cameron N-77 balloon	D. Berg
	G-CCST	PA-32R-301 Saratoga	A. R. Whibley
	G-CCSX	Skyranger 912(1)	T. Jackson
	G-CCSY	Mainair Pegasus Quik	G. J. Gibson
	G-CCTA	Zenair CH.601UL Zodiac	J. R. Hunt
	G-CCTC	Mainair Pegasus Quik	D. R. Purslow
	G-CCTD	Mainair Pegasus Quik	R. N. S. Taylor
	G-CCTE	Dyn'Aéro MCR-01 Banbi	C. J. McInnes
	G-CCTG	Van's RV-3B	E. R. J. Hicks
	G-CCTH	Cosmik EV-97 TeamEurostar UK	T. C. Hilder
	G-CCTI	Cosmik EV-97 TeamEurostar UK	TI Group
	G-CCTM	Mainair Blade	J. N. Hanso
	G-CCTO	Aerotechnik EV-97 Eurostar	T. A. Dobbins
	G-CCTP	Aerotechnik EV-97 Eurostar	P. E. Rose
	G-CCTR	Skyranger 912(1)	K. Mallin
	G-CCTT	Cessna 172S	Highland Aviation Training Ltd
	G-CCTU	Mainair Pegasus Quik	N. J. Lindsay
	G-CCTZ	Mainair Pegasus Quik 912S	S. Baker
	G-CCUA	Mainair Pegasus Quik	J. B. Crawford
	G-CCUB	Piper J-3C-65 Cub	G. Cormack
	G-CCUC	Skyranger J2.2(1)	R. Marrs
	G-CCUH	RAF 2000 GTX-SE	V. G. Freke
	G-CCUI	Dyn'Aéro MCR-01 Banbi	T. White
	G-CCUL	Europa XS	Europa 6
	G-CCUR	Mainair Pegasus Quantum 15-912	T. A. Daniel
	G-CCUT	Aerotechnik EV-97 Eurostar	W. P. Hearn
	G-CCUY	Europa	D. B. Neave
	G-CCVA	Aerotechnik EV-97 Eurostar	K. J. Scott
	G-CCVE	Raj Hamsa X'Air Jabiru (3)	G. J. Slater
	G-CCVF	Lindstrand LBL-105 balloon	Alan Patterson Design
	G-CCVH	Curtiss H-75A-1 (82:8)	The Fighter Collection
	G-CCVI	Zenair CH.701 SP	P. J. Bunce
	G-CCVK	Cosmik EV-97 TeamEurostar UK	J. Holditch
	G-CCVL	Zenair CH.601XL Zodiac	A. Y-T. Leungr & G. Constantine
	G-CCVM	Van's RV-7	M. J. Mothershaw
	G-CCVN	Jabiru SP-470	G-CCVN Syndicate
	G-CCVR	Skyranger 912(2)	M. J. Batchelor
	G-CCVS	Van's RV-6A	L. Jensen (G-CCVC)
	G-CCVU	Robinson R22 Beta II	HQ Aviation Ltd
	G-CCVX	Mainair Tri Flyer 330	J. A. Shufflebotham
	G-CCVZ	Cameron O-120 balloon	T. M. C. McCoy
	G-CCWC	Skyranger 912	E. S. Jones
	G-CCWH	MCR-01 Banbi	E. J. Partridge & J. M. Keane
	G-CCWL	Mainair Blade	A. German
	G-CCWM	Robin DR.400/180	J. L. Dixon
	G-CCWO	Mainair Pegasus Quantum 15-912	T. Robinson
	G-CCWP	Cosmik EV-97 TeamEurostar UK	Airsports

Reg	Type	Owner or Operator	Notes
G-CCWU	Skyranger 912(1)	A. R. Young	
G-CCWV	Mainair Pegasus Quik	C. Buttery	
G-CCWW	Mainair Pegasus Quantum 15-912	C. J. Eddies	
G-CCXA	Boeing Stearman A75N-1 Kaydet (669)	Skymax (Aviation) Ltd	
G-CCXB	Boeing Stearman B75N1 (699)	S. Kendall	
G-CCXC	Avion Mudry CAP-10B	J. E. Keighley	
G-CCXF	Cameron Z-90 balloon	A. J. M. Pollock	
G-CCXG	SE-5A (replica) (C5430)	C. Morris	
G-CCXH	Skyranger J2.2	M. J. O'Connor	
G-CCXK	Pitts S-1S Special	P. G. Bond	
G-CCXM	Skyranger 912(1)	P. Batchelor	
G-CCXN	Skyranger 912(1)	G. D. P. Clouting	
G-CCXO	Corby CJ-1 Starlet	RW Coldstore Construction Ltd	
G-CCXP	ICP Savannah Jabiru	D. Ballard	
G-CCXS	Montgomerie-Bensen B.8MR	A. Morgan	
G-CCXT	Mainair Pegasus Quik	C. F. Yaxley	
G-CCXV	Thruster T.600N 450	R. J. Humphries	
G-CCXW	Thruster T.600N 450	D. J. Atkinson	
G-CCXX	AG-5B Tiger	P. D. Lock	
G-CCXZ	Mainair Pegasus Quik	M. Innes	
G-CCYB	Escapade 912(1)	M. R. Grunwell	
G-CCYE	Mainair Pegasus Quik	P. M. Scrivener	
G-CCYG	Robinson R44 II	Ed Murray & Sons Ltd	
G-CCYJ	Mainair Pegasus Quik	J. Grey	
G-CCYL	MainairPegasus Quantum 15	D. Pattenden & S. Haines	
G-CCYM	Skyranger 912(2)	K. Roach, P. Hannah, M. M. Galloway & B. Skidmore	
G-CCYO	Christen Eagle II	P. C. Woolley	
G-CCYP	Colt 56A balloon	Magical Adventures Ltd	
G-CCYR	Ikarus C.42 FB80	Airbourne Aviation Ltd	
G-CCYS	Cessna F.182Q	C. J. Griffiths	
G-CCYU	Ultramagic S-90 balloon	J. Francis	
G-CCYY	PA-28-161 Cherokee Warrior II	Flightcontrol Ltd	
G-CCYZ	Dornier EKW C3605	CW Tomkins Ltd	
G-CCZB	Mainair Pegasus Quantum 15	J. A. Crofts	
G-CCZD	Van's RV-7	A. P. Hatton & E. A. Stokes	
G-CCZJ	Raj Hamsa X' Air Falcon 582	E. G. Williams	
G-CCZK	Zenair CH.601UL Zodiac	D. C. Woods	
G-CCZL	Ikarus C-42 FB80	Shadow Aviation Ltd	
G-CCZM	Skyranger 912S	N. A. Higgins	
G-CCZN	Rans S.6-ES Coyote II	S. Rose	
G-CCZO	Mainair Pegasus Quik	P. G. Penhaligan	
G-CCZR	Medway EclipseR	G. A. Hazell	
G-CCZS	Raj Hamsa X'Air Falcon 582	S. Siddiqui	
G-CCZT	Van's RV-9A	J. C. A. Wheeler	
G-CCZV	PA-28-151 Warrior	London School of Flying Ltd	
G-CCZX	Robin DR.400/180	Robin Flying Club Ltd	
G-CCZY	Van's RV-9A	W. G. E. James	
G-CCZZ	Aerotechnik EV-97 Eurostar	B. M Starck & J. P. Aitken	
G-CDAB	Glasair Super IISRG	G. Marsango	
G-CDAC	Cosmik EV-97 TeamEurostar	A. Munn	
G-CDAD	Lindstrand LBL-25A balloon	G. Gray	
G-CDAE	Van's RV-6A	The Alpha Echo Group	
G-CDAI	Robin DR.400/140B	D. Hardy & J. Sambrook	
G-CDAO	Mainair Pegasus Quantum 15 -912	T. G. Jones	
G-CDAP	Cosmik EV-97 TeamEurostar UK	D. P. Webb	
G-CDAR	Mainair Pegasus Quik	A. A. Gaskin	
G-CDAT	ICP MXP-740 Savannah Jabiru	R. J. Duckett	
G-CDAX	Mainair Pegasus Quik	L. Hurman	
G-CDAY	Skyranger 912	C. Ricketts	
G-CDAZ	Aerotechnik EV-97 Eurostar	K. M. Howell	
G-CDBA	Skyranger 912(1)	G-CDBA Group	
G-CDBB	Mainair Pegasus Quik	J. McLaughlin	
G-CDBC	Aviation Enterprises Magnum	A. M. Fleming	
G-CDBD	Jabiru J400	I. D. Rutherford	
G-CDBG	Robinson R22 Beta	Jepar Rotorcraft	
G-CDBJ	Yakovlev Yak-3	C. E. Bellhouse	
G-CDBK	Rotorway Executive 162F	Southern Helicopters Ltd	
G-CDBM	Robin DR.400/180	C. M. Simmonds	
G-CDBO	Skyranger 912	R. I. Ferguson	

Notes	Reg	Type	Owner or Operator
	G-CDBR	Stolp SA.300 Starduster Too	J. J. Warren
	G-CDBU	Ikarus C.42 FB100	G. A. Evans
	G-CDBV	Skyranger 912S	J. Devine
	G-CDBX	Europa XS	J. Marston
	G-CDBY	Dyn'Aero MCR-01 ULC	A. Thornton
	G-CDBZ	Thruster T.600N 450	Alan & Andy BZ
	G-CDCC	Aerotechnik EV-97 Eurostar	T. W. Carr
	G-CDCD	Van's RVF-9A	RV9ers
	G-CDCE	Avions Mudry CAP-10B	The Tiger Club (1990) Ltd
	G-CDCF	Pegasus Quik	S. E. Lyden
	G-CDCG	Ikarus C.42 FB UK	N. E. Ashton
	G-CDCH	Skyranger 912(1)	M. D. Protheroe
	G-CDCI	Pegasus Quik	R. J. Allarton
	G-CDCK	Pegasus Quik	K. Foyen
	G-CDCM	Ikarus C.42 FB UK	S. T. Allen
	G-CDCO	Ikarus C.42 FB UK	P. W. H. Streeter
	G-CDCP	Avtech Jabiru J400	G. G. Johnstone
	G-CDCR	Savannah Jabiru(1)	G. W. McKinstry
	G-CDCS	PA-12 Super Cruiser	F. R. A. Cummings
	G-CDCT	Cosmik EV-97 TeamEurostar UK	G. R. Nicholson
	G-CDCV	Robinson R44 II	3GR Comm Ltd
	G-CDCW	Escapade 912 (1)	W. B. Breakell
	G-CDDA	SOCATA TB20 Trinidad	N. W. Kean
	G-CDDB	Schemmp-Hirth Standard Cirrus	C. E. Hooper
	G-CDDG	PA-26-161 Cherokee Warrior II	Jaleasing Ltd
	G-CDDI	Thruster T.600N 450	I. W. Barlow
	G-CDDK	Cessna 172M	B. K. & W. G. Ranger
	G-CDDN	Lindstrand LBL 90A balloon	Flying Enterprises
	G-CDDO	Raj Hamsa X'Air 133(2)	S. Bain
	G-CDDP	Lazer Z.230	G-CDDP Flying Group
	G-CDDR	Skyranger 582(1)	S. E. Buckle
	G-CDDS	Zenair CH.601HD	P. R. Dalton
	G-CDDU	Skyranger 912(2)	V. P. Robson
	G-CDDW	Aeroprakt A.22 Foxbat	A. J. Hilton
	G-CDDX	Thruster T.600N 450	S. R. Davis
	G-CDDY	Van's RV-8	J. F. D. Hallam
	G-CDEF	PA-28-161 Cadet	Falcon Flying Services Ltd
	G-CDEH	ICP MXP-740 Savannah VG LS(1)	D. C. Crawley
	G-CDEM	Raj Hamsa X' Air 133	R. J. Froud
	G-CDEN	Pegasus Quantum 15-912	M. P. Shea
	G-CDEO	PA-28-180 Cherokee	Perranporth Flying Club Ltd
	G-CDEP	Cosmik EV-97 TeamEurostar	EP Group
	G-CDET	Culver LCA Cadet	J. Gregson
	G-CDEU	Lindstrand LBL-90B balloon	K. P. Storey
	G-CDEV	Escapade 912 (1)	G-CDEV Escapade Tailwheel Group
	G-CDEW	Pegasus Quik	S. D. Sparrow
	G-CDEX	Europa	K. Martindale
	G-CDFD	Scheibe SF.25C Falke	The Royal Air Force Gliding and Soaring Association
	G-CDFG	Mainair Pegasus Quik	A. G. Fish
	G-CDFJ	Skyranger 912(1)	G-CDFJ Flying Group
	G-CDFM	Raj Hamsa X'Air 582 (5)	W. A. Keel-Stocker
	G-CDFN	Thunder Ax7-77 balloon	E. Rullo/Italy
	G-CDFO	Mainair Pegasus Quik	The Foxtrot Oscars
	G-CDFR	Mainair Pegasus Quantum 15	P. D. J. Davies
	G-CDFU	Rans S.6-ES Coyote II	G. Mudd
	G-CDFW	Lovegrove Sheffy Gyroplane ★	Norfolk and Suffolk Aviation Museum/Flixton
	G-CDGA	Taylor JT.1 Monoplane	T. P. Eglinton
	G-CDGB	Rans S.6-116 Coyote	S. Penoyre
	G-CDGC	Mainair Pegasus Quik	E. A. McCabe
	G-CDGD	Mainair Pegasus Quik	T. A. Dockrell
	G-CDGE	Edge XT912-IIIB	M & G Flight
	G-CDGF	Ultramagic S-105 balloon	D. & K. Bareford
	G-CDGH	Rans S.6-ES Coyote	R. W. Keene
	G-CDGI	Thruster T600N 450	P. Asbridge
	G-CDGN	Cameron C-90 balloon	M. C. Gibbons
	G-CDGO	Mainair Pegasus Quik	C. R. Dunford
	G-CDGR	Zenair CH 701UL	J. H. Cameron-Pimblett
	G-CDGS	AG-5B Tiger	R. K. Hyatt
	G-CDGT	Montgomerie-Parsons Two Place g/p	J. B. Allan
	G-CDGU	VS.300 Spitfire I (X4276)	Peter Monk Ltd

Reg	Type	Owner or Operator	Notes
G-CDGW	PA-28-181 Archer III	B. F. Millet	
G-CDGX	Mainair Pegasus Quantum 15-912	S. R. Green	
G-CDGY	VS.349 Spitfire Mk VC	Warbird Experiences Ltd	
G-CDHA	Skyranger 912S(1)	S. R. Langtry	
G-CDHC	Slingsby T67C	R. S. Stent	
G-CDHE	Skyranger 912(2)	CDHE Group	
G-CDHG	Mainair Pegasus Quik	T. W. Pelan	
G-CDHJ	Lindstrand LBL-90B balloon	Lindstrand Hot Air Balloons Ltd	
G-CDHM	Mainair Pegasus Quantum 15	G. A. Gamblin	
G-CDHO	Raj Hamsa X'Air 133 (1)	C. J. Tomlin	
G-CDHR	Ikarus C.42 FB80	H. D. Colliver	
G-CDHU	Skyranger Swift 912 (1)	G-CDHU Flying Group	
G-CDHX	Aeroprakt A.22 Foxbat	M. D. Aston	
G-CDHY	Cameron Z-90 balloon	S. F. Caie	
G-CDHZ	Nicollier HN.700 Menestrel II	G. E. Whittaker	
G-CDIF	Mudry CAP-10B	J. D. Gordon	
G-CDIG	Aerotechnik EV-97 Eurostar	R. D. Masters	
G-CDIJ	Skyranger 912 (2)	J. Ridley & R. P. Carter	
G-CDIL	Mainair Pegasus Quantum 15-912	G. E. Blackstone	
G-CDIO	Cameron Z-90 balloon	Slowfly Montgolfiere SNC/Italy	
G-CDIR	Mainair Pegasus Quantum 15-912	M. Crane	
G-CDIT	Cameron Z-105 balloon	Bailey Balloons Ltd	
G-CDIU	Skyranger 912S(1)	A. C. McAllister	
G-CDIX	Ikarus C.42 FB.100	T. G. Greenhill & J. G. Spinks	
G-CDIY	Aerotechnik EV-97A Eurostar	R. E. Woolsey	
G-CDIZ	Escapade 912(3)	S. J. M. Morling	
G-CDJB	Van's RV-4	J. N. Giller	
G-CDJD	ICP MXP-740 Savannah Jabiru (4)	V. S. Jamwal	
G-CDJE	Thruster T.600N 450	R. J. Stamp	
G-CDJF	Flight Design CT2K	M. L. Twynham	
G-CDJG	Zenair 601UL Zodiac	G-CDJG Group	
G-CDJI	UltraMagic M-120 balloon	Ascension Cider Co.Ltd	
G-CDJJ	IAV Yakovlev Yak-52	Verdin Group Holdings Ltd	
G-CDJK	Ikarus C.42 FB 80	Hull Aero Club Ltd	
G-CDJL	Avtech Jabiru J400	M. C. Davies	
G-CDJP	Skyranger 912(2)	I. A. Cunningham	
G-CDJR	Cosmik EV-97 TeamEurostar	G. Carr	
G-CDJU	CASA 1.131E Jungmann Srs.1000	P. Gaskell	
G-CDJV	Beech A.36 Bonanza	B. C. Faulkner	
G-CDJY	Cameron C-80 balloon	British Airways PLC	
G-CDKE	Rans S6-ES Coyote II	J. E. Holloway	
G-CDKF	Escapade 912 (1)	K. R. Butcher	
G-CDKH	Skyranger 912S (1)	C. Lenaghan	
G-CDKI	Skyranger 912S (1)	J. M. Hucker	
G-CDKK	Mainair Pegasus Quik	P. M. Knight	
G-CDKL	Escapade 912 (2)	G. A. Barrall	
G-CDKM	Mainair Pegasus Quik	N. G. Stevens	
G-CDKN	ICP MXP-740 Savannah Jabiru (4)	T. Wicks	
G-CDKO	ICP MXP-740 Savannah Jabiru (4)	J. B. Silverstone	
G-CDKP	Avtech Jabiru UL-D Calypso	J. M. Poole	
G-CDKX	Skyranger J.2 .2 (1)	E. Lewis	
G-CDLA	Mainair Pegasus Quik	S. M. Smith	
G-CDLC	CASA 1.131E Jungmann 2000 (E3B-494:81-47)	R. D. Luder	
G-CDLD	Mainair Pegasus Quik 912S	W. Williams	
G-CDLG	Skyranger 912 (2)	CDLG Skyranger Group	
G-CDLI	Airco DH.9 (E8894)	Aero Vintage Ltd	
G-CDLJ	Mainair Pegasus Quik	J. S. James	
G-CDLK	Skyranger 912S (1)	P. M. Quinn	
G-CDLL	Dyn'Aéro MCR-01 ULC	R. F. Connell	
G-CDLS	Jabiru Aircrraft Jabiru J400	Teesside Aviators Group	
G-CDLW	Zenair ZH.601UL Zodiac	D. W. Allen	
G-CDLY	Cirrus SR20	Talama/France	
G-CDMA	PA-28-151 Cherokee Warrior	Falcon Flying Services Ltd	
G-CDMD	Robin DR.400/500	P. R. Liddle	
G-CDME	Van's RV-7	R. W. H. Cole	
G-CDMF	Van's RV-9A	D. Ridley	
G-CDMH	Cessna P.210N	A. M. Holman-West	
G-CDMJ	Mainair Pegasus Quik	M. J. R. Dean	
G-CDMK	Montgomerie-Bensen B8MR	P. Rentell	
G-CDML	Mainair Pegasus Quik	Flyingscool	

Notes	Reg	Type	Owner or Operator
	G-CDMN	Van's RV-9	T. A. Willcox & R. J. Watts
	G-CDMP	Skyranger 912(1)	J. A. Charlton
	G-CDMS	Ikarus C,42 FB 80	Airbourne Aviation Ltd
	G-CDMT	Zenair CH.601XL Zodiac	H. Drever
	G-CDMV	Skyranger 912S(1)	D. O'Keeffe & K. E. Rutter
	G-CDMX	PA-28-161 Cherokee Warrior II	Clifton Aviation Ltd
	G-CDMY	PA-28-161 Cherokee Warrior II	Redhill Air Services Ltd
	G-CDNA	Grob G.109A	Army Gliding Association
	G-CDND	GA-7 Cougar	IFA Instituto de Formacao Aeronautica LDA/Portugal
	G-CDNE	Skyranger Swift 912S(1)	St. Michael's Skyranger Syndicate
	G-CDNF	Aero Design Pulsar 3	D. Ringer
	G-CDNG	Cosamik EV-97 TeamEurostar UK	S. D. Hunter
	G-CDNH	Mainair Pegasus Quik	T. P. R. Wright
	G-CDNM	Cosmik EV-97 TeamEurostar UK	Athey's Moor Flying School Ltd
	G-CDNP	Cosmik EV-97 TeamEurostar UK	Eaglescott Eurostar Group
	G-CDNS	Westland Gazelle AH.1 (XZ321/D)	Falcon Aviation Ltd
	G-CDNW	Ikarus C.42 FB UK	W. Gabbott
	G-CDNY	Jabiru SP-470	G. Lucey
	G-CDOA	Cosmik EV-97 TeamEurostar UK	Mainair Microlight School Ltd
	G-CDOB	Cameron C-90 balloon	G. T. Holmes
	G-CDOC	Mainair Quik GT450	R. J. Carver
	G-CDOK	Ikarus C.42 FB 100	M. A. McClelland
	G-CDON	PA-28-161 Cherokee Warrior II	G-CDON Group
	G-CDOP	Mainair Pegasus Quik	G. M. Douglas
	G-CDOT	Ikarus C.42 FB 100	A. C. Anderson
	G-CDOV	Skyranger 912(2)	N. Grugan
	G-CDOY	Robin DR.400/180R	Lasham Gliding Society Ltd
	G-CDOZ	Cosmik EV-97 TeamEurostar UK	The Wizards of Oz
	G-CDPA	Alpi Pioneer 300	N. D. White
	G-CDPB	Skyranger 982(1)	A. W. Collett
	G-CDPD	Mainair Pegasus Quik	M. T. Batchelor
	G-CDPE	Skyranger 912(2)	M. J. Cook
	G-CDPG	Crofton Auster J1-A	G-CDPG Group
	G-CDPH	Tiger Cub RL5A LW Sherwood Ranger ST	P. Puddiphatt
	G-CDPL	Cosmik EV-97 TeamEurostar UK	C. I. D. H Garrison
	G-CDPN	Ultramagic S-105 balloon	M. A. Stelling
	G-CDPP	Ikarus C42 FB UK	H. M. Owen
	G-CDPS	Raj Hamsa X'Air 133	C. G. Chambers
	G-CDPV	PA-34-200T Seneca II	M & A Aviation Ltd
	G-CDPW	Mainair Pegasus Quantum 15-912	Hadair Flexwing Flyers
	G-CDPY	Europa	A. Burrill
	G-CDPZ	Flight Design CT2K	M. E. Henwick
	G-CDRC	Cessna 182Q	Warwickshire Aviation Ltd
	G-CDRD	AirBorne XT912-B Edge/Streak III-B	M. A. Medlock
	G-CDRG	Mainair Pegasus Quik	A. W. Leadley
	G-CDRH	Thruster T.600N	Carlisle Thruster Group
	G-CDRI	Cameron O-105 balloon	Snapdragon Balloon Group
	G-CDRJ	Tanarg/Ixess 15 912S(1)	Griffin Toomes Consulting Engineers Ltd
	G-CDRO	Ikarus C42 F880	GS Aviation (Europe) Ltd
	G-CDRP	Ikarus C42 FB80	D. S. Parker
	G-CDRR	Mainair Pegasus Quantum 15-912	S. D. Moran
	G-CDRS	Rotorway Executive 162F	R. C. Swann
	G-CDRT	Mainair Pegasus Quik	R. Tetlow
	G-CDRU	CASA 1.131E Jungmann 2000	M. R. Masters
	G-CDRV	Van's RV-9A	R. J. Woodford
	G-CDRW	Mainair Pegasus Quik	C. J. Meadows
	G-CDRY	Ikarus C42 FB100 VLA	R. A. Lister
	G-CDSA	Mainair Pegasus Quik	F. R. Simpson
	G-CDSB	Alpi Pioneer 200	F. M. Ward
	G-CDSC	Scheibe SF.25C Rotax-Falke	Devon & Somerset Motorglider Group
	G-CDSF	Diamond DA40D Star	Tesla Solutions Ltd
	G-CDSH	ICP MXP-740 Savannah Jabiru (5)	T. W. Whitty
	G-CDSK	Escapade Jabiru(3)	I. B. Lavelle
	G-CDSP	Cameron Racing Car-110 balloon	Magical Adventures Ltd
	G-CDSS	Mainair Pegasus Quik	R. N. S. Taylor
	G-CDTA	Cosmik EV-97 TeamEurostar UK	R. D. Stein
	G-CDTB	Mainair Pegasus Quantum 15-912	D. W. Corbett
	G-CDTG	Diamond DA.42 Twin Star	CTC Aviation Group Ltd
	G-CDTH	Schempp-Hirth Nimbus 4DM	S. J. Clark
	G-CDTI	Messerschmitt Bf.109E (4034)	Rare Aero Ltd

Reg	Type	Owner or Operator	Notes
G-CDTJ	Escapade Jabiru(5)	M. E. Gilbert	
G-CDTL	Avtech Jabiru J-400	M. I. Sistern	
G-CDTO	P & M Quik GT450	A. R. Watt	
G-CDTP	Skyranger 912S (1)	A. L. Thornton	
G-CDTR	P & M Quik GT450	S. M. Furner	
G-CDTU	Cosmik EV-97 TeamEurostar UK	G-CDTU Group	
G-CDTV	Tecnam P2002 EA Sierra	P. I. Morgans	
G-CDTX	Cessna F.152	Brinkley Aviation Ltd	
G-CDTY	Savannah Jabiru (5)	D. A. Cook	
G-CDTZ	Aeroprakt A.22 Foxbat	Colditz Group	
G-CDUH	P & M Quik GT450	N. F. Taylor	
G-CDUK	Ikarus C.42 FB UK	G-CDUK C42 Group	
G-CDUL	Skyranger 912S (2)	M. B. Wallbutton & M. P. D. Cook	
G-CDUS	Skyranger 912S (1)	East Durham Rangers	
G-CDUT	Jabiru J400	A. I. Eskander	
G-CDUU	P & M Quik GT450	A. J. Fillingham	
G-CDUV	Savannah Jabiru(5)	D. M. Blackman	
G-CDUW	Aeronca C3	N. K. Geddes	
G-CDUY	Thunder & Colt 77A balloon	Virgin Balloon Flights	
G-CDVA	Skyranger 912 (1)	R. Dilkes	
G-CDVD	Aerotechnik EV-97 Eurostar	M. A. Dagg	
G-CDVG	Pegasus Quik	I. A. Macadam	
G-CDVH	Pegasus Quantum 15-912	F. Godfrey	
G-CDVI	Ikarus C42 FB80	Airbourne Aviation Ltd	
G-CDVJ	Montgomerie-Bensen B8MR	P. Robinson	
G-CDVK	Savannah Jabiru (5)	R. J. Edgell	
G-CDVL	Alpi Pioneer 300	J. D. Clabon	
G-CDVN	P & M Quik GT450	P. Warrener	
G-CDVR	P & M Quik GT450	W. M. Horne	
G-CDVS	Europa XS	J. F. Lawn	
G-CDVT	Van's RV-6	P. J. Wood	
G-CDVU	Cosmik EV-97 TeamEurostar	Camfly Ltd	
G-CDVV	SA Bulldog Srs. 120/121 (XX626:02, W)	High G Props	
G-CDVZ	P & M Quik GT450	S. M. Green & M. D. Peacock	
G-CDWB	Skyranger 912(2)	C. Booth	
G-CDWD	Cameron Z-105 balloon	Bristol University Ballooning Society	
G-CDWE	Nord NC.856 Norvigie (N856)	T. Bland	
G-CDWG	Dyn'Aéro MCR-01 Club	A. W. Lowrie	
G-CDWI	Ikarus C42 FB80	G-CDWI Syndicate	
G-CDWJ	Flight Design CTSW	G. P. Rood	
G-CDWK	Robinson R44	Poly Commerce SARL/France	
G-CDWM	Skyranger 912S (1)	S. P. McVeigh & P. Fox	
G-CDWO	P & M Quik GT450	M. J. Robbins	
G-CDWR	P & M Quik GT450	I. C. Macbeth	
G-CDWT	Flight Design CTSW	R. Scammell	
G-CDWU	Zenair CH.601UL Zodiac	A. Barnett	
G-CDWX	Lindstrand LBL-77A balloon	L. P. Hooper	
G-CDWZ	P & M Quik GT450	C. L. M. Haywood	
G-CDXD	Medway SLA100 Executive	C. W. Day	
G-CDXF	Lindstrand LBL 31A balloon	R. K. Worsman	
G-CDXG	P & M Pegasus Quantum 15-912	I. C. Braybrook	
G-CDXI	Cessna 182P	E. G. & G. R. Woods	
G-CDXJ	Jabiru J400	J. C. Collingwood	
G-CDXK	Diamond DA42 Twin Star	Tesla Solutions Ltd	
G-CDXL	Flight Design CTSW	A. K. Paterson	
G-CDXM	P & M Quik	C. Wright	
G-CDXN	P & M Quik GT450	M. A. Elliott	
G-CDXP	Aerotechnik EV-97 Eurostar	J. C. Nudd & G. M. Machin	
G-CDXR	Replica Fokker DR.1 (403/17)	W. H. Greenwood	
G-CDXS	Aerotechnik EV-97 Eurostar	T. R. James	
G-CDXT	Van's RV-9	A. B. Wimble	
G-CDXU	Chilton DW.1A	M. Gibbs	
G-CDXV	Campbell Cricket Mk.6A	T. L. Morley	
G-CDXW	Cameron Orange 120 SS balloon	M. T. Joyce	
G-CDXY	Skystar Kitfox Mk.7	M. G. Porter	
G-CDYB	Rans S.6-ES Coyote II	J. A. Matthews	
G-CDYD	Ikarus C42 FB80	C42 Group DYD	
G-CDYL	Lindstrand LBL-77A balloon	J. S. Morge	
G-CDYM	Murphy Maverick 430	C. B. Hopkins	
G-CDYO	Ikarus C42 FB80	M. George	
G-CDYP	Cosmik EV-97 TeamEurostar UK	R. V. Buxton & R. Cranborne	

Notes	Reg	Type	Owner or Operator
	G-CDYT	Ikarus C42 FB80	P. Bayliss
	G-CDYU	Zenair CH.701UL	A. Gannon
	G-CDYX	Lindstrand LBL-77B balloon	R. A. Harris
	G-CDYY	Alpi Pioneer 300	J. A. Crook
	G-CDYZ	Van's RV-7	R. M. Holden
	G-CDZA	Alpi Pioneer 300	J. F. Dowe
	G-CDZB	Zenair CH.601UL Zodiac	A. C. Bell & S. S. Aujla
	G-CDZG	Ikarus C42-FB80	Mainair Microlight School Ltd
	G-CDZO	Lindstrand LBL-60X balloon	R. D. Parry
	G-CDZR	Nicollier HN.700 Menestrel II	S. J. Bowles & C. Antrobus
	G-CDZS	Kolb Twinstar Mk.3 Extra	P. J. Nolan & K. V. Hill
	G-CDZT	Beech B200 Super King Air	RVL Aviation Ltd
	G-CDZU	ICP MXP-740 Savannah Jabiru (5)	P. J. Cheyney
	G-CDZW	Cameron N-105 balloon	Backetorp Byggconsult AB
	G-CDZY	Medway SLA 80 Executive	D. L. & L. D. Pappin
	G-CDZZ	Rotorsport UK MT-03	D. J. Bell
	G-CEAK	Ikarus C42 FB80	Barton Heritage Flying Group
	G-CEAM	Cosmik EV-97 TeamEurostar UK	G-CEAM Group
	G-CEAN	Ikarus C42 FB80	G-CEAN Syndicate
	G-CEAO	Jurca MJ.5 Sirocco	P. S. Watts
	G-CEAR	Alpi Pioneer 300	S. H. Cassia
	G-CEAT	Zenair CH.601HDS Zodiac	T. B. Smith
	G-CEAU	Robinson R44	Mullahead Property Co Ltd
	G-CEAY	Ultramagic H-42 balloon	E. T. J. Shields
	G-CEBA	Zenair CH.601XL Zodiac	Lamb Holm Flyers
	G-CEBC	ICP MXP-740 Savannah Jabiru (5)	J. D. H. Robson
	G-CEBE	Schweizer 269C-1	Scott Aviation (Berkshire) Ltd
	G-CEBF	Aerotechnik EV-97A Eurostar	M. Lang
	G-CEBG	Balóny Kubícek BB26 balloon	M. E. White
	G-CEBH	Tanarg 912S/Bionix 15	G. McAnelly
	G-CEBI	Kolb Twinstar Mk.3	R. W. Livingstone
	G-CEBL	Balóny Kubícek BB20GP balloon	Associazione Sportiva Aerostatica Lombada/Italy
	G-CEBO	Ultramagic M-65C balloon	M. G. Howard
	G-CEBP	EV-97 TeamEurostar UK	M. J. Morson
	G-CEBZ	Zenair CH.601UL Zodiac	I. W. Robertson
	G-CECC	Ikarus C42 FB80	G. P. Burns
	G-CECF	Just/Reality Escapade Jabiru (3)	M. M. Hamer
	G-CECG	Jabiru UL-D	A. N. C. P. Lester
	G-CECH	Jodel D.150	W. R. & J. P. K. Prescott
	G-CECJ	Aeromot AMT-200S Super Ximango	A. & P. W. McEnery
	G-CECK	ICP MXP-740 Savannah Jabiru (5)	A. A. Ross
	G-CECL	Ikarus C42 FB80	R. Fitzgerald
	G-CECP	Skyranger 912(2)	Woobugly Flying Group
	G-CECS	Lindstrand LBL-105A balloon	R. P. Ashfo
	G-CECV	Van's RV-7	D. M. Stevens
	G-CECY	Aerotechnik EV-97 Eurostar	M. R. M. Welch
	G-CECZ	Zenair CH.601XL Zodiac	M. D. White
	G-CEDB	Reality Escapade Jabiru (5)	D. R. Appleton
	G-CEDC	Ikarus C42 FB100	L. M. Call
	G-CEDE	Flight Design CTSW	M. B. Horan
	G-CEDI	Skyranger 912(2)	G-CEDI Syndicate
	G-CEDJ	Aero Designs Pulsar XP	P. F. Lorriman
	G-CEDL	TEAM Minimax 91	A. J. Martin
	G-CEDN	P & M Quik	A. Falconbridge
	G-CEDT	Tanarg/Ixess 15 912S (2)	N. S. Brayn
	G-CEDV	Cosmik EV-97 TeamEurostar UK	G-CEDV Flying Group
	G-CEDX	Cosmik EV-97 TeamEurostar UK	Delta X-Ray Flying Group
	G-CEEC	Raj Hamsa X'Air Hawk	G-CEEC Group
	G-CEED	ICP MXP-740 Savannah Jabiru(5)	R. G. Whyte
	G-CEEG	Alpi Pioneer 300	D. McCormack
	G-CEEI	P & M Quik GT450	G. Kirsch
	G-CEEJ	Rans S-7S Courier	R. Dunn
	G-CEEK	Cameron Z-105 balloon	T. R. Wood & J. Campbell
	G-CEEN	PA-28-161 Cadet	North Weald Flight Training Ltd
	G-CEEO	Flight Design CTSW	S. Best & Z. Newton
	G-CEEP	Van's RV-9A	B. M. Jones
	G-CEER	ELA 07R	F. G. Shepherd
	G-CEEU	PA-28-161 Cadet	White Waltham Airfield Ltd
	G-CEEX	ICP MXP-740 Savannah Jabiru(5)	R. G. Whyte

Reg	Type	Owner or Operator	Notes
G-CEFA	Ikarus C42 FB100 VLA	D. K. Potter	
G-CEFB	Ultramagic H-31 balloon	M. Ekeroos	
G-CEFC	Super Marine Spitfire 26 (RB142)	D. R. Bishop	
G-CEFJ	Sonex	R. W. Chatterton	
G-CEFK	Cosmik EV-97 TeamEurostar UK	S. R. Pike	
G-CEFM	Cessna 152	Westair Flying Services Ltd	
G-CEFP	Jabiru J430	R. W. Brown & D. Kumar	
G-CEFS	Cameron C-100 balloon	A. Dunnington	
G-CEFT	Whittaker MW5-D Sorcerer	B. Outhwaite & M. Cottle	
G-CEFV	Cessna 182T Skylane	C. C. Clinkard	
G-CEFZ	EV-97 TeamEurostar uk	R. E. F. Melia	
G-CEGG	Lindstrand LBL-25A Cloudhopper balloon	M. W. A. Shemitt	
G-CEGH	Van's RV-9A	M. E. Creasey	
G-CEGI	Van's RV-8	Vertical Aerospace Group Ltd	
G-CEGJ	P & M Quik GT450	C. A. Mason	
G-CEGK	ICP MXP-740 Savannah VG Jabiru(1)	A. & C. Kimpton	
G-CEGL	Ikarus C42 FB80	G-CEGL Group	
G-CEGO	Aerotechnik EV-97A Eurostar	D. W. Allen, R. F. McLachlan & J. A. Charlton	
G-CEGP	Beech 200 Super King Air	Airfleet Solutions Ltd	
G-CEGS	PA-28-161 Cherokee Warrior II	Parachuting Aircraft Ltd	
G-CEGT	P & M Quik GT450	S. J. Fisher	
G-CEGU	PA-28-151 Cherokee Warrior	White Waltham Airfield Ltd	
G-CEGV	P & M Quik GT450	S. P. A. Morris	
G-CEGW	P & M Quik GT450	J. A. Wright	
G-CEGZ	Ikarus C42 FB80	M. J. Donnelly	
G-CEHD	Skyranger 912(2)	A. L. Lyons	
G-CEHE	Medway SLA 100 Executive	SLA 100 Group	
G-CEHG	Ikarus C42 FB100	P. E. Thompson	
G-CEHL	Cosmik EV-97 TeamEurostar UK	D. Cholmondeley	
G-CEHM	Rotorsport UK MT-03	1013 Aviation Ltd	
G-CEHN	Rotorsport UK MT-03	Red Hut Ltd	
G-CEHR	Auster AOP.9 (XP241)	M. H. Bichan	
G-CEHS	CAP.10B	M. D. Wynne	
G-CEHT	Rand KR-2	P. P. Geoghegan	
G-CEHV	Ikarus C42 FB80	G-CEHV Share Group	
G-CEHW	P & M Quik GT450	G-CEHW Group	
G-CEHX	Lindstrand LBL-9A balloon	P. Baker	
G-CEIA	Rotorsport UK MT-03	G-CEIA Syndicate	
G-CEIB	Yakovlev Yak-18A (03)	J. Smith	
G-CEID	Van's RV-7	A. Moyce	
G-CEIE	Flight Design CTSW	J. F. Heath	
G-CEIG	Van's RV-7	W. K. Wilkie	
G-CEII	Medway SLA80 Executive	L. J. Addington & W. M. Sharp	
G-CEIL	Reality Escapade 912(2)	T. N. Crawley	
C CEIO	BN-2T-4S Islander	Britten-Norman Aerospace Ltd	
G-CEIP	BN-2T-4S Islander	Britten-Norman Aerospace Ltd	
G-CEIR	BN-2T-4S Islander	Britten-Norman Aerospace Ltd	
G-CEIS	Jodel DR.1050	Prestwick Tailwheel Group	
G-CEIT	Van's RV-7	C. P. Davis	
G-CEIV	Tanarg/Ixess 15 912S(2)	S. J. Taft	
G-CEIW	Europa	R. Scanlan	
G-CEIX	Alpi Pioneer 300	I. M. Walton	
G-CEIZ	PA-28-161 Cherokee Warrior II	The Army Flying Association AAC	
G-CEJD	PA-28-161 Cherokee Warrior III	Blue Cloud Aviation Ltd	
G-CEJE	Wittman W.10 Tailwind	D. Beale	
G-CEJG	Ultramagic M-56 balloon	Dragon Balloon Co.Ltd	
G-CEJI	Lindstrand LBL-105A balloon	R. P. Nash	
G-CEJJ	P & M Quik GT450	D. A. Hendriksen	
G-CEJN	Mooney M.20F	Visual Visionary Ltd	
G-CEJW	Ikarus C42 FB80	A. G. Sparshott	
G-CEJX	P & M Quik GT450	A. J. Huntly	
G-CEJY	Aerospool Dynamic WT9 UK	R. Maude	
G-CEJZ	Cameron C-90 balloon	M. J. Woodcock	
G-CEKC	Medway SLA100 Executive	J. A. Robinson	
G-CEKD	Flight Design CTSW	CT Flying Group	
G-CEKG	P & M Quik GT450	C. R. Whitton	
G-CEKI	Cessna 172P	N. Houghton	
G-CEKJ	Aerotechnik EV-97A Eurostar	D. K. Short & G. Thompson	
G-CEKK	Skyranger Swift 912S(1)	M. S. Schofield	
G-CEKO	Robin DR400/100	Exavia Ltd	
G-CEKS	Cameron Z-105 balloon	Phoenix Balloons Ltd	

Notes	Reg	Type	Owner or Operator
	G-CEKT	Flight Design CTSW	R. L. Green
	G-CEKV	Europa	K. Atkinson
	G-CEKW	Jabiru J430	J430 Syndicate
	G-CELM	Cameron C-80 balloon	Hartland & Evans
	G-CEMA	Alpi Pioneer 200	N. Sigsworth
	G-CEMB	P & M Quik GT450	D. W. Logue
	G-CEMC	Robinson R44 Raven II	Express Charters Ltd
	G-CEME	Aerotechnik EV-97 Eurostar	A. Szczepanek
	G-CEMF	Cameron C-80 balloon	M. Marubbi
	G-CEMI	Europa XS	S. Meester
	G-CEMM	P & M Quik GT450	J. A. Walker
	G-CEMO	P & M Quik GT450	R. R. Vincent
	G-CEMR	Mainair Blade 912	P. J. Kirkpatrick
	G-CEMT	P & M Quik GT450	A. J. Fillingham
	G-CEMU	Cameron C-80 balloon	J. G. O'Connell
	G-CEMV	Lindstrand LBL-105A balloon	R. G. Turnbull
	G-CEMX	P & M Pegasus Quik	C. P. Dean
	G-CEMY	Alpi Pioneer 300	M. A. Gumeniuk & J. J. Bodnarec
	G-CENA	Dyn'Aero MCR-01 ULC Banbi	I. N. Drury
	G-CENB	Cosmik EV-97 TeamEurostar UK	The Scottish Aero Club Ltd
	G-CEND	Cosmik EV-97 TeamEurostar UK	Eurostar Syndicate
	G-CENE	Flight Design CTSW	Barton CT Group
	G-CENG	Skyranger 912(2)	R. A. Knight
	G-CENH	Tecnam P2002-EA Sierra	K. A. Perratt
	G-CENJ	Medway SLA 951	M. Ingleton
	G-CENL	P & M Quik GT450	P. Von Sydow & S. Baker
	G-CENM	Aerotechnik EV-97 Eurostar	N. D. Meer
	G-CENO	Aerospool Dynamic WT9 UK	J. R. Iveson
	G-CENP	Ace Magic Laser	A. G. Curtis
	G-CENS	Skyranger Swift 912S(1)	J. Spence
	G-CENW	Aerotechnik EV-97A Eurostar	November Whiskey Group
	G-CENX	Lindstrand LBL-360A	Wickers World Ltd
	G-CENZ	Aeros Discus/Alize	A. M. Singhvi
	G-CEOB	Pitts S-1 Special	C. Butler & G. G. Ferriman
	G-CEOC	Tecnam P2002-EA Sierra	J. E. Farnworth
	G-CEOG	PA-28R-201 Cherokee Arrow	A. J. Gardiner
	G-CEOH	Raj Hamsa X'Air Falcon ULP(1)	I. K. Hogg
	G-CEOM	Jabiru UL-450	I. G. Harrison
	G-CEON	Raj Hamsa X'Air Hawk	P. J. Disley
	G-CEOP	Aeroprakt A22-L Foxbat	G. F. Elvis
	G-CEOS	Cameron C-90 balloon	G. G. Scaife
	G-CEOU	Lindstrand LBL-31A balloon	R. D. Allen
	G-CEOW	Europa XS	A. P. Howells
	G-CEOX	Rotorsport UK MT-03	A. J. Saunders
	G-CEPL	Super Marine Spitfire Mk.26 (P9398)	S. R. Marsh
	G-CEPM	Jabiru J430	T. R. Sinclair
	G-CEPP	P & M Quik GT450	W. M. Studley
	G-CEPR	Cameron Z-90 balloon	Sport Promotion SRL/Italy
	G-CEPU	Cameron Z-77 balloon	G. Forgione/Italy
	G-CEPV	Cameron Z-77 balloon	John Aimo Balloons SAS/Italy
	G-CEPW	Alpi Pioneer 300	N. K. Spedding
	G-CEPX	Cessna 152	Devon & Somerset Flight Training Ltd
	G-CEPY	Ikarus C42 FB80	GS Aviation (Europe) Ltd
	G-CERB	SkyRanger Swift 912S(1)	I. M. Spence
	G-CERC	Cameron Z-350 balloon	Ballooning Network Ltd
	G-CERD	D.H.C.1 Chipmunk 22 (WK640)	L. E. Burnett
	G-CERE	Cosmik EV-97 TeamEurostar UK	M. Quinn & B. J. Digney
	G-CERF	Rotorsport UK MT-03	C. Taylor
	G-CERH	Cameron C-90 balloon	A. Walker
	G-CERI	Europa XS	N. Musgrave
	G-CERK	Van's RV-9A	P. E. Brown
	G-CERN	P & M Quik GT450	P. M. Jackson
	G-CERP	P & M Quik GT450	RP Syndicate
	G-CERV	P & M Quik GT450	S. T. Cain
	G-CERW	P & M Pegasus Quik	B. F. Levy
	G-CESA	Replica Jodel DR.1050	T. J. Bates
	G-CESD	SkyRanger Swift 912S(1)	B. R. Trotman
	G-CESH	Cameron Z-90 balloon	A. P. Jay
	G-CESI	Aeroprakt A22-L Foxbat	D. N. L. Howell
	G-CESJ	Raj Hamsa X'Air Hawk	G-CESJ Group
	G-CESM	TL2000UK Sting Carbon	Spilsted Sting Group

Reg	Type	Owner or Operator	Notes
G-CESR	P & M Quik GT450	A. A. Kennedy	
G-CEST	Robinson R44	Startrade Heli Gmbh & Co KG/Germany	
G-CESV	Cosmik EV-97 TeamEurostar UK	W. D. Kyle & T. J. Dowling	
G-CESW	Flight Design CTSW	R. M. Savage	
G-CESZ	CZAW Sportcruiser	G-CESZ Group	
G-CETB	Robin DR.400/180	QR Flying Club	
G-CETF	Flight Design CTSW	M. Cackett	
G-CETK	Cameron Z-145 balloon	J. C. M. Greatrix	
G-CETL	P & M Quik GT450	A. R. Young	
G-CETM	P & M Quik GT450	M. Calvert	
G-CETN	Hummelbird	A. A. Haseldine	
G-CETO	Sky Ranger Swift 912S(1)	S. C. Stoodley	
G-CETP	Van's RV-9A	D. Boxall & S. Hill	
G-CETR	Ikarus C42 FB80	R. S. Tullett	
G-CETS	Van's RV-7	TS Group	
G-CETU	Skyranger Swift 912S(1)	A. Raithby	
G-CETV	Skyranger Swift 912S(1)	C. J. Johnson	
G-CETX	Alpi Pioneer 300	D. R. Stansfield	
G-CETZ	Ikarus C42 FB100	Micro Aviation Ltd	
G-CEUH	P & M Quik GT450	J. A. Currie	
G-CEUJ	Skyranger Swift 912S(1)	J. R. C. Brightman & G. J. Burley	
G-CEUL	Ultramagic M-105 balloon	R. A. Vale	
G-CEUM	Ultramagic M-120 balloon	A. J. Gregory	
G-CEUN	Orlican Discus CS	The Royal Air Force Gliding and Soaring Association	
G-CEUU	Robinson R44 II	D. K. Richardson	
G-CEUV	Cameron C-90 balloon	M. S. Stevens & S. Goldring	
G-CEUW	Zenair CH.601XL Zodiac	A. N. Murira	
G-CEUZ	P & M Quik GT450	P. M. Williamson	
G-CEVA	Ikarus C42 FB80	The Scottish Flying Group	
G-CEVB	P & M Quik GT450	B. J. Anderson	
G-CEVC	Van's RV-4	P. A. Brook	
G-CEVD	Rolladen-Schneider LS3	H. P. Miller	
G-CEVE	Centrair 101A	M. C. Bailey	
G-CEVH	Cameron V-65 balloon	P. T. Likorish	
G-CEVJ	Alpi Pioneer 200-M	K. Worthington	
G-CEVM	Tecnam P2002-EA Sierra	J. A. Ellis	
G-CEVN	Rolladen-Schneider LS7	N. Gaunt & B. C. Toon	
G-CEVO	Grob G.109B	BR Aviation Ltd	
G-CEVP	P & M Quik GT450	P. J. Lowe	
G-CEVS	Cosmik EV-97 TeamEurostar UK	Golf Victor Sierra Flying Group	
G-CEVU	Savannah VG Jabiru(4)	I. C. May	
G-CEVV	Rolladen-Schneider LS3	LS3 307 Syndicate	
G-CEVX	Aeriane Swift Light PAS	P. Trueman	
G-CEVY	Rotorsport UK MT-03	Silver Birch Pet Jets Ltd	
G-CEVZ	Centrair ASW-20FL	J. F. Beringer	
G-CEWC	Schleicher ASK-21	London Gliding Club Proprietary Ltd	
G-CEWD	P & M Quik GT450	GS Aviation (Europe) Ltd	
G-CEWE	Schempp-Hirth Nimbus 2	G. J. Scott	
G-CEWF	Jacobs V35 Airchair balloon	G. F. & I. Chadwick & M. G. Roberts	
G-CEWH	P & M Quik GT450	G-CEWH Syndicate	
G-CEWI	Schleicher ASW-19B	S. R. Edwards	
G-CEWL	Alpi Pioneer 200	J. E. Merriman	
G-CEWM	DHC.6 Twin Otter 300	Isles of Scilly Skybus Ltd	
G-CEWO	Schleicher Ka 6CR	D. P. Westcott	
G-CEWP	Grob G.102 Astir CS	G-CEWP Flying Group	
G-CEWR	Aeroprakt A22-L Foxbat	S. Edwards	
G-CEWS	Zenair CH.701SP	A. I. Sutherland	
G-CEWT	Flight Design CTSW	K. Tuck	
G-CEWU	Ultramagic H-77 balloon	C. E. Aindow	
G-CEWW	Grob G.102 Astir CS	Lasham Gliding Society Ltd	
G-CEWX	Cameron Z-350 balloon	Bailey Balloons Ltd	
G-CEWY	Quicksilver GT500	N. Andrews	
G-CEWZ	Schempp-Hirth Discus bT	J. F. Goudie	
G-CEXL	Ikarus C42 FB80	Syndicate C42-1	
G-CEXM	Skyranger Swift 912S(1)	A. F. Batchelor	
G-CEXN	Cameron A-120 balloon	Dragon Balloon Company Ltd	
G-CEXX	Rotorsport UK MT-03	D. Goh	
G-CEYC	DG Flugzeugbau DG-505 Elan Orion	Edgehill Gliding Centre Ltd	
G-CEYE	PA-32R-300 Cherokee Lance	D. C. McH. Wilson	
G-CEYH	Cessna 152	Stapleford Flying Club Ltd	

Notes	Reg	Type	Owner or Operator
	G-CEYI	Cessna 152	E. J. Partridge
	G-CEYK	Europa XS	K. D. Taylor
	G-CEYN	Grob G.109B	G-CEYN Flying Group
	G-CEYP	North Wing Design Stratus/ATF	J. S. James
	G-CEYR	Rotorsport UK MT-03	S. R. Voller
	G-CEYY	Cosmik EV-97 TeamEurostar UK	N. J. James
	G-CEZA	Ikarus C42 FB80	P. J. Morton
	G-CEZB	Savannah VG Jabiru(1)	G. P. Martin
	G-CEZD	Cosmik EV-97 TeamEurostar UK	N. A. Janes
	G-CEZE	Skyranger Swift 912S	Newtownards Microlight Group
	G-CEZF	Cosmik EV-97 TeamEurostar UK	ZF Microlight Group
	G-CEZI	PA-28-161 Cadet	Redhill Air Services Ltd
	G-CEZK	Stolp S.750 Acroduster Too	R. I. M. Hague
	G-CEZL	PA-28-161 Cadet	Chalrey Ltd
	G-CEZM	Cessna 152	Modern Air (UK) Ltd
	G-CEZO	PA-28-161 Cadet	Redhill Air Services Ltd
	G-CEZR	Diamond DA.40D Star	Tesla Solutions Ltd
	G-CEZS	Zenair CH.601HDS Zodiac	G-CEZS Syndicate
	G-CEZT	P & M Aviation Quik GT450	A. A. Greig
	G-CEZU	CFM Streak Shadow SA	N. H. Richardson
	G-CEZW	Jodel D.150 Mascaret	J. C. Carter
	G-CEZX	P & M Aviation Quik GT450	Zulu Xray Group
	G-CEZZ	Flight Design CTSW	A. G. Hawkes
	G-CFAJ	Glaser-Dirks DG-300 Elan	J. P. Borland & R. S. Rand
	G-CFAK	Rotorsport UK MT-03	R. M. Savage
	G-CFAM	Schempp-Hirth Nimbus 3/24.5	T. M. Mitchell
	G-CFAO	Rolladen-Schneider LS4	V. R. Roberts
	G-CFAP	Interplane ZJ-Viera	P. I. Passmore
	G-CFAR	Rotorsport UK MT-03	A. D. Morrow
	G-CFAS	Escapade Jabiru(3)	C. G. N. Boyd
	G-CFAT	P & M Aviation Quik GT450	A. H. C. Morris
	G-CFAV	Ikarus C42 FB80	Airbourne Aviation Ltd
	G-CFAW	Lindstrand LBL-35A Cloudhopper balloon	A. Walker
	G-CFAX	Ikarus C42 FB80	R. E. Parker & B. Cook
	G-CFAY	Sky 120-24 balloon	G. B. Lescott
	G-CFBA	Schleicher ASW-20BL	D. A. Close
	G-CFBB	Schempp-Hirth Standard Cirrus	C. A. J. Allen
	G-CFBC	Schleicher ASW-15B	T. L. Straszewski
	G-CFBE	Ikarus C42 FB80	Andrewsfield Aviation Ltd
	G-CFBH	Glaser-Dirks DG-100G Elan	I. Richardson
	G-CFBL	Sky Ranger Swift 912S(1)	D. Hennings & M. A. Azeem
	G-CFBM	P & M Quantum 15-912	C. W. Welsh
	G-CFBN	Glasflugel Mosquito B	S. R. & J. Nash
	G-CFBT	Schempp-Hirth Ventus bT	P. R. Stafford-Allen
	G-CFBV	Schleicher ASK-21	London Gliding Club Proprietary Ltd
	G-CFBW	DG-100G Elan	M. C. Bailey
	G-CFBY	Sky Ranger Swift 912S(1)	K. Washbourne
	G-CFCA	Schempp-Hirth Discus b	J. A. Woolley
	G-CFCB	Centrair 101	C. R. Partington
	G-CFCD	SkyRanger Swift 912S(1)	D. & L. Payn
	G-CFCE	Raj Hamsa X'Air Hawk	B. M. Tibenham
	G-CFCF	Aerochute Dual	C. J. Kendal & S. G. Smith
	G-CFCI	Cessna F.172N	P. A. Spurrs
	G-CFCJ	Grob G.102 Astir CS	Banbury Gliding Club Ltd
	G-CFCK	Sky Ranger 912S(1)	J. Smith
	G-CFCL	Rotorsport UK MT-03	D. D. Taylor
	G-CFCM	Robinson R44	Newmarket Plant Hire Ltd
	G-CFCN	Schempp-Hirth Standard Cirrus	M. Jardine
	G-CFCP	Rolladen-Schneider LS6-a	M. A. Hall
	G-CFCR	Schleicher Ka-6E	R. F. Whittaker
	G-CFCS	Schempp-Hirth Nimbus 2C	C. Ashman & P. R. Johnson
	G-CFCT	Cosmik EV-97 TeamEurostar UK	Sutton Eurostar Group
	G-CFCV	Schleicher ASW-20	I. R. Gallacher
	G-CFCW	Rotorsport UK MT-03	C. M. Jones
	G-CFCX	Rans S-6-ES Coyote II	V. Asquith & S. Gennery
	G-CFCZ	P & M Quik GT450	P. K. Dale
	G-CFDA	Schleicher ASW-15	N. B. Coggins
	G-CFDE	Schempp-Hirth Ventus bT	R. G. Parker
	G-CFDF	Ultramagic S-90 balloon	Edinburgh University Hot Air Balloon Club
	G-CFDG	Schleicher Ka 6CR	M. A. Benham

Reg	Type	Owner or Operator	Notes
G-CFDI	Van's RV-6	M. W. Richardson	
G-CFDJ	Cosmik EV-97 TeamEurostar UK	M. Jones	
G-CFDK	Rans S-6-ES Coyote II	J. Fleming	
G-CFDL	P & M QuikR	B. Light	
G-CFDM	Schempp-Hirth Discus b	J. L. & T. G. M. Whiting	
G-CFDN	Sky Ranger Swift 912S(1)	Hadair Fixed Wing Flyers	
G-CFDO	Flight Design CTSW	M. Harris	
G-CFDP	Flight Design CTSW	N. Fielding	
G-CFDS	TL2000UK Sting Carbon	A. G. Cummings	
G-CFDT	Aerola Alatus-M	M. J. Reader-Hoer	
G-CFDX	PZL-Bielsko SZD-48-1 Jantar Standard 2	C. Rudy	
G-CFDY	P &M Quik GT450	J. Skidmore	
G-CFEB	Cameron C-80 balloon	N. C. A. Edmunds	
G-CFED	Van's RV-9	E. W. Taylor	
G-CFEE	EV-97 Eurostar	G-CFEE Flying Group	
G-CFEF	Grob G.102 Astir CS	Oxford University Gliding Club	
G-CFEG	Schempp-Hirth Ventus b/16.6	D. K. McCarthy	
G-CFEH	Centrair 101 Pegase	Booker Gliding Club Ltd	
G-CFEI	RAF 2000 GTX-SE	C. J. Watkinson	
G-CFEJ	Schempp-Hirth Discus b	S. E. Jones	
G-CFEK	Cameron Z-105 balloon	R. M. Penny (Plant Hire and Demolition) Ltd	
G-CFEL	Aerotechnik EV-97 Eurostar	F. D. S. Russell	
G-CFEM	P & M Aviation Quik GT450	A. M. King	
G-CFEN	PZL-Bielsko SZD-50-3 Puchacz	The Northumbria Gliding Club Ltd	
G-CFEO	Aerotechnik EV-97 Eurostar	J. B. Binks	
G-CFER	Schempp-Hirth Discus b	2024 Discus B Syndicate	
G-CFES	Schempp-Hirth Discus b	P. G. Webber	
G-CFET	Van's RV-7	J. Astor	
G-CFEV	P & M Pegasus Quik	E. Bowyer & A. Tucker	
G-CFEX	P & M Quik GT450	H. Wilson	
G-CFEY	Aerola Alatus-M	M. S. Hayman	
G-CFEZ	CZAW Sportcruiser	B. R. Whitehead	
G-CFFB	Grob G.102 Astir CS	Astir CS G-CFFB Syndicate	
G-CFFC	Centrair 101A	M. P. Capps	
G-CFFE	Cosmik EV-97 TeamEurostar UK	M. J. Buchanan	
G-CFFF	Pitts S-1S Special	P. J. Roy	
G-CFFG	Aerochute Dual	G. J. Pemberton	
G-CFFN	P & M Quik GT450	S. D. Cox	
G-CFFO	P & M Quik GT450	D. R. Langton	
G-CFFS	Centrair 101A	D. W. McCormick	
G-CFFU	Glaser-Dirks DG-101G Elan	M. W. Price	
G-CFFV	PZL-Bielsko SZD-51-1 Junior	Herefordshire Gliding Club Ltd	
G-CFFX	Schempp-Hirth Discus b	P. J. Richards	
G-CFFY	PZL-Bielsko SZD-51-1 Junior	Scottish Gliding Union Ltd	
G CFGA	VS Spitfire VIII	TSIB Ltd	
G-CFGC	Aeros Discus 15T	I. B. Currer	
G-CFGD	P & M Quik GT450	J. Featherstone	
G-CFGE	Stinson 108-1 Voyager (108-1601:H)	Windmill Aviation	
G-CFGF	Schempp-Hirth Nimbus 3T	C. J. Short	
G-CFGG	Rotorsport UK MT-03	G-CFGG Flying Group	
G-CFGH	Jabiru J160	J. P. Pullin	
G-CFGJ	VS.300 Spitfire I (N3200)	Imperial War Museum	
G-CFGM	Ikarus C42 FB80	G. P. Burns	
G-CFGO	Sky Ranger Swift 912S	K. J. & R. J. Steele	
G-CFGP	Schleicher ASW-19	Norfolk Gliding Club Ltd	
G-CFGR	Schleicher ASK-13	Dartmoor Gliding Society	
G-CFGT	P & M Aviation Quik GT450	G. P. Preston	
G-CFGU	Schempp-Hirth Standard Cirrus	N. S. March	
G-CFGV	P & M Quik GT450	R. Bennett	
G-CFGY	Rotorsport UK MT-03	A. R. Hawes	
G-CFGZ	Flight Design CTSW	A. J. L. Gordon	
G-CFHB	Micro Aviation B.22J Bantam	P. Rayson	
G-CFHC	Micro Aviation B.22J Bantam	L. Hurman	
G-CFHD	Schleicher ASW-20 BL	J. D. Johnson & F. B. Jeynes	
G-CFHF	PZL-Bielsko SZD-51-1	Black Mountains Gliding Club	
G-CFHI	Van's RV-9	M. Pekrzyk	
G-CFHK	Aeroprakt A22-L Foxbat	R. Bellew	
G-CFHL	Rolladen-Schneider LS4	Welsh Mountains Soaring Group	
G-CFHM	Schleicher ASK-13	Lasham Gliding Society Ltd	
G-CFHO	Grob G.103 Twin Astir II	The Surrey Hills Gliding Club Ltd	
G-CFHP	Ikarus C42 FB80	Perranporth Flying Club Ltd	

Notes	Reg	Type	Owner or Operator
	G-CFHR	Schempp-Hirth Discus b	Q5 Syndicate
	G-CFHS	Tchemma T01/77 balloon	J. Dyer
	G-CFHU	Robinson R22 Beta	Cameron and Brown Partnership
	G-CFHW	Grob G.102 Astir CS	D. J. Wedlock & S. P. Rudge
	G-CFHX	Schroeder Fire Balloons G22/24 balloon	T. J. Ellenrieder
	G-CFHY	Fokker Dr.1 Triplane replica (556/17)	P. G. Bond
	G-CFIC	Jodel DR.1050/M1	S. D. Kent & C. J. Turner
	G-CFIE	Rotorsport UK MT-03	The India Echo Flyers
	G-CFIF	Christen Eagle II	Eagle Group FGP
	G-CFIG	P & M Aviation Quik GT450	J. Whitfield
	G-CFIH	Piel CP.1320	T. B. Livermore
	G-CFII	DH.82A Tiger Moth	Avalon Ventures Ltd
	G-CFIJ	Christen Eagle II	V. Kiminius
	G-CFIK	Lindstrand LBL-60X balloon	L. Sambrook
	G-CFIL	P & M Aviation Quik GT450	S. N. Catchpole
	G-CFIM	P & M Aviation Quik GT450	G-CFIM Flying Group
	G-CFIT	Ikarus C42 FB100	D. Pettitt
	G-CFIU	CZAW Sportcruiser	G. Everett & D. Smith
	G-CFIW	Balony Kubicek BB20XR balloon	I. S. Bridge
	G-CFIZ	Sky Ranger 912(2)	Fizzy Flyers
	G-CFJB	Rotorsport UK MT-03	K. J. Whitehead
	G-CFJG	Sky Ranger Swift 912S(1)	M. B. Horan, C. A. S. Powell & A. R. Vincent
	G-CFJH	Grob G.102 Astir CS77	D. B. Harrison
	G-CFJJ	Sky Ranger Swift 912S(1)	M. W. Orr
	G-CFJK	Centrair 101A	G-CFJK Flying Group
	G-CFJL	Raj Hamsa X'Air Hawk	I. S. Doig
	G-CFJM	Rolladen-Schneider LS4-a	I. G. Sullivan
	G-CFJR	Glaser-Dirks DG-300 Club Elan	W. Palmer & C. B. Jones
	G-CFJS	Glaser-Dirks DG-300 Club Elan	K. L. Goldsmith
	G-CFJU	Raj Hamsa X'Air Hawk	G. D. Cackett
	G-CFJW	Schleicher K7	K7 Group
	G-CFJX	DG-300 Elan	Crown Service Gliding Club
	G-CFJZ	Schempp-Hirth SHK-1	C. I. Knowles
	G-CFKA	Rotorsport UK MT-03	M. J. L. Carter
	G-CFKB	CZAW Sportcruiser	KB Flying Group
	G-CFKD	Raj Hamsa X'Air Falcon Jabiru(2)	C. Prince
	G-CFKE	Raj Hamsa X'Air Hawk	W. E. Tinsley
	G-CFKG	Rolladen-Schneider LS4-a	B. W. B. Sonneveld
	G-CFKH	Zenair CH.601XL Zodiac	J. F. Boyce
	G-CFKJ	P & M Aviation Quik GT450	T. A. Dobbins
	G-CFKL	Schleicher ASW-20 BL	G. C. Stallard
	G-CFKM	Schempp-Hirth Discus b	Lasham Gliding Society Ltd
	G-CFKO	P & M Quik GT450	A. Maudsley
	G-CFKP	Performance Designs Barnstormer/Voyager	G. P. Foyle
	G-CFKR	P & M Pegasus Quik	R. D. Ballard
	G-CFKS	Flight Design CTSW	L. I. Bailey
	G-CFKT	Schleicher K 8B	C. A. Ward
	G-CFKU	P & M Aviation Quik GT450	P. W. Frost
	G-CFKW	Alpi Pioneer 200	J. M. Watts
	G-CFKX	Cameron Z-160 balloon	K. R. Karlstrom
	G-CFKY	Schleicher Ka 6CR	J. A. Timmis
	G-CFKZ	Europa XS	G-CFKZ Group
	G-CFLA	P & M Aviation Quik GT450	P. H. Woodward
	G-CFLC	Glaser-Dirks DG-300 Elan	A. M. Carden & R. Waddington
	G-CFLD	Ikarus C42 FB80	D. G. Gilchrist
	G-CFLE	Schempp-Hirth Discus b	D. A. Humphreys
	G-CFLF	Rolladen-Schneider LS4-a	C. J. Davison
	G-CFLG	CZAW Sportcruiser	G. R. Greensall
	G-CFLH	Schleicher K.8B	The Surrey Hills Gliding Club Ltd
	G-CFLI	Europa	A. & E. Bennett
	G-CFLL	Aerotechnik EV-97A Eurostar	I. Galea
	G-CFLM	P & M Pegasus Quik	The JAG Flyers
	G-CFLN	Sky Ranger Swift 912S(1)	D. Bletcher
	G-CFLO	Rotorsport UK MT-03	S. J. Bingham
	G-CFLP	Druine D.31 Turbulent	Eaglescott Turbulent Group
	G-CFLR	P & M Aviation Quik GT450	T. Fowler
	G-CFLW	Schempp-Hirth Standard Cirrus 75	S. A. Law
	G-CFLX	DG-300 Club Elan	The Felix Flying Group
	G-CFLZ	Scheibe SF-27A Zugvogel V	I. Tyler
	G-CFMA	BB03 Trya/BB103	S. Uzochukwu
	G-CFMC	Van's RV-9A	D. J. Forrest

Reg	Type	Owner or Operator	Notes
G-CFMD	P & M Aviation Quik GT450	S. A. C. Curtis	
G-CFMI	Sky Ranger 912(1)	P. Shelton	
G-CFMN	Schempp-Hirth Ventus cT	G. D. Clack & G. B. Baird	
G-CFMO	Schempp-Hirth Discus b	P. D. Bagnall	
G-CFMP	Europa XS	A. T. Cross & I. R. Caesar	
G-CFMR	Ultramagic V-14 balloon	G. J. Winker	
G-CFMS	Schleicher ASW-15	D. A. Logan	
G-CFMT	Schempp-Hirth Standard Cirrus	P. D. Whitters	
G-CFMU	Schempp-Hirth Standard Cirrus	T. J. Williamson	
G-CFMV	Aerola Alatus-M	P. J. Wood	
G-CFMW	Scheibe SF-25C	The Mike Whisky Flying Group	
G-CFMX	PA-28-161 Warrior II	Stapleford Flying Club Ltd	
G-CFNC	Flylight Dragonfly	W. G. Minns	
G-CFND	Schleicher Ka 6E	C. Scutt	
G-CFNE	PZL-Bielsko SZD-38A Jantar 1	T. Robson, J. Murray & I. Gordon	
G-CFNF	Robinson R44 II	Kuki Helicopter Sales Ltd	
G-CFNH	Schleicher ASW-19	Rattlesden Gliding Club Ltd	
G-CFNI	Airborne Edge XT912-B/Streak III-B	Flexaero Ltd	
G-CFNK	Slingsby T.65A Vega	I. P. Goldstraw	
G-CFNL	Schempp-Hirth Discus b	A. S. Ramsay & P. P. Musto	
G-CFNM	Centrair 101B Pegase	D. T. Hartley	
G-CFNO	Skyranger Swift 912S(1)	P. R. Hanman	
G-CFNP	Schleicher Ka 6CR	P. Pollard-Wilkins	
G-CFNR	Schempp-Hirth Discus b	L. A. Stimmel	
G-CFNT	Glaser-Dirks DG-600	G-CFNT Group	
G-CFNU	Rolladen Schneider LS4-a	R. J. Simpson	
G-CFNX	Ixess 13 modified Tanarg 912 Trike	D. A. Eastough	
G-CFNZ	Airborne Edge XT912-B/Streak III-B	C. J. Alderson	
G-CFOB	Schleicher ASW-15B	S. Whybrow	
G-CFOC	Glaser-Dirks DG200/17	R. J. Robinson & K. R. Snell	
G-CFOF	Scheibe SF-27A Zugvogel V	S. P. Melhuish	
G-CFOG	Ikarus C42 FB UK	P. D. Coppin	
G-CFOM	Scheibe SF27A	P. Drake	
G-CFON	Wittman W8 Tailwind	G-CFON Group	
G-CFOO	P & M Aviation Quik R	H. Parry-Jones	
G-CFOP	Cameron Hopping Bag 120 SS balloon	J. Ravibalan	
G-CFOR	Schleicher K 8B	Dorset Gliding Club Ltd	
G-CFOS	Flylight Dragonfly	B. C.C. Middleton	
G-CFOT	PZL-Bielsko SZD-48-3 Jantar Standard 3	A. M. Smith & J. Hemingway	
G-CFOU	Schleicher K7	Eaglescott ASK7 Group	
G-CFOV	CZAW Sportcruiser	J. G. Murphy	
G-CFOW	Skyranger Swift 912S(1)	Oscar Whiskey Syndicate	
G-CFOX	Marganski MDM-1	Born to Fly Trust	
G-CFOY	Schempp-Hirth Discus b	J. E. Thomas	
G-CFOZ	Rolladen-Schneider LS1-f	C. Booker	
G-CFPA	CZAW Sportcruiser	D. L. Nind	
G-CFPB	Schleicher ASW-15B	G-CFPB Syndicate	
G-CFPD	Rolladen-Schneider LS7	W. E. Lozowski	
G-CFPE	Schempp-Hirth Ventus cT	K. Barnes	
G-CFPH	Centrair ASW-20F	J. Hunt	
G-CFPI	P & M Aviation Quik GT450	E. J. Douglas	
G-CFPJ	CZAW Sportcruiser	S. R. Winter	
G-CFPL	Schempp-Hirth Ventus c	M. W. Black	
G-CFPM	PZL-Bielsko SZD-51-1 Junior	Kent Gliding Club Ltd	
G-CFPN	Schleicher ASW-20	J. J. Parker	
G-CFPP	Schempp-Hirth Nimbus 2B	D. W. North	
G-CFPS	Sky 25-16 balloon	G. B. Lescott	
G-CFPT	Schleicher ASW-20	L. Hornsey and L. Weeks Syndicate	
G-CFPW	Glaser-Dirks DG-600	P. B. Gray	
G-CFRC	Schempp-Hirth Nimbus 2B	A. J. Hollings	
G-CFRE	Schleicher Ka 6E	R. A. Foreshew	
G-CFRF	Lindstrand LBL-31A	RAF Halton Hot Air Balloon Club	
G-CFRH	Schleicher ASW-20CL	J. N. Wilton	
G-CFRI	Ultramagic N-355 balloon	Kent Ballooning	
G-CFRJ	Schempp-Hirth Standard Cirrus	M. F. Gilliland	
G-CFRK	Schleicher ASW-15B	FRK Syndicate	
G-CFRM	Skyranger Swift 912S(1)	R. K. & T. A. Willcox	
G-CFRN	Rotorsport UK MTO Sport	R. Marks	
G-CFRP	Centrair 101A Pegase	L. Bourne	
G-CFRR	Centrair 101A	S. B.Marlor	
G-CFRS	Scheibe Zugvogel IIIB	G-CFRS Flying Group	

Notes	Reg	Type	Owner or Operator
	G-CFRT	Cosmik EV-97 TeamEurostar UK	K. A. O'Neill
	G-CFRV	Centrair 101A	Cambridge University Gliding Club
	G-CFRX	Centrair 101A	Essex & Suffolk Gliding Club Ltd
	G-CFRY	Zenair CH 601UL	T. L. Whitcombe
	G-CFRZ	Schempp-Hirth Standard Cirrus	S. G. Lapworth
	G-CFSB	Tecnam P2002-RG Sierra	W. J. Gale and Son
	G-CFSD	Schleicher ASK-13	Dartmoor Gliding Society
	G-CFSF	P & M Aviation QuikR	C. J. Gordon
	G-CFSG	Van's RV-9	Foley Farm Flying Group
	G-CFSH	Grob G.102 Astir CS Jeans	Yorkshire Gliding Club (Proprietary) Ltd
	G-CFSJ	Jabiru J160	G-CFSJ Flying Group
	G-CFSL	Kubicek BB-26Z balloon	M. R. Jeynes
	G-CFSR	DG-300 Elan	A. P. Montague
	G-CFSS	Schleicher Ka 6E	FSS Syndicate
	G-CFSW	Skyranger Swift 912S(1)	C. T. Hanbury-Tenison
	G-CFSX	Savannah VG Jabiru(1)	M. E. Caton
	G-CFTB	Schleicher Ka-6CR	C. Boyd
	G-CFTC	PZL-Bielsko SZD-51-1 Junior	Seahawk Gliding Club
	G-CFTH	PZL-Bielsko SZD-50-3 Puchacz	Buckminster Gliding Club Ltd
	G-CFTI	Aerotechnik EV-97A Eurostar	R. J. Dance
	G-CFTJ	Aerotechnik EV-97A Eurostar	J. A. Turner
	G-CFTK	Grob G.102 Astir CS Jeans	Ulster Gliding Club Ltd
	G-CFTL	Schleicher ASW-20CL	B. Basson
	G-CFTM	Cameron C-80 balloon	P. A. Meecham
	G-CFTN	Schleicher K 8B	Mendip Gliding Club Ltd
	G-CFTO	Ikarus C42 FB80	Solent Flight Ltd
	G-CFTP	Schleicher ASW-20CL	T. Harrod & J. Andrewartha
	G-CFTR	Grob G.102 Astir CS77	The University of Nottingham Students Union
	G-CFTS	Glaser-Dirks DG-300 Club Elan	FTS Syndicate
	G-CFTT	Van's RV-7	P. J. Kinsella
	C-CFTU	Flylight Dragonfly	R. J. Cook
	G-CFTV	Rolladen-Schneider LS7-WL	J. N. Giles
	G-CFTW	Schempp-Hirth Discus b	230 Syndicate
	G-CFTX	Jabiru J160	J. Williamson & J. King
	G-CFTY	Rolladen-Schneider LS7-WL	S. Myall
	G-CFTZ	Aerotechnik EV-97 Eurostar	TZ Flyers
	G-CFUA	Van's RV-9A	I. M. Macleod
	G-CFUB	Schleicher Ka 6CR	D. & J. Osment
	G-CFUD	Skyranger Swift 912S(1)	J. A. Turner
	G-CFUE	Alpi Pioneer 300 Hawk	S. A. Ivell
	G-CFUG	Grob G.109B	Portsmouth Naval Gliding Centre
	G-CFUH	Schempp-Hirth Ventus c	C. G. T. Huck & S. E. Lucas
	G-CFUI	Hunt Wing/Avon 503(4)	R. F. G. Moyle
	G-CFUJ	Glaser-Dirks DG-300 Elan	T. J. Rusin & K. Z. Handzlik
	G-CFUL	Schempp-Hirth Discus b	Discus 803 Syndicate
	G-CFUN	Schleicher ASW-20CL	G-CFUN Group
	G-CFUP	Schempp-Hirth Discus b	Lasham Gliding Society Ltd
	G-CFUR	Schempp-Hirth Ventus cT	A. P. Carpenter
	G-CFUS	PZL-Bielsko SZD-51-1 Junior	Scottish Gliding Union Ltd
	G-CFUT	Glaser-Dirks DG-300 Club Elan	J. W. Ferrington
	G-CFUU	DG-300 Club Elan	J. P. Alexander
	G-CFUV	Rolladen-Schneider LS7-WL	C. H. Braithwaite
	G-CFUW	Rotorsport UK MTO Sport	D. Robertson
	G-CFUX	Cameron C-80 balloon	D. J. Lockhart
	G-CFUY	PZL-Bielsko SZD-50-3 Puchacz	The Bath, Wilts and North Dorset Gliding Club
	G-CFUZ	CZAW Sportcruiser	T. Dounias
	G-CFVC	Schleicher ASK-13	Mendip Gliding Club Ltd
	G-CFVE	Schempp-Hirth Nimbus 2	L. Mitchell
	G-CFVF	Air Creation 582(1)/Kiss 400	G. R. Wilson
	G-CFVH	Rolladen-Schneider LS7	C. C. & J. C. Marshall
	G-CFVJ	Cvjetkovic CA-65 Skyfly	N. D. Hunter
	G-CFVK	Skyranger 912(2)	R. J. McElvogue
	G-CFVL	Scheibe Zugvogel IIIB	M. T. Waite
	G-CFVM	Centrair 101A Pegase	S. H. North
	G-CFVN	Centrair 101A Pegase	S. J. Maddison
	G-CFVP	Centrair 101A Pegase	R. W. A. Bennett
	G-CFVR	Europa XS	D. & J. M. R. Royle
	G-CFVU	Schleicher ASK-13	UWE Students' Union
	G-CFVV	Centrair 101A Pegase	Cambridge Gliding Club Ltd
	G-CFVX	Cameron C-80 balloon	A. Hornshaw
	G-CFVY	Cameron A-120 balloon	C. A. Petre

Reg	Type	Owner or Operator	Notes
G-CFVZ	Schleicher Ka 6E	N. R. Bowers	
G-CFWA	Schleicher Ka 6CR	C. C. Walley	
G-CFWB	Schleicher ASK-13	Cotswold Gliding Club	
G-CFWD	Rotorsport UK MTO Sport	Gower Gyronautics	
G-CFWF	Rolladen-Schneider LS7	M. A. Bobula-Nowak	
G-CFWH	Scheibe SF27A	SF27A G-CFWH Group	
G-CFWJ	P & M Quik GT450	T. Porter & D. Whiteley	
G-CFWK	Schempp-Hirth Nimbus-3DT	G. S. Goudie	
G-CFWM	Glaser-Dirks DG-300 Club Elan	FWM Group	
G-CFWP	Schleicher ASW-19B	P. Chwiejczak	
G-CFWR	Skyranger 912(1)	D. Squire	
G-CFWS	Schleicher ASW-20C	B. N. M. House	
G-CFWT	PZL-Bielsko SZD-50-3 Puchacz	Bidford Gliding & Flying Club Ltd	
G-CFWU	Rolladen-Schneider LS7-WL	T. W. Arscott	
G-CFWV	Van's RV-7	D. K. Sington	
G-CFWW	Schleicher ASH-25E	N. A. C. Norman	
G-CFWY	Centrair 101A Pegase	G-CFWY Group	
G-CFXA	Grob G.104 Speed Astir IIB	Ringmer Speedy Syndicate	
G-CFXB	Schleicher K 8B	Dartmoor Gliding Society	
G-CFXC	Schleicher Ka 6E	M. Jenks	
G-CFXD	Centrair 101A Pegase	Husbands Bosworth Gliding Club Ltd	
G-CFXF	Magni M-16C Tandem Trainer	P. I. Jordan	
G-CFXG	Flylight Dragonfly	J. A. McRae	
G-CFXK	Flylight Dragonfly	N. R. Pettigrew	
G-CFXM	Schempp-Hirth Discus bT	G. R. E. Bottomley	
G-CFXN	CZAW Sportcruiser	P. J. Reilly	
G-CFXO	PZL-Bielsko SZD-50-3 Puchacz	Derbyshire & Lancashire Gliding Club Ltd	
G-CFXP	Lindstrand LBL-105A balloon	Shaun Bradley Project Services Ltd	
G-CFXR	Lindstrand LBL-105A balloon	Lindstrand Media Ltd	
G-CFXS	Schleicher Ka 6E	D. P. Aherne	
G-CFXT	Naval Aircraft Factory N3N-3 (4445/228)	S. K. Woodgate, R. A. Pike & J. L. Arnott	
G-CFXU	Schleicher Ka-6E	C. P. Long & D. M. Martinez-Normand	
G-CFXW	Schleicher K8B	The South Wales Gliding Club Ltd	
G-CFXX	P & M Quik R	G. Bates	
G-CFXY	Schleicher ASW-15B	P. W. Armstrong	
G-CFXZ	P & M Quik R	M. Naylor	
G-CFYA	PZL-Bielsko SZD-50-3 Puchacz	Cairngorm Gliding Club	
G-CFYB	Rolladen-Schneider LS7	A. T. Macdonald & V. P. Haley	
G-CFYC	Schempp-Hirth Ventus b	P. R. H. Starey	
G-CFYD	Aeroprakt A22-L Foxbat	A. P. Fenn	
G-CFYF	Schleicher ASK-21	London Gliding Club Proprietary Ltd	
G-CFYG	Glasflugel Club Libelle 205	FYG Syndicate	
G-CFYH	Rolladen-Schneider LS4-a	G. W. & C. A. Craig	
G-CFYI	Grob G.102 Astir CS	R. D. Dance	
G-CFYJ	Schempp-Hirth Standard Cirrus	F. J. Norton	
G-CFYK	Rolladen-Schneider LS7-WL	S. D. S. Smith & S. K. Haigh	
G-CFYL	PZL-Bielsko SZD-50-3 Puchacz	Bidford Gliding & Flying Club Ltd	
G-CFYM	Schempp-Hirth Discus bT	T. Wright	
G-CFYN	Schempp-Hirth Discus b	N. White & P. R. Foulger	
G-CFYO	P & M Quik R	M. A. Sandwith	
G-CFYR	LET L-23 Super Blanik	G-CFYR Group	
G-CFYS	Dynamic WT9 UK	J. Jones	
G-CFYU	Glaser-Dirks DG-100 Elan	H. S. Stewart & W. J. Prince	
G-CFYV	Schleicher ASK-21	The Bristol Gliding Club Proprietary Ltd	
G-CFYW	Rolladen-Schneider LS7	J. Douglass	
G-CFYX	Schempp-Hirth Discus b	D. A. Salmon	
G-CFYY	Schleicher ASK-13	Lasham Gliding Society Ltd	
G-CFYZ	Schleicher ASH-25	T. L. L. Clark	
G-CFZB	Glasflugel H201B Standard Libelle	J. C. Meyer	
G-CFZD	Jabiru J430	C. A. & C. D. Spence	
G-CFZF	PZL-Bielsko SZD-51-1 Junior	Devon and Somerset Gliding Club Ltd	
G-CFZI	Savannah Jabiru (5)	J. T., A. L. & O. D. Lewis	
G-CFZJ	VS.388 Seafire F.46	C. T. Charleston	
G-CFZK	Schempp-Hirth Standard Cirrus	Trustees of FZK	
G-CFZO	Schempp-Hirth Nimbus 3	954 Syndicate	
G-CFZP	PZL-Bielsko SZD-51-1 Junior	Midland Gliding Club Ltd	
G-CFZW	Glaser-Dirks DG-300 Club Elan	D. O'Flanagan & G. Stilgoe	
G-CFZX	Rotorsport UK MTO Sport	P. A. Robinson	
G-CFZZ	LET L-33 Solo	The Andreas L33 Group	
G-CGAA	Flylight Dragonfly	G. Adkins	

Notes	Reg	Type	Owner or Operator
	G-CGAB	AB Sportine LAK-12 Lietuva	W. T. Emery
	G-CGAC	P & M Quik GT450	G. Brockhurst
	G-CGAD	Rolladen-Schneider LS3	J. D. Brister
	G-CGAF	Schleicher ASK-21	Lasham Gliding Society Ltd
	G-CGAG	Scleicher ASK-21	Stratford on Avon Gliding Club Ltd
	G-CGAH	Schempp-Hirth Standard Cirrus	J. W. Williams
	G-CGAI	Raj Hamsa X'Air Hawk	C. P. Barber
	G-CGAK	Acrosport II	J. W. Wolfe
	G-CGAM	Schleicher ASK-21	T. R. Dews
	G-CGAN	Glasflugel H301 Libelle	C. J. Davison
	G-CGAO	DHC.1 Chipmunk 22 (1350)	G-CGAO Group
	G-CGAP	Schempp-Hirth Ventus bT	M. C. Bailey & T. M. Mitchell
	G-CGAR	Rolladen-Schneider LS6-c	A. Warbrick
	G-CGAS	Schempp-Hirth Ventus cT	GAS Syndicate
	G-CGAT	Grob G.102 Astir CS	Herefordshire Gliding Club Ltd
	G-CGAU	Glasflugel H201B Standard Libelle	G-CGAU Group
	G-CGAV	Scheibe SF-27A Zugvogel V	T. R. Wallace
	G-CGAX	PZL-Bielsko SZD-55-1 Promyk	Golf Alpha Xray Group
	G-CGAZ	P & M Quik R	I. Tulkan
	G-CGBB	Schleicher ASK-21	University of Edinburgh Sports Union
	G-CGBD	PZL-Bielsko SZD-50-3	The Northumbria Gliding Club Ltd
	G-CGBF	Schleicher ASK-21	London Gliding Club Pty Ltd
	G-CGBG	Rolladen-Schneider LS6-18w	P. M. M. Bonhomme
	G-CGBH	Raj Hamsa X'Air Hawk	S. E. McEwen
	G-CGBJ	Grob G.102 Astir CS	Banbury Gliding Club Ltd
	G-CGBL	Rolladen-Schneider LS7-WL	P. A. Roche
	G-CGBM	Flight Design CTSW	P. P. Duffy
	G-CGBN	Schleicher ASK-21	Essex and Suffolk Gliding Club Ltd
	G-CGBR	Rolladen-Schneider LS6-c	The Eagle Soaring Group
	G-CGBS	Glaser-Dirks DG-300 Club Elan	B. Fulton & J. Thomas
	G-CGBU	Centrair 101A Pegase	N. A. Betteridge
	G-CGBV	Schleicher ASK-21	Wolds Gliding Club Ltd
	G-CGBY	Rolladen-Schneider LS7-WL	R. J. Coles & M. G. Boasman
	G-CGBZ	Glaser-Dirks DG-500 Elan Trainer	Oxford Gliding Company Ltd
	G-CGCA	Schleicher ASW-19B	P. Armstrong
	G-CGCC	PZL-Bielsko SZD-51-1 Junior	Husbands Bosworth Gliding Club Ltd
	G-CGCD	Schempp-Hirth Standard Cirrus	Cirrus Syndicate
	G-CGCE	Magni M16C Tandem Trainer	A. J. A. Fowler
	G-CGCF	Schleicher ASK-23	Cotswold Gliding Club
	G-CGCH	CZAW Sportcruiser	M. R. Wallis
	G-CGCI	Sikorsky S-92A	Bristow Helicopters Ltd
	G-CGCK	PZL-Bielsko SZD-50-3 Puchacz	Kent Gliding Club Ltd (G-BTJV)
	G-CGCL	Grob G.102 Astir CS	Southdown Gliding Club Ltd
	G-CGCM	Rolladen-Schneider LS6-c	J. W. L. Clarke
	G-CGCN	MCR-01 Club	M. H. Rollins
	G-CGCO	Schempp-Hirth Cirrus VTC	R. McLean
	G-CGCP	Schleicher Ka-6CR	I. Burnham & W. T. Weir
	G-CGCR	Schleicher ASW-15B	N. J. Khan
	G-CGCS	Glasflugel Club Libelle 205	D. G. Coats
	G-CGCT	Schempp-Hirth Discus b	P. Allingham
	G-CGCU	PZL-Bielsko SZD-50-3 Puchacz	Peterbourgh & Spalding Gliding Club Ltd
	G-CGCV	Raj Hamsa X'Air Hawk	G. A. J. Salter
	G-CGCX	Schleicher ASW-15	M. A. Durden
	G-CGDA	Rolladen-Schneider LS3-17	J. S. Romanes
	G-CGDB	Schleicher K 8B	Buckminster Gliding Club Ltd
	G-CGDD	Bolkow Phoebus C	G. C. Kench
	G-CGDE	Schleicher Ka 6CR	K6 Syndicate
	G-CGDF	Schleicher Ka 6BR	G-CGDF Group
	G-CGDH	Europa XS	P. S. Mitchell
	G-CGDI	Aerotechnik EV-97A Eurostar	Delta India Group
	G-CGDK	Schleicher K 8B	Dartmoor Gliding Society
	G-CGDL	P & M Quik R	M. A. Lewis
	G-CGDM	Sonex Sonex	M. R. Evans
	G-CGDN	Rolladen-Schneider LS3-17	J. A. Steel
	G-CGDO	Grob G.102 Astir CS	P. Lowe & R. Bostock
	G-CGDR	Schempp-Hirth Discus CS	Discus G-CGDR Syndicate
	G-CGDS	Schleicher ASW-15B	B. Birk
	G-CGDT	Schleicher ASW-24	Tango 54 Syndicate
	G-CGDV	CSA Sportcruiser	S. R. Thomas & J. P. McCreedy
	G-CGDW	CSA PS-28 Sportcruiser	Onega Ltd
	G-CGDX	Orlican Discus CS	D. Bieniasz

Reg	Type	Owner or Operator	Notes
G-CGDY	Schleicher ASW-15B	L. White & P. Bannister	
G-CGDZ	Schleicher ASW-24	J. M. Norman	
G-CGEA	Schleicher Ka 6CR	Scottish Gliding Union Ltd	
G-CGEB	Grob G.102 Astir CS77	T. R. Dews	
G-CGEC	Flight Design CTLS 600 UK	S. Munday	
G-CGEE	Glasflugel H201B Standard Libelle	D. Plumb	
G-CGEG	Schleicher K 8B	The Windrushers Gliding Club Ltd	
G-CGEH	Schleicher ASW-15B	K. Fuks	
G-CGEJ	Alpi Pioneer 200-M	J. White	
G-CGEK	Ace Magic Laser	S. M. Smith	
G-CGEL	PZL-Bielsko SZD-50-3	The Northumbria Gliding Club Ltd	
G-CGEM	Schleicher Ka 6CR	GEM Syndicate	
G-CGEO	CSA Sportcruiser	The Jester Flying Group	
G-CGEP	Schempp-Hirth Standard Cirrus	J. Vickers	
G-CGEW	Rotorsport UK MTO Sport	GS Aviation (Europe) Ltd	
G-CGEX	P & M Quik GT450	A. C. Hayward	
G-CGEY	Julian CD Dingbat	A. H. H. Mole	
G-CGEZ	Raj Hamsa X'Air Hawk	Coyote Ugly Group	
G-CGFB	BB03 Trya/BB103	B. J. Fallows	
G-CGFG	Cessna 152	LAC Flying School	
G-CGFK	Ace Magic Laser	B. B. Adams	
G-CGFN	Cameron C-60 balloon	S. Dyer	
G-CGFO	Ultramagic H-42 balloon	P. Richardson	
G-CGFP	Pietenpol Aircamper	M. D. Waldron	
G-CGFU	Schempp-Hirth Mini-Nimbus C	D. J. L. Graham	
G-CGFY	Lindstrand LBL-105A balloon	Gone Ballooning	
G-CGFZ	Thruster T.600N 450	K. J. Crompton	
G-CGGC	P & M QuikR	Oakley Flyers	
G-CGGG	Robinson R44	Flying Pig & Elstree Helicopters (G-SJDI)	
G-CGGK	Westland Wasp HAS Mk.1 (XT434:455)	Fly Navy Heritage Trust Ltd	
G-CGGM	Cosmik EV-97 TeamEurostar UK	Golf Mike Group	
G-CGGO	Robin DR.400-180 Regent	G. I. J. Thomson & R. A. Hawkins	
G-CGGP	Autogyro MTOSport	J. Taylforth & G. P. Gibson	
G-CGGS	Robinson R44 II	Oakfield Investments Ltd	
G-CGGT	P & M Quik GT450	A. H. Beveridge	
G-CGGV	Rotorsport UK MTO Sport	S. Morris	
G-CGGW	Rotorsport UK MTO Sport	P. Adams	
G-CGGZ	UltraMagic S-90 balloon	R. A. Durham	
G-CGHA	P & M Quik R	V. Donskovas	
G-CGHB	NAMC CJ-6A (61367)	M. J. Harvey	
G-CGHG	P & M Quik GT450	J. & K. D. McAlpine	
G-CGHH	P & M Quik R	C. Pyle & N. Richardson	
G-CGHJ	Staaken Z-21A Flitzer	D. J. Ashley	
G-CGHK	Alpi Pioneer 300 Hawk	M. R. Foreman	
G-CGHL	Rotorsport UK MTOSport	P. K. Hinault	
G-CGHR	Magic Laser	N. P. Power	
G-CGHT	Dyn'Aero MCR-01 Banbi	R. P. Trives (G-POOP)	
G-CGHU	Hawker Hunter T.Mk.8C	Hawker Hunter Aviation Ltd	
G-CGHV	Raj Hamsa X'Air Hawk	H. Adams	
G-CGHW	Czech Sport Aircraft Sportcruiser	Sportcruiser 290 Ltd	
G-CGHZ	P & M Quik R	J. Rockey	
G-CGIA	Paramania Action/Adventure	A. E. C. Phillips	
G-CGIB	Magic Cyclone	S. B. Walters	
G-CGIC	Rotorsport MTO Sport	Gyro Copter HQ Ltd	
G-CGID	PA-31-350 Navajo Chieftain	T. Michaels	
G-CGIE	Flylight Dragonfly	N. S. Brayn	
G-CGIF	Flylight Dragonfly	R. D. Leigh	
G-CGIG	Lindstrand LBL-90A balloon	M. R. Stokoe	
G-CGIH	Cameron C-90 balloon	N. J. Dunnington	
G-CGIL	CZAW Sportcruiser	G-CGIL Group	
G-CGIM	Ace Aviation Magic Laser	C. Royle	
G-CGIN	Paramania Action GT/Adventure	A. E. C. Phillips	
G-CGIO	Medway SLA100 Executive	G-CGIO Syndicate	
G-CGIP	CZAW Sportcruiser	R. T. Miller	
G-CGIR	Remos GX	D. J. S. McClean	
G-CGIS	Cameron Parachutist-110 balloon	M. T. Joyce (G-RIPS)	
G-CGIV	Kolb Firefly	W. A. Emmerson	
G-CGIX	Rotorsport UK MTO Sport	J. W. G. Andrews	
G-CGIY	Piper J3C-65 (330244:C-46)	R. D. Myles	
G-CGIZ	Flight Design CTSW	J. Hilton	
G-CGJB	Schempp-Hirth Duo Discus T	G. J. Basey	

Notes	Reg	Type	Owner or Operator
	G-CGJC	Rotorsport UK MTO Sport	R. Hughes
	G-CGJD	AutoGyro Calidus	Danelander Ltd & Gyro Copter HQ Ltd
	G-CGJE	VS.361 Spitfire IX	Propshop Ltd
	G-CGJF	Fokker E.111 Replica (E37/17)	E. Paterson
	G-CGJJ	P & M Quik R	Juliet Juliet Group
	G-CGJL	CZAW Sportcruiser	G-CGJL Flying Group
	G-CGJM	Skyranger Swift 912S(1)	K. J. Underwood
	G-CGJN	Van's RV-7	T. Stavrou
	G-CGJP	Van's RV-10	G-CGIP Group
	G-CGJS	CZAW Sportcruiser	J. M. Tiley
	G-CGJT	CZAW Sportcruiser	D. F. Toller
	G-CGJW	RAF 2000 GTX-SE	S. V. Hessel
	G-CGJX	SA.341B Gazelle AH Mk.1	The Gazelle Squadron Display Team
	G-CGJZ	SA.341D Gazelle HT Mk.3 (XZ933)	The Gazelle Squadron Display Team
	G-CGKD	Grob G115E Tutor	Babcock Aerospace Ltd
	G-CGKE	Grob G115E Tutor	Babcock Aerospace Ltd
	G-CGKG	Grob G115E Tutor	Babcock Aerospace Ltd
	G-CGKH	Grob G115E Tutor	Babcock Aerospace Ltd
	G-CGKK	Grob G115E Tutor	Babcock Aerospace Ltd
	G-CGKL	Grob G115E Tutor	Babcock Aerospace Ltd
	G-CGKN	Grob G115E Tutor	Babcock Aerospace Ltd
	G-CGKP	Grob G115E Tutor	Babcock Aerospace Ltd
	G-CGKR	Grob G115E Tutor	Babcock Aerospace Ltd
	G-CGKS	Grob G115E Tutor	Babcock Aerospace Ltd
	G-CGKU	Grob G115E Tutor	Babcock Aerospace Ltd
	G-CGKW	Grob G115E Tutor	Babcock Aerospace Ltd
	G-CGKY	Cessna 182T	T. A. E. Dobell
	G-CGKZ	Sky Ranger Swift 912S(1)	M. Russell
	G-CGLB	Airdrome Dream Classic	R. D. Leigh
	G-CGLC	Czech Sport Aircraft Sportcruiser	J. S. Richmond
	G-CGLE	Flylight Dragonfly	B. Skelding
	G-CGLF	Magni M-16C Tandem Trainer	J. S. Walton
	G-CGLG	P & M Quik GT450	P. H. Evans
	G-CGLJ	TL 2000UK Sting Carbon	N. G. Bumford & P. J. Brown
	G-CGLK	Magni M-16C Tandem Trainer	R. M. Savage
	G-CGLM	Rotorsport UK MTO Sport	S. Purcell
	G-CGLN	Jabiru J430	A. J. Thomas
	G-CGLO	P & M Quik R	R. H. Lowndes
	G-CGLP	CZAW Sportcruiser	R. J. Field
	G-CGLR	Czech Sport Aircraft Sportcruiser	J. S. Fogel
	G-CGLT	Czech Sport Aircraft Sportcruiser	I. Jalowiecki
	G-CGLY	Rotorsport UK Calidus	R. J. Steel
	G-CGLZ	TL 2000UK Sting Carbon	Newtownards Microlight Group
	G-CGMA	Ace Magic Laser	J. N. Hanson
	G-CGMB	Embraer EMB-135ER	Eastern Airways International Ltd
	G-CGMD	Rotorsport UK Calidus	Danelander Ltd
	G-CGMG	Van's RV-9	D. J. Bone
	G-CGMH	Jodel D150A Mascaret	R. Maven & I. M. McKenzie
	G-CGMI	P & M Quik GT450	A. M. Sadd
	G-CGMK	Skyranger 582(1)	P. J. Smith & E. J. Wells
	G-CGML	TL 2000UK Sting Carbon	G. M. Park
	G-CGMM	CZAW Sportcruiser	TAF and Co
	G-CGMN	Skyranger Swift 912S	G-CGMN Flying Group
	G-CGMO	Ace Magic Laser	G. J. Latham
	G-CGMP	CZAW Sportcruiser	R. Hasler
	G-CGMR	Colt Bibendum-110 balloon	Mobberley Balloon Collection (G-GRIP)
	G-CGMV	Roko Aero NG 4HD	Solent Roko Group
	G-CGMW	Alpi Pioneer 200M	M. S. McCrudden
	G-CGMZ	P & M Quik R	G. C. C. Roberts
	G-CGNA	Cameron Super FMG-100 balloon	Cameron Balloons Ltd
	G-CGNC	Rotorsport UK MTO Sport	A. B. Scott
	G-CGNE	Robinson R44 II	Heli Air Ltd
	G-CGNG	CZAW Sportcruiser	R. P. Johnson
	G-CGNH	Reality Escapade Jabiru(3)	J. M. Ingram
	G-CGNI	Ikarus C42 FB80	The Sesh Bars Ltd
	G-CGNJ	Cameron Z-105 balloon	Loughborough Students Union Hot Air Balloon Club
	G-CGNM	Magni M-16C Tandem Trainer	J. W. Hall
	G-CGNO	P & M Quik GT450	Mid Anglia Microlights Ltd
	G-CGNS	Sky 65-24 balloon	R. L. Bovell
	G-CGNW	Scheibe SF-25C Falke	Army Gliding Association

Reg	Type	Owner or Operator	Notes
G-CGNX	Rotorsport UK MTO Sport	L. McCallum	
G-CGNZ	Europa XS	S. J. Carr	
G-CGOG	Aerotechnik EV-97 Eurostar	D. C. & S. G. Emmons	
G-CGOH	Cameron C-80 balloon	I. R. Jones	
G-CGOJ	Jodel D.11	J. Laszio	
G-CGOR	Jodel D.18	R. D. Cook	
G-CGOS	PA-28-161 Cherokee Warrior III	S. H. B. Smith	
G-CGOW	Cameron Z-77 balloon	M. R. Daley	
G-CGOX	Raj Hamsa X'Air Hawk	A. P. Laws	
G-CGPA	Ace Magic Cyclone	A. Williams	
G-CGPB	Magni M-24C	D. Beevers	
G-CGPC	P & M Pegasus Quik	D. W. Watson	
G-CGPD	Ultramagic S-90 balloon	S. Robinson	
G-CGPE	P & M Quik GT450	J. Hillyer	
G-CGPF	Flylight Dragonfly	C. G. Langham	
G-CGPG	Rotosport UK MTO Sport	E. Barnes	
G-CGPH	Ultramagic S-50 balloon	O. G. V. Stallwood & D. M. Feldhaus	
G-CGPJ	Robin DR.400-140	P. A. Bainbridge-Clayton	
G-CGPK	Rotorsport UK MT-03	Ellis Flying Group (G-RIFS)	
G-CGPL	Sonex Sonex	P. Robichaud	
G-CGPO	TL2000UK Sting Carbon	A. Pritchard	
G-CGPR	Czech Sport Aircraft Pipersport	J. T. Langford	
G-CGPS	Aerotechnik EV-97 Eurostar SL	N. J. Jordan	
G-CGPW	Raj Hamsa X'Air Hawk	G. J. Langston	
G-CGPX	Zenair CH.601XL Zodiac	A. James	
G-CGPY	Boeing A75L 300 Stearman (671)	Wingwalkers.co.uk Ltd	
G-CGPZ	Rans S-4 Coyote	G. J. Jones	
G-CGRB	Flight Design CTLS 600 UK	Heathcliff Associates Ltd	
G-CGRC	P & M Quik R	R. J. Cook	
G-CGRJ	Carnet Paramotor	M. Carnet	
G-CGRM	VS.329 Spitfire Mk.IIA	M. R. Oliver	
G-CGRN	Pazmany PL-4A	A. F. S. & T. C. Caldecourt	
G-CGRR	P & M Quik	C. R. Chapman	
G-CGRS	P & M Quik	J. Crosby	
G-CGRV	DG Flugzeugbau DG-1000M	BR Aviation Ltd	
G-CGRW	P & M Quik	R. D. J. Buchanan	
G-CGRY	Magni M-24C	D. A. Jaques	
G-CGRZ	Magni M-24C	C-More Flying School Ltd	
G-CGSA	Flylight Dragonfly	G. Sykes	
G-CGSC	BFC Challenger II	C. R. Dunford	
G-CGSD	Magni M-16C	M. I. Sellers	
G-CGSG	Cessna 421C	J. R. Shannon	
G-CGSH	Cosmik EV-97 TeamEurostar UK	D. B. Medland	
G-CGSI	Zenair CH.601HDS Zodiac	E. McHugh	
G-CGSO	P & M Quik GT450	B. Light	
G-CGSW	Flylight Motorfloater	R. D. Leigh	
G-CGSX	Aeroprakt A22-L Foxbat	M. A. McKillop	
G-CGSZ	Schempp-Hirth Ventus 2CM	D. J. Wilson	
G-CGTC	BN-2T-4S Islander	Police Service of Northern Ireland	
G-CGTD	Cosmik EV-97 TeamEurostar UK	G-CGTD Flying Group	
G-CGTE	Cherry BX-2	D. Roberts	
G-CGTT	AutoCyro MT 03	A. Stock	
G-CGTK	Magni M-24C	Tango Kilo Group	
G-CGTL	Alpi Pioneer 300	B. M. Davis	
G-CGTM	Cessna 172S	Skytrek Air Services	
G-CGTR	Skyranger Nynja 912S(1)	G-CGTR Syndicate	
G-CGTT	Aerotechnik EV-97 Eurostar SL	D. L. Walker	
G-CGTU	P & M Quik GT450	K. L. Polson	
G-CGTV	Savannah VG Jabiru(1)	B. L. Cook	
G-CGTX	CASA 1-131E Jungmann Srs 2000 (E3B-599:791-31)	G. Hunter & T. A. S. Rayner	
G-CGUD	Lindstrand LBL-77A balloon	J. Phillips	
G-CGUE	Aeroprakt A-22-L Foxbat	A. T. Hayward	
G-CGUG	P & M Quik R	G. Bennett	
G-CGUI	Clutton FRED Srs.II	I. Pearson	
G-CGUK	VS.300 Spitfire 1A (X4650)	Comanche Warbirds Ltd	
G-CGUP	P & M Quik GT450	D. J. Allen	
G-CGUR	P & M QuikR	M. J. Williams	
G-CGUU	Skyranger Nynja 912S(1)	K. P. Halden	
G-CGUW	Tecnam P2002-EA Sierra	D. J. Burton	
G-CGUY	Rotorsport UK Calidus	R. F. Harrison	

Notes	Reg	Type	Owner or Operator
	G-CGVA	Aeroprakt A-22-L Foxbat	M. E. Gilman
	G-CGVB	BN-2T-4S Islander	Britten-Norman Aerospace Ltd
	G-CGVD	Van's RV-12	A. D. Heath
	G-CGVE	Raj Hamsa X'Air Hawk	G. A. Robb
	G-CGVG	Flight Design CTSW	B. Cook
	G-CGVJ	Europa XS	D. Glowa
	G-CGVK	Autogyro UK Calidus	D. Robertson
	G-CGVP	Aerotechnik EV-97 Eurostar	M. Finch, G. J. P. & R. B. Skinner
	G-CGVS	Raj Hamsa X'Air Hawk	D. Matthews
	G-CGVT	Cosmik EV-97 TeamEurostar UK	Mainair Microlight School Ltd
	G-CGVX	Europa	M. P. Sambrook
	G-CGVY	Cameron Z-77 balloon	C. M. C. Nelmes
	G-CGVZ	Zenair CH.601XL Zodiac	K. A. Dilks
	G-CGWA	Ikarus C42 FB80 Bravo	M. Howland
	G-CGWC	Ultramagic H-31 balloon	K. Dodman
	G-CGWE	Aerotechnik EV-97A Eurostar	Prestwick Eurostar Flyers
	G-CGWF	Van's RV-7	M. S. Hill
	G-CGWG	Van's RV-7	G. Waters
	G-CGWH	CZAW Sportcruiser	G-CGWH Group
	G-CGWI	Spitfire Mk.26 (BL927:JH-I)	I. J. Hutchinson
	G-CGWK	Ikarus C42 FB80	B. H. Goldsmith
	G-CGWM	Flylight Dragonfly Lite	C. R. Dunford
	G-CGWP	Aeroprakt A22-L Foxbat	C. B. J. Barker
	G-CGWS	Raj Hamsa X'Air Hawk	I. S. McNulty
	G-CGWT	Skyranger Swift 912(1)	J. & R. J. Henderson
	G-CGWU	UltraMagic S-90 balloon	P. Pruchnickj & R. P. Allan
	G-CGWZ	P & M QuikR	E. J. Douglas
	G-CGXB	Glasair Super IIS RG	P. J. Brion
	G-CGXI	Ikarus C42 FB80	G. V. Aggett
	G-CGXL	Robin DR.400/180	C. D. W. Smith & P. D. Holt (G-GLKE)
	G-CGXN	American Legend Cub	P. L. Gaze
	G-CGXO	Lindstrand LBL-105A balloon	S. Cobley
	G-CGXP	Grob G.109B	P. R. Holloway
	G-CGXR	Van's RV-9A	M. S. Johnson
	G-CGXV	P & M Quik R	A. Nikulin
	G-CGXW	Grob G.109B	I. B. Kennedy
	G-CGXZ	AutoGyro MTO Sport	D. J. Hancock
	G-CGYA	Stoddard-Hamilton Glasair III	Aerocars Ltd
	G-CGYB	Cosmik EV-97 TeamEurostar UK	J. Waite
	G-CGYC	Eurofox 912(S)	G. I. & R. M. Doake
	G-CGYD	Fairey Firefly TT.1	Fly to Inspire Ltd
	G-CGYF	Gloster Gamecock II	Retro Track & Air (UK) Ltd
	G-CGYG	Eurofox 912(S)	Highland Eurofox Syndicate
	G-CGYH	Magni M-24C	J. L. Ward
	G-CGYI	Van's RV-12	M. J. Poole
	G-CGYJ	VS.361 Spitfire HF.IX (TD314)	Aero Legends Leasing Ltd
	G-CGYO	Van's RV-6A	M. Paterson, M. Sutherland & R. J. Kennedy
	G-CGYP	Skyranger 912(2)	Yankee Papa Group
	G-CGYR	Avro RJ-85	Trident Turboprop (Dublin) Ltd
	G-CGYT	Flylight Dragonfly	S. J. Varden
	G-CGYW	Sikorsky S-92A	Offshore Helicopter Services UK Ltd
	G-CGYY	MXP-740 Savannah VG Jabiru(1)	Carlisle Skyrangers
	G-CGYZ	P & M Quik GT450	M. Florence
	G-CGZE	Rotorsport UK MTO Sport	C. Musgreave
	G-CGZF	Cosmik EV-97 TeamEurostar UK	I. A. Goatcher
	G-CGZG	AutoGyro MTO Sport	Highland Aviation Training Ltd
	G-CGZI	SOCATA TB-21 Trinidad TC	Keith Hallam & Partners
	G-CGZJ	ITV Dakota XL	C. J. Lines
	G-CGZM	AutoGyro MTO Sport	J. W. Cope
	G-CGZN	Dudek Synthesis 31/Nirvana Carbon	P. M. Jones
	G-CGZP	Curtiss P-40F Kittyhawk	The Fighter Collection
	G-CGZT	Aeroprakt A22-L Foxbat	D. Jessop
	G-CGZU	VS.361 Spitfire F.IXc (LZ842:EF-F)	M. A. Bennett
	G-CGZV	Europa XS	I. M. Moxon
	G-CGZW	Scheibe SF-25C Falke	Denbigh Gliding
	G-CGZY	Cosmik EV-97 TeamEurostar UK	D. J. F. Rickwood
	G-CGZZ	Kubicek BB22E balloon	T. Taylor
	G-CHAB	Schleicher Ka 6CR	J. T. Emsley
	G-CHAE	Glasflugel H205 Club Libelle	R. W. Newton
	G-CHAF	PZL-Bielsko SZD-50-3 Puchacz	Seahawk Gliding Club

Reg	Type	Owner or Operator	Notes
G-CHAH	Europa	T. Higgins	
G-CHAJ	Cirrus SR22	R. J. Garbutt	
G-CHAN	Robinson R22 Beta	J. S. Everett	
G-CHAO	Rolladen-Schneider LS6-b	Cloud Nine Syndicate	
G-CHAR	Grob G.109B	Lleweni Parc Ltd	
G-CHAS	PA-28-181 Cherokee Archer II	G-CHAS Flying Group	
G-CHAW	Replica Fokker EIII (E33/15)	P. A. Harvie	
G-CHAX	Schempp-Hirth Standard Cirrus	J. Hunneman	
G-CHAY	Rolladen-Schneider LS7	N. J. Leaton	
G-CHBA	Rolladen-Schneider LS7	G-CHBA Group	
G-CHBC	Rolladen-Schneider LS6-c	A. Crowden	
G-CHBE	Glaser-Dirks DG-300 Club Elan	DG 356 Group	
G-CHBG	Schleicher ASW-24	Imperial College of Science, Technology and Medicine	
G-CHBH	Grob G.103C Twin III Acro	Imperial College of Science, Technology and Medicine	
G-CHBK	Grob G.103 Twin Astir II	Dartmoor Gliding Society Ltd	
G-CHBL	Grob G.102 Astir CS77	Bidford Gliding & Flying Club Ltd	
G-CHBM	Grob G.102 Astir CS77	Staffordshire Gliding Club Ltd	
G-CHBO	Schleicher Ka 6CR	The Vale of the White Horse Gliding Club	
G-CHBS	PZL-Bielsko SZD-41A Jantar Standard 1	P. J. Chaisty & D. Hendry	
G-CHBT	Grob G.102 Astir CS Jeans	Darlton Gliding Club Ltd	
G-CHBV	Schempp-Hirth Nimbus 2B	I. W. Myles	
G-CHBW	Jurca Spitfire (AD370:PJ-C)	T. A. Major	
G-CHBX	Lindstrand LBL-77A balloon	K. R. Karlstrom	
G-CHBZ	TL2000UK Sting Carbon	C. R. Ashley	
G-CHCG	AS.332L-2 Super Puma	Airbus Helicopters Ltd	
G-CHCH	AS.332L-2 Super Puma	Airbus Helicopters Ltd	
G-CHCU	AS.332L2 Super Puma II	Airbus Helicopters Ltd	
G-CHCY	EC.225LP Super Puma	Airbus Helicopters Ltd	
G-CHDA	Pilatus B4-PC11AF	HDA Syndicate	
G-CHDB	PZL-Bielsko SZD-51-1 Junior	Stratford on Avon Gliding Club Ltd	
G-CHDD	Centrair 101B Pegase 90	591 Glider Syndicate	
G-CHDH	Lindstrand LBL-77A balloon	R. D. Allen	
G-CHDJ	Schleicher ASW-20CL	G. E. G. Lambert & L. M. M. Sebreights	
G-CHDK	Magni M-16C Tandem Trainer	J. Gledhill	
G-CHDL	Schleicher ASW-20	S. R. Locke	
G-CHDM	P & M QuikR	A. Sheveleu	
G-CHDP	PZL-Bielsko SZD-50-3 Puchacz	Heron Gliding Club 'DP'	
G-CHDR	DG-300 Elan	M. J. Rice & P. F. Taylor	
G-CHDU	PZL-Bielsko SZD-51-1 Junior	Cambridge Gliding Club Ltd	
G-CHDV	Schleicher ASW-19B	J. R. Young & G. Olentsenko	
G-CHDX	Rolladen-Schneider LS7-WL	D. Holborn & R. T. Halliburton	
G-CHDY	Schleicher K 8B	V. Mallon	
G-CHDZ	Cameron O-120 balloon	W. D. MacKinnon	
G-CHEC	PZL-Bielsko SZD-55-1	D. Pye	
G-CHEE	Schempp-Hirth Discus b	The RAF Gliding & Soaring Association	
G-CHEF	Glaser-Dirks DG-500 Elan Trainer	Yorkshire Gliding Club (Proprietary) Ltd	
G-CHEG	AB Sportine Aviacija LAK-12	CHEG Ownership	
G-CHEH	Rolladen-Schneider LS7-WL	S. Brown	
G-CHEJ	Schleicher ASW-15B	T. K. Gooch	
G-CHEL	Colt 77B balloon	Chelsea Financial Services PLC	
G-CHEN	Schempp-Hirth Discus b	G-CHEN Group	
G-CHEO	Schleicher ASW-20	FU Syndicate	
G-CHEP	PZL-Bielsko SZD-50-3 Puchacz	Peterborough and Spalding Gliding Club Ltd	
G-CHER	PA-38-112 Tomahawk II	G. E. Fox	
G-CHEW	Rolladen-Schneider LS6-c18	C. I. Sullivan	
G-CHFA	Schempp-Hirth Ventus b/16.6	A. K. Lincoln	
G-CHFC	P & M Quik GTR	A. R. Mayes & J. M. Cole	
G-CHFF	Schempp-Hirth Standard Cirrus	Foxtrot 2 Group	
G-CHFG	Van's RV-6	RV Flying Group	
G-CHFH	PZL-Bielsko SZD-50-3	Trent Valley Gliding Club Ltd	
G-CHFL	Scheibe SF-25C Falke	Staffordshire Gliding Club Ltd	
G-CHFM	Cameron Z-120 balloon	Vista Ballooning Ltd	
G-CHFO	P & M Quik GTR	P. J. P. Doherty	
G-CHFT	Tanarg Bionix 15 912S(1)	N. C. Stubbs	
G-CHFU	P & M Quik GTR	A. J. Fell	
G-CHFV	Schempp-Hirth Ventus B/16.6	A. Cliffe & B. Pearson	
G-CHFX	Schempp-Hirth Nimbus 4T	R. F. Barber	
G-CHFZ	Skyranger Nynja 912S(1)	Skyview Systems Ltd	
G-CHGA	P & M Quik GTR	Flying for Freedom Ltd	

Notes	Reg	Type	Owner or Operator
	G-CHGB	Grob G.102 Astir CS	D. R. D. Murray
	G-CHGE	Cosmik EV-97 TeamEurostar UK	J. R. Mackay
	G-CHGF	Schleicher ASW-15B	HGF Flying Group
	G-CHGG	Schempp-Hirth Standard Cirrus	HGG Flying Group
	G-CHGK	Schempp-Hirth Discus bT	C. J. Tooze
	G-CHGL	Bell 206B JetRanger II	Vantage Aviation Ltd (G-BPNG/G-ORTC)
	G-CHGM	Groppo Trail	M. Stow
	G-CHGP	Rolladen-Schneider LS6-c	D. J. Miller
	G-CHGR	AB Sportline Aviacija LAK-12	M. R. Garwood
	G-CHGS	Schempp-Hirth Discus b	G-CHGS Syndicate
	G-CHGT	FFA Diamant 16.5	T. E. Lynch
	G-CHGV	Glaser-Dirks DG500/22 Elan	Hotel Golf Victor Syndicate
	G-CHGW	Centrair ASW-20F	J. L. Vincent
	G-CHGX	AB Sportine LAK-12 Lietuva	M. Jenks
	G-CHGY	Schleicher ASW-27-18	D. Breeze, V. Derrick & M. Oliver
	G-CHGZ	Schempp-Hirth Discus bT	G. C. Bell
	G-CHHB	Aeroprakt A22-LS Foxbat	J. G. O. Kane
	G-CHHC	Cameron A-300 balloon	Wickers World Ltd
	G-CHHH	Rolladen-Schneider LS6-c	R. A. Lovegrove
	G-CHHI	Van's RV-7	M. R. Turner
	G-CHHJ	Eurofox 912(1)	S. R. Kirkham
	G-CHHK	Schleicher ASW-19B	S. Whalley
	G-CHHL	Cameron C-80 balloon	H. G. Griffiths & W. A. Steel
	G-CHHN	Schempp-Hirth Ventus b/16.6	Ventus 979 Syndicate
	G-CHHO	Schempp-Hirth Discus bT	S. G. Jones
	G-CHHP	Schempp-Hirth Discus b	F. R. Knowles
	G-CHHR	PZL-Bielsko SZD-55-1 Promyk	J. & S. R. Nash
	G-CHHS	Schleicher ASW-20	O. D. A. Wheeler
	G-CHHT	Rolladen-Schneider LS6-c	M. A. Fellis & S. M. Hall
	G-CHHU	Rolladen-Schneider LS6-c	445 Syndicate
	G-CHHV	Junqua Ibis RJ.03	J. J. R. Joubert
	G-CHHW	AB Sportine LAK-12	A. J. Dibdin
	G-CHHY	Ace Magic Laser	J. L. Stone
	G-CHHZ	Schempp-Hirth Cirrus	B. J. Dawson
	G-CHID	Eurofox 912(1)	A. P. Scott & P. David
	G-CHIG	Grob G.109B	J. B. Marchant
	G-CHIH	Eurofox 912(S)	K. R. Nash
	G-CHII	CASA 1-131E Jungmann Srs 1000	R. J. Allan, A. J. Maxwell & N. Jones
	G-CHIJ	Ikarus C42 FB80	R. G. Herrod
	G-CHIM	Ultramagic H-31 balloon	G. B. Lescott
	G-CHIP	PA-28-181 Cherokee Archer II	Golden Lion Aviation Ltd
	G-CHIS	Robinson R22	A. R. Collett
	G-CHIT	AutoGyro MTO Sport	N. G. H. Staunton
	G-CHIV	P & M Quik R	G-CHIV Syndicate
	G-CHIW	Raj Hamsa X'Air Hawk	M. M. P. Evans
	G-CHIX	Robin DR.400/500	P. A. & R. Stephens
	G-CHIY	Flylight MotorFloater	S. Polley
	G-CHJB	Flylight Dragonfly	S. J. Robson
	G-CHJD	Schleicher Ka 6E	The Ruby Syndicate
	G-CHJE	Schleicher K 8B	Wing and a Prayer Bunch
	G-CHJF	Rolladen-Schneider LS6-c	G-CHJF Syndicate
	G-CHJG	Cosmik EV-97 TeamEurostar UK	D. J. Moore
	G-CHJK	Cessna T.206H Turbo Stationair	G. G. Weston
	G-CHJL	Schempp-Hirth Discus bT	Discus JL Group
	G-CHJM	Cameron C-80 balloon	C. L. Smith
	G-CHJN	Schempp-Hirth Standard Cirrus	P. M. Hardingham
	G-CHJO	Bushby-Long Midget Mustang M-1	N. R. Aldersley
	G-CHJP	Schleicher Ka-6CR	R. C. Berry
	G-CHJR	Glasflugel H201B Standard Libelle	R. P. G. Hayhoe
	G-CHJS	Schleicher ASW-27-18E	J. D. Spencer
	G-CHJT	Centrair ASW-20F	A. F. Irwin
	G-CHJV	Grob G.102 Astir CS	P. W. Armstrong
	G-CHJW	P & M Quik GTR	A. C. Rowlands
	G-CHJX	Rolladen-Schneider LS6-c	M. R. Haynes
	G-CHJY	Schempp-Hirth Standard Cirrus	Cirrus-459 Group
	G-CHKA	Schempp-Hirth Discus CS	J. E. Keen
	G-CHKB	Grob G.102 Astir CS77	C. D. Woodward
	G-CHKC	Schempp-Hirth Standard Cirrus	S. D. Chaffey
	G-CHKD	Schempp-Hirth Standard Cirrus	P. Jackson
	G-CHKF	Grob G.109B	CHKF Group
	G-CHKG	Skyranger Nynja 912S(1)	D. L. Turner

Reg	Type	Owner or Operator	Notes
G-CHKH	Schleicher ASW-28	D. F. McKinney	
G-CHKK	Schleicher K8B	The Surrey Hills Gliding Club Ltd	
G-CHKM	Grob G.102 Astir CS Jeans	Essex and Suffolk Gliding Club Ltd	
G-CHKN	Kiss 400-582(1)	P. J. Higgins	
G-CHKO	Skyranger Swift 912S(1)	S. McGuirk	
G-CHKR	Jastreb Standard Cirrus G/81	N. A. White	
G-CHKS	Jastreb Standard Cirrus G/81	B. J. Davies	
G-CHKU	Schempp-Hirth Standard Cirrus	J. A. Farr	
G-CHKX	Rolladen-Schneider LS4-B	R. Sutton	
G-CHKY	Schempp-Hirth Discus b	R. Overvliet	
G-CHKZ	CARMAM JP 15-36AR Aiglon	T. A. & A. J. Hollings	
G-CHLB	Rolladen-Schneider LS4-b	E. G. Leach & K. F. Rogers	
G-CHLC	Pilatus B4-PC11AF	E. Lockhart	
G-CHLD	AutoGyro MTO Sport	D. L. Sivyer	
G-CHLH	Schleicher K 8B	Edgehill Gliding Centree Ltd	
G-CHLI	Cosmik Aviation Superchaser	N. R. Beale	
G-CHLK	Glasflugel H.301 Libelle	P. M. Wells	
G-CHLM	Schleicher ASW-19B	Wolds Gliding Club Ltd	
G-CHLN	Schempp-Hirth Discus CS	Portsmouth Naval Gliding Centre	
G-CHLP	Schleicher ASK-21	Southdown Gliding Club Ltd	
G-CHLS	Schempp-Hirth Discus b	R. Roberts	
G-CHLV	Schleicher ASW-19B	R. A. Hall	
G-CHLY	Schempp-Hirth Discus CS	M. Roberts	
G-CHLZ	Skyranger Swift 912(1)	A. W. & M. R. Badminton	
G-CHMA	PZL-Bielsko SZD-51-1 Junior	The Welland Gliding Club Ltd	
G-CHMB	Glaser-Dirks DG-300 Elan	A. D. & P. Langlands	
G-CHMD	DG Flugzeugbau LS8-T	G. B. Monslow & A. P. Balkwill	
G-CHME	Glaser-Dirks DG-300 Elan	P. N. Hardwick	
G-CHMH	Schleicher K8B	L. R. Merritt	
G-CHMI	Lindstrand LBL-105A balloon	J. A. Lawton	
G-CHMK	Rolladen-Schneider LS6-18W	R. C. Hodge	
G-CHML	Schempp-Hirth Discus CS	I. D. Bateman	
G-CHMM	Glasflugel 304B	G. D. Acroyd	
G-CHMN	Raj Hamsa X'Air Falcon Jabiru(1)	F. C. Claydon	
G-CHMO	Orlican Discus CS	J. D. Ewence	
G-CHMP	Bellanca 7ACA Champ	I. J. Langley	
G-CHMS	Glaser-Dirks DG-100	S. Henshall, K. G. Fairburn & N. J. Johnson	
G-CHMT	Glasflugel Mosquito B	J. Taberham	
G-CHMV	Schleicher ASK-13	Darlton Gliding Club Ltd	
G-CHMW	Aerotechnik EV-97 Eurostar SL	B. A. Fairston & A. Stotter	
G-CHMX	Rolladen-Schneider LS4-a	HMX Syndicate	
G-CHMY	Schempp-Hirth Standard Cirrus	HMY Syndicate	
G-CHMZ	Fedorov ME7 Mechta	ME7 Syndicate	
G-CHNA	Glaser-Dirks DG-500/20 Elan	Tallard G-CHNA Syndicate	
G CHNB	Scheibe SF-28A	J. M. Alonso	
G-CHNC	Schleicher ASK-19B	R. D. Grieve	
G-CHND	Ultramagic H-65	N. Dykes	
G-CHNF	Schempp-Hirth Duo Discus	Booker Gliding Club Ltd	
G-CHNI	Magni M-24C	R. M. Frost	
G-CHNK	PZL-Bielsko SZD-51-1 Junior	The Surrey Hills Gliding Club Ltd	
G-CHNM	Standard Cirrus G/81	A. A. I. Emson	
G-CHNO	Cameron C-60 balloon	J. F. Till	
G-CHNR	P & M Quik GTR	M. L. Hill	
G-CHNT	Schleicher ASW-15	K. Tunnicliff	
G-CHNU	Schempp-Hirth Nimbus 4DT	D. E. Findon	
G-CHNV	Rolladen-Schneider LS4-b	G. R. Pilkington	
G-CHNW	Schempp-Hirth Duo Discus	G-CHNW Group	
G-CHNZ	Centrair 101A Pegase	C. R. Partington	
G-CHOA	Bell 206B-3 JetRanger III	Haverholme Farm Partnership	
G-CHOD	Schleicher ASW-20	S. E. Archer-Jones & A. Duerden	
G-CHOE	Robin DR400/140B	YP Flying Group	
G-CHOF	CARMAM M100S	P. E. Rice	
G-CHOG	AB Sportine LAK-12	J. M. Pursey	
G-CHOI	ReplicaWhite Monoplane 1912 Canard Pusher	J. Aubert	
G-CHOO	Ikarus C42 FB80	C. L. Bush	
G-CHOP	Westland-Bell 47G-3B1	H. Cole	
G-CHOR	Schempp-Hirth Discus b	R. T. C. Connors	
G-CHOT	Grob G.102 Astir CS77	Southdown Gliding Club Ltd	
G-CHOU	Cosmik EV-97 TeamEurostar UK	R. A. Betts	
G-CHOX	Europa XS	Chocs Away Ltd	
G-CHOY	Schempp-Hirth Mini Nimbus C	M. F. Stringfellow	

Notes	Reg	Type	Owner or Operator
	G-CHOZ	Rolladen-Schneider LS6-18W	I. Pendlebury
	G-CHPA	Robinson R22 Beta	Swift Helicopter Services Ltd
	G-CHPC	Schleicher ASW-20 CL	B. L. Liddard & P. J. Williams
	G-CHPD	Rolladen-Schneider LS6-c18	M. P. Day
	G-CHPE	Schleicher ASK-13	Dumfries and District Gliding Club
	G-CHPG	Cirrus SR-20	Guy Greenfield Architects & M. R. Hill
	G-CHPH	Schempp-Hirth Discus CS	L. Finlay
	G-CHPK	Van's RV-8	Vans Papa Kilo Group
	G-CHPL	Rolladen-Schneider LS4-b	Southdown Gliding Club Ltd
	G-CHPO	Schleicher Ka-6CR	T. Linsell
	G-CHPS	Skyranger 582(1)	C. H. Richards & A. S. Hand
	G-CHPT	Federov ME7 Mechta	Gem Aero Ltd
	G-CHPW	Schleicher ASK-21	Darlton Gliding Club Ltd
	G-CHPX	Schempp-Hirth Discus CS	G-CHRS Group
	G-CHPZ	P & M Quik GT450	R. Barry
	G-CHRC	Glaser-Dirks DG500/20 Elan	DG500-390 Syndicate
	G-CHRD	Flylight Dragonlite	I. A. Barclay
	G-CHRE	Nicollier HN.700 Menestrel II	M. K. A. Blyth
	G-CHRG	PZL-Bielsko SZD-51-1 Junior	Mendip Gliding Club Ltd
	G-CHRH	Schempp-Hirth Discus 2cT	R. G. Calvert
	G-CHRJ	Schleicher K 8B	The Gliding Heritage Centre
	G-CHRM	Ikarus C42 FB80 Bravo	Briongos MacKinnon Partnership
	G-CHRN	Schleicher ASK-18	K. Richards
	G-CHRT	Cosmik EV-97 TeamEurostar UK	C. Childs
	G-CHRU	Flylight Dragonlite Fox	J. R. Kendall
	G-CHRV	Van's RV-7	R. E. Tyers
	G-CHRW	Schempp-Hirth Duo Discus	R. A. Johnson
	G-CHRX	Schempp-Hirth Discus a	A. Spirling
	G-CHSB	Glaser-Dirks DG-303 Elan	P. J. Britten
	G-CHSD	Schempp-Hirth Discus b	G-CHSD Group
	G-CHSE	Grob G.102 Astir CS77	J. L. Rhodes
	G-CHSG	Scheibe SF27A	S. P. Melhuish
	G-CHSH	Scheibe Zugvogel IIIB	G-CHSH Group
	G-CHSK	Schleicher ASW-20CL	751 Syndicate
	G-CHSM	Schleicher ASK-13	K13 HSM
	G-CHSN	Schleicher Ka-6CR	S. Dulac
	G-CHSO	Schempp-Hirth Discus b	W. A. Baumann
	G-CHSP	UltraMagic M-65C balloon	S. Hemmings
	G-CHSS	Ikarus C42 FB80 Bravo	A. P. Burch
	G-CHST	Van's RV-9A	R. J. Charles
	G-CHSX	Scheibe SF-27A	Essex & Suffolk Gliding Club Ltd
	G-CHTA	AA-5A Cheetah	D. Byrne (G-BFRC)
	G-CHTB	Schempp-Hirth Janus	R. A. Markham
	G-CHTD	Grob G.102 Astir CS	Oxford Gliding Company Ltd
	G-CHTE	Grob G.102 Astir CS77	J. P. W. Towill
	G-CHTF	AB Sportline LAK-12	K. Richards
	G-CHTH	Zenair CH.701SP	R. E. Lasnier
	G-CHTI	Van's RV-12	S. Zani & D. Walls
	G-CHTJ	Schleicher ASK-13	Ulster Gliding Club Ltd
	G-CHTK	Hawker Sea Hurricane 1B (P2921/GZ-L)	Warbird Experiences Ltd (G-TWTD)
	G-CHTL	Schempp-Hirth Arcus T	38 Syndicate
	G-CHTM	Rolladen-Schneider LS8-18	G. Connolly
	G-CHTO	Rans S-7S	Robin Flying Club Ltd
	G-CHTR	Grob G.102 Astir CS	B. Mackenzie
	G-CHTS	Rolladen-Schneider LS8-18	A. T. Dowell
	G-CHTU	Schempp-Hirth Cirrus	Cirrus Syndicate
	G-CHTV	Schleicher ASK-21	Cambridge Gliding Club Ltd
	G-CHUC	Denney Kitfox Mk 2	K. T. Stewart
	G-CHUD	Schleicher ASK-13	Portmoak HUD Syndicate
	G-CHUE	Schleicher ASW-27	M. J. Smith
	G-CHUF	Schleicher ASK-13	The Welland Gliding Club Ltd
	G-CHUG	Europa	C. M. Washington
	G-CHUH	Schempp-Hirth Janus	B. J. Biskup
	G-CHUJ	Centrair ASW-20F	T. J. Chapman
	G-CHUN	Grob G.102 Astir CS Jeans	Staffordshire Gliding Club Ltd
	G-CHUO	Federov ME7 Mechta	Gem Aero Ltd
	G-CHUR	Schempp-Hirth Cirrus	P. King
	G-CHUS	Scheibe SF27A Zugvogel V	SF27 HUS Syndicate
	G-CHUT	Centrair ASW-20F	S. R. Phelps
	G-CHUU	Schleicher ASK-13	T. J. Wilkinson
	G-CHUX	P & M Aviation QuikR	C. Wright

Reg	Type	Owner or Operator	Notes
G-CHUY	Schempp-Hirth Ventus cT	P. R. Gammell	
G-CHUZ	Schempp-Hirth Discus bT	G. Starling	
G-CHVB	P & M Aviation Quik R	Victor Bravo Group	
G-CHVG	Schleicher ASK-21	Rattlesden Gliding Club Ltd	
G-CHVH	Pilatus B4-PC11AF	A. J. Cunningham	
G-CHVI	Cameron Z-210 balloon	Helena Maria Fragoso dos Santos SA/Portugal	
G-CHVJ	VS.349 Spitfire Vb	G. N. S. Farrant	
G-CHVK	Grob G.102 Astir CS	J. P. Flather	
G-CHVM	Glaser-Dirks DG-300	Glider Syndicate 393	
G-CHVO	Schleicher ASK-13	Anglia Gliding Club	
G-CHVP	Schleicher ASW-20	C. D. Sutherland	
G-CHVR	Schempp-Hirth Discus b	Yorkshire Gliding Club (Proprietary) Ltd	
G-CHVS	ICP MXP-740 Savannah VG Jabiru(1)	Sandtoft Ultralights	
G-CHVV	Rolladen-Schneider LS4-b	A. J. Bardgett	
G-CHVW	Scleicher ASK-13	Essex Gliding Club Ltd	
G-CHVX	Centrair ASW-20F	D. Coker	
G-CHVY	Ikarus C42 FB80	Victor Yankee Syndicate	
G-CHVZ	Schempp-Hirth Standard Cirrus	ABC Soaring	
G-CHWA	Schempp-Hirth Ventus 2c	C. Garton	
G-CHWB	Schempp-Hirth Duo Discus	Oscar 3 Syndicate	
G-CHWC	Glasflugel Standard Libelle 201B	Libelle HWC Group	
G-CHWD	Schempp-Hirth Standard Cirrus	M. R. Hoskins	
G-CHWE	Lindstrand LBL-77A balloon	B. P. Witter	
G-CHWF	Jastreb Standard Cirrus G/81	Team Cirrus 2ZC	
G-CHWG	Glasflugel Standard Libelle 201B	P. E. Edgar	
G-CHWH	Schempp-Hirth Ventus cT	The G-CHWH Syndicate	
G-CHWK	Aerochute Hummerchute	W. A. Kimberlin	
G-CHWL	Rolladen-Schneider LS8-18	D. S. Lodge	
G-CHWM	AutoGyro Cavalon	Devon Autogyro Ltd	
G-CHWN	Ikarus C42 FB100	P. P. Tame	
G-CHWP	Glaser-Dirks DG-100G Elan	N. J. Moxon	
G-CHWS	Rolladen-Schneider LS8-18	G. E. & H. B. Chalmers	
G-CHWT	Schleicher K 8B	I. M. Castle	
G-CHWW	Grob G.103A Twin II Acro	Staffordshire Gliding Club Ltd	
G-CHXA	Scheibe Zugvogel IIIB	J. I. D. Aggiss	
G-CHXB	Grob G.102 Astir CS77	I. J. Rayner	
G-CHXD	Schleicher ASW-27	J. Quartermaine & M. Jerman	
G-CHXE	Schleicher ASW-19B	M. P. Featherstone	
G-CHXF	Cameron A-140 balloon	H. M. Fragoso dos Santos SA/Portugal	
G-CHXG	CZAW Sportcruiser	R. J. Warne	
G-CHXH	Schempp-Hirth Discus b	Deesside Gliding Club (Aberdeenshire) Ltd	
G-CHXJ	Schleicher ASK-13	Cotswold Gliding Club	
G-CHXK	Scheibe SF-25A Falke 2000	Stratford on Avon Gliding Club Ltd	
G-CHXL	Van's RV-6	C. S. Randall	
G-CHXM	Grob G.102 Astir CS	University of Bristol Students Union	
G-CHXN	Balony Kubicek BB20GP balloon	D. R. Medcalf	
G-CHXO	Schleicher ASH-25	R. Johns	
G-CHXP	Schleicher ASK-13	Bowland Forest Gliding Club Ltd	
G-CHXR	Schempp-Hirth Ventus cT	560 Group	
G-CHXS	Cameron C-90 balloon	B. R. Whatley	
G-CHXT	Rolladen-Schneider LS-4a	LS4-A G-CHXT Syndicate	
G-CHXU	Schleicher ASW-19B	UCLU	
G-CHXV	Schleicher ASK-13	HXV Syndicate	
G-CHXW	Rolladen-Schneider LS8-18	H. A. & R. E. Scott	
G-CHXZ	Rolladen-Schneider LS4	55 Syndicate	
G-CHYB	Grob G.109B	C. J. Tooze	
G-CHYD	Schleicher ASW-24	E. S. Adlard	
G-CHYE	DG-505 Elan Orion	The Bristol Gliding Club Proprietary Ltd	
G-CHYF	Rolladen-Schneider LS8-18	R. E. Francis	
G-CHYH	Rolladen-Schneider LS3-17	A. McDermott	
G-CHYJ	Schleicher ASK-21	Highland Gliding Club Ltd	
G-CHYK	Centrair ASW-20FL	A. W. Thornhill	
G-CHYO	Ace Magic Laser	D. R. Purslow	
G-CHYP	PZL-Bielsko SZD-50-3 Puchacz	Rattlesden Gliding Club Ltd	
G-CHYR	Schleicher ASW-27	A. J. Manwaring	
G-CHYS	Schleicher ASK-21	Army Gliding Association	
G-CHYT	Schleicher ASK-21	Army Gliding Association	
G-CHYU	Schempp-Hirth Discus CS	Army Gliding Association	
G-CHYY	Schempp-Hirth Nimbus 3DT	A26 Syndicate	
G-CHYZ	Skystar Kitfox Vixen	R. H. Bastin	
G-CHZB	PZL-Swidnik PW-5 Smyk	Essex Gliding Club Ltd	

Notes	Reg	Type	Owner or Operator
	G-CHZD	Schleicher ASW-15B	C. P. Ellison & S. Barber
	G-CHZE	Schempp-Hirth Discus CS	Lasham Gliding Society Ltd
	G-CHZG	Rolladen-Schneider LS8-18	G. C. Brunschen
	G-CHZH	Schleicher Ka 6CR	O. J. Butcher
	G-CHZJ	Schempp-Hirth Standard Cirrus	P. Mucha
	G-CHZK	Europa XS	P. J. Harrod
	G-CHZL	Zenair CH.601XL Zodiac	E. Leggoe
	G-CHZM	Rolladen-Schneider LS4-a	W. S. H. Taylor
	G-CHZO	Schleicher ASW-27	R. A. Drake
	G-CHZR	Schleicher ASK-21	K21 HZR Group
	G-CHZS	Zenair CH.601HDS	M. J. Jackson
	G-CHZT	Groppo Trail	G. R. Purcell
	G-CHZU	Schempp-Hirth Standard Cirrus	D. J. Richmond
	G-CHZV	Schempp-Hirth Standard Cirrus	A. W. Rands
	G-CHZW	P & M Aviation Quik GTR	N. J. Braund
	G-CHZX	Schleicher K 8B	The Nene Valley Gliding Club Ltd
	G-CHZZ	Schleicher ASW-20L	P. M. Davey
	G-CIAE	Cameron TR-70 balloon	John Aimo Balloons SAS/Italy
	G-CIAF	TL3000 Sirius	A. L. Scott, P. Tierney & S. A. Linklater
	G-CIAI	Schempp-Hirth Arcus T	G-CIAI Group
	G-CIAJ	Hawker Hart B4A	Westh Flyg AB/Sweden
	G-CIAK	Groppo Trail	I. Markham
	G-CIAL	Cameron Z-77 balloon	A. A. Osman
	G-CIAN	Unicorn Ax6 balloon	G. A. & I. Chadwick
	G-CIAO	I.I.I. Sky Arrow 1450-L	P. L. Turner
	G-CIAR	P & M Aviation Quik GTR	C. R. Paterson
	G-CIAW	Ikarus C42 FB80	R. Hilton
	G-CIAX	CZAW Sportcruiser	S. Kelly
	G-CIAY	Cameron C-70 balloon	R. J. Gahan
	G-CIAZ	Eurofox 912(1)	M. P. Dale
	G-CIBC	Eurofox 912(S)	M. P. Brockington
	G-CIBG	Rolladen-Schneider LS4	G. D. Ackroyd
	G-CIBH	Van's RV-8A	W. B. Blair-Hickman
	G-CIBI	Lindstrand LBL-90A balloon	A. J. & S. J. M. Boyle
	G-CIBL	AutoGyro Cavalon	A. J. Tranter
	G-CIBM	Van's RV-8	G. P. Williams
	G-CIBN	Cameron Z-90 balloon	R. A. Lovell
	G-CIBO	Cessna 180K	CIBO Ops Ltd
	G-CIBR	P & M Quik GT450	K. D. Smith
	G-CIBT	P & M Quik R	G-CIBT Syndicate
	G-CIBU	Jabiru J160	D. J. Bly
	G-CIBV	Skyranger Swift 912S(1)	PPL (UK) Ltd
	G-CIBW	Westland Scout AH.1 (XT626)	Historic Aircraft Flight Trust
	G-CIBZ	Eurofox 912(S1)	K. N. Rigley & D. Thorpe
	G-CICA	Europa XS	R. J. Grainger
	G-CICC	Cessna 152	The Pilot Centre Ltd
	G-CICD	Colt 105A balloon	Mobberley Balloon Collection
	G-CICF	Ikarus C42 FB80	Deanland Flight Training Ltd
	G-CICG	Ikarus C42 FB80	G-CICG Group
	G-CICH	Sikorsky S-92A	Bristow Helicopters Ltd
	G-CICK	VS.509 Spitfire T IX (NH341)	Aero Legends Leasing Ltd
	G-CICM	Rotorsport UK Calidus	R. S. Dines
	G-CICN	Agusta-Bell Sioux H. Mk.1 (XT131)	Historic Aircraft Flight Trust
	G-CICP	DHC-2 Beaver AL.Mk.1 (XP820)	Historic Aircraft Flight Trust
	G-CICR	Auster AOP.Mk.9 (XR244)	Historic Aircraft Flight Trust
	G-CICU	Raj Hamsa X'Air Hawk	X'Air Group
	G-CICV	Rotorsport UK MTO Sport	J. Owen
	G-CICW	Flylight Dragonlite Fox	N. I. Hart
	G-CICY	PZL-Bielsko SZD-50-3 Puchasz	L. R. Saker
	G-CIDB	Flylight Dragon Chaser	D. M. Broom
	G-CIDC	Yakovlev Yak-18T	D. M. Cue
	G-CIDD	Bellanca 7ECA Citabria	C. R. Nichol
	G-CIDF	Autogyro MTOSport	F. Brand
	G-CIDG	P & M Aviation Quik GTR	G. N. Kenny
	G-CIDH	Cameron C-80 balloon	J. Johnson
	G-CIDO	Glaser-Dirks DG-600/18M	S. S. M. Turner
	G-CIDP	Sonex	P. I. Marshall
	G-CIDS	Ikarus C42 FB100	P. H. J. Fenn
	G-CIDT	Schleicher ASH-25E	G. D. E. Macdonald (G-KIGR)
	G-CIDU	Balony Kubicek BB22E balloon	A. M. Daniels

Reg	Type	Owner or Operator	Notes
G-CIDW	Aerotechnik EV-97 Eurostar	D. Workman	
G-CIDX	Sonex Sonex	J. P. Dilks	
G-CIDY	P & M Quik GTR	G. P. Wade	
G-CIDZ	Aerotechnik EV-97 Eurostar SL	L. M. Newnham	
G-CIEB	AutoGyro MTO Sport	K. A. Hastie	
G-CIED	Riply RP1/Aeros Fox 16T	I. D. Smith	
G-CIEE	Ikarus C42 FB100	A. C. Cotton	
G-CIEG	P & M Quik R	Flying Group G-CIEG	
G-CIEH	Eurofox 912(S)	J. H. Ellwood	
G-CIEI	Lindstrand LBL-HS-110 balloon	Spirit Operations Ltd (G-TRIB)	
G-CIEJ	AutoGyro MTO Sport	G-CIEJ Group	
G-CIEM	P & M Quik R	G. R. F. Daniel	
G-CIEN	Super Marine Spitfire Mk.26 (PL788)	P. J. Scullion	
G-CIEP	Flylight Dragon Chaser	R. Urquhart	
G-CIER	Cameron Z-160 balloon	J. Taylor	
G-CIET	Lindstrand LBL-31A balloon	C. A. Butter & S. I. Williams	
G-CIEW	AutoGyro Cavalon	M. J. Lloyd	
G-CIEY	Westland SA.341G Gazelle AH.Mk.1	Gazelle Flying Group A	
G-CIEZ	Bucker Bu.181B-1 Bestmann	A. C. Whitehead	
G-CIFA	Eurofox 912(1)	I. C. & P. H. White	
G-CIFB	Aerochute Dual	J. D. Abraham	
G-CIFC	SOCATA TB-200 Tobago XL	Lincoln Aero Club Ltd	
G-CIFD	Titan T-51 Mustang	B. J. Chester-Master	
G-CIFF	P &M Quik GT450	Light Flight Fox Fox Group	
G-CIFK	Raj Hamsa X'Air Hawk	Avair Flying Group	
G-CIFL	Van's RV-6	A. J. Maxwell	
G-CIFM	Flylight Dragon Chaser	D. A. Eastough	
G-CIFN	Ikarus C42 FB80	K. J. A. Farrance & U. Tokgoz	
G-CIFO	Eurofox 912(S)	Herefordshire Gliding Club Ltd	
G-CIFP	Cameron Frog-90 SS balloon	Spirit Operations Ltd	
G-CIFT	Autogyro MTO Sport	J. Reade & Sons	
G-CIFU	Rolladen-Schneider LS4	T. Parker	
G-CIFV	P & M Quik GTR	Over Farm GTR	
G-CIFY	PA-28-181 Archer III	M. K. Barnes (G-GFPA)	
G-CIFZ	Ikarus C42 FB80	Air Cornwall	
G-CIGA	Ultramagic H-42 balloon	I. Chadwick	
G-CIGB	Stinson L-1 Vigilant	G. & P. M. Turner	
G-CIGC	P & M Quik R	W. G. Craig	
G-CIGE	DHC-1 Chipmunk 22 (WK634:902)	Skyblue Aero Services Ltd	
G-CIGF	Slingsby T.61F Venture T.Mk.2	D. C. Gell	
G-CIGG	P & M Quik GTR	P. C. Smith	
G-CIGI	Lindstrand LBL-77A balloon	A. R. Pitt	
G-CIGS	Autogyro MTOSport	E. A. Blomfield-Smith	
G-CIGT	Skyranger Swift 912S(1)	N. S. Wells	
G-CIGU	Aerochute Dual	R. Griffiths	
G-CIGW	BRM Aero Bristell NG5 Speed Wing	G-CIGW Syndicate	
G-CIGY	Westland-Bell 47G-3B1	K. P. Mayes (G-BGXP)	
G-CIHA	P & M Quik R	C. R. Buckle	
G-CIHB	Colomban LC-30 Luciole	S. Kilpin	
G-CIHC	Cameron Z-105 balloon	Vista Ballooning Ltd	
G-CIHG	Cameron Z-90 balloon	Rien Jurg Promotions BV/Netherlands	
G-CIHI	Cameron V-77 balloon	P. Spellward	
G-CIHL	P & M Quik GTR	T. G. Jackson	
G-CIHM	Schleicher ASW-28018E	S. A. Kerby	
G-CIHO	Cameron Z-77 balloon	S. D. Wrighton	
G-CIHS	Fokker D.VII replica	J. A. & R. H. Cooper	
G-CIHT	Flylight Dragonlite Fox	M. D. Harper	
G-CIHU	Fokker D.VIII replica	J. A. & R. H. Cooper	
G-CIHW	AutoGyro Cavalon	A. E. Polkey & R. I. Broadhead	
G-CIHY	P & M Pegasus Quik	J. A. Cammack	
G-CIIA	P & M Quik R	K. A. Ritchie	
G-CIIB	Aerochute Dual	P. Dean	
G-CIIC	PA-18-150 Super Cub	Bianchi Aviation Film Services Ltd (G-PULL)	
G-CIIH	P & M Quik GTR	S. J. Leask	
G-CIIK	Yakovlev Yak-55	E. P. Bunnage-Flavell	
G-CIIL	BRM Aero Bristell NG5 Speed Wing	P. & C. Shardlow	
G-CIIM	Cessna F.172N	Abbotsinch Aviation Ltd	
G-CIIN	Ikarus C42 FB100	Mid Ulster Aviation Ltd	
G-CIIO	Curtis P-40C Warhawk (39-160:160 10AB)	Patina Ltd	
G-CIIT	Skyranger Swift 912S(1)	P. Higgins	
G-CIIU	TLAC Sherwood Ranger ST	M. W. Fitch	

Notes	Reg	Type	Owner or Operator
	G-CIIV	AMS-Flight Apis M	Callen-Lenz Associates Ltd
	G-CIIW	Piper J3L-65 Cub	G. R. French
	G-CIIZ	Flylight Dragonlite Fox	W. G. Brooks
	G-CIJA	P & M Quik GT450	A. Fern
	G-CIJB	Cameron Z-90 balloon	P. L. N. Dowlen
	G-CIJC	Sikorsky S-92A	Bristow Helicopters Ltd
	G-CIJE	Alisport Silent 2 Electro	C. C. Marshall
	G-CIJF	Schempp-Hirth Duo Discus T	Lasham Gliding Society Ltd
	G-CIJH	Alisport Silent Club	R. J. Marshall
	G-CIJJ	Cameron O-31 balloon	M. J. Woodcock
	G-CIJK	Zenair CH.750	A. M. Cameron
	G-CIJL	Cameron Z-105 balloon	British Balloon Flights
	G-CIJM	Cameron N-133 balloon	L. J. M. Muir
	G-CIJN	Boeing Stearman E-75 Kaydet (317)	P. Fernandes
	G-CIJO	P & M Quik GTR	B. N. Montila
	G-CIJR	P & M Pegasus Quantum 15-912	D. P. Gawlowski
	G-CIJT	Skyranger Nynja 912S(1)	G-CIJT Group
	G-CIJV	CASA 1-133 Jungmeister (LG+01)	R. A. Cumming
	G-CIJY	Wittman W.10 Tailwind	K. M. Bowen
	G-CIJZ	Zenair CH.750	S. A. Linklater, A. L. Scott & P. Tierney
	G-CIKA	P & M Quik Lite	S. A. Noble
	G-CIKB	Schempp-Hirth Duo Discus T	P. Morrison, N. L. Jones & J. C. Burrow
	G-CIKC	Cameron D-77 airship	Cameron Balloons Ltd
	G-CIKD	Alisport Silent 2 Targa	Whiskey 17
	G-CIKE	Aeroprakt A22-LS Foxbat Supersport 600	J. S. G. Down
	G-CIKG	Rotorsport UK Calidus	GS Aviation (Europe) Ltd
	G-CIKH	Eurofox 914	Deeside Gliding Club (Aberdeenshire) Ltd
	G-CIKI	P & M Pegasus Quik	D. Brown
	G-CIKJ	Ace Aviation Easy Riser Spirit	W. R. Astbury
	G-CIKK	Ace Magic Laser	D. R. Cooper
	G-CIKL	Ultramagic S-70 balloon	J. Taylor
	G-CIKM	Diamond DA.42 Twin Star	Plane Rentals Ltd
	G-CIKN	Lindstrand LBL-150A balloon	Helena Maria Fragoso Dos Santos SA/Portugal
	G-CIKR	Skyranger Nynja 912S(1)	Ulster Seaplane Association Ltd
	G-CIKS	Slingsby T.67 Mk.II Firefly	B7 Aviation Ltd
	G-CIKU	Flylight Dragonfly	N. S. Brayn
	G-CIKX	Robinson R66	Dynamiq Asset Holdings Ltd
	G-CILA	Eurofox 912(1)	M. J. Turner
	G-CILB	Alisport Silent 2 Electro	R. G. J. Tait
	G-CILD	Curtiss Model D replica	Wickenby Aerodrome LLP
	G-CILG	Van's RV-7A	M. F. Henderson
	G-CILI	Replica Nieuport 11 (A126)	R. E. Peirse
	G-CILL	BRM Aero Bristell NG5	P. J. Reilly
	G-CILO	Cameron TR-70 balloon	D. R. Firkins
	G-CILS	Rolladen-Schneider LS10-st	D. Hilton
	G-CILT	Ikarus C42 FB100	S. C. Wardle
	G-CILV	Dragon Chaser	C. J. Johnson
	G-CILW	Ace Aviation Easy Riser Touch	G. W. T. Farrington
	G-CILX	Stolp V-Star	S. R. Green
	G-CILY	Ikarus C42 FB80	T. W. Penn
	G-CIMB	Cessna 177RG	A. R. Willis
	G-CIMC	Hoffmann H.36 Dimona	Chris Dawes Ltd
	G-CIMD	Alpi Pioneer 400	Hardwick Flying Group
	G-CIMG	Aerochute Dual	M. R. Gaylor
	G-CIMI	Grob G.115	Kernow Flying Group Ltd
	G-CIMK	P & M Quik Lite	N. E. King
	G-CIML	Eurofox-M	W. H. McMinn
	G-CIMM	Cessna T.182 Turbo Skylane II	A. W. Oliver (G-PDHJ)
	G-CIMP	Scheibe SF.25C Falke	Southwest Motorgliders
	G-CIMS	Eurofox 912(1)	C. M. Sperring
	G-CIMT	Autogyro Cavalon	C. M. Evans & J. W. Blaylock
	G-CIMV	Groppo Trail	Atomite Ltd
	G-CIMX	Westland Scout AH.Mk.1 (XW283)	T. L. Hobbs
	G-CIMY	Sadler Vampire SV2	R. M. Williams
	G-CIMZ	Robinson R44 II	KHF Enterprises Ltd
	G-CINA	Cessna 152	APB Leasing Ltd
	G-CIND	Cameron C-70 balloon	N. J. Dunnington
	G-CING	Sherwood Ranger ST	D. R. Appleton
	G-CINH	P & M Quik R	P. A. Benham
	G-CINI	Rans S7S	D. R. P. Mole
	G-CINJ	Milholland Legal Eagle	N. S. Jeffrey

Reg	Type	Owner or Operator	Notes
G-CINK	Grob G.109	The Lyveden Motor Gliding Syndicate	
G-CINL	Skyranger Swift 912(S)1	B. Richardson	
G-CINM	Grob G.109B	Grob 109B Motorglider Syndicate	
G-CINN	Cameron Z-31 balloon	D. L. Peltan	
G-CINO	Grob G.109B	T. R. Dews	
G-CINV	Aeroprakt A22-LS Foxbat	R. Everitt	
G-CINX	Van's RV-7	C. D. Meek	
G-CINZ	Ace Aviation Magic/Cyclone	R. W. T. Gibbs	
G-CIOA	Murphy Rebel	O. P. Sparrow	
G-CIOD	P &M Quik Lite	D. D'Arcy-Ewing	
G-CIOF	Eurofox 914	Yorkshire Gliding Club (Proprietary) Ltd	
G-CIOG	Fresh Breeze Bullix Trike/Relax	M. R. Spray	
G-CIOJ	Eurofox 912(IS)	A. C. S. Paterson	
G-CIOK	Skyranger Swift 912(S)(1)	J. de Pree & B. Janson	
G-CIOL	P &M Quik GTR	R. R. Green	
G-CIOM	Magni M24C Orion	D. J. Gale	
G-CIOO	Van's RV-7	M. Albert-Recht	
G-CIOP	Aerospatiale AS.355F Ecureuil 2	RCR Aviation Ltd	
G-CIOR	Nicollier HN.700 Menestrel II	R. C. & R. P. C. Teverson	
G-CIOU	Cameron Z-70 balloon	P. K. Durgam	
G-CIOV	Ultramagic H-31 balloon	P. B. Dopson & H. Crawley	
G-CIOW	Westland SA.341C Gazelle HT Mk.2	S. Atherton	
G-CIOX	Flylight Foxcub	P. J. Cheyney	
G-CIOY	Beech G.36 Bonanza	Bonanzair Ltd	
G-CIOZ	Ikarus C42 FB100	C. L. G. Innocent	
G-CIPA	P & M Pegasus Quik	J. Rodgers	
G-CIPB	Messerschmitt Bf109E-4 (3579/14)	Biggin Hill Heritage Hangar Ltd	
G-CIPD	Cameron O-31 balloon	A. Dunnington	
G-CIPE	Boeing Stearman A75L300	Retro Track and Air (UK) Ltd	
G-CIPF	Alisport Silent 2 Electro	A. & M. Truelove	
G-CIPG	BRM Aero Bristell NG5 Speed Wing	G-CIPG Syndicate	
G-CIPL	Van's RV-9	R. Manning	
G-CIPM	P & M Quik R	M. R. Niznik	
G-CIPO	Ikarus C42 FB80	D. J. Brookfield	
G-CIPP	AutoGyro Calidus	S. McMellon	
G-CIPR	Skyranger Nynja 912(1)	J. M. Ross	
G-CIPS	Eurofox 912(1)	M. B. Jackson	
G-CIPT	BRM Aero Bristell NG5 Speed Wing	A. J. Radford	
G-CIPU	Cessna F.172F	G. Hinz/Germany	
G-CIPY	Cessna F.172 II	Brinkley Aviation Ltd	
G-CIPZ	Pazmany PL-4A	J. J. Hill	
G-CIRB	Aerotechnik EV-97 Eurostar SL	C. R. Williams	
G-CIRC	Such BM60-20 balloon	D. J. Tofton	
G-CIRE	Corby CJ-1 Starlet	J. Evans	
G-CIRG	Airbus Helicopters AS350B3 Ecureuil	Airbus Helicopters UK Ltd	
G-CIRH	Magni M16C Tandem Trainer	O. Levy	
G-CIRI	Cirrus SR20	Cirrus Flyers Group	
G-CIRL	Ultramagic S-90 balloon	O. G. V. Stallwood & D. M. Feldhaus	
G-CIRM	Van's RV-12	S. Dale	
G-CIRO	Cessna F.172H	H. G. Stroemer	
G-CIRP	Eurofox 912(S)	M. Petrie & S. D. Kellner	
G-CIRT	AutoGyro MTOSport	M. Pugh & J. Gleeson	
G-CIRV	Van's RV-7	R. J. Fray	
G-CIRW	Cessna FA.150K	Air Navigation and Trading Company Ltd	
G-CIRX	Cameron Z-150 balloon	Bristol International Balloon Fiesta Ltd	
G-CIRY	Aerotechnik EV-97 Eurostar SL	Hotel Victor Flying Group	
G-CIRZ	Ikarus C42 FB80	Mainair Microlight School Ltd	
G-CISB	Sackville AH56 balloon	B. D. Close	
G-CISC	Sackville AH77 balloon	T. I. Laws	
G-CISD	Sackville AH31 balloon	P. Coman	
G-CISE	Aero Designs Pulsar XP	S. C. Goozee	
G-CISF	Quad City Challenger II	S. A. Beddus	
G-CISG	Ikarus C42 FB80	M. Howland	
G-CISH	Thatcher CX4	J. R. Pullin	
G-CISI	P & M Quik GTR	Kent County Scout Council	
G-CISJ	Ultramagic H-31 balloon	R. P. Wade	
G-CISN	Flylight Foxcub	G. Nicholas	
G-CISO	Cessna 150G	Egoli Enterprises Ltd	
G-CISR	Flying K Sky Raider 1	J. A. Harris	
G-CISS	Ikarus C42 FB80	C-More Flying School	
G-CIST	P & M Quik GT450	N. E. King	

Notes	Reg	Type	Owner or Operator
	G-CISU	CM Sunbird	C. W. Mitchinson
	G-CISX	Cessna 172M	Praeluceo Property Ltd
	G-CISZ	Van's RV-7	R. O. Johnson, J. M. Fulton & M. Stewart
	G-CITC	Apollo Delta Jet 2	P. Broome
	G-CITD	Sportavia-Putzer Fournier RF-5	G-CITD Group
	G-CITE	Grob G.102 Astir CS Jeans	The Bath, Wilts & North Dorset Gliding Club Ltd
	G-CITF	EV-97 Eurostar SL	P. D. Street
	G-CITG	Skyranger Nynja 912S(1)	J. Attard
	G-CITH	Rans S-6-ES Coyote II	E. Espie
	G-CITK	Alisport Silent 2 Targa	A. M. Keyte
	G-CITL	Ace Magic Cyclone	S. F. Beardsell
	G-CITM	Magni M16C Tandem Trainer	Lambdatek Ltd
	G-CITO	P & M Quik	M. P. Jackson
	G-CITR	Cameron Z-105 balloon	A. Kaye
	G-CITS	Groppo Trail	L. B. Smith
	G-CITT	Mooney M.20J Model 201	J. M. Tiley
	G-CITV	AutoGyro Cavalon	C. P. Rowley
	G-CITW	Extra EA.400	LAC Marine Ltd
	G-CITX	AutoGyro MTOSport	M. Bragg
	G-CIUA	Ultramagic B-70 balloon	K. W. Graham
	G-CIUB	Cameron Z-90 balloon	M. N. Macleod
	G-CIUD	ACLA Sirocco SW FT	S. Siddiqui (G-ROCO)
	G-CIUF	Aviad Zigolo MG12	J. L. Burgoin, T. J. Franklin & S. J. Reeves
	G-CIUG	Eurofox 3K	J. V. Clewer
	G-CIUH	Cessna 152	Easy Aircrtaft Rental Ltd
	G-CIUM	PA-12 Super Cruiser	J. Havers & S. James
	G-CIUO	Ekolot KR-010 ELF	P. V. Griffiths
	G-CIUP	Europa XS	P. C. Matthews & P. Bridges
	G-CIUW	AT-16 Harvard IIB (FE511)	Collett Aviation Services Ltd
	G-CIUX	Auster AOP.Mk.9 (WZ679)	R. Warner
	G-CIUZ	P & M Quik GTR	D. Sisson
	G-CIVB	Boeing 747-436 ★	preserved Cotswold Airport
	G-CIVW	Boeing 747-436 ★	preserved Cotswold Airport
	G-CIWA	Skyranger Swift 912(1)	S. D. Lilley
	G-CIWB	Van's RV-6	G. D. Price
	G-CIWC	Raj Hamsa X'Air Hawk	G. A. J. Salter
	G-CIWG	Eurofox 915(IS)	A. Hegner
	G-CIWI	EV-97 Eurostar SL	Mademoiselle CIWI Group
	G-CIWL	Techpro Merlin 100UL	A. J. Glynn
	G-CIWN	Such BM42-16 balloon	C. Kunert & C. J. Battersby
	G-CIWO	AS.350B3 Ecureuil	R & J Helicopters LLP
	G-CIWP	Ikarus C42 FB100	G-CIWP Syndicate
	G-CIWT	Ikarus C42 FB80	J. W. Lorains
	G-CIWU	McDonnell Douglas MD.369E	A Shade Greener Finance Ltd
	G-CIWV	Van's RV-7	J. W. Baker
	G-CIWW	Sackville BM-56 balloon	R. P. Wade
	G-CIWX	Sackville 65 balloon	R. Frankham
	G-CIWY	Sackville 90 balloon	D. Sulcas
	G-CIWZ	Sackville 6BM-34 balloon	T. J. Wilkinson
	G-CIXB	Grob G.109B	The Full English
	G-CIXD	Cameron A-105 balloon	K. R. Karlstrom
	G-CIXE	Moravan Zlin Z-326 Trener Master	J. P. Armitage
	G-CIXG	Phantom X1	K. B. Woods
	G-CIXH	Schempp-Hirth Ventus 2a	P. M. Shelton
	G-CIXL	Air Creation Ifun 13 Pixel 250XC	M. Ford
	G-CIXM	Supermarine Spitfire Mk.26 (PL793)	S. W. Markham
	G-CIXN	CFM Shadow Series E	U. J. Anderson
	G-CIXP	Cessna 152	H. E. da Costa Alburquerque
	G-CIXR	Cameron Z-77 balloon	G. Kilsby
	G-CIXS	Zenair CH.701SP	J. M. Watts
	G-CIXT	Fox 13TL/Eurofly Snake	M. Tatt
	G-CIXU	Cameron Z-77 balloon	N. J. Langley
	G-CIXX	AutoGyro Cavalon	J. A. Hughes
	G-CIXY	Ikarus C42 FB80	T. H. Brown
	G-CIXZ	P & M Quik R	M. Finch & G. J. P. Skinner
	G-CIYC	Flylight Foxcub	D. P. Lee
	G-CIYG	Airbike Light Sport	J. A. Harris
	G-CIYJ	MD Helicopter Inc Hughes 369E	Studwelders Holdings Ltd
	G-CIYK	Free Spirit Biplane	J. C. Greenslade
	G-CIYL	Eurofox 912iS(1)	R. K. W. Moss
	G-CIYN	Skyranger Nynja 912S(1)	R. W. Sutherland

Reg	Type	Owner or Operator	Notes
G-CIYO	Groppo Trail	G. R. Williams	
G-CIYP	Eurofox 912(1)	J. Andrews	
G-CIYT	Flugastol	F. B. Rich	
G-CIYV	Van's RV-9A	M. S. Ashby	
G-CIYY	TLAC Sherwood Ranger XP	M. R. M. Welch	
G-CIYZ	P & M Quik R	T. E. Reed	
G-CIZA	Spacek SD-1 Minisport	K. P. Rusling	
G-CIZB	Magni M-24C Orion	B. F. Pearson	
G-CIZD	P & M Quik GT450	D. Orton	
G-CIZE	Cameron O-56 balloon	P. Spellward	
G-CIZF	Ozone Indy/Paramotor Flyer Trike	M. R. Gaylor	
G-CIZG	Robinson R66	Buildrandom Ltd	
G-CIZL	P & M Quik R	S. K. Green	
G-CIZM	Cameron Z-210 balloon	N. J. Dunnington	
G-CIZN	J-5B Cub Cruiser	M. Howells	
G-CIZO	PA-28-161 Cadet	Falcon Flying Services Ltd	
G-CIZP	AutoGyro Cavalon Pro	C. Coffield	
G-CIZR	Van's RV-9	A. F. Wankowski & H. C. Wankowska	
G-CIZS	Tipsy Nipper T.66 Series 2	S. R. Green	
G-CIZT	Ace Magic Cyclone	T. L. Squires	
G-CIZU	EV-97 Eurostar SL	E. K. McAlinden	
G-CIZV	P & M Quik R	G-CIZV Syndicate	
G-CIZW	Alisport Silent 2 Electro	J. R. Bisset & N. D. Gatward	
G-CJAF	Cessna 182T	Aerospace Resources	
G-CJAI	P & M Quik GT450	M. Ingleton	
G-CJAJ	P & M Quik GT450	D. Al-Bassam	
G-CJAK	Skyranger Nynja 912S(1)	A. K. Birt	
G-CJAL	Schleicher Ka 6E	JAL Syndicate	
G-CJAM	Ikarus C42 FB80	M. A. Camponi	
G-CJAO	Schempp-Hirth Discus b	R. W. Coombs	
G-CJAP	Ikarus C42 FB80	M. R. Theobald	
G-CJAR	Schempp-Hirth Discus bT	C. J. H. Donnelly	
G-CJAS	Glasflugel Standard Libelle 201B	M. J. Collett	
G-CJAT	Schleicher K8B	D. B. Harrison	
G-CJAU	White Sports Monoplane	J. Aubert	
G-CJAV	Schleicher ASK-21	Rattlesden Gliding Club Ltd	
G-CJAW	Glaser-Dirks DG-200/17	R. A. van H. Pennick	
G-CJAX	Schleicher ASK-21	Wolds Gliding Club Ltd	
G-CJAY	Mainair Pegasus Quik GT450	M. Ingleton	
G-CJAZ	Grob G.102 Astir CS Jeans	M. R. Dews	
G-CJBA	Alisport Silent 2 Electro	B. A. Fairston & A. Stotter	
G-CJBC	PA-28-180 Cherokee	J. B. Cave	
G-CJBD	Spacek SD-1 Minisport	D. Cox	
G CJBE	Ikarus C42 FB80	Micro Aviation Ltd	
G-CJBH	Eiriavion PIK-20D	Y. Kozheurov	
G-CJBI	Eurofox 912(iS)	M. B. Z. de Ferranti	
G-CJBJ	Schempp-Hirth Standard Cirrus	S. T. Dutton	
G-CJBK	Schleicher ASW-19B	A. R. Greensmith	
G-CJBL	Twamley Trike/Flylight Foxtug	R. W. Twamley	
G-CJBM	Schleicher ASK-21	The Burn Gliding Club Ltd	
G-CJBN	Sackville BM-65 balloon	M. Newman	
G-CJBO	Rolladen-Schneider LS8-18	N. Croxford	
G-CJBR	Schempp-Hirth Discus b	G-CJBR Group	
G-CJBT	Schleicher ASW-19B	E. Steffinlongo	
G-CJBU	BRM Aero Bristell NG5 Speed Wing	H. R. Pearson	
G-CJBV	IAV Bacau Yak-52	G. G. L. James	
G-CJBW	Schempp-Hirth Discus bT	G-CJBW Syndicate	
G-CJBX	Rolladen-Schneider LS4-a	A. P. Wheeler	
G-CJBZ	Grob G.102 Astir CS	The Royal Air Force Gliding Association	
G-CJCD	Schleicher ASW-24	B. Bobrovinkov	
G-CJCE	Ultramagic M-77C	G. A. Chadwick & J. W. Adams	
G-CJCF	Grob G.102 Astir CS77	The Northumbria Gliding Club Ltd	
G-CJCG	PZL-Swidnik PW-5 Smyk	R. J. Brown & H. S. van de Noort	
G-CJCH	AB Sportine Aviacija LAK-19T	A. G. Gibbs	
G-CJCJ	Schempp-Hirth Standard Cirrus	G-CJCJ Syndicate	
G-CJCK	Schempp-Hirth Discus bT	G. A. Friedrich	
G-CJCL	Aerotechnik EV-97B Eurostar SL	M. Dunlop	
G-CJCM	Schleicher ASW-27	Zulu Glasstek Ltd	
G-CJCN	Schempp-Hirth Standard Cirrus 75	G. D. E. Macdonald	
G-CJCO	Ikarus C42 FB80	GS Aviation (Europe) Ltd	

Notes	Reg	Type	Owner or Operator
	G-CJCR	Grob G.102 Astir CS	B. J. Harrison
	G-CJCT	Schempp-Hirth Nimbus 4T	E. W. Richards
	G-CJCU	Schempp-Hirth Standard Cirrus B	S. M. Slawinski
	G-CJCW	Grob G.102 Astir CS77	A. P. Daines
	G-CJCX	Schempp-Hirth Discus bT	A. D. Johnson
	G-CJDA	Ikarus C42 FB80	Mainair Microlight School Ltd
	G-CJDB	Cessna 525 Citationjet	Breed Aircraft Ltd
	G-CJDC	Schleicher ASW-27	P. G. Farrimond & R. J. Brimfield
	G-CJDD	Glaser-Dirks DG-200/17	N. P. Harrison
	G-CJDE	Rolladen-Schneider LS8-18	Army Gliding Association
	G-CJDG	Rolladen-Schneider LS6B	R. H. & A. Moss
	G-CJDJ	Rolladen-Schneider LS3	B. J. R. Moate
	G-CJDL	Pipistrel Apis 15M M FES	Callen-Lenz Associates Ltd
	G-CJDM	Schleicher ASW-15B	J. D. Morris
	G-CJDN	Cameron C-90 balloon	N. Ivison
	G-CJDP	Glaser-Dirks DG-200/17	G. K. Hutchinson
	G-CJDS	Schempp-Hirth Standard Cirrus 75	P. Nicholls
	G-CJDV	DG Flugzeugbau DG-300 Elan Acro	D. M. Lisk
	G-CJDW	Magni M-16C Tandem Trainer	R. W. D. Noon
	G-CJEA	Rolladen-Schneider LS8-18	M. W. Durham
	G-CJEB	Schleicher ASW-24	P. C. Scholz
	G-CJEC	PZL-Bielsko SZD-50-3 Puchasz	Cambridge Gliding Club Ltd
	G-CJED	Schempp-Hirth Nimbus 3/24.5	J. Edyvean
	G-CJEE	Schleicher ASW-20L	P. Woodcock
	G-CJEH	Glasflugel Mosquito B	CJEH Syndicate
	G-CJEI	UltraMagic M-77 balloon	D. Baker
	G-CJEJ	Skyranger Nynja 912(1)	G-CJEJ Rossall Skyranger
	G-CJEL	Schleicher ASW-24	C. W. Lewis
	G-CJEP	Rolladen-Schneider LS4-b	S. M. Platt
	G-CJER	Schempp-Hirth Standard Cirrus 75	C. Parvin
	G-CJEU	Glasflugel Standard Libelle	G. S. Morrison
	G-CJEW	Schleicher Ka 6CR	W. J. Prince
	G-CJEX	Schempp-Hirth Ventus 2a	D. S. Watt
	G-CJEY	Flylight Dragon Combat 12T	T. Southwell
	G-CJEZ	Glaser-Dirks DG-100	D. P. Spragg
	G-CJFA	Schempp-Hirth Standard Cirrus	J. Osment
	G-CJFC	Schempp-Hirth Discus CS	S. J. Jenkins
	G-CJFG	Aeriane Swift Light PAS	M. Jackson
	G-CJFH	Schempp-Hirth Duo Discus	The Royal Air Force Gliding and Soaring Association
	G-CJFJ	Schleicher ASW-20CL	A. M. McDeremott
	G-CJFN	DHC.8-402Q Dash Eight	NAC Aviation 23 Ltd
	G-CJFS	Pulse SSDR	M. Allan
	G-CJFT	Schleicher K-8B	The Surrey Hills Gliding Club Ltd
	G-CJFU	Schleicher ASW-19B	M. T. Stanley
	G-CJFW	Ace As-tec 15	S. E. Dancaster
	G-CJFX	Rolladen-Schneider LS8-a	M. J. Gatfield
	G-CJGB	Schleicher K 8B	L. R. Merritt
	G-CJGD	Scleicher K 8B	NICO Syndicate
	G-CJGE	Schleicher ASK-21	Midland Gliding Club Ltd
	G-CJGF	Schempp-Hirth Ventus c	R. D. Slater
	G-CJGG	P & M Quik GT450	S. J. Butler
	G-CJGH	Schempp-Hirth Nimbus 2C	G-CJGH Syndicate
	G-CJGJ	Schleicher ASK-21	Scottish Gliding Union Ltd
	G-CJGK	Eiri PIL-200	D. M. & J. P. Roberts
	G-CJGL	Schempp-Hirth Discus CS	The Royal Air Force Gliding and Soaring Association
	G-CJGM	Schempp-Hirth Discus CS	The Royal Air Force Gliding and Soaring Association
	G-CJGN	Schempp-Hirth Standard Cirrus	P. A. Shuttleworth
	G-CJGP	Breezer M400	A. P. Walker
	G-CJGR	Schempp-Hirth Discus bT	G. W. Kemp
	G-CJGS	Rolladen-Schneider LS8-18	T. Stupnik
	G-CJGT	AMS-Flight Apis M	Chris Dawes Ltd
	G-CJGU	Schempp-Hirth Mini-Nimbus B	M. D. Cobham
	G-CJGV	Flylight Foxcub	S. J. E. Smith
	G-CJGW	Schleicher ASK-13	Darlton Gliding Club Ltd
	G-CJGY	Schempp-Hirth Standard Cirrus	P. J. Shout
	G-CJHC	Kolb Firefly	I. C. White
	G-CJHF	Eurofox 912(iS)	BGC Eurofox Group
	G-CJHG	Grob G.102 Astir CS	P. L. E. Zelazowski

Reg	Type	Owner or Operator	Notes
G-CJHJ	Glasflugel Standard Libelle 201B	N. P. Marriott	
G-CJHL	Schleicher Ka 6E	J. R. Gilbert	
G-CJHM	Schempp-Hirth Discus b	E. N. Hellawell	
G-CJHN	Grob G.102 Astir CS Jeans	A. J. Morgan	
G-CJHO	Schleicher ASK-18	R43 Syndicate	
G-CJHP	Flight Design CTSW	S. J. Reader	
G-CJHR	Centrair SNC34C Alliance	The Borders (Milfield) Gliding Club Ltd	
G-CJHS	Schleicher ASW-19B	JHS Syndicate	
G-CJHT	Eurofox 3K	M. C. Gayton	
G-CJHV	Lindstrand LTL Series 1-31 balloon	Pegasus Ballooning	
G-CJHW	Glaser-Dirks DG-200	I. A. Rudy	
G-CJHY	Rolladen-Schneider LS8-18	S. J. Eyles	
G-CJHZ	Schleicher ASW-20	T. J. Stanley	
G-CJIB	Alisport Silent 2 Electro	G-CJIB Gransden Group	
G-CJID	Alisport Silent 2	A. K. Carver	
G-CJIE	Flylight Foxcub	B. R. Ward	
G-CJIH	Lindstrand LTL Series 1-105 balloon	R. M. Theil	
G-CJII	TLAC Sherwood Ranger ST	M. M. A. Darcy	
G-CJIK	Cameron Z-77 balloon	P. Greaves	
G-CJIL	Sackville BM-90 balloon	B. Crossland-Mead	
G-CJIN	Boeing Stearman A75L300 (4826:582)	A. Brooks	
G-CJIO	Rans S65 Sport	R. J. Almey	
G-CJIP	Aero 31 AM9 balloon	C. J. Sanger-Davies	
G-CJIR	Rotorway Executive 162F	Scotshouse Quarries Ltd (G-ESUS)	
G-CJIT	Ikarus C42 FB100	The SARM Group	
G-CJIX	Cameron O-31 balloon	D. J. Head	
G-CJJA	EV-97 Eurostar SL	G-CJJA Group	
G-CJJB	Rolladen-Schneider LS4	M. Tomlinson	
G-CJJC	Lindstrand LTL Series 1-105 balloon	J. E. Rose	
G-CJJD	Schempp-Hirth Discus bT	G-CJJD Syndicate	
G-CJJE	Schempp-Hirth Discus-a	A. Soffici	
G-CJJH	DG Flugzeugbau DG-800S	B. D. Allen	
G-CJJJ	Schempp-Hirth Standard Cirrus	J. J. Conway & T. B. Tomkins	
G-CJJK	Rolladen-Schneider LS8-18	A. D. Roch	
G-CJJL	Schleicher ASW-19B	G-CJJL Group	
G-CJJN	Robin HR.100/210 Safari II	A. Waters	
G-CJJP	Schempp-Hirth Duo Discus	494 Syndicate	
G-CJJS	PA-28-151 Cherokee Warrior	R. J. Whyam (G-VIVS)	
G-CJJT	Schleicher ASW-27	N. J. Laux	
G-CJJV	Van's RV-12	S. Eustace	
G-CJJW	Lambert Mission M108	D. S. James	
G-CJJX	Schleicher ASW-15B	Derbyshire & Lancashire Gliding Club Ltd	
G-CJJY	Aerochute SSDR	G. R. Britton	
G-CJJZ	Schempp-Hirth Discus bT	I. S. Gillbe	
G-CJKA	Schleicher ASK-21	East Sussex Gliding Club Ltd	
G-CJKB	PZL-Swidnik PW-5 Smyk	Loughborough Students Union	
G-CJKE	PZL-Swidnik PW-5 Smyk	D. Hertzberg	
G-CJKF	Glaser-Dirks DG-200	D. O. Sandells	
G-CJKG	Schleicher ASK-18	The Royal Air Force Gliding and Soaring Association	
G-CJKH	Ultramagic M-120 balloon	Cold Climate Expeditions Ltd	
G-CJKI	Ultramagic S-90 balloon	M. P. Rowley	
G-CJKJ	Schleicher ASK-21	The Royal Air Force Gliding and Soaring Association	
G-CJKK	Schleicher ASK-21	Army Gliding Association	
G-CJKM	Glaser-Dirks DG200/17	G. F. Coles & E. W. Russell	
G-CJKN	Rolladen-Schneider LS8-18	790 Syndicate	
G-CJKO	Schleicher ASK-21	The Royal Air Force Gliding and Soaring Association	
G-CJKP	Rolladen-Schneider LS4-b	D. A. Spencer	
G-CJKS	Schleicher ASW-19B	R. J. P. Lancaster	
G-CJKT	Schleicher ASK-13	Ulster Gliding Club Ltd	
G-CJKU	Schleicher ASK-18	Derbyshire & Lancashire Gliding Club Ltd	
G-CJKV	Grob G.103A Twin II Acro	The Welland Gliding Club Ltd	
G-CJKW	Grob G.102 Astir CS77	The Bath, Wilts and North Dorset Gliding Club Ltd	
G-CJKY	Schempp-Hirth Ventus cT	G. V. Matthews & M. P. Osborn	
G-CJKZ	Schleicher ASK-21	BR Aviation Ltd	
G-CJLA	Schempp-Hirth Ventus 2cT	S. G. Jones	
G-CJLC	Schempp-Hirth Discus CS	S. M. Stannard	
G-CJLD	Lambert Mission M108	P. R. Mailer	

Notes	Reg	Type	Owner or Operator
	G-CJLF	Schleicher ASK-13	V. Mallon
	G-CJLH	Rolladen-Schneider LS4	D. D. Keegan
	G-CJLI	PA-28-161 Cherokee Warrior II	W. Ali & Denderah Sa
	G-CJLJ	Rolladen-Schneider LS4-b	Army Gliding Association
	G-CJLK	Rolladen-Schneider LS7	D. N. Munro & S. Urry
	G-CJLL	Robinson R44 II	R. D. J. Alexander
	G-CJLM	Denney Kitfox 4-1050 Speedster	C. Kinder & T. Neale
	G-CJLN	Rolladen-Schneider LS8-18	The Royal Air Force Gliding and Soaring Association
	G-CJLO	Schleicher ASK-13	Bowland Forest Gliding Club Ltd
	G-CJLP	Schempp-Hirth Discus CS	J. G. Arnold
	G-CJLS	Schleicher K-8B	E. Ustenler
	G-CJLT	Cameron O-84 balloon	T. M. Lee
	G-CJLV	Schleicher Ka-6E	J. C. Cooper
	G-CJLW	Schempp-Hirth Discus CS	J. G. Arnold
	G-CJLX	Schempp-Hirth Standard Cirrus	S. France
	G-CJLY	Schleicher ASW-27	H. F. Pires da Ribeira
	G-CJLZ	Grob G.103A Twin II Acro	21 Syndicate
	G-CJMA	Schleicher ASK-18	D. A. Shipley
	G-CJMF	BRM Aero Bristell NG5 Speed Wing	C. J. Taunton
	G-CJMG	PZL-Bielsko SZD-51-1 Junior	Kent Gliding Club Ltd
	G-CJMJ	Schleicher ASK-13	S. A. Adlard
	G-CJMK	Schleicher ASK-18	R. W. Skuse
	G-CJML	Grob G.102 Astir CS77	The Royal Air Force Gliding and Soaring Association
	G-CJMN	Schempp-Hirth Nimbus 2	R. A. Holroyd
	G-CJMO	Rolladen-Schneider LS8-18	J. M. Hood
	G-CJMP	Schleicher ASK-13	The Surrey Hills Gliding Club Ltd
	G-CJMS	Schleicher ASK-21	The Royal Air Force Gliding and Soaring Association
	G-CJMU	Rolladen-Schneider LS8-18	O. E. Ramsay
	G-CJMV	Schempp-Hirth Nimbus-2C	M. P. Benson
	G-CJMW	Schleicher ASK-13	The Royal Air Force Gliding and Soaring Association
	G-CJMX	Schleicher ASK-13	The Nene Valley Gliding Club Ltd
	G-CJMY	PZL-Bielsko SZD-51-1 Junior	The Burn Gliding Club Ltd
	G-CJMZ	Schleicher ASK-13	The Vale of the White Horse Gliding Centre Ltd
	G-CJNA	Grob G.102 Astir CS Jeans	M. F.Defendi
	G-CJNB	Rolladen-Schneider LS8-18	B. B. Hughes
	G-CJNF	Schempp-Hirth Discus 2a	T. J. Milner
	G-CJNG	Glasflugel Standard Libelle 201B	S. J. Trowell
	G-CJNH	P & M Quik R	N. Hammerton
	G-CJNJ	Rolladen-Schneider LS8-18	A. B. Laws
	G-CJNK	Rolladen-Schneider LS8-18	Army Gliding Association
	G-CJNL	Jodel DR.1050M Replica	M. G. Dolphin
	G-CJNN	Schleicher K 8B	Buckminster Gliding Club Ltd
	G-CJNO	Glaser-Dirks DG-300 Elan	Yankee Kilo Group
	G-CJNP	Rolladen-Schneider LS6-b	E. & P. S. Fink
	G-CJNR	Glasflugel Mosquito B	R. Birch
	G-CJNU	Techpro Merlin 100UL	B. S. Carpenter
	G-CJNZ	Glaser-Dirks DG-100	S. Mudaliar
	G-CJOA	Schempp-Hirth Discus b	K. A. Jarrett
	G-CJOB	Schleicher K 8B	UWE Gliding Club
	G-CJOC	Schempp-Hirth Discus bT	F. J. Jones
	G-CJOD	Rolladen-Schneider LS8-18	The Royal Air Force Gliding and Soaring Association
	G-CJOE	Schempp-Hirth Standard Cirrus	A. B. Cresswell
	G-CJOJ	Schleicher K 8B	M. P. Webb
	G-CJOK	HpH Glasflugel 304 MS Shark	JOK Syndicate
	G-CJOL	Eurofox 3K	C. D. Waldron
	G-CJOM	Eurofox 3K	G. R. Postans
	G-CJON	Grob G.102 Astir CS77	The Royal Air Force Gliding and Soaring Association
	G-CJOO	Schempp-Hirth Duo Discus	A. & C. A. Sheldon
	G-CJOR	Schempp-Hirth Ventus 2cT	A. M. George & N. A. Maclean
	G-CJOS	Schempp-Hirth Standard Cirrus	G-CJOS Group
	G-CJOT	Ikarus C42 FB80	Cumulus International Services Ltd
	G-CJOV	Schleicher ASW-27	P. J. Stratten
	G-CJOW	Schempp-Hirth Cirrus VTC	North Wales Gliding Club Ltd
	G-CJOX	Schleicher ASK-21	Southdown Gliding Club Ltd
	G-CJOY	Zenair CH.601HDS Zodiac	G. M. Johnson

Reg	Type	Owner or Operator	Notes
G-CJOZ	Schleicher K 8B	Derbyshire and Lancashire Gliding Club Ltd	
G-CJPA	Schempp-Hirth Duo Discus	R. A. Markham	
G-CJPB	Skyranger Swift 582(1)	T. W. Thiele	
G-CJPC	Schleicher ASK-13	Shalbourne Soaring Society Ltd	
G-CJPE	Skyranger Nynja 912S(1)	B. J. Youngs	
G-CJPI	HPH Glasflugel 304S Jet	J. M. Whelan	
G-CJPJ	Grob G.104 Speed Astir IIB	W. F. Griffiths	
G-CJPK	Sgian Dubh	Sgian Dubh Flying Group	
G-CJPL	Rolladen-Schneider LS8-18	I. A. Reekie	
G-CJPM	Grob G.102 Astir CS Jeans	G-CJPM Syndicate	
G-CJPO	Schleicher ASK-18	The Royal Air Force Gliding and Soaring Association	
G-CJPP	Schempp-Hirth Discus b	D. M. Gill	
G-CJPR	Rolladen-Schneider LS8-18	D. M. Byass & J. A. McCoshim	
G-CJPT	Schleicher ASW-27	T. S. Stepleton	
G-CJPV	Schleicher ASK-13	Cyprus Gliding Group/Cyprus	
G-CJPW	Glaser-Dirks DG-200	A. W. Kitchen & L. Collinson	
G-CJPX	Schleicher ASW-15	M. A. Durden	
G-CJPY	Schleicher ASK-13	The Royal Air Force Gliding and Soaring Association	
G-CJPZ	Schleicher ASK-18	R. W. Skuse	
G-CJRA	Rolladen-Schneider LS8-18	J. Williams	
G-CJRB	Schleicher ASW-19B	J. W. Baxter	
G-CJRC	Glaser-Dirks DG-300 Elan	P. J. Sillett	
G-CJRE	Scleicher ASW-15	R. A. Starling	
G-CJRF	PZL-Bielsko SZD-50-3 Puchacz	Wolds Gliding Club Ltd	
G-CJRG	Schempp-Hirth Standard Cirrus	F. M. Grosche	
G-CJRJ	PZL-Bielsko SZD-50-3 Puchacz	Derbyshire & Lancashire Gliding Club Ltd	
G-CJRK	Cameron Z-31 balloon	D. D. Maltby	
G-CJRL	Glaser-Dirks DG-100G Elan	Southampton University Gliding Club	
G-CJRM	Grob G.102 Astir CS	A. R. Moore	
G-CJRN	Glaser-Dirks DG-200/17	T. G. Roberts	
G-CJRO	Cameron Z-105 balloon	BWS Standfast Fire and Security Systems	
G-CJRS	BRM Aero Bristell NG5 Speed Wing	A. Watt	
G-CJRT	Schempp-Hirth Standard Cirrus	M. Strickland & J. A. D. Fowkes	
G-CJRU	Schleicher ASW-24	I. G. Walker & D. Tait	
G-CJRV	Schleicher ASW-19B	J. A. Bartlett	
G-CJRX	Schleicher ASK-13	The Royal Air Force Gliding and Soaring Association	
G-CJRZ	Ikarus C42 FB80	D. W. Cross	
G-CJSA	Nanchang NAMC CJ-6A (CT130)	J. N. Ware & M. Elmes	
G-CJSB	Republic RC-3 Seabee	J. A. & R. H. Cooper	
G-CJSC	Schempp-Hirth Nimbus-3DT	S. G. Jones	
G-CJSD	Grob G.102 Astir CS	The Royal Air Force Gliding and Soaring Association	
G-CJSE	Schempp-Hirth Discus b	Imperial College of Science, Technology and Medicine	
G-CJSG	Schleicher Ka 6E	A. J. Emck	
G-CJSH	Grob G.102 Club Astir IIIB	Lasham Gliding Society Ltd	
G-CJSL	Schempp-Hirth Ventus cT	M. J. Newbery	
G-CJSM	Van's RV-8	S. T. G. Lloyd	
G-CJSN	Schleicher K 8B	Cotswold Gliding Club	
G-CJSP	PA-28-180 Cherokee Archer	K. J. Perryman	
G-CJSS	Schleicher ASW-27	G. K. & S. R. Drury	
G-CJST	Rolladen-Schneider LS1-c	A. M. Walker	
G-CJSU	Rolladen-Schneider LS8-18	J. G. Bell	
G-CJSV	Schleicher ASK-13	The Royal Air Force Gliding and Soaring Association	
G-CJSX	AMS-Flight DG-500	Oxford Gliding Company Ltd	
G-CJSY	Sackville BM-34 balloon	M. Newman	
G-CJSZ	Schleicher ASK-18	C. Weston	
G-CJTA	Autogyro MTOSport	J. M. Gibson Executor of the Estate of W. C. Walters & G. M. Johnson	
G-CJTB	Schleicher ASW-24	T. Davies	
G-CJTC	AutoGyro Calidus	C. J. Rose	
G-CJTD	Techpro Aviation Merlin 100UL	J. Murphy	
G-CJTE	Eurofox 3K	C. M. Theakstone	
G-CJTG	Hoffman H36 Dimona II	Mendip Dimona Group	
G-CJTH	Schleicher ASW-24	J. Bodzsar	
G-CJTI	Aerochute Industries Hummerchute	S. T. P. Askew	
G-CJTJ	Schempp-Hirth Mini-Nimbus B	B. L. Hudson	

Notes	Reg	Type	Owner or Operator
	G-CJTK	DG Flugzeugbau DG-300 Elan Acro	A. Drury
	G-CJTM	Rolladen-Schneider LS8-18	A. D. Holmes
	G-CJTN	Glaser-Dirks DG-300 Elan	P. R. Gardner & S. F. Ducker
	G-CJTO	Glasflugel H303A Mosquito	P. J. Gilll
	G-CJTP	Schleicher ASW-20L	C. A. Sheldon & R. Abercrombie
	G-CJTS	Schempp-Hirth Cirrus VTC	G-CJTS Cirrus Group
	G-CJTT	Aerochute Industries Hummerchute	D. C. Bichan
	G-CJTU	Schempp-Hirth Duo Discus T	I. Hayward
	G-CJTX	EV-97 Eurostar SL	G-TX Group
	G-CJTY	Rolladen-Schneider LS8-a	JTY Syndicate
	G-CJUB	Schempp-Hirth Discus CS	P. S. Smith
	G-CJUD	Denney Kitfox Mk.3	I. C. Pearson
	G-CJUF	Schempp-Hirth Ventus 2cT	A. L. Farr
	G-CJUJ	Schleicher ASW-27	T. K. Gooch
	G-CJUK	Grob G.102 Astir CS	Oxford Gliding Company Ltd
	G-CJUN	Schleicher ASW-19B	M. P. S. Roberts
	G-CJUR	Valentin Mistral C	East Sussex Gliding Club Ltd
	G-CJUT	Skyranger Nynja 912S(1)	A. Jackson
	G-CJUU	Schempp-Hirth Standard Cirrus	A. B. Cresswell
	G-CJUV	Schempp-Hirth Discus b	Lasham Gliding Society Ltd
	G-CJUX	Aviastroitel AC-4C	J. R. Stiles & A. Jarvis
	G-CJUY	SNS-8 Hiperlight	J. K. Parnaby
	G-CJUZ	Schleicher ASW-19B	J. M. Hough & M. R. Baldwin
	G-CJVA	Schempp-Hirth Ventus 2cT	M. S. Armstrong
	G-CJVB	Schempp-Hirth Discus bT	R. J. Simpson
	G-CJVC	PZL-Bielsko SZD-51-1 Junior	York Gliding Centre (Operations) Ltd
	G-CJVD	Team Minimax 1600	D. R. Thompson
	G-CJVE	Eiriavion PIK-20D	S. R. Wilkinson
	G-CJVG	Schempp-Hirth Discus bT	C. A. Edwards
	G-CJVH	Lindstrand LTL Series 1-105 balloon	Nottingham & Derby Hot Air Balloon Club
	G-CJVI	Techpro Merlin 100UL	P. A. Tarplee
	G-CJVK	Skyranger Nynja 912S(1)	H. G. Reid
	G-CJVL	DG-300 Elan	A. T. Vidion & M. S. Hoy
	G-CJVM	Schleicher ASW-27	G. K. Payne
	G-CJVN	Lindstrand Racer 65 balloon	Slowfly Montgolfiere SNC/Italy
	G-CJVP	Glaser-Dirks DG-200	L. M. Wilkinson & R. W. Iddon
	G-CJVS	Schleicher ASW-28	W. J. Veitch
	G-CJVU	Standard Cirrus CS-11-75L	S. R. Prideaux
	G-CJVV	Schempp-Hirth Janus C	A. P. Balkwill
	G-CJVW	Schleicher ASW-15	G. M. S. Smith
	G-CJVX	Schempp-Hirth Discus CS	988 Group '988'
	G-CJVZ	Schleicher ASK-21	Yorkshire Gliding Club (Proprietary) Ltd
	G-CJWA	Schleicher ASW-28	B-I. Manoiu
	G-CJWB	Schleicher ASK-13	East Sussex Gliding Club Ltd
	G-CJWD	Schleicher ASK-21	London Gliding Club Proprietary Ltd
	G-CJWE	Harvard 4 (481273)	M. J. S. Wright
	G-CJWG	Schempp-Hirth Nimbus 3	880 Syndicate
	G-CJWH	Lindstrans LTL series 1-90 balloon	Flintnine Fasteners Ltd
	G-CJWI	Streak Shadow	C. Hannan
	G-CJWJ	Schleicher ASK-13	The Vale of the White Horse Gliding Centre Ltd
	G-CJWK	Schempp-Hirth Discus bT	722 Syndicate
	G-CJWL	Hawker Hunter Mk.58A	Hawker Hunter Aviation Ltd
	G-CJWM	Grob G.103 Twin Astir II	The South Wales Gliding Club Ltd
	G-CJWP	Bolkow Phoebus B1	A. Fidler
	G-CJWR	Grob G.102 Astir CS	Cairngorn Gliding Club
	G-CJWT	Glaser-Dirks DG-200	K. R. Nash
	G-CJWU	Schempp-Hirth Ventus bT	B. C. P. & C. Crook
	G-CJWW	Spitfire Mk.26 (MH526:LO-D)	J. L. Apsley
	G-CJWY	Cameron O-31 balloon	Cameron Balloons Ltd
	G-CJXA	Schempp-Hirth Nimbus 3	P. T. Johnson & J. T. Newbery
	G-CJXB	Centrair 201B Marianne	A. C. Cherry
	G-CJXC	Wassmer WA28	A. P. Montague
	G-CJXD	Ultramagic H-77 balloon	S. Dyer
	G-CJXF	Skyranger Swift 912(1)	D. H. Nash
	G-CJXG	Eiriavion PIK-20D	G-CJXG Group
	G-CJXJ	Cameron Z-105 balloon	Bristol University Hot Air Ballooning Society
	G-CJXK	Cameron O-31 balloon	A. P. Jay
	G-CJXL	Schempp-Hirth Discus CS	CJXL Syndicate
	G-CJXM	Schleicher ASK-13	Husbands Bosworth Gliding Club Ltd
	G-CJXN	Centrair 201B	C. E. Metcalfe
	G-CJXO	Flylight Dragonfly	P. C. Knowles

Reg	Type	Owner or Operator	Notes
G-CJXP	Glaser-Dirks DG-100	N. L. Morris	
G-CJXR	Schempp-Hirth Discus b	Cambridge Gliding Club Ltd	
G-CJXT	Schleicher ASW-24B	JXT Syndicate	
G-CJXW	Schempp-Hirth Duo Discus T	R. A. Beatty & R. R. Bryan	
G-CJXX	Pilatus B4-PC11AF	C. B. Shepperd	
G-CJXY	Neukom Elfe S4A	Rufforth Elfe S4A Syndicate	
G-CJYC	Grob G.102 Astir CS	W. Fisher	
G-CJYF	Schempp Hirth Discus CS	H. R. Fraser	
G-CJYI	PA-28-140 Cherokee	Bluebird Aviation	
G-CJYJ	Cameron O-31 balloon	P. Spellward	
G-CJYL	AB Sportine Aviacija LAK-12	S. Camerotto	
G-CJYM	Ultramagic S-90 balloon	M. A. Wrigglesworth	
G-CJYO	Glaser-Dirks DG-100G Elan	D. W. Wilde	
G-CJYP	Grob G.102 Club Astir II	M. Lessmann	
G-CJYR	Schempp-Hirth Duo Discus T	CJYR Flying Group	
G-CJYS	Schempp-Hirth Mini Nimbus C	A. Jenkins	
G-CJYU	Schempp-Hirth Ventus 2cT	P. D. Brown	
G-CJYY	Spitfire Mk.26 (X4496)	D. A. Whitmore	
G-CJYZ	Cameron Z-120 balloon	K. R. Karlstrom	
G-CJZB	Glaser-Dirks DG-500 Elan Orion	The Borders (Milfield) Gliding Club Ltd	
G-CJZD	Eurofox 912(S)	R. Maddocks-Born	
G-CJZE	Schleicher ASK-13	Bowland Forest Gliding Club Ltd	
G-CJZG	Schempp-Hirth Discus bT	I. K. G. Mitchell	
G-CJZH	Schleicher ASW-20 CL	P. Swallow	
G-CJZK	Glaser-Dirks DG-505 Elan Orion	Devon and Somerset Gliding Club Ltd	
G-CJZL	Schempp-Hirth Mini Nimbus B	J. F. Wells	
G-CJZM	Schempp-Hirth Ventus 2a	N. McLaughlin	
G-CJZN	Schleicher ASW-28	D. M. Rushton	
G-CJZO	RAF BE2e replica (A2943)	O. Wulff	
G-CJZW	Van's RV-12	H. M. & M. A. Child	
G-CJZZ	Rolladen-Schneider LS7	7Up Syndicate	
G-CKAA	Whittaker MW9 Plank	M. W. J. Whittaker	
G-CKAB	Eurofox 912(S)	Trent Valley Gliding Club Ltd	
G-CKAC	Glaser-Dirks DG-200	J. P. Crump	
G-CKAE	Centrair 101A Pegase	J. R. Gilbert	
G-CKAI	Griffin RG28 balloon	R. G. Griffin	
G-CKAM	Glasflugel Club Libelle 205	P. A. Cronk & R. C. Tallowin	
G-CKAN	PZL-Bielsko SZD-50-3 Puchacz	The Bath Wilts and North Dorset Gliding Club Ltd	
G-CKAP	Schempp-Hirth Discus CS	H. A. Johnston & R. Gollings	
G-CKAR	Schempp-Hirth Duo Discus T	977 Syndicate	
G-CKAS	Schempp-Hirth Ventus 2cT	R. H. Westlake	
G-CKAT	Cessna F.152	JMT Servicios Aereos LDA/Portugal	
G-CKAU	DG Flugzeugbau DG-303 Elan Acro	G. Earle	
G-CKAX	AMS-Flight DG-500 Elan Orion	York Gliding Centre (Operations) Ltd	
G-CKAY	Grob G.102 Astir CS	P. Fowler & R. G. Skerry	
G-CKBA	Centrair 101A Pegase	M. Nowak	
G-CKBC	Rolladen-Schneider LS6-c18	A. W. Lyth	
G-CKBD	Grob G.102 Astir CS	Peterborough & Spalding Gliding Club Ltd	
G-CKBE	Van's RV-8	B. E. Smith	
G-CKBF	AMS-Flight DG-303 Elan	C. M. J. Page & S. H. Williams	
G-CKBG	Schempp Hirth Ventus 2cT	Syndicate 71	
G-CKBH	Rolladen-Schneider LS6	D. Stobie	
G-CKBJ	Ultramagic H-31 balloon	R. D. Parry	
G-CKBL	Grob G.102 Astir CS	M. Lessmann	
G-CKBM	Schleicher ASW-28	P. J. Brown	
G-CKBN	PZL-Bielsko SZD-55-1 Promyk	M. D. Etherington	
G-CKBP	Smudger 77 balloon	C. E. Smith	
G-CKBT	Schempp-Hirth Standard Cirrus	P. Gould	
G-CKBU	Schleicher ASW-28	G. C. Metcalfe	
G-CKBV	Schleicher ASW-28	G-CKBV Syndicate	
G-CKBX	Schleicher ASW-27	M. Wright	
G-CKCB	Rolladen-Schneider LS4-a	The Bristol Gliding Club Proprietary Ltd	
G-CKCD	Schempp-Hirth Ventus 2cT	P. R. Gammell	
G-CKCE	Schempp-Hirth Ventus 2cT	Ventus 24 Group	
G-CKCH	Schempp-Hirth Ventus 2cT	A. J. Limb & M. Boasman	
G-CKCI	Guimbal Cabri G2	Meadowland Aviation LLP	
G-CKCM	Glasflugel Standard Libelle 201B	A. Davey	
G-CKCP	Grob G.102 Astir CS	Norfolk Gliding Club Ltd	
G-CKCT	Schleicher ASK-21	Kent Gliding Club	
G-CKCV	Schempp-Hirth Duo Discus T	WE4 Group	

Notes	Reg	Type	Owner or Operator
	G-CKCZ	Schleicher ASK-21	Booker Gliding Club Ltd
	G-CKDA	Schempp-Hirth Ventus 2B	D. T. Bray
	G-CKDD	Eurofox 2K	W. M. Holmes
	G-CKDE	Grob G.109B	G-CKDE Syndicate
	G-CKDF	Schleicher ASK-21	Portsmouth Naval Gliding Centre
	G-CKDG	BB03 Tyra/BB103	Z. G. Nagygyorgy
	G-CKDJ	Sonex	G. F. Frend
	G-CKDK	Rolladen-Schneider LS4-a	M. C. & P. A. Ridger
	G-CKDM	Zenair CH.750	M. R. Cleveley
	G-CKDN	Schleicher ASW-27B	A. F. W. Watson
	G-CKDO	Schempp-Hirth Ventus 2cT	M. W. Edwards
	G-CKDP	Schleicher ASK-21	Kent Gliding Club
	G-CKDS	Schleicher ASW-27	G. D. Morris & A. J. Rees
	G-CKDU	Glaser-Dirks DG-200/17	K. Brandon
	G-CKDV	Schempp-Hirth Ventus B/16.6	M. A. Codd
	G-CKDW	Schleicher ASW-27	C. Colton
	G-CKDX	Glaser-Dirks DG-200	D. J. Hayday
	G-CKDY	Glaser-Dirks DG-100	W. M. Elliott & S. P. Lesson
	G-CKEA	Schempp-Hirth Cirrus 18	S. G. Jessup
	G-CKEB	Schempp-Hirth Standard Cirrus	S. P. Melhuish
	G-CKED	Schleicher ASW-27B	A. & R. Maskell
	G-CKEE	Grob G.102 Astir CS	Essex and Suffolk Gliding Club Ltd
	G-CKEG	Cameron Z-105 balloon	First Flight
	G-CKEH	Kolb Twister Mk.III Xtra	Condor Engineering Group Ltd
	G-CKEI	Diamond DA.40NG Star	D. B. Smith
	G-CKEJ	Schleicher ASK-21	London Gliding Club Proprietary Ltd
	G-CKEK	Schleicher ASK-21	Devon and Somerset Gliding Club Ltd
	G-CKER	Schleicher ASW-19B	M. A. Johnson
	G-CKES	Schempp-Hirth Cirrus 18	C. N. Smith
	G-CKET	Rolladen-Schneider LS8-t	M. B. Jefferyes & J. C. Taylor
	G-CKEV	Schempp-Hirth Duo Discus	The Royal Air Force Gliding and Soaring Association
	G-CKEY	PA-28-161 Warrior II	Warwickshire Leasing Ltd
	G-CKEZ	DG Flugzeugbau LS8	D. A. Jesty
	G-CKFA	Schempp-Hirth Standard Cirrus 75	P. Storey
	G-CKFB	Schempp-Hirth Discus-2T	P. L. & P. A. G. Holland
	G-CKFD	Schleicher ASW-27B	R. M. Theil
	G-CKFF	Zenair CH.701SP	Batch 701 Group LLP
	G-CKFG	Grob G.103A Twin II Acro	The Surrey Hills Gliding Club Ltd
	G-CKFH	Schempp-Hirth Mini Nimbus	C. J. Friar
	G-CKFK	Schempp-Hirth Standard Cirrus 75	G-CKFK Syndicate
	G-CKFL	Rolladen-Schneider LS4	D. O'Brien & D. R. Taylor
	G-CKFN	DG Flugzeugbau DG1000	Yorkshire Gliding Club (Proprietary) Ltd
	G-CKFP	Schempp-Hirth Ventus 2cxT	D. A. Smith
	G-CKFS	Schleicher ASK-14	G. K. Stanford
	G-CKFT	Schempp-Hirth Duo Discus T	Duo Discus Syndicate
	G-CKFV	DG Flugzeugbau LS8-t	C. J. Teagle
	G-CKFW	Mauchline Quaich	Quaich Flying Group
	G-CKFY	Schleicher ASK.21	Cambridge Gliding Club
	G-CKGA	Schempp-Hirth Ventus 2cxT	D. R. Campbell
	G-CKGC	Schempp-Hirth Ventus 2cxT	J. McLaughlin
	G-CKGD	Schempp-Hirth Ventus 2cxT	J. Brand
	G-CKGF	Schempp-Hirth Duo Discus T	Duo 233 Group
	G-CKGG	Grob G.109B	G-CKGG Syndicate
	G-CKGH	Grob G.102 Club Astir II	The G-CKGH Group
	G-CKGI	Ultramagic M-77C balloon	W. C. Wood
	G-CKGJ	Nicollier HN.700 Menestrel II	J. R., S. J. & T. M. Rickett
	G-CKGK	Schleicher ASK-21	The Royal Air Force Gliding & Soaring Association
	G-CKGL	Schempp-Hirth Ventus 2cT	T. R. Dews
	G-CKGM	Centrair 101A Pegase	KGM Syndicate
	G-CKGS	Ikarus C42 FB80	GS Aviation (Europe) Ltd
	G-CKGV	Schleicher ASW-20	A. H. Reynolds
	G-CKGX	Schleicher ASK-21	Husbands Bosworth Gliding Club Ltd
	G-CKGY	Scheibe Bergfalke IV	B. R. Pearson
	G-CKHB	Rolladen-Schneider LS3	A. A. I. Emson
	G-CKHC	DG Flugzeugbau DG.505	C. A. Boyle
	G-CKHD	Schleicher ASW-27B	R. L. Smith
	G-CKHE	AB Sportine Aviacija LAK-17AT	V. S. Bettle
	G-CKHH	Schleicher ASK-13	The South Wales Gliding Club Ltd
	G-CKHI	P & M Quik R	G-CKHI Syndicate

Reg	Type	Owner or Operator	Notes
G-CKHK	Schempp-Hirth Duo Discus T	Duo Discus Syndicate	
G-CKHM	Centrair 101A Pegase 90	J. A. Tipler	
G-CKHN	PZL SZD-51-1 Junior	The Nene Valley Gliding Club Ltd	
G-CKHO	Flight Design CT-Supralight	J. A. Horn	
G-CKHR	PZL-Bielsko SZD-51-1 Junior	Wolds Gliding Club Ltd	
G-CKHS	Rolladen-Schneider LS7-WL	M. Lawson & D. Wallis	
G-CKHV	Glaser-Dirks DG-100	The Asasets G-CKHV Trust	
G-CKHW	PZL SZD-50-3 Puchacz	Derbyshire and Lancashire Gliding Club Ltd	
G-CKHY	P &M Hyper GTR	C. Young	
G-CKHZ	Aeriane Swift Light PAS	C. J. Wallbank	
G-CKIG	Flylight Fox Tug	Malvern Aerotow Club	
G-CKIO	PA-28-151 Cherokee Warrior	W. Ali & N. A. Ishaq	
G-CKIT	Cameron C-60 balloon	Turner Balloons Ltd	
G-CKIU	Scheibe SF-25C Rotax-Falke	G. S. S. Rizk & P. Huber	
G-CKIX	Eurofox 3K	A. J. Ferguson	
G-CKIY	Best Off Skyranger Nynja 912S(1)	D. Lamb & N. Elahi	
G-CKIZ	Eurofly Minifox	R. M. Patwardhan	
G-CKJB	Schempp-Hirth Ventus bT	KJB Group	
G-CKJC	Schempp-Hirth Nimbus 3T	A. C. Wright	
G-CKJE	DG Flugzeugbau LS8-18	M. D. Wells	
G-CKJF	Schempp-Hirth Standard Cirrus	R. W. Skuse	
G-CKJG	Schempp-Hirth Cirrus VTC	P. D. Gibbons	
G-CKJI	Skyranger Nynja 912S(1)	A. Sawdon	
G-CKJJ	DG Flugzeugbau DG-500 Elan Orion	Ulster Gliding Club Ltd	
G-CKJL	Scleicher ASK-13	Lincolnshire Gliding Club Ltd	
G-CKJM	Schempp-Hirth Ventus cT	A. I. Mutch	
G-CKJN	Schleicher ASW-20	R. Logan	
G-CKJP	Schleicher ASK-21	The Royal Air Force Gliding and Soaring Association	
G-CKJT	Ultramagic H-42 balloon	J. Taylor	
G-CKJV	Schleicher ASW-28-18E	A. C. Price	
G-CKJZ	Schempp-Hirth Discus bT	T. J. Brunskill	
G-CKKB	Centrair 101A Pegase	W. B. Wood & G. C. Taffs	
G-CKKC	DG Flugzeugbau DG-300 Elan Acro	Charlie Kilo Kilo Charlie Syndicate	
G-CKKE	Schempp-Hirth Duo Discus T	R. A. Vaughan	
G-CKKF	Schempp-Hirth Ventus 2cT	M. S. Davidson	
G-CKKH	Schleicher ASW-27	P. L. Hurd	
G-CKKO	Ultramagic H-77 balloon	I. C. Steward	
G-CKKP	Schleicher ASK-21	Bowland Forest Gliding Club Ltd	
G-CKKR	Schleicher ASK-13	A. M. Smith	
G-CKKX	Rolladen-Schneider LS4-A	Lleweni Parc Ltd	
G-CKKY	Schempp-Hirth Duo Discus T	P. D. Duffin	
G-CKLA	Schleicher ASK-13	Booker Gliding Club Ltd	
G-CKLC	Glasflugel H206 Hornet	W. Ellis	
G-CKLD	Schempp-Hirth Discus 2cT	G-CKLD Syndicate	
G-CKLE	Autogyro MTOsport 2017	J. R. Wilkinson	
G-CKLG	Rolladen-Schneider LS4	P. M. Scheiwiller	
G-CKLI	PA-28R-180 Cherokee Arrow	C. J. Bannocks	
G-CKLK	Autogyro MTOsport 2017	R. Peach	
G-CKLL	Waco YKS-7	K. D. Pearce	
G-CKLN	Rolladen-Schneider LS4-A	Army Gliding Association	
G-CKLP	Schleicher ASW-28-18	P. F. Baker	
G-CKLS	Rolladen-Schneider LS4	C. I. Ellis	
G-CKLT	Schempp-Hirth Nimbus 3/24.5	M. C. Bailey	
G-CKLV	Schempp-Hirth Discus 2cT	KLV Syndicate	
G-CKLW	Schleicher ASK-21	Yorkshire Gliding Club	
G-CKLY	DG Flugzeugbau DG-1000T	D6 Flying Group	
G-CKMB	AB Sportline Aviacija LAK-19T	D. J. McKenzie	
G-CKME	DG Flugzeugbau LS8-T	S. M. Smith	
G-CKMF	Centrair 101A Pegase	D. L. M. Jamin	
G-CKMG	Glaser-Dirks DG-101G Elan	D. J. Blackman	
G-CKMH	Kavanagh Balloons EX-65 balloon	L. J. M. Muir	
G-CKMI	Schleicher K8C	V. Mallon	
G-CKMJ	Schleicher Ka 6CR	V. Mallon	
G-CKMK	Sportine Aviacija LAK-17AT	P. M. Yeoman & Medaviate Ltd	
G-CKML	Schempp-Hirth Duo Discus T	G-CKML Group	
G-CKMM	Schleicher ASW-28-18E	R. G. Munro	
G-CKMO	Rolladen-Schneider LS7-WL	S. P. van der Stichele	
G-CKMP	AB Sportine Aviacija LAK-17A	J. L. McIver	
G-CKMT	Grob G103C	Essex & Suffolk Gliding Club Ltd	
G-CKMV	Rolladen-Schneider LS3-17	P. A. T. Guthrie	

Notes	Reg	Type	Owner or Operator
	G-CKMW	Schleicher ASK-21	The Royal Air Force Gliding & Soaring Association
	G-CKMX	Van's RV-7	W. Stotton
	G-CKMZ	Schleicher ASW-28-18E	Deesside ASW28 Group
	G-CKNB	Schempp-Hirth Standard Cirrus	N. A. C. E. Barnes
	G-CKNC	Caproni Calif A21S	Calif 240 Syndicate
	G-CKND	DG Flugzeugbau DG-1000T	KND Group
	G-CKNE	Schempp-Hirth Standard Cirrus 75-VTC	G. D. E. Macdonald
	G-CKNF	DG Flugzeugbau DG-1000T	DG 1000 Syndicate
	G-CKNG	Schleicher ASW-28-18E	NG209 Group
	G-CKNK	Glaser-Dirks DG.500	Cotswold Gliding Club
	G-CKNL	Schleicher ASK-21	Buckminster Gliding Club Ltd
	G-CKNM	Scleicher ASK-18	Derbyshire & Lancashire Gliding Club Ltd
	G-CKNO	Schempp-Hirth Ventus 2cxT	R. T. Starling
	G-CKNR	Schempp-Hirth Ventus 2cxT	R. J. Torr
	G-CKNS	Rolladen-Schneider LS4-A	I. R. Willows
	G-CKNV	Schleicher ASW-28-18E	The KNV Group
	G-CKOD	Schempp-Hirth Discus BT	D. Ascroft
	G-CKOE	Schleicher ASW-27-18	R. C. Bromwich
	G-CKOF	Boeing 787-9	Norse Atlantic UK Ltd
	G-CKOH	DG Flugzeugbau DG-1000T	A. D. & P. Langlands
	G-CKOI	AB Sportine Aviacija LAK-17AT	C. G. Corbett
	G-CKOK	Schempp-Hirth Discus 2cT	P. Topping
	G-CKOL	Schempp-Hirth Duo Discus T	Oscar Lima Syndicate
	G-CKOM	Schleicher ASW-27-18	J. & W. T. Craig
	G-CKON	Schleicher ASW-27-18E	XE Flying Group
	G-CKOO	Schleicher ASW-27-18E	G-CKOO Flying Group
	G-CKOR	Glaser-Dirks DG-300 Elan	W. Xu
	G-CKOT	Schleicher ASK-21	Ulster Gliding Club Ltd
	G-CKOU	AB Sportine Aviacija LAK-19T	A. W. Thornhill & A. M. McDermott
	G-CKOW	DG-505 Elan Orion	Southdown Gliding Club Ltd
	G-CKOX	AMS-Flight DG-505 Elan Orion	Seahawk Gliding Club
	G-CKOY	Schleicher ASW-27-18E	G-CKOY Group
	G-CKOZ	Schleicher ASW-27-18E	E. W. Johnston
	G-CKPA	AB Sportline Aviacija LAK-19T	M. J. Hargreaves
	G-CKPE	Schempp-Hirth Duo Discus	Portsmouth Naval Gliding Centre
	G-CKPF	Champion 7GCBC Citabria	M. J. Searle
	G-CKPG	Schempp-Hirth Discus 2cT	KPG Syndicate
	G-CKPJ	Neukom S-4D Elfe	W. B. Hartnett
	G-CKPK	Schempp-Hirth Ventus 2cxT	F. K. Russell & R. F. Brown
	G-CKPN	PZL-Bielsko SZD-51-1 Junior	Rattlesden Gliding Club Ltd
	G-CKPO	Schempp-Hirth Duo Discus xT	Sierrraindia Ltd
	G-CKPP	Schleicher ASK-21	Banbury Gliding Club Ltd
	G-CKPU	Schleicher ASW-27-18E	J. C. Ferguson
	G-CKPV	Schempp-Hirth Mini-Nimbus B	J. A. Allan
	G-CKPX	ZS Jezow PW-6U	North Wales Gliding Club Ltd
	G-CKPY	Schempp-Hirth Duo Discus xT	M. Tomlinson & D. T. S. Walsh
	G-CKPZ	Schleicher ASW-20	T. C. J. Hogarth
	G-CKRB	Schleicher ASK-13	Derbyshire and Lancashire Gliding Club Ltd
	G-CKRC	Schleicher ASW-28-18E	G-CKRC Flying Group
	G-CKRD	Schleicher ASW-27-18E	R. F. Thirkell
	G-CKRF	Glaser-Dirks DG-300 Elan	P. M. Allen
	G-CKRJ	Schleicher ASW-27-18E	J. J. Marshall
	G-CKRK	Guimbal Cabri G2	Lyza Aviation Ltd
	G-CKRL	Europa XS	D. M. Cope
	G-CKRR	Schleicher ASW-15B	D. C. Krings
	G-CKRU	ZS Jezow PW-6U	Essex Gliding Club Ltd
	G-CKRV	Schleicher ASW-27-18E	W. J. Head
	G-CKRW	Schleicher ASK-21	The Royal Air Force Gliding and Soaring Association
	G-CKRX	Jezow PW-6U	Essex Gliding Club Ltd
	G-CKRZ	Skyranger Nynja 912S(1)	R. J. Clarke
	G-CKSC	Czech Sport Aircraft Sportcruiser	Czechmate Syndicate
	G-CKSD	Rolladen-Schneider LS8-a	J. H. Cox
	G-CKSE	Cessna 208B Grand Caravan	Wingglider Ltd
	G-CKSF	Antares 18T	J. R. Kinder
	G-CKSK	Pilatus B4-PC11	K. Steinmair
	G-CKSL	Schleicher ASW-15B	Sierra Lima Group
	G-CKSM	Schempp-Hirth Duo Discus T	KSM Syndicate
	G-CKSR	Boeing Stearman D75N	C. R. Maher
	G-CKSS	Lange Antares 18T	P. S. Birkett

Reg	Type	Owner or Operator	Notes
G-CKST	Boeing Stearman B75N1	T. W. Gilbert	
G-CKSV	Boeing Stearman A75	T. W. Gilbert	
G-CKSW	Cameron O-26 balloon	S. G. Whatley	
G-CKSX	Schleicher ASW-27-18E	E. Sparrow & S. Pozerskis	
G-CKSY	Rolladen-Schneider LS-7-WL	CKSY Syndicate	
G-CKTA	Aerochute Hummerchute	W. A. Kimberlin	
G-CKTB	Schempp-Hirth Ventus 2cT	M. H. Player	
G-CKTC	Schleicher Ka 6CR	J. M. Blaszczyk	
G-CKTD	Colomban MC-30 Luciole	D. K. Lawry	
G-CKTE	Eurofox 3K	D Wood Developments Ltd	
G-CKTG	Balony Kubicek BB26E balloon	Nova Balloon Service Ltd	
G-CKTK	Denney Kitfox Model 4-1200	C. D. Sutherland	
G-CKTL	Aerochute Hummerchute	R. D. Knight	
G-CKTM	Pitts S-1 Special	A. S. Porter	
G-CKTN	BRM Aero Bristell NG5 Speed Wing	I. M. MacKay	
G-CKTS	Jodel D.9 Bebe	P. R. Harvey	
G-CKTT	P & M Quik GTR	R. J. Whitmarsh	
G-CKTW	Cameron O-31 balloon	M. & S. Mitchell	
G-CKTX	Van's RV-7	M. M. McElrea	
G-CKUH	CZAW Sportcruiser	I. C. Waddell	
G-CKUJ	ATEC 212 Solo	Mission Capital Ltd	
G-CKUK	Ultramagic Shemilt Eco 50 balloon	Thames Valley Balloons Ltd	
G-CKUL	Ace As-Tec 13	S. M. Smith	
G-CKUN	Bareford DB-6R balloon	D. Bareford	
G-CKUO	Aeroprakt A22-LS Foxbat	P. Gosney	
G-CKUP	Cameron Z-77 balloon	Wickers World Ltd	
G-CKUR	Skyranger Swift 912(1)	R. F. Pearce	
G-CKUS	Conway Viper	D. B. Conway	
G-CKUV	PA-34-220T Seneca V	Craigard Property Trading Ltd (G-VYND)	
G-CKUW	Colt 21A balloon	Airship and Balloon Company Ltd	
G-CKUX	Magic Laser	J. L. Jordan	
G-CKUZ	Boeing 737-46J	West Atlantic UK Ltd	
G-CKVC	Rotorsport UK Cavalon	R. E. Davies	
G-CKVD	Rolladen-Schneider LS-1f	G. M. Spreckley	
G-CKVE	Aero 31 AM9 balloon	A. Marshall	
G-CKVF	Aeroprakt A22-LS Foxbat	R. J. Davey	
G-CKVG	Ikarus C42 FB80	GS Aviation (Europe) Ltd	
G-CKVI	Cameron A-120 balloon	G. B. Davies	
G-CKVJ	Titan T-51 Mustang (44-63684)	C. Firth	
G-CKVM	Eurofox 3K	K. & P. Bowland	
G-CKVP	Rotorsport UK Calidus	P. M. Bidston	
G-CKVT	Schempp-Hirth Ventus 3T	S. G. Jones	
G-CKVV	PA-28-181 Cherokee Archer II	A. S. Bamrah	
G-CKVX	Breezer M400	M. W. Houghton	
G-CKVY	Eurofox 2K	A. E. Kay	
G-CKVZ	Rotorsport UK Cavalon Pro	J. Sinclair & Son Ltd	
G-CKWG	Spacek SD-1 Minisport	M. M. Wheeler	
G-CKWH	Cameron Ronald 105 balloon	L. Bingley & D. Bovington	
G-CKWJ	Lindstrand LBL-77A balloon	M. A. Stelling & M. J. Smith	
G-CKWM	Van's RV-8	C. A. G. Schofield	
G-CKWN	Boeing 787-9	Norse Atlantic UK Ltd	
G-CKWO	Eurofox 912(S)	G. J. Slater	
G-CKWP	Boeing 787-9	Norse Atlantic UK Ltd	
G-CKWR	Magni M.16C Tandem Trainer	P. Cullimore	
G-CKWS	Boeing 787-9	Norse Atlantic UK Ltd	
G-CKWW	Cameron Sport 50 balloon	Cameron Balloons Ltd	
G-CKWX	Ikarus C42 FB100	M. J. Slack	
G-CKWZ	Grob G.109B	CKWZ Group	
G-CKXA	Cameron Sprt 90 balloon	S. Church	
G-CKXC	Skyranger Swift 912(1)	M. T. Dawson	
G-CKXD	PZL-Bielsko SZD-22C Mucha Standard	A. Mazan	
G-CKXE	Cameron Sport 90 balloon	R. A. Johnson	
G-CKXF	Auster J/5G Cirrus Autocar	R. B. Webber	
G-CKXG	Cameron C-70 balloon	J. T. Wilkinson	
G-CKXH	Ultramagic M-65C balloon	D. Bareford	
G-CKXI	Mooney M20E	S. Wellings	
G-CKXL	Sikorsky S-92A	Bristow Helicopters Ltd	
G-CKXM	Eurofox 3K	J. A. Walker	
G-CKXP	Aerochute Hummerchute	G. Stokes	
G-CKXR	Lindstrand LTL Series 1-105 balloon	R. J. Rivers-Scott	
G-CKXT	Balony Kubicek BB22 balloon	S. Venegoni	

Notes	Reg	Type	Owner or Operator
	G-CKXU	PA-28-181 Cherokee Archer II	S. P. Adshead
	G-CKXV	PA-28-181 Cherokee Archer III	S. P. Adshead
	G-CKXX	PA-32R-301 Saratoga SP	Warbird Experiences Ltd
	G-CKXY	Boeing Stearman A75N1	SI Aviation Services Ltd
	G-CKXZ	Team Himax 1700R	S. Richens
	G-CKYA	Autogyro MTOsport 2017	R. J. Fitzpatrick
	G-CKYB	Autogyro MTOsport 2017	V. S. Hussain
	G-CKYF	Eurofox 912(S)	Wolds Gliding Club Ltd
	G-CKYG	Eurofox 3K	F. S. Ogden
	G-CKYI	DAR Solo 120	Aeroplanes DAR (Bulgaria) Group
	G-CKYJ	PA-28RT-201 Arrow IV	Altus Flying Group
	G-CKYL	Ikarus C42 FB80	MAS Design Products Ltd
	G-CKYM	VS.361 Spitfire LF.IX	M. A. Bennett
	G-CKYN	Colomban MC-15 Cri-Cri	M. Hajdukiewicz
	G-CKYO	Schempp-Hirth Ventus 3T	D. M. Bray & A. J. Holswilder
	G-CKYS	P & M Quik GT450	P. G. Eastlake
	G-CKYU	Lindstrand LBL-31A balloon	G. B. Dey
	G-CKYX	Cameron O-31 balloon	W. Rousell & J. Tyrrell
	G-CKYZ	Eurofly Minifox	F. Kratky
	G-CKZA	TAF Sling 4	J. Smith
	G-CKZB	Spacek SD-1 Minisport	C. J. Lines
	G-CKZD	Eurofox 3K	Breeze Aviation Services Ltd
	G-CKZE	Medway SLA80 Executive	D. W. Power & D. James
	G-CKZF	P & M Quik GTR	W. G. Nott-Bower
	G-CKZG	Apco Cruiser 550/Parajet Explorer	G. B. N. Cardozo
	G-CKZH	Van's RV-12	R. D. Masters
	G-CKZI	Techpro Merlin 100UK	M. Housley
	G-CKZJ	Kubicek BB26E balloon	M. R. Crossley
	G-CKZL	PA-28RT-201 Cherokee Arrow IV	Magna Carta Aviation Ltd
	G-CKZM	Aerochute Hummerchute	G. J. Pemberton
	G-CKZP	TL2000UK Sting Carbon S4	M. C. Bayley
	G-CKZR	Steen Skybolt	N. Musgrave
	G-CKZT	PA-28-235 Cherokee Pathfinder	R. Zybert
	G-CKZU	Air Creation Tanarg/Bionix 13	D. A. Easstough
	G-CKZX	Stoddard-Hamilton GlaStar	P. M. Harrison
	G-CKZY	HpH Glasflugel 304 ES Shark	D. L. J. Thomas
	G-CKZZ	Magni M.16C Tandem Trainer	O. L. B. Brooking
	G-CLAC	PA-28-161 Cherokee Warrior II	G-CLAC Group
	G-CLAD	Cameron V-90 balloon	L. H. Davies
	G-CLAF	Kubicek BB-9EF balloon	Nova Balloon Services Ltd
	G-CLAI	Ikarus C42 FB100	P. E. Thompson
	G-CLAJ	Robin DR400-180R	Kent Gliding Club Ltd
	G-CLAK	TLAC Sherwood Scout	The Light Aircraft Company Ltd
	G-CLAL	Ikarus C42 FB100	C. I. Law
	G-CLAM	DAR Solo 120	Ferrari Flying Group
	G-CLAO	Van'sa RV-7	T. J. B. Dugan
	G-CLAP	Cessna 152	British Aviation Academy Ltd
	G-CLAT	P & M Quik R	W. R. C. Williams-Wynne
	G-CLAV	Europa	M. George
	G-CLAY	Bell 206B JetRanger 3	Luxury Aviation Ltd (G-DENN)
	G-CLAZ	Autogyro Cavalon	J. Deutsch
	G-CLBD	Cameron Z-120 balloon	M. E. Dunstan
	G-CLBG	Van's RV-7	T. Groves
	G-CLBH	Lindstrand LTL Series SS balloon	A. M. Holly
	G-CLBI	Extra EA.300/S	Airdisplays.com Ltd
	G-CLBK	Ultramagic H-77 balloon	M. A. Wrigglesworth
	G-CLBN	P & M QuikR	S. L. Williams
	G-CLBP	Lindstrand LTL Series 1-180 balloon	Spirit Operations Ltd
	G-CLBR	Parajet Explorer/Apco Cruiser 500	G. B. N. Cardozo
	G-CLBS	Flylight Foxtug	Cambridge Aerotow Club
	G-CLBT	BRM Bristell NG5 Speed Wing	C. W. Thompson
	G-CLBV	Aeriane P Swift	A. Nelson
	G-CLBX	Messerschmitt Bf.109E-4/7	C. T. Charleston
	G-CLBY	Robinson R44 II	B. R. Alexander
	G-CLCA	Extra EA.300/LC	N. J. Wakefield
	G-CLCD	Advance Iota Mk.4	S. Siddiqui
	G-CLCJ	T-6 Harvard 4M (EX490)	T. W. Gilbert
	G-CLCK	PA-28RT-201T Turbo Arrow IV	M. Ali
	G-CLCL	Van's RV-7	R. M. Powell
	G-CLCM	Lambert Mission M108	K. L. Shern, L. D. L. & V. Soutter

Reg	Type	Owner or Operator	Notes
G-CLCO	Groppo Trail Mk.2	C. Gartland	
G-CLCP	Bell 505 Jet Ranger X	D. M. Hunter	
G-CLCS	VS Spitfire HF.IX	Fly to Inspire Ltd	
G-CLCT	VS Spitfire F.Mk.XIVE	Fly to Inspire Ltd	
G-CLCW	Zenair CH.701SP	A. M. Leonard	
G-CLCZ	Ultramagic M-105 balloon	Kent Ballooning	
G-CLDA	Mission M108	D. R. & C.A. Ho	
G-CLDB	EV-97 Eurostar SL 912(1)	V. R. Nolan	
G-CLDC	Aerotechnik EV-97 Eurostar	A. Maudsley	
G-CLDD	PA-32R-300 Cherokee Lance	J. L. Mossman	
G-CLDE	Jabiru UL-450	E. Bentley	
G-CLDH	Pietenpol Air Camper	S. Eustace	
G-CLDI	Just SuperSTOL	S. G. Shilling	
G-CLDJ	Lindstrand LTL Racer 60	R. D. Parry	
G-CLDK	PA-28-161 Cherokee Warrior II	Henshaw Aviation Ltd	
G-CLDL	Robin DR.400-180R	Lasham Gliding Society Ltd	
G-CLDM	Skyranger Swift 912(1)	The Delta Mike Syndicate	
G-CLDN	Skyranger Swift 912(1)	A. R. Pluck	
G-CLDR	Raj Hamsa X'Air Hawk	J. E. Merriman	
G-CLDT	Eurofox 3K	J. E. Course	
G-CLDW	Autogyro Calidus	G. A. Reid	
G-CLDX	Boeing Stearman B75N1 Kaydet	T. W. Gilbert	
G-CLDY	Spacek SD-1 Minisport	CLDY Flying Group	
G-CLDZ	Autogyro Calidus	N. R. Osborne	
G-CLEA	PA-28-161 Cherokee Warrior II	Freedom Aviation Ltd	
G-CLEE	Rans S.6-ES Coyote II	J. R. Mosey	
G-CLEH	Aeroprakt A-32M Vixxen	C. A. Pollard	
G-CLEI	Eurofox 2K	P. A. C. Cronin	
G-CLEL	Raj Hamsa X'Air 582(11)	G. M. Cruise-Smith, D. J. Howarth & B. J. Morton	
G-CLEN	Boeing Stearman A.75N1 Kaydet	T. W. Gilbert	
G-CLEO	Zenair CH.601HD	W. L. Collett	
G-CLER	Flylight Foxcub	J. J. A. K. Smith	
G-CLES	Scheicher ASW-27-18E	A. P. Brown	
G-CLEU	Glaser-Dirks DG-200	D. T. Freeman	
G-CLEV	Ikarus C42 FB80	S. A. Harvey & M. T. Cook	
G-CLEW	P & M QuikR	A. Atkin	
G-CLEX	Flylight Dragon/Grif HX11	C. J. Johnson	
G-CLEY	Skyranger Nynja 912S(1)	Exodus Airsports Ltd	
G-CLFA	TL200UK Sting Carbon S4	D. Durrans	
G-CLFB	Rolladen-Schneider LS4-A	S. Prin	
G-CLFD	Brandli BX-2 Cherry	R. H. Rawles	
G-CLFF	Cameron Z-42	P. Lesser	
G-CLFG	TL3000 Sirius	R. E. Scott	
G-CLFH	Schleicher ASW-20C	C. S. Foster & M. P. Cieslak	
G-CLFI	Messerschmitt Bf 109G-2	Fighter Aviation Engineering Ltd	
G-CLFJ	P & M Quik GTR	Flying for Freedom Ltd	
G-CLFK	Eurofox 912(S)	D. W. , A. & J. Murcott	
G-CLFL	Kubicek BB-S/Mascot	M. J. Axtell	
G-CLFM	Glasair GlaStar Sportsman	D. F. P. Finan & P. W. Carlton	
G-CLFN	Messerschmitt Bf.109F-4	Fighter Aviation Engineering Ltd	
G-CLFU	Messerschmitt Bf.109F-4/Z	Fighter Aviation Engineering Ltd	
G-CLFX	Schempp-Hirth Duo Discus T	M. P. Kemp	
G-CLFY	PA-28-181 Cherokee Archer II	G-CLFY Group	
G-CLFZ	Schleicher ASW-18E	C. F. Cownden	
G-CLGA	PA-28-161 Cherokee Warrior II	T. W. Gilbert	
G-CLGB	Ultramagic M-77 balloon	R. A. Durham	
G-CLGC	Schempp-Hirth Duo Discus	London Gliding Club Proprietary Ltd	
G-CLGD	Aeroprakt A-32 Vixxen	J. R. Bell	
G-CLGF	Sikorsky S-92A	Bristow Helicopters Ltd	
G-CLGG	AutoGyro Cavalon	D. J. Gavan	
G-CLGI	Stoddard-Hamilton Glastar	J. L. Bone	
G-CLGK	Ultramagic M-105 balloon	S. J. Thomas	
G-CLGL	Schempp-Hirth Ventus 2c	L. I. W. Pesonen	
G-CLGO	Westland SA.341C Gazelle HT.Mk.2 (XZ939)	Gazelle Squadron Flying Group	
G-CLGP	Ultramagic B-70 balloon	J. A. Viner	
G-CLGR	Glasflugel Club Libelle 205	G-CLGR Syndicate	
G-CLGT	Rolladen-Schneider LS4	N. M. Hill & L. Laks	
G-CLGU	Schleicher ASW-27-18	G. S. Lapworth	
G-CLGW	Centrair 101A Pegase	B. D. Hilton	
G-CLGX	Sackville BM-56 balloon	N. A. Carr	
G-CLGY	Ultramagic H-31 balloon	D. K. Hempleman-Adams	

Notes	Reg	Type	Owner or Operator
	G-CLGZ	Schempp-Hirth Duo Discus T	Tango 3 Syndicate
	G-CLHF	Scheibe Bergfalke IV	Andreas Gliding Club Ltd
	G-CLHG	Schempp-Hirth Discus b	R. I. G. Smith
	G-CLHI	Eurofox 3K	GS Aviation (Europe) Ltd
	G-CLHK	Fokker DVI replica	A. J. Gibson
	G-CLHL	Boeing Stearman B75N1 Kaydet	T. W. Gilbert
	G-CLHM	Flylight Fox Cub	W. D. Foster
	G-CLHN	Cessna F.150M	M. D. Wilson & F. W. Sandwell
	G-CLHO	Westland SA.341D Gazelle HT.Mk.3	The Gazelle Squadron Display Team Ltd
	G-CLHP	Flylight Peabee	T. L. Squires
	G-CLHR	BN-2B-26 Islander	Britten-Norman Aircraft Ltd
	G-CLHS	Ultramagic M-65C balloon	D. Bareford
	G-CLHT	Flylight Peabee Red Line	G. W. Cameron
	G-CLHU	Alisport Silent IN	P. M. Yeoman
	G-CLHV	Cameron Z-105 balloon	The Belmont Estate (Farm) Ltd
	G-CLHW	Sikorsky S-92A	Bristow Helicopters Ltd
	G-CLHY	Miles M.14A Hawk Trainer 3 (N3827)	RAF Station Czechoslovakia SRO/Czech Republic
	G-CLHZ	Europa XS	M. E. Henwick
	G-CLID	Skyranger Nynja 912S(1)	A. J. Kerr
	G-CLIF	Ikarus C42 FB UK	E. R. Sims
	G-CLIH	Supermarine 300 Spitfire 1 (P9372/QJ-G)	G. F. T. Van Eerd
	G-CLIJ	Schleicher Ka 6E	G. D. Ackroyd
	G-CLIL	Lindstrand LTL Series 1-120 balloon	Spirit Operations Ltd
	G-CLIM	Hoffman H.36 Dimona	R. C. Bettany
	G-CLIN	Ikarus C42 FB100	R. S.O'Carroll
	G-CLIR	Aero Adventure Aventura UL	Ulster Seaplane Association Ltd
	G-CLIS	Medway Rumour	M. Ingleton
	G-CLIW	Cessna 208B Grand Caravan	Windglider Ltd
	G-CLIZ	Van's RV-8	R. D. Morcom
	G-CLJA	Ikarus C42 FB80	Adventure Aviation Ltd
	G-CLJC	Scottish Aviation Bulldog Srs.120/121	Excelis Ltd
	G-CLJD	Scottish Aviation Bulldog Srs.120/121 (AS0023)	Excelis Ltd
	G-CLJE	Schleicher ASH-25M	Juliet Echo Syndicate
	G-CLJI	Supermarine Spitfire Mk.26 (R6923/QJ-S)	M. R. Love & P. Wilding
	G-CLJL	Kubicek BB22Z	A. G. A. Barclay-Faulkner
	G-CLJN	Boeing 787-9	Norwegian Air UK
	G-CLJO	Cameron O-105 balloon	L. Dalberto
	G-CLJP	Cessna F.172G	P. R. Logiewa
	G-CLJR	Robinson R44 II	G-CLJR Flying Group
	G-CLJS	PA-32R-301T Turbo Sarastoga SP	A. Chafer
	G-CLJT	Sackville BM-56 LW balloon	B. Crossland-Mead
	G-CLJU	Wassmer WA.40 Super IV	A. P. Sellars
	G-CLJX	UTVA U-66	Blackstone Aviation
	G-CLJY	Tecnam P2002-JF Sierra	E. J. Lamb
	G-CLJZ	Schleicher ASH-31Mi	J. C. Thompson
	G-CLKB	Cessna 172N	W. T. D. Gillam
	G-CLKC	Cameron O-31 balloon	S. J. Roake
	G-CLKF	Schempp-Hirth Cirrus VTC	G. D. Ackroyd
	G-CLKH	Pietenpol Air Camper	K. Redfearn
	G-CLKJ	Aurore MB.02 Souricette	C. F. Janes
	G-CLKK	Schleicher ASH-31 Mi	P. M. Wells
	G-CLKL	Robinson R44	WPS Aviation
	G-CLKM	Taylor JT.2 Titch	J. E. Lewis
	G-CLKN	Super Marine Spitfire Mk.26	I. V. Staines
	G-CLKR	ICA-Brasov IS-28M2A	M. J. Lane
	G-CLKT	Mead BM-77 balloon	C. Timbrell
	G-CLKU	Schleicher Ka 6E	R. A. Foreshew
	G-CLKV	Bucker Bu.131 Jungmann (A-35)	N. Barnard
	G-CLKX	DHC-1 Chipmunk 22	M. Harvey
	G-CLKY	Lambert Mission M108	M. A. Wood
	G-CLLA	Skyranger Swift 912(1)	P. M. Dewhurst
	G-CLLB	Schempp-Hirth Discus 2cT	R. A.Vaughan
	G-CLLC	HpH Glasflugel 304 S Jet	F16 Group
	G-CLLD	Robin DR400/180RP	C. J. O. Fox
	G-CLLE	Schleicher ASG 32 Mi	O. J. Walters
	G-CLLG	Spacek SD-1 Minisport	M. A. Fowler
	G-CLLH	HpH Glasflugel 304 S Jet	J. Haigh
	G-CLLI	DHC.1 Chipmunk 22 (WG458)	Eshott Airfield
	G-CLLK	Avions Max Holste MH 1521 (30-QA)	J. M. B. Prior
	G-CLLL	Schleicher ASW-27-18E	D. M. Rusbridgel

Reg	Type	Owner or Operator	Notes
G-CLLN	Pietenpol Air Camper	D. Scott	
G-CLLO	Bristell NG5 Speed Wing	J. & N. A. Quintin	
G-CLLR	PA-28-140 Cherokee	Stars Fly Ltd	
G-CLLS	Sackville BM-56 balloon	T. J. Wilkinson	
G-CLLV	Schleicher ASW-28-18E	S. J. Kohnstamm	
G-CLLW	Boeing A75N1 Stearman	T. W. Gilbert	
G-CLLX	Schempp-Hirth Duo Discus T	J. F. Paterson	
G-CLLY	Rolladen-Schneider LS6-C18	P. W. Brown	
G-CLMA	Van's RV-12	M. Wilkinson	
G-CLMB	Schempp-Hirth Discus-2c FES	A. E. & G. J. Hoile	
G-CLMC	Isaacs Spitfire	G. R. J. Caunter	
G-CLMD	AB Sportine Aviacija LAK-17B FES	P. G. Whipp	
G-CLME	Schempp-Hirth Ventus 2cT	K. Beale	
G-CLMF	Glaser-Dirks DG-200	I. Godding	
G-CLMG	Alisport Silent-IN	O. J. Anderson	
G-CLMH	Pipistrel Alpha BCAR-S 164	Micro Leasing Ltd	
G-CLMI	Pipistrel Alpha BCAR-S 164	Golden Wings Aviation Ltd	
G-CLML	Kitfox Mk.7	C. S. & P. S. Foster	
G-CLMM	Cameron Sport-70 balloon	Cameron Balloons Ltd	
G-CLMN	Griffin RG56	R. G. Griffin	
G-CLMO	Schleicher ASW-28-18E	B. Bobrovnikov	
G-CLMR	Aerotechnik EV-97 Eurostar	M. H. Harding	
G-CLMS	Sackville BM-56 balloon	L. S. Crosland-Mead	
G-CLMU	Schleicher Ka.6BR	N. J. Pusey	
G-CLMV	Glasflugel 304 S Jet	J. J. Perkes	
G-CLMW	Lambert Mission M108	D. W. Collins	
G-CLMY	Glaser-Dirks DG-300	G-CLMY Group	
G-CLMZ	Fairchild 24W-41A	A. C. Whitehead	
G-CLNA	Cessna 152	Brinkley Aviation Ltd	
G-CLNB	Cessna 152	Brinkley Aviation Ltd	
G-CLNC	Cessna 152	Brinkley Aviation Ltd	
G-CLND	Airdrome Dream Classic	R. W. Frost	
G-CLNG	Schleicher ASW-27-18	G-CLNG Flying Group	
G-CLNI	DHC.1 Chipmunk 22 (WK608)	Fly Navy Heritage Trust Ltd	
G-CLNJ	Hawker Sea Fury FB.Mk.11 (VR930)	Fly Navy Heritage Trust Ltd	
G-CLNK	Avions Transort ATR-72-211F	West Atlantic UK Ltd	
G-CLNN	Skyranger Swift 912(1)	Colin Flying Group	
G-CLNO	KFA Safari	S. J. Simpson	
G-CLNP	Stolp SA.500 Starlet	B. J. Towers	
G-CLNS	Sackville BM-56 balloon	T. J. Wilkinson	
G-CLNU	Bucker Bu181 Bestmann	P. S. Watts	
G-CLNV	North American P-51D Mustang	W Air Collection (G-MSTG)	
G-CLNW	Skyranger Swift 912S(1)	G-CLNW Group	
G-CLNX	Balony Kubicek BB18E balloon	Nova Balloon Services Ltd	
G-CLNY	Balony Kubicek BB20Z balloon	Yorkshire Balloon Flights Ltd	
G-CLNZ	Sherwood Ranger ST (A6906)	P. Nicholls	
G-CLOA	Best BlueTwo	A. J. Best	
G-CLOB	Pietenpol Air Camper	G-CLOB Group	
G-CLOC	Schleicher ASK-13	Norfolk Gliding Club Ltd	
G-CLOF	Kubicek BB22	Volare con Noi/Italy	
G-CLOG	Schleicher ASW-27-18E	R. E. D. Bailey	
G-CLOH	Greatrix O-50 balloon	J. C. M. Greatrx	
G-CLOI	Skyranger Nynja	D. M. Lonnen	
G-CLOJ	Greatrix O-90 balloon	J. C. M. Greatrx	
G-CLOK	Ultramagic B-60 balloon	E. C. Meek	
G-CLOL	Schleicher ASK-21	Lasham Gliding Society Ltd	
G-CLOM	Greatrix O-105 balloon	J. C. M. Greatrx	
G-CLON	HPH Glasflugel 304S Jet	P. D. Ruskin	
G-CLOO	Grob G.103 Twin Astir	R. G. J. Tait	
G-CLOU	Skyranger Nynja	Flylight Airsports Ltd	
G-CLOV	Schleicher ASK-21	Scottish Gliding Union Ltd	
G-CLOX	Ultramagic B-26 balloon	E. C. Meek	
G-CLOY	Squadron SE5 (F5621/K)	J. M. Blackiston	
G-CLOZ	KFA Explorer	P. Marsden	
G-CLPA	Flylight BivvyBee	G. J. Latham	
G-CLPB	Rolladen-Schneider LS6c-18W	C. J. Harrison	
G-CLPC	Cameron Sport-70 balloon	M. J. Woodcock	
G-CLPD	Cameron Sport-50 balloon	A. Dunnington	
G-CLPE	Schempp-Hirth Discus bT	K. Kawalec	
G-CLPL	Rolladen-Schneider LS7-WL	W. M. Davies	
G-CLPM	Robin DR400/180S	M. A. Pettican & D. M. Hook	

Notes	Reg	Type	Owner or Operator
	G-CLPN	Replica Nieuport 11 (N594:3982)	R. A. H. Vary
	G-CLPP	Van's RV-7	J. P. Chaplin
	G-CLPS	Skyranger Nynja	G-CLPS Flying Group
	G-CLPT	Ikarus C42 FB100	Mid Anglia Microlights Ltd
	G-CLPU	Schleicher ASW-27-18E	D. J. Wilkinson
	G-CLPV	Schleicher ASK-21	Portsmouth Naval Gliding Centre
	G-CLPW	Camewron O-31 balloon	C. R. Rawson
	G-CLPX	Grob G.103C Twin III Acro	The South Wales Gliding Club Ltd
	G-CLPY	Van's RV-7	A. Spencer
	G-CLPZ	Jonker JS-MD Single	W. M. Coffee
	G-CLRA	Schleicher ASW-27-18E	C. A. Hunt & C. P. J. Gibson
	G-CLRB	Sonex Onex	Condor Aviation International Ltd
	G-CLRC	Schleicher ASW-27-18E	W. R. Tandy
	G-CLRD	PZL-Bielsko SZD-51-1 Junior	Devon & Somerset Gliding Club Ltd
	G-CLRF	Schleicher ASW-27-18E	C. G. Starkey
	G-CLRG	North American P-51D-5-NA Mustang	D. H. Grace
	G-CLRH	HPH Glasflugel 304 S Jet	The Shark Group
	G-CLRI	Zenair CH.750 Cruzer	Dawn to Dusk Flyers
	G-CLRJ	Schempp-Hirth Discus bT	M. S. Smith
	G-CLRK	Sky 77-24 balloon	William Clark & Son (Parkgate) Ltd
	G-CLRM	Skyranger Swift 912S(1)	R. A., R. S. & S. Mott
	G-CLRN	Glaser-Dirks DG-100G Elan	G. D. Hume
	G-CLRO	Glaser-Dirks DG-300 Elan	P. E. Kerman
	G-CLRP	Schempp-Hirth Janus B	S. M. Grant & W. I. H. Hall
	G-CLRR	Zenair CH.750 Cruzer	Nuncats CIC
	G-CLRS	Schleicher ASW-27-18E	G-CLRS Flying Group
	G-CLRT	Schleicher ASK-21	Cotswold Gliding Club
	G-CLRU	Aeriane Swift Light E	W. True
	G-CLRW	PA-28R-201 Cherokee Arrow III	F. Miskov
	G-CLRY	Rolladen Schneider LS4	D. J. Blackman
	G-CLRZ	Rolladen-Schneider LS-1f	C. B. Hill
	G-CLSC	Sportstar SLM	C. F. Pote
	G-CLSD	Alisport Silent 2 Electro	D. A. & R. J. Cox
	G-CLSE	Skyranger Nynja 912S(1)	R. H. Mulligan
	G-CLSF	Van's RV-12	Kernow RV Ltd
	G-CLSG	Rolladen-Schneider LS4-b	C. Marriott & C. J. Taunton
	G-CLSH	Schleicher ASK-21	Lasham Gliding Society Ltd
	G-CLSJ	HPH Glasflugel 304S Jet	C. M. Lewis
	G-CLSK	Flylight BivvyBee	M. Warren
	G-CLSL	Glaser-Dirks DG-500 Elan Trainer	V. R. Roberts
	G-CLSM	DH.85 Leopard Moth ('G-AUSM')	D. C. Reid
	G-CLSN	Embraer ERJ190-100LR	Eastern Airways (UK) Ltd
	G-CLSO	Schempp-Hirth Nimbus 3T	R. S. Rose
	G-CLSP	SAAB 91B Safir	N. C. Stone
	G-CLSR	Grob G103 Twin Astir	The Nene Valley Gliding Club Ltd
	G-CLSS	Schempp-Hirth Arcus T	J. A. Inglis & C. Luton
	G-CLSU	Schempp-Hirth Ventus-2c FES	C. C. Brown
	G-CLSV	Flylight Dragon/Aeros Fox 13T	J. R. Kendall
	G-CLSW	Schleicher ASW-20BL	A. J. Brown
	G-CLSX	Bucker Bu.133C Jungmeister	A. Burroughes
	G-CLSY	Schempp-Hirth SHK-1	J. R. Stiles
	G-CLSZ	DG Flugzeugbau DG-800B	D. J. Pilkington
	G-CLTA	HpH Glasflugel 304ES	R. R. Bryan
	G-CLTC	Schempp-Hirth Janus CE	C. A. Willson & P. J. D. Smith
	G-CLTD	Schleicher K.8B	G. D. Western
	G-CLTE	Magni M24C Plus	C. Wakerley & D. Bevan
	G-CLTF	Schempp-Hirth Discus a	L. Runhaar
	G-CLTG	Glaser-Dirks DG-100	T. Pearson
	G-CLTJ	Sportine Aviacija LAK-17B FES	R. A. F. King
	G-CLTL	Schleicher ASW-19B	N. M. L. Claiden
	G-CLTN	Schempp-Hirth Ventus-2c FES	C. R. Thornhill
	G-CLTO	Schleicher ASW-27-18E	J. Pack
	G-CLTP	Rolladen-Schneider LS3-17	N. Smirnov
	G-CLTS	Schempp-Hirth Arcus T	M. J. Cook & D. C. Little
	G-CLTW	Glasflugel 304ES	S. Murdoch
	G-CLTX	Sportine Aviacija LAK-17B FES Mini	D. R. Bennett
	G-CLTY	Fisher 404XP	S-J Huxtable
	G-CLUD	Grob G.102 Club Astir IIIB	Lasham Gliding Society Ltd
	G-CLUE	PA-34-200T Seneca II	P. Wilkinson
	G-CLUG	Schleicher K.8B	The Nene Valley Gliding Club Ltd
	G-CLUH	PA-28-180 Cherokee Archer	Joe Bill Aviation Ltd

Reg	Type	Owner or Operator	Notes
G-CLUI	Bristell NG5 Classic HD	M. Charlick	
G-CLUJ	Sportine Aviacija LAK-17B FES Mini	N. R. Bray	
G-CLUK	Schleicher ASK-23B	London Gliding Club Proprietary Ltd	
G-CLUM	Sackville BM-56 balloon	A. E. Austin	
G-CLUN	Vans RV-3B	J. A. Harris	
G-CLUO	Schempp-Hirth Duo Discus T	Duo Discus G-CLUO Syndicate	
G-CLUP	Schleicher ASH-25	A. K. Laylee & G. G. Dale	
G-CLUU	Ultramagic H-65 balloon	Eighty Eight Digital Ltd	
G-CLUV	Schleicher ASK-23B	Midland Gliding Club Ltd	
G-CLUX	Cessna F.172N	E. J. O'Rafferty	
G-CLUY	Ultramagic M-145 balloon	C. W. Wood	
G-CLUZ	Schempp-Hirth Discus 2c FES	G-CLUZ Group	
G-CLVA	Rolladen-Scneider LS3-a	J. Franke	
G-CLVB	Cessna 172R	Chalrey Ltd	
G-CLVD	Schempp-Hirth Discus 2c FES	J. Brand	
G-CLVE	Eurofox 3K	L. H. Beeson	
G-CLVG	Schempp-Hirth Ventus 3T	A. R. MacGregor	
G-CLVI	Glasair Sportsman	Amanda Investments Ltd	
G-CLVJ	DG Flugzeugbau DG-505 Elan Orion	Husbands Bosworth Gliding Club Ltd	
G-CLVL	Schempp-Hirth Arcus T	G-CLVL Syndicate	
G-CLVM	Schleicher ASK-21	York Gliding Centre (Operations) Ltd	
G-CLVO	SZD-54-2 Perkoz	Deeside Gliding Club (Aberdeenshire) Ltd	
G-CLVP	PZL-Bielsko SZD-42-2 Jantar 2B	J2B Flying Group	
G-CLVR	Skyranger Nynja 912S(1)	ECAM Actions Group	
G-CLVS	HpH Glasflugel 304 ES Shark	R. G. Corbin & S. E. Buckley	
G-CLVU	Schleicher ASK-21	Stratford on Avon Gliding Club Ltd	
G-CLVV	Cameron O-31 balloon	H. G. Griffiths & S. I. Williams	
G-CLVW	Rolladen-Schneider LS4-a	P. Atkinson & L. Hume	
G-CLVX	Cameron Sport-70 balloon	H. G. Griffiths & W. A. Steel	
G-CLVY	Cameron Sport 80 balloon	N. J. Bland	
G-CLWA	Schleicher LS8-a	M. D. A. Brown	
G-CLWB	PA-28-161 Cherokee Warrior III	Norwich Aviation Centre Ltd	
G-CLWC	PZL SZD-54-2 Perkoz	Essex and Suffolk Gliding Club Ltd	
G-CLWD	PA-28-161 Cherokee Warrior II	WBW Services Ltd (G-OONY)	
G-CLWG	Albatross QuikR	G-CLWG Syndicate	
G-CLWH	Zlin Z.381	P. S. Watts	
G-CLWI	Welsh W-1	F. P. Welsh	
G-CLWJ	Schleicher ASW-27-18E	P. Johnson	
G-CLWK	DHC-1 Chipmunk 22	Historic Aircraft Flight Trust	
G-CLWK	DHC-1 Chipmunk 22 (WD325/N)	Historic Aircraft Flight Trust	
G-CLWL	Schempp-Hirth Discus BT	N. H. Wal	
G-CLWM	Schempp-Hirth Ventus 3T	W. J. Murray	
G-CLWN	Cameron Clown SS balloon	Magical Adventures Ltd (G-UBBE)	
G-CLWO	Pipistrel Virus SW 121	Fly About Aviation Ltd	
G-CLWP	Sportine Aviacija LAK-17B FES	J. A. Thomson	
G-CLWR	Rolladen-Schneider LS8-a	M. D. A. Brown	
G-CLWT	TLAC Sherwood Scout	Kingsmuir Group	
G-CLWU	Boeing D75N1 Stearman	T. W. Gilbert	
G-CLWW	Pipistrel Virus SW 121	Chicken Roundabout Finance Ltd	
G-CLWY	Skyranger Swift	G-CLWY Group	
G-CLWZ	Schempp-Hirth Ventus-2c	M. J. & T. J. Webb	
G-CLXD	Spitfire LF.IX (ML205:DB/M)	Great British Aircraft Company	
G-CLXD	DHC.1 Chipmunk 22	M. Harvey	
G-CLXE	Cameron Sport 105 balloon	G. G. Scaife	
G-CLXF	Flylight Foxcub	B. Skelding	
G-CLXG	Lange E1 Antares	J. A. Inglis	
G-CLXH	Grob G.103C Twin III Acro	Staffordshire Gliding Club Ltd	
G-CLXK	Hoffmann H36 Dimona	K. M. Charlton	
G-CLXL	Shawtrike Paramotor	G. B. Shaw	
G-CLXM	Westland SA.341B Gazelle AH.1	The Gazelle Squadron Display Team Ltd	
G-CLXN	Schempp-Hirth Ventus-3T	R. J. Nicholls	
G-CLXO	Schempp-Hirth Ventus-3M	J. P. Galloway	
G-CLXP	Westland SA.341B Gazelle AH.1	The Gazelle Squadron Display Team Ltd	
G-CLXR	Westland SA.341B Gazelle AH.1	The Gazelle Squadron Display Team Ltd	
G-CLXU	Europa	P. Bailey, M. J. Gregory & P. J. Tiller	
G-CLXW	Schempp-Hirth Ventus-3T	J. S. McCullagh	
G-CLXX	Eurofox 2K	R. C. Tadman	
G-CLXZ	Aeriane Swift Light E	M. Jackson	
G-CLYA	Ikarus C42 FB80	British Young Pilots	
G-CLYB	Schempp-Hirth Ventus-3F	C. A. Edwards	
G-CLYC	M & D Flugzeugbau JS-MD Single	R. A. Cheetham	

Notes	Reg	Type	Owner or Operator
	G-CLYD	Schempp-Hirth Ventus-3F	S. Hutchinson
	G-CLYE	Rolladen-Schneider LS4A	Deeside Gliding Club (Aberdeenshire) Ltd
	G-CLYF	Schleicher ASW-27-18E	P. L. Turner
	G-CLYH	Van's RV-12iS	D. M. Kane
	G-CLYJ	Ikarus C42 FB100	Blue Bay Hotel Estates (Kinross) Ltd
	G-CLYL	PZL SZD-51-1	Cambridge Gliding Club Ltd
	G-CLYM	Schleicher AS-33 Es	P. J. O'Connell & M. C. Foreman
	G-CLYO	Schleicher AS-33 Es	J. E. Gatfield
	G-CLYP	Iksarus C42 FB100	G. J. Prisk
	G-CLYR	M & D JS-MD 3 Rapture	I. G. Macarthur
	G-CLYS	Van's RV-6	J. A. Cuff
	G-CLYU	Embraer ERJ190-100LR	Tipperary Aircraft Leasing Ltd
	G-CLYW	Airdrome Dream Classic	J. Fleming
	G-CLYY	Dyn'Aero MCR-01 VLA Sportster	S. A. Wilson
	G-CLYZ	Eurofox 3K	D. Murphy
	G-CLZA	Zenair CH.601HDS Zodiac	S. Foreman
	G-CLZB	Schleicher ASK-21B	Husbands Bosworth Gliding Club Ltd
	G-CLZD	Offpiste Discovery Tandem 210	J. Soper
	G-CLZE	Skyranger Swift 912S(1)	R. P. Hall
	G-CLZF	Centrair 101D Pegase	T. Skorzewski
	G-CLZG	Schempp-Hirth Ventus-3T	S. G. Jones
	G-CLZH	Schempp-Hirth Discus bT	R. A. Davis
	G-CLZI	Cameron Z-133 balloon	Poplar Insulation Ltd
	G-CLZK	Schempp-Hirth Ventus 3M	D. Latimer
	G-CLZL	Van's RV-10	C. J. Heathcote
	G-CLZO	Sportstar SLM	Close Encounters Film Action
	G-CLZP	Skyranger Nynja	M. C. Brenard
	G-CLZR	Lindstrand LTL Series 1-105 balloon	L. E. A. Mejia
	G-CLZS	Allstar PZL SZD-54-2 Perkoz	Scottish Gliding Union Ltd
	G-CLZT	Aero 31 AM9 balloon	R. J. Clements
	G-CLZV	Rotorsport UK Cavalon	C. G. Gilbert
	G-CLZW	TLAC Sherwood Ranger ST	W. T. Davis
	G-CLZX	Schempp-Hirth Ventus 3M	D. J. Pilkington
	G-CLZZ	Magni M24C Plus	C. R. Lear
	G-CMAA	Eurofox 3K	T. Lowe
	G-CMAB	Ultramagic M-90 balloon	J. J. Davis
	G-CMAD	Air Creation Tanarg Bionix 912S(2)	J. P. Quinlan
	G-CMAE	Van's RV-4	C. D. Mitchell
	G-CMAG	Schleicher AS-33 ES	G-CMAG Syndicate
	G-CMAH	Cessna 152	Brinkley Aviation Ltd
	G-CMAI	Cessna 152	Brinkley Aviation Ltd
	G-CMAJ	Cessna 152	Brinkley Aviation Ltd
	G-CMAK	Cessna 152	Brinkley Aviation Ltd
	G-CMAN	Ultramagic M-77 balloon	E. C. Meek
	G-CMAP	Van's RV-7	N. G. Goodacre
	G-CMAR	Cameron Sport-90 balloon	M. S. Jennings
	G-CMAV	CCF T-6 Harvard Mk.4	T. W. Gilbert
	G-CMAW	Ikarus C42B FB80	G. J. Slater
	G-CMAX	Eurofox 2K	Black Mountains Gliding Club
	G-CMAY	Clutton Fred Series II	M. J. Sharp & M. G. Dolphin
	G-CMAZ	Diamond P-120 balloon	A. M. Holly
	G-CMBD	AutoGyro MTOsport 2017	Bath Sports & Aviation Ltd
	G-CMBE	Westland Wasp HAS.1 (NZ 3909)	Dragonfly Aviation (G-KANZ)
	G-CMBG	Ikarus C42C FB100	G. F. Smith
	G-CMBH	Sikorsky S-92A	Bristow Helicopters Ltd
	G-CMBJ	Ultramagic H-77 balloon	Nightingale House Hospice
	G-CMBK	Raj Hamsa X'Air Hawk	W. B. Russell
	G-CMBN	Schleicher ASK21 Mi	R. Feeney
	G-CMBO	Aeroprakt A-32 Vixxen	J. P. Mimnagh
	G-CMBT	Cameron Z-90 balloon	A. M. Holly
	G-CMBU	Cameron Z-90 balloon	Hop Auctions.com Ltd
	G-CMBV	Wade DB-6RS	D. M. Wade
	G-CMBW	Cameron Sport-60 balloon	S. J. Thomas
	G-CMBZ	Diamond S-77 balloon	A. M. Holly
	G-CMCA	Condor 137R	Condor Aviation International Ltd
	G-CMCB	Eurofox 3K	M. Brown
	G-CMCE	Cameron Z-77 balloon	Airship & Balloon Company Ltd
	G-CMCF	Cessna F.182Q	D. J. Lee
	G-CMCG	Tecnam P2010 TDI	Jaggs Consultants Ltd
	G-CMCH	Cameron Cloud Baby-100 balloon	Cameron Balloons Ltd

Reg	Type	Owner or Operator	Notes
G-CMCI	Smudger 30	A. M. Farrant	
G-CMCJ	Kolb Twinstar Mk.III Xtra	C. F. Janes	
G-CMCK	Balony Kubicek BB30Z balloon	Nova Balloon Services Ltd	
G-CMCN	Flylight BivyBee	C. J. Tomlin	
G-CMCO	Rand KR-2	F. J. Snell	
G-CMCP	Cessna 120	A. J. Brophy	
G-CMCR	Cessna F.177RG	S. M. Dufton (G-AYSX)	
G-CMCS	Cessna 177B	N. T. Williams	
G-CMCU	Skyranger Nynja 912S(1)	P. J. Whiteaker	
G-CMCV	Avro RJ85	Executive Jet Support Ltd	
G-CMCW	Atos VQ190 Race/Adam Trike	M.Dodd	
G-CMCX	Bucker Bu.133C Jungmeister (U-88)	D. E. Starkey	
G-CMCY	Tecnam P2012 Traveller	Oriens Aviation Ltd	
G-CMCZ	PA-28-181 Cherokee Archer III	T. W. Gilbert	
G-CMDA	Grif 3DC/Eurofly Snake	W. J. Court	
G-CMDB	Ultramagic N-425 balloon	Spirit Operations Ltd	
G-CMDC	Ultramagic M-120 balloon	Spirit Operations Ltd	
G-CMDD	Skyranger Nynja 912S(1)	S. D. J. Harvey	
G-CMDE	Ultramagic M-130 balloon	J. C. M. Greatrix	
G-CMDF	Ultramagic M-120 balloon	Spirit Operations Ltd	
G-CMDG	P & M Quik R	N. W. Laird	
G-CMDH	Ultramagic M-120 balloon	Spirit Operations Ltd	
G-CMDK	P-51D Mustang (413779/WD-C)	Warbird Experiences Ltd (G-SHWN)	
G-CMDL	Aeropro 13TL/Seadragon	J. M. Pearce	
G-CMDM	Van's RV-9A	M. W. Cave	
G-CMDN	Sopwith Strutter replica (F2211)	Aviation Preservation Society of Scotland	
G-CMDO	Westland Sea King HC.Mk.4 (ZA314/WT)	A. D, Whitehouse	
G-CMDP	Europa XS	B. Mackay & P. J. Kember	
G-CMDS	Van's RV-8	S. T. G. Lloyd	
G-CMDT	Ace Aviation Magic/As-Tec 13	D. A. Morgan	
G-CMDV	Skyranger Nynja	N. R. Smith & L. J. Lambert	
G-CMDW	Eurofox 3K	B. S. Keene	
G-CMDY	Ikarus C42 FB100	J. Richards	
G-CMDZ	Robinson R44	R. R. Orr	
G-CMEC	Flylight Dragon/Ace Aviation Cyclone	G. Cousins	
G-CMEE	Ikarus C42 FB100	G. M. Roberts	
G-CMEF	Ikarus C42 FB100	Bristol Flying	
G-CMEG	Sportstar SLM	G-CMEG Sportstar Syndicate	
G-CMEK	Lindstrand LTL Series 2-70	S. A. Simington	
G-CMEL	Skyranger Nynja	D. B. Gibbins	
G-CMEO	Bloop 4	M. D. Burns	
G-CMEP	PA-28-161 Cherokee Warrior III	Norwich Aviation Centre Ltd	
G-CMER	MBB Bolkow BO.209 Monsun	Recovair Ltd	
G-CMET	Eurofox 3K	R. J. Mitchell	
G-CMEU	BAe. 146-100 ★	Imperial War Museum/Duxford	
G-CMEV	Eurofox 2K	Husbands Bosworth Gliding Club Ltd	
G-CMEW	Aerospool Dynamic WT9 UK	M. W. Frost	
G-CMEX	Ultramagic M-90 balloon	J. J. Davis	
G-CMEY	Cameron TR-65 balloon	K. R. Karlstrom	
G-CMEZ	Eurofox 2K	Cotswold Gliding Club	
G-CMFA	Van's RV-8	A. G. & E. A. Hill (G-HILZ)	
G-CMFB	Hawker Seahawk FGA6 (WV908)	Fly Navy Heritage Trust Ltd	
G-CMFD	Bristell NG Classic HD	Burt Bros (Hosiery) Ltd	
G-CMFE	Skyranger Swift 912S(1)	P. Martin	
G-CMFF	PA-28-161 Cherokee Warrior II	T. W. Gilbert	
G-CMFG	Van's RV-12IS	M. N. & N. D. Stannard	
G-CMFJ	PA-28-151 Cherokee Warrior	E. J. Lamb	
G-CMFK	Westland SA.341D Gazelle HT.Mk.3 (XW906)	The Gazelle Squadron Display Team Ltd	
G-CMFL	Avions Transport ATR-72-212A	Emerald Airlines UK Ltd	
G-CMFM	Westland Sea King HC.Mk.4	Heli-Lift Services	
G-CMFN	Westland Sea King HU.Mk.5	Lift West (Helicopters) Ltd	
G-CMFO	Westland SA.341D Gazelle HCC.Mk.4 (XZ935)	The Gazelle Squadron Display Team Ltd	
G-CMFP	Cameron Z-140 balloon	Bailey Balloons Ltd	
G-CMFR	Eurofox 3K	J. Summers & D. Arkwright	
G-CMFT	Skyranger Nynja 912(1)	A. Atkin	
G-CMFU	Spacek SD-1 Minisport	F. J. Brown	
G-CMFV	Ultra-UAS	Windracers Ltd	
G-CMFW	Cameron Whisky Bottle-90 balloon	D. P. Busby & N. Ivison	
G-CMFX	Cameron Krush Bottle-105 balloon	D. P. Busby & N. Ivison	
G-CMFY	BAe.146-100	Aircraft Maintenance Services Ltd	
G-CMFZ	Van's RV-10	K. Brown	

Notes	Reg	Type	Owner or Operator
	G-CMGA	Thorp T-18	R. G. Marshall
	G-CMGD	Grob G109B	Aerobility
	G-CMGF	Grob G109B	Aerobility
	G-CMGI	Grob G109B	Aerobility
	G-CMGJ	Grob G109B	Aerobility
	G-CMGK	Grob G109B	T. R. Dews
	G-CMGL	Grob G109B	Aerobility
	G-CMGM	Grob G109B	T. R. Dews
	G-CMGN	Grob G109B	T. R. Dews
	G-CMGS	Grob G109B	T. R. Dews
	G-CMGT	Grob G109B	Aerobility
	G-CMGW	Grob G109B	Aerobility
	G-CMGY	Grob G109B	T. R. Dews
	G-CMHB	Grob G109B	Aerobility
	G-CMHC	Grob G109B	T. R. Dews
	G-CMHD	Grob G109B	T. R. Dews
	G-CMHE	Grob G109B	T. R. Dews
	G-CMHF	Grob G109B	T. R. Dews
	G-CMHG	Grob G109B	T. R. Dews
	G-CMHH	Grob G109B	Arngrob
	G-CMHI	Grob G109B	T. R. Dews
	G-CMHL	Grob G109B	T. R. Dews
	G-CMHM	Grob G109B	T. R. Dews
	G-CMHN	Grob G109B	T. R. Dews
	G-CMHP	Grob G109B	T. R. Dews
	G-CMHS	Grob G109B	T. R. Dews
	G-CMHU	Grob G109B	Aerobility
	G-CMHY	Grob G109B	T. R. Dews
	G-CMHZ	Grob G109B	Wiltshire Ventures Group
	G-CMIA	Grob G109B	Aerobility
	G-CMIC	Grob G109B	Aerobility
	G-CMID	Grob G109B	G. S. Lapworth
	G-CMIE	Grob G109B	T. R. Dews
	G-CMIF	Grob G109B	Aerobility
	G-CMIH	Grob G109B	Aerobility
	G-CMIL	Grob G109B	Aerobility
	G-CMIM	Grob G109B	Aerobility Holdings CIC
	G-CMIO	Beagle B.121 Pup Series 1	C. J. Barrett
	G-CMIP	Percival P.546 Provost T.Mk.1 (WW447)	A. D. M. Edie
	G-CMIW	Stinson L-5 Sentinel	C. P. Duffy
	G-CMIX	Murphy Renegade 912	F. Overall
	G-CMIZ	J-3C-65 Cub	A. S. Vogel
	G-CMJA	Apollo Deltajet 500/Aeros Stingray	Exodus Aircraft Ltd
	G-CMJB	CFM Streak Shadow	C. I. Chegwen
	G-CMJC	Cessna 195A	Von Otto Ltd
	G-CMJD	Apollo Deltajet 500/Aeros Stingray	J. A. Davies
	G-CMJE	Diamond S-120 balloon	A. M. Holly
	G-CMJG	Cameron C-70 balloon	G. J. Madelin & J. A. Lawton
	G-CMJH	Eurofox 3K	BR Aviation Ltd
	G-CMJI	Ikarus C42B FB80	Ampsair Leasing Ltd
	G-CMJJ	Avions Transport ATR-72-212A	Emerald Airlines UK Ltd
	G-CMJL	Avions Transport ATR-72-212A	Emerald Airlines UK Ltd
	G-CMJM	Avions Transport ATR-72-212A	Emerald Airlines UK Ltd
	G-CMJN	Avions Transport ATR-72-212A	Emerald Airlines UK Ltd
	G-CMJO	Pilatus PC-9A	SR Aviation Ltd
	G-CMJP	TL3000 Sirius 600	E. Watson
	G-CMJS	Skyranger Nynja	Hadair Flight Training Ltd
	G-CMJU	Ikarus C42C FB100	R. K.N Nayak
	G-CMJW	Exodus Deltajet 500 Stingray	R. Higton
	G-CMJX	Tecnam P-Mentor	Oriens Aviation Ltd
	G-CMJY	Flylight Dragonfly	A. I. Lea
	G-CMJZ	Diamond DA50C	DP Aero Ltd
	G-CMKA	Ultramagic N-425 balloon	The Wild Pig Group Ltd
	G-CMKB	Bard 32 balloon	R. G. Griffin
	G-CMKC	Spacek SD-1 Minisport	C. B. Jones
	G-CMKD	Europa	D. J. Southward
	G-CMKE	Van's RV-8	M. V. Linney
	G-CMKH	Van's RV-7	A. E. N. Nicholas
	G-CMKI	Cessna 152	T. W. Gilbert
	G-CMKJ	PA-28-161 Warrior II	T. W. Gilbert
	G-CMKK	Zenair CH.750	A. Roddam

Reg	Type	Owner or Operator	Notes
G-CMKL	Van's RV-12	A. B. Dean	
G-CMKM	Cameron Z-105 balloon	The Balloon Company Ltd	
G-CMKN	Ikarus C42C FB80 Charlie	M. C. Edwards	
G-CMKR	Ikarus C42C FB100	Progress Vehicle Management Ltd	
G-CMKV	Ikarus C42C FB100	M. R. Badminton	
G-CMKW	Zenair CH750	A. Alaziaq	
G-CMKX	Cessna 172N	Redhill Air Services Ltd	
G-CMKY	Beech 76 Duchess	Redhill Air Services Ltd	
G-CMKZ	Fokker Dr.1 Triplane replica	P. G. Bond	
G-CMLB	Eurofox 3K	D. Drew	
G-CMLC	Beech 76 Duchess	Redhill Air Services Ltd	
G-CMLD	Skyranger Nynja 912S(1)	A. J. Hubbard	
G-CMLE	Pegasus Sport QuikR	GS Aviation (Europe) Ltd	
G-CMLF	Diamond S-105 balloon	A. M. Holly	
G-CMLG	Skyranger Swift	Athey's Moor Flying School Ltd	
G-CMLH	Diamond P-90L balloon	L. P. Hooper	
G-CMLJ	Europa	G. D. Bailey	
G-CMLK	Ace Spirit 70/Touch 70	Ace Aviation	
G-CMLL	Van's RV-12	J. Edgeworth	
G-CMLM	Van's RV-7	M. G. Jefferies	
G-CMLR	Cameron Z-105 balloon	The Royal Crescent Hotel & Spa	
G-CMLV	TL2000 Sting S4	J. C. Rose	
G-CMLX	Skyranger Nynja	R. C. Green	
G-CMLY	Eurofox 2K	The Bath, Wilts and North Dorset Gliding Club	
G-CMLZ	KFA Explorer	P. Marsden	
G-CMMA	Westland Gazelle AH.Mk.1	S. Atherton	
G-CMMD	McQuick GT300	I. A. Macadam	
G-CMMG	Rolladen-Schneider LS8-e	G. Cooksey	
G-CMMH	CASA 1-133 Jungmeister	Retro Track and Air (UK) Ltd	
G-CMMJ	Kubicek BB-16EF balloon	C. G. Dobson	
G-CMMK	Avions Transport ATR-72-212A	Emerald Airlines UK Ltd	
G-CMML	Evektor Sportstar RTC	Kensington Aviation Isle of Man Ltd	
G-CMMN	Avions Transport ATR-212A	Emerald Airlines UK Ltd	
G-CMMO	Eurofox 3K	Banbury Gliding Club Ltd	
G-CMMS	Kubicek BB22E balloon	K. F. Lowry	
G-CMMT	Avions Transport ATR-72-212A	Emerald Airlines UK Ltd	
G-CMMU	Fisher FP404	D. A. Balbert	
G-CMMV	Ultramagic N-210 balloon	Spirit Operations Ltd	
G-CMMW	Exodus Deltajet 500 Stingray	B. Birtle	
G-CMMX	Aerospatiale SA.341G Gazelle 1	K. O. Soerlie	
G-CMMY	Ikarus C42C FB80	The Redhill C42 Group	
G-CMMZ	Eurofox 3K	M. B. Solomon	
G-CMND	Cameron Z-140 balloon	The Balloon Company Ltd	
G-CMNF	Kubicek BB60Z balloon	Fly Away Ballooning Ltd	
G-CMNG	Ikarus C42C FB100	Royal Air Force Microlight Flying Association	
G-CMNH	Flylight Adam/PB2	C. Lomas	
G-CMNI	Skyranger Nynja 912S(1)	GB Engineering (NI) Ltd	
G-CMNJ	North American T-28A Trojan	Twyford Aviation Services (UK) Ltd	
G-CMNK	DHC.1 Chipmunk 22	Vintage Aircraft Factory Ltd	
G-CMNL	Skyranger Swift 912S(1)	M. A. Sandwith	
G-CMNM	Diamond P-70 balloon	A. M. Holly	
G-CMNN	Ultramagic N-180 balloon	The Hot Air Balloon Company (Global) Ltd	
G-CMNO	TLAC Sherwood Scout	The Light Aircraft Company Ltd	
G-CMNP	Exodus Deltajet 500 Stingray	N. Blackman	
G-CMNR	Cameron O-65 balloon	Sade Balloons Ltd, A. A. Leggate & E. H. & H. M. Savage	
G-CMNS	Pipistrel Virus SW127 BCAR-S	C. D. Barry	
G-CMNT	Avealto Subscale HAPS	Avealto Ltd	
G-CMNU	KFA Safari	D. J. Marchand	
G-CMNV	Sikorsky S-92A	Bristow Helicopters Ltd	
G-CMNW	Diamond DA.62	247 Aviation Ltd	
G-CMNX	Fresh Breeze Relax Evo 25/X-One Trike	J. D. Sings	
G-CMNY	Spacek SD-1 Minisport	W. Tunna	
G-CMNZ	Chilton DW.1A	R. Hodgson	
G-CMOA	Cessna 152	T. W. Gilbert	
G-CMOB	Eurofox 2K	J. M. Clarke	
G-CMOC	Tecnam P-Mentor	Cloud Global Ltd	
G-CMOD	VS Spitfire IXT	Pays Air Service Holdings Pty. Ltd	
G-CMOF	Tecnam P-Mentor	Cloud Global Ltd	
G-CMOG	Sling 2	D. C. Green	
G-CMOI	Flylight Exodus Deltajet 500 Stingray	D. T. Mackenzie	

Notes	Reg	Type	Owner or Operator
	G-CMOJ	Lancair 320	G. R. Phillips
	G-CMOK	Diamond P-90 balloon	A. M. Holly
	G-CMOL	Flylight Exodus Deltajet 500 Stingray	J. P. Floyd
	G-CMOM	PA-28-161 Cadet	Falcon Flying Services Ltd
	G-CMON	Van's RV-7	F. McMullan
	G-CMOO	Cameron Z-31 balloon	S. Church
	G-CMOP	Flylight Adam	Flylight Airsports Ltd
	G-CMOR	Skyranger 912(2)	C. A. W. Harvey
	G-CMOS	Cessna T.303 Crusader	Stenball Holdings Ltd
	G-CMOV	Flylight Nine	C. J. Johnson
	G-CMOW	Schleicher AS-33 ES	P. F. Brice
	G-CMOY	Flylight Exodus Deltajet 500 Stingray	B. J. Holloway
	G-CMOZ	Van's RV-6	J. C. Secker
	G-CMPA	PA-28RT-201Arrow IV	G. J. Melen (G-BREP)
	G-CMPB	Flylight Adam/PB2	L. A. Harper
	G-CMPC	Titan T-51 Mustang	S. J. Perkins
	G-CMPD	TLAC Sherwood Scout	D. H. Pattison
	G-CMPE	Ikarus C42 FB100	The Light Aircraft Company Ltd
	G-CMPF	Ikarus C42 FB100	G. A. Wright
	G-CMPG	Apollo Deltajet 500/Aeros Stingray	M. Howland
	G-CMPJ	Marquart MA5 Charger	Aviation Park Group Ltd
	G-CMPL	Ikarus C42 FB100	C. Lee
	G-CMPM	Skyranger Nynja	J. D. Fielding & J. C. Mundy
	G-CMPN	Flylight Exodus Deltajet 500 Stingray	N. H. N. Douglas
	G-CMPO	Magni M24C Plus	J. P. Cigrang
	G-CMPR	Guimbal Cabri G2	CJS Helicopters Ltd
	G-CMPT	Auster 5J2 Arrow	N. B. Morrison
	G-CMPV	Bristell NG5 Classic HD	D. T. Ellington
	G-CMPW	Flylight Exodus Deltajet 500 Stingray	T. J. Burrow
	G-CMPX	Flylight Nine	P. D. E. Batterton
	G-CMPZ	Autogyro MTOSport	J. C. Doherty
	G-CMRB	Replica SE5A	M. W. Bodger
	G-CMRC	Cessna 152	Brinkley Aviation Ltd (G-SCFG)
	G-CMRE	Ikarus C42C FB100	Balado Airfield Ltd
	G-CMRF	Flylight Nine	G. M. Fowler
	G-CMRG	Cessna 170B	R. A. Gammons
	G-CMRH	Diamond Peacock-77 (Animal-1) balloon	A. M. Holly
	G-CMRJ	Magni M245C Plus	R. D. Armishaw
	G-CMRK	Harris SSDR	J. A. Harris
	G-CMRL	Tharme Pippit	C. T. Tharme
	G-CMRO	Cameron O-31 balloon	Phoenix Balloons Ltd
	G-CMRP	Micro Aviation Raptor	M. Hilton
	G-CMRR	PA-18-150 Super Cub	G. M. Oliver
	G-CMRT	Techpro Merlin 106	Livelink Aerospace Ltd
	G-CMRV	Flylight PeaBee Red Line	T. A. Dockrell
	G-CMRW	Flylight Nine	C. Garton
	G-CMRY	Flylight Adam/PB2	F. Molloy
	G-CMRZ	Flylight Exodus Deltajet 500 Stingray	W. G. Reynolds
	G-CMSA	Aerospatiale AS.350B2 Ecureuil	Wavendon Social Housing Ltd
	G-CMSB	Cameron O-90 balloon	Phoenix Balloons Ltd
	G-CMSC	Hawker Hurricane IIb	Pays Air Service Holdings Pty Ltd
	G-CMSD	Diamond S-90 balloon	A. M. Holly
	G-CMSE	Skyranger Nynja 912S(1)	S. M. Eyers
	G-CMSF	Supermarine Spitfire LF.XVIE	Warbird Experiences Ltd
	G-CMSG	Tecnam P2010 TDI	GMSA Air Charters Ltd
	G-CMSH	Skyranger Swift 912S(1)	A. M. Sutton
	G-CMSI	TLAC Sherwood Cub	Hangar 1 Ltd
	G-CMSJ	Stratus P-17/Echoplus	S. B. Wilkes
	G-CMSK	Magni M-22C	P. R. Gloyens
	G-CMSL	Eurofox 3K	P. S. Milling
	G-CMSM	Bristell NG5 Speed Wing	G. E. Collard
	G-CMSP	Bucker Bu.131 Jungmann	N. Barnard
	G-CMSR	Agusta A109E Power	Castle Air Ltd
	G-CMSS	Skystar Kitfox Mk. 7	P. Johnson
	G-CMSU	Agusta A.109E	Castle Air Ltd
	G-CMSW	Skyranger Nynja	W. Long
	G-CMSZ	Cameron Z-105 balloon	T. Simpson
	G-CMTA	Flylight Adam	R. J. Cook
	G-CMTB	Diamond DA.50C	Aerial Exposure Ltd
	G-CMTC	Trendak Tercel	Forward Aviation Ltd
	G-CMTD	Eurofox 3K	R. G. Hearsey

Reg	Type	Owner or Operator	Notes
G-CMTE	Flylight Exodus Deltajet 500 Stingray	C. S. Traher	
G-CMTG	PA-28-161 Cherokee Warrior II	T. W. & W. S. Gilbert	
G-CMTH	Team Himax 1700R	S. M. Hall	
G-CMTI	Vun	J. J. D. Clarke	
G-CMTJ	Van's RV-12iS	M. F. El-Deen	
G-CMTK	Cessna 152	T. W. Gilbert	
G-CMTL	KFA Safari	A. R. F. Blinch	
G-CMTM	Cameron O-38 balloon	D. J. Groombridge	
G-CMTN	Van's RV-12IS	M. J. Dooley	
G-CMTS	CM Sunbird	C. W. Mitchinson	
G-CMTU	Cameron Z-105 balloon	D. R. Firkins	
G-CMTV	Bristell NG5 Speed Wing	W. J. Miazek	
G-CMTW	Cameron Z-210 balloon	The Balloon Company Ltd	
G-CMTX	Flylight Nine	J. R. Kendall	
G-CMTY	KFA Safari	G. Lewis	
G-CMTZ	Pipistrel Alpha BCAR-S-164A	The Tizzy Flying Group	
G-CMUB	Flylight Nine	Flylight Airsports Ltd	
G-CMUC	Cessna 172F	R. F. G. Moyle	
G-CMUE	Flylight Peabee/Aeros Adam 13T	I. D. Baxter	
G-CMUF	Diamond S-105 balloon	A. M. Holly	
G-CMUH	KFA Safari	R. J. Hopkins	
G-CMUI	Aeronca 11AC Chief	I. M. Maddock	
G-CMUJ	Van's RV-6A	D. Gani	
G-CMUK	Rockwell Commander 112TC	R. Forman & G. Slater (G-ERIC)	
G-CMUL	P & M Quik GT450	GS Aviatioin (Europe) Ltd	
G-CMUM	Cameron O-38 balloon	P. Spellward	
G-CMUO	Ultramagic T-150 balloon	Zebedee Balloon Service Ltd (G-OMOO)	
G-CMUP	Eurofox 2K	R. H. Cornwell	
G-CMUS	La Mouette Cosmos/Chronos 16	I. A. Macadam	
G-CMUT	Yates Lakes	M. J. A. Yates	
G-CMUV	Leonardo AW109SP Grand New	Galegrove 2 LBG	
G-CMUW	Flylight Adam	C. N. Clegg	
G-CMUZ	Flylight Exodus Deltajet 500 Stingray	D. P. Clarke	
G-CMVA	Skyranger Nynja 912S	T. A. Burgess	
G-CMVB	Cameron Z-105 balloon	The Balloon Company Ltd	
G-CMVC	Zenair CH750 Cruzer	G. S. Carter (G-CMVS)	
G-CMVD	Ikarus C42 FB100	Progress Flying School Ltd	
G-CMVE	Skyranger Nynja	C. L. Moore	
G-CMVF	Cameron Z-105 balloon	D. Hu	
G-CMVG	Flylight Nine	C. I. Farwell	
G-CMVH	Skyranger Nynja 912S(1)	J. D. Buchanan	
G-CMVI	Cameron Z-90 balloon	Phoenix Balloons Ltd	
G-CMVK	Eurofox 2K	R. T. Pearson	
G-CMVL	Flylight Exodus Deltajet 500 Stingray	Kent County Scout Council	
C CMVM	Skyrangor Nynja 912S(1)	S. Rance	
G-CMVO	Flylight Nine	N. C. Grayson	
G-CMVP	Montgomerie-Bensen B8MR	R. S. Sanby	
G-CMVT	Eurofox 3K	M. R. Buchanan	
G-CMVU	Skyranger Nynja 912S	T. J. Chapman	
G-CMVW	Flylight Adam13T/Peabee	I. M. Goddard	
G-CMVV	Van's RV-9	G. Hardwick	
G-CMVX	Flylight Fox Cub	S. Polley	
G-CMVY	TLAC Bobcat 600	The Light Aircraft Company Ltd	
G-CMVZ	Skyranger Nynja 912S(1)	N. P. Morton	
G-CMWA	Skyranger Nynja 912S(1)	C. R. Smith	
G-CMWB	Cameron Z-77 balloon	A. A. Osman	
G-CMWC	Pipistrel Alpha BCAR-S 164A	Flyabout Aviation Ltd	
G-CMWD	Flylight Exodus Deltajet 500 Stingray	K. Loder	
G-CMWE	Eurofox 2K	K. P. I. Kent	
G-CMWF	Ultramagic N-210 balloon	Spirit Operations Ltd	
G-CMWG	Diamond DA.62	247 Aviation Ltd	
G-CMWH	Flylight Nine	M. B. Horan	
G-CMWI	Embraer ERJ190-100STD	Eastern Airways (UK) Ltd	
G-CMWK	Grob G.102 Astir CS	Buckminster Gliding Club Ltd	
G-CMWM	Van's RV-7	R. S. Rose	
G-CMWN	Bell 47J-2 Ranger	Eliexpress SRLS	
G-CMWO	Eurofox 3K	S. B. Williams (G-CMOT)	
G-CMWP	Glaser-Dirks DG-400	A. P. L. Binks	
G-CMWS	Groppo Trail 600	U. Izzo & M. D. Aliotta	
G-CMWT	Pipistrel Alpha BCAR-S 164A	M. E. Hughes	
G-CMWU	Eurofox 2K	D. E. R. Jones	

Notes	Reg	Type	Owner or Operator
	G-CMWV	Avian Riot-13	E. J. McDowell
	G-CMWW	Flylight Nine	T. Southwell
	G-CMWY	Spacek SRO SD-1 Minisport	T. C. Barnby
	G-CMWZ	Flylight Adam	D. J. Seymour
	G-CMXE	Airbus Helicopters MBB-BK 117 D-3	Airbus Helicopters UK Ltd
	G-CMXF	Airbus Helicopters MBB-BK 117 D-3	Airbus Helicopters UK Ltd
	G-CMXG	Cameron Z-120 balloon	R. P. Nash
	G-CMXI	Cameron Z-69 balloon	J. A. Leahy
	G-CMXN	Westland Gazelle AH.1	Falcon Aviation Ltd
	G-CMXP	Westland Gazelle AH.1	Falcon Aviation Ltd
	G-CMXR	Cameron Sport-80 balloon	Cameron Balloons Ltd
	G-CMXU	Affordaplane	J. Riley
	G-CMXV	Aeroprakt A-32 Vixxen	Fly Far Aviation Ltd
	G-CMXZ	Ikarus C42 FB80	ZX Flying Group (G-SHCK)
	G-CMYA	Zall Jihlaven JA-400 Skyleader 400	Inditu Air Services Ltd
	G-CMYB	Van's RV-8	P. S. Oglesby (G-CMSV)
	G-CMYC	Ultramagic M-120 balloon	Spirit Operations Ltd
	G-CMYD	Cameron Z-120 balloon	The Hot Air Balloon Company (Global) Ltd
	G-CMYE	Aeros Fox 13T/Dragon	S. B. Walters
	G-CMYG	Cameron O-26 balloon	J. A. Lawton & G. J. Madelin
	G-CMYH	Eurofox 3K	Highland Gliding Club Ltd
	G-CMYI	Affordaplane	R. J. Ripley
	G-CMYJ	Tecnam P-Mentor	Aeros Leasing Ltd
	G-CMYK	Kubicek BB60Z balloon	Yorkshire Balloon Flights Ltd
	G-CMYL	Tecnam P-Mentor	Aeros Leasing Ltd
	G-CMYM	Eurofox 2K	I. M. Norfield
	G-CMYN	Schleicher ASK-21B	Midland Gliding Club Ltd
	G-CMYO	Van's RV-12iS	M. A. Streatfield
	G-CMYP	Replica Heath LNA-40 Parasol	S. T. G. Ingram
	G-CMYR	Eurocopter AS.365N3 Dauphin 2	Ministry of Defence
	G-CMYS	Van's RV-9A	H. M. Lees & T. J. Lawrence
	G-CMYT	Eurofox 2K	C. M. Scott
	G-CMYU	Flylight Exodus Deltajet 500 Stingray	K. I. Making
	G-CMYV	Van's RV-8	K. W. Baker & D. E. James (G-LUDM)
	G-CMYW	Westland Gazelle AH.1	S. Atherton
	G-CMYX	Cameron Sport-80 balloon	J. Vonka
	G-CMYZ	AutoGyro Calidus	Rotorsport Sales & Service Ltd
	G-CMYY	Flylight Exodus Deltajet 500 Stingray	P. Szymanski
	G-CMZA	Commander 114B	WT Group
	G-CMZB	Eurofox 3K	R. J. Bird
	G-CMZD	Aeroprakt A-32 Vixxen	Blue Bay Hotel Estates (Kinross) Ltd
	G-CMZE	Sling 4 TSI	D. M. Newton
	G-CMZG	Flylight Exodus Deltajet 500 Stingray	N. C. Mitchell
	G-CMZI	Embraer ERJ190-100STD	Air Kilroe Ltd
	G-CMZJ	Hughes 369D	Eliexpress SRLS/Italy
	G-CMZK	Chilton DW.1A	R. Y. Kendal
	G-CMZL	Raj Hamsa X'Air Hawk	G. A. J. Salter
	G-CMZN	Cameron Sport-60 balloon	L. P. Hooper
	G-CMZP	Tecnam P2010 TDI	Oriens Aviation Ltd
	G-CMZR	Cameron Z-225 balloon	B. Melzer
	G-CMZS	Rans S7S Coiurier	D. H. Pattison
	G-CMZT	Douglas C-47A-90-DL	Icarus Foundation/Greece
	G-CMZU	Replica Spitfire Mk.1	G. J. Davis
	G-CMZV	Aeroprakt A-32 Vixxen	R. Everitt
	G-CMZW	Windracers Ultra-UAS	Windracers Ltd
	G-CMZZ	PA-28-151 Cherokee Warrior	Kensington Aviation Isle of Man Ltd
	G-CNAA	Flylight Nine	Flylight Airsports Ltd
	G-CNAB	Avtech Jabiru UL	S. E. Buckle & J. Mitchell
	G-CNAC	Van's RV-9A	K. C. Evans
	G-CNAD	Wade BM-34	D. M. Wade
	G-CNAG	Tecnam P-Mentor	Aeros Leasing Ltd
	G-CNAH	Airbus Helicopters MBB-BK 117 D-3	Babcock Mission Critical Services Onshore Ltd
	G-CNAI	Airbus Helicopters MBB-BK 117 D-3	Babcock Mission Critical Services Onshore Ltd
	G-CNAJ	Flylight Exodus Deltajet 500 Stingray	A. L. Johnson
	G-CNAK	Sling 4 TSI	CNAK Group
	G-CNAL	Skyranger Nynja	A. Gilruth
	G-CNAM	Van's RV-7	J. Graham
	G-CNAN	Cameron Z-105 balloon	The Hot Air Balloon Company (Global) Ltd
	G-CNAO	Van's RV-12IS	R. J. Dawson
	G-CNAP	Eurofox 3K	Deeside Gliding Club (Aberdeenshire) Ltd

Reg	Type	Owner or Operator	Notes
G-CNAR	Pegasus Sport QuikR	S. P. Pearson	
G-CNAS	Flylight Exodus Deltajet 500 Stingray	A. P. Seal	
G-CNAT	Kubicek BB26Z balloon	M. Mutton	
G-CNAU	Airbus Helicopters EC130 T2	Airbus Helicopters	
G-CNAV	DG Flugzeugbau DG-1000S	Wolds Gliding Club Ltd	
G-CNAX	Tecnam P-Mentor	Aeros Leasing Ltd	
G-CNAY	Airbus Helicopters EC130 T2	Airbus Helicopters	
G-CNAZ	Windracers Ultra-UAS	Windracers Ltd	
G-CNBA	Cameron Z-105 balloon	Atmosphere Hot Air Balloons Ltd	
G-CNBB	Cameron T-70 balloon	Cameron Balloons Ltd	
G-CNBD	VS Spitfire F Mk.IV	Warbird Experiences Ltd	
G-CNBF	Aerospatiale SA.318C Alouette II Astazou	Eliexpress SRLS/Italy	
G-CNBG	Kubicek BB30E balloon	K. J. Parsons	
G-CNBH	Zenair CH.750	T. I. Carlin	
G-CNBI	Gyro Technic GT-VX2	R. F. G. Moyle	
G-CNBJ	Bell 505 Jet Ranger X	Arimpex Perience SL	
G-CNBM	DH.87B Hornet Moth	R. A. Meyer	
G-CNBN	PA-18A-135 Super Cub	B. A. Nicholson	
G-CNBP	Diamond S-77 balloon	A. M. Holly	
G-CNBR	Diamond S-77 balloon	A. M. Holly	
G-CNBS	Kubicek BB22E balloon	Nova Balloon Services Ltd	
G-CNBU	Diamond S-105 balloon	A. M. Holly	
G-CNBY	Diamond S-77 balloon	A. M. Holly	
G-CNBZ	Diamond S-120 balloon	A. M. Holly	
G-CNCA	Cameron Sport-105 balloon	I. R. Jones	
G-CNCC	Cameron Sport-105 balloon	The Hot Air Balloon Company (Global) Ltd	
G-CNCD	Cameron Z-105 balloon	First Flight Ballooning Ltd	
G-CNCE	Ozone Power Triox 2	Blakcro Ltd	
G-CNCF	Ikarus C42 FB100 Bravo	The Light Aircraft Company Ltd	
G-CNCM	Cameron Sport-90 balloon	Cameron Balloons Ltd	
G-CNCN	Rockwell Commander 112CA	Astec Holdings (UK) Ltd	
G-CNCO	Flylight Fox13TL Foxcub	C. M. Russell	
G-CNCR	Diamond F-70 balloon	A. M. Holly	
G-CNCW	Diamond S-77 balloon	A. M. Holly	
G-CNCX	Cameron O-31 balloon	D. J. Head	
G-CNDC	Magni M24C Plus	D. Croston	
G-CNEM	Cessna 152	Brinkley Aviation Ltd (G-BNPY)	
G-CNEW	Aeroprakt A22-L2 Foxbat	J. Pearce	
G-CNLL	Leonardo AW169	Cornwall Air Ambulance Trust	
G-CNPW	Kubicek BB20E balloon	D. M. Hoddinott	
G-COAT	Cameron Z-90 balloon	D. W. Torrington	
G-COBS	Diamond DA.42 M-NG	Thales UK Ltd	
G-COCG	Eurofox 3K	S. G. Dawson	
G-CODA	Hughes 369F	Whirlybirds Helicopters Ltd (G-CIYJ)	
G-COGS	Bell 407	R. B. Matthews	
G-COIN	Bell 206B JetRanger 2	J. P. Niehorster	
G-COLA	Beech F33C Bonanza	J. R. C. Spooner (G-BUAZ)	
G-COLF	BRM Bristell NG-5 Speed Wing	C. Firth	
G-COLI	Rotorsport UK MT-03	G. D. Smith	
G-COLR	Colt 69A balloon ★	British School of Ballooning/Lancing	
G-COLS	Van's RV-7A	I. A. Cunningham	
G-COLY	Eurofox 912(S)	N. D. Hoult	
G-COMB	PA-30-160 Twin Comanche	Scaffold Orkney Ltd (G-AVBL)	
G-COMP	Cameron N-90 balloon	Computacenter Ltd	
G-CONB	Robin DR.400/180	Flight Software Services Ltd (G-BUPX)	
G-CONC	Cameron N-90 balloon	A. A. Brown	
G-CONL	SOCATA TB10 Tobago	Flightplan Aviation Ltd	
G-CONN	Eurocopter EC.120B Colibri	M. J. Connors (G-BZMK)	
G-CONR	Champion 7GCBC Scout	Aerofoyle Group	
G-CONS	Groppo Trail	S. E. J. M. McDonald	
G-CONV	Convair CV-440-54 ★	Reynard Nursery/Carluke	
G-COOT	Taylor Coot A	P. M. Napp	
G-COPP	Schleicher ASW-27-18E	J. B. Giddins	
G-COPR	Robinson R44 II	Barrmill Plant Services Ltd	
G-COPS	Piper J-3C-65 Cub	R. W. Sproat	
G-CORA	Europa XS	A. M. C. Dams (G-ILUM)	
G-CORB	SOCATA TB20 Trinidad	Corvid Aviation Ltd	
G-CORD	Slingsby T.66 Nipper 3	P. S. Gilmour (G-AVTB)	
G-CORI	Hughes 369E	CJS Helicopters Ltd (G-SOOH/G-BRTL)	
G-CORS	Noorduyn AT-16-ND Harvard IIB (KF183)	Rolls-Royce PLC	

Notes	Reg	Type	Owner or Operator
	G-CORW	PA-28-180 Cherokee C	R. P. Osborne & C. A. Wilson (G-AVRY)
	G-CORY	Guimbal Cabri G2	CJS Helicopters Ltd (G-PERU)
	G-COSA	Sling 4 TSI	G-COSA Group
	G-COSF	PA-28-161 Warrior II	Stapleoffice Ltd
	G-COSM	Flylight Skyranger Nynja	Royal Air Force Microlight Flying Association
	G-COTT	Cameron 60 Cottage SS balloon	Dragon Balloon Co Ltd
	G-COUZ	Raj Hamsa X'Air 582(2)	S. McGowan
	G-COVA	PA-26-161 Cherokee Warrior III	Coventry (Civil) Aviation Ltd (G-CDCL)
	G-COVC	PA-28-161 Cherokee Warrior II	Coventry (Civil) Aviation Ltd
	G-COVR	Diamond DA62	Quadano (Jersey) Ltd
	G-COVZ	Cessna F.150M	R. A. Doherty (G-BCRT)
	G-COWW	Jodel DR.1050	N. C. Scanlan (G-ATAG)
	G-COXE	Cub Crafters CC19-180 XCub	Red Beast Aviation LLP
	G-COXI	Xtremeair XA42	ABD Networks LLP
	G-COXS	Aeroprakt A.22 Foxbat	S. Cox
	G-COZE	Cozy	R. S. Goodwin
	G-COZI	Rutan Cozy III	R. Machin
	G-CPAF	Diamond S-90 balloon	R. Pugh
	G-CPAO	Eurocopter EC.135P2+	West Yorkshire Combined Authority National Police Air Service
	G-CPAS	Eurocopter EC.135P2+	West Yorkshire Combined Authority National Police Air Service
	G-CPCD	CEA DR.221	P. J. Taylor
	G-CPDA	DH.106 Comet 4C (XS235) ★	C. Walton Ltd/Bruntingthorpe
	G-CPDW	Avions Mudry CAP-10B	Green Lane Veterinary & Farming Ltd
	G-CPIO	Avions Mudry CAP-10B	R. M. Midgley (G-BXRC)
	G-CPJB	Rolladen-Schneider LS8-e	P. M. Barnes
	G-CPLG	AutoGyro Cavalon Pro	M. E. Wakefield
	G-CPLH	Guimbal Cabri G2	Helicentre Aviation Ltd
	G-CPMK	DHC.1 Chipmunk 22 (WZ847)	P. A. Walley
	G-CPMS	SOCATA TB20 Trinidad	A. N. Dugard
	G-CPMW	PA-32R-301 Saratoga II HP	P. D. Wheelen
	G-CPPG	Alpi Pioneer 400	P. B. Godfrey
	G-CPPM	North American Harvard II (3091)	S. D. Wilch
	G-CPSS	Cessna 208B Grand Caravan	Army Parachute Aircraft Company Ltd
	G-CPTM	PA-28-151 Cherokee Warrior	T. J. & C. Mackay (G-BTOE)
	G-CPTZ	Leonardo AW169	Sloane Helicopters Ltd
	G-CPXC	Avions Mudry CAP-10C	JRW Aerobatics Ltd
	G-CRAB	Skyranger 912 (2)	C. D. Bloomfield
	G-CRAR	CZAW Sportcruiser	S. A. Korour
	G-CRBV	Balóny Kubíček BB26 balloon	G. C. Dare
	G-CRDL	Robinson R44 II	Cradel Aviation Ltd (G-ILLD)
	G-CRED	Eurofox 3K	R. C. Whittaker
	G-CREG	TAF Sling 4 TSI	C. M. Macbeth
	G-CRES	Denney Kitfox Mk 3	I. Foster
	G-CREY	SeaRey Amphibian	A. D. Sutton
	G-CRGD	PA-34-220T Seneca V	P. B. Foster (G-VYND)
	G-CRIC	Colomban MC.15 Cri-Cri	R. S. Stoddart-Stones
	G-CRIK	Colomban MC.15 Cri-Cri	N. Huxtable
	G-CRIL	Rockwell Commander 112B	Rockwell Aviation Group
	G-CRIS	Taylor JT.1 Monoplane	C. R. Steer
	G-CRJW	Schleicher ASW-27-18E	R. J. Welford
	G-CRNL	Fairchild M62A-4 Cornell (FJ662)	CRNL Aviation Ltd (G-CEVL)
	G-CROE	Robin HR200/120B	R. J. Williamson (G-MFLA/G-HHUK)
	G-CROI	Robin HR200/120B	R. J. Williamson (G-MFLE/G-BYLH)
	G-CROL	Maule MXT-7-180	J. R. Pratt
	G-CROS	Avro RJ85	Executive Jet Support Ltd
	G-CROX	Robin R2112 Alpha	R. J. Williamson (G-CBNG)
	G-CROY	Europa	M. T. Austin
	G-CRSR	Czech Sport Aircraft Sportcruiser	G-CRSR Flying Group
	G-CRUE	Van's RV-7	C. Arnold
	G-CRUI	CZAW Sportcruiser	J. Massey
	G-CRUM	Westland Scout AH.1 (XV137)	G. Greenall
	G-CRUX	Boeing 737-MAX8	Ascend Airways Ltd
	G-CRUZ	Cessna T.303	S. J. & J. J. Ollier
	G-CRVC	Van's RV-14	I. A. Sweetland
	G-CRWL	Leonardo AW.169	Cornwall Air Ambulance Trust
	G-CRWZ	CZAW Sportcruiser	T. J. Gayton-Polley
	G-CRZA	CZAW Sportcruiser	A. W. K. Van der Schatte Olivier

Reg	Type	Owner or Operator	Notes
G-CRZE	Ultramagic M-105 balloon	Fresh Air Ltd	
G-CRZR	Czech Sport PS-28 Cruiser	Fife Cruiser Group (G-EGHA)	
G-CSAC	Eurofox 3K	C. S. A. Costa	
G-CSAM	Van's RV-9A	N. J. L. Heald	
G-CSAV	Thruster T.600N 450	J. T. Engelbert	
G-CSAW	CZAW Sportcruiser	B. C. Fitzgerald-O'Connor	
G-CSCS	Cessna F.172N	L. E. Winstanley	
G-CSDJ	Avtech Jabiru UL	K. A. McDonnell	
G-CSDR	Corvus CA22	Crusader Syndicate	
G-CSET	Van's RV-7	C. Matthews	
G-CSGT	PA-28-161 Cherokee Warrior II	W. Ali & Denderah S A (G-BPHB)	
G-CSHB	Czech Sport PS-28 Cruiser	Ulster Flying Club (1961) Ltd	
G-CSHW	Bell 206B-3 Jet Ranger III	P. Bennedsen	
G-CSIX	PA-32-300 Cherokee Six	DMB Collection Ltd	
G-CSKW	Van's RV-7	G-CSKW Group (G-CDJW)	
G-CSLE	Agusta A.109E Power	Castle Air Ltd (G-SPRI/G-EMHC)	
G-CSLG	Robinson R66	C. R, S. E. & L. A. Hewgill (G-PDDY)	
G-CSLL	PA-28R-201 Arrow III	C. Hope (G-FROS)	
G-CSLS	SOCATA TB-10 Tobago	Cavendish Aviation UK Ltd	
G-CSLY	SOCATA TB-20 Trinidad	Cavendish Aviation UK Ltd	
G-CSMK	EV-97A Eurostar	T. J. Miller	
G-CSPR	Van's RV-6A	Casper Group	
G-CSUE	Savannah VG Jabiru (5)	J. R. Stratton & B. J. Jeffery	
G-CSZM	Zenair CH.601XL Zodiac	C. Budd	
G-CTAB	Bellanca 7GCAA Citabria	North West Aerobatics Ltd (G-BFHP)	
G-CTAV	EV-97 Eurostar	K. R. Porter	
G-CTCB	Diamond DA42 Twin Star	Tesla Solutions Ltd (G-CDTG)	
G-CTCC	Diamond DA42 Twin Star	Tesla Solutions Ltd (G-OCCZ)	
G-CTCE	Diamond DA42 Twin Star	Tesla Solutions Ltd	
G-CTCF	Diamond DA42 Twin Star	Tesla Solutions Ltd	
G-CTCG	Diamond DA42 Twin Star	Leading Edge Aviation Ltd	
G-CTCH	Diamond DA42 Twin Star	Tesla Solutions Ltd	
G-CTCL	SOCATA TB10 Tobago	Double S Group (G-BSIV)	
G-CTDH	Flight Design CT2K	A. D. Thelwall	
G-CTDW	Flight Design CTSW	T. A. Fineman	
G-CTED	Van's RV-7A	J. J. Nicholson	
G-CTEE	Flight Design CTSW	T. R. Grief (G-CLEG)	
G-CTFS	Westland SA.341C Gazelle HT2	The Gazelle Squadron Displayt Team (G-OJCO/G-LEDR/G-CBSB)	
G-CTIO	SOCATA TB20 Trinidad	I. R. Hunt	
G-CTIX	VS.509 Spitfire T.IX (P9386:QV-K)	Spitfire Productions Ltd	
G-CTKL	Noorduyn AT-16 Harvard IIB (54137)	M. R. Simpson	
G-CTLS	Flight Design CTLS 600UK	G. P. Masters	
G-CTNG	Cirrus SR20	J. Crackett	
G-CTOY	Denney Kitfox Mk 3	R. P. Hogg & R. Nelson	
G-CTSC	Diamond DA.40NG Star	Tesla Solutions Ltd	
G-CTSL	Flight Design CT-Supralight	J. E. Lander	
G-CTSM	Diamond DA.40NG Star	Tesla Solutions Ltd	
G-CTSO	Diamond DA.40NG Star	Romeo Golf Aviation Ltd	
G-CTSP	Diamond DA.40NG Star	Tesla Solutions Ltd	
G-CTST	Diamond DA.40NG Star	Tesla Solutions Ltd	
G-CTSV	Diamond DA.42 Twin Star	Tesla Solutions Ltd	
G-CTTS	English Electric Canberra B.Mk.2	Vulcan to the Sky Trust (G-BVWC)	
G-CTWO	Schempp-Hirth Standard Cirrus	R. J. Griffin	
G-CTZO	SOCATA TB20 Trinidad GT	G-CTZO Group	
G-CUAV	Apollo Deltajet 500/Aeros Stingray	ACR Flight Training Ltd	
G-CUBA	PA-32R-301T Turbo Saratoge	M. Atlass	
G-CUBB	PA-18-180 Super Cub	J. McCullough	
G-CUBI	PA-18-125 Super Cub	G. T. Fisher	
G-CUBJ	PA-18-150 Super Cub (18-5395:CDG)	S. A. Lockyer	
G-CUBN	PA-18-150 Super Cub	N. J. R. Minchin	
G-CUBS	Piper J-3C-65 Cub	Sunbeam Aviation (G-BHPT)	
G-CUBT	PA-18-95 Super Cub (51-15555)	A. Thomas (G-OSPS/G-AWRH)	
G-CUBW	WAG-Aero Acro Trainer	B. G. Plumb, A. G. Bourne & D. P. Dyer	
G-CUBZ	PA-18-135 Super Cub	A. J. L. Eves (G-BMAY)	
G-CUMU	Schempp-Hirth Discus b	D. J. Blackman	
G-CUPP	Pitts S-2A	Avmarine Ltd	
G-CURV	Avid Speedwing	K. S. Kelso	

Notes	Reg	Type	Owner or Operator
	G-CUSS	Van's RV-7	J. W. Beaty
	G-CUTE	Dyn'Aéro MCR-01	J. M. Keane
	G-CUTH	P & M Quik R	A. R. & S. Cuthbertson
	G-CVBA	Rolladen-Schneider LS6-18W	J. S. Moore
	G-CVBF	Cameron A-210 balloon	Virgin Balloon Flights Ltd
	G-CVET	Flight Design CTLS 600UK	S. J. Sykes (G-CGVR)
	G-CVII	Dan Rihn DR.107 One Design	One Design Group
	G-CVLN	Autogyro Cavalon	M. Groom (G-CIAT)
	G-CVMI	PA-18-150 Super Cub	J. S. Peplow & E. V. Moffatt
	G-CVST	Jodel D.140E	Forge Consulting Ltd
	G-CVZT	Schempp-Hirth Ventus 2cT	A. & M. C. Conboy
	G-CWAG	Sequoia F. 8L Falco	D. R. Austin
	G-CWAL	Raj Hamsa X'Air 133	L. R. Morris
	G-CWAW	AOT JA-400 Skyleader 400	A. J. & C. R. Williams
	G-CWAY	Ikarus C42 FB100	M. Conway
	G-CWBM	Phoenix Currie Wot	R. S. Acton (G-BTVP)
	G-CWDB	Flylight Exodus Deltajet 500 Stingray	D. W. C. Beer
	G-CWDW	Cessna 182T	P. J. Webb (G-PCBC)
	G-CWEB	P & M Quik GT450	G-CWEB Syndicate
	G-CWFT	Cessna 172N	Avalon Ventures Ltd
	G-CWIC	Mainair Pegasus Quik	G-CWIC Group
	G-CWIX	Supermarine 361 Spitfire LF.Ixe	Boultbee Flight Academy Ltd
	G-CWLC	Schleicher ASH-25	G-CWLC Group
	G-CWMC	P & M Quik GT450	S. A. Harvey
	G-CWOW	Balony Kubicek BB45Z balloon	Skybus Ballooning
	G-CWTD	Aeroprakt A22 Foxbat	Newtownards Microlight Group
	G-CWTT	Cessna 182T	A. P. Walker
	G-CWVY	P & M Pegasus Quik	M. T. Batchelor
	G-CXCX	Cameron N-90 balloon	Cathay Pacific Airways (London) Ltd
	G-CXDE	Eurofox 2K	D. Evans
	G-CXDZ	Cassutt Speed Two	J. A. H. Chadwick
	G-CXIP	Thruster T.600N	P. H. Thomas
	G-CXIV	Thatcher CX4	I. B. Melville
	G-CXSM	Cessna 172R	S. Eustathiou (G-BXSM)
	G-CXTE	BRM Aero Bristell NG5 Speed Wing	M. Langmead
	G-CYFR	PA-36-350P Malibu Mirage	Benjarron Aviation Ltd (G-JTBP)
	G-CYGI	HAPI Cygnet SF-2A	C. B. Jones
	G-CYLL	Sequoia F.8L Falco	N. J. Langrick & A. J. Newall
	G-CYMA	GA-7 Cougar	Grade Digital Ltd (G-BKOM)
	G-CYPC	Cessna 208B Grand Caravan	The Cyprus Combined Services Parachute Club
	G-CYPM	Cirrus SR22	Ice Helicopters
	G-CYRA	Kolb Twinstar Mk. 3 (Modified)	S. J. Fox (G-MYRA)
	G-CYRL	Cessna 182T	Zone Travel Ltd
	G-CZAC	Zenair CH.601XL	A. Best
	G-CZCZ	Avions Mudry CAP-10B	M. Farmer
	G-CZMI	Skyranger Swift 912(1)	D. G. Baker
	G-CZNE	BN-2B-20 Islander	Cormack (Aircraft Services) Ltd (G-BWZF)
	G-CZOS	Cirrus SR20	Cambridge Flying Company Ltd
	G-CZSC	CZAW Sportcruiser	A. D. Berryman
	G-DAAN	Eurocopter EC 135P2+	Devon Air Ambulance Trading Co.Ltd
	G-DAAS	Airbus Helicopters MBB BK 117 D-2	Devon Air Ambulance Trading Co.Ltd
	G-DAAW	MBB Bolkow BO209 Monsun 160RV	A. J. Court & N. A. Brown
	G-DAAY	Ultramagic B-70 balloon	Longleat Enterprises Ltd
	G-DAAZ	PA-28RT-201T Turbo Arrow IV	Cambrian Flying Group Ltd
	G-DABS	Robinson R22 II	T. Campbell
	G-DACA	P.57 Sea Prince T.1 (WF118) ★	P. G. Vallance Ltd/Charlwood
	G-DACE	Corben Baby Ace D	P. King (G-BTSB)
	G-DACF	Cessna 152 II	T. M. & M. L. Jones (G-BURY)
	G-DADA	Rotorsport UK MT-03	J. C. Hilton-Johnson
	G-DADD	Reality Escapade 912(2)	P. S. Balmer
	G-DADG	PA-18-150 Super Cub	F. J. Cox
	G-DADJ	Glaser-Dirks DG-200	M. A. Hunton
	G-DADX	Apollo DeltaJet 500/Aeros Stingray	G. D. Hall
	G-DADZ	CZAW Sportcruiser	Meon Flying Group

Reg	Type	Owner or Operator	Notes
G-DAFC	Bristell NG5 Speedwing	R. B. C. Stalker	
G-DAGF	EAA Acrosport II	M. G. Pahle	
G-DAGJ	Zenair CH.601HD Zodiac	C. A. Larkins	
G-DAGN	Ikarus C42 FB80	N. L. James	
G-DAIR	Luscombe 8A Silvaire	D. F. Soul (G-BURK)	
G-DAKK	Douglas C-47A	R. G. T. de Man	
G-DAKM	Diamond DA.40D Star	Plane Rentals Ltd	
G-DAKO	PA-28-236 Dakota	S. J. McBride	
G-DAKT	PA-28-236 Dakota	K. A. Sherwood (G-CSBD/G-CSBO)	
G-DAMB	Sequoia F.8L Falco	S. O. Foxlee (G-OGKB)	
G-DAME	Vans RV-7	S. James	
G-DAMO	Rotorway Executive 162F	D. Wellman (G-CCMU)	
G-DAMS	Skyranger Nynja 912S(1)	Dambusters Ltd	
G-DAMY	Europa	U. A. Schliessler & R. J. Kelly	
G-DANA	Jodel DR.200 (replica)	Cheshire Eagles (G-DAST)	
G-DANB	Sherwood Ranger ST	W. A. Douthwaite	
G-DAND	SOCATA TB10 Tobago	Coventry Aviators Flying Group	
G-DANJ	Cameron TR-65 balloon	D. J. Gregory	
G-DANL	Beech 76 Duchess	L. C. P. Montoya (G-GPAT)	
G-DANO	Cessna 182Q	D. T. Pangbourne (G-BNRY)	
G-DANP	Van's RV-7	I. D. Foley	
G-DANY	Avtech Jabiru UL	D. A. Crosbie	
G-DASG	Schleicher ASW-27-18E	E. Alston	
G-DASH	Rockwell Commander 112	S. M. Upton (G-BDAJ)	
G-DASS	Ikarus C.42 FB100	Fly 365	
G-DATR	Agusta-Bell 206B-3 JetRanger 3	P. J. Spinks (G-JLEE/G-JOKE/G-CSKY/G-TALY)	
G-DAVB	Aerosport Scamp ★	Montrose Air Station Heritage Centre	
G-DAVE	Jodel D.112	I. D. Worthington	
G-DAVH	Cessna 150H	C. Burton (G-BRBH)	
G-DAVM	Akrotech Europe CAP.10B	D. Moorman	
G-DAVS	AB Sportine Aviacija LAK-17AT	G-DAVS Syndicate	
G-DAWG	SA Bulldog Srs 120/121 (XX522)	M. A. Hanson	
G-DAXA	Robinson R44 II	HQ Aviation Ltd (G-ROYM)	
G-DAYA	Bombardier CL600-2B16 Challenger 604	Gama Aviation (UK) Ltd (G-RCAV)	
G-DAYD	Agusta A109S Grand	Altitude Charters (IOM) Ltd (G-SKBL/G-PDAY/G-CDWY)	
G-DAYF	Agusta AW109SP Grand New	Altitude Charters (IOM) Ltd (G-SKBH)	
G-DAYI	Europa	R. S. Cullum	
G-DAYO	Beech A36 Bonanza	A36 Ltd	
G-DAYZ	Pietenpol Air Camper	G. W. Hilferty	
G-DAZO	Diamond DA.20-A1 Katana	Cubair Flight Training Ltd	
G-DAZW	Zenair CH.750 Cruzer	D. Weston	
G-DAZZ	Van's RV-8	Wishangar RV8	
G-DBCA	Airbus A.319-131	British Airways plc	
G-DBCB	Airbus A.319-131	British Airways plc	
G-DBCC	Airbus A.319-131	British Airways plc	
G-DBCD	Airbus A.319-131	British Airways plc	
G-DBCE	Airbus A.319-131	British Airways plc	
G-DBCF	Airbus A.319-131	British Airways plc	
G-DBCG	Airbus A.319-131	British Airways plc	
G-DBCH	Airbus A.319-131	British Airways plc	
G-DBCJ	Airbus A.319-131	British Airways plc	
G-DBCK	Airbus A.319-131	British Airways plc	
G-DBDM	Eurofox 3K	D. W. Buggins & L. Brehm	
G-DBEE	Jabiru J430	A. G. Bridger	
G-DBEN	Schleicher ASW-15	Oscar 8 Syndicate	
G-DBGB	Diamond P-50 balloon	A. M. Holly	
G-DBHI	Bell 505 Jet Ranger X	D. B. Hamilton	
G-DBIN	Medway SLA 80 Executive	P. D. J. Purdy	
G-DBIT	Cameron A-210 balloon	J. C. M. Greatrix	
G-DBJD	PZL-Bielsko SZD-9BIS Bocian 1D	The Gliding Heritage Centre	
G-DBLU	Leonardo AW139	Flexjet Helicopters	
G-DBNH	Schleicher Ka 6CR	The Bath, Wilts and North Dorset Gliding Club Ltd	
G-DBNK	Eurocopter EC.120B Colibri	De Banke Aviation LLP (G-PERF)	
G-DBOD	Cessna 172S	Goodwood Road Racing Co Ltd	
G-DBOI	Diamond S-77 balloon	A. M. Holly	
G-DBOL	Schleicher Ka 6CR	G-DBOL Group	
G-DBRT	Slingsby T.51 Dart	A. R. Gate	
G-DBRU	Slingsby T.51 Dart	G-DBRU Group	
G-DBSA	Slingsby T.51 Dart	The Gliding Heritage Centre	

Notes	Reg	Type	Owner or Operator
	G-DBSB	TL2000UK Sting Carbon S4	M. D. Lulham
	G-DBSD	Bombardier BD700-2A12 Global 7500	Conciege U Ltd
	G-DBSL	Slingsby T.51 Dart	W. R. Davis
	G-DBSN	Diamond P-60 balloon	C. G. Dobson
	G-DBUZ	Schleicher Ka 6CR	J. J. Hartwell
	G-DBVB	Schleicher K7	S. W. Kahn
	G-DBVR	Schleicher Ka 6CR	A. L. Hoskin
	G-DBVX	Schleicher Ka 6CR	Y. Marom
	G-DBVZ	Schleicher Ka 6CR	S. J. Bradley
	G-DBWC	Schleicher Ka 6CR	A. R. Gate
	G-DBWJ	Slingsby T.51 Dart 17R	T. J. Horsley
	G-DBWM	Slingsby T.51 Dart 17R	I. D. Walton
	G-DBWO	Slingsby T.51 Dart	C. R. Stacey
	G-DBWP	Slingsby T-51 Dart 17R	S. P. Withey & A. J. Whiteman
	G-DBWS	Slingsby T-51 Dart 17R	R. D. Broome
	G-DBXG	Slingsby T.51 Dart 17R	T. H. Knapton
	G-DBXS	Europa XS	G. D. Bird
	G-DBYC	Slingsby T.51 Dart 17R	R. L. Horsnell & N. A. Jaffray
	G-DBYG	Slingsby T.51 Dart 17R	The Portmoak Collection
	G-DBYL	Schleicher Ka 6CR	The Surrey Hills Gliding Club Ltd
	G-DBYM	Schleicher Ka 6CR	S. F. Smith
	G-DBYU	Schleicher Ka-6CR	M. C. Jones
	G-DBYX	Schleicher Ka-6E	I. Bannister
	G-DBZF	Slingsby T.51 Dart 17R	A. Powell, P.Molloy & N. Hanney
	G-DBZJ	Slingsby T.51 Dart 17R	P. Lindberg
	G-DCAE	Schleicher Ka 6E	N. J. Weston
	G-DCAG	Schleicher Ka 6E	715 Syndicate
	G-DCAM	Eurocopter AS.355NP Ecureuil 2	Cameron Charters LLP
	G-DCAO	Schempp-Hirth SHK-1	R. A. Morriss
	G-DCAR	Magni M24C Plus	R. Carey
	G-DCAS	Schleicher Ka 6E	J. M. Preller
	G-DCAZ	Slingsby T-51 Dart 17R	D. A. & J. M. L. Bullock
	G-DCBA	Slingsby T.51 Dart 17R	K. T. Kreis
	G-DCBI	Schweizer 269C-1	A & W Demolition (Bracknell)
	G-DCBM	Schleicher Ka 6CR	S. C. Male
	G-DCBP	SZD-24C Foka	The Gliding Heritage Centre
	G-DCBW	Schleicher ASK-13	Stratford on Avon Gliding Club Ltd
	G-DCBY	Schleicher Ka 6CR	R. G. Appleboom
	G-DCCA	Schleicher Ka 6E	P. N. Maddocks
	G-DCCB	Schempp-Hirth SHK-1	CCB Syndicate
	G-DCCD	Schleicher Ka 6E	Charlie Charlie Delta Group
	G-DCCE	Schleicher ASK-13	The Welland Gliding Club Ltd
	G-DCCG	Schleicher Ka 6E	R. J. Playle
	G-DCCL	Schleicher Ka 6E	T. J. Brunskill
	G-DCCM	Schleicher ASK-13	Trent Valley K13 Group
	G-DCCP	Schleicher ASK-13	Lima 99 Syndicate
	G-DCCR	Schleicher Ka 6E	G-DCCR Syndicate
	G-DCCT	Schleicher ASK-13	East Sussex Gliding Club Ltd
	G-DCCU	Schleicher Ka 6E	J. L. Hasker
	G-DCCV	Schleicher Ka 6E	S. P. Evans
	G-DCCW	Schleicher ASK-13	Midland Gliding Club Ltd
	G-DCCX	Schleicher ASK-13	Trent Valley Gliding Club Ltd
	G-DCCY	Schleicher ASK-13	Dartmoor Gliding Society
	G-DCCZ	Schleicher ASK-13	Midland Gliding Club Ltd
	G-DCDA	Schleicher Ka 6E	Ka6E-DCDA Group
	G-DCDC	Lange E1 Antares	J. D. Williams
	G-DCDF	Schleicher Ka 6E	CDF Syndicate
	G-DCDG	FFA Diamant 18	J. Cashin & D. McCarty
	G-DCDO	Ikarus C42 FB80	M. Cheetham
	G-DCDW	Diamant 18	D. R. Chapman
	G-DCDZ	Schleicher Ka 6E	J. A. H. Shaw & G. M. Spelman
	G-DCEB	PZL-Bielsko SZD-9BIS Bocian 1E	G-DCEB Syndicate
	G-DCEC	Schempp-Hirth Cirrus	CEC Group
	G-DCEM	Schleicher Ka 6E	S. G. Jessup
	G-DCEO	Schleicher Ka 6E	C. L. Lagden
	G-DCEW	Schleicher Ka 6E	A. M. Cowey
	G-DCFA	Schleicher ASK-13	Dorset Gliding Club Ltd
	G-DCFF	Schleicher K 8B	Derbyshire and Lancashire Gliding Club Ltd
	G-DCFG	Schleicher ASK-13	The Nene Valley Gliding Club Ltd
	G-DCFK	Schempp-Hirth Cirrus	P. D. Whitters

Reg	Type	Owner or Operator	Notes
G-DCFL	Schleicher Ka 6E	6E Syndicate	
G-DCFS	Glasflugel Standard Libelle 201B	J. E. Hoy	
G-DCFW	Glasflugel Standard Libelle 201B	A. Hill	
G-DCFX	Glasflugel Standard Libelle 201B	A. S. Burton	
G-DCFY	Glasflugel Standard Libelle 201B	D. P. Taylor	
G-DCGB	Schleicher Ka 6E	M. A. Howitt	
G-DCGD	Schleicher Ka 6E	A. T. Green	
G-DCGE	Schleicher Ka 6E	O. J. Anderson & B. Silke	
G-DCGH	Schleicher K 8B	M. F. Jenkins	
G-DCGM	FFA Diamant 18	J. G. Batch	
G-DCGO	Schleicher ASK-13	Black Mountains Gliding Club	
G-DCGT	Schempp-Hirth SHK-1	T. Callier	
G-DCGY	Schempp-Hirth Cirrus	S. H. Fletcher	
G-DCHB	Schleicher Ka 6E	577 Syndicate	
G-DCHJ	Bolkow Phoebus C	The Gliding Heritage Centre	
G-DCHL	PZL-Bielsko SZD-30	N. A. C. E. Barnes	
G-DCHT	Schleicher ASW-15	D. Edwards	
G-DCHU	Schleicher K 8B	G-DCHU Syndicate	
G-DCHW	Schleicher ASK-13	Dorset Gliding Club Ltd	
G-DCHZ	Schleicher Ka 6E	T. P. Browning	
G-DCJB	Bolkow Phoebus C	R. Idle	
G-DCJF	Schleicher K-8B	G. Smith	
G-DCJJ	Bolkow Phoebus C	P. N. Maddocks	
G-DCJK	Schempp-Hirth SHK-1	G. G. Dale	
G-DCJM	Schleicher K-8B	Midland Gliding Club Ltd	
G-DCJN	Schempp-Hirth SHK-1	SHK V55 Syndicate	
G-DCJR	Schempp-Hirth Cirrus	C. Thirkell	
G-DCJY	Schleicher Ka 6CR	T. H. Robinson	
G-DCKD	PZL-Bielsko SZD-30	The Gliding Heritage Centre	
G-DCKK	Cessna F.172N	DCKK Group	
G-DCKL	Schleicher Ka 6E	C. J. Sturdy	
G-DCKP	Schleicher ASW-15	M. W. Black	
G-DCKY	Glasflugel Standard Libelle 201B	M. N. K. Willcox	
G-DCKZ	Schempp-Hirth Standard Cirrus	A. Rattray & J. W. Barrett	
G-DCLL	Van's RV-14	D. J. Cullen	
G-DCLM	Glasflugel Standard Libelle 201B	R. L. Smith	
G-DCLO	Schempp-Hirth Cirrus	Bravo Delta Group	
G-DCLP	Glasflugel Standard Libelle 201B	K. Stokes	
G-DCLZ	Schleicher Ka 6E	S. K. Westrope	
G-DCMI	Mainair Pegasus Quik	F. Omaraie-Hamdanie	
G-DCMK	Schleicher ASK-13	Black Mountains Gliding Club	
G-DCMN	Schleicher K 8B	The Bristol Gliding Club Proprietary Ltd	
G-DCMO	Glasflugel Standard Libelle 201B	D. M. Arnold	
G-DCMR	Glasflugel Standard Libelle 201B	S. F. Bellamy	
G DCMW	Glasflugel Standard Libelle 201B	J. K. Davidson	
G-DCNC	Schempp-Hirth Standard Cirrus	M. D. Cobham	
G-DCNE	Glasflugel Standard Libelle 201B	M. D. Worthington	
G-DCNG	Glasflugel Standard Libelle 201B	S. J. Sanderson	
G-DCNJ	Glasflugel Standard Libelle 201B	P. I. Jameson	
G-DCNM	PZL-Bielsko SZD-9bis Bocian 1E	Bocian Syndicate	
G-DCNP	Glasflugel Standard Libelle 201B	I. G. Carrick & D. J. Shepherd	
G-DCNS	Slingsby T.59A Kestrel	J. D. Westgarth	
G-DCNW	Slingsby T.59F Kestrel	P. King	
G-DCOC	PZL-Bielsko SZD-30 Pirat	The Welland Gliding Club Ltd	
G-DCOE	Van's RV-6	R. E. Welch	
G-DCOJ	Slingsby T.59A Kestrel	M. C. Bailey	
G-DCOR	Schempp-Hirth Standard Cirrus	H. R. Ford	
G-DCOY	Schempp-Hirth Standard Cirrus	RPG	
G-DCPB	Eurocopter MBB-BK 117C-1	West Yorkshire Combined Authority National Police Air Service	
G-DCPD	Schleicher ASW-17	ASW17 Group	
G-DCPF	Glasflugel Standard Libelle 201B	T. J. Reeve	
G-DCPM	Glasflugel Standard Libelle 201B	P. E. Jessop & A. M. Carpenter	
G-DCPU	Schempp-Hirth Standard Cirrus	J. A. Thomson	
G-DCRB	Glasflugel Standard Libelle 201B	P. J. Carpenter	
G-DCRH	Schempp-Hirth Standard Cirrus	P. E. Thelwall	
G-DCRN	Schempp-Hirth Standard Cirrus	J. P. Eldem	
G-DCRO	Glasflugel Standard Libelle 201B	G. R. Williams & T. P. Smith	
G-DCRS	Glasflugel standard Libelle 201B	D. T. Bury	
G-DCRV	Glasflugel Standard Libelle 201B	D. Williams	
G-DCRW	Glasflugel Standard Libelle 201B	G-DCRW Syndicate	

Notes	Reg	Type	Owner or Operator
	G-DCSB	Slingsby T.59F Kestrel	W. Fischer
	G-DCSD	Slingsby T.59D Kestrel	L. P. Davidson
	G-DCSF	Slingsby T.59F Kestrel 19	R. Birch
	G-DCSI	Robinson R44 II	Select Engineering (UK) Ltd (G-TGDL)
	G-DCSJ	Glasflugel Standard Libelle 201B	P. J. Gill
	G-DCSK	Slingsby T.59D Kestrel	Kestrel CSK Group
	G-DCSN	Pilatus B4-PC11AF	J. S. Firth
	G-DCSP	Pilatus B4-PC11	S. J. Norman
	G-DCSR	Glasflugel Standard Libelle 201B	G-DCSR Flying Group
	G-DCTB	Schempp-Hirth Standard Cirrus	G-DCTB Group
	G-DCTJ	Slingsby T.59D Kestrel	J. Young & R. J. Aylesbury
	G-DCTL	Slingsby T.59D Kestrel	E. S. E. Hibbard
	G-DCTM	Slingsby T.59D Kestrel	C. Swain
	G-DCTO	Slingsby T.59D Kestrel	G-DCTO Gliding Syndicate
	G-DCTP	Slingsby T.59D Kestrel	D. C. Austin
	G-DCTR	Slingsby T.59D Kestrel	K. M. Charlton
	G-DCTT	Schempp-Hirth Standard Cirrus	N. I. van Genugten
	G-DCTU	Glasflugel Standard Libelle 201B	P. M. Davies & R. Cobb
	G-DCTV	PZL-Bielsko SZD-30	M. Cudmore & R. Walters
	G-DCTX	PZL-Bielsko SZD-30	A. M. Bennett
	G-DCUB	Pilatus B4-PC11	G. M. Taylor
	G-DCUC	Pilatus B4-PC11	G. M. Cumner
	G-DCUD	Yorkshire Sailplanes YS53 Sovereign	T. J. Wilkinson
	G-DCUJ	Glasflugel Standard Libelle 201B	M. P. Tooley
	G-DCUS	Schempp-Hirth Cirrus VTC	G. D. Ackroyd
	G-DCUT	Pilatus B4 PC11AF	A. L. Walker
	G-DCVE	Schempp-Hirth Cirrus VTC	S. Hardy
	G-DCVK	Pilatus B4-PC11AF	M. Frank
	G-DCVL	Glasflugel Standard Libelle 201B	J. Williams
	G-DCVR	PZL-Bielsko SZD-30 Pirat	M. T. Pitorak
	G-DCVV	Pilatus B4-PC11AF	D. W. Poll
	G-DCVW	Slingsby T.59D Kestrel	J. J. Green & J. A. Tonkin
	G-DCVY	Slingsby T.59D Kestrel	N. Dickenson
	G-DCWB	Slingsby T.59D Kestrel	I. J. Ashdown
	G-DCWD	Slingsby T.59D Kestrel	G. J. Palmer
	G-DCWE	Glasflugel Standard Libelle 201B	L. J. Maksymowicz
	G-DCWF	Slingsby T.59D Kestrel	P. F. Nicholson
	G-DCWG	Glasflugel Standard Libelle 201B	T. D. Farquhar
	G-DCWH	Schleicher ASK-13	York Gliding Centre (Operations) Ltd
	G-DCWR	Schempp-Hirth Cirrus VTC	CWR Group
	G-DCWS	Schempp-Hirth Cirrus VTC	Cirrus G-DCWS Syndicate
	G-DCWT	Glasflugel Standard Libelle 201B	A. A. Tills
	G-DCWX	Glasflugel Standard Libelle	Dorset Gliding Club Ltd
	G-DCWY	Glasflugel Standard Libelle 201B	S. J. Taylor
	G-DCXH	PZL-Bielsko SZD-36A Cobra 15	J. Dudzik
	G-DCXI	Slingsby T.61F Venture T.2	611 Vintage Flight (G-BUDB)
	G-DCXK	Glasflugel Standard Libelle 201B	P. Dolan
	G-DCXV	Yorkshire Sailplanes YS-53 Sovereign	The Gliding Heritage Centre
	G-DCYA	Pilatus B4 PC-11	B4-072 Group
	G-DCYC	Pilatus B4 PC-11	D. P. Aherne
	G-DCYG	Glasflugel H201B Standard Libelle	G. S. Wheldon
	G-DCYM	Schempp-Hirth Standard Cirrus	L. A. Woodforth & R. J. M. Balfour
	G-DCYO	Schempp-Hirth Standard Cirrus	M. J. Layton
	G-DCYP	Schempp-Hirth Standard Cirrus	A. F. Scott
	G-DCYT	Schempp-Hirth Standard Cirrus	W. A. L. Leader
	G-DCYZ	Schleicher K 8B	UWE Students Union
	G-DCZD	Pilatus B4 PC-11AF	T. Dale
	G-DCZG	PZL-Bielsko SZD-30	J. T. Pajdak
	G-DCZN	Schleicher ASW-15B	J. R. Walters
	G-DCZR	Slingsby T.59D Kestrel	A. H. Wales
	G-DCZS	Slingsby T.59D Kestrel	O. W. L. Killean
	G-DCZU	Slingsby T.59D Kestrel	R. A. Morris
	G-DDAC	PZL-Bielsko SZD-36A	R. J. A. Colenso
	G-DDAD	Robinson R44	Andrew's Whirlybirds Ltd
	G-DDAJ	Shempp-Hirth Nimbus 2	J. J. Mion
	G-DDAN	PZL-Bielsko SZD-30	J. M. A. Shannon
	G-DDAP	SZL-Bielsko SZD-30	T. H. Knapton
	G-DDAS	Schempp-Hirth Standard Cirrus	N. K. Shead
	G-DDAW	Schleicher Ka 6CR	D. A. Whitticase
	G-DDBB	Slingsby T.51 Dart 17R	A. J. A. Forrest

Reg	Type	Owner or Operator	Notes
G-DDBC	Pilatus B4-PC11	J. H. France & G. R. Harris	
G-DDBD	Europa XS	R. B. Skinner	
G-DDBG	ICA IS-29D	P. S. Whitehead	
G-DDBK	Slingsby T.59D Kestrel	P. J. Howarth	
G-DDBN	Slingsby T.59D Kestrel	B. C. McKiernan	
G-DDBV	PZL-Bielsko SZD-30	M. D. Pateman, E. R. Dineen & S. E. Chew	
G-DDCA	PZL-Bielsko SZD-36A Cobra 15	M. T. Pitorak	
G-DDCC	Glasflugel Standard Libelle 201B	J. R. Glen	
G-DDDA	Schempp-Hirth Standard Cirrus	G-DDDA Group	
G-DDDB	Schleicher ASK-13	Shenington Gliding Club	
G-DDDE	PZL-Bielsko SZD-38A Jantar 1	Jantar One Syndicate	
G-DDDK	PZL-Bielsko SZD-30 Pirat	D. Fehse	
G-DDDL	Schleicher K8B	The Windrushers Gliding Club Ltd	
G-DDDM	Schempp-Hirth Cirrus	H. D. Maddams	
G-DDDR	Schempp-Hirth Standard Cirrus	A. J. Davis	
G-DDDY	P & M Quik GT450	K. T. Howley	
G-DDEB	Slingsby T.59D Kestrel	K. M. Fresson	
G-DDEG	ICA IS-28B2	C. A. Bailey	
G-DDEO	Glasflugel H205 Club Libelle	N. Dickenson	
G-DDEV	Schleicher Ka-6CR	P. Weaver	
G-DDEW	ICA-Brasov IS-29D	P. S. Whitehead	
G-DDFC	Schempp-Hirth Standard Cirrus	Davies & Smith Cirrus Syndicate	
G-DDFE	Molino PIK-20	M. A. Roff-Jarrett	
G-DDFK	Molino PIK-20B	B. H. & M. J. Fairclough	
G-DDFR	Grob G.102 Astir CS	The Windrushers Gliding Club Ltd	
G-DDFU	PZL-Bielsko SZD-38A Jantar 1	Jantar 38A Group	
G-DDGA	Schleicher K-8B	The Welland Gliding Club Ltd	
G-DDGE	Schempp-Hirth Standard Cirrus	D. F. Adams	
G-DDGG	Schleicher Ka 6E	N. F. Holmes & F. D. Platt	
G-DDGK	Schleicher Ka 6CR	K. A. Hale	
G-DDGV	Breguet 905S Fauvette	J. N. Lee	
G-DDGY	Schempp-Hirth Nimbus 2	N. D. Paveley	
G-DDHA	Schleicher K 8B	Shalborne Soaring Society Ltd	
G-DDHG	Schleicher Ka 6CR	M. W. Roberts	
G-DDHJ	Glaser-Dirks DG-100	G. E. McLaughlin	
G-DDHK	Glaser-Dirks DG-100	K. Dillon & R. Allcoat	
G-DDHL	Glaser-Dirks DG-100	G. J. Bishop	
G-DDHT	Schleicher Ka 6E	P. J. Flack	
G-DDHW	Schempp-Hirth Nimbus 2	M. J. Carruthers & D. Thompson	
G-DDHX	Schempp-Hirth Standard Cirrus B	J. Franke	
G-DDJB	Schleicher K-8B	Portsmouth Naval Gliding Centre	
G-DDJD	Grob G.102 Astir CS	M. Oddone	
G-DDJF	Schempp-Hirth Duo Discus T	R. J. H. Fack	
G-DDJK	Schleicher ASK-18	Dorset Gliding Club Ltd	
G-DDJN	Eiriavion PIK 20B	M. Ireland & S. Lambourne	
G-DDJR	Schleicher Ka 6CR	K6CR Syndicate	
G-DDJX	Grob G.102 Astir CS	Trent Valley Gliding Club Ltd	
G-DDKD	Glasflugel Hornet	A. C. Deacon	
G-DDKE	Schleicher ASK-13	The South Wales Gliding Club Ltd	
G-DDKG	Schleicher Ka 6CR	V. Skochko	
G-DDKL	Schempp-Hirth Nimbus 2	G. J. Croll	
G-DDKM	Glasflugel Hornet	R. S. Lee	
G-DDKR	Grob G.102 Astir CS	Banbury Gliding Club Ltd	
G-DDKS	Grob G.102 Astir CS	A. Docherty	
G-DDKU	Grob G.102 Astir CS	R. H. Lee	
G-DDKV	Grob G.102 Astir CS	Husbands Bosworth Gliding Club Ltd	
G-DDKW	Grob G.102 Astir CS	M. Rudnicki, A. H. Mair & N. T. Bale	
G-DDKX	Grob G.102 Astir CS	The South Wales Gliding Club Ltd	
G-DDLA	Pilatus B4 PC-11	G-DDLA Pilatus Group	
G-DDLB	Schleicher ASK-18	A. W. Thornhill	
G-DDLC	Schleicher ASK-13	Lasham Gliding Society Ltd	
G-DDLE	Schleicher Ka 6E	G. Martin	
G-DDLG	Schempp-Hirth Standard Cirrus 75	S. Naylor	
G-DDLH	Grob G.102 Astir CS77	M. D. & M. E. Saunders	
G-DDLJ	Eiriavion PIK-20B	R. J. Pye	
G-DDLM	Grob G.102 Astir CS	DDLM Syndicate	
G-DDLP	Schleicher Ka 6CR	A. C. Claydon	
G-DDLS	Schleicher K 8B	North Devon Gliding Club	
G-DDLY	Eiriavioin PIK-20D	D. J. Neale	
G-DDMB	Schleicher K 8B	Crown Service Gliding Club	
G-DDMH	Grob G.102 Astir CS	C. K. Lewis	

Notes	Reg	Type	Owner or Operator
	G-DDMK	Schempp-Hirth SHK-1	SHK593 Syndicate
	G-DDML	Schleicher K-7	Z. A. Mallam
	G-DDMM	Schempp-Hirth Nimbus 2	T. Linee
	G-DDMN	Glasflugel Mosquito	M. D. Etherington
	G-DDMO	Schleicher Ka 6E	R. H. Kronenburg
	G-DDMP	Grob G.102 Astir CS	Kingswood Syndicate
	G-DDMR	Grob G.102 Astir CS	Mendip Gliding Club Ltd
	G-DDMS	Glasflugel Standard Libelle 201B	S. P. Lewis
	G-DDMV	NA T-6G Texan (493209)	Aero Legends Leasing Ltd
	G-DDNC	Grob G.102 Astir CS	Lasham Gliding Society Ltd
	G-DDND	Pilatus B4-PC11AF	C. J. Goldsworthy
	G-DDNE	Grob G.102 Astir CS77	Dartmoor Gliding Society
	G-DDNG	Schempp-Hirth Nimbus 2	P. D. Wright
	G-DDNK	Grob G.102 Astir CS	P. Ogram & Syndicate
	G-DDNU	PZL-Bielsko SZD-42-1 Jantar 2	J. M. Thiel
	G-DDNV	Schleicher ASK-13	The Surrey Hills Gliding Club Ltd
	G-DDNW	Schleicher Ks 6CR	G-DDNW Group
	G-DDNX	Schleicher Ka 6CR	D. Jefferies & R. A. Robertson
	G-DDNZ	Schleicher K 8B	G. Brind
	G-DDOA	Schleicher ASK-13	Essex and Suffolk Gliding Club Ltd
	G-DDOC	Schleicher Ka 6CR	W. St. G. V. Stoney
	G-DDOE	Grob G.102 Astir CS77	Heron Gliding Club
	G-DDOF	Schleicher Ka 6CR	G-DDOF Group
	G-DDOG	SA Bulldog Srs 120/121 (XX524:04)	Deltaero Ltd
	G-DDOK	Schleicher Ka 6E	R. S. Hawley & S. Y. Duxbury
	G-DDOU	Eiriavion PIK-20D	J. M. A. Shannon
	G-DDPA	Schleicher ASK-18	M. Best
	G-DDPH	Schempp-Hirth Mini-Nimbus B	J. W. Murdoch
	G-DDPJ	Grob G.102 Astir CS77	DPJ Syndicate
	G-DDPK	Glasflugel H303A Mosquito	H. Nolz
	G-DDPL	Eiriavion PIK-20D	437 Syndicate
	G-DDPO	Grob G.102 Astrir CS77	Yorkshire Gliding Club (Proprietary) Ltd
	G-DDPY	Grob G.102 Astir CS77	C. A. Bailey
	G-DDRA	Schleicher Ka 6CR	K6CR Group Shobdon
	G-DDRB	Glaser-Dirks DG-100	M. C. Bailey
	G-DDRD	Schleicher Ka 6CR	Essex & Suffolk Gliding Club Ltd
	G-DDRE	Schleicher Ka 6CR	DRE Syndicate
	G-DDRJ	Schleicher ASK-13	Lasham Gliding Society Ltd
	G-DDRL	Scheibe SF26A	J. A. Erskine
	G-DDRN	Glasflugel H303A Mosquito	K. J. King
	G-DDRO	Grob G.103 Twin Astir	Twin Astir 258 Syndicate
	G-DDRT	Eiriavion PIK-20D	N. Braithwaite
	G-DDRV	Schleicher K 8B	DRV Syndicate
	G-DDRW	Grob G.102 Astir CS	The Royal Air Force Gliding & Soaring AssociationI
	G-DDRY	Schleicher Ka 6CR	M. K. Bradford
	G-DDRZ	Schleicher K-8B	East Sussex Gliding Club Ltd
	G-DDSG	Schleicher Ka 6CR	S. McGuirk
	G-DDSH	Grob G.102 Astir CS77	Bidford Gliding & Flying Club Ltd
	G-DDSJ	Grob G.103 Twin Astir II	Herefordshire Gliding Club Ltd
	G-DDSL	Grob G.103 Twin Astir	Dartmoor Gliding Society
	G-DDSP	Schempp-Hirth Mini Nimbus B	DDSP Group
	G-DDST	Schleicher ASW-20L	H. A. Bloxham
	G-DDSU	Grob G.102 Astir CS77	Yorkshire Gliding Club (Proprietary) Ltd
	G-DDSX	Schleicher ASW-19B	G-DDSX Group '877'
	G-DDSY	Schleicher Ka-6CR	A. Hill
	G-DDTA	Glaser-Dirks DG-200	M. A. Jaworski
	G-DDTC	Schempp-Hirth Janus B	Darlton Gliding Club Ltd
	G-DDTE	Schleicher ASW-19B	G. R. Purcell
	G-DDTG	Schempp-Hirth SHK-1	M. W. Roberts
	G-DDTK	Glasflugel Mosquito B	M. G. Entwisle
	G-DDTM	Glaser-Dirks DG-200	S. V. Jones
	G-DDTN	Schleicher K 8B	C. G. & G. N. Thomas
	G-DDTP	Schleicher ASW-20	Crown Service Gliding Club
	G-DDTS	CARMAM M-100S	J. P. Dyne
	G-DDTU	Schempp-Hirth Nimbus 2B	M. D. Miskimmin
	G-DDTV	Glasflugel Mosquito B	D. R. Allan
	G-DDTW	PZL-Bielsko SZD-30 Pirat	NDGC Pirat Syndicate
	G-DDTX	Glasflugel Mosquito B	P. T. S. Nash
	G-DDTY	Glasflugel H303 Mosquito B	A. A. Landau
	G-DDUB	Glasflugel H303 Mosquito B	J. E. Ritchie

Reg	Type	Owner or Operator	Notes
G-DDUE	Schleicher ASK-13	The Nene Valley Gliding Club Ltd	
G-DDUH	Scheibe L-Spatz 55	R. J. Aylesbury & J. Young	
G-DDUK	Schleicher K-8B	Edgehill Gliding Centre Ltd	
G-DDUL	Grob G.102 Astir CS77	Husbands Bosworth Gliding Club Ltd	
G-DDUR	Schleicher Ka 6CR	B. N. Bromley	
G-DDUS	Schleicher Ka 6E	D.E. Findon	
G-DDUT	Schleicher ASW-20	M. E. Doig & E. T. J. Murphy	
G-DDUY	Glaser-Dirks DG-100	I. D. Symon	
G-DDVA	Schempp-Hirth Nimbus 2B	L. W. Bishop	
G-DDVB	Schleicher ASK-13	Essex and Suffolk Gliding Club Ltd	
G-DDVC	Schleicher ASK-13	W. S. H. Taylor	
G-DDVG	Schleicher Ka-6CR	G-DDVG Banana Group	
G-DDVK	PZL-Bielsko SZD-48 Jantar Standard 2	R. Goodchild & R. A. Child	
G-DDVL	Schleicher ASW-19	J. Gavin, P. K. Newman & G. Prophet	
G-DDVM	Glasflugel H205 Club Libelle	M. W. Bennett	
G-DDVN	Eiriavion PIL-20D-78	P. V. Ibbotson	
G-DDVP	Schleicher ASW-19	VP Syndicate	
G-DDVS	Schempp-Hirth Standard Cirrus	W. T. J. Wilson	
G-DDVV	Schleicher ASW-20L	D. M. & T. A. Zawisza	
G-DDVX	Schleicher ASK-13	Edgehill Gliding Centre Ltd	
G-DDVY	Schempp-Hirth Cirrus	G. Martin	
G-DDVZ	Glasflugel H303 Mosquito B	L. J. W. Norman & D. J. Richardson	
G-DDWB	Glasflugel H303 Mosquito B	K. C. Springate	
G-DDWC	Schleicher Ka 6E	G-DDWC Syndicate	
G-DDWJ	Glaser-Dirks DG-200	A. P. Kamp & P. R. Desmond	
G-DDWL	Glasflugel Mosquito B	H. A. Stanford	
G-DDWN	Schleicher K7 Rhonadler	K. A. Ford	
G-DDWP	Glasflugel Mosquito B	D. W. Jones	
G-DDWR	Glasflugel Mosquito B	W. H. Greenwood	
G-DDWS	Eiriavion PIK-20D	D. G. Slocombe	
G-DDWT	Slingsby T.65C Vega	C. M. Tims	
G-DDWU	Grob G.102 Astir CS	Astir G-DDWU Syndicate	
G-DDWW	Slingsby T.65A Vega	D. M. Thomas	
G-DDWZ	Schleicher ASW-19B	P. Woodcock	
G-DDXB	Schleicher ASW-20	81 Syndicate	
G-DDXD	Slingsby T.65A Vega	G-DDXD Flying Group	
G-DDXE	Slingsby T.65 Vega 17L	A. G. A. Parker	
G-DDXF	Slingsby T.65A Vega	I. E. Russell	
G-DDXG	Slingsby T.65A Vega	S. P. Melhuish	
G-DDXH	Schleicher Ka 6E	G. C. Grainger & C. D. Bingham	
G-DDXJ	Grob G.102 Astir CS77	DXJ Syndicate	
G-DDXK	Centrair ASW-20F	E. & A. Townsend	
G-DDXL	Schempp-Hirth Standard Cirrus	A. C. Bridges	
G-DDXN	Glaser-Dirks DG-200	J. A. Johnston	
G DDXW	Glasflugel Mosquito B	G-DDXW Group	
G-DDXX	Schleicher ASW-19B	J. Bodzsar	
G-DDYC	Schleicher Ka 6CR	C. M. Tunnicliffe	
G-DDYE	Schleicher ASW-20L	G. Cook	
G-DDYF	Grob G.102 Astir CS77	York Gliding Centre (Operations) Ltd	
G-DDYH	Glaser-Dirks DG-200	W. A. B. Roberts	
G-DDYJ	Schleicher Ka 6CR	T. J. Wilkinson	
G-DDYL	CARMAM JP 15 36AR	J. M. Caldwell	
G-DDYU	Schempp-Hirth Nimbus -2C	C. B. Shepperd	
G-DDZA	Slingsby T.65 Vega 17L	A. W. Roberts	
G-DDZB	Slingsby T.65A Vega	D. A. Dodds	
G-DDZF	Schempp-Hirth Standard Cirrus	J. D. E. Macdonald	
G-DDZM	Slingsby T.65A Vega	A. Mattano	
G-DDZN	Slingsby T.65 Vega 17L	A. C. Giles	
G-DDZP	Slingsby T.65A Vega	M. T. Crews	
G-DDZT	Eiriavion PIK-20D	PIK-20D 106 Group	
G-DDZU	Grob G.102 Astir CS	P. Clarke	
G-DDZV	Scheibe SF-27A	N. Newham	
G-DDZW	Schleicher Ka 6CR	S. W. Naylor	
G-DDZY	Schleicher ASW-19B	I. L. Pattingale	
G-DEAE	Schleicher ASW-20L	R. Burghall	
G-DEAF	Grob G.102 Astir CS77	The Borders (Milfield) Gliding Club Ltd	
G-DEAG	Slingsby T.65A Vega	P. Hadfield	
G-DEAJ	Schempp-Hirth Nimbus 2	A. O'Keefe	
G-DEAK	Glasflugel H303 Mosquito B	T. A. L. Barnes	
G-DEAM	Schempp-Hirth Nimbus 2B	Alpha Mike Syndicate	

Notes	Reg	Type	Owner or Operator
	G-DEAR	Eiriavion PIK-20D	G-DEAR Group
	G-DEAT	Eiriavion PIK-20D	D. J. Knights
	G-DEAV	Schempp-Hirth Mini-Nimbus C	G. Cuthill
	G-DEAW	Grob G.102 Astir CS77	EAW Group
	G-DEBT	Pioneer 300	N. J. T. Tonks & A. J. Lloyd
	G-DEBX	Schleicher ASW-20	S. M. Economou & R. M Harris
	G-DECE	Robinson R22	Helimech Ltd (G-DHGS)
	G-DECF	Schleicher Ka 6CR	E. L. Burns
	G-DECJ	Slingsby T.65A Vega	P. J. Flack
	G-DECL	Slingsby T.65 Vega 17L	J. M. Sherman
	G-DECM	Slingsby T.65 Vega 17L	F. Wilson
	G-DECO	Dyn'Aéro MCR-01 Club	A. P. Wheelwright & A. W. Bishop
	G-DECP	Rolladen-Schneider LS3-17	LS3-17 ECP Syndicate
	G-DECR	P & M Quik R	D. J. Lawrence
	G-DECS	Glasflugel H303 Mosquito B	G. Richardson
	G-DECW	Schleicher ASK-21	Norfolk Gliding Club Ltd
	G-DECZ	Schleicher ASK-21	Booker Gliding Club Ltd
	G-DEDG	Schleicher Ka 6CR	M. Wood
	G-DEDH	Glasflugel H303 Mosquito B	I. L. Pattingale
	G-DEDJ	Glasflugel H303 Mosquito B	D. M. Ward
	G-DEDM	Glaser-Dirks DG-200	Echo Delta Mike Group
	G-DEDN	Glaser-Dirks DG-100G	DG 280 Syndicate
	G-DEDU	Schleicher ASK-13	The South Wales Gliding Club Ltd
	G-DEDX	Slingsby T.65D Vega	G. Kirkham
	G-DEDY	Slingsby T.65D Vega	G. Spelman & J. Shaw
	G-DEDZ	Slingsby T.65C Vega	R. C. R. Copley
	G-DEEA	Slingsby T.65C Vega	D. A. Scott
	G-DEEC	Schleicher ASW-20L	J. D. Johnson & F. B. Jeynes
	G-DEED	Schleicher K-8B	Oxford Gliding Company Ltd
	G-DEEF	Rolladen-Schneider LS3-17	P. C. Morgan
	G-DEEG	Slingsby T.65C Vega	S. J. Glassett
	G-DEEH	Schleicher ASW-19	J. J. Lelusz
	G-DEEJ	Schleicher ASW-20L	T. R. Dews
	G-DEEK	Schempp-Hirth Nimbus 2C	G. D. Palmer
	G-DEEM	Schleicher K-8	The South Wales Gliding Club Ltd
	G-DEEN	Schempp-Hirth Standard Cirrus 75	G-DEEN Flying Group
	G-DEEO	Grob G.102 Club Astir II	G-DEEO Group
	G-DEEP	Wassmer WA.26P Squale	Wassmer G-DEEP Group
	G-DEES	Rolladen-Schneider LS3-17	J. B. Illidge
	G-DEEX	Rolladen-Schneider LS3-17	G-DEEX Flying Group
	G-DEEZ	Denney Kitfox Mk.3	D. A. Slater
	G-DEFA	Schleicher ASW-20L	Eight Eighties Syndicate
	G-DEFB	Schempp-Hirth Nimbus 2C	D. J. Blackman
	G-DEFE	Centrair ASW-20F	ASW20FL 586 Syndicate
	G-DEFF	Schempp-Hirth Nimbus 2C	C. Roney
	G-DEFS	Rolladen-Schneider LS3	F. C. & J. E. Roberts
	G-DEFV	Schleicher ASW-20	A. R. McKillen
	G-DEFW	Slingsby T.65C Sport Vega	H. Yildiz
	G-DEFZ	Rolladen-Schneider LS3-a	EFZ Syndicate
	G-DEGE	Rolladen-Schneider LS3-a	N. L. Lorga
	G-DEGF	Slingsby T.65D Vega	Shalbourne Soaring Society Ltd
	G-DEGH	Slingsby T.65C Vega	D. Sissons & D. Bowns
	G-DEGJ	Slingsby T.65C Vega	Sport Vega Syndicate AD Assets
	G-DEGK	Schempp-Hirth Standard Cirrus	D. A. Parker
	G-DEGN	Grob G.103 Twin Astir II	Staffordshire Gliding Club Ltd
	G-DEGP	Schleicher ASW-20L	J. R. Paine
	G-DEGS	Schempp-Hirth Nimbus 2CS	A. Klapa
	G-DEGT	Slingsby T.65 Vega 17L	A. C. Giles
	G-DEGW	Schempp-Hirth Mini-Nimbus C	Nimbus G-DEGW Syndicate
	G-DEGX	Slingsby T.65C Vega	I. J. Riley
	G-DEGZ	Schleicher ASK-21	Oxford Gliding Co.Ltd
	G-DEHC	Akaflieg Braunschweig SB-5B	G-DEHC Syndicate
	G-DEHG	Slingsby T.65C Vega	S. R. Hopkins
	G-DEHH	Schempp-Hirth Ventus a	S. J. Naisby
	G-DEHK	Rolladen-Schneider LS4	J. J. M. Ingram & E. M. Bunting
	G-DEHM	Schleicher Ka 6E	W. D. Blakey
	G-DEHO	Schleicher ASK-21	Lasham Gliding Society Ltd
	G-DEHP	Schempp-Hirth Nimbus 2C	D. J. King
	G-DEHT	Schempp-Hirth Nimbus 2C	Six Nine Group
	G-DEHU	Glasflugel 304	R. A. Rowntree & K. Malone
	G-DEHY	Slingsby T.65 Vega 17L	I. P. Stork

Reg	Type	Owner or Operator	Notes
G-DEHZ	Schleicher ASW-20L	I. R. Russell	
G-DEJB	Slingsby T.65C Vega	DEV Group	
G-DEJC	Slingsby T.65C Vega	I. Powis	
G-DEJE	Slingsby T.65C Vega	Crown Service Gliding Club	
G-DEJF	Schleicher K 8B	Cotswold Gliding Club	
G-DEJR	Schleicher ASW-19B	C. Godding & T. J. Andrews	
G-DEJY	PZL-Bielsko SZD-9bis Bocian 1D	G-DEJY Group	
G-DEKA	Cameron Z-90 balloon	P. G. Bogliaccino	
G-DEKC	Schleicher Ka 6E	P. G. Smith & N. P. Aldred	
G-DEKF	Grob G.102 Club Astir III	The Bristol Gliding Club Proprietary Ltd	
G-DEKG	Schleicher ASK-21	Army Gliding Association	
G-DEKJ	Schempp-Hirth Ventus b	I. J. Metcalfe	
G-DEKS	Scheibe SF27A Zugvogel V	T. Emms	
G-DEKU	Schleicher ASW-20L A. J. Gillson		
G-DEKV	Rolladen-Schneider LS4	S. L. Helstrip	
G-DEKW	Schempp-Hirth Nimbus 2B	V. Luscombe-Mahoney	
G-DEKX	Schleicher Ka 6E	Davies &Smith K6E Syndicate	
G-DELA	Schleicher ASW-19B	S. G. Jones	
G-DELB	Robinson R-22 Beta ★	South Yorkshire Aircraft Museum/Doncaster	
G-DELD	Slingsby T65C Vega	C. R. Leggett	
G-DELG	Schempp-Hirth Ventus b/16.6	A. Jelden	
G-DELN	Grob G.102 Astir CS Jeans	Bowland Forest Gliding Club Ltd	
G-DELO	Slingsby T.65D Vega	I. Surley & M. Soulsby	
G-DELR	Schempp-Hirth Ventus b	Swindon Ventus B Flying Group	
G-DELU	Schleicher ASW-20L	P. G. Roberts	
G-DELZ	Schleicher ASW-20L	I. J. Ashdown	
G-DEME	Glaser-Dirks DG-200/17	A. Kidd	
G-DEMF	Rolladen-Schneider LS4	N. Le Gras	
G-DEMG	Rolladen-Schneider LS4	Stratford on Avon Gliding Club	
G-DEMH	Cessna F.172M (modified)	M. Hammond (G-BFLO)	
G-DEMN	Slingsby T.65D Vega	J. C. Jenks	
G-DEMP	Slingsby T.65C Vega	S. J. Drew	
G-DEMR	Slingsby T.65C Vega	Llantysilio Team	
G-DEMT	Rolladen-Schneider LS4	M. R. Fox	
G-DEMU	Glaser-Dirks DG-202/17	A. Butterfield & N. Swinton	
G-DEMZ	Slingsby T65A Vega	K. Western & K. D. Hatcher G-BGCA)	
G-DENC	Cessna F.150G	G-DENC Cessna Group (G-AVAP)	
G-DEND	Cessna F.150M	Hull Aero Club Ltd (G-WAFC/G-BDFI)	
G-DENI	PA-32-300 Cherokee Six	A. Bendkowski (G-BAIA)	
G-DENJ	Schempp-Hirth Ventus b/16.6	S. Boyden	
G-DENO	Glasflugel Standard Libelle 201B	D. M. Bland	
G-DENS	Binder CP.301S Smaragd	Garston Smaragd Group	
G-DENU	Glaser-Dirks DG-100G	N. M. C. Robinson	
G-DENX	PZL-Bielsko SZD-48 Jantar Standard 2	J. M. Hire	
G-DEOB	PZL-Bielsko SZD-30	R. M. Golding	
G-DEOD	Grob G.102 Astir CS77	Lasham Gliding Society Ltd	
G-DEOE	Schleicher ASK-13	Essex Gliding Club Ltd	
G-DEOJ	Centrair ASW-20FL	C. J. Bowden	
G-DEOK	Centrair 101A Pegase	C. M. Scott	
G-DEOM	Carman M100S	S. W. Hutchinson	
G-DEON	Schempp-Hirth Nimbus 3	117 Syndicate	
G-DEOT	Grob G.103A Twin II Acro	East Sussex Gliding Club Ltd	
G-DEOU	Pilatus B4-PC11AF	J. E. Lambert	
G-DEOV	Schempp-Hirth Janus C	Burn Gliding Club Ltd	
G-DEOW	Schempp-Hirth Janus C	383 Syndicate	
G-DEOZ	Schleicher K 8B	Cotswold Gliding Club	
G-DEPD	Schleicher ASK-21	London Gliding Club Proprietary Ltd	
G-DEPF	Centrair ASW-20FL	D. A. Noble	
G-DEPG	CARMAM M100S	J. Kohlmetz	
G-DEPP	Schleicher ASK-13	Mendip Gliding Club Ltd	
G-DEPS	Schleicher ASW-20L	G-DEPS Syndicate	
G-DEPT	Schleicher K-8B	Bowland Forest Gliding Club Ltd	
G-DEPU	Glaser-Dirks DG-101G Elan	J. F. Rogers	
G-DEPX	Schempp-Hirth Ventus b/16.6	M. E. S. Thomas	
G-DERA	Centrair ASW-20FL	R. J. Lockett	
G-DERH	Schleicher ASK-21	The Burn Gliding Club Ltd	
G-DERJ	Schleicher ASK-21	The Royal Air Force Gliding and Soaring Association	
G-DERO	Van's RV-10	D. Atkinson	
G-DERR	Schleicher ASW-19B	University of Edinburgh Sports Union	
G-DERS	Schleicher ASW-19B	Booker Gliding Club Ltd	

Notes	Reg	Type	Owner or Operator
	G-DERV	Cameron Truck SS balloon	J. M. Percival
	G-DERX	Centrair 101A Pegase	M. Nowak
	G-DESB	Schleicher ASK-21	Oxford University Gliding Club
	G-DESC	Rolladen-Schneider LS4	J. Crawford & J. M. Staley
	G-DESH	Centrair 101A	J. E. Moore
	G-DESO	Glaser-Dirks DG-300 Elan	G. R. P. Brown
	G-DESU	Schleicher ASK-21	Banbury Gliding Club Ltd
	G-DETA	Schleicher ASK-21	P. Hawkins
	G-DETG	Rolladen-Schneider LS4	A. Parish
	G-DETJ	Centrair 101A	S. C. Phillips
	G-DETM	Centrair 101A	M. C. Bailey
	G-DETV	Rolladen-Schneider LS4	P. Fabian
	G-DETY	Rolladen-Schneider LS4	G-DETY Group
	G-DETZ	Schleicher ASW-20CL	The 20 Syndicate
	G-DEUC	Schleicher ASK-13	North Wales Gliding Club Ltd
	G-DEUD	Schleicher ASW-20C	R. Tietema
	G-DEUF	PZL-Bielsko SZD-50-3	Shalbourne Soaring Society Ltd
	G-DEUH	Rolladen-Schneider LS4	B. Winchester
	G-DEUJ	Schempp-Hirth Ventus b/16.6	S. J. Zielonka
	G-DEUK	Centrair ASW-20FL	P. A. Clark
	G-DEUS	Schempp-Hirth Ventus b/16.6	R. J. Whitaker
	G-DEUV	PZL-Bielsko SZD-42-2 Jantar 2B	G. V. McKirdy
	G-DEUY	Schleicher ASW-20BL	ASW20BL-G-DUEY Group
	G-DEVF	Schempp-Hirth Nimbus 3T	S. W. Naylor
	G-DEVH	Schleicher Ka 10	C. W. & K. T. Matten
	G-DEVJ	Schleicher ASK-13	Lasham Gliding Society Ltd
	G-DEVK	Grob G.102 Astir CS	Peterborough and Spalding Gliding Club Ltd
	G-DEVM	Centrair 101A	R. Schouchana
	G-DEVO	Centrair 101A	G-DEVO Pegase Glider
	G-DEVP	Schleicher ASK-13	Black Mountains Gliding Club
	G-DEVS	PA-28-180 Cherokee	G-DEVS 180 Group (G-BGVJ)
	G-DEVV	Schleicher ASK-23	Midland Gliding Club Ltd
	G-DEVW	Schleicher ASK-23	London Gliding Club Proprietary Ltd
	G-DEVX	Schleicher ASK-23	London Gliding Club Proprietary Ltd
	G-DEWE	Flight Design CTSW	R. L. Green
	G-DEWG	Grob G.103A Twin II Acro	Herefordshire Gliding Club Ltd
	G-DEWI	Rotorsport UK MTO Sport	D. V. Nockels
	G-DEWP	Grob G.103A Twin II Acro	Bowland Forest Gliding Club Ltd
	G-DEWR	Grob G.103A Twin II Acro	The Bristol Gliding Club Proprietary Ltd
	G-DEWS	Grob G.109B	T. R. Dews
	G-DEWZ	Grob G.103A Twin II Acro	T. R. Dews
	G-DEXA	Grob G.103A Twin II Acro	Trent Valley Gliding Club Ltd
	G-DEXP	ARV Super 2	R. W. Clarke
	G-DEXT	Robinson R44 II	Berkley Properties Ltd
	G-DFAF	Schleicher ASW-20L	N. Baldock
	G-DFAR	Glasflugel H205 Club Libelle	R. G. Appleboom
	G-DFAT	Schleicher ASK-13	Dorset Gliding Club Ltd
	G-DFAW	Schempp-Hirth Ventus b/16.6	J. Hanlon
	G-DFBD	Schleicher ASW-15B	J. J. Mion
	G-DFBE	Rolladen-Schneider LS6	E. C. Syson & P. H. Fanshawe
	G-DFBJ	Schleicher K 8B	Bidford Gliding & Flying Club Ltd
	G-DFBO	Schleicher ASW-20BL	A. M. Cridge
	G-DFBY	Schempp-Hirth Discus b	S. V. Ogden
	G-DFCD	Centrair 101A	G. J. Bass
	G-DFCK	Schempp-Hirth Ventus b	S. A. Adlard
	G-DFCM	Glaser-Dirks DG-300	A. Davis & I. D. Roberts
	G-DFCW	Schleicher ASK-13	Black Mountains Gliding Club
	G-DFCY	Schleicher ASW-15	M. R. Shaw
	G-DFDF	Grob G.102 Astir CS	W. D. Harrop
	G-DFDO	EV-97 Eurostar SL	C. D. Taylor
	G-DFDW	Glaser-Dirks DG-300	B. G. Wainwright & A. D. Noble
	G-DFEB	Grob G.102 Club Astir III	Lasham Gliding Society Ltd
	G-DFES	Schempp-Hirth Discus 2c FES	C. J. Short
	G-DFEX	Grob G.102 Astir CS77	S. Hay
	G-DFFP	Schleicher ASW-19B	A. J. Sayer
	G-DFGJ	Schleicher Ka 6CR	G. D. S. Caldwell
	G-DFGT	Glaser-Dirks DG-300 Elan	M. J. Love
	G-DFHS	Schempp-Hirth Ventus cT	154 Group
	G-DFHY	Scheibe SF-27A	J. M. Pursey
	G-DFJO	Schempp-Hirth Ventus cT	FJO Syndicate

Reg	Type	Owner or Operator	Notes
G-DFKA	Schleicher Ka 6CR	The Bath Wilts & North Dorset Gliding Club Ltd	
G-DFKH	Schleicher Ka 6CR	Bellarena Ka6 Group	
G-DFKX	Schleicher Ka 6CR	Dorset Gliding Club Ltd	
G-DFOG	Rolladen-Schneider LS7	R. B. Porteous	
G-DFOV	CARMAM JP 15-36AR Aiglon	T. H. Knapton	
G-DFSA	Grob G.102 Astir CS	Astir 498 Syndicate	
G-DFTF	Schleicher Ka-6CR	J. Preller	
G-DFTJ	PZL-Bielsko SZD-48-1 Jantar Standard 2	P. Nock	
G-DFUF	Scheibe SF-27A Zugvogel V	S. P. Melhuish	
G-DFUN	Van's RV-6	G-DFUN Flying Group	
G-DFXE	Rolladen-Schneider LS7	J. A. Linger	
G-DFXR	Sportine Aviacija LAK-12	I. P. Freestone	
G-DGAL	Ikarus C42 FB80 Bravo	R. J. Hawkins	
G-DGAV	P & M Quik R	M. D. Howe	
G-DGAW	Schleicher Ka 6CR	D. J. Robinson	
G-DGDJ	Rolladen-Schneider LS4-a	G-DGDJ Group	
G-DGDW	Scheibe SF-27A Zugvogel V	G. Wardle	
G-DGEF	Schleicher Ka 6CR	Lee K6CR Group	
G-DGFD	Robinson R44 II	Hawkwind Helicopters Ltd (G-CGNF)	
G-DGFY	Flylight Dragonfly	B. F. Johnson	
G-DGHI	Dyn'Aéro MCR-01 Club	J. M. Keane	
G-DGIO	Glaser-Dirks DG-100G Elan	D. A. Perriam	
G-DGKB	Centrair ASW-20F	T. R. Dews	
G-DGMT	III Sky Arrow 650 T	W. B. Russell	
G-DGON	Taylor JT.2 Titch	H. R. Hawkins (G-RKET/G-BIBK)	
G-DGPS	Diamond DA-42 Twin Star	Cloud Global Ltd	
G-DGRE	Guimbal Cabri G2	Helicentre Aviation Ltd	
G-DGSC	CZAW Sportcruiser	N. K. Foster	
G-DGST	Beech 95-B55 Baron	Mvsquared Ltd (G-BXDF)	
G-DHAA	Glasflugel H201B Standard Libelle	P. W. Jennings	
G-DHAD	Glasflugel H201B Standard Libelle	R. Hines	
G-DHAH	Aeronca 7BCM Champion	M. Rogan (G-JTYE)	
G-DHAL	Schleicher ASK-13	Dumfries & District Gliding Club	
G-DHAM	Robinson R44 II	VNE Group Ltd	
G-DHAP	Schleicher Ka 6E	T. Turner & R. King	
G-DHAT	Glaser-Dirks DG-200/17	G-DHAT Group	
G-DHBZ	DH.82A Tiger Moth	H. M. M. Haines (G-BWIK)	
G-DHCA	Grob G.103 Twin Astir	P. W. Armstrong	
G-DHCC	DHC.1 Chipmunk 22 (WG321:G)	Liberty Aviation Ltd	
G-DHCE	Schleicher ASW-19B	A. M. Wilmot	
G-DHCF	PZL-Bielsko SZD-50-3	Shalbourne Soaring Society Ltd	
G-DHCJ	Grob G.103A Twin II Acro	Peterborough and Spalding Gliding Club Ltd	
C DHCL	Schompp Hirth Discus b	M. S. Woodhead	
G-DHCO	Glasflugel Standard Libelle 201B	M. J. Birch	
G-DHCR	PZL-Bielsko SZD-51-1	East Sussex Gliding Club Ltd	
G-DHCU	DG-300 Club Elan	G-DHCU Syndicate	
G-DHCV	Schleicher ASW-19B	London Gliding Club Proprietary Ltd	
G-DHCW	PZL-Bielsko SZD-51-1	Edgehill Gliding Centre Ltd	
G-DHCX	Schleicher ASK-21	Devon and Somerset Gliding Club Ltd	
G-DHCY	Glaser-Dirks DG-300 Club Elan	M. J. Carter	
G-DHCZ	DHC.2 Beaver 1	Fly to Inspire Ltd (G-BUCJ)	
G-DHDH	Glaser-Dirks DG-200	R. G. Sangster	
G-DHDV	DH.104 Dove 8 (VP981)	Aero Legends Leasing Ltd	
G-DHEB	Schleicher Ka 6CR	D. K. Archer	
G-DHEM	Schempp-Hirth Discus CS	473 Syndicate	
G-DHER	Schleicher ASW-19B	A. A. May	
G-DHES	Centrair 101A	G. H. Lawrence & G. S. Sanderson	
G-DHET	Rolladen-Schneider LS6-c18	A. Lake & M. D. Langford	
G-DHEV	Schempp-Hirth Cirrus	C. N. Smith	
G-DHGL	Schempp-Hirth Discus b	E. A. Martin	
G-DHHD	PZL-Bielsko SZD-51-1	Scottish Gliding Union Ltd	
G-DHKL	Schempp-Hirth Discus bT	D. C. & K. J. Mockford	
G-DHLE	Boeing 767-3JHF	DHL Air (UK) Ltd	
G-DHLJ	Boeing 767-3JHF	DHL Air (UK) Ltd	
G-DHLK	Boeing 767-3JHF	DHL Air (UK) Ltd	
G-DHLM	Boeing 767-324ER(F)	DHL Air (UK) Ltd (G-OOBK)	
G-DHLO	Boeing 767-316ER	DHL Air (UK) Ltd	
G-DHLP	Boeing 767-316ER(F)	DHL Air (UK) Ltd	
G-DHLR	Boeing 767-316F	DHL Air (UK) Ltd	

Notes	Reg	Type	Owner or Operator
	G-DHLS	Boeing 767-316ER(F)	DHL Air (UK) Ltd
	G-DHLU	Boeing 777F	DHL Air (UK) Ltd
	G-DHLV	Boeing 777F	DHL Air (UK) Ltd
	G-DHLW	Boeing 777F	DHL Air (UK) Ltd
	G-DHLX	Boeing 777F	DHL Air (UK) Ltd
	G-DHLY	Boeing 777F	DHL Air (UK) Ltd
	G-DHMC	Boeing 777FZB	DHL Air (UK) Ltd
	G-DHMD	Boeing 777FZB	DHL Air (UK) Ltd
	G-DHMP	Schempp-Hirth Discus b	G. K. Drury
	G-DHNX	Rolladen-Schneider LS4-b	V. Lusis
	G-DHOC	Scheibe Bergfalke II-55	The Gliding Heritage Centre
	G-DHOK	Schleicher ASW-20CL	S. D. Minson
	G-DHOP	Van's RV-9A	C. Partington
	G-DHPA	Issoire E-78 Silene	P. Woodcock
	G-DHPM	OGMA DHC.1 Chipmunk 20 (1365)	P. G. Winterbottom
	G-DHPR	Schempp-Hirth Discus b	Seahawk Gliding Club
	G-DHRR	Schleicher ASK-21	Bowland Forest Gliding Club Ltd
	G-DHSJ	Schempp-Hirth Discus b	D. Byrne
	G-DHSR	AB Sportine LAK-12 Lietuva	A. G. A. Parker
	G-DHTG	Grob G.102 Astir CS	North Wales Gliding Club Ltd
	G-DHYL	Schempp-Hirth Ventus 2a	P-R. N. Murray
	G-DHYS	Titan T-51 Mustang (414907:CY-S)	A. A. Whitewick
	G-DHZF	DH.82A Tiger Moth (N9192)	R. J. Doughton (G-BSTJ)
	G-DHZP	Rolladen-Schneider LS8-18	A. D. May & D. J. Bennett
	G-DIAS	Hill Helicopters HX50	Hill Helicopters Ltd
	G-DICK	Thunder Ax6-56Z balloon	C. J. & S. M. Davies
	G-DIDG	Van's RV-7	B. R. Alexander
	G-DIDY	Thruster T600N 450	T. J. Wilkinson
	G-DIGA	Robinson R66	C. S. Ringer
	G-DIGI	PA-32-300 Cherokee Six	Security Unlimited Group
	G-DIGS	Hughes 369HE	W Aircollection (G-DIZZ)
	G-DIGZ	Hughes 369D	Mackinnon Construction Ltd (G-MCDD)
	G-DIII	Pitts S-2B Special	J. A. Coutts (G-STUB)
	G-DIIO	Schempp-Hirth Arcus M	K2 Aviation Ltd
	G-DIKY	Murphy Rebel	Stoke Golding Flyers
	G-DIME	Rockwell Commander 114	H. B. Richardson
	G-DINA	AA-5B Tiger	Portway Aviation Ltd
	G-DINO	Pegasus Quantum 15	A. Powell (G-MGMT)
	G-DIPI	Cameron 80 Tub SS balloon	M. T. Joyce
	G-DIPZ	Colt 17A Cloudhopper balloon	M. T. Joyce
	G-DIRK	Glaser-Dirks DG.400	M. A. Bennett
	G-DISA	SA Bulldog Srs 120/125	I. W. Whiting
	G-DISO	Jodel 150	C. R. Coates
	G-DISP	AutoGyro Calidus	P. J. Troy-Davies
	G-DITW	Tecnam P2006T	CFS Aeroproducts Ltd
	G-DIYA	TAF Sling 4 TSI	G-DIYA Flying Group
	G-DIZI	Reality Escapade 912(2)	J. C. Carter
	G-DIZO	Jodel D.120A	N. M. Harwood (G-EMKM)
	G-DIZY	PA-28R-201T Turbo Cherokee Arrow III	Dizy Aviation Ltd
	G-DJAA	Schempp-Hirth Janus B	Bidford Gliding & Flying Club Ltd
	G-DJAC	Schempp-Hirth Duo Discus	G-DJAC Group
	G-DJAD	Schleicher ASK-21	The Borders (Milfield) Gliding Club Ltd
	G-DJAH	Schempp-Hirth Discus b	The Borders (Milfield) Gliding Club Ltd
	G-DJAN	Schempp-Hirth Discus b	N. F. Perren
	G-DJAY	Avtech Jabiru UL-450	M. A. Grant & G. J. Colfer
	G-DJBC	Ikarus C42 FB100	Bluecool Water Dispensers
	G-DJBX	Eurofox 912(IS)	D. J. Barrott
	G-DJEB	HpH Glasflugel 304 ES Shark	P. D. Candler
	G-DJET	Diamond DA42 Twin Star	Plane Rentals Ltd
	G-DJGG	Schleicher ASW-15B	R. E. Perry
	G-DJHP	Valentin Mistral C	P. B. Higgs
	G-DJJA	PA-28-181 Cherokee Archer II	Interactive Aviation Ltd
	G-DJLL	Schleicher ASK-13	D. W. J. Lee
	G-DJMC	Schleicher ASK-21	The Royal Air Force Gliding and Soaring Association
	G-DJNC	ICA-Brasov IS-28B2	Delta Juliet November Group
	G-DJNE	DG Flugzeugbau DG-808C	112 Syndicate (G-DGRA)
	G-DJNH	Denney Kitfox Mk 3	S. Borthwick
	G-DJSM	Eurocopter AS.350B3 Ecureuil	Meoble Estate (G-CICZ)

Reg	Type	Owner or Operator	Notes
G-DJST	Ixess 912(1)	G-DJST Flying Group	
G-DJVY	Scintex CP.1315-C3 Super Emeraude	A. P. Goodwin	
G-DJWS	Schleicher ASW-15B	G-DJWS Syndicate	
G-DKBA	DKBA AT 0301-0 balloon	I. Chadwick	
G-DKDK	Cessna 525 Citation M2	Catreus AOC Ltd	
G-DKDP	Grob G.109	C. I. Knowles	
G-DKEN	Rolladen-Schneider LS4-a	G-DKEN Syndicate	
G-DKEY	PA-28-161 Cherokee Warrior II	Praelueo Property Ltd	
G-DKFU	Schempp-Hirth Ventus 2cxT	P. F. Whitehead (G-CKFU)	
G-DKLD	Aerospool WT9 Dynamic LSM	G. A. Cockrell	
G-DKNA	Aero L-159E	Draken	
G-DKNB	Aero L-159E	Draken	
G-DKNC	Aero L-159E	Draken	
G-DKND	Aero L-159E	Draken	
G-DKNE	Aero L-159E	Draken	
G-DKNF	Aero L-159E	Draken	
G-DKNG	Aero L-159E	Draken	
G-DKNH	Aero L-159E	Draken	
G-DKNI	Aero L-159E	Draken	
G-DKNJ	Aero L-159E	Draken	
G-DKNK	Aero L-159E	Draken	
G-DKNL	Aero L-159E	Draken	
G-DKNM	Aero L-159E	Draken	
G-DKNN	Aero L-159E	Draken	
G-DKNO	Aero L-159E	Draken	
G-DKNR	Aero L-159E	Draken	
G-DKNT	Aero L-159E	Draken	
G-DKNY	Robinson R44 II	Redfern Share Holdings Ltd	
G-DKSK	TL2000UK Sting Carbon S4	D. J. Brook	
G-DKTA	PA-28-236 Dakota	Dakota Flying Group	
G-DLAD	Cessna 208 Caravan I	Avonvale Ltd	
G-DLAF	Bristell NG5 Speed Wing	A. French & G. Dangerfield	
G-DLCB	Europa	G. F. Perry	
G-DLDL	Robinson R22 Beta	Bath & West Aviation LLP	
G-DLEE	SOCATA TB9 Tampico Club	V. J. Friery (G-BPGX)	
G-DLFN	Aero L-29 Delfin	Verdin Group Holdings Ltd	
G-DLGC	PZL-Bielsko SZD-50-3 Puchacz	Derbyshire and Lancashire Gliding Club Ltd	
G-DLOE	Schleicher ASW-27-18E	R. E. Robertson	
G-DLOM	SOCATA TB20 Trinidad	P. A Rieck	
G-DLOT	Glasflugel 304S Jet	Shark G-DLOT Syndicate	
G-DLRA	BN-2T Islander	Britten-Norman Aerospace Ltd (G-BJYU)	
G-DLRL	Glasflugel 304SJet	T. P. Browning	
G-DLTY	HpH Glasflugel 304 ES	J. M. Gilboy	
G-DLTZ	Bell 505 Jet Ranger X	Lockheli Ltd	
G-DLUT	HpH Glasflugel 304 ES	M. R. Baldwin & J. M. Hough	
G-DMAB	Schempp-Hirth Arcus T	M. A. Boulton	
G-DMAC	Avtech Jabiru SP-430	C. J. Pratt	
G-DMAH	SOCATA TB20 Trinidad	S. D. Pike	
G-DMAM	Schleicher AS 33 ES	J. W. White	
G-DMAP	M & D Flugzeugbau JS-MD 3	A. & M. Truelove	
G-DMAR	Schleicher ASW-17	S. France	
G-DMAW	Glasflugel 304 ES Shark	T. J. Highton	
G-DMAX	Strojirny Prvni Petilesky L-13 Blanik	The Welland Gliding Club Ltd	
G-DMBC	Schleicher AS-33ES	M. E. Newland-Smith	
G-DMBD	Schleicher ASK-21B	Wolds Gliding Club Ltd	
G-DMBE	Schempp-Hirth Ventus-2c FES	J. L. Whiting	
G-DMBJ	Schempp-Hirth Ventus 2cT	D. A. Hope	
G-DMBL	PZL PW-5 Smyk	C. E. Metcalfe	
G-DMBO	Van's RV-7	C. J. Goodwin	
G-DMBP	Schleicher ASK-21	Lasham Gliding Society Ltd	
G-DMBT	Schleicher AS-33 ME	D. Bowes	
G-DMCA	Douglas DC-10-30 ★	Forward fuselage/Manchester Airport Viewing Park	
G-DMCB	Schempp-Hirth Ventus-2cT	S. C. Williams	
G-DMCC	Lange Antares 18T	T. J. Wills	
G-DMCF	M & D Flugzeugbau JS-MD-3	A. J. Davis	
G-DMCI	Ikarus C42 FB100	C-More G-DCMI Group	
G-DMCP	Tecnam P2008-JC	R. J. Alderson	

Notes	Reg	Type	Owner or Operator
	G-DMCR	Schempp-Hirth Arcus M	DP Aero Ltd
	G-DMCS	PA-28R Cherokee Arrow 200-II	Arrow Associates (G-CPAC)
	G-DMCT	Flight Design CT2K	A. M. Sirant
	G-DMCU	Schempp-Hirth Arcus M	I. C. Lees
	G-DMCW	Magni M-24C	B. A. Carnegie (G-CGVF)
	G-DMCX	Schempp-Hirth Ventus 3T	G. A. Glazebrook
	G-DMDA	Allstar PZL SZD-54-2	East Sussex Gliding Club Ltd
	G-DMDE	Schempp-Hirth Arcus M	DP Aero Ltd
	G-DMDM	TL3000 Sirius 600	D and C Murrell Ltd
	G-DMEE	Cameron Z-105 balloon	B. J. Ross
	G-DMIX	Flylight Nine	D. A. Morgan
	G-DMND	Diamond DA42 Twin Star	Tesla Solutions Ltd
	G-DMNG	Diamond DA42M-NG Twin Star	DEA Aviation Ltd (G-PEEK)
	G-DMOB	Robinson R66	O'Brien Motorsport Ltd (G-HKPC)
	G-DMON	Xtremeair XA-42 Sbach 342	R. M. Hockey
	G-DMPI	Agusta A.109E Power	Bath & West Aviation LLP (G-FVIP/G-HCFC)
	G-DMPL	Van's RV-7A	J. P. Hall
	G-DMSS	Westland Gazelle HT.3 (XW858:C)	G. Wood
	G-DMWW	CFM Shadow Srs DD	M. Whittle
	G-DNBH	Raj Hamsa X'Air Hawk	D. R. Western
	G-DNGO	Ivanov Dingo	J. B. Silverstone
	G-DNGR	Colt 31A balloon	M. J. & T. J. Turner
	G-DNKS	Ikarus C42 FB80	D. N. K. & M. A. Symon
	G-DNOP	PA-46-350P Malibu Mirage	Campbell Aviation Ltd
	G-DOBS	Van's RV-8	BS Flying Group
	G-DOCB	Boeing 737-436 ★	Cranfield University instructional airframe
	G-DODG	Aerotechnik EV-97A Eurostar	G-DODG Flying Group
	G-DOFY	Bell 206B JetRanger 3	Adventure 001 Ltd
	G-DOGA	Diamond DA50C	Zinck Aviation Ltd
	G-DOGG	SA Bulldog Srs 120/121 (XX638)	P. Sengupta
	G-DOGI	Robinson R22 Beta	A. R. Parcell (G-BVGS)
	G-DOGZ	Horizon 1	M. J. Nolan
	G-DOIG	CZAW Sportcruiser	C. J. May
	G-DOIN	Skyranger 912(S)1	I. B. Lavelle
	G-DOLI	Cirrus SR20	Chiltern Cirrus Ltd
	G-DOLS	PA-28-236 Dakota	N. Sheldrake (G-FRGN)
	G-DOLY	Cessna T.303	KW Aviation Ltd (G-BJZK)
	G-DOMC	Van's RV-8	L. J. Clarke
	G-DOMS	Aerotechnik EV-97A Eurostar	R. K. & C. A. Stewart
	G-DONE	Bell 505 Jet Ranger X	Vivio Developments Ltd
	G-DONN	Cessna 550 Citation II	OPES MRF 2013 Ltd (G-MLBC/G-CGOA/ G-JMDW)
	G-DONR	Cameron O-31 balloon	G. Gray
	G-DONT	Xenair CH.601XL Zodiac	M. S. Woodhead
	G-DOOG	TL 2000 Sting S4	G. R. Cassie
	G-DOPE	Mainair Blade	D. R. Sealey (G-MZAR)
	G-DORO	Robin DR.400-140B	Denbigh Gliding
	G-DOSB	Diamond DA42 Twin Star	Acrobat Ltd
	G-DOSC	Diamond DA42 Twin Star	Acrobat Ltd
	G-DOSS	Exodus Deltajet 500 Stingray	R. N. Gamble & A. W. Trew
	G-DOTI	DG Flugzeugbau DG-1001M	G. C. Lewis (G-LOLI)
	G-DOTS	Dornier Do.27A-4	Liberty Aviation Ltd
	G-DOTT	CFM Streak Shadow	R. J. Bell
	G-DOTY	Van's RV-7	J. W. Scott
	G-DOUZ	Van's RV-12	J and G Aerospace Ltd
	G-DOUN	Agusta A109S Grand	Eagle Moon Ltd
	G-DOVE	Cessna 182Q	P. Puri
	G-DOVS	Robinson R44 II	A. P. Bedford
	G-DOZI	Ikarus C.42 FB100	G-DOZI Group
	G-DOZZ	Sky Ranger Swift 912S(1)	M. C. Webb
	G-DPAE	Diamond DA.40NG	DPAero Ltd
	G-DPAZ	Diamond DA.40NG	DPAero Ltd
	G-DPER	M & D Flugzeugbau JS-MD	M. P. Clark
	G-DPRV	Van's RV-7A	G. G. Ferriman/C. W. Kirk
	G-DRAA	Bombardier Aerospace Learjet 60XR	Draken
	G-DRAK	Bombardier CL600-2B16 Challenger 604	FR Aviation Ltd
	G-DRAL	Bombardier CL600-2B16 Challenger 604	Draken

Reg	Type	Owner or Operator	Notes
G-DRAM	Cessna FR.172F (floatplane)	H. R. Mitchell	
G-DRAT	Slingsby T.51 Dart 17R	W. R. Longstaff	
G-DRAW	Colt 77A balloon	Notfot Services Ltd	
G-DRCC	Cosmik EV-97 TeamEurostar UK	C. J. Corbin (G-SLNM)	
G-DRCS	Schleicher ASH-25E	C. R. Smithers	
G-DREG	Superchaser	N. R. Beale	
G-DREI	Fokker DR.1 Triplane Replica (425/17)	R. A. H. Vary	
G-DRGC	P & M Quik GT450	D. R. G. Cornwell	
G-DRGL	PA-18-135 Super Cub	Goodwood Road Racing Company Ltd (G-BLIH)	
G-DRGS	Cessna 182S	A. C. Averill	
G-DRHK	Kubicek BB22XR	A. Hook	
G-DRIO	Jodel DR.1050M	B. N. Stevens (G-BXIO)	
G-DRJH	Hill Helicopters HX50	Dynamiq Engineering Ltd	
G-DRLA	Leonardo AW109SP Grand New	Sloane Helicopters Ltd	
G-DRMM	Europa	T. J. Harrison	
G-DROP	Cessna U.206C	K. Brady (G-UKNO/G-BAMN)	
G-DRPK	Reality Escapade	J. M. Carter	
G-DRRT	Slingsby T.51 Dart 17R	The Gliding Heritage Centre (G-DBXH)	
G-DRSV	CEA DR.315 (modified)	M. D. Anstey	
G-DRTA	Boeing 737-85P	Jet 2.com	
G-DRTB	Boeing 737-85N	Jet 2.com	
G-DRTC	Boeing 737-808	Jet 2.com	
G-DRTD	Boeing 737-808	Jet 2.com	
G-DRTE	Boeing 737-8K5	Jet 2.com	
G-DRTF	Boeing 737-85P	Jet 2.com	
G-DRTG	Boeing 737-8BK	Jet 2.com	
G-DRTH	Boeing 737-8BK	Jet 2.com	
G-DRTI	Boeing 737-8FH	Jet 2.com	
G-DRTJ	Boeing 737-86N	Jet 2.com	
G-DRTK	Boeing 737-8KN	Jet 2.com	
G-DRTL	Boeing 737-8AL	Jet 2.com	
G-DRTM	Boeing 737-85P	Jet 2.com	
G-DRTN	Boeing 737-86N	Jet 2.com	
G-DRTO	Boeing 737-8JP	Jet 2.com	
G-DRTP	Boeing 737-8AL	Jet 2.com	
G-DRTR	Boeing 737-86N	Jet 2.com	
G-DRTT	Boeing 737-8Q8	Jet 2.com	
G-DRTU	Boeing 737-86N	Jet 2.com	
G-DRTV	Boeing 737-8AL	Jet 2.com	
G-DRTW	Boeing 737-86N	Jet 2.com	
G-DRTX	Boeing 737-8AL	Jet 2.com	
G-DRTY	Boeing 737-8AS	Jet 2.com	
G-DRTZ	Boeing 737-8AS	Jet 2.com	
G-DRYS	Cameron N-90 balloon	C. A. Butter	
G-DRZF	CEA DR.360	P. K. Kaufeler	
G-DSAA	Leonardo AW169	The Dorset & Somerset Air Ambulance Charity	
G-DSFT	PA-28R-200 Cherokee Arrow II	J. Jones (G-LFSE/G-BAXT)	
G-DSGC	PA-25-235C Pawnee	Notsa Aviation	
G-DSID	PA-34-220T Seneca III	I. M. Worthington	
G-DSJT	Cessna 182T	D. S. J. Tait	
G-DSKI	Aerotechnik EV-97 Eurostar	G-DSKI Group	
G-DSKY	Diamond DA.42 Twin Star	Twinstar Aviation Ltd (G-CDSZ)	
G-DSLL	Pegasus Quantum 15-912	D. T. Evans	
G-DSMA	P & M Aviation Quik R	DSMA Flying Group	
G-DSOO	Glaser-Dirks DG-500M	C. Rau	
G-DSPZ	Robinson R44 II	Focal Point Communications Ltd	
G-DSRV	Van's RV-7	S. J. Boynett	
G-DSUE	Eurofox 912(S)	D. M. Garrett	
G-DSVN	Rolladen-Schneider LS8-18	O. G. Butlin	
G-DTAR	P & M Aviation Quik GT450	The Scottish Aero Club Ltd	
G-DTCP	PA-32R-300 Cherokee Lance	Hattersley Consulting Ltd (G-TEEM)	
G-DTFF	Cessna T.182T Turbo Skylane	Ridgway Aviation Ltd	
G-DTOF	Schempp-Hirth Discus 2c FES	K. Neave & C. F. M. Smith	
G-DTOY	Ikarus C.42.FB100	C. W. Laske	
G-DTPC	Van's RV-9A	P. M. Clayton & D. Turner	
G-DTSA	Aermacchi MB339-CB	SDTS	
G-DTSB	Aermacchi MB339-CB	SDTS	
G-DTSC	Aermacchi MB339-CB	SDTS	
G-DTSD	Aermacchi MB339-CB	SDTS	

Notes	Reg	Type	Owner or Operator
	G-DTSI	TAF Sling 4 TSI	G. L. Davies
	G-DTSM	Cosmik EV-97 TeamEurostar UK	M. S. Ashby
	G-DTUG	Wag-Aero Super Sport	J. H. Stewart
	G-DUBI	Lindstrand LBL-120A balloon	M. B. Vennard
	G-DUDE	Van's RV-8	J. P. Marriott
	G-DUDI	Rotorsport UK MTO Sport	J. M. Thwaites
	G-DUDP	KFA Safari	Kiltinney Farm Group
	G-DUDZ	Robin DR.400/180	W. J. Lee (G-BXNK)
	G-DUFF	Rand Robinson KR-2	J. I. B. Duff
	G-DUGE	Ikarus C42 FB UK	D. Stevenson
	G-DUMP	Customcraft A25	Department of Doing Ltd
	G-DUNK	Cessna F172M Skyhawk	Devon and Somerset Flight Training Ltd
	G-DUNS	Lindstrand LBL-90A balloon	A. J. & A. R. Brown
	G-DUOT	Schempp-Hirth Duo Discus T	G-DUOT Soaring Group
	G-DURO	Europa	C. A. Larkins
	G-DURX	Thunder 77A balloon	P. Coman & D. J. Stagg
	G-DUSK	DH.115 Vampire T.11 (XE856) ★	Bournemouth Aviation Museum
	G-DUST	Stolp SA.300 Starduster Too	P. JH. Whitehouse
	G-DUVL	Cessna F.172N	VL Flying Group
	G-DVBF	Lindstrand LBL-210A balloon	Virgin Balloon Flights
	G-DVCI	Ultramagic H-31 balloon	Davinci Associates Ltd
	G-DVII	Leonardo AW139	Executive Jet Charter Ltd
	G-DVIO	Leonardo AW139	Executive Jet Charter Ltd
	G-DVIP	Agusta A.109E Power	Castle Air Ltd
	G-DVMI	Van's RV-7	North West RV Flyers
	G-DVON	DH.104 Devon C.2 (VP955)	C. L. Thatcher
	G-DVOR	Diamond DA.62	Flight Calibration Services Ltd
	G-DVOY	CZAW Sportcruiser	P. Marsden (G-TDKI)
	G-DVTA	Cessna T.206H	Macrae Aviation Ltd
	G-DWCB	Chilton DW.1A	C. M. Barnes
	G-DWCE	Robinson R44 II	3CR Comm Ltd
	G-DWGI	Leonardo AW139	Executive Jet Charter
	G-DWIA	Chilton D.W.1A	D. Elliott
	G-DWIB	Chilton D.W.1B (replica)	J. Jennings
	G-DWJF	Skyranger Nynja 912S (1)	G-DWJF Nynja Group
	G-DWMS	Avtech Jabiru UL-450	M. D. Brown
	G-DWRU	Chilton DW.1A	K. J. Steele
	G-DWSR	Chilton DW.1A	S. J. Rickett
	G-DWYP	Skyranger Nynja 912S(1)	G-DWYP Nynja Syndicate
	G-DXLT	Schempp-Hirth Duo Discus xLT	G-DXLT Group
	G-DYKE	Dyke JD.2 Delta	M. S. Bird
	G-DYNA	Dynamic WT9 UK	J. C. Stubbs
	G-DYNC	Cirrus SR22	N. Yu (G-RAYY)
	G-DYNM	Aerospool Dynamic WT9 UK	R. E. Cotterrell
	G-DYUP	Europa	A. Hunter
	G-DZDZ	Rolladen-Schneider LS4	I. G. MacArthur
	G-DZKY	Diamond DA.40D Star	Go 2 Aviation Ltd (G-CEZP)
	G-DZZY	Champion 8KCAB	Paul's Planes Ltd
	G-EAGA	Sopwith Dove (replica)	A. Wood
	G-EAOU†	Vickers Vimy (replica)(NX71MY)	Greenco (UK) Ltd
	G-EASD	Avro 504L	G. M. New
	G-EASQ†	Bristol Babe (replica) (BAPC87) ★	Bristol Aero Collection (stored)/Kemble
	G-EAVX	Sopwith Pup	K. A. M. Baker
	G-EBED†	Vickers 60 Viking (replica) (BAPC114)★	Brooklands Museum of Aviation/Weybridge
	G-EBHB	Avro 504K (E2977)	T. W. Harris
	G-EBHX	DH.53 Humming Bird	The Shuttleworth Collection
	G-EBIA	RAF SE-5A (F904)	The Shuttleworth Collection
	G-EBIB	RAF SE-5A ★	Science Museum/South Kensington
	G-EBIC	RAF SE-5A (F938) ★	RAF Museum/Hendon
	G-EBIR	DH.51	The Shuttleworth Collection
	G-EBJE	Avro 504K (E449)	RAF Museum/Hendon
	G-EBJG	Parnall Pixie IIIH	Midland Aircraft Preservation Society
	G-EBJI	Hawker Cygnet (replica)	R. A. Fleming

Reg	Type	Owner or Operator	Notes
G-EBJO	ANEC IIH	The Shuttleworth Collection	
G-EBKY	Sopwith Pup (9917)	The Shuttleworth Collection	
G-EBLV	DH.60 Cirrus Moth	Richard Shuttleworth Trustees	
G-EBMB	Hawker Cygnet I ★	RAF Museum/Cosford	
G-EBNV	English Electric Wren	The Shuttleworth Collection	
G-EBQP	DH.53 Humming Bird (J7326) ★	P. L. Kirk & T. G. Pankhurst	
G-EBWD	DH.60X Hermes Moth	The Shuttleworth Collection	
G-EBZM	Avro 594 Avian IIIA ★	The Aeroplane Collection/Hooton Park	
G-EBZN	DH.60X Moth	J. Hodgkinson (G-UAAP)	
G-ECAC	Alpha R21620U	Bulldog Aviation Ltd	
G-ECAD	Cessna FA.152	Andrewsfield Aviation Ltd (G-JEET/G-BHMF)	
G-ECAE	Royal Aircraft Factory SE.5A (C8996)	West Flyg AB	
G-ECAF	Robin HR.200-120B	Bulldog Aviation Ltd (G-BZET)	
G-ECAG	Robin HR.200-120B	Bulldog Aviation Ltd (G-MFLD/G-BXDT)	
G-ECAK	Cessna F.172M	Bulldog Aviation Ltd (G-BENK)	
G-ECAM	EAA Acrosport II	C. England	
G-ECAN	DH.84 Dragon	Norman Aeroplane Trust	
G-ECAP	Robin HR.200-120B	Bulldog Aviation Ltd (G-NSOF)	
G-ECAR	Robin HR.200-120B	Bulldog Aviation Ltd (G-MFLB/G-BXOR)	
G-ECAY	PA-28R-201T Turbo Cherokee Arrow III	Bulldog Aviation Ltd (G-SHAY/G-JEFS/G-BFDG)	
G-ECBI	Schweizer 269C-1	JBS-Helicopters Ltd	
G-ECDB	Schleicher Ka 6E	J. Pool	
G-ECDF	DH.83C Fox Moth	Airtime Aerobatics Ltd (G-CGUO)	
G-ECDS	DH.82A Tiger Moth	G-ECDS Tiger Moth Group Ltd	
G-ECDX	DH.71 Tiger Moth (replica)	Airtime Aerobatics Ltd	
G-ECEA	Schempp-Hirth Cirrus	G-ECEA Group	
G-ECET	Cessna T.182T	W. J. Forrest	
G-ECGC	Cessna F.172N	D. H. G. Penney	
G-ECGO	Bölkow Bö.208C1 Junior	P. Norman & N. T. Oakman	
G-ECHL	Cirrus SR20	A9 Leasing LLP	
G-ECJM	PA-28R-201T Turbo Cherokee Arrow III	Regishire Ltd (G-FESL/G-BNRN)	
G-ECJV	Airbus A.320-214	easyJet Airline Co.Ltd	
G-ECKB	Escapade 912(2)	C. M. & C. P. Bradford	
G-ECLB	Airbus A.340-642	European Cargo Ltd (G-VFIT)	
G-ECLC	Airbus A.340-642	European Cargo Ltd (G-VRED)	
G-ECLD	Airbus A.340-642	European Cargo Ltd (G-VWIN)	
G-ECLE	Airbus A.340-642	European Cargo Ltd	
G-ECLF	Airbus A.340-541	Priority 1 Leasing Ltd	
G-ECLH	Airbus A.340-642	Priority 1 Leasing Ltd	
G-ECLJ	Airbus A.340-642	Priority 1 Leasing Ltd	
G-ECLK	Airbus A.340-642	Priority 1 Leasing Ltd	
G-ECLM	Airbus A.340-642	Priority 1 Leasing Ltd	
G-ECLN	Airbus A.340-642	European Cargo Ltd (G-VWEB)	
G-ECLW	Glasflugel Standard Libelle 201B	S. Leach	
G-ECMK	PA-18-150 Super Cub	K. Pogwizd	
G-ECOL	Schempp-Hirth Nimbus 2	M. Upex & L. I. Rigby	
G-ECOX	Pietenpol Air Camper	T. D. Wood	
G-ECPA	Glasflugel H201B Standard Libelle	M. J. Witton	
G-ECRM	Slingsby T.67M Firefly Mk II	CRM Aviation Europe Ltd (G-BNSP)	
G-ECTF	Comper CLA.7 Swift Replica	P. R. Cozens	
G-ECUB	PA-18-150 Super Cub	G-ECUB Flying Group (G-CBFI)	
G-ECVZ	Staaken Z-1S Flitzer	J. Cresswell	
G-ECXL	PZL-Bielsko SZD-30 Pirat	S. E. Chew	
G-EDAM	Ultramagic M-77C balloon	A. M. Holly	
G-EDAV	SA Bulldog Srs 120/121 (XX534:B)	Edwalton Aviation Ltd	
G-EDBD	PZL-Bielsko SZD-30 Pirat	S. P. Burgess	
G-EDDD	Schempp-Hirth Nimbus 2	C. A. Mansfield (G-BKPM)	
G-EDDS	CZAW Sportcruiser	D. A. Jackson	
G-EDDV	PZL-Bielsko SZD-38A Jantar 1	S. R. Bruce	
G-EDEE	Ikarus C.42 FB100	N. A. Mitchell & J. A. Cruikshank	
G-EDEL	PA-32-300 Cherokee Six D	J. Francis	
G-EDFS	Pietenpol Air Camper	J. G. Russell	
G-EDGA	PA-28-161 Cherokee Warrior II	The RAF Halton Aeroplane Club Ltd	
G-EDGE	Jodel 150	A. D. Edge	
G-EDGI	PA-28-161 Cherokee Warrior II	H. K. & T. W. Gilbert	
G-EDGY	Flight Test Edge 540	P. M. Gale	
G-EDII	Boeing E75 Stearman	Ethel (Two) Ltd	
G-EDLY	Airborne Edge 912/Streak IIIB	S. G. A. Milburn & S. Hall	
G-EDMK	Boeing A75L 300 Stearman	T. W. Harris	

Notes	Reg	Type	Owner or Operator
	G-EDRE	Lindstrand LBL 90A balloon	Edren Homes Ltd
	G-EDRV	Van's RV-6A	N. R. Horn
	G-EDSU	Sackville BM-56 balloon	S. A. Kidd & E. C. Lubbock
	G-EDTO	Cessna FR.172F	Vayu Aviation Services Ltd
	G-EDVK	RH78 Tiger Light	M. Peters (G-MZGT)
	G-EDVL	PA-28R Cherokee Arrow 200-II	Redhill Air Services Ltd (G-BXIN)
	G-EDWA	Agusta A.109E Power	Bath & West Aviation LLP
	G-EDZZ	Ikarus C42 FB100 Bravo	Microavionics UK Ltd
	G-EEAA	Pietenpol Air Camper	P. G. Humphrey
	G-EEAD	Slingsby T.65A Vega	J. D. Bodian
	G-EEAH	Bolkow BO.208C Junior	S. L. Buckingham
	G-EEBA	Slingsby T.65 Vega 17L	A. G. A. Parker
	G-EEBF	Schempp-Hirth Mini Nimbus C	M. Pingel
	G-EEBK	Schempp-Hirth Mini Nimbus C	D. P. Bennison
	G-EEBL	Schleicher ASK-13	Lincolnshire Gliding Club Ltd
	G-EEBN	Centrair ASW-20FL	S. MacArthur & R. Carlisle
	G-EEBR	Glaser-Dirks DG200/17	EBR Glider Syndicate
	G-EEBS	Scheibe Zugvogel IIIA	W. R. Davis
	G-EEBZ	Schleicher ASK-13	Buckminster Gliding Club Ltd
	G-EECC	Aerospool Dynamic WT9 UK	C. V. Ellingworth
	G-EECO	Lindstrand LBL-25A balloon	A. Jay
	G-EEDE	Centrair ASW-20F	G. M. Cumner
	G-EEER	Schempp-Hirth Mini Nimbus C	S. Massey
	G-EEES	Cessna 310R II	Modern Air (UK) Ltd (G-RVLZ)
	G-EEEZ	Champion 8KCAB	P. J. Webb
	G-EEFK	Centrair ASW-20FL	N. Dickenson
	G-EEFT	Schempp-Hirth Nimbus 2B	S. A. Adlard
	G-EEGL	Christen Eagle II	S. L. Nicholson
	G-EEGU	PA-28-161 Cherokee Warrior II	Tor Financial Consulting Ltd
	G-EEHA	Sonex	T. J. Fane de Salis
	G-EEKA	Glaser-Dirks DG-202/17	D. M. Betts
	G-EEKE	Skyranger Swift 912(1)	N. Jamieson
	G-EEKK	Cessna 152	A. D. R. Northeast (G-BNSW)
	G-EEKZ	P & M Quik GTR	A. P. Douglas-Dixon
	G-EELS	Cessna 208B Caravan 1	Glass Eels Ltd
	G-EELT	Rolladen-Schneider LS4	ELT Syndicate
	G-EELY	Schleicher Ka 6CR	K6 ELY Syndicate
	G-EENI	Europa	M. P. Grimshaw
	G-EENK	Schleicher ASK-21	Cotswold Gliding Club
	G-EENT	Glasflugel 304	M. Hastings & P. D. Morrison
	G-EENW	Schleicher ASW-20L	G. P. T. White
	G-EENZ	Schleicher ASW-19B	C. J. & G. J. Walker
	G-EEPJ	Pitts S-1S Special	R. J. Porter
	G-EERR	Eurocopter AS.350B3 Ecureuil	Cariad Investments Ltd (G-OOWS)
	G-EERV	Van's RV-6	J. M. Pipping
	G-EERY	Robinson R22	EGB (Helicopters) Ltd
	G-EESA	Europa	E. J. Wallington (G-HIIL)
	G-EESY	Rolladen-Schneider LS4	S. G. D. Gaze
	G-EETH	Schleicher K.8B	Bowland Forest Gliding Club Ltd
	G-EEUP	SNCAN Stampe SV.4C	A. M. Wajih
	G-EEVL	Grob G.102 Astir CS77	BR Aviation Ltd
	G-EEWA	Beech F.33A Bonanza	P. J. Barnett
	G-EEYE	Mainair Blade 912	B. J. Egerton
	G-EEZR	Robinson R44	Swift Helicopter Services Ltd
	G-EEZZ	Zenair CH.601XL Zodiac	A. G. Andrew
	G-EFAO	Scintex CP.301-C1 Emeraude	T. A. S. Rayner
	G-EFBP	Cessna FR.172K	Sierra Mike Juliet Flying Group
	G-EFCG	Eurofox 912(S)	C. A. White
	G-EFCM	PA-28-180 Cherokee D	Charlie Mike Syndicate
	G-EFER	PA-18-150 Super Cub	E. D. Haig-Thomas
	G-EFFH	Cessna T.210L Turbo Centurion	R. Paletar
	G-EFGT	Eurofox 2K	G. T. Taylor
	G-EFIZ	Pitts S-2B Special	R. S. Goodwin & G. V. Paino
	G-EFJD	MBB Bo.209 Monsun	M. H. D. Smith
	G-EFLT	Glasflugel Standard Libelle 201B	P. A. Tietema
	G-EFLY	Centrair ASW-20FL	S. A. Whitaker
	G-EFNH	Cessna FR.182	C. J. & V. J. Crawford
	G-EFOE	Bolkow BO.207	J. A. Webb
	G-EFOF	Robinson R22 Beta	Helicopter & Pilot Services Ltd

Reg	Type	Owner or Operator	Notes
G-EFON	Robinson R22 II	Burton Aviation Ltd (G-SCHO)	
G-EFOX	Eurofox 912(2)	H. J. Parker	
G-EFRP	Bower Fly Baby 1A	R. A. Phillips (G-BFRD)	
G-EFSD	Eurofox 912(IS)	S. E. Dancaster	
G-EFSF	Cessna FR.172K	A. Vaughan	
G-EFSM	Slingsby T.67M Firefly 260	Anglo Europe Aviation Ltd (G-BPLK)	
G-EFTE	Bölkow Bö.207	B. Morris & R. L. Earl	
G-EFUN	Bishop & Castelli E-Go	Giocas Ltd	
G-EFVS	Wassmer WA.52 Europa	F. A. Bakir	
G-EGAG	SOCATA TB20 Trinidad	J. J. Sinnott	
G-EGAL	Christen Eagle II	Prestwick Eagle Group	
G-EGBJ	PA-28-161 Cherokee Warrior II	Henshaw Aviation Ltd (G-CPFM/G-BNNS)	
G-EGBP	American Champion 7ECA Citabria Aurora	Freedom Aviation Ltd (G-IRGJ)	
G-EGBS	Van's RV-9A	Shobdon RV-9A Group	
G-EGBW	PA-28-161 Cherokee Warrior II	D. N. Sluman	
G-EGCA	Rans S-6-ES Coyote II	P. A. Linford	
G-EGCD	Cessna 172S	Avro Flying Group (G-PFCL)	
G-EGCK	Grob G.115C	Beagle Flight Consultancy Ltd	
G-EGEG	Cessna 172R	Echo Golf Flying Ltd	
G-EGES	Lindstrand LBL Triangle balloon	Lighter Than Air Ltds	
G-EGEN	Piel CP301A Emeraude	Croft Aviators Flying Group	
G-EGGI	Ikarus C.42FB UK	T. R. E. Goldfield & J. Stocking	
G-EGGS	Robin DR.400/180	G-EGGS Syndicate	
G-EGGZ	Sky Ranger Swift 912S(1)	B. J. Howlett & G. H. H. Wiedermann	
G-EGHP	Ikarus C42 FB80	Airbourne Aviation Ltd (G-CFHP)	
G-EGHW	MBB Bolkow BO.209 Monsun 150FV	N. Wright	
G-EGIA	UltraMagic M-65C balloon	A. Dizioli/Italy	
G-EGIB	PA-28-181 Cherokee Archer II	P. A. Venton	
G-EGIL	Christen Eagle II	S. J. Perkins	
G-EGJJ	P & M Quik GTR	T. J. Drew	
G-EGLA	Cessna 172M	Cornwall Flying Club Ltd (G-CGFJ)	
G-EGLE	Christen Eagle II	D. Thorpe	
G-EGLK	CSA PS-28 Cruiser	J. R. Hornby	
G-EGLL	PA-28-161 Cherokee Warrior II	Airways Aero Associations Ltd (G-BLEJ)	
G-EGLS	PA-28-181 Cherokee Archer III	M. Wallace	
G-EGLT	Cessna 310R	Modern Air (UK) Ltd (G-BHTV)	
G-EGPD	PA-28-181 Cherokee Archer II	Alexander Air Ltd	
G-EGPF	PA-28R-201 Cherokee Arrow III	Abbotsinch Aviation Ltd	
G-EGPG	PA-18-135 Super Cub	G. Cormack (G-BWUC)	
G-EGPH	Groppo Trail	H. R. Abraham	
G-EGSC	Rotorway Executive 162F	D. R. Fessey (G-JONG)	
G-EGSF	Robinson R22	Helimech Ltd (G-HMEK/G-HIEL)	
G-EGSJ	Jabiru J400	C. N. & K. J. Stephen (G-MGRK)	
G-EGSL	Cessna F.152	Andrewsfield Aviation Ltd	
G-EGSR	Van's RV-7A	S. J. Carr	
G-EGSX	PA-28-161 Cherokee Warrior II	North Weald Flight Training Ltd	
G-EGTB	PA-28-161 Cherokee Warrior II	Henshaw Aviation Ltd (G-BPWA)	
G-EGTF	EV-97 Eurostar SL	C. R. Wark	
G-EGTU	Cessna F.152 II	Devon and Somerset Flight Training Ltd (G-BGLR/G-HFCL)	
G-EGUR	Jodel D.140B	A. V. Harmer	
G-EGWN	American Champion 7ECA	Freedom Aviation Ltd	
G-EGZM	Cessna FR.172K	P. Riley	
G-EHAP	Fournier RF7	J. A. Hallam	
G-EHAT	Leonardo AW169	Essex & Herts Air Ambulance Trust	
G-EHAV	Glasflugel Standard Libelle 201B	G. M. Brooks	
G-EHAZ	PA-28-161 Cherokee Warrior III	Freedom Aviation Ltd (G-CEEY)	
G-EHBJ	CASA 1.131E Jungmann 2000	E. P. Howard	
G-EHCB	Schempp-Hirth Nimbus 3DT	G-EHCB Group	
G-EHCC	PZL-Bielsko SZD-50-3 Puchacz	Heron Gliding Club	
G-EHDS	CASA 1.131E Jungmann 2000	I. C. Underwood (G-DUDS)	
G-EHEH	Lindstrand LTL Series 1 balloon	M. A. Webb & J. Pierson	
G-EHGF	PA-28-181 CherokeeArcher II	S. J. Colson	
G-EHIC	Jodel D.140B	G-EHIC Group	
G-EHIL	EH Industries EH101 ★	The Helicopter Museum/Weston-super-Mare	
G-EHLE	Ikarus C42C FB100	E. Hardiman & L. Eccles	
G-EHLT	DH.82A Tiger Moth	R. C. P. Brookhouse (G-BHLT)	
G-EHLX	PA-28-181 Cherokee Archer II	Synergy Flight Centres Ltd	
G-EHMF	Isaacs Fury II	G. W. Hilferty	

Notes	Reg	Type	Owner or Operator
	G-EHMJ	Beech S35 Bonanza	A. J. Daley
	G-EHZT	Zlin Z.526F Trener Master	K. Harness
	G-EIAP	Jodel DR.1050	P. M. Irvine
	G-EIAR	Jodel DR250/160	D. G. Holman
	G-EIDY	Airbus A.330-302	Aer Lingus (UK) Ltd
	G-EIGT	Van's RV-8	M. J. Benham
	G-EIKY	Europa	J. D. Milbank
	G-EILA	Airbus A.330-302	Aer Lingus (UK) Ltd
	G-EIMS	Bell 505 Jet Ranger X	N. V. Cook
	G-EINI	Europa XS	D. G. Parsons (G-KDCC)
	G-EISG	Beech A36 Bonanza	R. J. & B. Howard
	G-EISO	SOCATA MS.892A Rallye Commodore ★	Sammy Miller Motorcycle Museum/New Milton
	G-EITE	Luscombe 8F Silvaire	C. P. Davey
	G-EIZO	Eurocopter EC 120B	Blok (UK) Ltd
	G-EJAE	GlaserDirks DG-200	S. D. Foster & I. J. Harris
	G-EJAS	Skystar Kitfox Model 7	D. A. Holl
	G-EJBB	Focke Wulf FW44J Stieglitz (BB+EJ)	Oldstead Aero LLP
	G-EJBI	Bolkow Bo.207	A. A. R. Moore
	G-EJCA	Airbus A.320-214	easyJet Airline Co.Ltd
	G-EJCC	Airbus A.320-214	easyJet Airline Co.Ltd
	G-EJCD	Airbus A.320-214	easyJet Airline Co.Ltd
	G-EJCE	Airbus A.320-214	easyJet Airline Co.Ltd
	G-EJCF	Airbus A.320-214	easyJet Airline Co.Ltd
	G-EJCG	Airbus A.320-214	easyJet Airline Co.Ltd
	G-EJCH	Airbus A.320-214	easyJet Airline Co.Ltd
	G-EJCI	Airbus A.320-214	easyJet Airline Co.Ltd
	G-EJCJ	Airbus A.320-214	easyJet Airline Co.Ltd
	G-EJCK	Airbus A.320-214	easyJet Airline Co.Ltd
	G-EJCL	Airbus A.320-214	easyJet Airline Co.Ltd
	G-EJCM	Airbus A.320-214	easyJet Airline Co.Ltd
	G-EJCO	Airbus A.320-214	easyJet Airline Co.Ltd
	G-EJCP	Airbus A.320-214	easyJet Airline Co.Ltd
	G-EJCR	Airbus A.320-214	easyJet Airline Co.Ltd
	G-EJGO	Z.226HE Trener	S. K. T. Neofytou
	G-EJHH	Schempp-Hirth Standard Cirrus	I. S. Simmonds
	G-EJIM	Schempp-Hirth Discus 2cT	N. A. L. Stuart
	G-EJIT	Diamond P-60 balloon	Evos Group Ltd
	G-EJMK	Pitts S-1S Special	M. J. Collett (G-CCFO)
	G-EJMX	Bell 505 Jet Ranger X	EJ Mackelden & Sons (Bobbing) Ltd
	G-EJRS	PA-28-161 Cadet	Carlisle Flight Traing Ltd
	G-EJTC	Robinson R44	N. Parkhouse
	G-EJWI	Flight Design CTLS 600UK	D. D. J. Rossdale
	G-EKBA	SOCATA TB-200 Tobago XL	A. Demetriou & S. Gray
	G-EKEY	Schleicher ASW-20 CL	A. N. Mayer
	G-EKHW	PA-28R-201T Turbo Cherokee Arrow IV	D. V. Shaw
	G-EKIM	Alpi Pioneer 300	T. P. Nettleton
	G-EKIR	PA-28-262 Cadet	Aeros Leasing Ltd
	G-EKJD	Cessna FR.172J	Juliet Delta Flying Group
	G-EKKL	PA-28-161 Cherokee Warrior II	C G Aviation Ltd
	G-EKOS	Cessna FR.182 RG	S. Charlton
	G-EKTN	Beech 95-B55 Baron	N. S. Cooper (G-IPEP/G-FABM/G-JOND/G-BMVC)
	G-EKTP	SAAB 91D Safir	J. M. C. Loureiro
	G-EKUB	TLAC Sherwood eKUB	The Light Aviation Company Ltd
	G-ELAK	Sportine Aviacija LAK-17B FES	G. N. Fraser
	G-ELBB	Pipistrel Alpha BCAR-S 164	G-ELBB Group
	G-ELBE	Van's RV-7	E. G. Jones & I. E. Blackburn
	G-ELBW	Van's RV-14	P. J. Foreman
	G-ELCH	Commandeer 114B	L. Ormsby
	G-ELDR	PA-32-260 Cherokee Six	R. S. Wilson
	G-ELEC	Westland WG.30 ★	The Helicopter Museum/Weston-super-Mare (G-BKNV)
	G-ELEE	Cameron Z-105 balloon	M. A. Stelling
	G-ELEN	Robin DR.400/180	Foster ELEN Group
	G-ELII	Kubicek BB26E balloon	M. R. Stokoe
	G-ELIS	PA-34-200T Seneca II	Air Medic Services Ltd & A. Gougas (G-BOPV)
	G-ELKA	Christen Eagle II	M. R. Smith

Reg	Type	Owner or Operator	Notes
G-ELKE	Cirrus SR-20	L. & N. P. L. Turner	
G-ELKI	Diamond DA.40 NG Star	Euro Flight Training Ltd	
G-ELKO	Diamond DA.42 NG Twin Star	Euro Flight Training Ltd	
G-ELLI	Bell 206B JetRanger 3	T. J. Ricketts	
G-ELMH	NA AT-6D Harvard III (42-84555:EP-H)	S. J. L. Jones	
G-ELMR	Kubicek BB85Z balloon	Yorkshire Balloon Flights Ltd	
G-ELNA	TL2000UK Sting Carbon S4	P. Crolla	
G-ELRI	Champion 7GCBC Citabria	J. H. D. Newman	
G-ELRT	Sopwith Pup (N6161)	T. A. Bechtolsheimer	
G-ELSB	Robin DR.400-180R	Cambridge Gliding Club Ltd	
G-ELSE	Diamond DA.42 Twin Star	Twinstar Ops Ltd	
G-ELSR	Robin DR400/180R	Viscount Cobham	
G-ELUE	PA-28-161 Cherokee Warrior II	Freedom Aviation Ltd	
G-ELUN	Robin DR.400/180R	Cotswold DR.400 Syndicate	
G-ELVN	Van's RV-7	M. Rothwell	
G-ELWK	Van's RV-12	J. Devlin	
G-ELXE	Cessna 182T	A. W. Oliver	
G-ELYS	Cessna FA.150K	J. A. Whiston (G-BIBN)	
G-ELZN	PA-28-161 Cherokee Warrior II	ZN Flying Group	
G-ELZY	PA-28-161 Cherokee Warrior II	Redhill Air Services Ltd	
G-EMAA	Eurocopter EC 135T2+	Babcock Mission Critical Services Onshore Ltd	
G-EMAC	Robinson R22 Beta	Helicopter & Pilot Services Ltd (G-CBDB)	
G-EMAT	Diamond DA.62	Galaxy Flair Ltd	
G-EMCA	Commander Aircraft 114B	S. Roberts	
G-EMCG	M & D Flugzeugbau JS-MD 3	T. J. Scott	
G-EMCP	Schempp-Hirth Arcus M	Yorkshire Arcus	
G-EMCS	HpH 304TS Twin Shark	T. J. Highton	
G-EMCV	Learjet 45	247 Aviation Ltd	
G-EMCW	HpH 304TS Twin Shark	M. Gibson	
G-EMCX	Learjet 45	247 Aviation Ltd	
G-EMCY	Learjet 45	247 Aviation Ltd	
G-EMCZ	Learjet 45	247 Aviation Ltd	
G-EMDM	Diamond DA40-P9 Star	D. J. Munson	
G-EMEB	Airbus EC175B	CHC Scotia Ltd	
G-EMEC	Airbus EC175B	CHC Scotia Ltd	
G-EMED	Airbus EC175B	CHC Scotia Ltd	
G-EMEF	Sikorsky S-92A	CHC Scotia Ltd	
G-EMEG	Sikorsky S-92A	CHC Scotia Ltd	
G-EMEH	Airbus EC175B	CHC Scotia Ltd	
G-EMEI	Airbus EC175B	CHC Scotia Ltd (G-CLTB)	
G-EMEK	Airbus EC175B	CHC Scotia Ltd (G-MCSE)	
G-EMHF	Leonardo AW109SP Grand New	East Midlands Helicopters	
G-EMHK	MBB Bö.209 Monsun 150FV	C. Elder (G-BLRD)	
G-EMHN	Agusta A109S Grand	Burton Aviation Ltd	
G-EMID	Eurocopter EC 135P2	West Yorkshire Combined Authority National Police Air Service	
G-EMIN	Europa	S. A. Lamb	
G-EMJA	CASA 1.131E Jungmann 2000	T. A. Fulcher	
G-EMKT	Cameron Z-105 balloon	Webster Adventures Ltd	
G-EMLE	Aerotechnik EV-97 Eurostar	A. R. White	
G-EMLG	Bombardier BD700-1A10 Global 6000	Concierge U Ltd	
G-EMLY	Pegasus Quantum 15	S. J. Reid	
G-EMMR	Van's RV-10	P. G. Reid	
G-EMMX	P & M Quik GT450	S. J. Reader	
G-EMMY	Rutan Vari-Eze	M. J. Tooze	
G-EMNN	Focke-Wulf FW.44J Stieglitz	Olstead Aero LLP	
G-EMOL	Schweizer 269C-1	A & W Demolition (Bracknell)	
G-EMSA	Czech Sport Aircraft Sportcruiser	A. C. & M. A. Naylor	
G-EMSI	Europa	P. W. L. Thomas	
G-EMSS	Airbus MBB-BK 117 D-2	Babcock Mission Critical Services Onshore Ltd	
G-EMSY	DH.82A Tiger Moth	Tiger Flights (G-ASPZ)	
G-ENBW	Robin DR.400-180R	P. S. Carder & B. Elliott	
G-ENCE	Partenavia P.68B	Exeter Flights Ltd (G-OROY/G-BFSU)	
G-ENDG	Ikarus C42C FB100	N. D. Hoult	
G-ENEA	Cessna 182P	ATI Group	
G-ENEE	CFM Streak Shadow SA	S. G. Smith	
G-ENGO	Steen Skybolt	J. P. Gilbert & A. C. Hill	
G-ENGR	Head AX8-105 balloon	S. Dyer	
G-ENIA	Staaken Z-21 Flitzer	A. F. Wankowski	

Notes	Reg	Type	Owner or Operator
	G-ENID	Reality Escapade ULP(1)	R. D. Thomasson
	G-ENIE	Tipsy T.66 Nipper 3	M. J. Freeman
	G-ENII	Cessna F.172M	P. J. Gatland (G-CIGD)
	G-ENIO	Pitts S-2C Special	Advanced Flying (London) Ltd
	G-ENKO	Yakovlev Yak-18T	D. Ischenko
	G-ENKY	Skyranger Swift 912S(1)	J. Brumpton & R. Urquhart
	G-ENLI	Tecnam P2010 TDI	S. Barden
	G-ENNA	PA-28-161 Cherokee Warrior II	Falcon Flying Serices Ltd (G-ESFT)
	G-ENOA	Cessna F.172F	W. K. & D. Macleod & S. Eardley (G-ASZW)
	G-ENRE	Avtech Jabiru SPL-450	Kernow Flying Group Ltd
	G-ENRG	Embraer EMB-5590 Praetor 600	London Executive Aviation Ltd
	G-ENST	CZAW Sportcruiser	Enstone Flyers
	G-ENTL	P & M QuikR	D. A. Hopkinson
	G-ENTO	American General AG-5B Tiger	G-ENTO Group
	G-ENTT	Cessna F.152 II	T. W. Gilbert (G-BHHI)
	G-ENTW	Cessna F.152 II	Eagle Flying Ltd (G-BFLK)
	G-EODS	Airbus A.330-343F	Geodis Air Network sas/Titan Airways Ltd
	G-EOFW	Pegasus Quantum 15-912	G-EOFW Microlight Group
	G-EOFZ	TL 2000 Sting S4	G. T. Leedham
	G-EOGE	Gefa-Flug AS105GD airship (hot air)	Cameron Balloons Ltd
	G-EOHL	Cessna 182L	Branton Knight Ltd
	G-EOID	Aeroprakt A22-L Foxbat	J. Pearce
	G-EOIN	Zenair CH.701UL	G-EOIN Group
	G-EOJB	Robinson R44 II	Difuria Contractors Ltd (G-EDES)
	G-EOLD	PA-28-161 Cherokee Warrior II	Phoenix Aviation Ltd
	G-EORG	PA-38-112 Tomahawk	G. W. & T. W. Gilbert
	G-EORJ	Europa	P. E. George
	G-EOSM	Apollo Deltajet 500/Aeros Stingray	G. M. Douglas
	G-EPAR	Robinson R22 Beta II	Jepar Rotorcraft
	G-EPEE	JA400 Skyleader 400	R. Engelhard
	G-EPIC	Jabiru UL-450	T. Chadwick
	G-EPIM	Cessna R172K	A. H. Creaser
	G-EPOC	Jabiru UL-450	S. Cope
	G-EPSN	Ultramagic M-105 balloon	G. Everett
	G-EPTR	PA-28R Cherokee Arrow 200-II	ACS Aviation Ltd
	G-EPWR	Pipistrel Virus SW 128	BAE Systems (Operations) Ltd
	G-ERAF	Pipistrel Virus SW 128	Chicken Roundabout Finance Ltd
	G-ERAS	Cameron O-31 balloon	E. M. F. Worsman
	G-ERCO	Ercoupe 415D	E. G. Girardey
	G-ERDA	Staaken Z-21A Flitzer	J. Cresswell
	G-ERDS	DH.82A Tiger Moth	W. A. Gerdes
	G-ERDW	Enstrom F-28F Falcon	G. Georgiev/Bulgaria
	G-ERFC	S.E.5A replica (C1096)	T. W. Harris
	G-ERFS	PA-28-161 Cherokee Warrior II	North Wales Flight Academy Ltd
	G-ERGP	Pilatus PC-12/47E	Solid Rock Aviation GP Ltd
	G-ERGT	P & M Quik GT450	G-ERGT Group
	G-ERIW	Staaken Z-21 Flitzer	R. I. Wasey
	G-ERJR	Agusta A109C	3GRCOMM Ltd (G-DBOY)
	G-ERMN	Staaken Z-21 Flitzer	S. R. Pock (G-WIDZ)
	G-ERNI	PA-28-181 Cherokee Archer II	J. Gardener & N. F. P. Hopwood (G-OSSY)
	G-EROB	Europa XS	R. J. Bull (G-RBJW)
	G-EROE	Avro 504K Replica	British Aviation 100
	G-EROS	Cameron H-34 balloon	M. J. Axtell
	G-ERRI	Lindstrand LBL-77A balloon	S. M. Jones
	G-ERTA	Pietenpol Air Camper	H. M. Theron
	G-ERTE	Skyranger 912S (1)	S. J. Gibson
	G-ERTI	Staaken Z-21A Flitzer	T. D. Gardner
	G-ERYN	Ikarus C42 FB100	M. J. Donnelly
	G-ERYR	P & M Aviation Quik GT450	R. D. Ellis
	G-ESAA	Caudron C68	AREC 68 Group
	G-ESAR	Leonardo AW139	Helioperations
	G-ESCA	Escapade Jabiru (1)	G. W. E. & R. H. May
	G-ESCC	Escapade 912	G. & S. Simons
	G-ESCP	Escapade 912(1)	A. Palmer
	G-ESET	Eurocopter EC.130B4 Ecureuil	Hogs Head Transportation Ltd
	G-ESGA	Reality Escapade	D. W. & S. J. McAllister
	G-ESGC	Eurofox 2K	East Sussex Gliding Club Ltd

Reg	Type	Owner or Operator	Notes
G-ESHR	Van's RV-12iS	D. Crocker	
G-ESJA	Sud SA.318C Alouette Astazou	G. Gudbergsson	
G-ESKA	Escapade 912 (2)	C. G. Thompson	
G-ESKR	Skyranger Nynja	Flylight Airsports Ltd	
G-ESME	Cessna R.182 II (15211)	G. C. Cherrington (G-BNOX)	
G-ESMI	Cameron Z-90 balloon	The Hot Air Balloon Company (Global) Ltd	
G-ESMK	Bucker Bu131 Jungmann	T. W. Harris	
G-ESSL	Cessna R.182	Flightplan Aviation Ltd	
G-ESTR	Van's RV-6	J. P. M. & P. M. White	
G-ETAC	Dornier 228-212	Aurigny Air Services Ltd	
G-ETBT	PA-38-112 Tomahawk	Highland Aviation Training Ltd	
G-ETBY	PA-32 Cherokee Six 260	G-ETBY Group (G-AWCY)	
G-ETDC	Cessna 172P	R. Forman & G. Slater	
G-ETET	PA-46-600TP Meridian M600	Livingstone Aviation Ltd	
G-ETGO	Groppo Trail Mk.2	A. R. Pitcher	
G-ETHO	Leonardo AW109SP	Jetheli Ltd	
G-ETHL	Flylight Adam	Q. F. Irving	
G-ETIM	Eurocopter EC 120B	Tenterfield (Holdings) Ltd	
G-ETIN	Robinson R22 Beta	Swift Helicopter Services Ltd	
G-ETIV	Robin DR.400/180	C. A. Prior	
G-ETKT	Robinson R44 II	K. R. Taylor	
G-ETLX	PA-28R-200 Cherokee Arrow II	Blue Skys Aviation Ltd	
G-ETME	Nord 1002 Pingouin (KG+EM)	S. H. O'Connell	
G-ETNT	Robinson R44	Irwin Plant Sales	
G-ETOY	CASA 1-131E Jungmann Series 2000	L. B. Clark & B. A. Hinsley	
G-ETPA	Pilatus PC-21	QinetiQ Ltd	
G-ETPB	Pilatus PC-21	QinetiQ Ltd	
G-ETPE	Airbus AS.350B3 Ecureuil	QinetiQ Ltd	
G-ETPF	Airbus AS.350B3 Ecureuil	QinetiQ Ltd	
G-ETPG	Airbus AS.350B3 Ecureuil	QinetiQ Ltd	
G-ETPH	Airbus AS.350B3 Ecureuil	QinetiQ Ltd	
G-ETPI	Agusta A.109E Power	QinetiQ Ltd	
G-ETPJ	Agusta A.109E Power	QinetiQ Ltd (G-ESLH)	
G-ETPK	Avro RJ70	QinetiQ Ltd (G-BVRJ)	
G-ETPL	Avro RJ100	QinetiQ Ltd (G-BZAY)	
G-ETPM	Diamond DA.42M-NG Twin Star	QinetiQ Ltd (G-LTPA)	
G-ETPN	Agusta A109S Grand	QinetiQ Ltd	
G-ETPO	Agusta A109S Grand	QinetiQ Ltd	
G-ETPP	Leonardo AW.139	QinetiQ Ltd	
G-ETPR	Beech B300 King Air 350	QinetiQ Ltd	
G-ETTO	Skyranger Swift 912S	N. S. Dell	
G-ETUG	Eurofox 912(S)	The Nortumbria Gliding Club Ltd	
G-ETWO	Guimbal Cabri G2	Helicentre Aviation Ltd	
G-EUAB	Europa XS	B. A. Stephens-Simonazzi	
G-EUAN	Jabiru UL-D	S. J. Hood & S. Gilbouret	
G-EUEL	Europa Elite	Europa Aircraft (2004) Ltd	
G-EUFO	Rolladen-Schneider LS7-WL	M. J. Mingay	
G-EUFX	Eurofox 912(IS)(1)	P. S. Harvey	
G-EUJG	Avro 594 Avian IIIA	M. D. Souch	
G-EUKS	Westland Widgeon III	M. D. Souch	
G-EUNG	Europa NG	D. I. Stanbridge	
G-EUOE	Airbus A.319-131	British Airways	
G-EUOF	Airbus A.319-131	British Airways	
G-EUOG	Airbus A.319-131	British Airways	
G-EUPD	Airbus A.319-131	British Airways	
G-EUPG	Airbus A.319-131	British Airways	
G-EUPJ	Airbus A.319-131	British Airways	
G-EUPK	Airbus A.319-131	British Airways	
G-EUPN	Airbus A.319-131	British Airways	
G-EUPO	Airbus A.319-131	British Airways	
G-EUPP	Airbus A.319-131	British Airways	
G-EUPR	Airbus A.319-131	British Airways	
G-EUPS	Airbus A.319-131	British Airways	
G-EUPU	Airbus A.319-131	British Airways	
G-EUPW	Airbus A.319-131	British Airways	
G-EUPZ	Airbus A.319-131	British Airways	
G-EUSO	Robin DR.400/140 Major	Weald Air Services Ltd	
G-EUUA	Airbus A.320-232	British Airways	
G-EUUB	Airbus A.320-232	British Airways	

Notes	Reg	Type	Owner or Operator
	G-EUUC	Airbus A.320-232	British Airways
	G-EUUD	Airbus A.320-232	British Airways
	G-EUUE	Airbus A.320-232	British Airways
	G-EUUF	Airbus A.320-232	British Airways
	G-EUUG	Airbus A.320-232	British Airways
	G-EUUH	Airbus A.320-232	British Airways
	G-EUUI	Airbus A.320-232	British Airways
	G-EUUJ	Airbus A.320-232	British Airways
	G-EUUK	Airbus A.320-232	British Airways
	G-EUUL	Airbus A.320-232	British Airways
	G-EUUM	Airbus A.320-232	British Airways
	G-EUUN	Airbus A.320-232	British Airways
	G-EUUO	Airbus A.320-232	British Airways
	G-EUUP	Airbus A.320-232	British Airways
	G-EUUR	Airbus A.320-232	British Airways
	G-EUUS	Airbus A.320-232	British Airways
	G-EUUT	Airbus A.320-232	BA Euroflyer Ltd
	G-EUUU	Airbus A.320-232	British Airways
	G-EUUV	Airbus A.320-232	BA Euroflyer Ltd
	G-EUUW	Airbus A.320-232	BA Euroflyer Ltd
	G-EUUX	Airbus A.320-232	BA Euroflyer Ltd
	G-EUUY	Airbus A.320-232	BA Euroflyer Ltd
	G-EUUZ	Airbus A.320-232	British Airways
	G-EUXC	Airbus A.321-231	BA Euroflyer Ltd
	G-EUXD	Airbus A.321-231	BA Euroflyer Ltd
	G-EUXE	Airbus A.321-231	BA Euroflyer Ltd
	G-EUXF	Airbus A.321-231	BA Euroflyer Ltd
	G-EUXG	Airbus A.321-231	BA Euroflyer Ltd
	G-EUXH	Airbus A.321-231	BA Euroflyer Ltd
	G-EUXI	Airbus A.321-231	BA Euroflyer Ltd
	G-EUXJ	Airbus A.321-231	BA Euroflyer Ltd
	G-EUXK	Airbus A.321-231	BA Euroflyer Ltd
	G-EUXL	Airbus A.321-231	BA Euroflyer Ltd
	G-EUXM	Airbus A.321-231	BA Euroflyer Ltd
	G-EUYA	Airbus A.320-232	British Airways
	G-EUYB	Airbus A.320-232	British Airways
	G-EUYC	Airbus A.320-232	British Airways
	G-EUYD	Airbus A.320-232	British Airways
	G-EUYE	Airbus A.320-232	British Airways
	G-EUYF	Airbus A.320-232	British Airways
	G-EUYG	Airbus A.320-232	British Airways
	G-EUYH	Airbus A.320-232	British Airways
	G-EUYI	Airbus A.320-232	British Airways
	G-EUYJ	Airbus A.320-232	British Airways
	G-EUYK	Airbus A.320-232	British Airways
	G-EUYL	Airbus A.320-232	British Airways
	G-EUYM	Airbus A.320-232	British Airways
	G-EUYN	Airbus A.320-232	British Airways
	G-EUYO	Airbus A.320-232	British Airways
	G-EUYP	Airbus A.320-232	British Airways
	G-EUYR	Airbus A.320-232	British Airways
	G-EUYS	Airbus A.320-232	British Airways
	G-EUYT	Airbus A.320-232	British Airways
	G-EUYU	Airbus A.320-232	British Airways
	G-EUYV	Airbus A.320-232	British Airways
	G-EUYW	Airbus A.320-232	British Airways
	G-EUYX	Airbus A.320-232	British Airways
	G-EUYY	Airbus A.320-232	British Airways
	G-EVAA	Autogyro Cavalon	G-EVAA Syndicate
	G-EVAJ	Skyranger 912S(1)	A. B. Gridley
	G-EVBF	Cameron Z-350 balloon	Virgin Balloon Flights
	G-EVCA	Skyfly Axe	Skyfly Technologies Ltd
	G-EVEE	Robinson R44	C. C. Butt (G-REGE)
	G-EVEY	Thruster T.600N 450-JAB	The G-EVEY Flying Group
	G-EVIB	Cirrus SR22	G. H. Tempest-Hay
	G-EVIE	PA-28-181 Cherokee Warrior II	J. L. Patton (G-ZULU)
	G-EVIG	Cosmik EV-97 TeamEurostar UK	M. J. Brown
	G-EVII	Schempp-Hirth Ventus 2cT	M. Lawrence-Jones
	G-EVLE	Rearwin 8125 Cloudster	R. S. K. Solley (G-BVLK)
	G-EVMK	DHC-2 Beaver 1	T. W. Harris

Reg	Type	Owner or Operator	Notes
G-EVRO	Aerotechnik EV-97 Eurostar	J. E. Rourke	
G-EVSL	Aerotechnik EV-97 Eurostar SL	J. A. T. Dow	
G-EVSW	Evektor Sportstar	I. Shulver	
G-EVTA	Vertical Aerospace VA-1X	Vertical Aerospace Group Ltd	
G-EVTB	Vertical Aerospace VA-1X	Vertical Aerospace Group Ltd	
G-EVTL	Vertical Aerospace VA-1X	Vertical Aerospace Group Ltd	
G-EVTO	PA-28-161 Cherokee Warrior II	Redhill Air Services Ltd	
G-EWAD	Robinson R44 II	MG Helicopters Ltd & Select Engineering	
G-EWAN	Prostar PT-2C	C. G. Shaw	
G-EWBC	Avtec Jabiru SK	E. W. B. Comber	
G-EWEN	Eurofox 912(S)	M. H. Talbot	
G-EWES	Alpi Pioneer 300	I. J. Harvey	
G-EWEW	AB Sportine Aviacija LAK-19T	J. B. Strzebrakowski	
G-EWIZ	Pitts S-2E Special	R. S. Goodwin	
G-EWOK	Pitts S-11B Super Stinker	A. T. Cartwright	
G-EXAM	PA-28RT-201T Turbo Cherokee Arrow IV	H. S. Urquhart	
G-EXCC	Carbon Cub EX-2	M. S. Colebrook	
G-EXEC	PA-34-200 Seneca	Sky Air Travel Ltd	
G-EXES	Europa XS	M. W. Olliver	
G-EXGC	Extra EA.300/200	P. J. Bull	
G-EXHL	Cameron C-70 balloon	K. C. Tanner	
G-EXII	Extra EA.300	Z. Lidzius	
G-EXIL	Extra EA.300/S	G-Force Aerobatics LLP	
G-EXIT	MS.893E Rallye 180GT	G-EXIT Group	
G-EXLL	Zenair CH.601	M. R. Brumby	
G-EXLT	Extra EA.300/LT	J. W. Marshall	
G-EXNG	Extra NG	J. W. Marshall	
G-EXPO	PA-46R-350T Malibu Matrix	G-EXPO LLP	
G-EXTC	Experimental Aviation Berkut	P. Wyckaert	
G-EXTR	Extra EA.260	Airdisplays.com Ltd	
G-EXXD	PA-28R-201 Cherokee Arrow III	North Weald Flight Training Ltd & Smart Aircraft Ltd	
G-EXXL	Zenair CH.601XL Zodiac	R. Smith	
G-EYAK	Yakovlev Yak-50	P. N. A. Whitehead	
G-EYOR	Van's RV-6	S. I. Fraser	
G-EYVZ	Navion L-17A (47.911)	Lithica Navion LLP	
G-EZAJ	Airbus A.319-111	easyJet Airline Co.Ltd	
G-EZAN	Airbus A.319-111	easyJet Airline Co.Ltd	
G-EZAO	Airbus A.319-111	easyJet Airline Co.Ltd	
G-EZAR	Pegasus Quik	D. McCormack	
G-EZAU	Airbus A.319-111	easyJet Airline Co.Ltd	
G-EZAX	Airbus A.319-111	easyJet Airline Co.Ltd	
G-EZBH	Airbus A.319-111	easyJet Airline Co.Ltd	
G-EZBI	Airbus A.319-111	easyJet Airline Co.Ltd	
G-EZBJ	Airbus A.319-111	easyJet Airline Co.Ltd	
G-EZBO	Airbus A.319-111	easyJet Airline Co.Ltd	
G-EZBR	Airbus A.319-111	easyJet Airline Co.Ltd	
G-EZBT	Airbus A.319-111	easyJet Airline Co.Ltd	
G-EZBU	Airbus A.319-111	easyJet Airline Co.Ltd	
G-EZBV	Airbus A.319-111	easyJet Airline Co.Ltd	
G-EZBW	Airbus A.319-111	easyJet Airline.Co.Ltd	
G-EZBX	Airbus A.319-111	easyJet Airline Co.Ltd	
G-EZBY	Airbus A.319-111	easyJet Airline Co.Ltd	
G-EZBZ	Airbus A.319-111	easyJet Airline Co.Ltd	
G-EZDA	Airbus A.319-111	easyJet Airline Co.Ltd	
G-EZDG	Rutan Vari-Eze	W. S. Allen (G-EZOS)	
G-EZDH	Airbus A.319-111	easyJet Airline Co.Ltd	
G-EZDJ	Airbus A.319-111	easyJet Airline Co.Ltd	
G-EZDK	Airbus A.319-111	easyJet Airline Co.Ltd	
G-EZDL	Airbus A.319-111	easyJet Airline Co.Ltd	
G-EZDM	Airbus A.319-111	easyJet Airline Co.Ltd	
G-EZDN	Airbus A.319-111	easyJet Airline Co.Ltd	
G-EZDR	Airbus A.319-111	easyJet Airline Co.Ltd	
G-EZDV	Airbus A.319-111	easyJet Airline Co.Ltd	
G-EZDX	Airbus A.319-111	easyJet Airline Co.Ltd	
G-EZES	Airbus A.319-111	easyJet Airline Co Ltd	
G-EZEV	Airbus A.319-111	easyJet Airline Co Ltd	
G-EZFI	Airbus A.319-111	easyJet Airline Co.Ltd	

Notes	Reg	Type	Owner or Operator
	G-EZFR	Airbus A.319-111	easyJet Airline Co.Ltd
	G-EZFT	Airbus A.319-111	easyJet Airline Co.Ltd
	G-EZFU	Airbus A.319-111	easyJet Airline Co.Ltd
	G-EZFV	Airbus A.319-111	easyJet Airline Co.Ltd
	G-EZFW	Airbus A.319-111	easyJet Airline Co.Ltd
	G-EZGE	Airbus A.319-111	easyJet Airline Co.Ltd
	G-EZGG	Airbus A.319-111	easyJet Airline Co.Ltd
	G-EZGH	Airbus A.319-111	easyJet Airline Co.Ltd
	G-EZGI	Airbus A.319-111	easyJet Airline Co.Ltd
	G-EZGJ	Airbus A.319-111	easyJet Airline Co.Ltd
	G-EZGK	Airbus A.319-111	easyJet Airline Co.Ltd
	G-EZGN	Airbus A.319-111	easyJet Airline Co.Ltd
	G-EZGO	Airbus A.319-111	easyJet Airline Co.Ltd
	G-EZGR	Airbus A.319-111	easyJet Airline Co.Ltd
	G-EZGX	Airbus A.320-214	easyJet Airline Co.Ltd
	G-EZGY	Airbus A.320-214	easyJet Airline Co.Ltd
	G-EZIY	Airbus A.319-111	easyJet Airline Co.Ltd
	G-EZMT	Extra EA.300/200	Joff Ltd
	G-EZOA	Airbus A.320-214	easyJet Airline Co.Ltd
	G-EZOE	Airbus A.320-214	easyJet Airline Co.Ltd
	G-EZOF	Airbus A.320-214	easyJet Airline Co.Ltd
	G-EZOH	Airbus A.320-214	easyJet Airline Co.Ltd
	G-EZOI	Airbus A.320-214	easyJet Airline Co.Ltd
	G-EZOJ	Airbus A.320-214	easyJet Airline Co.Ltd
	G-EZOK	Airbus A.320-214	easyJet Airline Co.Ltd
	G-EZOM	Airbus A.320-214	easyJet Airline Co.Ltd
	G-EZOP	Airbus A.320-214	easyJet Airline Co.Ltd
	G-EZOT	Airbus A.320-214	easyJet Airline Co.Ltd
	G-EZOU	Airbus A.320-214	easyJet Airline Co.Ltd
	G-EZOX	Airbus A.320-214	easyJet Airline Co.Ltd
	G-EZPB	Airbus A.320-214	easyJet Airline Co.Ltd
	G-EZPD	Airbus A.320-214	easyJet Airline Co.Ltd
	G-EZPE	Airbus A.320-214	easyJet Airline Co.Ltd
	G-EZPV	Airbus A.320-214	easyJet Airline Co.Ltd
	G-EZPX	Airbus A.320-214	easyJet Airline Co.Ltd
	G-EZRT	Airbus A.320-214	easyJet Airline Co.Ltd
	G-EZRX	Airbus A.320-214	easyJet Airline Co.Ltd
	G-EZRY	Airbus A.320-214	easyJet Airline Co.Ltd
	G-EZRZ	Airbus A.320-214	easyJet Airline Co.Ltd
	G-EZTA	Airbus A.320-214	easyJet Airline Co.Ltd
	G-EZTB	Airbus A.320-214	easyJet Airline Co.Ltd
	G-EZTC	Airbus A.320-214	easyJet Airline Co.Ltd
	G-EZTD	Airbus A.320-214	easyJet Airline Co.Ltd
	G-EZTG	Airbus A.320-214	easyJet Airline Co.Ltd
	G-EZTH	Airbus A.320-214	easyJet Airline Co.Ltd
	G-EZTJ	Airbus A.320-214	easyJet Airline Co.Ltd
	G-EZTK	Airbus A.320-214	easyJet Airline Co.Ltd
	G-EZTL	Airbus A.320-214	easyJet Airline Co.Ltd
	G-EZTM	Airbus A.320-214	easyJet Airline Co.Ltd
	G-EZTN	Airbus A.320-214	easyJet Airline Co.Ltd
	G-EZTR	Airbus A.320-214	easyJet Airline Co.Ltd
	G-EZTT	Airbus A.320-214	easyJet Airline Co.Ltd
	G-EZTV	Airbus A.320-214	easyJet Airline Co.Ltd
	G-EZTX	Airbus A.320-214	easyJet Airline Co.Ltd
	G-EZTY	Airbus A.320-214	easyJet Airline Co.Ltd
	G-EZTZ	Airbus A.320-214	easyJet Airline Co.Ltd
	G-EZUA	Airbus A.320-214	easyJet Airline Co.Ltd
	G-EZUB	Zenair CH.601HD Zodiac	M. J. Jackson
	G-EZUC	Airbus A.320-214	easyJet Airline Co.Ltd
	G-EZUF	Airbus A.320-214	easyJet Airline Co.Ltd
	G-EZUI	Airbus A.320-214	easyJet Airline Co.Ltd
	G-EZUK	Airbus A.320-214	easyJet Airline Co.Ltd
	G-EZUL	Airbus A.320-214	easyJet Airline Co.Ltd
	G-EZUN	Airbus A.320-214	easyJet Airline Co.Ltd
	G-EZUO	Airbus A.320-214	easyJet Airline Co.Ltd
	G-EZUP	Airbus A.320-214	easyJet Airline Co.Ltd
	G-EZUR	Airbus A.320-214	easyJet Airline Co.Ltd
	G-EZUS	Airbus A.320-214	easyJet Airline Co.Ltd
	G-EZUT	Airbus A.320-214	easyJet Airline Co.Ltd
	G-EZUW	Airbus A.320-214	easyJet Airline Co.Ltd
	G-EZUZ	Airbus A.320-214	easyJet Airline Co.Ltd

Reg	Type	Owner or Operator	Notes
G-EZWA	Airbus A.320-214	easyJet Airline Co.Ltd	
G-EZWB	Airbus A.320-214	easyJet Airline Co.Ltd	
G-EZWC	Airbus A.320-214	easyJet Airline Co.Ltd	
G-EZWD	Airbus A.320-214	easyJet Airline Co.Ltd	
G-EZWH	Airbus A.320-214	easyJet Airline Co.Ltd	
G-EZWI	Airbus A.320-214	easyJet Airline Co.Ltd	
G-EZWK	Airbus A.320-214	easyJet Airline Co.Ltd	
G-EZWL	Airbus A.320-214	easyJet Airline Co.Ltd	
G-EZWP	Airbus A.320-214	easyJet Airline Co.Ltd	
G-EZWR	Airbus A.320-214	easyJet Airline Co.Ltd	
G-EZWS	Airbus A.320-214	easyJet Airline Co.Ltd	
G-EZWU	Airbus A.320-214	easyJet Airline Co.Ltd	
G-EZWX	Airbus A.320-214	easyJet Airline Co.Ltd	
G-EZWY	Airbus A.320-214	easyJet Airline Co.Ltd	
G-EZWZ	Airbus A.320-214	easyJet Airline Co.Ltd	
G-EZXO	Colt 56A balloon	K. Jakobsson/Sweden	
G-EZZA	Europa XS	J. C. R. Davey	
G-EZZE	CZAW Sportcruiser	P. Hade	
G-EZZL	Westland Gazelle HT.3	Regal Group UK (G-CBKC)	
G-EZZY	Aerotechnik EV-97A Eurostar	D. P. Creedy	
G-FABA	PA-31-350 Navajo Chieftain	Gulfjet Aviation Ltd (G-OJIL)	
G-FABS	Thunder Ax9-120 S2 balloon	R. Corrall & A. B. Court	
G-FABV	Embraer EMB-550 Phenom 100	Gill Airways Ltd	
G-FABX	Ultramagic N-210 balloon	Fly Away Ballooning Ltd	
G-FACE	Cessna 172S	Oxford Aviation Services Ltd	
G-FADD	Skyranger Nynja 912S(1)	F. A. Dimmock	
G-FADE	Airbus AS.350B3 Ecureuil	Vyadom Aviation Inc	
G-FADF	PA-18-150 Super Cub	O. J. Smith	
G-FAGK	DH.60M Moth	G. Cormack	
G-FAJC	Alpi Pioneer 300 Hawk	S. T. Phoenix	
G-FALC	Aeromere F.8L Falco	D. M. Burbridge (G-AROT)	
G-FAME	Starstreak Shadow SA-II	N. I. Hart	
G-FAMJ	Agusta A109S Grand	Castle Air Ltd (G-LETO)	
G-FANL	Cessna FR.172K XP-II	Poyston Aviation	
G-FARL	Pitts S-1E Special	J. P. Barrenechea	
G-FARO	Aero Designs Star-Lite SL.1	S. C. Goozee	
G-FARR	Jodel 150	S. J. Farr	
G-FARY	QAC Quickie Tri-Q	A. Bloomfield	
G-FATB	Rockwell Commander 114B	James D. Pearce & Co	
G-FATE	Falco F8L	G-FATE Flying Group	
G-FAZT	Stoddard-Hamilton Glasair II-SRG	T. Klarenbeek	
G-FBAR	Diamond DA.40 Star	Exceedingly Ltd	
G-FBAT	Aeroprakt A.22 Foxbat	M. Sothorloy	
G-FBCY	Skystar Kitfox Mk 7	A. J. L. Eves (G-FBOY)	
G-FBFB	PA-32R-301 Saratoga SP	H. & S, Notley (G-ROLF)	
G-FBII	Ikarus C.42 FB100	J. A. Lynch	
G-FBKF	Cessna 510 Citation Mustang	Jetcom SRL/Italy	
G-FBPS	Cessna 208B Grand Caravan	British Parachute Schools Ltd	
G-FBRN	PA-28-181 Cherokee Archer II	G. E. Fox	
G-FBSS	Aeroprakt A22 LS Foxbat	S. R. V. McNeill	
G-FBVI	DH.98 Mosquito FB.VI replica	The People's Mosquito Ltd	
G-FBWH	PA-28R-180 Cherokee Arrow	Whiskey Hotel Flying Group	
G-FCAC	Diamond DA.42 Twin Star	ACS Aviation Ltd (G-ORZA)	
G-FCAT	Zenair CH.750	M. A. Potter (G-CLYN)	
G-FCAV	Schleicher ASK-13	M. F. Cuming	
G-FCCC	Schleicher ASK-13	Edgehill Gliding Centre Ltd	
G-FCKD	Eurocopter EC 120B	Red Dragon Management LLP	
G-FCOM	Slingsby T.59F Kestrel	P. A. C. Wheatcroft & A. G. Truman	
G-FCSL	PA-32-350 Navajo Chieftain	Flight Calibration Services Ltd (G-CLAN)	
G-FCSP	Robin DR.400/180	J. D. McCarthy	
G-FCTK	DH.82C Tiger Moth (5084)	R. J. Doughton	
G-FCTY	DHC.1B-2-S5 Chipmunk (18072/072)	Rayburn Properties Ltd	
G-FCUK	Pitts S-1C Special	C. E. Styles	
G-FDDB	PA-32RT-300 Lance II	B. Nedjati-Gilani (G-NROY/G-LYNN/G-BGNY)	
G-FDHB	Bristol Scout Model C Replica (1264)	Bristol Scout Group	
G-FDHS	Leonardo AW109SP Grand New	Pendley Aviation LLP	
G-FDZD	Boeing 737-8K5	TUI Airways Ltd	

Notes	Reg	Type	Owner or Operator
	G-FDZR	Boeing 737-8K5	TUI Airways Ltd
	G-FDZS	Boeing 737-8K5	TUI Airways Ltd
	G-FDZX	Boeing 737-8K5	TUI Airways Ltd
	G-FDZY	Boeing 737-8K5	TUI Airways Ltd
	G-FDZZ	Boeing 737-8K5	TUI Airways Ltd
	G-FEAB	PA-28-181 Cherokee Archer III	R. W. Nash
	G-FEBB	Grob G.104 Speed Astir IIB	C. P. A. Jones
	G-FEBJ	Schleicher ASW-19B	N. C. Day
	G-FEBU	DG Flugzeugbau DG-1000S	University of Bristol
	G-FECK	Raj Hamsa X'Air Jabiru(3)	R. J. Spence (G-CDSN)
	G-FECO	Grob G.102 Astir CS77	Stratford on Avon Gliding Club
	G-FEEN	Cewssna F.182Q	J. J. M. Feeney
	G-FEET	Mainair Pegasus Quik	G. Burns
	G-FEGN	PA-28-236 Dakota	G-FEGN Group Ltd
	G-FELC	Cirrus SR22	D. Norman
	G-FELD	Rotorsport UK MTO Sport	S. Pearce
	G-FELL	Europa	M. C. Costin & J. A. Inglis
	G-FELX	CZAW Sportcruiser	T. F. Smith
	G-FERO	Zenair CH.701SP	P. M. Porter
	G-FERV	Rolladen-Schneider LS4	S. Walker
	G-FESB	Pipistrel Apis 15M M FES	B. N. Searle
	G-FESH	Allstar PZL SZD-54 2 Perkoz	Cairngorm Gliding Club
	G-FESS	Pegasus Quantum 15-912	P. M. Fessi (G-CBBZ)
	G-FESX	Schempp-Hirth Discus 2C FES	P. K. Carpenter
	G-FEVS	PZL-Bielsko SZD-50-3 Puchacz	Norfolk Gliding Club Ltd
	G-FEWG	Fuji FA.200-160	Cirrus UK Training Ltd (G-BBNV)
	G-FFAB	Cameron N-105 balloon	G. A. Boyle
	G-FFAF	Cessna F.150L	Bnett Aviation Ltd
	G-FFBG	Cessna F.182Q	Synnova Aviation Ltd
	G-FFFA	P & M PulsR	I. A. Macadam
	G-FFFB	P & M Quik GTR	Flying for Freedom Ltd
	G-FFFF	Zenair CH.750	J. Bate
	G-FFFT	Lindstrand LBL-31A balloon	G. B. Dey
	G-FFIT	Pegasus Quik	M. J. Hyde
	G-FFMV	Diamond DA.42 M-NG Twin Star	FR Aviation Ltd t/a Draken
	G-FFRA	Dassault Falcon 20DC	FR Aviation Ltd t/a Draken
	G-FFRL	Eurocopter EC120B Colibri	BEMC Corporate Hire Ltd
	G-FFRV	Van's RV-10	J. M. Bostock
	G-FFUN	Pegasus Quantum 15	M. D. & R. M. Jarvis
	G-FFWD	Cessna 310R	T. S. Courtman (G-TVKE/G-EURO)
	G-FGAZ	Schleicher Ka 6E	S. E. Chew
	G-FGRP	Agusta A.109E Power	PRF (Agusta) Ltd (G-JBCB/G-PLPL/G-TMWC)
	G-FGSI	Montgomerie-Bensen B8MR	F. G. Shepherd
	G-FHAS	Scheibe SF.25E Super Falke	Upwood Motorglider Group
	G-FHFX	Wmbraer EMB-550 Praetor 600	Flexjet Ltd
	G-FHJS	HA-420 Hondajet	Astrajet Ltd
	G-FHJT	HA-420 Hondajet	Bookajet Aircraft Management Ltd
	G-FIAT	PA-28 Cherokee 140	LS Airmotive Ltd (G-BBYW)
	G-FICS	Flight Design CTSW	N. Harris
	G-FIDO	Skyranger Nynja 912S(1)	G. J. Pearce
	G-FIFA	Cessna 404 Titan	RVL Aviation Ltd (G-TVIP/G-KIWI/G-BHNI)
	G-FIFE	Cessna FA.152	CG Aviation Ltd (G-BFYN)
	G-FIFI	SOCATA TB20 Trinidad	The Foxtrot India Group (G-BMWS)
	G-FIFT	Ikarus C.42 FB 100	S. R. Moore
	G-FIGB	Cessna 152	A. J. Gomes
	G-FINA	Cessna F.150L	K. M. Rigby (G-BIFT)
	G-FIND	Cessna F.406	RVL Aviation Ltd
	G-FINT	Piper L-4B Grasshopper (43583)	G. & H. M. Picarella
	G-FINZ	I.I.I Sky Arrow 650T	K. A. Daniels
	G-FITC	Pilatus PC-12/47E	Elstree Ink Ltd
	G-FITY	Europa XS	Lios Cathain Group
	G-FIXR	Flylight Skyranger Nynja 912S	P. S. Bates
	G-FIXX	Van's RV-7	P. C. Hambilton
	G-FIZY	Europa XS	B. C. W. Easdown (G-DDSC)
	G-FIZZ	PA-28-161 Cherokee Warrior II	G-FIZZ Group

Reg	Type	Owner or Operator	Notes
G-FJCE	Thruster T600T	P. F. McConville	
G-FJMS	Partenavia P.68B	Ravenair Aircraft Ltd (G-SVHA)	
G-FJTH	Aeroprakt A.22 Foxbat	A. J. Tuson	
G-FKKR	Fokker D.VII replica	P. D. & S. E. Ford	
G-FKNH	PA-15 Vagabond	M. J. Mothershaw	
G-FKOS	PA-28-181 Cherokee Archer II	SVM Glasgow	
G-FLAG	Colt 77A balloon	J. Phillips	
G-FLAV	PA-28-161 Cherokee Warrior II	G. E. Fox	
G-FLAX	Eurofox 914	Lleweni Parc Ltd	
G-FLBX	Eurofox 914	Bumblebee Group	
G-FLBY	Ikarus C42 FB100 Bravo	Air Cornwall	
G-FLCA	Fleet Model 80 Canuck	S. P. Evans	
G-FLDG	Skyranger 912	G. E. Parker	
G-FLEA	SOCATA TB10 Tobago	N. J. Thomas	
G-FLEE	Ivanov ZJ-Viera	T. H. Knapton	
G-FLEW	Lindstrand LBL-90A balloon	H. C. Loveday	
G-FLIA	AutoGyro Calidus	I. H. Clarke	
G-FLIE	TL2000 Sting S4	A. J. Byford & S. R. Wilkinson	
G-FLIK	Pitts S-1S Special	R. P. Millinship	
G-FLIP	Cessna FA.152	Invicta Aero Club Ltd (G-BOES)	
G-FLIS	Magni M.16C	W. R. Roach	
G-FLKE	Scheibe SF.25C Falke	The Royal Air Force Gliding & Soaring Association	
G-FLKS	Scheibe SF.25C Falke	London Gliding Club Propietary Ltd	
G-FLOE	Robinson R66	Air DM Ltd	
G-FLOH	Cessna 208B Grand Caravan	British Parachute Schools Ltd	
G-FLOR	Europa	D. Jones	
G-FLOW	Cessna 172N	P. H. Archard	
G-FLOX	Europa	N. T. Read	
G-FLPI	Rockwell Commander 112	J. B. Thompson	
G-FLUZ	Rolladen-Schneider LS8-18	D. M. King	
G-FLXI	Pilatus PC-12/47E	Flexifly Aircraft Hire Ltd	
G-FLXY	PA-28-181 Cherokee Archer	Flexifly Aircraft Hire Ltd	
G-FLXZ	PA-28-181 Cherokee Archer	Flexifly Aircraft Hire Ltd	
G-FLYB	Ikarus C42 FB100	Air Sea Land Ltd	
G-FLYC	Ikarus C.42 FB100	Solent Flight Ltd	
G-FLYG	Slingsby T.67C	G. Laden	
G-FLYJ	EV-97 Eurostar SL	G-FLYJ Group	
G-FLYK	Beech B.200 Super King Air	D. T. A. Rees	
G-FLYO	EV-97 Eurostar SL	N. A. & P. A. Allwood	
G-FLYP	Beagle B.206 Srs 2	A. T. J. Darrah (G-AVHO)	
G-FLYT	Europa	K. F. & R. Richardson	
G-FLYW	Beech B.200 Super King Air	Poyston Aviation (G-LIVY/C-PETR)	
G-FLZR	Staaken Z-21 Flitzer	I. V. Staines	
G-FMAC	Allstar PZL SZD-54-2 Perkoz	Deeside Gliding Cliub (Aberdeenshire) Ltd	
G-FMAM	PA-28-151 Cherokee Warrior (modified)	I. Denham-Brown (G-BBXV)	
G-FMBS	Inverted US 12	W. P. Wright	
G-FMGB	Cameron Z-90 balloon	John Aimo Balloons SAS/Italy	
G-FMGG	Maule M5-235C Lunar Rocket	E. Bierbaum (C RACC)	
G-FMLY	Commander 114B	Falcon Flying Group (G-VICS)	
G-FNEY	Cessna F.177RG	F. Ney	
G-FNLD	Cessna 172N	A. J. Brown & R. C. Laming	
G-FNOT	Scheibe SF.25C Falke 2000	The TMG Syndicate (Milfield)	
G-FOCX	Eurofox 2K	P. R. Simmonds-Short	
G-FOEW	M + R BM-77	N. M. Musson & J. M. Retallick	
G-FOFO	Robinson R44 II	Countrywide Commercial Ltd	
G-FOGI	Europa XS	C. M. Carrington-Smith	
G-FOHN	Schempp-Hirth Ventus 2b	J. C. Bastin (G-XJON)	
G-FOKK	Fokker DR1 (replica) (477/17)	P. D. & S. E. Ford	
G-FOKR	Fokker E.III (replica) (422/15)	R. D. Myles	
G-FOKS	Eurofox 912(S)	E. R. Scougall	
G-FOKX	Eurofox 912(S)	Trent Valley Eurofox Group	
G-FOKZ	Eurofox 912(IS)	D. J. MacPherson	
G-FOLY	Aerotek Pitts S-2A Modified	C. T. Charleston	
G-FOMO	Bombardier BD700-1A10 Global 6000	London Executive Aviation Ltd	
G-FOOJ	Fuji FA-200-160 Aero Subaru	Euro Aircraft Leasing Ltd	

Notes	Reg	Type	Owner or Operator
	G-FOOT	Robinson R44 I	Swift Helicopter Services Ltd
	G-FOPP	Lancair 320	Great Circle Design Ltd
	G-FORA	Schempp-Hirth Ventus cT	K. R. Walton & G. D. Tucker
	G-FORB	Bristell NG5 Speed Wing	A. Forbes
	G-FORD	SNCAN Stampe SV.4C	P. H. Meeson
	G-FORG	AA-5B Tiger	J. D. de Jager (G-WINK)
	G-FORH	J-3C-90 Cub	D. A. & R-R. J. Cadman
	G-FORZ	Pitts S-1S Special	N. W. Parkinson
	G-FOST	Leonardo AW139	Helioperations
	G-FOSY	MS.880B Rallye Club	A. G. Foster (G-AXAK)
	G-FOTN	Van's RV-7	M. T. Manwaring
	G-FOWL	Colt 90A balloon	M. R. Stokoe
	G-FOWR	Bell 206L-3 Long Ranger III	GBF Aviation Ltd (G-CDYR)
	G-FOXA	PA-28-161 Cadet	Leicestershire Aero Club Ltd
	G-FOXB	Aeroprakt A.22 Foxbat	G. D. McCullough
	G-FOXC	Denney Kitfox Mk 3	T. Willford & R. M. Bremner
	G-FOXD	Denney Kitfox Mk 2	Solent Fox Flying Group
	G-FOXF	Denney Kitfox Mk 4	J. H. H. Turner
	G-FOXH	Schempp-Hirth Ventus-2a	O. M. McCormack
	G-FOXI	Denney Kitfox	I. M. Walton
	G-FOXL	Zenair CH.601XL Zodiac	R. W. Taylor
	G-FOXM	Bell 206B JetRanger 2	Hessle Dock Company Ltd (G-STAK/G-BNIS)
	G-FOXO	Eurofox 912(S)	S. A. Richardson
	G-FOXP	Cessna 208 Caravan 1	British Parachute Schools Ltd
	G-FOXS	Denney Kitfox Mk 2	R. Holmes
	G-FOXT	Aeros Ant/Fox 13TL	R. Bower
	G-FOXU	Eurofox 912S(1)	T. C. Hilder
	G-FOXV	Aeroprakt A22-LS Foxbat	D. F. P. Finan (G-CHSY)
	G-FOXW	Aeropro Eurofox 912(1)	A. P. Whitmarsh
	G-FOXX	Denney Kitfox	J. Skelson
	G-FOXZ	Denney Kitfox	S. C. Goozee
	G-FOZY	Van's RV-7	J. R. Parkinson (G-COPZ)
	G-FPEH	Guimbal Cabri G2	Elstree Helicopters Ltd
	G-FPIG	PA-28-151 Cherokee Warrior	G. F. Strain (G-BSSR)
	G-FPLD	Beech 200 Super King Air	Thales UK Ltd
	G-FPRD	Cirrus SR22	F. Pearson & R. G. Drury
	G-FPSA	PA-28-161 Cherokee Warrior II	Falcon Flying Services (G-RSFT/G-WARI)
	G-FRAD	Dassault Falcon 20E	FR Aviation Ltd t/a Draken (G-BCYF)
	G-FRAF	Dassault Falcon 20E	FR Aviation Ltd t/a Draken
	G-FRAG	PA-32-300E Cherokee Six	Frag Aviation Ltd
	G-FRAH	Dassault Falcon 20DC	FR Aviation Ltd t/a Draken
	G-FRAI	Dassault Falcon 20E	FR Aviation Ltd t/a Draken
	G-FRAJ	Dassault Falcon 20E	FR Aviation Ltd t/a Draken
	G-FRAK	Dassault Falcon 20DC	FR Aviation Ltd t/a Draken
	G-FRAL	Dassault Falcon 20DC	FR Aviation Ltd t/a Draken
	G-FRAN	Piper J-3C-90 Cub (480321:H-44)	Essex L-4 Group (G-BIXY)
	G-FRAP	Dassault Falcon 20DC	FR Aviation Ltd t/a Draken
	G-FRAR	Dassault Falcon 20DC	FR Aviation Ltd t/a Draken
	G-FRAS	Dassault Falcon 20C	FR Aviation Ltd t/a Draken
	G-FRAT	Dassault Falcon 20C	FR Aviation Ltd t/a Draken
	G-FRAU	Dassault Falcon 20C	FR Aviation Ltd t/a Draken
	G-FRAW	Dassault Falcon 20ECM	FR Aviation Ltd t/a Draken
	G-FRCE	Folland Gnat T.Mk.1 (XS104)	Red Gnat Ltd
	G-FRCX	P & M Quik GTR	N. J. Perrell
	G-FRDY	Dynamic WT9 UK	J. A. Lockert
	G-FREY	Cirrus SR20	M. J. Jones & S. M. L. Pegg
	G-FRGP	Leonardo AW109SP Grand New	SDI Aviation Ltd
	G-FRJB	Britten Sheriff SA-1 ★	Aeropark/East Midlands
	G-FRNK	Skyranger Swift 912(1)	G. Lace
	G-FROB	Diamond DA.40 NG	B. A. Collins
	G-FROM	Ikarus C.42 FB100	D. P. Tidmas
	G-FRSB	Dassault Falcon 20F-5	Cobham Aviation Services UK
	G-FRSX	VS.388 Seafire F.46 (LA564)	Seafire Displays Ltd
	G-FRYA	Robinson R44 II	Helicentre Aviation Ltd (G-EJRC)
	G-FSAR	Agusta Westland AW189	Bristow Helicopters Ltd
	G-FSBW	Eurofox 912S(1)	N. G. Heywood
	G-FSID	North American P-51D-30-NT Mustang	517 Ltd
	G-FSKY	Skyranger Nynja	The Scottish Aero Club Ltd

Reg	Type	Owner or Operator	Notes
G-FSZY	TB-10 Tobago	R. Arquier	
G-FTAC	PA-28-161 Cherokee Warrior II	Burraq Aviation Ltd	
G-FTAD	PA-28-161 Cherokee Warrior II	Tesla Solutions Ltd	
G-FTAF	PA-28-161 Cherokee Warrior II	Oxfordshire Sportflying Ltd (G-BOKB)	
G-FTAI	Boeing 757-256	2 Excel Aviation Ltd (G-POWH)	
G-FTAX	Cessna 421C	Gold Air International Ltd (G-BFFM)	
G-FTFX	Embraer EMB-550 Praetor 600	Flexjet Ltd	
G-FTIL	Robin DR.400/180R	S. M. Pink & S. Hardy	
G-FTRO	Cessna F.152	S. D. Braddon	
G-FTUS	Ultramagic F-12 Paquete balloon	A. M. Holly	
G-FUEL	Robin DR.400/180	S. L. G. Darch	
G-FUEU	Pitts S-1C Special	R. Harrison	
G-FUJE	Fuji FA-200-180 Aero Subaru	C. Killops	
G-FUKM	Westland Gazelle AH.1 (ZA730)	Falcon Aviation Ltd	
G-FULL	PA-28R Cherokee Arrow 200-II	Stapleford Flying Club Ltd (G-HWAY/G-JULI)	
G-FUND	Thunder Ax7-65Z balloon	G. B. Davies	
G-FUNN	Plumb BGP-1A	N. F. Shorter	
G-FURI	Isaacs Fury II	S. M. Johnston	
G-FURO	Furio	Falcotec Ltd	
G-FURZ	Sky Ranger Nynja 912S(1)	S. M. Bridgwood	
G-FUSE	Cameron N-105 balloon	J. C. M. Greatrix	
G-FUUN	Silence SA.180 Twister	A. W. McKee	
G-FUXM	Supermarine Spitfire Mk.26B	The Mitchell and Royce Spitfire	
G-FUZZ	PA-18-95 Super Cub (51-15319)	M. G. Cline	
G-FVEE	Monnett Sonerai 1	J. S. Baldwin	
G-FVEL	Cameron Z-90 balloon	Fort Vale Engineering Ltd	
G-FVUK	Cameron Sport-90 balloon	Fort Vale Engineering Ltd	
G-FWJR	Ultramagic M-56 balloon	Harding and Sons Ltd	
G-FWKS	Tanarg/Ixess 15 912S(2)	M. A. Coffin (G-SYUT)	
G-FWLR	Flylight PeaBee Yellow Line	G. M. Fowler	
G-FWPW	PA-28-236 Dakota	Channel Islands Aircraft Maintenance Ltd	
G-FWRK	Cameron Z-0105 balloon	Sky High Ballooning Ltd	
G-FXBA	Aeroprakt A22-LS Foxbat	R. G. G. Pinder	
G-FXBT	Aeroprakt A.22 Foxbat	T. G. F. Trenchard & T. Willford	
G-FXCT	Sikorsky S-92A	Flexjet Helicopters (G-LAWX)	
G-FXER	Raytheon 400A	Flexjet Ltd	
G-FXII	VS.366 Spitfire F.XII (EN224)	Twyford Aviation Services (UK) Ltd	
G-FXVA	Sikorsky S-76C	Flexjet Helicopters	
G-FXVC	Sikorsky S-76C	Flexjet Helicopters(G-XXEB)	
G-FXXC	Rutan Long Ez	C. J. Fox	
G-FYAN	Williams Westwind MLB	M. D. Williams	
G-FYAO	Williams Westwind MLB	M. D. Williams	
G-FYAU	Williams Westwind Mk 2 MLB	M. D. Williams	
G-FYAV	Osprey Mk 4E2 MLB	C. D. Egan & C. Stiles	
G-FYBX	Portswood Mk XVI MLB	I. Chadwick	
G-FYCL	Osprey Mk 4G MLB	P. J. Rogers	
G-FYCV	Osprey Mk 4D MLB	M. Thomson	
G-FYDF	Osprey Mk 4DV	K. A. Jones	
G-FYDI	Williams Westwind Two MLB	M. D. Williams	
G-FYDN	European 8C MLB	P. D. Ridout	
G-FYDO	Osprey Mk 4D MLB	N. L. Scallan	
G-FYDP	Williams Westwind Three MLB	M. D. Williams	
G-FYDS	Osprey Mk 4D MLB	N. L. Scallan	
G-FYEK	Unicorn UE.1C MLB	D. & D. Eaves	
G-FYEO	Eagle Mk 1 MLB	M. E. Scallan	
G-FYEV	Osprey Mk 1C MLB	M. E. Scallan	
G-FYEZ	Firefly Mk 1 MLB	M. E. & N. L. Scallan	
G-FYFI	European E.84DS MLB	M. Stelling	
G-FYFJ	Williams Westland 2 MLB	M. D. Williams	
G-FYFN	Osprey Saturn 2 MLB	J. & M. Woods	
G-FYFW	Rango NA-55 MLB	Rango Balloon and Kite Company	
G-FYFY	Rango NA-55RC MLB	Rango Balloon and Kite Company	
G-FYGC	Rango NA-42B MLB	L. J. Wardle	
G-FYGJ	Airspeed 300 MLB	N. Wells	
G-FYGM	Saffrey/Smith Princess MLB	A. Smith	

Notes	Reg	Type	Owner or Operator
	G-FZZA	General Avia F22-A	W. A. Stewart
	G-FZZI	Cameron H-34 balloon	Magical Adventures Ltd
	G-GAAL	Cessna 560XL Citation XLS	London Executive Aviation Ltd (G-DEIA)
	G-GAAZ	Cessna F.172N	M. Haller
	G-GABI	Lindstrand LBL-35A Cloudhopper balloon	R. D. Sargeant
	G-GABS	Cameron TR-70 balloon	L. A. & M. R. Hulbert
	G-GACA	P.57 Sea Prince T.1 (WP308:572CU) ★	Gatwick Aviation Museum/Charlwood
	G-GACB	Robinson R44 II	East Midlands Helicopters Engineering Ltd
	G-GACE	Flylight Nine	Ace Aviation
	G-GAGE	Cameron Z-105 balloon	A. J. Thompson
	G-GAIA	TAF Sling 2	M. Dutton
	G-GAII	Hawker Hunter GA.11 (XE685)	S. W. Turley
	G-GAJB	AA-5B Tiger	G-GAJB Group (G-BHZN)
	G-GALB	PA-28-161 Cherokee Warrior II	Gamston Flying School Ltd
	G-GALI	Agusta Westland AW.109SP Grand New	Gall Air LLP (G-HLSA/G-HCOM)
	G-GAMA	Beech 58 Baron	Gama Aviation (UK) Ltd (G-WWIZ/G-BBSD)
	G-GAMB	Game Composites GB1 Gamebird	A. R. Haynes
	G-GAME	Cessna T.303	P. Wadsley
	G-GAMM	Agusta AW109SP Grand New	Hadleigh Aviation LLP (G-CHFD)
	G-GAND	Agusta-Bell 206B Jet Ranger	R. Henderson (G-AWMK)
	G-GAOH	Robin DR.400 / 2 +2	Yeovilton Flying Club
	G-GAOM	Robin DR.400 / 2+2	Marine & Aviation Ltd
	G-GAPC	Cirrus SR22T	A. P. Cunningham
	G-GARE	Cessna 560XL Citation XLS	Virtus Aviation Ltd
	G-GARI	Ace Aviation Touch/Buzz	G. B. Shaw
	G-GASI	Ballonbau Worner NL-STU/1000 balloon	M. A. & D. J. Scholes
	G-GASP	PA-28-181 Cherokee Archer II	G-GASP Flying Group
	G-GAST	Van's RV-8	G. M. R. Abrey
	G-GATH	Airbus A.320-232	BA Euroflyer Ltd
	G-GATK	Airbus A.320-232	BA Euroflyer Ltd
	G-GATL	Airbus A.320-232	BA Euroflyer Ltd
	G-GATM	Airbus A.320-232	BA Euroflyer Ltd
	G-GATN	Airbus A.320-232	BA Euroflyer Ltd
	G-GATP	Airbus A.320-232	BA Euroflyer Ltd
	G-GATR	Airbus A.320-232	BA Euroflyer Ltd
	G-GATS	Airbus A.320-232	BA Euroflyer Ltd
	G-GATT	Robinson R44 II	B. W. Faulkner
	G-GATU	Airbus A.320-232	BA Euroflyer Ltd
	G-GAVH	P & M Quik	S. Dixon
	G-GAVV	Flight Design CTSL	G. Hardman
	G-GAWA	Cessna 140	C140 Group (G-BRSM)
	G-GAXC	Robin R2160 Alpha Sport	JW Aviation Ltd
	G-GAZA	Aérospatiale SA.341G Gazelle 1	Excel Charter Ltd (G-RALE/G-SFTG)
	G-GAZN	P & M Quik GT450	C. Hughes
	G-GAZO	Ace Magic Cyclone	J. Mooney
	G-GAZZ	Aérospatiale SA.341G Gazelle 1	Cheqair Ltd
	G-GBAO	Robin R1180TD	E. R. Hall
	G-GBAS	Diamond DA.62	Flight Calibration Services Ltd
	G-GBBB	Schleicher ASH-25	BB Glider Syndicate
	G-GBBT	Ultramagic M-90 balloon	S. J. Nicholls
	G-GBCC	Ikarus C42 FB100	J. A. Lynch
	G-GBEE	Mainair Pegasus Quik	K. A. Knowles
	G-GBET	Ikarus C42 FB UK	P. K. Meech (G-BDBMK/G-MROY)
	G-GBFI	Kreimendahl K-10 Shoestring	T. Jarvis
	G-GBFR	Cessna F.177RG	Airspeed Aviation Ltd
	G-GBGA	Scheibe SF.25C Falke	The Royal Air Force Gliding and Soaring Association
	G-GBGB	Ultramagic M.105 balloon	S. A. Nother
	G-GBGF	Cameron Dragon SS balloon	Magical Adventures Ltd (G-BUVH)
	G-GBLP	Cessna F.172M	Leading Edge Flight Training Ltd (G-GWEN)
	G-GBMM	Agusta A109S Grand	Orchard Holdings Ltd (G-GRND)
	G-GBNI	Airbus A.321-251NX	Titan Airways Ltd (G-POWT)
	G-GBNZ	Eurofox 912(iS)	C. F. Pote
	G-GBOB	Alpi Pioneer 300 Hawk	J. A. Harris
	G-GBPP	Rolladen-Schneider LS6-c18	G. J. Lyons
	G-GBRB	PA-28 Cherokee 180C	Bravo Romeo Group
	G-CBRI	Skyranger Nynja 912S	R. A. J. Parris
	G-GBRV	Van's RV-9A	J. S. Chaggar (G-THMB)
	G-GBSD	TL2000UK Sting Carbon S4	Sting Air Ltd

Reg	Type	Owner or Operator	Notes
G-GBSL	Beech 76 Duchess	M. H. Cundey & R. D. A. Berliand (G-BGVG)	
G-GBTV	Eurocopter AS.355N Ecureuil II	Cheshire Helicopters Ltd	
G-GBUA	Aeroprakt A-32 Vixxen	D. J. Sladden (G-DREW)	
G-GBUE	Robin DR.400/120A	J. A. Kane (G-BPXD)	
G-GBUN	Cessna 182T	G. M. Bunn	
G-GBVN	Robin DR400/180	Bicester Robin Crew	
G-GBVX	Robin DR400/120A	P. Murphy & G. H. Johns	
G-GBXL	Just Superstol XL	M. P. Wilkinson	
G-GCAC	Europa XS T-G	D. S. Tarmey & L. S. Roberts	
G-GCAT	PA-28-140 Cherokee B	A. M. S. Sher (G-BFRH)	
G-GCDA	Cirrus SR20	Cirrus RRST Group	
G-GCDB	Cirrus SR20	Golf Golf Ltd	
G-GCEA	P & M Quik	D. L. Marshall	
G-GCIY	Robin DR.400-140B	M. S. Lonsdale	
G-GCJA	Rolladen-Schneider LS8-18	N. T. Mallender	
G-GCKI	Mooney M.20K	T. W. Gilbert	
G-GCLC	PA-18-150 Super Cub	P. J. Harvey (G-BAKV)	
G-GCMS	Exodus Deltajet 500 Stingray	C. M. Saysell	
G-GCMW	Grob G.102 Astir CS	Portsmouth Naval Gliding Centre	
G-GCUF	Robin DR400/160	Bolter's Dowry Ltd	
G-GCVV	Cirrus SR22	Daedalus Aviation (Services) Ltd	
G-GCYC	Cessna F.182Q	The Cessna 180 Group	
G-GDAC	AA-5A Cheetah	D. S. Tarmey	
G-GDAV	Robinson R44 II	G. H. Weston	
G-GDEF	Robin DR.400/120	J. M. Shackleton	
G-GDER	Robin R.1180TD	Berkshire Aviation Services Ltd	
G-GDFC	Boeing 737-8K2	Jet 2	
G-GDFD	Boeing 737-8K5	Jet 2	
G-GDFF	Boeing 737-85P	Jet 2	
G-GDFG	Boeing 737-36Q	Jet 2	
G-GDFJ	Boeing 737-804	Jet 2 (G-CDZI)	
G-GDFK	Boeing 737-36N	Jet 2 (G-STRE/G-XBHX)	
G-GDFL	Boeing 737-36N	Jet 2	
G-GDFM	Boeing 737-36N	Jet 2	
G-GDFN	Boeing 737-33V	Jet 2 (G-EZYH)	
G-GDFO	Boeing 737-3U3	Jet 2 (G-THOP)	
G-GDFP	Boeing 737-8Z9	Jet 2	
G-GDFR	Boeing 737-8Z9	Jet 2	
G-GDFS	Boeing 737-86N	Jet 2	
G-GDFT	Boeing 737-36Q	Jet 2 (G-TOYM/G-OHAJ)	
G-GDFU	Boeing 737-8K5	Jet 2	
G-GDFV	Boeing 737-85F	Jet 2	
G-GDFW	Boeing 737-8K5	Jet 2	
G-GDFX	Boeing 737-8K5	Jet 2	
G-GDFY	Boeing 737-86Q	Jet 2	
G-GDFZ	Boeing 737-86Q	Jet 2	
G-GDHI	Boeing 737-8K5	Jet 2	
G-GDIA	Cessna F.152	Skytrek Flying School Ltd	
G-GDJM	Autogyro Cavalon	D. Howell	
G-GDKI	Robin DR400/120	W. H. Cole	
G-GDKR	Robin DR400/140B	Hampshire Flying Group	
G-GDOG	PA-28R-200 Cherokee Arrow	The Mutley Crew Group (G-BDXW)	
G-GDRV	Van's RV-6	J. G. Holmes	
G-GDSO	Autogyro Cavalon	P. Setterfield	
G-GDSP	Leonardo A109S Trekker	DSP Helicopters	
G-GDTU	Avions Mudry CAP-10B	R. W. H. Cole	
G-GECO	Hughes 369HS	Southern Heli Ops Ltd (G-TVEE/G-GCXK)	
G-GEEP	Robin R.1180TD	The Aiglon Flying Group	
G-GEHL	Cessna 172S	K. A. & M. Whittaker	
G-GEHP	PA-28RT-201 Cherokee Arrow IV	J. D. C. Lea	
G-GEJS	Extra EA300/LT	G. Sealey	
G-GELB	Hill Helicvopters HX50	Hill Helicopters Ltd	
G-GELI	Colt 31A balloon	M. Rowlands (G-CDFI)	
G-GEMX	P & M Quik GT450	L. A. Harris	
G-GEOS	Diamond HK.36 TTC-ECO Super Dimona	University Court (School of Geosciences) of the University of Edinburgh	
G-GERI	Robinson R44 1	Robraven Ltd	
G-GETU	Leonardo AW169	Leonardo SPA	

Notes	Reg	Type	Owner or Operator
	G-GEZZ	Bell 206B JetRanger II	Phoenix Building Systems Ltd
	G-GFCA	PA-28-161 Cadet	S. Danson
	G-GFCB	PA-28-161 Cadet	Falcon Flying Services Ltd
	G-GFEF	Schempp-Hirth Ventus 3T	D. P. Francis
	G-GFIB	Cessna F.152 II	Westair Flying Services Ltd (G-BPIO)
	G-GFIG	Cessna 152	The Pilot Centre Ltd (G-BNOZ)
	G-GFKY	Zenair CH.250	R. G. Kelsall
	G-GFLY	Cessna F.150L	Speur Aviation Ltd
	G-GFNO	Robin ATL	M. J. Pink
	G-GFOA	PA-28-161 Cherokee Warrior II	P. M. Jones
	G-GFRA	PA-28RT-201T Turbo Cherokee Arrow IV	Ravenair Aircraft Ltd (G-LROY/G-BNTS)
	G-GFTA	PA-28-161 Cherokee Warrior III	Guernsey Flying Training Ltd
	G-GFUN	Eurofox 2K	L. S. Williams
	G-GFZG	PA-28-140 Cherokee E	Guar Flying Group
	G-GGBD	PA-32R-301T Turbo Saratoga	M. R. Crossley
	G-GGDV	Schleicher Ka 6E	I. L. Pattingale
	G-GGEM	PA-28-161 Cherokee Warrior III	Hull Aero Club Ltd
	G-GGHZ	Robin ATL	M. J. Pink
	G-GGJK	Robin DR.400/140B	Headcorn Jodelers
	G-GGPC	Bell 407	Figgle LLP
	G-GGRH	Robinson R44	Heli Air Ltd
	G-GGRN	PA-28R-201 Cherokee Arrow III	J. P. Durnford
	G-GGRR	SA Bulldog Srs 120/121 (XX614:V)	J. D. Howard (G-CBAM)
	G-GGRV	Van's RV-8	C. F. O'Neill
	G-GGTR	Pegasus Quik GTR	T. D. Lee
	G-GGTT	Agusta-Bell 47G-4A	P. R. Smith
	G-GGWP	Stemme S12	K. Segerstrale
	G-GGZZ	Aviat A-1B Husky	Honesdale Ltd
	G-GHEE	Aerotechnik EV-97 Eurostar	P. R. Howson
	G-GHER	AS.355N Ecureuil II	Gallagher Air LLP
	G-GHOP	Cameron Z-77 balloon	David P Hopkins
	G-GHRW	PA-28RT-201 Cherokee Arrow IV	P. Cowley (G-ONAB/G-BHAK)
	G-GHST	Ikarus C42C FB100	The Ikarus Flying Group
	G-GHSV	Beech 200 Super King Air	Atlantic Bridge Aviation Lt
	G-GHZJ	SOCATA TB9 Tampico	P. K. Hayward
	G-GIAN	Ikarus C42 FB100	C. A. Hasell
	G-GIAS	Ikarus C42 FB80	Athey's Moor Flying School Ltd
	G-GIGZ	Van's RV-8	N. G. Rhind & K. A. A. McDonald
	G-GIMT	Diamond DA.62	Diamond Flight Training Co.Ltd
	G-GIPC	PA-32R-301 Saratoga SP	GIPC Flying Group
	G-GIRY	AG-5B Tiger	Romeo Yankee Flying Group
	G-GIWT	Europa XS	A. Twigg
	G-GJCD	Robinson R22 Beta	J. C. Lane
	G-GJIM	Diamond DA.62	J. Hartley
	G-GJOA	Eurofox 2K	G. B. Porter
	G-GKAT	Enstrom 280C	D. G. Allsop & A. J. Clark
	G-GKEA	Hughes 369E	Forties Aviation LLP
	G-GKFC	RL-5A LW Sherwood Ranger	J. S. Greenroyd (G-MYZI)
	G-GKKI	Avions Mudry CAP 231EX	D. R. Farley
	G-GKRC	Cessna 180K	W. J. Pitts
	G-GKUE	SOCATA TB-9 Tampico Club	M. Ali & Denderah SA
	G-GLAA	Eurocopter EC135 T2	PDG Helicopters and PDG Aviation Services
	G-GLAB	Eurocopter EC135 T2+	PDG Helicopters and PDG Aviation Services (G-CFFR)
	G-GLAD	Gloster G.37 Gladiator II (N5903:H)	Patina Ltd
	G-GLAK	AB Sportine LAK-12	M. Tolson
	G-GLAW	Cameron N-90 balloon	A. S. Davidson
	G-GLCM	PA-32R-300 Cherokee Lance	S. Lane
	G-GLED	Cessna 150M	Westminster Academies Ltd
	G-GLHI	Skyranger 912	K. R. Hine
	G-GLII	Great Lakes 2T-1A-2	T. J. Richardson
	G-GLLY	Bell 505 Jet Ranger X	A. J. Reynard
	G-GLOC	Extra EA.300/200	Modern Air (UK) Ltd
	G-GLSA	EV-97 Eurostar SL	G-GLSA Group

Reg	Type	Owner or Operator	Notes
G-GLST	Great Lakes Sport Trainer	T. Boehmerle & A. Hofmann	
G-GLUC	Van's RV-6	N. I. Claughton	
G-GLUE	Cameron N-65 balloon	L. J. M. Muir	
G-GLVZ	Magni M24C Plus	A. C. S. M. Hart	
G-GMAE	Beech B.200 Super King Air	Gama Aviation (UK) Ltd	
G-GMAF	Beech B.200 Super King Air	Gama Aviation (UK) Ltd	
G-GMAH	Airbus MBB BK117 D-2	Gama Aviation (UK) Ltd	
G-GMAX	SNCAN Stampe SV.4C	M. E. Carrell (G-BNXW)	
G-GMCM	AS.350B3 Ecureuil	Steda Ltd	
G-GMGH	Robinson R66	M. G. Holland	
G-GMIB	Robin DR400/500	P. M. Shelton & I. Johansson	
G-GMKA	PA-28-140 Cherokee F	GMK Aviation Services Ltd (G-KALI/G-BASL)	
G-GMKB	PA-28RT-201T Turbo Cherokee Arrow IV	GMK Aviation Services Ltd (G-OPEP)	
G-GMSI	SOCATA TB9 Tampico	M. L. Rhodes	
G-GNEE	Ikarus C42C FB100 Charlie	J. M. Morris & C. J. Hayward	
G-GNHL	Eurofox 2K	Devon & Somerset Gliding Club Ltd	
G-GNJR	Kubicek BB26E balloon	A. & S. J. Stevens	
G-GNJW	Ikarus C.42	N. C. Pearse	
G-GNRV	Van's RV-9A	N. K. Beavins	
G-GNSS	Diamond DA.62	Flight Calibration Services Ltd	
G-GOAC	PA-34-200T Seneca II	J. P. de C. P. Calhamar/Portugal	
G-GOAL	Lindstrand LBL-105A balloon	I. Chadwick	
G-GOAT	Airbus AS.350B3 Ecureuil	Axe Asset Managemnent Ltd	
G-GODV	CAP Aviation CAP232	G-GODV Group	
G-GOER	Bushby-Long Midget Mustang	S. L. Goldspink	
G-GOES	Robinson R44-II	Helicentre Ltd	
G-GOGB	Lindstrand LBL ,90A	J. Dyer (G-CDFX)	
G-GOGW	Cameron N-90 balloon	D. J. Sayer	
G-GOHI	Cessna 208 Caravan 1 amphibian	Headcorn Parachute Club Ltd	
G-GOLF	SOCATA TB10 Tobago	S. M. Dufton	
G-GOLX	Europa XS	D. M. Hook (G-CROB)	
G-GOMC	Cirrus SR22T	V. P. Ferguson	
G-GOMS	Robinson R66	Bri-Stor Systems Ltd	
G-GOOF	Flylight Dragonfly	M. G. Preston	
G-GOPR	Cameron Z-90 balloon	Flying Enterprises	
G-GORD	Robin DR.401	J. G. Bellerby (G-JSMH)	
G-GORE	CFM Streak Shadow	P. F. Stares	
G-GORV	Van's RV-8	G-GORV Group	
G-GOSL	Robin DR.400/180	R. M. Gosling (G-BSDG)	
G-GOSS	Jodel DR.221	Avon Flying Group	
G-GOST	PA-28-181 Cherokee Archer LX	Morgan Land Sea Air LLP	
G-GOTI	PA-20-161 Cherokee Warrior III	Guernsey Flying Training Ltd	
G-GOUP	Robinson R22 Beta	AKP Aviation Ltd (G-DIRE)	
G-GOXC	HpH Glasflugel 304 S Jet	A. G. Reid	
G-GOXL	AS.355F2 Ecureuil II	Excel Charter Ltd (G-KHCG/G-SDAY/ G-SYPA/G-BPRE)	
G-GPAG	Van's RV-6	J. & N. Salmon	
G-GPMW	PA-28RT-201T Turbo Cherokee Arrow IV	G-GPMW Ltd	
G-GPOT	Agusta AW109SP Grand New	Castle Air Ltd (G-GOSP)	
G-GPSI	Grob G.115	C. R. Edwards	
G-GPWE	Ikarus C42 FB100	P. W. Ellis	
G-GRAK	Westland SA.341B Gazelle AH.Mk.1	Excel Charter Ltd	
G-GREC	Sequoia F.8L Falco	D. O'Donnell	
G-GRIN	Van's RV-6	E. Andersen	
G-GRIZ	PA-18-135 Super Cub (modified)	P. N. Elkington (G-BSHV)	
G-GRLS	Skyranger Swift 912S(1)	Batch End Flying Group	
G-GRLW	Jabiru J400	S. Rickard & J. Boniface (G-NMBG)	
G-GROE	Grob G.115A	Vu JV19 Ltd	
G-GROW	Cameron N-77 balloon	Derbyshire Building Society	
G-GRPA	Ikarus C.42 FB100	G-GRPA Group	
G-GRRR	SA Bulldog Srs 120/122	Horizons Europe Ltd (G-BXGU)	
G-GRUN	Leonardo AW109SP Grand New	Pendley Aviation LLP	
G-GRVE	Van's RV-6	G-GRVE Group	
G-GRVY	Van's RV-8	A. Page	
G-GRWL	Lilliput Type 4 balloon	A. E. & D. E. Thomas	
G-GRYN	Rotorsport UK Calidus	J. Taylforth	

Notes	Reg	Type	Owner or Operator
	G-GRYZ	Beech F33A Bonanza	J. Kawadri & M. Kaveh
	G-GRZZ	Robinson R44 II	A. P. Sellars
	G-GSAL	Fokker E.III Reolica (416/15)	Grass Strip Aviation Ltd
	G-GSAR	Agusta AW.139	Helioperations
	G-GSAS	Airbus MBB BK117 D-2	Gama Aviation Ltd
	G-GSCD	Jodel D.140E	W. H. Greenwood
	G-GSCV	Ikarus C42 FB UK	A. P. & P. R. Santus
	G-GSFS	Cessna 152	Cherokee Aviation Ltd
	G-GSGS	HpH Glasflugel 304 ES	G. E. Smith
	G-GSIX	PA-32-300 Cherokee Six	N. Venn
	G-GSMR	Bell 206B Jet Ranger III	Amiben Holdings Ltd (G-BXNS)
	G-GSPY	Robinson R44 II	Corbeau II Ltd
	G-GSST	Grob G.102 Astir CS77	Highland Gliding Club Ltd
	G-GSYL	PA-28RT-201T Turbo Cherokee Arrow IV	S. J. Sylvester (G-DAAH)
	G-GSYS	PA-34-220T Seneca V	GSR Aviation Ltd
	G-GSTN	Airbus Helicopters EC130 T2	GB Helicopters
	G-GTAX	PA-31-350 Navajo Chieftain	Hadagain Investments Ltd (G-OIAS)
	G-GTFB	Magni M-24C	Rotormurf Ltd
	G-GTFC	P & M Quik	C. Curtin
	G-GTGT	P & M Quik GT.450	Jarvy Enterprises Ltd
	G-GTHM	PA-38-112 Tomahawk	D. R. Clyde
	G-GTJD	P & M Quik GT450	A. J. Bacon
	G-GTNA	Robinson R66	A. N. Abel (G-LROK)
	G-GTOM	Alpi Pioneer 300	S. C. Oliphant & J. Watkins
	G-GTRE	P & M Quik GTR	M. J. Austin
	G-GTRR	P & M Quik GTR	M. R. Wallis
	G-GTSD	P & M Quik GT450	T. H. Beales
	G-GTSO	P & M Quik GT450	D. Jones
	G-GTTP	P & M Quik GT450	L. M. Westwood
	G-GTUG	PA-25-235 Pawnee D	S. J. Nolan & J. N. Nichoills (G-BHUU)
	G-GTWL	Eurofox 912 (iS)	D. C. Dollery
	G-GTWO	Schleicher ASW-15	G2 Syndicate
	G-GUAR	PA-28-161 Cherokee Warrior II	Guar Flying Group
	G-GUIN	Ultramagic B-70 balloon	A. M. Holly
	G-GULP	I.I.I. Sky Arrow 650T	L. J. Betts
	G-GULZ	Christen Eagle II	Screaming Eagle Flying Group
	G-GUMM	Aviat A-1B	S. J. Beaty (G-LTMM)
	G-GUNZ	Van's RV-8	M. J. S. Wright
	G-GURU	PA-28-161 Cherokee Warrior II	G-GURU Ltd
	G-GVII	Gulfstream GVIII	Executive Jet Charter Ltd
	G-GVPI	Evans VP-1 srs.2	G. Martin
	G-GVSL	Aerotechnik EV-97 Eurostar SL	G. Verity
	G-GWAC	Eurocopter EC.135 T2+	Babcock Mission Critical Services Onshore Ltd (G-WASN)
	G-GWFT	Rans S-6-ES Coyote II	R. R. Davies & A. E. Williams
	G-GWIZ	Colt Clown SS balloon	Magical Adventures Ltd
	G-GWMB	Pacific Aerospace PAC 750XL	Hinton Skydiving Centre Ltd
	G-GWOW	Cirrus SR22T	G. R. Bartlett
	G-GWTF	Van's RV-14	M. W. Harris
	G-GWVV	Cirrus SR20	Daedalus Aviation (Services) Ltd
	G-GXII	Supermarine 366 Spitfire F.XII	366 Holdings Ltd
	G-GXVV	Cirrus SR20	Daedalus Aviation (Services) Ltd
	G-GYAK	Yakovlev Yak-50	O. Luehring
	G-GYAV	Cessna 172N	Southport & Merseyside Aero Club (1979) Ltd
	G-GYRA	AutoGyro Calidus	D. B. Roberts
	G-GYRO	Campbell Cricket	J. W. Pavitt
	G-GYTO	PA-28-161 Cherokee Warrior III	White Waltham Airfield Ltd
	G-GZDO	Cessna 172N	Eagle Flying Ltd
	G-GZIP	Rolladen-Schneider LS8-18	D. S. S. Haughton
	G-HAAH	Schempp-Hirth Ventus 2cT	R. Davey & J. E. M. Herman
	G-HAAR	Eurofox 912(S)	Longside Flying Group
	G-HABI	SkyRanger 912S(1)	D. R. White

Reg	Type	Owner or Operator	Notes
G-HABT	Supermarine Aircraft Spitfire Mk.26 (BL735:BT-A)	Wright Grumman Aviation Ltd	
G-HACA	Percival Type K Vega Gull	G. C. Smith	
G-HACE	Van's RV-6A	B. F. Hill	
G-HACK	PA-18-150 Super Cub	Intrepid Aviation Co	
G-HADD	P & M Quik R	L. A. Wood	
G-HAEF	Cosmik EV-97 TeamEurostar UK	C-More Flying School	
G-HAFG	Cessna 340A	Sportno Drustvo Letalski Center Maribor/Slovenia	
G-HAHU	Yakovlev Yak-18T	N. C. Lewton	
G-HAIG	Rutan LongEz	P. R. Dalton	
G-HAII	Bristell NG5 Classic HD	Gosk Ltd	
G-HAIR	Robin DR.400/180	S. P. Copson	
G-HAJJ	Glaser-Dirks DG.400	W. G. Upton & J. G. Kosak	
G-HALC	PA-28R-200 Cherokee Arrow	Halcyon Aviation Ltd	
G-HALJ	Cessna 140	Modern Air (UK) Ltd	
G-HALL	PA-22-160 Tri-Pacer	A. A. M. Wafaa (G-ARAH)	
G-HALS	Robinson R44 II	Adventure 001 Ltd (G-CEKA)	
G-HALT	Mainair Pegasus Quik	M. B. Edwards	
G-HAMD	Eurofox 3K	A. M. Lewis	
G-HAMI	Fuji FA.200-180	HAMI Group (G-OISF/G-BAPT)	
G-HAMP	Bellanca 7ACA Champ	R. J. Grimstead	
G-HAMR	PA-28-161 Cherokee Warrior II	CG Aviation Ltd	
G-HAMS	Pegasus Quik	D. R. Morton	
G-HAMW	Eurofox 3K	A. M. Walton	
G-HANC	Robinson R22	AA Helicopters Ltd (G-CHIS)	
G-HANS	Robin DR.400 2+2	The Cotswold Aero Club Ltd	
G-HANY	Agusta-Bell 206B JetRanger 3	Heliflight (UK) Ltd (G-ESAL/G-BHXW/G-JEKP)	
G-HAPA	Embraer EMB-550 Legacy 500	Centreline AV Ltd (G-RORA)	
G-HAPE	Pietenpol Aircamper	J. P. Chape	
G-HAPI	Lindstrand LBL-105A balloon	K. S. Hull	
G-HAPY	DHC.1 Chipmunk 22A (WP803)	Astrojet Ltd	
G-HAPZ	Pipistrel Alpha BCAR-S 164	Smiley Wings Aviatioin Ltd (G-CLYT)	
G-HARE	Cameron N-77 balloon	D. H. Sheryn & C. A. Buck	
G-HARG	Embraer EMB-550 Legacy 500	Centreline AV Ltd	
G-HARI	Raj Hamsa X'Air V2 (2)	XAir Group	
G-HARN	PA-28-181 Cherokee Archer II	Dennis Flying Group (G-DENK/G-BXRJ)	
G-HARR	Robinson R22 Beta	Sloane Charter	
G-HART	Cessna 152 (tailwheel)	J. R. Chapman (G-BPBF)	
G-HARY	Alon A-2 Aircoupe	H. J. & J. J. Grose (G-ATWP)	
G-HATH	Techpro Merlin 100UL	N. R. Hathaway	
G-HATZ	Hatz CB-1	S. P. Rollason	
G-HAUL	Westland WG.30 Srs 300 ★	The Helicopter Museum/Weston-super-Mare	
G-HAUT	Schempp-Hirth Mini Nimbus C	A. D. Peacock	
G-HAWC	BAe. Hawk T.Mk.1	I 39 Aviation Ltd	
G-HAYE	Mudry CAP 232	H. A. M. Tallini (G-SKEW)	
G-HAYS	Skyranger Swift 912S(1)	F. J. M. & S. F. Blatchford (G-CFBS)	
G-HAYY	Czech Sport Aircraft Sportcruiser	Sportcrew YY	
G-HAYZ	Airbus AS.350B3 Ecureuil	350 Air Ltd (G-0CLZN)	
G-HAZA	Diamond DA.42NG Twin Star	R. W. F. Jackson	
G-HAZD	Cameron Z-56 balloon	L. S. Crossland-Mead	
G-HAZL	Skyranger Nynja 912S(1)	J. A. Walker	
G-HAZZ	Eurocopter AS.350B3 Ecureuil	Cheshire Helicopters Ltd (G-IANW)	
G-HBBC	DH.104 Dove 8	Roger Gawn 2007 Family Trust (G-ALFM)	
G-HBBH	Ikarus C42 FB100	Golf Bravo Hotel Group	
G-HBEE	Lindstrand LTL Series 2-80 balloon	R. P. Waite	
G-HBOS	Scheibe SF-25C Rotax-Falke	Husbands Bosworth Gliding Club Ltd	
G-HBOX	Supermarine 361 Spitfire LF.1X	A. C. Monk	
G-HBRB	Ikarus C42 FB100 Bravo	Progress Vehicle Management Ltd	
G-HBTG	Ascent Eurofox 2K	Husbands Bosworth Gliding Club	
G-HCAC	Schleicher Ka 6E	Ka 6E 994 Group	
G-HCBW	Sequoia Falco F.8L	M. A. Searle	
G-HCEN	Guimbal Cabri G2	Helicentre Aviation Ltd	
G-HCIF	PA-28-180 Cherokee C	Glasgow Flying Club Ltrd (G-AVVV)	
G-HCKT	Zenair CH.601HDS Zodiac	M. G. Petrie	
G-HCNX	Eurocopter EC.155B1	Silvercrest Aviation LP Inc	
G-HCOS	Ultramagic M-120 balloon	Hampshire Balloons Ltd	
G-HCPD	Cameron C-80 balloon	H. Crawley& P. Dopson	
G-HCUB	J-5B Cub Cruiser	A. F. Ratcliffe (G-CIZN)	

Notes	Reg	Type	Owner or Operator
	G-HCUP	Magni M-22C Voyager	A. Harcup
	G-HCUS	Lindstrand LTL Series 2-80	D. G. Such & M. Tomlin
	G-HDAE	DHC.1 Chipmunk 22 (WP964)	Airborne Classics Ltd
	G-HDEW	PA-32R-301 Saratoga SP	G. Kirk
	G-HDSP	Leonardo A109S Grand	Sloane Helicopters Ltd
	G-HDUO	Ultramagic M-56 balloon	F. R. Battersby
	G-HEAL	Lindstrand LTL Series 1-31 balloon	D. R. Rawlings
	G-HEAN	AS.355NP Ecureuil 2	Brookview Developments Ltd
	G-HEBO	BN-2B-20 Islander	G. Cormack (G-BUBK)
	G-HEBS	BN-2B-26 Islander	Hebridean Air Services Ltd (G-BUBJ)
	G-HECB	Fuji FA.200-160	H. E. W. E. Bailey (G-BBZO)
	G-HECK	Robinson R44 II	Helivation Aviation Ltd (G-ILLG)
	G-HECT	Flight Design CTLS 600 UK	M. A. Coffin
	G-HEDL	Extra EA.300/LC	Fresco Solar Shading LLP
	G-HEHE	Eurocopter EC.120B Colibri	HE Group Ltd
	G-HEKL	Percival Mew Gull Replica	D. Beale
	G-HELA	SOCATA TB10 Tobago	Future Flight
	G-HELE	Bell 206B JetRanger 3	B. E. E. Smith (G-OJFR)
	G-HELL	Sonex	T. J. Shaw
	G-HELN	PA-18 Super Cub (MM-52 2392:EI-69)	Helen Group
	G-HEMC	Airbus Helicopters MBB BK-117D-3	Babcock Mission Critical Services Onshore Ltd
	G-HEMN	Eurocopter EC135 T2+	Babcock Mission Critical Services Onshore Ltd
	G-HEMZ	Agusta A109S Grand	Sloane Helicopters Ltd
	G-HENT	SOCATA Rallye 110ST	T. D. Nathan
	G-HENY	Cameron V-77 balloon	Zebedee Balloon Service Ltd
	G-HENZ	Autogyro Cavalon	A. Henson
	G-HEOI	Eurocopter EC135 P2+	West Yorkshire Combined Authority National Police Air Service
	G-HERC	Cessna 172S	Cambridge Aero Club Ltd
	G-HERD	Lindstrand LBL-77B balloon	S. W. Herd
	G-HERZ	Robinson R44	Elstree Helicopters Ltd (G-OBHE/G-PRET)
	G-HETY	Eurofox 914	Yorkshire Gliding Club (Proprietary) Ltd
	G-HEVI	Boeing 737-3M8	TAG Aviation (Stansted) Ltd (G-EZYB)
	G-HEVR	Ikarus C42 FB80	Flight Sport Aviation LLP
	G-HEWI	Piper J-3C-90 Cub	Denham Grasshopper Flying Group (G-BLEN)
	G-HEWZ	Hughes 369HS	P. A. Emery (G-LEEJ)
	G-HEXE	Colt 17A balloon	A. Dunnington
	G-HEYY	Cameron 72 Bear SS balloon	Magical Adventures Ltd
	G-HFAV	PA-28-181 Cherokee Archer DX	HFA Ventures Ltd
	G-HFBM	Curtiss Robin C-2	D. M. Forshaw
	G-HFCB	Cessna F.150L	Easy Aircraft Rental Ltd
	G-HFCF	SOCATA TB-20 Trinidad	A. P. Shoobert
	G-HFCT	Cessna F.152	Stapleford Flying Club Ltd
	G-HFLW	Airbus Helicopters MBB-BK 117 D-3	Seven Up Aviation Ltd
	G-HFRH	DHC-1 Chipmunk 22 (WK635)	PL Photography Ltd
	G-HFZA	Dornier 228-200	Zeroavia Ltd (G-SAYE)
	G-HGPI	SOCATA TB20 Trinidad	M. J. Jackson
	G-HGRB	Robinson R44	DC Attachments Ltd (G-BZIN)
	G-HHAA	HS. Buccaneer S.2B (XX885)	Hawker Hunter Aviation Ltd
	G-HHAC	Hawker Hunter F.58 (J-4021)	Hawker Hunter Aviation Ltd (G-BWIU)
	G-HHDR	Cessna 182T	I. D. Brierley
	G-HHEM	Leonardo AW169	Essex & Herts Air Ambulance Trust
	G-HHII	Hawker Hurricane IIB (BE505: XP-L)	Hurriback Ltd (G-HRLO)
	G-HHPM	Cameron Z-105 balloon	J. Armstrong
	G-HIAL	Viking DHC-6-400 Twin Otter	Loganair Ltd
	G-HIBB	Jabiru J430	C. M. Hibbert
	G-HIBM	Cameron N-145 balloon	Alba Ballooning Ltd
	G-HICU	Schleicher ASW-27-18E	N. A. Hoare & M. T. Davenport
	G-HIGA	Cessna 172P	LAC Flying School (G-BRZS)
	G-HIGB	Robin R2120U	High-G Flight Training (G-CBVB)
	G-HIGC	Robin R2120U	High-G Flight Training (G-CBLE)
	G-HIJK	Cessna 421C	Acrobat Ltd (G-OSAL)
	G-HIJN	Ikarus C.42 FB80	J. D. Avey
	G-HILI	Van's RV-3B	A. G. & E. A. Hill
	G-HILO	Rockwell Commander 114	Alpha Golf Flying Group

Reg	Type	Owner or Operator	Notes
G-HILS	Cessna F.172H	A. M. Smith (G-AWCH)	
G-HILT	SOCATA TB10 Tobago	L. Windle	
G-HILY	Zenair CH.600 Zodiac	P. J. Brookman (G-BRII)	
G-HIMM	Cameron Z-105 balloon	C. M. D. Haynes	
G-HINZ	Avtec Jabiru SK	N. T. Blackbourn	
G-HIOW	Airbus Helicopters EC.135T3	Babcock Mission Critical Services Onshore Ltd	
G-HIPE	Sorrell SNS-7 Hiperbipe	T. A. Cleaver (G-ISMS)	
G-HIRE	GA-7 Cougar	W. Ali (G-BGSZ)	
G-HISP	Hispano HA-1112 M1L Buchon	Ultimate Warbird Flights Ltd	
G-HITC	Airbus Helicopters AS.350B3	Ferns Surfacing Ltd	
G-HITG	Airbus Helicopters AS.350B3	Elstree Ink Ltd	
G-HITH	Airbus Helicopters AS.350B3	Airbus Helicopters UK Ltd	
G-HITT	Hawker Hurricane 1 (P3717:SW-P)	Northwilds Ltd	
G-HIVE	Cessna F.150M	Peterborough Flying School Ltd (G-BCXT)	
G-HIYA	Skyranger 912(2)	R. D. & C. M. Parkinson	
G-HIZZ	Robinson R22 II	Elstree Helicopters Ltd (G-CNDY/G-BXEW)	
G-HJBM	Honda HA-420 Hondajet	Bookajet Aircraft Management Ltd	
G-HJDP	Bell 505 Jet Ranger X	VNE Group Ltd	
G-HJSM	Schempp-Hirth Nimbus 4DM	60 Syndicate (G-ROAM)	
G-HJSS	AIA Stampe SV.4C (modified)	R. S. Ward (G-AZNF)	
G-HJUK	Honda HA-420 Hondajet	Bookajet Ltd	
G-HKAA	Schempp-Hirth Duo Discus T	J. Randall	
G-HKCC	Robinson R66	Nightingales Aviation	
G-HKCF	Enstrom 280C-UK	HKC Helicopter Services (G-MHCF/G-GSML/ G-BNNV)	
G-HKHK	Robinson R66	HQ Aviation Ltd	
G-HKHM	Hughes 369B	HQ Aviation Ltd	
G-HLCF	Starstreak Shadow SA-II	N. Hart	
G-HLEE	Sky Ranger J2.2(1)	P. G. Hill	
G-HLOB	Cessna 172S	Goodwood Road Racing Co.Ltd	
G-HLYA	Airbus A.321-211	Jet 2.com (G-TCDD)	
G-HLYB	Airbus A.321-211	Jet 2.com (G-TCDE)	
G-HLYF	Airbus A.321-211	Jet 2.com	
G-HLYH	Airbus A.321-251NX	Jet 2.com	
G-HLYI	Airbus A.321-251NX	Jet 2.com	
G-HLYJ	Airbus A.321-251NX	Jet 2.com	
G-HLYK	Airbus A.321-251NX	Jet 2.com	
G-HLYL	Airbus A.321-251NX	Jet 2.com	
G-HLYM	Airbus A.321-251NX	Jet 2.com	
G-HLYN	Airbus A.321-251NX	Jet 2.com	
G-HLYO	Airbus A.321-251NX	Jet 2.com	
G-HMAA	Airbus MBB-BK117 D-3	Babcock Mission Critical Services	
G-HMCA	Cosmik EV-97 TeamEurostar UK	A. D. Kenmuir	
G-HMCB	Skyranger Swift 912S(1)	L. N. Blyth	
G-HMCD	Ikarus C42 FB80	G. J. Stamp	
G-HMCE	Ikarus C42 FB80	RAF Microlight Flying Association	
G-HMCF	EV-97 Eurostar SL mictolight	RAF Microlight Flying Association	
C HMCH	EV-97 Eurostar SI	RAF Microlight Flying Association	
G-HMEC	Robinson R22	Helimech Ltd (G-BWTH)	
G-HMED	PA-28-161 Cherokee Warrior III	Eglinton Flying Club Ltd	
G-HMGA	Beech 200 Super King Air	ACH London Ltd	
G-HMGC	Beech 200 Super King Air	ACH London Ltd (G-OGAT)	
G-HMGD	Diamond DA.62	AMPA Ltd	
G-HMGE	Diamond DA.62	AMPA Ltd	
G-HMGF	Beech B300 Super King Air 350	ACH Manthorpe Ltd	
G-HMGG	Beech B300 Super King Air 350	AHC Manthorpe Ltd	
G-HMGH	Beech B300 Super King Air 350	AMPA Ltd	
G-HMGI	Beech B300 Super King Air 350	AMPA Ltd	
G-HMHM	Rotorsport UK MTO Sport	J. W. Harmon	
G-HMJB	PA-34-220T Seneca III	W. B. Bateson	
G-HMLB	Van's RV-8	P. R. Upshall	
G-HMPS	CZAW Sportcruiser	G. P. D. Clover	
G-HMPT	Agusta-Bell 206B JetRanger 2	Yorkshire Helicopters	
G-HNEY	Bombardier BD700-2A12 Global 7500	Concierge U Ltd	
G-HNGE	Ikarus C42 FB80	D. Coward	
G-HNTR	Hawker Hunter T.7 (XL571:V) ★	Yorkshire Air Museum/Elvington	

Notes	Reg	Type	Owner or Operator
	G-HODD	Schleicher ASW-27-18E	A. K. Eckton & K. Tipples
	G-HODL	Boeing 737-82R	Ascend Airways Ltd
	G-HODR	Skyranger Swift 912S(1)	A. W. Hodder
	G-HOFF	P & M Aviation Quik GT450	L. Mazurek
	G-HOFM	Cameron N-56 balloon	Magical Adventures Ltd
	G-HOGA	Airbus EC130 T2	Airbus Helicopters
	G-HOGB	Airbus EC130 T2	Hogs Head Transportation Ltd
	G-HOGC	Airbus EC130 T2	Hogs Head Transportation Ltd
	G-HOGS	Cameron 90 Pig SS balloon	Magical Adventures Ltd
	G-HOJO	Schempp-Hirth Discus 2a	S. G. Jones
	G-HOLA	PA-28-201T Turbo Dakota	R. & K. Everson (G-BNYB)
	G-HOLE	P & M Quik GT450	B. Birtle (G-CEBD)
	G-HOLM	Eurocopter EC.120B Colibri	Heligroup Operations Ltd
	G-HOMA	Cessna F.172H	M. K. N. Khan
	G-HONK	Cameron O-105 balloon	M. A. Green
	G-HONY	Lilliput Type 1 Srs A balloon	A. E. & D. E. Thomas
	G-HOOF	Beech B.200GT King Air 250	Twofifi Ltd
	G-HOON	Pitts S-1S Special	M. C. Staite
	G-HOOZ	Kettlety N-77 balloon	H. D. Jones
	G-HOPA	Lindstrand LBL-35A balloon	L. J. M. Muir
	G-HOPE	Beech F33A Bonanza	T. W. Gilbert
	G-HOPR	Lindstrand LBL-25A balloon	K. C. Tanner
	G-HOPY	Van's RV-6A	R. C. Hopkinson
	G-HORK	Pioneer 300 Hawk	R. Y. Kendal
	G-HOSS	Beech F33A Bonanza	A. C. Renouf
	G-HOTA	Cosmik EV-97 TeamEurostar UK	W. Chang
	G-HOTB	Eurocopter EC155 B1	Multiflight Ltd (G-CEXZ)
	G-HOTC	AutoGyro MTOSport	N. W. G. Wade (G-CINW)
	G-HOTM	Cameron C-80 balloon	M. G. Howard
	G-HOTR	P & M Quik GTR	M. E. Fowler
	G-HOTZ	Colt 77B balloon	C. J. & S. M. Davies
	G-HOUR	Max Holste MH.1521 C1 Broussard	Bremont Watch Company Ltd
	G-HOUS	Colt 31A balloon ★	The British Balloon Museum and Library
	G-HOWD	Magni M-24C Orion	M. G. Howard
	G-HOWL	RAF 2000 GTX-SE gyroplane	C. J. Watkinson
	G-HOXN	Van's RV-9	GHOXN Flying Group
	G-HPCB	Ultramagic S-90 balloon	D. & K. Bareford
	G-HPIN	Bell 429	Harpin Ltd
	G-HPSF	Rockwell Commander 114B	R. W. Scandrett
	G-HPUX	Hawker Hunter T.7 (XL587)	Hawker Hunter Aviation Ltd
	G-HPWA	Van's RV-8	M. de Ferranti
	G-HRAF	Schleicher ASK-13	K13 – HRAF Syndicate (G-DETS)
	G-HRDY	Cameron Z-105 balloon	Flying Enterprises
	G-HRLI	Hawker Hurricane 1 (V7497)	Hawker Restorations Ltd & Hurricane Restoration Ltd
	G-HRND	Cessna 182T	R. H. Wicks
	G-HROI	Rockwell Commander 112A	Inter-European Aviation Ltd
	G-HRST	Cessna FR.172H	G. A. E. Waring
	G-HRVS	Van's RV-8	D. J. Harvey
	G-HRYZ	PA-28-180 Cherokee Archer	LS Airmotive Ltd (G-WACR/G-BCZF)
	G-HSDL	Westland Gazelle AH. Mk 1	Howard Stott Demolition Ltd
	G-HSEB	Pegasus Quantum 15-912	C. R. Dunford (G-BYNO)
	G-HSKE	Aviat A-18 Husky	R. B. Armitage & S. L. Davis
	G-HSKI	Aviat A-1B	C. H. M. Brown
	G-HSOO	Hughes 369HE	A Shade Greener Finance Ltd (G-BFYJ)
	G-HSTH	Lindstrand LBL. HS-110 balloon	R. P. Wade, T. G. Read & J. Kenny
	G-HSTI	Robinson R44 II	H S Thirsk & Son (G-SHAF)
	G-HSVI	Cessna FR.172J	A. Scott
	G-HTAX	PA-31-350 Navajo Chieftain	Hadagain Investments Ltd
	G-HTFU	Gippsland GA8-TC 320 Airvan	Skydiving Aircraft Ltd
	G-HTML	P & M Aviation Quik R	FlyingsCool
	G-HTRL	PA-34-220T Seneca III	Techtest Ltd (G-BXXY)
	G-HTSI	Sling 4 TSI	G. L. Holford
	G-HTWE	Rans S6-116	G. R. Hill
	G-HUBB	Partenavia P.68B	Ravenair Aircraft Ltd
	G-HUBO	Cameron Z-105 balloon	Huboo Technologies Ltd

Reg	Type	Owner or Operator	Notes
G-HUCH	Cameron 80 Carrots SS balloon	Magical Adventures Ltd (G-BYPS)	
G-HUDS	P & M Quik GTR	S. J. M. Morling	
G-HUEW	Europa XS	Europa 94 Group	
G-HUEY	Bell UH-1H	MX Jets Ltd	
G-HUEZ	Hughes 369E	Falcon Helicopters Ltd (G-WEBI)	
G-HUFF	Cessna 182P	Cousins Holdings Ltd	
G-HUGB	Bell 47G-5	UGB Aviation Ltd (G-LHCI/G-SOLH/G-AZMB)	
G-HUKA	MDH Hughes 369E	Muskany Ltd (G-OSOO)	
G-HUKS	Balony Kubicek BB22XR balloon	Wharf Farm Ltd	
G-HULK	Skyranger 912(2)	L. C. Stockman	
G-HULL	Cessna F.150M	Hull Aero Club Ltd	
G-HUMB	BXM Hopper Shape	L. S. Crossland-Mead	
G-HUME	EAA Acrosport 2	G. Home	
G-HUMH	Van's RV-9A	D. F. Daines	
G-HUML	Hummel UltraCruiser	Albion Aero Services Ltd	
G-HUMM	Bell 407	Century Aviation Ltd	
G-HUNI	Bellanca 7GCBC Scout	Paul's Planes Ltd	
G-HUPW	Hawker Hurricane 1 (R4118:UP-W)	J. Brown	
G-HURI	CCF Hawker Hurricane XIIA (R4175:RF-R)	Historic Aircraft Collection Ltd	
G-HUSH	Hughes 269C	Cirrus UK Training Ltd & JBS-Helicopters Ltd	
G-HUTY	Van's RV-7	S. A. Hutt	
G-HUWE	Hughes 369HS	P. R. Butler (G-TCEE/G-AZVM)	
G-HUWW	PA-34-200T Seneca II	Watson Aviation (Gloucester) LLP	
G-HUXX	Hughes 369E	Iris Aviation Ltd	
G-HUXY	Cessna 152	Iris Aviation Ltd	
G-HVBF	Lindstrand LBL-210A balloon	Virgin Balloon Flights	
G-HVER	Robinson R44 II	Equation Associates Ltd	
G-HVRZ	Eurocopter EC 120B	J. S. Tobias	
G-HWKI	Bell 47G-5	C. C. Butt	
G-HWKS	Robinson R44	Rapid International (Holdings) Ltd (G-ETFF/ G-HSLJ)	
G-HWOW	Robinson R44	J. Pratt	
G-HWPK	TAF Sling 4	A. P. & D. Alvis	
G-HXJT	Glasflugel 304 S Jet	H. Hingley	
G-HXTD	Robin DR.400/180	S. R. Evans	
G-HYBD	Gramex Song	P. A. Robertson	
G-HYBR	TAF Sling 4	Boeing United Kingdom Ltd	
G-HYGN	Ballonbau Worner NL-STU/510 gas balloon	The Hydrogen Balloon Group	
G-HYLA	Balony Kubicek BB26E balloon	J. A. Viner	
G-HYPE	TAF Sling 4 TSi	P. J. Fly	
G-HYUK	BN-2B-26 Islander	Cranfield Aerospace Solutions Ltd (G-BUBP)	
G-HZRD	AgustaWestland AW.119 Mk.II	SaxonAir Helicopters	
G-IACA	Sikorsky S-92A	Bristow Helicopters Ltd	
G-IACD	Sikorsky S-92A	Bristow Helicopters Ltd	
G-IACE	Sikorsky S-92A	Bristow Helicopters Ltd	
G-IACF	Sikorsky S-92A	Bristow Helicopters Ltd	
G-IADX	Supermarine 300 Spitfire Ia	M. Weston (G-CMDX)	
G-IAGL	Eurocopter EC.120B Colibri	T Clark Aviation LLP (G-UYFI)	
G-IAGO	Groppo Trail Mk.2	J. Jones & J. W. Armstrong	
G-IAHS	Cosmik EV-97 TeamEurostar UK	P. A. & M. W. Aston	
G-IAJJ	Robinson R44 II	P. J. R. Holt	
G-IAJS	Ikarus C.42 FB UK	A. J. Slater	
G-IAMP	Cameron H-34 balloon	W. D. Mackinnon	
G-IANB	Glaser-Dirks DG-800B	I. S. Bullous	
G-IANC	SOCATA TB10 Tobago	Kemble Flyers Ltd (G-BIAK)	
G-IANH	SOCATA TB10 Tobago	Severn Valley Aero Group	
G-IANI	Europa XS T-G	S. M. Webster	
G-IANJ	Cessna F.150K	Poyston Aviation (G-AXVW)	
G-IANM	AB Sportine LAK-17AT	M. Roberts	
G-IANP	Schleicher ASK-18	I. L. Pattingale	
G-IANZ	P & M Quik GT450	A. J. Morrell	
G-IARC	Stoddard-Hamilton Glastar	A. A. Craig	
G-IASA	Beech B.200 Super King Air	IAS Medical Ltd	
G-IASB	Beech B.200GT Super King Air	Stearman G-IIIG Group	

Notes	Reg	Type	Owner or Operator
	G-IASC	Beech B.200 Super King Air	IAS Medical Ltd (G-CLOW)
	G-IASM	Beech B.200 Super King Air	2Excel Aviation Ltd (G-OEAS)
	G-IBAZ	Ikarus C.42 FB100	B. R. Underwood
	G-IBBC	Cameron Sphere-105 balloon	L. J. Whitelock
	G-IBBJ	Rotorsport UK Cavalon	D. A. Smith
	G-IBBS	Europa	R. H. Gibbs
	G-IBBY	Jodel D.150	D. R. Gibby (G-BACL)
	G-IBCF	Cameron Z-105 balloon	Cash 4 Cars
	G-IBEA	PA-28-181 Cherokee Archer LX	J. Dobson
	G-IBED	Robinson R22A	Swift Helicopter Services Ltd (G-BMHN)
	G-IBEE	Pipistrel Apis	T. J. Franklin
	G-IBEN	Van's RV-7	B. A. Fawke (G-CHIR)
	G-IBFP	VPM .M.16 Tandem Trainer	B. F. Pearson
	G-IBFW	PA-28R-201 Cherokee Arrow III	The Foxtrot Whiskey Flying Group
	G-IBIG	Bell 206B JetRanger 3	Cloud Telematics LLP (G-BORV)
	G-IBII	Pitts S-2A Special	First Light Aviation Ltd (G-XATS)
	G-IBLP	P & M Quik GT450	P. G. Evans
	G-IBMS	Robinson R44	R. R. Deakin
	G-IBNH	Westland Gazelle HT Mk.2	Buckland Newton Hire Ltd (G-SWWM)
	G-IBOO	DG Flugzeugbau DG-808C	P. J. Gill (G-SMAJ/G-TRTM)
	G-IBSY	VS.349 Spitfire Mk.VC (EE602/DV-V)	Fighter Aviation Engineering Ltd (G-VMIJ)
	G-IBUZ	CZAW Sportcruiser	D. D. Finlay-Maxwell
	G-ICAN	Zenair CH.750	A. M. Cameron
	G-ICAS	Pitts S-2B Special	A. K. Halvorsen
	G-ICBM	Stoddard-Hamilton Glasair III Turbine	W. S. S. Curtis
	G-ICDM	Jabiru UL-450	P. J. Hellyer (G-CEKM)
	G-ICDP	Cessna F.150L	Praeluceo Property Ltd
	G-ICEL	Robinson R66	Ice Helicopters Ltd
	G-ICER	Leonardo AW169	Iceland International Ltd
	G-ICES	Thunder Ax6-56 balloon ★	British Balloon Museum & Library Ltd
	G-ICET	Robinson R44	Elstree Aviation Centre Ltd
	G-ICEZ	Robinson R44	Chelsea Green (VI) Ltd
	G-ICGA	PA-28-140 Cherokee E	Eco-Additives Sp ZOO/Poland
	G-ICMT	Aerotechnik EV-97 Eurostar	R. Haslam
	G-ICOM	Cessna F.172M	Stuart Taylor Aviation Ltd (G-BFXI)
	G-ICOR	Lindstrand LTL Series 2-60 balloon	R. G. Griffin
	G-ICRM	Slingsby T.67M-200 Firefly	CRM Aviation Europe Ltd (G-HONG)
	G-ICRR	Aeronca 11AC Chief	Chieftain's Flying Group
	G-ICRS	Ikarus C.42 FB UK Cyclone	S. Stockill
	G-ICRT	Robinson R44 II	Macrae Aviation Ltd
	G-ICRV	Van's RV-7	I. A. Coates
	G-ICUT	Maule MX-7-180A Super Rocket	T. Clarke
	G-ICWT	Pegasus Quantum 15-912	Whisky Tango Group
	G-IDAY	Skyfox CA-25N Gazelle	G. G. Johnstone
	G-IDEB	AS.355F1 Ecureuil 2	Excel Charter Ltd (G-ORMA/G-SITE/G-BPHC)
	G-IDFE	Bell 505 Jet Ranger X	Pwersense LLP
	G-IDID	SA. Bulldog Srs.120/121 (XX699/F)	N. J. Tucker (G-CBCV)
	G-IDII	Dan Rihn DR.107 One Design	G. G. Ferriman
	G-IDMG	Robinson R44	Aecus Aviation Ltd
	G-IDOL	Aerotechnik EV-97 Eurostar	IDOL Group
	G-IDOO	Grob G.109B	Aerobility
	G-IDRS	Van's RV-8	Firmbeam Ltd
	G-IDTO	PA-28RT-201 Turbo Cherokee Arrow IV	G. Cresdee
	G-IDUL	Alpi Pioneer 300	M. A. McConville & M. Ruddy
	G-IEEF	Raj Hamsa X'Air Hawk	P. J. Major
	G-IEJH	Jodel 150A	A. Turner & D. Worth (G-BPAM)
	G-IFAB	Cessna F.182Q	H. E. Thomas & A. Bruce
	G-IFBP	AS.350B2 Ecureuil	Airbourne Solutions Ltd
	G-IFDA	Van's RV-6A	C. Callicott
	G-IFES	Schempp-Hirth Discus 2c FES	J. M. Bevan
	G-IFFR	PA-32 Cherokee Six 300	Brendair (G-BWVO)
	G-IFFY	Flylight Dragonfly	R. D. Leigh
	G-IFIF	Cameron TR-60 balloon	M. G. Howard
	G-IFII	Van's RV-8	J. Rowlinson (G-SPRC)
	G-IFIT	PA-31-350 Navajo Chieftain	Dart Group PLC (G-NABI/G-MARG)
	G-IFLP	PA-34-200T Seneca II	B. & J. S. Miller

Reg	Type	Owner or Operator	Notes
G-IFMI	Bombardier BD700-1A10 Global 6500	Ifimi Ltd	
G-IFOS	Ultramagic M-90 balloon	I. J. Sharpe	
G-IFRV	Van's RV-8A	P. S. Gilmour	
G-IFWD	Schempp-Hirth Ventus cT	C. J. Hamilton	
G-IGBF	Van's RV-8	B. J. Flippence	
G-IGEL	Cameron N-90 balloon	Computacenter Ltd	
G-IGES	DHC-1 Chipmunk 22 (WP872)	G. R. Charlton	
G-IGET	Skyranger Nynja 912S(1)	CK Group	
G-IGGL	SOCATA TB10 Tobago	Cavendish Aviation UK Ltd (G-BYDC)	
G-IGHT	Van's RV-8	Miratoni Ltd	
G-IGIE	SIAI Marchetti SF.260	Flew LLP	
G-IGII	Europa	J. M. Gibson, Executor of the estate of W. C. Walters	
G-IGIS	Bell 206B JetRanger II	Wood Advisory Ltd (G-CHGL/G-BPNG/G-ORTC)	
G-IGLE	Cameron V-90 balloon	G-IGLE Group	
G-IGLI	Schempp-Hirth Duo Discus T	C. Fox	
G-IGLL	AutoGyro MTO Sport	I. M. Donnellan	
G-IGLY	P & M Aviation Quik GT450	R. Davies	
G-IGLZ	Champion 8KCAB	C. A. Parsons	
G-IGRT	TL2000 Sting S4	S. Jolles	
G-IHCI	Europa	G. A. Rodmell (G-VKIT)	
G-IHHI	Extra EA.300/SC	Airdisplays.com Ltd	
G-IHOP	Cameron Z-31 balloon	N. W. Roberts	
G-IHOT	Cosmik EV-97 TeamEurostar UK	J. R. Grundy	
G-IHXD	Cessna F.150M	Air Navigation & Trading Co.Ltd	
G-IIAC	Aeronca 11AC Chief	T. D. Coulthard, J. McMillan & W. A. Parrish (G-BTPY)	
G-IIAI	Mudry CAP.232	DEP Promotions Ltd	
G-IIAL	Aerospool Dynamic WT9 UK	A. Howell (G-GCJH)	
G-IIAN	Aero Designs Pulsar	I. G. Harrison	
G-IIBB	Bell 505 Jet Ranger X	First Blue Aviation Ltd	
G-IICC	Van's RV-4	P. R. Fabish & J. C. Carter (G-MARX)	
G-IICT	Schempp-Hirth Ventus 2Ct	P. McLean	
G-IICX	Schempp-Hirth Ventus 2cxT	M. J. M. Turnbull	
G-IIDC	Midget Mustang	D. Cooke (G-IIMT/G-BDGA)	
G-IIDD	Van's RV-8	T. I. Williams	
G-IIDI	Extra EA.300/L	Power Aerobatics Ltd (G-XTRS)	
G-IIDR	Ikarus C42 FB100	I. A. Harper & S. G. Penk	
G-IIDW	Flylight Dragon Combat 12T	G. Allison	
G-IIDY	Aerotek Pitts S-2B Special	The S-2B Group (G-BPVP	
G-IIEX	Extra EA.300/L	S. G. Jones	
G-IIFM	Edge 360	F. L. McGee	
G-IIFX	Marganski MDM-1	Glider FX	
G-IIGB	Game Composites GB1 Gamebird	Airtime Aerobatics Ltd	
G-IIGI	Van's RV-4	C. J. L. Wolf	
G-IIGL	Christen Eagle II	R. C. Berger (G-RIFY)	
G-IIHX	Bushby-Long Midget Mustang	AJDW Consultancy Ltd	
G-IIHZ	Avions Mudry CAP 231	S. P. Reeve (G-OZZO)	
G-IIID	Dan Rihn DR.107 One Design	G-IIID Group	
G-IIIE	Aerotek Pitts S-2B Special	R. M. C. R. de Aguiar/Portugal	
G-IIIJ	American Champion 8GCBC	J. D. May	
G-IIIL	Pitts S-1T Special	I. F. Thompson	
G-IIIM	Stolp SA.100 Starduster	R. O. Johnson	
G-IIIN	Pitts S-1C Special	R. P. Evans	
G-IIIR	Pitts S-1S Special	P. J. & W. M. Hodgkins	
G-IIIV	Pitts Super Stinker 11-260	S. D. Barnard	
G-IIIX	Pitts S-1S Special	D. F. Friel (G-LBAT/G-UCCI/G-BIYN)	
G-IIIY	Boeing A75N1 Stearman	Aero-Super-Batics Ltd	
G-IIJC	Midget Mustang	J. M. Keane (G-CEKU)	
G-IIJI	Xtremeair XA-42 Sbach 342	G. H. Willson	
G-IIJM	Extra NG	Airdisplays.com Ltd	
G-IILL	Vans RV-7	C. P. Wilkinson	
G-IILX	Extra EA.300/LC	Collett Aviation Services Ltd	
G-IILY	Robinson R44 I	JS Berry Contractors Ltd (G-DCSG/G-TRYG)	
G-IIMI	Extra EA.300/L	Firebird Aerobatics Ltd	
G-IINI	Van's RV-9A	N. W. Thomas	
G-IINK	Cirrus SR22	N. P. Kingdon	

Notes	Reg	Type	Owner or Operator
	G-IIOE	Schempp-Hirth Ventus-3E	Southern Sailplanes
	G-IIOI	Extra EA.300/L	S. G. Jones (G-OLAD/G-JJIL)
	G-IIOO	Schleicher ASW-27-18E	N. A. Taylor
	G-IIPI	Steen Skybolt	J. Burglass (G-BVXE/G-LISA)
	G-IIPT	Robinson R22 Beta	Swift Helicopter Services Ltd (G-FUSI)
	G-IIRI	Xtreme Air Sbach 300	S. P. Wood
	G-IIRV	Van's RV-7	B. O. Harvey
	G-IIRW	Van's RV-8	A. A. Wordsworth
	G-IISC	Extra EA.300/SC	G-IISC Group
	G-IIWI	Van's RV-14	G. C. J. Cooper (G-CLYG)
	G-IIXA	Xtremeair XA41 Sbach 300	Aerobatics Ltd
	G-IIXF	Van's RV-7	C. A. & S. Noujaim
	G-IIXI	Extra EA.300/L	B. Nielsen
	G-IIXZ	Schleicher ASG-32 Mi	P. M. Wells
	G-IIYI	Boeing Stearman A75N1	V. S. EW. Norman
	G-IIYK	Yakovlev Yak-50	Eaglescott Yak 50 Group
	G-IIZE	Zivko Edge 540	Palenque Jewellery Ltd
	G-IIZI	Extra EA.300	M. G. Jefferies
	G-IJAC	Light Aero Avid Speedwing Mk 4	I. J. A. Charlton
	G-IJAG	Cessna 182T Skylane	N. J. Ratcliffe
	G-IJMC	Magni M-16 Tandem Trainer	R. F. G. Moyle (G-POSA/G-BVJM)
	G-IKAH	Slingsby T.51 Dart 17R	K. A. Hale
	G-IKBP	PA-28-161 Cherokee Warrior II	Merseyflight Ltd
	G-IKES	Stoddard-Hamilton GlaStar	M. Stow
	G-IKEV	Jabiru UL-450	A. D. Keen
	G-IKON	Van's RV-4	N. C. Spooner
	G-IKRK	Europa	M. W. Bodger
	G-IKRS	Ikarus C42 FB UK	K. J. Warburton
	G-IKUS	Ikarus C42 FB UK	M. J. Wilson
	G-ILBG	Cessna 525A Citationjet CJ2	Catreus AOC Ltd
	G-ILBO	Rolladen-Schneider LS3-A	J. P. Gilbert
	G-ILBT	Cessna 182T	G. E. Gilbert
	G-ILDA	VS.361 Spitfire HF.IX (SM520 : KJ-1)	Boultbee Flight Academy Ltd (G-BXHZ)
	G-ILEE	Colt 56A balloon	H. G. Wadey
	G-ILES	Cameron O-90 balloon	G. N. Lantos
	G-ILEW	Schempp Hirth Arcus M	Lleweni Parc Ltd
	G-ILFA	BN-2B-26 Islander	D. Brem-Wilson (G-BSWO)
	G-ILFF	Leonardo AW109SP Grand New	Hero's Ltd
	G-ILHR	Cirrus SR22	R. R. Tyler
	G-ILIB	PZL-Bielsko SZD-36A	D. Poll
	G-ILIS	Mudry CAP232	I. M. Zidane (G-IIRP)
	G-ILLL	Robinson R66	D. Gill (G-JDUN)
	G-ILLY	PA-28-181 Cherokee Archer II	R. A. & G. M. Spiers
	G-ILLZ	Europa XS	R. S. Palmer
	G-ILMC	Aeroprakt A-32 Vixen	K. Tumilty
	G-ILNJ	Cameron O-31 balloon	I. R. Jones
	G-ILRS	Ikarus C.42 FB UK	J. J. Oliver & D. Archibald
	G-ILSE	Corby CJ-1 Starlet	S. Stride
	G-ILUA	Alpha R2160I	A. R. Haynes
	G-ILYA	Agusta-Bell 206B Jet Ranger II	Aerospeed Ltd (G-MHMH/G-HOLZ/G-CDBT)
	G-ILZZ	PA-31 Navajo	T. D. Nathan & I. Kazi
	G-IMAB	Europa XS	I. D. Gale
	G-IMAG	Colt 77A balloon ★	Balloon Preservation Group
	G-IMBI	QAC Quickie 1	P. Churcher (G-BWIT)
	G-IMBJ	QAC Quickie	P. Churcher (G-WAHL)
	G-IMBO	CEA Jodel DR.250/160	H. S. J. Ochtman
	G-IMCD	Van's RV-7	I. G. McDowell
	G-IMCH	Lindstrand LTL Series SS Cube balloon	A. M. Holly
	G-IMEA	Beech 200 Super King Air	2 Excel Aviation Ltd (G-OWAX)
	G-IMEL	RAF 2000 GTX-SE	S. L. Morris
	G-IMIK	PA-28-180 Cherokee C	M. K. Kent (G-ATNB)
	G-IMLW	Autogyro Cavalon	M. L. Watson
	G-IMME	Zenair CH.701SP	T. R. Sinclair
	G-IMMI	Escapade Kid	P. J. Tanulak
	G-IMNY	Escapade 912	D. S. Bremner
	G-IMOK	Hoffmann HK-36R Super Dimona	G-IMOK Syndicate
	G-IMPS	Skyranger Nynja 912S	B. J. Killick

Reg	Type	Owner or Operator	Notes
G-IMPT	Eurofox 2K	Popham Tailwheel Eurofox Group	
G-IMPX	Rockwell Commander 112B	R. G. Cook	
G-INAS	PA-28-181 Cherokee Archer II	D. N. F. & R. Barrington-Bullock (G-BRNV)	
G-INCA	Glaser-Dirks DG.400	L. E. Ingram	
G-INDC	Cessna T.303	G. Mexias	
G-INDX	Robinson R44	L. G. Milne	
G-INDY	Robinson R44	Lincoln Aviation	
G-INES	Zenair CH.650B	P. W. Day & N. J. Brownlow	
G-INGA	Thunder Ax8-84 balloon	M. L. J. Ritchie	
G-INGS	American Champion 8KCAB	The Leicestershire Aro Club Ltd	
G-INJA	Ikarus C42 FB UK	G. Sloan	
G-INNY	SE-5A (replica) (F5459:Y)	J. M. Gammidge	
G-INSR	Cameron N-90 balloon	P. J. Waller	
G-INTS	Van's RV-4	G. C. Bridges	
G-INTV	AS.355F2 Ecureuil 2	AZB Heli (Charters) Ltd (G-JETU)	
G-INXS	Robinson R22	Kuki Helicopter Sales Ltd (G-OBIO)	
G-INYS	TLAC Sherwood Scout	S. D. Pain	
G-INZZ	Cameron Z-105 balloon	The Bath Gin Company Ltd	
G-IOCJ	PA-28R-200 Cherokee Arrow	Too Low Terrain Ltd (G-RONG)	
G-IOFR	Lindstrand LBL-105A balloon	RAF Halton Hot Air Balloon Club	
G-IOIA	I.I.I. Sky Arrow 650T	G-IOIA Group	
G-IOOI	Robin DR.400-160	N. B. Mason & R. P. Jones	
G-IOOP	Christen Eagle II	I. Smith	
G-IOOS	Agusta A.109S Grand	Hundred Percent Aviation Ltd	
G-IORV	Van's RV-10	J. E. Howe	
G-IOSH	Sikorsky S-76C	Starspeed Ltd	
G-IOSI	Jodel DR.1051	G-IOSI Group	
G-IOSL	Van's RV-9	S. Leach (G-CFIX)	
G-IOSO	Jodel DR.1050	U. Izzo & M. D. Aliotta	
G-IOVE	BRM Bristell NG5 Speedwing	S. D. Austen	
G-IOWE	Europa XS	P. G. & S. J. Jeffers	
G-IPAT	Jabiru SP-470	J. G. Cook	
G-IPCE	Guimbal Cabri G2	T. Gallop & J. Cook	
G-IPDP	Pilatus PC-12/47G	Ravenair Aircraft Ltd	
G-IPEN	UltraMagic M-90 balloon	R. A. Benham	
G-IPGL	AgustaWestland AW109SP Grand New	IPGL No.7 Ltd	
G-IPIG	Elan 550/Pegasus Cosmos Fly Away 01	R. Frankham	
G-IPII	Steen Skybolt	J. Burglass	
G-IPJF	Robinson R44 II	Specialist Group International Ltd (G-RGNT/ G-DMCG)	
G-IPKA	Alpi Pioneer 300	L. A. & M. F. Humphries	
G-IPLY	Cessna 550 Citation Bravo	International Plywood (Aviation) Ltd (G-OPEM)	
G-IPOD	Europa XS	J. Wighton (G-CEBV)	
G-IPPS	Gippsland GA8 Airvan	Boultbee Flight Academy Ltd (G-VANA)	
G-IPSI	Grob G.109B	G-IPSI Flying Group (G-BMLO)	
G-IPSY	Rutan Vari-Eze ★	Science Museum/Wroughton	
G-IPUP	Beagle B.121 Pup 2	T. S. Walker	
G-IRAF	RAF 2000 GTX SE gyroplane	Condor Aviation International Ltd	
G-IRAK	SOCATA TB-10 Tobago	Flying Feather Ltd	
G-IRAL	Thruster T600N 450	J. Giraldez	
G-IRED	Ikarus C42 FB80	Mid Kent Aviation	
G-IRJE	Diamond DA.62	NALJets Ltd	
G-IRJX	Avro RJX-100 ★	Runway Visitor Park/Manchester	
G-IRLE	Schempp-Hirth Ventus cT	D. J. Scholey	
G-IRLI	P & M Quik GTR	N. Griffin	
G-IRLY	Colt 90A balloon	J. A. Viner	
G-IROB	SOCATA TB-10 Tobago	G. L. Davies	
G-IROD	Rotorsport UK MTO Sport	R. A. R. Stringer (G-FELD)	
G-IROH	Magni N24C Plus	CFP Mann Ltd	
G-IROI	Rotorsport UK MTO Sport	Oscar India Syndicate (G-KIMH)	
G-IROJ	Magni M-16C Tandem Trainer	Kernow RV Ltd	
G-IROK	Magni M-16C Tandem Trainer	G-IROK Flying Group	
G-IRON	Europa XS	T. A. Beever & J. D. Park	
G-IROS	Rotorsport UK Calidus	S. Hall	
G-IROW	Magni VPM M16 Tandem Trainer	Danelander Ltd (G-DBDB)	
G-IROX	Magni M-24C Orion	B. Minihane	
G-IRPC	Cessna 182Q	A. T. Jeans (G-BSKM)	

Notes	Reg	Type	Owner or Operator
	G-IRPW	Europa XS	R. P. Wheelwright
	G-IRRB	SOCATA TB-10 Tobago	R. Bone
	G-IRTY	VS.361 Spitfire LF.IX	Anpartsselskabet AF 19.9.2006 APS
	G-IRVI	Van's RV-14	M. W. Albery
	G-IRYC	Schweizer 269C-1	A & W Demolition (Bracknell)
	G-ISAC	Isaacs Spitfire (TZ164:OI-A)	A. James
	G-ISAS	Airbus MBB BK117 D-2	Gama Aviation (UK) Ltd
	G-ISAX	PA-28-181 Cherokee Archer III	Spectrum Flying Group
	G-ISBD	Alpi Pioneer 300 Hawk	M. I. White & B. W. Webb
	G-ISCD	Czech Sport Aircraft Sportcruiser	R. V. Bowles
	G-ISDN	Boeing Stearman A75N1 (14)	V. Boddy
	G-ISEL	Skyranger 912 (1)	P. A. Robertson
	G-ISEW	P & M Quik GT450	R. & T. Raffle
	G-ISHA	PA-28-161 Cherokee Warrior III	LAC Flying School
	G-ISJE	Pilatus PC-12/47E	247 Aviation Ltd
	G-ISLK	Aerospatiale ATR-72-212A	Executive Jet Support Ltd
	G-ISLL	Aerospatiale ATR-72-212A	Red-Tail Aviation Ltd
	G-ISLM	Aerospatiale ATR-72-212A	Abelo Assets 22 Ltd
	G-ISLN	Aerospatiale ATR-72-212A	Highclere Turboprop Leasing 2 Ltd
	G-ISLP	Aerospatiale ATR-72-212A	JAH2022A ATR72 MSN 1167,LLC
	G-ISLR	Cirrus SR22T	Tollund Ltd
	G-ISMA	Van's RV-7	D. King (G-STAF)
	G-ISMC	Cessna F.152	Stapleford Flying Club Ltd
	G-ISMO	Robinson R22 Beta	Kuki Helicopter Sales Ltd
	G-ISOB	Cameron O-31 balloon	A. C. Booth
	G-ISPH	Bell 206B JetRanger 2	S. P. Hagan (G-OPJM)
	G-ISPM	Leonardo AW109SP Grand New	Sloane Helicopters Ltd
	G-ISRV	Van's RV-7	S. A. Ivell
	G-ISSG	DHC.6-310 Twin Otter	Isles of Scilly Skybus Ltd
	G-ISZA	Aerotek Pitts S-2A Special	E. P. Morrow (G-HISS/G-BLVU)
	G-ITAF	SIAI-Marchetti SF.260AM	N. A. Whatling & W. R. Tandy
	G-ITAR	Magni M-16C Tandem Trainer	Hartis Autogyro Syndicate
	G-ITII	Aerotech Pitts S-2A Special	Hurricane Restoration Ltd
	G-ITOI	Cameron N-90 balloon	Flying Pictures Ltd
	G-ITOR	Robinson R44 II	Duro Design & Build Ltd
	G-ITST	Europa	M. Reindl
	G-ITVM	Lindstrand LBL-105A balloon	Elmer Balloon Team
	G-ITWB	DHC.1 Chipmunk 22	I. T. Whitaker-Bethe
	G-IUII	Aerostar Yakovlev Yak-52	Cosmos Technology Ltd
	G-IUMB	Schleicher ASW-20L	M. S. Szymkowicz
	G-IVER	Europa XS	I. Phillips
	G-IVES	Europa	D. R. Ockleton (G-JOST)
	G-IVET	Europa	K. J. Fraser
	G-IVII	Van's RV-7	M. A. N. Newall
	G-IVON	Skyranger Nynja 912(1)	L. N. Givens (G-CIHV)
	G-IVOR	Aeronca 11AC Chief	South Western Aeronca Group
	G-IVYY	Ikarus C42 FB100	J. W. D. Blythe
	G-IWAW	Robinson R66	W2 Helicopters Ltd (G-CLWX)
	G-IWIN	Raj Hamsa X'Air Hawk	C. G. Chambers
	G-IWON	Cameron V-90 balloon	D. P. P. Jenkinson (G-BTCV)
	G-IWRD	PA-28-180 Cherokee B	I. D. Ward
	G-IXII	Christen Eagle II	S. Hall (G-BPZI)
	G-IXXI	Schleicher ASW-27-18E	D. C. Hodgson
	G-IXXY	Magic Cyclone	L. Hogan
	G-IYRO	RAF 2000 GTX-SE	J. P. Mellett (G-BXDD)
	G-IZEN	Schleicher AS-33 ES	Z. Marczynski
	G-IZIT	Rans S.6-116 Coyote II	M. R. Ayder & M. Gray
	G-IZRV	Van's RV-12	D. J. Mountain & H. W. Hall
	G-IZZI	Cessna T.182T	E. B. & K. S. Bowlt
	G-IZZT	Cirrus SR22T	H. G. Dilloway
	G-IZZZ	Champion 8KCAB	P. J. Randell
	G-JAAB	Jabiru UL	I. A. Smith

Reg	Type	Owner or Operator	Notes
G-JAAM	Diamond DA62	Fly Private Ltd	
G-JAAP	Aeroprakt A-32 Vixxen	J. Rademaker	
G-JABE	Jabiru UL-D	K. J. Reynolds	
G-JABJ	Jabiru J400	South Essex Flying Group	
G-JABS	Jabiru UL-450	Jabiru Flying Group	
G-JABU	Jabiru J430	S. D. Miller	
G-JABY	Jabiru UL-450	D. R. Watson	
G-JABZ	Jabiru UL-450	D. K. Chaplin	
G-JACA	PA-28-161 Cherokee Warrior II	The Pilot Centre Ltd	
G-JACB	PA-28-181 Cherokee Archer III	P. R. Coe (G-PNNI)	
G-JACH	PA-28-181 Cherokee Archer III	Alderney Flight Training Ltd (G-IDPH)	
G-JACL	Tecnam P2010	Jersey Jet Centre Ltd	
G-JACM	Tecnam P2008-JC	Jersey Jet Centre Ltd	
G-JACN	Tecnam P2008-JC	Jersey Jet Centre Ltd	
G-JACS	PA-28-181 Cherokee Archer III	Modern Air (UK) Ltd	
G-JADJ	PA-28-181 Cherokee Archer III	Hull Aero Club	
G-JADN	Pilatus PC-12/47E	Zinck Aviation Ltd	
G-JADW	Ikarus C42 FB80	G-JADW Group	
G-JAEE	Van's RV-6A	J. A. E. Edser	
G-JAFS	PA-32R-301 Saratoga II HP	Sandholme Properties Ltd (G-VMFC)	
G-JAGA	Embraer EMB-505 Phenom 300	London Executive Aviation Ltd	
G-JAGS	Cessna FRA.150L	M. Bonsall (G-BAUY)	
G-JAIR	Mainair Blade	G. Spittlehouse	
G-JAJA	Robinson R44 II	J. D. Richardson	
G-JAJB	AA-5A Cheetah	N. S. Brookes	
G-JAJP	Jabiru UL	J. Anderson	
G-JAKF	Robinson R44 Raven II	P. A. Burkitt	
G-JAKM	Cirrus SR22 GTS	GKM Aviation Ltd (G-SPWP)	
G-JAKS	PA-28 Cherokee 160	J. L. & M. Harper (G-ARVS)	
G-JAKX	Cameron Z-69 balloon	J. A. Hibberd	
G-JAME	Zenair CH 601UL	G. L. Daniels & K. Davies (G-CDFZ)	
G-JAMP	PA-28-151 Cherokee Warrior	Lapwing Flying Group Ltd (G-BRJU)	
G-JAMY	Europa XS	J. P. Sharp	
G-JAMZ	P & M QuikR	S. Cuthbertson	
G-JANA	PA-28-181 Cherokee Archer II	London School of Flying Ltd	
G-JANB	Colt Flying Bottle SS balloon	Justerini & Brooks Ltd	
G-JANF	BRM Aero Bristell NG5 Speed Wing	B. Frederiks	
G-JANI	Robinson R44	JT Helicopters Ltd	
G-JANN	PA-34-220T Seneca III	D. J. Whitcombe	
G-JANS	Cessna FR.172J	R. G. Scott	
G-JAOC	Sky Ranger Swift 912S(1)	G. C. McLaughlin	
G-JARY	PA-24-260 Comanche	N3UN Ltd (G-BRXW)	
G-JASS	Beech B200 Super King Air	ACH (Witham) Ltd	
G-JAVO	PA-28-161 Cherokee Warrior II	Victor Oscar Ltd (G-BSXW)	
G-JAWC	Pegasus Quantum 15-912	S. K. Turner	
G-JAWZ	Pitts S-1S Special	A. R. Harding	
G-JAYD	Europa XS	J. R. Davis (G-RDHS)	
G-JAYI	Auster J/1 Autocrat	S. R. Pock	
G-JAYK	Robinson R44 II	AMH Heli LLP (G-MACU/G-SEFI)	
G-JAYS	Skyranger 912S(1)	S. O. Scott	
G-JAYZ	CZAW Sportcruiser	J. J. A. Williams	
G-JBAN	P & M Quik GT450	A. Nourse	
G-JBBH	Eurocopter AS.350B3 Ecureuil	Bartram Land Ltd (G-LODZ)	
G-JBBZ	AS.350B3 Ecureuil	D. Donnelly	
G-JBDH	Robin DR.400/180	A. I. Anderson	
G-JBEE	Robinson R44	Beeston Manor Ltd (G-CGWD)	
G-JBIB	Diamond DA.62	WILC74 Ltd	
G-JBKA	Robinson R44	J. G. Harrison	
G-JBOB	Schempp-Hirth Discus 2c FES	O. J. Bosanko & J. M. Robson	
G-JBRD	Mooney M.20K	Godspeed MS LLP	
G-JBRE	Rotorsport UK MT-03	P. A. Remfry	
G-JBRS	Van's RV-8	C. Jobling	
G-JBSP	Avtech Jabiru SP-470	C. K. James	
G-JBUZ	Robin DR400/180R Remorqueur	D. A. Saywell	
G-JBVP	Eurofox 3K	J. A. Valentine & B. J. Partridge	
G-JBVW	American Champion 8KCAB Super Decathlon	J. B. Van Wyk	
G-JCAN	Bombardier BD700-1A10 Global 6500	Voluxis Ltd	
G-JCBS	Piper J-3C-65 Cub	M. E. W. Fairhead (G-CUBY/G-BTZW)	
G-JCIH	Van's RV-7A	M. A. Hughes & D. F. Chamberlain	

Notes	Reg	Type	Owner or Operator
	G-JCJC	Colt Flying Jeans SS balloon	Magical Adventures Ltd
	G-JCKT	Stemme S.10VT	M. B. Jefferyes & J. C. Taylor
	G-JCOP	Eurocopter AS.350B3 Ecureuil	Cheshire Helicopters Ltd
	G-JCWM	Robinson R44 II	M. L. J. Goff
	G-JCWS	Reality Escapade 912(2)	S. E. Lyden
	G-JDBC	PA-34-200T Seneca II	First Air Ltd (G-BDEF)
	G-JDEL	Jodel 150	K. F. & R. Richardson (G-JDLI)
	G-JDOG	Cessna 305C Bird Dog (24541/BMG)	BC Arrow Ltd
	G-JDPB	PA-28R-201T Turbo Cherokee Arrow III	BC Arrow Ltd (G-DNCS)
	G-JDRD	Alpi Pioneer 300	RD Pioneer Flying Group
	G-JDSP	Bell 505 Jet Ranger X	D and S P Holdings LLP
	G-JEAO	BAe.146-100 ★	deHavilland Aircraft Heritage Centre/London Colney
	G-JEBS	Cessna 172S	Integrated Hi-Tech Ltd
	G-JEDH	Robin DR.400/180	Regent Aero Group
	G-JEEP	Aerotechnik EV-97 Eurostar	W. D. Franks (G-CBNK)
	G-JEFY	Avtech Jabiru UL-450	G. S. Bulpitt (G-BZYK)
	G-JEJH	Jodel DR.1050 Ambassadeur	Bredon Hill Flying Group
	G-JEMI	Lindstrand LBL-90A balloon	S. W. K. Smeeton
	G-JEMM	Jodel DR.1050 replica	The Piper Flyers
	G-JEMP	BRM Aero Bristell NG5 Speed Wing	W. Precious
	G-JEMS	Ultramagic S-90 balloon	J. E. McDonald
	G-JEMZ	Ultramagic H-31 balloon	C. M. Duggan
	G-JENK	Ikarus C42 FB80	G-JENK Chatteris 2015
	G-JEOL	Slingsby T67C Firefly	London Transport Flying Training Ltd
	G-JERK	Commonwealth Aircraft CA18 Mk.21 (44-15152:QI-T)	Fighter Aviation Engineering Ltd
	G-JERR	Eurofox 3K	J. Robertson
	G-JESS	PA-28R-201T Turbo Cherokee Arrow III	R. E. Trawicki (G-REIS)
	G-JETH	Hawker Sea Hawk FGA.6 (XE489) ★	Gatwick Aviation Museum/Charlwood
	G-JETM	Gloster Meteor T.7 (VZ638) ★	Gatwick Aviation Museum/Charlwood
	G-JETV	HPH Glasflugel 304 S Jet	N. Le Gras
	G-JEWL	Van's RV-7	J. S. Jewell
	G-JEZZ	Skyranger 912S(1)	I. J. Harvey
	G-JFAN	P & M Quik R	P. R. Brooker & G. R. Hall
	G-JFDI	Dynamic WT9 UK	D. Cholmondely
	G-JFER	Rockwell Commander 114B	D. T. Woodward (G-HPSE)
	G-JFLO	Aerospool Dynamic WT9 UK	P. A. Bass
	G-JFLY	Schleicher ASW-24	W. E. Lozowski
	G-JFMK	Zenair CH.701SP	J. D. Pearson
	G-JFPG	Leonardo AW109SP Grand New	AW Jenkinson Business Services Ltd
	G-JFRV	Van's RV-7A	J. Wilson & F. Glendon
	G-JFWI	Cessna F.172N	R. P. van der Hoorn
	G-JGAR	Robinson R44 II	Sloane Charter (G-DMRS)
	G-JGBI	Bell 206L-4 LongRanger	Dorbcrest Homes Ltd
	G-JGLG	Tecnam P2010	Lima Juliett Golf Ltd
	G-JGMN	CASA 1.131E Jungmann 2000	P. D. Scandrett
	G-JGRV	Van's RV-14A	J. Greenhalgh
	G-JGSI	Pegasus Quantum 15-912	G-JGSI Group
	G-JHAA	Csameron Z-90 balloon	B. T. Lewis
	G-JHAC	Cessna FRA.150L	G. D. Williamson (G-BACM)
	G-JHDD	Czech Sport Aircraft Sportcruiser	G-JHDD Syndicate
	G-JHEW	Robinson R22 Beta	Heli Air Ltd
	G-JHKP	Europa XS	N. I. Claughton
	G-JHLE	P & M Quik GTR	G. Colby
	G-JHLP	Flylight Dragon Chaser	S. J. Culpin & S. A. Lawson
	G-JHNY	Cameron A.210 balloon	Spirit Operations Ltd
	G-JHPC	Cessna 182T	G-JHPC Group
	G-JHYS	Europa	G-JHYS Group
	G-JIFI	Schempp-Hirth Duo Discus T	620 Syndicate
	G-JIII	Stolp SA.300 Starduster Too	VT10 Aero Company
	G-JIIL	Pitts S-2AE Special	A. M. Southwell
	G-JIIO	Schempp-Hirth Arcus M	S. G. Jones
	G-JILI	Van's RV-7	H. R. Hawkins
	G-JIMA	Cameron Z-105 balloon	Bristol and Avon Transport and Recycling Ltd

Reg	Type	Owner or Operator	Notes
G-JIMB	Beagle B.121 Pup 1	K. D. H. Gray & P. G. Fowler (G-AWWF)	
G-JIMC	Van's RV-7	J. Chapman	
G-JIMH	Cessna F.152 II	The Flying School Ltd (G-SHAH)	
G-JIMM	Europa XS	J. Cherry	
G-JIMP	Messerschmitt Bf 109G-2	M. R. Oliver	
G-JIMX	Skyranger Nynja 912S(1)	J. Henderson	
G-JIMZ	Van's RV-4	P. S. Waghorne	
G-JINI	Cameron V-77 balloon	I. R. Warrington	
G-JINT	Robinson R44 II	Axe Asset Management Ltd	
G-JJAN	PA-28-181 Cherokee Archer II	Blueplane Ltd	
G-JJEN	PA-28-181 Cherokee Archer III	K. M. R. Jenkins	
G-JJER	PA-28-161 Cherokee Warrior II	FBO Skywalker Ltd (G-GFCE/G-BVIH/G-BNJP)	
G-JJGI	SNCAN Stampe SV.4A	D. J. Pearson	
G-JJIL	Extra EA.300/L	M. M. Choim	
G-JJMM	Magni M24C Plus	International Road Safety Training Ltd	
G-JJSN	Robinson R44 II	Heatherway Taverns Ltd	
G-JKBN	CFM Starstreak Shadow SS-D	J. A. Cook	
G-JKEE	Diamond DA.42NG Twin Star	Morgan Land and Sea Ltd	
G-JKEL	Van's RV-7	H. P. Jardon & R. W. Mullard (G-LNNE)	
G-JKER	Monnett Sonnerai 2	D. Messenger (G-BGEH)	
G-JKHT	Robinson R22	J K Helicopter Training Ltd (G-OTUA/G-LHCA)	
G-JKJA	Agusta A109E Power	Myheli Ltd	
G-JKMH	Diamond DA42 Twin Star	Cloud Global Ltd	
G-JKMI	Diamond DA42 Twin Star	Tesla Solutions Ltd (G-KELV)	
G-JKRV	Schempp-Hirth Arcus T	Syndicate 291	
G-JKSN	Skyranger Nynja 912S(1)	G-JKSN Group	
G-JLAT	Aerotechnik EV-97 Eurostar	N. E. Watts	
G-JLGE	Gefa-Flug AS105GD Airship	Magical Adventures Ltd	
G-JLIA	Cameron O-90 balloon	M. Thompson	
G-JLIN	PA-28-161 Cadet	Falcon Flying Services Ltd	
G-JLRW	Beech 76 Duchess	Aviation South West Ltd	
G-JMAC	BAe Jetstream 4100 ★	Speke Aerodrome Heritage Group (G-JAMD/ G-JXLI)	
G-JMAL	Jabiru UL-D	K. Lewis	
G-JMAN	Mainair Blade 912S	A. P. Pearce	
G-JMAW	Beech B200GT King Air	Martin-Baker Aircraft Company Ltd	
G-JMBJ	Magni M24C Orion	N. M. Éclair-Heath	
G-JMCH	Boeing 737-476	West Atlantic UK Ltd (G-RAJG)	
G-JMCS	Boeing 737-4YO	West Atlantic UK Ltd	
G-JMDI	Schweizer 269C	A & W Demolition (Bracknell) (G-FLAT)	
G-JMGP	Aero L-39ZO Albatros	L39 Aviation Ltd	
G-JMIA	PA-28-180 Cherokee E	E. C. Griffith (G-AYEE)	
G-JMKE	Cessna 172S	M. C. Plomer-Roberts & H. White	
G-JMNN	CASA 1-131E Jungmann	B. S. Charters	
G-JMON	Agusta A109A-II	Falcon Aviation Ltd (G-RFDS/G-BOLA)	
G-JMRT	Ikarus C42 FB80	Ulster Flying Group	
G-JMRV	Van's RV-7	C. T. Gotke	
G-JNAP	Ace Aviation Magic/As-Tec 13	A. R. Lewis	
G-JNAR	Ace Aviation Easy Riser Touch	G. Cousins	
G-JNDY	Game Composites GB1	Skydance Aviation Ltd	
G-JNET	Robinson R22 Beta	R. L. Hartshorn	
G-JNGA	Agusta AW109SP Grand New	Castle Air Ltd	
G-JNNB	Colt 90A balloon	N. A. P. Godfrey	
G-JNSC	Schempp-Hirth Janus CT	R. C. Tatlow	
G-JNUS	Schempp-Hirth Janus C	N. A. Peatfield	
G-JOBA	P & M Quik GT450	S. P. Durnall	
G-JODB	Jodel D.9 Bebe	M. R. Routh	
G-JODE	Jodel D.150	B. R. Vickers	
G-JODL	Jodel D.1050/M	A. J. Almosawi	
G-JOED	Lindstrand LBL-77A balloon	G. R. Down	
G-JOET	Aeropro Eurofox 912(S)	J. A. Thomas	
G-JOHA	Cirrus SR20	M. J. Robinson	
G-JOID	Cirrus SR20	I. F. Doubtfire	
G-JOKR	Extra EA.300/L	Airdisplays.com Ltd	
G-JOLY	Cessna 120	Robhurst Aviation Ltd	

Notes	Reg	Type	Owner or Operator
	G-JONL	CZAW Sportcruiser	P. Weston
	G-JONM	PA-28-181 Cherokee Archer III	C. C. Wilson-Hart
	G-JONO	Colt 77A balloon★	British Balloon Museum and Library
	G-JONT	Cirrus SR22	J. A. Green
	G-JONX	Eurofox 912(1)	A. J. South
	G-JONY	Cyclone AX2000	A. Zelcs
	G-JOOL	Mainair Blade 912	P. C. Collins
	G-JORD	Robinson R44 II	G. Riddell
	G-JOTC	BAe.146-300QT	Fairfield Aviation Ltd (G-TNTM/G-BSLZ)
	G-JOTR	Avro RJ-85	Executive Jet Support Ltd (G-CHFE)
	G-JOVE	Sackville BM-56 balloon	J. A. Scott
	G-JOYT	PA-28-181 Cherokee Archer II	Alan Cathcart Ltd (G-BOVO)
	G-JOYZ	PA-28-181 Cherokee Archer III	Zulu Group
	G-JOZI	AS.350BA Ecureuil	SAS Altra Services
	G-JPBA	Van's RV-6	S. B. Austin
	G-JPHH	Tecnam P2010 TDI	J. Hinton
	G-JPIT	Pitts S-2SE Special	R. S. Goodwin
	G-JPJR	Robinson R44 II	Longstop Investments Ltd
	G-JPMA	Avtech Jabiru UL	M. Bastin
	G-JPOT	PA-32R-301 Saratoga SP	The Big 6 Flyers Ltd (G-BIYM)
	G-JPRO	P.84 Jet Provost T.5A (XW433)	J. A. Campbell
	G-JPWM	Skyranger 912 (2)	R. S. Waters & M. Pittock
	G-JRBC	PA-28-140 Cherokee	Homewhenaway Ltd
	G-JRCR	Bell 206L-1 LongRanger II	RSCP Management Ltd (G-EYRE/G-STVI)
	G-JREE	Maule MX-7-180	C. R. P. Briand
	G-JRER	Tecnam P2006T	3GRCOMM Ltd
	G-JRHH	Diamond DA.42NG Twin Star	J. Hale
	G-JRLR	Sackville BM-65 balloon	J. S. Russon
	G-JRME	Jodel D.140E	M. J. Applewhite
	G-JROO	Agusta-Bell 206B JetRanger II	S. Hancock (G-VJMJ/G-PEAK/ G-BLJE)
	G-JRSH	Cirrus SR22T	JF Aviation Ltd
	G-JRVA	Van's RV-6	A. C. Batchelar
	G-JRVB	Van's RV-8	J. W. Salter
	G-JRXV	Bell 505 Jet Ranger X	Scotbeef Ltd
	G-JRZE	Skyranger Nynja	J. R. A. Russell
	G-JSAK	Robinson R22 Beta II	Swift Helicopter Services Ltd
	G-JSAW	Robinson R66	GT40 Aviation Ltd
	G-JSCA	PA-28RT-201 Cherokee Arrow IV	G-JSCA Flying Group (G-ICSA)
	G-JSCB	Eurocopter EC.120B Colibri	S. J. B. Brooks (G-OLDO/G-HIGI)
	G-JSEY	Bollonbau Worner NL-STU/1000	M. Leblanc
	G-JSFC	Tecnam P2008-JC	Stapleford Flying Club Ltd
	G-JSIC	M & D Flugzeugbau JS-MD 1C	A. G. W. Hall
	G-JSKY	Ikarus C42 FB80	M. S. Westman
	G-JSLE	M & D Flugzeugbau JS-MD 3	L. M. P. Wells
	G-JSMA	Gloster Meteor T.Mk.7.5 (WL419)	Martin-Baker Aircraft Company Ltd
	G-JSPL	Jabiru UL-450	G-JSPL Group
	G-JSPR	Glaser-Dirks DG400	I. P. Freestone
	G-JSRK	HpH Glasflugel 304SJet	Great White Syndicate
	G-JSRV	Van's RV-6	M. K. Holmes
	G-JSSD	HP.137 Jetstream 3001 ★	Museum of Flight/East Fortune
	G-JSUE	Van's RV-7A	A. Jenkins
	G-JTBL	Tecnam P2010	S. M. Malone
	G-JTBX	Bell 206B Jet Ranger III	G. Reidy (G-EWAW/G-DORB)
	G-JTII	Pitts S-1S Special	J. C. Tempest
	G-JTPC	Aeromot AMT-200 Super Ximango	J. T. Potter & G. C. Alexander
	G-JTSA	Robinson R44 II	D. Gregor
	G-JUDD	Jabiru UL-450	A. M. Wynn
	G-JUDE	Robin DR.400/180	Bravo India Flying Group Ltd
	G-JUDY	AA-5A Cheetah	The Bield Flying Group
	G-JUFS	SOCATA TB-9 Tampico	A. C. Cooper-Evans
	G-JUGE	Cosmik EV-97 TeamEurostar UK	The Golf Echo Group
	G-JUGS	Autogyro MTOSport	S. J. M. Hornsby
	G-JUJU	Chilton DW1A	R. A. Pike & S. K. Woodgate
	G-JULE	P & M Quik GT450	P. J. Nolan
	G-JULL	Stemme S.10VT	J. P. C. Fuchs
	G-JULU	Cameron V-90 balloon	J. M. Muscat

Reg	Type	Owner or Operator	Notes
G-JULZ	Europa XS	J. S. Firth	
G-JUNG	CASA 1.131E Jungmann 1000	I. V. Staines	
G-JUNO	Fokker D.VII Replica	S. J. Green	
G-JUNR	Bolkow BO.208C Junior	The 3 Amigos	
G-JURG	Rockwell Commander 114A	A. G. Bell	
G-JUST	Beech F33A Bonanza	N. M. R. Richards	
G-JVBF	Lindstrand LBL-210A balloon	Virgin Balloon Flights	
G-JVBP	Cosmik EV-97 Team Eurostar UK	Otherton Blue Skies Syndicate	
G-JVET	Eurofox 912(IS)	B. J. Finch	
G-JWBI	Agusta-Bell 206B JetRanger 2	The Cloudy Bay Trading Company (G-RODS/ G-NOEL/G-BCWN)	
G-JWDB	Ikarus C.42 FB80	D. C. Acroyd	
G-JWDS	Cessna F.150G	G. Sayer (G-AVNB)	
G-JWDW	Ikarus C42 FB80	D. A. & J. W. Wilding	
G-JWEE	Van's RV-14A	J. C. A. Wheeler	
G-JWIV	Jodel DR.1051	C. M. Fitton	
G-JWJW	CASA 1-131E Jungmann Srs.2000	G. Haye	
G-JWMA	Gloster Meteor T.Mk.7 (WA638)	Martin-Baker Aircraft Co.Ltd	
G-JWNW	Magni M-16C Tandem Trainer	K. A. O'Neill	
G-JWPP	Eurofox 912(S)	J. D. Brownlow	
G-JWRN	Robinson R44 II	Wood Advisory Ltd (G-JSCH)	
G-JWXS	Europa XS T-G	J. Wishart	
G-JYRO	Rotorsport UK MT-03	A. Richards	
G-JZBA	Boeing 737-8MG	Jet 2.com	
G-JZBB	Boeing 737-8MG	Jet 2.com	
G-JZBC	Boeing 737-8MG	Jet 2.com	
G-JZBD	Boeing 737-8MG	Jet 2.com	
G-JZBE	Boeing 737-8MG	Jet 2.com	
G-JZBF	Boeing 737-8MG	Jet 2.com	
G-JZBG	Boeing 737-8MG	Jet 2.com	
G-JZBH	Boeing 737-8MG	Jet 2.com	
G-JZBI	Boeing 737-8MG	Jet 2.com	
G-JZBJ	Boeing 737-8MG	Jet 2.com	
G-JZBK	Boeing 737-8MG	Jet 2.com	
G-JZBL	Boeing 737-8MG	Jet 2.com	
G-JZBM	Boeing 737-8MG	Jet 2.com	
G-JZBN	Boeing 737-8MG	Jet 2.com	
G-JZBO	Boeing 737-8MG	Jet 2.com	
G-JZBP	Boeing 737-8MG	Jet 2.com	
G-JZBR	Boeing 737-8MG	Jet 2.com	
G-JZBS	Boeing 737-8MG	Jet 2.com	
G-JZBT	Boeing 737-883	Jet 2.com	
G-JZBU	Boeing 737-85P	Jet 2.com	
G-JZBV	Boeing 737-85P	Jet 2.com	
G-JZBW	Boeing 737-85P	Jet 2.com	
G-JZBX	Boeing 737-8HX	Jet 2.com	
G-JZBZ	Boeing 737-86J	Jet 2.com	
G-JZCA	Airbus A.321-251NX	Jet 2.com	
G-JZCB	Airbus A.321-251NX	Jet 2.com	
G-JZCC	Airbus A.321-251NX	Jet 2.com	
G-JZCD	Airbus A.321-251NX	Jet 2.com	
G-JZCE	Airbus A.321-251NX	Jet 2.com	
G-JZDA	Boeing 737-82R	Jet 2.com	
G-JZDB	Boeing 737-8KN	Jet 2.com	
G-JZDC	Boeing 737-82R	Jet 2.com	
G-JZDD	Boeing 737-8JP	Jet 2.com	
G-JZDE	Boeing 737-8H6	Jet 2.com	
G-JZDF	Boeing 737-8H6	Jet 2.com	
G-JZDG	Boeing 737-8H6	Jet 2.com	
G-JZDH	Boeing 737-8AL	Jet 2.com	
G-JZHA	Boeing 737-8K5	Jet 2.com	
G-JZHB	Boeing 737-8K5	Jet 2.com	
G-JZHC	Boeing 737-8K5	Jet 2.com	
G-JZHD	Boeing 737-808	Jet 2.com	
G-JZHE	Boeing 737-8K2	Jet 2.com	
G-JZHF	Boeing 737-8K2	Jet 2.com	
G-JZHG	Boeing 737-85P	Jet 2.com	

Notes	Reg	Type	Owner or Operator
	G-JZHH	Boeing 737-85P	Jet 2.com
	G-JZHJ	Boeing 737-8MG	Jet 2.com
	G-JZHK	Boeing 737-8MG	Jet 2.com
	G-JZHL	Boeing 737-8MG	Jet 2.com
	G-JZHM	Boeing 737-8MG	Jet 2.com
	G-JZHN	Boeing 737-8MG	Jet 2.com
	G-JZHO	Boeing 737-8MG	Jet 2.com
	G-JZHP	Boeing 737-8MG	Jet 2.com
	G-JZHR	Boeing 737-8MG	Jet 2.com
	G-JZHS	Boeing 737-8MG	Jet 2.com
	G-JZHT	Boeing 737-8MG	Jet 2.com
	G-JZHU	Boeing 737-8MG	Jet 2.com
	G-JZHV	Boeing 737-8MG	Jet 2.com
	G-JZHW	Boeing 737-8MG	Jet 2.com
	G-JZHX	Boeing 737-8MG	Jet 2.com
	G-JZHY	Boeing 737-8MG	Jet 2.com
	G-JZHZ	Boeing 737-8MG	Jet 2.com
	G-KAEW	Fairey Gannet AEW Mk.3 (XL500) ★	South Wales Aviation Museum/St. Athan
	G-KAIR	PA-28-181 Cherokee Archer II	Invicta Aero Club Ltd
	G-KALE	Diamond DA62	G-KALE Aviation Ltd
	G-KALI	PA-28-140 Cherokee F	Glasgow Prestwick Flight Centre (G-GMKA/ G-BASL)
	G-KALM	Aeroprakt A22-LS Foxbat	P. B. Sloan (G-CLNM)
	G-KALP	Schleicher ASW-24	H. E. Gokalp
	G-KAMY	AT-6D Harvard III (285068)	T. J. Manna
	G-KANF	Bell 505 Jet Ranger X	Kane Haulage Ltd
	G-KAOM	Scheibe SF.25C Falke	Falke G-KAOM Syndicate
	G-KAOS	Van's RV-7	I. A. Harding
	G-KAPW	P.56 Provost T.1 (XF603)	The Shuttleworth Collection
	G-KARA	Brügger MB.2 Colibri	C. L. Hill (G-BMUI)
	G-KARE	Pilatus PC-12/47E	Ping Air Ltd
	G-KARK	Dyn'Aéro MCR-01 Club	M. J. Dawson
	G-KARL	Guimbal Cabri G2	Helicentre Aviation Ltd
	G-KARN	Rotorway Executive 90	U. G. P. Nimz (G-VART/G-BSUR)
	G-KART	PA-28-161 Cherokee Warrior II	Romeo Tango Aviation Ltd
	G-KASW	Rotorsport UK Calidus	R. A. Clarkson
	G-KASX	VS.384 Seafire Mk.XVII (SX336)	Fly Navy Heritage Trust Ltd (G-BRMG)
	G-KATO	Sonex	J. M. Greenway
	G-KATT	Cessna 152 II	C. M. de C. C. Cabral/Portugal (G-BMTK)
	G-KATZ	Flight Design CT2K	A. N. D. Arthur
	G-KAVI	Cessna 182T	C. S. Jundu
	G-KAWA	Denney Kitfox Mk 2	R. J. Holmes
	G-KAXT	Westland Wasp HAS.1 (XT787)	Fly Navy Heritage Trust Ltd
	G-KAXW	Westland Scout AH.1 (XW612)	Military Vehicle Solutions Ltd (G-BXRR)
	G-KAYD	Boeing Stearman A75N1	R. H. Butterfield
	G-KAYI	Cameron Z-90 balloon	R. Bayly
	G-KAYX	Skyranger Nynja 912(1)	R. N. J. Hughes
	G-KBBS	PA-28-161 Cherokee Warrior II	K. Bartholomew (G-ISDB/G-BWET)
	G-KBEB	Cessna 182P	K. N. S. Hennah
	G-KBOJ	Autogyro MTOSport	K. M. G. Barnett
	G-KBOS	Flight Design CTSW	G. N. S. Farrant (G-KBOX)
	G-KBWP	Schempp-Hirth Arcus T	G-KBWP Gliding Group
	G-KCHG	Schempp-Hirth Ventus Ct	A. Davey
	G-KCIG	Sportavia RF-5B	Deeside Fournier Group
	G-KCIN	PA-28-161 Cadet	The Pilot Centre Ltd (G-CDOX)
	G-KCMI	PA-46-600TP Meridian M600	British European Aviation Ltd
	G-KCUB	Piper J-3F-50 Cub	S. J. Hornsby (G-AGAT)
	G-KCWJ	Schempp-Hirth Duo Discus T	G-KCWJ Group
	G-KDCD	Thruster T.600N 450	M. N. Watson
	G-KDEN	Ikarus C42 FB80	K. H. Denham
	G-KDHU	Bristell NG5 Classic HD	N. W. McConachie
	G-KDIX	Jodel D.9 Bébé	S. J. Johns
	G-KDKD	Pipistrel Virus SW 128	Aerovolt UK Ltd
	G-KDLO	Schempp-Hirth Duo Discus T	M. Jordy, A. W. Thornhill, J. Tillson & A. West
	G-KDOG	SA Bulldog Srs 120/121 (XX624:E)	Redcat Aviation Services Ltd
	G-KDRU	Van's RV-9	C. B. Linton
	G-KDRZ	PA-28-181 Cherokee Archer LX	Kittyhawk Flight Academy Ltd

Reg	Type	Owner or Operator	Notes
G-KEAM	Schleicher ASH 26E	J. W. Paterson & A. A. Docherty	
G-KEAY	AutoGyro MTO Sport	R. Keay	
G-KEDK	Schempp-Hirth Discus bT	S. G. Vardigans	
G-KEEF	Commander Aircraft 112A	G-KEEF Group	
G-KEEN	Stolp SA.300 Starduster Too	M. J. W. & A. J. Harris	
G-KEES	PA-28 Cherokee 180	C. N. Ellerbrook	
G-KEGZ	Diamond P-90 balloon	Ascension Cider Company Ltd	
G-KELL	Van's RV-6	P. R. Watkins	
G-KELP	Aeroprakt A22-LS Foxbat	R. W. Swift	
G-KELT	Airbus A.320-251N	Acropolis Aviation Ltd	
G-KELX	Van's RV-6	J. J. Damp (G-HAMY)	
G-KELZ	Van's RV-8	Brown Dog Aviation Ltd (G-DJRV)	
G-KEMC	Grob G.109	R. D. Grieve & K. B. Stedman	
G-KEMD	Westland SA.341B Gazelle AH.Mk.1	Calport Ltd (G-CHBR)	
G-KEMI	PA-28-181 Cherokee Archer III	D. Baverstock	
G-KEMJ	Schempp-Hirth Duo Discus T	H. Anderson	
G-KENC	Ikarus C42 FB100	K. Clark	
G-KENG	Rotorsport UK MT-03	R. G. Appleboom	
G-KENK	Cameron TR-70 balloon	Raven Aviation Ltd	
G-KENL	Sackville BM-65 balloon	K. F. Lowry	
G-KENM	Luscombe 8EF Silvaire	L. M. Goodsell & M. J. Hawkins	
G-KENR	Balony Kubicek BB20XR balloon	K. R. Karlstrom	
G-KENW	Robin DR400/500	K. J. White	
G-KENX	Cameron Sport-90 balloon	K. R. Karlstrom	
G-KENZ	Rutan Vari-Eze	K. M. McConnel I (G-BNUI)	
G-KEPE	Schempp-Hirth Nimbus 3DT	Nimbus Syndicate PE	
G-KEPP	Rans S.6-ES Coyote II	J. J. Donnelly	
G-KESS	Glaser-Dirks DG-400	A. J. Swan	
G-KEST	Steen Skybolt	G-KEST Syndicate	
G-KESY	Slingsby T.59D Kestrel	B. Cross	
G-KETH	Agusta-Bell 206B JetRanger 2	DAC Leasing Ltd	
G-KEVA	Ace Magic Cyclone	J. C. Birkbeck	
G-KEVB	PA-28-181 Cherokee Archer III	Victor Bravo Flying Ltd	
G-KEVF	Bristell NG5 Classic HD	K. J. Faint	
G-KEVG	Rotorsport UK MT-03	VG Gyro Flying Group	
G-KEVH	Jabiru UL-450	K. L. Harris & M R. Livermore (G-CBPP)	
G-KEVI	Jabiru J400	P. Horth, D. W. Brown & D. J. Macleod	
G-KEVJ	TAF Sling 4 TSI	K. Jobling	
G-KEVL	Rotorway Executive 162F	Elrick & Gunn Ltd (G-CBIK)	
G-KEVS	P 7 M Quik GT450	J. Durber	
G-KEVX	Jabiru J400	K. L. Harris (G-JABI)	
G-KEVZ	P & M Quik R	K. Mallin	
G-KEWT	Ultramagic M.90 balloon	R. D. Parry	
G-KEYS	PA-23-250 Aztec	W. M. Giles	
G-KEYY	Cameron N-77 balloon	L. J. Whitelock (G-BORZ)	
G-KEZZ	Robinson R44 II	Swift Helicopter Services Ltd (G-CMEN)	
G-KFAS	KFA Safari	S. Favell	
G-KFCA	Ikarus C42 FB80	S. Balasubramaniam	
G-KFCN	Skyranger Nynja	Kemble Flying Centre Ltd	
G-KFCW	Flylight Skyranger Nynja	Kemble Flying Centre Ltd	
G-KFLY	Flight Design CT&W	J. J. Brutnell (G-LFLY)	
G-KFOG	Van's RV-7	K. Fogarty	
G-KFOX	Denney Kitfox	R. A. Hampshire	
G-KFTI	Pilatus PC-12/47E	Daki Aviation Ltd	
G-KFVG	Schempp-Hirth Arcus M	M. T. Burton	
G-KGAO	Scheibe SF.25C Falke 1700	Midland Gliding Club Ltd	
G-KGAW	Scheibe SF.25C	Rattlesden Gliding Club Ltd	
G-KGKG	Embraer EMB-135BJ Legacy 600	London Executive Aviation Ltd	
G-KGMM	Schempp-Hirth Ventus 2cT	G. Smith	
G-KGRP	Agusta A109E Power Elite	CE Aviation UK Ltd (G-ZIPE)	
G-KHCC	Schempp-Hirth Ventus Bt	S. R. Thompson	
G-KHDW	Jabiru J430	D. I. Walters-Davies (G-CCGG)	
G-KHEA	Scheibe SF.25B Falke	P. A. Cronk	
G-KHOP	Zenair CH.601HDS Zodiac	J. F. Woodham	
G-KHPI	Schleicher ASW-28-18E	P. W. Copland & J. M. Hutchinson	
G-KHRE	MS.893E Rallye 150SV	Romeo Echo Group	
G-KIAB	Scheibe SF-25C Falke 2000	York Gliding Centre Ltd	

Notes	Reg	Type	Owner or Operator
	G-KIAN	PA-28R-201 Cherokee Arrow III	Brinkley Aviation Ltd
	G-KIAU	Scheibe SF.25C Falke 2000	East Sussex Gliding Club Ltd
	G-KICK	Pegasus Quantum 15-912	M. J. Hunt
	G-KIDD	Jabiru J430	R. L. Lidd (G-CEBB)
	G-KIEV	DKBA AT 0300-0 balloon	The Volga Balloon Team
	G-KIGL	Bristell NG5 Classic HD	NG5 Aviation Ltd
	G-KIII	Extra EA.300/L	Extra 200 Ltd
	G-KIKI	PA-28-181 Cherokee Archer II	Flight Training London (G-BSIZ)
	G-KILL	Westland Gazelle AH.Mk.1	Excel Helicopters
	G-KIMA	Zenair CH.601XL Zodiac	P. J. Chandler
	G-KIMB	Robin DR.300/140	CK Aviation Services Ltd
	G-KIMD	Sling Aircraft Sling HW	P. B. Harrison
	G-KIMI	PA-46-500TP Malibu Meridian	S. N. Mitchell & M. Konstantinovic
	G-KIMK	Partenavia P.68B	R. Turrell & P. Mason (G-BCPO)
	G-KIMM	Europa XS	M. J. Sharp
	G-KIMS	Ikarus C42 FB100	M. P. Rodda
	G-KIMY	Robin DR.400/140B	R. H. Joy
	G-KIMZ	PA-28-160 Cherokee D	Ravenair Aircraft Ltd (G-AWDP)
	G-KIND	Cirrus SR20	Up (EGBO) Ltd
	G-KINL	Grumman FM-2 Wildcat (AX733/K)	T. W. Harris (G-CHPN)
	G-KINT	Scheibe SF.25C Falke 2000	G-KINT Syndicate
	G-KINZ	Autogyro MTOsport	M. Law
	G-KION	Cessna 525 Citationjet	Naljets Ltd
	G-KIPY	Van's RV-7	T. R. Fray
	G-KIRB	Europa XS	M. H. Wylde (G-OIZI)
	G-KIRT	Stoddard-Hamilton GlaStar	A. Cook & G. D. Smith
	G-KISP	Rolladen-Schneider LS10-st	D. J. Crosby
	G-KISS	Rand-Robinson KR-2	B. L. R. J. Keeping
	G-KITH	Alpi Pioneer 300	K. G. Atkinson
	G-KITI	Pitts S-2E Special	J. C. W. Seward
	G-KITS	Europa XS	D. W. Logan
	G-KIZZ	Kiss 450-582	D. L. Price
	G-KJBS	Czech Sport Sportcruiser	S. Styles
	G-KJJR	Schempp-Hirth Ventus 2cT	R. J. L. Maisonpierre
	G-KJSW	Van's RV-14	S. G. Wooler
	G-KJTT	Cessna 182A	S. E. Heale
	G-KKAM	Schleicher ASW-22BLE	D. P. Taylor
	G-KKCT	Flight Design CTSL	K. Kirby
	G-KKER	Jabiru UL-450	C. G. Langham
	G-KKKK	SA Bulldog Srs 120/121 (XX513:10)	M. Cowan (G-CCMI)
	G-KKRN	Robinson R22	HQ Aviation Ltd (G-WFWS/G-LINS/G-DMCD/G-OOLI)
	G-KKRV	Van's RV-7	K. C. Hobday & K. J. Bladen
	G-KKSX	Rolladen-Schneider LS8-t	P. D. Kaye
	G-KKTG	Cessna 182R	Chartland Aviation Ltd
	G-KKXR	Kubicek BB16XR balloon	Virgin Balloon Flights
	G-KLAW	Christen Eagle II	L. F. Pella
	G-KLCK	Airbus AS.350B3 Ecureuil	Skyhook Helicopters
	G-KLDA	Eurocopter EC135 P2+	Castle Air Ltd
	G-KLLY	Airbus AS.350B2 Ecureuil	Performance Focus Ltd
	G-KLMS	Groppo Trail	K. Luby
	G-KLNH	Leonardo AW109SP Grand New	Elstree Ink Ltd
	G-KLNM	Aibus AS.350B3 Ecureuil	Klyne Air Ltd (G-OGLE/G-CIEU)
	G-KLUB	Scheibe SF.25C Rotax-Falke	L. Ingram
	G-KLYE	Skyranger Swift 912S(1)	P. P. Fegan
	G-KLYM	TAF Sling 4 TSI	S. Klymenko
	G-KMAK	P & M Quik GT450	F. Godfrey
	G-KMIR	Schleicher ASH-31 Mi	A. Darlington
	G-KMJK	DG Flugzeugbau DG-808C	N. Burke, L. Rayment & D. W. Smith
	G-KMKM	AutoGyro MTO Sport	S. W. Kinsey
	G-KMLA	Cirrus SR20	KML Aviation OY/Finland
	G-KMRV	Van-s RV-9A	P. P. Duffy
	G-KMTE	Cirrus SR22	KeyMT Installation Ltrd
	G-KNCG	PA-32-301FT 6X	M. C. Plomer-Roberts & T. Moore
	G-KNEE	Ultramagic M-77C balloon	M. A.Green
	G-KNEK	Grob G.109B	Syndicate 109

Reg	Type	Owner or Operator	Notes
G-KNIB	Robinson R22 Beta II	HQ Aviation Ltd	
G-KNSH	Cessna 182T	K. N. S. Hennah	
G-KNYT	Robinson R44	Brosters Environmental Ltd	
G-KOBH	Schempp-Hirth Discus bT	C. F. M. Smith & K. Neave	
G-KOCO	Cirrus SR22	G. Riddell	
G-KOFM	Glaser-Dirks DG.600/18M	A. Mossman	
G-KOKO	Cirrus SR22T	R. K. Fitzgerald	
G-KOLB	Kolb Twinstar Mk 3A	Condor Aviation International Ltd	
G-KOLI	WSK PZL-110 Koliber 150	G-KOLI Group	
G-KOLO	Dassault Falcon 8X	Centreline AV Ltd	
G-KOOK	Robinson R44 II	Kuki Helicopter Sales Ltd (G-HAGL)	
G-KOOL	DH.104 Devon C2 (VP967) ★	Yorkshire Air Museum/Elvington	
G-KORE	Sportavia SFS31 Milan	J. R. Edyvean	
G-KOSC	Supermarine 329 Spitfire IIB (P8331/RF-M)	S. A. Booth	
G-KOTA	PA-28-236 Dakota	M. D. Rush	
G-KOYY	Schempp-Hirth Nimbus 4T	D. J. Hopgood	
G-KPEM	Schempp-Hirth Ventus 3T	O. J. Walters	
G-KRAN	Scheibe SF25C Rotax-Falke	Southdown Gliding Club Ltd	
G-KRBY	Van's RV-8	P. Kirby	
G-KRES	Stoddard-Hamilton Glasair IIS RG	A. D. Murray	
G-KRIB	Robinson R44 II	Omega Environmental Services Ltd	
G-KRMT	Eurofox 3K	P. J. P. Doherty	
G-KRTO	Rand KR-2	A. R. Moller	
G-KRUZ	CZAW Sportcruiser	A. W. Shellis & P. Whittingham	
G-KRWR	Glaser-Dirks DG-600/18M	A. D. W. Hislop	
G-KSHI	Beech A36 Bonanza	Hangar 11 Collection	
G-KSIR	Stoddard-Hamilton Glasair IIS RG	K. M. Bowen	
G-KSKS	Cameron N-105 balloon	A. Kaye	
G-KSKY	Sky 77-24 balloon	M. W. Durham	
G-KSMC	Ikarus C42C FB100	P. McCarthy	
G-KSSC	Leonardo AW169	Specialist Aviation Services Ltd	
G-KSST	Agusta AW.169	Specialist Aviation Services Ltd	
G-KSSX	Schleicher ASW-27-18E	L. M. Brady	
G-KSVB	PA-24-260 Comanche	A. R. Elliott	
G-KTCH	Magni M16C Tandem Trainer	L. H. J. Spiller	
G-KTEA	Robin DR.400-140B	A. B. English	
G-KTOM	Europa XS	T. O. Koochitt	
G-KTOW	Ikarus C42 FB100	J. G. Parkin	
G-KTTY	Denney Kitfox Model 3	T. Pennington (G-LESJ)	
G KTWO	Cessna 182T	S. J. Geary	
G-KUBE	Robinson R44 II	Pentacle Ltd (G-VEIT)	
G-KUBY	PA-18-150 Super Cub (452454)	Fly to Inspire Ltd	
G-KUDU	Sling HW	T. D. R. Hardy	
G-KUGA	Sling 4 TSI	A. P. Ringrose	
G-KUGG	Schleicher ASW-27-18E	J. W. L. Otty	
G-KUIK	Mainair Pegasus Quik	P. Nugent	
G-KUIP	CZAW Sportcruiser	Cumbernauld Flyers SC	
G-KULA	Skyranger 912S(1)	G. S. Cridland	
G-KUPP	Flight Design CTSW	Cloudbase Group	
G-KUTI	Flight Design CTSW	R. Trister	
G-KUUI	J-3C-65 Cub	V. S. E. Norman	
G-KVAN	Flight Design CTSW	K. Brown (G-IROE)	
G-KVBF	Cameron A-340HL balloon	Virgin Balloon Flights	
G-KVIP	Beech 200 Super King Air	Centreline AV Ltd	
G-KVRB	PA-46-701TP M700	British European Aviation Ltd	
G-KWAK	Scheibe SF.25C	Mendip Gliding Club Ltd	
G-KWET	Cessna 150L	Vision Aerospace Ltd (G-CSFC)	
G-KWFL	EV-97 Eurostar SL	K. M. Waugh & A. P. Portsmouth	
G-KWKI	QAC Quickie Q.200	W. S. Allen	
G-KWKR	P & M QuikR	R. M. Vernon	
G-KWKX	P & M Quik R	M. G. Evans	
G-KWPW	Guimbal Cabri G2	Flying Pig & Elstree Helicopters (G-RJVH)	

Notes	Reg	Type	Owner or Operator
	G-KXMS	Schempp-Hirth Ventus cT	H. Hamid
	G-KXXI	Schleicher ASK-21	Edgehill Gliding Centre Ltd
	G-KYLA	Cirrus SR22	J. Bannister
	G-KYLE	Thruster T600N 450	Thruster G-KYLE Pilot Training Group
	G-KYTE	PA-28-161 Cherokee Warrior II	G. Whitlow (G-BRRN)
	G-KYTT	PA-18-150 Super Cub	F. Actis
	G-KZEN	Lange E1 Antares	I. C. Baker
	G-LAAA	Airbus Helicopters EC.135 T3	London's Air Ambulance Ltd
	G-LAAB	Airbus Helicopters EC.135 T3	London's Air Ambulance Ltd
	G-LAAC	Cameron C-90 balloon	S. Dyer
	G-LAAI	Druine D.5 Turbi	D. Silsbury
	G-LABS	Europa	B. I. Knight
	G-LACB	PA-28-161 Cherokee Warrior II	LAC Flying School
	G-LADS	Rockwell Commander 114	D. F. Soul
	G-LAIR	Stoddard-Hamilton Glasair IIS FT	E. P. Howard
	G-LAKA	Bombardier BD700-1A11 Global 5500	Jet Concierge Club
	G-LAKB	JSC Sportine Aviacija LAK-17B FES	J. B. Marchant
	G-LAKI	Jodel DR.1050	E. C. R. Holland (G-JWBB)
	G-LALA	Cessna FA.150K	W. Ali
	G-LAMI	PA-46-350P Malibu Mirage	R. E. Thompson & Co (Vacuum) Ltd
	G-LAMM	Europa	S. A. Lamb
	G-LAMP	Cameron 110 Lightbulb SS balloon	D. M. Hoddinott
	G-LAMS	Cessna F.152 II	APB Leasing Ltd
	G-LAMU	Diamond DA62	R. C. Sharp
	G-LANC	Avro 683 Lancaster X (KB889) ★	Imperial War Museum/Duxford
	G-LANE	Cessna F.172N	Gala Motors Ltd
	G-LAOL	PA-28RT-201 Cherokee Arrow IV	Arrow Flying Group
	G-LAPL	Scheibe SF25C Rotax-Falke	L. Ingram
	G-LAPW	PA-46-350P Malibu Mirage	A. J. Pritchard (G-PTEA)
	G-LARA	Robin DR.400/180	K. D. & C. A. Brackwell
	G-LARD	Robinson R66	Perry Farming Company
	G-LARE	PA-39 Twin Comanche	Glareways (Neasden) Ltd
	G-LARK	Helton Lark 95	Lark Group
	G-LARR	AS.350B3 Squirrel	TSL Contractors Ltd
	G-LASR	Stoddard-Hamilton Glasair II	G. Lewis
	G-LASS	Rutan Vari-Eze	T. White
	G-LAUD	Cessna 208 Caravan 1	Laudale Estate LLP
	G-LAVN	Guimbal Cabri G2	Helicentre Aviation Ltd
	G-LAWA	Agusta Westland AW139	Castle Air Ltd (G-VIPG)
	G-LAZL	PA-28-161 Cherokee Warrior II	Highland Aviation Training Ltd
	G-LAZZ	Stoddard-Hamilton Glastar	D. F. P. Finan & P. W. Carlton
	G-LBAC	Cosmik EV-97 TeamEurostar UK	A. Cox
	G-LBDC	Bell 206B JetRanger III	Duagh Leasing LLP
	G-LBMM	PA-28-161 Cherokee Warrior II	Reyviation Ltd
	G-LBRC	PA-28RT-201 Cherokee Arrow IV	D. J. V. Morgan
	G-LBRR	Eurocopter AS.350B3 Ecureuil	Skyhook Helicopters
	G-LBRT	Beech D.17S	T. W. Gilbert
	G-LBUK	Lindstrand LBL-77A balloon	Virgin Balloon Flights
	G-LBUZ	Aerotechnick EV-97A Eurostar	D. P. Tassart
	G-LCAB	Embraer ERJ190-100LR	BA Cityflyer Ltd
	G-LCAC	Embraer ERJ190-100LR	BA Cityflyer Ltd
	G-LCAD	Embraer ERJ190-100LR	BA Cityflyer Ltd
	G-LCAE	Embraer ERJ190-100LR	BA Cityflyer Ltd
	G-LCAF	Embraer ERJ190-100LR	BA Cityflyer Ltd
	G-LCAG	Embraer ERJ190-100LR	BA Cityflyer Ltd
	G-LCAH	Embraer ERJ190-100LR	BA Cityflyer Ltd
	G-LCGL	Comper CLA.7 Swift (replica)	R. A. Fleming
	G-LCKY	Flight Design CTSW	D. Subhani
	G-LCMW	TL 2000UK Sting Carbon	B. J. Tyre
	G-LCPL	AS.365N-2 Dauphin 2	AS Aerospace Ltd
	G-LCPX	Eurocopter EC155 B1	Charterstyle Ltd (G-WINV/G-WJCJ)
	G-LCUB	PA-18-95 Super Cub	The Tiger Club 1990 Ltd (G-AYPR)
	G-LCYJ	Embraer ERJ190-100LR	BA Cityflyer Ltd
	G-LCYK	Embraer ERJ190-100LR	BA Cityflyer Ltd
	G-LCYL	Embraer ERJ190-100LR	BA Cityflyer Ltd
	G-LCYM	Embraer ERJ190-100LR	BA Cityflyer Ltd

Reg	Type	Owner or Operator	Notes
G-LCYN	Embraer ERJ190-100LR	BA Cityflyer Ltd	
G-LCYO	Embraer ERJ190-100LR	BA Cityflyer Ltd	
G-LCYP	Embraer ERJ190-100LR	BA Cityflyer Ltd	
G-LCYR	Embraer ERJ190-100LR	BA Cityflyer Ltd	
G-LCYS	Embraer ERJ190-100LR	BA Cityflyer Ltd	
G-LCYT	Embraer ERJ190-100LR	BA Cityflyer Ltd	
G-LCYU	Embraer ERJ190-100LR	BA Cityflyer Ltd	
G-LCYV	Embraer ERJ190-100LR	BA Cityflyer Ltd	
G-LCYZ	Embraer ERJ190-100LR	BA Cityflyer Ltd	
G-LDAH	Skyranger 912 (1)	S. Davies	
G-LDER	Schleicher ASW-22	P. Shrosbree & D. Starer	
G-LDGA	Diamond DA.42NG Twin Star	Twinstar4hire Ltd	
G-LDGB	Diamond DA.42NG Twin Star	Twinstar4hire Ltd	
G-LDGC	Diamond DA.40D Star	Twinstar4hire Ltd (G-OCCU)	
G-LDGD	Diamond DA.40D Star	Leading Edge Aviation Ltd (G-TULA)	
G-LDGF	Diamond DA.42NG Twin Star	Twinstar4hire Ltd	
G-LDGG	Diamond DA.42NG Twin Star	Twinstar4hire Ltd	
G-LDGH	Diamond DA.40NG Star	P. R. Hornyak	
G-LDGU	Slingsby T67M-200 Firefly	Leading Edge Aviation Ltd (G-BYRY)	
G-LDMC	Schleicher AS-33 ES	M. Clarke	
G-LDNG	Diamond DA.62	Twinstar4Hire Ltd	
G-LDSA	TAF Sting 4	L. J. d'Sa	
G-LDWS	Jodel D.150	C. A. & L. J. Bailey (G-BKSS)	
G-LDYS	Colt 56A balloon	M. J. Myddelton	
G-LEAF	Cessna F.406	RVL Aviation Ltd	
G-LEAH	Alpi Pioneer 300	J. M. Gibson Executor of the Estate of W. C. Walters	
G-LEAM	PA-28-236 Dakota	G-LEAM Group (G-BHLS)	
G-LEAS	Sky 90-24 balloon	C. I. Humphrey	
G-LEAT	Ultramagic B-70 balloon	Longleat Enterprises Ltd	
G-LEAX	Cessna 560XL Citation XLS	London Executive Aviation Ltd	
G-LEBE	Europa	J. D. C. Henslow	
G-LECY	Pipistrel Virus SW 128	G-LECY Aviation Ltd	
G-LEDE	Zenair CH.601UL Zodiac	A. Tucker	
G-LEED	Denney Kitfox Mk 2	O. C. Rash	
G-LEEE	Jabiru UL-450	T. Bailey	
G-LEEH	Ultramagic M-90 balloon	Sport Promotion SRL/Italy	
G-LEEK	Reality Escapade	S. E. Lyden	
G-LEEN	Aero Designs Pulsar XP	R. B. Hemsworth (G-BZMP/G-DESI)	
G-LEEX	Hughes 369D	LPJ Aviation Ltd	
G-LEEZ	Bell 206L-1 LongRanger 2	Heli-Lift Services (G-BPCT)	
G-LEGC	Embraer EMB-135BJ Legacy	London Executive Aviation Ltd	
G-LECD	Vickers-Armstrong Spitfire T.IX	Aero Legends Leasing Ltd (MJ444/DK-H)	
G-LEGG	Cessna F.182Q	W. A. L. Mitchell (G-GOOS)	
G-LEGO	Cameron O-77 balloon	P. M. Traviss	
G-LEGY	Flight Design CTLS 600 UK	T. R. Grief	
G-LELE	Lindstrand LBL-31A balloon	A. P. Wallace & M. T. Wiltshire	
G-LEME	PA-28-181 Cherokee Archer II	A. S. Bamrah (G-BSIM)	
C LEMI	Van's RV-8	C. R. Robert	
G-LEMM	Ultramagic Z-90 balloon	I. Vastano/Italy	
G-LEMP	P & M Quik R	E. M. & A. M. Brewis	
G-LENB	Flylight Adam	G. M. P. Stokes	
G-LENF	Mainair Blade 912S	A. P. Douglas-Dixon	
G-LENI	AS.355F1 Ecureuil	Helicopter Services Ltd (G-ZFDB/G-BLEV)	
G-LENN	Cameron V-56 balloon	R. Parr	
G-LENO	Flylight Exodus Deltajet 500 Stingray	C. Fender	
G-LENZ	Cirrus SR20	Renneta Ltd	
G-LEOD	Pietenpol Aircamper	E. Gordon	
G-LEOS	Robin DR.400/120	Exavia Ltd	
G-LEPR	Eurofox 3K	G-LEPR Group	
G-LESF	Jabiru UL-450	Lord L. J. Field (G-ODGS)	
G-LESO	Boeing 737-MAX8	Ascend Airways Ltd	
G-LESZ	Denney Kitfox Mk 5	G. M. Park	
G-LETS	Van's RV-7	M. O'Hearne	
G-LEVI	Aeronca 7AC Champion	G-LEVI Group	
G-LEXS	Agusta A.109E Power	Blade 5 Ltd (G-IVJM/G-MOMO)	
G-LEXX	Van's RV-8	S. Emery	
G-LEXY	Van's RV-8	A. J. Tailby & A. J. L. Eves	

Notes	Reg	Type	Owner or Operator
	G-LEZE	Rutan LongEz	C. M. Pearson
	G-LFES	AB Sportine LAK-17B FES	C. J. Tooze
	G-LFEZ	AB Sportine LAK-17B FES	G-LFEZ Syndicate
	G-LFIX	VS.509 Spitfire T.IX (ML407/NL-D)	Ultimate Warbird Flights Ltd
	G-LFSA	PA-38-112 Tomahawk	Ravenair Aircraft Ltd (G-BSFC)
	G-LFSC	PA-28-140 Cherokee	Bristol Flying Club Ltd (G-BGTR)
	G-LFSG	PA-28-180 Cherokee E	NE PC IT Ltd (G-AYAA)
	G-LFSI	PA-28-140 Cherokee	Merseyflight Ltd (G-AYKV)
	G-LFSJ	PA-28-161 Cherokee Warrior II	Praeluceo Property Ltd (G-BPHE)
	G-LFSL	PA-38-112 Tomahawk II	Leading Edge Flight Training Ltd (G-BNSL)
	G-LFSN	PA-38-112 Tomahawk	Ravenair Aircraft Ltd (G-BNYV)
	G-LFSO	PA-38-112 Tomahawk	Abbotsinch Aviation Ltd (G-BGRM)
	G-LFST	PA-28-180 Cherokee E	Ravenair Aircraft Ltd (G-BSGD)
	G-LFSU	PA-38-112 Tomahawk II	Liverpool Flying School Ltd (G-BNNU)
	G-LFSW	PA-28-161 Cherokee Warrior II	Perranporth Flying Club Ltd (G-BSGL)
	G-LFTM	KFA Safari	R. A. Stephens & L. Goldsbrough
	G-LFVB	VS.349 Spitfire LF.Vb (EP120)	Patina Ltd
	G-LFVC	VS.349 Spitfire VC (JG891)	Comanche Warbirds Ltd
	G-LFVE	VS.349 Spitfire LF.Vb	Aircraft Restoration Company Ltd (G-CJWO)
	G-LGAN	PA-28-181 Cherokee Archer III	D. Hepworth
	G-LGCA	Robin DR.400/180R	London Gliding Club Proprietary Ltd
	G-LGCB	Robin DR.400/180R	London Gliding Club Proprietary Ltd
	G-LGCC	Robin DR 400/180R	London Gliding Club Proprietary Ltd (G-BNXI)
	G-LGCD	Robin DR 400/180R	London Gliding Club Proprietary Ltd (G-EHMM)
	G-LGEZ	Rutan Long-EZ	P. C. Elliott
	G-LGIS	Dornier 228-202K	Aurigny Air Services Ltd
	G-LGLG	Cameron Z-210 balloon	Flying Circus SRL/Spain
	G-LHAB	TAF Sling 2	A. P. Beggin
	G-LHCB	Robinson R22 Beta	Helipower Hire Ltd (G-SIVX)
	G-LHER	Czech Sport Aircraft Piper Sport	S. J. Tootell
	G-LHXA	Diamond DA.42NG Twin Star	Tesla Solutions Ltd
	G-LHXB	Diamond DA.42NG Twin Star	Atlantic Flight Training Ltd
	G-LHXC	Diamond DA.42NG Twin Star	Romeo Golf Aviation Ltd
	G-LHXD	Diamond DA.42NG Twin Star	Romeo Golf Aviation Ltd
	G-LIBB	Cameron V-77 balloon	R. J. Mercer
	G-LIBI	Glasflugel Standard Libelle 201B	O. Spreckley
	G-LIBS	Hughes 369HS	R. J. H. Strong
	G-LIBY	Glasflugel Standard Libelle 201B	R. P. Hardcastle
	G-LICK	Cessna 172N II	Sky Back Ltd (G-BNTR)
	G-LIDA	Hoffmann H36 Dimona	W. D. & S. M. Inglis
	G-LIFB	Aeroprakt A-32M Vixxen	N. J. Wright
	G-LIIZ	Boeing Stearman D75N1 Kaydet (44)	M. L. Blaze (G-DINS/G-RJAH)
	G-LIKE	Europa	N. G. Henry (G-CHAV)
	G-LIKK	Robinson R66 Turbine	G-LIKK Ltd
	G-LIKY	Aviat A-1C-180 Husky	L. W. H. Griffith
	G-LILB	Van's RV-3B	E. R. J. Hicks & A. R. Williams
	G-LILM	Extra NG	M. J. de Morgan
	G-LILO	Bell 505 Jet Ranger X	S. J. E. Wills
	G-LILY	Bell 206B JetRanger 3	T. S. Brown (G-NTBI)
	G-LIMO	Bell 206L-1 LongRanger	Prism Shift Ltd
	G-LIMP	Cameron C-80 balloon	Balloons over Yorkshire Ltd
	G-LIMR	Bristell NG5 Classic HD	C. J. Adey
	G-LINJ	Robinson R44 II	Helicentre Ltd (G-ODCR)
	G-LINN	Europa XS	G. J. Port
	G-LINY	Robinson R44 II	Helicentre Aviation Ltd
	G-LINZ	Robinson R44 II	Helicentre Aviation Ltd
	G-LIOA	Lockheed 10A ElectraH (NC5171N) ★	Science Museum/South Kensington
	G-LION	PA-18 Super Cub 135 (R-167)	North Wales Flight Academy Ltd
	G-LIOT	Cameron O-77 balloon	N. D. Eliot
	G-LIPS	Cameron 90 Lips SS balloon	M. T. Joyce & T. P. Balson (G-BZBV)
	G-LISS	AutogGyro UK Calidus	Gyronauts Flying Club Ltd
	G-LITN	Murphy Renegade 912	G. R. Litton
	G-LITO	Agusta A109S Grand	Castle Air Ltd
	G-LITS	P & M Quik R	L. Hogan
	G-LITT	Bell 407	Hirecopter Ltd
	G-LITZ	Pitts S-1E Special	H. J. Morton
	G-LIVH	Piper J-3C-65 Cub (330238:A-24)	B. L. Procter

Reg	Type	Owner or Operator	Notes
G-LIVS	Schleicher ASH-26E	R. N. John	
G-LIZI	PA-28-160 Cherokee	Peterborough Flying School Ltd (G-ARRP)	
G-LIZY	Westland Lysander III (V9673) ★	Imperial War Museum/Duxford	
G-LJMJ	Cirrus SR22T	P. M. C. Jordan	
G-LKAM	Sonaca S200	Blueplane Ltd	
G-LKDM	Sonaca S200	Blueplane Ltd	
G-LKSM	Sonaca S200	Blueplane Ltd	
G-LKVA	Tecnam P2010	JTA Aviation Ltd	
G-LKZZ	PA-28R-201 Cherokee Arrow III	Blackbushe Aviation	
G-LLBE	Lindstrand LBL-360A balloon	K. S. Hull	
G-LLEW	Aeromot AMT-200S Super Ximango	M. P. Brockington & K. Richards	
G-LLLL	Rolladen-Schneider LS8-18	P. C. Fritche	
G-LLMW	Diamond DA42 Twin Star	Ming W. L.	
G-LLNT	Schleicher ASW-27-18E	N. D. Tillett	
G-LLOY	Alpi Pioneer 300	N. J. A. Tsappis	
G-LLLY	Enstrom 480B	AR-Pats LLP	
G-LLWP	Aeroprakt A-32M Vixxen	J. G. Porter (G-VXXI)	
G-LLYN	Eurofox 912(IS)	D. M. Griffiths	
G-LMAO	Cessna F.172N	Think N Fly	
G-LMCB	Raj Hamsa X'Air Hawk	T. C. Rushton	
G-LMHA	Bombardier BD700-1A10 Global 6500	Jet Concierge Club	
G-LMLV	Dyn'Aéro MCR-01	S. I. Hatherall	
G-LMRA	Avions Transport ATR-42-500	Loganair Ltd	
G-LMRB	Avions Transport ATR-42-500	Loganair Ltd	
G-LMRD	Avions Transport ATR-42-500	Loganair Ltd (G-HUET)	
G-LMRE	Avions Transport ATR-42-500	Loganair Ltd	
G-LMRV	Avions Transport ATR-72-212A	Loganair Ltd	
G-LMRX	Avions Transport ATR-72-212A	Loganair Ltd	
G-LMRY	Avions Transport ATR-72-202F	Loganair Ltd	
G-LMRZ	Avions Transport ATR-72-212A	Loganair Ltd	
G-LMSA	Avions Transport ATR-42-500	Loganair Ltd	
G-LMSB	Avions Transport ATR-42-500	Loganair Ltd	
G-LMTA	Avions Transport ATR-72-212A	Loganair Ltd	
G-LMTB	Avions Transport ATR-72-212A	Loganair Ltd	
G-LMTC	Avions Transport ATR-72-212A	Loganair Ltd	
G-LMTD	Avions Transport ATR-72-212A	Loganair Ltd	
G-LMTE	Avions Transport ATR-72-212A	Loganair Ltd	
G-LMTF	Avions Transport ATR-72-212A	Loganair Ltd	
G-LMTG	Avions Transport ATR-72-212A	Loganair Ltd	
G-LMTH	Avions Transport ATR-72-212A	Loganair Ltd	
G-LMTI	Avions Transport ATR-72-212A	Loganair Ltd	
G-LMTJ	Avions Transport ATR-72-212A	Loganair Ltd	
G-LNAC	Leonardo AW169	Specialist Aviation Services Ltd	
G-LNCC	Leonardo AW169	Heliservice UK Ltd	
G-LNCR	Lancair 235	Cavendish Aviation UK Ltd (G-BSRI)	
G-LNCT	MDH MD-900 Explorer	Specialist Aviation Services Ltd	
G-LNDA	BRM Bristell NG5 Speed Wing	D. J. Medcraft	
G-LNIG	Flylight Dragonfly	A. J. Cox	
G-LNKX	Westland Lynx AH Mk.7	A. D. Whitehouse	
G-LNWZ	Hawker Hurricane 1 (P3966/VY-X)	White Waltham Airfield Ltd	
G-LOAD	Dan Rihn DR.107 One Design	M. J. Clark	
G-LOAM	Flylight MotorFloater	I. C. White	
G-LOAN	Cameron N-77 balloon	P. R. Hutchinson	
G-LOBO	Cameron O-120 balloon	Solo Aerostatics	
G-LOBX	Bombardier BD700-2A12 Global 7500	ARC Aviation Ltd	
G-LOBY	Bombardier BD700-2A12 Global 7500	Concierge U Ltd	
G-LOCC	Flylight Adam	D. A. Hendriksen	
G-LOCH	Piper J-3C-65 Cub	M. C. & M. R. Greenland	
G-LOEZ	Rutan LongEz	C. J. Perkins (G-BLRH)	
G-LOGI	Robinson R66	LA Helicopters Ltd	
G-LOGN	PA-28-181 Cherokee Archer III	Corporate Aviation UK Ltd	
G-LOIS	Jabiru UL	R. J. Green	
G-LOKI	Ultramagic M-77C balloon	L. J. M. Muir	
G-LOLZ	Robinson R22 Beta	Swift Helicopter Services Ltd	
G-LOMN	Cessna 152	Brinkley Aviation Ltd	

Notes	Reg	Type	Owner or Operator
	G-LONE	Bell 206L-1 LongRanger	Central Helicopters Ltd
	G-LOOC	Cessna 172S	Goodwood Road Racing Co.Ltd
	G-LOON	Cameron C-60 balloon	C. Williamson
	G-LOOP	Pitts S-1D Special	N. J. Tomlinson
	G-LORC	PA-28-161 Cadet	Advanced Flight Training Ltd
	G-LORD	PA-34-200T Seneca II	The Flying Griggin GmbH/Germany
	G-LORN	Avions Mudry CAP-10B	M. J. Caskey
	G-LORR	PA-28-181 Cherokee Archer III	Shropshire Aero Club Ltd
	G-LORY	Thunder Ax4-31Z balloon	L. J. Wigfield
	G-LOSM	Gloster Meteor NF.11 (WM167)	D. G. Thomas
	G-LOSY	Aerotechnik EV-97 Eurostar	M. L. Willmington
	G-LOTI	Bleriot XI (replica) ★	Brooklands Museum Trust Ltd
	G-LOTY	P & M Aviation Pegasus Quik	L. Hewitt
	G-LOUD	Schleicher ASW-27-18E	T. Stuart
	G-LOUS	EV-97 Eurostar SL	S. E. Bettley & M. D. Jealous
	G-LOWE	Monett Sonerai I	P. A. Hall
	G-LOWZ	P & M Quik GT450	N. S. Martin
	G-LOYA	Cessna FR.172J	R. I. Dawson (G-BLVT)
	G-LOYD	Aérospatiale SA.341G Gazelle 1	S. Athgerton (G-SFTC)
	G-LOYW	Airbus MBB BK-117 D-2	Gama Aviation (UK) Ltd (G-YOAA)
	G-LPAD	Lindstrand LBL-105A balloon	G. R. Down
	G-LPIN	P & M Aviation Quik R	G. P. D. Coan
	G-LRBW	Lindstrand LBL HS-110 Hot-Air Airship	Flydade
	G-LREE	Grob G.109B	Husbands Bosworth Gliding Club Ltd
	G-LRMJ	Cirrus SR22	AQ GCI Ltd
	G-LRNC	PA-28-161 Cherokee Warrior II	UP (EGBO) Ltd (G-BOFZ)
	G-LSCM	Cessna 172S	Pooler-LMT Ltd
	G-LSCP	Rolladen-Schneider LS6-18W	M. F. Collins & L. G. Blows
	G-LSCW	Gulfstream 550	Langley Aviation Ltd
	G-LSED	Rolladen-Schneider LS6-c	K. Atkinson & T. Faver
	G-LSFB	Rolladen-Schneider LS7-WL	G. K. Stanford
	G-LSFR	Rolladen-Schneider LS4-a	A. Mulder
	G-LSFT	PA-28-161 Cherokee Warrior II	Falcon Flying Services Ltd (G-BXTX)
	G-LSGB	Rolladen-Schneider LS6-b	A. Rieder
	G-LSGM	Rolladen-Schneider LS3-17	N. G. English
	G-LSHI	Colt 77A balloon	J. H. Dobson
	G-LSIF	Rolladen-Schneider LS1-f	G. P. T. White & D. Heslop
	G-LSIO	DG Flugzeugbau LS10-ST	C. Darlow
	G-LSIV	Rolladen-Schneider LS4	G. M. O'Hagan
	G-LSIX	Rolladen-Schneider LS6-18W	D. P. Masson
	G-LSJE	Escapade Jabiru(1)	L. S. J. Webb
	G-LSKV	Rolladen-Schneider LS8-18	H. L. Wilson
	G-LSKY	Mainair Pegasus Quik	M. Gudgeon
	G-LSLS	Rolladen-Schneider LS4	288 Syndicate
	G-LSPH	Van's RV-8	R. S. Partridge-Hicks
	G-LSTA	Stoddard-Hamilton Glastar	Lampy Investments Ltd
	G-LSTR	Stoddard-Hamilton Glastar	R. J. Wesley
	G-LSVI	Rolladen-Schneider LS6-c18	R. B. Porteous
	G-LSXG	Rolladen-Scneider LS6-b	S. M. Kenyon-Roberts (G-DFRA)
	G-LTBR	Courtford DB-3 balloon	A. B. Court
	G-LTFB	PA-28-140 Cherokee	C. Marker
	G-LTSB	Cameron LTSB-90 balloon	ABC Flights Ltd
	G-LTWA	Robinson R44	L. T. W. Alderman
	G-LUAS	SIAI Marchetti SF.260D	SF260 Ltd
	G-LUBY	Jabiru J430	P. R. Brown
	G-LUCK	Cessna F.150M	A. W. C. Knight
	G-LUCL	Colomban MC-30 Luciole	A. McQueen
	G-LUED	Aero Designs Pulsar	J. Cook
	G-LUEK	Cessna 182T	S. R. Greenall
	G-LUEY	Rans S-7S Courier	T. N. Jerry
	G-LUGS	Agusta A109S Grand	Myheli Ltd (G-FRZN)
	G-LUKA	Beech G.58 Baron	Bentley O-S Ltd
	G-LUKE	Rutan LongEz	M. A. Hatch-Roy
	G-LULA	Cameron C-90 balloon	T. S. Davis
	G-LULV	Diamond DA-42 Twin Star	B. A. & M. L. M. Langevad
	G-LUMI	Cirrus SR22T	A9 Leasing LLP

Reg	Type	Owner or Operator	Notes
G-LUNE	Mainair Pegasus Quik	D. Muir	
G-LUNG	Rotorsport UK MT-03	P. Krysiak	
G-LUNT	Van's RV-7	C. C. Lunt	
G-LUNY	Pitts S-1S Special	G-LUNY Group	
G-LUON	Schleicher ASW-27-18E	A. D. Le Roux & P. Davis	
G-LUSC	Luscombe 8E Silvaire	C. D. Carder	
G-LUSI	Luscombe 8F Silvaire	P. H. Isherwood	
G-LUSK	Luscombe 8F Silvaire	M. A. Lamprell & P. J. Laycock (G-BRGG)	
G-LUSO	Pilatus PC-121/47E	247 Aviation Ltd.	
G-LUST	Luscombe 8E Silvaire	C. J. Watson & M. R. Griffiths	
G-LUUP	Pilatus B4-PC11AF	B. L. Coopere (G-ECSW)	
G-LUUX	Agusta A109E	Castle Air Ltd	
G-LUXE	BAe 146-301	United Kingdom Research & Innovation (G-SSSH)	
G-LVCY	Colomban MC-30 Luciole	C. Wright	
G-LVIE	Robinson R44 II	Luviair Ltd (G-GEST)	
G-LVLY	Agusta A109S Grand	Castle Air Ltd (G-EMHE)	
G-LVME	Cessna F.152 II	Superior Air SA/Greece (G-BGHI)	
G-LVPL	Edge XT912 B/Streak III-B	V. D. Carmichael	
G-LVRS	PA-28-181 Cherokee Archer II	M. Manzouri (G-ZMAM/G-BNPN)	
G-LWLW	Diamond DA.40D Star	Virage Aviation LLP (G-CCLV)	
G-LXBB	Aerospool Dynmamic WT9 LSM	LX Aviation Ltd	
G-LXUS	Alpi Pioneer 300	J. Oswald	
G-LXVI	Schempp-Hirth Arcus T	S. G. Holland & M. G. Lynes	
G-LXXI	PA-18-135 Super Cub (42617/617)	P. J. & R. V. Tucker	
G-LXXV	Boeing E75L 300 Stearman	Mid America (UK) Ltd (G-CLWV)	
G-LYDA	Hoffmann H-36 Dimona	G-LYDA Flying Group	
G-LYDF	PA-31-350 Navajo Chieftain	Gulfjet Aviation Ltd	
G-LYFA	IDABacau Yakovlev Yak-52	Fox Alpha Group	
G-LYFT	Magni M24C Plus	L. Baring	
G-LYNC	Robinson R22 Beta II	P. M. Phillips	
G-LYND	PA-25-235 Pawnee	York Gliding Centre (Operations) Ltd (G-ASFX/ G-BSFZ)	
G-LYNI	Aerotechnik EV-97 Eurostar	M. E. Booth	
G-LYNJ	Bell 407	Jones Brothers (Henllan) Ltd	
G-LYNK	CFM Shadow Srs DD	A. Crowe	
G-LYNX	Westland WG.13 Lynx ★	The Helicopter Museum/Weston-super-Mare	
G-LYPG	Jabiru UL	A. J. Geary	
G-LYPH	Rolladen-Schneider LS8-18-st	S. & S. Barter	
G-LYRA	Robinson R44 II	EBG (Helicopters) Ltd	
G-LYTE	Thunder Ax7-77 S1 balloon	R. G. Turnbull	
G-LYZA	Guimbal Cabri G2	Lyza Aviation Ltd (G-IZOO)	
G-LYZY	Westland Lysander IIIA (V9546/MA-D)	Patina Ltd	
G-LZED	AutoGyro MTO Sport	L. Zivanovic	
G-LZII	Laser Z200	K. G. Begley	
G-LZRI	Embraer EMB-550 Praetor 600	Centreline AV Ltd	
G-LZZI	Airbus MBB BK117 D-3	Wycombe Management Services LLP	
G-MAAL	TLAC Shark 600	Mid Anglia Aviation Ltd	
G-MAAN	Europa XS	P. S. Mann	
G-MAAT	Flight Design CTLS	M. J. Cackett (G-CONA/G-CGED)	
G-MABE	Cessna F.150L	Aviolease Ltd (G-BLJP)	
G-MABL	Quik GTR	M. Tomlinson	
G-MACC	Cub Crafters Carbon Cub EX-2	M. W. Albery	
G-MACH	SIAI-Marchetti SF.260	Cheyne Motors Ltd	
G-MACI	Van's RV-7	N. J. F. Campbell	
G-MACR	Cirrus SR22T	Lismore Instruments Ltd	
G-MACY	Boeing 767-204	Maersk Air Cargo UK Ltd (G-SATR/G-BPFV)	
G-MACZ	Boeing 767-25E	Maersk Air Cargo UK Ltd	
G-MADC	Grif 3DC/Eurofly Snake	N. C. Milnes	
G-MADV	P & M Quik GT450	Flylight Airsports Ltd	
G-MADX	AgustaWestland AW.119 Mk.II	SaxonAir Helicopters	
G-MADZ	Bell 505 Jet Ranger X	Overby Ltd	
G-MAFA	Cessna F.406	Directflight Ltd (G-DFLT)	
G-MAFB	Cessna F.406	Directflight Ltd	
G-MAFF	BN-2T Turbine Islander	Islander Aircraft Ltd (G-BJED)	

Notes	Reg	Type	Owner or Operator
	G-MAGC	Cameron Grand Illusion SS balloon	Magical Adventures Ltd
	G-MAGG	Pitts S-1SE Special	J. J. Radcliffe
	G-MAGK	Schleicher ASW-20L	A. G. K. Mackenzie
	G-MAGN	Magni M-24C	R. Subberwal
	G-MAGZ	Robin DR.400/500	M. Farrugia
	G-MAHY	Cessna 182T	G. J. Mahoney (G-SKEN)
	G-MAIE	PA-32RT-301T Turbo Saratoga II TC	S. James
	G-MAIN	Mainair Blade 912	J. C. Seal
	G-MAJA	BAe Jetstream 4102	Eastern Airways
	G-MAJB	BAe Jetstream 4102	Eastern Airways (G-BVKT)
	G-MAJC	BAe Jetstream 4102	Eastern Airways (G-LOGJ)
	G-MAJD	BAe Jetstream 4102	Eastern Airways (G-WAWR)
	G-MAJG	BAe Jetstream 4102	Eastern Airways (G-LOGL)
	G-MAJJ	BAe Jetstream 4102	Eastern Airways (G-WAFT)
	G-MAJK	BAe Jetstream 4102	Eastern Airways
	G-MAJL	BAe Jetstream 4102	Eastern Airways
	G-MAJR	DHC.1 Chipmunk 22 (WP805)	C. Adams
	G-MAJT	BAe Jetstream 4100	Eastern Airways
	G-MAJU	BAe Jetstream 4100	Eastern Airways
	G-MAJW	BAe Jetstream 4100	Eastern Airways
	G-MAJY	BAe Jetstream 4100	Eastern Airways
	G-MAJZ	BAe Jetstream 4100	Eastern Airways
	G-MAKE	Rotorsport UK Calidus	W. H. Allchin
	G-MAKK	Aeroprakt A-22-L Foxbat	M. A. McKillop
	G-MAKM	Bristell B23-915	M. A. K. McKay
	G-MAKO	Shark Aero Shark 600	J. W. D. Blythe
	G-MAKS	Cirrus SR22	M. C. Fox & D. A. Abel
	G-MALC	AA-5 Traveler	J. C. Thompson (G-BCPM)
	G-MALE	Balony Kubicek BB-S Skyballs SS balloon	A. M. Holly
	G-MALT	Colt Flying Hop SS balloon	P. J. Stapley
	G-MAMM	Ikarus C42 FB80	J. Nestor & R. W. Skelton
	G-MAMZ	Ikarus C42 FB80	Mid Anglia Microlights Ltd
	G-MANH	BAe ATP	Atlantic Airlines Ltd (G-LOGC/G-OLCC)
	G-MANX	FRED Srs 2	S. Styles
	G-MANZ	Robinson R44 II	S. M. Hill
	G-MAPY	PA-31-350 Chieftain	Blue Sky Investments Ltd (G-BXUV)
	G-MARE	Schweizer 269C	A & W Demolition (Bracknell)
	G-MARL	Autogyro Calidus	R. J. Platt & K. J. Jamieson
	G-MARZ	Thruster T.600N 450	R. J. Waldron
	G-MASC	Jodel 150A	K. F. & R. Richardson
	G-MASF	PA-28-181 Cherokee Archer II	J. D. C. Lea
	G-MASH	Westland-Bell 47G-4A	C. C. Butt (G-AXKU)
	G-MASS	Cessna 152 II	MK Aero Support Ltd (G-BSHN)
	G-MATB	Robin DR.400-160	J. & M. J. Bacon (G-BAFP)
	G-MATO	Dassault Falcon 7X	SDI Aviation Ltd
	G-MATS	Colt GA-42 airship	P. A. Lindstrand
	G-MATT	Robin R.2160	Vu JV19 Ltd (G-BKRC)
	G-MATZ	PA-28-140 Cherokee	Midland Air Training School (G-BASI)
	G-MAUS	Europa XS	A. P. Ringrose
	G-MAVK	Pitts S-1S	W. A. F. Hilton & J. N. Ponsford
	G-MAVS	Flylight Skyranger Nynja	Wanafly Airports Ltd
	G-MAXA	PA-32-301FT 6X	L. Bennett & Son Ltd
	G-MAXD	Robinson R44 1	RSM Aviation Ltd
	G-MAXG	Pitts S-1S Special	The Assets of G-MAXG Group
	G-MAXI	PA-34-200T Seneca II	Draycott Seneca Syndicate Ltd
	G-MAXS	Mainair Pegasus Quik 912S	S. Cooper
	G-MAXT	PA-28RT-201T Turbo Cherokee Arrow IV	M. Toninelli/Italy
	G-MAXV	Van's RV-4	P. G. Winters
	G-MAYZ	Van's RV-8	M. J. Allen
	G-MAZA	Rotorsport UK MT-03	V. N. Boneva
	G-MAZO	Mitchell Wing B-10	Ancient Aviation Ltd
	G-MAZY†	DH.82A Tiger Moth ★	Newark Air Museum/Newark
	G-MBAA	Hiway Skytrike Mk 2	M. J. Aubrey
	G-MBAB	Hovey Whing-Ding II	M. J. Aubrey
	G-MBAD	Weedhopper JC-24A	M. Stott
	G-MBAF	R. J. Swift 3	C. G. Wrzesien
	G-MBBJ	Hiway Demon	M. J. Aubrey
	G-MBBZ	Volmer VJ-24 ★	Newark Air Museum/Newark
	G-MBCG	Solar Wings Typhoon/Tri-Pacer 250 ★	Lakeland Motor Museum/Ulverston
	G-MBCJ	Mainair Sports Tri-Flyer	R. A. Smith

Reg	Type	Owner or Operator	Notes
G-MBCL	Sky-Trike/Typhoon	P. J. Callis	
G-MBDL	AES Lone Ranger ★	North East Aircraft Museum	
G-MBDM	Southdown Sigma Trike	A. R. Prentice	
G-MBEP	American Aerolights Eagle 215B	M. J. Aubrey	
G-MBFO	Eipper Quicksilver MX	R. A. Szczepanik	
G-MBHE	American Aerolights Eagle	R. J. Osborne	
G-MBHK	Flexiform Skytrike	A. L. Virgoe	
G-MBIO	American Eagle 215B	D. J. Lewis	
G-MBIT	Hiway Demon Skytrike	K. S. Hodgson	
G-MBJK	American Aerolights Eagle	B. W. Olley	
G-MBKY	American Aerolight Eagle	M. J. Aubrey	
G-MBKZ	Hiway Skytrike	L. Magill	
G-MBLU	Southdown Lightning L.195	C. R. Franklin	
G-MBMG	Rotec Rally 2B	J. R. Pyper	
G-MBMM	TAF Sling 4 TSI	Shoreham Sling TSI Group	
G-MBOF	Pakes Jackdaw	M. J. Aubrey	
G-MBOH	Microlight Engineering Mistral	T. J. Gayton-Polley	
G-MBPB	Pterodactyl Ptraveller	T. D. Dawson	
G-MBPX	Eurowing Goldwing SP	V. H. Hallam	
G-MBRD	American Aerolights Eagle	R. J. Osborne	
G-MBSJ	American Aerolights Eagle 215B	T. J. Gayton-Polley	
G-MBSX	Ultraflight Mirage II	A. D. Russell	
G-MBTH	Whittaker MW4	T. A. Willcox	
G-MBTJ	Solar Wings Microlight	H. A. Comber	
G-MBUD	Skycraft Scout 2 ★	Norfolk and Suffolk Aviation Museum/Flixton	
G-MBUE	MBA Tiger Cub 440 ★	Newark Air Museum/Newark	
G-MBVE	Hiway Super Scorpion/Sky-Trike ★	Newark Air Museum/Newark	
G-MBWI	Microlite Lafayette 1 ★	M. J. Aubrey	
G-MBWL	Huntair Pathfinder Mk.1	A. D. Russell	
G-MBYK	Huntair Pathfinder Mk.1	S. McGirr	
G-MBZO	Tri-Pacer 330	A. N. Burrows	
G-MBZV	American Aerolights Eagle	M. J. Aubrey	
G-MCAD	Cessna T.206H	Semer LLP	
G-MCAP	Cameron C-80 balloon	J. A. Hibberd	
G-MCAW	Sling 4 TSI	M. C. Watkiss	
G-MCCF	Thruster T.600N	I. J. Webb	
G-MCCY	IAV Bacau Yak-52	D. P. McCoy	
G-MCDB	VS.361 Spitfire LF.IX	Peter Monk Ltd	
G-MCEL	Pegasus Quantum 15-912	F. Hodgson	
G-MCFC	Leonardo AW139	Castle Air Ltd	
G-MCFK	P & M Quik GT450	F. A. A. Kay	
G-MCGE	Sikorsky S-92A	Bristow Helicopters Ltd	
G-MCGF	Sikorsky S-92A	Bristow Helicopters Ltd	
G-MCGG	Sikorsky S-92A	Bristow Helicopters Ltd	
G-MCGH	Sikorsky S-92A	Bristow Helicopters Ltd	
G-MCGI	Sikorsky S-92A	Bristow Helicopters Ltd	
G-MCGJ	Sikorsky S-92A	Bristow Helicopters Ltd	
G-MCGK	Sikorsky S-92A	Bristow Helicopters Ltd	
G-MCGL	Sikorsky S-92A	Bristow Helicopters Ltd	
G-MCGM	Agusta AW189	Bristow Helicopters Ltd	
G-MCGO	Agusta AW189	Bristow Helicopters Ltd	
G-MCGP	Agusta AW189	Bristow Helicopters Ltd	
G-MCGR	Agusta AW189	Bristow Helicopters Ltd	
G-MCGS	Agusta AW189	Bristow Helicopters Ltd	
G-MCGT	Agusta AW189	Bristow Helicopters Ltd	
G-MCGU	Leonardo AW189	Bristow Helicopters Ltd	
G-MCGV	Leonardo AW189	Bristow Helicopters Ltd	
G-MCGX	Leonardo MW189	Bristow Helicopters Ltd	
G-MCGY	Sikorsky S-92A	Bristow Helicopters Ltd	
G-MCGZ	Sikorsky S-92A	Bristow Helicopters Ltd	
G-MCJL	Pegasus Quantum 15-912	RM Aviation Ltd	
G-MCLA	Robinson R44	S. M. McLarty (G-OHJV)	
G-MCLE	Cirrus SR22T	J-B. A. Moens	
G-MCLJ	Cirrus SR22T	J. F. McLean(G-ZIVA)	
G-MCLK	Van's RV-10	S. J. Simpson	
G-MCME	TL2000 Sting S4	S. J. Haley	
G-MCNY	Cameron Z-105 balloon	Sky Rainbow UK Ltd	
G-MCOW	Lindstrand LBL-77A balloon	S. & S. Villiers	
G-MCOX	Fuji FA.200-180AO	Notsa Aviation Ltd	
G-MCPR	PA-32-301T Turbo Saratoga	M. L. Roberts (G-MOLL)	

Notes	Reg	Type	Owner or Operator
	G-MCRO	Dyn'Aero MCR-01	J. M. Keane
	G-MCRV	Van's RV-14A	M. W. Clarke
	G-MCSC	Agusta Westland AW139	Offshore Helicopter Services UK Ltd
	G-MCSD	Agusta Westland AW139	Offshore Helicopter Services UK Ltd
	G-MCSF	Airbus Helicopters EC175B	Offshore Helicopter Services UK Ltd
	G-MCSG	Airbus Helicopters EC175B	Offshore Helicopter Services UK Ltd
	G-MCSH	Airbus Helicopters EC175B	Offshore Helicopter Services UK Ltd
	G-MCSI	Sikorsky S-92A	Offshore Helicopter Services UK Ltd
	G-MCSJ	Sikorsky S-92A	Offshore Helicopter Services UK Ltd
	G-MCSK	Sikorsky S-92A	Offshore Helicopter Services UK Ltd
	G-MCSN	Airbus Helicopters EC175B	Offshore Helicopter Services UK Ltd (G-EMEA)
	G-MCSO	Airbus Helicopters EC175B	Offshore Helicopter Services UK Ltd
	G-MCSP	Airbus Helicopters EC175B	Offshore Helicopter Services UK Ltd
	G-MCSW	North American P-51D Mustang (414237/HO-W)	Warbird Experiences Ltd
	G-MCTO	Flylight Dragon Chaser	R. J. Humphries
	G-MCUB	Reality Escapade	M. A. Appleby
	G-MCVE	Ikarus C42 FB80	A. & J. McVey
	G-MCVY	Flight Design CT2K	A. & J. McVey (G-CBNA)
	G-MDAC	PA-28-181 Cherokee Archer II	Blackbushe Aviation
	G-MDAM	Fuji FA.200-180 Aero Subaru	Romeo Whisky Ltd
	G-MDAY	Cessna 170B	P. H. Dickinson
	G-MDBC	Pegasus Quantum 15-912	J. D. Ryan
	G-MDDE	Hughes 369E	Flitwick Helicopters Ltd
	G-MDMX	Hughes 369E	M. Hunt (G-CHRI)
	G-MDSE	Pilatus PC-12/47E	Select Aircrafts Ltd
	G-MDSZ	Pilatus PC-12/47E	Select Aircrafts Ltd
	G-MDYG	Diamond DA.40NG Star	Meddyg Care Group Holdings Ltd
	G-MEAS	Diamond S120 balloon	A. M. Holly & R. A. Pugh
	G-MEDK	Airbus A.320-232	BA Euroflyer Ltd
	G-MEDY	Pilatus PC-12/47E	Oriens Aviation Ltd
	G-MEEE	Schleicher ASW-20L	T. E. Macfadyen
	G-MEEP	Robinson R44 II	C. P. Marshall (G-PAMY)
	G-MEGG	Europa XS	R. L. Hitchcock
	G-MEGN	Beech B200 Super King Air	Dragonfly Aviation Services Ltd
	G-MEGZ	Ikarus C42 FB100	GMEGZ Pilots
	G-MEIS	CASA 1-133 Jungmeister	B. S. Charters
	G-MELL	CZAW Sportcruiser	G. A. & J. A. Mellins
	G-MELS	PA-28-181 Cherokee Archer III	P. J. Sowood
	G-MELT	Cessna F.172H	Falcon Aviation Ltd (G-AWTI)
	G-MEME	PA-28R-201 Cherokee Arrow III	N. D. Arjan
	G-MENU	Robinson R44 II	Brinkley Aviation Ltd
	G-MEOW	CFM Streak Shadow	G. J. Moor
	G-MERE	Lindstrand LBL-77A balloon	R. D. Baker
	G-MERF	Grob G.115A	G-MERF Group
	G-MERL	PA-28RT-201 Cherokee Arrow IV	J. Gubbay & D. Brennan
	G-MESH	CZAW Sportcruiser	M. E. S. Heaton
	G-METH	Cameron C-90 balloon	A. & D. Methley
	G-MEUP	Cameron A-120 balloon	J. M. Woodhouse
	G-MFAC	Cessna F.172H	S. F. Turner & K. J. Peacock (G-AVGZ)
	G-MFEF	Cessna FR.172J	D. R. Bide
	G-MFHI	Europa	Hi Fliers
	G-MFLI	Cameron V-90 balloon	J. M. Percival
	G-MFLJ	P & M Quik GT450	D. L. Wright
	G-MFLM	Cessna F.152 II	AT Aviation Sales Ltd (G-BFFC)
	G-MFLY	Mainair Rapier	J. J. Tierney
	G-MFMF	Bell 206B JetRanger 3	Polo Aviation Ltd (G-BJNJ)
	G-MFMM	Scheibe SF.25C Falke	J. E. Selman
	G-MFNC	Eurofly Minifox	N. W. Charles
	G-MFOX	Eurofox 912(1)	G. M. Cruise-Smith
	G-MFUX	Eurofly Minifox	Fun Flying Ltd
	G-MGBF	Pitts S-2C Special	George J Goff Ltd
	G-MGBG	Cessna 310Q	Cotswold Aero Maintenance Ltd (G-AYND)
	G-MGCK	Whittaker MW6-S FT	J. Channer
	G-MGDL	Pegasus Quantum 15	M. J. Buchanan
	G-MGEC	Rans S.6-ESD-XL Coyote II	D. Williams & S. P. Tkaczyk
	G-MGEF	Pegasus Quantum 15	S. P. Jarvis

Reg	Type	Owner or Operator	Notes
G-MGFC	Eurofox 912(1)	R. Smith	
G-MGFK	Pegasus Quantum 15	M. P. Bawden	
G-MGGG	Pegasus Quantum 15	R. A. Beauchamp	
G-MGGV	Pegasus Quantum 15-912	I. S. Duffy	
G-MGIC	Ace Magic Cyclone	N. Hart	
G-MGKG	Leonardo AW109SP Grand New	KPD 79 Ltd	
G-MGNI	Magni M.16C Tandem Trainer	S. J. Peal	
G-MGOD	Medway Raven	N. R. Andrew, A. Wherrett & D. J. Millward	
G-MGOO	Renegade Spirit UK Ltd	J. Aley	
G-MGPA	Ikarus C42 FB100	S. Ashley	
G-MGPH	CFM Streak Shadow	N. I. Hart (G-RSPH)	
G-MGPS	Leonardo AW169	Specialist Aviation Services Ltd	
G-MGTG	Pegasus Quantum 15	P. T. Seaward (G-MZIO)	
G-MGTW	CFM Shadow Srs DD	J. H. H. Turner	
G-MGWH	Thruster T.300	Bluestreak Thruster Group	
G-MGWI	Robinson R44	Hields Aviation (G-BZEF)	
G-MHAN	Just Superstol	SCF Fabrication Ltd (G-HONO)	
G-MHCE	Enstrom F-28A	K.W. Soendergaard (G-BBHD)	
G-MHCM	Enstrom 280FX	Sky Fly LP Inc (G-IBWF/G-ZZWW/G-BSIE)	
G-MHGS	Stoddard-Hamilton Glastar	A. Lane	
G-MHIX	Supermarine 509 Spitfire Tr.9	Ultimate Warbird Flights Ltd	
G-MHMR	Pegasus Quantum 15-912	N. S. Martin & K. Bigland	
G-MHPS	Glasair Sportsman	P. Powell-Shedden	
G-MHRV	Van's RV-6A	M. R. Harris	
G-MIAN	Skyranger Nynja 912S(1)	I. P. Stubbins	
G-MICB	Exodus Deltajet 500 Stingray	B. Michnay	
G-MICH	Robinson R22 Beta	Tiger Helicopters Ltd (G-BNKY)	
G-MICI	Cessna 182S	The Magic Carpet Flying Company (G-WARF)	
G-MICK	Cessna F.172N	D. H. G. Penney	
G-MICX	Air Creation Tanarg/Bionix 13 912S(1)	M. J. Moulton	
G-MICY	Everett Srs 1 gyroplane	G. M. V. Richardson	
G-MIDD	PA-28-140 Cherokee	Midland Air Training School (G-BBDD)	
G-MIDO	Airbus A.320-232	BA Euroflyer Ltd	
G-MIFF	Robin DR.400/180	Westfield Flying Group	
G-MIII	Extra EA.300/L	Ujamaflip Ltd	
G-MIIO	Schempp-Hirth Ventus 3M	S. G. Jones	
G-MIKE	Brookland Hornet	M. H. J. Goldring	
G-MIKI	Rans S.6-ESA Coyote II	S. P. Slade	
G-MILE	Cameron N-77 balloon	Miles Air Ltd	
G-MILF	Harmon Rocket II	E. Stinton	
G-MILR	Aeroprakt A22-LS Foxbat	Myrtlegrove Aviation Services	
G-MIMU	CFM Shadow Series CD	R. G. Johnston (G-MYXY)	
G-MINJ	Diamond DA.42 Twin Star	Barkley Consulting BV/Belgium (G-ITFL)	
G-MINN	Lindstrand LBL-90A balloon	S. M. & D. Johnson (G-3KKC/G-OHUB)	
G-MINT	Pitts S-1S Special	T. R. G. Barnby	
G-MIOO	M.100 Student ★	Museum of Berkshire Aviation/Woodley (G-APLK)	
G-MIRV	Van's RV-8	D. J. M. White	
G-MISH	Cessna 182R	A. C. Hill & A. A. D. McKerrell (G-RFAB/G-BIXT)	
G-MISJ	CZAW Sportcruiser	B. P. Clarke	
G-MITE	Raj Hamsa X'Air Falcon	H. J. & E. Merriman	
G-MITY	Mole Mite	R. H. Mole	
G-MITZ	Cameron N-77 balloon	Colt Car Co Ltd	
G-MJAD	Eipper Quicksilver MX	J. McCullough	
G-MJAJ	Eurowing Goldwing	M. J. Aubrey	
G-MJAM	Eipper Quicksilver MX	P. R. Szczepanik	
G-MJAN	Hiway Skytrike	G. M. Sutcliffe	
G-MJBL	American Aerolights Eagle	B. W. Olley	
G-MJCF	Maxair Sports Hummer ★	Newark Air Museum/Newark	
G-MJCU	Tarjani	J. K. Ewing	
G-MJDE	Huntair Pathfinder	P. Rayson	
G-MJDJ	Hiway Skytrike Demon	A. J. Cowan	
G-MJDP	Eurowing Goldwing	A. D. Russell	
G-MJDW	Eipper Quicksilver MX ★	Newark Air Museum/Newark	
G-MJEO	American Aerolights Eagle	A. M. Shaw	
G-MJER	Flexiform Striker	D. S. Simpson	
G-MJFM	Huntair Pathfinder	M. J. Aubrey	
G-MJFX	Skyhook TR-1	M. R. Dean	
G-MJFZ	Hiway Demon/Tri-flyer	A. W. Lowrie	

Notes	Reg	Type	Owner or Operator
	G-MJHV	Hiway Demon 250	A. G. Griffiths
	G-MJJA	Huntair Pathfinder	D. H. Edwards
	G-MJJK	Eipper Quicksilver MXII	J. McCullough
	G-MJKP	Super Scorpion/Sky-Trike ★	South Yorkshire Aircraft Museum/Doncaster
	G-MJKX	Ultralight Skyrider Phantom	G. R. Moore
	G-MJOC	Huntair Pathfinder	A. J. Glynn
	G-MJOE	Eurowing Goldwing	R. J. Osborne
	G-MJPB	Manuel Ladybird	J. Aubert
	G-MJPE	Hiway Demon Skytrike	T. G. Elmhirst
	G-MJPV	Eipper Quicksilver MX	F. W. Ellis
	G-MJRA	Mainair Tri-Flyer 330 ★	Yorkshire Air Museum/Elvington
	G-MJSF	Skyrider Airsports Phantom	M. J. Whiteman-HaywoodR. P. Stonor
	G-MJSL	Dragon 200	M. J. Aubrey
	G-MJSP	Romain Tiger Cub 440	A. R. Sunley
	G-MJST	Pterodactyl Ptraveller	T. D. Dawson
	G-MJSU	Flylite Tiger Cub ★	Norfolk and Suffolk Aviation Museum/Flixton
	G-MJSZ	DH Wasp	J. J. Hill
	G-MJTM	Aerostructure Pipistrelle 2B	A. M. Sirant
	G-MJTX	Skyrider Airsports Phantom	P. D. Coppin
	G-MJTY	Huntair Pathfinder Mk.1	A. S. Macdonald
	G-MJTZ	Skyrider Airsports Phantom	B. J. Towers
	G-MJUF	MBA Super Tiger Cub 440	D. G. Palmer
	G-MJUW	MBA Tiger Cub 440	D. G. Palmer
	G-MJUX	Skyrider Airsports Phantom	A. R. Garman
	G-MJVF	CFM Shadow series CD	J. A. Cook
	G-MJVI	Rooster 1 Series 4 ★	Norfolk and Suffolk Aviation Museum/Flixton
	G-MJVN	Ultrasports Puma 440	R. McGookin
	G-MJVP	Eipper Quicksilver MX II	G. J. Ward
	G-MJVU	Eipper Quicksilver MX II	A. Young
	G-MJVY	Dragon Srs 150	J. C. Craddock
	G-MJWB	Eurowing Goldwing	D. G. Palmer
	G-MJWF	Tiger Cub 440	R. A. & T. Maycock
	G-MJYV	Mainair Triflyer 2 Seat	H. L. Phillips
	G-MJYW	Wasp Gryphon III	P. D. Lawrence
	G-MJYX	Mainair Tri-Flyer/Hiway Demon	K. G. Grayson & R. D. Leigh
	G-MJZK	Southdown Puma Sprint 440	R. J. Osborne
	G-MJZX	Hummer TX	M. J. Aubrey
	G-MKAK	Colt 77A balloon	M. J. Axtell
	G-MKAS	PA-28-140 Cherokee	Zeroavia Ltd (G-BKVR)
	G-MKER	P & M QuikR	D. S. Clews
	G-MKEV	Aerotechnik EV-97 Eurostar	K. Laud
	G-MKHB	Eurofox 912(iS)	A. P. W. Roediger
	G-MKVT	Supermarine 349 Spitfire VC	Helifan Pty Ltd
	G-MKXI	VS.365 Spitfire PR.XI (PL965)	Hangar 11 Collection
	G-MKZG	Super Marine Spitfire Mk.26	D. G. Richardson
	G-MLAL	Jabiru J400	P. E. Barker
	G-MLAW	P & M Quik GT450	R. D. McKellar
	G-MLHI	Maule MX-7-180 Star Rocket	M. N. P. Saunders (G-BTMJ)
	G-MLKA	Aeroprakt A.32 Vixxen	P. M. Mason
	G-MLKE	P & M Aviation Quik R	G. Oliver
	G-MLLI	PA-32RT-300 Lance II	M. Steward (G-JUPP/G-BNJF)
	G-MLLR	Bell 505 Jet Ranger X	Miller Brothers Services Ltd
	G-MLRO	Kubicek BB22Z	C. T. E. Wetters (G-SODA/G-CIWE)
	G-MLSY	BRM Bristell NG5 Speed Wing	T. E. Mills
	G-MLTA	UltraMagic M-77 balloon	C. A. Timson
	G-MLUG	Bell 505 Jet Ranger X	MJL Plant Hire (Cornwall) Ltd (G-DUNO)
	G-MLWI	Thunder Ax7-77 balloon	C. A. Butter
	G-MLXP	Europa	T. Cook
	G-MLZZ	Sky Ranger Swift 912S(1)	F. Murphy & S. Holmes
	G-MMAG	MBA Tiger Cub 440	M. J. Aubrey
	G-MMAM	MBA Tiger Cub 440	I. Pearson
	G-MMAR	Mainair Gemini/Southdown Puma Sprint	B. A. Fawkes
	G-MMBU	Eipper Quicksilver MXII	A. Young
	G-MMCB	Huntair Pathfinder III ★	Science Musem/Wroughton
	G-MMDJ	Mainair Tri-Flyer 250/Solar Wings Typhoon	A. M. Webb
	G-MMDK	Flexiform Striker/Tri-Flyer ★	South Yorkshire Aircraft Museum/Doncaster
	G-MMDO	Hornet Invader/Southdown Sprint	H. M. Roberts
	G-MMFV	Flexiform Striker	R. A. Walton

Reg	Type	Owner or Operator	Notes
G-MMGF	MBA Tiger Cub 440	M. D. Etherington	
G-MMGL	MBA Tiger Cub 440	H. E. Dunning	
G-MMGT	Solar Wings Typhoon	H. Cook	
G-MMGV	Whittaker MW5 Sorcerer	M. W. J. Whittaker & G. N. Haffey	
G-MMHN	MBA Tiger Cub 440	M. J. Aubrey	
G-MMHS	SMD Viper	C. J. Meadows	
G-MMIE	MBA Tiger Cub 440	B. M. Olliver	
G-MMJD	Southdown Puma Sprint	D. J. Durston	
G-MMJV	MBA Tiger Cub 440	D. G. Palmer	
G-MMKA	Ultrasports Panther Dual	R. S. Wood	
G-MMKM	Flexiform Dual Striker	S. W. Hutchinson	
G-MMKP	MBA Tiger Cub 440	J. W. Beaty	
G-MMKX	Skyrider Phantom 330	G. J. Lampitt	
G-MMLE	Eurowing Goldwing SP	M. J. Aubrey	
G-MMLK	MBA Tiger Cub 440	M. J. Aubrey	
G-MMLM	MBA Tiger Cub 440 ★	Montrose Air Station Heritage Centre/Montrose	
G-MMMG	Eipper Quicksilver MXL	J. B. Silverstone	
G-MMMH	Hadland Willow	M. J. Hadland	
G-MMML	Dragon 150	M. J. Aubrey	
G-MMNA	Eipper Quicksilver MXII	G. A. Marples	
G-MMNC	Eipper Quicksilver MX	W. S. Toulmin	
G-MMOK	Solar Wings Panther XL	R. F. Foster	
G-MMPH	Southdown Puma Sprint	J. Siddle	
G-MMPL	Lanashire Micro-Trike 440/Flexiform Dual Striker (modified)	P. D. Lawrence	
G-MMPZ	Teman Mono-Fly	H. Smith	
G-MMRH	Highway Skytrike	A. M. Sirant	
G-MMRN	Southdown Puma Sprint	D. C. Read	
G-MMSP	Mainair Gemini/Flash	J. Whiteford	
G-MMSS	Lightning/Tri-Pacer	G. A. Hazell	
G-MMSZ	Medway Half Pint/Aerial Arts 130SX	A. M. Sutton	
G-MMTD	Mainair Tri-Flyer 330	W. E. Teare	
G-MMTY	Fisher FP.202U	M. A. Welch	
G-MMUV	Southdown Puma Sprint	D. C. Read	
G-MMUX	Gemini Sprint	D. R. Gregson	
G-MMVI	Southdown Puma Sprint	G. R. Williams	
G-MMVS	Skyhook Pixie	B. W. Olley	
G-MMWG	Greenslade Mono-Trike	G-MMWG Group	
G-MMWL	Eurowing Foldwing ★	Norfolk and Suffolk Aviation Museum/Flixton	
G-MMXU	Mainair Gemini/Flash	T. J. Franklin	
G-MMZA	Mainair Gemini/Flash	G. T. Johnston	
G-MNAE	Mainair Gemini/Flash	K. B. Woods	
G-MNAZ	Solar Wings Pegasus XL-R	R. W. houldsworth	
G-MNBA	Solar Wings Pegasus XL-R	V. C. Chambers	
G-MNBB	Solar Wings Pegasus XL-R	A. A. Sawera	
G-MNBP	Mainair Gemini/Flash	B. J. James	
G-MNBS	Mainair Gemini/Flash	S. M. Hall	
G-MNCA	Hiway Demon 175	M. A. Sirant	
G-MNCF	Mainair Gemini/Flash	C. F. Janes	
G-MNCM	CFM Shadow Srs C	A. Gibson	
G-MNCS	Skyrider Airsports Phantom	I. G. Poutney	
G-MNDE	Medway Half Pint	C. G. Chambers	
G-MNDU	Midland Sirocco 377GB	M. A. Collins	
G-MNDY	Southdown Puma Sprint	A. M. Coupland	
G-MNER	CFM Shadow Srs B	S. P. Jarvis	
G-MNEY	Mainair Gemini/Flash	D. A. Spiers	
G-MNFG	Southdown Puma Sprint	M. Ingleton	
G-MNFL	AMF Microlight Chevvron	J. Pool	
G-MNFM	Mainair Gemini/Flash	P. M. Fidell	
G-MNGK	Mainair Gemini/Flash	A. R. Hawes	
G-MNHJ	Solar Wings Pegasus XL-R	C. Council	
G-MNHK	Solar Wings Pegasus XL-R	S. P. Williams	
G-MNHZ	Mainair Gemini/Flash	I. O. S. Ross	
G-MNII	Mainair Gemini/Flash	R. F. Finnis	
G-MNIK	Pegasus Photon	M. Belemet	
G-MNJD	Southdown Puma Sprint	S. D. Smith	
G-MNJJ	Solar Wings Pegasus Flash	P. A. Shelley	
G-MNJS	Southdown Puma Sprint	E. A. Frost	
G-MNJX	Medway Hybred 44XL	P. J. Mason	
G-MNKD	Solar Wings Pegasus Photon	A. M. Sirant	

Notes	Reg	Type	Owner or Operator
	G-MNKE	Solar Wings Pegasus Photon	H. C. Lowther
	G-MNKG	Solar Wings Pegasus Photon	M. E. Gilbert
	G-MNKK	Solar Wings Pegasus Photon	M. E. Gilbert
	G-MNKM	MBA Tiger Cub 440	A. R. Sunley
	G-MNKN	Skycraft Scout Mk.3-3R	M. A. Aubrey
	G-MNKP	Solar Wings Pegasus Flash	W. J. Grimwood
	G-MNLT	Southdown Raven	J. L. Stachini
	G-MNMG	Mainair Gemini/Flash	N. A. M. Beyer-Kay
	G-MNMM	Aerotech MW5 Sorcerer	S. F. N. Warnell
	G-MNMU	Southdown Raven	M. J. Curley
	G-MNMV	Mainair Gemini/Flash	E. J. Reilly
	G-MNMW	Aerotech MW6 Merlin	T. A. Willcox
	G-MNMY	Cyclone 70	N. R. Beale
	G-MNNA	Southdown Raven	D. & G. D. Palfrey
	G-MNNF	Mainair Gemini/Flash	W. J. Gunn
	G-MNNG	Solar Wings Photon	K. B. Woods
	G-MNNL	Mainair Gemini/Flash II	C. L. Rumney
	G-MNNM	Mainair Scorcher	S. R. Leeper
	G-MNNO	Southdown Raven	M. J. Robbins
	G-MNNS	Eurowing Goldwing	N. K. Geddes
	G-MNPZ	Mainair Scorcher Solo	S. Stevens
	G-MNRD	Ultraflight Lazair IIIE	Sywell Lazair Group
	G-MNRT	Sirocco 377GB ★	Newark Air Museum/Newark
	G-MNSJ	Mainair Gemini/Flash	P. Cooney
	G-MNTP	CFM Shadow Srs B	C. Krajewski & B. C. McKiernan
	G-MNTV	Mainair Gemini/Flash II	A.M. Sirant
	G-MNVE	Solar Wings Pegasus XL-R	M. P. Aris
	G-MNVI	CFM Shadow Srs B	D. R. C. Pugh
	G-MNVJ	CFM Shadow Srs CD	R. Delaney
	G-MNVK	CFM Shadow Srs B	S. J. Myatt
	G-MNVO	Hovey Whing-Ding II	C. Wilson
	G-MNVW	Mainair Gemini/Flash II	J. C. Munro-Hunt
	G-MNVZ	Solar Wings Pegasus Photon	J. J. Russ
	G-MNWG	Southdown Raven X	D. Murray
	G-MNWI	Mainair Gemini/Flash II	P. Dickinson
	G-MNWW	Solar Wings Pegasus XL-R	G-MNWW Group
	G-MNWY	CFM Shadow Srs C	S. R. Potts
	G-MNXX	CFM Shadow Srs BD	R. Sinclair-Brown
	G-MNYD	Aerial Arts 110SX Chaser	C. J. Meadows
	G-MNYF	Aerial Arts 110SX Chaser	R. W. Twamley
	G-MNYP	Southdown Raven X	A. G. Davies
	G-MNYU	Pegasus XL-R	G. L. Turner
	G-MNZJ	CFM Shadow Srs BD	W. Hepburn
	G-MNZW	Southdown Raven X	T. A. Willcox
	G-MOAC	Beech F33A Bonanza	G-MOAC Group
	G-MODE	Eurocopter EC 120B	P. G. Barker
	G-MOEL	Schempp-Hirth Arcus M	B. J. Flewett
	G-MOES	Van's RV-8	M. R. Overall
	G-MOFB	Cameron O-120 balloon	D. M. Moffat
	G-MOGN	BRM Bristell NG5 Speedwing	M. J. Green
	G-MOGS	CZAW Sportcruiser	J. M. Oliver
	G-MOJI	Lindstrand LTL Series SS balloon	S. Dyer
	G-MOKE	Cameron V-77 balloon	O. P. F. LeClercq/France
	G-MOLA	Cosmik EV-97 TeamEurostar UK	J. C. Miller
	G-MOMA	Thruster T.600N 450	Compton Abbas Microlight Group (G-CCIB)
	G-MOOR	SOCATA TB10 Tobago	Davidson Training Solutions Ltd (G-MILK)
	G-MOOS	P.56 Provost T.1 (XF690)	Yeo Pro Group (G-BGKA)
	G-MOOV	CZAW Sportcruiser	D. J. Elliston
	G-MOPP	Robinson R44 II	D. T. Carslaw
	G-MOPS	Sky Ranger Swift 912S	R. N. McSharry
	G-MOSH	PA-28R-201 Cherokee Arrow III	S. J. Griggs
	G-MOSY	Cameron O-84 balloon	D. R. Firkins
	G-MOTA	Bell 206B JetRanger 3	J. W. Sandle
	G-MOTH	DH.82A Tiger Moth (K2567)	P. T. Szluha
	G-MOTI	Robin DR.400/500	Tango India Flying Group
	G-MOTW	Meyers OTW-145	J. K. Padden
	G-MOUR	HS. Gnat T.1 (XR992)	Heritage Aircraft Ltd
	G-MOUT	Cessna 182T	C. Mountain
	G-MOUZ	Cameron O-26 balloon	T. J. Orchard & M. E. Banks
	G-MOVI	PA-32R-301 Saratoga SP	J. E. Bray (G-MARI)

G-AAMX DH.60M Gypsy Moth. *Peter R. March*

G-ACXE L-25C Swallow. *Peter R. March*

G-ANKV/C8500 DH.82A Tiger Moth. *Andrew March*

G-ANTK Avro York. *Peter R. March*

G-BFMF Cassutt Racer IIIM. *Andrew March*

G-BMRJ Boeing 757-236F of DHL Air. *Allan S. Wright*

G-CJWE/481273 Harvard 4. *Peter R. March*

G-CMMT Avions Transport ATR-72-212A of Emerald Airlines UK. *Allan S. Wright*

G-CMTB Diamond DA.50C. *Allan S. Wright*

G-ECDX DH.71 Tiger Moth replica. *Peter R. March*

G-EODS Airbus A.330-343F of Geodis Air Network. *Allan S. Wright*

G-EVTA Vertical Aerospace VA-1X. *Peter R. March*

G-LKDM Sonaca S200. *Allan S. Wright*

G-SOLE Cessna 525 Citation M2. *Allan S. Wright*

A7-BFN Boeing 777-FDZ of Qatar Cargo. *Allan S. Wright*

D-AASH DHC.8Q-402 Dash Eight of Avanti Air. *Allan S. Wright*

HL7646 Boeing 747-419F of AirZeta. *Allan S. Wright*

PH-YHS Airbus A.321-251NX of Transavia. *Allan S. Wright*

SX-DVS Airbus A.320-232 of Aegean Airlines. *Allan S. Wright*

TC-LPG Airbus A.321-271NX of Turkish Airlines. *Allan S. Wright*

UK32104 Airbus A.321-253NX of Uzbekistan Airways *Allan S. Wright*

YL-ABG Airbus A.220-300 of Air Baltic. *Allan S. Wright*

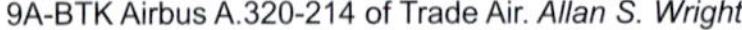

7T-VKS Boeing 737-7KS of Air Algerie. *Allan S. Wright*

9A-BTK Airbus A.320-214 of Trade Air. *Allan S. Wright*

Reg	Type	Owner or Operator	Notes
G-MOVR	Extra EA.300/LC	George J Goff Ltd (G-GOFF)	
G-MOWG	Aeroprakt A22-L Foxbat	H. C. M. Lowery	
G-MOWL	Robinson R44 II	MOAV Ltd	
G-MOWW	Cameron Z-105 balloon	Prestige Grounds Ltd	
G-MOYA	Vans RV-10	S. Moya	
G-MOYR	Eurofox 912(S)	The Northumbria Gliding Club Ltd	
G-MOZE	P & M Quik GTR	M. R. Mosley	
G-MOZI	Glasflugel Mosquito	T. T. Turan	
G-MOZZ	Avions Mudry CAP-10B	N. Skipworth	
G-MPAA	PA-28-181 Cherokee Archer III	Shropshire Aero Club Ltd	
G-MPAS	Agusta A109SP Grand New	Castle Air Ltd (G-KRNO)	
G-MPAT	Cosmik EV-97 TeamEurostar UK	P. J. Dale	
G-MPDF	TL2000 Sting S4	G. M. Prowling	
G-MPFC	Grumman AA-5B	Shipping & Airlines Ltd (G-ZARI/G-BHVY)	
G-MPHY	Ikarus C42 FB100	P. Murphy	
G-MPLA	Cessna 182T	Maguire Aviation Ltd	
G-MPLB	Cessna 182T	W. E. Buchanan	
G-MPLD	Cessna 182T	AKM Aviation Ltd	
G-MPLE	Cessna 182T	S. L. Martineau-Casau	
G-MPLF	Cessna 182T	Aereo Pangea Ltd	
G-MPRL	Cessna 210M	Mike Stapleton & Co.Ltd	
G-MPSA	Eurocopter MBB BK-117C-2	West Yorkshire Combined Authority National Police Air Service	
G-MPSB	Eurocopter MBB BK-117C-2	West Yorkshire Combined Authority National Police Air Service	
G-MPSC	Eurocopter MBB BK-117C-2	West Yorkshire Combined Authority National Police Air Service	
G-MRAG	Cessna 182T	C. M. Alonso	
G-MRAM	Mignet HM.1000 Balerit	R. A. Marven	
G-MRDS	CZAW Sportcruiser	J. Metcalfe & P. McCusker	
G-MRED	Christavia Mk 1	Mister Ed Group	
G-MREL	Rotorsport UK Cavalon	M. R. Love	
G-MRGT	Skyranger Swift 912S(1)	C. Summerfield	
G-MRJC	AutoGyro Cavalon	T. Woodcock	
G-MRJJ	Mainair Pegasus Quik	G. J. Hitchcox	
G-MRJP	Silence Twister	M. C. Reeve	
G-MRKM	Carbon Cub EX-2	R. C. Loveland	
G-MRKS	Robinson R44	TJD Trade Ltd (G-RAYC)	
G-MRKT	Lindstrand LBL-90A balloon	R. M. Stanley	
G-MRLI	Sikorsky S-92A	Bristow Helicopters Ltd (G-CKGZ)	
G-MRLL	North American P-51D-5-NA Mustang (413521:5Q-B)	Marinell Ltd	
G-MRLN	Sky 240-24 balloon	M. Wady	
G-MRLS	AutoGyro Calidus	C. N. Fleming	
G-MRME	Gefa-Flug AS 105 GD airship	Airship Over Atlanta Ltd	
G-MROC	Pegasus Quantum 15-912	P. Hill	
G-MROD	Van's RV-7A	K. Dreier	
G-MROS	Pipistrel Alpha BCAR-S 164	MKR Aviation Ltd	
G-MRPH	Murphy Rebel	P. & B. S. Metson	
G-MRRL	AgustaWestland AW109SP Grand New	GB Helicopters	
G-MRSB	Robinson R44 II	Beketts Aviation LLP	
G-MRSS	Ikarus C42 FB80	P. D. Alford	
G-MRSW	Lindstrand LBL-90A balloon	M. A. Derbyshire (G-CHWU)	
G-MRTJ	Enstrom 280FX Shark	M. Jones	
G-MRVL	Van's RV-7	T. W. Wielkopolski	
G-MRVN	PZL-Bielsko SZD-50-3	The Bath, Wilts and North Dorset Gliding Club Ltd	
G-MRVP	Van's RV-6	J. M. Whitham & D. Caldwell	
G-MRZZ	Robinson R44 II	ALT Nuvem Ltd (G-DENY)	
G-MSAL	MS.733 Alcyon (143)	M. Isbister t/a Alcyon Flying Group	
G-MSAV	ICP MXP-740 Savannah VG Camit (1)	J. G. Miller	
G-MSBI	Cessna F.406 Caravan II	RVL Aviation Ltd	
G-MSCB	Skyranger Nynja	S. M. Spencer	
G-MSCL	AutoGyro Cavalon	Power Management Engineering Ltd	
G-MSES	Cessna 150L	D. Petrauskab	
G-MSGI	Magni M-24C	Orion Cotswolds Aviation Ltd	
G-MSIX	Glaser-Dirks DG.800B	G-MSIX Group	
G-MSKY	Ikarus C.42 FB100 VLA	G-MSKY Group	
G-MSMK	Aeroprakt A-32M Vixxen	M. A. J. Spiers	

Notes	Reg	Type	Owner or Operator
	G-MSOF	Cessna 172N	Excelis Ltd
	G-MSON	Cameron Z-90 balloon	Regional Property Services Ltd
	G-MSOO	Revolution Mini 500 helicopter	R. H. Ryan
	G-MSPR	Robinson R66	MSPR Aviation LLP
	G-MSPY	Pegasus Quantum 15-912	B. E. Wagenhauser
	G-MSVI	Agusta A.109S Grand	JPM Ltd (G-ETOU)
	G-MSVO	Agusta A.109S Grand	JPM Ltd
	G-MTAC	Mainair Gemini/Flash II	B. T. Bradshaw
	G-MTAV	Solar Wings Pegasus XL-R	S. Fairweather
	G-MTAZ	Solar Wings Pegasus XL-R	M. O'Connell
	G-MTBE	CFM Shadow Srs BD	A. P. Jones
	G-MTBN	Southdown Raven X	A. J. & S. E. Crosby-Jones
	G-MTBO	Southdown Raven X	G. P. Lane
	G-MTBP	Aerotech MW5B Sorcerer	C. G. Chambers
	G-MTBR	Aerotech MW5B Sorcerer	R. Poulter
	G-MTBS	Aerotech MW5B Sorcerer	D. J. Pike
	G-MTCM	Southdown Raven X	J. C. Rose
	G-MTCP	Aerial Arts Chaser 110SX	C. J. Meadows
	G-MTDD	Aerial Arts Chaser 110SX	C. J. Meadows
	G-MTDF	Mainair Gemini/Flash II	P. G. Barnes
	G-MTDR	Mainair Gemini/Flash II	D. J. Morriss
	G-MTDU	CFM Shadow Srs CD	P. S. Sweet
	G-MTDW	Mainair Gemini/Flash II	S. R. Leeper
	G-MTEK	Mainair Gemini/Flash II	M. O'Hearne
	G-MTER	Solar Wings Pegasus XL-R	S. J. Nix
	G-MTES	Solar Wings Pegasus XL-R	R. J. Turner
	G-MTEY	Mainair Gemini/Flash II	B. H. L. Prior
	G-MTFG	AMF Microlight Chevvron 2-32C	J. C. Gates
	G-MTFK	Flexiform Striker/Moult Trike ★	Norfolk and Suffolk Aviation Museum/Flixton
	G-MTFN	Aerotech MW5 Sorcerer	S. M. King
	G-MTFU	CFM Shadow Srs CD	J. E. Roy
	G-MTGB	Thruster TST Mk 1	M. J. Aubrey
	G-MTGD	Thruster TST Mk 1	R. H. Hatfield
	G-MTGF	Thruster TST Mk 1	N. Hay
	G-MTGR	Thruster TST Mk 1	S. C. Stinchcombe
	G-MTGV	CFM Shadow Srs CD	D. J. Flanagan
	G-MTGW	CFM Shadow Srs CD	C. Krajewski
	G-MTHN	Solar Wings Pegasus XL-R	G. E. Murphy
	G-MTHT	CFM Shadow Srs BD	A. P. Jones
	G-MTHV	CFM Shadow Srs CD	P. W. Margetson
	G-MTIE	Solar Wings Pegasus XL-R	P. Wibberley
	G-MTIJ	Solar Wings Pegasus XL-R	M. J. F. Gilbody
	G-MTJC	Mainair Gemini/Flash IIA	T. A. Dockrell
	G-MTJN	Midland Ultralights Sirocco 377GB	A. R. Hawes
	G-MTJV	Mainair Gemini/Flash IIA	D. C. Dunn
	G-MTKA	Thruster TST Mk 1	M. J. Coles & S. R. Williams
	G-MTKI	Solar Wings Pegasus XL-R	M. Wady
	G-MTKR	CFM Shadow Srs CD	Shadow Group
	G-MTKW	Mainair Gemini/Flash IIA	J. H. McIvor
	G-MTKX	Mainair Gemini/Flash IIA	S. P. Disney
	G-MTLC	Mainair Gemini/Flash IIA	R. J. Alston
	G-MTLG	Solar Wings Pegasus XL-R	D. Young
	G-MTLN	Thruster TST Mk 1	P. W. Taylor
	G-MTLT	Solar Wings Pegasus XL-R	K. M. Mayling
	G-MTLX	Medway Hybred 44XLR	D. A. Coupland
	G-MTMA	Mainair Gemini/Flash IIA	S. Cunningham
	G-MTMC	Mainair Gemini/Flash IIA	A. A. Abdulrahman
	G-MTMF	Solar Wings Pegasus XL-R	H. T. M. Smith
	G-MTMR	Hornet Dual Trainer/Raven	D. J. Smith
	G-MTMX	CFM Shadow Srs BD	P. Hemmings
	G-MTND	Medway Hybred 44XLR	Butty Boys Flying Group
	G-MTNF	Medway Hybred 44XLR	P. A. Bedford
	G-MTNI	Mainair Gemini/Flash IIA	D. R. McDougall
	G-MTNK	Weedhopper JC-24B	S. D. Hutchinson
	G-MTNR	Thruster TST Mk 1	A. M. Sirant
	G-MTNU	Thruster TST Mk 1	T. H. Brearley
	G-MTNV	Thruster TST Mk 1	J. B. Russell
	G-MTOA	Solar Wings Pegasus XL-R	R. A. Bird
	G-MTOH	Solar Wings Pegasus XL-R	H. Cook
	G-MTOJ	Solar Wings Pegasus XL-R	J. Hennessy

Reg	Type	Owner or Operator	Notes
G-MTON	Solar Wings Pegasus XL-R	D. J. Willett	
G-MTOY	Solar Wings Pegasus XL-R	XL2 Group	
G-MTPE	Solar Wings Pegasus XL-R	S. O. Huid	
G-MTPF	Solar Wings Pegasus XL-R	G-MTPF Group	
G-MTPL	Solar Wings Pegasus XL-R	N. A. Martin	
G-MTPM	Solar Wings Pegasus XL-R	V. K. Snell	
G-MTPU	Thruster TST Mk 1	N. Hay	
G-MTRC	Midlands Ultralights Sirocco 377G	D. Thorpe	
G-MTRM	Solar Wings Pegasus XL-R	C. H. Edwards	
G-MTRS	Solar Wings Pegasus XL-R	W. R. Edwards	
G-MTRX	Whittaker MW5 Sorcerer	K. R. Emery	
G-MTSC	Mainair Gemini/Flash IIA	J. Kilpatrick	
G-MTSJ	Thruster TST Mk 1	J. D. Buchanan	
G-MTSK	Thruster TST Mk 1	C. Nicholson	
G-MTSM	Thruster TST Mk 1	M. A. Horton	
G-MTSS	Solar Wings Pegasus XL-R	V. Marchant	
G-MTTF	Aerotech MW6 Merlin	P. Cotton	
G-MTTI	Mainair Gemini/Flash IIA	G-MTTI Flying Group	
G-MTTN	Ultralight Flight Phantom	F. P. Welsh	
G-MTTP	Mainair Gemini/Flash IIA	A. Ormson	
G-MTTU	Solar Wings Pegasus XL-R	A. Friend	
G-MTUA	Solar Wings Pegasus XL-R	S. P. Cooper	
G-MTUC	Thruster TST Mk 1	N. S. Chittenden	
G-MTUN	Solar Wings Pegasus XL-Q	M. J. O'Connor	
G-MTUY	Solar Wings Pegasus XL-Q	H. C. Lowther	
G-MTVP	Thruster TST Mk 1	J. M. Evans	
G-MTVT	Thruster TST Mk.1	W. H. J. Knowles	
G-MTVX	Solar Wings Pegasus XL-Q	D. A. Foster	
G-MTWK	CFM Shadow Srs BD	M. Cooper	
G-MTWR	Mainair Gemini/Flash IIA	J. B. Hodson	
G-MTWS	Mainair Gemini/Flash IIA	A. Robins	
G-MTWX	Mainair Gemini/Flash IIA	K. Walsh	
G-MTWZ	Thruster TST Mk 1	M. J. Aubrey	
G-MTXA	Thruster TST Mk 1	J. D. Avey	
G-MTXD	Thruster TST Mk 1	L. N. Hancock	
G-MTXK	Solar Wings Pegasus XL-Q	D. R. G. Whitelaw	
G-MTXM	Mainair Gemini/Flash IIA	H. J. Vinning	
G-MTXO	Whittaker MW6	C. A. Harper & R. E. Arnold	
G-MTXR	CFM Shadow Srs BD	G. E. Arnott	
G-MTYC	Solar Wings Pegasus XL-Q	C. I. D. H. Garrison	
G-MTYI	Solar Wings Pegasus XL-Q	Q Group	
G-MTYL	Solar Wings Pegasus XL-Q	S. Cooper	
G-MTYV	Southdown Raven X	S. R. Jones	
G-MTZB	Thruster TST Mk 1	J. G. O. Williams	
G-MTZC	Thruster TST Mk 1	J. H. Brady	
G-MTZE	Thruster TST Mk 1	B. S. P. Finch	
G-MTZF	Thruster TST Mk 1	J. D. Buchanan	
G-MTZG	Mainair Gemini/Flash IIA	A. P. Fenn	
G-MTZL	Mainair Gemini/Flash IIA	N. S. Brayn	
G-MTZS	Solar Wings Pegasus XL-Q	J. F. Nichols	
G-MTZX	Mainair Gemini/Flash IIA	W. R. C. Williams-Wynne	
G-MTZY	Mainair Gemini/Flash IIA	M. D. Leslie	
G-MTZZ	Mainair Gemini/Flash IIA	G. J. Cadden	
G-MUCK	Lindstrand LBL 77A	C. J. Wootton	
G-MUDD	Hughes 369E	Derwen Aggregates Ltd	
G-MUDX	AutoGyro Cavalon	P. R. Biggs (G-CJVT)	
G-MUDY	PA-18-150 Super Cub	C. J. de Sousa e Morgado (G-OTUG)	
G-MUIR	Cameron V-65 balloon	J. M. Muir	
G-MUJD	Van's RV-12	M. F. El-Deen	
G-MUKY	Van's RV-8	I. E. K. Mackay	
G-MULE	Zenair CH.701UL	H. S. Urquhart (G-ZENA)	
G-MULR	Boeing 737-MAX8	Ascend Airways Ltd	
G-MUMY	Vans RV-4	M. Frame	
G-MUNI	Mooney M.20J	P. R. Williams	
G-MUON	Schleicher ASH-31 MI	P. C. Naegeli	
G-MUPP	Lindstrand LBL-90A balloon	Future Energy Performance	
G-MURG	Van's RV-6	D. S. Lawer	
G-MUSH	Robinson R44 II	Topgrade Propertry Management Ltd	
G-MUSM	Colt 77A balloon	The British Balloon Museum and Library Ltd	
G-MUSO	Rutan LongEz	D. J. Gay	

Notes	Reg	Type	Owner or Operator
	G-MUTE	Colt 31A balloon	G. B. Dey
	G-MUTS	Jurca MJ.100 Spitfire (X4683:EB-N)	S. M. Johnston & M. S. Rogerson (G-CDPM)
	G-MUTT	CZAW Sportcruiser	R. S. O'Carroll & R. J. Johnstone
	G-MUTZ	Jabiru J430	N. C. Dean
	G-MUZI	Magni M24C Plus	J. M. Weston
	G-MUZM	Extra EA300/SX	M. J. de Morgan
	G-MUZY	Titan T-51 Mustang (472218:WZ-I)	A. D. Bales
	G-MVAH	Thruster TST Mk 1	M. W. H. Henton
	G-MVAI	Thruster TST Mk 1	D. P. McCoy
	G-MVAM	CFM Shadow Srs CD	C. P. Barber
	G-MVAN	CFM Shadow Srs BD	R. W. Frost
	G-MVAR	Solar Wings Pegasus XL-R	A. J. Thomas
	G-MVBC	Aerial Arts Tri-Flyer 130SX	D. Beer
	G-MVBN	Mainair Gemini/Flash IIA	S. R. Potts
	G-MVBO	Mainair Gemini/Flash IIA	M. Bailey
	G-MVCA	Solar Wings Pegasus XL-R	R. Walker
	G-MVCC	CFM Shadow Srs BD	R. T. O. Vittoz
	G-MVCL	Solar Wings Pegasus XL-Q	T. E. Robinson
	G-MVCT	Solar Wings Pegasus XL-Q	G. S. Lampitt
	G-MVCW	CFM Shadow Srs BD	D. A. Coupland
	G-MVDE	Thruster TST Mk 1	M. N. Watson
	G-MVDH	Thruster TST Mk 1	R. J. Whettem
	G-MVDK	Aerial Arts Chaser S	P. D. Curtis
	G-MVDP	Aerial Arts Chaser S	G. J. Slater
	G-MVEG	Solar Wings Pegasus XL-R	A. M. Shaw
	G-MVEH	Mainair Gemini/Flash IIA	D. Evans
	G-MVEI	CFM Shadow Srs BD	R. L. Morgan
	G-MVEN	CFM Shadow Srs BD	K. Briggs
	G-MVER	Mainair Gemini/Flash IIA	J. R. Davis
	G-MVES	Mainair Gemini/Flash IIA	R. M. Rose
	G-MVET	Mainair Gemini/Flash IIA	D. Hurst
	G-MVFD	Solar Wings Pegasus XL-Q	D. Bilan
	G-MVFE	Solar Wings Pegasus XL-Q	S. J. Weeks
	G-MVFF	Solar Wings Pegasus XL-Q	A. Makepiece
	G-MVFH	CFM Shadow Srs BD	I. M. Brookes
	G-MVFJ	Thruster TST Mk 1	D. Bilan
	G-MVFL	Thruster TST Mk 1	E. J. Wallington
	G-MVFM	Thruster TST Mk 1	G. J. Boyer
	G-MVFO	Thruster TST Mk 1	A. Whittaker
	G-MVFT	Solar Wings Pegasus XL-R	R. E. Parker
	G-MVFX	Thruster TST Mk 1	A. M. Dalgetty
	G-MVGA	Aerial Arts Chaser S	Golf Alpha Group
	G-MVGC	AMF Chevvron 2-32	W. Fletcher
	G-MVGF	Aerial Arts Chaser S	P. J. Higgins
	G-MVGI	Aerial Arts Chaser S	P. D. Curtis
	G-MVGK	Aerial Arts Chaser S	D. J. Smith
	G-MVGO	Solar Wings Pegasus XL-R	R. J. Turner
	G-MVGP	Solar Wings Pegasus XL-R	J. W. Norman
	G-MVHB	Powerchute Raider	G. A. Marples
	G-MVHE	Mainair Gemini/Flash IIA	T. J. McMenamin
	G-MVHG	Mainair Gemini/Flash IIA	C. Clarkson
	G-MVHJ	Thruster TST Mk 1	S. P. Jarvis
	G-MVHK	Thruster TST Mk 1	D. J. Gordon
	G-MVHP	Solar Wings Pegasus XL-Q	J. B. Gasson
	G-MVHR	Solar Wings Pegasus XL-Q	J. M. Hucker
	G-MVIB	Mainair Gemini/Flash IIA	A. & S. Rosser
	G-MVIE	Aerial Arts Chaser S	C. J. Meadows
	G-MVIG	CFM Shadow Srs BD	H. M. Roberts
	G-MVIH	Mainair Gemini/Flash IIA	T. M. Gilesnan
	G-MVIN	Noble Hardman Snowbird Mk.IV	G. W. T. Farrington
	G-MVIP	AMF Chevvron 232	P-M. Cavallucci
	G-MVIR	Thruster TST Mk 1	T. Dziadkiewicz
	G-MVIX	Mainair Gemini/Flash IIA	A. J. Howard
	G-MVJF	Aerial Arts Chaser S	V. S. Vellacott
	G-MVJG	Aerial Arts Chaser S	T. H. Scott
	G-MVJJ	Aerial Arts Chaser S	C. W. Potts
	G-MVJK	Aerial Arts Chaser S	D. A. Morgan
	G-MVJN	Solar Wings Pegasus XL-Q	A. F. Sedcole
	G-MVJP	Solar Wings Pegasus XL-Q	S. H. Bakowski
	G-MVKL	Solar Wings Pegasus XL-R	B. J. Morton

Reg	Type	Owner or Operator	Notes
G-MVKN	Solar Wings Pegasus XL-Q	D. Bilan	
G-MVKO	Solar Wings Pegasus XL-Q	A. P. Gunston	
G-MVLA	Aerial Arts Chaser S	S. G. Beeson	
G-MVLC	Aerial Arts Chaser S	B. R. Barnes	
G-MVLE	Aerial Arts Chaser S	J. M. Hucker	
G-MVLF	Chaser S 508	A. Matheu/Spain	
G-MVLJ	CFM Shadow Srs CD	D. R. C. Pugh	
G-MVLL	Mainair Gemeni/Flash IIA	A. A. Sawera	
G-MVLS	Aerial Arts Chaser S	P. K. Dale	
G-MVLX	Solar Wings Pegasus XL-Q	D. J. Harber	
G-MVLY	Solar Wings Pegasus XL-Q	I. B. Osborn	
G-MVMA	Solar Wings Pegasus XL-Q	M. Peters	
G-MVMC	Solar Wings Pegasus XL-Q	M. W. Holmes	
G-MVML	Aerial Arts Chaser S	K. B. Woods	
G-MVMR	Mainair Gemini/Flash IIA	P. W. Ramage	
G-MVMX	Mainair Gemini/Flash IIA	E. A. Dygutowicz	
G-MVNE	Powerchute Raider	A. E. Askew	
G-MVNK	Powerchute Raider	A. E. Askew	
G-MVNR	Aerotech MW5 (K) Sorcerer	A. A. Haseldine	
G-MVNS	Aerotech MW5 (K) Sorcerer	A. M. Sirant	
G-MVNT	Aerotech MW5 (K) Sorceror ★	South Yorkshire Aircraft Museum/Doncaster	
G-MVNY	Mainair Gemini/Flash IIA	M. K. Buckland	
G-MVNZ	Mainair Gemini/Flash IIA	D. A. Ballard	
G-MVOA	Aerial Arts Chaser S 447	W. A. Emmerson	
G-MVOD	Aerial Arts Chaser 110SX	N. R. Beale	
G-MVOP	Aerial Arts Chaser S	D. Thorpe	
G-MVOR	Mainair Gemini/Flash IIA	P. T. & R. M. Jenkins	
G-MVOT	Thruster TST Mk 1	D. R. Hoy	
G-MVOV	Thruster TST Mk 1	I. Garforth	
G-MVPA	Mainair Gemini/Flash IIA	D. Hume	
G-MVPC	Mainair Gemini/Flash IIA	W. O. Flannery	
G-MVPD	Mainair Gemini/Flash IIA	P. Thelwel	
G-MVPF	Medway Hybred 44XLR	G. H. Crick	
G-MVPK	CFM Shadow Srs CD	B. R. Swindon	
G-MVPM	Whittaker MW6 Merlin	K. W. Curry	
G-MVPS	Solar Wings Pegasus XL-Q	J. Hough	
G-MVPW	Solar Wings Pegasus XL-R	G. R. Thomas	
G-MVPX	Solar Wings Pegasus XL-Q	J. R. Appleton	
G-MVRD	Mainair Gemini/Flash IIA	J. D. Pearce	
G-MVRG	Aerial Arts Chaser S	T. M. Stiles	
G-MVRH	Solar Wings Pegasus XL-Q	K. Farr	
G-MVRM	Mainair Gemini/Flash IIA	P. A. Smith	
G-MVRO	CFM Shadow Srs CD	Flux Aviation Ltd	
G-MVRR	CFM Shadow Srs BD	S. P. Christian	
G-MVRS	CFM Shadow Srs BD	Aero Venture	
G-MVRT	CFM Shadow Srs CD	A. M. Wyndham	
G-MVRW	Solar Wings Pegasus XL-Q	C. A. Hamps	
G-MVRZ	Medway Hybred 44XLR	P. J. Higgins	
G-MVSG	Aerial Arts Chaser S	M. Roberts	
G-MVSJ	Aviasud Mistral 532	Mistral MVSJ Syndicate	
G-MVSL	Aerial Arts Chaser 5	D. M. Pearson	
G-MV3O	Mainair Gemini/Flash IIA	D. W. Brown	
G-MVTD	Whittaker MW6 Merlin	G. R. Reynolds	
G-MVTL	Aerial Arts Chaser S	N. D. Meer	
G-MVUA	Mainair Gemini/Flash IIA	K. D. Sinclair-Russell	
G-MVUB	Thruster T.300	A. K. Grayson	
G-MVUC	Medway Hybred 44XLR	B. Pounder	
G-MVUF	Solar Wings Pegasus XL-Q	G. P. Blakemore	
G-MVUI	Solar Wings Pegasus XL-Q	P. E. Hadley & K. Casserley	
G-MVUJ	Solar Wings Pegasus XL-Q	R. S. Deering	
G-MVUO	AMF Chevvron 2-32	W. D. M. Turtle	
G-MVUP	Aviasud Mistral 532GB	M. J. Houghton	
G-MVUU	Hornet ZA	K. W. Warn	
G-MVVK	Solar Wings Pegasus XL-R	A. J. Martin	
G-MVVT	CFM Shadow Srs CD	S. J. Huxtable	
G-MVVV	AMF Chevvron 2-32	J. S. Firth	
G-MVVZ	Powerchute Raider	G. A. Marples	
G-MVWJ	Powerchute Raider	N. J. Doubek	
G-MVWS	Thruster T.300	I. G. Poutney	
G-MVWW	Aviasud Mistral	A. S. Evans	
G-MVXA	Brewster I MW6 (modified SS)	J. C. Gates	

Notes	Reg	Type	Owner or Operator
	G-MVXP	Aerial Arts Chaser S	J. C. Longmore
	G-MVXR	Mainair Gemini/Flash IIA	D. M. Bayne
	G-MVXX	AMF Chevvron 232	T. R. James
	G-MVYE	Thruster TST Mk 1	M. J. Aubrey
	G-MVYI	Hornet R-ZA	K. W. Warn
	G-MVYW	Noble Hardman Snowbird Mk IV	T. J. Harrison
	G-MVYX	Noble Hardman Snowbird Mk IV	R. McBlain
	G-MVYY	Aerial Arts Chaser S508	G. H. Crick
	G-MVZA	Thruster T.300	A. I. Milne
	G-MVZC	Thruster T.300	S. Dougan
	G-MVZD	Thruster T.300	P. Heckles
	G-MVZI	Thruster T.300	G. R. Moore
	G-MVZM	Aerial Arts Chaser S	P. Leigh
	G-MVZO	Medway Hybred 44XLR	S. J. Taft
	G-MVZP	Murphy Renegade Spirit UK	The North American Syndicate
	G-MVZT	Solar Wings Pegasus XL-Q	C. J. Meadows
	G-MVZU	Solar Wings Pegasus XL-Q	I. Swallow
	G-MVZV	Solar Wings Pegasus XL-Q	K. Mudra
	G-MVZX	Renegade Spirit UK	G. Holmes
	G-MVZZ	AMF Chevvron 232	W. A. L. Mitchell
	G-MWAB	Mainair Gemini/Flash IIA	J. E. Buckley
	G-MWAC	Solar Wings Pegasus XL-Q	H. Lloyd-Hughes & D. Jones
	G-MWAE	CFM Shadow Srs BD	S. J. Robson
	G-MWAJ	Murphy Renegade Spirit UK	L. D. Blair
	G-MWAR	Thruster T.300	N. Allen
	G-MWAT	Solar Wings Pegasus XL-Q	C. A. Reid
	G-MWBI	Medway Hybred 44XLR	G. E. Coates
	G-MWBJ	Medway Sprint	C. C. Strong
	G-MWBP	Hornet R-ZA	P. Wilcox
	G-MWBS	Hornet RS-ZA	P. D. Jaques
	G-MWBT	Hornet R-ZA	W. Finley & K. W. Warn
	G-MWCF	Solar Wings Pegasus XL-R	S. P. Tkaczyk
	G-MWCG	Microflight Spectrum (modified)	R. J. Hood
	G-MWCH	Rans S.6 Coyote	J. H. Pfaff
	G-MWCK	Powerchute Kestrel	A. E. Askew
	G-MWCM	Powerchute Kestrel	A. E. Askew
	G-MWCN	Powerchute Kestrel	A. E. Askew
	G-MWCO	Powerchute Kestrel	J. R. E. Gladstone
	G-MWCP	Powerchute Kestrel	A. E. Askew
	G-MWCY	Medway Hybred 44XLR	J. K. Masters
	G-MWCZ	Medway Hybed 44XLR	D. Botha
	G-MWDB	CFM Shadow Srs BD	T. D. Dawson
	G-MWDK	Solar Wings Pegasus XL-R	F. J. Windeth
	G-MWDN	CFM Shadow Srs BD	J. J. J. Roberts
	G-MWDZ	Eipper Quicksilver MXL II	R. G. Cook
	G-MWEG	Solar Wings Pegasus XL-Q	E. R. Muneta
	G-MWEK	Whittaker MW5 Sorcerer	D. W. & M. L. Squire
	G-MWEN	CFM Shadow Srs BD	C. Dawn
	G-MWEO	Whittaker MW5 Sorcerer	Friends of Partytime Garden
	G-MWEP	Rans S.4 Coyote	E. J. Wallington
	G-MWEZ	CFM Shadow Srs CD	G-MWEZ Group
	G-MWFC	Team Mini-Max	D. G. Blair (G-BTXC)
	G-MWFD	TEAM mini-MAX	C. O'Mahoney
	G-MWFF	Rans S.4 Coyote	P. J. Greenrod
	G-MWFL	Powerchute Kestrel	G. A. Marples
	G-MWFT	MBA Tiger Cub 440	J. R. Ravenhill
	G-MWFU	Quad City Challenger II UK	P. J. Brookman
	G-MWFV	Quad City Challenger II UK	M. Liptrot
	G-MWFW	Rans S.4 Coyote	C. Dewhurst
	G-MWGI	Whittaker MW5 (K) Sorcerer	J. Aley
	G-MWGJ	Whittaker MW5 (K) Sorcerer	I. Pearson
	G-MWGK	Whittaker MW5 (K) Sorcerer	S. Craven
	G-MWGR	Solar Wings Pegasus XL-Q	D. Bilan
	G-MWHF	Solar Wings Pegasus XL-Q	N. J. Troke
	G-MWHH	TEAM mini-MAX	D. R. Blissett
	G-MWHR	Mainair Gemini/Flash IIA	J. E. S. Harter
	G-MWHS	AMF Microlight Chevvron 2-32C	J. Pool
	G-MWHX	Solar Wings Pegasus XL-Q	N. P. Kelly
	G-MWIC	Whittaker MW5-C Sorcerer	P. J. Cheyney
	G-MWIE	Solar Wings Pegasus XL-Q	C. S. McKenzie

Reg	Type	Owner or Operator	Notes
G-MWIF	Rans S.6-ESD Coyote II	S. M. Hudson	
G-MWIP	Whittaker MW6 Merlin	B. J. Merret & D. Beer	
G-MWIU	Pegasus Quasar TC	W. Hepburn	
G-MWIX	Solar Wings Pegasus Quasar TC	M. Walker	
G-MWIZ	CFM Shadow Srs BD	J. M. Boden	
G-MWJD	Solar Wings Pegasus Quasar	S. Meester	
G-MWJF	CFM Shadow Srs BD	A. J. Briars	
G-MWJN	Solar Wings Pegasus XL-Q	J. C. Corrall	
G-MWKE	Hornet R-ZA	K. W. Warn	
G-MWKX	Microflight Spectrum	C. R. Ions	
G-MWLD	CFM Shadow Srs CD	A. P. Love	
G-MWLE	Solar Wings Pegasus XL-R	D. Stevenson	
G-MWLG	Solar Wings Pegasus XL-R	A. R. Hawes	
G-MWLN	Whittaker MW6-S Fatboy Flyer	S. J. Field	
G-MWLP	Mainair Gemini/Flash IIA	K. M. Husecken	
G-MWLS	Medway Hybred 44XLR	A. G. H. Carr	
G-MWLU	Solar Wings Pegasus XL-R	R. M. Vernon	
G-MWLW	TEAM mini-MAX	C. D. Barnes	
G-MWLZ	Rans S.4 Coyote	Hedge Hopper Flying Group	
G-MWMF	Powerchute Kestrel	P. J. Blundell	
G-MWMI	SolarWings Pegasus Quasar TC	R. A. Khosravi	
G-MWML	SolarWings Pegasus Quasar	F. A. Collar	
G-MWMN	Solar Wings Pegasus XL-Q	P. A. Arnold & N. A. Rathbone	
G-MWMO	Solar Wings Pegasus XL-Q	D. S. F. McNair	
G-MWMV	Solar Wings Pegasus XL-R	M. Nutting	
G-MWMW	Renegade Spirit UK	D. M. Casey	
G-MWMX	Mainair Gemini/Flash IIA	P. G. Hughes/Ireland	
G-MWMY	Mainair Gemini/Flash IIA	K. Mudra	
G-MWNB	Solar Wings Pegasus XL-Q	G. W. F. J. Dear	
G-MWND	Tiger Cub Developments RL.5A	B. Plunkett	
G-MWNO	AMF Microlight Chevvron 2-32C	J. Pool	
G-MWNP	AMF Microlight Chevvron 2-32C	I. A. J. Lappin	
G-MWNR	Renegade Spirit UK	RJR Flying Group	
G-MWOD	Powerchute Kestrel	T. Morgan	
G-MWOI	Solar Wings Pegasus XL-R	B. T. Geoghegan	
G-MWOJ	Mainair Gemini/Flash IIA	W. W. Hammond	
G-MWON	CFM Shadow Series CD	D. B. Conway	
G-MWOV	Whittaker MW6 Merlin	C. F. James	
G-MWPH	Microflight Spectrum	C. G. Chambers	
G-MWPN	CFM Shadow Srs CD	W. R. H. Thomas	
G-MWPP	CFM Streak Shadow	R. B. J. Gordon	
G-MWPR	Whittaker MW6 Merlin	S. F. N. Warnell	
G-MWPZ	Renegade Spirit UK	Price Aviation & Transport	
G-MWRE	Mainair Gemini/Flash IIA	M. R. Gaylor	
G-MWRF	Mainair Gemini/Flash IIA	N. Hay	
G-MWRH	Mainair Gemini/Flash IIA	A. A. Abdulrahman	
G-MWRL	CFM Shadow Srs.CD	D. MacRae	
G-MWRN	Solar Wings Pegasus XL-R	R. Lewis-Evans	
G-MWRR	Mainair Gemini/Flash IIA	J. M. MacDonald	
G-MWSA	TEAM mini-MAX	A. R. Stratton	
G-MWSC	Rans S.6-ESD Coyote II	F. J. D. Heathfield	
G-MWSD	Solar Wings Pegasus XL-Q	A. M. Harley	
G-MWSF	Solar Wings Pegasus XL-R	J. J. Freeman	
G-MWSI	Solar Wings Pegasus Quasar TC	S. Chambers	
G-MWSJ	Solar Wings Pegasus XL-Q	R. J. Collison	
G-MWSK	Solar Wings Pegasus XL-Q	J. Doogan	
G-MWSO	Solar Wings Pegasus XL-R	M. A. Clayton	
G-MWSY	Whittaker MW5 Sorcerer	M. S. Getson	
G-MWSZ	CFM Shadow Srs CD	K. Pearce	
G-MWTC	Solar Wings Pegasus XL-Q	M. M. Chittenden	
G-MWTJ	CFM Shadow Srs CS	Shadow Tango Juliet Group	
G-MWTL	Solar Wings Pegasus XL-R	G. P. Lane	
G-MWTN	CFM Shadow Srs CD	M. J. Broom	
G-MWTO	Mainair Gemini/Flash IIA	M. B. Ryder-Jarvis	
G-MWTP	CFM Shadow Srs CD	N. P. St. J. Ramsay	
G-MWTT	Rans S.6-ESD Coyote II	L. E. Duffin	
G-MWUA	CFM Shadow Srs CD	P. A. James	
G-MWUD	Solar Wings Pegasus XL-R	G. P. Lane	
G-MWUI	AMF Chevvron 2-32C	W. Fletcher	
G-MWUK	Rans S.6-ESD Coyote II	P. M. Ferreira Abreu	
G-MWUL	Rans S.6-ESD Coyote II	D. M. Bayne	

Notes	Reg	Type	Owner or Operator
	G-MWUN	Rans S.6-ESD Coyote II	J. Parke
	G-MWUU	Solar Wings Pegasus XL-R	P. E. Hadley
	G-MWUV	Solar Wings Pegasus XL-R	XL Group
	G-MWUW	Solar Wings Pegasus XL-R	Ultraflight Microlights Ltd
	G-MWUX	Solar Wings Pegasus XL-Q	B. D. Attwell
	G-MWVA	Solar Wings Pegasus XL-Q	W. Frosina
	G-MWVE	Solar Wings Pegasus XL-R	W. A. Keel-Stocker
	G-MWVG	CFM Shadow Srs CD	R. W. Appleby
	G-MWVL	Rans S.6-ESD Coyote II	D. A. Crosbie
	G-MWVP	Renegade Spirit UK	P. K. Dale
	G-MWVT	Mainair Gemini/Flash IIA	P. J. Newman
	G-MWVZ	Mainair Gemini/Flash IIA	R. W. Twamley
	G-MWWB	Mainair Gemini/Flash IIA	D. McAulay
	G-MWWD	Renegade Spirit	R. M. Hughes
	G-MWWH	Solar Wings Pegasus XL-Q	R. G. Wall
	G-MWWI	Mainair Gemini/Flash IIA	M. A. S. Nesbitt
	G-MWWS	Thruster T.300	J. H. Milne
	G-MWWV	Solar Wings Pegasus XL-Q	R. W. Livingstone
	G-MWWZ	Cyclone Chaser S	P. K. Dale
	G-MWXG	Solar Wings Pegasus Quasar TC	J. A. Horn
	G-MWXH	Solar Wings Pegasus Quasar IITC	R. P. Wilkinson
	G-MWXP	Solar Wings Pegasus XL-Q	A. P. Attfield
	G-MWXV	Mainair Gemini/Flash IIA	T. A. Daniel
	G-MWXX	Aerial Arts Chaser S.447	N. R. Beale
	G-MWXY	Cyclone Chaser S 447	P. D. Curtis
	G-MWYC	Solar Wings Pegasus XL-Q (modified)	J. Urrutia
	G-MWYD	CFM Shadow Srs C	W. J. I. Robb
	G-MWYG	Mainair Gemini/Flash IIA	J. H. McIvor
	G-MWYL	Mainair Gemini/Flash IIA	A. J. Hinks
	G-MWYM	Cyclone Chaser S 1000	C. J. Meadows
	G-MWYS	CGS Hawk 1 Arrow	Ulster Seaplane Association Ltd
	G-MWYT	Mainair Gemini Flash IIA	C. Richards
	G-MWYV	Mainair Gemini/Flash IIA	R. Tomlinson
	G-MWZF	Solar Wings Pegasus Quasar IITC	K. A. Donoghue
	G-MWZO	Solar Wings Pegasus Quasar IITC	A. Robinson
	G-MWZZ	Solar Wings Pegasus XL-R	The Microlight School Ltd
	G-MXII	Pitts Model 12	D. C. Mowat
	G-MXMX	PA-46R-350T Malibu Matrix	Feabrex Ltd
	G-MXPH	BAC.167 Strikemaster Mk 84 (311)	167 Aviation Ltd (G-SARK)
	G-MXPI	Robinson R44 II	HQ Aviation Ltd (G-CGAE)
	G-MXVI	VS.361 Spitfire LF.XVIe (TE184:9N-B)	P. D. E. Freedman
	G-MYAB	Solar Wings Pegasus XL-R	A. Davis
	G-MYAC	Solar Wings Pegasus XL-Q	M. E. Gilman
	G-MYAF	Solar Wings Pegasus XL-Q	J. H. S. Booth
	G-MYAH	Whittaker MW5 Sorcerer	A. R. Hawes
	G-MYAM	Renegade Spirit UK	G. R. Litton
	G-MYAN	Whittaker MW5 (K) Sorcerer	A. F. Reid
	G-MYAR	Thruster T.300	G. Hawkins
	G-MYAS	Mainair Gemini/Flash IIA	J. R. Davis
	G-MYAT	TEAM mini-MAX	C. J. Gillam
	G-MYAZ	Renegade Spirit UK	R. Smith
	G-MYBA	Rans S.6-ESD Coyote II	A. M. Hughes
	G-MYBB	Maxair UK Drifter	M. Ingleton
	G-MYBC	CFM Shadow Srs CD	J. Aubert
	G-MYBF	Solar Wings Pegasus XL-Q	R. F. Kindon
	G-MYBJ	Mainair Gemini/Flash IIA	I. P. Maltas
	G-MYBM	TEAM mini-MAX	B. Hunter
	G-MYBR	Solar Wings Pegasus XL-Q	M. J. Larbey & G. T. Hunt
	G-MYBT	Solar Wings Pegasus Quasar IITC	T. J. Wiltshire
	G-MYBW	Solar Wings Pegasus XL-Q	P. K. Dale
	G-MYCA	Whittaker MW6 Merlin	C. M. Byford
	G-MYCB	Cyclone Chaser S 447	S. D. Voysey
	G-MYCE	Solar Wings Pegasus Quasar IITC	S. W. Barker
	G-MYCL	Mainair Mercury	P. B. Cole
	G-MYCO	Renegade Spirit UK	T. P. Williams
	G-MYCP	Whittaker MW6 Merlin	K. R. Emery
	G-MYCT	Team Minimax 91	S. R. Grant
	G-MYCX	Powerchute Kestrel	S. J. Pugh-Jones
	G-MYDA	Powerchute Kestrel	A. E. Askew

Reg	Type	Owner or Operator	Notes
G-MYDE	CFM Shadow Srs CD	D. N. L. Howell	
G-MYDN	Quad City Challenger II	T. C. Hooks	
G-MYDT	Thruster T.300	A. J. L. Eves	
G-MYDU	Thruster T.300	J. M. Murphy	
G-MYDV	Mainair Gemini /Flash IIA	S. J. Mazilis	
G-MYDX	Rans S.6-ESD Coyote II	A. Tucker	
G-MYDZ	Mignet HM.1000 Balerit	D. S. Simpson	
G-MYEA	Solar Wings Pegasus XL-Q	A. M. Taylor	
G-MYEI	Cyclone Chaser S503	D. J. Hyatt	
G-MYEJ	Cyclone Chaser S447	A. W. Lowrie	
G-MYEK	Solar Wings Pegasus Quasar IITC	The Microlight School Ltd	
G-MYEM	Solar Wings Pegasus Quasar IITC	D. J. Moore	
G-MYEN	Solar Wings Pegasus Quasar IITC	T. J. Feeney	
G-MYEO	Solar Wings Pegasus Quasar IITC	A. R. Young	
G-MYEP	CFM Shadow Srs. CD	S. T. Dixon	
G-MYER	Cyclone AX3/503	T. F. Horrocks	
G-MYFA	Powerchute Kestrel	M. Phillips	
G-MYFH	Quad City Challenger II	T. D. Wolstenholme	
G-MYFL	Solar Wings Pegasus Quasar IITC	C. S. Boyd	
G-MYFO	Cyclone Airsports Chaser S	M. H. Broadbent	
G-MYFP	Mainair Gemini/Flash IIA	A. O'Connor	
G-MYFV	Cyclone AX3/503	I. J. Webb	
G-MYGD	Cyclone AX3/503	G. M. R. Keenan	
G-MYGF	TEAM mini-MAX	P. J. Tanulak	
G-MYGK	Cyclone Chaser S 508	P. C. Collins	
G-MYGM	Quad City Challenger II	S. J. Luck	
G-MYGO	CFM Shadow Series CD	D. B. Bullard	
G-MYGP	Rans S.6-ESD Coyote II	The Spirit of Goole	
G-MYGR	Rans S.6-ESD Coyote II	S-J. Huxtable	
G-MYGT	Solar Wings Pegasus XL-R	Condors Aerotow Syndicate	
G-MYGU	Solar Wings Pegasus XL-R	J. A. Sims	
G-MYHJ	Cyclone AX3/503	D. H. Edwards	
G-MYHK	Rans S.6-ESD Coyote II	R. A. Durance	
G-MYHL	Mainair Gemini/Flash IIA	O. G. Houghton	
G-MYHM	Cyclone AX3/503	D. R. Appleton	
G-MYHN	Mainair Gemini/Flash IIA	J. D. Moon	
G-MYHP	Rans S.6-ESD Coyote II	D. M. Smith	
G-MYIA	Quad City Challenger II	I. Pearson	
G-MYIF	CFM Shadow Srs CD	P. J. Edwards	
G-MYIH	Mainair Gemeni Flash IIA	A. Phillips	
G-MYII	TEAM mini-MAX	G. H. Crick	
G-MYIK	Kolb Twinstar Mk 3	A. A. Ross	
G-MYIL	Cyclone Chaser S 508	R. A. Rawes	
G-MYIP	CFM Shadow Srs CD	R. Newell	
G-MYIS	Rans S.6-ESD Coyote II	I. E. Evorott & M. Stott	
G-MYIU	Cyclone AX3/503	Ulster Seaplane Association Ltd	
G-MYIZ	TEAM mini-MAX 2	J. C. Longmore	
G-MYJC	Mainair Gemini/Flash IIA	M. N. Irven	
G-MYJD	Rans S.6-ESD Coyote II	U. Chakravorty	
G-MYJF	Thruster T.300	D. G. Wigley	
G-MYJG	Thruster T.300	S. A. Rice	
G-MYJJ	Solar Wings Pegasus Quasar IITC	G. Stewart	
G-MYJM	Mainair Gemini/Flash IIA	J. G. Treanor	
G-MYJU	Solar Wings Pegasus Quasar IITC	C. Lamb	
G-MYJX	Whittaker MW8 ★	South Yorkshire Aircraft Museum/Doncaster	
G-MYJZ	Whittaker MW5D Sorcerer	P. A. Aston	
G-MYKB	Kolb Twinstar Mk 3	T. Antell	
G-MYKD	Cyclone Chaser S 508	S. D. Pain	
G-MYKE	CFM Shadow Srs BD	MKH Engineering	
G-MYKF	Cyclone AX3/503	M. A. Collins	
G-MYKG	Mainair Gemini/Flash IIA	B. D. Walker	
G-MYKJ	TEAM mini-MAX	R. J. Hood	
G-MYKO	Whittaker MW6-S Fat Boy Flyer	J. A. Weston	
G-MYKR	Solar Wings Pegasus Quasar IITC	R. F. Davis	
G-MYKS	Solar Wings Pegasus Quasar IITC	Hire & Higher Ltd	
G-MYKV	Mainair Gemini/Flash IIA	P. J. Gulliver	
G-MYKZ	TEAM mini-MAX	C. A. Vickers & D. P. Busby	
G-MYLC	Solar Wings Pegasus Quantum 15	M. D. Morris	
G-MYLE	Solar Wings Pegasus Quantum 15	Quantum Quartet	
G-MYLG	Mainair Gemini/Flash IIA	I. C. Campbell	
G-MYLH	Solar Wings Pegasus Quantum 15	A. V. Poeira	

Notes	Reg	Type	Owner or Operator
	G-MYLI	Solar Wings Pegasus Quantum 15	A. M. Keyte
	G-MYLM	Solar Wings Pegasus Quasar IITC	P. J. Bamford
	G-MYLN	Kolb Twinstar Mk 3	J. F. Joyes
	G-MYLR	Mainair Gemini/Flash IIA	A. L. Lyall
	G-MYLS	Mainair Mercury	W. K. C. Davies
	G-MYLT	Mainair Blade	J. McCafferty
	G-MYLV	CFM Shadow Srs CD	R. G. M-J Proost & B. R. Cannell
	G-MYLW	Rans S6-ESD Coyote II	G. N. Simons
	G-MYMH	Rans S.6-ESD Coyote II	M. Wady
	G-MYMI	Kolb Twinstar Mk.3	F. J. Brown
	G-MYMK	Mainair Gemini/Flash IIA	C. L. M. Haywood
	G-MYMM	Ultraflight Fun 18S	N. P. Power
	G-MYMN	Whittaker MW6 Merlin	R. E. Arnold
	G-MYMS	Rans S.6-ESD Coyote II	C. F. M. Cheasman
	G-MYMW	Cyclone AX3/503	A. J. North
	G-MYMZ	Cyclone AX3/503	A. R. Hawes
	G-MYNB	Solar Wings Pegasus Quantum 15	J. L. Stone
	G-MYNE	Rans S.6-ESD Coyote II	A. R. Hawes
	G-MYNF	Mainair Mercury	S. Carter
	G-MYNI	TEAM mini-MAX	I. Pearson
	G-MYNK	Solar Wings Pegasus Quantum 15	M. T. Cain
	G-MYNL	Solar Wings Pegasus Quantum 15	A. D. Bales
	G-MYNN	Solar Wings Pegasus Quantum 15	V. Loy
	G-MYNP	Solar Wings Pegasus Quantum 15	K. A. Davidson
	G-MYNS	Solar Wings Pegasus Quantum 15	P. Hunt
	G-MYNX	CFM Streak Shadow SA	S. P. Fletcher
	G-MYNY	Kolb Twinstar Mk 3	A. Vaughan
	G-MYOA	Rans S6-ESD Coyote II	A. J. Gibson
	G-MYOG	Kolb Twinstar Mk 3	T. A. Womersley
	G-MYOH	CFM Shadow Srs CD	D. Howarth
	G-MYOL	Air Creation Fun 18S GTBIS	Condors Aerotow Syndicate
	G-MYON	CFM Shadow Srs CD	E. H. Jenkins
	G-MYOS	CFM Shadow Srs CD	C. A. & E. J. Bowles
	G-MYOU	Solar Wings Pegasus Quantum 15	D. J. Tasker
	G-MYPA	Rans S.6-ESD Coyote II	J. D. Avey
	G-MYPH	Solar Wings Pegasus Quantum 15	B. J. Briddick
	G-MYPI	Solar Wings Pegasus Quantum 15	P. L. Jarvis
	G-MYPL	CFM Shadow Srs CD	G. I. Madden
	G-MYPM	Cyclone AX3/503	A. A. Ahmed
	G-MYPN	Solar Wings Pegasus Quantum 15	L. S. Hyslop
	G-MYPR	Cyclone AX3/503	B. A. Donnelly
	G-MYPS	Whittaker MW6 Merlin	I. S. Bishop
	G-MYPT	CFM Shadow Srs CD	J. Tuck
	G-MYPW	Mainair Gemini/Flash IIA	P. Lacon & K. Tunnicliff
	G-MYRD	Mainair Blade	D. P. Wildman
	G-MYRE	Cyclone Chaser S	S. W. Barker
	G-MYRF	Solar Wings Pegasus Quantum 15	S. D. Lines
	G-MYRG	TEAM mini-MAX	A. R. Hawes
	G-MYRK	Renegade Spirit UK	G. R. Howitt
	G-MYRL	TEAM mini-MAX	J. N. Hanson
	G-MYRP	Letov LK-2M Sluka	R. M. C. Hunter
	G-MYRS	Solar Wings Pegasus Quantum 15	M. Howland
	G-MYRW	Mainair Mercury	G. C. Hobson
	G-MYRZ	Solar Wings Pegasus Quantum 15	R. E. Forbes
	G-MYSA	Cyclone Chaser S508	P. W. Dunn & A. R. Vincent
	G-MYSB	Solar Wings Pegasus Quantum 15	The Microlight School Ltd
	G-MYSC	Solar Wings Pegasus Quantum 15	K. R. White
	G-MYSJ	Mainair Gemini/Flash IIA	G. J. Cadden
	G-MYSK	Team Minimax 91	T. D. Wolstenholme
	G-MYSL	Aviasud Mistral	R. D. Ainley
	G-MYSR	Solar Wings Pegasus Quantum 15	G. Stewart
	G-MYSU	Rans S.6-ESD Coyote II	W. Matthews
	G-MYSY	Solar Wings Pegasus Quantum 15	G. E. Murphy
	G-MYTB	Mainair Mercury	P. J. Higgins
	G-MYTD	Mainair Blade	D. B. Meades
	G-MYTI	Solar Wings Pegasus Quantum 15	K. M. Gaffney
	G-MYTJ	Solar Wings Pegasus Quantum 15	L. Blight
	G-MYTL	Mainair Blade	P. P. Tomley
	G-MYTN	Solar Wings Pegasus Quantum 15	Air Cornwall
	G-MYTP	Arrowflight Hawk II	R. J. Turner
	G-MYTT	Quad City Challenger II	P. W. Brush

Reg	Type	Owner or Operator	Notes
G-MYTU	Mainair Blade	A. P. Pearce	
G-MYTY	CFM Streak Shadow Srs M	P. Crossman	
G-MYUA	Air Creation Fun 18S GTBIS	A. Shaw	
G-MYUC	Mainair Blade	R. Moss	
G-MYUF	Renegade Spirit	J. T. Chappell	
G-MYUH	Solar Wings Pegasus XL-Q	K. S. Daniels	
G-MYUI	Cyclone AX3/503	G. J. Hanlon	
G-MYUJ	Murphy Maverick 430	P. J. Porter (G-ONFL)	
G-MYUN	Mainair Blade	L. J. Teasdale	
G-MYUO	Solar Wings Pegasus Quantum 15	E. J. Hughes	
G-MYUP	Letov LK-2M Sluka	N. M. Barriskell	
G-MYUV	Pegasus Quantum 15	G. P. Lane	
G-MYUW	Mainair Mercury	G. C. Hobson	
G-MYVA	Kolb Twinstar Mk 3	E. Bayliss	
G-MYVB	Mainair Blade	K. R. Gay	
G-MYVG	Letov LK-2M Sluka	A. Evans	
G-MYVI	Air Creation Fun 18S GTBIS	D. Rowland	
G-MYVJ	Pegasus Quantum 15	A. I. McPherson & P. W. Davidson	
G-MYVK	Cyclone Pegasus Quantum 15	T. P. C. Hague	
G-MYVM	Pegasus Quantum 15	G. J. Gibson	
G-MYVO	Mainair Blade	Victor Oscar Group	
G-MYVP	Rans S.6-ESD Coyote II	S. F. Dreyer	
G-MYWC	Hunt Wing/Hunt Avon Skytrike	T. Wilbor	
G-MYWE	Thruster T.600T	J. B. Grotrian	
G-MYWF	CFM Shadow Srs CD	J. Preller	
G-MYWG	Pegasus Quantum 15	S. L. Greene	
G-MYWI	Pegasus Quantum 15	P. Mansfield	
G-MYWJ	Pegasus Quantum 15-912	L. M. Sams & I. Clarkson	
G-MYWK	Pegasus Quantum 15	J. A. Wright	
G-MYWL	Pegasus Quantum 15	R. P. McGuffie	
G-MYWM	CFM Shadow Srs CD	N. McKinley	
G-MYWO	Pegasus Quantum 15	K. Grimley	
G-MYWR	Pegasus Quantum 15	The Microlight School Ltd	
G-MYWS	Cyclone Chaser S 447	M. H. Broadbent	
G-MYWU	Pegasus Quantum 15	P. L. Owen	
G-MYWV	Rans S.4C Coyote	R. J. Hood	
G-MYWW	Pegasus Quantum 15	C. Clarkson	
G-MYWY	Pegasus Quantum 15	J. P. Rooms & R. Cox	
G-MYXA	TEAM mini-MAX 91	A. C. Aiken	
G-MYXB	Rans S6-ESD Coyote II	M. J. Gaffney	
G-MYXD	Pegasus Quasar IITC	A. Knight	
G-MYXE	Pegasus Quantum 15	G. A. Reeve	
G-MYXH	Cyclone AX3/503	D. Maayan	
G-MYXL	Mignet HM.1000 Balerit	R. W. Hollamby	
G MYXO	Letov LK-2M Sluka	R M C. Hunter	
G-MYXT	Pegasus Quantum 15	L. A. Washer	
G-MYXU	Thruster T.300	D. W. Wilson	
G-MYXV	Quad City Challenger II	T. S. Savage	
G-MYXW	Pegasus Quantum 15	J. Uttley	
G-MYXZ	Pegasus Quantum 15	Opes Independent Financial Advisers Ltd	
G-MYYC	Pegasus Quantum 15	T. R. E. Goldfield	
G-MYYF	Quad City Challenger II	L. E. J. Wojciechowski	
G-MYYH	Mainair Blade	D. J. Dodd	
G-MYYI	Pegasus Quantum 15	C. M. Day	
G-MYYK	Pegasus Quantum 15	N. Ionita	
G-MYYL	Cyclone AX3/503	T. S. Walker	
G-MYYR	TEAM mini-MAX 91	D. R. Blissett	
G-MYZB	Pegasus Quantum 15	I. K. Priestley	
G-MYZC	Cyclone AX3/503	R. Loveday	
G-MYZF	Cyclone AX3/503	Ulster Seaplane Association Ltd	
G-MYZG	Cyclone AX3/503	D. L. R. Davies	
G-MYZH	Chargus Titan 38	T. J. Gayton-Polley	
G-MYZL	Pegasus Quantum 15	R. F. Greaves	
G-MYZP	CFM Shadow Srs DD	I. G. Poutney	
G-MYZR	Rans S.6-ESD XL Coyote II	N. R. Beale	
G-MYZV	Rans S.6-ESA Coyote II	I. M. Charlwood	
G-MYZY	Pegasus Quantum 15	L. Hurman	
G-MZAB	Mainair Blade	J. C. Ring	
G-MZAF	Mainair Blade	K. Walker	
G-MZAG	Mainair Blade	M. J. P. Sanderson	

Notes	Reg	Type	Owner or Operator
	G-MZAK	Mainair Mercury	I. Rawson
	G-MZAM	Mainair Blade	J. Wilkinson
	G-MZAN	Pegasus Quantum 15	P. M. Leahy
	G-MZAS	Mainair Blade	T. Carter
	G-MZBD	Rans S-6-ESD-XL Coyote II	S. W. Osborne
	G-MZBF	Letov LK-2M Sluka	V. Simpson
	G-MZBH	Rans S.6-ESD Coyote II	E. J. D. Heathfield
	G-MZBK	Letov LK-2M Sluka	R. M. C. Hunter
	G-MZBL	Mainair Blade	C. J. Rubery
	G-MZBN	CFM Shadow Srs B	W. J. Buskell
	G-MZBS	CFM Shadow Srs D	T. P. Ryan
	G-MZBT	Pegasus Quantum 15	I. A. Macadam
	G-MZBU	Rans S.6-ESD Coyote II	M. Khalid
	G-MZBW	Quad City Challenger II UK	R. M. C. Hunter
	G-MZBY	Pegasus Quantum 15	GS Aviation (Europe) Ltd
	G-MZCB	Cyclone Chaser S 447	A. R. Vincent & P. W. Dunn
	G-MZCE	Mainair Blade	I. C. Hindle
	G-MZCF	Mainair Blade	C. Hannanby
	G-MZCI	Pegasus Quantum 15	R. J. Hemmings
	G-MZCK	AMF Chevvron 2-32C	S. Mebarki
	G-MZCM	Pegasus Quantum 15	J. L. Smith
	G-MZCS	TEAM mini-MAX	J. Aley
	G-MZCT	CFM Shadow Srs CD	W. G. Gill
	G-MZCV	Pegasus Quantum 15	V. P. Z. Krause
	G-MZCW	Pegasus Quantum 15	K. L. Baldwin
	G-MZCX	Huntwing Avon Skytrike	A. I. Sutherland
	G-MZCY	Pegasus Quantum 15	G. Murphy
	G-MZDB	Pegasus Quantum 15	N. L. Halton
	G-MZDC	Pegasus Quantum 15	N. J. Millward
	G-MZDD	Pegasus Quantum 15	J. Ellis
	G-MZDF	Mainair Blade	M. Liptrot
	G-MZDI	Whittaker MW6-S Fat Boy Flyer	C. M. Byford (G-BUNN)
	G-MZDK	Mainair Blade	R. H. de Castro Ribeiro
	G-MZDM	Rans S.6-ESD Coyote II	M. E. Nicholas
	G-MZDS	Cyclone AX3/503	M. J. Cooper
	G-MZDV	Pegasus Quantum 15	Griffin Toomes Consulting Engineers Ltd
	G-MZDY	Pegasus Quantum 15	S. K. Turner
	G-MZDZ	Hunt Wing	E. W. Laidlaw
	G-MZEA	BFC Challenger II	G. S. Cridland
	G-MZEB	Mainair Blade	R. A. Campbell
	G-MZEC	Pegasus Quantum 15	A. B. Godber
	G-MZEE	Pegasus Quantum 15	N. Brigginshaw
	G-MZEM	Pegasus Quantum 15	L. H. Black
	G-MZEN	Rans S.6-ESD Coyote II	P. A. Harvie
	G-MZES	Letov LK-2M Sluka	D. S. Coutts
	G-MZEU	Rans S-6-ESD XL Coyote II	P. Wilcox
	G-MZFA	Cyclone AX2000	G. S. Highley
	G-MZFD	Mainair Rapier	R. G. Wyatt
	G-MZFE	Hunt Wing	G. J. Latham
	G-MZFF	Hunt Wing	B. J. Adamson
	G-MZFH	AMF Chevvron 2-32C	Eagle Flying Group
	G-MZFL	Rans S.6-ESD Coyote IIXL	J. J. Lynch
	G-MZFO	Thruster T.600N	G. L. Thomas
	G-MZFS	Mainair Blade	P. L. E. Zelakowski
	G-MZFU	Thruster T.600N	M. I. Garner
	G-MZFX	Cyclone AX2000	AX Group
	G-MZFY	Rans S.6-ESD Coyote IIXL	L. G. Tserkezos
	G-MZFZ	Mainair Blade	D. J. Bateman
	G-MZGA	Cyclone AX2000	S. M. Rawson
	G-MZGC	Cyclone AX2000	T. J. McMenamin
	G-MZGD	Rans S.5 Coyote II	P. J. Greenrod
	G-MZGG	Pegasus Quantum 15	J. M. Chapman
	G-MZGH	Hunt Wing/Avon 462(3)	J. H. Cole
	G-MZGL	Mainair Rapier	A. Robins
	G-MZGN	Pegasus Quantum 15	J. B. Peacock
	G-MZGO	Pegasus Quantum 15-912	A. A. Annaev
	G-MZGR	TEAM mini-MAX	K. G. Seeley
	G-MZGU	Arrowflight Hawk II (UK)	M. C. Holmes
	G-MZGY	Thruster T.600N 450	G. E. Norton
	G-MZHA	Thruster T.600N	C. J. Green
	G-MZHB	Mainair Blade	J. F. Davies

Reg	Type	Owner or Operator	Notes
G-MZHD	Thruster T.600N	J. Walsh & A. R. Sunley	
G-MZHF	Thruster T.600N	B. M. O'Brien	
G-MZHI	Pegasus Quantum 15	M. A. Gardiner	
G-MZHJ	Mainair Rapier	G. Standish	
G-MZHM	Team Himax 1700R ★	Ulster Aviation Society Heritage Collection, Long Kesh	
G-MZHN	Pegasus Quantum 15	F. W. Ferichs	
G-MZHO	Quad City Challenger II	J. Pavelin	
G-MZHP	Pegasus Quantum 15	W. J. Flood	
G-MZHR	Cyclone AX2000	T. P. Williams	
G-MZHS	Thruster T.600T	G-MZHS Group	
G-MZHV	Thruster T.600T	A. N. Schutte	
G-MZHW	Thruster T.600N	A. J. Glynn	
G-MZHY	Thruster T.600N	B. W. Webster	
G-MZIB	Pegasus Quantum 15	S. Murphy	
G-MZID	Whittaker MW6 Merlin	C. P. F. Sheppard	
G-MZIH	Mainair Blade 912	N. J. Waller	
G-MZIJ	Pegasus Quantum 15	Quantum 2 Group	
G-MZIK	Pegasus Quantum 15	J. H. Cole	
G-MZIL	Mainair Rapier	B. L. Cook	
G-MZIT	Mainair Blade 912	M. A. Robinson	
G-MZIU	Pegasus Quantum 15-912	E. A. McCabe	
G-MZIV	Cyclone AX2000	M. L. Williams	
G-MZIZ	Renegade Spirit UK (G-MWGP)	D. L. Price	
G-MZJF	Cyclone AX2000	D. J. Lewis	
G-MZJG	Pegasus Quantum 15	A. R. Hawes	
G-MZJI	Rans S-6-ESD-XL Coyote II	J. P. Hunsdale	
G-MZJJ	Murphy Maverick	M. F. Farrer	
G-MZJK	Mainair Blade	P. G. Angus	
G-MZJL	Cyclone AX2000	A. R. Hawes	
G-MZJM	Rans S.6-ESD XL Coyote II	D. J. Shaw	
G-MZJO	Pegasus Quantum 15	P. S. Hall	
G-MZJP	Whittaker MW6-S Fatboy Flyer	R. C. Funnell & D. J. Burton	
G-MZJT	Pegasus Quantum 15	N. Hammerton	
G-MZJX	M,ainair Blade	G. D. McCullough	
G-MZJY	Pegasus Quantum 15	P. G. Ratcliffe	
G-MZJZ	Mainair Blade	Lima Zulu Owner Syndicate	
G-MZKA	Pegasus Quantum 15	M. Richardson	
G-MZKC	Cyclone AX2000	D. J. Pike	
G-MZKD	Pegasus Quantum 15	T. M. Frost	
G-MZKE	Rans S.6-ESD XL Coyote II	G. E. Moore	
G-MZKF	Pegasus Quantum 15	A. H., D. P. & V. J. Tidmas	
G-MZKG	Mainair Blade	N. S. Rigby	
G-MZKH	CFM Shadow Srs DD	S. P. H. Calvert	
G-MZKI	Mainair Rapier	D. L. Aspinall	
G-MZKL	Pegasus Quantum 15	D. Gilmartin	
G-MZKN	Mainair Rapier	O. P. Farrell	
G-MZKS	Thruster T.600N	P. J. O'Carroll	
G-MZKU	Thruster T.600N	A. S. Day	
G-MZKW	Quad City Challenger II	L. E. J. Wojciechohowski	
G-MZKY	Pegasus Quantum 15	A. P. Lang	
G-MZLD	Pegasus Quantum 15	L. Sokoli	
G-MZLE	Maverick (G-BXSZ)	M. W. Hands	
G-MZLF	Pegasus Quantum 15	S. Seymour	
G-MZLI	Mignet HM.1000 Balerit	A. G. Barr	
G-MZLJ	Pegasus Quantum 15	M. J. Hyde	
G-MZLL	Rans S.6-ESD Coyote II	D. W. Adams	
G-MZLM	Cyclone AX2000	P. E. Hadley	
G-MZLN	Pegasus Quantum 15	P. A. Greening	
G-MZLP	CFM Shadow Srs D	D. J. Gordon	
G-MZLT	Pegasus Quantum 15	B. Jackson	
G-MZLV	Pegasus Quantum 15	A. D. McCormick	
G-MZLW	Pegasus Quantum 15	J. H. Cornish	
G-MZLX	Micro Aviation B.22S Bantam	V. J. Vaughan	
G-MZLY	Letov LK-2M Sluka	W. McCarthy	
G-MZMC	Pegasus Quantum 15	J. J. Baker	
G-MZME	Medway Eclipser	C. F. Janes	
G-MZMF	Pegasus Quantum 15	P. S. Constable	
G-MZMG	Pegasus Quantum 15	C. J. Meadows	
G-MZMH	Pegasus Quantum 15	A. K. Hole	
G-MZMJ	Mainair Blade	V. M. Szolin	

Notes	Reg	Type	Owner or Operator
	G-MZMK	Chevvron 2-32C	R. W. Appleby
	G-MZML	Mainair Blade 912	C. J. Meadows
	G-MZMN	Pegasus Quantum 912	M. D. Tredgold
	G-MZMO	TEAM mini-MAX 91	North East Flight Training Ltd
	G-MZMT	Pegasus Quantum 15	R. C. Dowle & S. P. Clements
	G-MZMU	Rans S.6-ESD Coyote II	D. W. Adams
	G-MZMV	Mainair Blade	M. J. Booth
	G-MZMW	Mignet HM.1000 Balerit	M. E. Whapham
	G-MZMY	Mainair Blade	J. W. Galloway
	G-MZMZ	Mainair Blade	D. T. Page
	G-MZNA	Quad City Challenger II UK	S. Hennessy
	G-MZNB	Pegasus Quantum 15	M. J. Hilton
	G-MZNC	Mainair Blade 912	A. J. Harrison
	G-MZNG	Pegasus Quantum 15	B. A. Dawson
	G-MZNH	CFM Shadow Srs DD	F. A. Bakir
	G-MZNJ	Mainair Blade	R. A. Hardy
	G-MZNR	Pegasus Quantum 15	N. J. Clemens
	G-MZNS	Pegasus Quantum 15	T. Eaton & S. D. P. Bridge
	G-MZNT	Pegasus Quantum 15-912	The Microlight School Ltd
	G-MZNV	Rans S.6-ESD Coyote II	A. P. Thomas
	G-MZOC	Mainair Blade	A. S. Davies
	G-MZOD	Pegasus Quantum 15	G. P. Burns
	G-MZOE	Cyclone AX2000	B. E. Wagenhauser
	G-MZOF	Mainair Blade	R. M. Ellis
	G-MZOG	Pegasus Quantum 15-912	Jarvy Enterprises Ltd
	G-MZOH	Whittaker MW5D Sorcerer	I. Pearson
	G-MZOK	Whittaker MW6 Merlin	G-MZOK Syndicate
	G-MZOS	Pegasus Quantum 15-912	T. G. Ryan
	G-MZOV	Pegasus Quantum 15	B. E. Wagenhauser
	G-MZOW	Pegasus Quantum 15-912	G. P. Burns
	G-MZOX	Letov LK-2M Sluka	N. R. Beale
	G-MZOY	TEAM Mini-MAX 91	P. R. & S. E. Whitehouse
	G-MZOZ	Rans S.6-ESA Coyote II	G. L. Daniels
	G-MZPH	Mainair Blade	C. A. Hamps
	G-MZRC	Pegasus Quantum 15	M. Hopkins
	G-MZRS	CFM Shadow Srs CD	C. A. Larkins
	G-MZSP	Spacek SD-1 Minisport	A. M. Hughes
	G-MZTG	Titan T-51 Mustang	A. R. Evans
	G-NABA	TL 3000 Sirius 600	J. Devoy
	G-NACA	Norman NAC-2 Freelance 180	P. J. L. Caruth
	G-NACI	Norman NAC-1 Freelance 180	I. & M. Williams (G-AXFB)
	G-NACL	Norman NAC-6 Fieldmaster	EPA Aircraft Co Ltd (G-BNEG)
	G-NACO	Norman NAC-6 Fieldmaster	EPA Aircraft Co Ltd
	G-NACP	Norman NAC-6 Fieldmaster	EPA Aircraft Co Ltd
	G-NADE	Bell 505 Jet Ranger X	M. E. Rost
	G-NADN	PA-23-250 Aztec F	N. M. T. Sparks (G-XSFT/G-CPPC/G-BGBH)
	G-NADS	TEAM mini-MAX 91	N. P. St.J Ramsay
	G-NAGG	Rotorsport UK MT-03	C. A. Clements
	G-NAHW	Steen Skybolt	M. T. J. Hadland
	G-NALC	Eurocopter AS.355NP Ecureuil 2	L. Zaccheo
	G-NALD	Aeroprakt A.32 Vixxen	D. J. Medcraft
	G-NANO	Avid Speed Wing	S. F. Beardsell
	G-NAPP	Van's RV-7	R. C. Meek
	G-NAPS	Schleicher ASH-31 Mi	D. M. Byass & J. A. McCoshim
	G-NARD	Aeros Ltd Fox 13T/Demoiselle 15	R. B. Hewing
	G-NARG	Tanarg/Ixess 15 912S (1)	D. A. Eastough
	G-NARL	Zlin Savage Shock Cub	P. C. Woolley
	G-NATI	Corby CJ-1 Starlet	S. P. Evans
	G-NATT	Rockwell Commander 114A	Northgleam Ltd
	G-NBCA	Pilatus PC-12/47E	Narm Aviation Ltd
	G-NBDD	Robin DR.400/180	McAully Flying Group Ltd
	G-NBOX	Ikarus C42 FB100 Bravo	N. Hammerton
	G-NBPL	Aerospatiale AS.355F2 Ecureuil 2	Nigel Brunt Properties Ltd
	G-NBSI	Cameron N-77 balloon	Nottingham Hot-Air Balloon Club
	G-NCDC	Skyranger Nynja 912S(1)	C. D. Church
	G-NCFC	PA-38-112 Tomahawk II	N. J. Butler (G-BNOA)
	G-NCKK	Pegasus Sport QuikR	N. C. Farley
	G-NCKS	Westland WG.13 Lynx AH.Mk.7 (XZ179)	G. P. Hinkley

Reg	Type	Owner or Operator	Notes
G-NCKY	Westland WG.13 Lynx AH.Mk.7	Gazelle Squadron Flying Group	
G-NCKZ	Westland WG.13 Lynx HMA.Mk.8	Landguard Point Ltd	
G-NCLA	Van's RV-12iS	J. Price	
G-NCUB	Piper J-3C-65 Cub	R. J. Willies (G-BGXV)	
G-NDAD	Medway SLA100 Executive	R. D. Pyne	
G-NDJS	Jonker JS1-C Revelation	A. J. Davis	
G-NDOT	Thruster T.600N	P. C. Bailey	
G-NDPA	Ikarus C42 FB UK	Grandpa's Flying Group	
G-NEAT	Europa	P. F. D. Foden	
G-NEDS	Skyranger Nynja 912S(1)	J. Hunter	
G-NEEE	Cessna F.172M	Easy Aircraft Rental Ltd (G-BCZM)	
G-NEEL	Rotorway Executive 90	I. C. Bedford	
G-NEEV	TL3000 Sirius 600	M. P. Neve	
G-NEIL	Thunder Ax3 Maxi Sky Chariot balloon	N. Ivison	
G-NEIO	Diamond DA.40NG Star	N. R. Scarles	
G-NELI	PA-28R-180 Cherokee Arrow	MK Aero Support Ltd	
G-NELS	Robinson R44	Heliwarns Aviation Ltd	
G-NEMO	Raj Hamsa X'Air Jabiru (4)	C. D. Swift	
G-NEON	PA-32 Cherokee Six 300B	T. F. Rowley	
G-NEOP	Airbus A.321-251NX	British Airways PLC	
G-NEOR	Airbus A.321-251NX	British Airways PLC	
G-NEOS	Airbus A.321-251NX	British Airways PLC	
G-NEOT	Airbus A.321-251NX	British Airways PLC	
G-NEOU	Airbus A.321-251NX	British Airways PLC	
G-NEOV	Airbus A.321-251NX	British Airways PLC	
G-NEOW	Airbus A.321-251NX	British Airways PLC	
G-NEOX	Airbus A.321-251NX	Briitish Airways PLC	
G-NEOY	Airbus A.321-251NX	British Airways PLC	
G-NEOZ	Airbus A.321-251NX	Briitish Airways PLC	
G-NESA	Europa XS	A. M. Kay	
G-NESE	Tecnam P2002-JF	G. Rumbles	
G-NESH	Robinson R44 II	Helicentre Aviation Ltd	
G-NESW	PA-34-220T Seneca III	G. C. U. Guida	
G-NESY	PA-18-95 Super Cub	M. L. J. Goff	
G-NETR	AS.355F1 Twin Squirrel	PDG Helicopters and PDG Aviation Services (G-JARV/G-OGHL)	
G-NETS	DHC.6-300 Twin Otter	Isles of Scilly Skybus Ltd (operated by Aurigny Air Services)	
G-NEUS	Brugger MB.2 Colibri	S. B. Robson	
G-NEVE	Ikarus C42 FB100	A. S. Bennett	
G-NEWA	Rans S-6-ES Coyote II	J. Cook	
G-NEWB	Agusta AW109SP Grand New	Apollo Air Services Ltd (G-SGRP)	
G-NEWG	Boeing 737-70N	21T Ltd (G-STRF)	
G-NEWT	Beech 35 Bonanza	Brinkley Aircraft Services Ltd (G-APVW)	
G-NEWZ	Bell 206B JetRanger 3	H. P. L. Frost	
G-NFLA	BAe Jetstream 3102	Cardiff University (G-BRGN/G-BLHC)	
G-NFLB	SAAB 340B	Cranfield University	
G-NFLC	HP.137 Jetstream 1H (G-AXUI) ★	Instructional airframe/Perth	
G-NFLY	Tecnam P2002-EA Siorra	Cavok Aviation Bridgwater	
G-NFNF	Robin DR.400/180	W. R. Cobb	
G-NFON	Van's RV-8	N. F. O'Neill	
G-NFVB	Cameron Z-105 balloon	N. S. Amor	
G-NGAA	Bristell NG5 Speed Wing	Jet Applications Ltd	
G-NGBB	Bristell NG5 Speed Wing	S. T. Georgiou	
G-NGCC	Bristell NG5 Speed Wing	G. C. Coull	
G-NGII	Bristell NG5 Speed Wing	S. A. Wilson	
G-NGLL	Bristell NG5 Speed Wing	F. Sayyah & A. J. Palmer	
G-NGLZ	Bell 206B-3 Jet Ranger III	N. A. Allen (G-STVZ/G-XCBI)	
G-NGSA	Extra NG	Addy Aviation LLP	
G-NGTC	Extra NG	Skyboard Aerobatics Ltd	
G-NHAA	AS.365N-2 Dauphin 2 ★	The Great North Air Ambulance Service (ground trainer) /Urlay Nook (G-MLTY)	
G-NHAD	AS.365N-2 Dauphin 2	The Great North Air Ambulance Service (G-SSKP/G-CIUC)	
G-NHAE	AS.365N-3 Dauphin 2	The Great North Air Ambulance Service (G-DOLF)	

Notes	Reg	Type	Owner or Operator
	G-NHRJ	Europa XS	R. J. Dawson
	G-NHVB	Agusta Westland AW139	NHV Helicopters Ltd (G-SNSK)
	G-NHVC	Agusta Westland AW139	NHV Helicopters Ltd
	G-NHVD	Agusta Westland AW169	NHV Helicopters Ltd
	G-NHVF	Airbus EC.175B	NHV Helicopters Ltd
	G-NHVG	Airbus EC.175B	NHV Helicopters Ltd
	G-NHVI	Airbus EC.175B	NHV Helicopters Ltd
	G-NHVJ	Airbus EC.175B	NHV Helicopters Ltd
	G-NHVP	Agusta Westland AW139	NHV Helicopters Ltd
	G-NHVR	Airbus EC175B	NHV Helicopters Ltd
	G-NHVT	Leonardo AW169	NHV Helicopters Ltd
	G-NHVU	Airbus EC175B	NHV Helicopters Ltd
	G-NHVV	Airbus EC175B	NHV Helicopters Ltd
	G-NHVX	Agusta Westland AW139	NHV Helicopters Ltd
	G-NIAA	Beech B.200 Super King Air	Woodgate Aviation (IoM) Ltd
	G-NIAB	Beech B.200 Super King Air	Woodgate Aviation (IoM) Ltd
	G-NIAC	TL2000UK Sting Carbon S4	R. R. Clarke
	G-NICC	Cosmik EV-97 Team Eurostar UK	C. Wileman
	G-NICI	Robinson R44	M. S. Goodwin
	G-NICS	Sky Ranger Swift 912S(1)	I. A. Forrest
	G-NICU	Leonardo AW169	Sloane Helicopters Ltd
	G-NICX	Europa XS	N. Kenney
	G-NIDG	Aerotechnik EV-97 Eurostar	Skydrive Ltd
	G-NIEN	Van's RV-9A	K. N. P. Higgs
	G-NIGC	Jabiru UL-450	C. K. Fry
	G-NIGE	Luscombe 8E Silvaire	Garden Party Ltd (G-BSHG)
	G-NIGM	Taylor JT.1 Monoplane	C. S. Hales
	G-NIIX	Skyranger Nynja	The Microlight School Ltd
	G-NIKA	Cessna 525 Citation	Comis Air Ltd
	G-NIKB	Skyranger Swift 912(1)	N. D. Brown
	G-NIKE	PA-28-181 Cherokee Archer II	Falcon Flying Services Ltd
	G-NIKK	Diamond Katana DA20-C1	D. J. & S. N. Taplin
	G-NIKL	Robinson R22	Helicopter Services Ltd (G-BTNA)
	G-NIKS	Eurofox 912(1)	A. H. Aljassar
	G-NILT	EV-97 Eurostar SL	G. I. Nelson
	G-NIMA	Balóny Kubíček BB30Z balloon	S. Dyer
	G-NIMB	Schempp-Hirth Nimbus 2C	P. D. Wright
	G-NIME	Cessna T.206H Turbo Stationair	J. G. Whittle
	G-NINC	PA-28-180 Cherokee	North Wales Flight Academy Ltd
	G-NIND	PA-28-180 Cherokee	Spirit of Flight Ltd
	G-NINJ	Skyranger Nynja 912S(1)	G. W. Naismith
	G-NIOG	Robinson R44 II	Helicopter Sharing Ltd
	G-NIOS	PA-32R-301 Saratoga SP	Plant Aviation
	G-NIPP	Slingsby T.66 Nipper 3	N. J. Riddin (G-AVKJ)
	G-NIPR	Slingsby T.66 Nipper 3	P. A. Gibbs (G-AVXC)
	G-NIPS	Tipsy T.66 Nipper 2	C. M. Evans & J. W. Blaylock
	G-NIXX	Skyranger 912(1)	E. W. Barnett (G-CDYJ)
	G-NJAA	Cessna 560XL Citation XLS	Netjets Europe Sociedade Unipessoal Lda/Portugal
	G-NJAB	Cessna 560XL Citation XLS	Netjets Europe Sociedade Unipessoal Lda/Portugal
	G-NJAC	Cessna 560XL Citation XLS	Netjets Europe Sociedade Unipessoal Lda/Portugal
	G-NJAE	Dassault Falcon 2000EX	Netjets Europe Sociedade Unipessoal Lda/Portugal
	G-NJAF	Dassault Falcon 2000EX	Netjets Europe Sociedade Unipessoal Lda/Portugal
	G-NJAH	Cessna 560XL Citation XLS	Netjets Europe Sociedade Unipessoal Lda/Portugal
	G-NJAI	Cessna 560XL Citation XLS	Netjets Europe Sociedade Unipessoal Lda/Portugal
	G-NJAJ	Cessna 560XL Citation XLS	Netjets Europe Sociedade Unipessoal Lda/Portugal
	G-NJAK	Cessna 560XL Citation XLS	Netjets Europe Sociedade Unipessoal Lda/Portugal
	G-NJBA	Rotorway Executive 162F	N. J. Beehoo
	G-NJCZ	Czech Sport Pipersport	Aerocruz Ltd
	G-NJET	Schempp-Hirth Ventus cT	P. S. Carder
	G-NJNH	Robinson R66	Hawesbates LLP

Reg	Type	Owner or Operator	Notes
G-NJOY	PA-28-181 Cherokee Archer III	M. J. Groves	
G-NJPG	Skyranger Nynja 912S(1)	P. Gibbs	
G-NJPW	P & M Quik GT450	Golf Papa Whiskey Group	
G-NJSH	Robinson R22 Beta	Hawesbates LLP	
G-NJSP	Jabiru J430	N. J. S. Pitman	
G-NJTC	Aeroprakt A22-L Foxbat	I. R. Russell	
G-NLCB	Ultramagic N-425 balloon	Virgin Balloon Flights	
G-NLDR	AS.355F2 Ecureuil 2	PDG Helicopters and PDG Aviation Services (G-PDGS)	
G-NLEE	Cessna 182Q	R. J. Houghton	
G-NLMB	Zenair CH.601UL Zodiac	N. Lamb	
G-NLSE	AS.355F2 Ecureuil 2	PDG Helicopters and PDG Aviation Services (G-ULES/G-OBHL/G-HARO/G-DAFT/ G-BNNN)	
G-NMBS	Schempp-Hirth Nimbus-3/24.5	D. S. Bramwell (G-DFBM)	
G-NMCC	Aviat A-1C-180 Husky	D. C. Mowat	
G-NMCL	Eurofox 912(S)	N. R. McLeod	
G-NMMB	Van's RV-10	M. S. Bamber & N. R. MacLennan	
G-NMMC	Robinson R44 II	BBR Leasing Ltd (G-GIBB)	
G-NMOS	Cameron C-80 balloon	A. O. H. Harvey	
G-NMRV	Van's RV-6	G. W. Street	
G-NNAC	PA-18-135 Super Cub	PAW Flying Services Ltd	
G-NNEE	North American SNJ-5 Harvard	Eagles 11 Ltd (G-DHHF)	
G-NNJA	Skyranger Nynja	J. Murphy & D. Cookson	
G-NNNA	Stolp SA.300 Starduster Too	R. Farrer (G-BUPB)	
G-NNON	Mainair Blade	D. R. Kennedy	
G-NOCK	Cessna FR.182RG II	Shropshire Knockers Flying Group (G-BGTK)	
G-NODE	AA-5B Tiger	Ultranomad Sro	
G-NOIL	BN-2A-26 Islander	Aerospace Resources Ltd (G-BJWO/G-BAXC)	
G-NOLA	Boeing 737-MAX8	Ascend Airways Ltd	
G-NOLR	Leonardo AW109SP	East Midlands Helicopters	
G-NONE	Dyn'Aéro MCR-01 ULC	M. A. Collins	
G-NORA	Ikarus C.42 FB UK	N. A. Rathbone	
G-NORB	Saturne S110K hang glider	R. N. Pearce	
G-NORD	SNCAN NC.854 (7)	Group Nord	
G-NORG	Gefa-Flug AS105GD airship	Creative Capital Group Ltd (G-BZUR)	
G-NORK	Bell 206B-3 JetRanger III	R. S. Forsyth	
G-NOSE	Cessna 402B	Litorali SRL/Italy (G-MPCU)	
G-NOTE	PA-28-181 Cherokee Archer III	J. Beach	
G-NOTS	Skyranger 912S(1)	S. F. N. Warnell	
G-NOWW	Mainair Blade 912	S. Orton	
G-NOXY	Robinson R44	T A Knox Shopfitters Ltd (G-VALV)	
G-NPKJ	Van's RV-6	D. & S. A. Firth	
G-NPPL	Ikarus C42 FB100	Papa Lima Group	
G-NPTA	Boeing 737-86N(BCF)	West Atlantic UK Ltd	
G-NPTB	Boeing 737-83N(F)	West Atlantic UK Ltd	
G-NPTD	Boeing 737-83N(F)	West Atlantic UK Ltd	
G-NPTH	Boeing 737-43Q(SF)	West Atlantic UK Ltd	
G-NPTI	Boering 737-8F2	West Atlantic UK Ltd	
G-NPTX	Boeing 737-4C9(F)	West Atlantic UK Ltd	
G-NRFK	Van's RV-8	C. N. Harper	
G-NRMA	Dan Rihn DR.107 One Design	T. A. Lewis	
G-NRRA	SIAI-Marchetti SF.260 (BF8431)	G. Boot	
G-NSBB	Ikarus C.42 FB-100 VLA	Bravo Bravo Flying Group	
G-NSCA	Airbus MBB BK117 D-3	Babcock Mission Critical Services Onshore Ltd	
G-NSFS	VS.361 Spitfire IX	Norwegian Spitfire Foundation	
G-NSKB	Aeroprakt A22-L Foxbat	N. F. Smith	
G-NSKY	Alpi Pioneer 400	W. T. D. Gillam	
G-NSSA	TLAC Sherwood Ranger XP	A. R. Stanley	
G-NSTG	Cessna F.150F	Westair Flying Services Ltd (G-ATNI)	
G-NSYS	Eurocopter EC135 T1	Novas Aerospace Ltd (G-CEYF/G-HARP)	
G-NTPS	BRM Aero Bristell NG5	N. D. H. Stokes	
G-NTSI	TAF Sling 4 TSI	N. J. Trowsdale	

Notes	Reg	Type	Owner or Operator
	G-NTWK	AS.355F2 Twin Squirrel	PDG Helicopters and PDG Aviation Services (G-FTWO/G-OJOR/G-BMUS)
	G-NUFC	Skyranger Swift 912S(1)	J. F. Garbutt
	G-NUGC	Grob G.103A Twin II Acro	The University of Nottingham Students Union
	G-NUKA	PA-28-181 Cherokee Archer II	London Flight Experience Ltd
	G-NULA	Flight Design CT2K	S. L. Cogger
	G-NULL	Airbus Helicopters AS.350 B3	O. A. O' Donovan
	G-NUTA	Christen Eagle II	E. M. & M. C. W. Johns
	G-NUTT	Mainair Pegasus Quik	I. E. Barry
	G-NVBF	Lindstrand LBL-210A balloon	Virgin Balloon Flights
	G-NWAA	Eurocopter EC.135T2+	Babcock Mission Critical Services Onshore Ltd
	G-NWEM	Eurocopter EC.135T2+	Babcock Mission Critical Services Onshore Ltd (G-SSXX/G-SSSX)
	G-NWFA	Cessna 150M	North Weald Flying Group Ltd (G-CFBD)
	G-NWFB	Cessna 152	North Weald Flight Training Ltd (G-BTYT)
	G-NWFC	Cessna 172P	North Weald Flying Group Ltd
	G-NWFG	Cessna 172P	North Weald Flying Group Ltd
	G-NWFS	Cessna 172P	North Weald Flying Group Ltd (G-TYMS)
	G-NWFT	Cessna F.172N	North Weald Flight Training Ltd (G-BURD)
	G-NWFX	Cessna F.152	North Weald Flight Training Ltd (G-CIUU)
	G-NWHF	CCF Harvard IV	Fly Navy Heritge Trust Ltd (G-BSBG)
	G-NWOI	Eurocopter EC135 P2+	West Yorkshire Combined Authority National Police Air Service
	G-NWPR	Cameron N-77 balloon	A. B. Court
	G-NWRD	Flylight Adam	N. A. Ward
	G-NXOE	Cessna 172S	Goodwood Road Racing Co.Ltd
	G-NYMB	Schempp-Hirth Nimbus 3	Nimbus Syndicate
	G-NYMF	PA-25-235 Pawnee	Bristol Gliding Club Pty Ltd
	G-NYMP	Eurofox 2K	The Bristol Gliding Club Proprietary Ltd
	G-NYNA	Van's RV-9A	J. S. Langberg
	G-NYNE	Schleicher ASW-27-18E	J. Eccles
	G-NYNJ	Skyranger Nynja 912S)1)	N. J. Sutherland
	G-NZIC	LeVier Cosmic Wind	J. C. Tempest
	G-NZOC	LeVier Cosmic Wind	R. S. Grace (G-AYRJ)
	G-NZSS	Boeing Stearman N2S-5 (43517:227)	R. W. Davies
	G-OAAA	PA-28-161 Cherokee Warrior II	Red Hill Air Services Ltd
	G-OABB	Jodel D.150	K. Manley
	G-OABO	Enstrom F-28A	C. R. Taylor (G-BAIB)
	G-OABR	AG-5B Tiger	F. & M. Hopper
	G-OACE	Valentin Taifun 17E	I. F. Wells
	G-OACI	MS.893E Rallye 180GT	J. M. & S. Bain
	G-OADY	Beech 76 Duchess	S. Uerguen
	G-OAFA	Cessna F.172M	Warwickshire Leasing Ltd (G-BFZV)
	G-OAFG	Pipistrel Alpha BCAR-S 164	A. F. Greenhalgh
	G-OAFS	PA-32R-301T Turbo Saratoga	AFS Aviation Ltd (G-SVPN)
	G-OAGA	Eurocopter EC.225LP Super Puma	CHC Scotia Ltd
	G-OAGI	FLS Aerospace Sprint 160	A. L. Breckell (G-FLSI)
	G-OAHC	Beech F33C Bonanza	SI Aviation Services Ltd (G-BTTF)
	G-OAHL	Eurocopter AS.355N Ecureuil II	Helicompany Ltd
	G-OAJL	Ikarus C.42 FB100	M. J. Donnelly
	G-OAJS	PA-39-160 Twin Comanche	M. C. Bellamy (G-BCIO)
	G-OALC	AS.355F2 Ecureuil II	Alcaline UK Ltd (G-VONG)
	G-OALD	SOCATA TB20 Trinidad	Gold Aviation
	G-OALE	Balony Kubicek BB22XR balloon	C. W. Brown
	G-OALH	Tecnam P92-EA Echo	D. G. I. Wheldon
	G-OALI	AS.355F1 Ecureuil II	Helispares Ltd (G-WDKR/G-NEXT/G-OMAV)
	G-OALP	Alpi Pioneer 300 Hawk	Cavendish Aviation UK Ltd
	G-OALT	Diamond S-77 balloon	Evos Group Ltd
	G-OALZ	IAV Bacau Yak-52	Y. Ryzhenkov
	G-OAMF	Pegasus Quantum 15-912	T. A. Dobbins
	G-OAML	Cameron AML-105 balloon	Stratton Motor Co (Norfolk) Ltd
	G-OANI	PA-28-161 Cherokee Warrior II	Falcon Flying Services
	G-OANN	Zenair CH.601HD	H. S. Fowler
	G-OAPR	Brantly B.2B ★	The Helicopter Museum/Weston-super-Mare

Reg	Type	Owner or Operator	Notes
G-OARA	PA-28R-201 Cherokee Arrow III	Synergy Flight Centres Ltd	
G-OARB	Brown BM-56 balloon	A. J. & A. R. Brown	
G-OARC	PA-28RT-201 Cherokee Arrow IV	G-MC Aviation (G-BMVE)	
G-OARS	Cessna 172S	De Hertog Juweeldesign GCV/Belgium	
G-OART	PA-23-250 Aztec D	T. W. Gilbert (G-AXKD)	
G-OARU	PA-28R-201 Cherokee Arrow III	J. R. Colthurst	
G-OASA	Flight Design CTSW	O. E. W. & S. M. Achurch (G-CGHE)	
G-OASB	Avions Transport ATR-72-212AF	ASL Airlines UK Ltd	
G-OASH	Robinson R22 Beta	J. C. Lane	
G-OASK	Eurofox 912(S)	Aero Space Scientific Educational Trust	
G-OASM	HpH Glasflugel 304 ES Shark	A. S. Miller	
G-OASP	AS.355F2 Twin Squirrel	Helicopter & Pilot Services Ltd	
G-OASW	Schleicher ASW-27	M. P. W. Mee	
G-OATE	Mainair Pegasus Quantum 15-912	A. Roberts	
G-OATL	Agusta Westland AW109SP Grand New	Helicompany Ltd (G-EMHJ)	
G-OATR	Avions Transport ATR-72-212A	Aurigny Air Services Ltd	
G-OATV	Cameron V-77 balloon	A. W. & E. P. Braund-Smith	
G-OATW	Airbus A.321-253NX	Titan Airways Ltd (G-GBNI)	
G-OATY	Pipistrel Alpha BCAR-S 164	Chicken Roundabout Finance Ltd	
G-OATZ	Van's RV-12	J. W. Armstrong	
G-OAUD	Robinson R44	Stenball Holdings Ltd (G-CDHV)	
G-OAUR	Dornier 228-212	Aurigny Air Services Ltd	
G-OAVC	Cessna F.177RG	Avionicare Ltd (G-BBJV)	
G-OAWM	Cirrus SR20	Cambridge Flying Company Ltd (G-GCDD)	
G-OAWS	Colt 77A balloon	L. Menzies	
G-OBAB	Lindstrand LBL-35A Cloudhopper balloon	M. A. Green	
G-OBAD	EV-97 Eurostar SL	M. J. Robbins	
G-OBAK	PA-28R-201T Turbo Cherokee Arrow III	G-OBAK Group Aviation	
G-OBAL	Mooney M.20J	G-OBAL Group	
G-OBAN	Jodel D.140B	L. P. Keegan (G-ATSU)	
G-OBAZ	Skyranger 912(2)	K. A. O'Neill	
G-OBBI	Guimbal Cabri G2	Helispeed Solutions Ltd	
G-OBBO	Cessna 182S	M. J. Smith	
G-OBCP	Balony Kubicek BB40Z balloon	OB Experiences Ltd	
G-OBDA	Diamond Katana DA20-A1	I. T. & N. R. J. Bradford	
G-OBDN	PA-28-161 Cherokee Warrior II	R. M. Bennett	
G-OBEE	Boeing Stearman A75N-1 (3397:174)	R. H. Mackay	
G-OBET	Sky 77-24 balloon	P. M. Watkins & S. M. Carden	
G-OBFE	Sky 120-24 balloon	J. Sonnabend	
G-OBIC	Robin DR.400/180R	Norfolk Gliding Club Ltd (G-OTIB)	
G-OBIL	Robinson R22 Beta	B. B. Kennedy	
G-OBJB	Lindstrand LBL-90A balloon	Fly Away Ballooning Ltd	
G-OBJM	Taylor JT.1 Monoplane	M. F. Pocock	
G-OBJP	Pegasus Quantum 15-912	C. I. Comers	
G-OBJT	Europa	A. Burill (G-MUZO)	
G-OBLC	Beech 76 Duchess	Air Navigation & Trading Company Ltd	
G-OBLN	DH.115 Vampire T.Mk.11 (XE665) ★	South Wales Aviation Museum/St. Athan	
G-OBLR	Cessna R.172K	T. Shorland	
G-OBMS	Cessna F.172N	Mike Sierra Group	
G-OBOE	Skyranger Nynja	Medaviate Ltd & I. R. & M. P. Tooley	
G-OBOF	Remos GX	D. Hawkino	
G-OBPP	Schleicher ASW-27-18E	A. C. P. Taylor	
G-OBRO	Alpi Pioneer 200M	A. Brown	
G-OBRY	Cameron N-180 balloon	A. C. K. Rawson & J. J. Rudoni	
G-OBSM	Robinson R44 Raven	Cutting Edge Helicopters Ltd (G-CDSE)	
G-OBSR	Partenavia P68	Ravenair Aircraft Ltd	
G-OBTS	Cameron C-80 balloon	D. Pearce	
G-OBTO	Cub Crafters CC19-180 XCub	G. Oberholzer	
G-OBUC	PA-34-220T Seneca III	Eurotzt SRL/Romania	
G-OBUP	DG Flugzeugbau DG-808C	C. J. Lowrie	
G-OBUU	Replica Comper CLA Swift	J. A. Pothecary & R. H. Hunt	
G-OBUY	Colt 69A balloon	E. K. Read	
G-OBUZ	Van's RV-6	A. F. Hall	
G-OBYT	Agusta-Bell 206A JetRanger	J. S. Everett (G-BNRC)	
G-OCAC	Robin R-2112	The Cotswold Aero Club Ltd (G-EWHT)	
G-OCAD	Sequoia F.8L Falco	D. R. Vale	
G-OCAF	Robinson R44	Heli Air Ltd	
G-OCAK	Bombardier BD700-1A10 Global Express	Gama Aviation (UK) Ltd	
G-OCAM	AA-5A Cheetah	J. Khambatta & G. Fenton (G-BLHO)	

Notes	Reg	Type	Owner or Operator
	G-OCBI	Schweizer 269C-1	A and W Demolition (Bracknell)
	G-OCCF	Diamond DA40D Star	Tesla Solutions Ltd
	G-OCCG	Diamond DA40D Star	North Weald Flight Training Ltd
	G-OCCH	Diamond DA40D Star	Innovative Aviation (Leeds) Ltd
	G-OCCN	Diamond DA40D Star	Tesla Solutions Ltd
	G-OCCX	Diamond DA42 Twin Star	Aeros Leasing Ltd
	G-OCDC	Sky Ranger Nynja 912S(1)	R. J. Almey
	G-OCDP	Flight Design CTSW	M. A. Beadman
	G-OCDW	Jabiru UL-450	P. R. Smith
	G-OCEH	Robinson R44	Cutting Edge Helicopters Ltd
	G-OCFD	Bell 206B JetRanger 3	Rushmere Helicopters LLP (G-WGAL/G-OICS)
	G-OCGC	Robin DR.400-180R	Cambridge Gliding Club Ltd
	G-OCGD	Cameron O-26 balloon	C. G. Dobson
	G-OCHM	Robinson R44	C. M. Beighton
	G-OCLV	Robinson R44 II	Adventure 001 Ltd
	G-OCMS	Cosmik EV-97 TeamEurostar UK	C. M. Saysell
	G-OCMT	Cosmik EV-97 TeamEurostar UK	P. Crowhurst
	G-OCOK	American Champion 8KCAB Super Decathlon	R. C. Fines
	G-OCOL	Sportstar SLM	C. J. & J. A. Aldous
	G-OCON	Robinson R44	P. Kelly
	G-OCOV	Robinson R22 Beta	Central Helicopters Ltd
	G-OCOX	Worner NL-STU/1000 gas balloon	The Hydrogen Balloon Group
	G-OCPC	Cessna FA.152	Praeluceo Property Ltd
	G-OCRL	Europa	R. J. Lewis (G-OBEV)
	G-OCRM	Slingsby T.67M Firefly II	CRM Aviation Europe Ltd (G-BUUB)
	G-OCRZ	CZAW Sportcruiser	P. Marsden
	G-OCTI	PA-32 Cherokee Six 260	M. B. Dyos (G-BGZX)
	G-OCTO	Van's RV-8	P. M. Wells
	G-OCTS	Cameron Z-90 balloon	A. Collett
	G-OCTU	PA-28-161 Cadet	Neon Moose Aviation Ltd
	G-OCUB	Piper J-3C-90 Cub	Zebedee Flying Group
	G-OCXI	Van's RV-8	W. M. Buchanan
	G-OCZA	CZAW Sportcruiser	S. M. Dawson
	G-ODAC	Cessna F.152 II	T. M. Jones (G-BITG)
	G-ODAF	Lindstrand LBL-105A balloon	T. J. Horne
	G-ODAK	PA-28-236 Dakota	Flydak LLP
	G-ODAL	PA-24-250 Comanche	Alta Volant Ltd
	G-ODAY	Cameron N-56 balloon	British Balloon Museum & Library
	G-ODBN	Lindstrand LBL Flowers SS balloon	Magical Adventures Ltd
	G-ODCH	Schleicher ASW-20L	T. R. Freeland
	G-ODDB	Hill Helicopters HX50	Hill Helicopters Ltd
	G-ODDZ	Schempp-Hirth Duo Discus T	P. A. King
	G-ODEE	Van's RV-6	J. Redfearn
	G-ODEL	Falconar F-11-3	G. F. Brummell
	G-ODGC	Eurofox 912(iS)	G-ODGC Flying Group
	G-ODHB	Robinson R44	First Blue Aviation Ltd
	G-ODHC	DHC.1B-2-S5 Chipmunk	P. M. Wells
	G-ODIN	Avions Mudry CAP-10B	CAP Ten
	G-ODIP	Aviat A-1C-180 Husky	A. J. White
	G-ODIZ	AutoGyro Cavalon	P. Williams
	G-ODJD	Raj Hamsa X'Air 582 (7)	N. M. Toulson
	G-ODJF	Lindstrand LBL-90B balloon	Helena Dos Santos SA/Portugal
	G-ODJG	Europa	A. G. Andrew
	G-ODJH	Mooney M.20C	R. M. Schweitzer/Netherlands (G-BMLH)
	G-ODLD	Cameron Z-600 balloon	Red Bull Company Ltd
	G-ODMT	Safari	D. G. Childs, R. M. Jameson & T. M. Pearson
	G-ODNM	Hughes 369E	Lomas Helicopters (G-DNWH/G-MRAJ)
	G-ODRT	Cameron Z-105 balloon	N. W. N. Townshend
	G-ODSA	Bell 429	Starspeed Ltd
	G-ODTW	Europa	D. T. Walters
	G-ODUD	PA-28-181 Cherokee Archer II	S. Barlow, R. N. Ingle & R. J. Murray (G-IBBO)
	G-ODUO	Schempp-Hirth Duo Discus	3D Syndicate
	G-ODVB	CFM Shadow Srs DD	L. J. E. Moss
	G-ODWS	Silence SA.180 Twister	T. R. Dews
	G-OECO	Flylight Dragonfly	P. A. & M. W. Aston
	G-OEDP	Cameron N-77 balloon	M. J. Betts
	G-OEFL	Pipistrel Virus SW128	Chicken Roundabout Finance Ltd
	G-OEGG	Cameron Egg-65 SS balloon	C. G. Timbrell
	G-OEGL	Christen Eagle II	E. Mason
	G-OEGO	E-Go	Cambridge Business Travel

Reg	Type	Owner or Operator	Notes
G-OEKO	Pipistrel Virus SW 128	Chicken Roundabout Finance Ltd	
G-OEKS	Ikarus C42 FB80	M. J. Harrison	
G-OELC	Pipistrel Virus SW 128	Chicken Roundabout Finance Ltd	
G-OELZ	Wassmer WA.52 Europa	S. L. Lewis & G. R. Thomas	
G-OEMZ	Pietenpol Air Camper	C. Brockis (G-IMBY)	
G-OEND	Leonardo AW189	Bristow Helicopters Ltd	
G-OERR	Lindstrand LBL-60A balloon	C. Davis	
G-OERS	Cessna 172N	N. J. Smith & A. Stevens (G-SSRS)	
G-OESC	Aquila AT01	Osterreichischer Sportflieger/Austria (G-OZIO)	
G-OESP	Robinson R44 II	Scariff Plant Hire Ltd (G-CGND)	
G-OESY	Easy Raider J2.2 (1)	J. Gray	
G-OETI	Bell 206B JetRanger 3	Jaspa (G-RMIE/G-BPIE)	
G-OETS	Ultramagic M-105 balloon	ETS (SW) Ltd	
G-OEVA	PA-32-260 Cherokee Six	Egoli Enterprises Ltd (G-FLJA/G-AVTJ)	
G-OEWE	Cameron Sport 80	N. C. A. Edmunds	
G-OEZI	Easy Raider J2.2(2)	M. G. Read	
G-OEZY	Europa	D. B. Lennie	
G-OFAA	Cameron Z-105 balloon	R. A. Schwab	
G-OFAL	Ozone Roadster/Bailey Quattro	Malcolm Roberts Ltd	
G-OFAS	Robinson R22 Beta	Castle Air Academy Ltd	
G-OFBT	Cameron O-84 balloon	A. A. & W. S. Calvert	
G-OFBU	Ikarus C.42 FB UK	Old Sarum C42 Group	
G-OFDR	PA-28-161 Cadet	Electric Scribe 2000 Ltd	
G-OFDT	Mainair Pegasus Quik	C. Lomas	
G-OFER	PA-18-150 Super Cub	White Watham Airfield Ltd	
G-OFES	Alisport Silent 2 Electro	K. F. Byrne	
G-OFFA	Pietenpol Air Camper	D. & G. A. Shepherd	
G-OFFO	Extra EA.300/L	2 Excel Aviation Ltd	
G-OFFS	PA-38-112 Tomahawk	Brimpton Flying Group (G-BMSF)	
G-OFGC	Aeroprakt A22-L Foxbat	R. G. Whyte	
G-OFIT	SOCATA TB10 Tobago	GFI Aviation Group (G-BRIU)	
G-OFIX	Grob G.109B	T. R. Dews	
G-OFJC	Eiriavion PIK-20E	D. M. Thomas	
G-OFLI	Colt 105A balloon	Virgin Airship & Balloon Co Ltd	
G-OFLT	EMB-110P1 Bandeirante ★	Rescue trainer/Aveley, Essex (G-MOBL/G-BGCS)	
G-OFLX	Embraer EMB-145LR	BAE Systems (Corporate Travel) Ltd	
G-OFNC	Balony Kubicek BB17XR balloon	M. R. Jeynes	
G-OFOM	BAe 146-100	Executive Jet Support Ltd (G-BSLP/G-BRLM)	
G-OFRB	Everett gyroplane	J. P. Comerford	
G-OFRO	Mudry CAP 232	P. J. Tomlinson & D. A. McAinsh	
G-OFRY	Cessna 152	Devon and Somerset Flight Training Ltd	
G-OFSP	CZAW Sportcruiser	L. Dempsey	
G-OFTR	Pipistrel Virus SW 128	Chicken Roundabout Finance Ltd	
G-OFWD	Pipistrel Virus SW 128	Chicken Roundabout Finance Ltd	
G-OFZY	Eurocopter AS.355N Ecureuil II	Atlas Helicopters Ltd (G-ORDH)	
G-OGAL	Van's RV-14	D. A. Gittins (G-CLMP)	
G-OGAN	Europa	A. H. Lloyd	
G-OGAR	PZL SZD-45A Ogar	J. F. C. Sergeant	
G-OGAS	Westland WG.30 Srs 100 ★	(stored)/Yeovil (G-BKNW)	
G-OGEM	PA-28-181 Cherokee Archer II	Coventry (Civil) Aviation Ltd	
G-OGEO	Aérospatiale SA.341G Gazelle 1	G. Steel (G-BXJK)	
G-OGEZ	Robinson R44 II	G. K. Jewson	
G-OGFC	Aerospatiale ATR-72-600	Aurigney Air Services Ltd	
G-OGGB	Grob G.102 Astir CS	M. P. Webb	
G-OGGS	Thunder Ax8-84 balloon	G. Gamble & Sons (Quorn) Ltd	
G-OGGY	Aviat A.1B	J. H. Garrett-Cox	
G-OGIL	Short SD3-30 Variant 100 ★	North East Land Sea and Air Museum/ Sunderland (G-BITV)	
G-OGIN	Kubicek BB40Z	A. B. Court	
G-OGJC	Robinson R44 II	Telecom Advertising & Promotions Ltd	
G-OGJM	Cameron C-80 balloon	G. F. Madelin	
G-OGLY	Cameron Z-105 balloon	H. M. Ogston	
G-OGOD	P & M Quik GT450	L. McIlwaine	
G-OGOS	Everett gyroplane	N. A. Seymour	
G-OGPN	Cassutt Special	S. Alexander (G-OMFI/G-BKCH)	
G-OGRL	Van's RV-7	J. S. Allison	
G-OGRN	Pipistrel Virus SW128	Fly About Aviation Ltd	
G-OGSA	Avtech Jabiru SPL-450	G-OGSA Group	
G-OGTC	Guimbal Cabri G2	G. A. Richardson (G-VVBH)	

Notes	Reg	Type	Owner or Operator
	G-OGTR	P & M Quik GTR	K. J. Bowles
	G-OGUN	Eurocopter AS.350B2 Ecureuil	Nuport Aviation Ltd (G-SMDJ)
	G-OGZZ	Van's RV-8	M. A. Jones
	G-OHAC	Cessna F.182Q	Maguirelzatt Partners LLP
	G-OHAK	Aeroprakt A.22 Foxbat	A. R. Hackshall (G-CHAD)
	G-OHAL	Pietenpol Air Camper	A. Ryan-Fecitt
	G-OHAM	Robinson R44 II	Hamsters Wheel Productions Ltd (G-GBEN/ G-CDJZ)
	G-OHAS	Robinson R66	Heli Air Scotland Ltd
	G-OHCP	AS.355F1 Twin Squirrel	Staske Construction Ltd (G-BTVS/G-STVE/G-TOFF/G-BKJX)
	G-OHDC	Colt Film Cassette SS balloon ★	Balloon Preservation Group
	G-OHDK	Glasflugel 304S Shark	K. Manley & A. Vine
	G-OHGC	Scheibe SF.25C Falke	Southwest Motorgliders
	G-OHII	Van's RV-7	Green Earth Ltd
	G-OHIO	Dyn'Aero MCR-01	J. M. Keane
	G-OHIR	PA-28-161 Cherokee Warrior II	B. & J. S. Miller (G-BGPL)
	G-OHJE	Alpi Pioneer 300 Hawk	Abergavenny Flying Group
	G-OHJK	Boieing 737-82R	ASL Airlines UK Ltd
	G-OHKS	Pegasus Quantum 15-912	L. J. Nelson
	G-OHLI	Robinson R44 II	NCS Partnership
	G-OHLV	Sackville BM-65 balloon	H. & L. D. Vaughan
	G-OHMS	AS.355F1 Twin Squirrel	RCR Aviation Ltd
	G-OHOH	Diamond DA42NG Twin Star	A. D. Friday
	G-OHOV	Rotorway Executive 162F	F. Hahn
	G-OHRA	Jabiru J430	H. R. Apps
	G-OHSB	Sikorsky S-92A	Offshore Helicopter Services UK Ltd
	G-OHSE	Airbus Helicopters EC175B	Offshore Helicopter Services UK Ltd
	G-OHST	Rotorway A600 Talon	I. C. Bedford
	G-OHUR	Hurricane 315	M. Ingleton
	G-OHWK	Bell 206L-1 LongRanger II	Elite Helicopters (G-PWIT/G-DWMI)
	G-OIBO	PA-28-180 Cherokee	M. Kraemer & J. G. C. Schneider (G-AVAZ)
	G-OIFM	Cameron 90 Dude SS balloon	Magical Adventures Ltd
	G-OIHC	PA-32R-301 Saratoga IIHP	N. J. Lipczynski (G-PUSK)
	G-OIIO	Robinson R22 Beta	Wattlesborough Helicopters Ltrd (G-ULAB)
	G-OIIY	Ultramagic S-70 balloon	T. B. Davis
	G-OIMC	Cessna 152 II	East Midlands Flying School Ltd
	G-OINN	UltraMagic H-31 balloon	G. Everett
	G-OINT	Balony Kubicek BB20XR balloon	M. A. Green
	G-OIOB	Mudry CAP.10B	E. N. Macpherson
	G-OIOZ	Thunder Ax9-120 S2 balloon	D. Venegoni
	G-OIPM	Agusta A109E Pwer	Air Elite Aviation Ltd
	G-OISY	Hill Helicopters HX50	Hill Helicopters Ltd
	G-OIVN	Liberty XL-2	I. Shaw
	G-OJAB	Avtech Jabiru SK	A. K. Robinson
	G-OJAC	Mooney M.20J	Hornet Engineering Ltd
	G-OJAG	Cessna 172S	Valhalla Aviation LLP
	G-OJAN	Robinson R22 Beta	J. C. Lane (G-SANS/G-BUHX)
	G-OJAS	Auster J/1U Workmaster	C. E. Tyers
	G-OJBB	Enstrom 280FX	M. Jones
	G-OJBM	Cameron N-90 balloon	B. J. Bettin
	G-OJBW	Lindstrand LBL J & B Bottle SS balloon	M. T. Joyce
	G-OJCW	PA-32RT-300 Lance II	P. G. Dobson
	G-OJDA	EAA Acrosport II	R. J. Almey
	G-OJDB	Airbus AS.350B3 Ecureuil	Valley Court Ltd (G-LEOG/G-CIRG)
	G-OJDC	Thunder Ax7-77 balloon	A. Heginbottom
	G-OJDG	Robinson R44 II	J. D. Garton
	G-OJEH	PA-28-181 Cherokee Archer II	P. C. Lilley
	G-OJFA	Pilatus PC-12/47E	Jetfly Aviation UK Ltd
	G-OJGC	Van's RV-4	J. G. Claridge
	G-OJGT	Maule M.5-235C	Newnham Joint Flying Syndicate
	G-OJHC	Cessna 182P	WF Aviation
	G-OJHL	Europa	M. D. Burns & G. Rainey
	G-OJIM	PA-28R-201T Turbo Cherokee Arrow III	Ethel (One) Ltd
	G-OJJP	Learjet 45	Zenith Aviation Ltd (G-OPUL)
	G-OJJV	P & M Pegasus Quik	M. Heron
	G-OJKM	Rans S.7 Courier	C. J. Palmer
	G-OJLD	Van's RV-7	J. L. Dixon

Reg	Type	Owner or Operator	Notes
G-OJLH	TEAM mini-MAX 91	R. J. Hood (G-MYAW)	
G-OJMS	Cameron Z-90 balloon	Turner Balloons Ltd	
G-OJNE	Schempp-Hirth Nimbus 3T	M. R. Garwood	
G-OJON	Taylor JT.2 Titch	Freelance Aviation Ltd	
G-OJRM	Cessna T.182T	Romeo Mike Group	
G-OJSD	Eurofox 912(S)	J. D. Sinclair-Day	
G-OJSH	Thruster T.600N 450 JAB	A. Whittaker	
G-OJTO	Avian 2/180	ARC Aerosystems Ltd	
G-OJVA	Van's RV-6	J. A. Village	
G-OJVL	Van's RV-6	S. E. Tomlinson	
G-OJWB	Hawker 800XP	Langford Lane Ltd	
G-OJWS	PA-28-161 Cherokee Warrior II	A. M. S. Sher	
G-OKAY	Pitts S-1E Special	I. S. Smith	
G-OKCP	Lindstrand LBL Battery SS balloon	C. L. Hayden & M. T. Joyce (G-MAXX)	
G-OKDM	TL3000 Sirius 600	D. B. Gibbons	
G-OKED	Cessna 150L	LAC Flying School	
G-OKEN	PA-28R-201T Turbo Cherokee Arrow III	L. James & J. D. Hood	
G-OKER	Van's RV-7	W. J. Harrison & A. Shuttleworth	
G-OKEV	Europa	G. L. Quenault	
G-OKEW	UltraMagic M-65C balloon	Hampshire Balloons Ltd	
G-OKFA	KFA Safari	J. M., M. S. & P. J. Shenton	
G-OKID	Reality Escapade Kid	V. H. Hallam	
G-OKIM	Sykyranger 912 (2)	P. J. Callis	
G-OKIS	Tri-R Kis	T. E. Reeder	
G-OKLY	Cessna F.150K	W. Ali & Denderah SA (G-ECBH)	
G-OKMA	Tri-R Kis	K. Miller	
G-OKOK	Robin DR.400/140B	A. D. Friday	
G-OKPS	Skyranger Nynja 912S(1)	G-OKPS Group	
G-OKTA	Ikarus C42 FB80	Avion Training & Consultancy Ltd	
G-OKTI	Aquila AT01	P. H. Ferdinand	
G-OKUB	TLAC Sherwood Kub	The Light Aircraft Company Ltd	
G-OKYA	Cameron V-77 balloon	R. J. Pearce	
G-OLAA	Alpi Pioneer 300 Hawk	P. Ritchie	
G-OLAJ	Robinson R44 II	Bliss Aviation Ltd & Switchdata Investments Ltd (G-FCUM)	
G-OLAU	Robinson R22 Beta	Whizzard Helicopters	
G-OLAW	Lindstrand LBL-25A balloon	R. A. Vale	
G-OLCJ	Cessna 172P	Devon & Somerset Flight Training Ltd (G-BNRR)	
G-OLCP	AS.355N Twin Squirrel	Cheshire Helicopters Ltd (G-CLIP)	
G-OLCY	Lindstrand LTL Series 1-105 balloon	I. Chadwick & S. Richards-Chadwick	
G-OLDG	Cessna T.182T	H. W. Palmer (G-CBTJ)	
G-OLDM	Pegasus Quantum 15-912	J. W. Holme	
G-OLDP	Mainair Pegasus Quik	G. J. Gibson	
G-OLEA	PA-28-151 Cherokee Warrior	London School of Flying Ltd	
G-OLEC	Alisport Silent 2 Electro	N. Parry	
G-OLED	Eurofox 912(S)	J. J. & S. J. M. Ledingham	
G-OLEG	Yakovlev Yak-3UA	A. M. Holman-West	
G-OLEM	Jodel D.18	M. Peters (G-BSBP)	
G-OLEW	Vans RV-7	S. W. Abbott	
G-OLFB	Pegasus Quantum 15-912	J. S. Dunlop	
G-OLFT	Rockwell Commander 114	R. Morgan	
G-OLFX	Schempp-Hirth Ventus 2cT	T. P. Cook & C. J. Curtis	
G-OLFZ	P & M Quik GT450	A. J. Boyd	
G-OLGE	Cirrus SR20	Bliss Aviation Ltd and Switchdata Investments Ltd	
G-OLHR	Cassutt Racer IIIM	P. A. Hall & A. R. Lewis (G-BNJZ)	
G-OLIC	Tecnam P2008-JC	Stapleford Flying Club Ltd	
G-OLIV	Beech B.200 Super King Air	Dragonfly Aviation Services Ltd (G-RAFN)	
G-OLOU	Bell 206B-3 Jet Ranger III	Helitrip Charter LLP	
G-OLOV	Eurofox 912S(1)	Aero Space Scientific Educational Trust	
G-OLPM	P & M Quik R	M. D. Freeman	
G-OMAA	Eurocopter EC.135 T2+	Midlands Air Ambulance Charity	
G-OMAG	Cessna 182B	J. W. N. Sharpe	
G-OMAH	Cessna 182H	A & F Haulage Ltd (G-PUGS)	
G-OMAL	Thruster T.600N 450	M. I. Gardner	
G-OMAO	SOCATA TB-20 Trinidad	Alpha Oscar Group (G-GDGR)	
G-OMAT	PA-28-140 Cherokee	Midland Air Training School (G-JIMY/G-AYUG)	
G-OMBE	Beech A23-24 Musketeer Super III	Empreso Property Ventures Ltd (G-IBFF/G-AXCJ)	
G-OMCB	TL2000UK Sting Carbon S4	P. J. Ely	

Notes	Reg	Type	Owner or Operator
	G-OMCH	PA-28-161 Cherokee Warrior III	Chalrey Ltd
	G-OMCM	Airbus Helicopters AS.350B3 Ecureuil	T. J. Morris Ltd (G-CKYE)
	G-OMDD	Thunder Ax8-90 S2 balloon	M. L. Berry
	G-OMDH	Hughes 369E	Stilgate Ltd
	G-OMDR	Agusta-Bell 206B JetRanger II	Castle Air Ltd (G-HRAY/G-VANG/G-BIZA)
	G-OMEN	Cameron Z-90 balloon	M. G. Howard
	G-OMER	Avtech Jabiru UL-450	A. Phillips (G-GPAS)
	G-OMEZ	Zenair CH.601HDS	L. A. Barton
	G-OMGR	Cameron Z-105 balloon	M. J. Axtell
	G-OMHC	PA-28RT-201 Arrow IV	GTEWS Ltd
	G-OMHI	Mills MH-1	J. P. Mills
	G-OMIA	MS.893A Rallye Commodore 180	S. R. Winter & M. S. Johnson
	G-OMIB	Diamond Alien-48 (Character 1) balloon	L. P. Hooper
	G-OMIC	Bucker Bu.133C Jungmeister	B. P. M. Nielson
	G-OMIK	Europa	Mikite Flying Group
	G-OMIW	Pegasus Quik	A. J. Ladell
	G-OMJA	PA-28-181 Cherokee Archer II	Aerobility
	G-OMJT	Rutan LongEz	D. A. Daniel
	G-OMLC	EAA Acrosport II	M. A. C. Chapman
	G-OMMM	Colt 90A balloon	A. & M. Frayling
	G-OMNI	PA-28R-200 Cherokee Arrow II	The Cotswold Aero Club Ltd (G-BAWA)
	G-OMPH	Van's RV-7	R. J. Luke
	G-OMPW	Mainair Pegasus Quik	M. P. Wimsey
	G-OMRB	Cameron V-77 balloon	I. J. Jevons
	G-OMRC	Van's RV-10	A. W. Collett
	G-OMRP	Flight Design CTSW	M. E. Parker
	G-OMSA	Flight Design CTSW	G-OMSA Syndicate
	G-OMST	PA-28-161 Cherokee Warrior III	T. T. Waters (G-BZUA)
	G-OMTM	Cirrus SR22T	Sirom Aviation Ltd
	G-OMTX	Bombardier BD700-1A11 Global 5000	OMTX Aviation LP Inc
	G-OMUM	Rockwell Commander 114	M. J. P. Lynch
	G-OMYR	Europa	P. S. Myers (G-BVGF)
	G-ONAA	North American Rockwell OV-10B Bronco (99+18)	Liberty Aviation Ltd
	G-ONAF	Naval Aircraft Factory N3N-3 (4406:12)	J. P. Birnie
	G-ONAN	Bensen B.8MV	Department of Doing Ltd (G-BKBS)
	G-ONAT	Grob G.102 Astir CS77	N. A. Toogood
	G-ONAV	PA-31-310 Turbo Navajo C	Panther Aviation Ltd (G-IGAR)
	G-ONCB	Lindstrand LBL-31A balloon	B. J. Alford
	G-ONCS	Slingsby T.66 Nipper 3	S. D. Atherton (G-AZBA)
	G-ONEE	Boeing 747-433F	One Air Ltd
	G-ONEF	Boeing 747-428F	One Air Ltd (G-CLBA)
	G-ONEG	Boeing 777F	One Air Ltd
	G-ONEH	Boeing 777F	One Air Ltd
	G-ONET	PA-28-180 Cherokee E	Easy Aircraft Rental Ltd (G-AYAU)
	G-ONEZ	Glaser-Dirks DG-200/17	One Zulu Group
	G-ONGC	Robin DR.400/180R	The Burn Gliding Club Ltd
	G-ONHH	Forney F-1A Aircoupe	R. D. I. Tarry (G-ARHA)
	G-ONHL	SZD-54-2 Perkoz	Devon and Somerset Gliding Club Ltd
	G-ONIC	Evektor EV-97 Sportstar Max	D. M. Jack
	G-ONIG	Murphy Elite	N. S. Smith
	G-ONKA	Aeronca K	S. W. Osborne
	G-ONNE	Westland Gazelle HT.3 (XW858:C)	S. N. Muir (G-DMSS)
	G-ONOA	PA-28R-200 Cherokee Arrow II	Ono Aviation Ltd
	G-ONSW	Skyranger Swift 912S(1)	N. S. Wells
	G-ONTV	Agusta-Bell 206B-3 JetRanger III	Adventure 001 Ltd (G-GOUL)
	G-ONTY	Sud SE.3130 Alouette II	Lark Aviation (G-CICS)
	G-ONUN	Van's RV-6A	Honey Badger Capital Holdings Ltd
	G-ONVG	Guimbal Cabri G2	Vantage Aviation Ltd
	G-ONYX	Bell 206B-3 JetRanger III	Orchid Homes Ltd (G-BXPN)
	G-OOAK	Jabiru J430	Rooviators Group
	G-OOCI	Robinson R44	O. P. Chapman (G-JARM)
	G-OOCP	SOCATA TB-10 Tobago	R. M. Briggs (G-BZRL)
	G-OODE	SNCAN Stampe SV.4C	G-OODE Flying Group (G-AZNN)
	G-OODI	Pitts S-1D Special	C. Hutson & M. J. McCulloch (G-BBBU)
	G-OODW	PA-28-181 Cherokee Archer II	Redhill Air Services Ltd
	G-OOEY	Balony Kubicek BB-222 balloon	A. W. Holly
	G-OOEZ	Rutan Long-Ez	B. K. Ashworth (G-IEZI/G-RAEM)
	G-OOFE	Thruster T.600N 450	A. J. Thomas

Reg	Type	Owner or Operator	Notes
G-OOGY	P & M Quik R	Cambridge Road Professional Services Ltd	
G-OOIO	AS.350B3 Ecureuil	Hovering Ltd	
G-OOKE	Skyranger Nynja 912(1)	J. P. & P. A. Cooke	
G-OOLD	Funk B85C	A. D. Pearce & P. King	
G-OOLE	Cessna 172M	J. Edmondson (G-BOSI)	
G-OOMA	PA-28-161 Cherokee Warrior II	UP (EGBO) Ltd (G-BRBB)	
G-OOMF	PA-18-150 Super Cub	M. J. Coles	
G-OONE	Mooney M.20J	K. A. Stewart	
G-OONZ	P & M Aviation Quik	G-OONZ Group	
G-OOOL	Cameron Sphere-105 balloon	Cameron Balloons Ltd	
G-OOON	PA-34-220T Seneca III	R. Paris	
G-OOPY	CSA PS-28 Cruiser	V. Barnes	
G-OORB	Diamond DA.40D Star	ABD Networks LLP	
G-OORV	Van's RV-6	C. Sharples	
G-OOSH	Zenair CH.601UL Zodiac	A. Harding	
G-OOSY	DH.82A Tiger Moth (DE971)	S. Philpott & C. Stopher	
G-OOTC	PA-28R-201T Turbo Cherokee Arrow III	G-OOTC Group (G-CLIV)	
G-OOUK	Cirrus SR22	Seventy Ninth Air Two Ltd	
G-OOXP	Aero Designs Pulsar XP	C. N. Hannan	
G-OOZE	Diamond DA.62	Aerium Flight LLP	
G-OPAM	Cessna F.152 II (tailwheel)	PJC Leasing Ltd (G-BFZS)	
G-OPAR	Van's RV-6	L. V. Adams (G-CGNR)	
G-OPAT	Beech 76 Duchess	Golf Alpha Tango Ltd	
G-OPAW	Cameron Z-105 balloon	Lighter Than Air Ltd	
G-OPAZ	Pazmany PL.2	A. D. Wood	
G-OPBW	Cameron nZ-150 balloon	Polar Bear Windows Ltd	
G-OPCB	Van's RV-7	P. C. Burgess	
G-OPCG	Cessna 182T	S. K. Pomfret	
G-OPEJ	TEAM Minimax 91A	A. W. McBlain	
G-OPET	PA-28-181 Cherokee Archer II	London Flight Experience Ltd	
G-OPFA	Pioneer 300	S. Eddison & R. Minett	
G-OPHT	Schleicher ASH-26E	J. S. Wand	
G-OPIC	Cessna FRA.150L	T. E. Kiy (G-BGNZ)	
G-OPIK	Eiri PIK-20E	P. Goodchild	
G-OPIT	CFM Streak Shadow Srs SA	I. J. Guy	
G-OPJD	PA-28RT-201T Turbo Cherokee Arrow IV	J. M. McMillan	
G-OPJK	Europa	P. J. Kember	
G-OPJS	Pietenpol Air Camper	P. J. Shenton	
G-OPKF	Cameron 90 Bowler SS balloon	D. K. Fish	
G-OPLC	DH.104 Dove 8	O. J. Kilkenny (G-BLRB)	
G-OPME	PA-23-250 Aztec	R. G. Pardo (G-ODIR/G-AZGB)	
G-OPMJ	Cessna F.172M	T. E. Dighton (G-BIIB)	
G-OPMT	Lindstrand LBL-105A balloon	K. R. Karlstrom	
G-OPPO	Groppo Trail	Groppo Group	
G-OPRC	Europa X3	M. J. Ashby-Arnold & D. Lee	
G-OPSF	PA-38-112 Tomahawk	P. I. Higham (G-BGZI)	
G-OPSG	Eurofox 912(S)	P. S. Gregory	
G-OPSL	PA-32R-301 Saratoga SP	P. R. Tomkins (G-IMPW)	
G-OPSS	Cirrus SR20	Clifton Aviation Ltd	
G-OPST	Cessna 182R	Sierra Tango Flying Group Ltd	
G-OPTH	Van's RV-7	P. T. Hunt	
G-OPTI	PA-28-161 Cherokee Warrior II	K. Hinton	
G-OPTZ	Pitts S-2A Special	J. L. Dixon (G-SKNT/G-PEAL)	
G-OPUB	Slingsby T.67M Firefly 160	A. L. Barker (G-DLTA/G-SFTX)	
G-OPUG	Czech Sport PS-28 Cruiser	Pentaction Ltd	
G-OPUK	PA-28-161 Cherokee Warrior III	D. J. King	
G-OPUP	Beagle B.121 Pup 2	F. A. Zubiel (G-AXEU)	
G-OPVM	Van's RV-9A	M. R. Green	
G-OPWR	Cameron Z-90 balloon	Flying Enterprises	
G-OPWS	Mooney M.20K	D. Vreto	
G-ORAE	Van's RV-7	R. W. Eaton	
G-ORAF	CFM Streak Shadow	G. A. Carter	
G-ORAI	Avions ATR-72-212A	Aurigny Air Services Ltd	
G-ORAM	Thruster T600N 450	D. W. Wilson	
G-ORAR	PA-28-181 Cherokee Archer III	P. N. & S. M. Thornton	
G-ORAS	Clutton FRED Srs 2	A. I. Sutherland	
G-ORAT	Pipistrel Virus SW 121A Explorer	Chicken Roundabout Finance Ltd	
G-ORAU	Aerotechnik EV-97 Eurostar	W. R. C. Williams-Wynne	
G-ORAY	Cessna F.182Q II	M. Parrinder (G-BHDN)	

Notes	Reg	Type	Owner or Operator
	G-ORBK	Robinson R44 II	Select Engineering (UK) Ltd (G-CCNO)
	G-ORBS	Mainair Blade	M. T. Butler
	G-ORBT	BRM Bristell NG5 Speed Wing	R. B. Thomas
	G-ORCA	Van's RV-4	K. N. Williams
	G-ORCB	Cessna 152 II	Devon and Somerset Flight Training Ltd (G-BMXB)
	G-ORCC	AutoGyro Calidus	J. Marshall
	G-ORCD	Agusta A.109S Grand	Interoceans Company Ltd (G-GBMM/G-GRND)
	G-ORCV	Cameron Z-120 balloon	A. Collett
	G-ORCW	Schempp-Hirth Ventus 2cT	J. C. A. Garland
	G-ORDM	Cessna 182T	The Cambridge Aero Club Ltd (G-KEMY)
	G-ORDS	Thruster T.600N 450	C. D. Swift
	G-OREZ	Cessna 525 Citation M2	Helitrip Charter LLP
	G-ORGB	Ultramagic H-77 balloon	A. D. McCutcheon
	G-ORGN	Kubicek BB30Z balloon	Nova Balloon Services Ltd
	G-ORIB	Eurofox 912(IS)	J. McAlpine
	G-ORIG	Glaser-Dirks DG.800A	R. Kalin
	G-ORIK	Flylight Skyranger Nynja	R. P. Hall
	G-ORJM	Ultramagic M-77 balloon	R. J. Maud
	G-ORKA	EAA Acrosport II	M. R. H. Wishart (G-BPGH)
	G-ORKY	AS.350B2 Ecureuil	PDG Helicopters and PDG Aviation Services
	G-ORLA	P & M Pegasus Quik	J. Summers
	G-ORLY	AA-5B Tiger	Community Air Support Service (SCIO) (G-DONI/G-BLLT)
	G-ORMB	Robinson R22 Beta	Heli Air Ltd
	G-ORMW	Ikarus C.42 FB100	ORMW Syndicate
	G-ORNG	Magni M16C Tandem Trainer	Gyromania Ltd
	G-ORNH	Lindstrand LTL Series 2-50 balloon	A. M. Holly
	G-OROD	PA-18-150 Super Cub	B. W. Faulkner
	G-OROS	Ikarus C.42 FB80	G-OROS Group
	G-ORPC	Europa XS	P. W. Churms
	G-ORRG	Robin DR.400-180 Regent	Oaksey Flying Group
	G-ORSE	Ikarus C42 FB100 Bravo	D. R. Pesticcio
	G-ORSM	Bell 206B-3 JetRanger III	RSM Av Ltd (G-MOTA)
	G-ORUG	Thruster T.600N 450	M. W. Glencross
	G-ORUN	Reality Escapade	M. J. Clark
	G-ORVB	McCulloch J-2 ★	The Helicopter Museum/Weston-super-Mare (G-HEKY)
	G-ORVE	Van's RV-6	M. J. Jackson
	G-ORVG	Van's RV-6	RV6 Group
	G-ORVI	Van's RV-6	B. O. Harvey
	G-ORVR	Partenavia P.68B	Ravenair Aircraft Ltd (G-BFBD)
	G-ORVS	Van's RV-9	G. L. Boast
	G-ORVX	Van's RV-10	C. D. Meek (G-OHIY)
	G-ORVZ	Van's RV-7	C. Taylor
	G-ORWS	Van's RV-14A	R. G. Bromiley
	G-ORYG	Rotorsport UK Cavalon	A. G. Jones
	G-OSAF	Agusta Bell 206B-3 Jet Ranger III	Adventure 001 Ltd (G-OCST/G-BMKM)
	G-OSAI	PA-28-181 Cherokee Archer II	Falcon Flying Services Ltd (G-BYKL)
	G-OSAR	Bell 206L-1 LongRanger	Tauromachian Ltd
	G-OSAT	Cameron Z-105 balloon	A. V. & M. R. Noyce
	G-OSAX	Pipistrel Virus SW121A	Chicken Roundabout Finance Ltd
	G-OSCC	PA-32-300 Cherokee Six	BG & G Airlines Ltd (G-BGFD)
	G-OSCO	TEAM mini-MAX 91	L. J. Jones
	G-OSDF	Schempp-Hirth Ventus a	S. D. Foster
	G-OSEM	Robinson R44 II	Sloane Charter
	G-OSEP	Mainair Blade 912	J. D. Smith
	G-OSFB	Diamond HK.36TTC Super Dimona	Oxfordshire Sportflying Ltd
	G-OSFS	Cessan F.177RG	D. G. Wright & D. J. Cunningham
	G-OSGC	Eurofox 914	Scottish Gliding Union Ltd
	G-OSGU	Eurofox 912(S)	Scottish Gliding Union Ltd
	G-OSGX	Grob G109B	Aerosparx (G-CMGU)
	G-OSHK	Schempp-Hirth SHK-1	P. B. Hibbard
	G-OSHL	Robinson R22 Beta	Sloane Helicopters Ltd
	G-OSIC	Pitts S-1C Special	P. J. Hebdon (G-BUAW)
	G-OSII	Cessna 172N	G-OSII Group (G-BIVY)
	G-OSIM	Flylight Peabee Red Line	P. T. Lathrope
	G-OSIS	Pitts S-1S Special	D. S. T. Eggleton
	G-OSIV	TAF Sling 4	R. J. Crosson
	G-OSJT	PA-32R-301 Saratoga II HP	S-J. Thirsk (G-OSJC/G-GOBD/G-OARW)

Reg	Type	Owner or Operator	Notes
G-OSKR	Skyranger 912 (2)	T. A. Reed	
G-OSKY	Cessna 172M	Skyhawk Leasing Ltd	
G-OSLD	Europa XS	S. Percy & C. Davies	
G-OSLO	Schweizer 269C	A. H. Helicopter Services Ltd	
G-OSMD	Bell 206B JetRanger 2	TR Aviation Services Ltd (G-LTEK/G-BMIB)	
G-OSND	Cessna FRA.150M	Group G-OSND (G-BDOU)	
G-OSNJ	North American SNJ-5 Texan (85061:7F 061)	Smoking Hole LLP (G-CHIA)	
G-OSNX	Grob G.109B	R. J. Barsby	
G-OSOD	P & M Quik GTR	R. Gellert	
G-OSON	P & M QuikR	R. Parr	
G-OSOX	Grob G.109B	Aerosparx Ltd	
G-OSPD	Cosmik EV-97 TeamEurostar UK	R. A. Stewart-Jones	
G-OSPH	Ikarus C42 FB100	J. E. Midder	
G-OSPP	Robinson R44	Danelander Ltd	
G-OSPX	Grob G109B	Aerosparx (G-BMHR)	
G-OSRA	Boeing 727-2S2F	T2 Aviation Ltd	
G-OSRB	Boeing 727-2S2F	T2 Aviation Ltd	
G-OSRL	Learjet 45	S. R. Lloyd	
G-OSRS	Cameron A-375 balloon	Wickers World Ltd	
G-OSRX	Grob G.109B	Aerosparx Ltd (G-CMHR)	
G-OSSA	Cessna Tu.206B	Skydive St.Andrews Ltd	
G-OSST	Colt 77A balloon	A. A. Brown	
G-OSTC	AA-5A Cheetah	C. J. Aucken	
G-OSTL	Ikarus C.42 FB 100	Z. O. Hammerton	
G-OSTX	Grob G.109B	Aerosparx Ltd (G-CKXB)	
G-OSUS	Mooney M.20K	D. Sutton	
G-OSUT	Scheibe SF-25C Rotax-Falke	Yorkshire Gliding Club (Pty.) Ltd	
G-OSVN	AutoGyro Cavalon	Gyroteers G-OSVN	
G-OSZB	Christen Pitts S-2B Special	K. A. Fitton & A. M. Gent (G-OGEE)	
G-OSZD	Allstar PZL SZD-59	Born To Fly Trust	
G-OTAL	ARV Super 2	M. Kolev (G-BNGZ)	
G-OTAM	Cessna 172M	G. V. White	
G-OTAN	PA-18-135 Super Cub (54-2445)	A. & J. D. Owen	
G-OTAW	BRM Bristell NG5 Speed Wing	J. Nanthakumar	
G-OTAY	Tecnam P2006T	Nyuki Ltd (G-ZOOG)	
G-OTBM	Schempp-Hirth Arcus M	TBM Estates Ltd	
G-OTCH	Streak Shadow	R. M. M. & A. G. Moura	
G-OTCT	Cameron Z-105 balloon	Lighter Than Air Ltd	
G-OTCV	Skyranger 912S (1)	A. G. Harman, P. Jackson, S. D. Lines & S. Davies	
G-OTCZ	Schempp-Hirth Ventus 2cT	G. D. Morris	
G-OTEC	Tecnam P2002 Sierra Deluxe	D. P. Budworth	
G-OTED	Robinson R22 ★	The Helicopter Museum/Weston-super-Mare (G-BMYR)	
G-OTFT	PA-38-112 Tomahawk	P. Tribble (G-BNKW)	
G-OTGA	PA-28R-201 Cherokee Arrow III	V. Ramani & M. Harbhajanka	
G-OTHE	Enstrom 280C-UK Shark	K. P. Groves (G-OPJT/G-BKCO)	
G-OTHL	Robinson R-22★	Gatwick Aviation Museum/Charlwood	
G-OTIM	Bensen B.8MV	T. J. Deane	
G-OTIV	Aerospool Dynamic WT9 UK	K. Wensley	
G-OTJH	Pegasus Quantum 15-912	S. Chapman	
G-OTJT	Glasflugel 304 S Jet	N. J. L. Busvine	
G-OTLC	Grumman AA-5 Traveller	L. P. Keegan & S. R. Cameron (G-BBUF)	
G-OTME	SNCAN Nord 1002 Pingouin II	C. R. A. Scrope	
G-OTNA	Robinson R44 II	PFH Asset Management Ltd	
G-OTOE	Aeronca 7AC Champion	D. & N. Cheney (G-BRWW)	
G-OTOO	Stolp SA.300 Starduster Too	I. M. Castle	
G-OTOP	P & M Quik R	I. J. Richardson	
G-OTOW	Cessna 175BX	C. J. P. Wilkes (G-AROC)	
G-OTPL	Pilatus PC-12/47E	Duagh Leasing LLP (G-RABB)	
G-OTRT	Robinson R44 II	TRT Aviation Ltd (G-CFEC)	
G-OTRV	Van's RV-6	C. A. Hawkins	
G-OTRY	Schleicher ASW-24	A. H. Beckingham	
G-OTSI	Sling 4 TSI	T. D. R. Hardy	
G-OTSP	AS.355F1 Twin Squirrel	Excel Charter Ltd (G-XPOL/G-BPRF)	
G-OTSS	TL2000 Sting S4	B. C. Gotts	
G-OTST	Diamond DA.42 NG	BAE Systems (Operations) Ltd	
G-OTTI	Cameron Otti-34 balloon	P. Spellward	
G-OTTK	PA-28-180 Cherokee E	TK2 Flying Club (G-GALA/G-AYAP)	
G-OTTR	Kitfox Series 7 Super Sport	R. A. Devey	

Notes	Reg	Type	Owner or Operator
	G-OTTS	Ikarus C42 FB100 Bravo	Air Cornwall
	G-OTTY	Rotorsport UK Calidus	GS Aviation (Europe) Ltd
	G-OTUI	SOCATA TB20 Trinidad	H. Graff (G-KKDL/G-BSHU)
	G-OTUM	Skyranger Nynja LS 912S(1)	J. B. Edwards
	G-OTUN	AerotechnikEV-97A Eurostar	L. R. Morris
	G-OTVR	PA-34-220T Seneca V	M. Barr
	G-OTWS	Schempp-Hirth Duo Discus XLT	R. J. H. Fack
	G-OTYE	Aerotechnik EV-97 Eurostar	A. B. Godber
	G-OTYP	PA-28-180 Cherokee	T. C. Lewis
	G-OTZZ	AutoGyro Cavalon	J. C. Collingwood
	G-OUDA	Aeroprakt A22-L Foxbat	A. R. Cattell
	G-OUEG	Bombardier BD700-1A10 Global 6000	Catreus AOC Ltd
	G-OUGH	Yakovlev Yak-52	Optimum Promotions Ltd (G-LAOK)
	G-OUIK	Mainair Pegasus Quik	M. D. Evans
	G-OURO	Shaw Europa	S. J. Westley
	G-OURT	Lindstrand LTL Series Racer 56 balloon	A. B. Court
	G-OUTY	Diamond DA.50C	S. D. Paver
	G-OUVI	Cameron O-105 balloon	Bristol University Hot Air Ballooning Society
	G-OVAL	Ikarus C.42 FB100	N. G. Tomes
	G-OVBF	Cameron A-250 balloon	Virgin Balloon Flights
	G-OVBL	Lindstrand LBL-150A balloon	R. J. Henderson
	G-OVEG	Diamond DA.20-C1 Katana	F. Frandsen
	G-OVEL	Pipistrel Virus SW.128	Chicken Roundabout Finance Ltd
	G-OVFM	Cessna 120	P. A. Harvie
	G-OVFR	Cessna F.172N	Marine and Aviation Ltd
	G-OVII	Van's RV-7	T. J. Richardson
	G-OVIN	Rockwell Commander 112TC	Ovin Ltd
	G-OVLA	Ikarus C.42 FB	R. R. Till
	G-OVLS	Pipistrel Virus SW 128	Chicken Roundabout Finance Ltd
	G-OVLX	Pipistrel Virus SW 121	Fly About Aviation Ltd
	G-OVMC	Cessna F.152 II	Swiftair Maintenance Ltd
	G-OVNE	Cessna 401A ★	City of Norwich Aviation Museum/Norwich
	G-OVOL	Skyranger Swift 912S(1)	K. B. Woods
	G-OVON	PA-18 Super Cub	T. A. Willcox & R. J. Watts
	G-OVPM	Europa NG	P. Munford
	G-OWAG	Cameron TR-70 balloon	M. G. Howard
	G-OWAI	Schleicher ASK-21	Scottish Gliding Union
	G-OWAP	PA-28-161 Cherokee Warrior II	CG Aviation Ltd (G-BXNH)
	G-OWAR	PA-28-161 Cherokee Warrior II	Bickertons Aerodromes Ltd
	G-OWAZ	Pitts S-1C Special	P. E. S. Latham (G-BRPI)
	G-OWBA	Alpi Pioneer 300 Hawk	D. B. Hothi
	G-OWDY	Van's RV-7	Cloud Surfers Ltd
	G-OWEE	Bell 505 Jet Ranger X	Claygate Ltd
	G-OWEN	K & S Jungster	R. C. Owen
	G-OWGC	Slingsby T.61F Venture T.2	Golf Charlie Group
	G-OWIB	Diamond Alien-48 (Character-1) balloon	L. P. Hooper
	G-OWLL	Ultramagic M-105 balloon	R. P. E. Phillips
	G-OWLS	Magni M.24C Orion	K. D. Woods
	G-OWLY	Cameron C-70 balloon	M. E. Banks
	G-OWOF	Cameron Z-0105 balloon	Lighter Than Air Ltd
	G-OWOW	Cessna 152 II	T. W. Gilbert (G-BMSZ)
	G-OWPS	Ikarus C42 FB100	Webb Plant Sales
	G-OWRC	Cessna F.152 II	Unimat SA/France
	G-OWRT	Cessna 182G	Tripacer Group
	G-OWST	Cessna 172S	A. L. Wrennall (G-WABH)
	G-OWTF	Pitts S-2B Special	D. P. Curtis (G-BRVT)
	G-OWTN	Embraer EMB-145EP	BAE Systems (Corporate Air Travel) Ltd
	G-OWWW	Europa	A. J. Brown
	G-OXBA	Cameron Z-160 balloon	Virgin Balloon Flights
	G-OXBC	Cameron A-140 balloon	J. E. Rose
	G-OXFB	PA-34-220T Seneca V	CAE Aviation Academy (Oxford) Ltd
	G-OXFD	PA-34-220T Seneca V	Falcon Flying Services Ltd
	G-OXFE	PA-34-220T Seneca V	CAE Aviation Academy (Oxford) Ltd
	G-OXFF	PA-34-220T Seneca V	Flyjet Importaceo e Exportacao de Aeronaves e Pecas Ltda/Brazil
	G-OXII	Van's RV-12	C. A. Acland
	G-OXIV	Van's RV-14	M. Browning

Reg	Type	Owner or Operator	Notes
G-OXPS	Falcon XPS	J. C. Greenslade (G-BUXP)	
G-OXVI	VS.361 Spitfire LF.XVIe (TD248:CR-S)	Spitfire Ltd	
G-OYAK	Yakovlev C-11 (9 white)	M. G. Jefferies	
G-OYGC	Eurofox	York Gliding Centre (Operations) Ltd	
G-OYIO	Robin DR.400/120	Exavia Ltd	
G-OYTE	Rans S.6ES Coyote II	K. C. Noakes	
G-OZEE	Light Aero Avid Speedwing Mk 4	G. D. Bailey	
G-OZIE	Jabiru J400	S. A. Bowkett	
G-OZIP	Christen Eagle II	B. S. Davis	
G-OZJX	PA-28-161 Cherokee Warrior II	J. Zhang (G-BNTD)	
G-OZOE	Lindstrand LBL Cornetto	C. L. Hayden & M. T. Joyce	
G-OZOI	Cessna R.182	J. R. G. & F. L. G. Fleming (G-ROBK)	
G-OZON	PA-32R-301T Saratoga II TC	W. P. Best	
G-OZOZ	Schempp-Hirth Nimbus 3DT	G-OZOZ Flying Group	
G-OZSB	Geta-Flug AS.105GD airship	Wings of Time Ltd	
G-OZZE	Lambert Mission M108	Lambert Aircraft Engineering BVBA/Belgium	
G-OZZI	Jabiru SK	A. H. Godfrey	
G-OZZT	Cirrus SR-22T	B. O'Brien & T. B. Levine	
G-PAAL	PA-32-301FT 6X	Premier Aviation (Alderney) Ltd	
G-PACE	Robin R.1180T	M. A. Pettican	
G-PACO	Sikorsky S-76C	Cardinal Helicopter Services	
G-PACR	PA-22-150 Caribbean	A. P. J. Tester (G-ARFB)	
G-PACT	PA-28-181 Cherokee Archer III	A. Parsons	
G-PADE	Escapade 912 (2)	P. D. Mickleburgh	
G-PAFF	AutoGyro MTO Sport	S. R. Paffett	
G-PAIB	PA-18-135 Super Cub	G. Cormack (G-LIBC/G-KAMP)	
G-PAID	Ultramagic M-65C balloon	J. W. Tyrrell	
G-PAIG	Grob G.109B	M. E. Baker	
G-PAIZ	PA-12 Super Cruiser	B. R. Pearson	
G-PAJU	Rans S-4 Coyote	A. R. Dobrowolski (G-MWES)	
G-PALI	Czech Sport Aircraft Piper Sport	MPG Aviation Ltd	
G-PALT	AutoGyro MTO Sport	A. R. Hawes	
G-PAMH	Pilatus PC-24	Regency Jet Ltd	
G-PAPI	Ikarus C42 FB80	Avon Training and Consultancy Ltd	
G-PAPJ	Van's RV-8	M. J. Collett	
G-PARG	Pitts S-1C Special	H. J. Morton	
G-PASA	MBB Bolkow Bo.105D ★	The Helicopter Museum/Weston-super-Mare (G-BGWP)	
G-PASB	MBB Bolkow Bo.105D ★	The Helicopter Museum/Weston-super-Mare (G-BDMC)	
G-PASH	AS.355F1 Twin Squirrel	Excel Charter Ltd	
C-PASL	AS.355F2 Ecureuil 2	C-E, Giblain/France	
G-PASN	Enstrom F-28F	N. Pasha (G-BSHZ)	
G-PATF	Europa	Condor Aviation International Ltd	
G-PATG	Cameron O-90 balloon	N. & S. Symonds	
G-PATJ	Ikarus C42 FB80	R. J. Collison	
G-PATN	SOCATA TB10 Tobago	A. Kumar (G-LUAR)	
G-PATO	Zenair CH.601UL Zodiac	K. R. Browne	
C-PATP	Lindstrand LBL-77A balloon	P. Pruchnickyj	
G-PATS	Europa	R. A. Harrison	
G-PATX	Lindstrand LBL-90A balloon	M. R. Noyce & R. P. E. Phillips	
G-PATZ	Europa	C. W. & S. R. Potts	
G-PAUK	Eurocopter AS.355N Ecureuil 2	Pursuit Aviation UK Ltd	
G-PAWA	PA-28-180 Cherokee C	Lanpro Group (G-AVRU)	
G-PAWS	AA-5A Cheetah	R. E. Dagless	
G-PAWW	Ultramagic M-90 balloon	A. M. Holly	
G-PAWZ	Sky Ranger Swift 912S(1)	G-PAWZ Syndicate	
G-PAXX	PA-20-135 Pacer (modified)	C. W. Monsell	
G-PAYD	Robin DR.400/180	P. Bigland	
G-PAZY	Pazmany PL.4A	M. Richardson (G-BLAJ)	
G-PBAL	Autogyro MTOsport	P. S. Ball	
G-PBAT	Czech Sport Aircraft Sportcruiser	P. M. W. Bath	
G-PBAY	Robinson R44 II	Briktec Ltd (G-ENSX/G-CLII)	
G-PBDG	Glaser-Dirks DG-300	B. G. & P. W. McDermid (G-DJAB)	
G-PBEC	Van's RV-7	P. G. Reid	
G-PBEE	Robinson R44	A. Ragin	
G-PBEL	CFM Shadow Srs DD	S. Fairweather	

Notes	Reg	Type	Owner or Operator
	G-PBII	DR.107 One Design	D. J. Taudevin
	G-PBIV	Falco F.8L	P. D. Baisden (G-RJAM)
	G-PBIX	VS.361 Spitfire LF XVI E	The Suffolk Spitfire Ltd (G-XVIA)
	G-PBOT	Avions Transport ATR-72-212A	Aurigny Air Services Ltd
	G-PBWS	Schleicher ASH-31Mi	A. R. J. Hughes
	G-PBYA	Consolidated PBY-5A Catalina (433915)	Catalina Aircraft Ltd
	G-PCAT	SOCATA TB10 Tobago	S. J. Allen (G-BHER)
	G-PCCC	Alpi Pioneer 300	G-PCCC Flying Group
	G-PCCM	Alpi Pioneer 200M	M. G. Freeman
	G-PCGC	Allstar PZL SZD-54-2 Perkoz	Cambridge Gliding Club Ltd
	G-PCIZ	Pilatus PC-12/47E	Limbourne Ltd
	G-PCJS	Diamond DA.42NG Twin Star	P. J. Cooper & G. E. J. Sealey
	G-PCMC	P & M Quik R	C. Smith
	G-PCOP	Beech B200 Super King Air	Albert Batlett and Sons (Airdrie) Ltd
	G-PCTF	Pilatus PC-24	Regency Jet Ltd
	G-PCTW	Pilatus PC-12/47E	Yellow Skies LLP
	G-PCUB	Piper L-21B Super Cub	B. A. Nicholson
	G-PDBY	Enstrom 480	Metafin Ltd (G-IJBB/G-LIVA/G-PBTT)
	G-PDGF	AS.350B2 Ecureuil	PDG Helicopters and PDG Aviation Services (G-FROH)
	G-PDGG	Aeromere F.8L Falco Srs 3	T. W. Gilbert
	G-PDGI	AS.350B2 Ecureuil	PDG Helicopters and PDG Aviation Services (G-BVJE)
	G-PDGO	AS.365N2 Dauphin II	PDG Helicopters and PDG Aviation Services
	G-PDGP	AS.355F2 Ecureuil 2	PDG Helicopters and PDG Aviation Services (G-ZITZ)
	G-PDGR	AS.350B2 Ecureuil	PDG Helicopters and PDG Aviation Services (G-RICC/G-BTXA)
	G-PDGT	AS.355F2 Ecureuil 2	PDG Helicopters and PDG Aviation Services (G-BOOV)
	G-PDOC	PA-44-180 Seminole	Medicare (G-PVAF)
	G-PDOG	Cessna O-1E Bird Dog (24550)	R. J. Dalley
	G-PDPD	Eurocopter EC.120B Colibri	Clayland Estates Ltd (G-SKLR/G-VIPR)
	G-PDRO	Schleicher ASH-31 Mi	P. Crawley
	G-PDSI	Cessna 172N	DA Flying Group
	G-PEAR	P &M Pegasus Quik	N. D. Major
	G-PECK	PA-32-300 Cherokee Six D	K. H. McCune (G-ETAV/G-MCAR/G-LADA/ G-AYWK)
	G-PECX	Eurofox 912S(2)	Airbourne Aviation Ltd
	G-PEEP	Skyranger Nynja	K. Perryman & C. S. Wilson
	G-PEGE	Skyranger 912	I. H. F. Smith
	G-PEGI	PA-34-200T Seneca II	New Euroline Ltd
	G-PEGY	Europa	A. Carter
	G-PEJM	PA-28-181 Cherokee Archer III	S. J. Clark
	G-PEKT	SOCATA TB20 Trinidad	The WERY Flying Group
	G-PEMB	Avions Transport ATR-72-212A	Aurigny Air Services Ltd
	G-PEMD	Diamond DA.50C	Meraki Flight Ltd
	G-PERC	Cameron N-90 balloon	I. R. Warrington
	G-PERD	Agusta Westland AW.139	CHC Scotia Ltd
	G-PERR	Cameron 60 Bottle SS balloon ★	British Balloon Museum/Newbury
	G-PEST	Hawker Tempest II (MW401)	Fighter Aviation Engineering Ltd
	G-PETH	PA-24-260C Comanche	J. V. Hutchinson & W. T. G. Ponnet
	G-PETO	Hughes 369HM	P. E. Tornberg (G-HAUS/G-KBOT/G-RAMM)
	G-PETR	PA-28-140 Cherokee	LS Aiurmotive Ltd (G-BCJL)
	G-PEVA	Aeroprakt A-32M Vixxen	J. P. Nestor & R. C. Tener
	G-PFAA	EAA Biplane Model P	T. A. Fulcher
	G-PFAF	FRED Srs 2	M. S. Perkins
	G-PFAH	Evans VP-1	J. A. Scott
	G-PFAP	Currie Wot/SE-5A (C1904:Z)	J. H. Seed
	G-PFAR	Isaacs Fury II (K2059)	T. Jarvis
	G-PFAT	Monnett Sonerai II	H. B. Carter
	G-PFAW	Evans VP-1	R. F. Shingler
	G-PFKD	Yakovlev Yak-12M	R. D. Bade
	G-PFLY	Cirrus SR22T	R. G. Macdowall
	G-PFSL	Cessna F.152	P. A. Simon
	G-PFTA	Cessna F.152 II	Pilot Flight Training Ltd (G-BHIN)

Reg	Type	Owner or Operator	Notes
G-PGDG	Van's RV-10	A. Solleveld	
G-PGEE	PA-18-95 Super Cub	P. S. Gilmour (G-BIYJ)	
G-PGFG	Tecnam P92-EM Echo	T. Farncombe	
G-PGGY	Robinson R44 II	B. V. Fisher	
G-PGHM	Air Creation 582(2) /Kiss 450	M. Nazm	
G-PGSI	Pierre Robin R2160	P. Spencer	
G-PHAA	Cessna F.150M	W. B. Bateson (G-BCPE)	
G-PHAB	Cirrus SR22	Warriner Aviation Ltd (G-MACL)	
G-PHAT	Cirrus SR20	T. W. Wielkopolski	
G-PHFR	Druine D.31 Turbulent	R. A. H. Vary (G-BWID)	
G-PHIZ	PA-30 Twin Comanche	T. J. & G. M. Laundy	
G-PHNX	Schempp-Hirth Duo Discus Xt	72 Syndicate '72'	
G-PHOR	Cessna FRA.150L Aerobat	M. Bonsall (G-BACC)	
G-PHOX	Aeroprakt A22-L Foxbat	J. D. Webb	
G-PHSI	Colt 90A balloon	P. H. Strickland	
G-PHTG	SOCATA TB10 Tobago	L. P. L. Dawes	
G-PHUN	Cessna FRA.150L Aerobat	M. Bonsall (G-BAIN)	
G-PHVM	Van's RV-8	E. M, K. H. & S. W. Haskins	
G-PHYL	Denney Kitfox Mk 4	T. Holland	
G-PHYS	Jabiru SP-470	A. J. Black	
G-PHYZ	Jabiru J430	R. J. Almey	
G-PIAF	Thunder Ax7-65 balloon	L. Battersley	
G-PICO	Cameron O-31 balloon	J. F. Trehern	
G-PICX	P & M Aviation QuikR	A. Lindsay	
G-PIEL	CP.301A Emeraude	E. B. Atalay (G-BARY)	
G-PIET	Pietenpol Air Camper	P. Batchelor & J. Granell	
G-PIGI	Aerotechnik EV-97 Eurostar	Pigs Might Fly Group	
G-PIGS	SOCATA Rallye 150ST	R. L. Hodgson (G-BDWB)	
G-PIGZ	Cameron Z-315 balloon	Wickers World Ltd	
G-PIII	Pitts S-1D Special	M. O'Leary (G-BETI)	
G-PIIT	Pitts S-2 Special	J. Law	
G-PIKD	Eiriavion PIK-20D-78	G-PIKD Syndicate	
G-PIKE	Robinson R22 Mariner	Sloane Helicopters Ltd	
G-PILE	Rotorway Executive 90	J. B. Russell	
G-PILL	Light Aero Avid Flyer Mk 4	Guardian 81 Flying Group	
G-PILY	Pilatus B4 PC-11	M. T. Cook & L. A. Martin	
G-PILZ	AutoGyro MT-03	MAMRFG Ltd	
G-PIMM	Ultramagic M-77 balloon	G. Everett	
G-PINO	AutoGyro MTO Sport	D. Eaton	
G-PINT	Cameron 65 Barrel SS balloon	D. K. Fish	
G-PINX	Lindstrand Pink Panther SS balloon	Magical Adventures Ltd/USA	
G-PION	Alpi Pioneer 300	A. A. Mortimer	
G-PIPD	AS.355F1 Eourouil 2	Heli Air Ltd (G-NBEL /G-SKYW/G-RTIS/G-TALI)	
G-PIPR	PA-18-95 Super Cub	R. & T. Kellett (G-BCDC)	
G-PIPS	Van's RV-4	P. G. Noonan	
G-PIPZ	BRM Aero Bristell NG5 Speed Wing	T. W. Lorimer	
G-PITS	Pitts S-2AE Special	P. N. A. & S. N. Whithead	
G-PITZ	Pitts S-2A Special	G-PITZ Group	
G-PIVI	Pipistrel Virus SW127 912S(1)	PIVI Pilots Group	
G-PIXE	Colt 31A balloon	J. L. Hinton	
G-PIXI	Pegasus Quantum 15-912	D. S. F. McNair	
G-PIXL	Robinson R44 II	Flying TV Ltd	
G-PIXY	Supermarine Aircraft Spitfire Mk.26 (RK855)	D. J. Howell & D. J. Bennett	
G-PJCD	AgustaWestland AW139	Bond Helicopters Ltd	
G-PJCM	Agusta AW139	Bond Helicopters Ltd	
G-PJCN	Agusta AW139	Bond Helicopters Ltd	
G-PJCS	Agusta AW139	Bond Helicopters Ltd	
G-PJMT	Lancair 320	H. Meyerhofer/Austria	
G-PJSY	Van's RV-6	P. J. York	
G-PJTM	Cessna FR.172K II	J. R. Emery (G-BFIF)	
G-PKHA	Pilatus PC-12/47E	Ravenair Aircraft Ltd	
G-PKSE	Jodel D.11 (modified)	R. J. Young	
G-PKUP	Ikarus C42C FB100	C. E. Storey	
G-PLAD	Kolb Twinstar Mk.III Xtra	T. J. Wiltshire	
G-PLAN	Cessna F.150L	Praeluceo Property Ltd	
G-PLAR	Vans RV-9A	M. P. Board	

Notes	Reg	Type	Owner or Operator
	G-PLAZ	Rockwell Commander 112	Flightline Aviation Ltd (G-RDCI/G-BFWG)
	G-PLEE	Cessna 182Q	A. P. Thomson
	G-PLIP	Diamond DA.40D Star	Leading Edge Aviation Ltd
	G-PLJR	Pietenpol Air Camper	N. Keveren
	G-PLOP	Magni M-24C	R. E. Balderson
	G-PLOT	Eurofox 2K	J. M. Harbottle
	G-PLOW	Hughes 269B	D. W. Walton (G-AVUM)
	G-PLPC	Schweizer Hughes 269C	WF Aviation
	G-PLPM	Europa XS	P. L. P. Mansfield
	G-PMAM	Cameron V-65 balloon	D. G. Such & G. N. Evans
	G-PMCM	PA-46-600TP M600	Executive Light Aircraft Leasing LLP
	G-PMCW	PA-32R-301 Saratoga II HP	Warbird Experiences Ltd
	G-PMMC	Leonardo AW139	Bond Helicopters Ltd
	G-PMNF	VS.361 Spitfire HF.IX (TA805:FX-M)	P. R. Monk
	G-PNAD	Lindstrand LBL Box SS balloon	M. T. Joyce & C. L. Hayden (G-PLLT)
	G-PNGB	Partenavia P-68B	Ravenair Aircraft
	G-PNGC	Schleicher ASK-21	Portsmouth Naval Gliding Centre
	G-PNZE	Sikorsky S-76C+	Starspeed Ltd
	G-PODD	Robinson R66	Jamiroquai Ltd
	G-PODZ	TL3000 Sirius 600	Mapperley Glamping Ltd
	G-POET	Robinson R44 II	Air Caernarfon Ltd
	G-POLA	Eurocopter EC 135 P2+	West Yorkshire Combined Authority National Police Air Service
	G-POLB	Eurocopter EC 135 T2+	West Yorkshire Combined Authority National Police Air Service (G-SURY)
	G-POLC	Eurocopter EC 135 T2+	West Yorkshire Combined Authority National Police Air Service (G-CPSH)
	G-POLD	Eurocopter EC 135 T2+	West Yorkshire Combined Authority National Police Air Service (G-NMID)
	G-POLF	Eurocopter EC 135 T2+	West Yorkshire Combined Authority National Police Air Service (G-ESEX)
	G-POLG	Eurocopter EC 135 T2+	West Yorkshire Combined Authority National Police Air Service (G-LASU)
	G-POLH	Eurocopter EC 135 T2+	West Yorkshire Combined Authority National Police Air Service (G-WCAO)
	G-POLJ	Eurocopter EC 135 T2+	West Yorkshire Combined Authority National Police Air Service (G-NEAU)
	G-POLL	Skyranger 912 (1)	S. Spence
	G-POLR	P & M Quik R	D. Sykes
	G-POLS	Airbus Helicopters EC 135 T3	Babcock Mission Critical Services Onshore Ltd
	G-POLU	Eurocopter EC135 T2+	West Yorkshire Combined Authority National Police Air Service (G-XMII)
	G-POLV	Vulcanair P-68R	West Yorkshire Combined Authority National Police Air Service
	G-POLW	Vulcanair P-68R	West Yorkshire Combined Authority National Police Air Service
	G-POLX	Vulcanair P-68R	West Yorkshire Combined Authority National Police Air Service
	G-POLY	Cameron N-77 balloon	S. Church & S. Jenkins
	G-POLZ	Vulcanair P-68R	West Yorkshire Combined Authority National Police Air Service
	G-POMP	Cameron Bearskin 100 balloon	Lighter Than Air Ltd
	G-POOH	Piper J-3C-65 Cub	R. Kane
	G-POOL	ARV Super 2	A. J. Gibson
	G-POPA	Beech A36 Bonanza	T. G. Malton
	G-POPE	Eiri PIK-20E-1	G-POPE Syndicate
	G-POPG	Eurofox 2K	J. C. W. Smith
	G-POPW	Cessna 182S	M. S. Archer
	G-POPY	Sky Ranger Swift 912S(1)	J. Young
	G-POPZ	Druine D.31A Turbulent	S. A. Blanchard
	G-PORG	AB Sportine Aviacija LAK-17AT	M. P. Day
	G-PORK	AA-5B Tiger	S. D. Pryke (G-BFHS)
	G-POSH	Colt 56A balloon	T. Knight (G-BMPT)
	G-POSY	Pitts S-25 Special	Tailpin Holdings Ltd
	G-POTA	Extra EA.300/LT	R. P. Bickmann
	G-POTR	Agusta 109E Power	Castle Air Ltd (G-OFTC)
	G-POUX	Pou du Ciel-Bifly	J. I. Popplewell
	G-POWK	Airbus A.320-233	Titan Airways Ltd

Reg	Type	Owner or Operator	Notes
G-POWL	Cessna 182R	Oxford Aeroplane Company Ltd	
G-POWM	Airbus A.320-232	Titan Airways Ltd	
G-POWN	Airbus A.321-211	Titan Airways Ltd	
G-POWU	Airbus A.321-211	Titan Airways Ltd	
G-POWX	Embraer ERJ190-100LR	Titan Airways Ltd	
G-POYA	Cessna 525 Citationjet	Poyston Aviation	
G-POZA	Escapade Jabiru ULP (2)	M. R. Jones	
G-PPBZ	Autogyro Calidus	Dept of Doing Ltd	
G-PPIO	Cameron C-90 balloon	A. G. Martin	
G-PPLG	Rotorsport UK MT-03	Gyro Syndicate PPLG	
G-PPLL	Van's RV-7A	D. Bull & T. Harrison	
G-PPOD	Europa XS	C. Rodriguez-Garcia	
G-PPPP	Denney Kitfox Mk 3	J. Moss	
G-PPPT	Leonardo AW109SP Grand New	Gainon Aeronautics Ltd	
G-PRAG	Brügger MB.2 Colibri	Colibri Flying Group	
G-PRAH	Flight Design CT2K	G. P. Blakemore	
G-PRAY	Lindstrand LTL Series 2-60 balloon	S. Dyer	
G-PRBB	HpH Glasflugel 304ES	P. J. Belcher	
G-PRDH	AS.355F2 Ecureuil 2	Claremont Air Services	
G-PRDY	Van's RV-8	I. Smith	
G-PREY	Pereira Osprey II	Condor Aviation International Ltd (G-BEPB)	
G-PRID	Supermarine 353 Spitfire PR.IV (AA810)	Spitfire AA810 Restoration Ltd	
G-PRIV	VS.353 Spitfire PR.IV	J. Smith	
G-PRKZ	Allstar PZL SZD-54-2 Perkoz	Buckminster Gliding Club Ltd	
G-PROS	Van's RV-7A	A. J. & S. A. Sutcliffe	
G-PROV	P.84 Jet Provost T.52A (T.4)	Swords Aviation	
G-PROW	Aerotechnik EV-97 Eurostar	Quantum Syndicate	
G-PRXI	VS.365 Spitfire PR.XI (PL983)	Fly to Inspire Ltd	
G-PSAX	Lindstrand LBL-77B balloon	M. V. Farrant & I. Risbridger	
G-PSCA	Eurocopter EC135 T2+	Babcock Mission Critical Services Onshore Ltd. (G-WASC)	
G-PSFG	Robin R.21601	Mardenair Ltd (G-COVD/G-BYOF)	
G-PSGC	PA-25-260 Pawnee (modified)	Peterborough & Spalding Gliding Club Ltd (G-BDDT)	
G-PSHK	Schempp-Hirth SHK-1	P. Gentil	
G-PSHU	Eurocopter EC135 T2+	Babock Mission Critical Services Onshore Ltd (G-WONN)	
G-PSIR	Jurca MJ.77 Gnatsum (474008 'VF-R')	P. W. Carlton & D. F. P. Finan	
G-PSJS	Robinson R22 II	G. E. J. Sealey (G-PBRL)	
G-PSKY	Skyranger 912S(1)	P. W. Curnock & J. W. Wilcox	
G-PSLT	Cameron Z-105 balloon	Flying Enterprises	
C PSMS	Eurofox 912(S)	I. W. Harriman	
G-PSNI	Eurocopter EC 135T2	Police Service of Northern Ireland	
G-PSNO	Eurocopter MBB BK-117C-2	Police Service of Northern Ireland	
G-PSNR	MBB-BK 117 C-2	Police Service of Northern Ireland (G-LFRS)	
G-PSPT	TL2000 Sling 54	Arts & Travel Ltd	
G-PSRT	PA-28-151 Cherokee Warrior	R. W. Nash (G-BSGN)	
G-PSUE	CFM Shadow Srs CD	M. J. Burton (G-MYAA)	
G-PSZB	Pitts S-2B	SEAFS Group	
G-PTAG	Europa	M. A. Coffin	
G-PTAR	Skyranger 912S(1)	P. Vergette	
G-PTBA	Boeing Stearman A-75 (466)	Mach Eight 3 Ltd	
G-PTEK	Van's RV-9A	P. K. Eckersley	
G-PTFE	Bristell NG5 Speed Wing	J. C. O'Donnell	
G-PTIX	VS.361 Spitfire IX (PT879)	Hangar 11 Collection (G-AYDE)	
G-PTOO	Bell 206L-4 LongRanger 4	Helicompany Ltd	
G-PTPA	Pipistrel Virus SW 115	Cold Air Flying Machines Ltd	
G-PTPW	Zenair CH.601XL Zodiac	R. N. Hall	
G-PTRE	SOCATA TB20 Trinidad	W. M. Chesson (G-BNKU)	
G-PTRK	Eurocopter AS350B3 Ecureuil	GE Plant Ltd (G-SPVK/G-CERU)	
G-PTSI	TAF Sling 4 TSI	P. Harrison	
G-PTTA	Cessna F.152	North Weald Flight Training Ltd (G-BJVT)	
G-PTTE	Cessna 152	AT Aviatioin Sales Ltd (G-BXTB)	
G-PTTS	Aerotek Pitts S-2A	P. & J. Voce	
G-PTZZ	Ryan PT-22A	M. P. Blokland	
G-PUDL	PA-18-150 Super Cub	C. M. Edwards	

Notes	Reg	Type	Owner or Operator
	G-PUDS	Europa	A. Roberts
	G-PUFF	Thunder Ax7-77A balloon	Intervarsity Balloon Club
	G-PUGZ	P & M Aviation Quik GT450	I. M. Spence
	G-PUKA	Jabiru Aircraft Jabiru J400	D. P. Harris
	G-PULR	Pitts S-2AE	Ayre to Air
	G-PUNK	Thunder Ax8-105 balloon	S. C. Kinsey
	G-PUNT	Robinson R44 II	Flight Checks Ltd
	G-PUPY	Europa XS	D. A. Cameron
	G-PURE	Cameron can 70 SS balloon	Mobberley Balloon Collection
	G-PURL	PA-32R-301 Saratoga II	A. P.H. & E. Hay
	G-PURP	Lindstrand LBL-90 balloon	T. W. Harris
	G-PURR	AA-5A Cheetah	G-PURR Group (G-BJDN)
	G-PURS	Rotorway Executive	J. & D. Parke
	G-PUSA	Gefa-Flug AS105GD Hot Air Airship	Skyking Aviation Ltd
	G-PUSH	Rutan Long-Ez	K. W. Scrivens
	G-PUSI	Cessna T.303	C. Smith & S. Devin
	G-PUSS	Cameron N-77 balloon	B. D. Close
	G-PVBF	Lindstrand LBL-260S balloon	Virgin Balloon Flights
	G-PVCV	Robin DR400/140	Bustard Flying Club Ltd
	G-PVET	DHC.1 Chipmunk 22 (WB565)	Connect Properties Ltd
	G-PVIP	Cessna 421C	Passion 4 Autos Ltd
	G-PVSS	P & M Quik GT450	M. S. Eglin
	G-PWAL	Eurofox 912(1)	I. M. Archer
	G-PWBE	DH.82A Tiger Moth	Aero Legends Leasing Ltd
	G-PWEF	Magni M.24C Orion	P. W. D. Walshe
	G-PWFW	Tecnam P2010	F. C. & P. A. Winters
	G-PWII	Van's RV-8	P. G. Wilson (G-CMEJ)
	G-PWUL	Van's RV-6	The G-PWUL Group
	G-PXMI	Agusta A109C	T. E. A. Edgell (G-BWNZ)
	G-PYAK	Yakovlev Yak-18T	Fairwind Aero Ltd
	G-PYNE	Thruster T.600N 450	R. Dereham
	G-PYPE	Van's RV-7	R. & L. Pyper
	G-PYRO	Cameron N-65 balloon	A. C. Booth
	G-PZAS	Schleicher ASW-27-18	A. J. Birkbeck
	G-PZPZ	P & M Pegasus Quantum 15-912	M. G. Makin
	G-RAAM	PA-28-161 Cherokee Warrior II	A. S. Bamrah (G-BRSE)
	G-RAAY	Taylor JT.1 Monoplane	R. Bowden (G-BEHM)
	G-RABS	Alpi Pioneer 300	Conquest Aircraft Group Ltd
	G-RACK	Ikarus C42 FB80	G. P. Burns (G-CFIY)
	G-RACO	PA-28R-200 Cherokee Arrow	M. J. Sweeney
	G-RACR	Ultramagic M-65C balloon	R. A. Vale
	G-RACY	Cessna 182S	C. M. Bishop & N. K. Wright
	G-RADA	Soko P-2 Kraguj	Airfield Aviation Ltd
	G-RADI	PA-28-181 Cherokee Archer II	DI Archer Group
	G-RAEF	Schempp-Hirth SHK-1	K. W. Summers
	G-RAES	Boeing 777-236	British Airways
	G-RAFA	Grob G.115	Vu H40 Ltd
	G-RAFB	Grob G.115	RAF College Flying Club Ltd
	G-RAFC	Robin R.2112	RAF Charlie Group
	G-RAFE	Thunder Ax7-77 balloon	Giraffe Balloon Syndicate
	G-RAFG	Slingsby T.67C Firefly	R. C. P. Brookhouse
	G-RAFK	Beech B.200 Super King Air	Serco Ltd
	G-RAFL	Beech B.200 Super King Air	Serco Ltd
	G-RAFR	Skyranger 912S(1)	M. Ellis
	G-RAFS	Thruster T.600N 450	J. R. Gardiner
	G-RAFT	Rutan LongEz	H. M. & S. Roberts
	G-RAFV	Avid Speedwing	G. Forno (G-MOTT)
	G-RAFW	Mooney M.20E	L. Schreuder (G-ATHW)
	G-RAFY	Sky Ranger Swift 912S(1)	L. J. Fenn
	G-RAFZ	RAF 2000 GTX-SE	V. G. Freke
	G-RAGE	Wilson Cassutt IIIM	D. H. Grace (G-BEUN)
	G-RAGS	Pietenpol Air Camper	D. J. Messenger
	G-RAGT	PA-32-301FT Cherokee Six	Oxhill Aviation
	G-RAHA	Schempp-Hirth Standard Cirrus	A. D. Patrick
	G-RAIZ	Van's RV-10	R. A. Edgson

Reg	Type	Owner or Operator	Notes
G-RAJP	Ikarus C42C FB100	C. E. Storey	
G-RAJV	Bombardier BD700-1A10 Global Express	Catreus AOC Ltd (G-CEYL)	
G-RAMI	Bell 206B JetRanger 3	Yorkshire Helicopters	
G-RAML	PA-34-220T Seneca III	A. M. S. Sher (G-BWDT/G-BKHS)	
G-RAMP	Piper J-3C-65 Cub	M. F. D. Bartley	
G-RAMS	PA-32R-301 Saratoga SP	Mike Sierra LLP	
G-RANL	Leonardo AW.169SP Grand New	East Midlands Helicopters	
G-RANN	Beech B.300 Super King Air 350	Flycorp Aviation LLP	
G-RAPH	Cameron O-77 balloon	P. A. Sweatman	
G-RAPL	Schempp-Hirth Duo Discus T	G-RAPL Duo XLT Syndicate	
G-RARA	AutoGyro MTO Sport	Gyro School Pro Ltd	
G-RARB	Cessna 172N	Rare Bird Flying Group	
G-RARE	Thunder Ax5-42 SS balloon ★	Balloon Preservation Group	
G-RASA	Diamond DA42 Twin Star	Southern Sailplanes Ltd	
G-RASH	Grob G.109E	G-RASH Syndicate	
G-RASL	Beech 76 Duchess	A. J. Gomes (G-GCCL)	
G-RASP	Aeroprakt A.32 Vixxen	T. Booth	
G-RATC	Van's RV-4	N. A. Preston & R. J. Ellingworth	
G-RATD	Van's RV-8	I. Zidane	
G-RATE	AA-5A Cheetah	J. B. Mills & M. A. Cummings (G-BIFF)	
G-RATH	Rotorway Executive 162F	D. W. J. Lee	
G-RATI	Cessna F.172M	N. F. Collins (G-PATI/G-WACZ/G-BCUK)	
G-RATT	Eurofox 915iS	Rattlesden Gliding Club Ltd	
G-RATV	PA-28RT-201T Turbo Cherokee Arrow IV	Tango Victor Ltd (G-WILS)	
G-RATZ	Europa	B. Hulme	
G-RAVE	Southdown Raven X	M. J. Robbins (G-MNZV)	
G-RAVN	Robinson R44	Flying Lobster Aviation Ltd	
G-RAVT	DG Flugzeugbau LS8-E	D. Jokinen	
G-RAWM	Robinson R44 II	HQ Aviation Ltd	
G-RAWS	Rotorway Executive 162F	R. P. Robinson & P. J. Wood	
G-RAYB	P & M Quik GT450	R. Blatchford	
G-RAYH	Zenair CH.701UL	N. J. Barnes	
G-RAYO	Lindstrand LBL-90A balloon	J. M. Owen	
G-RAYZ	Tecnam P2002-EA Sierra	S. J. Perkins	
G-RAZE	Bell 407GXi	H C Services Ltd	
G-RAZI	SIAI-Marchetti SF.260	P. A. Freeland	
G-RAZY	PA-28-181 Archer II	T. H. Pemberton (G-REXS)	
G-RAZZ	Maule MX-7-180	R. Giles	
G-RBBB	Europa	T. J. Hartwell	
G-RBCT	Schempp-Hirth Ventus 2Ct	RB Syndicate	
G-RBEL	Murphy Rebel	D. & M. T. Parsonage	
G-RBFX	Eurofox 912(iS)	R. D. Alberg	
G-RBHB	Ikarus C42 FB100	R. M. & H. K. Bilbe	
G-RBIL	SA.341D Gazelle HT Mk.3	R. B. Illingworth (G-CGIY)	
G-RBLL	Murphy Rebel	Batch Rebel Group LLP	
G-RBOS	Colt AS-105 airship ★	Science Museum/Wroughton	
G-RBRB	Schleicher AS-33ES	Bailey Aviation	
G-RBRI	Robinson R44 II	Helicentre Aviation Ltd (G-RWGS)	
G-RBSN	Ikarus C.42 FB80	P. B. & M. Robinson	
G-RBWW	BRM Aero Bristell NG5 Speed Wing	W. Woods & R. J. Baker	
G-RCED	Rockwell Commander 114	M. Soltan	
G-RCHE	Cessna 182T	N. J. Morgan (G-PTRI)	
G-RCHY	Aerotechnik EV-97 Eurostar	Group Archie	
G-RCIE	J-3C-65 Cub	R. P. Marks (G-CCOX)	
G-RCKT	Harmon Rocket II	K. E. Armstrong	
G-RCMC	Murphy Renegade 912	The Renegades	
G-RCMF	Cameron V-77 balloon	J. M. Percival	
G-RCMP	PA-28RT-201T Turbo Cherokee Arrow IV	Southeast Air Ltd	
G-RCOH	Cameron Cube 105 SS balloon	A. M. Holly	
G-RCRC	P & M Quik	R. M. Brown	
G-RCRM	Slingsby T.67M-260 Firefly	CRM Aviation Europe Ltd (G-BWXF)	
G-RCSR	Replica de Havilland DH.88 Comet	K. Fern	
G-RCST	Jabiru J430	P. M. Jones	
G-RCUB	PA-18-95 Super Cub	D. Bennett (G-BPJH)	
G-RCUS	Schempp-Hirth Arcus T	Arcus G-RCUS Syndicate	
G-RDAD	Reality Escapade ULP(1)	N. C. Allen	
G-RDAR	Van's RV-7	R. P. Marks	
G-RDAY	Van's RV-9	R. M. Day	

Notes	Reg	Type	Owner or Operator
	G-RDCO	Jabiru J430	A. H. & F. A. Macaskill
	G-RDDM	Cessna 182T	J. W. Buitelaar
	G-RDEN	Cameron Z-105 balloon	Hillmount Bangor Ltd
	G-RDMS	Zenair CH.650B	M. R. Shewan
	G-RDNS	Rans S.6-S Super Coyote	S. R. Green
	G-RDNY	AutoGyro Cavalon	C. Rodney
	G-RDPH	P & M Quik R	R. S. Partidge-Hicks
	G-RDRD	Autogyro Cavalon	The Station Ltd
	G-RDRL	Reaction Drive Rotorcraft	Genesis Aerotech Ltd
	G-RDWN	Leonardo AW109SP Grand New	Southern Air Charter Ltd
	G-READ	Colt 77A balloon	P. Bayton
	G-REAF	Jabiru J400	S. J. Carr
	G-REAS	Van's RV-6A	T. J. Smith
	G-REBB	Murphy Rebel	P. T. Catanach
	G-RECL	Cameron Z-105 balloon	P. Bowles
	G-RECW	PA-28-181 Cherokee Archer II	R. E. C. Washington (G-BOBZ)
	G-REDC	Pegasus Quantum 15-912	S. Houghton
	G-REDX	Experimental Aviation Berkut	W. S. Allen
	G-REDZ	Thruster T.600T 450	B. S. W. & T. W. Davis
	G-REEC	Sequoia F.8L Falco	K. J. E. Augustinus/Belgium
	G-REED	Mainair Blade 912S	S. B. Brady
	G-REEF	Mainair Blade 912S	P. C. Askew
	G-REER	Centrair 101A Pegase	A. R. Thomas
	G-REES	Jodel D.140C	G-REES Flying Group
	G-REGC	Zenair CH.601XL Zodiac	Golf Golf Charlie Group
	G-REGL	Robinson R44 II	HFM Consulting Ltd (G-REGJ/G-OPTF)
	G-REGO	Diamond S-90 balloon	S. J. Chatfield
	G-REGS	Thunder AX7-77 balloon	A. J. Gregory
	G-REGY	Groppo Trail Mk.2	T. P. Beare
	G-REGZ	Aeroprakt A-22L Foxbat	T. E. Snoddy & L. J. McKelvie
	G-RELL	D.62B Condor	H. A. Thomas (G-OPJH/G-AVDW)
	G-REMH	Bell 206B-3 JetRanger III	Flightpath Ltd
	G-RENE	Renegade 912	R. J. Grimwood
	G-RENT	Robinson R22 ★	Ulster Aviation Society/Long Kesh
	G-RESA	Leonardo AW139	Bristow Helicopters Ltd
	G-RESB	Leonardo AW139	Bristow Helicopters Ltd
	G-RESE	Leonardo AW139	Bristow Helicopters Ltd
	G-RESF	Leonardo AW139	Bristow Helicopters Ltd
	G-RESG	Dyn'Aéro MCR-01 Club	R. E. S. Greenwood
	G-RESH	Leonardo AW139	Bristow Helicopters Ltd
	G-RESI	Leonardo AW139	Bristow Helicopters Ltd
	G-RESS	Cessna T.182T	W. E. Buchanan
	G-REST	Beech P35 Bonanza	N. J. Taaffe (G-ASFJ)
	G-RESU	Airbus Helicopters MBB BK-117D-3	Babcock Mission Critical Services Onshore Ltd
	G-RETA	CASA 1.131 Jungmann 2000	M. R. Turner (G-BGZC)
	G-RETH	Rutan Cozy	G. T. Bowker (G-OGJS)
	G-REVE	Van's RV-6	S. D. Foster
	G-REVO	Skyranger 912(2)	D. A. Wilson
	G-REVV	Van's RV-7	T. J. Franklin & P. J. Roy
	G-REWS	Bell 505 Jet Ranger X	Quadano Ltd
	G-REXA	Beech B.200GT Super King Air	RVL Aviation Ltd
	G-REXB	Beech B.200GT Super King Air	RVL Aviation Ltd
	G-REYE	Robinson R44 I	Redeye.com Ltd
	G-REZA	Skyranger Swift 912S(1)	R-A. Khosravi
	G-RFAD	Sportavia-Putzer Fournier RF4D	M. P. Dentith
	G-RFIO	Aeromot AMT-200 Super Ximango	M. D. Evans
	G-RFLO	Ultramagic M-105 balloon	Flying Enterprises
	G-RFLY	Extra EA.300/L	J. P. Taylor
	G-RFOX	Denney Kitfox Mk 3	G. Hawkins
	G-RFRV	Van's RV-9A	Radley Farm RV Group (G-RVWJ)
	G-RFSB	Sportavia RF-5B	G-RFSB Group
	G-RGAH	Diamond DA.40NG Star	Romeo Golf Aviation Ltd
	G-RGAL	Diamond DA.40D Star	Romeo Golf Aviation Ltd
	G-RGAM	Diamond DA.40NG Star	Romeo Golf Aviation Ltd
	G-RGCL	Auster J1 Autocrat	R. G. Callaway-Lewis
	G-RGTS	Schempp-Hirth Discus b	G. R. Green
	G-RGUS	Fairchild 24A-46A Argus III (KK527)	A. R. Willis

Reg	Type	Owner or Operator	Notes
G-RHAM	Skyranger 582(1)	L. Smart & P. Gibson	
G-RHCB	Schweizer 269C-1	P. R. Butler	
G-RHOD	Just Superstol	C. S. & K. D. Rhodes	
G-RHYM	PA-31-310 Turbo Navajo B	2 Excel Aviation Ltd (G-BJLO)	
G-RIBA	P & M Quik GT450	R. J. Murphy	
G-RICE	Robinson R22	Glenntrade Ltd	
G-RICO	AG-5B Tiger	Delta Lima Flying Group	
G-RIDA	Eurocopter AS.355NP Ecureuil 2	Airbourne Solutions Ltd	
G-RIDB	Bell 429	National Grid Electricity Transmission PLC	
G-RIDC	Bell 429	National Grid Electricity Transmission PLC	
G-RIDE	Stephens Akro	R. Mitchell	
G-RIDG	Van's RV-7	M. W. Hyde	
G-RIEF	DG Flugzeugbau DG-1000T	G-RIEF Syndicate	
G-RIET	Hoffmann H.36 Dimona	Dimona Syndicate	
G-RIEV	Rolladen-Schneider LS8-18	R. D. Grieve	
G-RIFD	HpH Glasflugel 304ES	RIFD Syndicate	
G-RIFN	Avion Mudry CAP-10B	D. E. Starkey & R. A. J. Spurrell	
G-RIFZ	M 7 D Flugzeugbau JS-MD 3 RES	D. Griffiths	
G-RIGH	PA-32R-301 Saratoga IIHP	Air Elite Aviation Ltd	
G-RIHN	Dan Rihn DR.107 One Design	P. J. Burgess	
G-RIII	Vans RV-3B	J. F. Dowe	
G-RIIV	Van's RV-4	Gloucester RV Group	
G-RIKI	Mainair Blade 912	A. Warnock	
G-RIKS	Europa XS	H. Foster	
G-RIKY	Mainair Pegasus Quik	S. Clarke	
G-RILA	Flight Design CTSW	P. A. Mahony	
G-RIME	Lindstrand LBL-25A balloon	N. Ivison	
G-RIMM	Westland Wasp HAS.1 (XT435:430)	J. M. Heath	
G-RINN	Mainair Blade	M. R. Hawkins	
G-RINS	Rans S.6-ESA Coyote II	A. M. Parnell & T. J. Vickers	
G-RINT	CFM Streak Shadow	D. Grint	
G-RINZ	Van's RV-7	R. C. May (G-UZZL)	
G-RIOT	Silence SA.180 Twister	P. M. Wells (G-SWIP)	
G-RIPA	Partenavia P.68 Observer 2	Ravenair Aircraft Ltd	
G-RIPH	VS.384 Seafire F.XVII	Seafire Displays Ltd (G-CDTM)	
G-RISA	PA-28-180 Cherokee C	Vu JV41 Ltd (G-ATZK)	
G-RISH	Rotorway Exeecutive 162F	T. Gilmartin	
G-RISY	Van's RV-7	D. I. Scott	
G-RITT	P & M Quik	N. C. Farley	
G-RIVE	Jodel D.153	R. J. D. Mellor	
G-RIVR	Thruster T.600N 450	S. W. Turley	
G-RIVT	Van's RV-6	J. M. Keane	
G-RIXA	J-3C-65 Cub	R. J. Hunter	
G-RIXE	Europa XS	W. M. Bell & S. J. Brooks	
G-RIZK	Schleicher ASW-27-18E	P. Lund	
G-RIZZ	PA-28-161 Cherokee Warrior II	W. Ali & Denderah SA	
G-RJMC	Eurofox 2K	M. G. F. Cawson	
G-RJRC	Commander114B	R. M. Jowitt	
G-RJRJ	Aerotechnik EV-97A Eurostar	D. P. Myatt	
G-RJWW	Maule M5-235C Lunar Rocket	N. Ibrahim (G-BRWG)	
G-RJWX	Europa XS	G. R. Thomas	
G-RKEL	Agusta-Bell 206B JetRanger 3	Nunkeeling Ltd	
G-RKID	Van's RV-6A	I. Shaw	
G-RKKT	Cessna FR.172G	K. L. Irvine (G-AYJW)	
G-RKUS	Arcus T	Arcus Syndicate	
G-RLDX	Cameron A-375 balloon	Bailey Balloons Ltd	
G-RLMW	Tecnam P2002-EA Sierra	S. P. Hoskins	
G-RLON	BN-2A Mk III-2 Trislander ★	Solent Sky Museum/Southampton (G-ITEX/ G-OCTA/G-BCXW)	
G-RLWG	Ryan ST3KR (687)	R. A. Fleming	
G-RLXA	Elixir	Rubric Aviation Ltd	
G-RMAA	Airbus MBB BK117 D-2	Midlands Air Ambulance Charity	
G-RMAC	Europa	P. J. Lawless	
G-RMAN	Aero Designs Pulsar	I. Psaila	
G-RMAR	Robinson R66	Marfleet Civil Engineering Ltd (G-NSEV)	
G-RMAV	Ikarus C42 FB80	RM Aviation Ltd	

Notes	Reg	Type	Owner or Operator
	G-RMAX	Cameron C-80 balloon	J. Kenny
	G-RMBH	Leonardo A109S Trekker	D & S P Holdings LLP
	G-RMCA	Van's RV-10	R. A. Arrowsmith (G-CKYK)
	G-RMCD	Cirrus SR22T	R. G. Macdowall
	G-RMCS	Cessna 182R	R. W. C. Sears
	G-RMHE	Aerospool Dynamic WT9 UK	D. R. Lewis
	G-RMIT	Van's RV-4	J. P. Kloos
	G-RMMT	Europa XS	N. Schmitt
	G-RMPI	Whittaker MW5D Sorcerer	D. R. Speight
	G-RMPS	Van's RV-12	R. B. C. Stalker & D. W. Halkett
	G-RMPY	Aerotechnik EV-97 Eurostar	N. R. Beale
	G-RMRV	Van's RV-7A	R. Morris
	G-RMUG	Cameron Nescafe Mug 90 SS balloon	The British Balloon Museum & Library Ltd
	G-RNAC	IDA Bacau Yakovlev Yak-52	Chewton Glen Aviation
	G-RNAF	BAC 167 Strikemaster Mk.80 (NZ6300)	NWMAS Leasing Ltd (G-FLYY)
	G-RNCA	Aeronca 11AC Chief	C. J. Perkins
	G-RNDD	Robin DR.400/500	G-RNDD Flying Group
	G-RNDE	Kubicek BB-S/Grenade balloon	Grenade (UK) Ltd
	G-RNDX	Embraer 550 Praetor 600	Voluxis Ltd
	G-RNFA	BAe. Sea Harrier FA.Mk.2	Fly Harrier Ltd
	G-RNGD	Murphy Renegade Spirit UK	W. D. Foster
	G-RNGS	Airbus MBB BK117 D-2	QinetiQ Ltd
	G-RNJW	Robinson R66	Blade Motor Group Ltd (G-WWMF)
	G-RNKK	Air Creation Tanarg/Bionix 15 912S(2)	K. Kirby
	G-RNMZ	Fairey Swordfish Mk.II	White Waltham Airfield Ltd
	G-RNRM	Cessna A.185F	Skydive St. Andrews Ltd
	G-RNTB	BAe. Harrier T.Mk.8	Fly Harrier Ltd
	G-RNVR	DHC-1 Chipmunk 22	Fly Navy Heritage Trust Ltd (G-CNVH)
	G-ROAD	Robinson R44 II	Blue Thunder Sound Ltd
	G-ROAT	Robinson R44 II	R. D. Jordan
	G-ROBA	Grob G.115D-2 Heron	Adastral Flying Displays Ltd (G-BVHF)
	G-ROBD	Europa	Condor Aviation International Ltd
	G-ROBG	P & M Quik GT450	R. D. Richardson
	G-ROBJ	Robin DR.500/200i	J. D. May
	G-ROBN	Pierre Robin R1180T	E. R. Hall
	G-ROBT	Hawker Hurricane I (P2902:DX-X)	Fighter Aviation Engineering Ltd
	G-ROBX	Cameron Sport-80 balloon	R. P. Cross
	G-ROBZ	Grob G109B	T. T. Turan
	G-ROCH	Cessna T.303	Yorkshire Land Ltd
	G-ROCR	Schweizer 269C	M. Wilkinson
	G-RODD	Cessna 310R II	Alpha Properties (London) Ltd (G-TEDD/G-MADI)
	G-RODG	Jabiru UL	A. I. Freeman
	G-RODI	Isaacs Fury (K3731)	C. F. Pote
	G-RODJ	Ikarus C42 FB80	Medaviate Ltd
	G-RODO	Europa XS	R. M. Carson (G-ROWI)
	G-RODW	Eurofox 2K	S. Holland
	G-RODZ	Van's RV-3A	R. C. Bunce
	G-ROFS	Groppo Trail	D. Gani
	G-ROGY	Cameron 60 Concept balloon	S. A. Laing
	G-ROHI	Yakovlev Yak-18T	R. Jaggi (G-RGTX)
	G-ROKO	Roko-Aero NG-4HD	C. D. Sidoli
	G-ROKY	Groppo Trail	J. Webb
	G-ROLL	Pitts S-2A Special	P. H. Meeson
	G-ROLY	Cessna F.172N	Hields Aviation (G-BHIH)
	G-ROME	I.I.I. Sky Arrow 650TC	T. J. G. Reijn
	G-ROMK	Magni M16C Tandem Trainer	J. A. Ingram
	G-ROMP	Extra 230H	The G-ROMP Group
	G-ROMT	Robinson R44 II	Groundsure Ltd (G-RALA)
	G-RONA	Europa	A. J. Rex
	G-RONI	Cameron V-77 balloon	R. E. Simpson
	G-RONS	Robin DR.400/180	Robin Flying Club Ltd
	G-RONW	FRED Srs 2	R. W. Frost
	G-RONZ	Ikarus C42 FB80 Bravo	R. F. Dean
	G-ROOG	Extra EA.300/LT	Fly (Fu Lai) Aviation Ltd
	G-ROOK	Cessna F.172P	Rolim Ltd
	G-ROON	Sikorsky S-76C	Rooney Air Ltd
	G-ROOO	Jabiru J430	R. J. Almey (G-HJZN)
	G-ROOV	Europa XS	P. W. Hawkins

Reg	Type	Owner or Operator	Notes
G-ROPO	Groppo Trail	W. Wennington	
G-ROPP	Groppo Trail	D. A. Small	
G-RORE	Embraer EMB-550 Praetor 600	Perinto LP Inc	
G-RORI	Folland Gnat T.1 (XR538)	Heritage Aircraft Ltd	
G-RORY	Piaggio FWP.149D	M. Edwards (G-TOWN)	
G-ROSI	Thunder Ax7-77 balloon	J. E. Rose	
G-ROSK	Ultramagic M-90 balloon	C. M. Jones	
G-ROSS	Practavia Pilot Sprite	Condor Aviation International Ltd	
G-ROTI	Luscombe 8A Silvaire	R. Ludgate & L. Prebble	
G-ROTS	CFM Streak Shadow Srs SA	J. Edwards	
G-ROVA	Aviat A-1B Husky Pup	Jigsaw Aviation Ltd	
G-ROVE	PA-18-135 Super Cub (R-156)	S. J. Gaveston	
G-ROVY	Robinson R22 Beta	East Midlands Helicopters Engineering Ltd	
G-ROWA	Aquila AT01	O. Bryan	
G-ROWL	AA-5B Tiger	M. S. Rapin	
G-ROWS	PA-28-151 Cherokee Warrior	Air Academy	
G-ROXI	Cameron C-90 balloon	D. Marshall	
G-ROXT	PA-28-140 Cherokee	M. U. Khan	
G-ROYC	Jabiru UL450	R. P. Stoner	
G-ROYP	Robinson R22	R. M. Price	
G-ROZE	Magni M-24C	A. B. Gowland	
G-ROZZ	Ikarus C.42 FB 80	N. J. James	
G-RPAF	Europa XS	I. Simpson & M. Foster	
G-RPAR	Aeroprakt A-32 Vixxen	A. P. and S. M. Parris and Son	
G-RPAX	CASA 1-133 Jungmeister (35-23)	M. J. de Morgan	
G-RPCC	Europa XS	R. P. Churchill-Coleman	
G-RPEZ	Rutan LongEz	M. P. Dunlop	
G-RPPO	Groppo Trail	R. Vianello	
G-RPRP	P & M Quik R	R. M. Brown	
G-RPRV	Van's RV-9	T. A. Willcox	
G-RRAK	Enstrom 480B	P. J. Began (G-RIBZ)	
G-RRAT	CZAW Sportcruiser	G. Sipson	
G-RRCU	CEA DR.221B Dauphin	Merlin Flying Club Ltd	
G-RRED	PA-28-181 Cherokee Archer II	J. P. Reddington	
G-RRFF	VS.329 Spitfire Mk.IIB	Retro Track & Air (UK) Ltd	
G-RRGN	VS.390 Spitfire PR.XIX (PS853)	Rolls-Royce PLC (G-MXIX)	
G-RRJR	Eurofox 2K	P. Anderson	
G-RROB	Robinson R44 II	D. J. Evans	
G-RROK	Cessna FR.172E	C. Payne (G-AWDR)	
G-RRRV	Van's RV-6	Plane Trading Ltd	
G-RRRZ	Van's RV-8	S. Whatmough	
G-RRSR	Piper J-3C-65 Cub (480173:57-H)	R. W. Roberts	
G-RRST	Supermarine 300 Spitfire Mk.1	G. J. Davis	
G-RRVV	Van's RV-8	M. W. Albery	
G-RRVX	Van's RV-10	T. B. Ellison	
G-RSAF	BAC.167 Strikemaster 80A (417)	NWMAS Leasing Ltd	
G-RSAM	P & M Quik GTR	D. J. Bromley	
G-RSCU	Agusta A.109E	Sloane Helicopters Ltd	
G-RSHI	PA-34-220T Seneca V	R. S. Hill and Sons	
G-RSJW	Cessna FR.172K	R. J. Shell Ltd & J. Wood (G-EFSF)	
G-RSKR	PA-28-161 Cherokee Warrior II	Henshaw Aviation Ltd (G-BOJY)	
G-RSKY	Skyranger 912(2)	P. Lister	
G-RSMC	Medway SLA 100 Executive	W. S. C. Toulmin	
G-RSSF	Denney Kitfox Mk 2	T. Holland	
G-RTFM	Jabiru J400	A. H. Hamilton	
G-RTHS	Rans S-6-ES Coyote II	R. G. Hughes	
G-RTMS	Rans S.6 ES Coyote II	C. J. Arthur	
G-RTMY	Ikarus C.42 FB 100	Orman (Carrolls Farm) Ltd	
G-RTNA	Beech B.300C King Air 350C	Raytheon Systems Ltd	
G-RTRV	V an's RV-9A	C. P. Giddins	
G-RUBB	AA-5B Tiger	M. J. Goodfellow	
G-RUBY	PA-28RT-201T Turbo Cherokee Arrow IV	Arrow Aircraft Group (G-BROU)	
G-RUCK	Bell 206B-3 JetRanger III	J. A. Ruck	
G-RUES	Robin HR.100/210	R. H. R. Rue	
G-RUFF	Mainair Blade 912	P. Mulvey	
G-RUKA	Boeing 737-8AS	Ryanair UK Ltd	

Notes	Reg	Type	Owner or Operator
	G-RUKB	Boeing 737-8AS	Ryanair UK Ltd
	G-RUKC	Boeing 737-8AS	Ryanair UK Ltd
	G-RUKD	Boeing 737-8AS	Ryanair UK Ltd
	G-RUKE	Boeing 737-8AS	Ryanair UK Ltd
	G-RUKF	Boeing 737-8AS	Ryanair UK Ltd
	G-RUKG	Boeing 737-8AS	Ryanair UK Ltd
	G-RUKH	Boeing 737-8AS	Ryanair UK Ltd
	G-RUKI	Boeing 737-8AS	Ryanair UK Ltd
	G-RUKJ	Boeing 737-8AS	Ryanair UK Ltd
	G-RUKK	Boeing 737-8AS	Ryanair UK Ltd
	G-RUKM	Boeing 737-8AS	Ryanair UK Ltd
	G-RUKN	Boeing 737-8AS	Ryanair UK Ltd
	G-RUKO	Boeing 737-8AS	Ryanair UK Ltd
	G-RUMM	Grumman F8F-2P Bearcat (121714:201B)	Patina Ltd
	G-RUMN	AA-1A Trainer	Northair Aviation Ltd
	G-RUMW	Grumman FM-2 Wildcat (JV579:F)	Patina Ltd
	G-RUNS	P & M Quik GT450	S. Nicol
	G-RUNT	Cassutt Racer IIIM	L. S. Kingman
	G-RUPS	Cameron TR-70 balloon	R. M. Stanley
	G-RUSL	Van's RV-6A	S. W. Osborne
	G-RUSO	Robinson R22 Beta	R. M. Barnes-Gorell
	G-RUVE	Van's RV-8	J. P. Brady & D. J. Taylor
	G-RUVI	Zenair CH.601UL	P. G. Depper
	G-RUVY	Van's RV-9A	A. Strachan
	G-RVAA	Van's RV-7	A. J. Almosawi
	G-RVAB	Van's RV-7	I. M. Belmore & A. T. Banks
	G-RVAC	Van's RV-7	A. F. S. & B. Caldecourt
	G-RVAG	Van's RV-8	A. M. Leviston & V. Millard
	G-RVAH	Van's RV-7	The Regent Group
	G-RVAL	Van's RV-8	P. D. Scandrett
	G-RVAM	Van's RV-9A	A. H. Miller (G-RVLC)
	G-RVAN	Van's RV-6	C. Richards
	G-RVAR	Van's RV-8	B. A. Ridgway
	G-RVAW	Van's RV-6	M. E. & R. E. Lee
	G-RVBA	Van's RV-8A	D. P. Richard
	G-RVBC	Van's RV-6A	B. J. Clifford
	G-RVBF	Cameron A-340 balloon	Virgin Balloon Flights
	G-RVBH	Van's RV-8	J. L. & M. R. Hunter
	G-RVBI	Van's RV-8	R. J. Lea
	G-RVBJ	Van's RV-8A	Thrive Group Holdings Ltd
	G-RVBK	Van's RV-8	K. R. H. Wingate
	G-RVBL	Van's RV-7	B. R. & L. W. Cornes
	G-RVBP	Van's RV-7	B. J. A. Polwin
	G-RVBZ	Van's RV-7	R. A. Broad
	G-RVCB	Van's RV-3	R. C. Bunce
	G-RVCE	Van's RV-6A	P. G. Reid
	G-RVCH	Van's RV-8A	JB Aviation Ltd
	G-RVCI	Van's RV-7	I. T. Corse (G-JSTS)
	G-RVCL	Van's RV-6	N. A. Onions
	G-RVCM	Van's RV-7	M. D. & C. Barnard
	G-RVDB	Van's RV-7	D. Broom
	G-RVDC	Van's RV-8	D. Stephens
	G-RVDD	Van's RV-14	D. M. Dash
	G-RVDG	Van's RV-9	D. M. Gill
	G-RVDH	Van's RV-8	R. D. Masters (G-ONER)
	G-RVDJ	Van's RV-6	M. W. Meynell
	G-RVDR	Van's RV-6A	L. J. Woodrow & K. A. Attwood
	G-RVDW	Van's RV-14	D, J. Wynne
	G-RVEA	BRM Aero Bristell NG5 Speed Wing	R. V. Emerson
	G-RVEM	Van's RV-7A	Plummet Aviation Ltd (G-CBJU)
	G-RVER	Van's RV-4	M. D. Falconer
	G-RVET	Van's RV-6	D. R. Coleman
	G-RVFB	Van's RV-8	L. W. Taylor
	G-RVFP	Van's RV-7	B. J. A. Polwin
	G-RVFT	Van's RV-8	R. H. W. A. Westerhuis
	G-RVGA	Van's RV-6A	R. Emery
	G-RVGO	Van's RV-10	Tapeformers Ltd
	G-RVGR	Van's RV-8A	G. Robertson
	G-RVHD	Van's RV-7	N. Lamb
	G-RVIA	Van's RV-6A	K. R. W. Scull & J. Watkins

Reg	Type	Owner or Operator	Notes
G-RVIB	Van's RV-6	R. D. Myles	
G-RVIC	Van's RV-6A	I. T. Corse	
G-RVII	Van's RV-7	M. J. H. White	
G-RVIL	Van's RV-4	S. C. Hipwell	
G-RVIN	Van's RV-6	M. Lawton	
G-RVIO	Van's RV-10	J. H. Garrett-Cox G-DGEW	
G-RVIS	Van's RV-8	M. W. Edwards	
G-RVIT	Van's RV-6	P. J. Shotbolt	
G-RVIV	Van's RV-4	S. B. Robson	
G-RVIW	Van's RV-9	C. R. James	
G-RVIX	Van's RV-9A	J. R. Holt & C. S. Simmons	
G-RVIZ	Van's RV-12	Chelwood Flying Group	
G-RVJG	Van's RV-7	J. W. Ellis (G-JTEM)	
G-RVJH	Van's RV-14	J. Hancock	
G-RVJL	Van's RV-6	A. R. Williams & S. P. Ayers	
G-RVJM	Van's RV-6	M. D. Challoner	
G-RVJO	Van's RV-9A	P. D. Chandler	
G-RVJP	Van's RV-9A	Oystercatcher Flying Group Ltd	
G-RVJS	Van's RV-8	J. Stringer	
G-RVJW	Van's RV-4	J. M. Williams	
G-RVLG	Cessna F.406	RVL Aviation Ltd	
G-RVLL	Van's RV-6	S. C. Hipwell	
G-RVLX	Cessna F.406 Caravan II	RVL Aviation Ltd	
G-RVLY	Cessna F.406 Caravan II	RVL Aviation Ltd (G-BPSX)	
G-RVMB	Van's RV-9A	The Mike Bravo Flying Group	
G-RVMM	Van's RV-7	M. Malone	
G-RVMS	Van's RV-7	M. P. C. Sweeney	
G-RVMT	Van's RV-6	D. R. Hardy & R. W. Thomas	
G-RVMZ	Van's RV-8	A. E. Kay	
G-RVNA	PA-38-112 Tomahawk	Ravenair Aircraft Ltd (G-DFLY)	
G-RVNC	PA-38-112 Tomahawk	Ravenair Aircraft Ltd (G-BTJK)	
G-RVND	PA-38-112 Tomahawk	E. L. Fox (G-BTAS)	
G-RVNE	Partenavia P.68B	Ravenair Aircraft Ltd (G-SAMJ)	
G-RVNF	PA-34-200T Seneca II	Ravenair Aircraft Ltd (G-GAFA)	
G-RVNG	Partenavia P.68B	Ravenair Aircraft Ltd (G-BMOI)	
G-RVNH	Van's RV-9A	Brimpton Flying Group Ltd	
G-RVNI	Van's RV-6A	G-RVNI Group	
G-RVNJ	Partenavia P.68B	Flight Calibration Services Ltd	
G-RVNK	Partenavia P.68B	Ravenair Aircraft Ltd (G-BHBZ)	
G-RVNM	Partenavia P.68B	Ravenair Aircraft Ltd (G-BFBU)	
G-RVNP	Partenavia P.68B	Ravenair Aircraft Ltd	
G-RVNR	Partenavia P.68B	Ravenair Aircraft Ltd	
G-RVNS	Van's RV-4	G. D. Connolly (G-CBGN)	
G-RVNV	Van's RV-9	M. Owen & N. D. McAllister (G-IRAR)	
G-RVNX	PA-28-180 Cherokee D	Ravenair Aircraft Ltd (G-AWTL)	
G-RVOM	Van's RV-8	C. J. Watson, B. M. Dines & S. P. Fletcher	
G-RVPH	Van's RV-8	E. M. Yard	
G-RVPL	Van's RV-8	M. B. Summers	
G-RVPM	Van's RV-4	D. P. Lightfoot (G-RVDS)	
G-RVPW	Van's RV-6A	C. G. Deeley	
G-RVRA	PA-28-140 Cherokee	J. D. C. Lea (G-OWVA)	
G-RVRD	PA-34-200T Seneca II	Romeo Bravo Aviation Ltd (G-BTAJ)	
G-RVRE	Partenavia P.68B	Flight Calibration Services Ltd	
G-RVRK	PA-38-112 Tomahawk	Ravenair Aircraft Ltd (G-BGZW)	
G-RVRM	PA-38-112 Tomahawk	Ravenair Aircraft Ltd (G-BGEK)	
G-RVRN	PA-28-161 Cherokee Warrior II	Ravenair Aircraft Ltd (G-BPID)	
G-RVRO	PA-38-112 Tomahawk II	Ravenair Aircraft Ltd (G-BOUD)	
G-RVRP	Van's RV-7	R. C. Parris	
G-RVRT	PA-28-140 Cherokee C	Full Sutton Flying Centre Ltd (G-AYKX)	
G-RVRU	PA-38-112 Tomahawk	Ravenair Aircraft Ltd (G-NCFE/G-BKMK)	
G-RVRV	Van's RV-4	P. Jenkins	
G-RVRX	Partenavia P.68B	Ravenair Aircraft Ltd (G-PART)	
G-RVRY	PA-38-112 Tomahawk	Ravenair Aircraft Ltd (G-BTND)	
G-RVSA	Van's RV-6A	M. R. Badminton	
G-RVSB	Van's RV-6	S. Beard	
G-RVSD	Van's RV-9A	C. S. Higgins	
G-RVSE	Van's RV-6	K. R. H. Wingate (G-USRV)	
G-RVSG	Van's RV-9A	S. Gerrish	
G-RVSK	Van's RV-9A	D. A. Kenworthy	
G-RVSP	Van's RV-7	S. P. Wakeham & P. Nayeri	
G-RVSR	Van's RV-8	R. K. & S. W. Elders	

Notes	Reg	Type	Owner or Operator
	G-RVST	Van's RV-6	A. F. Vizoso (G-BXYX)
	G-RVSX	Van's RV-6	S. A. Holy
	G-RVTA	Van's RV-7	A. G. Andrew
	G-RVTB	Van's RV-7	T. M. Bootyman (G-CIWM)
	G-RVTD	Van's RV-14	S. J. Farrant
	G-RVTE	Van's RV-6	E. McShane & T. Feeny
	G-RVTN	Van's RV-10	P. M. Richer & S. J. Haley
	G-RVTP	Van's RV-7	T. Phillips
	G-RVTT	Van's RV-7	R. L. Mitcham
	G-RVTW	Van's RV-12	A. P. Watkins
	G-RVTX	Van's RV-8	M. J. Tetlow
	G-RVUK	Van's RV-7	P. D. G. Grist
	G-RVVI	Van's RV-6	P. J. Pengilly
	G-RVXA	Van's RV-10	J. A. Holland
	G-RVXP	Van's RV-3B	A. N. Buchan
	G-RVZZ	Van's RV-7	D. R. Gilbert
	G-RWAY	Rotorway Executive 162F	E. Z. Amaira (G-URCH)
	G-RWCA	PA-18-150 Super Cub	R. J. Williamson
	G-RWDI	Van's RV-8	R. W. Davies (G-NISH)
	G-RWIA	Robinson R22 Beta	S. A. Wolski (G-BOEZ)
	G-RWIN	Rearwin 175	S. F. Smith
	G-RWOD	Dan Rihn DR.107 One Design	R. S. Wood
	G-RWSS	Denney Kitfox Mk 2	D. Reilly
	G-RWWW	WS-55 Whirlwind HCC.12 (XR486)★	IHM/Weston-super-Mare
	G-RYDR	Rotorsport UK MT-03	U. Junger
	G-RYFF	Agusta A. 109S Grand	Bandersnatch Ltd Partnership Inc (G-DEUP/G-FUFU)
	G-RYMA	Boeing 737-8200	Ryanair UK Ltd
	G-RYNS	PA-32-301FT Cherokee Six	D. A. Earle
	G-RYON	Mudry CAP-231	Ryan Lincoln Jetson (RLJ) Aviation (G-CPII)
	G-RYPE	DG Flugzeugbau DG-1000T	DG-1000T Partners
	G-RYPH	Mainair Blade 912	P. J. Kirkpatrick
	G-RZEE	Schleicher ASW-19B	R. Christopherson
	G-SAAA	Flight Design CTSW	J. J. Bodnarec
	G-SAAR	Agusta Westland AW-189	Bristow Helicopters Ltd
	G-SABA	PA-28R-201T Turbo Cherokee Arrow III	Saba Flying Group (G-BFEN)
	G-SACH	Stoddard-Hamilton Glastar	R. S. Holt
	G-SACI	PA-28-161 Cherokee Warrior II	PJC (Leasing) Ltd
	G-SACM	TL2000UK Sting Carbon	N. Turck
	G-SACN	Scheibe SF-25C Falke	The RAF Gliding and Soaring Association
	G-SACO	PA-28-161 Cherokee Warrior II	Stapleford Flying Club Ltd
	G-SACR	PA-28-161 Cadet	Sherburn Aero Club Ltd
	G-SACS	PA-28-161 Cadet	Sherburn Aero Club Ltd
	G-SACT	PA-28-161 Cadet	Sherburn Aero Club Ltd
	G-SACW	Aero AT-3 R100	J. Burndred
	G-SADB	Diamond DA.42M Twin Star	Skyborne Aviation Training Ltd
	G-SADK	Diamond DA.40D Star	Romeo Golf Aviation Ltd
	G-SAEA	Vickers Armstrongs Spitfire LF XVI E	M. Harris
	G-SAEB	Supermarine Spitfire LF XVI E	M. Harris
	G-SAFI	CP.1320 Super Emeraude	C. S. Carleton-Smith
	G-SAGA	Grob G.109B	M. C. Downey
	G-SAGE	Luscombe 8A Silvaire	C. Howell (G-AKTL)
	G-SAHI	Trago Mills SAH-1	Aerial Vocations Ltd
	G-SAIG	Robinson R44 II	J. H. Garrioch t/a Jaspa
	G-SAJA	Schempp-Hirth Discus 2	J. G. Arnold
	G-SAJC	Embraer EMB 145EP	Loganair Ltd (G-RJXF)
	G-SAJD	Embraer EMB 145EP	Loganair Ltd (G-RJXI)
	G-SAJE	Embraer EMB 145EP	Loganair Ltd (G-RJXH)
	G-SAJF	Embraer EMB-145EP	Loganair Ltd (G-RJXE)
	G-SAJG	Embraer EMB 145EP	Loganair Ltd (G-EMBI)
	G-SAJH	Embraer EMB 145EP	Loganair Ltd (G-EMBJ)
	G-SAJI	Embraer EMB 145EP	Loganair Ltd (G-EMBN)
	G-SAJJ	Embraer EMB 145EP	Loganair Ltd (G-RJXB)
	G-SAJK	Embraer EMB 145EP	Loganair Ltd (G-RJXC)
	G-SAJL	Embraer EMB 145EP	Loganair Ltd (G-RJXA)
	G-SAJM	Diamond DA.42 Twin Star	Skyborne Aviation Training Ltd (G-CJFO)
	G-SAJN	Embraer EMB 145EP	Loganair Ltd (G-RJXD)

Reg	Type	Owner or Operator	Notes
G-SAJT	Embraer EMB 135ER	BAE Systems (Corporate Air Travel) Ltd (G-RJXL)	
G-SALA	PA-32-300 Cherokee Six	Sala Aviation Ltd	
G-SALW	Diamond DA.42 Twin Star	Skyborne Aviation Training Ltd	
G-SAMB	Diamond DA.42 Twin Star	Skyborne Aviation Training Ltd	
G-SAMC	Ikarus C42 FB100	C. A. & C. D. Spence	
G-SAMG	Grob G.109B	A. A. May & P. M. Scheiwiller G-SAMG	
G-SAMZ	Cessna 150D	A. J. Taylor (G-ASSO)	
G-SANJ	Guimbal Cabri G2	Wizzjet Aviation Ltd	
G-SANT	Schempp-Hirth Discus bT	S. Cervantes (G-JPIP)	
G-SAOC	Schempp-Hirth Discus 2cT	The Royal Air Force Gliding and Soaring Association	
G-SAPA	Robinson R66	C. R, L. A & S. E. Hewgill	
G-SAPC	Diamond DA.42 Twin Star	Skyborne Aviation Training Ltd (G-COMS)	
G-SAPI	PA-28-181 Cherokee Archer II	Biggleswade Flying Group Ltd	
G-SAPM	SOCATA TB20 Trinidad	G-SAPM Flying Group (G-EWFN)	
G-SARA	PA-28-181 Cherokee Archer II	Clifton Aviation Ltd	
G-SARJ	P & M Quik GT450	M. Carter	
G-SARM	Ikarus C.42 FB80	G-SARM Group	
G-SARP	Cessna R182RG	Top Gun Indomitable Aces, Unipessoal LDA/Portugal	
G-SARV	Van's RV-4	Hinton Flying Group	
G-SASC	Beech B200C Super King Air	Gama Aviation (UK) Ltd	
G-SASD	Beech B200C Super King Air	Gama Aviation (UK) Ltd	
G-SASF	Scheibe SF-25C Rotor-Falke	The RAF Gliding and Soaring Association	
G-SASG	Schleicher ASW-27-18E	The 29E Syndicate	
G-SASI	CZAW Sportcruiser	K. W. Allan	
G-SASK	PA-31P Pressurised Navajo	Middle East Business Club Ltd (G-BFAM)	
G-SASM	Westland Scout AH.Mk.1 (XV138)	Armourgeddon Holdings Ltd	
G-SASO	MD Helicopters MD.900 Explorer	Specialist Aviation Services Ltd	
G-SASS	MBB-BK 117D-2	Babcock Mission Critical Services Onshore Ltd	
G-SATI	Cameron Sphere 105 SS balloon	M. A. Sterling	
G-SATL	Cameron Sphere 105 SS balloon	M. A. Sterling	
G-SATM	Diamond DA.42M Twin Star	Skyborne Aviation Training Ltd	
G-SATN	PA-25-260 Pawnee C	London Gliding Club Proprietary Ltd	
G-SAUK	Rans S-6-ES Coyote II	D. C. March	
G-SAUL	Robin HR.200-160	J. C. Wignall	
G-SAUP	Slingsby T.67M-200 Firefly	Chris Wade Aviation Ltd (G-ONES)	
G-SAUR	Moravan Zlin Z-242L	Skyborne Aviation Training Ltd	
G-SAVI	Bell 505 Jet Ranger X	Saviate LP Inc (G-TOWY)	
G-SAVY	Savannah VG Jabiru(1)	S. P. Yardley	
G-SAWG	Scheibe SF.25C Falke	The RAF Gliding and Soaring Association Ltd	
G-SAWI	PA-32RT-300T Turbo Lance II	F. Grima/Malta	
G-SAWS	Ultramagic M-90 balloon	G. A. Butler & Sons Ltd	
G-SAXL	Schempp-Hirth Duo Discus T	The Royal Air Force Gliding and Soaring Association	
G-SAXT	Schempp-Hirth Duo Discus Xt	The Royal Air Force Gliding and Soaring Association	
G-SAYS	RAF 2000 GTX-SE gyroplane	N. Cannavo	
G-SAYX	Cessna 152	Aero Club de Portugal/Portugal	
G-SAZM	Piper J-3C-65 Cub	A. L. M. O'Hare	
G-SAZY	Jabiru J400	I. A. Pereira	
G-SAZZ	CP.328 Super Emeraude	D. J. Long	
G-SBAG	Phoenix Currie Wot	R. W. Clarke (G-BFAH)	
G-SBDB	Remos GX	A. M. Peters	
G-SBII	Steen Skybolt	K. G., P. D. & P. J. Begley	
G-SBNM	Bombardier BD700-1A10 Global 6500	Concierge U Ltd	
G-SBOL	Steen Skybolt	Angus Skybolt	
G-SBOY	PA-28-181 Cherokee Archer III	W. E. Morgan (G-LACD/G-BYBG)	
G-SBRK	Aero AT-3 R100	Lesa Aviation Ltd	
G-SBRV	Zenair CH.250 Zenith	B. R. Vickers	
G-SBSB	Diamond DA.40NG Star	Diamond Aviation Training Ltd	
G-SBST	Pilatus PC-9A	SR Aviation Ltd	
G-SBUG	Van's RV-4	B. C. Faulkner	
G-SBUS	BN-2A-26 Islander	Isles of Scilly Skybus Ltd (G-BMMH)	
G-SBVT	Schempp-Hirth Ventus-3T	S. Barter	
G-SCAA	Eurocopter EC135 T2	Babcock Mission Critical Services Onshore Ltd (G-SASB)	
G-SCCA	Cessna 510 Citation Mustang	SCCA Ltd	
G-SCCZ	CZAW Sportcruiser	S. R. Thomas & J. P. McCreedy	

Notes	Reg	Type	Owner or Operator
	G-SCFC	Ultramagic S-90 balloon	J. S. Russon
	G-SCHI	Eurocopter AS.350B2 Ecureuil	Rigby Group (RG) plc
	G-SCIP	SOCATA TB20 Trinidad GT	D. E. Kingsnorth
	G-SCIR	PA-31 Navajo C	2 Excel Aviation Ltd
	G-SCLN	Pilatus PC-12/47E	Oriens Flight Operations Ltd
	G-SCLX	FLS Aerospace Sprint 160	Aero Sprint Group (G-PLYM)
	G-SCMG	Ikarus C42 FB80	C. J. Bishop & B. N. Thresher
	G-SCMR	PA-31 Navajo	2 Excel Aviation Ltd
	G-SCNN	Schempp-Hirth Standard Cirrus	G. C. Short
	G-SCOF	Eurocopter AS.355N Ecureuil 2	Helicompany Ltd (G-LINE)
	G-SCOL	Gippsland GA-8 Airvan	Parachuting Aircraft Ltd
	G-SCOP	SOCATA TB-9 Tampico	P. R. Keeling
	G-SCPD	Escapade 912 (1)	C. W. Potts
	G-SCPI	CZAW Sportcruiser	Barton Sportcruiser Group
	G-SCPL	PA-28-140 Cherokee	Falcon Flying Services Ltd (G-BPVL)
	G-SCRZ	CZAW Sportcruiser	R. Vora
	G-SCSC	CZAW Sportcruiser	R. Powers
	G-SCTA	Westland Scout AH.1 (XV126)	T. L. Hobbs
	G-SCTR	PA-31 Navajo C	2 Excel Aviation Ltd
	G-SCUB	PA-18-135 Super Cub (542447)	R. A. Stephens
	G-SCUL	Rutan Cozy	K. R. W. Scull
	G-SCZR	CZAW Sportcruiser	R. S. O'Carroll & R. J. Johnston
	G-SDAT	Flight Design CTSW	S. P. Pearson
	G-SDFM	Aerotechnik EV-97 Eurostar	G-SDFM Eurostar Group
	G-SDIM	Spacek SD-1 Minisport	W. A. Ritchie
	G-SDOA	Eurofox 912(S)	G. J. Slater
	G-SDOB	Tecnam P2002-EA Sierra	K. A. Knowles
	G-SDOI	Aeroprakt A.22 Foxbat	A. Assianian
	G-SDOZ	Tecnam P92-EA Echo Super	E. Gallacher
	G-SDRV	Van's RV-8	S. M. Dawson
	G-SDTL	Guimbal Cabri G2	Advanced Aviation & Marine Services Ltd
	G-SDTO	Stolp SA.300 Starduster Too	M. J. Golder
	G-SEAF	Hawker Sea Fury FB.11	Patina Ltd (G-BWOL)
	G-SEAI	Cessna U.206G	O. J. Kilkenny
	G-SEAK	Westland Sea King HAR.3	Lift West (Helicopters) Ltd
	G-SEAT	Colt 42A balloon	T. G. Read
	G-SEBN	Skyranger 912S(1)	B. Cook & R. E. Parker
	G-SEBS	Ultramagic M-77 balloon	F9 (Holdings) Ltd
	G-SECS	Ikarus C42 FB80	A. J. Baker
	G-SEDC	Fairchild 24W-46 Argus	P. C. Franzini
	G-SEDO	Cameron N-105 balloon	I. M. Ashpole
	G-SEED	Piper J-3C-65 Cub	J. H. Seed
	G-SEEE	Pegasus Quik GT450	Flying for Freedom Ltd
	G-SEEK	Cessna T.210N	A. Hopper
	G-SEEU	Robinson R44 II	Heli Air Ltd
	G-SEHK	Cessna 182T	Golf HK Ltd
	G-SEJW	PA-28-161 Cherokee Warrior II	Tor Financial Consulting Ltd
	G-SEKR	ISA 180 Seeker	Northern Aircraft Company Ltd
	G-SELA	Cessna 152	Glasgow Prestwick Flight Centre Ltd (G-FLOP)
	G-SELB	PA-28-161 Cherokee Warrior II	POM Flight Training Ltd (G-LFSK)
	G-SELC	Diamond DA42 Twin Star	Stapleford Flying Club Ltd
	G-SELF	Europa	The South East London Flying Group
	G-SELL	Robin DR.400/180	A. J. Harding
	G-SELY	Agusta-Bell 206B JetRanger 3	M. D. Tracey
	G-SEMR	Cessna T206H Turbo Stationair	Cardelis LLP
	G-SENE	PA-34-200T Seneca II	S & T Aviation Ltd
	G-SENS	Eurocopter EC.135T2+	Saville Air Services
	G-SENX	PA-34-200T Seneca II	First Air Ltd (G-DARE/G-WOTS/G-SEVL)
	G-SENZ	Eurocopter EC.120B Colibri	Senzati Ltd (G-DLUX/G-IGPW/G-CBRI)
	G-SEPT	Cameron N-105 balloon	J. J. Holmes
	G-SERL	SOCATA TB10 Tobago	G. C. Jarvis (G-LANA)
	G-SERV	Cameron N-105 balloon	S. J. Colin
	G-SETG	PA-28RT-201 Cherokee Arrow IV	LS Airmotive Ltd
	G-SETI	Cameron Sky 80-16 balloon	R. P. Allan
	G-SEUK	Cameron TV-80 ss balloon	Mobberley Balloon Collection
	G-SEVA	SE-5A (replica) (F141:G) ★	Montrose Air Station Heritage Centre
	G-SEVN	Van's RV-7	N. Reddish
	G-SEXE	Scheibe SF.25C Falke	G-SEXE Syndicate
	G-SEXX	PA-28-161 Cherokee Warrior II	Weald Air Services Ltd

Reg	Type	Owner or Operator	Notes
G-SEXY	AA-1 Yankee ★	Speke Aviation Heritage Group (G-AYLM)	
G-SEZA	Schleicher ASW-20C	R. M. Housden	
G-SFAR	Ikarus C42 FB100	Ulster Flying Club (1961) Ltd	
G-SFCM	P & M PulsR	J. D. Harrison	
G-SFLA	Ikarus C42 FB100	Solent Flight Ltd	
G-SFLB	Ikarus C42 FB80	Solent Flight Ltd	
G-SFSA	American Champion 8KCAB	A. C. Petteford	
G-SFSL	Cameron Z-105 balloon	A. J. Gregory	
G-SFTZ	Slingsby T.67M Firefly 160	Slingsby T.67M Group	
G-SGCA	Aeropro Eurofox 2K	Southdown Gliding Club Ltd	
G-SGCB	Eurofox 2K	Southdown Gliding Club Ltd	
G-SGEN	Ikarus C.42 FB 80	G. A. Arturi	
G-SGFE	Liberty XL-2	I. Fidler (G-OLAR)	
G-SGNT	Skylark	N. H. Townsend	
G-SGSE	PA-28-181 Cherokee Archer II	U. Patel (G-BOJX)	
G-SGTS	Viking DHC.6-400 Twin Otter	Loganair Ltd	
G-SGWA	Ikarus C42 FB100	A. J. Williams	
G-SHAD	Cameron Z-90 balloon	R. Parr	
G-SHAK	Cameron Cabin SS balloon	Magical Adventures Ltd (G-ODIS)	
G-SHAR	Cessna 182T Skylane	G. N. Clarkson	
G-SHAZ	Guimbal Cabri G2	Elite Helicopters	
G-SHBA	Cessna F.152	Paul's Planes Ltd	
G-SHBH	Ultramagic H-77 balloon	S. W. Herd	
G-SHED	PA-28-181 Cherokee Archer II	G-SHED Flying Group (G-BRAU)	
G-SHEE	P & M Quik GT450	C. J. Millership	
G-SHEZ	Mainair Pegasus Quik	R. J. Wells	
G-SHHH	Glaser-Dirks DG-100G	G-SHHH Group	
G-SHIM	CFM Streak Shadow	P. D. Babin	
G-SHIP	PA-23-250 Aztec ★	Midland Air Museum/Coventry	
G-SHKI	Ikarus C42 FB80	K. S. Daniels & G. R. Barker	
G-SHLS	Agusta A109E Power	Sloane Helicopters Ltd	
G-SHMB	Aero L-39ZA Albatross	L39 Aviation Ltd	
G-SHMI	Evektor EV-97 Team EuroStar UK	Mike India Flying Group	
G-SHMN	Alpi Pioneer 300 Hawk	A. R. McKillen (G-GKEV)	
G-SHNC	TLAC Shark 600 UK	N. W. Charles	
G-SHOC	Zenair CH.701SP	A. Mitchell (G-WFIT/G-OBAP)	
G-SHOW	MS.733 Alycon	P. Cartwright & F. A. Forster	
G-SHRK	Enstrom 280C-UK	Shark Helicopters Ltd (G-BGMX)	
G-SHRS	Boeing 737-8B5F	BAE Systems (Corporate Air Travel) Ltd	
G-SHRT	Robinson R44 II	Hingley Aviation Ltd	
G-SHRU	Guimbal Cabri G2	A. Verma (G-UMBL)	
G-SHSH	Europa	S. G. Hayman & J. Price	
G-SHSP	Cessna 172S	Shropshire Aero Club Ltd	
G-SHUC	Rans S-6-ESA Coyote II	E. W. Calvin (G-MYKN)	
G-SHUF	Mainair Blade	R. A. Needham	
G-SHUG	PA-28R-201T Turbo Cherokee Arrow III	G-SHUG Ltd	
G-SHUI	Cessna 680A Citation Latitude	Air Charter Scotland Ltd	
G-SHUV	Aerosport Woody Pusher	J. R. Wraigh	
G-SHWF	GAC/NLH 56K12G balloon	G. A. & I. Chadwick	
G-SHWK	Cessna 172S	Cambridge Aero Club Ltd	
G-SIBK	Raytheon Beech A36 Bonanza	W. Robson	
G-SICA	BN-2B-20 Islander	Shetland Leasing and Property Development Ltd (G-SLAP)	
G-SICB	BN-2B-20 Islander	Shetlands Islands Council (G-NESU/G-BTVN)	
G-SIGN	PA-39-160 Twin Comanche	D. Buttle	
G-SIIE	Christen Pitts S-2B Special	Wild Thing (G-SKYD)	
G-SIII	Extra EA.300	Owners of G-SIII	
G-SIIO	Schempp-Hirth Ventus 3T	P. J. Harvey	
G-SIIX	PA-32-260 Cherokee Six	EV Aviation Ltd (G-CHFK)	
G-SIJJ	North American P-51D-NA Mustang	R. W. Tyrell	
G-SIJW	SA Bulldog Srs 120/121 (XX630:5)	M. Miles	
G-SILS	Pietenpol Skyscout	D. Silsbury	
G-SIMM	Ikarus C.42 FB 100 VLA	G. P. Watts & A. P. Wilkinson	
G-SIMY	PA-32-300 Cherokee Six	I. Simpson (G-OCPF/G-BOCH)	
G-SINK	Schleicher ASH-25	K. Atkinson	
G-SINN	EV-97 Eurostar SL	Northern Flying Group	
G-SIPA	SIPA 903	A. C. Leak & G. S. Dilland (G-BGBM)	

Notes	Reg	Type	Owner or Operator
	G-SIPP	Lindstrand lbl-35a Cloudhopper balloon	A. R. Rich
	G-SIRD	Robinson R44 II	TKN International Ltd
	G-SIRE	Sky Ranger Swift 912S(1)	P. W. F. Coleman
	G-SIRO	Dassault Falcon 900EX	Condor Aviation LLP
	G-SIRS	Cessna 560XL Citation Excel	London Executive Aviation Ltd
	G-SIRT	Leonardo AW109SP Grand New	Gall Air LLP
	G-SISI	Schempp-Hirth Duo Discus	R. Puritz
	G-SISU	P & M Quik GT450	P. J. Doherty
	G-SISX	Pitts S-1S Special	A. J. & C. A. J. Millson
	G-SITA	Pegasus Quantum 15-912	P. N. Thompson
	G-SIVJ	Westland Gazelle HT.2	Skytrace (UK) Ltd (G-CBSG)
	G-SIXC	Douglas DC-6B ★	The DC-6 Diner/Coventry
	G-SIXD	PA-32-300 Cherokee Six D	G-SIXD Group
	G-SIXE	PA-32-260 Cherokee Six	Aerobility
	G-SIXP	Cameron Sport-90 balloon	Sarnia Balloon Group
	G-SIXT	PA-28-161 Warrior II	Airways Aero Associations Ltd (G-BSSX)
	G-SIXX	Colt 77A balloon	S. Drawbridge
	G-SIXY	Van's RV-6	C. J. Hall & C. R. P. Hamlett
	G-SIZZ	Jabiru J400	K. J. Betteley
	G-SJBB	Robin DR400/140B	SJ Aircraft
	G-SJBI	Pitts S-2C Special	S. L. Walton
	G-SJEF	AutoGyro Cavalon	J. Smith
	G-SJEN	Ikarus C42 FB80 ★	Museum of Flight/East Fortune
	G-SJKR	Lindstrand LBL-90A balloon	P. Richardson
	G-SJMW	SD-1 Minisport	M. A. Wood
	G-SJPC	Van's RV-8	J. T. Garrett
	G-SJPI	Dynamic WT9 UK	D. C. Maybury
	G-SKAN	Cessna F.172M	M. Richardson & J. Williams (G-BFKT)
	G-SKAZ	Aero AT-3 R100	The Moray Flying Club (1990)
	G-SKCI	Rutan Vari-Eze	O. J. Wheeldon
	G-SKFY	Robinson R44 II	Skyfly Air Ltd (G-GRGE)
	G-SKIE	Steen Skybolt	R. Farrer
	G-SKKY	Cessna 172S Skyhawk	Skytrek Air Services
	G-SKNC	AutoGyro MTOSport	C. J. Rose
	G-SKNG	Westlasnd Sea King HAR Mk.3 (XZ597)	Lift West (Helicopters) Ltd
	G-SKOT	Cameron V-42 balloon	S. A. Laing
	G-SKPG	Best Off Skyranger 912 (2)	T. Farncombe
	G-SKPH	Yakovlev Yak-50	R. S. Partridge-Hicks & I. C. Austin (G-BWWH)
	G-SKPP	Eurocopter EC.120B Colbri	Bliss Aviation Ltd & Switchdata Investments Ltd (G-MKII)
	G-SKRA	Sky Ranger 912S (1)	J. S. Peer
	G-SKRG	Sky Ranger 912 (2)	W. J. Dowty
	G-SKSW	Sky Ranger Swift 912S	J. & J. A. Pegram
	G-SKTN	Avro 696 Shackleton MR.Mk.2 (WR963) ★	Yorkshire Air Museum/Elvington
	G-SKUA	Stoddard-Hamilton Glastar	K. M. Bowen (G-LEZZ/G-BYCR)
	G-SKUB	TLAC Sherwood Cub	J. D. Cotterill
	G-SKYC	Slingsby T.67M Firefly	K. Taylor (G-BLDP)
	G-SKYF	SOCATA TB10 Tobago	W. L. McNeil
	G-SKYL	Cessna 182S	R. G. Gee
	G-SKYO	Slingsby T.67M-200	Skyboard Aerobatics Ltd
	G-SKYT	I.I.I. Sky Arrow 650TC	W. M. Bell & S. J. Brooks
	G-SLAY	Diamond DA40 NG	Fabro Verde Ltd
	G-SLBD	Sling 2	B. Davies
	G-SLCE	Cameron C-80 balloon	A. M. Holly
	G-SLCT	Diamond DA42NG Twin Star	Stapleford Flying Club Ltd
	G-SLEA	Mudry/CAARP CAP-10B	M. J. M. Jenkins, N. R. Thorburn, R. Harris & I. Cameron
	G-SLGG	TAF Sling 4 TSI	A. J. Pactat
	G-SLGZ	TAF Sling 2	P. G. Hooper
	G-SLIP	Reality Easy Raider J2.2(3)	J. Riley & E. C. Murgatroyd
	G-SLIV	TAF Sling 4	Sling Syndicate G-SLIV
	G-SLNG	TAF Sling 4	R. S. D. Wheeler & R. J. H. Davis
	G-SLNT	Flight Design CTSW	G-SLNT Syndicate
	G-SLPC	TAF Sling 4 TSI	Aakos Ltd
	G-SLVA	Pilatus PC-24	Select Aircrafts Ltd
	G-SLWN	Cameron TR-84 balloon	Ballooning Ltd (G-CMZM)
	G-SLYR	Gnat Mk.1	Heritage Aircraft Ltd
	G-SLYY	Ultramagic M-105 balloon	J. A. Lawton

Reg	Type	Owner or Operator	Notes
G-SLZT	TAF Sling 2	D. J. Pilkington	
G-SMAR	Schempp-Hirth Arcus M	Highland Gliding Club Ltd	
G-SMAT	SA Bulldog Srs.120/121 (XX658:07)	Skysmart MRO Ltd (G-BZPS)	
G-SMBM	Pegasus Quantum 15-912	B. Cook	
G-SMDH	Europa XS	A. P. Wilkie & S. M. Thomas	
G-SMIG	Cameron O-65 balloon	R. D. Parry	
G-SMIL	Lindstrand LBL-105A balloon	A. L. Wade	
G-SMKM	Cirrus SR20	SR Bus Ltd	
G-SMKR	Eurofox 912(S)	S. M. Kenyon-Roberts	
G-SMLE	Robinson R44 II	English Braids Ltd	
G-SMLI	Groppo Trail	A. M. Wilson	
G-SMLZ	Groppo Trail Mk.2	A. M. Wilson	
G-SMMA	Cessna F.406 Caravan II	Secretary of State for Scotland per Environmental and Rural Affairs Department	
G-SMMB	Cessna F.406 Caravan II	Secretary of State for Scotland per Environmental and Rural Affairs Department	
G-SMMF	Lindstrand LBL-77A balloon	M. & S. Mitchell	
G-SMRS	Cessna 172F	M. R. Sarling	
G-SMRY	Sikorsky S-76C	Starspeed Ltd	
G-SMSP	Super Marine Spitfire Mk.26B (JG241:ZX-J)	S. J. D. Hall	
G-SMYK	PZL-Swidnik PW-5 Smyk	P. R. Gammell	
G-SNCA	PA-34-200T Seneca II	Social Infrastructure Ltd	
G-SNDR	Supermarine S5 Replica	W. B. Hosie	
G-SNDS	Cirrus SR20	Shu Aviation Ltd	
G-SNDZ	Cirrus SR22T	Sands Wealth Management Ltd	
G-SNEL	Aeriane Swift Light PAS	A. Snell	
G-SNEV	CFM Streak Shadow SA	A. Child	
G-SNGZ	TAF Sling 2	M. L. Roland	
G-SNKE	Ultramagic M-90 balloon	J. J. Davis	
G-SNOP	Europa	M. L. Robinson-Boulton (G-DESL/G-WWWG)	
G-SNOT	Xtremeair XA42	S. B. R. Lovering	
G-SNOW	Cameron V-77 balloon	I. Welsford	
G-SNOZ	Europa	J. D. Amos (G-DONZ)	
G-SNSG	Agusta Westland AW139	Waypoint Asset Co.3 Ltd	
G-SNSI	Agusta Westland AW139	CHC Scotia Ltd (G-FTOM)	
G-SNSY	Agusta Westland AW139	CHC Scotia Ltd (G-NHVN)	
G-SNUG	Skyranger 912S(1)	G. L. Hayes & L. Searle	
G-SNUZ	PA-28-161 Cherokee Warrior II	Freedom Aviation Ltd	
G-SNXA	Sonex	S. K. Ridge	
G-SOAF	BAC.167 Strikemaster Mk. 82A (425)	Strikemaster Flying Club	
G-SOBI	PA-28-181 Cherokee Archer II	G-SOBI Flying Group	
G-3OCK	Mainair Pegasus Quik	K. R. McCartney	
G-SOCT	Yakovlev Yak-50 (AR-B)	M. P. Blokland	
G-SOKO	Soko P-2 Kraguj (30149)	D. G. Hart (G-BRXK)	
G-SOLA	Aero Designs Star-Lite SL.1	G. P. Thomas	
G-SOLE	Cessna 525 Citation M2	Catreus AOC Ltd	
G-SONA	SOCATA TB10 Tobago	G-SONA Group (G-BIBI)	
G-SONX	Sonex	K. A. W. Ashcroft	
G-COOC	Hughes 369HS	R.J.H. Strong (G-BRRX)	
G-SOOS	Colt 21A balloon	P. J. Stapley	
G-SOOT	PA-28-180 Cherokee	R. J. Hunter (G-AVNM)	
G-SOOZ	Rans S-6-ES Coyote II	T. A. Waudby	
G-SOPC	Replica Sopwith Camel	C. I. Law & P. Hoeft	
G-SORA	Glaser-Dirks DG.500/22	G-SORA Syndicate	
G-SORG	Diamond DA50C	Diamond Flight Training Co.Ltd	
G-SOUT	Van's RV-8	J. M. Southern (G-CDPJ)	
G-SOVB	Learjet 45	Zenith Aviation Ltd (G-OLDJ)	
G-SOVH	Cessna 525 Citationjet	Saxonair Charter Ltd	
G-SOVJ	Cessna 525 Citationjet	Saxonair Charter Ltd	
G-SOVR	Cessna 525 Citationjet	Saxonair Charter Ltd	
G-SPAM	Avid Aerobat (modified)	M. Durcan	
G-SPCI	Cessna 182P	K. Brady (G-GUMS/G-CBMN)	
G-SPCY	Embraer EMB-135BJ Legacy 650	London Executive Aviation Ltd (G-OTGL)	
G-SPCZ	CZAW Sportcruiser	C. P. Davis	
G-SPDY	Raj Hamsa X'Air Hawk	D. R. Sutton	
G-SPED	Alpi Pioneer 300	R. B. Shaw	
G-SPFX	Rutan Cozy	B. D. Tutty	

Notes	Reg	Type	Owner or Operator
	G-SPHU	Eurocopter EC 135T2+	Babcock Mission Critical Services Onshore Ltd
	G-SPID	Ultramagic S-90 balloon	A. Fawcett
	G-SPIN	Pitts S-2A Special	P. Avery
	G-SPIP	SNCAN Stampe SV.4C	A. G. Solleveld (G-BTIO)
	G-SPIT	VS.379 Spitfire FR.XIV (MV268)	Fighter Aviation Engineering Ltd (G-BGHB)
	G-SPIV	Agusta A109E Power	Myheli Ltd
	G-SPJT	Cessna 550 Citation Bravo	Dragonfly Aviation Services Ltd
	G-SPLU	Skyranger Nynja	S. W. Plume
	G-SPMI	Dassault Falcon 6X	Trinity Aviation Ltd
	G-SPMM	Skyranger Swift 912S(1)	A. W. Paterson
	G-SPOG	Jodel DR.1050	S. M. S. Smith (G-AXVS)
	G-SPOK	Robinson R22	Heliraptor Ltd (G-BOCN)
	G-SPRK	Van's RV-4	S. A. Reid
	G-SPRX	Van's RV-4	Sunset Displays Ltd
	G-SPRY	Diamond S-105 balloon	Perfect Paint
	G-SPTR	Robinson R44 II	M. A. Beadman
	G-SPTT	Diamond DA.40D Star	Acrobat Ltd (G-OCCS)
	G-SPTX	Dassault Falcon 7X	Concierge U Ltd
	G-SPUN	Grob G.115D	Modern Air (UK) Ltd
	G-SPUT	Yakovlev Yak-52	D. J. Hopkinson (G-BXAV)
	G-SPVI	SOCATA TB.20 Trinidad	Teegee Group
	G-SPXX	VS.356 Spitfire F.22	P. R. Arnold
	G-SPYZ	Robinson R66	HQ Aviation Ltd
	G-SRAH	Schempp-Hirth Mini-Nimbus C	R. A. Hall
	G-SRCB	Van's RV-12	C. Burgess
	G-SRII	Easy Raider 503	K. Myles
	G-SROE	Westland Scout AH.1 (XP907)	Saunders-Roe Helicopter Ltd
	G-SROY	PA-28-180 Cherokee E	Falcon Flying Services (G-DLTR/G-AYAV)
	G-SRRA	Tecnam P2002-EA Sierra	J. Dunn
	G-SRTW	Cirrus SR22	NRS Aviation Ltd
	G-SRWN	PA-28-161 Cherokee Warrior II	Turweston Flying Club Ltd (G-MAND/G-BRKT)
	G-SRXX	Cirrus SR20	A9 Leasing LLP
	G-SRYY	Europa XS	Foxball Ltd
	G-SRZZ	Cirrus SR22	A. Bodaghi
	G-SSCL	MDH Hughes 369E	Heli-Odyssey LLP
	G-SSDI	SD-1 Minisport	R. N. Griffiths
	G-SSDR	Scooter	J. Attard
	G-SSIX	Rans S.6-116 Coyote II	M. A. Cayford
	G-SSKY	BN-2B-26 Islander	Isles of Scilly Skybus Ltd (G-BSWT)
	G-SSTI	Cameron N-105 balloon	A. A. Brown
	G-SSVB	VS.349 Spitfire LF.Vb	T. W. Gilbert (G-CGBI)
	G-SSWV	Sportavia Fournier RF-5B	Fournier Flying Group
	G-SSXL	Just Superstol XL	P. T. Price
	G-STAC	Lindstrand LTL Series 1-105 balloon	R. K. Scott
	G-STAV	Cameron O-84 balloon	A. Pollock
	G-STAY	Cessna FR.172K	STAY Flying Group
	G-STBA	Boeing 777-336ER	British Airways PLC
	G-STBB	Boeing 777-36NER	British Airways PLC
	G-STBC	Boeing 777-36NER	British Airways PLC
	G-STBD	Boeing 777-36NER	British Airways PLC
	G-STBE	Boeing 777-36NER	British Airways PLC
	G-STBF	Boeing 777-336ER	British Airways PLC
	G-STBG	Boeing 777-336ER	British Airways PLC
	G-STBH	Boeing 777-336ER	British Airways PLC
	G-STBI	Boeing 777-336ER	British Airways PLC
	G-STBJ	Boeing 777-336ER	British Airways PLC
	G-STBK	Boeing 777-336ER	British Airways PLC
	G-STBL	Boeing 777-336ER	British Airways PLC
	G-STBM	Boeing 777-300ER	British Airways PLC
	G-STBN	Boeing 777-300ER	British Airways PLC
	G-STBO	Boeing 777-300ER	British Airways PLC
	G-STBP	Boeing 777-300ER	British Airways PLC
	G-STBT	Cameron N-42 balloon	L. J. Wigfield (G-BVLC)
	G-STDO	BRM Aero Bristell NG Speed Wing	R. de Pascalis
	G-STEA	PA-28R-200 Cherokee Arrow	D. W. Breden
	G-STEE	Aerotechnik EV-97 Eurostar	S. G. Beeson
	G-STEM	Stemme S.10V	A. M. Booth
	G-STEN	Stemme S.10 (4)	R. S. Stuart

Reg	Type	Owner or Operator	Notes
G-STES	Europa XS	C. J. Lowrie	
G-STEU	Rolladen-Schneider LS6-18W	F. K. Russell	
G-STFO	TL.2000UK Sting Carbon S4	K. Handley	
G-STIX	Van's RV-7	R. D. S. Jackson	
G-STJP	TL2000 Sting S4	J. M. Palmer	
G-STKM	BAC 167 Strikemaster Mk.80A	Viper Classic Aircraft Ltd	
G-STNE	Westland Bell 47G-3B-1	H. Cole	
G-STNG	TL2000UK Sting Carbon	P. S. Ganczakowski	
G-STOD	ICP MXP-740 Savannah VG Jabiru(1)	L. J. Boardman	
G-STOO	Stolp Starduster Too	A. K. Robinson	
G-STOW	Cameron 90 Wine Box SS balloon	Flying Enterprises	
G-STPK	Lambert Mission M108	S. T. P. Kember	
G-STPL	Vickers Supermarine Spitfire 1	517 Ltd	
G-STRG	Cyclone AX2000	D. R. Thompson	
G-STRK	CFM Streak Shadow SA	E. McCall	
G-STRV	Van's RV-14	S. D. Hicks	
G-STSN	Stinson 108-3 Voyager	M. S. Colebrook (G-BHMR)	
G-STUA	Aerotek Pitts S-2A Special	E. J. Attenborough	
G-STUE	Europa	Stones Aviation Holdings Ltd	
G-STUI	Pitts S-2AE	S. L. Goldspink & J-M. M. Munn	
G-STUM	Diamond DA.50C	Reclamet Ltd	
G-STUN	TL2000UK Sting Carbon	D. Russell (G-KEVT)	
G-STUU	Bristell NG5 Speed Wing	S. M. Spencer	
G-STUY	Robinson R44 II	Central Helicopters Ltd	
G-STUZ	Lambert Mission M108	C. J. Finnigan	
G-STVL	Lindstrand LBL-77A balloon	L. S. Targett-Parker & A. T. Brown	
G-STVO	Bell 505 Jet Ranger X	Mediatech Consulting Ltd (G-JBHL)	
G-STVT	CZAW Sportcruiser	S. Taylor	
G-STWO	ARV Super 2	R. E. Griffiths	
G-STZZ	TL2000UK Sting Carbon	M. Salt	
G-SUAU	Cameron C-90 balloon	A. Heginbottom	
G-SUCT	Robinson R22 II	Irwin Plant Sales	
G-SUED	Thunder Ax8-90 balloon	P. T. Lickorish (G-PINE)	
G-SUEG	Diamond DA.40 NG Star	Sue Air	
G-SUEI	Diamond DA.42 Twin Star	Sue Air	
G-SUEL	P & M Quik GT450	G-SUEL Syndicate	
G-SUEM	Diamond DA.42 Twin Star	Sue Air	
G-SUEO	Diamond DA.40NG Star	Sue Air	
G-SUER	Bell 206B JetRanger	Aerospeed Ltd (G-CBYX)	
G-SUET	Bell 206B JetRanger	Claysmore AS Ltd (G-BLZN)	
G-SUEV	Diamond DA.40NG Star	Sue Air	
G-SUEY	Bell 206L-1 Long Ranger	Aerospeed Ltd	
G-SUEZ	Agusta-Bell 206B JetRanger 2	Aerospeed Ltd	
G-SUFK	Eurocopter EC 135P2+	West Yorkshire Combined Authority National Police Air Service	
G-SUGR	Embraer EMB-135BJ Legacy 650	Air Charter Scotland Ltd	
G-SUGS	Steen Skybolt	M. D. Sugden	
G-SUKI	PA-38-112 Tomahawk	Merseyflight Ltd (G-RVNB/G-BPNV)	
G-SUKK	Sukhoi Su-29	M. Benshemesh	
G-SULU	Skyranger 912(2)	S. J. Taft (G-SOPH)	
G-SUMM	Skyranger Nynja 912S(1)	A. Summers	
G-SUMO	Skyranger Nynja LS 912S(1)	J. A. Hunt	
G-SUMX	Robinson R22 Beta	Swift Helicopter Services Ltd	
G-SUNB	Airbus A.321-251NX	Jet 2.com	
G-SUNC	Airbus A.321-251NX	Jet 2.com	
G-SUND	Airbus A.321-251NX	Jet 2.com	
G-SUNE	Airbus A.321-251NX	Jet 2.com	
G-SUNF	Airbus A.321-251NX	Jet 2.com	
G-SUNG	Airbus A.321-251NX	Jet 2.com	
G-SUNH	Airbus A.321-251NX	Jet 2.com	
G-SUNJ	Airbus A.321-251NX	Jet 2.com	
G-SUNK	Airbus A.321-251NX	Jet 2.com	
G-SUNL	Airbus A.321-251NX	Jet 2.com	
G-SUNM	Airbus A.321-251NX	Jet 2.com	
G-SUNN	Robinson R44	Virage Aviation LLP	
G-SUNO	Airbus A.321-251NX	Jet 2.com	
G-SUNP	Airbus A.321-251NX	Jet 2.com	
G-SUNR	Airbus A.321-251NX	Jet 2.com	
G-SUNS	Airbus A.321-251NX	Jet 2.com	
G-SUNU	Airbus A.321-251NX	Jet 2.com	

Notes	Reg	Type	Owner or Operator
	G-SUNV	Airbus A.321-251NX	Jet 2.com
	G-SUNW	Airbus A.321-251NX	Jet 2.com
	G-SUNX	Airbus A.321-251NX	Jet 2.com
	G-SUNZ	Airbus A.321-251NX	Jet 2.com
	G-SUPA	PA-18-150 Super Cub	Turweston Flying Club Ltd
	G-SURV	BN-2T-4S Islander	Britten-Norman Aerospace Ltd (G-BVHZ)
	G-SUSE	Europa XS	P. R. Tunney
	G-SUSH	Schleicher ASK-21Mi	S. M. Chapman
	G-SUSI	Cameron V-77 balloon	J. H. Dryden
	G-SUTD	Jabiru UL-D	W. J. Lister & S. Brady
	G-SUTE	Van's RV-8A	S. Woolmington
	G-SUTY	Robinson R44 II	Willpower South West Ltd (G-HOCA)
	G-SUZN	PA-28-161 Cherokee Warrior II	A. J. Gomes
	G-SVAN	Cessna 208B Grand Caravan	Parachuting Caravan Leasing Ltd
	G-SVAS	PA-18-150 Super Cub	Richard Shuttleworth Trustees
	G-SVDG	Jabiru SK	A. J. Purcell
	G-SVEN	Centrair 101A Pegase	G7 Group
	G-SVET	Yakovlev Yak-50	The Assets of the Svetlana Group
	G-SVGL	SNCAN Stampe SV-4A	G. W. Lynch
	G-SVIP	Cessna 421B Golden Eagle II	R. P. Bateman
	G-SVIV	SNCAN Stampe SV.4C	J. E. Keighley
	G-SVNH	Savannah VG Jabiru(1)	K. Harmston (G-CFKV)
	G-SVNN	Cirrus SR22	Aasco Air LLP
	G-SVNT	Learjet 45	Saxonair Charter Ltd
	G-SVNX	Dassault Falcon 7X	Executive Jet Charter Ltd
	G-SWAB	Tiger Cub RL5A Sherwood Ranger XP	D. S. Brown
	G-SWAI	Swift SWO1A	Swift Aircraft Ltd
	G-SWAK	Oldfield Baby Lakes	B. Bryan
	G-SWAT	Robinson R44 II	M. A. Corbett
	G-SWAY	PA-18 Super Cub	S. J. Gaveston & R. L. Brinklow
	G-SWCT	Flight Design CTSW	T. Christian
	G-SWEE	Beech 95-B55 Baron	T. Slotover (G-AZDK)
	G-SWEL	Hughes 369HS	M. A. Crook & A. E. Wright (G-RBUT)
	G-SWIF	VS.541 Swift F.7 (XF114) ★	Solent Sky, Southampton
	G-SWIG	Robinson R44	Autorotation Ltd
	G-SWNS	Robinson R44 II	EBG (Helicopters) Ltd (G-PROJ)
	G-SWON	Pitts S-1S Special	S. L. Goldspink
	G-SWOT	Currie Wot (C3011:S)	M. C. Boddington
	G-SWOW	Cirrus SR22	WOW Aviation LLP
	G-SWRD	Boeing 737-3L9	21T Ltd (G-OGBE)
	G-SWRE	Tecnam P2002-EA Sierra	W. Swire
	G-SWSW	Schempp-Hirth Ventus bT	R. Kalin
	G-SWYF	Skyranger Swift 912(1)	C. Moore & K. J. Bradley
	G-SWYM	CZAW Sportcruiser	R. W. Beal
	G-SXIX	Rans S.19	R. J. Almey
	G-SXVI	Vickers Supermarine Spitfire Mk.XVI	Warbird Experiences Ltd
	G-SYDH	Bell 206B-3 Jet Ranger III	SJH North West Ltd (G-BXNT)
	G-SYFW	Focke-Wulf Fw.190 replica (2+1)	M. V. Brown
	G-SYLA	Beech B200 King Air	ACH Scylla Ltd
	G-SYLJ	Embraer RJ135BJ	Blue Wings Ltd
	G-SYLL	PA-31-350 Navajo Chieftain	Lane Airways Ltd (G-BVYF/G-SAVE)
	G-SYLV	Cessna 208B Grand Caravan	Go Sailing Ltd
	G-SYTH	Flylight Fox 13T/PeaBee	S. Bayne
	G-SYWL	Aero AT-3 R100	Cabaero ASviation Ltd
	G-SZTD	TAF Sling 2	P. A. Kirkham
	G-TAAB	Cirrus SR22	Ddraig Aviation LLP
	G-TAAC	Cirrus SR20	Team TAAC
	G-TAAS	Agusta AW.109SP Grand New	Sloane Helicopters Ltd
	G-TAAT	PA-32-301FT 6X	A. D. Trotter
	G-TACC	SOCATA TB-20 Trinidad	F. Taccogna (G-GVFR/G-CEPT/G-BTEK)
	G-TACK	Grob G.109B	A. P. Mayne
	G-TADI	Magni M.24C Orion	REB Ltd
	G-TADS	Mead BM-77 balloon	R. D. Stagg
	G-TAFF	CASA 1.131E Jungmann 1000	A. J. E. Smith (G-BFNE)
	G-TAJB	Airbus MBB BK-117 D-3	Blythe HCI Ltd

Reg	Type	Owner or Operator	Notes
G-TALA	Cessna 152 II	Tatenhill Aviation Ltd (G-BNPZ)	
G-TALB	Cessna 152 II	Tatenhill Aviation Ltd (G-BORO)	
G-TALC	Cessna 152	Tatenhill Aviation Ltd (G-BPBG)	
G-TALD	Cessna F.152	Tatenhill Aviation Ltd (G-BHRM)	
G-TALE	PA-28-181 Cherokee Archer II	Tatenhill Aviation Ltd (G-BJOA)	
G-TALG	PA-28-151 Cherokee Warrior	Tatenhill Aviation Ltd (G-BELP)	
G-TALH	PA-28-181 Cherokee Archer II	Tatenhill Aviation Ltd (G-CIFR)	
G-TALJ	Grumman AA-5 Traveler	The Lima Juliet Group (G-BBUE)	
G-TALN	Rotorway A600 Talon	J. White	
G-TALO	Cessna FA.152	Tatenhill Aviation Ltd (G-BFZU)	
G-TALP	Cessna 172N	Tatenhill Aviation Ltd (G-BOUF)	
G-TALR	Cessna 152	The Leicestershire Aero Club Ltd (G-FIGA)	
G-TALS	Cessna F.152 II	Tatenhill Aviation Ltd (G-BIOK)	
G-TALZ	PA-24-250 Comanche	Tatenhill Aviation Ltd (G-ARBO)	
G-TAMI	Diamond DA.40 Star	Leading Edge Aviation Ltd	
G-TAMS	Beech A23-24 Musketeer Super	C. P. Allen	
G-TANA	Tanarg 912S(2)/Ixess 15	S. S. Smy	
G-TANG	Tanarg 912S(2)/Ixess 15	N. L. Stammers	
G-TANJ	Raj Hamsa X'Air 582(5)	P. J. Greenrod	
G-TANY	EAA Acrosport 2	P. J. Tanulak	
G-TAPS	PA-28RT-201T Turbo Cherokee Arrow IV	R. L. Nunn, T. R. Edwards & T. G. Sarson	
G-TARN	Pietenpol Air Camper	P. J. Heilbron	
G-TARR	P & M Quik	A. Edwards	
G-TART	PA-28-236 Dakota	N. K. G. Prescot	
G-TATR	Replica Travelair R Type	R. A. Seeley	
G-TATT	Gardan GY-20 Minicab	Tatt's Group	
G-TAUT	Pipistrel Alpha BCAR-S 164	M. Tautz	
G-TAWA	Boeing 737-8K5	TUI Airways Ltd	
G-TAWB	Boeing 737-8K5	TUI Airways Ltd	
G-TAWC	Boeing 737-8K5	TUI Airways Ltd	
G-TAWD	Bocing 737-8K5	TUI Airways Ltd	
G-TAWG	Boeing 737-8K5	TUI Airways Ltd	
G-TAWH	Boeing 737-8K5	TUI Airways Ltd	
G-TAWI	Boeing 737-8K5	TUI Airways Ltd	
G-TAWJ	Boeing 737-8K5	TUI Airways Ltd	
G-TAWK	Boeing 737-8K5	TUI Airways Ltd	
G-TAWM	Boeing 737-8K5	TUI Airways Ltd	
G-TAWO	Boeing 737-8K5	TUI Airways Ltd	
G-TAWP	Boeing 737-8K5	TUI Airways Ltd	
G-TAWS	Boeing 737-8K5	TUI Airways Ltd	
G-TAWU	Boeing 737-8K5	TUI Airways Ltd	
G-TAWV	Boeing 737-8K5	TUI Airways Ltd	
G-TAWW	Boeing 737-8K5	TUI Airways Ltd	
G-TAWX	Boeing 737-8K5	TUI Airways Ltd	
G-TAWY	Boeing 737-8K5	TUI Airways Ltd	
G-TAWZ	Boeing 737-8K5	TUI Airways Ltd	
G-TAXI	PA-23-250 Aztec E	S. Waite	
G-TAYC	Gulfstream G450	Executive Jet Charter Ltd	
G-TAYI	Grob G.115	K. P. Widdowson (G-DODO)	
G-TAYL	Pitts S-1S Special	R. S. Taylor	
G-TAZZ	Dan Rihn DR.107 One Design	N. J. Riddin	
G-TBAG	Murphy Renegade II	M. R. Tetley	
G-TBDI	Ikarus C42 FB100 Bravo	Progress Vehicle Management Ltd	
G-TBET	Ultramagic M-77 balloon	H. Crawley & P. Dopson	
G-TBEZ	Guimbal Cabri G2	Bez Aviation Ltd	
G-TBHH	AS355F2 Twin Squirrel	Alpha Properties (London) Ltd (G-HOOT/ G-SCOW/ G-POON/G-MCAL)	
G-TBGO	SOCATA TB-10 Tobago	P. P. W. Lowe (G-RIAM)	
G-TBIO	SOCATA TB10 Tobago	High Flight Training Solutions Ltd	
G-TBLB	P & M Quik GT450	R. S. Morley	
G-TBLC	Rans S-6-ES Coyote II	R. S. Marriott	
G-TBMR	P & M Aviation Quik GT450	I. A. Macadam	
G-TBXX	SOCATA TB20 Trinidad	Aeroplane Ltd	
G-TBYD	Raj Hamsa X'Air Falcon D(1)	A. Tucker	
G-TCAN	Colt 69A balloon	H. C. J. Williams	
G-TCHI	VS.509 Spitfire Tr.9 (BS410/PK-A)	Angels 13 Ltd	
G-TCHO	VS Spitfire Mk.IX	B. Phillips	
G-TCHZ	VS.329 Spitfire IIA (P7819)	M. B. Phillips	
G-TCNM	Tecnam P92-EA Echo	G-TCNM Flying Group	

BRITISH CIVIL AIRCRAFT MARKINGS

Notes	Reg	Type	Owner or Operator
	G-TCNY	Mainair Pegasus Quik	B. J. Wardle
	G-TCTC	PA-28RT-200 Cherokee Arrow IV	P. Salemis
	G-TCUB	Piper J-3C-65 Cub (modified)	C. Kirk
	G-TDJP	Van's RV-8	D. J. Pearson
	G-TDOG	SA Bulldog Srs 120/121 (XX538:O)	R. F. M. Jones
	G-TDSA	Cessna F.406 Caravan II	RVL Aviation Ltd
	G-TDSE	Grob G109B	T. R. Dews (G-CMIN)
	G-TDVB	Dyn' Aero MCR-01ULC	A. Thornton
	G-TDYN	Aerospool Dynamic WT9 UK	N. Lilley
	G-TEBZ	PA-28R-201 Cherokee Arrow III	Aeros Leasing Ltd
	G-TECC	Aeronca 7AC Champion	N. J. Orchard-Armitage
	G-TECE	Tecnam P92-EA Echo-Super	D. A. Lawrence (G-CBYZ)
	G-TECH	Rockwell Commander 114	C. A. Bradley-Case (G-BEDH)
	G-TECI	Tecnam P2002-JF	G-TECI Flying Club Ltd
	G-TECM	Tecnam P92-EA Echo	N. Stamford
	G-TECO	Tecnam P92-EM Echo	A. N. Buchan
	G-TECS	Tecnam P2002-EA Sierra	D. J. Rogerson, M. G. Woodbridge & N. G. Hotson
	G-TECT	Tecnam P2006T	Cabledraw Ltd
	G-TEDB	Cessna F.150L	R. Nightingale (G-AZLZ)
	G-TEDI	Skyranger J2.2(1)	M. J. Sunter
	G-TEDW	Kiss 450-582 (2)	G-TEDW Group
	G-TEDY	Evans VP-1	N. K. Marston (G-BHGN)
	G-TEEF	Diamond P-90 balloon	A. M. Holly
	G-TEFC	PA-28-140 Cherokee	D. H. G. Penney
	G-TEGS	Bell 206B JetRanger III	North West Helicopters Ltd
	G-TEHL	CFM Streak Shadow SA-M	A. A. Sawera (G-MYJE)
	G-TEKG	Tekever AR5 Evolution Mk.2.3	Tekever Ltd
	G-TEKM	Tekever AR5 Evolution Mk.2.3	Tekever Ltd
	G-TEKN	Tekever AR5 Evolution Mk.2	Tekever Ltd
	G-TEKV	Tekever AR5 Evolution Mk.2	Tekever Ltd
	G-TEKW	Tekever AR5 Evolution Mk.2.3	Tekever Ltd
	G-TEMB	Tecnam P2000-EA Sierra	N. G. Stopps & G. L. Luckett
	G-TEMP	PA-28-180 Cherokee	Easy Aircraft Rental Ltd (G-AYBK)
	G-TEMT	Hawker Tempest II (PR533/SR-V)	Fighter Aviation Engineering Ltd
	G-TEMU	Cirrus SR22T	T. O. Nivala
	G-TENN	Van's RV-10	P. F. Rothwell
	G-TENT	Auster J/1N Alpha	R. Callaway-Lewis (G-AKJU)
	G-TERD	Zenair CH.750	Condor Engineering Group Ltd (G-CIMN)
	G-TERN	Europa	J. Smith
	G-TERO	Van's RV-7	A. Phillips
	G-TERR	Mainair Pegasus Quik	M. Faulkner
	G-TERY	PA-28-181 Cherokee Archer II	CS Courier Transport Ltd (G-BOXZ)
	G-TESD	Diamond DA.40D Star	Tesla Solutions Ltd
	G-TESG	Diamond DA.42 Twin Star	Tesla Solutions Ltd
	G-TESH	Diamond DA.40D Star	Tesla Solutions Ltd
	G-TESI	Tecnam P2002 EA Sierra	C. C. Burgess
	G-TESJ	Diamond DA.40D Star	Tesla Solutions Ltd
	G-TESM	Diamond DA.42 Twin Star	Tesla Solutions Ltd
	G-TESN	Diamond DA.42 Twin Star	Tesla Solutions Ltd
	G-TESR	Tecnam P2002-RG Sierra	Tecnam RG Group
	G-TEWS	PA-28-140 Cherokee	Ovin Ltd (G-KEAN/G-AWTM)
	G-TEXN	North American T-6G Texan (KF402:HT-Y)	R. A. van Meeuwen (G-BHTH)
	G-TEZZ	CZAW Sportcruiser	A. G. Sindrey
	G-TFAM	PA-46-350T Malibu Matrix	Take Flight Asset Management (G-UDMS)
	G-TFCC	Cub Crafters Carbon Cub SS CC11-160	Warbird Experiences Ltd
	G-TFIX	Mainair Pegasus Quantum 15-912	T. G. Jones
	G-TFLX	P & M Quik GT450	B. M. Thompson
	G-TFLY	Air Creation Kiss 450-582 (1)	A. J. Ladell
	G-TFOG	Skyranger 912(2)	A. Brier
	G-TFRB	Air Command 532 Elite ★	Yorkshire Air Museum/Elvington
	G-TFUN	Valentin Taifun 17E	North West Taifun Group
	G-TFWE	Flylight BivvyBee	I. F. Bruce
	G-TGER	AA-5B Tiger	D. W. Winsper (G-BFZP)
	G-TGGR	Eurocopter EC 120B	Messiah Corporation Ltd
	G-TGJH	Evans VP-1 series 2	G. T. Gohl
	G-TGLG	AutoGyro Calidus	T. R. Galloway

Reg	Type	Owner or Operator	Notes
G-TGMG	Robinson R44 II	KPD 79 Ltd (G-PTRL)	
G-TGPG	Boeing 737-3YO	European Aviation Ltd	
G-TGRA	Agusta A109A	Tiger Helicopters Ltd	
G-TGRC	Robinson R22 Beta	Tiger Aviation Ltd (G-RSWW)	
G-TGRD	Robinson R22 Beta II	Tiger Aviation Ltd (G-OPTS)	
G-TGRE	Robinson R22 Alpha	Tiger Aviation Ltd (G-SOLD)	
G-TGRS	Robinson R22 Beta	Tiger Aviation Ltd (G-DELL)	
G-TGRX	Robinson R44	Tiger Aviation Ltd (G-TOLS/G-CBOT)	
G-TGRZ	Bell 206B JetRanger 3	Tiger Aviation Ltd (G-BXZX)	
G-TGTT	Robinson R44 II	Cloud Telematics LLP	
G-TGUK	Ultramagic F-38 Helmet balloon	A. M. Holly	
G-TGUL	Earthstar Thundergull J	P. J. Reilly	
G-TGVP	Cunliffe-Owen Seafire Mk.XV	T. A. V. Percy	
G-THAT	Raj Hamsa X'Air Falcon 912 (1)	M. C. Sawyer	
G-THDA	Leonardo A109S Grand	Sloane Helicopters Ltd	
G-THDR	Leonardo AW109SP Grand New	Thunder Aviation Limited Partnership	
G-THEO	TEAM mini-MAX 91	A. W. Gunn	
G-THFW	Bell 206B-3 JetRanger III	Fly Heli Wales Ltd	
G-THIN	Cessna FR.172E	T. B. Sumner (G-BXYY)	
G-THNG	Jabiru J430	C. H. Richardson (G-CGOL)	
G-THOM	Thunder Ax-6-56 balloon	Virgin Balloon Flights	
G-THOT	Jabiru SK	S. G. Holton	
G-THSL	PA-28R-201 Cherokee Arrow III	A. Jahanfar	
G-THUD	Bell 505 Jet Ranger X	Solaris Consulting Ltd	
G-THUN	Republic P-47D-40-RA Thunderbolt (549192)	Fighter Aviation Engineering Ltd	
G-TIAB	Schleicher ASW-27	R. G. Cox (G-CKCN)	
G-TIAC	Tiger Cub RL5A LW Sherwood Ranger	R. F. S. Thomson	
G-TIBF	Balony Kubicek BB34Z balloon	G. B.Lescott	
G-TIBS	SOCATA TB.20 Trinidad	E. A. Asimakis	
G-TICH	Taylor JT.2 Titch	J. C. Gazzard	
G-TICO	Cameron O-77 balloon	J. F. Trehern	
G-TIDS	Jodel 150	T. Brown	
G-TIDY	Sky Ranger Nynja 912S(1)	B. P. Wright & C. Fox	
G-TIFG	Ikarus C42 FB80	B. Flood	
G-TIFY	Hawker Typhoon IB	Hawker Typhoon Preservation Group	
G-TIGA	DH.82A Tiger Moth	The deHavilkland Educational Trust (G-AOEG)	
G-TIII	Pitts S-2A Special	R. Harrison	
G-TIIO	Schempp-Hirth Arcus M	S. G. Jones (G-KFFD)	
G-TILE	Robinson R22 Beta	Heli Air Ltd	
G-TILY	Sackville BM-56 balloon	T. I. Laws	
G-TIMA	Van's RV-7	T. J. Arnold	
G-TIMC	Robinson R44	T. Clark Aviation LLP (G-CDUR)	
G-TIMG	Beagle Terrier 3	T. M. Trowell	
G TIMK	PA 28 181 Cherokee Archer II	I. R. Wellesley-Harding	
G-TIMP	Aeronca 7BCM Champion	R. B. Valler	
G-TIMS	Falconar F-12A	T. Sheridan	
G-TIMX	Head AX8-88B balloon	J. Edwards & S. McMahon	
G-TIMY	Gardan GY-80 Horizon 160	J. A. McAnaney	
G-TINK	Robinson R22 Beta	Helimech Ltd	
G-TINT	Aerotechnik EV-97 Team Eurostar UK	I. A. Cunningham	
G-TIPJ	Cameron Z-77 balloon	J. R. Lawson	
G-TIPP	Aeroprakt A22-LS Foxbat	E. Fogarty	
G-TIPR	Eurocopter AS.350B2 Ecureuil	Thames Materials Holdings Ltd (G-PATM)	
G-TIPS	Nipper T.66 Srs.3	F. V. Neefs	
G-TIPY	Czech Sport PS-28 Cruiser	I. C. Tandy	
G-TIVV	Aerotechnik EV-97 Eurostar UK	Victor Victor Group	
G-TIZY	TAF Sling 4 TSI	Connecting Lines Ltd	
G-TJAE	Diamond DA.42	Tesla Solutions Ltd	
G-TJAL	Jabiru SPL-430	M. R. Williamson	
G-TJAV	Mainair Pegasus Quik	C. N. Clegg	
G-TJAY	PA-22-135 Tri-Pacer	D. Pegley	
G-TJCL	P &M QuikR	N. Cross	
G-TJDM	Van's RV-6A	J. D. Michie	
G-TJFF	VR Plus/Adam Trike	A. J. Fillingham	
G-TJPK	Leonardo AW109SP Grand New	Botany Aviation Ltd	
G-TKAY	Europa	A. M. Kay	
G-TKEV	P & M Quik R	N. F. Dee	

Notes	Reg	Type	Owner or Operator
	G-TKHE	PA-28R-201T Turbo Cherokee Arrow IV	C. H. Smith (G-EPTL)
	G-TKIS	Tri-R Kis	T. J. Bone
	G-TKNO	UltraMagic S-50 balloon	H. G. Board
	G-TLAC	Sherwood Ranger ST	The Light Aircraft Company Ltd
	G-TLAG	Lightwing AC4	The Light Aircraft Company Ltd
	G-TLDI	TL3000 Sirius 600	D. J. Curtis (G-CMLA)
	G-TLDK	PA-22-150 Caribbean	M. R. Masters
	G-TLDL	Medway SLA 100 Executive	J. G. Cook
	G-TLDM	TL 3000 Sirius 600	L. R. Stevenson
	G-TLET	PA-28-161 Cadet	ADR Aviation (G-GFCF/G-RHBH)
	G-TLFR	TL 2000 Sting S4	J. Page
	G-TLMA	Lindstrand LTL 1-105 balloon	A. M. Holly
	G-TLMI	Robinson R66	HQ Aviation Ltd
	G-TLNU	TL 3000 Sirius 600	Steven Haynes Aviation Ltd
	G-TLST	TL 2000UK Sting Carbon S4	W. H. J. Knowles
	G-TLTL	Schempp-Hirth Discus CS	E. K. Armitage
	G-TMAX	Evektor Sportstar Max	G-TMAX Group
	G-TMCB	Skyranger 912 (2)	J. R. Davis
	G-TMCF	Leonardo A109S Trekker	MCF Aviation Ltd
	G-TMHK	PA-38-112 Tomahawk	G. E. Fox (G-GALL/G-BTEV)
	G-TMPV	Hawker Tempest V	Anglia Aircraft Restorations Ltd
	G-TMRL	Zenair CH.750	A. D. J. Morris
	G-TNEA	Airbus A.321-251NX	British Airways PLC
	G-TNEB	Airbus A.321-251NX	British Airways PLC
	G-TNEC	Airbus A.321-251NX	British Airways PLC
	G-TNED	Airbus A.321-251NX	British Airways PLC
	G-TNEE	Airbus A.321-251NX	British Airways PLC
	G-TNEF	Airbus A.321-251NX	British Airways PLC
	G-TNEG	Airbus A.321-251NX	British Airways PLC
	G-TNEH	Airbus A.321-251NX	British Airways PLC
	G-TNEI	Airbus A.321-251NX	British Airways PLC
	G-TNEJ	Airbus A.321-251NX	British Airways PLC
	G-TNGO	Van's RV-6	J. D. M. Willis
	G-TNJB	P & M Quik R	Micro Aviation Ltd
	G-TNRG	Deltajet 2/Ixess 15 912S(2)	D. A. Eastough
	G-TNTN	Thunder Ax6-56 balloon	H. M. Savage & A. A. Leggate
	G-TNUP	Avions Max Holste MH.1521C1 Broussard (154/315-CM)	M. J. Babbage
	G-TOBI	Cessna F.172K	M. Buxton (G-AYVB)
	G-TODC	Bolkow BO.207	T. A. Cleaver
	G-TODD	ICA IS-28M2A	C. I. Roberts & C. D. King
	G-TOES	PA-28-161 Cherokee Warrior II	Freedom Aviation Ltd
	G-TOFT	Colt 90A balloon	C. S. Perceval
	G-TOGO	Van's RV-6	N. A. Onions
	G-TOKN	Diamond DA.62	Tokencard Ltd
	G-TOLL	PA-28R-201 Cherokee Arrow III	Arrow Heart Ltd
	G-TOLY	Robinson R22 Beta	Helicopter & Pilot Services Ltd (G-NSHR)
	G-TOMJ	Flight Design CT2K	M. E. Blandy
	G-TOML	Cessna F.150M	T. J. Caston & S. Magrabi (G-CSBM)
	G-TOMX	MCR-01 VLA Sportster	P. T. Knight
	G-TONE	Pazmany PL-4	P. I. Morgans
	G-TONN	Mainair Pegasus Quik	T. D. Evans
	G-TOOB	Schempp-Hirth Discus 2b	M. F. Evans
	G-TOOO	Guimbal Cabri G2	Helicentre Aviation Ltd
	G-TOPB	Cameron Z-140 balloon	Anana Ltd
	G-TOPC	AS.355F1 Twin Squirrel	Helispares Ltd
	G-TOPE	TLAC Shark 600 UK	N. Fleming
	G-TOPK	Europa XS	K. A. Hartley
	G-TOPM	Agusta-Bell 206B-2 JetRanger 2	A & W Demolition (Bracknell) (G-CCBL)
	G-TOPP	Van's RV-10	D. Topp & S. E. Coles
	G-TORC	PA-28R-200 Cherokee Arrow	Falcon Flying Services Ltd
	G-TORI	Zenair CH.701SP	R. W. H. Watson (G-CCSK)
	G-TORN	Flight Design CTSW	N. C. Harper
	G-TORO	Skyranger Nynja 912S(1)	L. J. E. Moss & C. Fenwick
	G-TOSH	Robinson R22 Beta	Heli Air Ltd
	G-TOTO	Cessna F.177RG	Airspeed Aviation Ltd (G-OADE/G-AZKH)
	G-TOUR	Robin R.2112	M. A. Henley

Reg	Type	Owner or Operator	Notes
G-TOWA	Zenair CH.750 Cruzer	C. M. Barnes	
G-TOWS	PA-25-260 Pawnee	Lasham Gliding Society Ltd	
G-TOYZ	Bell 206B JetRanger 3	Adventure 001 Ltd (G-RGER)	
G-TPAL	P & M Aviation Quik GT450	R. Robertson	
G-TPEE	Van's RV-7	N. A. Durham	
G-TPHY	Supermarine S.6 replica	W. B. Hosie	
G-TPPW	Van's RV-7	Ultimate Warbird Flights Ltd	
G-TPSL	Cessna 182S	A. N. Purslow	
G-TPSY	Champion 8KCAB Super Decathlon	Aerial Advantage Ltd (G-CEOE)	
G-TPTP	Robinson R44	Advanced IT Services Nottingham Ltd	
G-TPTR	Agusta Bell 206B Jet Ranger II ★	The Helicopter Museum/Weston-super-Mare (G-LOCK)	
G-TPWX	Heliopolis Gomhouria Mk.6 (TP+WX)	Cirrus Aircraft UK Ltd	
G-TRAC	Robinson R44	C. J. Sharples	
G-TRAM	Pegasus Quantum 15-912	P. & R. M. Smith	
G-TRBN	HpH 304S Shark	G. A. & H. B. Chalmers	
G-TRBO	Schleicher ASW-28-18E	R. M. Taylor	
G-TRDS	Guimbal Cabri G2	Helicentre Aviation Ltd	
G-TREB	Cessna 182T	Camel Aviation Ltd	
G-TREC	Cessna 421C	Sovereign Business Integration PLC (G-TLOL)	
G-TREE	Bell 206B JetRanger 3	Heliflight (UK) Ltd	
G-TREK	Jodel D.18	R. H. Mole	
G-TREL	Van's RV-14	J. E. Gattrell	
G-TREW	Balony Kubicek BB22Z balloon	C. Timbrell	
G-TREX	Alpi Pioneer 300	R. A. Thomson	
G-TRIG	Cameron Z-90 balloon	Hedge Hoppers Balloon Group	
G-TRIN	SOCATA TB20 Trinidad	M. J. Porter	
G-TRJB	Beech A36 Bonanza	G. A. J. Bowles	
G-TRKY	Van's RV-9	R. J. Bower	
G-TRLL	Groppo Trail	A. M. Wilson	
G-TRMC	Van's RV-7	M. S. Colebrook & T. J. Richardson	
G-TRNG	Agusta A109E Power	Dolores Aviation Ltd (G-NWOY/G-JMXA)	
G-TROW	Ikarus C42 FB80	Blue Socks Aviation Ltd	
G-TROY	NA T-28A Fennec (517692)	G. G. L. James	
G-TRTL	Skyranger Nynja LS 912S(1)	J. T. & J. W. Whicher	
G-TRUE	MDH Hughes 369E	N. E. Bailey	
G-TRUK	Stoddard-Hamilton Glasair RG	T. R. Whittome	
G-TRUU	PA-34-220T Seneca III	A. I. Freeman (G-BOJK/G-BRUF)	
G-TRUX	Colt 77A balloon	P. M. Traviss	
G-TRVR	Van's RV-7	The Richard Ormonde Shuttleworth Remembrance Trust	
G-TRVW	Van's RV-7	Guernsey Aviation & Marine Ltd (G-CNHB)	
G-TSAC	Tecnam P2002-EA Sierra	P. E. Riding	
G-TSAS	PA-28-181 Cherokee Archer II	M. E. McElhinney (G-MALA/G-BIIU)	
G-TSBY	Robinson R44 II	MacGen Power Generation Ltd	
G-TSDA	Aquila AT-01-100A	Praeluceo Property Ltd	
G-TSDB	Aquila AT-01-100A	Praeluceo Property Ltd	
G-TSDC	Aquila AT-01-100A	Praeluceo Property Ltd	
G-TSDE	Aquila AT-01-100A	Praeluceo Property Ltd	
G-TSDI	Spacek SD-1 Minisport	M. Innes	
G-TSDS	PA-32R-301 Saratoga SP	M. J. Hadley (G-TRIP/G-HOSK)	
G-TSFC	Tecnam P2008-JC	Stapleford Flying Club Ltd	
G-TSGA	PA-28R-201 Cherokee Arrow III	I. R. Lockhart & J. N. Bailey (G-ONSF/G-EMAK)	
G-TSGJ	PA-28-181 Cherokee Archer II	Golf Juliet Flying Club	
G-TSHO	Ikarus C42 FB80	P. A. J. Woolford & J. P. Sonander	
G-TSII	TAF Sling 4 TSI	S. A. Lamb	
G-TSIM	Titan T-51 Mustang	P. T. Claiden	
G-TSIX	AT-6C Harvard IIA (111836:JZ-6)	Bulldog Aviation Ltd	
G-TSKD	Raj Hamsa X'Air Jabiru J.2.2.	T. Sexton & K. B. Dupuy	
G-TSKS	Cosmik EV-97 TeamEurostar UK	S. Singh	
G-TSLC	Schweizer 269C-1	AH Helicopter Services Ltd	
G-TSOB	Rans S.6-ESA Coyote II	A. S. R. Galley	
G-TSOG	TLAC Sherwood Ranger XP	R. W. Kraike	
G-TSOL	EAA Acrosport 1	H. Stuart (G-BPKI)	
G-TSOO	Hughes 369D	D. W. Walton	
G-TSUE	Europa	H. J. C. Maclean	
G-TSWI	Lindstrand LBL-90A balloon	Miles Air Ltd	
G-TSWZ	Cameron Z-77 balloon	Business First Centre	

Notes	Reg	Type	Owner or Operator
	G-TTAT	ICP MXP-740 Savannah VG Jabiru(1)	D. Varley & D. J. Broughall
	G-TTCK	Cessna 525B Citationjet CJ3	Naljets Ltd
	G-TTEC	PA-32-301FT 6X	R. D. W. Evans
	G-TTFG	Colt 77B balloon	T. J. & M. J. Turner (G-BUZF)
	G-TTGV	Bell 206L-4 LongRanger IV	Langley Aviation Ltd (G-JACI)
	G-TTKP	Enstrom 280FX Shark	R. P. Bateman (G-HDIX)
	G-TTNA	Airbus A.320-251N	British Airways PLC
	G-TTNB	Airbus A.320-251N	British Airways PLC
	G-TTNC	Airbus A.320-251N	British Airways PLC
	G-TTND	Airbus A.320-251N	British Airways PLC
	G-TTNE	Airbus A.320-251N	British Airways PLC
	G-TTNF	Airbus A.320-251N	British Airways PLC
	G-TTNG	Airbus A.320-251N	British Airways PLC
	G-TTNH	Airbus A.320-251N	British Airways PLC
	G-TTNI	Airbus A.320-251N	British Airways PLC
	G-TTNJ	Airbus A.320-251N	British Airways PLC
	G-TTNK	Airbus A.320-251N	British Airways PLC
	G-TTNL	Airbus A.320-251N	British Airways PLC
	G-TTNM	Airbus A.320-251N	British Airways PLC
	G-TTNN	Airbus A.320-251N	British Airways PLC
	G-TTNO	Airbus A.320-251N	British Airways PLC
	G-TTNP	Airbus A.320-251N	British Airways PLC
	G-TTNR	Airbus A.320-251N	British Airways PLC
	G-TTNS	Airbus A.320-251N	British Airways PLC
	G-TTNT	Airbus A.320-251N	British Airways PLC
	G-TTNU	Airbus A.320-251N	British Airways PLC
	G-TTNV	Airbus A.320-251N	British Airways PLC
	G-TTNW	Airbus A.320-251N	British Airways PLC
	G-TTNX	Airbus A.320-251N	British Airways PLC
	G-TTNY	Airbus A.320-251N	British Airways PLC
	G-TTNZ	Airbus A.320-251N	British Airways PLC
	G-TTOB	Airbus A.320-232	British Airways PLC
	G-TTOE	Airbus A.320-232	British Airways PLC
	G-TTOM	Zenair CH.601HD Zodiac	D. P. Demmery
	G-TTOY	CFM Streak Shadow SA	J. Softley
	G-TTRE	Schleicher AS-33 Es	R. C. W. Ellis
	G-TTRL	Van's RV-9A	J. E. Gattrell
	G-TTSA	Airbus A.320-251N	British Airways PLC
	G-TTSB	Airbus A.320-251N	British Airways PLC
	G-TTSC	Airbus A.320-251N	British Airways PLC
	G-TTSD	Airbus A.320-251N	British Airways PLC
	G-TTSE	Airbus A.320-251N	British Airways PLC
	G-TTSF	Airbus A.320-251N	British Airways PLC
	G-TTSG	Airbus A.320-251N	British Airways PLC
	G-TTSH	Airbus A.320-251N	British Airways PLC
	G-TTSI	Airbus A.320-251N	British Airways PLC
	G-TTSJ	Airbus A.320-251N	British Airways PLC
	G-TTUG	Eurofox 912(IS)	Buckminster Gliding Club Ltd (G-WTUG)
	G-TTXL	Cameron A-400 balloon	Wickers World Ltd
	G-TUBB	Jabiru UL	A. H. Bower
	G-TUCK	Van's RV-8	N. G. R. Moffat
	G-TUGC	Eurofox 2K	Ulster Gliding Club Ltd
	G-TUGD	Eurofox 3K	Denbigh Gliding
	G-TUGG	PA-18-150 Super Cub	The South Wales Gliding Club Ltd
	G-TUGI	CZAW Sportcruiser	T. J. Wilson
	G-TUGY	Robin DR.400/180	GY Group
	G-TUGZ	Robin DR.400/180R	Buckminster Gliding Club Ltd
	G-TUIA	Boeing 787-8	TUI Airways Ltd
	G-TUIB	Boeing 787-8	TUI Airways Ltd
	G-TUIC	Boeing 787-8	TUI Airways Ltd
	G-TUID	Boeing 787-8	Orix Aviation Systems Ltd
	G-TUIE	Boeing 787-8	TUI Airways Ltd
	G-TUIF	Boeing 787-8	TUI Airways Ltd
	G-TUIH	Boeing 787-8	TUI Airways Ltd
	G-TUII	Boeing 787-8	TUI Airways Ltd
	G-TUIJ	Boeing 787-9	TUI Airways Ltd
	G-TUIL	Boeing 787-9	TUI Airways Ltd
	G-TUIM	Boeing 787-9	TUI Airways Ltd
	G-TUIN	Boeing 787-9	TUI Airways Ltd
	G-TUIO	Boeing 787-9	TUI Airways Ltd

Reg	Type	Owner or Operator	Notes
G-TUIP	Boeing 787-9	TUI Airways Ltd	
G-TUKF	Boeing 737-8AS	TUI Airways Ltd	
G-TUKO	Boeing 737-8K5	TUI Airways Ltd	
G-TUKR	Boeing 737-8K5	TUI Airways Ltd	
G-TUKS	Boeing 737-8K2	TUI Airways Ltd	
G-TUKT	Boeing 737-8JP	TUI Airways Ltd	
G-TUKW	Boeing 737-8K5	TUI Airways Ltd	
G-TUKX	Boeing 737-8K5	TUI Airways Ltd	
G-TUMA	Boeing 737-MAX8	TUI Airways Ltd	
G-TUMB	Boeing 737-MAX8	TUI Airways Ltd	
G-TUMC	Boeing 737-MAX8	TUI Airways Ltd	
G-TUMD	Boeing 737-MAX8	TUI Airways Ltd	
G-TUMF	Boeing 737-MAX8	TUI Airways Ltd	
G-TUMG	Boeing 737-MAX8	TUI Airways Ltd	
G-TUMH	Boeing 737-MAX8	TUI Airways Ltd	
G-TUMK	Boeing 737-MAX8	TUI Airways Ltd	
G-TUML	Boeing 737-MAX8	TUI Airways Ltd	
G-TUMM	Boeing 737-MAX8	TUI Airways Ltd	
G-TUMN	Boeing 737-MAX8	TUI Airways Ltd	
G-TUMO	Boeing 737-MAX8	TUI Airways Ltd	
G-TUMP	Boeing 737-MAX8	TUI Airways Ltd	
G-TUMS	Boeing 737-MAX8	TUI Airways Ltd	
G-TUMT	Boeing 737-MAX8	TUI Airways Ltd	
G-TUMU	Boeing 737-MAX8	TUI Airways Ltd	
G-TUMW	Boeing 737-MAX8	TUI Airways Ltd	
G-TUMX	Boeing 737-MAX8	TUI Airways Ltd	
G-TUMY	Boeing 737-MAX8	TUI Airways Ltd	
G-TUMZ	Boeing 737-MAX8	TUI Airways Ltd	
G-TUNL	Robinson R44 II	Kilkern Ltd (G-TCAL)	
G-TUOA	Boeing 737-MAX8	TUI Airways Ltd	
G-TUOB	Boeing 737-MAX8	TUI Airways Ltd	
G-TUOD	Boeing 737-MAX8	TUI Airways Ltd	
G-TUPA	Boeing 737-MAX8	TUI Airways Ltd	
G-TUPB	Boeing 737-MAX8	TUI Airways Ltd	
G-TUPC	Boeing 737-MAX8	TUI Airways Ltd	
G-TUPD	Boeing 737-MAX8	TUI Airways Ltd	
G-TUPE	Boeing 737-MAX8	TUI Airways Ltd	
G-TURT	Ultramagic S-90 balloon	C. J. Freeman	
G-TUTU	Cameron O-105 balloon	A. C. K. Rawson & J. J. Rudoni	
G-TVAB	Aerospatiale AS.355F2 EWcureuil 2	A2B Heli (Charters) Ltd (G-IALC/G-VVBA/ G-DBOK)	
G-TVBF	Lindstrand LBL-310A balloon	Virgin Balloons Flights	
G-TVCO	Gippsland GA-8 Airvan	P. Ligertwood	
G-TVGB	Airbus AS.350B3 Ecureuil	GB Helicopters	
G-TVGC	Schempp-Hirth Janus A	Trent Valley Gliding Club Ltd	
G-TVHB	Eurocopter EC 135 P2+	West Yorkshire Combined Authority National Police Air Service	
G-TVHD	AS.355F2 Ecureuil 2	AZB Heli (Charters) Ltd	
G-TVLY	Eurocopter EC.135 T2+	Thames Valley Air Ambulance (G-DVAA)	
G-TVSI	Campbell Cricket Replica	G. Smith	
G-TVSK	Ultramagic D-50 balloon	S. Dyer	
G-TWAL	Rutan Long-Ez	T. Walsh (G-BNCZ)	
G-TWAZ	Rolladen-Schneider LS7-WL	E. J. Skelhorn	
G-TWEL	PA-28-181 Cherokee Archer II	International Aerospace Engineering Ltd	
G-TWIS	Silence Twister	C. S. & K. D. Rhodes	
G-TWIT	Robinson R44 II	R. S. Rai	
G-TWIX	PA-16 Clipper	M. B. Blackmore, B. L. Procter & B. M. Vigor	
G-TWIZ	Rockwell Commander 114	M. A. Lorne	
G-TWLV	Van's RV-12	J. D. N. Cooke	
G-TWOC	Schempp-Hirth Ventus 2cT	G-TWOC Syndicate	
G-TWOO	Extra EA.300/200	North West Aerobatics Ltd (G-MRKI)	
G-TWRL	Pitts S-1S Special	M. G. Duffy	
G-TWSR	Silence Twister	J. A. Hallam	
G-TWSS	Silence Twister	T. R. Dews	
G-TWST	Silence Twister	J. E. Gatfield (G-ZWIP)	
G-TWTR	Robinson R44 II	Helicopter Services Ltd	
G-TWTW	Denney Kitfox Mk.2	R. M. Bremner	
G-TWWC	Boeing B75N1 Stearman	The Wing Walk Company Ltd (G-IYII)	

Notes	Reg	Type	Owner or Operator
	G-TXAS	Cessna A.150L	T. H. Scott (G-HFCA)
	G-TYAK	IDA Bacau Yakovlev Yak-52	S. J. Ducker
	G-TYER	Robin DR.400/500	C. A. White
	G-TYGA	AA-5B Tiger	Three Musketeers Flying Group (G-BHNZ)
	G-TYGR	Skyranger Swift 912S(1)	G-TYGR Group
	G-TYKE	Jabiru UL-450	P. E. Hadley
	G-TYNE	SOCATA TB20 Trinidad	N. V. Price
	G-TYRE	Cessna F.172M	J. S. C. English
	G-TZBW	Hawker 850XP	Voluxis Ltd
	G-TZED	SOCATA TB-200 Tobago XL	T. A. Clarke
	G-TZII	Thorp T.211B	M. J. Newton
	G-UACA	Skyranger Swift 912(1)	Light Flight GUACA Syndicate
	G-UANO	DHC.1 Chipmunk 22 (1367)	R. J. Stirk (G-BYYW)
	G-UANT	PA-28-140 Cherokee	Air Navigation & Trading Co Ltd
	G-UAPA	Robin DR.400/140B	NF-Air, Unipessoal Lda/Portugal
	G-UAPS	Van's RV-12IS	P. N. O'Hare
	G-UART	Moravan Zlin Z-242L	I. R. Pinkstone (G-EKMN)
	G-UASA	Schiebel Camcopter S-100	Bristow Helicopters Ltd
	G-UASB	Schiebel Camcopter S-100	Bristow Helicopters Ltd
	G-UASD	Schiebel Camcopter S-100	Bristow Helicopters Ltd
	G-UASE	Schiebel Camcopter S-100	Bristow Helicopters Ltd
	G-UAUK	Aeroprakt A-32M Vixxen	Tarnhelm Ltd
	G-UAVA	PA-30 Twin Comanche	Verdin Group Holdings Ltd
	G-UBET	Eurocopter AS.355N Ecureuil II	Balladoole Estate and Aviation Ltd (G-NMCF)
	G-UBIX	Robinson R44 II	R. J. Birt
	G-UBOO	Schleicher ASW-27-18E	J. P. Davies
	G-UCAM	PA-31-350 Navajo Chieftain	Blue Sky Investments Ltd (G-NERC/G-BBXX)
	G-UCAN	Tecnam P2002-JF Sierra	Aerobility
	G-UCLU	Schleicher ASK-21	University College London Union
	G-UDET	Replica Fokker E.111 (105/15)	M. J. Clark
	G-UDGE	Thruster T.600N	G-UDGE Syndicate (G-BYPI)
	G-UDIX	Schempp-Hirth Duo Discus T	G-UDIX Syndicate
	G-UFAW	Raj Hamsa X'Air 582 (15)	J. Norton
	G-UFCG	Cessna 172S	Ulster Flying Club (1961) Ltd
	G-UFCN	Cessna 152	Ulster Flying Club (1961) Ltd
	G-UFCP	Cessna F.152 II	E. J. Lamb (G-PTTB/G-WACT/G-BKFT)
	G-UFFY	Condor Ofica FUD	Condor Aviation International Ltd
	G-UFLY	Cessna F.150H	B. R. Hitchmough (G-AVVY)
	G-UFOE	Grob G.115	Capital SFLU Group Ltd
	G-UHGB	Bell 205A-1	Heli-Lift Services
	G-UHIH	Bell UH-1H Iroquois (72-21509)	MSS Holdings Ltd
	G-UHOP	UltraMagic H-31 balloon	C. J. Wootton
	G-UIDO	Robinson R22 II	EBG (Helicopters) Ltd
	G-UIII	Extra EA.300/200	M. Thomas
	G-UIKR	P & M Quik R	A. M. Sirant
	G-UILD	Grob G.109B	K. Butterfield
	G-UILT	Cessna T.303	P. Bentley (G-EDRY)
	G-UIMB	Guimbal Cabri G2	D. D. Saint
	G-UINN	Stolp SA.300 Starduster Too	A. Dunne
	G-UINZ	Ultramagic B-70 balloon	A. M. Holly
	G-UIRO	AutoGyro MT-03	S. D. Kellner (G-CFAG)
	G-UISE	Van's RV-8	J. A. Green
	G-UJAB	Jabiru UL	C. A. Thomas
	G-UJEA	Airbus A.320-251N	easyJet Airline Co.Ltd
	G-UJEB	Airbus A.320-251N	easyJet Airline Co.Ltd
	G-UJEC	Airbus A.320-251N	easyJet Airline Co.Ltd
	G-UJGK	Jabiru UL	W. G. Upton & J. G. Kosak
	G-UKAL	Cessna F.406 Caravan II	Aero Lease UK
	G-UKCS	PA-31 Navajo	2 Excel Aviation Ltd
	G-UKOZ	Jabiru SK	G. D. Burnett

Reg	Type	Owner or Operator	Notes
G-UKPA	Cessna 208B Grand Caravan	UK Parachute Services Ltd	
G-UKPB	Cessna 208B Grand Caravan	UK Parachute Services Ltd	
G-UKPS	Cessna 208 Caravan 1	UK Parachute Services Ltd	
G-UKRB	Colt 105A balloon	Virgin Airship & Balloon Co Ltd	
G-UKRV	Van's RV-7A	Netwasp.net Ltd	
G-UKTV	AS.355F2 Ecureuil 2	A2B Heli (Charters) Ltd (G-JESE/G-EMHH/ G-BYKH)	
G-UKUK	Head Ax8-105 balloon	P. A. George	
G-UKWA	Kubicek BB26Z balloon	G. P. Walton	
G-ULAS	DHC.1 Chipmunk 22 (WK517)	Chipmunk G-ULAS Ltd	
G-ULCC	Schleicher ASH-30 MI	G-ULCC Flying Club	
G-ULHI	SA Bulldog Srs.100/101	J. G. Claridge (G-OPOD/G-AZMS)	
G-ULIT	Boeing 737-MAX8	Ascend Airways Ltd	
G-ULLI	Skyranger Nynja LS 912S(1)	A. J. Hollidge	
G-ULPR	TLAC Shark 600 UK	F. P. Smiddy	
G-ULPS	Everett Srs 1 gyroplane	I. Pearson (G-BMNY)	
G-ULPY	Mooney M.20K Mooney 231	Brisk Aviation Ltd	
G-ULRK	Sequoia F.8L Falco	U. K. S. S. N. M. Lawson	
G-ULSY	Ikarus C.42 FB 80	B. Cook & R. E. Parker	
G-ULTB	Airbus MBB BK117 D-2	Starspeed Ltd	
G-ULTC	Airbus MBB BK117 D-2	Starspeed Ltd	
G-ULTR	Cameron A-105 balloon	R. K. Scott	
G-ULUL	Rotorsport UK Calidus	P. J. Tyler (G-HTBT)	
G-ULZE	Robinson R22	HQ Aviation Ltd (G-BUBW)	
G-UMBO	Thunder Ax7-77A balloon	Virgin Airship & Balloon Co Ltd	
G-UMBS	Solo Aerostatics DE-12/70 balloon	E. A. Butter	
G-UMBY	Hughes 369E	HQ Aviation Ltd	
G-UMMI	PA-31-310 Turbo Navajo	2 Excel Aviation Ltd (G-BGSO)	
G-UMMS	Cosmik EV-97 TeamEurostar UK	G. W. Carwardine (G-ODRY)	
G-UMMY	Skyranger J2.2(2)	Northern Ranger	
G-UMPY	Europa	G. D. Bird	
G-UNAC	PA-32R-301T Saratoga II TC	A. C. Campbell	
G-UNDD	PA-23 Aztec 250E	G. J. & D. P. Deadman (G-BATX)	
G-UNER	Lindstrand LBL-90A balloon	E. J. Attenborough	
G-UNES	Van's RV-6	C. A. Greatrex	
G-UNET	Boeing 747-433F	One Air Ltd	
G-UNGE	Lindstrand LBL-90A balloon ★	Bristol Balloon Collection (G-BVPJ)	
G-UNGO	Pietenpol Air Camper	A. R. Wyatt	
G-UNGY	Diamond -77 balloon	A. M. Holly	
G-UNIA	Leonardo AW.169	Uni-Fly Heliworx Ltd	
G-UNIB	Leonardo AW.169	Uni-Fly Heliworx Ltd	
G-UNIH	Leonardo AW.139	Uni-Fly Heliworx Ltd	
G-UNIN	Schempp-Hirth Ventus b	R. K. Forrest	
G-UNIV	Montgomerie JM Gyroplane ★	Museum of Flight/East Fortune	
G-UNIX	VPM M16 Tandem Trainer	A. P. Wilkinson	
G-UNJA	Pipistrel Alpha BCAR-S 164	Fly About Aviation Ltd	
G-UNKY	Ultramagic S-50 balloon	A. M. Holly	
G-UNNA	Jabiru UL-450WW	C. Thurgar-Dawson & M. Farthing	
G-UNNN	Aeropro Eurofox 3K	S. P. S. Dornan	
G-UNNR	Schempp-Hirth Arcus T	Arcus 18 Group	
G-UNNS	Westland SA.341B Gazelle AH.1	Burnhart Ltd (G-KEMH)	
G-UNRL	Lindstrand LBL-RR21 balloon	Lindstrand Media Ltd	
G-UNZZ	Bell 206L Long Ranger	K. Hayes (G-DSTN/G-CYRS)	
G-UORO	Europa	D. Dufton	
G-UPFS	Waco UPS-7	D. N. Peters & N. R. Finlayson	
G-UPHI	Skyranger Swift 912S(1)	M. B. Harper, J. Scott & C. Simmonds	
G-UPID	Bowers Fly Baby 1A	Bowers Fly Baby Group	
G-UPIZ	BRM Aero Bristell NG5 Speed Wing	M. P. Rainford	
G-UPOI	Cameron TR-84 S1 balloon	Cameron Balloons Ltd	
G-UPTA	Skyranger 912S (1)	O. J. & S. M. Hoddinott	
G-UPUZ	Lindstrand LBL-120A balloon	C.J. Sanger-Davies	
G-URGH	Extra EA.300/LC	Adastral Flying Displays Ltd	
G-URMS	Europa	C. Parkinson (G-DEBR)	
G-UROP	Beech 95-B55 Baron	Wallis Health Consultants Ltd	
G-URRR	Air Command 582 Sport	L. Armes	

Notes	Reg	Type	Owner or Operator
	G-URUH	Robinson R44	Heli Air Ltd
	G-USAA	Cessna F.150G	Aeros Leasing Ltd (G-OIDW)
	G-USAI	Agusta-Bell 47J-2A Ranger	Hields Aviation
	G-USHI	PA-28-140 Cherokee Cruiser	M. Rajain (G-BZWG)
	G-USIL	Thunder Ax7-77 balloon	Window On The World Ltd
	G-USKY	Aviat A-1B Husky	Pooler-LMT Ltd
	G-USTH	Agusta A109A-II	Stratton Motor Co.(Norfolk) Ltd
	G-UTSI	Rand-Robinson KR-2	K. B. Gutridge
	G-UUPP	Cameron Z-70 balloon	D. J. Scholes
	G-UURO	Aerotechnik EV-97 Eurostar	R. G. Leaning
	G-UUUU	Ikarus C42 FB100	Airbourne Aviation Ltd
	G-UVBF	Lindstrand LBL-400A balloon	Virgin Balloon Flights
	G-UWAS	SA Bulldog Srs 120/121 (XX625)	Transair (UK) Ltd (G-CBAB)
	G-UWEB	Cameron Z-120 balloon	GWE Business West Ltd
	G-UXLA	Learjet 40	Zenith Aviation Ltd
	G-UYAK	Yakovlev Yak-18T	C. A. Brightwell
	G-UZED	Airbus A.320-251N	easyJet Airline Co.Ltd
	G-UZEE	Airbus A.320-251N	easyJet Airline Co.Ltd
	G-UZEF	Airbus A.320-251N	easyJet Airline Co.Ltd
	G-UZEG	Airbus A.320-251N	easyJet Airline Co.Ltd
	G-UZEH	Airbus A.320-251N	easyJet Airline Co.Ltd
	G-UZHA	Airbus A.320-251N	easyJet Airline Co.Ltd
	G-UZHB	Airbus A.320-251N	easyJet Airline Co.Ltd
	G-UZHC	Airbus A.320-251N	easyJet Airline Co.Ltd
	G-UZHD	Airbus A.320-251N	easyJet Airline Co.Ltd
	G-UZHE	Airbus A.320-251N	easyJet Airline Co.Ltd
	G-UZHF	Airbus A.320-251N	easyJet Airline Co.Ltd
	G-UZHH	Airbus A.320-251N	easyJet Airline Co.Ltd
	G-UZHI	Airbus A.320-251N	easyJet Airline Co.Ltd
	G-UZHJ	Airbus A.320-251N	easyJet Airline Co.Ltd
	G-UZHK	Airbus A.320-251N	easyJet Airline Co.Ltd
	G-UZHL	Airbus A.320-251N	easyJet Airline Co.Ltd
	G-UZHM	Airbus A.320-251N	easyJet Airline Co.Ltd
	G-UZHN	Airbus A.320-251N	easyJet Airline Co.Ltd
	G-UZHO	Airbus A.320-251N	easyJet Airline Co.Ltd
	G-UZHP	Airbus A.320-251N	easyJet Airline Co.Ltd
	G-UZHR	Airbus A.320-251N	easyJet Airline Co.Ltd
	G-UZHS	Airbus A.320-251N	easyJet Airline Co.Ltd
	G-UZHT	Airbus A.320-251N	easyJet Airline Co.Ltd
	G-UZHU	Airbus A.320-251N	easyJet Airline Co.Ltd
	G-UZHV	Airbus A.320-251N	easyJet Airline Co.Ltd
	G-UZHW	Airbus A.320-251N	easyJet Airline Co.Ltd
	G-UZHX	Airbus A.320-251N	easyJet Airline Co.Ltd
	G-UZHY	Airbus A.320-251N	easyJet Airline Co.Ltd
	G-UZHZ	Airbus A.320-251N	easyJet Airline Co.Ltd
	G-UZLA	Airbus A.320-251N	easyJet Airline Co.Ltd
	G-UZLB	Airbus A.320-251N	easyJet Airline Co.Ltd
	G-UZLC	Airbus A.320-251N	easyJet Airline Co.Ltd
	G-UZLD	Airbus A.320-251N	easyJet Airline Co.Ltd
	G-UZLF	Airbus A.320-251N	easyJet Airline Co.Ltd
	G-UZLK	Airbus A.320-251N	easyJet Airline Co.Ltd
	G-UZLL	Airbus A.320-251N	easyJet Airline Co.Ltd
	G-UZLM	Airbus A.320-251N	easyJet Airline Co.Ltd
	G-UZLO	Airbus A.320-251N	easyJet Airline Co.Ltd
	G-UZLP	Airbus A.320-251N	easyJet Airline Co.Ltd
	G-UZLR	PA-28-140 Airbus A.320-251N	easyJet Airline Co.Ltd
	G-UZLS	Airbus A.320-251N	easyJet Airline Co.Ltd
	G-UZLT	Airbus A.320-251N	easyJet Airline Co.Ltd
	G-UZLV	Airbus A.320-251N	easyJet Airline Co.Ltd
	G-UZLW	Airbus A.320-251N	easyJet Airline Co.Ltd
	G-UZLX	Airbus A.320-251N	easyJet Airline Co.Ltd
	G-UZLY	Airbus A.320-251N	easyJet Airline Co.Ltd
	G-UZLZ	Airbus A.320-251N	easyJet Airline Co.Ltd

Reg	Type	Owner or Operator	Notes
G-UZMA	Airbus A.321-251NX	easyJet Airline Co.Ltd	
G-UZMB	Airbus A.321-251NX	easyJet Airline Co.Ltd	
G-UZMC	Airbus A.321-251NX	easyJet Airline Co.Ltd	
G-UZMD	Airbus A.321-251NX	easyJet Airline Co.Ltd	
G-UZME	Airbus A.321-251NX	easyJet Airline Co.Ltd	
G-UZMF	Airbus A.321-251NX	easyJet Airline Co.Ltd	
G-UZMG	Airbus A.321-251NX	easyJet Airline Co.Ltd	
G-UZMH	Airbus A.321-251NX	easyJet Airline Co.Ltd	
G-UZMI	Airbus A.321-251NX	easyJet Airline Co.Ltd	
G-UZMJ	Airbus A.321-251NX	easyJet Airline Co.Ltd	
G-UZMK	Airbus A.321-251NX	easyJet Airline Co.Ltd	
G-UZML	Airbus A.321-251NX	easyJet Airline Co.Ltd	
G-UZMM	Airbus A.321-251NX	easyJet Airline Co.Ltd	
G-UZUP	Aerotechnik EV-97A Eurostar	G-UZUP Flying Group	
G-UZZI	Lancair LC41-550FG Corvalis TT	The Wyck Estate Ltd	
G-VAAV	P & M Quik R	M. Kent	
G-VAGA	PA-15 Vagabond	G. V. Corcoran (G-CCEE)	
G-VAHH	Boeing 787-9	Virgin Atlantic Airways Ltd	
G-VALG	EV-97 Eurostar SL	J. A. Shufflebotham	
G-VALH	Robin DR.401-155CDI	A. L. M. O'Hare	
G-VALK	Beech 200 Super King Air	Airfleet Solutions Ltd (G-ROWN/G-BHLC)	
G-VALL	PA-32R-300 Cherokee Lance	J. A. Brown (G-BHBG)	
G-VALS	Pietenpol Air Camper	G-VALS Flying Group	
G-VALZ	Cameron N-120 balloon	J. D. & K. Griffiths	
G-VANC	Gippsland GA-8 Airvan	Irish Skydiving Club Ltd	
G-VANN	Van's RV-7A	G-VANN Flying Group	
G-VANS	Van's RV-4	R. J. Marshall	
G-VANU	PA-28RT-201 Turbo Cherokee Arrow IV	Falcon Flying Services Ltd	
G-VANX	Gippsland GA-8 Airvan	Tape It Up Ltd	
G-VANZ	Van's RV-6A	M. Wright	
G-VARG	Varga 2150A Kachina	J. M. Denton	
G-VARK	Van's RV-7	S. Morris	
G-VASS	Autogyro MTOsport 2017	V. S. Hussain (G-LFLF)	
G-VAZE	Robinson R44	DMC Heli-Hire Ltd	
G-VBAA	Cameron A-400 balloon	Virgin Balloon Flights	
G-VBAB	Cameron A-400 balloon	Virgin Balloon Flights	
G-VBAD	Cameron A-300 balloon	Virgin Balloon Flights	
G-VBAE	Cameron A-400 balloon	Virgin Balloon Flights	
G-VBAF	Cameron A-300 balloon	Virgin Balloon Flights	
G-VBAG	Cameron A-400 balloon	Virgin Balloon Flights	
G-VBAH	Cameron A-400 balloon	Virgin Balloon Flights	
G-VBAI	Cameron A-400 balloon	Virgin Balloon Flights	
G-VBAJ	Cameron A-400 balloon	Virgin Balloon Flights	
G-VBAK	Cameron A-400 balloon	Virgin Balloon Flights	
G-VBAL	Cameron A-400 balloon	Virgin Balloon Flights	
G-VBAM	Cameron A-400 balloon	Virgin Balloon Flights	
G-VBAN	Cameron A-400 balloon	Virgin Balloon Flights	
G-VBAO	Cameron A-400 balloon	Virgin Balloon Flights	
G-VBAP	Cameron A-400 balloon	Virgin Balloon Flights	
G-VBAR	Cameron A-400 balloon	Virgin Balloon Flights	
G-VBAS	Cameron A-400 balloon	Virgin Balloon Flights	
G-VBAT	Cameron A-400 balloon	Virgin Balloon Flights	
G-VBAU	Cameron A-400 balloon	Virgin Balloon Flights	
G-VBAV	Cameron A-400 balloon	Virgin Balloon Flights	
G-VBAW	Cameron A-400 balloon	Virgin Balloon Flights	
G-VBAX	Cameron A-400 balloon	Virgin Balloon Flights	
G-VBAY	Cameron A-400 balloon	Virgin Balloon Flights	
G-VBAZ	Cameron A-400 balloon	Virgin Balloon Flights	
G-VBBA	Cameron A-300 balloon	Virgin Balloon Flights	
G-VBBB	Cameron A-300 balloon	Virgin Balloon Flights	
G-VBBC	Cameron A-300 balloon	Virgin Balloon Flights	
G-VBBD	Cameron A-400 balloon	Virgin Balloon Flights	
G-VBBE	Cameron A-400 balloon	Virgin Balloon Flights	
G-VBBF	Cameron A-400 balloon	Virgin Balloon Flights	
G-VBBG	Cameron A-400 balloon	Virgin Balloon Flights	
G-VBBH	Cameron A-400 balloon	Virgin Balloon Flights	
G-VBBI	Cameron A-400 balloon	Virgin Balloon Flights	
G-VBBJ	Cameron A-400 balloon	Virgin Balloon Flights	
G-VBBK	Cameron A-400 balloon	Virgin Balloon Flights	

Notes	Reg	Type	Owner or Operator
	G-VBCA	Cirrus SR22	C. A. S. Atha
	G-VBDT	Cessna FR.172J	R. A. Ballard
	G-VBEL	Boeing 787-9	Virgin Atlantic Airways Ltd
	G-VBEZ	Rutan LongEz	V. Baltzopoulos (G-BMHA)
	G-VBFA	Ultramagic N-250 balloon	Virgin Balloon Flights
	G-VBFB	Ultramagic N-355 balloon	Virgin Balloon Flights
	G-VBFC	Ultramagic N-250 balloon	Virgin Balloon Flights
	G-VBFD	Ultramagic N-250 balloon	Virgin Balloon Flights
	G-VBFE	Ultramagic N-255 balloon	Virgin Balloon Flights
	G-VBFF	Lindstrand LBL-360A balloon	Virgin Balloon Flights
	G-VBFG	Cameron Z-350 balloon	Virgin Balloon Flights
	G-VBFH	Cameron Z-350 balloon	Virgin Balloon Flights
	G-VBFI	Cameron Z-350 balloon	Virgin Balloon Flights
	G-VBFJ	Cameron Z-350 balloon	Virgin Balloon Flights
	G-VBFK	Cameron Z-350 balloon	Virgin Balloon Flights
	G-VBFL	Cameron Z-400 balloon	Virgin Balloon Flights
	G-VBFM	Cameron Z-375 balloon	Virgin Balloon Flights
	G-VBFN	Cameron Z-375 balloon	Virgin Balloon Flights
	G-VBFO	Cameron Z-375 balloon	Virgin Balloon Flights
	G-VBFP	Ultramagic N-425 balloon	Virgin Balloon Flights
	G-VBFR	Cameron Z-375 balloon	Virgin Balloon Flights
	G-VBFS	Cameron Z-375 balloon	Virgin Balloon Flights
	G-VBFU	Cameron A-400 balloon	Virgin Balloon Flights
	G-VBFV	Cameron Z-400 balloon	Virgin Balloon Flights
	G-VBFW	Cameron Z-77 balloon	Virgin Balloon Flights
	G-VBFX	Cameron Z-400 balloon	Virgin Balloon Flights
	G-VBFY	Cameron Z-400 balloon	Virgin Balloon Flights
	G-VBFZ	Cameron A-300 balloon	Virgin Balloon Flights
	G-VBMD	Eurocopter AS.350B3 Ecureuil	T. B. McDeremott (G-FAIT)
	G-VBOB	Airbus A.350-1041	Virgin Atlantic Airways Ltd
	G-VBOW	Boeing 787-9	Virgin Atlantic Airways Ltd
	G-VBPM	Cirrus SR22	S. Perkes
	G-VBZZ	Boeing 787-9	Virgin Atlantic Airways Ltd
	G-VCIO	EAA Acro Sport II	J. W. Graham-White
	G-VCJH	Robinson R22 Beta	Pickup & Son Ltd
	G-VCML	Beech 58 Baron	St. Angelo Aviation Ltd
	G-VCRM	Slingsby T.67M Firefly Mk.II	CRM Aviation Europe Ltd (G-BUUC)
	G-VCRU	Boeing 787-9	Virgin Atlantic Airways Ltd
	G-VCRZ	Schleicher ASH-31 MI	C. A. & S. C. Noujaim
	G-VCUB	PA-18-150 Super Cub	J. C. Morrison
	G-VCXA	Schempp-Hirth Ventus 2cT	J. Best
	G-VCXT	Schempp-Hirth Ventus 2cT	E. Joseph
	G-VDIA	Boeing 787-9	Virgin Atlantic Airways Ltd
	G-VDIR	Cessna T.310R	J. Driver
	G-VDOG	Cessna 305C Bird Dog (24582)	J. A. Watt
	G-VDOT	Airbus A.350-1041	Virgin Atlantic Airways Ltd
	G-VECD	Robin R.1180T	B. Lee
	G-VEGA	Slingsby T.65A Vega	R. A. Rice (G-BFZN)
	G-VEII	Airbus A.330-941	Virgin Atlantic
	G-VELA	SIAI-Marchetti S.205-22R	Alta Volant Ltd
	G-VELJ	Airbus A.350-1041	Virgin Atlantic Airways Ltd
	G-VENC	Schempp-Hirth Ventus 2cT	A. James
	G-VERA	Gardan GY-201 Minicab	D. K. Shipton
	G-VERO	PA-46-600TP Meridian M600	G-VERO LLP
	G-VETC	Lambert Mission M108	C. J. Cheetham
	G-VETT	Guimbal Cabri G2	Helicentre Aviation Ltd
	G-VEVE	Airbus A.350-1041	Virgin Atlantic Airways Ltd
	G-VEYE	Robinson R22	K. A. Jones (G-BPTP)
	G-VEYR	Airbus A.330-941	Virgin Atlantic Airways Ltd
	G-VEZE	Rutan Vari-Eze	J. M. Keane
	G-VFAN	Boeing 787-9	Virgin Atlantic Airways Ltd
	G-VFAS	PA-28R-200 Cherokee Arrow	Camborne Insurance Services Ltd (G-MEAH/G-BSNM)
	G-VFDS	Van's RV-8	S. B. Shirley
	G-VFUN	Flylight Adam	M. Turner (G-THRN)
	G-VGAG	Cirrus SR20 GTS	TBIO Ltd

Reg	Type	Owner or Operator	Notes
G-VGEM	Airbus A.330-343	Virgin Atlantic Airways Ltd	
G-VGFS	Cameron Z-90 balloon	Western Commodities Ltd	
G-VGMC	Eurocopter AS.355N Ecureuil II	UK Asset Services Ltd (G-HEMH)	
G-VGMP	Airbus Helicopters AS.350B3 Ecureuil	Finlay Machinery LLP	
G-VGVG	Savannah VG Jabiru(1)	M. A. Jones	
G-VICA	Tipsy Nipper T.66 Series 2	V. Asquith (G-ARXN)	
G-VICC	PA-28-161 Cherokee Warrior II	Freedom Aviation Ltd (G-JFHL)	
G-VIDA	Eurofox 3K	Fox Flying Group	
G-VIFF	BAe. Sea Harrier FA2 (ZH798)	Jet Art Aviation Ltd	
G-VIIA	Boeing 777-236	British Airways	
G-VIIB	Boeing 777-236	British Airways	
G-VIIC	Boeing 777-236	British Airways	
G-VIID	Boeing 777-236	British Airways	
G-VIIE	Boeing 777-236	British Airways	
G-VIIF	Boeing 777-236	British Airways	
G-VIIG	Boeing 777-236	British Airways	
G-VIIH	Boeing 777-236	British Airways	
G-VIIJ	Boeing 777-236	British Airways	
G-VIIK	Boeing 777-236	British Airways	
G-VIIL	Boeing 777-236	British Airways	
G-VIIM	Boeing 777-236	British Airways	
G-VIIN	Boeing 777-236	British Airways	
G-VIIO	Boeing 777-236	British Airways	
G-VIIP	Boeing 777-236	British Airways	
G-VIIR	Boeing 777-236	British Airways	
G-VIIS	Boeing 777-236	British Airways	
G-VIIT	Boeing 777-236	British Airways	
G-VIIU	Boeing 777-236	British Airways	
G-VIIV	Boeing 777-236	British Airways	
G-VIIW	Boeing 777-236	British Airways	
G-VIIX	Boeing 777-236	British Airways	
G-VIIY	Boeing 777-236	British Airways	
G-VIIZ	CZAW Sportcruiser	N. I. Hart	
G-VILL	Lazer Z.200 (modified)	S. A. Youngman (G-BOYZ)	
G-VINA	Aeroprakt A-22L Foxbat	J. M. Davidson	
G-VINI	Sikorsky S-92A	Offshore Helicopter Services Ltd	
G-VINP	Sikorsky S-92A	Offshore Helicopter Services Ltd	
G-VINT	Sikorsky S-92A	Offshore Helicopter Services UK Ltd	
G-VIOF	Gulfstream VI (G650)	Executive Jet Charter Ltd	
G-VIPA	Cessna 182S	Stallingborough Aviation Ltd	
G-VIPH	Agusta A109C	Cheqair Ltd(G-BVNH/G-LAXO)	
G-VIPR	Eurocopter EC 120B Colibri	EFL Helicopters Ltd	
G-VIPU	PA-31-350 Navajo Chieftain	Gulfjet Ltd	
G-VIPW	PA-31-350 Navajo Chieftain	Flight Calibration Services Ltd	
G-VITE	Robin R.1180T	G-VITE Flying Group	
G-VITL	Lindstrand LBL-105A balloon	M. J. Axtell	
G-VIVE	Leonardo AW.109SP Grand New	Oxford Helicopter Services LLP	
G-VIVO	Nicollier HN 700 Menestrel II	I. P. Reader	
G-VIXI	Aeroprakt A-32 Vixxen	M. T. Taylor	
G-VIXN	DH.110 Sea Vixen FAW.2 (XS587) ★	Gatwick Aviation Museum/Charlwood	
G-VIXX	Alpi Pioneer 300	N. Harrison (G-CESE/G-CERJ)	
G-VIXY	Aeroprakt A-32 Vixxen	A. Everitt	
G-VIZZ	Sportavia RS.180 Sportsman	G-VIZZ Flying Group	
G-VJAM	Airbus A.350-1041	Virgin Atlantic Airways Ltd	
G-VJAZ	Airbus A.330-941	Virgin Atlantic Airways Ltd	
G-VJET	Avro 698 Vulcan B.2 (XL426) ★	Vulcan Restoration Trust	
G-VJTA	Cessna 560XL Citation XLS+	Saxonair Charter Ltd	
G-VJTB	Cessna 560XL Citation Excel	Saxonair Charter Ltd	
G-VJZZ	Volmer VJ-22 Sportsman	J. A. Wardlow	
G-VKRP	PA-32R-301 Saratoga IITC	R. G. Poxon	
G-VLCN	Avro 698 Vulcan B.2 (XH558) ★	Vulcan to the Sky Trust	
G-VLCT	Velocity SE FG	Hangar Homes Ltd	
G-VLDY	Airbus A.330-941N	Virgin Atlantic Airways Ltd	
G-VLET	Ikarus C42 FB100	J. W. D. Blythe	
G-VLIB	Airbus A.350-1041	Virgin Atlantic Airways Ltd	
G-VLTT	Diamond DA.42 Twin Star	R. H. Butterfield	
G-VLUV	Airbus A.330-343	Virgin Atlantic Airways Ltd	

Notes	Reg	Type	Owner or Operator
	G-VLUX	Airbus A.350-1041	Virgin Atlantic Airways Ltd
	G-VMAP	Boeing 787-9	Virgin Atlantic Airways Ltd
	G-VMCG	PA-38-112 Tomahawk	Pure Aviation Support Services Ltd (G-BSVX)
	G-VMJM	SOCATA TB10 Tobago	D. J. Bryan (G-BTOK)
	G-VMOZ	Van's RV-8	R. A. & R. M. Willings (G-CIKP)
	G-VMSO	Autogyro Cavalon	P. J. Harle
	G-VMVM	Cessna Z-77 balloon	K. R. Karlstrom
	G-VNAM	Cessna 305A Bird Dog (0-14781)	O-1 Aviation Ltd & L. J. Gregoire
	G-VNAV	Diamond DA.62	Flight Calibration Services Ltd
	G-VNEA	Tecnam P-Mentor	VNE Group Ltd
	G-VNEB	Tecnam P-Mentor	VNE Group Ltd
	G-VNEC	Cessna 172S	VNE Group Ltd
	G-VNER	Agusta AW109SP Grand New	Heliservice UK Ltd (G-MOAL)
	G-VNEW	Boeing 787-9	Virgin Atlantic Airways Ltd
	G-VNOM	DH.112 Venom FB.50 (J-1632) ★	de Havilland Heritage Museum/London Colney
	G-VNON	Escapade Jabiru (5)	A. J. Martin
	G-VNOR	Bombardier CL600-2B16 Challenger 650	Luxaviation United Kingdom
	G-VNTS	Schempp-Hirth Ventus bT	9H Syndicate
	G-VNVR	Airbus A.350-1041	Virgin Atlantic Airways Ltd
	G-VNYL	Boeing 787-9	Virgin Atlantic Airways Ltd
	G-VOAR	PA-28-181 Cherokee Archer III	Carlisle Flight Training Ltd
	G-VOCA	Extra EA.230	D. N. H. Gallagher (G-IEII)/G-CBUA)
	G-VODA	Cameron N-77 balloon	H. Cusden
	G-VOID	PA-28RT-201 Cherokee Arrow IV	D. J. Wood
	G-VOIP	Westland SA.341G Gazelle	C3 Property Consultants Ltd
	G-VOLO	Alpi Pioneer 300	R. S. Kennedy & A. Donnelly
	G-VONI	PA-32R-301T Saratoga II TC	W. S. Stanley
	G-VONK	AS.355F1 Squirrel	Airbourne Solutions Ltd (G-BLRI/G-NUTZ)
	G-VONR	Fisher FP 303	R. J. Whettem
	G-VONY	Cessna T182T	Fairbank Investments Ltd
	G-VOOH	Boeing 787-9	Virgin Atlantic Airways Ltd
	G-VOOM	Pitts S-1S Special	VOOM Syndicate
	G-VORN	Aerotechnik EV-97 Eurostar	J. Parker (G-ODAV)
	G-VOUS	Cessna 172S	Flyglass Ltd
	G-VOWS	Boeing 787-9	Virgin Atlantic Airways Ltd
	G-VPIE	Airbus A.330-941	Virgin Atlantic Airways Ltd
	G-VPOP	Airbus A.350-1041	Virgin Atlantic Airways Ltd
	G-VPPL	SOCATA TB20 Trinidad	Cherokee Aviation Ltd (G-BPAS)
	G-VPRD	Airbus A.350-1041	Virgin Atlatic Airways Ltd
	G-VPSJ	Europa	D. A. Dunn
	G-VRAB	Van's RV-8	I. M. Belmore & R. A. Brown
	G-VRAY	Airbus A.330-343	Virgin Atlantic Airways Ltd
	G-VRIF	Airbus A.330-941	Virgin Atlantic Airways Ltd
	G-VRNB	Airbus A.350-1041	Virgin Atlantic Airways Ltd
	G-VROE	Avro 652A Anson T.21 (WD413)	G. G. L. James (G-BFIR)
	G-VROM	Boeing 747-443	Celestial Aviation Trading 8 Ltd
	G-VROS	Boeing 747-443	Virgin Atlantic Airways Ltd
	G-VRRV	Van's RV-12	Southampton University Aviation Society
	G-VRVB	Van's RV-8	R. J. Verrall (G-CETI)
	G-VSGE	Cameron O-105 balloon	P. M. Oggioni/Italy
	G-VSGG	Schempp-Hirth Ventus 2b	S. G. Gaunt
	G-VSIX	Schempp-Hirth Ventus 2cT	J. M. Brooke
	G-VSOZ	Yakovlev Yak-18T	Boomerang Media Ltd
	G-VSPY	Boeing 787-9	Virgin Atlantic Airways Ltd
	G-VSRB	Airbus A.330-941	Virgin Atlantic Airways Ltd
	G-VSTR	Stolp SA-900 V-Star	R. H. Mackay
	G-VSXY	Airbus A.330-343	Virgin Atlantic Airways Ltd
	G-VTAL	Beech V35 Bonanza	D. N. Sluman
	G-VTCT	Schempp-Hirth Ventus-2cT	T. M. World
	G-VTEA	Airbus A.350-1041	Virgin Atlantic Airways Ltd
	G-VTGE	Bell 206L LongRanger	Orchardleigh Helicopters Ltd (G-ELIT)
	G-VTII	DH.115 Vampire T.11 (XX507:74)	M. B. Hooton
	G-VTLY	Bombardier BD700-1A10 Global 6000	Concierge U Ltd
	G-VTOL	Hawker Siddeley Harrier T.52 ★	Brooklands Museum of Aviation/Weybridge

Reg	Type	Owner or Operator	Notes
G-VTOM	Airbus A.330-941	Virgin Atlantic Airways Ltd	
G-VTUS	Schempp-Hirth Ventus 2cT	Ventus 02 Syndicate	
G-VUFO	Airbus A.330-343	Virgin Atlantic Airways Ltd	
G-VULC	Avro 698 Vulcan B.2A (XM655) ★	Radarmoor Ltd/Wellesbourne	
G-VVBF	Colt 315A balloon	Virgin Balloon Flights	
G-VVBO	Bell 206L-3 LongRanger III	Nugent Aviation Ltd	
G-VVRV	Van's RV-9A	I. G. Garban (G-ENTS)	
G-VVTV	Diamond DA42 Twin Star	Zero Four Five Aviation Ltd	
G-VVVV	Skyranger 912 (2)	J. Thomas	
G-VVWW	Enstrom 280C Shark	P. J. Odendaal	
G-VWAG	Airbus A.330-343	Virgin Atlantic Airways Ltd	
G-VWHO	Boeing 787-9	Virgin Atlantic Airways Ltd	
G-VWOO	Boeing 787-9	Virgin Atlantic Airways Ltd	
G-VXEN	Aeroprakt A-32M Vixxen	J. R. Elcocks (G-CMBI)	
G-VXGC	Aeroprakt A-32M Vixxen	J. M. Fearn	
G-VXNN	Aeroprakt A-32 Vixxen	P. J. Williams	
G-VXXN	Aeroprakt A-32 Vixxen	J. W. Shanks	
G-VXXY	Aeroprakt A-32 Vixxen	G. P. & C. J. Wiley	
G-VYAK	Yakovlev Yak-18T	A. I. McRobbie	
G-VYGJ	Airbus A.330-243	Air Tanker Ltd	
G-VYGK	Airbus A.330-243	Air Tanker Ltd	
G-VYGL	Airbus A.330-243	Air Tanker Ltd	
G-VYGM	Airbus A.330-243	Air Tanker Ltd	
G-VYUM	Boeing 787-9	Virgin Atlantic Airways Ltd	
G-VZED	Magni M.16C Tandem Trainer	K. J. McDonald	
G-VZIG	Boeing 787-9	Virgin Atlantic Airways Ltd	
G-VZIM	Alpha R2160	I. M. Hollingsworth	
G-VZVZ	Bell 505 Jet Ranger X	Jet Ranger Aviation Ltd	
G-WACB	Cessna F.152 II	MMC Aircraft Ltd	
G-WACE	Cessna F.152 II	Airways Aero Associations Ltd	
G-WACF	Cessna 152 II	Airways Aero Associations Ltd	
G-WACU	Cessna FA.152	APB Leasing Ltd (G-BJZU)	
G-WACW	Cessna 172P	Civil Service Flying Club (Biggin Hill) Ltd	
G-WACY	Cessna F.172P	The Vintage Wings Aviation Co.Ltd	
G-WADD	Airbus Helicopters EC120B Colibri	G. Riley	
G-WADF	Tanarg/Bionix 13 912S(2)	S. G. Haines & D. J. Pattenden	
G-WADZ	Lindstrand LBL-90A balloon	A. K. C., J. E. H., M. H. & Y. K. Wadsworth (G-CGVN)	
G-WAFI	Van's RV-12iS	M. N. Fotherby & B. M. Lloyd	
G-WAGA	Wag-Aero Wagabond	A. I. Sutherland (G-BNJA)	
G-WAGG	Robinson R22 Beta II	Geoge J Goff Ltd	
G-WAGN	Stinson 108-3 Voyager	S. E. H. Ellcome	
G-WAHT	Albatross D.Va-1 replica (D2263)	O. Wulff	
G-WAIR	PA-32-301 Saratoga	Finningley Aviation	
G-WAIT	Cameron V-77 balloon	M. A. Stelling	
G-WAKY	Cyclone AX2000	G. M. R. Keenan	
G-WALZ	Skyranger Nynja 912S(1)	N. G. Heppleston	
G-WAMS	PA-28R-201 Cherokee Arrow	Stapleford Flying Club Ltd	
G-WANA	P & M Quik	G-WANA Flying Group	
G-WAPA	Robinson R44 II	D. N. Watson	
G-WARB	PA-28-161 Cherokee Warrior III	The Flying School Ltd	
G-WARD	Taylor JT.1 Monoplane	R. P. J. Hunter	
G-WARE	PA-28-161 Cherokee Warrior II	I. D. Wakeling	
G-WARP	Cessna 182F Sylane	J. R. Nicholas (G-ASHB)	
G-WARR	PA-28-161 Cherokee Warrior II	S. A. Tessandier	
G-WARS	PA-28-161 Cherokee Warrior III	Stars Fly Ltd	
G-WARV	PA-28-161 Cherokee Warrior III	Bickertons Aerodromes Ltd	
G-WARW	PA-28-161 Cherokee Warrior III	SBR Aviation Ltd	
G-WARX	PA-28-161 Cherokee Warrior III	White Waltham Airfield Ltd	
G-WARY	PA-28-161 Cherokee Warrior III	P. N. Footitt	
G-WASF	Magni M22C Voyager	W. O. Fogden	
G-WATP	PA-28R-200 Cherokee Arrow	A. Stuart (G-BFZH)	
G-WATR	Christen A1 Husky	Clipper Aviation Ltd	
G-WAVA	Robin HR.200/120B	Carlisle Flight Training Ltd	

Notes	Reg	Type	Owner or Operator
	G-WAVE	Grob G.109B	D. Sibthorp & P. C. Lyons
	G-WAVV	Robon HR200/120B	Carlisle Flight Training Ltd (G-GORF)
	G-WAVY	Grob G.109B	G-WAVY Group
	G-WAWW	P & M Quik GT450	S. P. Hodges
	G-WAYS	Lindstrand LBL-105A balloon	Branded Seagulls Ltd
	G-WAZE	Leonardo AW109SP Grand New	Newshore Holdings Ltd
	G-WAZP	Skyranger 912 (2)	K. P. Smith
	G-WBEV	Cameron N-77 balloon	T. J. & M. Turner (G-PVCU)
	G-WBLY	Mainair Pegasus Quik	A. J. Lindsey
	G-WBRD	Avro Curtiss 1911 Replica	Cooper Aerial Surveys Engineering Ltd & The Lakes Flying Company Ltd
	G-WBRN	Robinson R66	HQ Aviation Ltd
	G-WBTS	Falconar F-11	P. J. Tanulak (G-BDPL)
	G-WCAT	Colt Flying Mitt SS balloon	I. Chadwick
	G-WCKM	Skyranger Swift 912(1)	A. Chowdhury
	G-WCME	Grumman FM-2 Wildcat	Wildcat WP Ltd
	G-WCMI	Grumman FM-2 Wildcat	Wildcat WP Ltd
	G-WCMO	Grumman FM-2 Wildcat	Wildcat WP Ltd
	G-WCUB	PA-18-150 Super Cub	P. A. Walley
	G-WDCL	Agusta A.109E Power	Wickford Development Company Ltd (G-WELY)
	G-WDEB	Thunder Ax-7-77 balloon	A. Heginbottom
	G-WDGC	Rolladen-Schneider LS8-18	W. D. G. Chappel (G-CEWJ)
	G-WDNS	Balony Kubicek BB22Z balloon	Nova Balloon Services Ltd
	G-WDST	Westland Scout AH.1	Colne Aviation Ltd
	G-WDUS	Skyranger Nynja 912S(1)	A. F. Lack
	G-WDZY	Bristell NG5 Classic HD	K. P. Widdowson
	G-WEAH	Boeing 737-MAX8	Ascend Airways Ltd
	G-WEAT	Robinson R44 II	P. J. Hollywood
	G-WEBY	Ace Magic Cyclone	B. W. Webster
	G-WECG	AS.355NP Ecureuil 2	Burnhart Ltd (G-MXCO)
	G-WEEK	Skyranger 912(2)	P. McAteer
	G-WEEV	Van's RV-8	Double Whisky Flying Group (G-JBTR)
	G-WEFR	Alpi Pioneer 200-M	Alpi Flying Group
	G-WEND	PA-28RT-201 Cherokee Arrow IV	A. J. Wallace
	G-WENU	Airbus Helicopters MBB-BK117 D-2	Gama Aviation (UK) Ltd
	G-WENY	Zenair CH.750 Cruzer	P. W. Porter
	G-WEPW	Skyranger Swift 912S(1)	D. C. Mackin
	G-WERY	SOCATA TB20 Trinidad	R-Aviation SARL/France
	G-WESS	Lindstrand LTL Series 1-90 balloon	A. R. A. Moore
	G-WESX	CFM Streak Shadow	M. Catania
	G-WETI	Cameron N-31 balloon	C. A. Butter & J. J. T. Cooke
	G-WEWI	Cessna 172	T. J. Wassell (G-BSEP)
	G-WEZZ	Taylor JT.1 Monoplane	W. A. Tierney (G-BDRF)
	G-WFFW	PA-28-161 Cherokee Warrior II	S. Letheren & D. A. Jelly
	G-WFLY	Mainair Pegasus Quik	S. Turton
	G-WFWA	PA-28-161 Cherokee Warrior II	Wings for Warriors (G-BPMR)
	G-WGCS	PA-18-95 Super Cub	G-WGCS Group
	G-WGMN	Schleicher AS 33 ES	A. G. K. Neofytou
	G-WGSI	Tanarg/Ixess 13 912S(1)	M. Nazm
	G-WGWK	Boeing A.75L 300 Stearman	The Wing Walk Company Ltd (G-BNIW)
	G-WHAA	TLAC Sherwood Ranger ST	Progress Vehicle Management Ltd
	G-WHAT	Colt 77A balloon	M. A. Scholes
	G-WHEE	Pegasus Quantum 15-912	G-WHEE Group
	G-WHEN	Tecnam P92-EM Echo	F. G. Walker
	G-WHIL	Balony Kubicek BB-S Cup SS balloon	A. M. Holly
	G-WHIP	Agusta Westland AW119 Mk.II	SaxonAir Helicopters
	G-WHOG	CFM Streak Shadow	B. R. Cannell
	G-WHOO	Rotorway Executive 162F	M. P. Lumbis
	G-WHPG	Ikarus C42 FB80	C. P. Roche
	G-WHRL	Schweizer 269C	A. Harvey
	G-WHST	AS.350B2 Ecureuil	Toppesfield Ltd (G-BWYA)
	G-WHTE	TLAC Shark 600 UK	The Light Aircraft Company Ltd
	G-WHYS	ICP MXP-740 Savannah VG Jabiru(1)	K. R. T. Stewart

Reg	Type	Owner or Operator	Notes
G-WIBB	Jodel D.18	C. J. Bragg	
G-WIBS	CASA 1-131E Jungmann 2000	C. Willoughby	
G-WICH	Clutton FRED Srs II	D. R. G. Griffith	
G-WIFE	Cessna R.182 RG II	Wife 182 Group (G-BGVT)	
G-WIFI	Cameron Z-90 balloon	A. R. Rich	
G-WIGI	Aeroprakt A22-LS Foxbat	K. E., M. & P. Wigginton	
G-WIGS	Yeoman Dynamic WT9 UK	A. Wiggins (G-DYMC)	
G-WIGY	Pitts S-1S Special	R. E. Welch (G-ITTI)	
G-WIGZ	Van's RV-7	E. J. Wiggin (G-OVEY)	
G-WIII	Schempp-Hirth Ventus bT	I. G. Carrick & R. S. Wood	
G-WIIZ	Augusta-Bell 206B JetRanger 2	Eliexpress SRLS/Italy	
G-WIKD	Van's RV-8	E. P. Morrow	
G-WIKI	Europa XS	A. H. Smith & S. P. Kirton	
G-WILB	Ultramagic M-105 balloon	Nottingham & Derby Hot Air Balloon Club	
G-WILC	Robinson R66	WILC74 Ltd	
G-WILD	Pitts S-1T Special	M. J. Collett	
G-WILG	PZL-104 Wilga 35	M. H. Bletsoe-Brown (G-AZYJ)	
G-WILN	Tecnam P2006T	W Flight Hire Ltd	
G-WILT	Ikarus C42 FB80	R. L. Green	
G-WILZ	Flylight Skyranger Nynja	S. A. Wills	
G-WIMP	Colt 56A balloon	D. M. Wade	
G-WINE	Thunder Ax7-77Z balloon ★	Balloon Preservation Group/Lancing	
G-WINH	Cosmik EV-97 TeamEurostar UK	M. Kolev	
G-WINI	SA Bulldog Srs.120/121 (XX546:03)	A. Bole (G-CBCO)	
G-WINN	Stolp SA300 Starduster Too	G-WINN Group	
G-WINO	Eurofox 912S(1)	G. Holmes	
G-WINY	Diamond S-77 balloon	A. R. A. Moore	
G-WINZ	Lindstrand LTL Penguin balloon	A. M. Holly	
G-WIRL	Robinson R22 Beta	Swift Helicopter Services Ltd	
G-WISD	Fowler SSDR Wisp	M. Fowler	
G-WISZ	Steen Skybolt	G. S. Reid	
G-WIXI	Avions Mudry CAP-10B	A. G. Hatton	
G-WIZI	Enstrom 280FX	K. D. Longhurst & T. J. Dray	
G-WIZR	Robinson R22 Beta II	Helimech Ltd	
G-WIZS	Mainair Pegasus Quik	I. B. Jones	
G-WIZZ	Agusta-Bell 206B JetRanger 2	A. P. Sellars	
G-WJAC	Cameron TR-70 balloon	L. J. Wigfield	
G-WJCM	CASA 1.131E Jungmann 2000 (S5+B06)	D. K. Keays (G-BSFB)	
G-WJET	HpH Glasflugel 304 S Jet	P. Thomson	
G-WJSG	P & M Quik GT450	W. J. Hardy	
G-WKDB	Ikarus C42 FB80 Bravo	W. Broadbent	
G-WKNS	Europa XS	A. L. Wickens	
G-WKTC	Diamond DA.42M-NG Twin Star	DEA Aviation Ltd	
G-WKTH	Diamond DA.62	DEA Aviation Ltd	
G-WKTL	Beech 200T King Air	DEA Aviation Ltd	
G-WKTO	Beech E.90 King Air	DEA Aviation Ltd	
G-WKTS	Beech E.90 King Air	DEA Aviation Ltd	
G-WLAC	PA-18-150 Super Cub	White Waltham Airfield Ltd (G-HAHA/G-BSWE)	
C WLDN	Robinson R44 Raven	J. N. Webster	
G-WLDO	Flylight Adam	P. M. Coppola	
G-WLGC	PA-28-181 Cherokee Archer III	E. F. Mangion (G-FLUX)	
G-WLKR	Embraer EMB-550 Legacy 500	Air Charter Scotland Ltd	
G-WLKS	Schleicher ASW-20L	G-WLKS Syndicate (G-IUMB)	
G-WLLS	Rolladen-Schneider LS8-18	L & A Wells	
G-WLLW	Schleicher AS.33 ES	G. P. Stingemore	
G-WLRS	Supermarine 236 Walrus Mk.1 (W2718)	T. W. Harris (G-RNLI)	
G-WLSN	Skyranger 912S (1)	A. R. Wilson	
G-WLTS	Bell 429	Wiltshire & Bath Air Ambulance Charity	
G-WLVE	Cameron Buddy-90 SS balloon	J. R. Lawson	
G-WMBL	P & M Quik R	S. J. E. Smith	
G-WMTM	AA-5B Tiger	R. J. Sivier	
G-WNCH	Beech B200 Super King Air	HR Smith Aviation Ltd (G-OMGI)	
G-WNDB	Windracers Ultra-UAS	Windracers Ltd	
G-WNDC	Windracers Ultra-UAS	Windracers Ltd	
G-WNDD	Pitts S-1T Special	CK Aviation Services Ltd	
G-WNDE	Windracers Ultra-UAS	Windracers Ltd	

Notes	Reg	Type	Owner or Operator
	G-WNDF	Windracers Ultra-UAS	Windracers Ltd
	G-WNDG	Windracers Ultra-UAS	Windracers Ltd
	G-WNDH	Windracers Ultra-UAS	Windracers Ltd
	G-WNDJ	Windracers Ultra-UAS	Windracers Ltd
	G-WNDK	Windracers Ultra-UAS	Windracers Ltd
	G-WNDR	University of Southampton Ultra-UAS	Windracers Ltd
	G-WNSC	Eurocopter AS.332L2 Super Puma	Airbus Helicopters Ltd
	G-WNSF	Sikorsky S-92A	CHC Scotia Ltd
	G-WNSG	Sikorsky S-92A	CHC Scotia Ltd
	G-WNST	Sikorsky S-92A	CHC Scotia Ltd
	G-WNSV	Sikorsky S-92A	CHC Scotia Ltd
	G-WNTR	PA-28-161 Cherokee Warrior II	Fleetlands Flying Group (G-BFNJ)
	G-WOBL	Flylight Nine	J. D. Rooney
	G-WOBR	Airbus Helicopters MBB-BK117 D-2	Gama Aviation (UK) Ltd
	G-WOFM	Agusta A109E Power	Quicksilver Charter LLP (G-NWRR)
	G-WOFT	Agusta A109E Power	Bath & West Aviation LLP
	G-WOLF	PA-28-140 Cherokee	A. L. Durrant
	G-WONE	Schempp-Hirth Ventus 2cT	J. P. Wright
	G-WOOD	Beech 95-B55A Baron	M. S. Choskey (G-AYID)
	G-WOOF	Enstrom 480	Netcopter.co.uk Ltd & Curvature Ltd
	G-WOOL	Colt 77A balloon	D. P. MacGregor
	G-WOOO	CZAW Sportcruiser	J. R. Powell
	G-WORD	Bell 505 Jet Ranger X	G. H. Wilson
	G-WOTW	Ultramagic M-77 balloon	S. M. Jones
	G-WOWI	Van's RV-7	H. A. Bloxham
	G-WOWO	Cirrus SR22	Archer Six Ltd
	G-WOWS	Cirrus SR22T	M. J. Matthews
	G-WPDA	Eurocopter EC135 P1	National Grid Helicopters Ltd
	G-WPDB	Eurocopter EC135 P1	National Grid Helicopters Ltd
	G-WPDC	Eurocopter EC135 P1	National Grid Helicopters Ltd
	G-WPDD	Eurocopter EC135 P1	National Grid Helicopters Ltd
	G-WPDE	Eurocopter EC135P2+	National Grid Helicopters Ltd
	G-WPNS	BN-2T-4S Defender 4000	Cranfield Aerospace Solutions Ltd (G-GMPB/G-BWPU)
	G-WRAP	Diamond S.120 balloon	R. D. Stagg
	G-WREN	Pitts S-2A Special	W. Ali
	G-WRFM	Enstrom 280C-UK Shark	A. J. Clark (G-CTSI/G-BKIO)
	G-WRIT	Colt 77A balloon	G. Pusey
	G-WRLY	Robinson R22 Beta	Burman Aviation Ltd (G-OFJS/G-BNXJ)
	G-WROL	MBB-BK 117 D-2	Gama Aviation (UK) Ltd (G-OLWG)
	G-WSEX	Westland Wessex HU.Mk.5 (XT761)	A. D. Whitehouse
	G-WSMW	Robinson R44	Chunnel Plant Hire & Contractors Ltd (G-SGPL)
	G-WSSX	Ikarus C42 FB100	S. H. Duboulay
	G-WSTO	Eurocopter AS.355NP Ecureuil II	GB Helicopters (G-WSTR/G-NPTV)
	G-WSTY	Lindstrand LBL-77A balloon	C. & C. Westwood
	G-WTFH	Van's RV-6	N. M. R. Richards
	G-WTSN	Van's RV-8	S. R. Watson
	G-WTWO	Aquila AT01	J. P. Wright
	G-WUFF	Europa	G-WUFF Group
	G-WUKM	Airbus A.321-271NX	Wizz Air UK Ltd
	G-WUKN	Airbus A.321-271NX	Wizz Air UK Ltd
	G-WUKO	Airbus A.321-271NX	Wizz Air UK Ltd
	G-WUKP	Airbus A.321-271NX	Wizz Air UK Ltd
	G-WUKR	Airbus A.321-271NX	Windz Air UK Ltd
	G-WUKS	Airbus A.321-271NX	Wizz Air UK Ltd
	G-WUKT	Airbus A.321-271NX	Wizz Air UK Ltd
	G-WUKU	Airbus A.321-271NX	Wizz Air UK Ltd
	G-WUKV	Airbus A.321-271NX	Wizz Air UK Ltd
	G-WUKW	Airbus A.321-271NX	Wizz Air UK Ltd
	G-WUKX	Airbus A.321-271NX	Wizz Air UK Ltd
	G-WUKY	Airbus A.321-271NX	Wizz Air UK Ltd
	G-WUKZ	Airbus A.321-271NX	Wizz Air UK Ltd
	G-WULF	Replica WAR Focke-Wulf 190 (1)	B. Hunter
	G-WUNA	Airbus A.321-271NX	Wizz Air UK Ltd
	G-WUNB	Airbus A.321-271NX	Wizz Air UK Ltd

Reg	Type	Owner or Operator	Notes
G-WUNC	Airbus A.321-271NX	Wizz Air UK Ltd	
G-WUND	Airbus A.321-271NX	Wizz Air UK Ltd	
G-WUNE	Airbus A.321-271NX	Wizz Air UK Ltd	
G-WVBF	Lindstrand LBL-210A balloon	Virgin Balloon Flights Ltd	
G-WVEN	Extra EA300/200	R. J. Hunter	
G-WVIP	Beech B.200 Super King Air	Newbery Metals Ltd	
G-WWAL	PA-28R-180 Cherokee Arrow	White Waltham Airfield Ltd (G-AZSH)	
G-WWAY	Piper PA-28-181 Cherokee Archer II	S. F. Payne	
G-WWLK	Boeing Stearman A75N1 Kaydet	The Wing Walk Company Ltd	
G-WWVV	Lange Antares 18T	W. D. Inglis	
G-WWZZ	CZAW Sportcruiser	L. Hogan	
G-WXYZ	Zenair CH.750	G. S. Carter	
G-WYAT	CFM Streak Shadow Srs SA	J. L. Wolstenholme	
G-WYDN	Airbus MBB BK117 D-2	Gama Aviation (UK) Ltd (G-YAAC)	
G-WYKD	Tanarg/Ixess 15 912S(2)	M. R. Thorley	
G-WYLD	Cessna T.210N Turbo Centurion II	Vision Aerospace Ltd (G-EEWS)	
G-WYMM	PA-15 Vagabond	N. G. Busschsau (G-AWOF)	
G-WYND	Wittman W.8 Tailwind	R. S. Marriott	
G-WYNT	Cameron N-56 balloon	M. C. Edmunds	
G-WYSZ	Robin DR.400/100	Exavia Ltd (G-FTIM)	
G-WYVN	DG Flugzeugbau DG-1000S	Army Gliding Association	
G-WZAP	Embraer EMB-505 Phenom 300	Hagondale Ltd/Titan Airways	
G-WZOL	RL.5B LWS Sherwood Ranger	D. Lentell (G-MZOL)	
G-WZOY	Rans S.6-ESA Coyote II	K. W. Millett & W. T. D. Gillam	
G-XABC	Cameron Z-77 balloon	N. J. Langley	
G-XACE	Van's RV-14	Dataweb Business Services Ltd	
G-XALT	PA-38-112 Tomahawk	D. R. Clyde	
G-XALZ	Rans S6S-116 Super Six	R. J. Almey	
G-XARA	Czech Sport PS-28 Cruiser	C. W. D. Ross	
G-XARV	ARV Super 2	C. M. Rose (G-OPIG/G-BMSJ)	
G-XASH	Schleicher ASH-31 MI	R. C. Wilson	
G-XATW	Airbus A.321-253NX	Titan Airways Ltd	
G-XAVI	PA-28-161 Cherokee Warrior II	Freedom Aviation Ltd (G-SACZ)	
G-XAVV	Schempp-Hirth Ventus 2c	One Five Two Group	
G-XBAL	Skyranger Nynja 912S(1)	W. G. Gill & N. D. Ewer	
G-XBGA	Glaser-Dirks DG500/22 Elan	N. Kelly	
G-XBJT	Aerotechnik EV-97 Eurostar	M. G. & R. D. Scothern (G-WHOA/G-DATH)	
G-XDOX	Bell 206B JetRanger 3	Adventure 001 Ltd (G-OOHO/G-OCHC/G-KLEE/ G-SIZL/G-BOSW)	
G-XBXX	Lindstrand LTL Series 1-90 balloon	A. M. Holly	
G-XCAP	Mudry CAP-232	D. M. Britten	
G-XCCC	Extra EA.300/L	P. T. Fellows	
G-XCID	SAAB 91D Safir	M. P. Blokland	
G-XCIT	Alpi Pioneer 300	A. Thomas	
G-XCRI	Colomban MC-15 Cri-Cri	Calpurnia Consulting Ltd	
G-XCRJ	Van's RV-9A	H. A. Comber	
G-XCUB	PA-18-150 Super Cub	White Waltham Airfield Ltd	
G-XDCB	Bell 505 Jet Ranger X	DCB Aviation Ltd Partnership Inc (G-CMSY)	
G-XDEA	Diamond DA.42 Twin Star	Tesla Solutions Ltd	
G-XDMK	SA Bulldog Srs 120/121	T. W. Harris	
G-XDUO	Schempp-Hirth Duo Discus xT	The Duo Group	
G-XDWE	P & M Quik GT450	D. Sullivan	
G-XELL	Schleicher ASW-27-18E	S. R. Ell	
G-XENA	PA-28-161 Cherokee Warrior II	P. Brewer	
G-XERK	Van's RV-7	J. D. Kelsall	
G-XERO	CZAW Sportcruiser	M. R. & P. M. Mosley	
G-XFLY	Lambert Mission M212-100	Lambert Aircraft Engineering BVBA	
G-XFOX	Eurofox 912(S)	Fox Five Group	
G-XFTF	BRM Aero Bristell NG5	N. G. Parr	
G-XFYF	Guimbal Cabri G2	R. O'Donnell	

Notes	Reg	Type	Owner or Operator
	G-XGAB	Bristell NG5 Speed Wing	G. A. Beale
	G-XIFR	Lambert Mission M108	Lambert Aircraft Engineering BVBA
	G-XIII	Van's RV-7	Icarus Flying Group
	G-XIIO	Schempp-Hirth Ventus-3T	S. G. Jones
	G-XILM	TL-3000 Sirius	G. P. Curtis
	G-XIOO	Raj Hamsa X'Air 133 (1)	G. M. R. Keenan
	G-XITE	Bell 505 Jet Ranger X	Vantage Leasing Ltd
	G-XIVA	Van's RV-14A	R. Jones
	G-XIXI	Cosmik EV-97 TeamEurostar UK	J. A. C. Cockfield
	G-XIXT	AB Sportine LAK-19T	P. R. Thomas & W. M. Kay
	G-XIXX	Glaser-Dirks DG-300 Elan	G. E. Mitcheson
	G-XKKA	Diamond KH36 Super Dimona	G-XKKA Group
	G-XKRV	Skyranger Nynja LS 912S(1)	A. V. Francis
	G-XLAM	Skyranger 912S	X-LAM Skyranger Syndicate
	G-XLEA	Airbus A.380-841	British Airways
	G-XLEB	Airbus A.380-841	British Airways
	G-XLEC	Airbus A.380-841	British Airways
	G-XLED	Airbus A.380-841	British Airways
	G-XLEE	Airbus A.380-841	British Airways
	G-XLEF	Airbus A.380-841	British Airways
	G-XLEG	Airbus A.380-841	British Airways
	G-XLEH	Airbus A.380-841	British Airways
	G-XLEI	Airbus A.380-841	British Airways
	G-XLEJ	Airbus A.380-841	British Airways
	G-XLEK	Airbus A.380-841	British Airways
	G-XLEL	Airbus A.380-841	British Airways
	G-XLII	Schleicher ASW-27-18E	K. S. McPhee
	G-XLLL	AS.355F1 Twin Squirrel	Excel Charter Ltd (G-PASF/G-SCHU)
	G-XLNT	Zenair CH.601XL	M. D. Gorlov & A. C. Towill
	G-XLRA	Airbus A.321-271NY	Wizz Air UK Ltd
	G-XLRB	Airbus A.321-271NY	Wizz Air UK Ltd
	G-XLRD	Airbus A.321-271NY	Wizz Air UK Ltd
	G-XLTG	Cessna 182S	J. Driver & D. J. Blackburn
	G-XLXL	Robin DR.400/160	K. J. Edwards (G-BAUD)
	G-XMDM	Extra EA.300/SC	M. J. D. Morgan
	G-XMGO	Aeromot AMT-200S Super Ximango	C. & R. P. Beck
	G-XMNE	Evans Aion	Airofly Vtol Ltd
	G-XOOM	Van's RV-8	A. P. S. Maynard (G-RVEI)
	G-XPBI	Letov LK-2M Sluka	R. M. C. Hunter
	G-XPDA	Cameron Z-120 balloon	J. C. M. Greatrix
	G-XPII	Cessna R.172K	London Denham Aviation Ltd (G-DIVA)
	G-XPLR	Pipistrel Virus SW 121A	Triple J Aviation Engineering Ltd
	G-XPRT	Aeros Fox13TDS/Microlite Fly	I. D. Smith
	G-XPXP	Aero Designs Pulsar XP	P. J. Harvey
	G-XRAF	Raj Hamsa X'Air 582 (11)	V. Simpson
	G-XRAY	Rand-Robinson KR-2	R. S. Smith
	G-XRED	Pitts S-1C Special	J. E. Rands (G-SWUN/G-BSXH)
	G-XRLD	Cameron A-250 balloon	Aeolus Aviation GmbH/Germany
	G-XRVB	Van's RV-8	R. E. Kelly
	G-XRVX	Van's RV-10	R. J. Sheridan
	G-XRXR	Raj Hamsa X'Air 582 (5)	B. E. Wagenhauser
	G-XSAM	Van's RV-9A	Parachuting Aircraft Ltd
	G-XSAS	Airbus Helicopters MBB-BK 117 D-3	Gama Aviation (UK) Ltd
	G-XSCP	PA-46-600TP Meridian M600	British European Aviation Ltd
	G-XSDJ	Europa XS	R. J. Sheridan
	G-XSEA	Van's RV-8	H. M. Darlington
	G-XSEL	Silence Twister	Skyview Systems Ltd
	G-XSFT	PA-23-250 Aztec F	M. Lawrynowicz (G-NADN/G-CPPC/G-BGBH)
	G-XSRF	Europa NG	W. J. Murray
	G-XTAZ	Van's RV-7	G-XTAZ Group
	G-XTEE	Edge XT912-B/Streak III	C. F. Janes
	G-XTNI	AirBorne XT912-B/Streak	A. J. Parry

Reg	Type	Owner or Operator	Notes
G-XTRA	Extra EA.230	C. Butler	
G-XTUG	Lambert Mission M108	Lambert Aircraft Engineering BVBA/Belgium	
G-XTUN	Westland-Bell 47G-3B1 (XT223)	P. A. Rogers (G-BGZK)	
G-XUMA	Agusta AW109SP Grand New	Lagopus Aviation Ltd (G-IWPI)	
G-XVAT	Schleicher ASW-27	B. Pridgeon	
G-XVAX	Tecnam P2006T	M. A. Baldwin	
G-XVII	Schleicher ASW-17	C. A. & S. C. Noujaim (G-DCTE)	
G-XVIP	Beech 200 Super King Air	Gama Aviation (UK) Ltd (G-OCEG)	
G-XVMK	Beagle B.121 Pup 2	T. W. Harris (G-PUPP/G-BASD)	
G-XVOM	Van's RV-6	A. Baker-Munton	
G-XVXV	Pitts S-1 Special	R. O. Johnson (G-BXAU)	
G-XWBA	Airbus A.350-1041	British Airways PLC	
G-XWBB	Airbus A.350-1041	British Airways PLC	
G-XWBC	Airbus A.350-1041	British Airways PLC	
G-XWBD	Airbus A.350-1041	British Airways PLC	
G-XWBE	Airbus A.350-1041	British Airways PLC	
G-XWBF	Airbus A.350-1041	British Airways PLC	
G-XWBG	Airbus A.350-1041	British Airways PLC	
G-XWBH	Airbus A.350-1041	British Airways PLC	
G-XWBI	Airbus A.350-1041	British Airways PLC	
G-XWBJ	Airbus A.350-1041	British Airways PLC	
G-XWBK	Airbus A.350-1041	British Airways PLC	
G-XWBL	Airbus A.350-1041	British Airways PLC	
G-XWBM	Airbus A.350-1041	British Airways PLC	
G-XWBN	Airbus A.350-1041	British Airways PLC	
G-XWBO	Airbus A.350-1041	British Airways PLC	
G-XWBP	Airbus A.350-1041	British Airways PLC	
G-XWBR	Airbus A.350-1041	British Airways PLC	
G-XWBS	Airbus A.350-1041	British Airways PLC	
G-XWEB	Skyranger 912 (2)	G. V. Higgins & A. P. Dalgetty	
G-XXEE	Leonardo AW139	The King's Helicopter Flight	
G-XXEF	Leonardo AW139	The King's Helicopter Flight	
G-XXHP	Extra EA.300/L	A. R. Willis (G-BZFR)	
G-XXIV	Agusta-Bell 206B JetRanger 3	Adventure 001 Ltd	
G-XXIX	Schleicher ASW-27-18E	P. R. & A. H. Pentecost	
G-XXLB	Bell 407	Seafresh Group (Holdings) Ltd	
G-XXMB	Gippsaero GA8-TC320 Airvan	Hinton Skydiving Centre Ltd	
G-XXRS	Bombardier BD-700 Global Express	TAG Aviation (UK) Ltd	
G-XXRV	Van's RV-9	D. R. Gilbert & D. Slabbert	
G-XXTH	Bell 505 Jet Ranger X	Pegasus Grab Hire Holdings Ltd (G-XXLH)	
G-XXTR	Extra EA.300/L	The Shoreham Extra Group (G-ECCC)	
G-XXUK	Eurocopter EC 120B Colibri	Rotor Machine Ltd (G-LIZY/G-OTFL/G-IBRI)	
G-XXVB	Schempp-Hirth Ventus b	G. R. P. Brown	
G-XYJY	Skyranger 912(1)	A. V. Francis	
G-XZXZ	Robinson R44 II	Ashley Martin Ltd	
G-YAAA	Airbus MBB-BK117 D-3	Yorkshire Air Ambulance Ltd	
G-YAAK	Yakovlev Yak-50 (20)	D. J. Hopkinson (G-BWJT)	
G-YACC	Yakovlev Yak-18T	A. J. Wood	
G-YADA	Ikarus C42 FB100	H. L. Wilson	
G-YAIR	Airbus MBB-BK 117 D-3	Yorkshire Air Ambulance Ltd	
G-YAKE	Yakovlev Yak-52 (10)	Transair (UK) Ltd (G-BVVA)	
G-YAKF	Aerostar Yakovlev Yak-52	P. Hardisty	
G-YAKG	Yakovlev Yak-18T	A. G. Jones	
G-YAKH	IDA Bacau Yakovlev Yak-52	G-YAKH Group	
G-YAKI	IDA Bacau Yakovlev Yak-52 (100 blue)	Yak One Ltd	
G-YAKM	IDA Bacau Yakovlev Yak-50 (61 red)	Airborne Services Ltd	
G-YAKN	IDA Bacau Yakovlev Yak-52 (66 red)	Airborne Services Ltd	
G-YAKU	IDA Bacau Yakovlev Yak-50 (49 red)	D. J. Hopkinson (G-BXND)	
G-YAKX	IDA Bacau Yakovlev Yak-52 (27 red)	The X-Flyers Ltd	
G-YAKZ	IDA Bacau Yakovlev Yak-50 (33 red)	J. M. W. Breuer	
G-YANK	PA-28-181 Cherokee Archer II	M. Cason	
G-YARD	Robinson R44 II	Caffco Ltd	
G-YARR	Mainair Rapier	D. Yarr	
G-YARV	ARV Super 2	A. M. Oliver (G-BMDO)	

Notes	Reg	Type	Owner or Operator
	G-YAWW	PA-28RT-201T Turbo Cherokee Arrow IV	Barton Aviation Ltd
	G-YBAA	Cessna FR.172J	N. A. Baxter
	G-YBES	Eurocopter EC130 B4	Gybe Ho Air LLP
	G-YCAP	Mudry CAP 232	H. A. M. Tallini (G-HAYE/G-SKEW)
	G-YCMI	Sonex	S. T. Hatherall
	G-YCUB	PA-18-150 Super Cub	F. W. Rogers
	G-YDEA	DA-42 Twin Star	DEA Aviation Ltd
	G-YEAS	Schleicher AS 33 ES	A. P. C. Sampson
	G-YEBO	Cirrus SR22	G. J. Trew
	G-YEHA	Schleicher ASW-27	B. L. Cooper
	G-YELA	Van's RV-8	A. G. Solleveld
	G-YELL	Murphy Rebel	I. N. Scott
	G-YELO	Autogyro MT-03	Gyro Copter HQ Ltd
	G-YELP	TLAC Sherwood Ranger ST	J. Bishop
	G-YEOM	PA-31-350 Navajo Chieftain	Strata Aviation Services Ltd
	G-YETI	Europa	C. G. Sutton (G-CILF)
	G-YEWS	Rotorway Executive 152	R. Turrell & P. Mason
	G-YFLI	Rotorsport UK Cavalon	A. J. & S. F. Unwin (G-CGYX)
	G-YFOX	Dassault Falcon 2000EX	London Executive Aviation Ltd
	G-YIPY	PA-31-350 Navajo Chieftain	Atlantic Bridge Aviation Ltd (G-VIPY/G-POLO)
	G-YIRO	Campbell Cricket Mk.4	M. A. Ward (G-KGED)
	G-YJET	Montgomerie-Bensen B.8MR	P. D. Davis-Ratcliffe (G-BMUH)
	G-YKED	Yakovlev Yak-50	E. P. Bunnage-Flavell
	G-YKSO	Yakovlev Yak-50 (23)	A. M. Holman-West
	G-YKVV	Yakovlev Yak-55M	E. P. Bunnage-Flavell
	G-YMFC	Waco YMF	M. J. Brernchley
	G-YMMA	Boeing 777-236ER	British Airways
	G-YMMB	Boeing 777-236ER	British Airways
	G-YMMC	Boeing 777-236ER	British Airways
	G-YMMD	Boeing 777-236ER	British Airways
	G-YMME	Boeing 777-236ER	British Airways
	G-YMMF	Boeing 777-236ER	British Airways
	G-YMMG	Boeing 777-236ER	British Airways
	G-YMMH	Boeing 777-236ER	British Airways
	G-YMMI	Boeing 777-236ER	British Airways
	G-YMMJ	Boeing 777-236ER	British Airways
	G-YMMK	Boeing 777-236ER	British Airways
	G-YMML	Boeing 777-236ER	British Airways
	G-YMMN	Boeing 777-236ER	British Airways
	G-YMMO	Boeing 777-236ER	British Airways
	G-YMMP	Boeing 777-236ER	British Airways
	G-YMMR	Boeing 777-236ER	British Airways
	G-YMMS	Boeing 777-236ER	British Airways
	G-YMMT	Boeing 777-236ER	British Airways
	G-YMMU	Boeing 777-236ER	British Airways
	G-YNJA	Skyranger Nynja 912S(1)	C. A. Green
	G-YNYS	Cessna 172S Skyhawk	T. V. Hughes
	G-YOBI	Schleicher ASH-25	J. Kangurs
	G-YOGA	Commander 114B	Thargo Ltd
	G-YOGI	Robin DR.400/140B	G-YOGI Flying Group (G-BDME)
	G-YOLK	P & M Aviation Quik GT450	P. Jones
	G-YOLO	Aeroprakt A22-L2 Foxbat	J. W. Mann
	G-YOLT	Magni M16C Tandem Trainer	P. Wells
	G-YORE	CZAW Sportcruiser	R. Yore (G-CFNV)
	G-YORX	Airbus Helicopters MBB-BK-117D-3	Yorkshire Air Ambulance Ltd
	G-YOTS	IDA Bacau Yakovlev Yak-52	G-YOTS Group
	G-YOYO	Pitts S-1E Special	P. M. Jarvis (G-OTSW/G-BLHE)
	G-YPDN	Rotorsport UK MT-03	T. M. Jones
	G-YPSY	Andreasson BA-4B	J. P. Burrill

Reg	Type	Owner or Operator	Notes
G-YRAF	RAF 2000 GTX-SE gyroplane	J. R. Cooper	
G-YRAX	Magni M-24C	J. A. Robinson	
G-YRIL	Luscombe 8E Silvaire	I. de Groot	
G-YROA	Rotorsport UK MTO Sport	C. A. Smith	
G-YROC	Rotorsport UK MT-03	C. V. Catherall	
G-YROF	Magni M22C Voyager	M. S. Shenton	
G-YROG	Magni M24C Orion	Flygyro	
G-YROH	Rotorsport UK MTO Sport	M. Winship	
G-YROJ	RAF2000 GTX-SE	Condor Aviation International Ltd	
G-YROK	Magni M-16C	K. J. Yeadon	
G-YROL	Rotorsport UK Cavalon	S. A. Bexfield	
G-YROM	Rotorsport UK MT-03	A. Wallace	
G-YRON	Magni M-16C Tandem Trainer	H. E. Simons	
G-YROO	RAF 2000 GTX-SE gyroplane	A. R. Hawes	
G-YROP	Magni M-16C Tandem Trainer	Gyrop Group	
G-YROR	Magni M.24C	R. M. Stanley	
G-YROT	Rotorsport UK MTO Sport 2017	R. Wright	
G-YROU	Magni M24C Orion	S. W. Lowndes & R. Morris	
G-YROV	Rotorsport UK MT-03	Carnie Aviation Ltd (G-UMAS)	
G-YROY	Montgomerie-Bensen B8MR	I. L. McCullough	
G-YROZ	Rotorsport UK Calidus	A. M. Mackey	
G-YRRO	Rotorsport UK Calidus	J. D. Winder	
G-YRTE	Agusta A.109S Grand	Castle Air Ltd	
G-YRUS	Jodel D.140E	W. E. Massam (G-YRNS)	
G-YSAR	Agusta AW139	Helioperations	
G-YSHK	Ultramagic M-105 balloon	Hampshire Balloons Ltd	
G-YSIR	Van's RV-8	The Lord Rotherwick	
G-YSMO	Mainair Pegasus Quik	D. P. Pointer	
G-YSSS	Pilatus PC-24	TAG Aviation (UK) Ltd	
G-YTLY	Rans S-6-ES Coyote II	A. J. Gibson	
G-YUGE	Schempp-Hirth Ventus cT	C. Godding (G-CFNN)	
G-YUGG	Van's RV-8	S. J. Wood, A. J. Hurrell & B. R. Iddon	
G-YULL	PA-28-180 Cherokee	G-YULL Flying Group (G-BEAJ)	
G-YUMM	Cameron N-90 balloon	H. Stringer	
G-YUPI	Cameron N-90 balloon	MCVH SA/Belgium	
G-YURO	Europa ★	Yorkshire Air Museum/Elvington	
G-YVES	Alpi Pioneer 300	A. P. Anderson	
G-YVIP	Beech B200 Super King Air	Gama Aviation (UK) Ltd	
G-YXLX	ISF Mistral C	R. R. Penman	
G-YYES	Cirrus SR20	A9 Leasing LLP	
G-YYRO	Magni M-16C Tandem Trainer	A. Yin-Tuen Leung	
G-YYYY	MH.1521C-1 Broussard (208)	Aerosuperbatics Ltd	
G-YZYZ	Mainair Blade 912	A. M. Beale	
G-ZAAP	CZAW Sportcruiser	H. Page	
G-ZAAZ	Van's RV-8	P. A. Super	
G-ZABA	Kubicek BB26E	J. A. Viner	
G-ZABC	Sky 90-24 balloon	P. Donnelly	
G-ZABH	Dassault Falcon 900LX	Centreline AV Ltd	
G-ZACE	Cessna 172S	Duna Aviation Ltd	
G-ZACH	Robin DR.400/100	Robin Flying Club Ltd (G-FTIO)	
G-ZACK	Cirrus SR20	AP Asset Holdings Ltd & M. A. Malik	
G-ZADA	Skyranger 912S(1)	C. P. Lincoln	
G-ZAHS	Dassault Falcon 900EX	Centreline	
G-ZAKA	Diamond DA.40D Star	Plane Rentals Ltd	
G-ZANY	Diamond DA.40D Star	Altair Aviation Ltd	
G-ZAPY	Robinson R22 Beta	HQ Aviation Ltd (G-INGB)	
G-ZARV	ARV Super 2	P. R. Snowden	
G-ZASH	Ikarus C42 FB80	J. Bulpin	
G-ZATG	Diamond DA.42M Twin Star	DEA Aviation Ltd (G-DOSA)	
G-ZAVI	Ikarus C42 FB100	ZAVI Syndicate	
G-ZAZA	PA-18-95 Super Cub	G. J. Harry, The Viscount Goschen	
G-ZAZU	Diamond DA.42 Twin Star	Romeo Golf Aviation Ltd (G-GFDA/G-CEFX)	
G-ZAZZ	Lindstrand LBL-120A balloon	A. Reikertas/Lithuania	

Notes	Reg	Type	Owner or Operator
	G-ZBAP	Airbus A.320-214	First Star Speir Aviation 1 Ltd (G-OOPT/G-OOAT)
	G-ZBED	Robinson R22 Beta	M. J. Wearing
	G-ZBEN	IAV Bacau Yakovlev Yak-52	B. A. Nicholson
	G-ZBJA	Boeing 787-8	British Airways PLC
	G-ZBJB	Boeing 787-8	British Airways PLC
	G-ZBJC	Boeing 787-8	British Airways PLC
	G-ZBJD	Boeing 787-8	British Airways PLC
	G-ZBJE	Boeing 787-8	British Airways PLC
	G-ZBJF	Boeing 787-8	British Airways PLC
	G-ZBJG	Boeing 787-8	British Airways PLC
	G-ZBJH	Boeing 787-8	British Airways PLC
	G-ZBJI	Boeing 787-8	British Airways PLC
	G-ZBJJ	Boeing 787-8	British Airways PLC
	G-ZBJK	Boeing 787-8	British Airways PLC
	G-ZBJM	Boeing 787-8	British Airways PLC
	G-ZBKA	Boeing 787-9	British Airways PLC
	G-ZBKB	Boeing 787-9	British Airways PLC
	G-ZBKC	Boeing 787-9	British Airways PLC
	G-ZBKD	Boeing 787-9	British Airways PLC
	G-ZBKE	Boeing 787-9	British Airways PLC
	G-ZBKF	Boeing 787-9	British Airways PLC
	G-ZBKG	Boeing 787-9	British Airways PLC
	G-ZBKH	Boeing 787-9	British Airways PLC
	G-ZBKI	Boeing 787-9	British Airways PLC
	G-ZBKJ	Boeing 787-9	British Airways PLC
	G-ZBKK	Boeing 787-9	British Airways PLC
	G-ZBKL	Boeing 787-9	British Airways PLC
	G-ZBKM	Boeing 787-9	British Airways PLC
	G-ZBKN	Boeing 787-9	British Airways PLC
	G-ZBKO	Boeing 787-9	British Airways PLC
	G-ZBKP	Boeing 787-9	British Airways PLC
	G-ZBKR	Boeing 787-9	British Airways PLC
	G-ZBKS	Boeing 787-9	British Airways PLC
	G-ZBLA	Boeing 787-10	British Airways PLC
	G-ZBLB	Boeing 787-10	British Airways PLC
	G-ZBLC	Boeing 787-10	British Airways PLC
	G-ZBLD	Boeing 787-10	British Airways PLC
	G-ZBLE	Boeing 787-10	British Airways PLC
	G-ZBLF	Boeing 787-10	British Airways PLC
	G-ZBLG	Boeing 787-10	British Airways PLC
	G-ZBLH	Boeing 787-10	British Airways PLC
	G-ZBLI	Boeing 787-10	British Airways PLC
	G-ZBLJ	Boeing 787-10	British Airways PLC
	G-ZBLK	Boeing 787-10	British Airways PLC
	G-ZBLL	Boeing 787-10	British Airways PLC
	G-ZBLT	Cessna 182S	M. Bisek
	G-ZBOP	PZL-Bielsko SZD-36A Cobra 15	A. C. Wilson & J. L. Pattingale
	G-ZDCL	Zenair CH650B	C. J. Gaunt
	G-ZDEA	Diamond DA.42 Twin Star	DEA Aviation Ltd
	G-ZDEE	Eurofox 2K	J. D. & D. Cheesman
	G-ZEAA	Diamond DA.62	AMPA Ltd
	G-ZEAB	Diamond DA.62	AMPA Ltd
	G-ZEAC	Diamond DA.62	AMPA Ltd
	G-ZEBY	PA-28-140 Cherokee	I. Parkinson (G-BFBF)
	G-ZECH	CZAW Sportcruiser	Sportcruiser UK015
	G-ZEIN	Slingsby T.67M Firefly 260	James A Mutton Consulting Ltd
	G-ZENG	Embraer EMB-505 Phenom 300	Saxonair Charter Ltd
	G-ZENR	Zenair CH.601HD Zodiac	A. R. Keating (G-BRJB)
	G-ZENY	Zenair CH.601HD Zodiac	S. Bishop
	G-ZEPI	Colt GA-42 gas airship	P. A. Lindstrand (G-ISPY/G-BPRB)
	G-ZERO	AA-5B Tiger	N. R. Evans & D. K. Rose
	G-ZEVS	Cessna F.172H	D. M. White
	G-ZEZE	Cessna 182S	S. Bonham (G-LVES/G-ELIE)
	G-ZFOO	Tucano Replica	A. J. Palmer & D. Sayyah
	G-ZFOX	Denney Kitfox Mk.2	A. P. Gunston
	G-ZFZF	Van's RV-8	B. M. Gwynnett (G-EGRV/G-PHMG)
	G-ZGAB	BRM Aero Bristell NG5 Speed Wing	A. M. Oliver

Reg	Type	Owner or Operator	Notes
G-ZGZG	Cessna 182T	J. Noble	
G-ZGTK	Schleicher ASH-26E	Attitude Aerobatics Ltd (G-BWBY)	
G-ZHKF	Escapade 912(2)	C. D. & C. M. Wills	
G-ZHWH	Rotorway Executive 162F	A. P. Goddard	
G-ZIGY	Europa XS	K. D. Weston	
G-ZIII	Pitts S-2B Special	D. J. Taplin & I. Noakes (G-CDBH)	
G-ZINC	Cessna 182S	M. Mears (G-VALI)	
G-ZION	Cessna 177B	E. V. Hammersley	
G-ZIPA	Rockwell Commander 114A	D. R. Doe (G-BHRA)	
G-ZIPI	Robin DR.400/180	A. J. Cooper	
G-ZIPX	Sonex Onex	B. A. E. Stephenson	
G-ZIPY	Wittman W.8 Tailwind	R. W. Kilham	
G-ZIRA	Z-1RA Stummelflitzer	P. J. Dale	
G-ZIZY	TL2000UK Sting Carbon S4	C. E. & R. P. Reeves	
G-ZLNN	Moravan Zlin Z-326 Trener Master	P. A. Colman	
G-ZLSK	TLAC Sherwood Scout	P. J. Laycock	
G-ZNTH	Learjet 75	Zenith Aviation Ltd	
G-ZODY	Zenair CH.601UL Zodiac	Zodyfly Ltd	
G-ZOFG	PA-28-181 Cherokee Archer II	The Zero Oktas Flying Group	
G-ZOGG	Agusta A109S Grand	Myheli Ltd (G-MIHD/G-SAFA/G-PBWR/G-VERU)	
G-ZOIZ	Ultramagic M-105 balloon	S. Dyer	
G-ZOLA	Diamond DA42 NG Twin Star	Plane Rentals Ltd	
G-ZOMB	Ikarus C42 FB100	D. Brooksbank	
G-ZOOB	Tecnam P2008-JC	Century Aviation Ltd	
G-ZOOL	Cessna FA.152	A. S. C. Rathmell-Davey (G-BGXZ)	
G-ZORO	Europa	N. T. Read	
G-ZOSA	Champion 7GCAA	V. F. A. Stanley	
G-ZOZO	Cameron R-77 GB balloon	D. J. & M. A. Scholes	
G-ZPPY	PA-18-95 Super Cub	R. Sims (G-NICK)	
G-ZSDB	PA-28-236 Dakota	Dakota Air Services LLP (G-BPCX)	
G-ZSIX	Schleicher ASW-27-18E	F. J. Davies	
G-ZSKD	Cameron Z-90 balloon	M. J. Gunston	
G-ZSKY	Skyranger Swift 912S(1)	J. E. Lipinski	
G-ZTED	Europa	J. J. Kennedy	
G-ZTOO	Staaken Z-2 Flitzer	E. B. Toulson	
G-ZTUC	Eurofox 914	G. Donnelly (G-CICX)	
G-ZTWO	Staaken Z-2 Flitzer	S. J. Randle	
G-ZUFL	Lindstrand LBL-90A balloon	Zuffle Dog Balloon Team (G-CHLL)	
G-ZUFO	Thunder AX3 balloon	Bear Balloons (G-BKBD)	
G-ZUMI	Van's RV-8	D. R. Cairns	
G-ZVIP	Beech 200 Super King Air	Centreline AV Ltd (G-SAXN/G-OMNH)	
G-ZVKO	Edge 360	M. F. Henderson	
G-ZXCL	Extra EA.300/L	J. Rowlinson	
G-ZXEL	Extra EA.300/L	Extrael Ltd	
G-ZXLL	Extra EA.300/L	2 Excel Aviation Ltd	
G-ZYDA	Diamond DA.40NG	Golf Delta Alpha Ltd	
G-ZZAC	Aerotechnik EV-97 Eurostar	N. R. Beale	
G-ZZAJ	Schleicher ASH-26E	S. D. Barnard	
G-ZZDD	Schweizer 269C	Scott Aviation (Berkshire) Ltd (G-OCJK)	
G-ZZDG	Cirrus SR20 G2	B. Lane & N. Deeks	
G-ZZEL	Westland Gazelle AH.1	Yeet Helicopters Ltd	
G-ZZIJ	PA-28-180 Cherokee C	T. M. Barton (G-AVGK)	
G-ZZLE	Westland Gazelle AH.2 (XX436)	The Gazelle Squadron Display Team Ltd	
G-ZZMM	Enstrom 480B	Fly 7 Helicopters LLP (G-TOIL)	
G-ZZOE	Eurocopter EC 120B	J. F. H. James	
G-ZZOT	PA-34-220T Seneca V	Ravenair Aircraft Ltd	
G-ZZXX	P & M Quik GT450	Mid Anglia Microlights Ltd	

Notes	Reg	Type	Owner or Operator
	G-ZZZS	Eurocopter EC.120B Colibri	EBG (Helicopters) LtdRosegate Helicopter Services Ltd

G-VGAG Cirrus SR20. *Allan S. Wright*

G-WIGY Pitts S-1S Special. *Allan S. Wright*

Serial Carried	Civil Identity	Serial Carried	Civil Identity
1 (Soviet AF)	G-BZMY	781-32 (Spanish AF)	G-BPDM
1 (Luftwaffe)	G-WULF	854 (USAAC)	G-BTBH
1	G-BPVE	897:E (USN)	G-BJEV
6	G-CAMM	99+18 (Luftwaffe)	G-ONAA
6G+ED (Lutwaffe)	G-BZOB	1018 (Polish AF)	G-ISKA
7 (French AF)	G-NORD	1102:102 (USN)	G-AZLE
9 (Luftwaffe)	G-AWHH	1130 (Royal Saudi AF)	G-VPER
9 (Luftwaffe)	G-CCFW	1264	G-FDHB
9 (Soviet AF)	G-OYAK	1342 (Soviet AF)	G-BTZD
03 (Soviet AF)	G-CEIB	1350 (Portuguese AF)	G-CGAO
07 (Soviet AF)	G-BMJY	1365 (Portuguese AF)	G-DHPM
10 (Soviet AF)	G-YAKE	1367 (Portuguese AF)	G-UANO
10 (DOSAAF)	G-BTZB	1373 (Portuguese AF)	G-CBJG
10 (Luftwaffe)	G-AWHK	1377 (Portuguese AF)	G-BARS
11 (Luftwaffe)	G-AWHC	1747 (Portuguese AF)	G-BGPB
14 (USAAC)	G-ISDN	1801/18 (Luftwaffe)	G-BNPV
20 (Soviet AF)	G-YAAK	1803/18 (Luftwaffe)	G-BUYU
21 (Soviet AF)	G-CDBJ	2345 (RFC)	G-ATVP
23 (Soviet AF)	G-YKSO	3066	G-AETA
26 (USAAC)	G-BAVO	3091 (RCAF)	G-CPPM
26 (DOSAAF)	G-BVXK	3303 (Portuguese AF)	G-CBGL
27 (Soviet AF)	G-YAKX	3397:174 (USN)	G-OBEE
27 (Soviet AF)	G-YAKX	3579/14 (Luftwaffe)	G-CIPB
28 (Soviet AF)	G-BSSY	3681 (USAAC)	G-AXGP
33 (grey) (Soviet AF)	G-YAKH	3914 (USAAF)	G-BHZU
33 (red) (Soviet AF)	G-YAKZ	4034 (Luftwaffe)	G-CDTI
35-23 (Spanish AF)	G-RPAX	4406:12 (USN)	G-ONAF
43 (Soviet AF)	G-BWSV	4445:228 (USN)	G-CFXT
43:SC (USAF)	G-AZSC	4513:1 (French AF)	G-BFYO
44 (USAAC)	G-LIIZ	4826:882 (USN)	G-CJIN
49 (Soviet AF)	G-YAKU	5084: (RCAF)	G-FCTK
52 (DOSAAF)	G-BWVR	5964 (RFC)	G-BFVH
52 (Soviet AF)	G-CCJK	7198/18 (Luftwaffe)	G-AANJ
54 (French Army)	G-CGWR	8449M (RAF)	G-ASWJ
61 (Soviet AF)	G-YAKM	9917	G-EBKY
66 (Soviet AF)	G-YAKN	01420 (Polish AF but in Korean colours)	G-BMZF
68 (Chinese AF)	G-BVVG	0-14781 (US Army)	G-VNAM
78 (French Army)	G-BIZK	16037 (USAAC)	G-BSFD
82:8 (French AF)	G-CCVH	16693:693 (RCAF)	G-BLPG
92 (South African Navy)	G-BYCX	18072:072 (RCAF)	G-FCTY
100 (DOSAAF)	G-YAKI	18393:393 (RCAF)	G-BCYK
104 (South Arabian AF)	G-PROV	18671:671 (RCAF)	G-BNZC
105/15 (Luftwaffe)	G-UDET	24541:BMG (French Army)	G-JDOG
112 (USAAC)	G-BSWC	24550 (US Army)	G-PDOG
113 (Kuwait AF)	G-CFBK	24582 (US Army)	G-VDOG
143 (French Navy)	G-MSAL	26359 (USN)	G-BNXM
152/17 (Luftwaffe)	G-BVGZ	30146 (Yugoslav Army)	G-BSXD
154/315-CM (French Army)	G-TNUP	30140 (Yugoslav Army)	G-SOKO
161 (Irish Air Corps)	G-CCCA	31145:G-26 (USAAF)	G-BBLH
168 (RFC)	G-BFDE	3-1923 (USAAF)	G-BRHP
174 (Royal Netherlands Navy)	G-BEPV	31952 (USAAF)	G-BRPR
208 (French Army)	G-YYYY	42617:617 (USAAF)	G-LXXI
30-QA (French AF)	G-CLLK	43517:227 (USN)	G-NZSS
311 (Singapore AF)	G-MXPH	43583	G-FINT
317 (USAAC)	G-CIIN	56321:U-AB (Royal Norwegian AF)	G-BKPY
354	G-BZNK	61367	G-CGID
403/17 (Luftwaffe)	G-CDXR	80105 (US Air Service)	G-CCBN
416/15 (Luftwaffe)	G-GSAL	85061:7F-061 (USN)	G-OSNJ
417 (Oman AF)	G-RSAF	111836:JZ-6 (USN)	G-TSIX
422/15 (Luftwaffe)	G-AVJO	115042:TA-042 (USAF)	G-BGHU
422/15 (Luftwaffe)	G-FOKR	115227 (USN)	G-BKRA
425/17 (Luftwaffe)	G-DREI	115373 (USAAF)	G-AYPM
425 (Oman AF)	G-SOAF	115684 (USAAF)	G-BKVM
441 (USN)	G-BTFG	121714:201-B (USN)	G-RUMM
466 (USAAC)	G-PTBA	124485:DF-A (USAAF)	G-BEDF
477/17 (Luftwaffe)	G-FOKK	133908 (USAAF)	G-BGOR
503 (Hungarian AF)	G-BRAM	150225:123 (USMC)	G-AWOX
540 (USAAF)	G-BCNX	18-2001 (USAAF)	G-BIZV
556/17 (Luftwaffe)	G-CFHY	18-5395:CDG (French Army)	G-CUBJ
669 (USAAC)	G-CCXA	236657:D-72 (USAAF)	G-BGSJ
671 (USAAC)	G-CGPY	238410:A-44 (USAAF)	G-BHPK
687 (Royal Flying Corps)	G-AWYI	285068 (USAAF)	G-KAMY
687 (USAAC)	G-RLWG	314887 (USAAF)	G-AJPI
699 (USAAC)	G-CCXB	315509:W7-S (USAAF)	G-BHUB

Serial Carried	Civil Identity	Serial Carried	Civil Identity
329405:A-23 (USAAF)	G-BCOB	A17-48 (RAAF)	G-BPHR
329417 (USAAF)	G-BDHK	A-35 (Swiss AF)	G-CLKV
329471:F-44 (USAAF)	G-BGXA	A-57 (Swiss AF)	G-BECT
329594 (USAAF)	G-BROR	A58-606:ZP-W (RAAF)	G-AWGB
329601:D-44 (USAAF)	G-AXHR	A-806 (Swiss AF)	G-BTLL
329707:S-44 (USAAF)	G-BFBY	A126	G-CILI
329854:R-44 (USAAF)	G-BMKC	A2943	G-CJZO
329934:B-72 (USAAF)	G-BCPH	A6906	G-CLNZ
330238:A-24 (USAAF)	G-LIVH	A8226	G-BIDW
330244:C-46 (USAAF)	G-CGIY	A8936	G-BFWD
330314 (USAAF)	G-BAET	B595:W	G-BUOD
330372 (USAAF)	G-AISX	B1162:F	G-AEPH
330485:C-44 (USAAF)	G-AJES	B6401	G-AWYY
379994:J-52 (USAAF)	G-BPUR	B7270	G-BFCZ
413521:5Q-B (USAAF)	G-MRLL	C1096	G-ERFC
413779:WD-C (USAAF)	G-CMDK	C1904:Z	G-PFAP
414237:HO-W (USAAF)	G-MCSW	C3011:S	G-SWOT
414673:LH-I (USAAF)	G-BDWM	C4918	G-BWJM
414907:CY-S (USAAF)	G-DHYS	C4994	G-BLWM
433915 (USAAF)	G-PBYA	C5430	G-CCXG
436021 (USAAF)	G-BWEZ	C8500/16 (German Army)	G-ANKV
454467:J-44 (USAAF)	G-BILI	C8846:M	G-AVOU
454537:J-04 (USAAF)	G-BFDL	C8996	G-ECAE
454630 (USAAF)	G-BDOL	C9533:M	G-BUWE
461748:Y (USAF)	G-BHDK	D1851	G-BZSC
472216:HO-M (USAAF)	G-BIXL	D2263 (Luftwaffe)	G-WAHT
472218:WZ-I (USAAF)	G-MUZY	D5397/17 (Luftwaffe)	G-BFXL
474008:VF-R (USAAF)	G-PSIR	D8084	G-ACAA
479712:8-R (USAAF)	G-AHIP	E3B-153:781-75 (Spanish AF)	G-BPTS
479744:M-49 (USAAF)	G-BGPD	E3B-494:81-47 (Spanish AF)	G-CDLC
479878 (USAAF)	G-BEUI	E32B-599:791-31 (Spanish AF)	G-CGTX
479897:JD (USAAF)	G-BOXJ	E33/15 (Luftwaffe)	G-CHAW
480015:M-44 (USAAF)	G-AKIB	E37/15 (Luftwaffe)	G-CGJF
480133:B-44 (USAAF)	G-BDCD	E449	G-EBJE
480173:57-H (USAAF)	G-RRSR	E2977	G-EBHB
480321:H-44 (USAAF)	G-FRAN	E3273	G-ADEV
480480:E-44 (USAAF)	G-BECN	E8894	G-CDLI
480636:A-58 (USAAF)	G-AXHP	F141:G	G-SEVA
480723:E5-J (USAAF)	G-BFZB	F235:B	G-BMDB
480752:E-39 (USAAF)	G-BCXJ	F904	G-EBIA
481273 (US ANG)	G-CJWE	F938	G-EBIC
493209 (US ANG)	G-DDMV	F943	G-BIHF
517692 (USAAF)	G-TROY	F2211	G-CMDN
542447 (USAF)	G-SCUB	F5447:N	G-BKER
542454 (US ARMY)	G-KUBY	F5459:Y	G-INNY
549192 (USAAF)	G-THUN	F5621:K	G-CLOY
5-624KT (USN)	G-BPKT	F8010:Z	G-BDWJ
22-296	G-BLXT	F8614	G-AWAU
39-160:160 10AB (USAAF)	G-CIIO	G-48-1 (Class B)	G-ALSX
41-33275:CE (USAAF)	G-BICE	J-1605 (Swiss AF)	G-BLID
42-35870:129 (USN)	G-BWLJ	J-1632 (Swiss AF)	G-VNOM
42-38384 (USMC)	G-BHVV	J-1758 (Swiss AF)	G-BLSD
42-5772 (USAAF)	G-BSXT	J-1790 (Swiss AF)	G-BLKA
42-58678:IY (USAAF)	G-BRIY	J-4021 (Swiss AF)	G-HHAC
42-78044 (USAAF)	G-BRXL	J7326	G-EBQP
42-84555:EP-H (USAAF)	G-ELMH	J9941:57	G-ABMR
43-35943 (USN)	G-BKRN	K1786	G-AFTA
44-15152:QI-T (USAAF)	G-JERK	K2048	G-BZNW
44-63684 (USAAF)	G-CKVJ	K2050	G-ASCM
44-79609:44-S (USAAF)	G-BHXY	K2059	G-PFAR
44-79649:69-K (USSAF)	G-AIIH	K2065	G-AYJY
44-80594 (USAAF)	G-BEDJ	K2075	G-BEER
47-797:A-797 (USAAF)	G-BFAF	K2227	G-ABBB
47.911 (UA Army)	G-EYVZ	K2567	G-MOTH
51-15319 (USAAF)	G-FUZZ	K2572	G-AOZH
51-15527 (USN)	G-BKRA	K2585	G-ANKT
51-15555 (US Army)	G-CUBT	K2587	G-BJAP
54-2445 (USAAF)	G-OTAN	K3241	G-AHSA
72-21509 (US Army)	G-UHIH	K3661	G-BURZ
108-1601 (USAAF)	G-CFGE	K3731	G-RODI
146-11083:5 (USAAC)	G-BNAI	K4259:71	G-ANMO
A-10 (Swiss AF)	G-BECW	K5054	G-BRDV
A11-301 (RAN)	G-ARKG	K5533	G-AENP
A16-199:SF-R (RAAF)	G-BEOX	K5600	G-BVVI

Serial Carried	Civil Identity	Serial Carried	Civil Identity
K5673	G-BZAS	T9707	G-AKKR
K5674	G-CBZP	T9738	G-AKAT
K5682	G-BBVO	T9768	G-AIUA
K7271	G-CCKV	U-0247 (Class B identity)	G-AGOY
K7985	G-AMRK	U-80 (Swiss AF)	G-BUKK
K8203	G-BTVE	U-88 (Swiss AF)	G-CMCX
K8303:D	G-BWWN	U-95 (Swiss AF)	G-BVGP
L2301	G-AIZG	U-99 (Swiss AF)	G-AXMT
L6739:YP-Q	G-BPIV	V3388	G-AHTW
L6906	G-AKKY	V7497	G-HRLI
L7181	G-CBLK	V9312	G-CCOM
N500	G-BWRA	V9367:MA-B	G-AZWT
N594:3982	G-CLPN	V9546:MA-D	G-LYZY
N856 (French AF)	G-CDWE	V9673:MA-J	G-LIZY
N1854	G-AIBE	W2718	G-WLRS
N1977:8 (French AF)	G-BWMJ	W5856:A2A	G-BMGC
N3200	G-CFGJ	W9385:YG-L	G-ADND
N3788	G-AKPF	X4276	G-CDGU
N3827	G-CLHY	X4496	G-CCJY
N4877:MK-V	G-AMDA	X4650	G-CGUK
N5182	G-APUP	X4683:EB-N	G-MUTS
N5195	G-ABOX	X9407	G-AFFD
N5719	G-CBHO	Z2033:N/275	G-ASTL
N5903:H	G-GLAD	Z7015:7-L	G-BKTH
N6161	G-ELRT	Z7197	G-AKZN
N6290	G-BOCK	AA810	G-PRID
N6377	G-BPOB	AB196	G-CCGH
N6452	G-BIAU	AD370 : PJ-C	G-CHBW
N6466	G-ANKZ	AJ841	G-BJST
N6537	G-AOHY	AP506	G-ACWM
N6720:VX	G-BYTN	AP507:KX-P	G-ACWP
N6797	G-ANEH	AR501:DU-E	G-AWII
N6847	G-APAL	AS0023 (Armed Forces of Malta)	G-CLJD
N6965:FL-J	G-AJTW	AX733:K	G-KINL
N9192:RCO-N	G-DHZF	BB697	G-ADGT
N9328	G-ALWS	BB803	G-ADWJ
N9372	G-ANHK	BB807	G-ADWO
N9389	G-ANJA	BE505:XP-L	G-HHII
N9503	G-ANFP	BF8431 (Burkina Faso)	G-NRRA
P2902:DX-X	G-ROBT	BL735 (BT-A)	G-HABT
P2921:GZ-L	G-CHTK	BL927 (JH-I)	G-CGWI
P3717:SW-P	G-HITT	BS410: (PK-A)	G-TCHI
P3966	G-LNWZ	CT130 (Sri Lankan AF)	G-CJSA
P6382:C	G-AJRS	CT180 (Sri Lankan AF)	G-BXZB
P7308:XR-D	G-AIST	DE208	G-AGYU
P7819	G-TCHZ	DE470	G-ANMY
P8331:RF-M	G-KOSC	DE623	G-ANFI
P9372:QJ-G	G-CLIH	DE673	G-ADNZ
P9386:QV-K	G-CTIX	DE745	G-BTOG
P9398	G-CEPL	DE971	G-OOSY
R-151 (RNethAF)	G-BIYR	DE974	G-ANZZ
R-156 (RNethAF)	G-ROVE	DE992	G-AXXV
R-167 (RNethAF)	G-LION	DF112	G-ANRM
R1914	G-AHUJ	DF128:RCO-U	G-AOJJ
R4118:UP-W	G-HUPW	DG590	G-ADMW
R4175:RF-R	G-HURI	EE602:DV-V	G-IBSY
R4922	G-APAO	EM720	G-AXAN
R4959:59	G-ARAZ	EM726	G-ANDE
R5136	G-APAP	EM840	G-ANBY
R5172:FIJ-E	G-AOIS	EM973	G-ALNA
R5246	G-AMIV	EN224	G-FXII
R6923/QJ-S	G-CLJI	EP120:AE-A	G-LFVB
S1287	G-BEYB	ES.1-4 (Spanish AF)	G-BUTX
S1581:573	G-BWWK	EX490	G-CLCJ
T6830	G-ANJI	FE511	G-CIUW
T6953	G-ANNI	FE695:94	G-BTXI
T7109	G-AOIM	FE788	G-CTKL
T7281	G-ARTL	FE992 :ER-992 (RCAF)	G-BDAM
T7290	G-ANNK	FH153 (RCAF)	G-BBHK
T7794	G-ASPV	FJ662	G-CRNL
T7842	G-AMTF	FJ777 (RCAF)	G-BIXN
T7909	G-ANON	FK338	G-AJOZ
T7997	G-AHUF	FR886	G-BDMS
T8191	G-BWMK	FS628	G-AIZE

Serial Carried	Civil Identity	Serial Carried	Civil Identity
FT391	G-AZBN	RB142:DW-B	G-CEFC
FZ626:YS-DH	G-AMPO	RG333	G-AIEK
HB612	G-AJSN	RK855	G-PIXY
HB737	G-BCBH	RL962	G-AHED
HB751	G-BCBL	RM169	G-ANVY
HD-75 (R Belgian AF)	G-AFDX	RM221	G-ANXR
HG691	G-AIYR	RR232	G-BRSF
HM580	G-ACUU	RS02 (Belgian AF)	G-BDNI
JG241 (ZX-J)	G-SMSP	RS04 (Belgian AF)	G-BDNK
JG891	G-LFVC	RT486:PF-A	G-AJGJ
JV579:F	G-RUMW	RT520	G-ALYB
KB889:NA-I	G-LANC	RT610	G-AKWS
KF183	G-CORS	RX168	G-BWEM
KF402 (HT-Y)	G-TEXN	SM520:KJ-1	G-ILDA
KG651	G-AMHJ	SR661	G-CBEL
KK527	G-RGUS	SX336:105-VL	G-KASX
KN353	G-AMYJ	TA634:8K-K	G-AWJV
KP220	G-ANAF	TA719:6T	G-ASKC
LB264	G-AIXA	TA805:FX-M	G-PMNF
LB286	G-ARRK	TD248:CR-S	G-OXVI
LB312	G-AHXE	TD314:FX-P	G-CGYJ
LB352	G-AHCR	TE184:9N-B	G-MXVI
LB367	G-AHGZ	TJ343	G-AJXC
LB369	G-AHHY	TJ518	G-AJIH
LB375	G-AHGW	TJ534	G-AKSY
LF858	G-BLUZ	TJ565	G-AMVD
LS326	G-AJVH	TJ569	G-AKOW
LZ766	G-ALCK	TJ672:TS-D	G-ANIJ
LZ842:EF-F	G-CGZU	TS798	G-AGNV
MH434:ZD-B	G-ASJV	TW439	G-ANRP
MH526:LO-D	G-CJWW	TW467	G-ANIE
MJ444:DK-H	G-LEGD	TW501	G-ALBJ
MJ627:9G-Q	G-BMSB	TW511	G-APAF
MK912:SH-L	G-BRRA	TW519	G-ANHX
ML295:DB-M	G-CLXB	TW536:TS-V	G-BNGE
ML407:NL-D	G-LFIX	TW641	G-ATDN
MM51-15302:EI-51 (Italian Army)	G-BITP	TX176	G-AHKX
MM52-2392:EI-69 (Italian Army)	G-HELN	TX310	G-AIDL
MM6976:16-5 (Italian Air Force)	G-CBLS	TZ164:OI-A	G-ISAC
MP425	G-AITB	VF512:PF-M	G-ARRX
MS824 (French AF)	G-AWBU	VF516	G-ASMZ
MT166	G-BICD	VF526:T	G-ARXU
MT197	G-ANHS	VF557:H	G-ARHM
MT438	G-AREI	VL348	G-AVVO
MT818:WZ-JJ	G-AIDN	VL349	G-AWSA
MV268:JE-J	G-SPIT	VM360	G-APHV
MW401	G-PEST	VN799	G-CDSX
NH341	G-CICK	VP955	G-DVON
NJ633	G-AKXP	VP967	G-KOOL
NJ673	G-AOCR	VP981	G-DHDV
NJ689	G-ALXZ	VR192	G-APIT
NJ695	G-AJXV	VR249:FA-EL	G-APIY
NJ703	G-AKPI	VR259:M	G-APJB
NJ719	G-ANFU	VR930	G-CLNJ
NJ728	G-AIKE	VS610:K-L	G-AOKL
NJ889	G-AHLK	VS623	G-AOKZ
NL750	G-AOBH	VW993	G-ASCD
NM138	G-ANEW	VX113	G-ARNO
NM181	G-AZGZ	VX281	G-BCOW
NX534	G-BUDL	VX653	G-BUCM
NX611:LE-C/DX-C	G-ASXX	VX927	G-ASYG
NZ3909 (Royal New Zealand Navy)	G-CMBE	VZ638:HF	G-JETM
NZ6300 (Royal New Zealand AF)	G-RNAF	VZ728	G-AGOS
PG657	G-AGPK	WA576	G-ALSS
PL788	G-CIEN	WA577	G-ALST
PL793	G-CIXM	WA638	G-JWMA
PL965	G-MKXI	WB549:7	G-BAPB
PL983	G-PRXI	WB565:X	G-PVET
PP972:II-5	G-BUAR	WB569:R	G-BYSJ
PR533:SR-V	G-TEMT	WB585:M	G-AOSY
PS853:C	G-RRGN	WB588:D	G-AOTD
PT879	G-PTIX	WB615:E	G-BXIA
PV202	G-CCCA		
PV303:ON-B	G-CCJL		

Serial Carried	Civil Identity	Serial Carried	Civil Identity
WB654:U	G-BXGO	WP929:F	G-BXCV
WB671:910	G-BWTG	WP930:J	G-BXHF
WB702	G-AOFE	WP964	G-HDAE
WB703	G-ARMC	WP973	G-BCPU
WB711	G-APPM	WP983:B	G-BXNN
WB726:E	G-AOSK	WP984:H	G-BWTO
WB763:14	G-BBMR	WR963	G-SKTN
WD286	G-BBND	WT333	G-BVXC
WD292	G-BCRX	WT933	G-ALSW
WD310:B	G-BWUN	WV198:K	G-BJWY
WD325:N	G-CLWK	WV322:VL	G-BZSE
WD327	G-ATVF	WV493:29	G-BDYG
WD331:J	G-BXDH	WV514	G-BLIW
WD363:5	G-BCIH	WV783	G-ALSP
WD373:12	G-BXDI	WV908	G-CMFB
WD390:68	G-BWNK	WW447	G-CMIP
WD413	G-VROE	WZ507:74	G-VTII
WE569	G-ASAJ	WZ662	G-BKVK
WF118	G-DACA	WZ679	G-CIUX
WG308:8	G-BYHL	WZ706	G-BURR
WG316	G-BCAH	WZ847:F	G-CPMK
WG321:G	G-DHCC	WZ872	G-BZGB
WG322:H	G-ARMF	WZ879	G-BWUT
WG348	G-BBMV	WZ882:K	G-BXGP
WG350	G-BPAL	XD693:Z-Q	G-AOBU
WG407:67	G-BWMX	XE489	G-JETH
WG422:16	G-BFAX	XE685:861/VL	G-GAII
WG458	G-CLLI	XE856	G-DUSK
WG465	G-BCEY	XE956	G-OBLN
WG472	G-AOTY	XF114	G-SWIF
WG719	G-BRMA	XF597:AH	G-BKFW
WJ358	G-ARYD	XF603	G-KAPW
WJ368	G-ASZX	XF690	G-MOOS
WJ404	G-ASOI	XF785	G-ALBN
WJ945:21	G-BEDV	XF836:J-G	G-AWRY
WK163	G-CTTS	XG160:U	G-BWAF
WK512:A	G-BXIM	XG452	G-BRMB
WK514	G-BBMO	XH558	G-VLCN
WK517	G-ULAS	XJ389	G-AJJP
WK522	G-BCOU	XJ398	G-BDBZ
WK558:DH	G-ARMG	XJ729	G-BVGE
WK577	G-BCYM	XK417	G-AVXY
WK585	G-BZGA	XK940:911	G-AYXT
WK586:V	G-BXGX	XL426	G-VJET
WK608	G-CLNI	XL500	G-KAEW
WK609:93	G-BXDN	XL502	G-BMYP
WK611	G-ARWB	XL571:V	G-HNTR
WK624	G-BWHI	XL573	G-DVCI
WK628	G-BBMW	XL577	G-BXKF
WK630	G-BXDG	XL587	G-HPUX
WK633:A	G-BXEC	XL621	G-BNCX
WK634:902	G-CIGE	XL714	G-AOGR
WK635	G-HFRH	XL809	G-BLIX
WK640	G-CERD	XL929	G-BNPU
WL419	G-JSMA	XM424	G-BWDS
WL626:P	G-BHDD	XM479:54	G-BVEZ
WM167	G-LOSM	XM497	G-AOVF
WP308:572CU	G-GACA	XM553	G-AWSV
WP321	G-BRFC	XM575	G-BLMC
WP788	G-BCHL	XM655	G-VULC
WP790:T	G-BBNC	XM685:513/PO	G-AYZJ
WP795:901	G-BVZZ	XM819	G-APXW
WP800:2	G-BCXN	XN351	G-BKSC
WP803	G-HAPY	XN437	G-AXWA
WP805:D	G-MAJR	XN441	G-BGKT
WP809:78 RN	G-BVTX	XN459	G-BWOT
WP811	G-BCKN	XN637:03	G-BKOU
WP848	G-BFAW	XP241	G-CEHR
WP870:12	G-BCOI	XP254	G-ASCC
WP872	G-IGES	XP282	G-BGTC
WP896	G-BWVY	XP355	G-BEBC
WP903	G-BCGC	XP820	G-CICP
WP925:C	G-BXHA	XP907	G-SROE
WP928:D	G-BXGM	XR240	G-BDFH

Serial Carried	Civil Identity	Serial Carried	Civil Identity
XR241	G-AXRR	XX626:02, W	G-CDVV
XR244	G-CICR	XX628:9	G-CBFU
XR246	G-AZBU	XX629:V	G-BZXZ
XR267	G-BJXR	XX630:5	G-SIJW
XR486	G-RWWW	XX631:W	G-BZXS
XR538:01	G-RORI	XX636:Y	G-CBFP
XR595	G-BWHU	XX638	G-DOGG
XR673:L	G-BXLO	XX658:07	G-SMAT
XR724	G-BTSY	XX667:16	G-BZFN
XR944	G-ATTB	XX668:1	G-CBAN
XR992	G-MOUR	XX692:A	G-BZMH
XS104	G-FRCE	XX693:07	G-BZML
XS235	G-CPDA	XX694:E	G-CBBS
XS587	G-VIXN	XX695:3	G-CBBT
XT131	G-CICN	XX698:9	G-BZME
XT223	G-XTUN	XX699:F	G-IDID
XT420:606	G-CBUI	XX700:17	G-CBEK
XT434:455	G-CGGK	XX702:P	G-CBCR
XT435:430	G-RIMM	XX704	G-BCUV
XT626	G-CIBW	XX885	G-HHAA
XT671	G-BYRC	XZ179	G-NCKS
XT761	G-WSEX	XZ321:D	G-CDNS
XT787	G-KAXT	XZ329	G-BZYD
XT788:316	G-BMIR	XZ550	G-BTDA
XV126	G-SCTA	XZ563	G-BUDT
XV137	G-CRUM	XZ597	G-SKNG
XV138	G-SASM	XZ933	G-CGJZ
XV268	G-BVER	XZ934:U	G-CBSI
XW283	G-CIMX	XZ935	G-CMFO
XW324:K	G-BWSG	XZ939	G-CLGO
XW325:E	G-BWGF	ZA314:WT	G-CMDO
XW333:79	G-BVTC	ZA634:C	G-BUHA
XW422:3	G-BWEB	ZA656	G-BTWC
XW423:14	G-BWUW	ZA730	G-FUKM
XW433	G-JPRO	ZB627:A	G-CBSK
XW612	G-KAXW	ZH798	G-VIFF
XW635	G-AWSW	HKG-5 (Royal Hong Kong AAF)	G-BULL
XW784:VL	G-BBRN	HKG-6 (Royal Hong Kong AAF)	G-BPCL
XW858:C	G-ONNE	HKG-11 (Royal Hong Kong AAF)	G-BYRY
XW906	G-CMFK	HKG-13 (Royal Hong Kong AAF)	G-BXKW
XX436	G-ZZLE	2+1:7334 Luftwaffe)	G-SYFW
XX513:10	G-KKKK	3+ (Luftwaffe)	G-BAYV
XX515:4	G-CBBC	4+ (Luftwaffe)	G-BSLX
XX521:H	G-CBEH	07 (Russian AF)	G-BMJY
XX522:06	G-DAWG	F+IS (Luftwaffe)	G-BIRW
XX524:04	G-DDOG	BB+EJ (Luftwaffe)	G-EJBB
XX528:D	G-BZON	BG+KM (Luftwaffe)	G-ASTG
XX534:B	G-EDAV	BU+CC (Luftwaffe)	G-BUCC
XX537:C	G-CBCB	BU+CK (Luftwaffe)	G-BUCK
XX538:O	G-TDOG	DG+BE (Luftwaffe)	G-BHPL
XX546:03	G-WINI	DM+BK (Luftwaffe)	G-BPHZ
XX549:6	G-CBID	F8+CA (Luftwaffe)	G-ETME
XX550:Z	G-CBBL	LG+01 (Luftwaffe)	G-CIJV
XX551:E	G-BZDP	LG+03 (Luftwaffe)	G-AEZX
XX561:7	G-BZEP	KG+EM (Luftwaffe)	G-ETME
XX611:7	G-CBDK	NJ+C11 (Luftwaffe)	G-ATBG
XX614:V	G-GGRR	NM+AA (Luftwaffe)	G-BZJV
XX619:T	G-CBBW	S4+A07 (Luftwaffe)	G-BWHP
XX621:H	G-CBEF	S5+B06 (Luftwaffe)	G-WJCM
XX622:B	G-CBGZ	TP+WX (Luftwaffe)	G-TPWX
XX624:E	G-KDOG	57-H (USAAC)	G-AKAZ
XX625	G-UWAS	+14 (Luftwaffe)	G-BSMD

Reg	Type	Owner or Operator	Notes
M-AAAL	Gulfstream 650	ALM New Jet Ltd	
M-AAAM	Bombardier CL600-2B16 Challenger	Durstwell Ltd	
M-AABG	Bombardier BD700-1A11 Global 5000	AB Air Holdings	
M-AAMM	Gulfstream 45	Al-Sahab G450 Ltd	
M-ABCC	Bombardier BD700-1A10 Global 6000	Global Aviation Partners LP Inc	
M-ABFQ	Bombardier BD700-1A10 Global 6000	AGT International GmbH	
M-ABFR	Bombardier BD700-1A10 Global 6000	AGT International GmbH	
M-ABGG	Bombardier CL600-2B16 Challenger	Zarox Holdings Ltd	
M-ABGS	Bombardier CL600-2B16 Challenger 605	Viking Travel Services Ltd	
M-ABGV	Learjet 45	Aviation Leasing (IOM) Ltd	
M-ABIY	Airbus A.320-232	CIT Aerospace International	
M-ABJA	Learjet 45	Aviation Leasing (IOM) Ltd	
M-ABKB	Eurocopter EC.225LP Super Puma	Parilease SAS	
M-ABKR	Embraer ERJ170-200LR	Celestial Aviation Trading 71 Ltd	
M-ABKT	Embraer ERJ170-200LR	Celestial Aviation Trading 71 Ltd	
M-ABLL	Airbus A.330-343	GHY Aviation Lease 1739 Co.Ltd	
M-ABMC	Avions Transport ATR-72-212A	Constellation Aircraft Leasing Ltd	
M-ABNF	Avro RJ100	Executive Jet Support Ltd	
M-ABNU	Airbus A.320-214	Osprey Aircraft Leasing Ltd (Eighteen)	
M-ABNV	Embraer ERJ190-100LR	Aero Power Leasing Company Ltd	
M-ABOL	Boeing 737-86N	NBB-36804 Lease Partnership	
M-ABPE	Avions Transport ATR-72-212A	Turbo Aviation Two DAC	
M-ABRI	Avions Transport ATR-72-212A	Billund Leasing V Ltd	
M-ABRN	Avions Transport ATR-72-212A	Billund Leasing V Ltd	
M-ABRO	Avions Transport ATR-72-212A	Billund Leasing IX Ltd	
M-ABRT	Cessna 680 Citation Sovereign	Meridian Investment Holdings Ltd	
M-ABST	Bombardier BD700-1A10 Global 6500	Global Aviation Partners LP Inc	
M-ABSU	Bombardier BD100-1A10 Challenger 3500	Aviation Finance and Leasing Ltd	
M-ABTC	Embraer EMB-135ER	Lorizon Invest SAS	
M-ABTD	Airbus EC225LP Super Puma	Rotortrade SASU	
M-ABTE	Bombardier BD100-1A10 Challenger 3500	Aviation Finance and Leasing Ltd	
M-ABTM	Cessna 525 Citationjet CJ1	Gama Aviation (UK) Ltd	
M-ABTS	Airbus A.320-216	Wilmington Trust SP Services (Dublin) Ltd	
M-ABTV	Embraer EMB-145LR	IPEK Aviation Ltd	
M-ABTW	Embraer EMB-145LR	IPEK Aviation Ltd	
M-ABTX	Embraer EMB-145LR	IPEK Aviation Ltd	
M-ABUB	Leonardo AW169	Bradbury Aviation LLP	
M-ACPT	BAe. 125 Srs.1000	Remo Investments Ltd	
M-ADAM	Embraer EMB-135BJ Legacy 650	Wat Aviation Ltd	
M-ADEL	Bombardier CL600-2B16 Challenger 650	Pacific Energy Company Ltd	
M-AERO	Dassault Falcon 2000LX	Rirox Ltd	
M-AGMA	Bombardier BD700-1A10 Global Express	Sugar Mama Ltd	
M-AGRI	Bombardier BD700-1A11 Global 5000	Blezir Invest Ltd	
M-AJET	Bombardier BD700-1A10 Global 6500	Jetrology GmbH	
M-AJOR	Airbus MBB BK117 D-2	Major Aviation LLP	
M-AKAR	Sikorsky S-76C	Starspeed Ltd	
M-ALDI	Embraer ERJ190-100ECJ	Aliforti Ltd	
M-ALEN	Embraer EMB-135BJ Legacy	ATT Aviation Ltd	
M-ALEZ	Bombardier BD700-1A10 Global Express	Constellation Aircraft Leasing Ltd	
M-ALLB	Pilatus PC-12/47E	M. S. Bartlett	
M-ALSH	Bombardier BD700-1A10 Global Express	Mirgab Aviation Ltd	
M-ALTH	Bombardier BD700-1A10 Global 6000	Shine Ever Holdings Ltd	
M-ALUN	BAe 125 Srs.700A	Briarwood Products Ltd	
M-AMAN	Pilatus PC-12	Pilatus PC-12 Centre UK Ltd	
M-AMBA	Gulfstream GVII-G600	Hampshire Aviation LLP	
M-AMBR	Bombardier BD700-1A11 Global 5000	Baz Group Ltd	
M-AMNM	Bombardier BD700-1A11 Global 5000	Marco Polo Aviation Ltd	
M-ANAP	Embraer EMB-505 Phenom	Equiom (Isle of Man) Ltd	
M-ANDY	Embraer EMB-135BJ Legacy 650	SOA Aviation Ltd	
M-ANFR	Gulfstream GVI	Selevan Management Ltd	
M-ANIL	Bombardier CL600-2B16 Challenger 604	Seven Nine Invest Ltd	
M-ANTA	Gulfstream GVII-G600	Hampshire Aviation LLP	
M-APLE	Bombardier BD700-1A10 Global 6000	Waylawn Ltd	
M-ARCO	Gulfstream GV-SP	GS Ltd	
M-ARDI	Gulfstream 650	Comet Limited Partnership Inc	
M-ARDN	Dassault Falcon 7X	East Coast Aviation Leasing Ltd	
M-ARIA	Bombardier BD700-1A11 Global 5000	Pabis IOM LP Inc	
M-ARIE	Hawker 800XP	Surf-Air Ltd	
M-ARKS	Diamond DA62	M. K. Simpson	
M-ARKZ	Bombardier CL600-2B16 Challenger	Markz Jet Ltd	
M-ARNZ	Pilatus PC-24	BAE Systems Ltd	

Notes	Reg	Type	Owner or Operator
	M-ARTY	Pilatus PC-12/47E	Creston (UK) Ltd
	M-ARVA	Bombardier BD700-1A10 Global 6000	Newjourney Trading Ltd
	M-ARWA	Cessna 425	TC Aviation AG
	M-ASBA	Bombardier BD100-1A10 Challenger 3500	Aviation Finance & Leasing Ltd
	M-ASTR	Eurocopter EC.155 B1	5-15 Global Energy Italia SRL
	M-ATCH	Dassault Falcon 2000EX	Dassault Leasing Ltd
	M-ATEX	Dassault Falcon 7X	Maritime Investment and Shipping Company II Ltd
	M-AURA	Hawker 900XP	Vitash Investments Pte Ltd
	M-AXIM	CessnaT.206H Turbo Stationair	C. D. B. Cope
	M-AZIA	Cessna 525C CitationJet CJ4	Hunting Star Ltd
	M-BAEP	Bombardier CL600-2B16 Challenger	Swift Cloud Aviation Services Ltd
	M-BCOL	Avions Transport ATR-72-212A	Blue Turbo Two Finance LLC
	M-BDWK	Eurocopter EC.155B1	Fertitta Entertainment Holdings LLC
	M-BEEF	Airbus Helicopters EC.135 T3	Acorn Mobility Services Ltd
	M-BETS	Rockwell Commander 695A	Aldersey Aviation Ltd
	M-BETY	Dornier Do.328-310	Funfte XR-GmbH
	M-BHOY	Dassault Falcon 7X	Cravant Ltd
	M-BIBE	Embraer EMB-505 Phenom 500	Embibe Ltd
	M-BIGG	Bombardier BD700-2A12 Global 7500	Horizon Airlines Ltd
	M-BIZZ	Gulfstream GVI	AC Executive Aircraft (2025) Ltd
	M-BLUE	Bombardier BD700-1A10 Global 6500	Telvor Aviation Ltd
	M-BRAB	Diamond DA.42M Twin Star	Bravura Group of Companies Ltd
	M-BRAC	Diamond DA.42M Twin Star	Bravura Group of Companies Ltd
	M-BRAD	Diamond DA.42M Twin Star	Bravura Group of Companies Ltd
	M-BRAV	Pilatus PC-12/47E	Bravura PC12 Company Ltd
	M-CAIR	Agusta A109E Power	Castle Air Ltd
	M-CDBM	Bell B.200GT Super King Air	BAE Systems Ltd
	M-CDJC	Beech B.200GT Super King Air	BAE Systems Marine Ltd
	M-CDMS	Beech B.200GT Super King Air	BAE Systems Marine Ltd
	M-CDOM	Aerospatiale ATR-72-212A	Fastjet Air Four Ltd
	M-CELT	Bombardier BD700-1A11 Global 6500	Ulmaria Ltd
	M-CESC	Cessna 560XL	Cessna Spanish Citation Service Center SL
	M-CESD	Cessna 560XL	Cessna Spanish Citation Service Center SL
	M-CITY	Daher SOCATA TBM-700N	TBM 960 Aviation Ltd
	M-CKAY	Learjet 40	Danish Aircraft Management APS
	M-CLUB	Cessna 525 Citationjet	Nextasea 1 Ltd
	M-CNZI	Bombardier BD700-1A10 Global 6000	Lavenda Services Inc
	M-COOL	Cessna 510 Citation Mustang	E. Keats
	M-CPAY	Dassault Falcon 900LX	Puru Aviation Ltd
	M-CRDL	Gulfstream 450	Samika Ltd
	M-CUZU	Dassault Falcon 900EX	Curzon Aviation Ltd
	M-CVGL	Bombardier BD700-1A11 Global 5000	Aircraft Operations Ltd
	M-DADA	Bombardier BD700-1A10 Global 6000	STC Aviation Services Ltd
	M-DANS	Gulfstream GVI	DSWA 1 LP Inc
	M-DAWN	Beech B200GT King Air	Dawn Meats Group UC
	M-DEEP	Leonardo AW109SP Grand New	Sloane Helicopters Ltd
	M-DEND	Bombardier BD100-1A10 Challenger 300	Campino Ltd
	M-DIVE	Pilatus PC-24	Blackthorn Aviation Ltd
	M-DKVL	Gulfstream 450	Fiordani Holding Ltd
	M-DMVR	Leonardo AW169	Vmadeleine Ltd
	M-DOGA	Airbus Helicopters EC135 T3	GUL Ltd
	M-DSTZ	Bombardiewer CL600-2B16 Challenger 650	Cameron Industries Consult Inc
	M-DSUN	Bombardier BD700-1A10 Global 6000	Splendiferous Global Ltd
	M-DUBS	Dassault Falcon 7X	6D Ltd
	M-DVJJ	Gulfstream VI	The Peters Family G650ER Company Ltd
	M-DWWW	Bombardier CL600-2B19 Challenger	Dragon Asset Global Investment Group Ltd
	M-EADE	Bombardier CL600-2B16 Challenger	Hadleigh Aviation LLP
	M-EAGL	Dassault Falcon 900EX	Faycroft Finance
	M-ECJI	Dassault Falcon 10	Fleet International Aviation and Finance Ltd
	M-EDIA	Dassault Falcon 7X	M-EDIA Aviation Ltd
	M-EGGA	Beech B200 Super King Air	Langley Aviation Ltd
	M-EGWD	Cessna 750 Citation X	GIV Airways Ltd
	M-EKSL	Airbus A.330-243F	DHL Air Ltd
	M-ELAS	Gulfstream 280	Aventurine Aviation Ltd
	M-ELIS	Bell 407GX	Leisure Parks Ltd
	M-ELON	Embraer EMB-505 Phenom 300	Sleepwell Aviation Ltd
	M-ELOW	Embraer EMB-505 Phenom 300	Sleepwell Aviation Ltd
	M-ENON	Gulfstream GVII-G500	Sobha Jet Ltd
	M-ETAL	Piaggio P.180 Avanti	GFG Aviation Ltd
	M-EVAN	Bombardier BD100-1A10 Challenger 300	Marcus Evans (Aviation) Ltd
	M-EXPL	Eurocopter AS.355N Ecureuil 2	Select Plant Hire Co.Ltd

Reg	Type	Owner or Operator	Notes
M-FLYI	Cessna 525 Citationjet CJ4	Avtrade Ltd	
M-FROG	Beech 390 Premier 1	White and Cope Aviation LLP	
M-FRSH	Airbus Helicopters EC135 P3	Airbus Helicopters UK Ltd	
M-FRZN	Bombardier CL600-2B16 Challenger	Iceland Foods Ltd	
M-FTHD	Dassault Falcon 2000EX	Eagle Reach Group Ltd	
M-FUAD	Gulfstream VI	Future Aviation (IOM) Ltd	
M-GABY	Bombardier BD700-1A10 Global Express	Manerk Holdings SA	
M-GACB	Dassault Falcon 10	Valiant Aviation Ltd	
M-GAGA	Gulfstream 650ER	Advance Global Development Ltd	
M-GALX	IAI Gilfstream 200	Worldwide Investment One Ltd	
M-GCAP	Piaggio P.180 Avanti	Greensill Capital (IOM) Ltd	
M-GDRS	Hawker 850XP	Surf-Air Ltd	
M-GETS	Pilatus PC-12/47E	3FS Aviation Ltd	
M-GIPH	Dassault Falcon 10	Regourd Aviation SAS	
M-GLRY	Dassault Falcon 8X	Silver Peregrine Ltd	
M-GSIR	Dassault Falcon 900DX	Sublime Holdings Ltd	
M-GZOO	IAI Gulfstram 200	Multiflight Charter Services LLP	
M-HERI	Gulfstream V-SP	Heri Aviation Ltd	
M-HISA	Leonardo AW139	RBHF Services Ltd	
M-HOME	Bombardier BD700-1A10 Global 6000	Symphony Master (IOM) Ltd	
M-HSCZ	Gulfstream 650ER	Shine Wealth Consultants Ltd	
M-HUGO	Avions Transport ATR-72-212A	Blue Turbo Two Finance LLC	
M-IAMI	Falcon 7X	Delane Finance Ltd	
M-IBAO	ATR-72-212A	Injet Leasing Company Ltd	
M-IBAS	Bombardier CL600-2B16 Challenger 605	AJ Aircraft 1 Ltd	
M-ICRO	Cessna 525C Citationjet CJ4	Pektron Group Ltd	
M-IFFY	Cessna 510 Citation Mustang	Xead Aviation Ltd	
M-IGHT	Learjet 60	High Wing Aviation Ltd	
M-IGWT	Bombardier BD700-1A10	Business Encore (IOM) Ltd	
M-IIII	Gulfstream 650ER	Talisman Aviation Ltd	
M-IKEY	Airbus Helicopters AS.365N3	Whirligig Ltd	
M-ILLA	Beech 400XP	Sunshine Aviation Ltd	
M-ILLS	Bell 429	Nigel Brunt Properties Ltd	
M-ILTA	Dassault Falcon 900LX	Delta Technical Services Ltd	
M-INES	Agusta AW109SP Grand New	GFG 109 Ltd	
M-INKE	Gulfstream G600	Hampshire Aviation LLP	
M-INNI	Learjet 60	M-INNI Aviation Ltd	
M-INOR	Bell 429	Major Aviation LLP	
M-IRAS	Airbus A.320-251N	STC Jet Ltd	
M-ISRA	Agusta A109E Power	Perfectway Services Ltd	
M-JACK	Beech B200GT King Air	Jetstream Aviation Ltd	
M-JAZZ	Cessna 680 Citation Sovereign	G-150 Aeronautics Ltd	
M-JCBA	Leonardo AW139	J C Bamford Excavators Ltd	
M-JCBB	Bombardier BD700-1A12 Global 7500	J C Bamford Excavators Ltd	
M-JCBC	Leonardo AW139	J C Bamford Excavators Ltd	
M-JCBD	Sikorsky S-76A	J C Bamford Excavators Ltd	
M-JETT	Dassault Falcon 200	Piraeus Leasing Chrimatodotikes Mishoseis SA	
M-JETZ	Dassault Falcon 2000EX	Avtorita Holdings Ltd	
M-JGUK	Bombardier BD700-1A10 Global 6000	Jetcraft Global (UK) Ltd	
M-JGVJ	Bombardier BD700-1A11 Global 5000	Aquatics Ventures Holdings Ltd	
M-JHCI	Cessna 525C Citationjet CJ4	Dowdeswell Aviation LLP	
M-JJTL	Pilatus PC-12/47E	L. Uggia, J. P. Huth & K. Giannamore	
M-JSMN	Bombardier BD700-1A11 Global 5000	Jasmin Aviation Ltd	
M-JSTA	Bombardier BD700-1A11 Global 5000	Jetsteff Aviation Ltd	
M-JSDT	Bombardier BD700-1A10 Global 6500	Star Bar and Café Mpumalaga (Pty) Ltd	
M-JSTR	Bombardier BD700-1A11 Global 5000	Jetsteff Aviation Ltd	
M-KAPP	Agusta A109C	Flexible Trading	
M-KASI	BN-2T-4S Islander	Kalusair Services Inc	
M-KBSD	Bombardier BD700-1A11 Global 5000	Faraotis Holdings Ltd	
M-KELI	Embraer EMB-505 Phenom 300	Kelly Airways Ltd	
M-KELY	Embraer EMB-500 Phenom 100	Kelly Air Ltd	
M-KING	Learjet 40	Kings Leisure Ltd	
M-KGKG	Embraer EMB-550 Praetor 600	Trosa Praetor Ltd	
M-KINK	Cessna 425 Conquest 1	TC Aviation AG	
M-KSSN	Gulfstream 650	NS Aviation Ltd	
M-KWOW	Bombardier BD700-1A11 Global 5000	Shurooq Aviation Ltd	
M-LDME	ATR-72-212A	Elix Assets 7 Ltd	
M-LDYS	Airbus MBB-BK117 D-3	Starspeed Ltd	
M-LEAD	Dassault Falcon 8X	Arirang Aviation IOM Ltd	
M-LEKT	Robin DR.400/180	T. D. Allan, P. & J. P. Bromley	
M-LENR	Beech B.200GT Super King Air	BAE Systems Marine Ltd	

Notes	Reg	Type	Owner or Operator
	M-LEOG	Leonardo AW109SP Grand New	Leo Aviation Ltd
	M-LIFT	Sikorsky S-76A	A. D. Whitehouse
	M-LILY	Airbus A.318-112	Lili Jet (Cayman) Ltd
	M-LION	Hawker 900XP	Lion Invest and Trade Ltd
	M-LJCR	Dassault Falcon 7X	Quinjet Ltd
	M-LJGI	Dassault Falcon 7X	Ven Air Unlimited Company
	M-LLIN	Bombardier BD700-1A10 Global 6000	Tian Yi Ltd
	M-LLMW	Beech Super King Air 300	Trosa Ltd
	M-LOOK	Bombardier CL600-2B16 Challenger	Kennington Ltd
	M-LOVE	Embraer EMB-550 Praetor 600	APCO Infratech Private Ltd
	M-LWCW	Bombardier BD700-2A12 Global 7500	Eircraft Ltd
	M-LWSG	Bombardier BD700-1A10 Global 6000	Lynx Aircraft Ltd
	M-MAEE	Gulfstream 450	Royston Sky Holdings Ltd
	M-MANX	PA-34-220T Seneca V	HUAS Investments Ltd
	M-MAXX	Bombardier BD700-1A10 Global 6000	Max Smart Development Ltd
	M-MBFF	Bombardier BD700-1A11 Global 5000	Itom Rotorcrafts (Pty) Ltd
	M-MBLU	Bombardier BD700-1A10 Global 6000	Asaj Holdings LLC
	M-MCBE	Cessna 525 Citation M2	M Two Aviation LP Inc
	M-MDBD	Bombardier BD700-1A10 Global Express	Cozuro Holdings Ltd
	M-MEVA	Cessna 560 Citation Ultra	AVEM'R
	M-MFLN	Cessna 425 Corsair	Curlywings GmbH
	M-MIKE	Cessna 525C Citationjet CJ4	Aviation by Westminster Ltd
	M-MMGM	Bombardier CL600-2B16 Challenger 604	Satelite IOM Ltd
	M-MSVI	Cessna 525B Citationjet CJ3	JPM Ltd
	M-MYNA	Bombardier BD700-1A10 Global 6000	Tibit Ltd
	M-NACK	Hawker 800XP	Camissa One (Pty) Ltd
	M-NBAY	Airbus MBB BK 117 D-2	Mestico Ltd
	M-NELS	Gulfstream 450	Citylink Partners Ltd
	M-NGSN	Pilatus PC-12/47E	N. Stolt-Nielson
	M-NICE	Gulfstream 200	M-NICE Ltd
	M-NLYY	PA-42-1000 Cheyenne 400LS	Factory Leasing Ltd
	M-NNNN	Gulfstream 650	Matrix Aviation 650 Ltd
	M-NORN	Embraer EMB-505 Phenom 300	Cross Aviation Ltd
	M-NREN	Embraer EMB-505 Phenom 300	Cross Aviation Ltd
	M-NWVM	Boeing 737-76V	MWWMMWM Ltd
	M-OBIL	Cessna 525C Citationjet C14	Popken Fashion Services GmbH
	M-OCHI	Bombardier BD700-1A10 Global Express	Colour Air Ltd
	M-OCNY	Bombardier BD100-1A10 Challenger 350	RH-Flugdienst GmbH & Co KG
	M-OCOM	Bombardier CL600-2B16 Challenger 604	Focus Holdings Ltd
	M-ODEL	Gulfstream 450	Hampshire Aviation LLP
	M-OGMC	Gulfstream G700	Northolt Aviation Ltd
	M-OIWA	Bombardier BD100-1A10 Challenger	Delta A/S
	M-OJOS	Airbus Helicopters EC135 T3	Seven Nine Invest Ltd
	M-OLEG	Embraer 135BJ Legacy	Hermitage Air Ltd
	M-OLLY	Cessna 525 Citationjet CJ1	MBK Maschinenbau GmbH/Bohnet GmbH
	M-OLOT	Bombardier CL600-2B16 Challenger	Kellie Aviation Ltd
	M-OMAN	Dassault Falcon 7X	RUWI Ltd
	M-ONDE	Eurocopter MBB BK 117C2	Peyton Ltd
	M-ONEM	Gulfstream 550	G550 Ltd
	M-ONEY	Cessna 525 Citation M2	Century Aviation Ltd
	M-OOMR	Dassault Falcon 50EX	Oomrang Air LLC
	M-OONL	Bombardier BD700-1A10 Global Express	Parker Holdings Ltd
	M-OPED	Sikorsky S-76C	Nordic Aircrafts Holding Ltd
	M-OPHS	Gulfstream 550	Islands Aviation Ltd
	M-ORAD	Dassault Falcon 7X	Swift New Jet Ltd
	M-ORZE	Eurocopter EC135 P2+	G650 Management Ltd
	M-OUNT	Dassault Falcon 8X	Abelia Ltd
	M-OUSE	Cessna 510 Citation Mustang	Mouse (IOM) Ltd
	M-OVIE	Gulfstream 650	Hampshire Aviation LLP
	M-PAPA	Airbus Helicopters EC130 T2	Papa Fly Ltd
	M-PCPC	Pilatus PC-12/45	Treetops Aviation LLP
	M-PDCS	Dassault Falcon 2000EX	Six Daughters Ltd
	M-PECL	Bombardier BD700-1A12 Global 7500	Pacific Energy Company Ltd
	M-PHML	American General AG-5B Tiger	I. J. Ross & J. R. Shannon
	M-PINK	Hawker 4000	R S Aviation Ltd
	M-PLGL	Bell 407	Pure Leisure (North West) LLP
	M-PORT	Bombardier BD700-1A11 Global 5000	Sirom Aviation Ltd
	M-POWR	Beech C.90A King Air	Northside Aviation Ltd
	M-PTGG	Dassault Falcon 8X	Prime Galaxy International Ltd
	M-PURE	Airbus MBB BK117 D-2	Nelida Ltd
	M-PVIL	Dassault Falcon 6X	Sky6X Ltd

Reg	Type	Owner or Operator	Notes
M-PZPZ	Gulfstream IV	A. I. Eze	
M-RAFI	Bombardier BD700-2A12 Global 7500	JCG 7000 Holdings Ltd	
M-RARE	Cessna T.210M	Rare Air (IOM) Ltd	
M-RBHF	Leonardo AW139	RBHF Services Ltd	
M-RBIG	Learjet 45	Volantair LP Inc	
M-RBUS	Airbus A.319-115CJ	Belville Investment Ltd	
M-REEE	Dassault Falcon 7X	B. C. Ecclestone	
M-REEM	AS.355NP Ecureuil 2	Kingdom 5-KR-267 Ltd	
M-RISE	Boeing 757-23N	Talos Aviation Ltd	
M-RKAY	Raytheon 390 Premier 1A	Sunseeker Corporate Aviation Ltd	
M-RLIV	Bombardier CL600-2B16 Challenger	Mobyhold Ltd	
M-RRRR	Bombardier BD700-1A11 Global 6000	Prestige Investments Ltd	
M-RSAR	Piaggio P.180 Avanti II	Aerovista Holdings Ltd	
M-RTEE	Learjet 40	Nextasea 2 Ltd	
M-RTFS	Dassault Falcon 7X	CIM Corporate Services Ltd	
M-SAFE	Pilatus PC-12/47E	Arirang Aviation IoM Ltd	
M-SAIL	Pilatus PC-12/47E	G. G. & L. G. Gordon	
M-SAJJ	Gulfstream V-SP	Horizon Aviation Ltd	
M-SAPD	Bombardier BD700-1A10 Global 6000	Sapetro Aviation (BVI) Ltd	
M-SAPT	Bombardier BD700-1A11 Global 5000	Sapetro Aviation Ltd	
M-SCDM	Gulfstream GVI	Isle Ventures Ltd	
M-SCMG	Dassault Falcon 7X	BlueSky International Management Ltd	
M-SEAO	Cessna 750 Citation X	Viewdart Ltd	
M-SETT	Bombardier BD700-1A11 Global 5000	Lodging 2020 LP Inc	
M-SEVN	Bombardier CL600-2B16 Challenger	Persimmon Trading Ltd	
M-SEXY	Embraer EMB-135BJ Legacy 650	Gerfaut Capital Ltd	
M-SFOZ	Dassault Falcon 2000	Alaman for Jets Ltd	
M-SFPL	Bombardier BD700-1A10 Global 6000	Jasoom Development Ltd	
M-SGCR	Cessna 550 Citation Bravo	Labraid Ltd	
M-SHRM	AgustaWestlandAW139	Frozendale Ltd	
M-SIYU	Bombardier BD700-1A1A Global Express	Cutlass Ltd	
M-SKSM	Bombardier BD700-1A11 Global	Tesker Management Ltd	
M-SKYF	Bombardier CL600-2B16 Challenger 650	Skyfly Aviation Ltd	
M-SKTO	Airbus Helicopters H160-B	T J Morris Ltd	
M-SNER	Dassault Falcon 2000EX	Wincor Aviation Establishment	
M-SOBR	Gulfstream 450	Sobha & BR Aviation Ltd	
M-SOZO	Gulfstream VI	Greenshill Capital II (IoM) Ltd	
M-SPEC	Beech B300 King Air 350	Specsavers Corporate Aircraft Leasing Ltd	
M-SPEK	Beech B300 King Air 360	Specsavers Corporate Aircraft Leasing Ltd	
M-SPEL	Beech B300 King Air 350	Specsavers Corporate Aircraft Leasing Ltd	
M-SPOR	Beech B200 King Air	Select Plant Hire Co.Ltd	
M-SSML	IAI Gulfstream 200	Shimali Ltd	
M-SSYS	Cessna 525C CitationJet CJ4	Fimway Asset Holdings Ltd	
M-SULT	Learjet 45	Ridgemont (Pty) Ltd	
M-3UNY	Dassault Falcon 7X	Harmony Flight International Ltd	
M-SURE	Dassault Falcon 7X	Arirang Aviation IOM Ltd	
M-SURF	Pilatus PC-12/47E	JJTL Ltd	
M-SVGN	Cessna 680 Citation Sovereign	Vocalion Ltd	
M-SZSZ	Gulfstream IV	HDL Smart Technology Ltd	
M-TENG	Dassault Falcon 6X	Jet Pro Ltd	
M-TGAU	Gulfstream IV	One Aviation SA	
M-TNDR	Cessna S550 Citation II	Tinadar Jets Ltd	
M-TNGO	Bombardier CL600-02B16 Challenger 605	Tango IOM Ltd	
M-TOMY	Embraer EMB-500 Phenom 100	TGTA Ltd	
M-TRBS	Bombardier CL600-2B16 Challenger	Arrow Management Property Corp	
M-UATG	Bombardier CL600-2B16 Challenger 650	Cloud Services Ltd	
M-UGIC	Gulfstream 550	Cityville Capital Ltd	
M-ULTI	Bombardier BD700-1A10 Global Express	Multibird Overseas Ltd	
M-VENA	Eurocopter AS365N3 Dauphin 2	Anglo Beef Processors Ireland ULC	
M-VENB	Eurocopter AS365N3 Dauphin 2	Ven Air ULC	
M-VGAL	Dassault Falcon 900EX	Charter Air Ltd	
M-VLCC	Cessna 525A Citationjet CJ2	Shiphold Management Services Ltd	
M-VNES	Hawker 800XP	Vivines Ltd	
M-VRNY	Gulfstream 550	Mirtos Ltd	
M-WAFA	Dassault Falcon 8X	Borbonicus Ltd	
M-WHAT	Eurocopter EC.135T2+	Starspeed Ltd	
M-WIND	Gulfstream 650	Nursam Invest SA	
M-WINT	Pilatus PC-12/43E	Air Winton Ltd	
M-WPCW	Airbus A.330-343	Caixabank SA	
M-XHEC	Eurocopter EC155B	Flambards Ltd	
M-YAIC	Embraer EMB-505 Phenom 300	AIC Spolka Akcyjna	

Notes	Reg	Type	Owner or Operator
	M-YAVA	Cessna 550 Citation Bravo	Jet Rent
	M-YBBJ	Boeing 737-7HE BBJ	Hamilton Jets Ltd
	M-YBLS	Pilatus PC-12/45	B. L. Schroder
	M-YBUS	Airbus A.320-214ACJ	STC Flight Ltd
	M-YFLY	Pilatus PC-12/47E	Fly High Ltd
	M-YGIG	Gulfstream 650	AC Executive Aircraft (2017) Ltd
	M-YIGO	Raytheon Hawker 850XP	NNG Aviation Ltd
	M-YKBO	Embraer EMB-135BJ Legacy	Transeurope Air Establishment
	M-YMCM	Bell 429	T. J. Morris Ltd
	M-YNNS	Gulfstream GVIII	Aviation One Ltd
	M-YOIL	Bombardier BD700-1A10 Global 6000	Shelf Support Shiphold Ltd
	M-YSPC	Cessna 525 Citationjet	M-YSPC Ltd
	M-YTAF	Beech B.36TC Bonanza	FBS Aviation Ltd
	M-YTOY	Agusta A109S Grand	Megacorp Aircraft Holding Ltd
	M-YULI	Airbus A.319-115CJ	Fourstars Trading Ltd
	M-YWAY	Gulfstream IV	Blue Sky Leasing Ltd
	M-ZELL	Cessna 208 Caravan	Ridler Verwaltungs und Vermittlungs GmbH
	M-ZPGJ	Cessna 525C Citationjet CJ4	Sapphire Leap Ltd

M-DIVE Pilatus PC-24. *Allan S. Wright*

Reg	Type	Owner or Operator	Notes
2-ACSE	Airbus A.319-112	ACS Aero 2 Omega Ltd	
2-ACSF	Airbus A.319-112	ACS Aero 2 Omega Ltd	
2-ACSH	Airbus A.319-112	ACS Aero 2 Omega Ltd	
2-ACSL	Airbus A.319-111	ACS Aero 1 Alpha Ltd	
2-ACSN	Airbus A.320-214	ACS Aero 1 Beta Ltd	
2-AKOP	Commander 114B	M. A. Perry	
2-ALCA	Airbus A.220-300	UMB Bank National Association	
2-ALCB	Airbus A.220-300	UMB Bank National Association	
2-ALFR	Airbus A.330-343	Alfor Aviation & Technical Services Ltd	
2-ALPS	Dassault Falcon 50	Alpjets SA	
2-AMBO	IAI 1125 Astra SPX	Nexure Global Pte Ltd	
2-ANJA	Beech B.200 King Air	FSB Aviation Ltd	
2-ANLD	PA-34-220T Seneca V	D. & L. Medcraft	
2-ANVL	Dassault Falcon 7X	Gainon Aviation Ltd	
2-ARKA	Avions Transport ATR-72-212A	Red-Tail Aviation Ltd	
2-ARKB	Avions Transport ATR-72-212A	Portlaoise Aircraft Leasing Ltd	
2-ARKC	Avions Transport ATR-72-212A	Portlaoise Aircraft Leasing Ltd	
2-ATRN	ATR-72-212A	NAC Aviation 8 Ltd	
2-ATUP	Boeing 737-44P	Aero Plus International Holdings Ltd	
2-AZFR	Cessna 401B	R. E. H. Wragg	
2-BBJI	Boeing 737-7P3	Eskimo Holdings Ltd	
2-BHXG	Airbus A.340-313	Aerfin Ltd	
2-BIGG	Boeing 737-7HE	Volare Aviation GSY Ltd	
2-BILL	Eclipse EA.550	TAK Aviation LLC	
2-BLNR	Airbus A.330-343	AWAS Leasing One LLC	
2-BOYS	Commander 114B	private	
2-BREM	MBB Bolkow BO.105 DBS-5	Wessex Aviation Ltd	
2-BTPO	Boeing 737-86N(F)	UMB Bank National Association	
2-CABO	Agusta A.109E Power	Leprechaun Leasing LLC	
2-CAMO	Agusta A.109S	Volare Aviation GSY Ltd	
2-CAMP	Eclipse EA500	TAK Aviation LLC	
2-CATS	Agusta A.109E Power	My Heli Ltd	
2-CAZZ	Eclipse EA500	TAK Aviation LLC	
2-CHAL	Bombardier CL600-2B19 Challenger 850	Weramex DMCC	
2-CHOP	Agusta Bell 206A Jet Ranger	AT Aviation (Engineering) Ltd	
2-CLES	Bombardier CL600-2B16 Challenger 604	C & L Engine Solutions LLC	
2-CLEV	Cessna 525A Citationjet CJ2	Clevewood Aviation Ltd	
2-CLRK	Eclipse 500	Aeris Aviation Ltd	
2-CMDR	Airbus A.330-223	MSN 332 LLC	
2-COOK	Cessna 525 Citation M2	William Cook Aviation Ltd	
2-COOL	Piaggio P180 Avanti II	private	
2-CPDD	PZL M28 05	P. D. Sicherheit – Privat Defence and Education Services GmbH	
2-CRZY	Eurocopter EC.155B	redacted	
2-CYFR	Cirrus SR22T	2608AD Ltd	
2-DAVE	Eclipse EA.500	TAK Aviation Holdings Ltd	
2-DCBU	ATR-72-212A	Elix Assets 14 Ltd	
2-DEAL	PA-32-301XTC 6XT	private	
2-DEER	Boeing 787-8(BBJ)	Ocean Transportation Facility Investment Ltd	
2-DITO	PA-46-500TP Malibu Meridian	Citavia BV	
2-DIVT	Leonardo A.109S Trekker	Volare Aviation GSY Ltd	
2-DOCZ	Diamond DA 62	2DOGZ LLP	
2-DRDR	Cirrus Vision SF50	private	
2-DRNK	Eurocopter EC.155B	Eskimo Holdings Ltd	
2-DTAL	Canadair CRJ200LR	Lineage Holdings Inc	
2-DUSC	Airbus A.320-214	Accipiter Investments Aircraft 2 Ltd	
2-EALB	Airbus A.340-642	European Aviation Ltd	
2-EALC	Airbus A.340-642	Priority 1 Leasing Ltd	
2-EALD	Airbus A.340-641	European Cargo Ltd	
2-EALF	Airbus A.340-642	European Aviation Ltd	
2-EALH	Airbus A.340-541	Priority 1 Leasing Ltd	
2-EALI	Airbus A.340-541	Priority 1 Leasing Ltd	
2-EENS	Airbus A.319-133	ACM GMT VII Asset Co LLC	
2-EGJB	Cirrus SR22	private	
2-EIAY	Boeing 737-4Q8F	V66A-734 LLC	
2-EIAZ	Boeing 737-4Q8F	V67A-734 LLC	
2-EJEL	Cessna 550 Citation 2	HMPR SA	
2-EJIY	Boeing 737-8AS	UMB Bank, National Association	
2-ELLY	Cessna T.206H Turbo Stationair	private	
2-EMBB	Embraer ERJ190-100 IGW	DASI LLC	
2-EMBR	Embraer EMB-505 Phenom 300	X'Air Ltd	

Notes	Reg	Type	Owner or Operator
	2-EZBC	Airbus A.319-111	Heston Materials UAB
	2-EZRA	Boeing 737-8AS	TC Aviation Capital Ireland Ltd
	2-FAST	Bombardier CL600-2B16 Challenger 604	private
	2-FEEL	Cirrus Vision SF50	Brachert Aviation GbR
	2-FERY	Agusta A109S Grand	Fratomco Ltd
	2-FFLY	Cirrus SR22T	private
	2-FINC	Embraer ERJ170-100LR	AerFin Ltd
	2-FPLF	Beech B.350 Super King Air	Miralty Holdings Ltd
	2-FUNN	PA-32R-301T Saratoga II TC	Rainbow Self Storage Ltd
	2-FWCD	Airbus A.321-271NX	FW Aviation (Holdings) 8937 Ltd
	2-GALA	PA-31P-350 Mojave	Gala LG SA
	2-GAYE	Eclipse EA.500	TAK Aviation Holdings Inc
	2-GCNZ	Boeing 737-36Q	Aviapro Airplane Management LLC
	2-GEQI	Eurocopter EC.225LP	GD Helicopter Finance Ltd
	2-GEQL	Eurocopter EC.225LP	GD Helicopter Finance Ltd
	2-GEVT	Eurocopter EC.225LP	GD Helicopter Finance Ltd
	2-GEZL	Eurocopter EC.225LP	GD Helicopter Finance Ltd
	2-GEZP	Eurocopter EC.225LP	GD Helicopter Finance Ltd
	2-GGGT	Cessna 560 Citation Encore	TVPX Aircraft Solutions Inc
	2-GNKA	Eurocopter EC225LP Super Puma	Airbus Helicopters SAS
	2-GOLD	PA-28-235 Cherokee F	private
	2-GOOD	Diamond DA.62	MAJ Aviation Ltd
	2-GZTD	Boeing 737-73V	ECAF I 32418 DAC
	2-GZTS	Boeing 737-73V	Wilmington Trust SP Services (Dublin) Ltd
	2-HELI	Agusta AW109SP Grand New	TAK Aviation Holdings Inc
	2-HELX	Airbus EC.135	TAK Aviation Holdings Inc
	2-HELY	Airbus EC.135	TAK Aviation Holdings Inc
	2-HHZJ	Boeing 737-8K2	WWTAI AirOpCo II DAC
	2-HIPP	Dassault Falcon 7X	Red Falcon Ltd
	2-HLAB	Boeing 737-8Q8	KDAC Aircraft Trading Ltd
	2-HOVR	Agusta A109E Power	Eskimo Holdings Ltd
	2-HPGS	Airbus A.340-642	Priority 1 Leasing Ltd
	2-HSZN	Airbus A.330-941	Casamance Owner SARL
	2-HVUO	Boeing 737-8FE	BBAM Freighter B Leane 14 Ltd
	2-HWDN	Bombardier CL600-2B16 Challenger 604	Volare Aviation GSY Ltd
	2-IBZA	Bombardier CL600-2B16 Challenger 604	private
	2-IMMN	Diamond DA20-C1 Katana	Diamond Flight Training Co.Ltd
	2-INNA	Boeing 747-228F	Eagle Aviation Ltd
	2-ISLO	Avions Transport ATR-72-212A	Olsen Gruppen AS
	2-ISTH	Boeing 737-429F	V37X-737 LLC
	2-ISTM	Boeing 737-4Z9F	V56AC-734 LLC
	2-ISTS	Boeing 737-48E(F)	UMB Bank NA
	2-JALQ	Embraer ERJ190-100IGW	Drake Jet Leasing 6 DAC
	2-JALR	Embraer ERJ190-100IGW	Drake Jet Leasing 6 DAC
	2-JAYN	Airbus A.380-841	Airbus SA
	2-JECP	DHC-8-402Q Dash Eight	Regional One Inc
	2-JECR	DHC-8-402Q Dash Eight	Regional One Inc
	2-JECX	DHC-8-402Q Dash Eight	Regional One Inc
	2-JEFF	Eclipse EA.500	TAK Aviation Holdings Inc
	2-JEYL	Airbus A.380-841	Airbus SAS
	2-JEZA	Eclipse EA.500	Eclipse 2018 LLP
	2-JJPA	Airbus A.320-232	Tokyo Century Corporation
	2-JRSY	Embraer EMB-550 Praetor 600	Trustflight (Jersey) Ltd
	2-JSEG	Eclipse EA.500	Truly Classic LP Inc
	2-JUCE	Avions Transport ATR-72-212A	NAC Aviation 8 Ltd
	2-KISS	Eclipse EA.500	Hub Air Anstalt
	2-KMLI	Boeing 737-8AS	UMB Bank, National Association
	2-KNIL	Piper J-3C-65 Cub	private
	2-KOOL	PA-28-181 Archer II	Charlie Alpha Ltd
	2-KSFR	Bombardier BD700-1A10 Global 6000	Linden Lea Partnership
	2-KSRA	Bombardier CL600-2B19 CRJ200ER	EFTEC (UK) Ltd
	2-KYCM	Gulfstream 650ER	Business Aviation Services Guernsey Ltd
	2-LAND	Rockwell Commander 114B	88 Zulu Ltd
	2-LEAL	Dornier 228-300	ACG – Airlease Capital Group LDA
	2-LERA	Boeing 747-228F	Eagle Aviation Ltd
	2-LIDZ	Hawker 750	Valavan Holding Ltd
	2-LISS	Eclipse EA500	TAK Aviation Holdings Inc
	2-LOOK	PA-46-350P Malibu Mirage	private
	2-LIVE	Embraer EMB-500 Phenom 100	Stammair Guernsey Ltd
	2-LIVI	Embraer EMB505 Phenom 100	Stammar Guernsey Ltd
	2-LOVE	Beech A.36 Bonanza	Immuno Biotech Ltd

Reg	Type	Owner or Operator	Notes
2-MAPP	Cessna 421C	MBA Aviation Ltd	
2-MATO	Bombardier BD700-1A11 Global 5000	S & K Aviation Ltd	
2-MEDF	Boeing 737-8F2(F)	Oakstar Cargo Aviation No.2 DAC	
2-MINI	Eclipse EA500	TAK Aviation LLC	
2-MISO	Cessna 525A Citationjet CJ2	Metcalfe Food Concepts Ltd	
2-MLBU	PA-46-350P Malibu Mirage	private	
2-MMWD	Cessna A185E	Claymore AS Ltd	
2-MMXC	Airbus A.320-232	MSN 2090 Trust	
2-MSLA	Airbus A.320-271N	Bluesky 31 Leasing Company Ltd	
2-MSLB	Airbus A.320-271N	Bluesky 31 Leasing Company Ltd	
2-MSLC	Airbus A.320-271N	Bluesky 19 Leasing Company Ltd	
2-MSLD	Airbus A.320-271N	Bluesky 19 Leasing Company Ltd	
2-MSLE	Airbus A.320-271N	Bluesky 19 Leasing Company Ltd	
2-MSPI	Eurocopter EC.225LP	Airbus Helicopters SAS	
2-MUJJ	Eclipse 550	TAK Aviation LLC	
2-MUST	Cessna 510 Citation Mustang	W. F. McSweeney	
2-NAOM	Eclipse EA.500	TAK Aviation LLC	
2-NICE	Bombardier CL600-2B16 Challenger 601	Eskimo Holdings Ltd	
2-NITE	Bombardier CL600-2B16 Challenger 604	Air Tonite Ltd	
2-NNOO	Boeing 737-8U3	DAE 3 SPC Ltd	
2-NTUP	Agusta Westland AW139	Wilmington Trust SP Services (Dublin) Ltd	
2-NYAW	Dassault Falcon 50	H2M	
2-OJSE	Airbus A.330-202	Hinode Aviation Investments LLC	
2-ONEL	Learjet 75	One Private Charter Services Ltd	
2-OOOX	Dassault Falcon 2000	Falcon Air Ltd	
2-OOPC	Embraer EMB-500 Phenom 300	Embibe Ltd	
2-OWLC	PA-31 Turbo Navajo	Channel Airways Ltd	
2-PASF	Diamond DA.42	Tesla Solutions Ltd	
2-PBMY	Hawker 1000	Beunghar Ltd	
2-PBNW	Hawker 850XP	Merienda Holding Ltd	
2-PCBS	Bombardier CL600-2B16 Challenger 601	Volare Aviation Ltd	
2-PCIB	Airbus A.320-232	Manazel Al Mukhtara Trading Company	
2-PCIE	Airbus A.320-232	AerFin Ltd	
2-PETE	PA-32-300 Cherokee Six	P. Biggins	
2-PINK	Dassault Falcon 8X	Black Panther Aviation Ltd	
2-POOR	Bombardier CL600-2B16 Challenger 605	Global Fleet 695 Inc	
2-PROF	Robinson R66	HT Flight Ltd	
2-PRPD	Avions Transport ATR-72-212A	DAE 1077 LLC	
2-PSFI	Boeing 737-33A	European Aviation Ltd	
2-PTXC	SOCATA TBM-700C2	Coelus Flight Services Ltd	
2-PUBS	Bombardier BD700-1A11 Global 5000	Volare Aviation GSY Ltd	
2-RACE	Leonardo A109E Power	Eskimo Holdings Ltd	
2-REDY	SOCATA TBM-700	L T D Investments Ltd	
2-RIDE	SOCATA TBM-700	Gazelle Properties Ltd	
2-RLBC	Airbus A.340-541	Global Airways Ltd	
2-RLCA	Embraer ERJ190-100 IGV	Caisse Nationale de Sécurité Sociale	
2-RNWL	Cessna 525 M2	Norbert Blueskies Two Ltd	
2-ROYA	Airbus A.319-114	Royal Aircraft Maintenance Company DWC LLC	
2-ROYB	Airbus A.319-114	Royal Aircraft Maintenance Company DWC LLC	
2-ROYC	Airbus A.319-114	Royal Aircraft Maintenance Company DWC LLC	
2-ROYD	Airbus A.319-114	Royal Aircraft Maintenance Company DWC LLC	
2-ROYE	Airbus A.319-114	Royal Aircraft Maintenance Company DWC LLC	
2-ROYF	Airbus A.319-114	Royal Aircraft Maintenance Company DWC LLC	
2-RUFF	Kodiak 100	L T D Investments Ltd	
2-SACE	Avions Transport ATR-72-212A	Wellington Leasing No.36 Ltd	
2-SAIB	Avions Transport ATR-72-212A	Constellation Aircraft Leasing Ltd	
2-SAJD	Boeing 737-8Q8	Oakstar Cargo Aviation No.1 DAC	
2-SALE	Diamond DA.62	Morson Group Ltd	
2-SATC	Avions Transport ATR-72-212A	Red-Tail Aviation Ltd	
2-SHEE	Eclipse EA.500	TAK Aviation Holdings Inc	
2-SIAM	Bombardier CL600-2B16 Challenger 601	GMK Aviation Services Ltd	
2-SING	Cirrus SR22 GTS	private	
2-SIRI	Cirrus SR20	private	
2-SLOW	Agusta A109S Grand	Volare Aviation GSY Ltd	
2-SMRT	Bombardier CL600-2B19 Challenger 850	Volare Aviation GSY Ltd	
2-SMTD	Airbus A.320-233	Skylink 3-Aircraft Ltd	
2-SNOW	Falcon 7X	Black Panther Aviation Ltd	
2-SPSP	Agusta AW109SP Grand New	Tamcourt Services Ltd	
2-STEF	Avions Transport ATR-72-212	Blue Turbo Two Finance LLC	
2-STEV	SNCASE SE.3130 Alouette II	private	
2-SXTF	Airbus A.330-343	BOC Aviation Ltd	

Notes	Reg	Type	Owner or Operator
	2-TABS	Eclipse EA.500	TAK Aviation LLC
	2-TAKA	Eclipse EA.500	TAK Aviation LLC
	2-TBJS	Raytheon Hawker 1000	Faborel Holdings Ltd
	2-TBMI	SOCATA TBM-930	TBM Aviation Ltd
	2-TECY	Airbus A.320-233	AFG Aviation Ireland Ltd
	2-TESI	Diamond DA.40D	Tesla Solutions Ltd
	2-TESK	Diamond DA.40D	Tesla Solutions Ltd
	2-TJEH	Boeing 777-35RER	JIHB DAC
	2-TJEX	Boeing 777-35RER	JIHB DAC
	2-TKOC	Airbus A.320-216	Wilimington Trust SP Services (Dublin) Ltd
	2-TOAU	Avro RJ100	H & C Aero Ltd
	2-TOBI	Cirrus SR22T	private
	2-TONY	Boeing 737-8H6	K Aviation Leasing Corporation 1B DAC
	2-TSSA	Boeing 767-239ER	Weststar Ltd
	2-TSUT	DHC-8-402 Dash Eight	Regional One Inc
	2-TSUW	DHC-8-402 Dash Eight	Regional One Inc
	2-TSUX	DHC-8-402 Dash Eight	Regional One Inc
	2-TWCA	Boeing 737 8K9	TWC Aviation Capital Ltd
	2-TWCB	Boeing 737 8K9	TWC Aviation Capital Ltd
	2-TWGN	Airbus A.320-271N	Pembroke Aircraft Leasing 11 Ltd
	2-UARA	Airbus A.330-202	Moorgate Aircraft 2007 DAC
	2-UBLI	Airbus A.330-243	Hangrun Tech Pte. Ltd
	2-VBIG	Airbus A.318-112ACJ	European Aviation Ltd
	2-VNYK	Bombardier CRJ100ER	Zipa Hoilding Ltd
	2-VNYL	Bombardier CRJ200ER	Myrmarian Ltd
	2-VSLP	Airbus A.320-233	Asia Pacific Leasing Co SAS
	2-VVIP	Agusta A.109A II	Castle Air Ltd
	2-WEBS	Eclipse EA.500	TAK Aviation LLC
	2-WEFX	Avro RJ100	H & C Aero Ltd
	2-WIDE	Diamond DA.62	Too Wide Ltd
	2-WILD	Bombardier CL600-2B16 Challenger 604	Volare Aviation GSY Ltd
	2-WKTJ	Beech B.300 King Air 350	DEA Aviation Ltd
	2-WKTK	Beech B.200T King Air	Dynamic AvLease Inc
	2-WKTN	Beech B.200 King Air	DEA Aviation Ltd
	2-WKTP	Beech B.300 King Air 350	DEA Aviation Ltd
	2-WKTR	Beech B.200T King Air	Dynamic AvLease Inc
	2-WOOD	Cessna 550 Citation Bravo	Horizon Air LLP
	2-WWAA	Avions Transport ATR-72-212A	Wilmington Trust Company
	2-WWBB	Avions Transport ATR-72-212A	Wilmington Trust Company
	2-XAPA	Boeing 737-752	Wells Fargo Trust Company, National Association
	2-XEAR	Boeing 767-352ER	Aercap Ireland Capital Designated Activity Company
	2-XSEV	Avions Transport ATR-72-212A	Elix Assets 12 Ltd
	2-YAYA	Gulfstream IV	Weststar Ltd
	2-YJZH	Avions Transport ATR-72-212A	NAC Aviation 8 Ltd
	2-YYDJ	Avions Transport ATR-72-212A	NAC Aviation 8 Ltd
	2-YYDK	Avions Transport ATR-72-212A	NAC Aviation 8 Ltd
	2-YYDM	Avions Transport ATR-72-212A	NAC Aviation 8 Ltd
	2-YYGF	Embraer ERJ190-200IGW	Aldus Portfolio Leasing Ltd
	2-ZENP	Embraer EMB-505 Phenom	Barrio Ltd

Reg	Type († False registration)	Owner or Operator	Notes
EI-ABI	DH.84 Dragon	Aer Lingus Charitable Foundation (EI-FBK)	
EI-ABS	Boeing B75N1 Stearman	S. Bennett	
EI-AEE	Auster 3/1 Autocrat	O. & N. A. O'Sullivan	
EI-AEF	Cessna 120	J. Halligan	
EI-AEH	Luscombe 8F	D. Kelly	
EI-AEI	Aeronca 65-TACS	F. J. McMorrow	
EI-AEL	PA-16	G. Dolan	
EI-AEN	Cessna 170	Taildragger Aviation Ltd	
EI-AEP	Cessna 170B	private individual	
EI-AER	Gulfstream G.VI	Aercap Ireland Ltd	
EI-AET	Piper J3C-65 Cub	S. T. Scully	
EI-AEU	PA-22-150 Tri-Pacer	J. L. O'Toole	
EI-AEW	Stampe SV-4C	E. T. Larkin	
EI-AEX	Cessna F.172H	Leeside Flying Ltd	
EI-AEY	PA-22-160 Tri-Pacer	private individual	
EI-AEZ	SOCATA MS.885 Rallye	private individual	
EI-AFE	Piper J3C-65 Cub	4 of Cubs Flying Group	
EI-AFX	Cessna F.172L	Advanced Field Solutions Ltd	
EI-AFZ	DHC.1 Chipmunk 22	Gipsy Captains Group	
EI-AGJ	Auster J/1 Autocrat	T. G. Rafter	
EI-AHI	DH.82A Tiger Moth	High Fidelity Flyers	
EI-AII	Cessna 150F	L. Bagnell	
EI-AIR	PA-18-135 Super Cub	The Vintage Aircraft Flying Group	
EI-AKM	Piper J-3C-65 Cub	J. A. Kent	
EI-ALP	Avro 643 Cadet	J. C. O'Loughlin	
EI-AMK	Auster J/1 Autocrat	Iona National Airways	
EI-ANT	Champion 7ECA Citabria	T. Croke & ptnrs	
EI-ANY	PA-18 Super Cub 95	Bogavia Group	
EI-AOB	PA-28 Cherokee 140	Knock Flying Group	
EI-AOO	Cessna 150E	C. Sheridan	
EI-ARW	Jodel D.R.1050	J. Davy	
EI-AUM	Auster J/1 Autocrat	E. W. Hopkins	
EI-AVE	PA-18-95 Super Cub	A. R. Hassett & P. Morgan	
EI-AVM	Cessna F.150L	J. Nugent	
EI-AWP	DH.82A Tiger Moth	O. E. P. O'Sullivan	
EI-AWR	Malmö MFI-9 Junior	L. P. Murray	
EI-AYB	GY-80 Horizon 180	J. B. Smith	
EI-AYI	MS.880B Rallye Club	J. McNamara	
EI-AYN	BN-2A-8 Islander	Aer Arann	
EI-AYR	Schleicher ASK-16	B. O'Broin & ptnrs	
EI-AYT	MS.894A Rallye Minerva	K. A. O'Connor	
EI-AYY	Evans VP-1	Ballyboughal VP-1 Flying Group	
EI-BAJ	Stampe SV.4C	W. Rafter & Partners	
EI-BAV	PA-22-108 Colt	E. Finnamore	
EI-AZA	Booing 737-86N	ASL Airlines (Ireland) Ltd	
EI-AZB	Boeing 737-8ASF	ASL Airlines (Ireland) Ltd	
EI-AZC	Boeing 737-86J	ASL Airlines (Ireland) Ltd	
EI-AZD	Boeing 737-86QSF	ASL Airlines (Ireland) Ltd	
EI-AZE	Boeing 737-86Q	ASL Airlines (Ireland) Ltd	
EI-AZF	Boeing 737-84P	ASL Airlines (Ireland) Ltd	
EI-AZG	Boeing 737-86Q	ASL Airlines (Ireland) Ltd	
EI-BAV	PA-22 Colt 108	E. Finnamore	
EI-BBE	Champion 7FC Tri-Traveler	private individual	
EI-BBV	Piper J-3C-65 Cub	private individual	
EI-BCE	BN-2A-26 Islander	Aer Arann	
EI-BCF	Bensen B.8M	P. Flanagan	
EI-BCJ	Aeromere F.8L Falco 1 Srs 3	M. P. McLoughlin	
EI-BCK	Cessna F.172N II	National Flight Centre Ltd	
EI-BCM	Piper J-3C-65 Cub	M. Bergin & Partners	
EI-BCN	Piper J-3C-65 Cub	H. Diver	
EI-BCP	D.62B Condor	T. Delaney	
EI-BDL	Evans VP-2	P. Buggle	
EI-BDR	PA-28-180 Cherokee	M. Sinkovec	
EI-BEN	Piper J-3C-65 Cub	Ballyboughal L4 Flying Group	
EI-BFR	MS.880B Rallye	J. M. Fingleton	
EI-BHV	Champion 7EC Traveler	P. O'Donnell & ptnrs	
EI-BIB	Cessna F.152	Sligo Aeronautical Club Ltd	
EI-BID	PA-18 Super Cub 95	Ballyboughal Super Cub Group	
EI-BIK	PA-18 Super Cub 180	Dublin Gliding Club	
EI-BIO	Piper J-3C-65 Cub	H. Duggan & Partners	
EI-BJB	Aeronca 7AC Champion	P. Brennan	

Notes	Reg	Type († False registration)	Owner or Operator
	EI-BJC	Aeronca 7AC Champion	A. E. Griffin
	EI-BJK	MS.880B Rallye 110ST	Phoenix Flying Ltd
	EI-BJM	Cessna A.152	National Flight Centre Ltd
	EI-BJO	Cessna R.172K	The XP Group
	EI-BKC	Aeronca 15AC Sedan	G. Hendrick & M. Farrell
	EI-BKK	Taylor JT.1 Monoplane	D. Doyle
	EI-BMN	Cessna F.152 II	National Flight Centre Ltd
	EI-BMU	Monnet Sonerai IIL	N. O'Donnell
	EI-BNL	Rand-Robinson KR-2	K. Hayes
	EI-BNU	MS.880B Rallye Club	J. Cooke
	EI-BOV	Rand-Robinson KR-2	G. O'Hara & G. Callan
	EI-BPP	Quicksilver MX	J. A. Smith
	EI-BRU	Evans VP-1	C. O'Shea
	EI-BSB	Wassmer Jodel D.112	private individual
	EI-BSG	Bensen B.80	J. Todd
	EI-BSK	SOCATA TB9 Tampico	J. Byrne
	EI-BSL	PA-34-220T Seneca III	P. Sreenan
	EI-BSN	Cameron O-65 balloon	L. Duncan
	EI-BSO	PA-28 Cherokee 140B	S. Brazil
	EI-BSW	Solar Wings Pegasus XL-R	E. Fitzgerald
	EI-BSX	J-3C-65 Cub	J. O'Dwyer
	EI-BUC	Jodel D.9 Bébé	M. Blake
	EI-BUF	Cessna 210N	210 Group
	EI-BUG	SOCATA ST.10 Diplomate	J. Cooke
	EI-BUL	Whittaker MW5 Sorcerer	J. Culleton
	EI-BUT	MS.893A Commodore 180	T. Keating
	EI-BVJ	AMF Chevvron 232	A. Dunn
	EI-BVK	PA-38-112 Tomahawk	B. Lowe
	EI-BVT	Evans VP-2	P. Morrison
	EI-BVY	Zenith 200AA-RW	J. Matthews & M. Skelly
	EI-BYL	Zenith CH.250	I. Calton
	EI-BYX	Champion 7GCAA	P. J. Gallagher & P. Kearne
	EI-BYY	Piper J-3C-85 Cub	T. A. Byrne
	EI-CAC	Grob G.115A	C. Phillips
	EI-CAD	Grob G.115A	C. Phillips
	EI-CAE	Grob G.115A	R. M. Davies
	EI-CAN	Aerotech MW5 Sorcerer	V. A. Vaughan
	EI-CAU	AMF Chevvron 232	E. Cronin
	EI-CAX	Cessna P.210N	K. A. O'Connor
	EI-CBK	Aérospatiale ATR-42-310	Elix Assets 7 Ltd
	EI-CCF	Aeronca 11AC Chief	F. J. Feeney
	EI-CCM	Cessna 152 II	E. Hopkins
	EI-CDP	Cessna 182L	Irish Parachute Club
	EI-CDV	Cessna 150G	K. A. O'Connor
	EI-CEG	MS.893A Rallye 180GT	M. Jarrett
	EI-CES	Taylorcraft BC-65	G. Higgins
	EI-CFF	PA-12 Super Cruiser	J. & T. O'Dwyer
	EI-CFG	CP.301B Emeraude	F. Doyle
	EI-CFH	PA-12 Super Cruiser	G. Treacy
	EI-CFO	Piper J-3C-65 Cub	J. Brouder
	EI-CFY	Cessna 172N	National Flight Centre Ltd
	EI-CGF	Luton LA-5 Major	P. Jones
	EI-CGH	Cessna 210N	J. Greif-Wustenbecker
	EI-CGP	PA-28 Cherokee 140C	L. A. Tattan
	EI-CHR	CFM Shadow Srs BD	B. Kelly
	EI-CIG	PA-18 Super Cub 150	8 Ball Cub Club
	EI-CIM	Avid Flyer Mk IV	P. Swan
	EI-CIN	Cessna 150K	K. A. O'Connor
	EI-CJJ	Slingsby T-31M	J. J. Sullivan
	EI-CJS	Jodel D.120A	A. Flood
	EI-CJT	Slingsby Motor Cadet III	J. Tarrant
	EI-CKH	PA-18 Super Cub 95	J. J. Conran
	EI-CKI	Thruster TST Mk 1	S. Woodgates
	EI-CKJ	Cameron N-77 balloon	A. F. Meldon
	EI-CKZ	Jodel D.18	J. O'Brien
	EI-CLQ	Cessna F.172N	E. Finnamore
	EI-CML	Cessna 150M	private individual
	EI-CMN	PA-12 Super Cruiser	A. McNamee & ptnrs
	EI-CMR	Rutan LongEz	F. & C. O'Caoimh
	EI-CMT	PA-34-200T Seneca II	Atlantic Flight Training
	EI-CMU	Mainair Mercury	Bill O'Neill

Reg	Type († False registration)	Owner or Operator	Notes
EI-CMW	Rotorway Executive	B. McNamee	
EI-CNG	Air & Space 18A gyroplane	P. Joyce	
EI-CNU	Pegasus Quantum 15-912	private individual	
EI-COT	Cessna F.172N	Tojo Air Leasing	
EI-COW	ICP MXP-740 Savannah S	N. O'Callaghan	
EI-COY	Piper J-3C-65 Cub	The Real Seaplane Flying Group	
EI-CPI	Rutan LongEz	D. J. Ryan	
EI-CPP	Piper J-3C-65 Cub	W. Kennedy	
EI-CPX	I.I.I. Sky Arrow 650T	M. Tormey	
EI-CRB	Lindstrand LBL-90A balloon	J. & C. Concannon	
EI-CRX	SOCATA TB-9 Tampico	J. W. Leonard	
EI-CTL	Aerotech MW-5B Sorcerer	M. Wade	
EI-CUJ	Cessna 172N	The Hotel Bravo Flying Club	
EI-CUS	AB-206B JetRanger 3	H. Hassard	
EI-CUW	BN-2B-20 Islander	Aer Arann	
EI-CVL	Ercoupe 415CD	V. O'Rourke	
EI-CVW	Bensen B.8M	F. Kavanagh	
EI-CXC	Raj Hamsa X'Air 502T	D.White	
EI-CXN	Boeing 737-329	Transalpine Leasing Ltd	
EI-CXR	Boeing 737-329	Transalpine Leasing Ltd	
EI-CXV	Boeing 737-8CX	MASL Ireland(14)Ltd/MIAT Mongolian Airlines	
EI-CXY	Evektor EV-97 Eurostar	G. Doody & ptnrs	
EI-CXZ	Boeing 767-216ER	Transalpine Leasing Ltd	
EI-CZA	ATEC Zephyr 2000	D. Cassidy	
EI-DAA	Airbus A.330-202	Aer Lingus St Keeva	
EI-DBI	Raj Hamsa X'Air Mk.2 Falcon	D. Cornally	
EI-DBO	Air Creation Kiss 400	E. Spain	
EI-DBV	Rand Kar X' Air 602T	S. Scanlon	
EI-DCA	Raj Hamsa X'Air	S. Cahill	
EI-DCJ	Boeing 737-8AS	Ryanair	
EI-DCK	Boeing 737-8AS	Ryanair	
EI-DCL	Boeing 737-8AS	Ryanair	
EI-DCM	Boeing 737-8AS	Ryanair	
EI-DCN	Boeing 737-8AS	Ryanair	
EI-DCO	Boeing 737-8AS	Ryanair	
EI-DCP	Boeing 737-8AS	Ryanair	
EI-DCR	Boeing 737-8AS	Ryanair	
EI-DCW	Boeing 737-8AS	Ryanair	
EI-DCX	Boeing 737-8AS	Ryanair	
EI-DCY	Boeing 737-8AS	Ryanair	
EI-DCZ	Boeing 737-8AS	Ryanair	
EI-DDC	Cessna F.172M	P. Murphy & J. Sullivan	
EI-DDD	Aeronca 7AC	J. Sullivan & M. Quinn	
EI-DDJ	Raj Hamsa X'Air 582	I. Talt	
EI-DDP	Southdown International microlight	M. Mannion	
EI-DDR	Bensen B8V	P. MacCabe & Partners	
EI-DDX	Cessna 172S	Atlantic Flight Training	
EI-DEE	Airbus A.320-214	Aer Lingus St Fintan	
EI-DEF	Airbus A.320-214	Aer Lingus St Declan	
EI-DEG	Airbus A.320-214	Aer Lingus St Fachtna	
EI-DEH	Airbus A.320-214	Aer Lingus St Malachy	
EI-DEI	Airbus A.320-214	Aer Lingus St Kilian	
EI-DEJ	Airbus A.320-214	Aer Lingus St Oliver Plunkett	
EI-DEK	Airbus A.320-214	Aer Lingus St Eunan	
EI-DEL	Airbus A.320-214	Aer Lingus St Ibar	
EI-DEM	Airbus A.320-214	Aer Lingus St Canice	
EI-DEN	Airbus A.320-214	Aer Lingus St Kieran	
EI-DEO	Airbus A.320-214	Aer Lingus St Senan	
EI-DEP	Airbus A.320-214	Aer Lingus St Eugene	
EI-DER	Airbus A.320-214	Aer Lingus St Mel	
EI-DES	Airbus A.320-214	Aer Lingus St Pappin	
EI-DFM	Evektor EV-97 Eurostar	J. Gibbons	
EI-DFO	Airbus A.320-211	Windjet	
EI-DFS	Boeing 767-33AER	Transalpine Leasing Ltd	
EI-DFX	Air Creation Kiss 400	K. Hynes & S. P. McGirr	
EI-DFY	Raj Hamsa R100 (2)	P. McGirr & R Gillespie	
EI-DGA	Urban Air UFM-11UK Lambada	Dr. P. & D. Durkin	
EI-DGG	Raj Hamsa X'Air 582	P. A. Weldon	
EI-DGH	Raj Hamsa X'Air 582	C. D. & W. Baker	
EI-DGJ	Raj Hamsa X'Air 582	N. Brereton	
EI-DGK	Raj Hamsa X'Air 133	B. Chambers	

Notes	Reg	Type († False registration)	Owner or Operator
	EI-DGP	Urban Air UFM-11 Lambada	R. Linehan
	EI-DGT	Urban Air UFM-11UK Lambada	P. Walsh & Partners
	EI-DGV	ATEC Zephyr 2000	K. Higgins
	EI-DGW	Cameron Z-90 balloon	J. Leahy
	EI-DGX	Cessna 152 II	National Flight Centre Ltd
	EI-DGY	Urban Air UFM-11 Lambada	D. McMorrow
	EI-DHA	Boeing 737-8AS	Ryanair
	EI-DHD	Boeing 737-8AS	Ryanair
	EI-DHE	Boeing 737-8AS	Ryanair
	EI-DHF	Boeing 737-8AS	Ryanair
	EI-DHG	Boeing 737-8AS	Ryanair
	EI-DHH	Boeing 737-8AS	Ryanair
	EI-DHK	Boeing 737-8AS	STLC Europe Seventeen Leasing Ltd
	EI-DHN	Boeing 737-8AS	Ryanair
	EI-DHO	Boeing 737-8AS	Ryanair
	EI-DHR	Boeing 737-8AS	Ryanair
	EI-DHX	Boeing 737-8AS	Ryanair
	EI-DHZ	Boeing 737-8AS	Ryanair
	EI-DIA	Solar Wings Pegasus XL-Q	P. Byrne
	EI-DIY	Van's RV-4	J. A. Kent
	EI-DJF	Luscombe 8F	S. Forde
	EI-DKE	Air Creation Kiss 450-582	S. Smith & A. Duffy
	EI-DKJ	Thruster T.600N	private individual
	EI-DKK	Raj Hamsa X'Air Jabiru	M. Tolan
	EI-DKT	Raj Hamsa X'Air 582 (11)	P. & D. Darcy
	EI-DKU	Air Creation Kiss 450-582 (1)	P. Kirwan
	EI-DKW	Evektor EV-97 Eurostar	Ormand Flying Club
	EI-DKY	Raj Hamsa X'Air 582	M. Clarke
	EI-DKZ	Reality Aircraft Escapade 912 (1)	private individual
	EI-DLB	Boeing 737-8AS	Ryanair
	EI-DLC	Boeing 737-8AS	Ryanair
	EI-DLD	Boeing 737-8AS	Ryanair
	EI-DLI	Boeing 737-8AS	Ryanair
	EI-DLV	Boeing 737-8AS	Ryanair
	EI-DLW	Boeing 737-8AS	Ryanair
	EI-DLX	Boeing 737-8AS	Ryanair
	EI-DLY	Boeing 737-8AS	Ryanair
	EI-DMA	MS.892E Rallye 150	J. Burke
	EI-DMB	Best Off Skyranger 912S (1)	E. Spain
	EI-DMU	Whittaker MW6S Merlin	M. Heaton
	EI-DNM	Boeing 737-4S3	Transalpine Leasing Ltd
	EI-DNR	Raj Hamsa X'Air 582 (5)	private individual
	EI-DNV	Urban Air UFM-11UK Lambada	F. Maughan
	EI-DOB	Zenair CH-701	D. O'Brien
	EI-DOW	Mainair Blade 912	P. Byrne
	EI-DOY	PZL Koliber 150A	T. J. Britton
	EI-DPF	Boeing 737-8AS	Ryanair
	EI-DPH	Boeing 737-8AS	Ryanair
	EI-DPI	Boeing 737-8AS	Ryanair
	EI-DPJ	Boeing 737-8AS	Ryanair
	EI-DPK	Boeing 737-8AS	Ryanair
	EI-DPL	Boeing 737-8AS	Ryanair
	EI-DPN	Boeing 737-8AS	Ryanair
	EI-DPP	Boeing 737-8AS	Ryanair
	EI-DPR	Boeing 737-8AS	Ryanair
	EI-DPV	Boeing 737-8AS	Ryanair
	EI-DPY	Boeing 737-8AS	Ryanair
	EI-DPZ	Boeing 737-8AS	Ryanair
	EI-DRH	Mainair Blade	J. McErlain
	EI-DRL	Raj Hamsa X'Air Jabiru	N. Brunton
	EI-DRM	Urban Air UFM-10 Samba	private individual
	EI-DRT	Air Creation Tanarg 912	P. McMahon
	EI-DRU	Tecnam P92/EM Echo	P. Gallogly
	EI-DRW	Evektor EV-97R Eurostar	Eurostar Flying Club
	EI-DRX	Raj Hamsa X'Air 582 (5)	private individual
	EI-DSA	Airbus A.320-216	ITA Airways
	EI-DSU	Airbus A.320-216	ITA Airways
	EI-DSV	Airbus A.320-216	ITA Airways
	EI-DSW	Airbus A.320-216	ITA Airways
	EI-DSX	Airbus A.320-216	ITA Airways
	EI-DSY	Airbus A.320-216	ITA Airways

Reg	Type († False registration)	Owner or Operator	Notes
EI-DSZ	Airbus A.320-216	ITA Airways	
EI-DTA	Airbus A.320-216	ITA Airways	
EI-DTB	Airbus A.320-216	ITA Airways	
EI-DTE	Airbus A.320-216	ITA Airways	
EI-DTM	Airbus A.320-216	ITA Airways	
EI-DTN	Airbus A.320-216	ITA Airways	
EI-DTO	Airbus A.320-216	ITA Airways	
EI-DTS	PA-18 Super Cub	M. D. Murphy	
EI-DTT	ELA-07 R-100 Gyrocopter	N. Steele	
EI-DUH	Scintex CP.1310C3 Emeraude	W. Kennedy	
EI-DUJ	Evektor EV-97 Eurostar	E. Fitzpatrick	
EI-DUO	Airbus A.330-203	Aer Lingus	
EI-DUZ	Airbus A.330-203	Aer Lingus	
EI-DVE	Airbus A.320-214	Aer Lingus	
EI-DVG	Airbus A.320-214	Aer Lingus	
EI-DVH	Airbus A.320-214	Aer Lingus	
EI-DVI	Airbus A.320-214	Aer Lingus	
EI-DVK	Airbus A.320-214	Aer Lingus	
EI-DVL	Airbus A.320-214	Aer Lingus	
EI-DVM	Airbus A.320-214	Aer Lingus	
EI-DVN	Airbus A.320-214	Aer Lingus	
EI-DVO	Barnett J4B2	T. Brennan	
EI-DVZ	Robinson R44 II	M. O'Donovan	
EI-DWA	Boeing 737-8AS	Ryanair	
EI-DWC	Boeing 737-8AS	Ryanair	
EI-DWD	Boeing 737-8AS	Ryanair	
EI-DWE	Boeing 737-8AS	Ryanair	
EI-DWF	Boeing 737-8AS	Ryanair	
EI-DWG	Boeing 737-8AS	Ryanair	
EI-DWH	Boeing 737-8AS	Ryanair	
EI-DWK	Boeing 737-8AS	Ryanair	
EI-DWM	Boeing 737-8AS	Ryanair	
EI-DWO	Boeing 737-8AS	Ryanair	
EI-DWP	Boeing 737-8AS	Ryanair	
EI-DWR	Boeing 737-8AS	Ryanair	
EI-DWS	Boeing 737-8AS	Ryanair	
EI-DWT	Boeing 737-8AS	Ryanair	
EI-DWV	Boeing 737-8AS	Ryanair	
EI-DWW	Boeing 737-8AS	Ryanair	
EI-DWX	Boeing 737-8AS	Ryanair	
EI-DWY	Boeing 737-8AS	Ryanair	
EI-DXA	Ikarus C42	B. Chambers	
EI-DXL	CFM Shadow	F. Lynch	
EI-DXM	Raj Hamsa X'Air 582	B. Nugent	
EI-DXP	Cyclone AX3/503	J. Hennessey	
EI-DXS	CFM Shadow	R. W. Frost	
EI-DXT	UrbanAir UFM-10 Samba	N. Irwin	
EI-DXV	Thruster T.600N	P. Higgins	
EI-DXX	Raj Hamsa X'AIR 582(5)	E. D. Hanly & S. Macsweeney	
EI-DXZ	UrbanAir UFM-10 Samba	D. O'Leary	
EI-DYA	Boeing 737-8AS	Ryanair	
EI-DYC	Boeing 737-8AS	Ryanair	
EI-DYD	Boeing 737-8AS	Ryanair	
EI-DYE	Boeing 737-8AS	Ryanair	
EI-DYL	Boeing 737-8AS	Ryanair	
EI-DYO	Boeing 737-8AS	Ryanair	
EI-DYR	Boeing 737-8AS	Ryanair	
EI-DYV	Boeing 737-8AS	Ryanair	
EI-DYW	Boeing 737-8AS	Ryanair	
EI-DYX	Boeing 737-8AS	Ryanair	
EI-DYY	Boeing 737-8AS	Ryanair	
EI-DZA	Colt 21A balloon	P. Baker	
EI-DZB	Colt 21A balloon	P. Baker	
EI-DZE	UrbanAir UFM-10 Samba	J. P. Gilroy	
EI-DZK	Robinson R22B2 Beta	Skywest Aviation Ltd	
EI-DZL	Urban Air Samba XXL	M. Tormey	
EI-DZM	Robinson R44 II	E1-SUB Ltd	
EI-DZO	Dominator Gyroplane Ultrawhite	P. O'Reilly	
EI-DZS	BRM Land Africa	M. Whyte	
EI-EAK	Airborne Windsports Edge XT	M. O'Brien	
EI-EAM	Cessna 172R	Atlantic Flight Training Ltd	

Notes	Reg	Type († False registration)	Owner or Operator
	EI-EAV	Airbus A.330-302	Aer Lingus
	EI-EAW	Airborne Windsports Edge XT582	F. Heary
	EI-EAY	Raj Hamsa X'Air 582 (5)	West-Tech Aviation Ltd
	EI-EAZ	Cessna 172R	Waterford Aero Club Ltd
	EI-EBC	Boeing 737-8AS	Ryanair
	EI-EBD	Boeing 737-8AS	Ryanair
	EI-EBE	Boeing 737-8AS	Ryanair
	EI-EBF	Boeing 737-8AS	Ryanair
	EI-EBG	Boeing 737-8AS	Ryanair
	EI-EBK	Boeing 737-8AS	Ryanair
	EI-EBL	Boeing 737-8AS	Ryanair
	EI-EBN	Boeing 737-8AS	Ryanair
	EI-EBO	Boeing 737-8AS	Ryanair
	EI-EBP	Boeing 737-8AS	Ryanair
	EI-EBR	Boeing 737-8AS	Ryanair
	EI-EBS	Boeing 737-8AS	Ryanair
	EI-EBV	Boeing 737-8AS	Ryanair
	EI-EBW	Boeing 737-8AS	Ryanair
	EI-EBX	Boeing 737-8AS	Ryanair
	EI-EBY	Boeing 737-8AS	Ryanair
	EI-EBZ	Boeing 737-8AS	Ryanair
	EI-ECC	Cameron Z-90 balloon	J. J. Daly
	EI-ECG	BRM Land Africa	EI-ECG Flying Group
	EI-ECK	Raj Hamsa X'Air Hawk	N. Geh
	EI-ECM	Boeing 737-86N	Alrosa
	EI-ECP	Raj Hamsa X'Air Hawk	S. P. McGirr & J. McDaid
	EI-ECZ	Raj Hamsa X'Air Hawk	M. Tolan
	EI-EDB	Cessna 152	National Flight Centre Ltd
	EI-EDC	Cessna FA.152	National Flight Centre Ltd
	EI-EDI	Ikarus C42	G. Smith
	EI-EDJ	CZAW Sportcruiser	Croftal Ltd
	EI-EDP	Airbus A.320-214	Aer Lingus
	EI-EDR	PA-28R Cherokee Arrow 200	G. J. Brady
	EI-EDS	Airbus A.320-214	Aer Lingus
	EI-EEH	BRM Land Africa	R. Duffy
	EI-EEO	Van's RV-7	A. Butler
	EI-EES	ELA-07R	D. Doyle & Partners
	EI-EEU	Osprey II	P. Forde & S. Coughlan
	EI-EFD	Boeing 737-8AS	Ryanair
	EI-EFE	Boeing 737-8AS	Ryanair
	EI-EFF	Boeing 737-8AS	Ryanair
	EI-EFG	Boeing 737-8AS	Ryanair
	EI-EFH	Boeing 737-8AS	Ryanair
	EI-EFI	Boeing 737-8AS	Ryanair
	EI-EFJ	Boeing 737-8AS	Ryanair
	EI-EFK	Boeing 737-8AS	Ryanair
	EI-EFN	Boeing 737-8AS	Ryanair
	EI-EFO	Boeing 737-8AS	Ryanair
	EI-EFX	Boeing 737-8AS	Ryanair
	EI-EFZ	Boeing 737-8AS	Ryanair
	EI-EGA	Boeing 737-8AS	Ryanair
	EI-EGB	Boeing 737-8AS	Ryanair
	EI-EGC	Boeing 737-8AS	Ryanair
	EI-EGD	Boeing 737-8AS	Ryanair
	EI-EHF	Aeroprakt A22 Foxbat	K. Glynn
	EI-EHK	Magni Gyro M-22 Voyager	J. Heffernan
	EI-EHL	Air Creation Tanarg/Ixess 15 912S	S. Woods
	EI-EHM	Rand KR-2T	A. Lagun
	EI-EHY	Urban Air Samba XXL	C. N. Murphy & R. White
	EI-EIA	Airbus A.320-216	ITA Airways
	EI-EIB	Airbus A.320-216	ITA Airways
	EI-EIC	Airbus A.320-216	ITA Airways
	EI-EID	Airbus A.320-216	ITA Airways
	EI-EIE	Airbus A.320-216	ITA Airways
	EI-EIK	Airbus A.330-302	Aer Lingus
	EI-EIL	Airbus A.330-302	Aer Lingus
	EI-EIM	Airbus A.330-302	Aer Lingus
	EI-EIN	Airbus A.330-302	Aer Lingus
	EI-EJG	Airbus A.330-202	ITA Airways
	EI-EJH	Airbus A.330-202	ITA Airways
	EI-EJM	Airbus A.330-202	ITA Airways

Reg	Type († False registration)	Owner or Operator	Notes
EI-EJO	Airbus A.330-202	ITA Airways	
EI-EJP	Airbus A.330-202	ITA Airways	
EI-EKC	Boeing 737-8AS	Ryanair	
EI-EKD	Boeing 737-8AS	Ryanair	
EI-EKF	Boeing 737-8AS	Ryanair	
EI-EKG	Boeing 737-8AS	Ryanair	
EI-EKH	Boeing 737-8AS	Ryanair	
EI-EKI	Boeing 737-8AS	Ryanair	
EI-EKJ	Boeing 737-8AS	Ryanair	
EI-EKK	Boeing 737-8AS	Ryanair	
EI-EKL	Boeing 737-8AS	Ryanair	
EI-EKM	Boeing 737-8AS	Ryanair	
EI-EKN	Boeing 737-8AS	Ryanair	
EI-EKO	Boeing 737-8AS	Ryanair	
EI-EKP	Boeing 737-8AS	Ryanair	
EI-EKR	Boeing 737-8AS	Ryanair	
EI-EKS	Boeing 737-8AS	Ryanair	
EI-EKT	Boeing 737-8AS	Ryanair	
EI-EKW	Boeing 737-8AS	Ryanair	
EI-EKX	Boeing 737-8AS	Ryanair	
EI-EKY	Boeing 737-8AS	Ryanair	
EI-ELB	Raj Hamsa X'Air 582 (1)	G. McLaughlin	
EI-ELC	Ikarus C42B	A. Kilpatrick & M. Mullin	
EI-ELL	Medway Eclipser	P. McMahon	
EI-ELM	PA-18-95 Super Cub	O. D. Fitzgibbon	
EI-EMA	Boeing 737-8AS	Ryanair	
EI-EMB	Boeing 737-8AS	Ryanair	
EI-EMC	Boeing 737-8AS	Ryanair	
EI-EMD	Boeing 737-8AS	Ryanair	
EI-EME	Boeing 737-8AS	Ryanair	
EI-EMF	Boeing 737-8AS	Ryanair	
EI-EMH	Boeing 737-8AS	Ryanair	
EI-EMI	Boeing 737-8AS	Ryanair	
EI-EMJ	Boeing 737-8AS	Ryanair	
EI-EMK	Boeing 737-8AS	Ryanair	
EI-EML	Boeing 737-8AS	Ryanair	
EI-EMM	Boeing 737-8AS	Ryanair	
EI-EMN	Boeing 737-8AS	Ryanair	
EI-EMO	Boeing 737-8AS	Ryanair	
EI-EMT	PA-16 Clipper	G. Dolan	
EI-EMU	Cessna F.152	National Flight Centre Ltd	
EI-EMV	CZAW Sportcruiser	private	
EI-ENA	Boeing 737-8AS	Ryanair	
EI-ENE	Boeing 737-8AS	Ryanair	
EI-ENF	Boeing 737-8AS	Ryanair	
EI-ENG	Boeing 737-8AS	Ryanair	
EI-ENH	Boeing 737-8AS	Ryanair	
EI-ENI	Boeing 737-8AS	Ryanair	
EI-ENJ	Boeing 737-8AS	Ryanair	
EI-ENK	Boeing 737-8AS	Ryanair	
EI-ENL	Boeing 737-8AS	Ryanair	
EI-ENM	Boeing 737-8AS	Ryanair	
EI-ENN	Boeing 737-8AS	Ryanair	
EI-ENO	Boeing 737-8AS	Ryanair	
EI-ENP	Boeing 737-8AS	Ryanair	
EI-ENR	Boeing 737-8AS	Ryanair	
EI-ENT	Boeing 737-8AS	Ryanair	
EI-ENV	Boeing 737-8AS	Ryanair	
EI-ENW	Boeing 737-8AS	Ryanair	
EI-EOA	Raj Hamsa X'Air Jabiru	private individual	
EI-EOC	Van's RV-6	V. P. & N. O'Brien	
EI-EOF	Jabiru SP430	J. Bermingham	
EI-EOH	BRM Land Africa	M. McCarrick	
EI-EOI	Take Off Merlin 1100	N. Fitzmaurice	
EI-EOU	Evektor EV-97 Eurostar SL	S. Kearney	
EI-EOW	Flight Design CTSW	J. Moriarty	
EI-EPC	Boeing 737-8AS	Ryanair	
EI-EPD	Boeing 737-8AS	Ryanair	
EI-EPI	Medway Hybred 44XLR	H. J. Long	
EI-EPJ	Mainair/Gemini Flash IIA	L. Flannery	
EI-EPK	Pegasus Quantum 15-912	private individual	

Notes	Reg	Type († False registration)	Owner or Operator
	EI-EPP	PA-22-160	P. McCabe
	EI-EPW	MXP-740 Savannah Jabiru(5)	L. Reilly
	EI-EPY	UFM-11 Lambada	P. Kearney
	EI-EPZ	Jodel DR.1050M1	A. Dunne & Partners
	EI-ERE	Pegasus Quantum 15-912	M. Carter
	EI-ERI	Air Creation Clipper/Kiss 400-582(1)	E. Thompson
	EI-ERJ	Southdown Raven X	M. Hanley
	EI-ERL	Best Off Sky Ranger 912	N. Chachlakis
	EI-ERM	Ikarus C42B	J. & G. Deegan
	EI-ERO	Pegasus XL-R	M. Doyle
	EI-ERZ	Flight Design CT-2K	T. McHolmes
	EI-ESB	Urban Air Samba XXL	G. Creegan
	EI-ESC	BRM Land Africa	D. Killian
	EI-ESE	Zenair CH.601XL Zodiac	private individual
	EI-ESF	PA-22-160	G. Dolan
	EI-ESS	Boeing 737-8AS	Ryanair
	EI-EST	Boeing 737-8AS	Ryanair
	EI-ESV	Boeing 737-8AS	Ryanair
	EI-ETB	Ikarus C42B	P. Connolly
	EI-ETE	MS.880B Rallye	Wicklow Wings Ltd
	EI-ETF	Samba XXL	V. Vaughan
	EI-ETV	Raj Hamsa X'Air Hawk	P. Higgins & Partners
	EI-EVA	Boeing 737-8AS	Ryanair
	EI-EVB	Boeing 737-8AS	Ryanair
	EI-EVC	Boeing 737-8AS	Ryanair
	EI-EVE	Boeing 737-8AS	Ryanair
	EI-EVG	Boeing 737-8AS	Ryanair
	EI-EVH	Boeing 737-8AS	Ryanair
	EI-EVI	Boeing 737-8AS	Ryanair
	EI-EVJ	Boeing 737-8AS	Ryanair
	EI-EVK	Boeing 737-8AS	Ryanair
	EI-EVL	Boeing 737-8AS	Ryanair
	EI-EVM	Boeing 737-8AS	Ryanair
	EI-EVN	Boeing 737-8AS	Ryanair
	EI-EVO	Boeing 737-8AS	Ryanair
	EI-EVP	Boeing 737-8AS	Ryanair
	EI-EVR	Boeing 737-8AS	Ryanair
	EI-EVS	Boeing 737-8AS	Ryanair
	EI-EVT	Boeing 737-8AS	Ryanair
	EI-EVV	Boeing 737-8AS	Ryanair
	EI-EVX	Boeing 737-8AS	Ryanair
	EI-EWB	Ikarus C42B	E. Maguire
	EI-EWX	Aeropro Eurofox 912	R. E. Barrington
	EI-EWZ	MB-2 Colibri	Colibri Group
	EI-EXD	Boeing 737-8AS	Ryanair
	EI-EXE	Boeing 737-8AS	Ryanair
	EI-EXF	Boeing 737-8AS	Ryanair
	EI-EXY	Urban Air Samba XXL	R. G. Linehan & S. P. Sarsfield
	EI-EYI	PA-28-181	C. Rooney
	EI-EYJ	Cessna F.172N	Trim Flying Club Ltd
	EI-EYT	Ikarus C42B	Croom C42 Club
	EI-EYW	Thruster T600N 450	R. & S. Dunne
	EI-EZX	PA-22-108 Colt	The Piper Colt Group
	EI-EZY	Dominator Ultrawhite	J. Dowling
	EI-FAB	Eurocopter EC.120B	Billy Jet Ltd
	EI-FAD	Van's RV-7A	J. Lynch & Partners
	EI-FAM	Rans S-6ES Coyote II	N. Blair
	EI-FAT	Aerospatiale ATR-72-600	Emerald Airlines Ireland Ltd
	EI-FAV	Aerospatiale ATR-72-600	Emerald Airlines Ireland Ltd
	EI-FAZ	Urban Air UFM-10 Samba	J. Halpin
	EI-FBC	Cessna 172N	National Flight Centre Ltd
	EI-FBW	BRM Land Africa	J. Burke
	EI-FBX	BRM Land Africa Citius	P. Higgins
	EI-FBY	BRM Land Africa Citius	private individual
	EI-FBZ	Thruster T.600N	V. Vaughan
	EI-FCA	Urban Air UFM-11 Lambada	private individual
	EI-FCH	Boeing 737-83N	Alrosa
	EI-FCI	Zenair CH-601HD	J. Kenny
	EI-FDC	PZL-110 Koliber 150	R. Taggart
	EI-FDD	Cameron Z-105 balloon	The Travel Department
	EI-FDF	Urban Air Samba XXL	private individual

Reg	Type († False registration)	Owner or Operator	Notes
EI-FDO	Jabiru UL-D	O. Matthews	
EI-FDR	Bombardier CL600-2B16 Challenger	P. Collins	
EI-FDY	Ikarus C42	N. Dockery	
EI-FEJ	Pipistrel Virus 912	R. Armstrong	
EI-FEO	ELA-07S	H. Graham	
EI-FEP	Aviatika MAI-890	H. A. Humphreys	
EI-FET	Raj Hamsa X'Air 502T	A. Cunningham	
EI-FEU	Aviatika MAI-890	P. O'Donnell	
EI-FEV	Raj Hamsa X'Air 582	private individual	
EI-FEW	Van's RV-7	P. Hayes	
EI-FFA	Boeing 737-8K5	Fly4 Airlines	
EI-FFB	Boeing 737-8K5	Fly4 Airlines	
EI-FFC	Boeing 737-8K5	Fly4 Airlines	
EI-FFD	Boeing 737-8K5	Fly4 Airlines	
EI-FFN	Raj Hamsa X'Air 582	L. O'Brien & K. A. J. O'Doherty	
EI-FFT	Forney F-1A Aircoupe	private individual	
EI-FFV	AA-5 Traveler	K. A. J. O'Doherty	
EI-FFZ	Magni M16	S. Brennan	
EI-FGB	BRM Land Africa	M. & C. M. Duncan	
EI-FGF	Ikarus C42	private individual	
EI-FGG	Ikarus C42	EIFGG Group	
EI-FGU	Sky Ranger 912S(1)	A. Ryan	
EI-FGW	PA-22-108	private individual	
EI-FII	Cessna 172RG	National Flight Centre Ltd	
EI-FKM	Wassmer WA.81 Piranha	T. Delaney & J. B. Bolger	
EI-FLA	Rotor Flight Dominator	P. Flanagan	
EI-FLF	Rans S-6ES Coyote II	E. Tougher	
EI-FLH	BRM Land Africa	S. O'Neill	
EI-FLI	Urban Air Samba XXL	private individual	
EI-FLK	BRM Land Africa	P. O'Dowd	
EI-FLL	Ikarus C42	P. Timothy & A. O'Brien	
EI-FLO	Kitfox Mk.IV	M. Nee	
EI-FLS	Ikarus C42	J. & O. Houlihan	
EI-FLU	PA-22-108	M. Bergin	
EI-FLW	Ikarus C42	D. Browne	
EI-FLX	Raj Hamsa X'Air 582(5)	P. M. Noons, I. Bennett & P. J. Keating	
EI-FMA	Aeropro Eurofox 912 3K	P. Reilly	
EI-FMF	Bellanca 7GCAA	Citabria Flying Group	
EI-FMO	BRM Land Africa	J. Minogue	
EI-FNC	BRM Land Africa Citius	FNC Group	
EI-FNE	Javron PA-18	P. J. McKenna	
EI-FNG	Airbus A.330-302	Aer Lingus Ltd	
EI-FNH	Airbus A.330-302	Aer Lingus Ltd	
EI-FNJ	Airbus A.320-214	Aer Lingus Ltd	
EI-FNO	Aeropro Eurofox	M. P. Breen & D. Carr	
EI-FNS	Ikarus C42	G. Hanna & G. McGrane	
EI-FNT	Agusta AW.169	LCI Helicopters Twenty Six Ltd	
EI-FNW	Boeing 737-86B	ASL Airlines (Ireland) Ltd	
EI-FNX	Airbus A.330-243	I-Fly	
EI-FPF	Canadair CRJ900LR	Cityjet/SAS	
EI-FPG	Canadair CRJ900LR	Cityjet/SAS	
EI-FPP	Canadair CRJ900LR	Cityjet/SAS	
EI-FPS	Canadair CRJ900LR	Cityjet/SAS	
EI-FPW	Canadair CRJ900LR	Cityjet/SAS	
EI-FPX	Canadair CRJ900LR	Cityjet/SAS	
EI-FSA	TL3000 Sirius	M. J. Kirrane	
EI-FSE	Airbus A.330-243	I-Fly	
EI-FSF	Airbus A.330-243	DAE Leasing (Ireland) 16 Ltd	
EI-FST	Ikarus C42	C. A., D. M. & W. Baker	
EI-FSW	Rans S-6 ESD	A. J., A. & J. Cunningham	
EI-FSX	Pegasus Quantum 15	G. Hanna	
EI-FTX	Rans S-6ES Coyote II	private individual	
EI-FVF	Raj Hamsa X'Air 582(1)	F. Sarsfield & J. N. Burke	
EI-FXL	Robinson R44	National Flight Centre Ltd	
EI-FXW	Best Off Sky Ranger Swift 912(2)	M. Sheehy	
EI-FXX	Boeing 737-8EH	Poste Air Cargo	
EI-FXY	Boeing 737-8EH	Poste Air Cargo	
EI-FXZ	Roko Aero NG 4UL	H. A. Maguire	
EI-GAH	Ikarus C42B	Tibohine Flying Club Ltd	
EI-GAJ	Airbus A.330-302	Aer Lingus	

Notes	Reg	Type († False registration)	Owner or Operator
	EI-GAL	Airbus A.320-214	Aer Lingus
	EI-GAM	Airbus A.320-214	Aer Lingus
	EI-GCF	Airbus A.330-302	Aer Lingus
	EI-GCG	BRM Land Africa Citius	D. Bolger
	EI-GCJ	CSA Sportcruiser	S. Meagher, N. Mulligan, D. O'Reilly & M. D. Ryan
	EI-GCP	Sky Ranger 912(2)	J. Haverty and Partners
	EI-GCR	Agusta AW.189	LCI Helicopters Fourteen Ltd
	EI-GCT	ATEC Zephyr 2000	C. S. Kilpatrick & S. R. McGirr
	EI-GCU	Airbus A.330-223	I-Fly
	EI-GCV	Boeing 737-7CT	Alrosa
	EI-GCZ	Airbus A.330-223	I-Fly
	EI-GDJ	Piper J-4E	Ballyboughal J4 Flying Group
	EI-GEA	Canadair CRJ900ER	Cityjet/SAS
	EI-GEB	Canadair CRJ900ER	Cityjet/SAS
	EI-GEC	Canadair CRJ900ER	Cityjet/SAS
	EI-GED	Canadair CRJ900ER	Cityjet/SAS
	EI-GEF	Canadair CRJ900ER	Cityjet/SAS
	EI-GEH	Canadair CRJ900ER	Cityjet/SAS
	EI-GEN	Skyranger 912(2)	N. Furlong & A. Merrigan
	EI-GEO	ICP MXP-740 Savannah S	B. & S. Reilly
	EI-GER	Maule MX7-180A	R. Lanigan & J.Patrick
	EI-GEU	Boeing 777-31HER	Rossiya
	EI-GEY	Airbus A.330-202	Aer Lingus
	EI-GFR	Boeing 737-7CT	Alrosa
	EI-GFV	Jodel D.112	private individual
	EI-GGE	BRM Land Africa Citius	P. M. Fin
	EI-GGV	Thruster TST Mk.1	A. Ryan
	EI-GGX	Zenair CH.601UL	N. Farrell
	EI-GGY	P & M Quik GT450	private individual
	EI-GHA	Boeing 737-490	Poste Air Cargo
	EI-GHB	Boeing 737-490	Poste Air Cargo
	EI-GHC	Boeing 737-490F	Poste Air Cargo
	EI-GHH	Europa	Lee Aero Club
	EI-GHI	PA-22-150	Boyne Aircraft Holdings Ltd
	EI-GHR	ICP MXP-740 Savannah S	Funfly Aerosports Flying Club Ltd
	EI-GHS	ICP Ventura	R. F. Gibney
	EI-GHU	Agusta AW.119 Mk.II	Perspect Aviation DAC
	EI-GHW	Bell 505	Yoyo Capital Unlimited Company
	EI-GHZ	Cessna 208 Caravan	Grob Power Service Ltd
	EI-GIH	Boeing 737-86N	Alrosa
	EI-GIJ	Van's RV-9	D. Horan
	EI-GIO	Magni VPM M-16	P. M. Flanagan
	EI-GIR	Sky Ranger 912S(1)	private individual
	EI-GIU	Cessna F.172N	National Flight Centre Ltd
	EI-GJS	Boeing 737-800	Ryanair
	EI-GJT	Boeing 737-800	Ryanair
	EI-GKN	Cessna 172S	Atlantic Flight Training Ltd
	EI-GKZ	Mainair Gemeni/Flash II	M. A. Brady
	EI-GLB	Schleicher ASK-21	Dublin Gliding Club Ltd
	EI-GLC	Centrair 101A Pegase	P. Nowak
	EI-GLD	Schleicher ASK-13	Dublin Gliding Club Ltd
	EI-GLF	Schleicher K-8B	Dublin Gliding Club Ltd
	EI-GLG	Schleicher Ka 6CR	C. Sinclair
	EI-GLH	AB Sportine LAK-17A	S. Kinnear & B. O'Neill
	EI-GLL	Glaser-Dirks DG-200	K. McDonagh
	EI-GLM	Schleicher Ka-6CR	P. Denman, C. Craig & J. Finnan
	EI-GLO	Scheibe Zugvogel IIIB	J. Walsh, J. Murphy & N. Short
	EI-GLP	Olympia 2B	J. Cashin
	EI-GLT	Schempp-Hirth Discus b	D. Thomas
	EI-GLU	Schleicher Ka-6CR	K. Cullen & Partners
	EI-GLV	Schleicher ASW-19B	A. McDermott
	EI-GLZ	ASK-21	Dublin Gliding Club Ltd
	EI-GMB	Schleicher ASW-17	ASW-17 Group
	EI-GMC	Schleicher ASK-18	The Eighteen Group
	EI-GMD	Phoebus C	F. McDonnell & Partners
	EI-GMF	Schleicher ASK-13	Dublin Gliding Club Ltd
	EI-GMG	H201B Standard Libelle	The Dragonfliers
	EI-GMH	WAG-Aero Sport Trainer	J. Matthews
	EI-GMJ	Schleicher ASW-19B	L. Keegan
	EI-GMK	Glasflugel H.201B Standard Libelle	P. Moran

Reg	Type († False registration)	Owner or Operator	Notes
EI-GMM	Schleicher ASW-22	The 22 Group	
EI-GMO	Schleicher Ka 6E	C. Ainclair & W. Kilroy	
EI-GMP	Rolladen-Schneider LS1-D	O. Grogan	
EI-GMR	Rolladen-Schneider LS1-O	R. Staeps-Morgenstern	
EI-GMS	Schleicher K-8B	Dublin Gliding Club Ltd	
EI-GOD	PA-28-180 Cherokee	M. & P. M. Corrigan	
EI-GOJ	BFC Challenger II	N. O'Brien	
EI-GOT	Airbus A.330-323	I-Fly	
EI-GOU	Agusta AW.139	LCI Helicopters Eight Ltd	
EI-GPF	Ikarus C42C	K. Clarke	
EI-GPJ	Airbus A.330-343	I-Fly	
EI-GPM	Magni Gyro M24 Orion	B. McCafferty	
EI-GPN	Aerospatiale ATR-72-600	Emerald Airlines Ireland Ltd	
EI-GPO	Aerospatiale ATR-72-600	Emerald Airlines Ireland Ltd	
EI-GPP	Aerospatiale ATR-72-600	Emerald Airlines Ireland Ltd	
EI-GPR	Noble Hardman Snowbird Mk.IV	P. Cattigan & J. Selman	
EI-GPT	Robinson R22 Beta	Treaty Plant & Tool (Hire & Sales)	
EI-GPV	Ikarus C42B	private individual	
EI-GRA	Urban Air UFM-13 Lambada	J. Selman	
EI-GRB	J-3F-65 Cub	private owner	
EI-GRF	Raj Hamsa X'Air 582(6)	M. Duffy	
EI-GRG	Super J300 Joker	F. Lynch	
EI-GRH	Ikarus C42B	B. Britton	
EI-GRI	ICP MXP-740 Savannah S	private individual	
EI-GRM	Diamond DA.42M-NG	Atlantic Flight Training Ltd	
EI-GRN	Diamond DA.42M-NG	Atlantic Flight Training Ltd	
EI-GRR	Robin DR400/180	G. Lyons	
EI-GRU	PA-30	E. A. Treacy	
EI-GRV	Van's RV-7	M. D. Murphy, D. Donoghue & C. Keane	
EI-GRW	Piel CP3012B Super Emeraude	D. T. Cross	
EI-GRY	Mooney M.20R	DK Innovation Ltd	
EI-GSG	Boeing 737-800	Ryanair	
EI-GSH	Boeing 737-800	Ryanair	
EI-GSI	Boeing 737-800	Ryanair	
EI-GSJ	Boeing 737-800	Ryanair	
EI-GSK	Boeing 737-800	Ryanair	
EI-GSM	Cessna 182S	Westpoint Flying Group	
EI-GSS	Mainair Blade 912	P. A. McMahon	
EI-GST	Littlewing Autogyros Inc LW3	J. Todd	
EI-GSU	P & M Quik GT450	J. Ryan	
EI-GTB	ICP MXP-740 Savannah S	K. Sheridan, K. Hosna, A. Kenny & R. Donal	
EI-GTC	Robin HR.200/120B	Davy Baby Flying Group	
EI-GTX	Skyranger 912(2)	private individual	
EI-GUI	Robinson R44	Alchemist Aviation Ltd	
EI GUL	Aerospatiale ATR-72-212A	ASL Airlines Ireland Ltd	
EI-GUM	Aerospatiale ATR-72-212A	ASL Airlines Ireland Ltd	
EI-GUO	Aerospatiale ATR-72-212A	ASL Airlines Ireland Ltd	
EI-GUP	Aerospatiale ATR-72-212A	ASL Airlines Ireland Ltd	
EI-GUR	Aerospatiale ATR-72-212A	ASL Airlines Ireland Ltd	
EI-GUZ	ICP MXP-740 Savannah S	Funfly Aerosports Flying Club Company Ltd	
EI-GVB	PA-28-140	Sun Mingxia	
EI-GVC	Aerospool WT-9 Dynamic LSA	D. Conway	
EI-GVE	Airborne Windsports Edge XT-912 L-SST	J. McQuoid	
EI-GVG	Rockwell Commander 112A	Sylph Aviation Ltd	
EI-GVH	Airbus A.330-243	I-Fly	
EI-GVL	Cessna 172S	Waterford Aero Club Ltd	
EI-GVM	Robinson R22 Beta	J. Porter	
EI-GVN	Boeing 737-8K5	Poste Air Cargo	
EI-GVS	Murphy Rebel	M. Ryan & N. O'Brien	
EI-GVT	Beagle A.61 Terrier 3	N. O'Brien & F. Hopkins	
EI-GWF	Airbus A.330-323	I-Fly	
EI-GWH	Cessna F.150M	J. Nugent	
EI-GWI	ICP MXP-740 Savannah S	private individual	
EI-GWU	Cessna F.172N	Ormand Flying Club Ltd	
EI-GWY	Cessna 172R	Waterford Aero Club Ltd	
EI-GXG	Boeing 737-800	Ryanair	
EI-GXH	Boeing 737-800	Ryanair	
EI-GXI	Boeing 737-800	Ryanair	
EI-GXJ	Boeing 737-800	Ryanair	
EI-GXK	Boeing 737-800	Ryanair	

Notes	Reg	Type († False registration)	Owner or Operator
	EI-GXL	Boeing 737-800	Ryanair
	EI-GXM	Boeing 737-800	Ryanair
	EI-GXN	Boeing 737-800	Ryanair
	EI-GXR	Agusta AW.169	SMFL LCI Helicopters Two Ltd
	EI-GXS	Agusta AW.169	SMFL LCI Helicopters Two Ltd
	EI-GXX	Aeroprakt A.22L Foxbat	D. McGuire
	EI-GXY	Cessna F.172M	G. P. Dunne & M. E. White
	EI-GYA	Cessna 172S	Atlantic Flight Training Ltd
	EI-GYD	ICP MXP-740 Savannah S	Funfly Aerosports Flying Club Co.Ltd
	EI-GYK	Ikarus C42C	private individual
	EI-GYL	PA-22-160 Tri-Pacer	P. M. McCabe & M. E. White
	EI-GYN	ICP MXP-740 Savannah S	private individual
	EI-GYR	Magni M24	D. Crombie
	EI-GYS	Cessna 172S	Atlantic Flight Training Ltd
	EI-GYT	Cessna 172R	Atlantic Flight Training Ltd
	EI-GZO	Aeroprakt A.22L Foxbat	J. A. O'Sullivan, D. McNamara, P. O'Carroll & D. Owens-Murphy
	EI-GZV	Aerospatiale ATR-72-600	Emerald Airlines Ireland Ltd
	EI-HAB	Aerospatiale ATR-72-212A	ASL Airlines Ireland Ltd
	EI-HAC	Aerospatiale ATR-72-212A	ASL Airlines Ireland Ltd
	EI-HAD	Aerospatiale ATR-72-212A	ASL Airlines Ireland Ltd
	EI-HAE	Aerospatiale ATR-72-212A	ASL Airlines Ireland Ltd
	EI-HAF	Aerospatiale ATR-72-212A	ASL Airlines Ireland Ltd
	EI-HAG	Aerospatiale ATR-72-212A	ASL Airlines Ireland Ltd
	EI-HAL	Cessna 172S	Atlantic Flight Training Ltd
	EI-HAP	Cessna 172S	Atlantic Flight Training Ltd
	EI-HAS	Cessna 172S	Atlantic Flight Training Ltd
	EI-HAR	Ikarus C42C	M. Houston & A. Gurnett
	EI-HAT	Boeing 737-8200	Ryanair
	EI-HAU	Cessna 172S	Atlantic Flight Training Ltd
	EI-HAW	Boeing 737-8200	Ryanair
	EI-HAX	Boeing 737-8200	Ryanair
	EI-HAY	Boeing 737-8200	Ryanair
	EI-HDH	Aerospatiale ATR-72-212A	Emerald Airlines
	EI-HDI	Aerospatiale ATR-72-212A	Emerald Airlines
	EI-HDK	Aerospatiale ATR-72-212A	Emerald Airlines
	EI-HDV	SOCATA TB-10	T. J. Kluck
	EI-HDW	Best Off Sky Ranger	J. Marbach
	EI-HDX	Mainair Blade	T. Noonan
	EI-HEN	Boeing 737-8200	Ryanair
	EI-HES	Boeing 737-8200	Ryanair
	EI-HET	Boeing 737-8200	Ryanair
	EI-HEV	Boeing 737-8200	Ryanair
	EI-HEW	Boeing 737-8200	Ryanair
	EI-HEY	Boeing 737-8200	Ryanair
	EI-HEZ	Boeing 737-8200	Ryanair
	EI-HFA	DHC-1 Chipmunk 22	Irish Historic Flight Foundation Ltd
	EI-HFB	DHC-1 Chipmunk 22	Irish Historic Flight Foundation Ltd
	EI-HFC	DHC-1 Chipmunk 22	Irish Historic Flight Foundation Ltd
	EI-HFD	Boeing E75 Stearman	Irish Historic Flight Foundation Ltd
	EI-HFE	Cessna FR.172H	Irish Historic Flight Foundation Ltd
	EI-HGE	Boeing 737-8200	Ryanair
	EI-HGF	Boeing 737-8200	Ryanair
	EI-HGG	Boeing 737-8200	Ryanair
	EI-HGH	Boeing 737-8200	Ryanair
	EI-HGL	Boeing 737-8200	Ryanair
	EI-HGM	Boeing 737-8200	Ryanair
	EI-HGN	Boeing 737-8200	Ryanair
	EI-HGO	Boeing 737-8200	Ryanair
	EI-HGP	Boeing 737-8200	Ryanair
	EI-HGR	Boeing 737-8200	Ryanair
	EI-HGS	Boeing 737-8200	Ryanair
	EI-HGT	Boeing 737-8200	Ryanair
	EI-HGV	Boeing 737-8200	Ryanair
	EI-HGW	Boeing 737-8200	Ryanair
	EI-HGX	Boeing 737-8200	Ryanair
	EI-HGY	Boeing 737-8200	Ryanair
	EI-HGZ	Boeing 737-8200	Ryanair
	EI-HHA	Robin HR200/120B	R. Kellett
	EI-HHB	Raj Hamsa X'Air	private individual
	EI-HHC	Diamond DA.42	Atlantic Flight Training Ltd

Reg	Type († False registration)	Owner or Operator	Notes
EI-HHD	Diamond DA.42	Atlantic Flight Training Ltd	
EI-HHE	Van's RV-8	F. Lawless	
EI-HHG	Cessna FR.172K	K. P. Rogan	
EI-HHI	Airbus A.220-300	ITA Airways	
EI-HHJ	Airbus A.220-300	ITA Airways	
EI-HHK	Airbus A.220-300	ITA Airways	
EI-HHL	Airbus A.220-300	ITA Airways	
EI-HHM	Airbus A.220-300	ITA Airways	
EI-HHN	Airbus A.220-300	ITA Airways	
EI-HHO	Airbus A.220-300	ITA Airways	
EI-HHP	Airbus A.220-300	ITA Airways	
EI-HHR	Airbus A.220-300	ITA Airways	
EI-HHS	Airbus A.220-300	ITA Airways	
EI-HHT	Airbus A.220-300	ITA Airways	
EI-HHU	Airbus A.220-300	ITA Airways	
EI-HHV	Airbus A.220-300	ITA Airways	
EI-HHW	Airbus A.220-300	ITA Airways	
EI-HIA	Canadair CRJ1000	Cityjet	
EI-HIB	Canadair CRJ1000	Cityjet	
EI-HID	Canadair CRJ1000	Cityjet	
EI-HIE	Canadair CRJ1000	Cityjet	
EI-HIJ	Agusta AW.169	LCI Helicopters Six Ltd	
EI-HIL	Boeing 737-800	Neos	
EI-HIM	Boeing 737-800	Neos	
EI-HIN	AA-5A Cheetah	private individual	
EI-HIR	Ikarus C-42B	Tibohine Flying Club	
EI-HIS	Ikarus C-42CS	Ikarus Aviation Ireland Ltd	
EI-HIU	BRM Citius Land Africa	J. O'Connor	
EI-HIW	Volksplane Skyranger 912	S. Collins	
EI-HIY	Leonardo AB206B	D. Marron	
EI-HJC	Robinson R44 II	J. Butler	
EI-HJD	Airbus A.320-272N	ITA Airways	
EI-HJE	Airbus A.320-272N	ITA Airways	
EI-HJN	Airbus A.330-941	ITA Airways	
EI-HJO	Airbus A.330-941	ITA Airways	
EI-HJP	Airbus A.330-941	ITA Airways	
EI-HJR	Airbus A.330-941	ITA Airways	
EI-HJS	Airbus A.330-941	ITA Airways	
EI-HJT	Diamond DA.42 Twin Star	Atlantic Flight Training Ltd	
EI-HJU	Magni M16	J. A. Grattan	
EI-HJW	BRM Land Africa	private individual	
EI-HJY	Aeros Fox-13T	J. R. Killian	
EI-HKA	Airbus A.380-841	Airbus Financial Services Ltd	
EI-HKK	Robinson R44 II	private individual	
EI-HKM	ICP MXP-740 Savannah XL	P. Wrafter & J. Butler	
EI-HLA	Airbus A.220-100	ITA Airways	
EI-HLB	Airbus A.220-100	ITA Airways	
EI-HLC	Airbus A.220-100	ITA Airways	
EI-HLD	Airbus A.220-100	ITA Airways	
EI-HLE	Airbus A.220-100	ITA Airways	
EI-HLF	Tecnam P-Mentor	National Flight Centre Ltd	
EI-HLG	Robinson R44 II	Toriamos Co.Ltd	
EI-HLT	Slingsby T.07M 200 Firefly	private individual	
EI-HLU	Skyranger Nynja 912S(1)	private individual	
EI-HLX	Tecnam P-Mentor	National Flight Centre Ltd	
EI-HLY	BRM Citius	private individual	
EI-HLZ	Skyranger 912	private individual	
EI-HMC	ICP MXP-740 Savannah S	Funfly Aerosports Flying Club Company Limited	
EI-HMD	Tomark Viper SD-4 RTC	Newcastle Logistics Ltd	
EI-HME	Tomark Viper SD-4 RTC	Agata Aerospace Ireland Ltd	
EI-HMG	Tomark Viper SD-4 RTC	private individual	
EI-HMJ	Starstreak Shadow SA-II	private individual	
EI-HMS	Boeing 737-8200	Ryanair	
EI-HMT	Boeing 737-8200	Ryanair	
EI-HMU	Leonardo AW139	Lugano Aviation Ltd	
EI-HMV	Boeing 737-8200	Ryanair	
EI-HMW	Boeing 737-8200	Ryanair	
EI-HMX	Boeing 737-8200	Ryanair	
EI-HMY	Boeing 737-8200	Ryanair	
EI-HMZ	Boeing 737-8200	Ryanair	

IRELAND CIVIL REGISTRATIONS

Notes	Reg	Type († False registration)	Owner or Operator
	EI-HNA	Aerospatiale ATR-72-212A	Emerald Airlines Ireland Ltd
	EI-HND	Tomark Viper SD-4 RTC	private individual
	EI-HNE	Agusta Westland AW189	Bolsena Aviation Ltd
	EI-HNF	Slingsby T-67M260 Firefly	private individual
	EI-HNG	Cessna 172S	Atlantic Flight Training Ltd
	EI-HNH	MBB BK-117D-3	SMFL LCI Helicopters Seven Ltd
	EI-HNI	Thruster T600N 450	private individual
	EI-HNL	Tomark Viper SD-4 RTC	Newcastle Logistics Ltd
	EI-HNM	Ikarus C42B	private individual
	EI-HNN	Eurofox 912 PRO-3K	private individual
	EI-HNP	Diamond DA.42NG	Skyharbour Ltd
	EI-HNR	Ikarus C42	private individual
	EI-HNX	ICP Savannah S	private individual
	EI-HOA	Airbus A.320-271N	ITA Airways
	EI-HOB	Airbus A.320-271N	ITA Airways
	EI-HOC	Airbus A.320-272N	ITA Airways
	EI-HOD	Airbus A.320-272N	ITA Airways
	EI-HOE	Airbus A.320-272N	ITA Airways
	EI-HOF	Airbus A.320-272N	ITA Airways
	EI-HOG	Airbus A.320-272N	ITA Airways
	EI-HOH	Airbus A.320-272N	ITA Airways
	EI-HOI	Airbus A.320-272N	ITA Airways
	EI-HOJ	Airbus A.320-272N	ITA Airways
	EI-HOL	Airbus A.320-272N	ITA Airways
	EI-HOM	Airbus A.320-272N	ITA Airways
	EI-HON	Airbus A.320-272N	ITA Airways
	EI-HOU	ICP Savannah S	Funfly Aerosports Flying Club
	EI-HOW	Tomark Viper SD-4 RTC	private individual
	EI-HOX	Tomark Viper SD-4 RTC	Newcastle Logistics Ltd
	EI-HOY	Ikarus C42B	private individual
	EI-HPA	Airbus A.330-941	ITA Airways
	EI-HPB	Airbus A.330-941	ITA Airways
	EI-HPC	Czech Sportcruiser	private individual
	EI-HPF	Vulcanair P.68C	Atlantic Flight Training Ltd
	EI-HPG	Vulcanair P.68C	Atlantic Flight Training Ltd
	EI-HPJ	Aerospatiale ATR-72-212A	Emerald Airlines Ireland Ltd
	EI-HPK	Aerospatiale ATR-72-212A	Emerald Airlines Ireland Ltd
	EI-HPL	Ikarus C42B	Tibohine Flying Club
	EI-HPN	Ultramagic M-77 balloon	private individual
	EI-HPR	Ikarus C42B	private individual
	EI-HPS	Robinson R44 II	private individual
	EI-HPW	Tomark Viper SD-4 RTC	Newcastle Logistics Ltd
	EI-HRB	Boeing 737-86N	ASL Airlines (Ireland) Ltd
	EI-HRC	Boeing 737-8FH	ASL Airlines (Ireland) Ltd
	EI-HRD	Boeing 737-86J	ASL Airlines (Ireland) Ltd
	EI-HRE	Boeing 737-86J	ASL Airlines (Ireland) Ltd
	EI-HRF	Boeing 737-86J	ASL Airlines (Ireland) Ltd
	EI-HRG	Boeing 737-86N	ASL Airlines (Ireland) Ltd
	EI-HRH	Diamond DA.40NG Star	Atlantic Flight Training Ltd
	EI-HRI	Diamond DA.40NG Star	Atlantic Flight Training Ltd
	EI-HRJ	Diamond DA.40NG Star	Atlantic Flight Training Ltd
	EI-HRK	Cessna F.172M	private individual
	EI-HRL	Diamond DA.40NG Star	Atlantic Flight Training Ltd
	EI-HRN	Boeing 737-76N	Celestial Aviation Trading
	EI-HRP	Aeroprakt A22-L	private individual
	EI-HRS	Cessna 172S	private individual
	EI-HSA	Canadair CRJ900ER	Cityjet/SAS
	EI-HSC	Canadair CRJ900ER	Cityjet/SAS
	EI-HSD	Canadair CRJ900ER	Cityjet/SAS
	EI-HSE	Canadair CRJ900ER	Cityjet/SAS
	EI-HSF	Canadair CRJ900ER	Cityjet/SAS
	EI-HUM	Van's RV-7	G. Humphreys
	EI-HUN	Embraer ERJ190-400	Hunnu Air
	EI-HUU	Embraer ERJ190-400	Hunnu Air
	EI-HXA	Airbus A.321-271NX	ITA Airways
	EI-HXB	Airbus A.321-271NX	ITA Airways
	EI-HXC	Airbus A.321-271NX	ITA Airways
	EI-HXD	Airbus A.321-271NX	ITA Airways
	EI-HXE	Airbus A.321-271NX	ITA Airways
	EI-HXF	Airbus A.321-271NX	ITA Airways
	EI-HXG	Airbus A.321-271NX	ITA Airways

Reg	Type († False registration)	Owner or Operator	Notes
EI-IAL	Agusta AW.109SP	Ion Aviation Ltd	
EI-ICP	ICP MXP-740 Savannah S	Funfly Aerosports Ltd	
EI-ICS	Sikorsky S-92A	CHC Ireland Ltd	
EI-ICU	Sikorsky S-92A	CHC Ireland Ltd	
EI-IFA	Airbus A.350-941	ITA Airways	
EI-IFB	Airbus A.350-941	ITA Airways	
EI-IFC	Airbus A.350-941	ITA Airways	
EI-IFD	Airbus A.350-941	ITA Airways	
EI-IFE	Airbus A.350-941	ITA Airways	
EI-IFF	Airbus A.350-941	ITA Airways	
EI-IFP	Boeing 737-8200	Ryanair	
EI-IFR	Boeing 737-8200	Ryanair	
EI-IFS	Boeing 737-8200	Ryanair	
EI-IFT	Boeing 737-8200	Ryanair	
EI-IFV	Boeing 737-8200	Ryanair	
EI-IFW	Boeing 737-8200	Ryanair	
EI-IFX	Boeing 737-8200	Ryanair	
EI-IFY	Boeing 737-8200	Ryanair	
EI-IFZ	Boeing 737-8200	Ryanair	
EI-IGE	Boeing 737-8200	Ryanair	
EI-IGF	Boeing 737-8200	Ryanair	
EI-IGG	Boeing 737-8200	Ryanair	
EI-IGH	Boeing 737-8200	Ryanair	
EI-IGI	Boeing 737-8200	Ryanair	
EI-IGJ	Boeing 737-8200	Ryanair	
EI-IGK	Boeing 737-8200	Ryanair	
EI-IGL	Boeing 737-8200	Ryanair	
EI-IGM	Boeing 737-8200	Ryanair	
EI-IGO	Boeing 737-8200	Ryanair	
EI-IGV	Boeing 737-8200	Ryanair	
EI-IGW	Boeing 737-8200	Ryanair	
EI-IGX	Boeing 737-8200	Ryanair	
EI-IGY	Boeing 737-8200	Ryanair	
EI-IGZ	Boeing 737-8200	Ryanair	
EI-IHA	Boeing 737-8200	Ryanair	
EI-IHB	Boeing 737-8200	Ryanair	
EI-IHC	Boeing 737-8200	Ryanair	
EI-IHE	Boeing 737-8200	Ryanair	
EI-IHF	Boeing 737-8200	Ryanair	
EI-IHG	Boeing 737-8200	Ryanair	
EI-IHI	Boeing 737-8200	Ryanair	
EI-IHJ	Boeing 737-8200	Ryanair	
EI-IHK	Boeing 737-8200	Ryanair	
EI-IHM	Boeing 737-8200	Ryanair	
EI-IIN	Boeing 737-8200	Ryanair	
EI-IHO	Boeing 737-8200	Ryanair	
EI-IHP	Boeing 737-8200	Ryanair	
EI-IHR	Boeing 737-8200	Ryanair	
EI-IHS	Boeing 737-8200	Ryanair	
EI-IHT	Boeing 737-8200	Ryanair	
EI-IHV	Boeing 737-8200	Ryanair	
EI-IIW	Boeing 737-8200	Ryanair	
EI-IHX	Boeing 737-8200	Ryanair	
EI-IHY	Boeing 737-8200	Ryanair	
EI-IHZ	Boeing 737-8200	Ryanair	
EI-IJA	Boeing 737-8200	Ryanair	
EI-IJB	Boeing 737-8200	Ryanair	
EI-IJC	Boeing 737-8200	Ryanair	
EI-IJD	Boeing 737-8200	Ryanair	
EI-IJE	Boeing 737-8200	Ryanair	
EI-IJF	Boeing 737-8200	Ryanair	
EI-IJG	Boeing 737-8200	Ryanair	
EI-IJH	Boeing 737-8200	Ryanair	
EI-IJI	Boeing 737-8200	Ryanair	
EI-IJJ	Boeing 737-8200	Ryanair	
EI-IJK	Boeing 737-8200	Ryanair	
EI-IJL	Boeing 737-8200	Ryanair	
EI-IJM	Boeing 737-8200	Ryanair	
EI-IJN	Boeing 737-8200	Ryanair	
EI-IJO	Boeing 737-8200	Ryanair	
EI-IJP	Boeing 737-8200	Ryanair	

Notes	Reg	Type († False registration)	Owner or Operator
	EI-IJS	Boeing 737-8200	Ryanair
	EI-IJT	Boeing 737-8200	Ryanair
	EI-IJV	Boeing 737-8200	Ryanair
	EI-IJW	Boeing 737-8200	Ryanair
	EI-IJX	Boeing 737-8200	Ryanair
	EI-IJY	Boeing 737-8200	Ryanair
	EI-IJZ	Boeing 737-8200	Ryanair
	EI-IKA	Boeing 737-8200	Ryanair
	EI-IKC	Boeing 737-8200	Ryanair
	EI-IKD	Boeing 737-8200	Ryanair
	EI-IKE	Boeing 737-8200	Ryanair
	EI-IKH	Boeing 737-8200	Ryanair
	EI-IKI	Boeing 737-8200	Ryanair
	EI-IKJ	Boeing 737-8200	Ryanair
	EI-IKK	Boeing 737-8200	Ryanair
	EI-IKM	Boeing 737-8200	Ryanair
	EI-IKN	Boeing 737-8200	Ryanair
	EI-IKO	Boeing 737-8200	Ryanair
	EI-IKP	Boeing 737-8200	Ryanair
	EI-IKR	Boeing 737-8200	Ryanair
	EI-IKS	Boeing 737-8200	Ryanair
	EI-IKT	Boeing 737-8200	Ryanair
	EI-IKV	Boeing 737-8200	Ryanair
	EI-IKW	Boeing 737-8200	Ryanair
	EI-IKX	Boeing 737-8200	Ryanair
	EI-IKY	Boeing 737-8200	Ryanair
	EI-IKZ	Boeing 737-8200	Ryanair
	EI-ILA	Boeing 737-8200	Ryanair
	EI-ILB	Boeing 737-8200	Ryanair
	EI-ILC	Boeing 737-8200	Ryanair
	EI-ILD	Boeing 737-8200	Ryanair
	EI-ILE	Boeing 737-8200	Ryanair
	EI-ILF	Boeing 737-8200	Ryanair
	EI-ILG	Boeing 737-8200	Ryanair
	EI-ILH	Boeing 737-8200	Ryanair
	EI-ILI	Boeing 737-8200	Ryanair
	EI-ILJ	Boeing 737-8200	Ryanair
	EI-ILK	Boeing 737-8200	Ryanair
	EI-ILL	Boeing 737-8200	Ryanair
	EI-ILM	Boeing 737-8200	Ryanair
	EI-ILN	Boeing 737-8200	Ryanair
	EI-ILO	Boeing 737-8200	Ryanair
	EI-ILP	Boeing 737-8200	Ryanair
	EI-ILR	Boeing 737-8200	Ryanair
	EI-ILT	Boeing 737-8200	Ryanair
	EI-ILV	Boeing 737-8200	Ryanair
	EI-IMB	Airbus A.319-112	ITA Airways
	EI-IMF	Airbus A.319-112	ITA Airways
	EI-IMH	Airbus A.319-112	ITA Airways
	EI-IMM	Airbus A.319-112	ITA Airways
	EI-IMN	Airbus A.319-111	ITA Airways
	EI-IMO	Airbus A.319-112	ITA Airways
	EI-IMS	Airbus A.319-111	ITA Airways
	EI-IMV	Airbus A.319-111	ITA Airways
	EI-IMW	Airbus A.319-111	ITA Airways
	EI-IMX	Airbus A.319-111	ITA Airways
	EI-INA	Airbus A.320-271N	ITA Airways
	EI-INB	Airbus A.320-271N	ITA Airways
	EI-INC	Airbus A.320-271N	ITA Airways
	EI-IND	Airbus A.320-271N	ITA Airways
	EI-INE	Airbus A.320-271N	ITA Airways
	EI-ION	Agusta Westland AW139	Krypton Aviation Ltd
	EI-IRD	Agusta Westland AW189	Bristow Ireland Ltd
	EI-IRF	Beech B.200 Super King Air	Toexcel Ireland Ltd
	EI-IRG	Leonardo AW189	Bristow Ireland Ltd
	EI-IRO	Agusta Westland AW189	Bristow Ireland Ltd
	EI-IRR	Agusta Westland AW189	Bristow Ireland Ltd
	EI-IRS	Agusta Westland AW189	Bristow Ireland Ltd
	EI-IRT	Leonardo AW189	Bristow Ireland Ltd
	EI-IRW	Beech 200 King Air	Toexcel Ireland Ltd
	EI-ISA	Boeing 777-243ER	Aircraft Purchase Number 12 Ltd

Reg	Type († False registration)	Owner or Operator	Notes
EI-ISB	Boeing 777-243ER	Aircraft Purchase Number 12 Ltd	
EI-ISD	Boeing 777-243ER	Aircraft Purchase Number 12 Ltd	
EI-ISE	Boeing 777-243ER	Aircraft Purchase Number 12 Ltd	
EI-ISO	Boeing 777-243ER	Aircraft Purchase Number 12 Ltd	
EI-IXJ	Airbus A.321-112	Aircraft Purchase Number 11 Ltd	
EI-IXV	Airbus A.321-112	Aircraft Purchase Number 11 Ltd	
EI-IXZ	Airbus A.321-112	Aircraft Purchase Number 11 Ltd	
EI-JAM	Cessna 172RG	Mannion Automation Ltd	
EI-JEF	Aeriane E-Swift 3	private individual	
EI-JIM	Urban Air Samba XLA	J. Smith	
EI-JPK	Tecnam P2002-JF	Limerick Flying Club (Coonagh) Ltd	
EI-JSV	SOCATA TB20 Trinidad GT	J. J. Condron	
EI-KBA	Airbus A.320-232	FlyArystan	
EI-KBB	Airbus A.320-232	FlyArystan	
EI-KBC	Airbus A.320-232	FlyArystan	
EI-KBD	Airbus A.320-232	FlyArystan	
EI-KBE	Airbus A.320-232	FlyArystan	
EI-KBF	Airbus A.320-232	FlyArystan	
EI-KBG	Airbus A.320-232	FlyArystan	
EI-KBH	Airbus A.320-271N	Air Astana	
EI-KBI	Airbus A.320-271N	Air Astana	
EI-KBJ	Airbus A.320-271N	Air Astana	
EI-KBK	Airbus A.320-271N	Air Astana	
EI-KBL	Airbus A.320-271N	Air Astana	
EI-KBM	Airbus A.320-271N	Air Astana	
EI-KBN	Airbus A.320-232	FlyArystan	
EI-KBO	Airbus A.320-232	FlyArystan	
EI-KBP	Airbus A.320-271N	FlyArystan	
EI-KBR	Airbus A.320-271N	FlyArystan	
EI-KBS	Airbus A.320-271N	FlyArystan	
EI-KBT	Airbus A.320-271N	FlyArystan	
EI-KBU	Airbus A.320-271N	FlyArystan	
EI-KBV	Airbus A.320-271N	FlyArystan	
EI-KBW	Airbus A.320-271N	FlyArystan	
EI-KBX	Airbus A.320-232	FlyArystan	
EI-KBY	Airbus A.320-232	FlyArystan	
EI-KBZ	Airbus A.320-232	FlyArystan	
EI-KDA	Airbus A.321-231	Air Astana	
EI-KDB	Airbus A.321-231	Air Astana	
EI-KDC	Airbus A.321-271N	Air Astana	
EI-KDD	Airbus A.321-271N	Air Astana	
EI-KDE	Airbus A.321-271N	Air Astana	
EI-KDF	Airbus A.321-271N	Air Astana	
EI-KDG	Airbus A.321-271N	Air Astana	
EI-KDI	Airbus A.321 231	Air Astana	
EI-KDJ	Airbus A.321-271N	Air Astana	
EI-KDK	Airbus A.321-271N	Air Astana	
EI-KEA	Boeing 767-3KY	Air Astana	
EI-KEB	Boeing 767-3KY	Air Astana	
EI-KEC	Boeing 767-3KY	Air Astana	
EI-KEV	Raj Hamsa X'Air Jabiru(3)	P. Kearney	
EI-KFA	Airbus A.320 271N	FlyArystan	
EI-KFB	Airbus A.320-271N	FlyArystan	
EI-KFC	Airbus A.320-271N	FlyArystan	
EI-KFD	Airbus A.320-271N	FlyArystan	
EI-KFE	Airbus A.320-232	FlyArystan	
EI-KFF	Airbus A.320-232	FlyArystan	
EI-KFG	Airbus A.320-232	FlyArystan	
EI-KGH	Airbus A.320-232	FlyArystan	
EI-KFI	Airbus A.320-271N	FlyArystan	
EI-KGA	Airbus A.321-271NX	Air Astana	
EI-KGB	Airbus A.321-271NX	Air Astana	
EI-KGC	Airbus A.321-271NX	Air Astana	
EI-KGD	Airbus A.321-271NX	Air Astana	
EI-KGE	Airbus A.321-271NX	Air Astana	
EI-KGF	Airbus A.321-271NX	Air Astana	
EI-KGG	Airbus A.321-271NX	Air Astana	
EI-KGH	Airbus A.321-271NX	Air Astana	
EI-KGI	Airbus A.321-271NX	Air Astana	
EI-KGJ	Airbus A.321-271NX	Air Astana	
EI-KGK	Airbus A.321-271NX	Air Astana	

Notes	Reg	Type († False registration)	Owner or Operator
	EI-KHA	Embraer ERJ190-300STD	Air Astana
	EI-KHC	Embraer ERJ190-300STD	Azorra Aviation
	EI-KHD	Embraer ERJ190-300STD	Air Astana
	EI-KHE	Embraer ERJ190-300STD	Air Astana
	EI-KIA	Airbus A.320-271N	Air Astana
	EI-KIB	Airbus A.320-271N	Air Astana
	EI-KIC	Airbus A.320-271N	Air Astana
	EI-KID	Airbus A.320-271N	Air Astana
	EI-KIE	Airbus A.320-271N	Air Astana
	EI-LAD	Robinson R44 II	Helicopter Support Ireland Ltd
	EI-LCM	TBM-700N	Tara Flying Group
	EI-LDA	Airbus A.300F4-605R	ASL Airlines (Ireland) Ltd
	EI-LDB	Airbus A.300F4-605R	ASL Airlines (Ireland) Ltd
	EI-LDC	Airbus A.300F4-605R	ASL Airlines (Ireland) Ltd
	EI-LDD	Airbus A.300F4-605R	ASL Airlines (Ireland) Ltd
	EI-LDE	Airbus A.300F4-605R	ASL Airlines (Ireland) Ltd
	EI-LDF	Airbus A.300F4-605R	ASL Airlines (Ireland) Ltd
	EI-LDG	Airbus A.300F4-605R	ASL Airlines (Ireland) Ltd
	EI-LDH	Airbus A.300F4-605R	ASL Airlines (Ireland) Ltd
	EI-LFC	Tecnam P.2002-JF	Limerick Flying Club (Coonagh) Ltd
	EI-LID	Agusta AW.169	Vertical Aviation No.1 Ltd
	EI-LIL	CASA 1.131-E	private individual
	EI-LIM	Agusta AW.139	Westair Aviation
	EI-LKD	Airbus A.330-302	ASL Airlines (Ireland) Ltd
	EI-LKE	Airbus A.330-302F	ASL Airlines (Ireland) Ltd
	EI-LOW	AS.355N	Executive Helicopter Maintenance Ltd
	EI-LRA	Airbus A.321-253NX	Aer Lingus
	EI-LRB	Airbus A.321-253NX	Aer Lingus
	EI-LRC	Airbus A.321-253NX	Aer Lingus
	EI-LRD	Airbus A.321-253NX	Aer Lingus
	EI-LRE	Airbus A.321-253NX	Aer Lingus
	EI-LRF	Airbus A.321-253NX	Aer Lingus
	EI-LRG	Airbus A.321-253NX	Aer Lingus
	EI-LRH	Airbus A.321-253NX	Aer Lingus
	EI-LSA	Cub Crafters CC11-160	Directsky Aviation Ltd
	EI-LSN	Gulfstream VI	Gain Jet (Ireland) Ltd
	EI-LSY	Gulfstream V-SP	Gain Jet (Ireland) Ltd
	EI-MAA	Airbus A.330-243	MAS Air Cargo
	EI-MAF	Airbus A.330-343	MAS Air Cargo
	EI-MAW	PZL Koliber 160A	A. Whelehan
	EI-MAZ	Airbus A.330-343	MAS Air Cargo
	EI-MCG	Cessna 172R	Galway Flying Club
	EI-MCM	Gulfstream VIII	Westair Aviation Ltd
	EI-MGL	Boeing 787-9	Gulf Air
	EI-MIK	Eurocopter EC.120B	Executive Helicopter Maintenance Ltd
	EI-MIR	Roko Aero NG 4HD	A. Fegan
	EI-MNG	Boeing 737-MAX8	MIAT Mongolian Airlines
	EI-MPW	Robinson R44	Connacht Helicopters
	EI-MRB	Denney Kitfox Mk.2	D. Doyle
	EI-MTZ	Urban Air Samba XXL	M. Motz
	EI-MVA	Airbus A.220-100	ITA Airways
	EI-MVB	Airbus A.220-100	ITA Airways
	EI-MVC	Airbus A.220-100	ITA Airways
	EI-MVE	Airbus A.220-100	ITA Airways
	EI-MVF	Airbus A.220-100	ITA Airways
	EI-MXV	Best Off Nynja 450	EICD Ventures Ltd
	EI-MYY	Airbus A.330-243	MAS Air Cargo
	EI-NEO	Boeing 787-9	Neos
	EI-NEU	Boeing 787-9	Neos
	EI-NEW	Boeing 787-9	Neos
	EI-NFC	Tecnam P-Mentor	National Flight Centre Ltd
	EI-NFW	Cessna 172S	Galway Flying Club
	EI-NFX	Embraer EMB-550	Volare Acquisitions Ltd
	EI-NGX	Pilatus PC-12/47E	CaficovTrust Co.Ltd
	EI-NJA	Robinson R44 II	Nojo Aviation Ltd
	EI-NSA	Airbus A.320-251N	Aer Lingus
	EI-NSB	Airbus A.320-251N	Aer Lingus
	EI-NSC	Airbus A.320-251N	Aer Lingus
	EI-NSD	Airbus A.320-251N	Aer Lingus
	EI-NSE	Airbus A.320-251N	Aer Lingus
	EI-NSF	Airbus A.320-251N	Aer Lingus

Reg	Type († False registration)	Owner or Operator	Notes
EI-NSG	Airbus A.320-251N	Aer Lingus	
EI-NSH	Airbus A.320-251N	Aer Lingus	
EI-NUA	Boeing 787-9	Neos	
EI-NVL	Jora spol S. R. O. Jora	S. Farrell	
EI-NYE	Boeing 787-9	Neos	
EI-OSS	MBB-BK117 D-3	Airbus Helicopters UK Ltd	
EI-PCI	Bell 206B	Marketside Ltd	
EI-PGA	Dudek Hadron XX	F. Taylor	
EI-PGB	Dudek Hadron 28	C. Fowler	
EI-PGD	Paramania Reflex Wings Revolution 2	D. Keoghegan	
EI-PGI	Dudek Hadron 28	J. McGovern	
EI-PGJ	Swing Sting 2	A. Auffret	
EI-PGK	Ozone Power Spyder 26	O. Creagh	
EI-PGN	ITV Boxer	N. Burke	
EI-PGO	Fly Market Relax 25	M. N. Bendon	
EI-PGP	Paramania Reflex Wings Fusion 26	E. DeKhors	
EI-PGS	Dudek Universal 25.5	M. Markowicz	
EI-PGT	ITV Boxer	M. Hastings	
EI-PGV	Ozone Power Spyder 26	R. Tobin	
EI-PGW	Dudek Universal 1.1	C. Finn	
EI-PHA	Dudek Hadron XX	J. R. Killian	
EI-PHB	Dudek Snake 1.2	J. R. Killian	
EI-PHC	Ozone Roadster 3	P. J. Holthues & M. E. White	
EI-PHD	Dudek Nemo 4	J. R. Killian	
EI-PHF	Dudek Hdron 3	T. Puodziukynas	
EI-PHG	Dudek Universal 1.1 28	D. Guilfoyle	
EI-PHH	Dudek Hadron 3 paramotor	P. Murray	
EI-PHJ	Ozone Roadster 2	B. Sludds	
EI-PHK	Dudek Hadron 1.1	A. Kenny	
EI-PHL	Ozone Speedster 33 paramotor	S. Shannon	
EI-PHM	Dudek Universal paramotor	J. Ferris	
EI-PHN	Dudek Nucleon XX paramotor	S. Donohoe	
EI-PHO	BGD Magic Motor	J. R. Killian	
EI-PHP	BGD Cyclone 38	J. R. Killian	
EI-PHV	Dudek Snake 1.2 paramotor	L. Graham	
EI-PHW	Bruce Goldsmith Design Magic Motor paramotor	private individual	
EI-PHX	Dudek Solo paramotor	S. McCarrick	
EI-PHY	Dudek Hadron 3 paramotor	D. Prialgauskis	
EI-PIA	Ozone Spyder paramotor	private individual	
EI-PIC	Ozone Sirocco 3 26 paramotor	private individual	
EI-PID	Dudek Warp 2	private individual	
EI-PIF	Dudek Universal 25.5	private individual	
EI-PIH	Aeros Fox-13TI	private individual	
EI-PIK	Dudek Universal 1.1 31	private individual	
EI-PIL	ITV Daytona-26	private individual	
EI-PIM	Aeros Nine	private individual	
EI-PIN	ITV Piper 27.5	private individual	
EI-PIR	Ozone Power Viper XC20	private individual	
EI-PIT	Dudek paraglider Warp 2	private individual	
FI-PMI	Agusta-Bell 206B JetRanger III	Eirland Ltd	
EI-POP	Cameron Z-90 balloon	The Travel Department	
EI-PRO	Airbus Helicopters AS.365N2	Executive Helicopter Maintenance Ltd	
EI-PWC	Magni M-24 Orion	R. Macnioclais	
EI-RAY	Best Off Skyranger 912S	G. R. Breaden	
EI-RDB	Embraer ERJ170-200LR	A. P. C. Aircraft Purchase Company Ltd	
EI-RDC	Embraer ERJ170-200LR	A. P. C. Aircraft Purchase Company Ltd	
EI-RII	Robinson R44 II	Scorchdale Ltd	
EI-RLY	P & M Flight Design CTSW	private individual	
EI-RNA	Embraer ERJ190-100STD	A. P. C. Aircraft Purchase Company Ltd	
EI-RNB	Embraer ERJ190-100STD	A. P. C. Aircraft Purchase Company Ltd	
EI-ROK	Roko Aero NG 4UL	K. Harley	
EI-RYN	Tecnam P.2010 TDI	Aerflex DAC	
EI-RZA	Boeing 737-MAX8	Neos	
EI-RZB	Boeing 737-MAX8	Neos	
EI-RZC	Boeing 737-MAX8	Neos	
EI-RZD	Boeing 737-MAX8	Neos	
EI-RZE	Boeing 737-MAX8	Neos	
EI-RZF	Boeing 737-MAX8	Neos	
EI-RZG	Boeing 737-MAX8	Neos	

Notes	Reg	Type († False registration)	Owner or Operator
	EI-RZH	Boeing 737-MAX8	Neos
	EI-SAC	Cessna 172P	Sligo Aero Club
	EI-SCA	Airbus A.320-251N	Scandinavian Airlines Ireland Ltd
	EI-SCB	Airbus A.320-251N	Scandinavian Airlines Ireland Ltd
	EI-SCC	Airbus A.320-251N	Scandinavian Airlines Ireland Ltd
	EI-SCD	Airbus A.320-251N	Scandinavian Airlines Ireland Ltd
	EI-SCE	Airbus A.320-251N	Scandinavian Airlines Ireland Ltd
	EI-SCF	Airbus A.320-251N	Scandinavian Airlines Ireland Ltd
	EI-SCG	Airbus A.320-251N	Scandinavian Airlines Ireland Ltd
	EI-SDK	Piper J-5A Cub	Ballyboughal J5 Flying Group
	EI-SEA	SeaRey	J. Brennan
	EI-SIA	Airbus A.320-251N	Scandinavian Airlines Ireland Ltd
	EI-SIB	Airbus A.320-251N	Scandinavian Airlines Ireland Ltd
	EI-SIC	Airbus A.320-251N	Scandinavian Airlines Ireland Ltd
	EI-SID	Airbus A.320-251N	Scandinavian Airlines Ireland Ltd
	EI-SIE	Airbus A.320-251N	Scandinavian Airlines Ireland Ltd
	EI-SIF	Airbus A.320-251N	Scandinavian Airlines Ireland Ltd
	EI-SIG	Airbus A.320-251N	Scandinavian Airlines Ireland Ltd
	EI-SIH	Airbus A.320-251N	Scandinavian Airlines Ireland Ltd
	EI-SII	Airbus A.320-251N	Scandinavian Airlines Ireland Ltd
	EI-SIJ	Airbus A.320-251N	Scandinavian Airlines Ireland Ltd
	EI-SIK	Airbus A.320-251N	Scandinavian Airlines Ireland Ltd
	EI-SIL	Airbus A.320-251N	Scandinavian Airlines Ireland Ltd
	EI-SIM	Airbus A.320-251N	Scandinavian Airlines Ireland Ltd
	EI-SIN	Airbus A.320-251N	Scandinavian Airlines Ireland Ltd
	EI-SIO	Airbus A.320-251N	Scandinavian Airlines Ireland Ltd
	EI-SIP	Airbus A.320-251N	Scandinavian Airlines Ireland Ltd
	EI-SIR	Airbus A.320-251N	Scandinavian Airlines Ireland Ltd
	EI-SIS	Airbus A.320-251N	Scandinavian Airlines Ireland Ltd
	EI-SIT	Airbus A.320-251N	Scandinavian Airlines Ireland Ltd
	EI-SIU	Airbus A.320-251N	Scandinavian Airlines Ireland Ltd
	EI-SIV	Airbus A.320-251N	Scandinavian Airlines Ireland Ltd
	EI-SIW	Airbus A.320-251N	Scandinavian Airlines Ireland Ltd
	EI-SIY	Airbus A.320-251N	Scandinavian Airlines Ireland Ltd
	EI-SIZ	Airbus A.320-251N	Scandinavian Airlines Ireland Ltd
	EI-SKP	Cessna F.172P	National Flight Centre Ltd
	EI-SKS	Robin R.2160	private individual
	EI-SKU	PA-28RT-201 Cherokee Arrow IV	private individual
	EI-SKV	Robin R.2160	Shemburn Ltd
	EI-SKW	PA-28-161 Warrior II	private individual
	EI-SMK	Zenair CH701	S. King
	EI-SNG	ICP Ventura	S. Grehan
	EI-SPY	Denney Kitfox Mk.3	J. J. & T. Beirne
	EI-SRV	Van's RV-7	T. M. Doddy & K. Keigher
	EI-STJ	Boeing 737-490F	ASL Airlines (Ireland) Ltd
	EI-STW	Boeing 737-4MO	ASL Airlines (Ireland) Ltd
	EI-SYL	Groppo Trail	private individual
	EI-SYM	Van's RV-7	EI-SYM Group
	EI-TAT	Bombardier CL600-2B16	Bandon Aircraft Leasing Ltd
	EI-TCN	Diamond DA.62	Flight Calibration Services Europe Ltd
	EI-TEA	Airbus A.220-300	ITA Airways
	EI-TEB	Airbus A.220-300	ITA Airways
	EI-TEC	Airbus A.220-300	ITA Airways
	EI-TED	Airbus A.220-300	ITA Airways
	EI-TFC	Cessna 172R	Trim Flying Club Company Ltd
	EI-TGG	PA-32R-301Cherokee Six	T. G. Gordon
	EI-TIG	GA AA-5B Tiger	L. Burke
	EI-TIM	Piper J-5A	N. & C. Murphy
	EI-TKI	Robinson R22 Beta	J. McDaid
	EI-TON	M. B. Cooke 582 (5)	private individual
	EI-TVG	Boeing 737-7ZF	Hansel Jet Ireland Ltd
	EI-TYA	Airbus A.330-941	ITA Airways
	EI-TYB	Airbus A.330-941	ITA Airways
	EI-TYC	Airbus A.330-941	ITA Airways
	EI-TYD	Airbus A.330-941	ITA Airways
	EI-TYE	Airbus A.330-941	ITA Airways
	EI-TYF	Airbus A.330-941	ITA Airways
	EI-TYG	Airbus A.330-941	ITA Airways
	EI-UBN	Boeing 787-9	MIAT Mongolian Airlines
	EI-UFO	PA-22 Tri-Pacer 150 (tailwheel)	W. Treacy
	EI-UMA	Ampyx Power AP-3	Ampyx Power Ireland Ltd

Reg	Type († False registration)	Owner or Operator	Notes
EI-UMB	Ampyx Power AP-3	Ampyx Power Ireland Ltd	
EI-UPR	Slingsby T-67M-260 Firefly	Fastnet Jet Alliance Ltd	
EI-VAL	Tecnam P.2010 TDI	National Flight Centre Ltd	
EI-VII	Vans RV-7	B. Sheane	
EI-VLN	PA-18A-150	private individual	
EI-WAC	PA-23 Aztec 250E	Westair Aviation	
EI-WEE	Cessna 182T	Westwind Energy Engineering Ltd	
EI-WFD	Tecnam P.2002-JF	Limerick Flying Club (Coonagh) Co.Ltd	
EI-WFI	Bombardier CL600-2B16 Challenger	Midwest Atlantic/Westair	
EI-WHO	Robinson R44 II	Forbairt Orga Tearanta Ltd	
EI-WHY	Robinson R44 II	OKR Group Unlimited Company	
EI-WIG	Sky Ranger 912	K. Lannery	
EI-WMN	PA-23 Aztec 250F	Westair Aviation	
EI-WOT	Currie Wot	D. Doyle & Partners	
EI-WST	Tecnam P.2006T	National Flight Centre Ltd	
EI-XHA	Airbus Helicopters AS.350B3	Executive Helicopter Maintenance Ltd	
EI-XHB	Airbus Helicopters EC.155B	Executive Helicopter Maintenance Ltd	
EI-XHC	Airbus Helicopters AS.350B3	Executive Helicopter Maintenance Ltd	
EI-XHI	Airbus Helicopters EC.155B	Executive Helicopter Maintenance Ltd	
EI-XIN	Boeing 787-9	Neos	
EI-XIV	Van's RV-14A	private individual	
EI-XLR	Airbus A.321-253NY XLR	Aer Lingus	
EI-XLT	Airbus A.321-253NY XLR	Aer Lingus	
EI-XLU	Airbus A.321-253NY XLR	Aer Lingus	
EI-XLV	Airbus A.321-253NY XLR	Aer Lingus	
EI-XLW	Airbus A.321-253NY XLR	Aer Lingus	
EI-XTW	Airbus Helicopters AS.350B3	Aeroheli Ltd	
EI-YLG	Robin HR.200/120B	Leinster Aero Club	
EI-ZPG	Bell 407	Zeus Essential Holding Ltd	
EI-ZZZ	Bell222	Executive Helicopter Maintenance Ltd	
EJ-ADMI	Gulfstream VI	Gain Jet Ireland Ltd	
EJ-JMMM	Bombardier BD700-1A10	ACASS Ireland Ltd	
EJ-KGRP	Gulfstream V-SP	KGP Aviation Ltd	
EJ-MACK	Pilatus PC-24	Mack Aer Ltd	
EJ-REVA	Hawker 800XP	Gain Jet Ireland Ltd	
EJ-SCOT	Gulfstream IV-X	Acass Ireland Ltd	
EJ-VAIS	Pilatus PC-12/47E	CAFICO Trust Company Ltd	

EI-FFB Boeing 737 8K5 of Fly4 Airlines. *Allan S. Wright*

(Aircraft included in this section are those most likely to be seen at UK airports)

Notes	Reg	Type	Owner or Operator

A4O (Oman)

Reg	Type	Owner or Operator
A4O-SC	Boeing 787-9	Oman Air
A4O-SE	Boeing 787-9	Oman Air
A4O-SF	Boeing 787-9	Oman Air
A4O-SG	Boeing 787-9	Oman Air
A4O-SH	Boeing 787-9	Oman Air
A4O-SI	Boeing 787-9	Oman Air
A4O-SJ	Boeing 787-9	Oman Air
A4O-SK	Boeing 787-9	Oman Air
A4O-SL	Boeing 787-9	Oman Air

A6 (United Arab Emirates)

Reg	Type	Owner or Operator
A6-APC	Airbus A.380-841	Etihad Airways
A6-APD	Airbus A.380-841	Etihad Airways
A6-APE	Airbus A.380-841	Etihad Airways
A6-APF	Airbus A.380-841	Etihad Airways
A6-APG	Airbus A.380-841	Etihad Airways
A6-APH	Airbus A.380-841	Etihad Airways
A6-API	Airbus A.380-841	Etihad Airways
A6-APJ	Airbus A.380-841	Etihad Airways
A6-ATA	Airbus A.321-251NX	Air Arabia
A6-ATB	Airbus A.321-251NX	Air Arabia
A6-ATC	Airbus A.321-251NX	Air Arabia
A6-ATD	Airbus A.321-251NX	Air Arabia
A6-ATE	Airbus A.321-251NX	Air Arabia
A6-ATF	Airbus A.321-251NX	Air Arabia
A6-BLA	Boeing 787-9	Etihad Airways
A6-BLB	Boeing 787-9	Etihad Airways
A6-BLC	Boeing 787-9	Etihad Airways
A6-BLD	Boeing 787-9	Etihad Airways
A6-BLE	Boeing 787-9	Etihad Airways
A6-BLF	Boeing 787-9	Etihad Airways
A6-BLG	Boeing 787-9	Etihad Airways
A6-BLH	Boeing 787-9	Etihad Airways
A6-BLI	Boeing 787-9	Etihad Airways
A6-BLJ	Boeing 787-9	Etihad Airways
A6-BLK	Boeing 787-9	Etihad Airways
A6-BLL	Boeing 787-9	Etihad Airways
A6-BLM	Boeing 787-9	Etihad Airways
A6-BLN	Boeing 787-9	Etihad Airways
A6-BLO	Boeing 787-9	Etihad Airways
A6-BLP	Boeing 787-9	Etihad Airways
A6-BLQ	Boeing 787-9	Etihad Airways
A6-BLR	Boeing 787-9	Etihad Airways
A6-BLS	Boeing 787-9	Etihad Airways
A6-BLT	Boeing 787-9	Etihad Airways
A6-BLU	Boeing 787-9	Etihad Airways
A6-BLV	Boeing 787-9	Etihad Airways
A6-BLW	Boeing 787-9	Etihad Airways
A6-BLX	Boeing 787-9	Etihad Airways
A6-BLY	Boeing 787-9	Etihad Airways
A6-BLZ	Boeing 787-9	Etihad Airways
A6-BMA	Boeing 787-10	Etihad Airways
A6-BMB	Boeing 787-10	Etihad Airways
A6-BMC	Boeing 787-10	Etihad Airways
A6-BMD	Boeing 787-10	Etihad Airways
A6-BME	Boeing 787-10	Etihad Airways
A6-BMF	Boeing 787-10	Etihad Airways
A6-BMG	Boeing 787-10	Etihad Airways
A6-BMH	Boeing 787-10	Etihad Airways
A6-BMI	Boeing 787-10	Etihad Airways
A6-BMJ	Boeing 787-10	Etihad Airways
A6-BNA	Boeing 787-9	Etihad Airways
A6-BNB	Boeing 787-9	Etihad Airways
A6-BNC	Boeing 787-9	Etihad Airways
A6-BND	Boeing 787-9	Etihad Airways
A6-BNE	Boeing 787-9	Etihad Airways

Reg	Type	Owner or Operator	Notes
A6-BNF	Boeing 787-9	Etihad Airways	
A6-BNG	Boeing 787-9	Etihad Airways	
A6-BNH	Boeing 787-9	Etihad Airways	
A6-BNI	Boeing 787-9	Etihad Airways	
A6-BNJ	Boeing 787-9	Etihad Airways	
A6-BNK	Boeing 787-9	Etihad Airways	
A6-DDB	Boeing 777-FFX	Etihad Airways Cargo	
A6-DDC	Boeing 777-FFX	Etihad Airways Cargo	
A6-DDD	Boeing 777-FFX	Etihad Airways Cargo	
A6-DDE	Boeing 777-FFX	Etihad Airways Cargo	
A6-DDF	Boeing 777-F	Etihad Airways Cargo	
A6-EBM	Boeing 777-31HER	Emirates Airlines	
A6-EBR	Boeing 777-36NER	Emirates Airlines	
A6-EBU	Boeing 777-31HER	Emirates Airlines	
A6-EBY	Boeing 777-36NER	Emirates Airlines	
A6-ECA	Boeing 777-36NER	Emirates Airlines	
A6-ECE	Boeing 777-31HER	Emirates Airlines	
A6-ECF	Boeing 777-31HER	Emirates Airlines	
A6-ECG	Boeing 777-31HER	Emirates Airlines	
A6-ECH	Boeing 777-31HER	Emirates Airlines	
A6-ECI	Boeing 777-31HER	Emirates Airlines	
A6-ECJ	Boeing 777-31HER	Emirates Airlines	
A6-ECK	Boeing 777-31HER	Emirates Airlines	
A6-ECM	Boeing 777-36NER	Emirates Airlines	
A6-ECO	Boeinb 777-36NER	Emirates Airlines	
A6-ECQ	Boeing 777-31HER	Emirates Airlines	
A6-ECR	Boeing 777-31HER	Emirates Airlines	
A6-ECS	Boeing 777-31HER	Emirates Airlines	
A6-ECT	Boeing 777-31HER	Emirates Airlines	
A6-ECU	Boeing 777-31HER	Emirates Airlines	
A6-ECV	Boeing 777-31HER	Emirates Airlines	
A6-ECW	Boeing 777-31HER	Emirates Airlines	
A6-ECX	Boeing 777-31HER	Emirates Airlines	
A6-ECY	Boeing 777-31HER	Emirates Airlines	
A6-ECZ	Boeing 777-31HER	Emirates Airlines	
A6-EDF	Airbus A.380-861	Emirates Airlines	
A6-EDI	Airbus A.380-861	Emirates Airlines	
A6-EDJ	Airbus A.380-861	Emirates Airlines	
A6-EDK	Airbus A.380-861	Emirates Airlines	
A6-EDL	Airbus A.380-861	Emirates Airlines	
A6-EDM	Airbus A.380-861	Emirates Airlines	
A6-EDN	Airbus A.380-861	Emirates Airlines	
A6-EDO	Airbus A.380-861	Emirates Airlines	
A6-EDP	Airbus A.380-861	Emirates Airlines	
A6-EDQ	Airbus A.380-861	Emirates Airlines	
A6-EDR	Airbus A.380-861	Emirates Airlines	
A6-EDS	Airbus A.380-861	Emirates Airlines	
A6-EDT	Airbus A.380-861	Emirates Airlines	
A6-EDU	Airbus A.380-861	Emirates Airlines	
A6-EDV	Airbus A.380-861	Emirates Airlines	
A6-EDW	Airbus A.380-861	Emirates Airlines	
A6-EDX	Airbus A.380-861	Emirates Airlines	
A6-EDY	Airbus A.380-861	Emirates Airlines	
A6-EDZ	Airbus A.380-861	Emirates Airlines	
A6-EEA	Airbus A.380-861	Emirates Airlines	
A6-EEB	Airbus A.380-861	Emirates Airlines	
A6-EEC	Airbus A.380-861	Emirates Airlines	
A6-EED	Airbus A.380-861	Emirates Airlines	
A6-EEE	Airbus A.380-861	Emirates Airlines	
A6-EEF	Airbus A.380-861	Emirates Airlines	
A6-EEG	Airbus A.380-861	Emirates Airlines	
A6-EEH	Airbus A.380-861	Emirates Airlines	
A6-EEI	Airbus A.380-861	Emirates Airlines	
A6-EEJ	Airbus A.380-861	Emirates Airlines	
A6-EEK	Airbus A,380-861	Emirates Airlines	
A6-EEL	Airbus A.380-861	Emirates Airlines	
A6-EEM	Airbus A.380-861	Emirates Airlines	
A6-EEN	Airbus A.380-861	Emirates Airlines	
A6-EEO	Airbus A.380-861	Emirates Airlines	
A6-EEP	Airbus A.380-861	Emirates Airlines	
A6-EEQ	Airbus A.380-861	Emirates Airlines	

Notes	Reg	Type	Owner or Operator
	A6-EER	Airbus A.380-861	Emirates Airlines
	A6-EES	Airbus A.380-861	Emirates Airlines
	A6-EET	Airbus A.380-861	Emirates Airlines
	A6-EEU	Airbus A.380-861	Emirates Airlines
	A6-EEV	Airbus A.380-861	Emirates Airlines
	A6-EEW	Airbus A.380-861	Emirates Airlines
	A6-EEX	Airbus A.380-861	Emirates Airlines
	A6-EEY	Airbus A.380-861	Emirates Airlines
	A6-EEZ	Airbus A.380-861	Emirates Airlines
	A6-EFM	Boeing 777-F1H	Emirates SkyCargo
	A6-EFN	Boeing 777-F1H	Emirates SkyCargo
	A6-EFO	Boeing 777-F1H	Emirates SkyCargo
	A6-EFS	Boeing 777-F1H	Emirates SkyCargo
	A6-EFT	Boeing 777-F1H	Emirates SkyCargo
	A6-EFU	Boeing 777-F1H	Emirates SkyCargo
	A6-EFV	Boeing 777-F1H	Emirates SkyCargo
	A6-EFW	Boeing 777-F1H	Emirates SkyCargo
	A6-EFX	Boeing 777-F1H	Emirates SkyCargo
	A6-EFY	Boeing 777-F1H	Emirates SkyCargo
	A6-EFZ	Boeing 777-F1H	Emirates SkyCargo
	A6-EGA	Boeing 777-31HER	Emirates Airlines
	A6-EGB	Boeing 777-31HER	Emirates Airlines
	A6-EGC	Boeing 777-31HER	Emirates Airlines
	A6-EGD	Boeing 777-31HER	Emirates Airlines
	A6-EGE	Boeing 777-31HER	Emirates Airlines
	A6-EGF	Boeing 777-31HER	Emirates Airlines
	A6-EGG	Boeing 777-31HER	Emirates Airlines
	A6-EGH	Boeing 777-31HER	Emirates Airlines
	A6-EGI	Boeing 777-31HER	Emirates Airlines
	A6-EGJ	Boeing 777-31HER	Emirates Airlines
	A6-EGK	Boeing 777-31HER	Emirates Airlines
	A6-EGL	Boeing 777-31HER	Emirates Airlines
	A6-EGM	Boeing 777-31HER	Emirates Airlines
	A6-EGN	Boeing 777-31HER	Emirates Airlines
	A6-EGO	Boeing 777-31HER	Emirates Airlines
	A6-EGP	Boeing 777-31HER	Emirates Airlines
	A6-EGQ	Boeing 777-31HER	Emirates Airlines
	A6-EGR	Boeing 777-31HER	Emirates Airlines
	A6-EGS	Boeing 777-31HER	Emirates Airlines
	A6-EGT	Boeing 777-31HER	Emirates Airlines
	A6-EGU	Boeing 777-31HER	Emirates Airlines
	A6-EGV	Boeing 777-31HER	Emirates Airlines
	A6-EGW	Boeing 777-31HER	Emirates Airlines
	A6-EGX	Boeing 777-31HER	Emirates Airlines
	A6-EGY	Boeing 777-31HER	Emirates Airlines
	A6-EGZ	Boeing 777-31HER	Emirates Airlines
	A6-ENA	Boeing 777-31HER	Emirates Airlines
	A6-ENB	Boeing 777-31HER	Emirates Airlines
	A6-ENC	Boeing 777-31HER	Emirates Airlines
	A6-END	Boeing 777-31HER	Emirates Airlines
	A6-ENE	Boeing 777-31HER	Emirates Airlines
	A6-ENF	Boeing 777-31HER	Emirates Airlines
	A6-ENG	Boeing 777-31HER	Emirates Airlines
	A6-ENH	Boeing 777-31HER	Emirates Airlines
	A6-ENI	Boeing 777-31HER	Emirates Airlines
	A6-ENJ	Boeing 777-31HER	Emirates Airlines
	A6-ENK	Boeing 777-31HER	Emirates Airlines
	A6-ENL	Boeing 777-31HER	Emirates Airlines
	A6-ENM	Boeing 777-31HER	Emirates Airlines
	A6-ENN	Boeing 777-31HER	Emirates Airlines
	A6-ENO	Boeing 777-31HER	Emirates Airlines
	A6-ENP	Boeing 777-31HER	Emirates Airlines
	A6-ENQ	Boeing 777-31HER	Emirates Airlines
	A6-ENR	Boeing 777-31HER	Emirates Airlines
	A6-ENS	Boeing 777-31HER	Emirates Airlines
	A6-ENT	Boeing 777-31HER	Emirates Airlines
	A6-ENU	Boeing 777-31HER	Emirates Airlines
	A6-ENV	Boeing 777-31HER	Emirates Airlines
	A6-ENW	Boeing 777-31HER	Emirates Airlines
	A6-ENX	Boeing 777-31HER	Emirates Airlines
	A6-ENY	Boeing 777-31HER	Emirates Airlines

Reg	Type	Owner or Operator	Notes
A6-ENZ	Boeing 777-31HER	Emirates Airlines	
A6-EOA	Airbus A.380-861	Emirates Airlines	
A6-EOB	Airbus A.380-861	Emirates Airlines	
A6-EOC	Airbus A.380-861	Emirates Airlines	
A6-EOD	Airbus A.380-861	Emirates Airlines	
A6-EOE	Airbus A.380-861	Emirates Airlines	
A6-EOF	Airbus A.380-861	Emirates Airlines	
A6-EOG	Airbus A.380-861	Emirates Airlines	
A6-EOH	Airbus A.380-861	Emirates Airlines	
A6-EOI	Airbus A.380-861	Emirates Airlines	
A6-EOJ	Airbus A.380-861	Emirates Airlines	
A6-EOK	Airbus A.380-861	Emirates Airlines	
A6-EOL	Airbus A.380-861	Emirates Airlines	
A6-EOM	Airbus A.380-861	Emirates Airlines	
A6-EON	Airbus A.380-861	Emirates Airlines	
A6-EOO	Airbus A.380-861	Emirates Airlines	
A6-EOP	Airbus A.380-861	Emirates Airlines	
A6-EOQ	Airbus A.380-861	Emirates Airlines	
A6-EOR	Airbus A.380-861	Emirates Airlines	
A6-EOS	Airbus A.380-861	Emirates Airlines	
A6-EOT	Airbus A.380-861	Emirates Airlines	
A6-EOU	Airbus A.380-861	Emirates Airlines	
A6-EOV	Airbus A.380-861	Emirates Airlines	
A6-EOW	Airbus A.380-861	Emirates Airlines	
A6-EOX	Airbus A.380-861	Emirates Airlines	
A6-EOY	Airbus A.380-861	Emirates Airlines	
A6-EOZ	Airbus A.380-861	Emirates Airlines	
A6-EPA	Boeing 777-31HER	Emirates Airlines	
A6-EPB	Boeing 777-31HER	Emirates Airlines	
A6-EPC	Boeing 777-31HER	Emirates Airlines	
A6-EPD	Boeing 777-31HER	Emirates Airlines	
A6-EPE	Boeing 777-31HER	Emirates Airlines	
A6-EPF	Boeing 777-31HER	Emirates Airlines	
A6-EPG	Boeing 777-31HER	Emirates Airlines	
A6-EPH	Boeing 777-31HER	Emirates Airlines	
A6-EPI	Boeing 777-31HER	Emirates Airlines	
A6-EPJ	Boeing 777-31HER	Emirates Airlines	
A6-EPK	Boeing 777-31HER	Emirates Airlines	
A6-EPL	Boeing 777-31HER	Emirates Airlines	
A6-EPM	Boeing 777-31HER	Emirates Airlines	
A6-EPN	Boeing 777-31HER	Emirates Airlines	
A6-EPO	Boeing 777-31HER	Emirates Airlines	
A6-EPP	Boeing 777-31HER	Emirates Airlines	
A6-EPQ	Boeing 777-31HER	Emirates Airlines	
A6-EPR	Boeing 777-31HER	Emirates Airlines	
A6-EPS	Boeing 777-31HER	Emirates Airlines	
A6-EPT	Boeing 777-31HER	Emirates Airlines	
A6-EPU	Boeing 777-31HER	Emirates Airlines	
A6-EPV	Boeing 777-31HER	Emirates Airlines	
A6-EPW	Boeing 777-31HER	Emirates Airlines	
A6-EPX	Boeing 777-31HER	Emirates Airlines	
A6-EPY	Boeing 777-31HER	Emirates Airlines	
A6-EPZ	Boeing 777-31HER	Emirates Airlines	
A6-EQA	Boeing 777-31HER	Emirates Airlines	
A6-EQB	Boeing 777-31HER	Emirates Airlines	
A6-EQC	Boeing 777-31HER	Emirates Airlines	
A6-EQD	Boeing 777-31HER	Emirates Airlines	
A6-EQE	Boeing 777-31HER	Emirates Airlines	
A6-EQF	Boeing 777-31HER	Emirates Airlines	
A6-EQG	Boeing 777-31HER	Emirates Airlines	
A6-EQH	Boeing 777-31HER	Emirates Airlines	
A6-EQI	Boeing 777-31HER	Emirates Airlines	
A6-EQJ	Boeing 777-31HER	Emirates Airlines	
A6-EQK	Boeing 777-31HER	Emirates Airlines	
A6-EQL	Boeing 777-31HER	Emirates Airlines	
A6-EQM	Boeing 777-31HER	Emirates Airlines	
A6-EQN	Boeing 777-31HER	Emirates Airlines	
A6-EQO	Boeing 777-31HER	Emirates Airlines	
A6-EQP	Boeing 777-31HER	Emirates Airlines	
A6-ETA	Boeing 777-3FXER	Etihad Airways	
A6-ETE	Boeing 777-3FXER	Etihad Airways	

Notes	Reg	Type	Owner or Operator
	A6-ETG	Boeing 777-3FXER	Etihad Airways
	A6-ETH	Boeing 777-3FXER	Etihad Airways
	A6-ETI	Boeing 777-3FXER	Etihad Airways
	A6-ETJ	Boeing 777-3FXER	Etihad Airways
	A6-ETP	Boeing 777-3FXER	Etihad Airways
	A6-ETQ	Boeing 777-3FXER	Etihad Airways
	A6-ETS	Boeing 777-3FXER	Etihad Airways
	A6-EUA	Airbus A.380-861	Emirates Airlines
	A6-EUB	Airbus A.380-861	Emirates Airlines
	A6-EUC	Airbus A.380-861	Emirates Airlines
	A6-EUD	Airbus A.380-861	Emirates Airlines
	A6-EUE	Airbus A.380-861	Emirates Airlines
	A6-EUF	Airbus A.380-861	Emirates Airlines
	A6-EUG	Airbus A.380-861	Emirates Airlines
	A6-EUH	Airbus A.380-861	Emirates Airlines
	A6-EUI	Airbus A.380-861	Emirates Airlines
	A6-EUJ	Airbus A.380-861	Emirates Airlines
	A6-EUK	Airbus A.380-861	Emirates Airlines
	A6-EUL	Airbus A.380-861	Emirates Airlines
	A6-EUM	Airbus A.380-861	Emirates Airlines
	A6-EUN	Airbus A.380-861	Emirates Airlines
	A6-EUO	Airbus A.380-861	Emirates Airlines
	A6-EUP	Airbus A.380-861	Emirates Airlines
	A6-EUQ	Airbus A.380-861	Emirates Airlines
	A6-EUR	Airbus A.380-861	Emirates Airlines
	A6-EUS	Airbus A.380-861	Emirates Airlines
	A6-EUT	Airbus A.380-861	Emirates Airlines
	A6-EUU	Airbus A.380-861	Emirates Airlines
	A6-EUV	Airbus A.380-861	Emirates Airlines
	A6-EUW	Airbus A.380-861	Emirates Airlines
	A6-EUX	Airbus A.380-861	Emirates Airlines
	A6-EUY	Airbus A.380-861	Emirates Airlines
	A6-EUZ	Airbus A.380-861	Emirates Airlines
	A6-EVA	Airbus A.380-842	Emirates Airlines
	A6-EVB	Airbus A.380-842	Emirates Airlines
	A6-EVC	Airbus A.380-842	Emirates Airlines
	A6-EVD	Airbus A.380-842	Emirates Airlines
	A6-EVE	Airbus A.380-842	Emirates Airlines
	A6-EVF	Airbus A.380-842	Emirates Airlines
	A6-EVG	Airbus A.380-842	Emirates Airlines
	A6-EVH	Airbus A.380-842	Emirates Airlines
	A6-EVI	Airbus A.380-842	Emirates Airlines
	A6-EVJ	Airbus A.380-842	Emirates Airlines
	A6-EVK	Airbus A.380-842	Emirates Airlines
	A6-EVL	Airbus A.380-842	Emirates Airlines
	A6-EVM	Airbus A.380-842	Emirates Airlines
	A6-EVN	Airbus A.380-842	Emirates Airlines
	A6-EVO	Airbus A.380-842	Emirates Airlines
	A6-EVP	Airbus A.380-842	Emirates Airlines
	A6-EVQ	Airbus A.380-842	Emirates Airlines
	A6-EVR	Airbus A.380-842	Emirates Airlines
	A6-EVS	Airbus A.380-842	Emirates Airlines
	A6-EXA	Airbus A.350-941	Emirates Airlines
	A6-EXB	Airbus A.350-941	Emirates Airlines
	A6-EXC	Airbus A.350-941	Emirates Airlines
	A6-EXD	Airbus A.350-941	Emirates Airlines
	A6-EXE	Airbus A.350-941	Emirates Airlines
	A6-EXF	Airbus A.350-941	Emirates Airlines
	A6-EXG	Airbus A.350-941	Emirates Airlines
	A6-EXH	Airbus A.350-941	Emirates Airlines
	A6-EXI	Airbus A.350-941	Emirates Airlines
	A6-EXJ	Airbus A.350-941	Emirates Airlines
	A6-EXK	Airbus A.350-941	Emirates Airlines
	A6-EXL	Airbus A.350-941	Emirates Airlines
	A6-EXM	Airbus A.350-941	Emirates Airlines
	A6-EXN	Airbus A.350-941	Emirates Airlines
	A6-EXO	Airbus A.350-941	Emirates Airlines
	A6-EXP	Airbus A.350-941	Emirates Airlines
	A6-EXQ	Airbus A.350-941	Emirates Airlines
	A6-EXR	Airbus A.350-941	Emirates Airlines
	A6-EXS	Airbus A.350-941	Emirates Airlines

Reg	Type	Owner or Operator	Notes
A6-EXT	Airbus A.350-941	Emirates Airlines	
A6-EXU	Airbus A.350-941	Emirates Airlines	
A6-EXV	Airbus A.350-941	Emirates Airlines	
A6-EXW	Airbus A.350-941	Emirates Airlines	

A7 (Qatar)

Reg	Type	Owner or Operator	Notes
A7-ALA	Airbus A.350-941	Qatar Airways	
A7-ALB	Airbus A.350-941	Qatar Airways	
A7-ALC	Airbus A.350-941	Qatar Airways	
A7-ALD	Airbus A.350-941	Qatar Airways	
A7-ALE	Airbus A.350-941	Qatar Airways	
A7-ALF	Airbus A.350-941	Qatar Airways	
A7-ALG	Airbus A.350-941	Qatar Airways	
A7-ALH	Airbus A.350-941	Qatar Airways	
A7-ALI	Airbus A.350-941	Qatar Airways	
A7-ALJ	Airbus A.350-941	Qatar Airways	
A7-ALK	Airbus A.350-941	Qatar Airways	
A7-ALL	Airbus A.350-941	Qatar Airways	
A7-ALM	Airbus A.350-941	Qatar Airways	
A7-ALN	Airbus A.350-941	Qatar Airways	
A7-ALO	Airbus A.350-941	Qatar Airways	
A7-ALP	Airbus A.350-941	Qatar Airways	
A7-ALQ	Airbus A.350-941	Qatar Airways	
A7-ALR	Airbus A.350-941	Qatar Airways	
A7-ALS	Airbus A.350-941	Qatar Airways	
A7-ALT	Airbus A.350-941	Qatar Airways	
A7-ALU	Airbus A.350-941	Qatar Airways	
A7-ALV	Airbus A.350-941	Qatar Airways	
A7-ALW	Airbus A.350-941	Qatar Airways	
A7-ALX	Airbus A.350-941	Qatar Airways	
A7-ALY	Airbus A.350-941	Qatar Airways	
A7-ALZ	Airbus A.350-941	Qatar Airways	
A7-AME	Airbus A.350-941	Qatar Airways	
A7-AMF	Airbus A.350-941	Qatar Airways	
A7-AMG	Airbus A.350-941	Qatar Airways	
A7-AMH	Airbus A.350-941	Qatar Airways	
A7-AMI	Airbus A.350-941	Qatar Airways	
A7-AMJ	Airbus A.350-941	Qatar Airways	
A7-AMK	Airbus A.350-941	Qatar Airways	
A7-AML	Airbus A.350-941	Qatar Airways	
A7-ANA	Airbus A.350-1041	Qatar Airways	
A7-ANB	Airbus A.350-1041	Qatar Airways	
A7-ANC	Airbus A.350-1041	Qatar Airways	
A7-AND	Airbus A.350-1041	Qatar Airways	
A7-ANE	Airbus A.350-1041	Qatar Airways	
A7-ANF	Airbus A.350-1041	Qatar Airways	
A7-ANG	Airbus A.350-1041	Qatar Airways	
A7-ANH	Airbus A.350-1041	Qatar Airways	
A7-ANI	Airbus A.350-1041	Qatar Airways	
A7-ANJ	Airbus A.350-1041	Qatar Airways	
A7-ANK	Airbus A.350-1041	Qatar Airways	
A7-ANL	Airbus A.350-1041	Qatar Airways	
A7-ANM	Airbus A.350-1041	Qatar Airways	
A7-ANN	Airbus A.350-1041	Qatar Airways	
A7-ANO	Airbus A.350-1041	Qatar Airways	
A7-ANP	Airbus A.350-1041	Qatar Airways	
A7-ANQ	Airbus A.350-1041	Qatar Airways	
A7-ANR	Airbus A.350-1041	Qatar Airways	
A7-ANS	Airbus A.350-1041	Qatar Airways	
A7-ANT	Airbus A.350-1041	Qatar Airways	
A7-AOA	Airbus A.350-1041	Qatar Airways	
A7-AOB	Airbus A.350-1041	Qatar Airways	
A7-AOC	Airbus A.350-1041	Qatar Airways	
A7-AOD	Airbus A.350-1041	Qatar Airways	
A7-AOE	Airbus A.350-1041	Qatar Airways	
A7-AOF	Airbus A.350-1041	Qatar Airways	
A7-AOG	Airbus A.350-1041	Qatar Airways	
A7-AOH	Airbus A.350-1041	Qatar Airways	
A7-APC	Airbus A.380-861	Qatar Airways	
A7-APD	Airbus A.380-861	Qatar Airways	

Notes	Reg	Type	Owner or Operator
	A7-APE	Airbus A.380-861	Qatar Airways
	A7-APF	Airbus A.380-861	Qatar Airways
	A7-APG	Airbus A.380-861	Qatar Airways
	A7-APH	Airbus A.380-861	Qatar Airways
	A7-API	Airbus A.380-861	Qatar Airways
	A7-APJ	Airbus A.380-861	Qatar Airways
	A7-BAA	Boeing 777-3DZ ER	Qatar Airways
	A7-BAB	Boeing 777-3DZ ER	Qatar Airways
	A7-BAC	Boeing 777-3DZ ER	Qatar Airways
	A7-BAE	Boeing 777-3DZ ER	Qatar Airways
	A7-BAF	Boeing 777-3DZ ER	Qatar Airways
	A7-BAG	Boeing 777-3DZ ER	Qatar Airways
	A7-BAH	Boeing 777-3DZ ER	Qatar Airways
	A7-BAI	Boeing 777-3DZ ER	Qatar Airways
	A7-BAJ	Boeing 777-3DZ ER	Qatar Airways
	A7-BAK	Boeing 777-3DZ ER	Qatar Airways
	A7-BAL	Boeing 777-3DZ ER	Qatar Airways
	A7-BAM	Boeing 777-3DZ ER	Qatar Airways
	A7-BAN	Boeing 777-3DZ ER	Qatar Airways
	A7-BAO	Boeing 777-3DZ ER	Qatar Airways
	A7-BAP	Boeing 777-3DZ ER	Qatar Airways
	A7-BAQ	Boeing 777-3DZ ER	Qatar Airways
	A7-BAS	Boeing 777-3DZ ER	Qatar Airways
	A7-BAT	Boeing 777-3DZ ER	Qatar Airways
	A7-BAU	Boeing 777-3DZ ER	Qatar Airways
	A7-BAV	Boeing 777-3DZ ER	Qatar Airways
	A7-BAW	Boeing 777-3DZ ER	Qatar Airways
	A7-BAX	Boeing 777-3DZ ER	Qatar Airways
	A7-BAY	Boeing 777-3DZ ER	Qatar Airways
	A7-BAZ	Boeing 777-3DZ ER	Qatar Airways
	A7-BBA	Boeing 777-2DZ LR	Qatar Airways
	A7-BBB	Boeing 777-2DZ LR	Qatar Airways
	A7-BBC	Boeing 777-2DZ LR	Qatar Airways
	A7-BBF	Boeing 777-2DZ LR	Qatar Airways
	A7-BBG	Boeing 777-2DZ LR	Qatar Airways
	A7-BBH	Boeing 777-2DZ LR	Qatar Airways
	A7-BBI	Boeing 777-2DZ LR	Qatar Airways
	A7-BCA	Boeing 787-8	Qatar Airways
	A7-BCB	Boeing 787-8	Qatar Airways
	A7-BCC	Boeing 787-8	Qatar Airways
	A7-BCD	Boeing 787-8	Qatar Airways
	A7-BCE	Boeing 787-8	Qatar Airways
	A7-BCF	Boeing 787-8	Qatar Airways
	A7-BCG	Boeing 787-8	Qatar Airways
	A7-BCH	Boeing 787-8	Qatar Airways
	A7-BCI	Boeing 787-8	Qatar Airways
	A7-BCJ	Boeing 787-8	Qatar Airways
	A7-BCK	Boeing 787-8	Qatar Airways
	A7-BCL	Boeing 787-8	Qatar Airways
	A7-BCM	Boeing 787-8	Qatar Airways
	A7-BCN	Boeing 787-8	Qatar Airways
	A7-BCO	Boeing 787-8	Qatar Airways
	A7-BCP	Boeing 787-8	Qatar Airways
	A7-BCQ	Boeing 787-8	Qatar Airways
	A7-BCR	Boeing 787-8	Qatar Airways
	A7-BCS	Boeing 787-8	Qatar Airways
	A7-BCT	Boeing 787-8	Qatar Airways
	A7-BCU	Boeing 787-8	Qatar Airways
	A7-BCV	Boeing 787-8	Qatar Airways
	A7-BCW	Boeing 787-8	Qatar Airways
	A7-BCX	Boeing 787-8	Qatar Airways
	A7-BCY	Boeing 787-8	Qatar Airways
	A7-BCZ	Boeing 787-8	Qatar Airways
	A7-BDA	Boeing 787-8	Qatar Airways
	A7-BDB	Boeing 787-8	Qatar Airways
	A7-BDC	Boeing 787-8	Qatar Airways
	A7-BDD	Boeing 787-8	Qatar Airways
	A7-BEA	Boeing 777-3DZER	Qatar Airways
	A7-BEB	Boeing 777-3DZER	Qatar Airways
	A7-BEC	Boeing 777-3DZER	Qatar Airways
	A7-BED	Boeing 777-3DZER	Qatar Airways

Reg	Type	Owner or Operator	Notes
A7-BEE	Boeing 777-3DZER	Qatar Airways	
A7-BEF	Boeing 777-3DZER	Qatar Airways	
A7-BEG	Boeing 777-3DZER	Qatar Airways	
A7-BEH	Boeing 777-3DZER	Qatar Airways	
A7-BEI	Boeing 777-3DZER	Qatar Airways	
A7-BEJ	Boeing 777-3DZER	Qatar Airways	
A7-BEK	Boeing 777-3DZER	Qatar Airways	
A7-BEL	Boeing 777-3DZER	Qatar Airways	
A7-BEM	Boeing 777-3DZER	Qatar Airways	
A7-BEN	Boeing 777-3DZER	Qatar Airways	
A7-BEO	Boeing 777-3DZER	Qatar Airways	
A7-BEP	Boeing 777-3DZER	Qatar Airways	
A7-BEQ	Boeing 777-3DZER	Qatar Airways	
A7-BER	Boeing 777-3DZER	Qatar Airways	
A7-BES	Boeing 777-3DZER	Qatar Airways	
A7-BET	Boeing 777-3DZER	Qatar Airways	
A7-BEU	Boeing 777-3DZER	Qatar Airways	
A7-BEV	Boeing 777-3DZER	Qatar Airways	
A7-BEW	Boeing 777-3DZER	Qatar Airways	
A7-BEX	Boeing 777-3DZER	Qatar Airways	
A7-BFA	Boeing 777-FDZ	Qatar Airways Cargo	
A7-BFB	Boeing 777-FDZ	Qatar Airways Cargo	
A7-BFC	Boeing 777-FDZ	Qatar Airways Cargo	
A7-BFD	Boeing 777-FDZ	Qatar Airways Cargo	
A7-BFE	Boeing 777-FDZ	Qatar Airways Cargo	
A7-BFF	Boeing 777-FDZ	Qatar Airways Cargo	
A7-BFG	Boeing 777-FDZ	Qatar Airways Cargo	
A7-BFH	Boeing 777-FDZ	Qatar Airways Cargo	
A7-BFI	Boeing 777-FDZ	Qatar Airways Cargo	
A7-BFJ	Boeing 777-FDZ	Qatar Airways Cargo	
A7-BFK	Boeing 777-FDZ	Qatar Airways Cargo	
A7-BFL	Boeing 777-FDZ	Qatar Airways Cargo	
A7-BFM	Boeing 777-FDZ	Qatar Airways Cargo	
A7-BFN	Boeing 777-FDZ	Qatar Airways Cargo	
A7-BFO	Boeing 777-FDZ	Qatar Airways Cargo	
A7-BFP	Boeing 777-200F	Qatar Airways Cargo	
A7-BFQ	Boeing 777-200F	Qatar Airways Cargo	
A7-BFR	Boeing 777-200F	Qatar Airways Cargo	
A7-BFS	Boeing 777-200F	Qatar Airways Cargo	
A7-BFT	Boeing 777-200F	Qatar Airways Cargo	
A7-BFU	Boeing 777-200F	Qatar Airways Cargo	
A7-BFV	Boeing 777-200F	Qatar Airways Cargo	
A7-BFW	Boeing 777-200F	Qatar Airways Cargo	
A7-BFX	Boeing 777-200F	Qatar Airways Cargo	
A7-BFY	Boeing 777-200F	Qatar Airways Cargo	
A7-BFZ	Boeing 777-200F	Qatar Airways Cargo	
A7-BHA	Boeing 787-9	Qatar Airways	
A7-BHB	Boeing 787-9	Qatar Airways	
A7-BHC	Boeing 787-9	Qatar Airways	
A7-BHD	Boeing 787-9	Qatar Airways	
A7-BHE	Boeing 787-9	Qatar Airways	
A7-BHF	Boeing 787-9	Qatar Airways	
A7-BHG	Boeing 787-9	Qatar Airways	
A7-BHH	Boeing 787-9	Qatar Airways	
A7-BHI	Boeing 787-9	Qatar Airways	
A7-BHJ	Boeing 787-9	Qatar Airways	
A7-BHK	Boeing 787-9	Qatar Airways	
A7-BHL	Boeing 787-9	Qatar Airways	
A7-BHM	Boeing 787-9	Qatar Airways	
A7-BHN	Boeing 787-9	Qatar Airways	
A7-BHO	Boeing 787-9	Qatar Airways	
A7-BHP	Boeing 787-9	Qatar Airways	
A7-BHQ	Boeing 787-9	Qatar Airways	
A7-BHR	Boeing 787-9	Qatar Airways	
A7-BHS	Boeing 787-9	Qatar Airways	
A7-BHT	Boeing 787-9	Qatar Airways	
A7-BHU	Boeing 787-9	Qatar Airways	
A7-BHV	Boeing 787-9	Qatar Airways	
A7-BHW	Boeing 787-9	Qatar Airways	
A7-BHX	Boeing 787-9	Qatar Airways	
A7-BHY	Boeing 787-9	Qatar Airways	

Notes	Reg	Type	Owner or Operator
	A7-BHZ	Boeing 787-9	Qatar Airways
	A7-BTA	Boeing 777-200F	Qatar Airways Cargo
	A7-BTB	Boeing 777-200F	Qatar Airways Cargo
	A7-BTC	Boeing 777-200F	Qatar Airways Cargo
	A7-BUA	Boeing 787-8	Qatar Airways
	A7-BUB	Boeing 787-8	Qatar Airways

A9C (Bahrain)

Notes	Reg	Type	Owner or Operator
	A9C-FA	Boeing 787-9	Gulf Air
	A9C-FB	Boeing 787-9	Gulf Air
	A9C-FC	Boeing 787-9	Gulf Air
	A9C-FD	Boeing 787-9	Gulf Air
	A9C-FE	Boeing 787-9	Gulf Air
	A9C-FF	Boeing 787-9	Gulf Air
	A9C-FG	Boeing 787-9	Gulf Air
	A9C-FH	Boeing 787-9	Gulf Air
	A9C-FI	Boeing 787-9	Gulf Air
	A9C-FJ	Boeing 787-9	Gulf Air

AP (Pakistan)

Notes	Reg	Type	Owner or Operator
	AP-BGJ	Boeing 777-240ER	Pakistan International Airlines
	AP-BGK	Boeing 777-240ER	Pakistan International Airlines
	AP-BHV	Boeing 777-340ER	Pakistan International Airlines
	AP-BHW	Boeing 777-340ER	Pakistan International Airlines
	AP-BHX	Boeing 777-240ER	Pakistan International Airlines
	AP-BID	Boeing 777-340ER	Pakistan International Airlines
	AP-BMG	Boeing 777-2Q8ER	Pakistan International Airlines
	AP-BMH	Boeing 777-2Q8ER	Pakistan International Airlines
	AP-BMS	Boeing 777-3Q8ER	Pakistan International Airlines

B (China/Taiwan/Hong Kong)

Notes	Reg	Type	Owner or Operator
	B-HNR	Boeing 777-367ER	Cathay Pacific Airways
	B-KPA	Boeing 777-367ER	Cathay Pacific Airways
	B-KPD	Boeing 777-367ER	Cathay Pacific Airways
	B-KPE	Boeing 777-367ER	Cathay Pacific Airways
	B-KPF	Boeing 777-367ER	Cathay Pacific Airways
	B-KPI	Boeing 777-367ER	Cathay Pacific Airways
	B-KPO	Boeing 777-367ER	Cathay Pacific Airways
	B-KPQ	Boeing 777-367ER	Cathay Pacific Airways
	B-KPR	Boeing 777-367ER	Cathay Pacific Airways
	B-KPU	Boeing 777-367ER	Cathay Pacific Airways
	B-KPV	Boeing 777-367ER	Cathay Pacific Airways
	B-KPW	Boeing 777-367ER	Cathay Pacific Airways
	B-KPX	Boeing 777-367ER	Cathay Pacific Airways
	B-KPY	Boeing 777-367ER	Cathay Pacific Airways
	B-KPZ	Boeing 777-367ER	Cathay Pacific Airways
	B-KQC	Boeing 777-367ER	Cathay Pacific Airways
	B-KQF	Boeing 777-367ER	Cathay Pacific Airways
	B-KQH	Boeing 777-367ER	Cathay Pacific Airways
	B-KQI	Boeing 777-367ER	Cathay Pacific Airways
	B-KQJ	Boeing 777-367ER	Cathay Pacific Airways
	B-KQL	Boeing 777-367ER	Cathay Pacific Airways
	B-KQM	Boeing 777-367ER	Cathay Pacific Airways
	B-KQN	Boeing 777-367ER	Cathay Pacific Airways
	B-KQO	Boeing 777-367ER	Cathay Pacific Airways
	B-KQP	Boeing 777-367ER	Cathay Pacific Airways
	B-KQQ	Boeing 777-367ER	Cathay Pacific Airways
	B-KQR	Boeing 777-367ER	Cathay Pacific Airways
	B-KQS	Boeing 777-367ER	Cathay Pacific Airways
	B-KQT	Boeing 777-367ER	Cathay Pacific Airways
	B-KQU	Boeing 777-367ER	Cathay Pacific Airways
	B-KQV	Boeing 777-367ER	Cathay Pacific Airways
	B-KQW	Boeing 777-367ER	Cathay Pacific Airways
	B-KQX	Boeing 777-367ER	Cathay Pacific Airways
	B-KQY	Boeing 777-367ER	Cathay Pacific Airways
	B-KQZ	Boeing 777-367ER	Cathay Pacific Airways
	B-LIA	Boeing 747-467ERF	Cathay Pacific Airways

Reg	Type	Owner or Operator	Notes
B-LIB	Boeing 747-467ERF	Cathay Pacific Airways	
B-LIC	Boeing 747-467ERF	Cathay Pacific Airways	
B-LID	Boeing 747-467ERF	Cathay Pacific Airways	
B-LIE	Boeing 747-467ERF	Cathay Pacific Airways	
B-LIF	Boeing 747-467ERF	Cathay Pacific Airways	
B-LJA	Boeing 747-867F	Cathay Pacific Airways	
B-LJB	Boeing 747-867F	Cathay Pacific Airways	
B-LJC	Boeing 747-867F	Cathay Pacific Airways	
B-LJD	Boeing 747-867F	Cathay Pacific Airways	
B-LJE	Boeing 747-867F	Cathay Pacific Airways	
B-LJF	Boeing 747-867F	Cathay Pacific Airways	
B-LJG	Boeing 747-867F	Cathay Pacific Airways	
B-LJH	Boeing 747-867F	Cathay Pacific Airways	
B-LJI	Boeing 747-867F	Cathay Pacific Airways	
B-LJJ	Boeing 747-867F	Cathay Pacific Airways	
B-LJK	Boeing 747-867F	Cathay Pacific Airways	
B-LJL	Boeing 747-867F	Cathay Pacific Airways	
B-LJM	Boeing 747-867F	Cathay Pacific Airways	
B-LJN	Boeing 747-867F	Cathay Pacific Airways	
B-LMA	Airbus A.330-243(P2F)	Hong Kong Air Cargo	
B-LNV	Airbus A.330-243F	Hong Kong Air Cargo	
B-LNW	Airbus A.330-243F	Hong Kong Air Cargo	
B-LNX	Airbus A.330-243F	Hong Kong Air Cargo	
B-LNY	Airbus A.330-243F	Hong Kong Air Cargo	
B-LNZ	Airbus A.330-243F	Hong Kong Air Cargo	
B-LQA	Airbus A.350-941	Cathay Pacific Airways	
B-LQB	Airbus A.350-941	Cathay Pacific Airways	
B-LQC	Airbus A.350-941	Cathay Pacific Airways	
B-LQD	Airbus A.350-941	Cathay Pacific Airways	
B-LQE	Airbus A.350-941	Cathay Pacific Airways	
B-LQF	Airbus A.350-941	Cathay Pacific Airways	
B-LQG	Airbus A.350-941	Cathay Pacific Airways	
B-LQH	Airbus A.350-941	Cathay Pacific Airways	
B-LRA	Airbus A.350-941	Cathay Pacific Airways	
B-LRB	Airbus A.350-941	Cathay Pacific Airways	
B-LRC	Airbus A.350-941	Cathay Pacific Airways	
B-LRD	Airbus A.350-941	Cathay Pacific Airways	
B-LRE	Airbus A.350-941	Cathay Pacific Airways	
B-LRF	Airbus A.350-941	Cathay Pacific Airways	
B-LRG	Airbus A.350-941	Cathay Pacific Airways	
B-LRI	Airbus A.350-941	Cathay Pacific Airways	
B-LRJ	Airbus A.350-941	Cathay Pacific Airways	
B-LRK	Airbus A.350-941	Cathay Pacific Airways	
B-LRL	Airbus A.350-941	Cathay Pacific Airways	
B-LRM	Airbus A.350-941	Cathay Pacific Airways	
B-LRN	Airbus A.350-941	Cathay Pacific Airways	
B-LRO	Airbus A.350-941	Cathay Pacific Airways	
B-LRP	Airbus A.350-941	Cathay Pacific Airways	
B-LRQ	Airbus A.350-941	Cathay Pacific Airways	
B-LRR	Airbus A.350-941	Cathay Pacific Airways	
B-LRS	Airbus A.350-941	Cathay Pacific Airways	
B-LRT	Airbus A.350-941	Cathay Pacific Airways	
B-LRU	Airbus A.350-941	Cathay Pacific Airways	
B-LRV	Airbus A.350-941	Cathay Pacific Airways	
B-LRX	Airbus A.350-941	Cathay Pacific Airways	
B-LXA	Airbus A.350-1041	Cathay Pacific Airways	
B-LXB	Airbus A.350-1041	Cathay Pacific Airways	
B-LXC	Airbus A.350-1041	Cathay Pacific Airways	
B-LXD	Airbus A.350-1041	Cathay Pacific Airways	
B-LXE	Airbus A.350-1041	Cathay Pacific Airways	
B-LXF	Airbus A.350-1041	Cathay Pacific Airways	
B-LXG	Airbus A.350-1041	Cathay Pacific Airways	
B-LXH	Airbus A.350-1041	Cathay Pacific Airways	
B-LXI	Airbus A.350-1041	Cathay Pacific Airways	
B-LXJ	Airbus A.350-1041	Cathay Pacific Airways	
B-LXK	Airbus A.350-1041	Cathay Pacific Airways	
B-LXL	Airbus A.350-1041	Cathay Pacific Airways	
B-LXM	Airbus A.350-1041	Cathay Pacific Airways	
B-LXN	Airbus A.350-1041	Cathay Pacific Airways	
B-LXO	Airbus A.350-1041	Cathay Pacific Airways	
B-LXP	Airbus A.350-1041	Cathay Pacific Airways	

Notes	Reg	Type	Owner or Operator
	B-LXQ	Airbus A.350-1041	Cathay Pacific Airways
	B-LXR	Airbus A.350-1041	Cathay Pacific Airways
	B-20AA	Boeing 787-9	China Southern Airlines
	B-20AL	Boeing 787-9	Hainan Airlines
	B-20C6	Boeing 787-9	China Southern Airlines
	B-20CJ	Boeing 787-9	China Southern Airlines
	B-20D1	Boeing 787-9	Juneyao Airlines
	B-20D7	Boeing 787-9	China Southern Airlines
	B-20DT	Boeing 787-9	Juneyao Airlines
	B-20E8	Boeing 787-9	China Southern Airlines
	B-20EC	Boeing 787-9	Juneyao Airlines
	B-20EH	Boeing 787-9	China Southern Airlines
	B-20EL	Boeing 787-9	China Southern Airlines
	B-20EM	Boeing 777-F	China Southern Airlines Cargo
	B-20EN	Boeing 777-F	China Southern Airlines Cargo
	B-20EP	Boeing 787-9	China Southern Airlines
	B-20EQ	Boeing 787-9	Juneyao Airlines
	B-20EW	Boeing 787-9	China Southern Airlines
	B-30A9	Airbus A.350-941	China Southern Airlines
	B-30AL	Airbus A.350-941	China Southern Airlines
	B-30C0	Airbus A.350-941	China Southern Airlines
	B-30CE	Airbus A.350-941	China Southern Airlines
	B-30CW	Airbus A.350-941	China Eastern Airlines
	B-30EA	Airbus A.350-941	China Southern Airlines
	B-30F0	Airbus A.350-941	China Southern Airlines
	B-30F9	Airbus A.350-941	China Southern Airlines
	B-30FM	Airbus A.350-941	China Eastern Airlines
	B-32A8	Airbus A.350-941	China Eastern Airlines
	B-32AL	Airbus A.350-941	Air China
	B-32AS	Airbus A.350-941	Air China
	B-32AV	Airbus A.350-941	China Southern Airlines
	B-32CA	Airbus A.350-941	Air China
	B-32CE	Airbus A.350-941	Air China
	B-32CQ	Airbus A.350-941	China Southern Airlines
	B-32CR	Airbus A.350-941	China Southern Airlines
	B-32CZ	Airbus A.350-941	China Eastern Airlines
	B-32D0	Airbus A.350-941	China Eastern Airlines
	B-32D3	Airbus A.350-941	Air China
	B-32DJ	Airbus A.350-941	China Eastern Airlines
	B-32DL	Airbus A.350-941	Air China
	B-32DM	Airbus A.350-941	Air China
	B-32DN	Airbus A.350-941	Air China
	B-32DW	Airbus A.350-941	China Eastern Airlines
	B-32ED	Airbus A.350-941	China Southern Airlines
	B-32EE	Airbus A.350-941	China Southern Airlines
	B-32EW	Airbus A.350-941	China Southern Airlines
	B-32EZ	Airbus A.350-941	Air China
	B-32F0	Airbus A.350-941	Air China
	B-32F1	Airbus A.350-941	Air China
	B-32FP	Airbus A.350-941	China Eastern Airlines
	B-32FQ	Airbus A.350-941	China Eastern Airlines
	B-32FR	Airbus A.350-941	China Southern Airlines
	B-32GY	Airbus A.330-243P2F	Jiangxi Cargo Airlines
	B-32MG	Airbus A.330-243P2F	Jiangxi Cargo Airlines
	B-206K	Boeing 787-9	China Eastern Airlines
	B-207J	Boeing 787-9	Hainan Airlines
	B-207N	Boeing 787-9	Juneyao Airlines
	B-207U	Boeing 787-9	Hainan Airlines
	B-207V	Boeing 787-9	Hainan Airlines
	B-208A	Boeing 787-9	Juneyao Airlines
	B-208P	Boeing 787-9	China Eastern Airlines
	B-208S	Boeing 787-9	Hainan Airlines
	B-208T	Boeing 787-9	Hainan Airlines
	B-209D	Boeing 787-9	China Southern Airlines
	B-209E	Boeing 787-9	China Southern Airlines
	B-209N	Boeing 787-9	China Eastern Airlines
	B-209R	Boeing 787-9	Juneyao Airlines
	B-209X	Boeing 787-9	China Southern Airlines
	B-220D	Boeing 787-9	China Eastern Airlines
	B-220E	Boeing 777-F	China Cargo Airlines
	B-220F	Boeing 777-F	China Cargo Airlines

Reg	Type	Owner or Operator	Notes
B-221S	Boeing 777-F	China Cargo Airlines	
B-221W	Boeing 777-F	China Cargo Airlines	
B-222H	Boeing 777-F	China Cargo Airlines	
B-222J	Boeing 777-F	China Cargo Airlines	
B-222K	Boeing 777-F	China Cargo Airlines	
B-222N	Boeing 777-F	China Cargo Airlines	
B-222S	Boeing 777-F	Air China Cargo	
B-222V	Boeing 777-F	China Cargo Airlines	
B-222W	Boeing 777-F	China Southern Airlines Cargo	
B-222Z	Boeing 777-F	China Cargo Airlines	
B-223A	Boeing 777-F	China Cargo Airlines	
B-223F	Boeing 777-F	China Cargo Airlines	
B-223G	Boeing 777-F	China Southern Airlines Cargo	
B-223N	Boeing 777-F	China Southern Airlines Cargo	
B-223S	Boeing 777-F	Air China Cargo	
B-223T	Boeing 777-F	Air China Cargo	
B-225A	Boeing 777-F	Air China Cargo	
B-225C	Boeing 777-F	Air China Cargo	
B-226C	Boeing 777-F	China Southern Airlines Cargo	
B-226D	Boeing 777-F	China Southern Airlines Cargo	
B-226M	Boeing 787-9	Juneyao Airlines	
B-226N	Boeing 787-9	Juneyao Airlines	
B-226Q	Boeing 787-9	China Eastern Airlines	
B-226V	Boeing 777-F	China Cargo Airlines	
B-227G	Boeing 777-F	China Cargo Airlines	
B-227H	Boeing 777-F	Central Airlines	
B-227J	Boeing 787-9	China Eastern Airlines	
B-227K	Boeing 777-F	China Cargo Airlines	
B-227L	Boeing 787-9	China Southern Airlines	
B-227M	Boeing 777-F	China Cargo Airlines	
B-227T	Boeing 787-9	China Eastern Airlines	
B-228C	Boeing 777-F	China Cargo Airlines	
B-302E	Airbus A.330-343	Shenzhen Airlines	
B-303C	Airbus A.330-343	Hainan Airlines	
B-303N	Airbus A.330-343	Shenzhen Airlines	
B-303Z	Airbus A.330-343	Hainan Airlines	
B-304K	Airbus A.330-343	Hainan Airlines	
B-304L	Airbus A.330-343	Hainan Airlines	
B-304N	Airbus A.350-941	China Eastern Airlines	
B-305R	Airbus A.330-343	Capital Airlines	
B-305X	Airbus A.350-941	China Eastern Airlines	
B-306Y	Airbus A.350-941	China Eastern Airlines	
B-307A	Airbus A.350-941	Air China	
B-307C	Airbus A.350-941	Air China	
B-307Y	Airbus A.350-941	China Eastern Airlines	
B-308C	Airbus A.350-941	Air China	
B-308E	Airbus A.350-941	China Eastern Airlines	
B-308M	Airbus A.350-941	Air China	
B-308T	Airbus A.350-941	China Southern Airlines	
B-309T	Airbus A.330-343	Capital Airlines	
B-309W	Airbus A.350-941	China Southern Airlines	
B-320S	Airbus A.350-941	China Southern Airlines	
B-321J	Airbus A.350-941	China Eastern Airlines	
B-321M	Airbus A.350-941	Air China	
B-321N	Airbus A.350-941	Air China	
B-322H	Airbus A.350-941	Air China	
B-322Y	Airbus A.350-941	Air China	
B-322Z	Airbus A.350-941	Air China	
B-323H	Airbus A.350-941	China Eastern Airlines	
B-324R	Airbus A.350-941	China Southern Airlines	
B-324S	Airbus A.350-941	China Southern Airlines	
B-324W	Airbus A.350-941	China Eastern Airlines	
B-324X	Airbus A.350-941	China Eastern Airlines	
B-326Y	Airbus A.350-941	Air China	
B-327V	Airbus A.350-941	Air China	
B-328Q	Airbus A.350-941	Air China	
B-329E	Airbus A.350-941	China Eastern Airlines	
B-329K	Airbus A.350-941	Air China	
B-329S	Airbus A.350-941	China Southern Airlines	
B-1017	Airbus A.330-343	Shenzhen Airlines	
B-1020	Airbus A.330-343	Hainan Airlines	

Notes	Reg	Type	Owner or Operator
	B-1021	Airbus A.330-343	Hainan Airlines
	B-1022	Airbus A.330-343	Hainan Airlines
	B-1036	Airbus A.330-343	Shenzhen Airlines
	B-1042	Airbus A.330-343	Capital Airlines
	B-1043	Airbus A.330-243	Capital Airlines
	B-1048	Airbus A.330-343	Hainan Airlines
	B-1072	Airbus A.330-343	Shenzhen Airlines
	B-1080	Airbus A.350-941	Air China
	B-1081	Airbus A.350-941	Air China
	B-1082	Airbus A.350-941	Air China
	B-1083	Airbus A.350-941	Air China
	B-1085	Airbus A.350-941	Air China
	B-1086	Airbus A.350-941	Air China
	B-1096	Airbus A.330-343	Hainan Airlines
	B-1097	Airbus A.330-343	Hainan Airlines
	B-1098	Airbus A.330-343	Hainan Airlines
	B-1115	Boeing 787-9	Juneyao Airlines
	B-1119	Boeing 787-9	Hainan Airlines
	B-1128	Boeing 787-9	China Southern Airlines
	B-1132	Boeing 787-9	Hainan Airlines
	B-1133	Boeing 787-9	Hainan Airlines
	B-1135	Boeing 787-9	Hainan Airlines
	B-1138	Boeing 787-9	Hainan Airlines
	B-1167	Boeing 787-9	China Southern Airlines
	B-1168	Boeing 787-9	China Southern Airlines
	B-1169	Boeing 787-9	China Southern Airlines
	B-1242	Boeing 787-9	China Southern Airlines
	B-1243	Boeing 787-9	China Southern Airlines
	B-1266	Boeing 777-39LER	Air China
	B-1282	Boeing 777-39LER	Air China
	B-1293	Boeing 787-9	China Southern Airlines
	B-1297	Boeing 787-9	China Southern Airlines
	B-1341	Boeing 787-9	Hainan Airlines
	B-1342	Boeing 787-9	Hainan Airlines
	B-1343	Boeing 787-9	Hainan Airlines
	B-1345	Boeing 787-9	Hainan Airlines
	B-1428	Boeing 777-39LER	Air China
	B-1429	Boeing 777-39LER	Air China
	B-1430	Boeing 777-39LER	Air China
	B-1499	Boeing 787-9	Hainan Airlines
	B-1539	Boeing 787-9	Hainan Airlines
	B-1540	Boeing 787-9	Hainan Airlines
	B-1543	Boeing 787-9	Hainan Airlines
	B-1546	Boeing 787-9	Hainan Airlines
	B-2001	Boeing 777-39PER	China Eastern Airlines
	B-2002	Boeing 777-39PER	China Eastern Airlines
	B-2003	Boeing 777-39PER	China Eastern Airlines
	B-2005	Boeing 777-39PER	China Eastern Airlines
	B-2006	Boeing 777-39LER	Air China
	B-2010	Boeing 777-F1B	China Southern Airlines Cargo
	B-2020	Boeing 777-39PER	China Eastern Airlines
	B-2021	Boeing 777-39PER	China Eastern Airlines
	B-2022	Boeing 777-39PER	China Eastern Airlines
	B-2023	Boeing 777-39PER	China Eastern Airlines
	B-2025	Boeing 777-39PER	China Eastern Airlines
	B-2026	Boeing 777-F1B	China Southern Airlines Cargo
	B-2027	Boeing 777-F1B	China Southern Airlines Cargo
	B-2028	Boeing 777-F1B	China Southern Airlines Cargo
	B-2031	Boeing 777-39LER	Air China
	B-2032	Boeing 777-39LER	Air China
	B-2033	Boeing 777-39LER	Air China
	B-2035	Boeing 777-39LER	Air China
	B-2036	Boeing 777-39LER	Air China
	B-2037	Boeing 777-39LER	Air China
	B-2038	Boeing 777-39LER	Air China
	B-2039	Boeing 777-39LER	Air China
	B-2040	Boeing 777-39LER	Air China
	B-2041	Boeing 777-F1B	China Southern Airlines Cargo
	B-2042	Boeing 777-F1B	China Southern Airlines Cargo
	B-2043	Boeing 777-39LER	Air China
	B-2045	Boeing 777-39LER	Air China

Reg	Type	Owner or Operator	Notes
B-2046	Boeing 777-39LER	Air China	
B-2047	Boeing 777-39LER	Air China	
B-2071	Boeing 777-F1B	China Southern Airlines Cargo	
B-2072	Boeing 777-F1B	China Southern Airlines Cargo	
B-2073	Boeing 777-F1B	China Southern Airlines Cargo	
B-2075	Boeing 777-F1B	China Southern Airlines Cargo	
B-2076	Boeing 777-F	China Cargo Airlines	
B-2077	Boeing 777-F	China Cargo Airlines	
B-2079	Boeing 777-F6N	YunExpress	
B-2080	Boeing 777-F1B	China Southern Airlines Cargo	
B-2081	Boeing 777-F1B	China Southern Airlines Cargo	
B-2082	Boeing 777-F6N	YunExpress	
B-2085	Boeing 777-39LER	Air China	
B-2086	Boeing 777-39LER	Air China	
B-2087	Boeing 777-39LER	Air China	
B-2088	Boeing 777-39LER	Air China	
B-2089	Boeing 777-39LER	Air China	
B-2090	Boeing 777-39LER	Air China	
B-2091	Boeing 777-F	Air China Cargo	
B-2092	Boeing 777-F	Air China Cargo	
B-2093	Boeing 777-F	Air China Cargo	
B-2094	Boeing 777-F	Air China Cargo	
B-2095	Boeing 777-F	Air China Cargo	
B-2096	Boeing 777-F	Air China Cargo	
B-2097	Boeing 777-F	Air China Cargo	
B-2098	Boeing 777-F	Air China Cargo	
B-2725	Boeing 787-8	China Southern Airlines	
B-2726	Boeing 787-8	China Southern Airlines	
B-2727	Boeing 787-8	China Southern Airlines	
B-2732	Boeing 787-8	China Southern Airlines	
B-2733	Boeing 787-8	China Southern Airlines	
B-2735	Boeing 787-8	China Southern Airlines	
B-2736	Boeing 787-8	China Southern Airlines	
B-2737	Boeing 787-8	China Southern Airlines	
B-2787	Boeing 787-8	China Southern Airlines	
B-2788	Boeing 787-8	China Southern Airlines	
B-6070	Airbus A.330-243P2F	Air China Cargo	
B-6090	Airbus A.330-243P2F	Air China Cargo	
B-6091	Airbus A.330-243P2F	Air China Cargo	
B-6092	Airbus A.330-243P2F	Air China Cargo	
B-6093	Airbus A.330-243P2F	Air China Cargo	
B-6113	Airbus A.330-243P2F	Air China Cargo	
B-6115	Airbus A.330-243P2F	Air China Cargo	
B-6117	Airbus A.330-243P2F	Air China Cargo	
B-6060	Boeing 787-9	Hainan Airlines	
B-6998	Boeing 787-9	Hainan Airlines	
B-7302	Boeing 787-9	Hainan Airlines	
B-7343	Boeing 777-39PER	China Eastern Airlines	
B-7347	Boeing 777-39PER	China Eastern Airlines	
B-7349	Boeing 777-39PER	China Eastern Airlines	
B-7365	Boeing 777-39PER	China Eastern Airlines	
B-7367	Boeing 777-39PER	China Eastern Airlines	
B-7368	Boeing 777-39PER	China Eastern Airlines	
B-7369	Boeing 777-39PER	China Eastern Airlines	
B-7667	Boeing 787-9	Hainan Airlines	
B-7835	Boeing 787-9	Hainan Airlines	
B-7837	Boeing 787-9	Hainan Airlines	
B-7839	Boeing 787-9	Hainan Airlines	
B-7868	Boeing 777-39PER	China Eastern Airlines	
B-7869	Boeing 777-39LER	Air China	
B-7880	Boeing 787-9	Hainan Airlines	
B-7881	Boeing 777-39PER	China Eastern Airlines	
B-7882	Boeing 777-39PER	China Eastern Airlines	
B-7883	Boeing 777-39PER	China Eastern Airlines	
B-7952	Boeing 777-39LER	Air China	
B-7973	Boeing 777-39LER	Air China	
B-8019	Airbus A.330-243	Capital Airlines	
B-8221	Airbus A.330-243	Capital Airlines	
B-8596	Airbus A.330-243	Tianjin Airlines	
B-8659	Airbus A.330-243	Tianjin Airlines	
B-8678	Airbus A.330-343	Capital Airlines	

Notes	Reg	Type	Owner or Operator
	B-8679	Airbus A.330-343	Capital Airlines
	B-8776	Airbus A.330-243	Tianjin Airlines
	B-8865	Airbus A.330-343	Shenzhen Airlines
	B-8959	Airbus A.330-243	Tianjin Airlines
	B-8981	Airbus A.330-243	Capital Airlines
	B-8982	Airbus A.330-243	Capital Airlines
	B-16705	Boeing 777-35EER	EVA Airways
	B-16706	Boeing 777-35EER	EVA Airways
	B-16707	Boeing 777-35EER	EVA Airways
	B-16708	Boeing 777-35EER	EVA Airways
	B-16709	Boeing 777-35EER	EVA Airways
	B-16710	Boeing 777-35EER	EVA Airways
	B-16711	Boeing 777-35EER	EVA Airways
	B-16712	Boeing 777-35EER	EVA Airways
	B-16713	Boeing 777-35EER	EVA Airways
	B-16715	Boeing 777-35EER	EVA Airways
	B-16716	Boeing 777-35EER	EVA Airways
	B-16717	Boeing 777-35EER	EVA Airways
	B-16718	Boeing 777-35EER	EVA Airways
	B-16719	Boeing 777-35EER	EVA Airways
	B-16720	Boeing 777-35EER	EVA Airways
	B-16721	Boeing 777-35EER	EVA Airways
	B-16722	Boeing 777-36NER	EVA Airways
	B-16723	Boeing 777-36NER	EVA Airways
	B-16725	Boeing 777-35EER	EVA Airways
	B-16726	Boeing 777-35EER	EVA Airways
	B-16727	Boeing 777-35EER	EVA Airways
	B-16728	Boeing 777-36NER	EVA Airways
	B-16729	Boeing 777-36NER	EVA Airways
	B-16730	Boeing 777-36NER	EVA Airways
	B-16731	Boeing 777-36NER	EVA Airways
	B-16732	Boeing 777-36NER	EVA Airways
	B-16733	Boeing 777-36NER	EVA Airways
	B-16735	Boeing 777-36NER	EVA Airways
	B-16736	Boeing 777-36NER	EVA Airways
	B-16737	Boeing 777-36NER	EVA Airways
	B-16738	Boeing 777-36NER	EVA Airways
	B-16739	Boeing 777-36NER	EVA Airways
	B-16740	Boeing 777-36NER	EVA Airways
	B-18901	Airbus A.350-941	China Airlines
	B-18902	Airbus A.350-941	China Airlines
	B-18903	Airbus A.350-941	China Airlines
	B-18905	Airbus A.350-941	China Airlines
	B-18906	Airbus A.350-941	China Airlines
	B-18907	Airbus A.350-941	China Airlines
	B-18908	Airbus A.350-941	China Airlines
	B-18909	Airbus A.350-941	China Airlines
	B-18910	Airbus A.350-941	China Airlines
	B-18912	Airbus A.350-941	China Airlines
	B-18915	Airbus A.350-941	China Airlines
	B-18916	Airbus A.350-941	China Airlines
	B-18917	Airbus A.350-941	China Airlines
	B-18918	Airbus A.350-941	China Airlines
	B-18919	Airbus A.350-941	China Airlines

C (Canada)

Notes	Reg	Type	Owner or Operator
	C-FAJA	Boeing 787-9	Westjet
	C-FBWS	Boeing 737-MAX8	Westjet
	C-FCAE	Boeing 767-375ERBDSF	Cargojet Airways
	C-FCCJ	Boeing 767-323ERBDSF	Cargojet Airways
	C-FCPD	Boeing 767-316ER	Cargojet Airways
	C-FCTK	Boeing 737-MAX8	Westjet
	C-FDIJ	Boeing 767-39HERBDSF	Cargojet Airways
	C-FEGI	Boeing 787-9 (862)	Air Canada
	C-FEWJ	Boeing 737-MAX8	Westjet
	C-FGDT	Boeing 787-9 (835)	Air Canada
	C-FGDX	Boeing 787-9 (836)	Air Canada
	C-FGDZ	Boeing 787-9 (837)	Air Canada
	C-FGEI	Boeing 787-9 (838)	Air Canada
	C-FGEO	Boeing 787-9 (839)	Air Canada

Reg	Type	Owner or Operator	Notes
C-FGFZ	Boeing 787-9 (840)	Air Canada	
C-FGHZ	Boeing 787-9 (842)	Air Canada	
C-FGSJ	Boeing 767-39HERBCF	Cargojet Airways	
C-FHCM	Boeing 737-MAX8	Westjet	
C-FIBA	Boeing 737-MAX8	Westjet	
C-FITL	Boeing 777-333ER (731)	Air Canada	
C-FITU	Boeing 777-333ER (732)	Air Canada	
C-FITW	Boeing 777-3Q8ER (733)	Air Canada	
C-FIUA	Boeing 777-233LR (701)	Air Canada	
C-FIUF	Boeing 777-233LR (702)	Air Canada	
C-FIUJ	Boeing 777-233LR (703)	Air Canada	
C-FIUL	Boeing 777-333ER (734)	Air Canada	
C-FIUR	Boeing 777-333ER (735)	Air Canada	
C-FIUV	Boeing 777-333ER (736)	Air Canada	
C-FIUW	Boeing 777-333ER (737)	Air Canada	
C-FIVK	Boeing 777-233LR (704)	Air Canada	
C-FIVM	Boeing 777-333ER (738)	Air Canada	
C-FIVQ	Boeing 777-333ER (740)	Air Canada	
C-FIVR	Boeing 777-333ER (741)	Air Canada	
C-FIVS	Boeing 777-333ER (742)	Air Canada	
C-FIVW	Boeing 777-333ER (743)	Air Canada	
C-FIVX	Boeing 777-333ER (744)	Air Canada	
C-FJZS	Boeing 777-333ER (748)	Air Canada	
C-FKAU	Boeing 777-333ER (749)	Air Canada	
C-FKSV	Boeing 787-9 (843)	Air Canada	
C-FKWS	Boeing 737-MAX8	Westjet	
C-FMAJ	Boeing 767-332ERBDSF	Cargojet Airways	
C-FMIJ	Boeing 767-328ERBDSF	Cargojet Airways	
C-FNAX	Boeing 737-MAX8	Westjet	
C-FNND	Boeing 777-233LR (705)	Air Canada	
C-FNNH	Boeing 777-233LR (706)	Air Canada	
C-FNNQ	Boeing 777-333ER (745)	Air Canada	
C-FNNU	Boeing 777-333ER (746)	Air Canada	
C-FNNW	Boeing 777-333ER (747)	Air Canada	
C-FNOE	Boeing 787-9 (831)	Air Canada	
C-FNOG	Boeing 787-9 (832)	Air Canada	
C-FNOH	Boeing 787-9 (833)	Air Canada	
C-FNOI	Boeing 787-9 (834)	Air Canada	
C-FNPJ	Boeing 767-316ER	Cargojet Airways	
C-FNWD	Boeing 737-MAX8	Westjet	
C-FPCJ	Boeing 767-306ER	Cargojet Airways	
C-FPIJ	Boeing 767-33AERBDSF	Cargojet Airways	
C-FPQB	Boeing 787-9 (841)	Air Canada	
C-FQGG	Boeing 737-MAX8	Westjet	
C-FRAM	Boeing 777-333ER (739)	Air Canada	
C-FRAX	Boeing 737-MAX8	Westjet	
C-FRSA	Boeing 787-9 (844)	Air Canada	
C-FRSE	Boeing 787-9 (845)	Air Canada	
C-FRSI	Boeing 787-9 (846)	Air Canada	
C-FRSO	Boeing 787-9 (847)	Air Canada	
C-FRSR	Boeing 787-9 (848)	Air Canada	
C-FRTG	Boeing 787-9 (849)	Air Canada	
C-FRTU	Boeing 787-9 (850)	Air Canada	
C-FRTW	Boeing 787-9(851)	Air Canada	
C-FRYV	Boeing 737-MAX8	Westjet	
C-FSBV	Boeing 787-9 (852)	Air Canada	
C-FSCY	Boeing 737-MAX8 (502)	Air Canada	
C-FSDB	Boeing 737-MAX8 (503)	Air Canada	
C-FSDQ	Boeing 737-MAX8 (504)	Air Canada	
C-FSDW	Boeing 737-MAX8 (505)	Air Canada	
C-FSEQ	Boeing 737-MAX8 (506)	Air Canada	
C-FSES	Boeing 737-MAX8 (507)	Air Canada	
C-FSIL	Boeing 737-MAX8 (508)	Air Canada	
C-FSIP	Boeing 737-MAX8 (509)	Air Canada	
C-FSIQ	Boeing 737-MAX8 (510)	Air Canada	
C-FSJH	Boeing 737-MAX8 (511)	Air Canada	
C-FSJJ	Boeing 737-MAX8 (512)	Air Canada	
C-FSKZ	Boeing 737-MAX8 (513)	Air Canada	
C-FSLU	Boeing 737-MAX8 (514)	Air Canada	
C-FSNQ	Boeing 737-MAX8 (515)	Air Canada	
C-FSNU	Boeing 737-MAX8 (516)	Air Canada	

Notes	Reg	Type	Owner or Operator
	C-FSOC	Boeing 737-MAX8 (517)	Air Canada
	C-FSOI	Boeing 737-MAX8 (518)	Air Canada
	C-FTJV	Boeing 737-MAX8 (501)	Air Canada
	C-FVLQ	Boeing 787-9 (853)	Air Canada
	C-FVLU	Boeing 787-9 (854)	Air Canada
	C-FVLX	Boeing 787-9 (855)	Air Canada
	C-FVLZ	Boeing 787-9 (856)	Air Canada
	C-FVNB	Boeing 787-9 (857)	Air Canada
	C-FVND	Boeing 787-9 (858)	Air Canada
	C-FVNF	Boeing 787-9 (859)	Air Canada
	C-FXWJ	Boeing 737-MAX8	Westjet
	C-FXYK	Boeing 737-MAX8	Westjet
	C-FZWS	Boeing 737-MAX8	Westjet
	C-GAAJ	Boeing 767-323ERBDSF	Cargojet Airways
	C-GAJG	Boeing 767-323ERBDSF	Cargojet Airways
	C-GAMQ	Boeing 737-MAX8	Westjet
	C-GCAM	Boeing 737-MAX8	Westjet
	C-GCIJ	Boeing 767-306ERBDSF	Cargojet Airways
	C-GDDR	Boeing 737-MAX8	Westjet
	C-GEFA	Airbus A.330-343 (939)	Air Canada
	C-GEGC	Airbus A.330-343 (940)	Air Canada
	C-GEGI	Airbus A.330-343 (941)	Air Canada
	C-GEGP	Airbus A.330-343 (942)	Air Canada
	C-GEHF	Boeing 737-MAX8	Westjet
	C-GEWJ	Boeing 737-MAX8	Westjet
	C-GFAF	Airbus A.330-343 (931)	Air Canada
	C-GFAH	Airbus A.330-343 (932)	Air Canada
	C-GFAJ	Airbus A.330-343 (933)	Air Canada
	C-GFJD	Boeing 737-MAX8	Westjet
	C-GFUR	Airbus A.330-343 (934)	Air Canada
	C-GHKC	Airbus A.330-343 (943)	Air Canada
	C-GHKR	Airbus A.330-343 (935)	Air Canada
	C-GHKW	Airbus A.330-343 (936)	Air Canada
	C-GHKX	Airbus A.330-343 (937)	Air Canada
	C-GHLM	Airbus A.330-343 (938)	Air Canada
	C-GHPQ	Boeing 787-8 (801)	Air Canada
	C-GHPT	Boeing 787-8 (802)	Air Canada
	C-GHPU	Boeing 787-8 (803)	Air Canada
	C-GHPV	Boeing 787-8 (804)	Air Canada
	C-GHPX	Boeing 787-8 (805)	Air Canada
	C-GHPY	Boeing 787-8 (806)	Air Canada
	C-GHQQ	Boeing 787-8 (807)	Air Canada
	C-GHQY	Boeing 787-8 (808)	Air Canada
	C-GIWJ	Boeing 737-MAX8	Westjet
	C-GKKN	Boeing 787-9	Westjet
	C-GKUG	Airbus A.330-343 (944)	Air Canada
	C-GKUH	Airbus A.330-343 (945)	Air Canada
	C-GKWJ	Boeing 737-MAX8	Westjet
	C-GLWS	Boeing 737-MAX8	Westjet
	C-GMIY	Boeing 737-MAX8	Air Canada
	C-GMJI	Boeing 737-MAX8	Air Canada
	C-GMJV	Boeing 737-MAX8	Air Canada
	C-GMKS	Boeing 787-9	Westjet
	C-GMLS	Boeing 737-MAX8	Air Canada
	C-GOCJ	Boeing 767-316ERBDSF	Cargojet Airways
	C-GOFV	Airbus A.330-343 (946)	Air Canada
	C-GOFW	Airbus A.330-343 (947)	Air Canada
	C-GOIE	Airbus A.321-271NX	Air Transat
	C-GOIF	Airbus A.321-271NX	Air Transat
	C-GOIH	Airbus A.321-271NX	Air Transat
	C-GOIJ	Airbus A.321-271NX	Air Transat
	C-GOIK	Airbus A.321-271NX	Air Transat
	C-GOIM	Airbus A.321-271NX	Air Transat
	C-GOIO	Airbus A.321-271NX	Air Transat
	C-GOIP	Airbus A.321-271NX	Air Transat
	C-GOIR	Airbus A.321-271NX	Air Transat
	C-GOIS	Airbus A.321-271NX	Air Transat
	C-GOIW	Airbus A.321-271NX	Air Transat
	C-GOIX	Airbus A.321-271NX	Air Transat
	C-GOJC	Airbus A.321-271NX	Air Transat
	C-GOJQ	Airbus A.321-271NX	Air Transat

Reg	Type	Owner or Operator	Notes
C-GOKC	Airbus A.321-271NX	Air Transat	
C-GOKE	Airbus A.321-271NX	Air Transat	
C-GOKF	Airbus A.321-271NX	Air Transat	
C-GOKG	Airbus A.321-271NX	Air Transat	
C-GOKH	Airbus A.321-271NX	Air Transat	
C-GPAJ	Boeing 767-38AER(BDSF)	Cargojet Airways	
C-GPDJ	Boeing 767-3Q8ER(BDSF)	Cargojet Airways	
C-GPFT	Boeing 737-MAX8	Westjet	
C-GPTS	Airbus A.330-243	Air Transat	
C-GRAG	Boeing 737-MAX8	Westjet	
C-GRAX	Boeing 737-MAX8	Westjet	
C-GSWJ	Boeing 737-MAX8	Westjet	
C-GTSD	Airbus A.330-343	Air Transat	
C-GTSJ	Airbus A.330-243	Air Transat	
C-GTSR	Airbus A.330-243	Air Transat	
C-GTSW	Boeing 737-MAX8	Westjet	
C-GTSZ	Airbus A.330-243	Air Transat	
C-GUAJ	Boeing 767-35EERBCF	Cargojet Airways	
C-GUBA	Airbus A.330-243	Air Transat	
C-GUBC	Airbus A.330-243	Air Transat	
C-GUBD	Airbus A.330-243	Air Transat	
C-GUBF	Airbus A.330-243	Air Transat	
C-GUBH	Airbus A.330-243	Air Transat	
C-GUBL	Airbus A.330-243	Air Transat	
G-GUBO	Airbus A.330-343	Air Transat	
C-GUBT	Airbus A.330-243	Air Transat	
C-GUDH	Boeing 787-9	Westjet	
C-GUDO	Boeing 787-9	Westjet	
C-GUFR	Airbus A.330-243	Air Transat	
C-GUFU	Airbus A.330-243	Air Transat	
C-GUFZ	Airbus A.330-243	Air Transat	
C-GVIJ	Boeing 767-328ERBDSF	Cargojet Airways	
C-GURP	Boeing 787-9	Westjet	
C-GUWS	Boeing 737-MAX8	Westjet	
C-GWLK	Boeing 737-MAX8	Westjet	
C-GWUU	Boeing 787-9	Air Canada	
C-GXAJ	Boeing 767-323ERBDSF	Cargojet Airways	
C-GXAN	Airbus A.321-271NY XLR (302)	Air Canada	
C-GXAU	Airbus A.321-271NY XLR (303)	Air Canada	
C-GXAX	Boeing 737-MAX8	Westjet	
C-GXBK	Airbus A.321-271NY XLR (304)	Air Canada	
C-GXLR	Airbus A.321-271NY XLR (301)	Air Canada	
C-GXWJ	Boeing 737-MAX8	Westjet	
C-GYAJ	Boeing 767-35EERBCF	Cargojet Airways	
C-GYJW	Boeing 787-9 (861)	Air Canada	
C-GYRS	Boeing 787-9	Westjet	
C-GZSG	Boeing 737-MAX8	Westjet	

Note: Airline fleet number when carried on aircraft is shown in parentheses.

CN (Morocco)

Reg	Type	Owner or Operator	Notes
CN-MAX	Boeing 737-MAX8	Royal Air Maroc	
CN-MAY	Boeing 737-MAX8	Royal Air Maroc	
CN-NMH	Airbus A.320-214	Air Arabia Maroc	
CN-NMI	Airbus A.320-214	Air Arabia Maroc	
CN-NMJ	Airbus A.320-214	Air Arabia Maroc	
CN-NML	Airbus A.320-214	Air Arabia Maroc	
CN-NMN	Airbus A.320-214	Air Arabia Maroc	
CN-NMO	Airbus A.320-214	Air Arabia Maroc	
CN-NMP	Airbus A.320-214	Air Arabia Maroc	
CN-NMQ	Airbus A.320-214	Air Arabia Maroc	
CN-NMS	Airbus A.320-214	Air Arabia Maroc	
CN-NMT	Airbus A.320-214	Air Arabia Maroc	
CN-RAM	Boeing 787-9	Royal Air Maroc	
CN-RGB	Boeing 787-8	Royal Air Maroc	
CN-RGC	Boeing 787-8	Royal Air Maroc	
CN-RGE	Boeing 737-86N	Royal Air Maroc	
CN-RGF	Boeing 737-86N	Royal Air Maroc	
CN-RGG	Boeing 737-86N	Royal Air Maroc	
CN-RGH	Boeing 737-86N	Royal Air Maroc	

Notes	Reg	Type	Owner or Operator
	CN-RGI	Boeing 737-86N	Royal Air Maroc
	CN-RGJ	Boeing 737-8B6	Royal Air Maroc
	CN-RGK	Boeing 737-8B6	Royal Air Maroc
	CN-RGM	Boeing 737-8B6	Royal Air Maroc
	CN-RGN	Boeing 737-8B6	Royal Air Maroc
	CN-RGO	Embraer ERJ190-100AR	Royal Air Maroc
	CN-RGP	Embraer ERJ190-100AR	Royal Air Maroc
	CN-RGQ	Embraer ERJ190-100AR	Royal Air Maroc
	CN-RGR	Embraer ERJ190-100AR	Royal Air Maroc
	CN-RGS	Boeing 787-8	Royal Air Maroc
	CN-RGT	Boeing 787-8	Royal Air Maroc
	CN-RGU	Boeing 787-8	Royal Air Maroc
	CN-RGV	Boeing 737-85P	Royal Air Maroc
	CN-RGW	Boeing 737-8SH	Royal Air Maroc
	CN-RGX	Boeing 787-9	Royal Air Maroc
	CN-RGY	Boeing 787-9	Royal Air Maroc
	CN-RGZ	Boeing 787-9	Royal Air Maroc
	CN-RHA	Boeing 787-9	Royal Air Maroc
	CN-RHB	Boeing 787-9	Royal Air Maroc
	CN-RHC	Boeing 737-MAX8	Royal Air Maroc
	CN-RHD	Boeing 737-MAX8	Royal Air Maroc
	CN-RHE	Boeing 737-MAX8	Royal Air Maroc
	CN-RHF	Boeing 737-MAX8	Royal Air Maroc
	CN-RHG	Boeing 737-MAX8	Royal Air Maroc
	CN-RHH	Boeing 737-MAX8	Royal Air Maroc
	CN-RHI	Boeing 737-MAX8	Royal Air Maroc
	CN-RHJ	Boeing 737-MAX8	Royal Air Maroc
	CN-RHK	Boeing 737-MAX8	Royal Air Maroc
	CN-RHL	Boeing 737-MAX8	Royal Air Maroc
	CN-RHM	Boeing 737-MAX8	Royal Air Maroc
	CN-RNU	Boeing 737-8B6	Royal Air Maroc
	CN-RNZ	Boeing 737-8B6	Royal Air Maroc
	CN-ROA	Boeing 737-8B6	Royal Air Maroc
	CN-ROB	Boeing 737-8B6	Royal Air Maroc
	CN-ROC	Boeing 737-8B6	Royal Air Maroc
	CN-ROE	Boeing 737-8B6	Royal Air Maroc
	CN-ROH	Boeing 737-8B6	Royal Air Maroc
	CN-ROJ	Boeing 737-8B6	Royal Air Maroc
	CN-ROK	Boeing 737-8B6	Royal Air Maroc
	CN-ROL	Boeing 737-8B6	Royal Air Maroc
	CN-ROP	Boeing 737-8B6	Royal Air Maroc
	CN-ROR	Boeing 737-8B6	Royal Air Maroc
	CN-ROS	Boeing 737-8B6	Royal Air Maroc
	CN-ROT	Boeing 737-8B6	Royal Air Maroc
	CN-ROU	Boeing 737-8B6	Royal Air Maroc
	CN-ROY	Boeing 737-8B6	Royal Air Maroc
	CN-ROZ	Boeing 737-8B6	Royal Air Maroc

CS (Portugal)

Notes	Reg	Type	Owner or Operator
	CS-TAW	Embraer ERJ190-200LR	TAP Express
	CS-TAX	Embraer ERJ190-200LR	TAP Express
	CS-TAY	Embraer ERJ190-200LR	TAP Express
	CS-TJE	Airbus A.321-211	TAP Air Portugal
	CS-TJF	Airbus A.321-211	TAP Air Portugal
	CS-TJH	Airbus A.321-211	TAP Air Portugal
	CS-TJI	Airbus A.321-251N	TAP Air Portugal
	CS-TJJ	Airbus A.321-251N	TAP Air Oportugal
	CS-TJK	Airbus A.321-251N	TAP Air Portugal
	CS-TJL	Airbus A.321-251N	TAP Air Portugal
	CS-TJM	Airbus A.321-251N	TAP Air Portugal
	CS-TJN	Airbus A.321-251N	TAP Air Portugal
	CS-TJO	Airbus A.321-251N	TAP Air Portugal
	CS-TJP	Airbus A.321-251N	TAP Air Portugal
	CS-TJQ	Airbus A.321-251N	TAP Air Portugal
	CS-TJR	Airbus A.321-251N	TAP Air Portugal
	CS-TJS	Airbus A.321-251N	TAP Air Portugal
	CS-TJT	Airbus A.321-251N	TAP Air Portugal
	CS-TNJ	Airbus A.320-214	TAP Air Portugal
	CS-TNK	Airbus A.320-214	TAP Air Portugal
	CS-TNL	Airbus A.320-214	TAP Air Portugal

Reg	Type	Owner or Operator	Notes
CS-TNM	Airbus A.320-214	TAP Air Portugal	
CS-TNN	Airbus A.320-214	TAP Air Portugal	
CS-TNQ	Airbus A.320-214	TAP Air Portugal	
CS-TNR	Airbus A.320-214	TAP Air Portugal	
CS-TNS	Airbus A.320-214	TAP Air Portugal	
CS-TNT	Airbus A.320-214	TAP Air Portugal	
CS-TNU	Airbus A.320-214	TAP Air Portugal	
CS-TNV	Airbus A.320-214	TAP Air Portugal	
CS-TNW	Airbus A.320-214	TAP Air Portugal	
CS-TNX	Airbus A.320-214	TAP Air Portugal	
CS-TNY	Airbus A.320-214	TAP Air Portugal	
CS-TON	Airbus A.330-202	TAP Air Portugal	
CS-TOO	Airbus A.330-202	TAP Air Portugal	
CS-TOP	Airbus A.330-202	TAP Air Portugal	
CS-TPO	Embraer ERJ190-100LR	TAP Express	
CS-TPP	Embraer ERJ190-100LR	TAP Express	
CS-TPQ	Embraer ERJ190-100LR	TAP Express	
CS-TPR	Embraer ERJ190-100LR	TAP Express	
CS-TPS	Embraer ERJ190-100LR	TAP Express	
CS-TPT	Embraer ERJ190-100LR	TAP Express	
CS-TPU	Embraer ERJ190-100LR	TAP Express	
CS-TPV	Embraer ERJ190-100LR	TAP Express	
CS-TPW	Embraer ERJ190-100LR	TAP Express	
CS-TPX	Embraer ERJ190-100LR	TAP Express	
CS-TPY	Embraer ERJ190-100LR	TAP Express	
CS-TPZ	Embraer ERJ190-100LR	TAP Express	
CS-TTP	Airbus A.319-111	TAP Air Portugal	
CS-TTR	Airbus A.319-112	TAP Air Portugal	
CS-TTS	Airbus A.319-112	TAP Air Portugal	
CS-TTW	Embraer ERJ190-200IGW	TAP Express	
CS-TTX	Embraer ERJ190-200IGW	TAP Express	
CS-TTY	Embraer ERJ190-200IGW	TAP Express	
CS-TTZ	Embraer ERJ190-200IGW	TAP Express	
CS-TUA	Airbus A.330-941	TAP Air Portugal	
CS-TUB	Airbus A.330-941	TAP Air Portugal	
CS-TUC	Airbus A.330-941	TAP Air Portugal	
CS-TUD	Airbus A.330-941	TAP Air Portugal	
CS-TUE	Airbus A.330-941	TAP Air Portugal	
CS-TUF	Airbus A.330-941	TAP Air Portugal	
CS-TUG	Airbus A.330-941	TAP Air Portugal	
CS-TUH	Airbus A.330-941	TAP Air Portugal	
CS-TUI	Airbus A.330-941	TAP Air Portugal	
CS-TUJ	Airbus A.330-941	TAP Air Portugal	
CS-TUK	Airbus A.330-941	TAP Air Portugal	
CS-TUL	Airbus A.330-941	TAP Air Portugal	
CS-TUM	Airbus A.330-941	TAP Air Portugal	
CS-TUN	Airbus A.330-941	TAP Air Portugal	
CS-TUO	Airbus A.330-941	TAP Air Portugal	
CS-TUP	Airbus A.330-941	TAP Air Portugal	
CS-TUQ	Airbus A.330-941	TAP Air Portugal	
CS-TUR	Airbus A.330-941	TAP Air Portugal	
CS-TUS	Airbus A.330-941	TAP Air Portugal	
CS-TVA	Airbus A.320-251N	TAP Air Portugal	
CS-TVB	Airbus A.320-251N	TAP Air Portugal	
CS-TVC	Airbus A.320-251N	TAP Air Portugal	
CS-TVD	Airbus A.320-251N	TAP Air Portugal	
CS-TVE	Airbus A.320-251N	TAP Air Portugal	
CS-TVF	Airbus A.320-251N	TAP Air Portugal	
CS-TVG	Airbus A.320-251N	TAP Air Portugal	
CS-TVH	Airbus A.320-251N	TAP Air Portugal	
CS-TVI	Airbus A.320-251N	TAP Air Portugal	
CS-TVJ	Airbus A.320-251N	TAP Air Portugal	
CS-TVK	Airbus A.320-251N	TAP Air Portugal	
CS-TVL	Airbus A.320-251N	TAP Air Portugal	
CS-TVM	Airbus A.320-251N	TAP Air Portugal	
CS-TVN	Airbus A.320-251N	TAP Air Portugal	
CS-TVO	Airbus A.320-251N	TAP Air Portugal	
CS-TVP	Airbus A.320-251N	TAP Air Portugal	
CS-TVQ	Airbus A.320-251N	TAP Air Portugal	
CS-TXA	Airbus A.321-251NX	TAP Air Portugal	
CS-TXB	Airbus A.321-251NX	TAP Air Portugal	

Notes	Reg	Type	Owner or Operator
	CS-TXC	Airbus A.321-251NX	TAP Air Portugal
	CS-TXD	Airbus A.321-251NX	TAP Air Portugal
	CS-TXE	Airbus A.321-251NX	TAP Air Portugal
	CS-TXF	Airbus A.321-251NX	TAP Air Portugal
	CS-TXG	Airbus A.321-251NX	TAP Air Portugal
	CS-TXH	Airbus A.321-251NX	TAP Air Portugal
	CS-TXI	Airbus A.321-251NX	TAP Air Portugal
	CS-TXJ	Airbus A.321-251NX	TAP Air Portugal
	CS-TXK	Airbus A.321-251NX	TAP Air Portugal
	CS-TXL	Airbus A.321-251NX	TAP Air Portugal
	CS-TXM	Airbus A.321-251NX	TAP Air Portugal

D (Germany)

Notes	Reg	Type	Owner or Operator
	D-AALA	Boeing 777-FZN	AeroLogic
	D-AALB	Boeing 777-FZN	AeroLogic
	D-AALC	Boeing 777-FZN	AeroLogic
	D-AALD	Boeing 777-FZN	AeroLogic
	D-AALE	Boeing 777-FZN	AeroLogic
	D-AALF	Boeing 777-FZN	AeroLogic
	D-AALG	Boeing 777-FZN	AeroLogic
	D-AALH	Boeing 777-FZN	AeroLogic
	D-AALI	Boeing 777-FZN	AeroLogic
	D-AALJ	Boeing 777-FZN	AeroLogic
	D-AALK	Boeing 777-200F	AeroLogic
	D-AALL	Boeing 777-200F	AeroLogic
	D-AALM	Boeing 777-200F	AeroLogic
	D-AALN	Boeing 777-200F	AeroLogic
	D-AALO	Boeing 777-200F	AeroLogic
	D-AALP	Boeing 777-200F	AeroLogic
	D-AALQ	Boeing 777-200F	AeroLogic
	D-AALR	Boeing 777-200F	AeroLogic
	D-AALS	Boeing 777-200F	AeroLogic
	D-AALT	Boeing 777-200F	AeroLogic
	D-AALU	Boeing 777-200F	AeroLogic
	D-AALV	Boeing 777-200F	AeroLogic
	D-AALW	Boeing 777-200F	AeroLogic
	D-AALX	Boeing 777-200F	AeroLogic
	D-AALY	Boeing 777-200F	AeroLogic
	D-AALZ	Boeing 777-200F	AeroLogic
	D-AASG	DHC.8Q-402 Dash Eight	Avanti Air
	D-AASH	DHC.8Q-402 Dash Eight	Avanti Air
	D-ABGH	Airbus A.319-112	Lufthansa City Airlines
	D-ABGJ	Airbus A.319-112	Eurowings
	D-ABGK	Airbus A.319-112	Lufthansa City Airlines
	D-ABGN	Airbus A.319-112	Eurowings
	D-ABGP	Airbus A.319-112	Lufthansa City Airlines
	D-ABGQ	Airbus A.319-112	Eurowings
	D-ABHF	Airbus A.320-214	Eurowings
	D-ABHG	Airbus A.320-214	Eurowings
	D-ABKI	Boeing 737-86J	TUI fly
	D-ABKJ	Boeing 737-86J	TUI fly
	D-ABKM	Boeing 737-86J	TUI fly
	D-ABKN	Boeing 737-86J	TUI fly
	D-ABMQ	Boeing 737-86J	TUI fly
	D-ABMV	Boeing 737-86J	TUI fly
	D-ABNH	Airbus A.320-214	Eurowings
	D-ABNK	Airbus A.320-214	Eurowings
	D-ABNL	Airbus A.320-214	Eurowings
	D-ABNN	Airbus A.320-214	Eurowings
	D-ABNT	Airbus A.320-214	Eurowings
	D-ABNU	Airbus A.320-214	Eurowings
	D-ABPA	Boeing 787-9	Lufthansa
	D-ABPB	Boeing 787-9	Lufthansa
	D-ABPC	Boeing 787-9	Lufthansa
	D-ABPD	Boeing 787-9	Lufthansa
	D-ABPE	Boeing 787-9	Lufthansa
	D-ABPF	Boeing 787-9	Lufthansa
	D-ABPG	Boeing 787-9	Lufthansa
	D-ABPH	Boeing 787-9	Lufthansa
	D-ABPI	Boeing 787-9	Lufthansa

Reg	Type	Owner or Operator	Notes
D-ABPJ	Boeing 787-9	Lufthansa	
D-ABPK	Boeing 787-9	Lufthansa	
D-ABPL	Boeing 787-9	Lufthansa	
D-ABPM	Boeing 787-9	Lufthansa	
D-ABPO	Boeing 787-9	Lufthansa	
D-ABPP	Boeing 787-9	Lufthansa	
D-ABPQ	Boeing 787-9	Lufthansa	
D-ABPR	Boeing 787-9	Lufthansa	
D-ABPS	Boeing 787-9	Lufthansa	
D-ABPT	Boeing 787-9	Lufthansa	
D-ABPU	Boeing 787-9	Lufthansa	
D-ABQA	Boeing 787-9	Lufthansa	
D-ABTK	Boeing 747-430	Lufthansa	
D-ABTL	Boeing 747-430	Lufthansa	
D-ABVM	Boeing 747-430	Lufthansa	
D-ABVU	Boeing 747-430	Lufthansa	
D-ABVW	Boeing 747-430	Lufthansa	
D-ABVX	Boeing 747-430	Lufthansa	
D-ABVY	Boeing 747-430	Lufthansa	
D-ABVZ	Boeing 747-430	Lufthansa	
D-ABYA	Boeing 747-830	Lufthansa	
D-ABYC	Boeing 747-830	Lufthansa	
D-ABYF	Boeing 747-830	Lufthansa	
D-ABYG	Boeing 747-830	Lufthansa	
D-ABYH	Boeing 747-830	Lufthansa	
D-ABYI	Boeing 747-830	Lufthansa	
D-ABYJ	Boeing 747-830	Lufthansa	
D-ABYK	Boeing 747-830	Lufthansa	
D-ABYL	Boeing 747-830	Lufthansa	
D-ABYM	Boeing 747-830	Lufthansa	
D-ABYN	Boeing 747-830	Lufthansa	
D-ABYO	Boeing 747-830	Lufthansa	
D-ABYP	Boeing 747-830	Lufthansa	
D-ABYQ	Boeing 747-830	Lufthansa	
D-ABYR	Boeing 747-830	Lufthansa	
D-ABYS	Boeing 747-830	Lufthansa	
D-ABYT	Boeing 747-830	Lufthansa	
D-ABYU	Boeing 747-830	Lufthansa	
D-ABZE	Airbus A.320-216	Eurowings	
D-ABZI	Airbus A.320-216	Eurowings	
D-ABZK	Airbus A.320-216	Eurowings	
D-ABZL	Airbus A.320-216	Eurowings	
D-ABZN	Airbus A.320-216	Eurowings	
D-ACJJ	Embraer ERJ190-100LR	German Airways	
D-ACNA	Canadair CRJ900ER	Lufthansa CityLine	
D-ACNB	Canadair CRJ900ER	Lufthansa CityLine	
D-ACNC	Canadair CRJ900ER	Lufthansa CityLine	
D-ACND	Canadair CRJ900ER	Lufthansa CityLine	
D-ACNE	Canadair CRJ900ER	Lufthansa CityLine	
D-ACNF	Canadair CRJ900ER	Lufthansa CityLine	
D-ACNG	Canadair CRJ900ER	Lufthansa CityLine	
D-ACNH	Canadair CRJ900ER	Lufthansa CityLine	
D-ACNI	Canadair CRJ900ER	Lufthansa CityLine	
D-ACNJ	Canadair CRJ900ER	Lufthansa CityLine	
D-ACNK	Canadair CRJ900ER	Lufthansa CityLine	
D-ACNL	Canadair CRJ900ER	Lufthansa CityLine	
D-ACNM	Canadair CRJ900ER	Lufthansa CityLine	
D-ACNN	Canadair CRJ900ER	Lufthansa CityLine	
D-ACNO	Canadair CRJ900ER	Lufthansa CityLine	
D-ACNP	Canadair CRJ900ER	Lufthansa CityLine	
D-ACNQ	Canadair CRJ900ER	Lufthansa CityLine	
D-ACNR	Canadair CRJ900ER	Lufthansa CityLine	
D-ACNT	Canadair CRJ900ER	Lufthansa CityLine	
D-ACNU	Canadair CRJ900ER	Lufthansa CityLine	
D-ACNV	Canadair CRJ900ER	Lufthansa CityLine	
D-ACNW	Canadair CRJ900ER	Lufthansa CityLine	
D-ACNX	Canadair CRJ900ER	Lufthansa CityLine	
D-ACVG	Airbus A.330-243F	EAT Leipzig/DHL	
D-AEAA	Airbus A.300B4-622R	EAT Leipzig/DHL	
D-AEAB	Airbus A.300B4-622R	EAT Leipzig/DHL	
D-AEAC	Airbus A.300B4-622R	EAT Leipzig/DHL	

Notes	Reg	Type	Owner or Operator
	D-AEAD	Airbus A.300B4-622R	EAT Leipzig/DHL
	D-AEAE	Airbus A.300B4-622R	EAT Leipzig/DHL
	D-AEAF	Airbus A.300B4-622R	EAT Leipzig/DHL
	D-AEAG	Airbus A.300B4-622R	EAT Leipzig/DHL
	D-AEAH	Airbus A.300B4-622R	EAT Leipzig/DHL
	D-AEAI	Airbus A.300B4-622R	EAT Leipzig/DHL
	D-AEAJ	Airbus A.300B4-622R	EAT Leipzig/DHL
	D-AEAK	Airbus A.300B4-622R	EAT Leipzig/DHL
	D-AEAL	Airbus A.300B4-622R	EAT Leipzig/DHL
	D-AEAM	Airbus A.300B4-622R	EAT Leipzig/DHL
	D-AEAN	Airbus A.300B4-622R	EAT Leipzig/DHL
	D-AEAO	Airbus A.300B4-622R	EAT Leipzig/DHL
	D-AEAP	Airbus A.300B4-622R	EAT Leipzig/DHL
	D-AEAQ	Airbus A.300B4-622R	EAT Leipzig/DHL
	D-AEAR	Airbus A.300B4-622R	EAT Leipzig/DHL
	D-AEAS	Airbus A.300B4-622R	EAT Leipzig/DHL
	D-AEAT	Airbus A.300B4-622R	EAT Leipzig/DHL
	D-AEEA	Airbus A.321-251NX	Eurowings
	D-AEEB	Airbus A.321-251NX	Eurowings
	D-AEEC	Airbus A.321-251NX	Eurowings
	D-AEED	Airbus A.321-251NX	Eurowings
	D-AEEE	Airbus A.321-251NX	Eurowings
	D-AENA	Airbus A.320-251N	Eurowings
	D-AENB	Airbus A.320-251N	Eurowings
	D-AENC	Airbus A.320-251N	Eurowings
	D-AENE	Airbus A.320-251N	Eurowings
	D-AENF	Airbus A.320-251N	Eurowings
	D-AENG	Airbus A.320-251N	Eurowings
	D-AENH	Airbus A.320-251N	Eurowings
	D-AENI	Airbus A.320-251N	Eurowings
	D-AERA	Boeing 777-200F	AeroLogic
	D-AERB	Boeing 777-200F	AeroLogic
	D-AEUA	Airbus A.321-211P2F	Lufthansa CityLine
	D-AEUC	Airbus A.321-211P2F	Lufthansa CityLine
	D-AEUI	Airbus A.321-211P2F	Lufthansa CityLine
	D-AEUJ	Airbus A.321-211P2F	Lufthansa CityLine
	D-AEWJ	Airbus A.320-214	Eurowings
	D-AEWK	Airbus A.320-214	Eurowings
	D-AEWL	Airbus A.320-214	Eurowings
	D-AEWM	Airbus A.320-214	Eurowings
	D-AEWN	Airbus A.320-214	Eurowings
	D-AEWO	Airbus A.320-214	Eurowings
	D-AEWP	Airbus A.320-214	Eurowings
	D-AEWQ	Airbus A.320-214	Eurowings
	D-AEWR	Airbus A.320-214	Eurowings
	D-AEWS	Airbus A.320-214	Eurowings
	D-AEWT	Airbus A.320-214	Eurowings
	D-AEWU	Airbus A.320-214	Eurowings
	D-AEWV	Airbus A.320-214	Eurowings
	D-AEWW	Airbus A.320-214	Eurowings
	D-AGMP	Embraer ERJ190-100IGW	German Airways
	D-AGWA	Airbus A.319-132	Eurowings
	D-AGWB	Airbus A.319-132	Eurowings
	D-AGWC	Airbus A.319-132	Eurowings
	D-AGWD	Airbus A.319-132	Eurowings
	D-AGWE	Airbus A.319-132	Eurowings
	D-AGWF	Airbus A.319-132	Eurowings
	D-AGWG	Airbus A.319-132	Eurowings
	D-AGWH	Airbus A.319-132	Eurowings
	D-AGWI	Airbus A.319-132	Eurowings
	D-AGWJ	Airbus A.319-132	Eurowings
	D-AGWK	Airbus A.319-132	Eurowings
	D-AGWL	Airbus A.319-132	Eurowings
	D-AGWM	Airbus A.319-132	Eurowings
	D-AGWN	Airbus A.319-132	Eurowings
	D-AGWO	Airbus A.319-132	Eurowings
	D-AGWP	Airbus A.319-132	Eurowings
	D-AGWR	Airbus A.319-132	Eurowings
	D-AGWU	Airbus A.319-132	Eurowings
	D-AGWV	Airbus A.319-132	Eurowings
	D-AGWX	Airbus A.319-132	Eurowings

Reg	Type	Owner or Operator	Notes
D-AHLK	Boeing 737-8K5	TUI fly	
D-AIAA	Airbus A.321-211	Condor	
D-AIAB	Airbus A.321-211	Condor	
D-AIAC	Airbus A.321-211	Condor	
D-AIAD	Airbus A.321-211	Condor	
D-AIAF	Airbus A.321-211	Condor	
D-AIAG	Airbus A.321-211	Condor	
D-AIAI	Airbus A.321-211	Condor	
D-AIAS	Airbus A.321-211	Condor	
D-AIBA	Airbus A.319-114	Lufthansa	
D-AIBB	Airbus A.319-114	Lufthansa	
D-AIBC	Airbus A.319-114	Lufthansa	
D-AIBD	Airbus A.319-114	Lufthansa	
D-AIBE	Airbus A.319-114	Lufthansa	
D-AIBF	Airbus A.319-112	Lufthansa	
D-AIBG	Airbus A.319-112	Lufthansa	
D-AIBH	Airbus A.319-112	Lufthansa	
D-AIBI	Airbus A.319-112	Lufthansa	
D-AIBJ	Airbus A.319-112	Lufthansa	
D-AIBK	Airbus A.319-112	Lufthansa CityLine	
D-AIBL	Airbus A.319-112	Lufthansa CityLine	
D-AIBM	Airbus A.319-112	Lufthansa CityLine	
D-AIBN	Airbus A.319-112	Lufthansa CityLine	
D-AIBP	Airbus A.319-112	Lufthansa CityLine	
D-AIBQ	Airbus A.319-112	Lufthansa CityLine	
D-AICA	Airbus A.320-212	Condor	
D-AICG	Airbus A.320-212	Condor	
D-AICH	Airbus A.320-212	Condor	
D-AICI	Airbus A.320-212	Condor	
D-AICS	Airbus A.320-214	Condor	
D-AICT	Airbus A.320-214	Condor	
D-AICU	Airbus A.320-214	Condor	
D-AIDA	Airbus A.321-231	Lufthansa	
D-AIDB	Airbus A.321-231	Lufthansa	
D-AIDC	Airbus A.321-231	Lufthansa	
D-AIDD	Airbus A.321-231	Lufthansa	
D-AIDE	Airbus A.321-231	Lufthansa	
D-AIDF	Airbus A.321-231	Lufthansa	
D-AIDG	Airbus A.321-231	Lufthansa	
D-AIDH	Airbus A.321-231	Lufthansa	
D-AIDI	Airbus A.321-231	Lufthansa	
D-AIDJ	Airbus A.321-231	Lufthansa	
D-AIDK	Airbus A.321-231	Lufthansa	
D-AIDL	Airbus A.321-231	Lufthansa	
D-AIDM	Airbus A.321-231	Lufthansa	
D-AIDN	Airbus A.321-231	Lufthansa	
D-AIDO	Airbus A.321-231	Eurowings	
D-AIDP	Airbus A.321-231	Eurowings	
D-AIDQ	Airbus A.321-231	Eurowings	
D-AIDT	Airbus A.321-231	Eurowings	
D-AIDU	Airbus A.321-231	Eurowings	
D-AIDV	Airbus A.321-231	Eurowings	
D-AIDW	Airbus A.321-231	Lufthansa	
D-AIDX	Airbus A.321-231	Lufthansa	
D-AIEA	Airbus A.321-271NX	Lufthansa	
D-AIEB	Airbus A.321-271NX	Lufthansa	
D-AIEC	Airbus A.321-271NX	Lufthansa	
D-AIED	Airbus A.321-271NX	Lufthansa	
D-AIEE	Airbus A.321-271NX	Lufthansa	
D-AIEF	Airbus A.321-271NX	Lufthansa	
D-AIEG	Airbus A.321-271NX	Lufthansa	
D-AIEH	Airbus A.321-271NX	Lufthansa	
D-AIEI	Airbus A.321-271NX	Lufthansa	
D-AIEJ	Airbus A.321-271NX	Lufthansa	
D-AIEK	Airbus A.321-271NX	Lufthansa	
D-AIEL	Airbus A.321-271NX	Lufthansa	
D-AIEM	Airbus A.321-271NX	Lufthansa	
D-AIEN	Airbus A.321-271NX	Lufthansa	
D-AIEO	Airbus A.321-271NX	Lufthansa	
D-AIEP	Airbus A.321-271NX	Lufthansa	
D-AIEQ	Airbus A.321-271NX	Lufthansa	

Notes	Reg	Type	Owner or Operator
	D-AIFD	Airbus A.340-313X	Lufthansa
	D-AIFE	Airbus A.340-313X	Lufthansa
	D-AIFF	Airbus A.340-313X	Lufthansa
	D-AIGN	Airbus A.340-313X	Lufthansa
	D-AIGO	Airbus A.340-313X	Lufthansa
	D-AIGP	Airbus A.340-313X	Lufthansa
	D-AIGS	Airbus A.340-313X	Lufthansa
	D-AIGT	Airbus A.340-313X	Lufthansa
	D-AIGU	Airbus A.340-313X	Lufthansa
	D-AIGV	Airbus A.340-313X	Lufthansa
	D-AIGW	Airbus A.340-313X	Lufthansa
	D-AIGX	Airbus A.340-313X	Lufthansa
	D-AIGY	Airbus A.340-313X	Lufthansa
	D-AIGZ	Airbus A.340-313X	Lufthansa
	D-AIHF	Airbus A.340-642	Lufthansa
	D-AIHW	Airbus A.340-642	Lufthansa
	D-AIHX	Airbus A.340-642	Lufthansa
	D-AIHY	Airbus A.340-642	Lufthansa
	D-AIHZ	Airbus A.340-642	Lufthansa
	D-AIIA	Airbus A.320-251N	Lufthansa City Airlines
	D-AIIB	Airbus A.320-251N	Lufthansa City Airlines
	D-AIIC	Airbus A.320-251N	Lufthansa City Airlines
	D-AIID	Airbus A.320-251N	Lufthansa City Airlines
	D-AIIE	Airbus A.320-251N	Lufthansa City Airlines
	D-AIJA	Airbus A.320-271N	Lufthansa
	D-AIJB	Airbus A.320-271N	Lufthansa
	D-AIJC	Airbus A.320-271N	Lufthansa
	D-AIJD	Airbus A.320-271N	Lufthansa
	D-AIJE	Airbus A.320-271N	Lufthansa
	D-AIJH	Airbus A.320-271N	Lufthansa City Airlines
	D-AIJI	Airbus A.320-271N	Lufthansa City Airlines
	D-AIJJ	Airbus A.320-271N	Lufthansa City Airlines
	D-AIJM	Airbus A.320-271N	Lufthansa City Airlines
	D-AIJN	Airbus A.320-271N	Lufthansa City Airlines
	D-AIJP	Airbus A.320-271N	Lufthansa City Airlines
	D-AIJQ	Airbus A.320-271N	Lufthansa City Airlines
	D-AIJR	Airbus A.320-271N	Lufthansa City Airlines
	D-AIKI	Airbus A.330-343X	Lufthansa
	D-AIKL	Airbus A.330-343X	Lufthansa
	D-AIKN	Airbus A.330-343X	Lufthansa
	D-AIKP	Airbus A.330-343X	Lufthansa
	D-AIKQ	Airbus A.330-343X	Lufthansa
	D-AIKR	Airbus A.330-343X	Lufthansa
	D-AIKS	Airbus A.330-343X	Lufthansa
	D-AILA	Airbus A.319-114	Lufthansa
	D-AILB	Airbus A.319-114	Lufthansa CityLine
	D-AILC	Airbus A.319-114	Lufthansa
	D-AILD	Airbus A.319-114	Lufthansa
	D-AILE	Airbus A.319-114	Lufthansa
	D-AILF	Airbus A.319-114	Lufthansa
	D-AILH	Airbus A.319-114	Lufthansa
	D-AILI	Airbus A.319-114	Lufthansa
	D-AILK	Airbus A.319-114	Lufthansa
	D-AILL	Airbus A.319-114	Lufthansa
	D-AILM	Airbus A.319-114	Lufthansa
	D-AILN	Airbus A.319-114	Lufthansa
	D-AILP	Airbus A.319-114	Lufthansa CityLine
	D-AILS	Airbus A.319-114	Lufthansa CityLine
	D-AILT	Airbus A.319-114	Lufthansa CityLine
	D-AILU	Airbus A.319-114	Lufthansa
	D-AILW	Airbus A.319-114	Lufthansa CityLine
	D-AILX	Airbus A.319-114	Lufthansa CityLine
	D-AILY	Airbus A.319-114	Lufthansa
	D-AIMA	Airbus A.380-841	Lufthansa
	D-AIMB	Airbus A.380-841	Lufthansa
	D-AIMC	Airbus A.380-841	Lufthansa
	D-AIMH	Airbus A.380-841	Lufthansa
	D-AIMK	Airbus A.380-841	Lufthansa
	D-AIML	Airbus A.380-841	Lufthansa
	D-AIMM	Airbus A.380-841	Lufthansa
	D-AIMN	Airbus A.380-841	Lufthansa

Reg	Type	Owner or Operator	Notes
D-AINA	Airbus A.320-271N	Lufthansa	
D-AINB	Airbus A.320-271N	Lufthansa	
D-AINC	Airbus A.320-271N	Lufthansa	
D-AIND	Airbus A.320-271N	Lufthansa	
D-AINE	Airbus A.320-271N	Lufthansa	
D-AINF	Airbus A.320-271N	Lufthansa	
D-AING	Airbus A.320-271N	Lufthansa	
D-AINH	Airbus A.320-271N	Lufthansa	
D-AINI	Airbus A.320-271N	Lufthansa	
D-AINJ	Airbus A.320-271N	Lufthansa	
D-AINK	Airbus A.320-271N	Lufthansa	
D-AINL	Airbus A.320-271N	Lufthansa	
D-AINM	Airbus A.320-271N	Lufthansa	
D-AINN	Airbus A.320-271N	Lufthansa	
D-AINO	Airbus A.320-271N	Lufthansa	
D-AINP	Airbus A.320-271N	Lufthansa	
D-AINQ	Airbus A.320-271N	Lufthansa	
D-AINR	Airbus A.320-271N	Lufthansa	
D-AINT	Airbus A.320-271N	Lufthansa	
D-AINU	Airbus A.320-271N	Lufthansa	
D-AINV	Airbus A.320-271N	Lufthansa	
D-AINW	Airbus A.320-271N	Lufthansa	
D-AINX	Airbus A.320-271N	Lufthansa	
D-AINY	Airbus A.320-271N	Lufthansa	
D-AINZ	Airbus A.320-271N	Lufthansa	
D-AIOA	Airbus A.321-251NX	Lufthansa	
D-AIOB	Airbus A.321-251NX	Lufthansa	
D-AIOC	Airbus A.321-251NX	Lufthansa	
D-AIOD	Airbus A.321-251NX	Lufthansa	
D-AIQT	Airbus A.320-211	Lufthansa	
D-AIQU	Airbus A.320-211	Lufthansa	
D-AIQW	Airbus A.320-211	Lufthansa	
D-AIRA	Airbus A.321-131	Lufthansa	
D-AIRC	Airbus A.321-131	Lufthansa	
D-AIRH	Airbus A.321-131	Lufthansa	
D-AIRL	Airbus A.321-131	Lufthansa	
D-AIRM	Airbus A.321-131	Lufthansa	
D-AIRN	Airbus A.321-131	Lufthansa	
D-AIRO	Airbus A.321-131	Lufthansa	
D-AIRP	Airbus A.321-131	Lufthansa	
D-AIRR	Airbus A.321-131	Lufthansa	
D-AIRS	Airbus A.321-131	Lufthansa	
D-AIRT	Airbus A.321-131	Lufthansa	
D-AIRU	Airbus A.321-131	Lufthansa	
D-AIRW	Airbus A.321-131	Lufthansa	
D-AIRX	Airbus A.321-131	Lufthansa	
D-AIRY	Airbus A.321-131	Lufthansa	
D-AISB	Airbus A.321-231	Lufthansa	
D-AISC	Airbus A.321-231	Lufthansa	
D-AISD	Airbus A.321-231	Lufthansa	
D-AISF	Airbus A.321-231	Lufthansa	
D-AISG	Airbus A.321-231	Lufthansa	
D-AISH	Airbus A.321-231	Lufthansa	
D-AISI	Airbus A.321-231	Lufthansa	
D-AISJ	Airbus A.321-231	Lufthansa	
D-AISK	Airbus A.321-231	Lufthansa	
D-AISL	Airbus A.321-231	Lufthansa	
D-AISN	Airbus A.321-231	Lufthansa	
D-AISO	Airbus A.321-231	Lufthansa	
D-AISP	Airbus A.321-231	Lufthansa	
D-AISQ	Airbus A.321-231	Lufthansa	
D-AISR	Airbus A.321-231	Lufthansa	
D-AIST	Airbus A.321-231	Lufthansa	
D-AISU	Airbus A.321-231	Lufthansa	
D-AISV	Airbus A.321-231	Lufthansa	
D-AISW	Airbus A.321-231	Lufthansa	
D-AISX	Airbus A.321-231	Lufthansa	
D-AISZ	Airbus A.321-231	Lufthansa	
D-AIUA	Airbus A.320-214	Lufthansa	
D-AIUB	Airbus A.320-214	Lufthansa	
D-AIUC	Airbus A.320-214	Lufthansa	

Notes	Reg	Type	Owner or Operator
	D-AIUD	Airbus A.320-214	Lufthansa
	D-AIUE	Airbus A.320-214	Lufthansa
	D-AIUF	Airbus A.320-214	Lufthansa
	D-AIUG	Airbus A.320-214	Lufthansa
	D-AIUH	Airbus A.320-214	Lufthansa
	D-AIUI	Airbus A.320-214	Lufthansa
	D-AIUJ	Airbus A.320-214	Lufthansa
	D-AIUK	Airbus A.320-214	Lufthansa
	D-AIUL	Airbus A.320-214	Lufthansa
	D-AIUM	Airbus A.320-214	Lufthansa
	D-AIUN	Airbus A.320-214	Lufthansa
	D-AIUO	Airbus A.320-214	Lufthansa
	D-AIUP	Airbus A.320-214	Lufthansa
	D-AIVA	Airbus A.350-941	Lufthansa
	D-AIVB	Airbus A.350-941	Lufthansa
	D-AIVC	Airbus A.350-941	Lufthansa
	D-AIVD	Airbus A.350-941	Lufthansa
	D-AIVE	Airbus A.350-941	Lufthansa
	D-AIWA	Airbus A.320-214	Lufthansa
	D-AIWH	Airbus A.320-214	Lufthansa
	D-AIWI	Airbus A.320-214	Lufthansa
	D-AIWJ	Airbus A.320-214	Lufthansa
	D-AIWK	Airbus A.320-214	Lufthansa
	D-AIXA	Airbus A.350-941	Lufthansa
	D-AIXB	Airbus A.350-941	Lufthansa
	D-AIXC	Airbus A.350-941	Lufthansa
	D-AIXD	Airbus A.350-941	Lufthansa
	D-AIXE	Airbus A.350-941	Lufthansa
	D-AIXF	Airbus A.350-941	Lufthansa
	D-AIXG	Airbus A.350-941	Lufthansa
	D-AIXH	Airbus A.350-941	Lufthansa
	D-AIXI	Airbus A.350-941	Lufthansa
	D-AIXJ	Airbus A.350-941	Lufthansa
	D-AIXK	Airbus A.350-941	Lufthansa
	D-AIXL	Airbus A.350-941	Lufthansa
	D-AIXM	Airbus A.350-941	Lufthansa
	D-AIXN	Airbus A.350-941	Lufthansa
	D-AIXO	Airbus A.350-941	Lufthansa
	D-AIXP	Airbus A.350-941	Lufthansa
	D-AIXQ	Airbus A.350-941	Lufthansa
	D-AIXR	Airbus A.350-941	Lufthansa
	D-AIXS	Airbus A.350-941	Lufthansa
	D-AIXT	Airbus A.350-941	Lufthansa
	D-AIXU	Airbus A.350-941	Lufthansa
	D-AIXV	Airbus A.350-941	Lufthansa
	D-AIXW	Airbus A.350-941	Lufthansa
	D-AIXX	Airbus A.350-941	Lufthansa
	D-AIXY	Airbus A.350-941	Lufthansa
	D-AIXZ	Airbus A.350-941	Lufthansa
	D-AIZA	Airbus A.320-214	Lufthansa
	D-AIZB	Airbus A.320-214	Lufthansa
	D-AIZC	Airbus A.320-214	Lufthansa
	D-AIZD	Airbus A.320-214	Lufthansa
	D-AIZE	Airbus A.320-214	Lufthansa
	D-AIZF	Airbus A.320-214	Lufthansa
	D-AIZG	Airbus A.320-214	Lufthansa
	D-AIZH	Airbus A.320-214	Lufthansa
	D-AIZI	Airbus A.320-214	Lufthansa
	D-AIZJ	Airbus A.320-214	Lufthansa
	D-AIZM	Airbus A.320-214	Lufthansa
	D-AIZN	Airbus A.320-214	Lufthansa
	D-AIZO	Airbus A.320-214	Lufthansa
	D-AIZP	Airbus A.320-214	Lufthansa
	D-AIZQ	Airbus A.320-214	Lufthansa
	D-AIZR	Airbus A.320-214	Lufthansa
	D-AIZS	Airbus A.320-214	Lufthansa
	D-AIZT	Airbus A.320-214	Lufthansa
	D-AIZW	Airbus A.320-214	Lufthansa
	D-AIZX	Airbus A.320-214	Lufthansa
	D-AIZY	Airbus A.320-214	Lufthansa
	D-AIZZ	Airbus A.320-214	Lufthansa

Reg	Type	Owner or Operator	Notes
D-AJFK	Airbus A.330-343(P2F)	EAT Leipzig/DHL	
D-AJHW	Embraer ERJ190-100LR	German Airways	
D-AKJC	Embraer ERJ190-100SR	German Airways	
D-ALEJ	Airbus A.330-243F	EAT Leipzig/DHL	
D-ALEP	Boeing 757-2Q8F	EAT Leipzig/DHL	
D-ALER	Boeing 757-2Q8F	EAT Leipzig/DHL	
D-ALET	Boeing 757-28AF	EAT Leipzig/DHL	
D-ALEU	Boeing 757-23NF	EAT Leipzig/DHL	
D-ALFA	Boeing 777FBT	Lufthansa Cargo	
D-ALFB	Boeing 777FBT	Lufthansa Cargo	
D-ALFC	Boeing 777FBT	Lufthansa Cargo	
D-ALFD	Boeing 777FBT	Lufthansa Cargo	
D-ALFE	Boeing 777FBT	Lufthansa Cargo	
D-ALFF	Boeing 777FBT	Lufthansa Cargo	
D-ALFG	Boeing 777FBT	Lufthansa Cargo	
D-ALFH	Boeing 777FBT	Lufthansa Cargo	
D-ALFI	Boeing 777FBT	Lufthansa Cargo	
D-ALFJ	Boeing 777FBT	Lufthansa Cargo	
D-ALFK	Boeing 777FBT	Lufthansa Cargo	
D-ALFL	Boeing 777FBT	Lufthansa Cargo	
D-ALMA	Airbus A.330-243F	EAT Leipzig/DHL	
D-ALMD	Airbus A.330-243F	EAT Leipzig/DHL	
D-ALMF	Airbus A.330-343(P2)F	EAT Leipzig/DHL	
D-ALMG	Airbus A.330-343(P2)F	EAT Leipzig/DHL	
D-AMAA	Boeing 737-MAX8	TUI fly	
D-AMAB	Boeing 737-MAX8	TUI fly	
D-AMAD	Boeing 737-MAX8	TUI fly	
D-AMAE	Boeing 737-MAX8	TUI fly	
D-AMAF	Boeing 737-MAX8	TUI fly	
D-AMAH	Boeing 737-MAX8	TUI fly	
D-AMAX	Boeing 737-MAX8	TUI fly	
D-AMAY	Boeing 737-MAX8	TUI fly	
D-AMAZ	Boeing 737-MAX8	TUI fly	
D-AMWO	Embraer ERJ190-IGW	German Airways	
D-ANCA	Airbus A.320-271N	Condor	
D-ANCK	Airbus A.320-271N	Condor	
D-ANCL	Airbus A.320-271N	Condor	
D-ANCW	Airbus A.320-271N	Condor	
D-ANCX	Airbus A.320-271N	Condor	
D-ANCY	Airbus A.320-271N	Condor	
D-ANCZ	Airbus A.320-271N	Condor	
D-ANLA	Airbus A.321-271NX	Condor	
D-ANLB	Airbus A.321-271NX	Condor	
D-ANLC	Airbus A.321-271NX	Condor	
D-ANLD	Airbus A.321-271NX	Condor	
D-ANLE	Airbus A.321-271NX	Condor	
D-ANLI	Airbus A.321-271NX	Condor	
D-ANMW	Airbus A.321-271NX	Condor	
D-ANMX	Airbus A.321-271NX	Condor	
D-ANMY	Airbus A.321-271NX	Condor	
D-ANMZ	Airbus A.321-271NX	Condor	
D-APRI	Embraer ERJ190-100SR	German Airways	
D-ASGE	Airbus A.320-214	Condor	
D-ASTX	Airbus A.319-112	Lufthansa City Airlines	
D-ATCA	Airbus A.321-211	Condor	
D-ATCB	Airbus A.321-211	Condor	
D-ATCC	Airbus A.321-211	Condor	
D-ATCF	Airbus A.321-211	Condor	
D-ATCG	Airbus A.321-211	Condor	
D-ATCH	Airbus A.320-214	Condor	
D-ATUA	Boeing 737-8K5	TUI fly	
D-ATUF	Boeing 737-8K5	TUI fly	
D-ATUK	Boeing 737-8K5	TUI fly	
D-ATUN	Boeing 737-8K5	TUI fly	
D-ATUO	Boeing 737-8K5	TUI fly	
D-ATUR	Boeing 737-8K5	TUI fly	
D-ATUZ	Boeing 737-8K5	TUI fly	
D-ATYL	Boeing 737-8K5	TUI fly	
D-AWSI	Embraer ERJ190-100LR	German Airways	
D-AZFA	Embraer ERJ190-100LR	German Airways	
D-AZMK	Airbus A.300F4-622R	EAT Leipzig/DHL	

Notes	Reg	Type	Owner or Operator
	D-AZML	Airbus A.300F4-622R	EAT Leipzig/DHL
	D-AZMM	Airbus A.300F4-622R	EAT Leipzig/DHL
	D-AZMN	Airbus A.300F4-622R	EAT Leipzig/DHL
	D-AZMO	Airbus A.300F4-622R	EAT Leipzig/DHL
	D-AZMP	Airbus A.300F4-622R	EAT Leipzig/DHL
	D-AZMQ	Airbus A.300F4-622R	EAT Leipzig/DHL

EC (Spain)

Notes	Reg	Type	Owner or Operator
	EC-FTR	Boeing 757-256PCF	Cygnus Air
	EC-HUH	Airbus A.321-211	Iberia
	EC-HUI	Airbus A.321-211	Iberia
	EC-IEF	Airbus A.320-214	Iberia
	EC-IJN	Airbus A.321-212	Iberia
	EC-ILP	Airbus A.321-211	Iberia
	EC-ILQ	Airbus A.320-214	Iberia Express
	EC-ILR	Airbus A.320-214	Iberia Express
	EC-ILS	Airbus A.320-214	Iberia
	EC-ISI	Airbus A.320-214	Volotea Airlines
	EC-IXD	Airbus A.321-212	Iberia
	EC-IXE	Boeing 737-883	Swiftair/DHL
	EC-IXO	Boeing 737-883	Swiftair/DHL
	EC-IZH	Airbus A.320-214	Iberia
	EC-IZR	Airbus A.320-214	Iberia
	EC-JDM	Airbus A.321-213	Iberia
	EC-JDR	Airbus A.321-213	Iberia
	EC-JEJ	Airbus A.321-231	Iberia
	EC-JFG	Airbus A.320-214	Iberia Express
	EC-JFH	Airbus A.320-214	Iberia Express
	EC-JFN	Airbus A.320-214	Iberia Express
	EC-JGS	Airbus A.321-213	Iberia
	EC-JLI	Airbus A.321-211	Iberia
	EC-JQZ	Airbus A.321-211	Iberia
	EC-JRE	Airbus A.321-211	Iberia
	EC-JSY	Airbus A.320-214	Vueling Airlines
	EC-JTQ	Airbus A.320-214	Vueling Airlines
	EC-JTR	Airbus A.320-214	Vueling Airlines
	EC-JYX	Airbus A.320-214	Vueling Airlines
	EC-JZI	Airbus A.320-214	Vueling Airlines
	EC-JZM	Airbus A.321-211	Iberia
	EC-KCU	Airbus A.320-216	Vueling Airlines
	EC-KDG	Airbus A.320-214	Vueling Airlines
	EC-KDH	Airbus A.320-214	Vueling Airlines
	EC-KDT	Airbus A.320-216	Vueling Airlines
	EC-KDX	Airbus A.320-216	Vueling Airlines
	EC-KHM	Airbus A.319-111	Iberia
	EC-KHN	Airbus A.320-216	Vueling Airlines
	EC-KJD	Airbus A.320-216	Vueling Airlines
	EC-KLB	Airbus A.320-214	Vueling Airlines
	EC-KLD	Boeing 757-236PCF	Cygnus Air
	EC-KLT	Airbus A.320-214	Vueling Airlines
	EC-KMI	Airbus A.320-216	Volotea Airlines
	EC-KOH	Airbus A.320-214	Iberia Express
	EC-KRH	Airbus A.320-214	Vueling Airlines
	EC-KUB	Airbus A.319-111	Iberia
	EC-LAA	Airbus A.320-214	Iberia Express
	EC-LAB	Airbus A.320-214	Vueling Airlines
	EC-LEI	Airbus A.319-111	Iberia
	EC-LLJ	Airbus A.320-214	Vueling Airlines
	EC-LOB	Airbus A.320-232	Vueling Airlines
	EC-LOC	Airbus A.320-232	Vueling Airlines
	EC-LOP	Airbus A.320-214	Vueling Airlines
	EC-LPQ	Boeing 737-85P	Air Europa
	EC-LPR	Boeing 737-85P	Air Europa
	EC-LQX	Boeing 737-85P	Air Europa
	EC-LRG	Airbus A.320-214	Iberia
	EC-LTM	Boeing 737-85P	Air Europa
	EC-LUB	Airbus A.330-302	Iberia
	EC-LUK	Airbus A.330-302E	Iberia
	EC-LUL	Airbus A.320-216	Iberia
	EC-LUN	Airbus A.320-232	Vueling Airlines

Reg	Type	Owner or Operator	Notes
EC-LUO	Airbus A.320-232	Vueling Airlines	
EC-LUS	Airbus A.320-216	Iberia Express	
EC-LUT	Boeing 737-85P	Air Europa	
EC-LUX	Airbus A.330-302	Iberia	
EC-LVD	Airbus A.320-216	Iberia	
EC-LVO	Airbus A.320-214	Vueling Airlines	
EC-LVP	Airbus A.320-214	Vueling Airlines	
EC-LVQ	Airbus A.320-216	Iberia Express	
EC-LVR	Boeing 737-85P	Air Europa	
EC-LVS	Airbus A.320-214	Vueling Airlines	
EC-LVT	Airbus A.320-214	Vueling Airlines	
EC-LVU	Airbus A.320-214	Vueling Airlines	
EC-LVV	Airbus A.320-214	Vueling Airlines	
EC-LXK	Airbus A.330-302E	Iberia	
EC-LXQ	Airbus A.320-216	Iberia	
EC-LXV	Boeing 737-86N	Air Europa	
EC-LYE	Airbus A.320-216	Iberia Express	
EC-LYF	Airbus A.330-302E	Iberia	
EC-LYM	Airbus A.320-216	Iberia Express	
EC-LZJ	Airbus A.330-302E	Iberia	
EC-LZN	Airbus A.320-214	Vueling Airlines	
EC-LZX	Airbus A.330-302E	Iberia	
EC-MAA	Airbus A.330-302	Iberia	
EC-MAH	Airbus A.320-214	Vueling Airlines	
EC-MAI	Airbus A.320-214	Vueling Airlines	
EC-MAN	Airbus A.320-214	Vueling Airlines	
EC-MAO	Airbus A.320-214	Vueling Airlines	
EC-MBD	Airbus A.320-214	Vueling Airlines	
EC-MBE	Airbus A.320-214	Vueling Airlines	
EC-MBF	Airbus A.320-214	Vueling Airlines	
EC-MBK	Airbus A.320-214	Volotea Airlines	
EC-MBS	Airbus A.320-214	Vueling Airlines	
EC-MBT	Airbus A.320-214	Vueling Airlines	
EC-MBY	Airbus A.320-214	Vueling Airlines	
EC-MCS	Airbus A.320-216	Iberia	
EC-MCU	Airbus A.320-214	Vueling Airlines	
EC-MDK	Airbus A.320-214	Iberia	
EC-MDZ	Airbus A.320-232	Vueling Airlines	
EC-MEA	Airbus A.320-232	Vueling Airlines	
EC-MEL	Airbus A.320-232	Vueling Airlines	
EC-MEQ	Airbus A.320-232	Vueling Airlines	
EC-MER	Airbus A.320-232	Vueling Airlines	
EC-MES	Airbus A.320-232	Vueling Airlines	
EC-MEY	Boeing 737-476SF	Swiftair/DHL	
EC-MFK	Airbus A.320-232	Vueling Airlines	
EC-MFL	Airbus A.320-232	Vueling Airlines	
EC-MFM	Airbus A.320-232	Vueling Airlines	
EC-MFN	Airbus A.320-232	Vueling Airlines	
EC-MGE	Airbus A.320-232	Vueling Airlines	
EC-MGF	Airbus A.319-111	Vueling Airlines	
EC-MGY	Airbus A.321-231	Vueling Airlines	
EC-MGZ	Airbus A.321-231	Vueling Airlines	
EC-MHA	Airbus A.321-231	Vueling Airlines	
EC-MHB	Airbus A.321-231	Vueling Airlines	
EC-MHS	Airbus A.321-231	Vueling Airlines	
EC-MIQ	Airbus A.319-112	Vueling Airlines	
EC-MIR	Airbus A.319-112	Vueling Airlines	
EC-MJB	Airbus A.320-232	Vueling Airlines	
EC-MJC	Airbus A.320-232	Vueling Airlines	
EC-MJR	Airbus A.321-231	Vueling Airlines	
EC-MJU	Boeing 737-85P	Air Europa	
EC-MKI	Airbus A.330-202	Iberia	
EC-MKJ	Airbus A.330-202	Iberia	
EC-MKL	Boeing 737-85P	Air Europa	
EC-MKM	Airbus A.320-232	Vueling Airlines	
EC-MKN	Airbus A.320-232	Vueling Airlines	
EC-MKO	Airbus A.320-232	Vueling Airlines	
EC-MKV	Airbus A.319-112	Vueling Airlines	
EC-MKX	Airbus A.319-112	Vueling Airlines	
EC-MLB	Airbus A.330-202	Iberia	
EC-MLD	Airbus A.321-231	Vueling Airlines	

Notes	Reg	Type	Owner or Operator
	EC-MLE	Airbus A.320-232	Vueling Airlines
	EC-MLM	Airbus A.321-231	Vueling Airlines
	EC-MLP	Airbus A.330-202	Iberia
	EC-MMG	Airbus A.330-202	Iberia
	EC-MMH	Airbus A.321-231	Vueling Airlines
	EC-MMU	Airbus A.321-231	Vueling Airlines
	EC-MNK	Airbus A.330-202	Iberia
	EC-MNL	Airbus A.330-202	Iberia
	EC-MNZ	Airbus A.320-232	Vueling Airlines
	EC-MOG	Airbus A.320-232	Vueling Airlines
	EC-MOO	Airbus A.321-231	Vueling Airlines
	EC-MOU	Airbus A.330-202	Iberia
	EC-MOY	Airbus A.330-202	Iberia
	EC-MPS	Boeing 737-85P	Air Europa
	EC-MPV	Airbus A.321-231	Vueling Airlines
	EC-MQB	Airbus A.321-231	Vueling Airlines
	EC-MQE	Airbus A.320-232	Vueling Airlines
	EC-MQL	Airbus A.321-231	Vueling Airlines
	EC-MRF	Airbus A.321-231	Vueling Airlines
	EC-MSY	Airbus A.330-202	Iberia
	EC-MTC	Airbus A.319-111	Volotea Airlines
	EC-MTD	Airbus A.319-111	Volotea Airlines
	EC-MTE	Airbus A.319-112	Volotea Airlines
	EC-MTF	Airbus A.319-112	Volotea Airlines
	EC-MTM	Airbus A.319-111	Volotea Airlines
	EC-MTN	Airbus A.319-111	Volotea Airlines
	EC-MTV	Boeing 737-86J	AlbaStar
	EC-MUB	Boeing 737-86J	AlbaStar
	EC-MUC	Airbus A.319-112	Volotea Airlines
	EC-MUD	Airbus A.330-302	Iberia
	EC-MUF	Airbus A.320-214	Iberia Express
	EC-MUK	Airbus A.320-214	Iberia Express
	EC-MUM	Airbus A.320-214	Vueling Airlines
	EC-MUT	Airbus A.319-111	Volotea Airlines
	EC-MUU	Airbus A.319-111	Volotea Airlines
	EC-MUX	Airbus A.319-111	Volotea Airlines
	EC-MUY	Airbus A.319-111	Volotea Airlines
	EC-MVD	Airbus A.320-214	Vueling Airlines
	EC-MVE	Airbus A.320-214	Vueling Airlines
	EC-MVO	Airbus A.320-232	Vueling Airlines
	EC-MXG	Airbus A.320-232	Vueling Airlines
	EC-MXP	Airbus A.320-232	Vueling Airlines
	EC-MXU	Airbus A.320-251N	Iberia
	EC-MXV	Airbus A.350-941	Iberia
	EC-MXY	Airbus A.320-251N	Iberia
	EC-MYA	Airbus A.330-202	Iberia
	EC-MYB	Airbus A.320-214	Vueling Airlines
	EC-MYC	Airbus A.320-232	Vueling Airlines
	EC-MYX	Airbus A.350-941	Iberia
	EC-MZT	Airbus A.320-271N	Vueling Airlines
	EC-NAB	Boeing 737-81Q	AlbaStar
	EC-NAE	Airbus A.320-271N	Vueling Airlines
	EC-NAF	Airbus A.320-271N	Vueling Airlines
	EC-NAJ	Airbus A.320-271N	Vueling Airlines
	EC-NAV	Airbus A.320-271N	Vueling Airlines
	EC-NAX	Airbus A.320-271N	Vueling Airlines
	EC-NAY	Airbus A.320-271N	Iberia
	EC-NAZ	Airbus A.320-271N	Iberia
	EC-NBA	Airbus A.320-271N	Vueling Airlines
	EC-NBE	Airbus A.350-941	Iberia
	EC-NCB	Airbus A.319-111	Volotea Airlines
	EC-NCF	Airbus A.320-271N	Vueling Airlines
	EC-NCG	Airbus A.320-271N	Vueling Airlines
	EC-NCM	Airbus A.320-251N	Iberia
	EC-NCS	Airbus A.320-271N	Vueling Airlines
	EC-NCT	Airbus A.320-271N	Vueling Airlines
	EC-NCU	Airbus A.320-271N	Vueling Airlines
	EC-NCX	Airbus A.350-941	Iberia
	EC-NDA	Airbus A.320-271N	Vueling Airlines
	EC-NDB	Airbus A.320-271N	Vueling Airlines
	EC-NDC	Airbus A.320-271N	Vueling Airlines

Reg	Type	Owner or Operator	Notes
EC-NDG	Airbus A.319-112	Volotea Airlines	
EC-NDH	Airbus A.319-112	Volotea Airlines	
EC-NDN	Airbus A.320-251N	Iberia	
EC-NDR	Airbus A.350-941	Iberia	
EC-NEA	Airbus A.320-271N	Vueling Airlines	
EC-NER	Airbus A.320-251N	Iberia	
EC-NFH	Airbus A.320-271N	Iberia	
EC-NFI	Airbus A.320-271N	Iberia	
EC-NFJ	Airbus A.320-271N	Vueling Airlines	
EC-NFK	Airbus A.320-271N	Vueling Airlines	
EC-NFN	Boeing 757-223PCF	Cygnus Air	
EC-NFZ	Airbus A.320-251N	Iberia	
EC-NGB	Airbus A.319-111	Vueling Airlines	
EC-NGC	Boeing 737-809	AlbaStar	
EC-NGL	Airbus A.319-112	Volotea Airlines	
EC-NGP	Airbus A.321-251NX	Iberia Express	
EC-NGT	Airbus A.350-941	Iberia	
EC-NHF	Boeing 757-223PCF	Cygnus Air	
EC-NHP	Airbus A.319-111	Volotea Airlines	
EC-NIA	Airbus A.321-251NX	Iberia Express	
EC-NIF	Airbus A.321-251NX	Iberia Express	
EC-NIG	Airbus A.350-941	Iberia	
EC-NIJ	Airbus A.320-271N	Vueling Airlines	
EC-NIS	Airbus A.350-941	Iberia	
EC-NIX	Airbus A.320-271N	Vueling Airlines	
EC-NIY	Airbus A.320-271N	Vueling Airlines	
EC-NJI	Airbus A.321-251NX	Iberia Express	
EC-NJM	Airbus A.350-941	Iberia	
EC-NJU	Airbus A.320-251N	Iberia	
EC-NJY	Airbus A.320-251N	Iberia	
EC-NLJ	Airbus A.321-231	Privilege Style	
EC-NLK	Boeing 737-81M	AlbaStar	
EC-NLP	Airbus A.350-941	Iberia	
EC-NLU	Boeing 737-4Q8SF	Swiftair/DHL	
EC-NLV	Airbus A.321-211	Vueling Airlines	
EC-NLX	Airbus A.321-211	Vueling Airlines	
EC-NLY	Airbus A.321-211	Vueling Airlines	
EC-NMK	Boeing 737-406SF	Swiftair/DHL	
EC-NMZ	Airbus A.350-941	Iberia	
EC-NNY	Airbus A.320-214	Volotea Airlines	
EC-NNZ	Airbus A.320-214	Volotea Airlines	
EC-NOL	Airbus A.320-214	Volotea Airlines	
EC-NOM	Airbus A.320-214	Volotea Airlines	
EC-NON	Airbus A.320-216	Volotea Airlines	
EC-NOP	Airbus A.320-214	Volotea Airlines	
EC-NOQ	Airbus A.320-216	Volotea Airlines	
EC-NOR	Airbus A.320-216	Volotea Airlines	
EC-NOS	Airbus A.320-216	Volotea Airlines	
EC-NOY	Airbus A.320-214	Volotea Airlines	
EC-NPB	Airbus A.320-214	Volotea Airlines	
EC-NPC	Airbus A.320-214	Volotea Airlines	
EC-NQM	Airbus A.320-214	Volotea Airlines	
EC-NQN	Airbus A.320-214	Volotea Airlines	
EC-NSC	Airbus A.350-941	Iberia	
EC-NST	Airbus A.321-251NX	Iberia Express	
EC-NTA	Airbus A.320-251N	Iberia	
EC-NTI	Airbus A.320-251N	Iberia	
EC-NTL	Airbus A.320-216	Volotea Airlines	
EC-NTM	Airbus A.320-216	Volotea Airlines	
EC-NTO	Airbus A.320-251N	Iberia	
EC-NTP	Airbus A.320-251N	Iberia	
EC-NTQ	Airbus A.320-251N	Iberia	
EC-NTU	Airbus A.320-214	Volotea Airlines	
EC-NUD	Airbus A.321-271NX	Iberia Express	
EC-NUG	Boeing 737-883BDSF	Swiftair/DHL	
EC-NUO	Airbus A.320-214	Vueling Airlines	
EC-NUP	Airbus A.320-214	Vueling Airlines	
EC-NUY	Boeing 737-8GP	Air Europa	
EC-NVJ	Boeing 737-8K5	Air Europa	
EC-NVP	Boeing 737-8AS	Air Europa	
EC-NVR	Airbus A.350-941	Iberia	

Notes	Reg	Type	Owner or Operator
	EC-NVS	Airbus A.320-251N	Iberia
	EC-NXC	Airbus A.350-941	Iberia
	EC-NXD	Airbus A.350-941	Iberia
	EC-NXE	Airbus A.350-941	Iberia
	EC-NXU	Boeing 737-883BDSF	Swiftair/DHL
	EC-NYC	Airbus A.321-271NX	Vueling Airlines
	EC-NYD	Airbus A.321-271NX	Vueling Airlines
	EC-NYE	Airbus A.321-271NX	Vueling Airlines
	EC-NYF	Airbus A.321-271NX	Vueling Airlines
	EC-NYM	Boeing 757-223PCF	Cygnus Air
	EC-NZP	Airbus A.320-251N	Iberia
	EC-NZQ	Airbus A.320-251N	Iberia
	EC-OAS	Airbus A.321-251NX	Iberia Express
	EC-OAU	Airbus A.321-271NX	Iberia Express
	EC-OAV	Airbus A.350-941	Iberia
	EC-OAX	Airbus A.350-941	Iberia
	EC-OAY	Airbus A.350-941	Iberia
	EC-OBN	Boeing 737-83N	Swiftair
	EC-OBQ	Boeing 737-883	Swiftair/DHL
	EC-OBY	Airbus A.321-271NX	Iberia Express
	EC-OCC	Airbus A.321-271NX	Iberia Express
	EC-OCH	Airbus A.321-271NX	Iberia Express
	EC-OCI	Airbus A.321-271NX	Iberia Express
	EC-OCR	Airbus A.350-941	Iberia
	EC-OCS	Airbus A.320-251N	Iberia
	EC-OCT	Airbus A.321-231	Privilege Style
	EC-ODJ	Airbus A.320-232	Vueling Airlines
	EC-ODL	Airbus A.320-232	Vueling Airlines
	EC-ODM	Airbus A.320-232	Vueling Airlines
	EC-ODN	Airbus A.320-232	Vueling Airlines
	EC-OEH	Airbus A.320-216	Volotea Airlines
	EC-OEI	Airbus A.320-214	Volotea Airlines
	EC-OES	Airbus A.350-941	Iberia
	EC-OFH	Airbus A.320-216	Vueling Airlines
	EC-OFM	Airbus A.350-941	Iberia
	EC-OFU	Airbus A.320-214	Vueling Airlines
	EC-OFV	Airbus A.320-232	Vueling Airlines
	EC-OFX	Airbus A.320-214	Vueling Airlines
	EC-OFY	Airbus A.320-214	Vueling Airlines
	EC-OFZ	Airbus A.320-214	Vueling Airlines
	EC-OGC	Airbus A.320-232	Vueling Airlines
	EC-OGD	Airbus A.320-232	Vueling Airlines
	EC-OGE	Airbus A.320-232	Vueling Airlines
	EC-OGS	Boeing 737-MAX8	Air Europa
	EC-OID	Avions Transport ATR-72-600F	FedEx Feeder
	EC-OIE	Avions Transport ATR-72-600F	FedEx Feeder
	EC-OIF	Avions Transport ATR-72-600F	FedEx Feeder
	EC-OIL	Airbus A.321-253NY	Iberia
	EC-OJF	Airbus A.320-232	Vueling Airlines
	EC-OJG	Airbus A.320-232	Vueling Airlines
	EC-OJH	Airbus A.320-232	Vueling Airlines
	EC-OJN	Avions Transport ATR-72-600F	FedEx Feeder
	EC-OJT	Airbus A.320-214	Volotea Airlines
	EC-OJX	Boeing 737-8Z0	Swiftair/DHL
	EC-OKG	Airbus A.320-232	Vueling Airlines
	EC-OKH	Airbus A.320-232	Vueling Airlines
	EC-OKI	Airbus A.320-232	Vueling Airlines
	EC-OKJ	Airbus A.320-232	Vueling Airlines
	EC-OLE	Airbus A.321-253NY	Iberia
	EC-OLF	Airbus A.320-233	Vueling Airlines
	EC-ONR	Airbus A.321-253NY	Iberia
	EC-OOC	Airbus A.320-214	Volotea Airlines
	EC-OOJ	Airbus A.321-253NY	Iberia
	EC-OOL	Airbus A.350-941	Iberia
	EC-OOV	Airbus A.320-232	Vueling Airlines
	EC-OPA	Boeing 737-MAX8	Air Europa
	EC-OPX	Boeing 737-MAX8	Air Europa
	EC-OPY	Boeing 737-MAX8	Air Europa
	EC-OQC	Airbus A.320-232	Vueling Airlines
	EC-OQG	Airbus A.321-253NY	Iberia
	EC-OQH	Airbus A.321-253NY	Iberia

Reg	Type	Owner or Operator	Notes
EC-ORE	Airbus A.321-253NY	Iberia	
EC-ORJ	Boeing 737-MAX8	Air Europa	
EC-ORK	Boeing 737-MAX8	Air Europa	
EC-ORZ	Airbus A.321-253NY	Iberia	

ER (Moldova)

Reg	Type	Owner or Operator	Notes
ER-00001	Airbus A.321-211	Fly One	
ER-00003	Airbus A.321-211	Fly One	
ER-00004	Airbus A.320-214	Fly One	
ER-00005	Airbus A.320-214	Fly One	
ER-00008	Airbus A.320-233	Fly One	
ER-00009	Airbus A.321-211	Fly One	
ER-00010	Airbus A.320-214	Fly One	
ER-00011	Airbus A.320-232	Fly One	
ER-00012	Airbus A.320-214	Fly One	
ER-SKY	Airbus A.319-131	Hi Sky Europe	

ET (Ethiopia)

Reg	Type	Owner or Operator	Notes
ET-APS	Boeing 777-F	Ethiopian Cargo	
ET-APU	Boeing 777-F	Ethiopian Cargo	
ET-ARI	Boeing 777-F	Ethiopian Cargo	
ET-ARJ	Boeing 777-F	Ethiopian Cargo	
ET-ARK	Boeing 777-F	Ethiopian Cargo	
ET-ATQ	Airbus A.350-941	Ethiopian Airlines	
ET-ATR	Airbus A.350-941	Ethiopian Airlines	
ET-ATY	Airbus A.350-941	Ethiopian Airlines	
ET-AUA	Airbus A.350-941	Ethiopian Airlines	
ET-AUB	Airbus A.350-941	Ethiopian Airlines	
ET-AUC	Airbus A.350-941	Ethiopian Airlines	
ET-AUO	Boeing 787-9	Ethiopian Airlines	
ET-AUP	Boeing 787-9	Ethiopian Airlines	
ET-AUQ	Boeing 787-9	Ethiopian Airlines	
ET-AUR	Boeing 787-9	Ethiopian Airlines	
ET-AVB	Airbus A.350-941	Ethiopian Airlines	
ET-AVC	Airbus A.350-941	Ethiopian Airlines	
ET-AVD	Airbus A.350-941	Ethiopian Airlines	
ET-AVE	Airbus A.350-941	Ethiopian Airlines	
ET-AVN	Boeing 777-F	Ethiopian Cargo	
ET-AVQ	Boeing 777-F	Ethiopian Cargo	
ET-AVT	Boeing 777-F	Ethiopian Cargo	
ET-AWE	Boeing 777-F	Ethiopian Cargo	
ET-AWM	Airbus A.350-941	Ethiopian Airlines	
ET-AWN	Airbus A.350-941	Ethiopian Airlines	
ET-AWO	Airbus A.350-941	Ethiopian Airlines	
ET-AWP	Airbus A.350-941	Ethiopian Airlines	
ET-AXK	Boeing 787-9	Ethiopian Airlines	
ET-AXL	Boeing 787-9	Ethiopian Airlines	
ET-AXS	Boeing 787-9	Ethiopian Airlines	
ET-AXT	Boeing 787-9	Ethiopian Airlines	
ET-AYA	Airbus A.350-941	Ethiopian Airlines	
ET-AYB	Airbus A.350-941	Ethiopian Airlines	
ET-AYC	Boeing 787-9	Ethiopian Airlines	
ET-AYD	Boeing 787-9	Ethiopian Airlines	
ET-AYM	Airbus A.350-941	Ethiopian Airlines	
ET-AYN	Airbus A.350-941	Ethiopian Airlines	
ET-AZI	Airbus A.350-941	Ethiopian Airlines	
ET-AZN	Airbus A.350-941	Ethiopian Airlines	
ET-BAA	Boeing 777-F	Ethiopian Cargo	
ET-BAB	Boeing 777-F	Ethiopian Cargo	
ET-BAC	Boeing 777-F	Ethiopian Cargo	
ET-BAW	Airbus A.350-1041	Ethiopian Airlines	
ET-BAX	Airbus A.350-1041	Ethiopian Airlines	
ET-BAY	Airbus A.350-1041	Ethiopian Airlines	
ET-BAZ	Airbus A.350-1041	Ethiopian Airlines	
ET-BCD	Airbus A.350-941	Ethiopian Airlines	
ET-BCE	Airbus A.350-941	Ethiopian Airlines	

Notes	Reg	Type	Owner or Operator

EZ (Turkmenistan)

EZ-A778	Boeing 777-22KLR	Turkmenistan Airlines
EZ-A779	Boeing 777-22KLR	Turkmenistan Airlines
EZ-A781	Boeing 777-367ER	Turkmenistan Airlines
EZ-A782	Boeing 777-367ER	Turkmenistan Airlines

F (France)

F-GKXC	Airbus A.320-214	Air France
F-GKXG	Airbus A.320-214	Air France
F-GKXH	Airbus A.320-214	Air France
F-GKXI	Airbus A.320-214	Air France
F-GKXJ	Airbus A.320-214	Air France
F-GKXL	Airbus A.320-214	Air France
F-GKXM	Airbus A.320-214	Air France
F-GKXN	Airbus A.320-214	Air France
F-GKXO	Airbus A.320-214	Air France
F-GKXP	Airbus A.320-214	Air France
F-GKXQ	Airbus A.320-214	Air France
F-GKXR	Airbus A.320-214	Air France
F-GKXS	Airbus A.320-214	Air France
F-GKXT	Airbus A.320-214	Air France
F-GKXU	Airbus A.320-214	Air France
F-GKXV	Airbus A.320-214	Air France
F-GKXY	Airbus A.320-214	Air France
F-GKXZ	Airbus A.320-214	Air France
F-GMZC	Airbus A.321-111	Air France
F-GMZD	Airbus A.321-111	Air France
F-GNEO	Airbus A.320-252N	Transavia France
F-GRXF	Airbus A.319-111	Air France
F-GSPA	Boeing 777-228ER	Air France
F-GSPD	Boeing 777-228ER	Air France
F-GSPE	Boeing 777-228ER	Air France
F-GSPF	Boeing 777-228ER	Air France
F-GSPG	Boeing 777-228ER	Air France
F-GSPI	Boeing 777-228ER	Air France
F-GSPJ	Boeing 777-228ER	Air France
F-GSPK	Boeing 777-228ER	Air France
F-GSPL	Boeing 777-228ER	Air France
F-GSPM	Boeing 777-228ER	Air France
F-GSPN	Boeing 777-228ER	Air France
F-GSPO	Boeing 777-228ER	Air France
F-GSPP	Boeing 777-228ER	Air France
F-GSPQ	Boeing 777-228ER	Air France
F-GSPU	Boeing 777-228ER	Air France
F-GSPX	Boeing 777-228ER	Air France
F-GSPY	Boeing 777-228ER	Air France
F-GSPZ	Boeing 777-228ER	Air France
F-GSQA	Boeing 777-328ER	Air France
F-GSQB	Boeing 777-328ER	Air France
F-GSQC	Boeing 777-328ER	Air France
F-GSQD	Boeing 777-328ER	Air France
F-GSQE	Boeing 777-328ER	Air France
F-GSQF	Boeing 777-328ER	Air France
F-GSQG	Boeing 777-328ER	Air France
F-GSQH	Boeing 777-328ER	Air France
F-GSQI	Tboeing 777-328ER	Owr France
F-GSQJ	Boeing 777-328ER	Air France
F-GSQK	Boeing 777-328ER	Air France
F-GSQL	Boeing 777-328ER	Air France
F-GSQM	Boeing 777-328ER	Air France
F-GSQN	Boeing 777-328ER	Air France
F-GSQO	Boeing 777-328ER	Air France
F-GSQP	Boeing 777-328ER	Air France
F-GSQR	Boeing 777-328ER	Air France
F-GSQS	Boeing 777-328ER	Air France
F-GSQT	Boeing 777-328ER	Air France
F-GSQU	Boeing 777-328ER	Air France
F-GSQV	Boeing 777-328ER	Air France
F-GSQX	Boeing 777-328ER	Air France

Reg	Type	Owner or Operator	Notes
F-GSQY	Boeing 777-328ER	Air France	
F-GSTB	Airbus A.300-608ST Beluga	Airbus Transport International	
F-GSTC	Airbus A.300-608ST Beluga	Airbus Transport International	
F-GSTF	Airbus A.300-608ST Beluga	Airbus Transport International	
F-GTAJ	Airbus A.321-211	Air France	
F-GTAK	Airbus A.321-211	Air France	
F-GTAM	Airbus A.321-211	Air France	
F-GTAP	Airbus A.321-212	Air France	
F-GTAQ	Airbus A.321-211	Air France	
F-GTAS	Airbus A.321-211	Air France	
F-GTAT	Airbus A.321-211	Air France	
F-GTAU	Airbus A.321-211	Air France	
F-GTAY	Airbus A.321-211	Air France	
F-GTAZ	Airbus A.321-211	Air France	
F-GUGM	Airbus A.318-111	Air France	
F-GUGN	Airbus A.318-111	Air France	
F-GUGO	Airbus A.318-111	Air France	
F-GUGP	Airbus A.318-111	Air France	
F-GUOB	Boeing 777-F28	Air France Cargo	
F-GUOC	Boeing 777-F28	Air France Cargo	
F-GXLG	Airbus A.330-743L Beluga	Airbus Transport International	
F-GXLH	Airbus A.330-743L Beluga	Airbus Transport International	
F-GXLI	Airbus A.330-743L Beluga	Airbus Transport International	
F-GXLJ	Airbus A.330-743L Beluga	Airbus Transport International	
F-GXLN	Airbus A.330-743L Beluga	Airbus Transport International	
F-GXLO	Airbus A.330-743L Beluga	Airbus Transport International	
F-GZCA	Airbus A.330-203	Air France	
F-GZCF	Airbus A.330-203	Air France	
F-GZCG	Airbus A.330-203	Air France	
F-GZCI	Airbus A.330-203	Air France	
F-GZCK	Airbus A.330-203	Air France	
F-GZCM	Airbus A.330-203	Air France	
F-GZCN	Airbus A.330-203	Air France	
F-GZCO	Airbus A.330-203	Air France	
F-GZHA	Boeing 737-8GJ	Transavia France	
F-GZHB	Boeing 737-8GJ	Transavia France	
F-GZHC	Boeing 737-8GJ	Transavia France	
F-GZHE	Boeing 737-8K2	Transavia France	
F-GZHI	Boeing 737-8K2	Transavia France	
F-GZHJ	Boeing 737-8K2	Transavia France	
F-GZHK	Boeing 737-8K2	Transavia France	
F-GZHL	Boeing 737-8K2	Transavia France	
F-GZHM	Boeing 737-8K2	Transavia France	
F-GZHO	Boeing 737-8K2	Transavia France	
F-GZHP	Boeing 737-8K2	Transavia France	
F-GZHQ	Boeing 737-8K2	Transavia France	
F-GZHR	Boeing 737-8K2	Transavia France	
F-GZHT	Boeing 737-8K2	Transavia France	
F-GZHU	Boeing 737-8K2	Transavia France	
F-GZHX	Boeing 737-8K2	Transavia France	
F-GZHY	Boeing 737-8K2	Transavia France	
F-GZHZ	Boeing 737-85P	Transavia France	
F-GZNA	Boeing 777-328ER	Air France	
F-GZNB	Boeing 777-328ER	Air France	
F-GZNC	Boeing 777-328ER	Air France	
F-GZND	Boeing 777-328ER	Air France	
F-GZNE	Boeing 777-328ER	Air France	
F-GZNF	Boeing 777-328ER	Air France	
F-GZNG	Boeing 777-328ER	Air France	
F-GZNH	Boeing 777-328ER	Air France	
F-GZNI	Boeing 777-328ER	Air France	
F-GZNJ	Boeing 777-328ER	Air France	
F-GZNK	Boeing 777-328ER	Air France	
F-GZNL	Boeing 777-328ER	Air France	
F-GZNN	Boeing 777-328ER	Air France	
F-GZNO	Boeing 777-328ER	Air France	
F-GZNP	Boeing 777-328ER	Air France	
F-GZNQ	Boeing 777-328ER	Air France	
F-GZNR	Boeing 777-328ER	Air France	
F-GZNS	Boeing 777-328ER	Air France	
F-GZNT	Boeing 777-328ER	Air France	

Notes	Reg	Type	Owner or Operator
	F-GZNU	Boeing 777-328ER	Air France
	F-HBLA	Embraer ERJ190-100LR	Air France HOP
	F-HBLB	Embraer ERJ190-100LR	Air France HOP
	F-HBLC	Embraer ERJ190-100LR	Air France HOP
	F-HBLD	Embraer ERJ190-100LR	Air France HOP
	F-HBLE	Embraer ERJ190-100LR	Air France HOP
	F-HBLF	Embraer ERJ190-100LR	Air France HOP
	F-HBLG	Embraer ERJ190-100LR	Air France HOP
	F-HBLH	Embraer ERJ190-100LR	Air France HOP
	F-HBLI	Embraer ERJ190-100LR	Air France HOP
	F-HBLJ	Embraer ERJ190-100LR	Air France HOP
	F-HBLK	Embraer ERJ190-100STD	Air France HOP
	F-HBLL	Embraer ERJ190-100STD	Air France HOP
	F-HBLM	Embraer ERJ190-100STD	Air France HOP
	F-HBLN	Embraer ERJ190-100STD	Air France HOP
	F-HBLO	Embraer ERJ190-100STD	Air France HOP
	F-HBLP	Embraer ERJ190-100STD	Air France HOP
	F-HBLQ	Embraer ERJ190-100STD	Air France HOP
	F-HBLR	Embraer ERJ190-100STD	Air France HOP
	F-HBLS	Embraer ERJ190-100STD	Air France HOP
	F-HBLV	Embraer ERJ190-100STD	Air France HOP
	F-HBLX	Embraer ERJ190-100STD	Air France HOP
	F-HBLY	Embraer ERJ190-100STD	Air France HOP
	F-HBLZ	Embraer ERJ190-100STD	Air France HOP
	F-HBNB	Airbus A.320-214	Air France
	F-HBND	Airbus A.320-214	Air France
	F-HBNE	Airbus A.320-214	Air France
	F-HBNG	Airbus A.320-214	Air France
	F-HBNH	Airbus A.320-214	Air France
	F-HBNJ	Airbus A.320-214	Air France
	F-HBQA	Embraer ERJ190-100STD	Air France HOP
	F-HBQB	Embraer ERJ190-100STD	Air France HOP
	F-HBQC	Embraer ERJ190-100STD	Air France HOP
	F-HBQD	Embraer ERJ190-100STD	Air France HOP
	F-HBQE	Embraer ERJ190-100STD	Air France HOP
	F-HBXA	Embraer ERJ170-100LR	Air France HOP
	F-HBXB	Embraer ERJ170-100LR	Air France HOP
	F-HBXC	Embraer ERJ170-100LR	Air France HOP
	F-HBXD	Embraer ERJ170-100LR	Air France HOP
	F-HBXE	Embraer ERJ170-100LR	Air France HOP
	F-HBXF	Embraer ERJ170-100LR	Air France HOP
	F-HBXG	Embraer ERJ170-100LR	Air France HOP
	F-HBXH	Embraer ERJ170-100LR	Air France HOP
	F-HBXI	Embraer ERJ170-100LR	Air France HOP
	F-HBXJ	Embraer ERJ170-100LR	Air France HOP
	F-HBXN	Embraer ERJ170-100LR	Air France HOP
	F-HEPA	Airbus A.320-214	Air France
	F-HEPB	Airbus A.320-214	Air France
	F-HEPC	Airbus A.320-214	Air France
	F-HEPD	Airbus A.320-214	Air France
	F-HEPE	Airbus A.320-214	Air France
	F-HEPF	Airbus A.320-214	Air France
	F-HEPG	Airbus A.320-214	Air France
	F-HEPH	Airbus A.320-214	Air France
	F-HEPI	Airbus A.320-214	Air France
	F-HEPJ	Airbus A.320-214	Air France
	F-HEPK	Airbus A.320-214	Air France
	F-HOZA	Airbus A.220-300	Owner France
	F-HOZB	Airbus A.220-300	Air France
	F-HOZC	Airbus A.220-300	Air France
	F-HPNA	Airbus A.220-300	Air France
	F-HPNB	Airbus A.220-300	Air France
	F-HPNC	Airbus A.220-300	Air France
	F-HPND	Airbus A.220-300	Air France
	F-HPNE	Airbus A.220-300	Air France
	F-HPNF	Airbus A.220-300	Air France
	F-HPNG	Airbus A.220-300	Air France
	F-HPNH	Airbus A.220-300	Air France
	F-HPNI	Airbus A.220-300	Air France
	F-HPNJ	Airbus A.220-300	Air France
	F-HPNK	Airbus A.220-300	Air France

Reg	Type	Owner or Operator	Notes
F-HPNL	Airbus A.220-300	Air France	
F-HPNM	Airbus A.220-300	Air France	
F-HPNN	Airbus A.220-300	Air France	
F-HPNO	Airbus A.220-300	Air France	
F-HPNP	Airbus A.220-300	Air France	
F-HPNQ	Airbus A.220-300	Air France	
F-HPNR	Airbus A.220-300	Air France	
F-HPNS	Airbus A.220-300	Air France	
F-HPNT	Airbus A.220-300	Air France	
F-HPNU	Airbus A.220-300	Air France	
F-HPNV	Airbus A.220-300	Air France	
F-HPNX	Airbus A.220-300	Air France	
F-HPNY	Airbus A.220-300	Air France	
F-HPNZ	Airbus A.220-300	Air France	
F-HRBA	Boeing 787-9	Air France	
F-HRBB	Boeing 787-9	Air France	
F-HRBC	Boeing 787-9	Air France	
F-HRBD	Boeing 787-9	Air France	
F-HRBE	Boeing 787-9	Air France	
F-HRBF	Boeing 787-9	Air France	
F-HRBG	Boeing 787-9	Air France	
F-HRBH	Boeing 787-9	Air France	
F-HRBI	Boeing 787-9	Air France	
F-HRBJ	Boeing 787-9	Air France	
F-HTVA	Boeing 737-8K2	Transavia France	
F-HTVB	Boeing 737-8K2	Transavia France	
F-HTVC	Boeing 737-8K2	Transavia France	
F-HTVD	Boeing 737-8K2	Transavia France	
F-HTVE	Boeing 737-8K2	Transavia France	
F-HTVF	Boeing 737-8K2	Transavia France	
F-HTVG	Boeing 737-8K2	Transavia France	
F-HTVH	Boeing 737-8K2	Transavia France	
F-HTVI	Boeing 737-8K2	Transavia France	
F-HTVJ	Boeing 737-8K2	Transavia France	
F-HTVK	Boeing 737-8K2	Transavia France	
F-HTVL	Boeing 737-84P	Transavia France	
F-HTVM	Boeing 737-8K2	Transavia France	
F-HTVN	Boeing 737-8GJ	Transavia France	
F-HTVP	Boeing 737-8AL	Transavia France	
F-HTVQ	Boeing 737-8AL	Transavia France	
F-HTVR	Boeing 737-86J	Transavia France	
F-HTVS	Boeing 737-86J	Transavia France	
F-HTVT	Boeing 737-86J	Transavia France	
F-HTVU	Boeing 737-86J	Transavia France	
F-HTVV	Boeing 737-8JP	Transavia France	
F-HTVX	Boeing 737-8JP	Transavia France	
F-HTVY	Boeing 737-8JP	Transavia France	
F-HTVZ	Boeing 737-8JP	Transavia France	
F-HTYA	Airbus A.350-941	Air France	
F-HTYB	Airbus A.350-941	Air France	
F-HTYC	Airbus A.350-941	Air France	
F-HTYD	Airbus A.350-941	Air France	
F-HTYE	Airbus A.350-941	Air France	
F-HTYF	Airbus A.350-941	Air France	
F-HTYG	Airbus A.350-941	Air France	
F-HTYH	Airbus A.350-941	Air France	
F-HTYI	Airbus A.350-941	Air France	
F-HTYJ	Airbus A.350-941	Air France	
F-HTYK	Airbus A.350-941	Air France	
F-HTYL	Airbus A.350-941	Air France	
F-HTYM	Airbus A.350-941	Air France	
F-HTYN	Airbus A.350-941	Air France	
F-HTYO	Airbus A.350-941	Air France	
F-HTYP	Airbus A.350-941	Air France	
F-HTYQ	Airbus A.350-941	Air France	
F-HTYR	Airbus A.350-941	Air France	
F-HTYS	Airbus A.350-941	Air France	
F-HTYT	Airbus A.350-941	Air France	
F-HUVA	Airbus A.350-941	Air France	
F-HUVB	Airbus A.350-941	Air France	
F-HUVC	Airbus A.350-941	Air France	

Notes	Reg	Type	Owner or Operator
	F-HUVD	Airbus A.350-941	Air France
	F-HUVE	Airbus A.350-941	Air France
	F-HUVF	Airbus A.350-941	Air France
	F-HUVG	Airbus A.350-941	Air France
	F-HUVH	Airbus A.350-941	Air France
	F-HUVI	Airbus A.350-941	Air France
	F-HUVJ	Airbus A.350-941	Air France
	F-HUVK	Airbus A.350-941	Air France
	F-HUVL	Airbus A.350-941	Air France
	F-HUVM	Airbus A.350-941	Air France
	F-HUVN	Airbus A.350-941	Air France
	F-HUVO	Airbus A.350-941	Air France
	F-HUVP	Airbus A.350-941	Air France
	F-HUVQ	Airbus A.350-941	Air France
	F-HUVR	Airbus A.350-941	Air France
	F-HUVS	Airbus A.350-941	Air France
	F-HUVT	Airbus A.350-941	Air France
	F-HUVU	Airbus A.350-941	Air France
	F-HUYA	Boeing 737-8JP	Transavia France
	F-HUYB	Boeing 737-8JP	Transavia France
	F-HUYC	Boeing 737-8JP	Transavia France
	F-HUYD	Boeing 737-8JP	Transavia France
	F-HUYE	Boeing 737-8JP	Transavia France
	F-HUYF	Boeing 737-8JP	Transavia France
	F-HUYG	Boeing 737-8JP	Transavia France
	F-HUYH	Boeing 737-86N	Transavia France
	F-HUYI	Boeing 737-86N	Transavia France
	F-HUYJ	Boeing 737-86N	Transavia France
	F-HUYK	Boeing 737-883	Transavia France
	F-HUYL	Boeing 737-86N	Transavia France
	F-HUYM	Boeing 737-86N	Transavia France
	F-HUYN	Boeing 737-82R	Transavia France
	F-HUYO	Boeing 737-82R	Transavia France
	F-HUYP	Boeing 737-8GP	Transavia France
	F-HUYQ	Boeing 737-8GP	Transavia France
	F-HUYR	Boeing 737-8K5	Transavia France
	F-HUYS	Boeing 737-8K5	Transavia France
	F-HUYT	Boeing 737-8K5	Transavia France
	F-HUYU	Boeing 737-86N	Transavia France
	F-HUYV	Boeing 737-8K5	Transavia France
	F-HUYX	Boeing 737-8GP	Transavia France
	F-HUYY	Boeing 737-8GP	Transavia France
	F-HUYZ	Boeing 737-8GP	Transavia France
	F-HXSA	Airbus A.320-252N	Transavia France
	F-HXSB	Airbus A.320-252N	Transavia France
	F-HXSC	Airbus A.320-252N	Transavia France
	F-HXSD	Airbus A.320-252N	Transavia France
	F-HXSE	Airbus A.320-252N	Transavia France
	F-HXSF	Airbus A.320-252N	Transavia France
	F-HXSG	Airbus A.320-252N	Transavia France
	F-HXSH	Airbus A.320-252N	Transavia France
	F-HXSI	Airbus A.320-252N	Transavia France
	F-HXSJ	Airbus A.320-252N	Transavia France
	F-HXSK	Airbus A.320-252N	Transavia France
	F-HXSL	Airbus A.320-252N	Transavia France
	F-HXSM	Airbus A.320-252N	Transavia France
	F-HXSN	Airbus A.320-252N	Transavia France
	F-HXSO	Airbus A.320-252N	Transavia France
	F-HXSP	Airbus A.320-252N	Transavia France
	F-HXSQ	Airbus A.320-252N	Transavia France
	F-HXSR	Airbus A.320-252N	Transavia France
	F-HXST	Airbus A.320-252N	Transavia France
	F-HXSU	Airbus A.320-252N	Transavia France
	F-HXSV	Airbus A.320-252N	Transavia France
	F-HXSX	Airbus A.320-252N	Transavia France
	F-HZFM	Airbus A.320-214	Air France
	F-HZUA	Airbus A.220-300	Air France
	F-HZUB	Airbus A.220-300	Air France
	F-HZUC	Airbus A.220-300	Air France
	F-HZUD	Airbus A.220-300	Air France
	F-HZUE	Airbus A.220-300	Air France

Reg	Type	Owner or Operator	Notes
F-HZUF	Airbus A.220-300	Air France	
F-HZUG	Airbus A.220-300	Air France	
F-HZUH	Airbus A.220-300	Air France	
F-HZUI	Airbus A.220-300	Air France	
F-HZUJ	Airbus A.220-300	Air France	
F-HZUK	Airbus A.220-300	Air France	
F-HZUL	Airbus A.220-300	Air France	
F-HZUM	Airbus A.220-300	Air France	
F-HZUN	Airbus A.220-300	Air France	
F-HZUO	Airbus A.220-300	Air France	
F-HZUP	Airbus A.220-300	Air France	
F-HZUQ	Airbus A.220-300	Air France	
F-HZUR	Airbus A.220-300	Air France	
F-HZUS	Airbus A.220-300	Air France	
F-HZUT	Airbus A.220-300	Air France	
F-HZUU	Airbus A.220-300	Air France	
F-HZUV	Airbus A.220-300	Air France	
F-HZUX	Airbus A.220-300	Air France	
F-HZUY	Airbus A.220-300	Air France	
F-HZUZ	Airbus A.220-300	Air France	

HA (Hungary)

Reg	Type	Owner or Operator	Notes
HA-LDA	Airbus A.321-271NX	Wizz Air	
HA-LDB	Airbus A.321-271NX	Wizz Air	
HA-LDC	Airbus A.321-271NX	Wizz Air	
HA-LDG	Airbus A.321-271NX	Wizz Air	
HA-LDH	Airbus A.321-271NX	Wizz Air	
HA-LDI	Airbus A.321-271NX	Wizz Air	
HA-LDK	Airbus A.321-271NX	Wizz Air	
HA-LDL	Airbus A.321-271NX	Wizz Air	
HA-LDM	Airbus A.321-271NX	Wizz Air	
HA-LGA	Airbus A.321-271NX	Wizz Air	
HA-LGB	Airbus A.321-271NX	Wizz Air	
HA-LGD	Airbus A.321-271NX	Wizz Air	
HA-LGE	Airbus A.321-271NX	Wizz Air	
HA-LGF	Airbus A.321-271NX	Wizz Air	
HA-LGH	Airbus A.321-271NX	Wizz Air	
HA-LGI	Airbus A.321-271NX	Wizz Air	
HA-LGL	Airbus A.321-271NX	Wizz Air	
HA-LGM	Airbus A.321-271NX	Wizz Air	
HA-LGN	Airbus A.321-271NX	Wizz Air	
HA-LGO	Airbus A.321-271NX	Wizz Air	
HA-LGP	Airbus A.321-271NX	Wizz Air	
HA-LGQ	Airbus A.321-271NX	Wizz Air	
HA-LGR	Airbus A.321-271NX	Wizz Air	
HA-LGS	Airbus A.321-271NX	Wizz Air	
HA-LGT	Airbus A.321-271NX	Wizz Air	
HA-LGU	Airbus A.321-271NX	Wizz Air	
HA-LGV	Airbus A.321-271NX	Wizz Air	
HA-LGW	Airbus A.321-271NX	Wizz Air	
HA-LGX	Airbus A.321-271NX	Wizz Air	
HA-LGY	Airbus A.321-271NX	Wizz Air	
HA-LGZ	Airbus A.321-271NX	Wizz Air	
HA-LKG	Boeing 737-8CX	Smart Wings Hungary	
HA-LPJ	Airbus A.320-232	Wizz Air	
HA-LPM	Airbus A.320-232	Wizz Air	
HA-LTA	Airbus A.321-231	Wizz Air	
HA-LTB	Airbus A.321-231	Wizz Air	
HA-LTC	Airbus A.321-231	Wizz Air	
HA-LTD	Airbus A.321-231	Wizz Air	
HA-LTE	Airbus A.321-231	Wizz Air	
HA-LTF	Airbus A.321-231	Wizz Air	
HA-LTG	Airbus A.321-231	Wizz Air	
HA-LTH	Airbus A.321-231	Wizz Air	
HA-LTI	Airbus A.321-231	Wizz Air	
HA-LTJ	Airbus A.321-231	Wizz Air	
HA-LTK	Airbus A.321-231	Wizz Air	
HA-LTL	Airbus A.321-231	Wizz Air	
HA-LTM	Airbus A.321-231	Wizz Air	
HA-LVB	Airbus A.321-271NX	Wizz Air	

Notes	Reg	Type	Owner or Operator
	HA-LVC	Airbus A.321-271NX	Wizz Air
	HA-LVD	Airbus A.321-271NX	Wizz Air
	HA-LVE	Airbus A.321-271NX	Wizz Air
	HA-LVF	Airbus A.321-271NX	Wizz Air
	HA-LVG	Airbus A.321-271NX	Wizz Air
	HA-LVH	Airbus A.321-271NX	Wizz Air
	HA-LVI	Airbus A.321-271NX	Wizz Air
	HA-LVJ	Airbus A.321-271NX	Wizz Air
	HA-LVK	Airbus A.321-271NX	Wizz Air
	HA-LVO	Airbus A.321-271NX	Wizz Air
	HA-LVP	Airbus A.321-271NX	Wizz Air
	HA-LVQ	Airbus A.321-271NX	Wizz Air
	HA-LVT	Airbus A.321-271NX	Wizz Air
	HA-LVW	Airbus A.321-271NX	Wizz Air
	HA-LWC	Airbus A.320-232	Wizz Air
	HA-LWE	Airbus A.320-232	Wizz Air
	HA-LWM	Airbus A.320-232	Wizz Air
	HA-LWN	Airbus A.320-232	Wizz Air
	HA-LWQ	Airbus A.320-232	Wizz Air
	HA-LWU	Airbus A.320-232	Wizz Air
	HA-LWV	Airbus A.320-232	Wizz Air
	HA-LWY	Airbus A.320-232	Wizz Air
	HA-LXA	Airbus A.321-231	Wizz Air
	HA-LXB	Airbus A.321-231	Wizz Air
	HA-LXC	Airbus A.321-231	Wizz Air
	HA-LXD	Airbus A.321-231	Wizz Air
	HA-LXE	Airbus A.321-231	Wizz Air
	HA-LXF	Airbus A.321-231	Wizz Air
	HA-LXG	Airbus A.321-231	Wizz Air
	HA-LXH	Airbus A.321-231	Wizz Air
	HA-LXI	Airbus A.321-231	Wizz Air
	HA-LXJ	Airbus A.321-231	Wizz Air
	HA-LXL	Airbus A.321-231	Wizz Air
	HA-LXM	Airbus A.321-231	Wizz Air
	HA-LXN	Airbus A.321-231	Wizz Air
	HA-LXO	Airbus A.321-231	Wizz Air
	HA-LXP	Airbus A.321-231	Wizz Air
	HA-LXQ	Airbus A.321-231	Wizz Air
	HA-LXR	Airbus A.321-231	Wizz Air
	HA-LXS	Airbus A.321-231	Wizz Air
	HA-LXT	Airbus A.321-231	Wizz Air
	HA-LXU	Airbus A.321-231	Wizz Air
	HA-LXV	Airbus A.321-231	Wizz Air
	HA-LXW	Airbus A.321-231	Wizz Air
	HA-LXY	Airbus A.321-231	Wizz Air
	HA-LYF	Airbus A.320-232	Wizz Air
	HA-LYG	Airbus A.320-232	Wizz Air
	HA-LYK	Airbus A.320-232	Wizz Air
	HA-LYL	Airbus A.320-232	Wizz Air
	HA-LYS	Airbus A.320-232	Wizz Air
	HA-LYT	Airbus A.320-232	Wizz Air
	HA-LZE	Airbus A.321-271NX	Wizz Air
	HA-LZI	Airbus A.321-271NX	Wizz Air
	HA-LZJ	Airbus A.321-271NX	Wizz Air
	HA-LZK	Airbus A.321-271NX	Wizz Air
	HA-LZL	Airbus A.321-271NX	Wizz Air
	HA-LZM	Airbus A.321-271NX	Wizz Air
	HA-LZN	Airbus A.321-271NX	Owzz Air
	HA-LZO	Airbus A.321-271NX	Wizz Air
	HA-LZP	Airbus A.321-271NX	Wizz Air
	HA-LZQ	Airbus A.321-271NX	Wizz Air
	HA-LZR	Airbus A.321-271NX	Wizz Air
	HA-LZT	Airbus A.321-271NX	Wizz Air
	HA-LZU	Airbus A.321-271NX	Wizz Air
	HA-LZV	Airbus A.321-271NX	Wizz Air
	HA-LZW	Airbus A.321-271NX	Wizz Air
	HA-LZX	Airbus A.321-271NX	Wizz Air
	HA-LZY	Airbus A.321-271NX	Wizz Air

Reg	Type	Owner or Operator	Notes
HB (Switzerland)			
HB-AFJ	Aerospatiale ATR-72-202F	Zimex Aviation	
HB-AFN	Aerospatiale ATR-72-201F	Zimex Aviation	
HB-ALM	Aerospatiale ATR-72-202F	Zimex Aviation	
HB-AYE	Airbus A.320-251N	easyJet Switzerland	
HB-AYM	Airbus A.320-251N	easyJet Switzerland	
HB-AYN	Airbus A.320-251N	easyJet Switzerland	
HB-AYO	Airbus A.320-251N	easyJet Switzerland	
HB-AYP	Airbus A.320-251N	easyJet Switzerland	
HB-AYQ	Airbus A.320-251N	easyJet Switzerland	
HB-AYR	Airbus A.320-251N	easyJet Switzerland	
HB-AZA	Embraer ERJ190-300STD	Helvetic Airways	
HB-AZB	Embraer ERJ190-300STD	Helvetic Airways	
HB-AZC	Embraer ERJ190-300STD	Helvetic Airways	
HB-AZD	Embraer ERJ190-300STD	Helvetic Airways	
HB-AZE	Embraer ERJ190-300STD	Helvetic Airways	
HB-AZF	Embraer ERJ190-300STD	Helvetic Airways	
HB-AZG	Embraer ERJ190-300STD	Helvetic Airways	
HB-AZH	Embraer ERJ190-300STD	Helvetic Airways	
HB-AZI	Embraer ERJ190-400	Helvetic Airways	
HB-AZJ	Embraer ERJ190-400	Helvetic Airways	
HB-AZK	Embraer ERJ190-400	Helvetic Airways	
HB-AZL	Embraer ERJ190-400	Helvetic Airways	
HB-IFA	Airbus A.350-941	Swiss International	
HB-IFB	Airbus A.350-941	Swiss International	
HB-IHX	Airbus A.320-214	Edelweiss Air	
HB-IHY	Airbus A.320-214	Edelweiss Air	
HB-IHZ	Airbus A.320-214	Edelweiss Air	
HB-IFA	Airbus A.350-941	Swiss International	
HB-IFB	Airbus A.350-941	Swiss International	
HB-IJK	Airbus A.320-214	Swiss International	
HB-IJL	Airbus A.320-214	Swiss International	
HB-IJM	Airbus A.320-214	Swiss International	
HB-IJN	Airbus A.320-214	Swiss International	
HB-IJO	Airbus A.320-214	Swiss International	
HB-IJP	Airbus A.320-214	Swiss International	
HB-IJQ	Airbus A.320-214	Swiss International	
HB-IJR	Airbus A.320-214	Swiss International	
HB-IJU	Airbus A.320-214	Edelweiss Air	
HB-IJV	Airbus A.320-214	Edelweiss Air	
HB-IJW	Airbus A.320-214	Edelweiss Air	
HB-IOD	Airbus A.321-111	Swiss International	
HB-IOF	Airbus A.321-111	Swiss International	
HB-IOH	Airbus A.321-111	Swiss International	
HB-IOM	Airbus A.321-212	Swiss International	
HB-ION	Airbus A.321-212	Swiss International	
HB-IOO	Airbus A.321-212	Swiss International	
HB-JBA	Airbus A.220-100	Swiss International	
HB-JBB	Airbus A.220-100	Swiss International	
HB-JBC	Airbus A.220-100	Swiss International	
HB-JBD	Airbus A.220-100	Swiss International	
HB-JBE	Airbus A.220-100	Swiss International	
HB-JBF	Airbus A.220-100	Swiss International	
HB-JBG	Airbus A.220-100	Swiss International	
HB-JBH	Airbus A.220-100	Swiss International	
HB-JBI	Airbus A.220-100	Swiss International	
HB-JCA	Airbus A.220-300	Swiss International	
HB-JCB	Airbus A.220-300	Swiss International	
HB-JCC	Airbus A.220-300	Swiss International	
HB-JCD	Airbus A.220-300	Swiss International	
HB-JCE	Airbus A.220-300	Swiss International	
HB-JCF	Airbus A.220-300	Swiss International	
HB-JCG	Airbus A.220-300	Swiss International	
HB-JCH	Airbus A.220-300	Swiss Intwational	
HB-JCI	Airbus A.220-300	Swiss Intwational	
HB-JCJ	Airbus A.220-300	Swiss International	
HB-JCK	Airbus A.220-300	Swiss International	
HB-JCL	Airbus A.220-300	Swiss International	
HB-JCM	Airbus A.220-300	Swiss International	
HB-JCN	Airbus A.220-300	Swiss International	

Notes	Reg	Type	Owner or Operator
	HB-JCO	Airbus A.220-300	Swiss International
	HB-JCP	Airbus A.220-300	Swiss International
	HB-JCQ	Airbus A.220-300	Swiss International
	HB-JCR	Airbus A.220-300	Swiss International
	HB-JCS	Airbus A.220-300	Swiss International
	HB-JCT	Airbus A.220-300	Swiss International
	HB-JCU	Airbus A.220-300	Swiss International
	HB-JDA	Airbus A.320-271N	Swiss International
	HB-JDB	Airbus A.320-271N	Swiss International
	HB-JDC	Airbus A.320-271N	Swiss International
	HB-JDD	Airbus A.320-271N	Swiss International
	HB-JDE	Airbus A.320-271N	Swiss International
	HB-JDF	Airbus A.320-271N	Swiss International
	HB-JDG	Airbus A.320-271N	Swiss International
	HB-JDH	Airbus A.320-271N	Swiss International
	HB-JDI	Airbus A.320-271N	Swiss International
	HB-JDJ	Airbus A.320-271N	Swiss International
	HB-JDK	Airbus A.320-271N	Swiss International
	HB-JDL	Airbus A.320-271N	Swiss International
	HB-JDM	Airbus A.320-271N	Swiss International
	HB-JDN	Airbus A.320-271N	Swiss International
	HB-JHA	Airbus A.330-343	Swiss International
	HB-JHB	Airbus A.330-343	Swiss International
	HB-JHC	Airbus A.330-343	Swiss International
	HB-JHD	Airbus A.330-343	Swiss International
	HB-JHE	Airbus A.330-343	Swiss International
	HB-JHF	Airbus A.330-343	Swiss International
	HB-JHG	Airbus A.330-343	Swiss International
	HB-JHH	Airbus A.330-343	Swiss International
	HB-JHI	Airbus A.330-343	Swiss International
	HB-JHJ	Airbus A.330-343	Swiss International
	HB-JHK	Airbus A.330-343	Swiss International
	HB-JHL	Airbus A.330-343	Swiss International
	HB-JHM	Airbus A.330-343	Swiss International
	HB-JHN	Airbus A.330-343	Swiss International
	HB-JJK	Airbus A.320-214	Edelweiss Air
	HB-JJL	Airbus A.320-214	Edelweiss Air
	HB-JJM	Airbus A.320-214	Edelweiss Air
	HB-JJN	Airbus A.320-214	Edelweiss Air
	HB-JLP	Airbus A.320-214	Edelweiss Air
	HB-JLQ	Airbus A.320-214	Edelweiss Air
	HB-JLR	Airbus A.320-214	Edelweiss Air
	HB-JLS	Airbus A.320-214	Edelweiss Air
	HB-JLT	Airbus A.320-214	Edelweiss Air
	HB-JMA	Airbus A.340-313X	Swiss International
	HB-JMB	Airbus A.340-313X	Swiss International
	HB-JMH	Airbus A.340-313X	Swiss International
	HB-JMI	Airbus A.340-313X	Swiss International
	HB-JNA	Boeing 777-3DEER	Swiss International
	HB-JNB	Boeing 777-3DEER	Swiss International
	HB-JNC	Boeing 777-3DEER	Swiss International
	HB-JND	Boeing 777-3DEER	Swiss International
	HB-JNE	Boeing 777-3DEER	Swiss International
	HB-JNF	Boeing 777-3DEER	Swiss International
	HB-JNG	Boeing 777-3DEER	Swiss International
	HB-JNH	Boeing 777-3DEER	Swiss International
	HB-JNI	Boeing 777-3DEER	Swiss International
	HB-JNJ	Boeing 777-3DEER	Swiss International
	HB-JNK	Boeing 777-300ER	Swiss International
	HB-JNL	Boeing 777-300ER	Swiss International
	HB-JPA	Airbus A.321-271NX	Swiss International
	HB-JPB	Airbus A.321-271NX	Swiss International
	HB-JPC	Airbus A.321-271NX	Swiss International
	HB-JPD	Airbus A.321-271NX	Swiss International
	HB-JPE	Airbus A.321-271NX	Swiss International
	HB-JPF	Airbus A.321-271NX	Swiss International
	HB-JPG	Airbus A.321-271NX	Swiss International
	HB-JPH	Airbus A.321-271NX	Swiss International
	HB-JVA	Embraer ERJ190-200LR	Helvetic Airways
	HB-JVJ	Embraer ERJ190-200LR	Helvetic Airways
	HB-JVO	Embraer ERJ190-100LR	Helvetic Airways

Reg	Type	Owner or Operator	Notes
HB-JVP	Embraer ERJ190-100LR	Helvetic Airways	
HB-JVW	Embraer ERJ190-200LR	Helvetic Airways	
HB-JVX	Embraer ERJ190-100STD	Helvetic Airways	
HB-JVY	Embraer ERJ190-100STD	Helvetic Airways	
HB-JVZ	Embraer ERJ190-200LR	Helvetic Airways	
HB-JXA	Airbus A.320-214	easyJet Switzerland	
HB-JXB	Airbus A.320-214	easyJet Switzerland	
HB-JXD	Airbus A.320-214	easyJet Switzerland	
HB-JXE	Airbus A.320-214	easyJet Switzerland	
HB-JXF	Airbus A.320-214	easyJet Switzerland	
HB-JXJ	Airbus A.320-214	easyJet Switzerland	
HB-JXK	Airbus A.320-214	easyJet Switzerland	
HB-JXL	Airbus A.320-214	easyJet Switzerland	
HB-JXM	Airbus A.320-214	easyJet Switzerland	
HB-JXN	Airbus A.320-214	easyJet Switzerland	
HB-JXO	Airbus A.320-214	easyJet Switzerland	
HB-JXP	Airbus A.320-214	easyJet Switzerland	
HB-JXQ	Airbus A.320-214	easyJet Switzerland	
HB-JXR	Airbus A.320-214	easyJet Switzerland	
HB-JXS	Airbus A.320-214	easyJet Switzerland	
HB-JXT	Airbus A.320-214	easyJet Switzerland	
HB-JXU	Airbus A.320-214	easyJet Switzerland	
HB-JXV	Airbus A.320-214	easyJet Switzerland	
HB-JYA	Airbus A.320-214	easyJet Switzerland	
HB-JYD	Airbus A.320-214	easyJet Switzerland	
HB-JZR	Airbus A.320-214	easyJet Switzerland	
HB-JZX	Airbus A.320-214	easyJet Switzerland	
HB-JZY	Airbus A.320-214	easyJet Switzerland	
HB-JZZ	Airbus A.320-214	easyJet Switzerland	

HL (Korea)

Reg	Type	Owner or Operator	Notes
HL7202	Boeing 777-3B5EER	Korean Air	
HL7203	Boeing 777-3B5EER	Korean Air	
HL7204	Boeing 777-3B5EER	Korean Air	
HL7205	Boeing 777-3B5EER	Korean Air	
HL7417	Boeing 747-48EBCF	AirZeta	
HL7419	Boeing 747-48EF (SCD)	AirZeta	
HL7420	Boeing 747-48EF (SCD)	AirZeta	
HL7421	Boeing 747-48EBSF	AirZeta	
HL7423	Boeing 747-48EBSF	AirZeta	
HL7436	Boeing 747-48EF (SCD)	AirZeta	
HL7578	Airbus A.350-941	Asiana Airlines	
HL7579	Airbus A.350-941	Asiana Airlines	
HL7616	Boeing 747-446F	AirZeta	
HL7620	Boeing 747-419F	AirZeta	
HL7637	Boeing 747-8B5	Korean Air	
HL7638	Boeing 747-8B5	Korean Air	
HL7642	Boeing 747-8B5	Korean Air	
HL7644	Boeing 747-8B5	Korean Air	
HL7645	Boeing 747-419F	AirZeta	
HL7646	Boeing 747-419F	AirZeta	
HL7771	Airbus A.350-941	Asiana Airlines	
HL7782	Boeing 777-3B5ER	Korean Air	
HL7783	Boeing 777-3B5ER	Korean Air	
HL8005	Boeing 777-FB5	Korean Air Cargo	
HL8006	Boeing 777-3B5ER	Korean Air	
HL8007	Boeing 777-3B5ER	Korean Air	
HL8008	Boeing 777-3B5ER	Korean Air	
HL8009	Boeing 777-3B5ER	Korean Air	
HL8010	Boeing 777-3B5ER	Korean Air	
HL8011	Boeing 777-3B5ER	Korean Air	
HL8041	Boeing 777-3B5ER	Korean Air	
HL8042	Boeing 777-3B5ER	Korean Air	
HL8043	Boeing 777-FB5	Korean Air Cargo	
HL8044	Boeing 777-FB5	Korean Air Cargo	
HL8045	Boeing 777-FB5	Korean Air Cargo	
HL8046	Boeing 777-FB5	Korean Air Cargo	
HL8075	Boeing 777-FB5	Korean Air Cargo	
HL8076	Boeing 777-FB5	Korean Air Cargo	
HL8077	Boeing 777-FB5	Korean Air Cargo	

Notes	Reg	Type	Owner or Operator
	HL8078	Airbus A.350-941	Asiana Airlines
	HL8079	Airbus A.350-941	Asiana Airlines
	HL8208	Boeing 777-3B5ER	Korean Air
	HL8209	Boeing 777-3B5ER	Korean Air
	HL8210	Boeing 777-3B5ER	Korean Air
	HL8216	Boeing 777-3B5ER	Korean Air
	HL8217	Boeing 777-3B5ER	Korean Air
	HL8218	Boeing 777-3B5ER	Korean Air
	HL8226	Boeing 777-FB5	Korean Air Cargo
	HL8250	Boeing 777-3B5ER	Korean Air
	HL8251	Boeing 777-FB5	Korean Air Cargo
	HL8252	Boeing 777-FB5	Korean Air Cargo
	HL8274	Boeing 777-3B5ER	Korean Air
	HL8275	Boeing 777-3B5ER	Korean Air
	HL8285	Boeing 777-FB5	Korean Air Cargo
	HL8308	Airbus A.350-941	Asiana Airlines
	HL8346	Boeing 777-300ER	Korean Air
	HL8347	Boeing 777-300ER	Korean Air
	HL8359	Airbus A.350-941	Asiana Airlines
	HL8360	Airbus A.350-941	Asiana Airlines
	HL8361	Airbus A.350-941	Asiana Airlines
	HL8362	Airbus A.350-941	Asiana Airlines
	HL8381	Airbus A.350-941	Asiana Airlines
	HL8382	Airbus A.350-941	Asiana Airlines
	HL8383	Airbus A.350-941	Asiana Airlines
	HL8521	Airbus A.350-941	Asiana Airlines
	HL8522	Airbus A.350-941	Asiana Airlines

HS (Thailand)

Notes	Reg	Type	Owner or Operator
	HS-TKK	Boeing 777-3ALER	Thai Airways International
	HS-TKL	Boeing 777-3ALER	Thai Airways International
	HS-TKM	Boeing 777-3ALER	Thai Airways International
	HS-TKN	Boeing 777-3ALER	Thai Airways International
	HS-TKO	Boeing 777-3ALER	Thai Airways International
	HS-TKP	Boeing 777-3ALER	Thai Airways International
	HS-TKQ	Boeing 777-3ALER	Thai Airways International
	HS-TKR	Boeing 777-3ALER	Thai Airways International
	HS-TKU	Boeing 777-3D7ER	Thai Airways International
	HS-TKV	Boeing 777-3D7ER	Thai Airways International
	HS-TKW	Boeing 777-3D7ER	Thai Airways International
	HS-TKX	Boeing 777-3D7ER	Thai Airways International
	HS-TKY	Boeing 777-3D7ER	Thai Airways International
	HS-TKZ	Boeing 777-3D7ER	Thai Airways International
	HS-TTA	Boeing 777-300ER	Thai Airways International
	HS-TTB	Boeing 777-300ER	Thai Airways International
	HS-TTC	Boeing 777-300ER	Thai Airways International

HZ (Saudi Arabia)

Notes	Reg	Type	Owner or Operator
	HZ-AK11	Boeing 777-368ER	Saudi Arabian Airlines
	HZ-AK12	Boeing 777-368ER	Saudi Arabian Airlines
	HZ-AK13	Boeing 777-368ER	Saudi Arabian Airlines
	HZ-AK14	Boeing 777-368ER	Saudi Arabian Airlines
	HZ-AK15	Boeing 777-368ER	Saudi Arabian Airlines
	HZ-AK16	Boeing 777-368ER	Saudi Arabian Airlines
	HZ-AK17	Boeing 777-368ER	Saudi Arabian Airlines
	HZ-AK18	Boeing 777-368ER	Saudi Arabian Airlines
	HZ-AK19	Boeing 777-368ER	Saudi Arabian Airlines
	HZ-AK20	Boeing 777-368ER	Saudi Arabian Airlines
	HZ-AK21	Boeing 777-368ER	Saudi Arabian Airlines
	HZ-AK22	Boeing 777-368ER	Saudi Arabian Airlines
	HZ-AK23	Boeing 777-368ER	Saudi Arabian Airlines
	HZ-AK24	Boeing 777-368ER	Saudi Arabian Airlines
	HZ-AK25	Boeing 777-368ER	Saudi Arabian Airlines
	HZ-AK26	Boeing 777-368ER	Saudi Arabian Airlines
	HZ-AK27	Boeing 777-368ER	Saudi Arabian Airlines
	HZ-AK28	Boeing 777-368ER	Saudi Arabian Airlines
	HZ-AK29	Boeing 777-368ER	Saudi Arabian Airlines
	HZ-AK30	Boeing 777-368ER	Saudi Arabian Airlines

Reg	Type	Owner or Operator	Notes
HZ-AK31	Boeing 777-3FGER	Saudi Arabian Airlines	
HZ-AK32	Boeing 777-3FGER	Saudi Arabian Airlines	
HZ-AK33	Boeing 777-3FGER	Saudi Arabian Airlines	
HZ-AK34	Boeing 777-3FGER	Saudi Arabian Airlines	
HZ-AK35	Boeing 777-3FGER	Saudi Arabian Airlines	
HZ-AK36	Boeing 777-3FGER	Saudi Arabian Airlines	
HZ-AK37	Boeing 777-3FGER	Saudi Arabian Airlines	
HZ-AK38	Boeing 777-3FGER	Saudi Arabian Airlines	
HZ-AK39	Boeing 777-3FGER	Saudi Arabian Airlines	
HZ-AK40	Boeing 777-3FGER	Saudi Arabian Airlines	
HZ-AK41	Boeing 777-3FGER	Saudi Arabian Airlines	
HZ-AK42	Boeing 777-3FGER	Saudi Arabian Airlines	
HZ-AK43	Boeing 777-3FGER	Saudi Arabian Airlines	
HZ-AK44	Boeing 777-3FGER	Saudi Arabian Airlines	
HZ-AK45	Boeing 777-3FGER	Saudi Arabian Airlines	
HZ-AR11	Boeing 787-9	Saudi Arabian Airlines	
HZ-AR12	Boeing 787-9	Saudi Arabian Airlines	
HZ-AR13	Boeing 787-9	Saudi Arabian Airlines	
HZ-AR22	Boeing 787-9	Saudi Arabian Airlines	
HZ-AR23	Boeing 787-9	Saudi Arabian Airlines	
HZ-AR24	Boeing 787-10	Saudi Arabian Airlines	
HZ-AR25	Boeing 787-10	Saudi Arabian Airlines	
HZ-AR26	Boeing 787-10	Saudi Arabian Airlines	
HZ-AR27	Boeing 787-10	Saudi Arabian Airlines	
HZ-AR28	Boeing 787-10	Saudi Arabian Airlines	
HZ-AR29	Boeing 787-10	Saudi Arabian Airlines	
HZ-AR32	Boeing 787-10	Saudi Arabian Airlines	
HZ-AR33	Boeing 787-10	Saudi Arabian Airlines	
HZ-ARA	Boeing 787-9	Saudi Arabian Airlines	
HZ-ARB	Boeing 787-9	Saudi Arabian Airlines	
HZ-ARC	Boeing 787-9	Saudi Arabian Airlines	
HZ-ARD	Boeing 787-9	Saudi Arabian Airlines	
HZ-ARE	Boeing 787-9	Saudi Arabian Airlines	
HZ-ARF	Boeing 787-9	Saudi Arabian Airlines	
HZ-ARG	Boeing 787-9	Saudi Arabian Airlines	
HZ-ARH	Boeing 787-9	Saudi Arabian Airlines	
HZ-ASA	Airbus A.320-214	Saudi Arabian Airlines	
HZ-ASB	Airbus A.320-214	Saudi Arabian Airlines	
HZ-ASC	Airbus A.320-214	Saudi Arabian Airlines	
HZ-ASD	Airbus A.320-214	Saudi Arabian Airlines	
HZ-ASE	Airbus A.320-214	Saudi Arabian Airlines	
HZ-ASF	Airbus A.320-214	Saudi Arabian Airlines	
HZ-ASG	Airbus A.320-214	Saudi Arabian Airlines	
HZ-RXAA	Boeing 787-9	Riyadh Air	
HZ-RXX	Boeing 787-9	Riyadh Air	

I (Italy)

Reg	Type	Owner or Operator	Notes
I-ADJK	Embraer ERJ190-200LR	Air Dolomiti	
I-ADJL	Embraer ERJ190-200LR	Air Dolomiti	
I-ADJM	Embraer ERJ190-200LR	Air Dolomiti	
I-ADJN	Embraer ERJ190-200LR	Air Dolomiti	
I-ADJO	Embraer ERJ190-200LR	Air Dolomiti	
I-ADJP	Embraer ERJ190-200LR	Air Dolomiti	
I-ADJQ	Embraer ERJ190-200LR	Air Dolomiti	
I-ADJR	Embraer ERJ190-200LR	Air Dolomiti	
I-ADJS	Embraer ERJ190-200LR	Air Dolomiti	
I-ADJT	Embraer ERJ190-200LR	Air Dolomiti	
I-ADJU	Embraer ERJ190-200LR	Air Dolomiti	
I-ADJV	Embraer ERJ190-200LR	Air Dolomiti	
I-ADJW	Embraer ERJ190-200LR	Air Dolomiti	
I-ADJX	Embraer ERJ190-200LR	Air Dolomiti	
I-ADJY	Embraer ERJ190-200LR	Air Dolomit	
I-ADJZ	Embraer ERJ190-200LR	Air Dolomiti	
I-ADVG	Airbus A.220-100	ITA Airways	
I-ADVH	Airbus A.220-100	ITA Airways	
I-ENJA	Embraer ERJ190-200LR	Air Dolomiti	
I-JENB	Embraer ERJ190-200LR	Air Dolomiti	
I-JENC	Embraer ERJ190-100LR	Air Dolomiti	
I-JEND	Embraer ERJ190-100LR	Air Dolomiti	
I-JENE	Embraer ERJ190-100LR	Air Dolomiti	

Notes	Reg	Type	Owner or Operator
	I-JENF	Embraer ERJ190-100LR	Air Dolomiti
	I-JENG	Embraer ERJ190-100LR	Air Dolomiti
	I-JENH	Embraer ERJ190-100LR	Air Dolomiti
	I-JENI	Embraer ERJ190-100LR	Air Dolomiti
	I-JENJ	Embraer ERJ190-100LR	Air Dolomiti
	I-JENK	Embraer ERJ190-100LR	Air Dolomiti
	I-NEOU	Boeing 737-86N	Neos
	I-NEOZ	Boeing 737-86N	Neos

JA (Japan)

Notes	Reg	Type	Owner or Operator
	JA01WJ	Airbus A.350-1041	Japan Airlines
	JA02WJ	Airbus A.350-1041	Japan Airlines
	JA03WJ	Airbus A.350-1041	Japan Airlines
	JA04WJ	Airbus A.350-1041	Japan Airlines
	JA05WJ	Airbus A.350-1041	Japan Airlines
	JA06WJ	Airbus A.350-1041	Japan Airlines
	JA07WJ	Airbus A.350-1041	Japan Airlines
	JA08WJ	Airbus A.350-1041	Japan Airlines
	JA09WJ	Airbus A.350-1041	Japan Airlines
	JA10WJ	Airbus A.350-1041	Japan Airlines
	JA784A	Boeing 777-381ER	All Nippon Airways
	JA785A	Boeing 777-381ER	All Nippon Airways
	JA787A	Boeing 777-381ER	All Nippon Airways
	JA788A	Boeing 777-381ER	All Nippon Airways
	JA790A	Boeing 777-381ER	All Nippon Airways
	JA791A	Boeing 777-381ER	All Nippon Airways
	JA792A	Boeing 777-381ER	All Nippon Airways
	JA793A	Boeing 777-381ER	All Nippon Airways
	JA794A	Boeing 777-381ER	All Nippon Airways
	JA795A	Boeing 777-381ER	All Nippon Airways
	JA796A	Boeing 777-381ER	All Nippon Airways
	JA797A	Boeing 777-381ER	All Nippon Airways
	JA798A	Boeing 777-381ER	All Nippon Airways
	JA836J	Boeing 787-8	Japan Airlines
	JA837J	Boeing 787-8	Japan Airlines
	JA838J	Boeing 787-8	Japan Airlines
	JA839J	Boeing 787-8	Japan Airlines
	JA840J	Boeing 787-8	Japan Airlines
	JA841J	Boeing 787-8	Japan Airlines
	JA842J	Boeing 787-8	Japan Airlines
	JA843J	Boeing 787-8	Japan Airlines
	JA844J	Boeing 787-8	Japan Airlines
	JA845J	Boeing 787-8	Japan Airlines

JY (Jordan)

Notes	Reg	Type	Owner or Operator
	JY-AYR	Airbus A.320-232	Royal Jordanian
	JY-AYT	Airbus A.321-231	Royal Jordanian
	JY-AYV	Airbus A.321-231	Royal Jordanian
	JY-AYW	Airbus A.320-232	Royal Jordanian
	JY-AZC	Airbus A.320-232	Royal Jordanian
	JY-AZD	Airbus A.320-232	Royal Jordanian
	JY-BAA	Boeing 787-8	Royal Jordanian
	JY-BAB	Boeing 787-8	Royal Jordanian
	JY-BAC	Boeing 787-8	Royal Jordanian
	JY-BAE	Boeing 787-8	Royal Jordanian
	JY-BAF	Boeing 787-8	Royal Jordanian
	JY-BAG	Boeing 787-8	Royal Jordanian
	JY-BAH	Boeing 787-8	Royal Jordanian
	JY-RAA	Airbus A.320-271N	Royal Jordanian
	JY-RAB	Airbus A.320-271N	Royal Jordanian
	JY-RAC	Airbus A.320-271N	Royal Jordanian
	JY-RAD	Airbus A.320-271N	Royal Jordanian
	JY-RAE	Airbus A.320-271N	Royal Jordanian
	JY-RAF	Airbus A.320-271N	Royal Jordanian
	JY-RAG	Airbus A.320-271N	Royal Jordanian
	JY-RAH	Airbus A.320-271N	Royal Jordanian
	JY-RAI	Airbus A.320-271N	Royal Jordanian
	JY-RAJ	Airbus A.320-271N	Royal Jordanian

Reg	Type	Owner or Operator	Notes
JY-RAK	Airbus A.320-271N	Royal Jordanian	
JY-RAL	Airbus A.320-271N	Royal Jordanian	
JY-RAM	Airbus A.320-271N	Royal Jordanian	
JY-RAN	Airbus A.320-271N	Royal Jordanian	
JY-RAO	Airbus A.320-271N	Royal Jordanian	
JY-RAP	Airbus A.320-271N	Royal Jordanian	
JY-RAQ	Airbus A.320-271N	Royal Jordanian	

LN (Norway)

Reg	Type	Owner or Operator	Notes
LN-DYM	Boeing 737-8JP	Norwegian Air Shuttle	
LN-DYR	Boeing 737-8JP	Norwegian Air Shuttle	
LN-DYT	Boeing 737-8JP	Norwegian Air Shuttle	
LN-DYU	Boeing 737-8JP	Norwegian Air Shuttle	
LN-DYX	Boeing 737-8JP	Norwegian Air Shuttle	
LN-DYY	Boeing 737-8JP	Norwegian Air Shuttle	
LN-ENL	Boeing 737-8JP	Norwegian Air Shuttle	
LN-ENM	Boeing 737-8JP	Norwegian Air Shuttle	
LN-ENN	Boeing 737-8JP	Norwegian Air Shuttle	
LN-ENO	Boeing 737-8JP	Norwegian Air Shuttle	
LN-ENP	Boeing 737-8JP	Norwegian Air Shuttle	
LN-ENQ	Boeing 737-8JP	Norwegian Air Shuttle	
LN-ENR	Boeing 737-8JP	Norwegian Air Shuttle	
LN-ENS	Boeing 737-8JP	Norwegian Air Shuttle	
LN-ENT	Boeing 737-8JP	Norwegian Air Shuttle	
LN-ENU	Boeing 737-8JP	Norwegian Air Shuttle	
LN-ENV	Boeing 737-8JP	Norwegian Air Shuttle	
LN-FGE	Boeing 737-MAX8	Norwegian Air Shuttle	
LN-FGF	Boeing 737-MAX8	Norwegian Air Shuttle	
LN-FGG	Boeing 737-MAX8	Norwegian Air Shuttle	
LN-FGH	Boeing 737-MAX8	Norwegian Air Shuttle	
LN-FGI	Boeing 737-MAX8	Norwegian Air Shuttle	
LN-FGJ	Boeing 737-MAX8	Norwegian Air Shuttle	
LN-FNA	Boeing 787-9	Norse Atlantic Airways	
LN-FNB	Boeing 787-9	IndiGo	
LN-FNC	Boeing 787-9	IndiGo	
LN-FND	Boeing 787-9	Norse Atlantic Airways	
LN-FNE	Boeing 787-9	IndiGo	
LN-FNL	Boeing 787-9	IndiGo	
LN-LNO	Boeing 787-9	IndiGo	
LN-LNR	Boeing 787-9	IndiGo	
LN-NGD	Boeing 737-8JP	Norwegian Air Shuttle	
LN-NGK	Boeing 737-8JP	Norwegian Air Shuttle	
LN-NGM	Boeing 737-8JP	Norwegian Air Shuttle	
LN-NGZ	Boeing 737-8JP	Norwegian Air Shuttle	
LN-NHA	Boeing 737-8JP	Norwegian Air Shuttle	
LN-NHE	Boeing 737-8JP	Norwegian Air Shuttle	
LN-NHG	Boeing 737-8JP	Norwegian Air Shuttle	
LN-NIB	Boeing 737-8JP	Norwegian Air Shuttle	
LN-NIG	Boeing 737-8JP	Norwegian Air Shuttle	
LN-NIH	Boeing 737-8JP	Norwegian Air Shuttle	
LN-NII	Boeing 737-8JP	Norwegian Air Shuttle	
LN-NIK	Boeing 737-8FZ	Norwegian Air Shuttle	
LN-NIL	Boeing 737-8KN	Norwegian Air Shuttle	
LN-NIM	Boeing 737-8KN	Norwegian Air Shuttle	
LN-NIN	Boeing 737-81M	Norwegian Air Shuttle	
LN-NIO	Boeing 737-8Q8	Norwegian Air Shuttle	
LN-NIP	Boeing 737-86N	Norwegian Air Shuttle	
LN-NIQ	Boeing 737-86N	Norwegian Air Shuttle	
LN-NOD	Boeing 737-8Q8	Norwegian Air Shuttle	
LN-RDY	DHC.8-402 Dash Eight	Wideroe's Flyveselskap	
LN-RDZ	DHC.8-402 Dash Eight	Wideroe's Flyveselskap	
LN-RGL	Airbus A.320-251N	SAS	
LN-RGM	Airbus A.320-251N	SAS	
LN-RGN	Airbus A.320-251N	SAS	
LN-RGO	Airbus A.320-251N	SAS	
LN-RKM	Airbus A.330-343	SAS	
LN-RKN	Airbus A.330-343	SAS	
LN-RKO	Airbus A.330-343	SAS	
LN-RKR	Airbus A.330-343	SAS	
LN-RKS	Airbus A.330-343	SAS	

Notes	Reg	Type	Owner or Operator
	LN-RKT	Airbus A.330-343	SAS
	LN-RKU	Airbus A.330-343	SAS
	LN-WDF	DHC.8-402 Dash Eight	Wideroe's Flyveselskap
	LN-WDG	DHC.8-402 Dash Eight	Wideroe's Flyveselskap
	LN-WDH	DHC.8-402 Dash Eight	Wideroe's Flyveselskap
	LN-WDI	DHC.8-402 Dash Eight	Wideroe's Flyveselskap
	LN-WDJ	DHC.8-402 Dash Eight	Wideroe's Flyveselskap
	LN-WDK	DHC.8-402 Dash Eight	Wideroe's Flyveselskap
	LN-WDL	DHC.8-402 Dash Eight	Wideroe's Flyveselskap
	LN-WDM	DHC.8-402 Dash Eight	Wideroe's Flyveselskap
	LN-WDN	DHC.8-402 Dash Eight	Wideroe's Flyveselskap
	LN-WDO	DHC.8-402 Dash Eight	Wideroe's Flyveselskap
	LN-WDP	DHC.8-402 Dash Eight	Wideroe's Flyveselskap
	LN-WDR	DHC.8-402 Dash Eight	Wideroe's Flyveselskap
	LN-WDS	DHC.8-402 Dash Eight	Wideroe's Flyveselskap
	LN-WDT	DHC.8-402 Dash Eight	Wideroe's Flyveselskap
	LN-WDU	DHC.8-402 Dash Eight	Wideroe's Flyveselskap
	LN-WDV	DHC.8-402 Dash Eight	Wideroe's Flyveselskap
	LN-WEA	Embraer ERJ190-300STD	Wideroe's Flyveselskap
	LN-WEB	Embraer ERJ190-300STD	Wideroe's Flyveselskap
	LN-WEC	Embraer ERJ190-300STD	Wideroe's Flyveselskap

LX (Luxembourg)

Notes	Reg	Type	Owner or Operator
	LX-ECV	Boeing 747-4HQERF	Cargolux
	LX-GCL	Boeing 747-467F	Cargolux
	LX-ICL	Boeing 747-467f	Cargolux
	LX-JCV	Boeing 747-4EVERF	Cargolux
	LX-KCL	Boeing 747-4HAERF	Cargolux
	LX-LBA	Boeing 737-8C9	Luxair
	LX-LBB	Boeing 737-86J	Luxair
	LX-LBK	Boeing 737-MAX8	Luxair
	LX-LBL	Boeing 737-MAX8	Luxair
	LX-LBR	Boeing 737-7K2	Luxair
	LX-LBT	Boeing 737-706	Luxair
	LX-LCL	Boeing 747-4HAF	Cargolux
	LX-LEA	Embraer ERJ190-400STD	Luxair
	LX-LGE	DHC.8Q-402 Dash Eight	Luxair
	LX-LGF	DHC.8Q-402 Dash Eight	Luxair
	LX-LGG	DHC.8Q-402 Dash Eight	Luxair
	LX-LGM	DHC.8Q-402 Dash Eight	Luxair
	LX-LGN	DHC.8Q-402 Dash Eight	Luxair
	LX-LGQ	Boeing 737-7C9	Luxair
	LX-LGS	Boeing 737-7C9	Luxair
	LX-LGU	Boeing 737-8C9	Luxair
	LX-LGV	Boeing 737-8C9	Luxair
	LX-LQA	DHC.8Q-402 Dash Eight	Luxair
	LX-LQB	DHC.8Q-402 Dash Eight	Luxair
	LX-LQC	DHC.8Q-402 Dash Eight	Luxair
	LX-LQD	DHC.8Q-402 Dash Eight	Luxair
	LX-LQI	DHC.8Q-402 Dash Eight	Luxair
	LX-LQJ	DHC.8Q-402 Dash Eight	Luxair
	LX-MCL	Boeing 747-4HAF	Cargolux
	LX-NCL	Boeing 747-4EVF	Cargolux
	LX-OCV	Boeing 747-4R7F (SCD)	Cargolux
	LX-RCV	Boeing 747-4R7F (SCD)	Cargolux
	LX-SCV	Boeing 747-4R7F (SCD)	Cargolux
	LX-TCV	Boeing 747-4R7F (SCD)	Cargolux
	LX-UCV	Boeing 747-4R7F (SCD)	Cargolux Italia
	LX-VCA	Boeing 747-8R7F	Cargolux
	LX-VCB	Boeing 747-8R7F	Cargolux
	LX-VCC	Boeing 747-8R7F	Cargolux
	LX-VCD	Boeing 747-8R7F	Cargolux
	LX-VCE	Boeing 747-8R7F	Cargolux
	LX-VCF	Boeing 747-8R7F	Cargolux
	LX-VCG	Boeing 747-8R7F	Cargolux
	LX-VCH	Boeing 747-8R7F	Cargolux
	LX-VCI	Boeing 747-8R7F	Cargolux
	LX-VCJ	Boeing 747-8R7F	Cargolux
	LX-VCK	Boeing 747-8R7F	Cargolux
	LX-VCL	Boeing 747-8R7F	Cargolux

Reg	Type	Owner or Operator	Notes
LX-VCM	Boeing 747-8R7F	Cargolux	
LX-VCN	Boeing 747-8R7F	Cargolux	
LX-VCV	Boeing 747-4R7F (SCD)	Cargolux Italia	
LX-WCV	Boeing 747-4R7F (SCD)	Cargolux Italia	
LX-YCV	Boeing 747-4R7F	Cargolux Italia	

LY (Lithuania)

Reg	Type	Owner or Operator	Notes
LY-CAP	Airbus A.320-214	Getjet Airlines	
LY-CIN	Boeing 737-83N	Getjet Airlines	
LY-DAE	Airbus A.320-214	Getjet Airlines	
LY-DUE	Boeing 737-8FE	Getjet Airlines	
LY-FAS	Airbus A.320-214	Getjet Airlines	
LY-FOX	Airbus A.320-214	Getjet Airlines	
LY-GYM	Airbus A.320-214	Getjet Airlines	
LY-KUA	Boeing 737-83N	Getjet Airlines	
LY-MAL	Airbus A.320-214	Getjet Airlines	
LY-MLF	Airbus A.320-214	Avion Express	
LY-MLG	Airbus A.320-214	Avion Express	
LY-MLI	Airbus A.320-214	Avion Express	
LY-MLJ	Airbus A.320-232	Avion Express	
LY-MLK	Airbus A.320-214	Avion Express	
LY-MLN	Airbus A.320-214	Avion Express	
LY-NOW	Airbus A.320-232	Getjet Airlines	
LY-NVE	Airbus A.320-232	Avion Express	
LY-NVF	Airbus A.320-232	Avion Express	
LY-NVG	Airbus A.320-214	Avion Express	
LY-NVH	Airbus A.321-231	Avion Express	
LY-NVI	Airbus A.320-232	Avion Express	
LY-NVJ	Airbus A.320-232	Avion Express	
LY-NVL	Airbus A.320-232	Avion Express	
LV-NVM	Airbus A.320-214	Avion Express	
LY-NVN	Airbus A.320-214	Avion Express	
LY-SEI	Boeing 737-86N	Getjet Airlines	
LY-TAP	Airbus A.320-216	Getjet Airlines	
LY-TUI	Boeing 737-85P	Getjet Airlines	
LY-UNO	Boeing 737-8FE	Getjet Airlines	
LY-VEL	Airbus A.320-214	Avion Express	
LY-WIL	Airbus A.320-214	Getjet Airlines	
LY-WIZ	Airbus A.320-232	Getjet Airlines	
LY-WSA	Airbus A.321-211	Getjet Airlines	

LZ (Bulgaria)

Reg	Type	Owner or Operator	Notes
LZ-AMS	Airbus A.220-300	Bulgaria Air	
LZ-BUR	Embraer ERJ190-100IGW	Bulgaria Air	
LZ-CGA	Boeing 737-809F	Cargo Air	
LZ-CGB	Boeing 737-8K2F	Cargo Air	
LZ-CGC	Boeing 737-85SF	Cargo Air	
LZ-CGD	Boeing 737-8K5	Cargo Air	
LZ-CGE	Boeing 737-86JSF	Cargo Air	
LZ-CGQ	Boeing 737-3Y5SF	Cargo Air	
LZ-CGT	Boeing 737-4YOSF	Cargo Air	
LZ-CGU	Boeing 737-448SF	Cargo Air	
LZ-CGV	Boeing 737-405SF	Cargo Air	
LZ-CGW	Boeing 737-46JSF	Cargo Air	
LZ-CGX	Boeing 737-43QSF	Cargo Air	
LZ-CGY	Boeing 737-49RSF	Cargo Air	
LZ-CXA	Boeing 737-85F	Compass Air Cargo	
LZ-CXB	Boeing 737-86N	Compass Air Cargo	
LZ-CXC	Boeing 737-8CX	Compass Air Cargo	
LZ-CXD	Boeing 737-85R	Compass Air Cargo	
LZ-EAB	Airbus A.320-232	Electra Airways	
LZ-EAC	Airbus A.320-232	Electra Airways	
LZ-EAD	Airbus A.320-232	Electra Airways	
LZ-EAH	Airbus A.320-214	Electra Airways	
LZ-EAI	Airbus A.320-232	Electra Airways	
LZ-EAJ	Airbus A.320-214	Electra Airways	
LZ-EAK	Airbus A.320-214	Electra Airways	
LZ-EAL	Airbus A.320-214	Electra Airways	

Notes	Reg	Type	Owner or Operator
	LZ-FBB	Airbus A.319-112	Bulgaria Air
	LZ-FBG	Airbus A.320-214	Bulgaria Air
	LZ-FBH	Airbus A.320-214	Bulgaria Air
	LZ-FBI	Airbus A.320-214	Bulgaria Air
	LZ-FBK	Airbus A.320-214	Bulgaria Air
	LZ-FRA	Airbus A.220-300	Bulgaria Air
	LZ-LIS	Airbus A.220-100	Bulgaria Air
	LZ-LON	Airbus A.220-300	Bulgaria Air
	LZ-PAR	Airbus A.220-300	Bulgaria Air
	LZ-PLO	Embraer ERJ190-100IGW	Bulgaria Air
	LZ-ROM	Airbus A.220-300	Bulgaria Air
	LZ-SOF	Embraer ERJ190-100IGW	Bulgaria Air
	LZ-VAR	Embraer ERJ190-100IGW	Bulgaria Air
	LZ-VIE	Airbus A.220-100	Bulgaria Air

N (USA)

Notes	Reg	Type	Owner or Operator
	N128AM	Boeing 787-9	Aeromexico
	N169DZ	Boeing 767-332ER	Delta Air Lines
	N171DN	Boeing 767-332ER	Delta Air Lines
	N171DZ	Boeing 767-332ER	Delta Air Lines
	N172DZ	Boeing 767-332ER	Delta Air Lines
	N173DZ	Boeing 767-332ER	Delta Air Lines
	N174DN	Boeing 767-332ER	Delta Air Lines
	N174DZ	Boeing 767-332ER	Delta Air Lines
	N175DZ	Boeing 767-332ER	Delta Air Lines
	N176DZ	Boeing 767-332ER	Delta Air Lines
	N177DN	Boeing 767-332ER	Delta Air Lines
	N177DZ	Boeing 767-332ER	Delta Air Lines
	N178DN	Boeing 767-332ER	Delta Air Lines
	N178DZ	Boeing 767-332ER	Delta Air Lines
	N179DN	Boeing 767-332ER	Delta Air Lines
	N180DN	Boeing 767-332ER	Delta Air Lines
	N183AM	Boeing 787-9	Aeromexico
	N185DN	Boeing 767-332ER	Delta Air Lines
	N186DN	Boeing 767-332ER	Delta Air Lines
	N187DN	Boeing 767-332ER	Delta Air Lines
	N188DN	Boeing 767-332ER	Delta Air Lines
	N189DN	Boeing 767-332ER	Delta Air Lines
	N190DN	Boeing 767-332ER	Delta Air Lines
	N191DN	Boeing 767-332ER	Delta Air Lines
	N192DN	Boeing 767-332ER	Delta Air Lines
	N193DN	Boeing 767-332ER	Delta Air Lines
	N194DN	Boeing 767-332ER	Delta Air Lines
	N195DN	Boeing 767-332ER	Delta Air Lines
	N196DN	Boeing 767-332ER	Delta Air Lines
	N197DN	Boeing 767-332ER	Delta Air Lines
	N198DN	Boeing 767-332ER	Delta Air Lines
	N199DN	Boeing 767-332ER	Delta Air Lines
	N204UA	Boeing 777-222ER	United Airlines
	N206UA	Boeing 777-222ER	United Airlines
	N209UA	Boeing 777-222ER	United Airlines
	N216UA	Boeing 777-222ER	United Airlines
	N217UA	Boeing 777-222ER	United Airlines
	N218UA	Boeing 777-222ER	United Airlines
	N219UA	Boeing 777-222ER	United Airlines
	N220UA	Boeing 777-222ER	United Airlines
	N221UA	Boeing 777-222ER	United Airlines
	N222UA	Boeing 777-222ER	United Airlines
	N223UA	Boeing 777-222ER	United Airlines
	N224UA	Boeing 777-222ER	United Airlines
	N225UA	Boeing 777-222ER	United Airlines
	N226UA	Boeing 777-222ER	United Airlines
	N227UA	Boeing 777-222ER	United Airlines
	N228UA	Boeing 777-222ER	United Airlines
	N229UA	Boeing 777-222ER	United Airlines
	N300NY	Airbus A.321-253NY XLR	American Airlines
	N301NY	Airbus A.321-253NY XLR	American Airlines
	N301UP	Boeing 767-34AFER	United Parcel Service
	N302NY	Airbus A.321-253NY XLR	American Airlines
	N302UP	Boeing 767-34AFER	United Parcel Service

Reg	Type	Owner or Operator	Notes
N393NY	Airbus A.321-253NY XLR	American Airlines	
N303UP	Boeing 767-34AFER	United Parcel Service	
N304NY	Airbus A.321-253NY XLR	American Airlines	
N304UP	Boeing 767-34AFER	United Parcel Service	
N305NY	Airbus A.321-253NY XLR	American Airlines	
N305UP	Boeing 767-34AFER	United Parcel Service	
N306UP	Boeing 767-34AFER	United Parcel Service	
N306XR	Airbus A.321-253NY XLR	American Airlines	
N307UP	Boeing 767-34AFER	United Parcel Service	
N308UP	Boeing 767-34AFER	United Parcel Service	
N309UP	Boeing 767-34AFER	United Parcel Service	
N310UP	Boeing 767-34AFER	United Parcel Service	
N311UP	Boeing 767-34AFER	United Parcel Service	
N312UP	Boeing 767-34AFER	United Parcel Service	
N313NY	Airbus A.321-253NY XLR	American Airlines	
N313UP	Boeing 767-34AFER	United Parcel Service	
N314UP	Boeing 767-34AFER	United Parcel Service	
N315UP	Boeing 767-34AFER	United Parcel Service	
N316UP	Boeing 767-34AFER	United Parcel Service	
N317UP	Boeing 767-34AFER	United Parcel Service	
N318UP	Boeing 767-34AFER	United Parcel Service	
N319UP	Boeing 767-34AFER	United Parcel Service	
N320UP	Boeing 767-34AFER	United Parcel Service	
N322UP	Boeing 767-34AFER	United Parcel Service	
N323UP	Boeing 767-34AFER	United Parcel Service	
N324UP	Boeing 767-34AFER	United Parcel Service	
N325UP	Boeing 767-34AFER	United Parcel Service	
N326UP	Boeing 767-34AFER	United Parcel Service	
N327UP	Boeing 767-34AFER	United Parcel Service	
N328UP	Boeing 767-34AFER	United Parcel Service	
N329UP	Boeing 767-34AER	United Parcel Service	
N330UP	Boeing 767-34AER	United Parcel Service	
N331UP	Boeing 767-34AER	United Parcel Service	
N332UP	Boeing 767-34AER	United Parcel Service	
N334UP	Boeing 767-34AER	United Parcel Service	
N335UP	Boeing 767-34AF	United Parcel Service	
N336UP	Boeing 767-34AF	United Parcel Service	
N337UP	Boeing 767-34AF	United Parcel Service	
N338UP	Boeing 767-34AF	United Parcel Service	
N339UP	Boeing 767-34AF	United Parcel Service	
N340UP	Boeing 767-34AF	United Parcel Service	
N341UP	Boeing 767-34AF	United Parcel Service	
N342UP	Boeing 767-34AF	United Parcel Service	
N343UP	Boeing 767-34AF	United Parcel Service	
N344UP	Boeing 767-34AF	United Parcel Service	
N345UP	Boeing 767-34AF	United Parcel Service	
N346UP	Boeing 767-34AF	United Parcel Service	
N347UP	Boeing 767-34AF	United Parcel Service	
N348UP	Boeing 767-34AF	United Parcel Service	
N349UP	Boeing 767-34AF	United Parcel Service	
N350UP	Boeing 767-34AF	United Parcel Service	
N351UP	Boeing 767-34AF	United Parcel Service	
N352UP	Boeing 767-34AF	United Parcel Service	
N353UP	Boeing 767-34AF	United Parcel Service	
N354UP	Boeing 767-34AF	United Parcel Service	
N355UP	Boeing 767-34AF	United Parcel Service	
N356UP	Boeing 767-34AF	United Parcel Service	
N357UP	Boeing 767-34AF	United Parcel Operator	
N358UP	Boeing 767-34AF	United Parcel Service	
N359UP	Boeing 767-34AF	United Parcel Service	
N360UP	Boeing 767-34AF	United Parcel Service	
N361UP	Boeing 767-34AF	United Parcel Service	
N362UP	Boeing 767-346ER	United Parcel Service	
N363UP	Boeing 767-346ER	United Parcel Service	
N364UP	Boeing 767-346ER	United Parcel Service	
N365UP	Boeing 767-300F	United Parcel Service	
N366UP	Boeing 767-300F	United Parcel Service	
N367UP	Boeing 767-300F	United Parcel Service	
N368UP	Boeing 767-300F	United Parcel Service	
N369UP	Boeing 767-300F	United Parcel Service	
N370UP	Boeing 767-300F	United Parcel Service	

Notes	Reg	Type	Owner or Operator
	N371UP	Boeing 767-300F	United Parcel Service
	N372UP	Boeing 767-300F	United Parcel Service
	N373UP	Boeing 767-300F	United Parcel Service
	N374UP	Boeing 767-300F	United Parcel Service
	N375UP	Boeing 767-300F	United Parcel Service
	N376UP	Boeing 767-300F	United Parcel Service
	N377UP	Boeing 767-300F	United Parcel Service
	N378UP	Boeing 767-300F	United Parcel Service
	N379UP	Boeing 767-300F	United Parcel Service
	N380UP	Boeing 767-300F	United Parcel Service
	N381UP	Boeing 767-300F	United Parcel Service
	N382UP	Boeing 767-300F	United Parcel Service
	N383UP	Boeing 767-300F	United Parcel Service
	N384UP	Boeing 767-300F	United Parcel Service
	N385UP	Boeing 767-300F	United Parcel Service
	N386UP	Boeing 767-300F	United Parcel Service
	N387UP	Boeing 767-300F	United Parcel Service
	N388UP	Boeing 767-300F	United Parcel Service
	N389UP	Boeing 767-300F	United Parcel Service
	N390UP	Boeing 767-300F	United Parcel Service
	N391UP	Boeing 767-304ERF	United Parcel Service
	N392UP	Boeing 767-304ERF	United Parcel Service
	N393UP	Boeing 767-316ER	United Parcel Service
	N394UP	Boeing 767-381ERF	United Parcel Service
	N395UP	Boeing 767-316ER	United Parcel Aervice
	N396UP	Boeing 767-346ER	United Parcel Service
	N397UP	Boeing 767-346ER	United Parcel Service
	N401DZ	Airbus A.330-941	Delta Air Lines
	N402DX	Airbus A.330-941	Delta Air Lines
	N403DX	Airbus A.330-941	Delta Air Lines
	N404DX	Airbus A.330-941	Delta Air Lines
	N404KZ	Boeing 747-4KZF	Atlas Air
	N405DX	Airbus A.330-941	Delta Air Lines
	N405KZ	Boeing 747-4KZF	Atlas Air
	N406DX	Airbus A.330-941	Delta Air Lines
	N406KZ	Boeing 747-4KZF	Atlas Air
	N407DX	Airbus A.330-941	Delta Air Lines
	N407KZ	Boeing 747-4KZF	Atlas Air
	N408DX	Airbus A.330-941	Delta Air Lines
	N408MC	Boeing 747-47UF	Atlas Air
	N409DX	Airbus A.330-941	Delta Air Lines
	N409MC	Boeing 747-47UF	Atlas Air
	N410DZ	Airbus A.330-941	Delta Air Lines
	N411DX	Airbus A.330-941	Delta Air Lines
	N412DX	Airbus A.330-941	Delta Air Lines
	N412MC	Boeing 747-47UF	Atlas Air
	N413DX	Airbus A.330-941	Delta Air Lines
	N414DZ	Airbus A.330-941	Delta Air Lines
	N415DX	Airbus A.330-941	Delta Air Lines
	N415MC	Boeing 747-47UF	Atlas Air
	N416DX	Airbus A.330-941	Delta Air Lines
	N416MC	Boeing 747-47UF	Atlas Air
	N417DX	Airbus A.330-941	Delta Air Lines
	N418DX	Airbus A.330-941	Delta Air Lines
	N418MC	Boeing 747-47UF	Atlas Air
	N419DX	Airbus A.330-941	Delta Air Lines
	N419MC	Boeing 747-48EF	Atlas Air
	N420DX	Airbus A.330-941	Delta Air Lines
	N421DX	Airbus A.330-941	Delta Air Lines
	N422DZ	Airbus A.330-941	Delta Air Lines
	N423DX	Airbus A.330-941	Delta Air Lines
	N424DX	Airbus A.330-941	Delta Air Lines
	N425DX	Airbus A.330-941	Delta Air Lines
	N426DZ	Airbus A.330-941	Delta Air Lines
	N427DX	Airbus A.330-941	Delta Air Lines
	N428DX	Airbus A.330-941	Delta Air Lines
	N429DX	Airbus A.330-941	Delta Air Lines
	N429MC	Boeing 747-481	Atlas Air
	N430DX	Airbus A.330-941	Delta Air Lines
	N430GT	Boeing 747-4H6F	Atlas Air
	N431DX	Airbus A.330-941	Delta Air Lines

Reg	Type	Owner or Operator	Notes
N431GT	Boeing 747-4H6F	Atlas Air	
N432DX	Airbus A.330-941	Delta Air Lines	
N433DX	Airbus A.330-941	Delta Air Lines	
N434DX	Airbus A.330-941	Delta Air Lines	
N435DX	Airbus A.330-941	Delta Air Lines	
N436DX	Airbus A.330-941	Delta Air Lines	
N437DX	Airbus A.330-941	Delta Air Lines	
N438AM	Boeing 787-9	Aeromexico	
N438DX	Airbus A.330-941	Delta Air Lines	
N438GT	Boeing 747-409F	Atlas Air	
N439DX	Airbus A.330-941	Delta Air Lines	
N439GT	Boeing 747-409F	Atlas Air	
N445MC	Boeing 747-4B5ERF	Atlas Air	
N446AM	Boeing 787-9	Aeromexico	
N446MC	Boeing 747-4B5ERF	Atlas Air	
N450PA	Boeing 747-46NF	Atlas Air	
N451PA	Boeing 747-46NF	Atlas Air	
N452PA	Boeing 747-46NF	Atlas Air	
N471MC	Boeing 747-412BCF	Atlas Air	
N472MC	Boeing 747-45EF	Atlas Air	
N473MC	Boeing 747-45EF	Atlas Air	
N475MC	Boeing 747-47U	Atlas Air	
N476MC	Boeing 747-47U	Atlas Air	
N477MC	Boeing 747-47U	Atlas Air	
N485MC	Boeing 747-45EF	Atlas Air	
N486MC	Boeing 747-45EF	Atlas Air	
N487MC	Boeing 747-45EF	Atlas Air	
N489MC	Boeing 747-412F	Atlas Air	
N492MC	Boeing 747-47UF	Atlas Air	
N493MC	Boeing 747-47UF	Atlas Air	
N496MC	Boeing 747-47UF	Atlas Air	
N498MC	Boeing 747-47UF	Atlas Air	
N499MC	Boeing 747-47UF	Atlas Air	
N508KZ	Boeing 747-4ZKF	Atlas Air	
N537CA	Boeing 747-446F	National Airlines	
N569CA	Boeing 747-409F	National Airlines	
N641UA	Boeing 767-322ER	United Airlines	
N642UA	Boeing 767-322ER	United Airlines	
N643UA	Boeing 767-322ER	United Airlines	
N644UA	Boeing 767-322ER	United Airlines	
N647UA	Boeing 767-322ER	United Airlines	
N648UA	Boeing 767-322ER	United Airlines	
N649UA	Boeing 767-322ER	United Airlines	
N651UA	Boeing 767-322ER	United Airlines	
N652UA	Boeing 767-322ER	United Airlines	
N653UA	Boeing 767-322ER	United Airlines	
N654UA	Boeing 767-322ER	United Airlines	
N655UA	Boeing 767-322ER	United Airlines	
N656UA	Boeing 767-322ER	United Airlines	
N657UA	Boeing 767-322ER	United Airlines	
N658UA	Boeing 767-322ER	United Airlines	
N659UA	Boeing 767-322ER	United Airlines	
N660UA	Boeing 767-322ER	United Airlines	
N661UA	Boeing 767-322ER	United Airlines	
N662UA	Boeing 767-322ER	United Airlines	
N663CA	Boeing 747-4HAERF	National Airlines	
N663UA	Boeing 767-322ER	United Airlines	
N664UA	Boeing 767-322ER	United Airlines	
N665UA	Boeing 767-322ER	United Airlines	
N666UA	Boeing 767-322ER	United Airlines	
N667UA	Boeing 767-322ER	United Airlines	
N668UA	Boeing 767-322ER	United Airlines	
N669UA	Boeing 767-322ER	United Airlines	
N670UA	Boeing 767-322ER	United Airlines	
N671UA	Boeing 767-322ER	United Airlines	
N672UA	Boeing 767-322ER	United Airlines	
N673UA	Boeing 767-322ER	United Airlines	
N674UA	Boeing 767-322ER	United Airlines	
N675UA	Boeing 767-322ER	United Airlines	
N676UA	Boeing 767-322ER	United Airlines	
N677UA	Boeing 767-322ER	United Airlines	

Notes	Reg	Type	Owner or Operator
	N684UA	Boeing 767-3CBER	United Airlines
	N685UA	Boeing 767-3CBER	United Airlines
	N686UA	Boeing 767-3CBER	United Airlines
	N702CA	Boeing 747-412BCF	National Airlines
	N712GT	Boeing 777-F	Atlas Air
	N717AN	Boeing 777-323ER	American Airlines
	N718AN	Boeing 777-323ER	American Airlines
	N719AN	Boeing 777-323ER	American Airlines
	N720AN	Boeing 777-323ER	American Airlines
	N721AN	Boeing 777-323ER	American Airlines
	N722AN	Boeing 777-323ER	American Airlines
	N723AN	Boeing 777-323ER	American Airlines
	N724AN	Boeing 777-323ER	American Airlines
	N725AN	Boeing 777-323ER	American Airlines
	N726AN	Boeing 777-323ER	American Airlines
	N727AN	Boeing 777-323ER	American Airlines
	N728AN	Boeing 777-323ER	American Airlines
	N729AN	Boeing 777-323ER	American Airlines
	N729CA	Boeing 747-412BCF	National Airlines
	N730AN	Boeing 777-323ER	American Airlines
	N731AN	Boeing 777-323ER	American Airlines
	N732AN	Boeing 777-323ER	American Airlines
	N733AR	Boeing 777-323ER	American Airlines
	N734AR	Boeing 777-323ER	American Airlines
	N735AT	Boeing 777-323ER	American Airlines
	N736AT	Boeing 777-323ER	American Airlines
	N742AM	Boeing 787-9	Aeromexico
	N748AM	Boeing 787-9	Aeromexico
	N750AN	Boeing 777-223ER	American Airlines
	N751AN	Boeing 777-223ER	American Airlines
	N752AN	Boeing 777-223ER	American Airlines
	N753AN	Boeing 777-223ER	American Airlines
	N754AN	Boeing 777-223ER	American Airlines
	N755AN	Boeing 777-223ER	American Airlines
	N756AM	Boeing 777-223ER	American Airlines
	N756CA	Boeing 747-412BCF	National Airlines
	N757AN	Boeing 777-223ER	American Airlines
	N758AN	Boeing 777-223ER	American Airlines
	N759AN	Boeing 777-223ER	American Airlines
	N760AN	Boeing 777-223ER	American Airlines
	N761AJ	Boeing 777-223ER	American Airlines
	N762AN	Boeing 777-223ER	American Airlines
	N765AN	Boeing 777-223ER	American Airlines
	N766AN	Boeing 777-223ER	American Airlines
	N767AJ	Boeing 777-223ER	American Airlines
	N768AA	Boeing 777-223ER	American Airlines
	N770AN	Boeing 777-223ER	American Airlines
	N771AN	Boeing 777-223ER	American Airlines
	N772AN	Boeing 777-223ER	American Airlines
	N773AN	Boeing 777-223ER	American Airlines
	N774AN	Boeing 777-223ER	American Airlines
	N775AN	Boeing 777-223ER	American Airlines
	N776AN	Boeing 777-223ER	American Airlines
	N777AN	Boeing 777-223ER	American Airlines
	N778AN	Boeing 777-223ER	American Airlines
	N779AN	Boeing 777-223ER	American Airlines
	N780AN	Boeing 777-223ER	American Airlines
	N780AV	Boeing 787-8	AVIANCA
	N780HA	Boeing 787-9	Alaska Airlines
	N781AN	Boeing 777-223ER	American Airlines
	N781AV	Boeing 787-8	AVIANCA
	N781HA	Boeing 787-9	Alaska Airlines
	N782AM	Boeing 787-8	Aeromexico
	N782AN	Boeing 777-223ER	American Airlines
	N782AV	Boeing 787-8	AVIANCA
	N782HA	Boeing 787-9	Alaska Airlines
	N782UA	Boeing 777-222ER	United Airlines
	N783AM	Boeing 787-8	Aeromexico
	N783AN	Boeing 777-223ER	American Airlines
	N783AV	Boeing 787-8	AVIANCA
	N783HA	Boeing 787-9	Alaska Airlines

Reg	Type	Owner or Operator	Notes
N783UA	Boeing 777-222ER	United Airlines	
N784AN	Boeing 777-223ER	American Airlines	
N784AV	Boeing 787-8	AVIANCA	
N784HA	Boeing 787-9	Alaska Airlines	
N784UA	Boeing 777-222ER	United Airlines	
N785AN	Boeing 777-223ER	American Airlines	
N785AV	Boeing 787-8	AVIANCA	
N785UA	Boeing 777-222ER	United Airlines	
N786AN	Boeing 777-223ER	American Airlines	
N786AV	Boeing 787-8	AVIANCA	
N786UA	Boeing 777-222ER	United Airlines	
N787AL	Boeing 777-223ER	American Airlines	
N787UA	Boeing 777-222ER	United Airlines	
N788AN	Boeing 777-223ER	American Airlines	
N788UA	Boeing 777-222ER	United Airlines	
N789AN	Boeing 777-223ER	American Airlines	
N790AN	Boeing 777-223ER	American Airlines	
N791AN	Boeing 777-223ER	American Airlines	
N791AV	Boeing 787-8	AVIANCA	
N791UA	Boeing 777-222ER	United Airlines	
N792AN	Boeing 777-223ER	American Airlines	
N792AV	Boeing 787-8	AVIANCA	
N792UA	Boeing 777-222ER	United Airlines	
N793AN	Boeing 777-223ER	American Airlines	
N793AV	Boeing 787-8	AVIANCA	
N793UA	Boeing 777-222ER	United Airlines	
N794AN	Boeing 777-223ER	American Airlines	
N794AV	Boeing 787-8	AVIANCA	
N794UA	Boeing 777-222ER	United Airlines	
N795AN	Boeing 777-223ER	American Airlines	
N795AV	Boeing 787-8	AVIANCA	
N795UA	Boeing 777-222ER	United Airlines	
N796AN	Boeing 777-223ER	American Airlines	
N796AV	Boeing 787-8	AVIANCA	
N796UA	Boeing 777-222ER	United Airlines	
N797AN	Boeing 777-223ER	American Airlines	
N797UA	Boeing 777-222ER	United Airlines	
N798AN	Boeing 777-223ER	American Airlines	
N798UA	Boeing 777-222ER	United Airlines	
N799AN	Boeing 777-223ER	American Airlines	
N799UA	Boeing 777-222ER	United Airlines	
N800AN	Boeing 787-8	American Airlines	
N801AC	Boeing 787-8	American Airlines	
N801NW	Airbus A.330-323X	Delta Airlines	
N802AN	Boeing 787-8	American Airlines	
N802NW	Airbus A.330-323X	Delta Airlines	
N803AL	Boeing 787-8	American Airlines	
N803NW	Airbus A.330-323X	Delta Air Lines	
N804AN	Boeing 787-8	American Airlines	
N804NW	Airbus A.330-323X	Delta Air Lines	
N805AN	Boeing 787-8	American Airlines	
N805NW	Airbus A.330-323X	Delta Air Lines	
N806AA	Boeing 787-8	American Airlines	
N806NW	Airbus A.330-323X	Delta Air Lines	
N807AA	Boeing 787-8	American Airlines	
N807NW	Airbus A.330-323X	Delta Air Lines	
N808AN	Boeing 787-8	American Airlines	
N808NW	Airbus A.330-323X	Delta Air Lines	
N809AA	Boeing 787-8	American Airlines	
N809NW	Airbus A.330-323E	Delta Air Lines	
N810AN	Boeing 787-8	American Airlines	
N810NW	Airbus A.330-323E	Delta Air Lines	
N811AB	Boeing 787-8	American Airlines	
N811NW	Airbus A.330-323E	Delta Air Lines	
N812AA	Boeing 787-8	American Airlines	
N812NW	Airbus A.330-323E	Delta Air Lines	
N813AN	Boeing 787-8	American Airlines	
N813NW	Airbus A.330-323E	Delta Air Lines	
N814AA	Boeing 787-8	American Airlines	
N814NW	Airbus A.330-323E	Delta Air Lines	
N815AA	Boeing 787-8	American Airlines	

Notes	Reg	Type	Owner or Operator
	N815AM	Boeing 787-9	Aeromexico
	N815NW	Airbus A.330-323E	Delta Air Lines
	N816AA	Boeing 787-8	American Airlines
	N816NW	Airbus A.330-323E	Delta Air Lines
	N817AN	Boeing 787-8	American Airlines
	N817NW	Airbus A.330-323E	Delta Air Lines
	N818AL	Boeing 787-8	American Airlines
	N818NW	Airbus A.330-323E	Delta Air Lines
	N819AN	Boeing 787-8	American Airlines
	N819NW	Airbus A.330-323E	Delta Air Lines
	N820AL	Boeing 787-9	American Airlines
	N820NW	Airbus A.330-323E	Delta Air Lines
	N821AN	Boeing 787-9	American Airlines
	N821NW	Airbus A.330-323E	Delta Air Lines
	N822AN	Boeing 787-9	American Airlines
	N822NW	Airbus A.330-323E	Delta Air Lines
	N823AN	Boeing 787-9	American Airlines
	N823NW	Airbus A.330-302	Delta Air Lines
	N824AN	Boeing 787-9	American Airlines
	N824NW	Airbus A.330-302	Delta Air Lines
	N825AA	Boeing 787-9	American Airlines
	N825MH	Boeing 767-432ER	Delta Air Lines
	N825NW	Airbus A.330-302	Delta Air Lines
	N826AN	Boeing 787-9	American Airlines
	N826MH	Boeing 767-432ER	Delta Air Lines
	N826NW	Airbus A.330-302	Delta Air Lines
	N827AN	Boeing 787-9	American Airlines
	N827MH	Boeing 767-432ER	Delta Air Lines
	N827NW	Airbus A.330-302	Delta Air Lines
	N828AA	Boeing 787-9	American Airlines
	N828CA	Airbus A.330-243	National Airlines
	N828MH	Boeing 767-432ER	Delta Air Lines
	N828NW	Airbus A.330-302	Delta Air Lines
	N829AN	Boeing 787-9	American Airlines
	N829MH	Boeing 767-432ER	Delta Air Lines
	N829NW	Airbus A.330-302	Delta Air Lines
	N830AN	Boeing 787-9	American Airlines
	N830MH	Boeing 767-432ER	Delta Air Lines
	N830NW	Airbus A.330-302	Delta Air Lines
	N831AA	Boeing 787-9	American Airlines
	N831MH	Boeing 767-432ER	Delta Air Lines
	N831NW	Airbus A.330-302	Delta Air Lines
	N832AA	Boeing 787-9	American Airlines
	N832MH	Boeing 767-432ER	Delta Air Lines
	N833AA	Boeing 787-9	American Airlines
	N833MH	Boeing 767-432ER	Delta Air Lines
	N834AA	Boeing 787-9	American Airlines
	N834MH	Boeing 767-432ER	Delta Air Lines
	N835AN	Boeing 787-9	American Airlines
	N835MH	Boeing 767-432ER	Delta Air Lines
	N836AA	Boeing 787-9	American Airlines
	N836MH	Boeing 767-432ER	Delta Air Lines
	N837AN	Boeing 787-9	American Airlines
	N837MH	Boeing 767-432ER	Delta Air Lines
	N838AA	Boeing 787-9	American Airlines
	N838MH	Boeing 767-432ER	Delta Air Lines
	N839AA	Boeing 787-9	American Airlines
	N839MH	Tyoeing 767-432ER	Oelta Air Lines
	N840AN	Boeing 787-9	American Airlines
	N840FD	Boeing 777-FHT	Federal Express
	N840MH	Boeing 767-432ER	Delta Air Lines
	N841AN	Boeing 787-9	American Airlines
	N841FD	Boeing 777-200F	Federal Express
	N841MH	Boeing 767-432ER	Delta Air Lines
	N842AA	Boeing 787-9	American Airlines
	N842FD	Boeing 777-FHT	Federal Express
	N842MH	Boeing 767-432ER	Delta Air Lines
	N843AN	Boeing 787-9	American Airlines
	N843FD	Boeing 777-FHT	Federal Express
	N843MH	Boeing 767-432ER	Delta Air Lines
	N844FD	Boeing 777-FHT	Federal Express

Reg	Type	Owner or Operator	Notes
N844MC	Boeing 787-9	American Airlines	
N844MH	Boeing 767-432E	Delta Air Lines	
N845FD	Boeing 777-FHT	Federal Express	
N845MD	Boeing 787-9	American Airlines	
N845MH	Boeing 767-432ER	Delta Air Lines	
N846AN	Boeing 787-9	American Airlines	
N846FD	Boeing 777-200F	Federal Express	
N847FD	Boeing 777-200F	Federal Express	
N847MF	Boeing 787-9	American Airlines	
N848AN	Boeing 787-9	American Airlines	
N848FD	Boeing 777-200F	Federal Express	
N849AN	Boeing 787-9	American Airlines	
N849FD	Boeing 777-200F	Federal Express	
N850AN	Boeing 787-9	American Airlines	
N850FD	Boeing 777-2S2LRF	Federal Express	
N850GT	Boeing 747-87UF	Atlas Air	
N851FD	Boeing 777-2S2LRF	Federal Express	
N851GT	Boeing 747-87UF	Atlas Air	
N851MK	Boeing 787-9	American Airlines	
N851NW	Airbus A.330-223	Delta Air Lines	
N852FD	Boeing 777-2S2LRF	Federal Express	
N852GT	Boeing 747-87UF	Atlas Air	
N852ML	Boeing 787-9	American Airlines	
N852NW	Airbus A.330-223	Delta Air Lines	
N853FD	Boeing 777-2S2LRF	Federal Express	
N853GT	Boeing 747-87UF	Atlas Air	
N853NW	Airbus A.330-223	Delta Air Lines	
N854FD	Boeing 777-2S2LRF	Federal Express	
N854GT	Boeing 747-87UF	Atlas Air	
N854NW	Airbus A.330-223	Delta Air Lines	
N855FD	Boeing 777-2S2LRF	Federal Express	
N855GT	Boeing 747-87UF	Atlas Air	
N855NW	Airbus A.330-223	Delta Air Lines	
N856FD	Boeing 777-2S2LRF	Federal Express	
N856GT	Boeing 747-87UF	Atlas Air	
N856NW	Airbus A.330-223	Delta Air Lines	
N857FD	Boeing 777-2S2LRF	Federal Express	
N857GT	Boeing 747-87UF	Atlas Air	
N857NW	Airbus A.330-223	Delta Air Lines	
N858FD	Boeing 777-2S2LRF	Federal Express	
N858GT	Boeing 747-87UF	Atlas Air	
N858NW	Airbus A.330-223	Delta Air Lines	
N859FD	Boeing 777-2S2LRF	Federal Express	
N859GT	Boeing 747-87UF	Atlas Air	
N050NW	Airbus A.330-223	Delta Air Lines	
N860FD	Boeing 777-2S2LRF	Federal Express	
N860GT	Boeing 747-87UF	Atlas Air	
N860NW	Airbus A.330-223	Delta Air Lines	
N861FD	Boeing 777-2S2LRF	Federal Express	
N861GT	Boeing 747-87UF	Atlas Air	
N861NW	Airbus A.330-223	Delta Air Lines	
N862FD	Boeing 777-2S2LRF	Federal Express	
N863FD	Boeing 777-2S2LRF	Federal Express	
N864FD	Boeing 777-2S2LRF	Federal Express	
N864GT	Boeing 747-83QF	Atlas Air	
N865FD	Boeing 777-2S2LRF	Federal Express	
N865GT	Boeing 747-83QF	Atlas Air	
N866FD	Boeing 777-2S2LRF	Federal Express	
N867FD	Boeing 777-200F	Federal Express	
N868FD	Boeing 777-200F	Federal Express	
N868GT	Boeing 747-83QF	Atlas Air	
N869FD	Boeing 777-200F	Federal Express	
N870AX	Boeing 787-8	American Airlines	
N871AY	Boeing 787-8	American Airlines	
N870FD	Boeing 777-200F	Federal Express	
N871FD	Boeing 777-200F	Federal Express	
N872AN	Boeing 787-8	American Airlines	
N872FD	Boeing 777-200F	Federal Express	
N873BB	Boeing 787-8	American Airlines	
N873FD	Boeing 777-200F	Federal Express	
N874AN	Boeing 787-8	American Airlines	

Notes	Reg	Type	Owner or Operator
	N874FD	Boeing 777-200F	Federal Express
	N875BD	Boeing 787-8	American Airlines
	N875FD	Boeing 777-200F	Federal Express
	N876AL	Boeing 787-8	American Airlines
	N876FD	Boeing 777-2S2LRF	Federal Express
	N877BF	Boeing 787-8	American Airlines
	N877FD	Boeing 777-2S2LRF	Federal Express
	N878BG	Boeing 787-8	American Airlines
	N878FD	Boeing 777-2S2LRF	Federal Express
	N879BH	Boeing 787-8	American Airlines
	N879FD	Boeing 777-2S2LRF	Federal Express
	N880BJ	Boeing 787-8	American Airlines
	N880FD	Boeing 777-2S2LRF	Federal Express
	N881BK	Boeing 787-8	American Airlines
	N882BL	Boeing 787-8	American Airlines
	N882FD	Boeing 777-2S2LRF	Federal Express
	N883BM	Boeing 787-8	American Airlines
	N883FD	Boeing 777-2S2LRF	Federal Express
	N884AA	Boeing 787-8	American Airlines
	N884FD	Boeing 777-2S2LRF	Federal Express
	N885BP	Boeing 787-8	American Airlines
	N885FD	Boeing 777-2S2LRF	Federal Express
	N886BR	Boeing 787-8	American Airlines
	N886FD	Boeing 777-2S2LRF	Federal Express
	N887FD	Boeing 777-2S2LRF	Federal Express
	N888FD	Boeing 777-2S2LRF	Federal Express
	N889FD	Boeing 777-2S2LRF	Federal Express
	N890FD	Boeing 777-2S2LRF	Federal Express
	N891FD	Boeing 777-2S2LRF	Federal Express
	N892FD	Boeing 777-2S2LRF	Federal Express
	N893FD	Boeing 777-2S2LRF	Federal Express
	N894FD	Boeing 777-2S2LRF	Federal Express
	N895FD	Boeing 777-2S2LRF	Federal Express
	N896FD	Boeing 777-2S2LRF	Federal Express
	N897FD	Boeing 777-2S2LRF	Federal Express
	N898CA	Airbus A.330-243	National Airlines
	N898FD	Boeing 777-200F	Federal Express
	N899FD	Boeing 777-200F	Federal Express
	N910UP	Boeing 767-300F	United Parcel Service
	N912UP	Boeing 767-300F	United Parcel Service
	N913UP	Boeing 767-300F	United Parcel Service
	N914UP	Boeing 767-300F	United Parcel Service
	N915UP	Boeing 767-300F	United Parcel Service
	N916UP	Boeing 767-300F	United Parcel Service
	N917UP	Boeing 767-300F	United Parcel Service
	N918UP	Boeing 767-300F	United Parcel Service
	N919CA	Boeing 747-428BCF	National Airlines
	N919UP	Boeing 767-300F	United Parcel Service
	N920UP	Boeing 767-300F	United Parcel Service
	N921UP	Boeing 767-300F	United Parcel Service
	N922UP	Boeing 767-300F	United Parcel Service
	N923UP	Boeing 767-300F	United Parcel Service
	N924UP	Boeing 767-300F	United Parcel Service
	N925UP	Boeing 767-300F	United Parcel Service
	N926UP	Boeing 767-300F	United Parcel Service
	N936CA	Boeing 747-446BCF	National Airlines
	N952CA	Boeing 747-428BCF	National Airlines
	N964AM	Boeing 787-8	Aeromexico
	N965AM	Boeing 787-8	Aeromexico
	N966AM	Boeing 787-8	Aeromexico
	N967AM	Boeing 787-8	Aeromexico
	N1200K	Boeing 767-332ER	Delta Air Lines
	N1201P	Boeing 767-332ER	Delta Air Lines
	N1602	Boeing 767-332ER	Delta Air Lines
	N1603	Boeing 767-332ER	Delta Air Lines
	N1604R	Boeing 767-332ER	Delta Air Lines
	N1605	Boeing 767-332ER	Delta Air Lines
	N2105J	Airbus A.321-271NX	Jet Blue
	N2135U	Boeing 777-322ER	United Airlines
	N2136U	Boeing 777-322ER	United Airlines
	N2138U	Boeing 777-322ER	United Airlines

Reg	Type	Owner or Operator	Notes
N2140U	Boeing 777-322ER	United Airlines	
N2142J	Airbus A.321-271NX	Jet Blue	
N2142U	Boeing 777-322ER	United Airlines	
N2151J	Airbus A.321-271NX	Jet Blue	
N2156J	Airbus A.321-271NX	Jet Blue	
N2157J	Airbus A.321-271NX	Jet Blue	
N2165J	Airbus A.321-271NX	Jet Blue	
N2169J	Airbus A.321-271NX	Jet Blue	
N2180J	Airbus A.321-271NX	Jet Blue	
N2188J	Airbus A.321-271NX	Jet Blue	
N2193J	Airbus A.321-271NX	Jet Blue	
N2199J	Airbus A.321-271NX	Jet Blue	
N2205J	Airbus A.321-271NX	Jet Blue	
N2243U	Boeing 777-322ER	United Airlines	
N2250U	Boeing 777-300ER	United Airlines	
N2251U	Boeing 777-300ER	United Airlines	
N2331U	Boeing 777-322ER	United Airlines	
N2332U	Boeing 777-322ER	United Airlines	
N2333U	Boeing 777-322ER	United Airlines	
N2341U	Boeing 777-322ER	United Airlines	
N2352U	Boeing 777-300ER	United Airlines	
N2534U	Boeing 777-322ER	United Airlines	
N2639U	Boeing 777-322ER	United Airlines	
N2644U	Boeing 777-322ER	United Airlines	
N2645U	Boeing 777-322ER	United Airlines	
N2737U	Boeing 777-322ER	United Airlines	
N2747U	Boeing 777-322ER	United Airlines	
N2748U	Boeing 777-322ER	United Airlines	
N2749U	Boeing 777-300ER	United Airlines	
N2846U	Boeing 777-322ER	United Airlines	
N4022J	Airbus A.321-271NX	Jet Blue	
N4048J	Airbus A.321-271NX	Jet Blue	
N4058J	Airbus A.321-271NX	Jet Blue	
N4062J	Airbus A.321-271NX	Jet Blue	
N4064J	Airbus A.321-271NX	Jet Blue	
N4073J	Airbus A.321-271NX	Jet Blue	
N4074J	Airbus A.321-271NX	Jet Blue	
N4076J	Airbus A.321-271NX	Jet Blue	
N4077J	Airbus A.321-271NX	Jet Blue	
N4080J	Airbus A.321-271NX	Jet Blue	
N4083J	Airbus A.321-271NX	Jet Blue	
N12003	Boeing 787-10	United Airlines	
N12004	Boeing 787-10	United Airlines	
N12005	Boeing 787-10	United Airlines	
N12006	Boeing 787-10	United Airlines	
N12010	Boeing 787-10	United Airlines	
N12012	Boeing 787-10	United Airlines	
N12020	Boeing 787-10	United Airlines	
N12021	Boeing 787-10	United Airlines	
N12109	Boeing 757-224	United Airlines	
N12114	Boeing 757-224	United Airlines	
N12116	Boeing 757-224	United Airlines	
N12125	Boeing 757-224	United Airlines	
N13013	Boeing 787-10	United Airlines	
N13014	Boeing 787-10	United Airlines	
N13018	Boeing 787-10	United Airlines	
N13110	Boeing 757-224	United Airlines	
N13113	Boeing 757-224	United Airlines	
N13138	Boeing 757-224	United Airlines	
N13954	Boeing 787-9	United Airlines	
N14001	Boeing 787-10	United Airlines	
N14011	Boeing 787-10	United Airlines	
N14016	Boeing 787-10	United Airlines	
N14019	Boeing 787-10	United Airlines	
N14102	Boeing 757-224	United Airlines	
N14106	Boeing 757-224	United Airlines	
N14107	Boeing 757-224	United Airlines	
N14115	Boeing 757-224	United Airlines	
N14118	Boeing 757-224	United Airlines	
N14120	Boeing 757-224	United Airlines	
N14121	Boeing 757-224	United Airlines	

Notes	Reg	Type	Owner or Operator
	N15969	Boeing 787-9	United Airlines
	N16008	Boeing 787-10	United Airlines
	N16009	Boeing 787-10	United Airlines
	N16065	Boeing 767-332ER	Delta Air Lines
	N17002	Boeing 787-10	United Airlines
	N17015	Boeing 787-10	United Airlines
	N17017	Boeing 787-10	United Airlines
	N17104	Boeing 757-224	United Airlines
	N17105	Boeing 757-224	United Airlines
	N17122	Boeing 757-224	United Airlines
	N17126	Boeing 757-224	United Airlines
	N17128	Boeing 757-224	United Airlines
	N17133	Boeing 757-224	United Airlines
	N17139	Boeing 757-224	United Airlines
	N17254	Boeing 737-MAX8	United Airlines
	N17262	Boeing 737-MAX8	United Airlines
	N17264	Boeing 737-MAX8	United Airlines
	N17265	Boeing 737-MAX8	United Airlines
	N17172	Boeing 737-MAX8	United Airlines
	N17279	Boeing 737-MAX8	United Airlines
	N17285	Boeing 737-MAX8	United Airlines
	N17289	Boeing 737-MAX8	United Airlines
	N17294	Boeing 737-MAX8	United Airlines
	N17296	Boeing 737-MAX8	United Airlines
	N17300	Boeing 737-MAX8	United Airlines
	N17301	Boeing 737-MAX8	United Airlines
	N17302	Boeing 737-MAX8	United Airlines
	N17303	Boeing 737-MAX8	United Airlines
	N17309	Boeing 737-MAX8	United Airlines
	N17310	Boeing 737-MAX8	United Airlines
	N17311	Boeing 737-MAX8	United Airlines
	N17312	Boeing 737-MAX8	United Airlines
	N17314	Boeing 737-MAX8	United Airlines
	N17315	Boeing 737-MAX8	United Airlines
	N17316	Boeing 737-MAX8	United Airlines
	N17317	Boeing 737-MAX8	United Airlines
	N17320	Boeing 737-MAX8	United Airlines
	N17321	Boeing 737-MAX8	United Airlines
	N17322	Boeing 737-MAX8	United Airlines
	N17326	Boeing 737-MAX8	United Airlines
	N17327	Boeing 737-MAX8	United Airlines
	N17328	Boeing 737-MAX8	United Airlines
	N17329	Boeing 737-MAX8	United Airlines
	N17331	Boeing 737-MAX8	United Airlines
	N17333	Boeing 737-MAX8	United Airlines
	N17335	Boeing 737-MAX8	United Airlines
	N17336	Boeing 737-MAX8	United Airlines
	N17337	Boeing 737-MAX8	United Airlines
	N17338	Boeing 737-MAX8	United Airlines
	N17339	Boeing 737-MAX8	United Airlines
	N17341	Boeing 737-MAX8	United Airlines
	N17344	Boeing 737-MAX8	United Airlines
	N17346	Boeing 737-MAX8	United Airlines
	N17347	Boeing 737-MAX8	United Airlines
	N17349	Boeing 737-MAX8	United Airlines
	N17355	Boeing 737-MAX8	United Airlines
	N17356	Boeing 737-MAX8	United Airlines
	N17358	Typeing 737-MAX8	Ownited Airlines
	N17359	Boeing 737-MAX8	United Airlines
	N17361	Boeing 737-MAX8	United Airlines
	N17362	Boeing 737-MAX8	United Airlines
	N17363	Boeing 737-MAX8	United Airlines
	N17364	Boeing 737-MAX8	United Airlines
	N17373	Boeing 737-MAX8	United Airlines
	N17963	Boeing 787-9	United Airlines
	N18112	Boeing 757-224	United Airlines
	N18119	Boeing 757-224	United Airlines
	N19117	Boeing 757-224	United Airlines
	N19130	Boeing 757-224	United Airlines
	N19136	Boeing 757-224	United Airlines
	N19141	Boeing 757-224	United Airlines

Reg	Type	Owner or Operator	Notes
N19951	Boeing 787-9	United Airlines	
N19986	Boeing 787-9	United Airlines	
N20904	Boeing 787-8	United Airlines	
N21102	Boeing 787-8	United Airlines	
N21108	Boeing 757-224	United Airlines	
N22992	Boeing 787-9	United Airlines	
N22995	Boeing 787-9	United Airlines	
N23983	Boeing 787-9	United Airlines	
N23994	Boeing 787-9	United Airlines	
N24972	Boeing 787-9	United Airlines	
N24973	Boeing 787-9	United Airlines	
N24974	Boeing 787-9	United Airlines	
N24976	Boeing 787-9	United Airlines	
N24979	Boeing 787-9	United Airlines	
N24980	Boeing 787-9	United Airlines	
N24988	Boeing 787-9	United Airlines	
N24990	Boeing 787-9	United Airlines	
N24993	Boeing 787-9	United Airlines	
N25982	Boeing 787-9	United Airlines	
N26902	Boeing 787-8	United Airlines	
N26906	Boeing 787-8	United Airlines	
N26909	Boeing 787-8	United Airlines	
N26910	Boeing 787-8	United Airlines	
N26952	Boeing 787-9	United Airlines	
N26960	Boeing 787-9	United Airlines	
N26966	Boeing 787-9	United Airlines	
N26967	Boeing 787-9	United Airlines	
N26970	Boeing 787-9	United Airlines	
N26996	Boeing 787-9	United Airlines	
N27015	Boeing 777-224ER	United Airlines	
N27251	Boeing 737-MAX8	United Airlines	
N27252	Boeing 737-MAX8	United Airlines	
N27253	Boeing 737-MAX8	United Airlines	
N27255	Boeing 737-MAX8	United Airlines	
N27256	Boeing 737-MAX8	United Airlines	
N27258	Boeing 737-MAX8	United Airlines	
N27260	Boeing 737-MAX8	United Airlines	
N27261	Boeing 737-MAX8	United Airlines	
N27263	Boeing 737-MAX8	United Airlines	
N27266	Boeing 737-MAX8	United Airlines	
N27267	Boeing 737-MAX8	United Airlines	
N27268	Boeing 737-MAX8	United Airlines	
N27269	Boeing 737-MAX8	United Airlines	
N27270	Boeing 737-MAX8	United Airlines	
N27271	Boeing 737-MAX8	United Airlines	
N27273	Boeing 737-MAX8	United Airlines	
N27274	Boeing 737-MAX8	United Airlines	
N27276	Boeing 737-MAX8	United Airlines	
N27277	Boeing 737-MAX8	United Airlines	
N27283	Boeing 737-MAX8	United Airlines	
N27287	Boeing 737-MAX8	United Airlines	
N27290	Boeing 737-MAX8	United Airlines	
N27292	Boeing 737-MAX8	United Airlines	
N27304	Boeing 737-MAX8	United Airlines	
N27323	Boeing 737-MAX8	United Airlines	
N27334	Boeing 737-MAX8	United Airlines	
N27366	Boeing 737-MAX8	United Airlines	
N27901	Boeing 787-8	United Airlines	
N27903	Boeing 787-8	United Airlines	
N27908	Boeing 787-8	United Airlines	
N27957	Boeing 787-9	United Airlines	
N27958	Boeing 787-9	United Airlines	
N27959	Boeing 787-9	United Airlines	
N27964	Boeing 787-9	United Airlines	
N27965	Boeing 787-9	United Airlines	
N27997	Boeing 787-9	United Airlines	
N28912	Boeing 787-8	United Airlines	
N28987	Boeing 787-9	United Airlines	
N29124	Boeing 757-224	United Airlines	
N29129	Boeing 757-224	United Airlines	
N29907	Boeing 787-8	United Airlines	

Notes	Reg	Type	Owner or Operator
	N29961	Boeing 787-9	United Airlines
	N29968	Boeing 787-9	United Airlines
	N29971	Boeing 787-9	United Airlines
	N29975	Boeing 787-9	United Airlines
	N29977	Boeing 787-9	United Airlines
	N29978	Boeing 787-9	United Airlines
	N29981	Boeing 787-9	United Airlines
	N29984	Boeing 787-9	United Airlines
	N29985	Boeing 787-9	United Airlines
	N29989	Boeing 787-9	United Airlines
	N29991	Boeing 787-9	United Airlines
	N30913	Boeing 787-8	United Airlines
	N33103	Boeing 757-224	United Airlines
	N33132	Boeing 757-224	United Airlines
	N34131	Boeing 757-224	United Airlines
	N34137	Boeing 757-224	United Airlines
	N35953	Boeing 787-9	United Airlines
	N36962	Boeing 787-9	United Airlines
	N37018	Boeing 777-224ER	United Airlines
	N37257	Boeing 737-MAX8	United Airlines
	N37278	Boeing 737-MAX8	United Airlines
	N37295	Boeing 737-MAX8	United Airlines
	N37297	Boeing 737-MAX8	United Airlines
	N37305	Boeing 737-MAX8	United Airlines
	N37307	Boeing 737-MAX8	United Airlines
	N37308	Boeing 737-MAX8	United Airlines
	N37313	Boeing 737-MAX8	United Airlines
	N37318	Boeing 737-MAX8	United Airlines
	N37319	Boeing 737-MAX8	United Airlines
	N37324	Boeing 737-MAX8	United Airlines
	N37325	Boeing 737-MAX8	United Airlines
	N37342	Boeing 737-MAX8	United Airlines
	N37348	Boeing 737-MAX8	United Airlines
	N37351	Boeing 737-MAX8	United Airlines
	N37352	Boeing 737-MAX8	United Airlines
	N37353	Boeing 737-MAX8	United Airlines
	N37354	Boeing 737-MAX8	United Airlines
	N37365	Boeing 737-MAX8	United Airlines
	N37367	Boeing 737-MAX8	United Airlines
	N37368	Boeing 737-MAX8	United Airlines
	N37371	Boeing 737-MAX8	United Airlines
	N37372	Boeing 737-MAX8	United Airlines
	N38950	Boeing 787-9	United Airlines
	N38955	Boeing 787-9	United Airlines
	N41135	Boeing 757-224	United Airlines
	N41140	Boeing 757-224	United Airlines
	N45905	Boeing 787-8	United Airlines
	N45956	Boeing 787-9	United Airlines
	N47275	Boeing 737-MAX8	United Airlines
	N47280	Boeing 737-MAX8	United Airlines
	N47281	Boeing 737-MAX8	United Airlines
	N47282	Boeing 737-MAX8	United Airlines
	N47284	Boeing 737-MAX8	United Airlines
	N47288	Boeing 737-MAX8	United Airlines
	N47291	Boeing 737-MAX8	United Airlines
	N47293	Boeing 737-MAX8	United Airlines
	N47298	Boeing 737-MAX8	United Airlines
	N47330	Boeing 737-MAX8	Owned Airlines
	N47332	Boeing 737-MAX8	United Airlines
	N47340	Boeing 737-MAX8	United Airlines
	N47343	Boeing 737-MAX8	United Airlines
	N47345	Boeing 737-MAX8	United Airlines
	N47357	Boeing 737-MAX8	United Airlines
	N47360	Boeing 737-MAX8	United Airlines
	N47369	Boeing 737-MAX8	United Airlines
	N47370	Boeing 737-MAX8	United Airlines
	N48127	Boeing 757-224	United Airlines
	N51104	Boeing 787-9	United Airlines
	N57016	Boeing 777-224ER	United Airlines
	N57111	Boeing 757-224	United Airlines
	N57286	Boeing 737-MAX8	United Airlines

Reg	Type	Owner or Operator	Notes
N57299	Boeing 737-MAX8	United Airlines	
N58101	Boeing 757-224	United Airlines	
N59053	Boeing 767-424ER	United Airlines	
N61101	Boeing 787-9	United Airlines	
N61103	Boeing 787-9	United Airlines	
N61106	Boeing 787-9	United Airlines	
N66051	Boeing 767-424ER	United Airlines	
N66056	Boeing 767-424ER	United Airlines	
N66057	Boeing 767-424ER	United Airlines	
N67052	Boeing 767-424ER	United Airlines	
N67058	Boeing 767-424ER	United Airlines	
N67134	Boeing 757-224	United Airlines	
N67350	Boeing 737-MAX8	United Airlines	
N68061	Boeing 767-424ER	United Airlines	
N69020	Boeing 777-224ER	United Airlines	
N69059	Boeing 767-424ER	United Airlines	
N69063	Boeing 767-424ER	United Airlines	
N71108	Boeing 787-9	United Airlines	
N74007	Boeing 777-224ER	United Airlines	
N76010	Boeing 777-224ER	United Airlines	
N76021	Boeing 777-224ER	United Airlines	
N76054	Boeing 767-424ER	United Airlines	
N76055	Boeing 767-424ER	United Airlines	
N76062	Boeing 767-424ER	United Airlines	
N76064	Boeing 767-424ER	United Airlines	
N76065	Boeing 767-424ER	United Airlines	
N77006	Boeing 777-224ER	United Airlines	
N77012	Boeing 777-224ER	United Airlines	
N77014	Boeing 777-224ER	United Airlines	
N77019	Boeing 777-224ER	United Airlines	
N77022	Boeing 777-224ER	United Airlines	
N77066	Boeing 767-424ER	United Airlines	
N77259	Boeing 737-MAX8	United Airlines	
N78001	Boeing 777-224ER	United Airlines	
N78002	Boeing 777-224ER	United Airlines	
N78003	Boeing 777-224ER	United Airlines	
N78004	Boeing 777-224ER	United Airlines	
N78005	Boeing 777-224ER	United Airlines	
N78008	Boeing 777-224ER	United Airlines	
N78009	Boeing 777-224ER	United Airlines	
N78013	Boeing 777-224ER	United Airlines	
N78017	Boeing 777-224ER	United Airlines	
N78060	Boeing 767-424ER	United Airlines	
N79011	Boeing 777-224ER	United Airlines	
N81106	Boeing 787-9	United Airlines	
N81107	Boeing 787-9	United Airlines	
N91007	Boeing 787-10	United Airlines	

OD (Lebanon)

Reg	Type	Owner or Operator	Notes
OD-MEA	Airbus A.330-243	MEA - Middle East Airlines	
OD-MEB	Airbus A.330-243	MEA - Middle East Airlines	
OD-MEC	Airbus A.330-243	MEA - Middle East Airlines	
OD-MEE	Airbus A.330-243	MEA - Middle East Airlines	
OD-MRL	Airbus A.320-232	MEA - Middle East Airlines	
OD-MRM	Airbus A.320-232	MEA - Middle East Airlines	
OD-MRN	Airbus A.320-232	MEA - Middle East Airlines	
OD-MRO	Airbus A.320-232	MEA - Middle East Airlines	
OD-MRR	Airbus A.320-232	MEA - Middle East Airlines	
OD-MRS	Airbus A.320-232	MEA - Middle East Airlines	
OD-MRT	Airbus A.320-232	MEA - Middle East Airlines	
OD-M10	Airbus A.321-271NX	MEA - Middle East Airlines	

MEA also operate T7- registered Airbus A.321s

OE (Austria)

Reg	Type	Owner or Operator	Notes
OE-IAJ	Boeing 737-476F	ASL Airlines Belgium	
OE-IAM	Boeing 737-490SF	ASL Airlines Belgium	
OE-IBF	Airbus A.320-214	easyJet Europe	

Notes	Reg	Type	Owner or Operator
	OE-IBI	Boeing 737-490SF	ASL Airlines Belgium
	OE-IBL	Boeing 737-490F	ASL Airlines Belgium
	OE-IBO	Boeing 737-490SF	ASL Airlines Belgium
	OE-IBS	Airbus A.320-214	easyJet Europe
	OE-ICB	Airbus A.320-214	easyJet Europe
	OE-ICD	Airbus A.320-214	easyJet Europe
	OE-ICF	Airbus A.320-214	easyJet Europe
	OE-ICI	Airbus A.320-214	easyJet Europe
	OE-ICJ	Airbus A.320-214	easyJet Europe
	OE-ICK	Airbus A.320-214	easyJet Europe
	OE-ICL	Airbus A.320-214	easyJet Europe
	OE-ICM	Airbus A.320-214	easyJet Europe
	OE-ICN	Airbus A.320-214	easyJet Europe
	OE-ICP	Airbus A.320-214	easyJet Europe
	OE-ICR	Airbus A.320-214	easyJet Europe
	OE-ICT	Airbus A.320-214	easyJet Europe
	OE-ICW	Airbus A.320-214	easyJet Europe
	OE-IDD	Airbus A.320-214	easyJet Europe
	OE-IDO	Airbus A.320-214	easyJet Europe
	OE-IDS	Airbus A.320-214	easyJet Europe
	OE-IDT	Airbus A.320-214	easyJet Europe
	OE-IDU	Airbus A.320-214	easyJet Europe
	OE-IDX	Airbus A.320-214	easyJet Europe
	OE-IJA	Airbus A.320-214	easyJet Europe
	OE-IJD	Airbus A.320-214	easyJet Europe
	OE-IJE	Airbus A.320-214	easyJet Europe
	OE-IJH	Airbus A.320-214	easyJet Europe
	OE-IJL	Airbus A.320-214	easyJet Europe
	OE-IJO	Airbus A.320-214	easyJet Europe
	OE-IJQ	Airbus A.320-214	easyJet Europe
	OE-IJR	Airbus A.320-214	easyJet Europe
	OE-IJU	Airbus A.320-214	easyJet Europe
	OE-IJV	Airbus A.320-214	easyJet Europe
	OE-IJW	Airbus A.320-214	easyJet Europe
	OE-IJX	Airbus A.320-214	easyJet Europe
	OE-IJY	Airbus A.320-214	easyJet Europe
	OE-IJZ	Airbus A.320-214	easyJet Europe
	OE-IMC	Boeing 737-83NF	ASL Airlines Belgium
	OE-IMD	Boeing 737-83NF	ASL Airlines Belgium
	OE-INA	Airbus A.320-214	easyJet Europe
	OE-INB	Airbus A.320-214	easyJet Europe
	OE-INC	Airbus A.320-214	EasyJet Europe
	OE-IND	Airbus A.320-214	easyJet Europe
	OE-INE	Airbus A.320-214	easyJet Europe
	OE-INF	Airbus A.320-214	easyJet Europe
	OE-ING	Airbus A.320-214	easyJet Europe
	OE-INH	Airbus A.320-214	easyJet Europe
	OE-INI	Airbus A.320-214	easyJet Europe
	OE-INM	Airbus A.320-214	easyJet Europe
	OE-INO	Airbus A.320-214	easyJet Europe
	OE-INP	Airbus A.320-214	easyJet Europe
	OE-ISB	Airbus A.321-251NX	easyJet Europe
	OE-ISC	Airbus A.321-251NX	easyJet Europe
	OE-ISD	Airbus A.321-251NX	easyJet Europe
	OE-ISE	Airbus A.321-251NX	easyJet Europe
	OE-ISG	Airbus A.321-251NX	easyJet Europe
	OE-ISH	Airbus A.321-251NX	easyJet Europe
	OE-IUA	Airbus A.321-251NX	easyJet Ourope
	OE-IUB	Airbus A.321-251NX	easyJet Europe
	OE-IUC	Airbus A.321-251NX	easyJet Europe
	OE-IUD	Airbus A.321-251NX	easyJet Europe
	OE-IVA	Airbus A.320-214	easyJet Europe
	OE-IVB	Airbus A.320-214	easyJet Europe
	OE-IVC	Airbus A.320-214	easyJet Europe
	OE-IVD	Airbus A.320-214	easyJet Europe
	OE-IVE	Airbus A.320-214	easyJet Europe
	OE-IVF	Airbus A.320-214	easyJet Europe
	OE-IVI	Airbus A.320-214	easyJet Europe
	OE-IVL	Airbus A.320-214	easyJet Europe
	OE-IVQ	Airbus A.320-214	easyJet Europe
	OE-IVR	Airbus A.320-214	easyJet Europe

Reg	Type	Owner or Operator	Notes
OE-IVS	Airbus A.320-214	easyJet Europe	
OE-IVT	Airbus A.320-214	easyJet Europe	
OE-IVU	Airbus A.320-214	easyJet Europe	
OE-IVV	Airbus A.320-214	easyJet Europe	
OE-IVW	Airbus A.320-214	easyJet Europe	
OE-IVZ	Airbus A.320-214	easyJet Europe	
OE-IWA	Boeing 737-8AS	ASL Airlines Belgium	
OE-IWB	Boeing 737-8AS	ASL Airlines Belgium	
OE-IWE	Boeing 737-8AS	ASL Airlines Belgium/Federal Express	
OE-IWF	Boeing 737-8AS	ASL Airlines Belgium/Federal Express	
OE-IWW	Airbus A.320-214	easyJet Europe	
OE-IXA	Boeing 737-8AS	ASL Airlines Belgium/Federal Express	
OE-IXB	Boeing 737-8AS	ASL Airlines Belgium	
OE-IXC	Boeing 737-8AS	ASL Airlines Belgium	
OE-IXE	Boeing 737-8AS	ASL Airlines Belgium	
OE-IXF	Boeing 737-86N	ASL Airlines Belgium/Federal Express	
OE-IXH	Boeing 737-8AS	ASL Airlines Belgium	
OE-IXJ	Boeing 737-86N	ASL Airlines Belgium	
OE-IXK	Boeing 737-86N	ASL Airlines Belgium	
OE-IXM	Boeing 737-8EH	ASL Airlines Belgium	
OE-IXN	Boeing 737-8EH	ASL Airlines Belgium	
OE-IXO	Boeing 737-883	ASL Airlines Belgium	
OE-IXP	Boeing 737-808	ASL Airlines Belgium	
OE-IXR	Boeing 737-85R	ASL Airlines Belgium	
OE-IXS	Boeing 737-86N	ASL Airlines Belgium	
OE-IXV	Boeing 737-86N	ASL Airlines Belgium	
OE-IXW	Boeing 737-8F2	ASL Airlines Belgium	
OE-IZF	Airbus A.320-214	easyJet Europe	
OE-IZG	Airbus A.320-214	easyJet Europe	
OE-IZH	Airbus A.320-214	easyJet Europe	
OE-IZJ	Airbus A.320-214	easyJet Europe	
OE-IZL	Airbus A.320-214	easyJet Europe	
OE-IZN	Airbus A.320-214	easyJet Europe	
OE-IZQ	Airbus A.320-214	easyJet Europe	
OE-LAE	Boeing 767-3Z9ER	Austrian Airlines	
OE-LAY	Boeing 767-3Z9ER	Austrian Airlines	
OE-LAZ	Boeing 767-3Z9ER	Austrian Airlines	
OE-LBA	Airbus A.321-111	Austrian Airlines	
OE-LBB	Airbus A.321-111	Austrian Airlines	
OE-LBC	Airbus A.321-111	Austrian Airlines	
OE-LBD	Airbus A.321-111	Austrian Airlines	
OE-LBE	Airbus A.321-111	Austrian Airlines	
OE-LBF	Airbus A.321-111	Austrian Airlines	
OE-LBI	Airbus A.320-214	Austrian Airlines	
OE-LBJ	Airbus A.320-212	Austrian Airlines	
OE-LBK	Airbus A.320-214	Austrian Airlines	
OE-LBL	Airbus A.320-214	Austrian Airlines	
OE-LBM	Airbus A.320-214	Austrian Airlines	
OE-LBN	Airbus A.320-214	Austrian Airlines	
OE-LBO	Airbus A.320-214	Austrian Airlines	
OE-LBP	Airbus A.320-214	Austrian Airlines	
OE-LBQ	Airbus A.320-214	Austrian Airlines	
OE-LBR	Airbus A.320-214	Austrian Airlines	
OE-LBS	Airbus A.320-214	Austrian Airlines	
OE-LBT	Airbus A.320-214	Austrian Airlines	
OE-LBU	Airbus A.320-214	Austrian Airlines	
OE-LBV	Airbus A.320-214	Austrian Airlines	
OE-LBW	Airbus A.320-214	Austrian Airlines	
OE-LBX	Airbus A.320-214	Austrian Airlines	
OE-LBY	Airbus A.320-214	Austrian Airlines	
OE-LBZ	Airbus A.320-214	Austrian Airlines	
OE-LKC	Airbus A.319-111	easyJet Europe	
OE-LKD	Airbus A.319-111	easyJet Europe	
OE-LKF	Airbus A.319-111	easyJet Europe	
OE-LKK	Airbus A.319-111	easyJet Europe	
OE-LKL	Airbus A.319-111	easyJet Europe	
OE-LKM	Airbus A.319-111	easyJet Europe	
OE-LKO	Airbus A.319-111	easyJet Europe	
OE-LKP	Airbus A.319-111	easyJet Europe	
OE-LKQ	Airbus A.319-111	easyJet Europe	
OE-LKV	Airbus A.319-111	easyJet Europe	

Notes	Reg	Type	Owner or Operator
	OE-LKX	Airbus A.319-111	easyJet Europe
	OE-LKY	Airbus A.319-111	easyJet Europe
	OE-LNA	Boeing 757-23ASF	DHL Air Austria
	OE-LNB	Boeing 757-236PCF	DHL Air Austria
	OE-LNC	Boeing 757-28ASF	DHL Air Austria
	OE-LND	Boeing 757-23NPCF	DHL Air Austria
	OE-LNE	Boeing 757-23NPCF	DHL Air Austria
	OE-LNF	Boeing 757-236PCF	DHL Air Austria
	OE-LNG	Boeing 757-28ASF	DHL Air Austria
	OE-LNH	Boeing 757-236PCF	DHL Air Austria
	OE-LNI	Boeing 757-28APCF	DHL Air Austria
	OE-LNJ	Boeing 757-256PCF	DHL Air Austria
	OE-LNK	Boeing 757-223PCF	DHL Air Austria
	OE-LNL	Boeing 757-223PCF	DHL Air Austria
	OE-LNO	Boeing 757-223PCF	DHL Air Austria
	OE-LNQ	Boeing 757-223PCF	DHL Air Austria
	OE-LNR	Boeing 757-223PCF	DHL Air Austria
	OE-LNU	Boeing 757-256PCF	DHL Air Austria
	OE-LNW	Boeing 757-223PCF	DHL Air Austria
	OE-LNX	Boeing 757-223PCF	DHL Air Austria
	OE-LNZ	Boeing 757-223PCF	DHL Air Austria
	OE-LPA	Boeing 777-2Z9ER	Austrian Airlines
	OE-LPB	Boeing 777-2Z9ER	Austrian Airlines
	OE-LPC	Boeing 777-2Z9ER	Austrian Airlines
	OE-LPD	Boeing 777-2Z9ER	Austrian Airlines
	OE-LPE	Boeing 777-2Q8ER	Austrian Airlines
	OE-LPF	Boeing 777-2Q8ER	Austrian Airlines
	OE-LPL	Boeing 787-9	Austrian Airlines
	OE-LPM	Boeing 787-9	Austrian Airlines
	OE-LQA	Airbus A.319-111	easyJet Europe
	OE-LQB	Airbus A.319-111	easyJet Europe
	OE-LQC	Airbus A.319-111	easyJet Europe
	OE-LQD	Airbus A.319-111	easyJet Europe
	OE-LQE	Airbus A.319-111	easyJet Europe
	OE-LQF	Airbus A.319-111	easyJet Europe
	OE-LQG	Airbus A.319-111	easyJet Europe
	OE-LQI	Airbus A.319-111	easyJet Europe
	OE-LQJ	Airbus A.319-111	easyJet Europe
	OE-LQL	Airbus A.319-111	easyJet Europe
	OE-LQM	Airbus A.319-111	easyJet Europe
	OE-LQN	Airbus A.319-111	easyJet Europe
	OE-LQP	Airbus A.319-111	easyJet Europe
	OE-LQQ	Airbus A.319-111	easyJet Europe
	OE-LQR	Airbus A.319-111	easyJet Europe
	OE-LQS	Airbus A.319-111	easyJet Europe
	OE-LQT	Airbus A.319-111	easyJet Europe
	OE-LQU	Airbus A.319-111	easyJet Europe
	OE-LQW	Airbus A.319-111	easyJet Europe
	OE-LQX	Airbus A.319-111	easyJet Europe
	OE-LQZ	Airbus A.319-111	easyJet Europe
	OE-LSA	Airbus A.320-251N	easyJet Europe
	OE-LSF	Airbus A.320-251N	easyJet Europe
	OE-LSI	Airbus A.320-251N	easyJet Europe
	OE-LSJ	Airbus A.320-251N	easyJet Europe
	OE-LSK	Airbus A.320-251N	easyJet Europe
	OE-LSM	Airbus A.320-251N	easyJet Europe
	OE-LSN	Airbus A.320-251N	easyJet Europe
	OE-LSO	Airbus A.320-251N	easyJet Eur0pe
	OE-LSP	Airbus A.320-251N	easyJet Europe
	OE-LSQ	Airbus A.320-251N	easyJet Europe
	OE-LSR	Airbus A.320-251N	easyJet Europe
	OE-LST	Airbus A.320-251N	easyJet Europe
	OE-LSU	Airbus A.320-251N	easyJet Europe
	OE-LSV	Airbus A.320-251N	easyJet Europe
	OE-LSW	Airbus A.320-251N	easyJet Europe
	OE-LUE	Airbus A.320-251N	easyJet Europe
	OE-LUF	Airbus A.320-251N	easyJet Europe
	OE-LUG	Airbus A.320-251N	easyJet Europe
	OE-LVC	Boeing 737-883BCF	ASL Airlines Belgium
	OE-LVG	Airbus A.319-111	easyJet Europe
	OE-LVK	Airbus A.319-111	easyJet Europe

Reg	Type	Owner or Operator	Notes
OE-LWA	Embraer ERJ190-200LR	Austrian Airlines	
OE-LWB	Embraer ERJ190-200LR	Austrian Airlines	
OE-LWC	Embraer ERJ190-200LR	Austrian Airlines	
OE-LWD	Embraer ERJ190-200LR	Austrian Airlines	
OE-LWE	Embraer ERJ190-200LR	Austrian Airlines	
OE-LWF	Embraer ERJ190-200LR	Austrian Airlines	
OE-LWG	Embraer ERJ190-200LR	Austrian Airlines	
OE-LWH	Embraer ERJ190-200LR	Austrian Airlines	
OE-LWI	Embraer ERJ190-200LR	Austrian Airlines	
OE-LWJ	Embraer ERJ190-200LR	Austrian Airlines	
OE-LWK	Embraer ERJ190-200LR	Austrian Airlines	
OE-LWL	Embraer ERJ190-200LR	Austrian Airlines	
OE-LWN	Embraer ERJ190-200LR	Austrian Airlines	
OE-LWO	Embraer ERJ190-200LR	Austrian Airlines	
OE-LWP	Embraer ERJ190-200LR	Austrian Airlines	
OE-LWQ	Embraer ERJ190-200LR	Austrian Airlines	
OE-LXA	Airbus A.320-216	Austrian Airlines	
OE-LXB	Airbus A.320-216	Austrian Airlines	
OE-LXC	Airbus A.320-216	Austrian Airlines	
OE-LXD	Airbus A.320-216	Austrian Airlines	
OE-LXE	Airbus A.320-216	Austrian Airlines	
OE-LYA	Boeing 767-3Q8ER(BDSF)	DHL Air Austria	
OE-LYB	Boeing 767-304ER(BDSF)	DHL Air Austria	
OE-LYC	Boeing 767-304ER(BDSF)	DHL Air Austria	
OE-LYD	Boeing 767-304ER	DHL Air Austria	
OE-LZA	Airbus A.320-214	Austrian Airlines	
OE-LZB	Airbus A.320-214	Austrian Airlines	
OE-LZC	Airbus A.320-214	Austrian Airlines	
OE-LZD	Airbus A.320-214	Austrian Airlines	
OE-LZE	Airbus A.320-214	Austrian Airlines	
OE-LZF	Airbus A.320-214	Austrian Airlines	
OE-LZN	Airbus A.320-271N	Austrian Airlines	
OE-LZO	Airbus A.320-271N	Austrian Airlines	
OE-LZP	Airbus A.320-271N	Austrian Airlines	
OE-LZQ	Airbus A.320-271N	Austrian Airlines	
OE-LZR	Airbus A.320-271N	Austrian Airlines	

OH (Finland)

Reg	Type	Owner or Operator	Notes
OH-LKE	Embraer RJ190-100LR	Nordic Regional Airlines/Finnair	
OH-LKF	Embraer RJ190-100LR	Nordic Regional Airlines/Finnair	
OH-LKG	Embraer RJ190-100LR	Nordic Regional Airlines/Finnair	
OH-LKH	Embraer RJ190-100LR	Nordic Regional Airlines/Finnair	
OH-LKI	Embraer RJ190-100LR	Nordic Regional Airlines/Finnair	
OH-LKK	Embraer RJ190-100LR	Nordic Regional Airlines/Finnair	
OH-LKL	Embraer RJ190-100LR	Nordic Regional Airlines/Finnair	
OH-LKM	Embraer RJ190-100LR	Nordic Regional Airlines/Finnair	
OH-LKN	Embraer RJ190-100LR	Nordic Regional Airlines/Finnair	
OH-LKO	Embraer RJ190-100LR	Nordic Regional Airlines/Finnair	
OH-LKP	Embraer RJ190-100LR	Nordic Regional Airlines/Finnair	
OH-LKR	Embraer RJ190-100LR	Nordic Regional Airlines/Finnair	
OH-LVC	Airbus A.319-112	Finnair	
OH-LVD	Airbus A.319-112	Finnair	
OH-LVH	Airbus A.319-112	Finnair	
OH-LVI	Airbus A.319-112	Finnair	
OH-LVL	Airbus A.319-112	Finnair	
OH-LWA	Airbus A.350-941	Finnair	
OH-LWB	Airbus A.350-941	Finnair	
OH-LWC	Airbus A.350-941	Finnair	
OH-LWD	Airbus A.350-941	Finnair	
OH-LWE	Airbus A.350-941	Finnair	
OH-LWF	Airbus A.350-941	Finnair	
OH-LWG	Airbus A.350-941	Finnair	
OH-LWH	Airbus A.350-941	Finnair	
OH-LWI	Airbus A.350-941	Finnair	
OH-LWK	Airbus A.350-941	Finnair	
OH-LWL	Airbus A.350-941	Finnair	
OH-LWM	Airbus A.350-941	Finnair	
OH-LWN	Airbus A.350-941	Finnair	
OH-LWO	Airbus A.350-941	Finnair	
OH-LWP	Airbus A.350-941	Finnair	

Notes	Reg	Type	Owner or Operator
	OH-LWR	Airbus A.350-941	Finnair
	OH-LWS	Airbus A.350-941	Finnair
	OH-LWT	Airbus A.350-941	Finnair
	OH-LXA	Airbus A.320-214	Finnair
	OH-LXB	Airbus A.320-214	Finnair
	OH-LXC	Airbus A.320-214	Finnair
	OH-LXD	Airbus A.320-214	Finnair
	OH-LXF	Airbus A.320-214	Finnair
	OH-LXH	Airbus A.320-214	Finnair
	OH-LXI	Airbus A.320-214	Finnair
	OH-LXK	Airbus A.320-214	Finnair
	OH-LXL	Airbus A.320-214	Finnair
	OH-LXM	Airbus A.320-214	Finnair
	OH-LZE	Airbus A.321-211	Finnair
	OH-LZF	Airbus A.321-211	Finnair
	OH-LZG	Airbus A.321-231	Finnair
	OH-LZH	Airbus A.321-231	Finnair
	OH-LZK	Airbus A.321-231	Finnair
	OH-LZL	Airbus A.321-231	Finnair
	OH-LZM	Airbus A.321-231	Finnair
	OH-LZN	Airbus A.321-231	Finnair
	OH-LZO	Airbus A.321-231	Finnair
	OH-LZP	Airbus A.321-231	Finnair
	OH-LZR	Airbus A.321-231	Finnair
	OH-LZS	Airbus A.321-231	Finnair
	OH-LZT	Airbus A.321-231	Finnair
	OH-LZU	Airbus A.321-231	Finnair

OK (Czechia)

Notes	Reg	Type	Owner or Operator
	OK-SWA	Boeing 737-MAX8	Smartwings
	OK-SWB	Boeing 737-MAX8	Smartwings
	OK-SWC	Boeing 737-MAX8	Smartwings
	OK-SWD	Boeing 737-MAX8	Smartwings
	OK-SWE	Boeing 737-MAX8	Smartwings
	OK-SWF	Boeing 737-MAX8	Smartwings
	OK-SWH	Boeing 737-MAX8	Smartwings
	OK-SWI	Boeing 737-MAX8	Smartwings
	OK-SWJ	Boeing 737-MAX8	Smartwings
	OK-SWK	Boeing 737-MAX8	Smartwings
	OK-SWL	Boeing 737-MAX8	Smartwings
	OK-SWM	Boeing 737-MAX8	Smartwings
	OK-SWN	Boeing 737-MAX8	Smartwings
	OK-TSD	Boeing 737-8Q8	Smartwings
	OK-TSE	Boeing 737-81D	Smartwings
	OK-TSF	Boeing 737-8GJ	Smartwings
	OK-TSI	Boeing 737-9GJ	Smartwings
	OK-TSM	Boeing 737-9GJ	Smartwings
	OK-TSO	Boeing 737-8GQ	Smartwings
	OK-TSR	Boeing 737-82R	Smartwings
	OK-TSS	Boeing 737-8Q8	Smartwings
	OK-TST	Boeing 737-86N	Smartwings
	OK-TSU	Boeing 737-8FZ	Smartwings
	OK-TVF	Boeing 737-8FH	Smartwings
	OK-TVG	Boeing 737-8Q8	Smartwings
	OK-TVJ	Boeing 737-8Q8	Smartwings
	OK-TVL	Boeing 737-8FN	Smartwings
	OK-TVM	Boeing 737-8FN	Smartwings
	OK-TVR	Boeing 737-86N	Smartwings
	OK-TVS	Boeing 737-86N	Smartwings
	OK-TVT	Boeing 737-86N	Smartwings
	OK-TVU	Boeing 737-86N	Smartwings
	OK-TVV	Boeing 737-86N	Smartwings
	OK-TVW	Boeing 737-86Q	Smartwings
	OK-TVY	Boeing 737-8Q8	Smartwings

OM (Slovakia)

Notes	Reg	Type	Owner or Operator
	OM-FEX	Boeing 737-8Q8	AirExplore
	OM-IEX	Boeing 737-8BK	AirExplore

Reg	Type	Owner or Operator	Notes
OM-JEX	Boeing 737-8AS	AirExplore	
OM-KEX	Boeing 737-8BK	AirExplore	
OM-LEX	Boeing 737-8BK	AirExplore	
OM-MEX	Boeing 737-8GJ	AirExplore	
OM-NEX	Boeing 737-8KN	AirExplore	
OM-OEX	Boeing 737-82R	AirExplore	
OM-PEX	Boeing 737-8HX	AirExplore	
OM-TVH	Boeing 737-8Q8	Smartwings Slovakia	

OO (Belgium)

Reg	Type	Owner or Operator	Notes
OO-IWD	Boeing 737-8AS	ASL Airlines Belgium/Federal Express	
OO-JAF	Boeing 737-8K5	TUI Airlines Belgium	
OO-JAQ	Boeing 737-8K5	TUI Airlines Belgium	
OO-JAX	Boeing 737-8K5	TUI Airlines Belgium	
OO-JDL	Boeing 787-8K5	TUI Airlines Belgium	
OO-JEF	Boeing 737-8K5	TUI Airlines Belgium	
OO-MAX	Boeing 737-8MAX	TUI Airlines Belgium	
OO-SBA	Airbus A.320-251N	Brussels Airlines	
OO-SBB	Airbus A.320-251N	Brussels Airlines	
OO-SBC	Airbus A.320-251N	Brussels Airlines	
OO-SBD	Airbus A.320-251N	Brussels Airlines	
OO-SBE	Airbus A.320-251N	Brussels Airlines	
OO-SBF	Airbus A.320-251N	Brussels Airlines	
OO-SBG	Airbus A.320-271N	Brussels Airlines	
OO-SBH	Airbus A.320-271N	Brussels Airlines	
OO-SNB	Airbus A.320-214	Brussels Airlines	
OO-SNE	Airbus A.320-214	Brussels Airlines	
OO-SNF	Airbus A.320-214	Brussels Airlines	
OO-SNH	Airbus A.320-214	Brussels Airlines	
OO-SNI	Airbus A.320-214	Brussels Airlines	
OO-SNJ	Airbus A.320-214	Brussels Airlines	
OO-SNK	Airbus A.320-214	Brussels Airlines	
OO-SNL	Airbus A.320-214	Brussels Airlines	
OO-SNM	Airbus A.320-214	Brussels Airlines	
OO-SNN	Airbus A.320-214	Brussels Airlines	
OO-SNO	Airbus A.320-214	Brussels Airlines	
OO-SNP	Airbus A.320-214	Brussels Airlines	
OO-SNQ	Airbus A.320-214	Brussels Airlines	
OO-SSA	Airbus A.319-111	Brussels Airlines	
OO-SSB	Airbus A.319-111	Brussels Airlines	
OO-SSF	Airbus A.319-111	Brussels Airlines	
OO-SSJ	Airbus A.319-111	Brussels Airlines	
OO-SSL	Airbus A.319-112	Brussels Airlines	
OO-SSN	Airbus A.319-112	Brussels Airlines	
OO-SSO	Airbus A.319-111	Brussels Airlines	
OO-SSR	Airbus A.319-112	Brussels Airlines	
OO-SSU	Airbus A.319-111	Brussels Airlines	
OO-SSV	Airbus A.319-111	Brussels Airlines	
OO-SSW	Airbus A.319-111	Brussels Airlines	
OO-SSX	Airbus A.319-111	Brussels Airlines	
OO-SSY	Airbus A.319-111	Brussels Airlines	
OO-TCH	Airbus A.320-214	Brussels Airlines	
OO-TCQ	Airbus A.320-214	Brussels Airlines	
OO-TCV	Airbus A.320-212	Brussels Airlines	
OO-TMA	Boeing 737-MAX8	TUI Airlines Belgium	
OO-TMB	Boeing 737-MAX8	TUI Airlines Belgium	
OO-TME	Boeing 737-MAX8	TUI Airlines Belgium	
OO-TMF	Boeing 737-MAX8	TUI Airlines Belgium	
OO-TMG	Boeing 737-MAX8	TUI Airlines Belgium	
OO-TMS	Boeing 737-MAX8	TUI Airlines Belgium	
OO-TMT	Boeing 737-MAX8	TUI Airlines Belgium	
OO-TMZ	Boeing 737-MAX8	TUI Airlines Belgium	
OO-TNB	Boeing 737-8K5	TUI Airlines Belgium	
OO-TNC	Boeing 737-8K5	TUI Airlines Belgium	
OO-TUJ	Boeing 737-8K5	TUI Airlines Belgium	
OO-TUK	Boeing 737-86J	TUI Airlines Belgium	
OO-TUV	Boeing 737-86J	TUI Airlines Belgium	

Notes	Reg	Type	Owner or Operator

OY (Denmark)

	Reg	Type	Owner or Operator
	OY-JRK	Airbus A.320-231	Danish Air Transport
	OY-JRP	Airbus A.320-232	Danish Air Transport
	OY-JRS	Airbus A.320-232	Danish Air Transport
	OY-KAP	Airbus A.320-232	SAS
	OY-KAR	Airbus A.320-232	SAS
	OY-KAS	Airbus A.320-232	SAS
	OY-KBO	Airbus A.319-132	SAS
	OY-KBP	Airbus A.319-132	SAS
	OY-KBR	Airbus A.319-132	SAS
	OY-KBT	Airbus A.319-132	SAS
	OY-MAC	Boeing 777-F	Maersk Air Cargo
	OY-MAD	Boeing 777-F	Maersk Air Cargo
	OY-RCJ	Airbus A.320-214	Atlantic Airways
	OY-RCK	Airbus A.320-251N	Atlantic Airways
	OY-RCL	Airbus A.320-251N	Atlantic Airways
	OY-RCM	Airbus A.320-214	Atlantic Airways
	OY-RUH	Airbus A.320-232	Danish Air Transport
	OY-RUU	Airbus A.321-231	Danish Air Transport
	OY-RUY	Airbus A.320-232	Danish Air Transport
	OY-SRF	Boeing 767-219 (SF)	Star Air/Maersk Air Cargo
	OY-SRG	Boeing 767-219 (SF)	Star Air/Maersk Air Cargo
	OY-SRI	Boeing 767-25E (SF)	Star Air/Maersk Air Cargo
	OY-SRK	Boeing 767-204 (SF)	Star Air/Maersk Air Cargo
	OY-SRM	Boeing 767-25E (SF)	Star Air/Maersk Air Cargo
	OY-SRN	Boeing 767-219 (SF)	Star Air/Maersk Air Cargo
	OY-SRO	Boeing 767-25E (SF)	Star Air/Maersk Air Cargo
	OY-SRU	Boeing 767-36NER	Star Air/Maersk Air Cargo
	OY-SRV	Boeing 767-346ERF	Star Air/Maersk Air Cargo
	OY-SRW	Boeing 767-346ERF	Star Air/Maersk Air Cargo
	OY-SYA	Boeing 767-3P6ERF	Maersk Air Cargo
	OY-SYB	Boeing 767-3P6ERF	Maersk Air Cargo
	OY-SYC	Boeing 767-3P6ERF	Maersk Air Cargo
	OY-SYD	Boeing 767-3P6ERF	Maersk Air Cargo
	OY-TCD	Airbus A.321-211	Sunclass Airlines
	OY-TCE	Airbus A.321-211	Sunclass Airlines
	OY-TCF	Airbus A.321-211	Sunclass Airlines
	OY-TCH	Airbus A.321-211	Sunclass Airlines
	OY-TCI	Airbus A.321-211	Sunclass Airlines
	OY-TCN	Airbus A.321-211	Sunclass Airlines
	OY-VKA	Airbus A.321-251NX	Sunclass Airlines
	OY-VKB	Airbus A.321-251NX	Sunclass Airlines
	OY-VKE	Airbus A.321-251NX	Sunclass Airlines

PH (Netherlands)

	Reg	Type	Owner or Operator
	PH-AKA	Airbus A.330-303	KLM
	PH-AKB	Airbus A.330-303	KLM
	PH-AKD	Airbus A.330-303	KLM
	PH-AKE	Airbus A.330-303	KLM
	PH-AKF	Airbus A.330-303	KLM
	PH-AOA	Airbus A.330-203	KLM
	PH-AOB	Airbus A.330-203	KLM
	PH-AOC	Airbus A.330-203	KLM
	PH-AOD	Airbus A.330-203	KLM
	PH-AOE	Airbus A.330-203	KLM
	PH-AOF	Airbus A.330-203	KLM
	PH-AXA	Airbus A.321-252NX	KLM
	PH-AXB	Airbus A.321-252NX	KLM
	PH-AXC	Airbus A.321-252NX	KLM
	PH-AXD	Airbus A.321-252NX	KLM
	PH-AXE	Airbus A.321-252NX	KLM
	PH-AXF	Airbus A.321-252NX	KLM
	PH-AXG	Airbus A.321-252NX	KLM
	PH-AXH	Airbus A.321-252NX	KLM
	PH-AXI	Airbus A.321-252NX	KLM
	PH-AXK	Airbus A.321-252NX	KLM
	PH-AXL	Airbus A.321-252NX	KLM
	PH-AXM	Airbus A.321-252NX	KLM
	PH-AXN	Airbus A.321-252NX	KLM

Reg	Type	Owner or Operator	Notes
PH-AXP	Airbus A.321-252NX	KLM	
PH-AXR	Airbus A.321-252NX	KLM	
PH-AXT	Airbus A.321-252NX	KLM	
PH-AXU	Airbus A.321-252NX	KLM	
PH-AXV	Airbus A.321-252NX	KLM	
PH-AXW	Airbus A.321-252NX	KLM	
PH-AXY	Airbus A.321-252NX	KLM	
PH-AXZ	Airbus A.321-252NX	KLM	
PH-BCA	Boeing 737-8K2	KLM	
PH-BCB	Boeing 737-8BK	KLM	
PH-BCD	Boeing 737-8BK	KLM	
PH-BCE	Boeing 737-8CK	KLM	
PH-BCG	Boeing 737-8K2	KLM	
PH-BCH	Boeing 737-8K2	KLM	
PH-BCK	Boeing 737-8K2	KLM	
PH-BCL	Boeing 737-8K2	KLM	
PH-BGA	Boeing 737-8K2	KLM	
PH-BGB	Boeing 737-8K2	KLM	
PH-BGC	Boeing 737-8K2	KLM	
PH-BGF	Boeing 737-7K2	KLM	
PH-BGG	Boeing 737-706	KLM	
PH-BGH	Boeing 737-7K2	KLM	
PH-BGI	Boeing 737-7K2	KLM	
PH-BGM	Boeing 737-7K2	KLM	
PH-BGQ	Boeing 737-7K2	KLM	
PH-BHA	Boeing 787-9	KLM	
PH-BHC	Boeing 787-9	KLM	
PH-BHD	Boeing 787-9	KLM	
PH-BHE	Boeing 787-9	KLM	
PH-BHF	Boeing 787-9	KLM	
PH-BHG	Boeing 787-9	KLM	
PH-BHH	Boeing 787-9	KLM	
PH-BHI	Boeing 787-9	KLM	
PH-BHL	Boeing 787-9	KLM	
PH-BHM	Boeing 787-9	KLM	
PH-BHN	Boeing 787-9	KLM	
PH-BHO	Boeing 787-9	KLM	
PH-BHP	Boeing 787-9	KLM	
PH-BKA	Boeing 787-10	KLM	
PH-BKC	Boeing 787-10	KLM	
PH-BKD	Boeing 787-10	KLM	
PH-BKF	Boeing 787-10	KLM	
PH-BKG	Boeing 787-10	KLM	
PH-BKH	Boeing 787-10	KLM	
PH-BKI	Boeing 787-10	KLM	
PH-BKK	Boeing 787-10	KLM	
PH-BKL	Boeing 787-10	KLM	
PH-BKM	Boeing 787-10	KLM	
PH-BKO	Boeing 787-10	KLM	
PH-BKP	Boeing 787-10	KLM	
PH-BKQ	Boeing 787-10	KLM	
PH-BKR	Boeing 787-10	KLM	
PH-BKS	Boeing 787-10	KLM	
PH-BQA	Boeing 777-206ER	KLM	
PH-BQB	Boeing 777-206ER	KLM	
PH-BQC	Boeing 777-206ER	KLM	
PH-BQD	Boeing 777-206ER	KLM	
PH-BQE	Boeing 777-206ER	KLM	
PH-BQF	Boeing 777-206ER	KLM	
PH-BQG	Boeing 777-206ER	KLM	
PH-BQH	Boeing 777-206ER	KLM	
PH-BQI	Boeing 777-206ER	KLM	
PH-BQK	Boeing 777-206ER	KLM	
PH-BQL	Boeing 777-206ER	KLM	
PH-BQM	Boeing 777-206ER	KLM	
PH-BQN	Boeing 777-206ER	KLM	
PH-BQO	Boeing 777-206ER	KLM	
PH-BQP	Boeing 777-206ER	KLM	
PH-BVA	Boeing 777-306ER	KLM	
PH-BVB	Boeing 777-306ER	KLM	
PH-BVC	Boeing 777-306ER	KLM	

Notes	Reg	Type	Owner or Operator
	PH-BVD	Boeing 777-306ER	KLM
	PH-BVF	Boeing 777-306ER	KLM
	PH-BVG	Boeing 777-306ER	KLM
	PH-BVI	Boeing 777-306ER	KLM
	PH-BVK	Boeing 777-306ER	KLM
	PH-BVN	Boeing 777-306ER	KLM
	PH-BVO	Boeing 777-306ER	KLM
	PH-BVP	Boeing 777-306ER	KLM
	PH-BVR	Boeing 777-306ER	KLM
	PH-BVS	Boeing 777-306ER	KLM
	PH-BVU	Boeing 777-300ER	KLM
	PH-BVV	Boeing 777-300ER	KLM
	PH-BVW	Boeing 777-300ER	KLM
	PH-BXA	Boeing 737-8K2	KLM
	PH-BXB	Boeing 737-8K2	KLM
	PH-BXC	Boeing 737-8K2	KLM
	PH-BXD	Boeing 737-8K2	KLM
	PH-BXE	Boeing 737-8K2	KLM
	PH-BXF	Boeing 737-8K2	KLM
	PH-BXG	Boeing 737-8K2	KLM
	PH-BXH	Boeing 737-8K2	KLM
	PH-BXI	Boeing 737-8K2	KLM
	PH-BXL	Boeing 737-8K2	KLM
	PH-BXM	Boeing 737-8K2	KLM
	PH-BXN	Boeing 737-8K2	KLM
	PH-BXO	Boeing 737-9K2	KLM
	PH-BXP	Boeing 737-9K2	KLM
	PH-BXR	Boeing 737-9K2	KLM
	PH-BXS	Boeing 737-9K2	KLM
	PH-BXT	Boeing 737-9K2	KLM
	PH-BXU	Boeing 737-8BK	KLM
	PH-BXV	Boeing 737-8K2	KLM
	PH-BXW	Boeing 737-8K2	KLM
	PH-BXY	Boeing 737-8K2	KLM
	PH-BXZ	Boeing 737-8K2	KLM
	PH-CKA	Boeing 747-406ERF	KLM Cargo
	PH-CKB	Boeing 747-406ERF	KLM Cargo
	PH-CKC	Boeing 747-406ERF	KLM Cargo
	PH-EXE	Embraer ERJ190-100STD	KLM Cityhopper
	PH-EXF	Embraer ERJ190-100STD	KLM Cityhopper
	PH-EXG	Embraer ERJ170-200STD	KLM Cityhopper
	PH-EXH	Embraer ERJ170-200STD	KLM Cityhopper
	PH-EXI	Embraer ERJ170-200STD	KLM Cityhopper
	PH-EXJ	Embraer ERJ170-200STD	KLM Cityhopper
	PH-EXK	Embraer ERJ170-200STD	KLM Cityhopper
	PH-EXL	Embraer ERJ170-200STD	KLM Cityhopper
	PH-EXM	Embraer ERJ170-200STD	KLM Cityhopper
	PH-EXN	Embraer ERJ170-200STD	KLM Cityhopper
	PH-EXO	Embraer ERJ170-200STD	KLM Cityhopper
	PH-EXP	Embraer ERJ170-200STD	KLM Cityhopper
	PH-EXR	Embraer ERJ170-200STD	KLM Cityhopper
	PH-EXS	Embraer ERJ170-200STD	KLM Cityhopper
	PH-EXT	Embraer ERJ170-200STD	KLM Cityhopper
	PH-EXU	Embraer ERJ170-200STD	KLM Cityhopper
	PH-EXV	Embraer ERJ190-100STD	KLM Cityhopper
	PH-EXW	Embraer ERJ170-200STD	KLM Cityhopper
	PH-EXX	Embraer ERJ170-200STD	KLM Cityhopper
	PH-EXY	Embraer ERJ190-100STD	KLM Cityhopper
	PH-EXZ	Embraer ERJ170-200STD	KLM Cityhopper
	PH-EZC	Embraer ERJ190-100STD	KLM Cityhopper
	PH-EZD	Embraer ERJ190-100STD	KLM Cityhopper
	PH-EZE	Embraer ERJ190-100STD	KLM Cityhopper
	PH-EZF	Embraer ERJ190-100STD	KLM Cityhopper
	PH-EZG	Embraer ERJ190-100STD	KLM Cityhopper
	PH-EZH	Embraer ERJ190-100STD	KLM Cityhopper
	PH-EZL	Embraer ERJ190-100STD	KLM Cityhopper
	PH-EZM	Embraer ERJ190-100STD	KLM Cityhopper
	PH-EZN	Embraer ERJ190-100STD	KLM Cityhopper
	PH-EZO	Embraer ERJ190-100STD	KLM Cityhopper
	PH-EZP	Embraer ERJ190-100STD	KLM Cityhopper
	PH-EZR	Embraer ERJ190-100STD	KLM Cityhopper

Reg	Type	Owner or Operator	Notes
PH-EZS	Embraer ERJ190-100STD	KLM Cityhopper	
PH-EZX	Embraer ERJ190-100STD	KLM Cityhopper	
PH-EZY	Embraer ERJ190-100STD	KLM Cityhopper	
PH-HBJ	Boeing 737-82R	Transavia	
PH-HBK	Boeing 737-82R	Transavia	
PH-HBL	Boeing 737-82R	Transavia	
PH-HBM	Boeing 737-82R	Transavia	
PH-HBN	Boeing 737-82R	Transavia	
PH-HSA	Boeing 737-8K2	Transavia	
PH-HSB	Boeing 737-8K2	Transavia	
PH-HSC	Boeing 737-8K2	Transavia	
PH-HSD	Boeing 737-8K2	KLM	
PH-HSE	Boeing 737-8K2	KLM	
PH-HSF	Boeing 737-8K2	Transavia	
PH-HSG	Boeing 737-8K2	Transavia	
PH-HSI	Boeing 737-8K2	Transavia	
PH-HSJ	Boeing 737-8K2	Transavia	
PH-HSK	Boeing 737-8K2	Transavia	
PH-HSM	Boeing 737-8K2	Transavia	
PH-HSW	Boeing 737-8K2	Transavia	
PH-HXA	Boeing 737-8K2	Transavia	
PH-HXB	Boeing 737-8K2	Transavia	
PH-HXC	Boeing 737-8K2	Transavia	
PH-HXD	Boeing 737-8K2	Transavia	
PH-HXE	Boeing 737-8K2	Transavia	
PH-HXF	Boeing 737-8K2	Transavia	
PH-HXG	Boeing 737-8K2	Transavia	
PH-HXI	Boeing 737-8K2	Transavia	
PH-HXJ	Boeing 737-8K2	Transavia	
PH-HXK	Boeing 737-8K2	Transavia	
PH-HXL	Boeing 737-8K2	Transavia	
PH-HXM	Boeing 737-8K2	Transavia	
PH-HXN	Boeing 737-8K2	Transavia	
PH-HXO	Boeing 737-8K2	Transavia	
PH-HZG	Boeing 737-8K2	Transavia	
PH-HZI	Boeing 737-8K2	Transavia	
PH-HZL	Boeing 737-8K2	Transavia	
PH-HZN	Boeing 737-8K2	Transavia	
PH-HZO	Boeing 737-8K2	Transavia	
PH-HZW	Boeing 737-8K2	Transavia	
PH-MPS	Boeing 747-412BCF	Martinair Cargo	
PH-NXA	Embraer ERJ190-400STD	KLM Cityhopper	
PH-NXB	Embraer ERJ190-400STD	KLM Cityhopper	
PH-NXC	Embraer ERJ190-400STD	KLM Cityhopper	
PH-NXD	Embraer ERJ190-400STD	KLM Cityhopper	
PH-NXE	Embraer ERJ190-400STD	KLM Cityhopper	
PH-NXF	Embraer ERJ190-400STD	KLM Cityhopper	
PH-NXG	Embraer ERJ190-400STD	KLM Cityhopper	
PH-NXH	Embraer ERJ190-400STD	KLM Cityhopper	
PH-NXI	Embraer ERJ190-400STD	KLM Cityhopper	
PH-NXJ	Embraer ERJ190-400STD	KLM Cityhopper	
PH-NXK	Embraer ERJ190-400STD	KLM Cityhopper	
PH-NXL	Embraer ERJ190-400STD	KLM Cityhopper	
PH-NXM	Embraer ERJ190-400STD	KLM Cityhopper	
PH-NXN	Embraer ERJ190-400STD	KLM Cityhopper	
PH-NXO	Embraer ERJ190-400STD	KLM Cityhopper	
PH-NXP	Embraer ERJ190-400STD	KLM Cityhopper	
PH-NXR	Embraer ERJ190-400STD	KLM Cityhopper	
PH-NXS	Embraer ERJ190-400STD	KLM Cityhopper	
PH-NXT	Embraer ERJ190-400STD	KLM Cityhopper	
PH-NXU	Embraer ERJ190-400STD	KLM Cityhopper	
PH-NXV	Embraer ERJ190-400STD	KLM Cityhopper	
PH-NXW	Embraer ERJ190-400STD	KLM Cityhopper	
PH-NXX	Embraer ERJ190-400STD	KLM Cityhopper	
PH-NXY	Embraer ERJ190-400STD	KLM Cityhopper	
PH-NXZ	Embraer ERJ190-400STD	KLM Cityhopper	
PH-TFJ	Boeing 787-8	TUI fly Nederland	
PH-TFK	Boeing 787-8	TUI fly Nederland	
PH-TFL	Boeing 787-8	TUI fly Nederland	
PH-TFM	Boeing 787-8	TUI fly Nederland	
PH-TFN	Boeing 737-MAX8	TUI fly Nederland	

Notes	Reg	Type	Owner or Operator
	PH-TFO	Boeing 737-MAX8	TUI fly Nederland
	PH-TFP	Boeing 737-MAX8	TUI fly Nederland
	PH-TFR	Boeing 737-MAX8	TUI fly Nederland
	PH-TFT	Boeing 737-MAX8	TUI fly Nederland
	PH-TFU	Boeing 737-MAX8	TUI fly Nederland
	PH-YHA	Airbus A.321-252NX	Transavia
	PH-YHB	Airbus A.321-252NX	Transavia
	PH-YHC	Airbus A.321-252NX	Transavia
	PH-YHD	Airbus A.321-252NX	Transavia
	PH-YHE	Airbus A.321-252NX	Transavia
	PH-YHG	Airbus A.321-252NX	Transavia
	PH-YHH	Airbus A.321-252NX	Transavia
	PH-YHI	Airbus A.321-252NX	Transavia
	PH-YHP	Airbus A.321-251NX	Transavia
	PH-YHQ	Airbus A.321-251NX	Transavia
	PH-YHR	Airbus A.321-251NX	Transavia
	PH-YHS	Airbus A.321-251NX	Transavia
	PH-YHT	Airbus A.321-251NX	Transavia
	PH-YHU	Airbus A.321-251NX	Transavia
	PH-YHV	Airbus A.321-251NX	Transavia
	PH-YHW	Airbus A.321-251NX	Transavia
	PH-YHX	Airbus A.321-251NX	Transavia
	PH-YHY	Airbus A.321-251NX	Transavia
	PH-YHZ	Airbus A.321-251NX	Transavia

PP/PR/PT (Brazil)

Notes	Reg	Type	Owner or Operator
	PT-MUA	Boeing 777-32WER	LATAM Airlines
	PT-MUB	Boeing 777-32WER	LATAM Airlines
	PT-MUC	Boeing 777-32WER	LATAM Airlines
	PT-MUD	Boeing 777-32WER	LATAM Airlines
	PT-MUE	Boeing 777-32WER	LATAM Airlines
	PT-MUF	Boeing 777-32WER	LATAM Airlines
	PT-MUG	Boeing 777-32WER	LATAM Airlines
	PT-MUH	Boeing 777-32WER	LATAM Airlines
	PT-MUI	Boeing 777-32WER	LATAM Airlines
	PT-MUJ	Boeing 777-32WER	LATAM Airlines

S2 (Bangladesh)

Notes	Reg	Type	Owner or Operator
	S2-AJS	Boeing 787-8	Biman Bangladesh Airlines
	S2-AJT	Boeing 787-8	Biman Bangladesh Airlines
	S2-AJU	Boeing 787-8	Biman Bangladesh Airlines
	S2-AJV	Boeing 787-8	Biman Bangladesh Airlines
	S2-AJX	Boeing 787-9	Biman Bangladesh Airlines
	S2-AJY	Boeing 787-9	Biman Bangladesh Airlines

S5 (Slovenia)

Notes	Reg	Type	Owner or Operator
	S5-ABO	Airbus A.300B4-622RF	Solinair/MNG Airlines
	S5-ABW	Airbus A.300B4-605RF	Solinair/MNG Airlines

SE (Sweden)

Notes	Reg	Type	Owner or Operator
	SE-DMO	Airbus A.321-253NX	SAS
	SE-DMR	Airbus A.321-253NX	SAS
	SE-DMS	Airbus A.321-253NX	SAS
	SE-DOX	Airbus A.320-251N	SAS
	SE-DOY	Airbus A.320-251N	SAS
	SE-DOZ	Airbus A.320-251N	SAS
	SE-NAA	Boeing 737-MAX8	Norwegian Air Sweden AOC
	SE-NAB	Boeing 737-MAX8	Norwegian Air Sweden AOC
	SE-NAC	Boeing 737-MAX8	Norwegian Air Sweden AOC
	SE-NAD	Boeing 737-MAX8	Norwegian Air Sweden AOC
	SE-REH	Airbus A.330-343E	SAS
	SE-RFZ	Boeing 787-9	TUI fly Nordic
	SE-RLE	Boeing 757-223PCF	West Atlantic Sweden/Far Cargo
	SE-RLJ	Boeing 737-8Q8F	West Atlantic Sweden/Swiftair
	SE-RND	Boeing 737-MAX8	TUI fly Nordic
	SE-RNE	Boeing 737-MAX8	TUI fly Nordic

Reg	Type	Owner or Operator	Notes
SE-RNF	Boeing 737-MAX8	TUI fly Nordic	
SE-ROA	Airbus A.320-251N	SAS	
SE-ROB	Airbus A.320-251N	SAS	
SE-ROC	Airbus A.320-251N	SAS	
SE-ROD	Airbus A.320-251N	SAS	
SE-ROE	Airbus A.320-251N	SAS	
SE-ROF	Airbus A.320-251N	SAS	
SE-ROG	Airbus A.320-251N	SAS	
SE-ROI	Airbus A.320-251N	SAS	
SE-ROJ	Airbus A.320-251N	SAS	
SE-ROK	Airbus A.320-251N	SAS	
SE-ROL	Airbus A.320-251N	SAS	
SE-ROM	Airbus A.320-251N	SAS	
SE-RON	Airbus A.320-251N	SAS	
SE-ROO	Airbus A.320-251N	SAS	
SE-ROP	Airbus A.320-251N	SAS	
SE-ROR	Airbus A.320-251N	SAS	
SE-ROS	Airbus A.320-251N	SAS	
SE-ROT	Airbus A.320-251N	SAS	
SE-ROU	Airbus A.320-251N	SAS	
SE-ROX	Airbus A.320-251N	SAS	
SE-ROY	Airbus A.320-251N	SAS	
SE-ROZ	Airbus A.320-251N	SAS	
SE-RPD	Boeing 737-8JP	Norwegian Air Sweden AOC	
SE-RPE	Boeing 737-8JP	Norwegian Air Sweden AOC	
SE-RPF	Boeing 737-8JP	Norwegian Air Sweden AOC	
SE-RPG	Boeing 737-8JP	Norwegian Air Sweden AOC	
SE-RPH	Boeing 737-8JP	Norwegian Air Sweden AOC	
SE-RPI	Boeing 737-8JP	Norwegian Air Sweden AOC	
SE-RPJ	Boeing 737-8JP	Norwegian Air Sweden AOC	
SE-RPK	Boeing 737-8JP	Norwegian Air Sweden AOC	
SE-RPL	Boeing 737-8JP	Norwegian Air Sweden AOC	
SE-RPM	Boeing 737-8JP	Norwegian Air Sweden AOC	
SE-RPR	Boeing 737-8JP	Norwegian Air Sweden AOC	
SE-RPS	Boeing 737-8JP	Norwegian Air Sweden AOC	
SE-RPT	Boeing 737-8JP	Norwegian Air Sweden AOC	
SE-RPU	Boeing 737-8JP	Norwegian Air Sweden AOC	
SE-RRE	Boeing 737-8JP	Norwegian Air Sweden AOC	
SE-RRF	Boeing 737-8JP	Norwegian Air Sweden AOC	
SE-RRJ	Boeing 737-8JP	Norwegian Air Sweden AOC	
SE-RRO	Boeing 737-8JP	Norwegian Air Sweden AOC	
SE-RRP	Boeing 737-8JP	Norwegian Air Sweden AOC	
SE-RRS	Boeing 737-8JP	Norwegian Air Sweden AOC	
SE-RSC	Airbus A.350-941	SAS	
SE-RSD	Airbus A.350-941	SAS	
SE-RSE	Airbus A.350-941	SAS	
SE-RSF	Airbus A.350-941	SAS	
SE-RSG	Airbus A.350-941	SAS	
SE-RSH	Airbus A.350-941	SAS	
SE-RSI	Embraer ERJ190-200LR	SAS Link	
SE-RSJ	Embraer ERJ190-200LR	SAS Link	
SE-RSK	Embraer ERJ190-200LR	SAS Link	
SE-RSL	Embraer ERJ190-200LR	SAS Link	
SE-RSM	Embraer ERJ190-200LR	SAS Link	
SE-RSN	Embraer ERJ190-200LR	SAS Link	
SE-RSO	Embraer ERJ190-200LR	SAS Link	
SE-RSP	Embraer ERJ190-200LR	SAS Link	
SE-RSR	Embraer ERJ190-200LR	SAS Link	
SE-RSS	Embraer ERJ190-200LR	SAS Link	
SE-RST	Embraer ERJ190-200LR	SAS Link	
SE-RSU	Embraer ERJ190-200LR	SAS Link	
SE-RSV	Embraer ERJ190-200LR	SAS Link	
SE-RSX	Embraer ERJ190-200LR	SAS Link	
SE-RSY	Embraer ERJ190-200LR	SAS Link	
SE-RSZ	Embraer ERJ190-200LR	SAS Link	
SE-RTA	Boeing 737-MAX8	Norwegian Air Sweden AOC	
SE-RTB	Boeing 737-MAX8	Norwegian Air Sweden AOC	
SE-RTC	Boeing 737-MAX8	Norwegian Air Sweden AOC	
SE-RTD	Boeing 737-MAX8	Norwegian Air Sweden AOC	
SE-RTE	Boeing 737-MAX8	Norwegian Air Sweden AOC	
SE-RTF	Boeing 737-MAX8	Norwegian Air Sweden AOC	

Notes	Reg	Type	Owner or Operator
	SE-RTG	Boeing 737-MAX8	Norwegian Air Sweden AOC
	SE-RTH	Boeing 737-MAX8	Norwegian Air Sweden AOC
	SE-RTI	Boeing 737-MAX8	Norwegian Air Sweden AOC
	SE-RTJ	Boeing 737-MAX8	Norwegian Air Sweden AOC
	SE-RTK	Boeing 737-MAX8	Norwegian Air Sweden AOC
	SE-RTL	Boeing 737-MAX8	Norwegian Air Sweden AOC
	SE-RTM	Boeing 737-MAX8	Norwegian Air Sweden AOC
	SE-RTN	Boeing 737-MAX8	Norwegian Air Sweden AOC
	SE-RTO	Boeing 737-MAX8	Norwegian Air Sweden AOC
	SE-RTP	Boeing 737-MAX8	Norwegian Air Sweden AOC
	SE-RTR	Boeing 737-MAX8	Norwegian Air Sweden AOC
	SE-RTS	Boeing 737-MAX8	Norwegian Air Sweden AOC
	SE-RTT	Boeing 737-MAX8	Norwegian Air Sweden AOC
	SE-RTU	Boeing 737-MAX8	Norwegian Air Sweden AOC
	SE-RTV	Boeing 737-MAX8	Norwegian Air Sweden AOC
	SE-RTX	Boeing 737-MAX8	Norwegian Air Sweden AOC
	SE-RTY	Boeing 737-MAX8	Norwegian Air Sweden AOC
	SE-RTZ	Boeing 737-MAX8	Norwegian Air Sweden AOC
	SE-RUA	Airbus A.320-251N	SAS
	SE-RUB	Airbus A.320-251N	SAS
	SE-RUC	Airbus A.320-251N	SAS
	SE-RUD	Airbus A.320-251N	SAS
	SE-RUE	Airbus A.320-251N	SAS
	SE-RUF	Airbus A.320-251N	SAS
	SE-RUO	Airbus A.320-251N	SAS
	SE-RUP	Airbus A.320-251N	SAS
	SE-RUR	Airbus A.320-251N	SAS
	SE-RXA	Boeing 737-84P	Norwegian Air Sweden AOC
	SE-RXB	Boeing 737-84P	Norwegian Air Sweden AOC
	SE-RXC	Boeing 737-86N	Norwegian Air Sweden AOC
	SE-RXD	Boeing 737-86N	Norwegian Air Sweden AOC
	SE-RYC	Boeing 737-MAX8	Norwegian Air Sweden AOC
	SE-RZA	Airbus A.320-251N	SAS
	SE-RZB	Airbus A.320-251N	SAS
	SE-RZC	Airbus A.320-251N	SAS
	SE-RZD	Airbus A.320-251N	SAS
	SE-RZE	Airbus A.320-251N	SAS
	SE-RZX	Airbus A.320-251N	SAS
	SE-RZY	Airbus A.320-251N	SAS
	SE-RZZ	Airbus A.320-251N	SAS

SP (Poland)

Notes	Reg	Type	Owner or Operator
	SP-ENG	Boeing 737-8CX	Enter Air
	SP-ENL	Boeing 737-8CX	Enter Air
	SP-ENM	Boeing 737-8CX	Enter Air
	SP-ENN	Boeing 737-8CX	Enter Air
	SP-ENQ	Boeing 737-85R	Enter Air
	SP-ENT	Boeing 737-8AS	Enter Air
	SP-ENU	Boeing 737-83N	Enter Air
	SP-ENV	Boeing 737-8BK	Enter Air
	SP-ENW	Boeing 737-86J	Enter Air
	SP-ENX	Boeing 737-8Q8	Enter Air
	SP-ESA	Boeing 737-8AL	Enter Air
	SP-ESB	Boeing 737-86N	Enter Air
	SP-ESC	Boeing 737-8AS	Enter Air
	SP-ESD	Boeing 737-8AS	Enter Air
	SP-ESE	Boeing 737-8Q8	Enter Air
	SP-ESF	Boeing 737-8AS	Enter Air
	SP-ESG	Boeing 737-8Q8	Enter Air
	SP-ESH	Boeing 737-81M	Enter Air
	SP-ESI	Boeing 737-8Q8	Enter Air
	SP-ESK	Boeing 737-8Q8	Enter Air
	SP-ESL	Boeing 737-86N	Enter Air
	SP-ESM	Boeing 737-8Q8	Enter Air
	SP-ESN	Boeing 737-85R	Enter Air
	SP-ESO	Boeing 737-85C	Enter Air
	SP-EXA	Boeing 737-MAX8	Enter Air
	SP-EXB	Boeing 737-MAX8	Enter Air
	SP-EXC	Boeing 737-MAX8	Enter Air
	SP-EXD	Boeing 737-MAX8	Enter Air

Reg	Type	Owner or Operator	Notes
SP-EXE	Boeing 737-MAX8	Enter Air	
SP-EXF	Boeing 737-MAX8	Enter Air	
SP-EXG	Boeing 737-MAX8	Enter Air	
SP-EXH	Boeing 737-MAX8	Enter Air	
SP-EXI	Boeing 737-MAX8	Enter Air	
SP-EXK	Boeing 737-MAX8	Enter Air	
SP-EXL	Boeing 737-MAX8	Enter Air	
SP-LEA	Embraer ERJ190-400STD	LOT	
SP-LEB	Embraer ERJ190-400STD	LOT	
SP-LEC	Embraer ERJ190-400STD	LOT	
SP-LMA	Embraer ERJ190-100STD	LOT	
SP-LMB	Embraer ERJ190-100STD	LOT	
SP-LMC	Embraer ERJ190-100STD	LOT	
SP-LMD	Embraer ERJ190-100STD	LOT	
SP-LME	Embraer ERJ190-100STD	LOT	
SP-LMF	Embraer ERJ190-100STD	LOT	
SP-LMG	Embraer ERJ190-100STD	LOT	
SP-LMH	Embraer ERJ190-100STD	LOT	
SP-LNA	Embraer ERJ190-200LR	LOT	
SP-LNB	Embraer ERJ190-200LR	LOT	
SP-LNC	Embraer ERJ190-200LR	LOT	
SP-LND	Embraer ERJ190-200LR	LOT	
SP-LNE	Embraer ERJ190-200LR	LOT	
SP-LNF	Embraer ERJ190-200LR	LOT	
SP-LNG	Embraer ERJ190-200LR	LOT	
SP-LNH	Embraer ERJ190-200LR	LOT	
SP-LNI	Embraer ERJ190-200LR	LOT	
SP-LNK	Embraer ERJ190-200LR	LOT	
SP-LNL	Embraer ERJ190-200LR	LOT	
SP-LNM	Embraer ERJ190-200LR	LOT	
SP-LNN	Embraer ERJ190-200LR	LOT	
SP-LNO	Embraer ERJ190-200LR	LOT	
SP-LNQ	Embraer ERJ190-200LR	LOT	
SP-LRA	Boeing 787-8	LOT	
SP-LRB	Boeing 787-8	LOT	
SP-LRC	Boeing 787-8	LOT	
SP-LRD	Boeing 787-8	LOT	
SP-LRE	Boeing 787-8	LOT	
SP-LRF	Boeing 787-8	LOT	
SP-LRG	Boeing 787-8	LOT	
SP-LRH	Boeing 787-8	LOT	
SP-LSA	Boeing 787-9	LOT	
SP-LSB	Boeing 787-9	LOT	
SP-LSC	Boeing 787-9	LOT	
SP-LSD	Boeing 787-9	LOT	
SP-LSE	Boeing 787-9	LOT	
SP-LSF	Boeing 787-9	LOT	
SP-LSG	Boeing 787-9	LOT	
SP-LVA	Boeing 737-MAX8	LOT	
SP-LVB	Boeing 737-MAX8	LOT	
SP-LVC	Boeing 737-MAX8	LOT	
SP-LVD	Boeing 737-MAX8	LOT	
SP-LVF	Boeing 737-MAX8	LOT	
SP-LVG	Boeing 737-MAX8	LOT	
SP-LVH	Boeing 737-MAX8	LOT	
SP-LVI	Boeing 737-MAX8	LOT	
SP-LVK	Boeing 737-MAX8	LOT	
SP-LVL	Boeing 737-MAX8	LOT	
SP-LVM	Boeing 737-MAX8	LOT	
SP-LVN	Boeing 737-MAX8	LOT	
SP-LVO	Boeing 737-MAX8	LOT	
SP-LVP	Boeing 737-MAX8	LOT	
SP-LVQ	Boeing 737-MAX8	LOT	
SP-LVR	Boeing 737-MAX8	LOT	
SP-LVS	Boeing 737-MAX8	LOT	
SP-LVT	Boeing 737-MAX8	LOT	
SP-LWA	Boeing 737-89P	LOT	
SP-LWB	Boeing 737-89P	LOT	
SP-LWC	Boeing 737-89P	LOT	
SP-LWD	Boeing 737-89P	LOT	
SP-LWF	Boeing 737-86N	LOT	

Notes	Reg	Type	Owner or Operator
	SP-LWG	Boeing 737-86N	LOT
	SP-LYA	Boeing 737-MAX8	LOT
	SP-LYB	Boeing 737-MAX8	LOT
	SP-LYC	Boeing 737-MAX8	LOT
	SP-LYD	Boeing 737-MAX8	LOT
	SP-LYE	Boeing 737-MAX8	LOT
	SP-LYF	Boeing 737-MAX8	LOT
	SP-LYG	Boeing 737-MAX8	LOT
	SP-LYH	Boeing 737-MAX8	LOT
	SP-RKB	Boeing 737-8AS	Buzz (Ryanair)
	SP-RKC	Boeing 737-8AS	Buzz (Ryanair)
	SP-RKD	Boeing 737-8AS	Buzz (Ryanair)
	SP-RKE	Boeing 737-8AS	Buzz (Ryanair)
	SP-RKF	Boeing 737-8AS	Buzz (Ryanair)
	SP-RKG	Boeing 737-8AS	Buzz (Ryanair)
	SP-RKH	Boeing 737-8AS	Buzz (Ryanair)
	SP-RKI	Boeing 737-8AS	Buzz (Ryanair)
	SP-RKK	Boeing 737-8AS	Buzz (Ryanair)
	SP-RKL	Boeing 737-8AS	Buzz (Ryanair)
	SP-RKM	Boeing 737-8AS	Buzz (Ryanair)
	SP-RKN	Boeing 737-8AS	Buzz (Ryanair)
	SP-RKO	Boeing 737-8AS	Buzz (Ryanair)
	SP-RKP	Boeing 737-8AS	Buzz (Ryanair)
	SP-RKQ	Boeing 737-8AS	Buzz (Ryanair)
	SP-RKR	Boeing 737-8AS	Buzz (Ryanair)
	SP-RKS	Boeing 737-8AS	Buzz (Ryanair)
	SP-RKT	Boeing 737-8AS	Buzz (Ryanair)
	SP-RKU	Boeing 737-8AS	Buzz (Ryanair)
	SP-RKV	Boeing 737-8AS	Buzz (Ryanair)
	SP-RKW	Boeing 737-8AS	Buzz (Ryanair)
	SP-RKZ	Boeing 737-8AS	Buzz (Ryanair)
	SP-RNB	Boeing 737-8AS	Buzz (Ryanair)
	SP-RNC	Boeing 737-8AS	Buzz (Ryanair)
	SP-RND	Boeing 737-8AS	Buzz (Ryanair)
	SP-RNE	Boeing 737-8AS	Buzz (Ryanair)
	SP-RNF	Boeing 737-8AS	Buzz (Ryanair)
	SP-RNG	Boeing 737-8AS	Buzz (Ryanair)
	SP-RNH	Boeing 737-8AS	Buzz (Ryanair)
	SP-RNI	Boeing 737-8AS	Buzz (Ryanair)
	SP-RNK	Boeing 737-8AS	Buzz (Ryanair)
	SP-RNL	Boeing 737-8AS	Buzz (Ryanair)
	SP-RNM	Boeing 737-8AS	Buzz (Ryanair)
	SP-RNN	Boeing 737-8AS	Buzz (Ryanair)
	SP-RNO	Boeing 737-8AS	Buzz (Ryanair)
	SP-RNP	Boeing 737-8AS	Buzz (Ryanair)
	SP-RNQ	Boeing 737-8AS	Buzz (Ryanair)
	SP-RNR	Boeing 737-8AS	Buzz (Ryanair)
	SP-RNS	Boeing 737-8AS	Buzz (Ryanair)
	SP-RSA	Boeing 737-8AS	Buzz (Ryanair)
	SP-RSB	Boeing 737-8AS	Buzz (Ryanair)
	SP-RSC	Boeing 737-8AS	Buzz (Ryanair)
	SP-RSD	Boeing 737-8AS	Buzz (Ryanair)
	SP-RSE	Boeing 737-8AS	Buzz (Ryanair)
	SP-RSF	Boeing 737-8AS	Buzz (Ryanair)
	SP-RSG	Boeing 737-8AS	Buzz (Ryanair)
	SP-RSH	Boeing 737-8AS	Buzz (Ryanair)
	SP-RSI	Boeing 737-8AS	Buzz (Ryanair)
	SP-RSK	Boeing 737-8AS	Buzz (Ryanair)
	SP-RSL	Boeing 737-8AS	Buzz (Ryanair)
	SP-RSM	Boeing 737-8AS	Buzz (Ryanair)
	SP-RSN	Boeing 737-8AS	Buzz (Ryanair)
	SP-RSO	Boeing 737-8AS	Buzz (Ryanair)
	SP-RSP	Boeing 737-8AS	Buzz (Ryanair)
	SP-RSQ	Boeing 737-8AS	Buzz (Ryanair)
	SP-RSR	Boeing 737-8AS	Buzz (Ryanair)
	SP-RSS	Boeing 737-8AS	Buzz (Ryanair)
	SP-RST	Boeing 737-8AS	Buzz (Ryanair)
	SP-RSU	Boeing 737-8AS	Buzz (Ryanair)
	SP-RSV	Boeing 737-8AS	Buzz (Ryanair)
	SP-RSW	Boeing 737-8AS	Buzz (Ryanair)
	SP-RSZ	Boeing 737-8AS	Buzz (Ryanair)

Reg	Type	Owner or Operator	Notes
SP-RUM	Boeing 737-73S	Buzz (Ryanair)	
SP-RZA	Boeing 737-8200	Buzz (Ryanair)	
SP-RZB	Boeing 737-8200	Buzz (Ryanair)	
SP-RZC	Boeing 737-8200	Buzz (Ryanair)	
SP-RZD	Boeing 737-8200	Buzz (Ryanair)	
SP-RZE	Boeing 737-8200	Buzz (Ryanair)	
SP-RZF	Boeing 737-8200	Buzz (Ryanair)	
SP-RZG	Boeing 737-8200	Buzz (Ryanair)	
SP-RZH	Boeing 737-8200	Buzz (Ryanair)	
SP-RZI	Boeing 737-8200	Buzz (Ryanair)	
SP-RZK	Boeing 737-8200	Buzz (Ryanair)	
SP-RZL	Boeing 737-8200	Buzz (Ryanair)	
SP-RZM	Boeing 737-8200	Buzz (Ryanair)	
SP-RZN	Boeing 737-8200	Buzz (Ryanair)	
SP-RZO	Boeing 737-8200	Buzz (Ryanair)	
SP-RZP	Boeing 737-8200	Buzz (Ryanair)	
SP-RZQ	Boeing 737-8200	Buzz (Ryanair)	
SP-RZR	Boeing 737-8200	Buzz (Ryanair)	
SP-RZS	Boeing 737-8200	Buzz (Ryanair)	
SP-RZT	Boeing 737-8200	Buzz (Ryanair)	
SP-RZU	Boeing 737-8200	Buzz (Ryanair)	
SP-RZV	Boeing 737-8200	Buzz (Ryanair)	
SP-RZX	Boeing 737-8200	Buzz (Ryanair)	
SP-RZY	Boeing 737-8200	Buzz (Ryanair)	

SU (Egypt)

Reg	Type	Owner or Operator	Notes
SU-GCM	Boeing 737-866WIN	EgyptAir	
SU-GCN	Boeing 737-866WIN	EgyptAir	
SU-GCO	Boeing 737-866WIN	EgyptAir	
SU-GCR	Boeing 737-866WIN	EgyptAir	
SU-GCS	Boeing 737-866WIN	EgyptAir	
SU-GCZ	Boeing 737-866WIN	EgyptAir	
SU-GDA	Boeing 737-866WIN	EgyptAir	
SU-GDB	Boeing 737-866WIN	EgyptAir	
SU-GDC	Boeing 737-866WIN	EgyptAir	
SU-GDD	Boeing 737-866WIN	EgyptAir	
SU-GDE	Boeing 737-866WIN	EgyptAir	
SU-GDM	Boeing 777-36NER	EgyptAir	
SU-GDN	Boeing 777-36NER	EgyptAir	
SU-GDO	Boeing 777-36NER	EgyptAir	
SU-GDP	Boeing 777-36NER	EgyptAir	
SU-GDR	Boeing 777-36NER	EgyptAir	
SU-GDX	Boeing 737-866WIN	EgyptAir	
SU-GDY	Boeing 737-866WIN	EgyptAir	
SU-GDZ	Boeing 737-866WIN	EgyptAir	
SU-GEA	Boeing 737-866WIN	EgyptAir	
SU-GEB	Boeing 737-866WIN	EgyptAir	
SU-GEC	Boeing 737-866WIN	EgyptAir	
SU-GED	Boeing 737-866WIN	EgyptAir	
SU-GEE	Boeing 737-866WIN	EgyptAir	
SU-GEF	Boeing 737-866WIN	EgyptAir	
SU-GEG	Boeing 737-866WIN	EgyptAir	
SU-GEH	Boeing 737-866WIN	EgyptAir	
SU-GEI	Boeing 737-866WIN	EgyptAir	
SU-GEJ	Boeing 737-866WIN	EgyptAir	
SU-GEK	Boeing 737-866WIN	EgyptAir	
SU-GEL	Boeing 737-866WIN	EgyptAir	
SU-GEM	Boeing 737-866WIN	EgyptAir	
SU-GEN	Boeing 737-866WIN	EgyptAir	
SU-GER	Boeing 787-9	EgyptAir	
SU-GES	Boeing 787-9	EgyptAir	
SU-GET	Boeing 787-9	EgyptAir	
SU-GEU	Boeing 787-9	EgyptAir	
SU-GEV	Boeing 787-9	EgyptAir	
SU-GEW	Boeing 787-9	EgyptAir	
SU-GFJ	Airbus A.320-251N	EgyptAir	
SU-GFK	Airbus A.320-251N	EgyptAir	
SU-GFL	Airbus A.320-251N	EgyptAir	
SU-GFM	Airbus A.320-251N	EgyptAir	
SU-GFN	Airbus A.320-251N	EgyptAir	

Notes	Reg	Type	Owner or Operator
	SU-GFO	Airbus A.320-251N	EgyptAir
	SU-GFP	Airbus A.320-251N	EgyptAir
	SU-GFQ	Airbus A.320-251N	EgyptAir
	SU-GFR	Airbus A.321-251NX	EgyptAir
	SU-GFS	Airbus A.321-251NX	EgyptAir
	SU-GFT	Airbus A.321-251NX	EgyptAir
	SU-GFU	Airbus A.321-251NX	EgyptAir
	SU-GFV	Airbus A.321-251NX	EgyptAir
	SU-GFW	Airbus A.321-251NX	EgyptAir
	SU-GFX	Airbus A.321-251NX	EgyptAir
	SU-GFY	Boeing 787-9	EgyptAir
	SU-GFZ	Boeing 787-9	EgyptAir
	SU-GGA	Boeing 737-85R	EgyptAir
	SU-GGB	Boeing 737-81M	EgyptAir

SX (Greece)

Notes	Reg	Type	Owner or Operator
	SX-CHG	Airbus A-320-251N	Sky Express
	SX-CRE	Airbus A.320-251N	Sky Express
	SX-DGA	Airbus A.321-231	Aegean Airlines
	SX-DGB	Airbus A.320-232	Aegean Airlines
	SX-DGD	Airbus A.320-232	Aegean Airlines
	SX-DGE	Airbus A.320-232	Aegean Airlines
	SX-DGI	Airbus A.320-232	Aegean Airlines
	SX-DGJ	Airbus A.320-232	Aegean Airlines
	SX-DGY	Airbus A.320-232	Aegean Airlines
	SX-DGZ	Airbus A.320-232	Aegean Airlines
	SX-DNA	Airbus A.320-232	Aegean Airlines
	SX-DNB	Airbus A.320-232	Aegean Airlines
	SX-DNC	Airbus A.320-232	Aegean Airlines
	SX-DND	Airbus A.320-232	Aegean Airlines
	SX-DNE	Airbus A.320-232	Aegean Airlines
	SX-DNG	Airbus A.321-231	Aegean Airlines
	SX-DNH	Airbus A.321-231	Aegean Airlines
	SX-DVG	Airbus A.320-232	Aegean Airlines
	SX-DVH	Airbus A.320-232	Aegean Airlines
	SX-DVI	Airbus A.320-232	Aegean Airlines
	SX-DVJ	Airbus A.320-232	Aegean Airlines
	SX-DVL	Airbus A.320-232	Aegean Airlines
	SX-DVM	Airbus A.320-232	Aegean Airlines
	SX-DVN	Airbus A.320-232	Aegean Airlines
	SX-DVQ	Airbus A.320-232	Aegean Airlines
	SX-DVR	Airbus A.320-232	Aegean Airlines
	SX-DVS	Airbus A.320-232	Aegean Airlines
	SX-DVT	Airbus A.320-232	Aegean Airlines
	SX-DVV	Airbus A.320-232	Aegean Airlines
	SX-DVW	Airbus A.320-232	Aegean Airlines
	SX-DVX	Airbus A.320-232	Aegean Airlines
	SX-DVY	Airbus A.320-232	Aegean Airlines
	SX-DVZ	Airbus A.321-232	Aegean Airlines
	SX-GNA	Airbus A.320-251N	Sky Express
	SX-GRA	Airbus A.321-251N	Sky Express
	SX-GRB	Airbus A.321-251N	Sky Express
	SX-GRE	Airbus A.320-251N	Sky Express
	SX-IOA	Airbus A.320-251N	Sky Express
	SX-IOB	Airbus A.320-251N	Sky Express
	SX-IOC	Airbus A.320-251N	Sky Express
	SX-IOD	Airbus A.320-251N	Sky Express
	SX-IOG	Airbus A-320-251N	Sky Express
	SX-NAA	Airbus A.321-271NX	Aegean Airlines
	SX-NAB	Airbus A.321-271NX	Aegean Airlines
	SX-NAC	Airbus A.321-271NX	Aegean Airlines
	SX-NAD	Airbus A.321-271NX	Aegean Airlines
	SX-NAE	Airbus A.321-271NX	Aegean Airlines
	SX-NAF	Airbus A.321-271NX	Aegean Airlines
	SX-NAG	Airbus A.321-271NX	Aegean Airlines
	SX-NAH	Airbus A.321-271NX	Aegean Airlines
	SX-NAJ	Airbus A.321-271NX	Aegean Airlines
	SX-NAK	Airbus A.321-271NX	Aegean Airlines
	SX-NAL	Airbus A.321-271NX	Aegean Airlines
	SX-NAM	Airbus A.321-271NX	Aegean Airlines

Reg	Type	Owner or Operator	Notes
SX-NAO	Airbus A.321-271NX	Aegean Airlines	
SX-NAP	Airbus A.321-271NX	Aegean Airlines	
SX-NAQ	Airbus A.321-271NX	Aegean Airlines	
SX-NAR	Airbus A.321-271NX	Aegean Airlines	
SX-NAS	Airbus A.321-271NX	Aegean Airlines	
SX-NAU	Airbus A.321-271NX	Aegean Airlines	
SX-NEA	Airbus A.320-271N	Aegean Airlines	
SX-NEB	Airbus A.320-271N	Aegean Airlines	
SX-NEC	Airbus A.320-271N	Aegean Airlines	
SX-NED	Airbus A.320-271N	Aegean Airlines	
SX-NEE	Airbus A.320-271N	Aegean Airlines	
SX-NEF	Airbus A.320-271N	Aegean Airlines	
SX-NEG	Airbus A.320-271N	Aegean Airlines	
SX-NEH	Airbus A.320-271N	Aegean Airlines	
SX-NEI	Airbus A.320-271N	Aegean Airlines	
SX-NEJ	Airbus A.320-271N	Aegean Airlines	
SX-NEK	Airbus A.320-271N	Aegean Airlines	
SX-NEL	Airbus A.320-271N	Aegean Airlines	
SX-NEM	Airbus A.320-271N	Aegean Airlines	
SX-NEO	Airbus A.320-271N	Aegean Airlines	
SX-NEP	Airbus A.320-271N	Aegean Airlines	
SX-NEQ	Airbus A.320-271N	Aegean Airlines	
SX-NER	Airbus A.320-271N	Aegean Airlines	
SX-NES	Airbus A.320-271N	Aegean Airlines	
SX-NET	Airbus A.320-271N	Aegean Airlines	
SX-NEU	Airbus A.320-271N	Aegean Airlines	
SX-NEV	Airbus A.320-271N	Aegean Airlines	
SX-NIG	Airbus A.320-251N	Sky Express	
SX-TEC	Airbus A-320-251N	Sky Express	
SX-VSL	Airbus A.320-214	Sky Express	
SX-WEB	Airbus A.320-251N	Sky Express	

T7 (San Marino)

Reg	Type	Owner or Operator	Notes
T7-ME1	Airbus A.321-271NX	MEA - Middle East Airlines	
T7-ME2	Airbus A.321-271NX	MEA - Middle East Airlines	
T7-ME3	Airbus A.321-271NX	MEA - Middle East Airlines	
T7-ME4	Airbus A.321-271NX	MEA - Middle East Airlines	
T7-ME5	Airbus A.321-271NX	MEA - Middle East Airlines	
T7-ME6	Airbus A.321-271NX	MEA - Middle East Airlines	
T7-ME7	Airbus A.321-271NX	MEA - Middle East Airlines	
T7-ME8	Airbus A.321-271NX	MEA - Middle East Airlines	
T7-ME9	Airbus A.321-271NX	MEA - Middle East Airlines	

TC (Turkey)

Reg	Type	Owner or Operator	Notes
TC-AIS	Boeing 737-82R	Pegasus Airlines	
TC-AZP	Boeing 737-82R	Pegasus Airlines	
TC-COE	Boeing 737-86J	Corendon Air	
TC-COH	Boeing 737-8EH	Corendon Air	
TC-CON	Boeing 737-8JP	Corendon Air	
TC-COR	Boeing 737-8SH	Corendon Air	
TC-CPC	Boeing 737-82R	Pegasus Airlines	
TC-CPD	Boeing 737-82R	Pegasus Airlines	
TC-CPE	Boeing 737-82R	Pegasus Airlines	
TC-CPK	Boeing 737-82R	Pegasus Airlines	
TC-CRE	Boeing 737-82R	Pegasus Airlines	
TC-CRF	Boeing 737-82R	Pegasus Airlines	
TC-CRG	Boeing 737-82R	Pegasus Airlines	
TC-DCE	Airbus A.320-216	Pegasus Airlines	
TC-DCG	Airbus A.320-216	Pegasus Airlines	
TC-DCH	Airbus A.320-216	Pegasus Airlines	
TC-DCI	Airbus A.320-216	Pegasus Airlines	
TC-DCL	Airbus A.320-214	Pegasus Airlines	
TC-DCM	Airbus A.320-214	Pegasus Airlines	
TC-EIA	Airbus A.320-233	Turkish Airlines	
TC-FBO	Airbus A.320-214	Freebird Airlines	
TC-FBV	Airbus A.320-214	Freebird Airlines	
TC-FHC	Airbus A.320-214	Freebird Airlines	
TC-FHF	Airbus A.320-214	Freebird Airlines	

Notes	Reg	Type	Owner or Operator
	TC-FHG	Airbus A.320-214	Freebird Airlines
	TC-FHK	Airbus A.320-214	Freebird Airlines
	TC-FHL	Airbus A.320-214	Freebird Airlines
	TC-FHM	Airbus A.320-232	Freebird Airlines
	TC-FHN	Airbus A.320-214	Freebird Airlines
	TC-FHP	Airbus A.320-216	Freebird Airlines
	TC-FHZ	Airbus A.320-214	Freebird Airlines
	TC-GPA	Airbus A.321-231	AJet
	TC-GPB	Airbus A.321-231	AJet
	TC-GPC	Airbus A.321-231	Ajet
	TC-GPD	Airbus A.321-231	AJet
	TC-GPE	Airbus A.321-231	AJet
	TC-GPF	Airbus A.321-231	AJet
	TC-GPG	Airbus A.321-231	AJet
	TC-JCI	Airbus A.330-223F	Turkish Cargo
	TC-JDO	Airbus A.330-243F	Turkish Cargo
	TC-JDP	Airbus A.330-243F	Turkish Cargo
	TC-JDR	Airbus A.330-243F	Turkish Cargo
	TC-JDS	Airbus A.330-243F	Turkish Cargo
	TC-JFC	Boeing 737-8F2	AJet
	TC-JFD	Boeing 737-8F2	AJet
	TC-JFE	Boeing 737-8F2	AJet
	TC-JFF	Boeing 737-8F2	AJet
	TC-JFH	Boeing 737-8F2	AJet
	TC-JFJ	Boeing 737-8F2	AJet
	TC-JFK	Boeing 737-8F2	AJet
	TC-JFL	Boeing 737-8F2	AJet
	TC-JFM	Boeing 737-8F2	AJet
	TC-JFN	Boeing 737-8F2	AJet
	TC-JFO	Boeing 737-8F2	AJet
	TC-JFP	Boeing 737-8F2	AJet
	TC-JFR	Boeing 737-8F2	AJet
	TC-JFT	Boeing 737-8F2	AJet
	TC-JFU	Boeing 737-8F2	AJet
	TC-JFY	Boeing 737-8F2	AJet
	TC-JFZ	Boeing 737-8F2	AJet
	TC-JGC	Boeing 737-8F2	AJet
	TC-JGR	Boeing 737-8F2	AJet
	TC-JGS	Boeing 737-8F2	AJet
	TC-JGT	Boeing 737-8F2	AJet
	TC-JGU	Boeing 737-8F2	AJet
	TC-JGV	Boeing 737-8F2	AJet
	TC-JGY	Boeing 737-8F2	AJet
	TC-JHA	Boeing 737-8F2	AJet
	TC-JHB	Boeing 737-8F2	AJet
	TC-JHC	Boeing 737-8F2	AJet
	TC-JHD	Boeing 737-8F2	AJet
	TC-JHE	Boeing 737-8F2	AJet
	TC-JHF	Boeing 737-8F2	AJet
	TC-JHK	Boeing 737-8F2	Turkish Airlines
	TC-JHL	Boeing 737-8F2	Turkish Airlines
	TC-JHM	Boeing 737-8F2	Turkish Airlines
	TC-JHN	Boeing 737-8F2	Turkish Airlines
	TC-JHO	Boeing 737-8F2	Turkish Airlines
	TC-JHP	Boeing 737-8F2	Turkish Airlines
	TC-JHR	Boeing 737-8F2	Turkish Airlines
	TC-JHS	Boeing 737-8F2	Turkish Airlines
	TC-JHT	Boeing 737-8F2	Turkish Airlines
	TC-JHU	Boeing 737-8F2	Turkish Airlines
	TC-JHV	Boeing 737-8F2	Turkish Airlines
	TC-JHY	Boeing 737-8F2	Turkish Airlines
	TC-JHZ	Boeing 737-8F2	Turkish Airlines
	TC-JIO	Airbus A.330-223	Turkish Airlines
	TC-JIP	Airbus A.330-223	Turkish Airlines
	TC-JIR	Airbus A.330-223	Turkish Airlines
	TC-JIS	Airbus A.330-223	Turkish Airlines
	TC-JIT	Airbus A.330-223	Turkish Airlines
	TC-JJE	Boeing 777-3F2ER	Turkish Airlines
	TC-JJF	Boeing 777-3F2ER	Turkish Airlines
	TC-JJG	Boeing 777-3F2ER	Turkish Airlines
	TC-JJH	Boeing 777-3F2ER	Turkish Airlines

Reg	Type	Owner or Operator	Notes
TC-JJI	Boeing 777-3F2ER	Turkish Airlines	
TC-JJJ	Boeing 777-3F2ER	Turkish Airlines	
TC-JJK	Boeing 777-3F2ER	Turkish Airlines	
TC-JJL	Boeing 777-3F2ER	Turkish Airlines	
TC-JJM	Boeing 777-3F2ER	Turkish Airlines	
TC-JJN	Boeing 777-3F2ER	Turkish Airlines	
TC-JJO	Boeing 777-3F2ER	Turkish Airlines	
TC-JJP	Boeing 777-3F2ER	Turkish Airlines	
TC-JJR	Boeing 777-3F2ER	Turkish Airlines	
TC-JJS	Boeing 777-3F2ER	Turkish Airlines	
TC-JJT	Boeing 777-3F2ER	Turkish Airlines	
TC-JJU	Boeing 777-3F2ER	Turkish Airlines	
TC-JJV	Boeing 777-3F2ER	Turkish Airlines	
TC-JJY	Boeing 777-3F2ER	Turkish Airlines	
TC-JJZ	Boeing 777-3F2ER	Turkish Airlines	
TC-JKU	Boeing 737-8Q8	AJet	
TC-JKV	Boeing 737-8Q8	AJet	
TC-JKY	Boeing 737-86N	AJet	
TC-JLS	Airbus A.319-132	Turkish Airlines	
TC-JLT	Airbus A.319-132	Turkish Airlines	
TC-JLU	Airbus A.319-132	Turkish Airlines	
TC-JLV	Airbus A.319-132	Turkish Airlines	
TC-JLY	Airbus A.319-132	Turkish Airlines	
TC-JLZ	Airbus A.319-132	Turkish Airlines	
TC-JMH	Airbus A.321-232	Turkish Airlines	
TC-JMI	Airbus A.321-232	Turkish Airlines	
TC-JMJ	Airbus A.321-232	Turkish Airlines	
TC-JMK	Airbus A.321-232	Turkish Airlines	
TC-JML	Airbus A.321-231	Turkish Airlines	
TC-JMO	Airbus A.321-231	Turkish Airlines	
TC-JMP	Airbus A.321-231	AJet	
TC-JNA	Airbus A.330-203	Turkish Airlines	
TC-JNB	Airbus A.330-203	Turkish Airlines	
TC-JNC	Airbus A.330-203	Turkish Airlines	
TC-JND	Airbus A.330-203	Turkish Airlines	
TC-JNE	Airbus A.330-203	Turkish Airlines	
TC-JNH	Airbus A.330-343	Turkish Airlines	
TC-JNI	Airbus A.330-343	Turkish Airlines	
TC-JNJ	Airbus A.330-343	Turkish Airlines	
TC-JNK	Airbus A.330-343	Turkish Airlines	
TC-JNL	Airbus A.330-343	Turkish Airlines	
TC-JNM	Airbus A.330-343	Turkish Airlines	
TC-JNN	Airbus A.330-343	Turkish Airlines	
TC-JNO	Airbus A.330-343	Turkish Airlines	
TC-JNP	Airbus A.330-343	Turkish Airlines	
TC JNR	Airbus A.330 343	Turkish Airlines	
TC-JNS	Airbus A.330-303	Turkish Airlines	
TC-JNT	Airbus A.330-303	Turkish Airlines	
TC-JNZ	Airbus A.330-303	Turkish Airlines	
TC-JOA	Airbus A.330-303	Turkish Airlines	
TC-JOB	Airbus A.330-303	Turkish Airlines	
TC-JOD	Airbus A.330-303	Turkish Airlines	
TC JOE	Airbus A.330-303	Turkish Airlines	
TC-JOF	Airbus A.330-303	Turkish Airlines	
TC-JOG	Airbus A.330-303	Turkish Airlines	
TC-JOH	Airbus A.330-303	Turkish Airlines	
TC-JOI	Airbus A.330-303	Turkish Airlines	
TC-JOJ	Airbus A.330-303	Turkish Airlines	
TC-JOK	Airbus A.330-303	Turkish Airlines	
TC-JOL	Airbus A.330-303	Turkish Airlines	
TC-JOO	Airbus A.330-223F	Turkish Cargo	
TC-JOU	Airbus A.330-243F	Turkish Cargo	
TC-JOV	Airbus A.330-243F	Turkish Cargo	
TC-JOY	Airbus A.330-243F	Turkish Cargo	
TC-JOZ	Airbus A.330-243F	Turkish Cargo	
TC-JPH	Airbus A.320-232	Turkish Airlines	
TC-JPI	Airbus A.320-232	Turkish Airlines	
TC-JPJ	Airbus A.320-232	Turkish Airlines	
TC-JPK	Airbus A.320-232	Turkish Airlines	
TC-JPL	Airbus A.320-232	Turkish Airlines	
TC-JPM	Airbus A.320-232	Turkish Airlines	

OVERSEAS AIRLINERS

Notes	Reg	Type	Owner or Operator
	TC-JPN	Airbus A.320-232	Turkish Airlines
	TC-JPP	Airbus A.320-232	Turkish Airlines
	TC-JPR	Airbus A.320-232	Turkish Airlines
	TC-JPS	Airbus A.320-232	Turkish Airlines
	TC-JPT	Airbus A.320-232	Turkish Airlines
	TC-JPZ	Airbus A.320-232	Turkish Airlines
	TC-JRA	Airbus A.321-231	Turkish Airlines
	TC-JRB	Airbus A.321-231	Turkish Airlines
	TC-JRC	Airbus A.321-231	Turkish Airlines
	TC-JRD	Airbus A.321-231	Turkish Airlines
	TC-JRE	Airbus A.321-231	Turkish Airlines
	TC-JRF	Airbus A.321-231	Turkish Airlines
	TC-JRG	Airbus A.321-231	Turkish Airlines
	TC-JRH	Airbus A.321-231	Turkish Airlines
	TC-JRI	Airbus A.321-232	Turkish Airlines
	TC-JRJ	Airbus A.321-232	Turkish Airlines
	TC-JRK	Airbus A.321-231	Turkish Airlines
	TC-JRL	Airbus A.321-231	Turkish Airlines
	TC-JRM	Airbus A.321-232	Turkish Airlines
	TC-JRN	Airbus A.321-232	Turkish Airlines
	TC-JRO	Airbus A.321-231	Turkish Airlines
	TC-JRP	Airbus A.321-231	Turkish Airlines
	TC-JRR	Airbus A.321-231	Turkish Airlines
	TC-JRS	Airbus A.321-231	Turkish Airlines
	TC-JRT	Airbus A.321-231	Turkish Airlines
	TC-JRU	Airbus A.321-231	Turkish Airlines
	TC-JRV	Airbus A.321-232	Turkish Airlines
	TC-JRY	Airbus A.321-232	Turkish Airlines
	TC-JRZ	Airbus A.321-232	Turkish Airlines
	TC-JSA	Airbus A.321-232	Turkish Airlines
	TC-JSB	Airbus A.321-231	Turkish Airlines
	TC-JSC	Airbus A.321-231	Turkish Airlines
	TC-JSD	Airbus A.321-231	Turkish Airlines
	TC-JSE	Airbus A.321-231	Turkish Airlines
	TC-JSF	Airbus A.321-231	Turkish Airlines
	TC-JSG	Airbus A.321-231	Turkish Airlines
	TC-JSI	Airbus A.321-231	Turkish Airlines
	TC-JSJ	Airbus A.321-232	Turkish Airlines
	TC-JSK	Airbus A.321-232	Turkish Airlines
	TC-JSL	Airbus A.321-232	Turkish Airlines
	TC-JSM	Airbus A.321-231	Turkish Airlines
	TC-JSN	Airbus A.321-231	Turkish Airlines
	TC-JSO	Airbus A.321-231	Turkish Airlines
	TC-JSP	Airbus A.321-231	Turkish Airlines
	TC-JSR	Airbus A.321-231	Turkish Airlines
	TC-JSS	Airbus A.321-231	Turkish Airlines
	TC-JST	Airbus A.321-231	Turkish Airlines
	TC-JSU	Airbus A.321-231	Turkish Airlines
	TC-JSV	Airbus A.321-231	Turkish Airlines
	TC-JSY	Airbus A.321-231	Turkish Airlines
	TC-JSZ	Airbus A.321-231	Turkish Airlines
	TC-JTA	Airbus A.321-231	Turkish Airlines
	TC-JTD	Airbus A.321-231	Turkish Airlines
	TC-JTE	Airbus A.321-231	Turkish Airlines
	TC-JTF	Airbus A.321-231	Turkish Airlines
	TC-JTG	Airbus A.321-231	Turkish Airlines
	TC-JTH	Airbus A.321-231	Turkish Airlines
	TC-JTI	Airbus A.321-231	Turkish Airlines
	TC-JTJ	Airbus A.321-231	Turkish Airlines
	TC-JTK	Airbus A.321-231	Turkish Airlines
	TC-JTL	Airbus A.321-231	Turkish Airlines
	TC-JTM	Airbus A.321-231	Turkish Airlines
	TC-JTN	Airbus A.321-231	Turkish Airlines
	TC-JTO	Airbus A.321-231	Turkish Airlines
	TC-JTP	Airbus A.321-231	Turkish Airlines
	TC-JTR	Airbus A.321-231	Turkish Airlines
	TC-JTS	Airbus A.320-232	Turkish Airlines
	TC-JTT	Airbus A.320-232	Turkish Airlines
	TC-JTU	Airbus A.320-232	Turkish Airlines
	TC-JTV	Airbus A.320-232	Turkish Airlines
	TC-JTY	Airbus A.320-232	AJet

Reg	Type	Owner or Operator	Notes
TC-JVA	Boeing 737-8F2	Turkish Airlines	
TC-JVB	Boeing 737-8F2	Turkish Airlines	
TC-JVC	Boeing 737-8F2	Turkish Airlines	
TC-JVD	Boeing 737-8F2	Turkish Airlines	
TC-JVE	Boeing 737-8F2	Turkish Airlines	
TC-JVF	Boeing 737-8F2	Turkish Airlines	
TC-JVG	Boeing 737-8F2	Turkish Airlines	
TC-JVH	Boeing 737-8F2	Turkish Airlines	
TC-JVI	Boeing 737-8F2	Turkish Airlines	
TC-JVJ	Boeing 737-8F2	Turkish Airlines	
TC-JVK	Boeing 737-8F2	Turkish Airlines	
TC-JVL	Boeing 737-8F2	Turkish Airlines	
TC-JVM	Boeing 737-8F2	Turkish Airlines	
TC-JVN	Boeing 737-8F2	Turkish Airlines	
TC-JVO	Boeing 737-8F2	Turkish Airlines	
TC-JVP	Boeing 737-8F2	Turkish Airlines	
TC-JVR	Boeing 737-8F2	Turkish Airlines	
TC-JVS	Boeing 737-8F2	Turkish Airlines	
TC-JVT	Boeing 737-8F2	Turkish Airlines	
TC-JVU	Boeing 737-8F2	Turkish Airlines	
TC-JVV	Boeing 737-8F2	Turkish Airlines	
TC-JVY	Boeing 737-8F2	Turkish Airlines	
TC-JVZ	Boeing 737-8F2	Turkish Airlines	
TC-JYA	Boeing 737-9F2ER	Turkish Airlines	
TC-JYB	Boeing 737-9F2ER	Turkish Airlines	
TC-JYC	Boeing 737-9F2ER	Turkish Airlines	
TC-JYD	Boeing 737-9F2ER	Turkish Airlines	
TC-JYE	Boeing 737-9F2ER	Turkish Airlines	
TC-JYF	Boeing 737-9F2ER	Turkish Airlines	
TC-JYG	Boeing 737-9F2ER	Turkish Airlines	
TC-JYH	Boeing 737-9F2ER	Turkish Airlines	
TC-JYI	Boeing 737-9F2ER	Turkish Airlines	
TC-JYJ	Boeing 737-9F2ER	Turkish Airlines	
TC-JYL	Boeing 737-9F2ER	Turkish Airlines	
TC-JYM	Boeing 737-9F2ER	Turkish Airlines	
TC-JYN	Boeing 737-9F2ER	Turkish Airlines	
TC-JYO	Boeing 737-9F2ER	Turkish Airlines	
TC-JYP	Boeing 737-9F2ER	Turkish Airlines	
TC-JZE	Boeing 737-8F2	Turkish Airlines	
TC-JZF	Boeing 737-8F2	Turkish Airlines	
TC-JZG	Boeing 737-8F2	Turkish Airlines	
TC-JZH	Boeing 737-8F2	Turkish Airlines	
TC-JZJ	Boeing 737-8AS	AJet	
TC-JZK	Boeing 737-8AS	AJet	
TC-JZL	Boeing 737-8AS	AJet	
TC-JZN	Boeing 737-8JP	AJet	
TC-JZO	Boeing 737-8JP	AJet	
TC-JZR	Boeing 737-8JP	AJet	
TC-JZS	Boeing 737-8JP	AJet	
TC-JZT	Boeing 737-8JP	AJet	
TC-JZU	Boeing 737-8AS	AJet	
TC-JZV	Boeing 737-8AS	AJet	
TC-JZZ	Boeing 737-8KV	AJet	
TC-LAE	Boeing 737-MAX8	AJet	
TC-LAF	Boeing 737-MAX8	AJet	
TC-LAG	Boeing 737-MAX8	AJet	
TC-LAH	Boeing 737-MAX8	AJet	
TC-LAI	Boeing 737-MAX8	AJet	
TC-LAJ	Boeing 737-MAX8	AJet	
TC-LAK	Boeing 737-MAX8	AJet	
TC-LBA	Airbus A.320-271N	AJet	
TC-LBB	Airbus A.320-271N	AJet	
TC-LBC	Airbus A.321-231	Turkish Airlines	
TC-LBD	Airbus A.321-231	Turkish Airlines	
TC-LBF	Airbus A.320-271N	AJet	
TC-LBG	Airbus A.320-271N	AJet	
TC-LBH	Airbus A.320-271N	AJet	
TC-LBK	Airbus A.320-271N	AJet	
TC-LBM	Airbus A.320-232	Turkish Airlines	
TC-LBO	Airbus A.320-271N	Ajet	
TC-LBP	Airbus A.320-232	Turkish Airlines	

Notes	Reg	Type	Owner or Operator
	TC-LBR	Airbus A.320-271N	Ajet
	TC-LBS	Airbus A.320-271N	Ajet
	TC-LBT	Airbus A.320-271N	Ajet
	TC-LBU	Airbus A.320-232	Turkish Airlines
	TC-LBV	Airbus A.320-232	Turkish Airlines
	TC-LBZ	Airbus A.320-271N	Ajet
	TC-LCA	Boeing 737-MAX8	Turkish Airlines
	TC-LCB	Boeing 737-MAX8	Turkish Airlines
	TC-LCC	Boeing 737-MAX8	Turkish Airlines
	TC-LCD	Boeing 737-MAX8	Turkish Airlines
	TC-LCE	Boeing 737-MAX8	Turkish Airlines
	TC-LCF	Boeing 737-MAX8	Turkish Airlines
	TC-LCG	Boeing 737-MAX8	Turkish Airlines
	TC-LCH	Boeing 737-MAX8	Turkish Airlines
	TC-LCI	Boeing 737-MAX8	Turkish Airlines
	TC-LCJ	Boeing 737-MAX8	Turkish Airlines
	TC-LCK	Boeing 737-MAX8	Turkish Airlines
	TC-LCL	Boeing 737-MAX8	Turkish Airlines
	TC-LCM	Boeing 737-MAX8	Turkish Airlines
	TC-LCN	Boeing 737-MAX8	Turkish Airlines
	TC-LCO	Boeing 737-MAX8	Turkish Airlines
	TC-LCP	Boeing 737-MAX8	Turkish Airlines
	TC-LCR	Boeing 737-MAX8	Turkish Airlines
	TC-LCS	Boeing 737-MAX8	Turkish Airlines
	TC-LCT	Boeing 737-MAX8	Turkish Airlines
	TC-LCU	Boeing 737-MAX8	Turkish Airlines
	TC-LGA	Airbus A.350-941	Turkish Airlines
	TC-LGB	Airbus A.350-941	Turkish Airlines
	TC-LGC	Airbus A.350-941	Turkish Airlines
	TC-LGD	Airbus A.350-941	Turkish Airlines
	TC-LGE	Airbus A.350-941	Turkish Airlines
	TC-LGF	Airbus A.350-941	Turkish Airlines
	TC-LGG	Airbus A.350-941	Turkish Airlines
	TC-LGH	Airbus A.350-941	Turkish Airlines
	TC-LGI	Airbus A.350-941	Turkish Airlines
	TC-LGJ	Airbus A.350-941	Turkish Airlines
	TC-LGK	Airbus A.350-941	Turkish Airlines
	TC-LGL	Airbus A.350-941	Turkish Airlines
	TC-LGM	Airbus A.350-941	Turkish Airlines
	TC-LGN	Airbus A.350-941	Turkish Airlines
	TC-LGO	Airbus A.350-941	Turkish Airlines
	TC-LGP	Airbus A.350-941	Turkish Airlines
	TC-LGR	Airbus A.350-941	Turkish Airlines
	TC-LGS	Airbus A.350-941	Turkish Airlines
	TC-LGT	Airbus A.350-941	Turkish Airlines
	TC-LGU	Airbus A.350-941	Turkish Airlines
	TC-LGV	Airbus A.350-941	Turkish Airlines
	TC-LGY	Airbus A.350-941	Turkish Airlines
	TC-LGZ	Airbus A.350-941	Turkish Airlines
	TC-LHA	Airbus A.350-941	Turkish Airlines
	TC-LHB	Airbus A.350-941	Turkish Airlines
	TC-LHC	Airbus A.350-941	Turkish Airlines
	TC-LHD	Airbus A.350-941	Turkish Airlines
	TC-LHE	Airbus A.350-941	Turkish Airlines
	TC-LHF	Airbus A.350-941	Turkish Airlines
	TC-LHG	Airbus A.350-941	Turkish Airlines
	TC-LHH	Airbus A.350-941	Turkish Airlines
	TC-LHI	Airbus A.350-941	Owrkish Airlines
	TC-LHJ	Airbus A.350-941	Turkish Airlines
	TC-LJA	Boeing 777-3F2ER	Turkish Airlines
	TC-LJB	Boeing 777-3F2ER	Turkish Airlines
	TC-LJC	Boeing 777-3F2ER	Turkish Airlines
	TC-LJD	Boeing 777-3F2ER	Turkish Airlines
	TC-LJE	Boeing 777-3F2ER	Turkish Airlines
	TC-LJF	Boeing 777-3F2ER	Turkish Airlines
	TC-LJG	Boeing 777-3F2ER	Turkish Airlines
	TC-LJH	Boeing 777-3F2ER	Turkish Airlines
	TC-LJI	Boeing 777-3F2ER	Turkish Airlines
	TC-LJJ	Boeing 777-3F2ER	Turkish Airlines
	TC-LJK	Boeing 777-3F2ER	Turkish Airlines
	TC-LJL	Boeing 777-FF2	Turkish Cargo

Reg	Type	Owner or Operator	Notes
TC-LJM	Boeing 777-FF2	Turkish Cargo	
TC-LJN	Boeing 777-FF2	Turkish Cargo	
TC-LJO	Boeing 777-F	Turkish Cargo	
TC-LJP	Boeing 777-F	Turkish Cargo	
TC-LJR	Boeing 777-F	Turkish Cargo	
TC-LJS	Boeing 777-F	Turkish Cargo	
TC-LJT	Boeing 777-F	Turkish Cargo	
TC-LJU	Boeing 777-F	Turkish Cargo	
TC-LJV	Boeing 777-F	Turkish Cargo	
TC-LJY	Boeing 777-F	Turkish Cargo	
TC-LJZ	Boeing 777-F	Turkish Cargo	
TC-LKA	Boeing 777-36NER	Turkish Airlines	
TC-LKB	Boeing 777-36NER	Turkish Airlines	
TC-LKC	Boeing 777-3U8ER	Turkish Airlines	
TC-LKF	Boeing 777-31HER	Turkish Airlines	
TC-LLA	Boeing 787-9	Turkish Airlines	
TC-LLB	Boeing 787-9	Turkish Airlines	
TC-LLC	Boeing 787-9	Turkish Airlines	
TC-LLD	Boeing 787-9	Turkish Airlines	
TC-LLE	Boeing 787-9	Turkish Airlines	
TC-LLF	Boeing 787-9	Turkish Airlines	
TC-LLG	Boeing 787-9	Turkish Airlines	
TC-LLH	Boeing 787-9	Turkish Airlines	
TC-LLI	Boeing 787-9	Turkish Airlines	
TC-LLJ	Boeing 787-9	Turkish Airlines	
TC-LLK	Boeing 787-9	Turkish Airlines	
TC-LLM	Boeing 787-9	Turkish Airlines	
TC-LLN	Boeing 787-9	Turkish Airlines	
TC-LLO	Boeing 787-9	Turkish Airlines	
TC-LLP	Boeing 787-9	Turkish Airlines	
TC-LLR	Boeing 787-9	Turkish Airlines	
TC-LLS	Boeing 787-9	Turkish Airlines	
TC-LLT	Boeing 787-9	Turkish Airlines	
TC-LLU	Boeing 787-9	Turkish Airlines	
TC-LLV	Boeing 787-9	Turkish Airlines	
TC-LLY	Boeing 787-9	Turkish Airlines	
TC-LLZ	Boeing 787-9	Turkish Airlines	
TC-LMB	Boeing 787-9	Turkish Airlines	
TC-LMC	Boeing 787-9	Turkish Airlines	
TC-LMD	Boeing 787-9	Turkish Airlines	
TC-LME	Boeing 787-9	Turkish Airlines	
TC-LNC	Airbus A.330-303	Turkish Airlines	
TC-LND	Airbus A.330-303	Turkish Airlines	
TC-LNE	Airbus A.330-303	Turkish Airlines	
TC-LNF	Airbus A.330-303	Turkish Airlines	
TC-LNG	Airbus A.330-303	Turkish Airlines	
TC-LOA	Airbus A.330-343	Turkish Airlines	
TC-LOB	Airbus A.330-343	Turkish Airlines	
TC-LOC	Airbus A.330-343	Turkish Airlines	
TC-LOD	Airbus A.330-343	Turkish Airlines	
TC-LOE	Airbus A.330-343	Turkish Airlines	
TC-LOF	Airbus A.330-343	Turkish Airlines	
TC-LOG	Airbus A.330-343	Turkish Airlines	
TC-LOH	Airbus A.330-223	Turkish Airlines	
TC-LOM	Airbus A.330-243	Turkish Airlines	
TC-LON	Airbus A.330-302	Turkish Airlines	
TC-LPA	Airbus A.321-271NX	Turkish Airlines	
TC-LPB	Airbus A.321-271NX	Turkish Airlines	
TC-LPC	Airbus A.321-271NX	Turkish Airlines	
TC-LPD	Airbus A.321-271NX	Turkish Airlines	
TC-LPE	Airbus A.321-271NX	Turkish Airlines	
TC-LPF	Airbus A.321-271NX	Turkish Airlines	
TC-LPG	Airbus A.321-271NX	Turkish Airlines	
TC-LPH	Airbus A.321-271NX	Turkish Airlines	
TC-LPI	Airbus A.321-271NX	Turkish Airlines	
TC-LPJ	Airbus A.321-271NX	Turkish Airlines	
TC-LPK	Airbus A.321-271NX	Turkish Airlines	
TC-LPL	Airbus A.321-271NX	Turkish Airlines	
TC-LPM	Airbus A.321-271NX	Turkish Airlines	
TC-LPN	Airbus A.321-271NX	Turkish Airlines	
TC-LPO	Airbus A.321-271NX	Turkish Airlines	

Notes	Reg	Type	Owner or Operator
	TC-LPP	Airbus A.321-271NX	Turkish Airlines
	TC-LPR	Airbus A.321-271NX	Turkish Airlines
	TC-LPS	Airbus A.321-271NX	Turkish Airlines
	TC-LPT	Airbus A.321-271NX	Turkish Airlines
	TC-LPU	Airbus A.321-271NX	Turkish Airlines
	TC-LPV	Airbus A.321-271NX	Turkish Airlines
	TC-LPY	Airbus A.321-271NX	Turkish Airlines
	TC-LPZ	Airbus A.321-271NX	Turkish Airlines
	TC-LRA	Airbus A.321-271NX	Turkish Airlines
	TC-LRB	Airbus A.321-271NX	Turkish Airlines
	TC-LRC	Airbus A.321-271NX	Turkish Airlines
	TC-LRD	Airbus A.321-271NX	Turkish Airlines
	TC-LRE	Airbus A.321-271NX	Turkish Airlines
	TC-LSA	Airbus A.321-271NX	Turkish Airlines
	TC-LSB	Airbus A.321-271NX	Turkish Airlines
	TC-LSC	Airbus A.321-271NX	Turkish Airlines
	TC-LSD	Airbus A.321-271NX	Turkish Airlines
	TC-LSE	Airbus A.321-271NX	Turkish Airlines
	TC-LSF	Airbus A.321-271NX	Turkish Airlines
	TC-LSG	Airbus A.321-271NX	Turkish Airlines
	TC-LSH	Airbus A.321-271NX	Turkish Airlines
	TC-LSJ	Airbus A.321-271NX	Turkish Airlines
	TC-LSK	Airbus A.321-271NX	Turkish Airlines
	TC-LSL	Airbus A.321-271NX	Turkish Airlines
	TC-LSM	Airbus A.321-271NX	Turkish Airlines
	TC-LSN	Airbus A.321-271NX	Turkish Airlines
	TC-LSO	Airbus A.321-271NX	Turkish Airlines
	TC-LSP	Airbus A.321-271NX	Turkish Airlines
	TC-LSR	Airbus A.321-271NX	Turkish Airlines
	TC-LSS	Airbus A.321-271NX	Turkish Airlines
	TC-LST	Airbus A.321-271NX	Turkish Airlines
	TC-LSU	Airbus A.321-271NX	Turkish Airlines
	TC-LSV	Airbus A.321-271NX	Turkish Airlines
	TC-LSY	Airbus A.321-271NX	Turkish Airlines
	TC-LSZ	Airbus A.321-271NX	Turkish Airlines
	TC-LTA	Airbus A.321-271NX	Turkish Airlines
	TC-LTB	Airbus A.321-271NX	Turkish Airlines
	TC-LTC	Airbus A.321-271NX	Turkish Airlines
	TC-LTD	Airbus A.321-271NX	Turkish Airlines
	TC-LTE	Airbus A.321-271NX	Turkish Airlines
	TC-LTF	Airbus A.321-271NX	Turkish Airlines
	TC-LTG	Airbus A.321-271NX	Turkish Airlines
	TC-LTH	Airbus A.321-271NX	Turkish Airlines
	TC-LTI	Airbus A.321-271NX	Turkish Airlines
	TC-LTJ	Airbus A.321-271NX	Turkish Airlines
	TC-LTK	Airbus A.321-271NX	Turkish Airlines
	TC-LTL	Airbus A.321-271NX	Turkish Airlines
	TC-LTM	Airbus A.321-271NX	Turkish Airlines
	TC-LTN	Airbus A.321-271NX	Turkish Airlines
	TC-LTO	Airbus A.321-271NX	Turkish Airlines
	TC-LTP	Airbus A.321-271NX	Turkish Airlines
	TC-LTR	Airbus A.321-271NX	Turkish Airlines
	TC-LTS	Airbus A.321-251NX	AJet
	TC-LTT	Airbus A.321-251NX	AJet
	TC-LTU	Airbus A.321-271NX	AJet
	TC-LTV	Airbus A.321-271NX	AJet
	TC-LTY	Airbus A.321-271NX	AJet
	TC-LTZ	Airbus A.321-271NX	AJet
	TC-LUA	Airbus A.321-251NX	AJet
	TC-LUB	Airbus A.321-251NX	AJet
	TC-LUC	Airbus A.321-251NX	AJet
	TC-LUE	Airbus A.321-251NX	AJet
	TC-LUI	Airbus A.321-251NX	AJet
	TC-LUJ	Airbus A.321-251NX	AJet
	TC-LUK	Airbus A.320-271N	AJet
	TC-LUL	Airbus A.320-271N	AJet
	TC-LUM	Airbus A.321-251NX	AJet
	TC-LUN	Airbus A.320-271N	AJet
	TC-LUO	Airbus A.320-271N	AJet
	TC-LUP	Airbus A.321-271NX	Turkish Airlines
	TC-LUR	Airbus A.321-251NX	AJet

Reg	Type	Owner or Operator	Notes
TC-LUS	Airbus A.320-271N	AJet	
TC-LUU	Airbus A.320-271N	AJet	
TC-LUV	Airbus A.320-271N	AJet	
TC-LUY	Airbus A.320-271N	AJet	
TC-LUZ	Airbus A.320-271N	AJet	
TC-LYA	Boeing 737-MAX9	Turkish Airlines	
TC-LYB	Boeing 737-MAX9	Turkish Airlines	
TC-LYC	Boeing 737-MAX9	Turkish Airlines	
TC-LYD	Boeing 737-MAX9	Turkish Airlines	
TC-LYE	Boeing 737-MAX9	Turkish Airlines	
TC-MCM	Airbus A.330-343F	MNG Airlines	
TC-MCN	Airbus A.330-343F	MNG Airlines	
TC-MCO	Airbus A.330-343F	MNG Airlines	
TC-MCP	Airbus A.330-343F	MNG Airlines	
TC-MCU	Airbus A.330-243F	MNG Airlines	
TC-MCZ	Airbus A.330-243F	MNG Airlines	
TC-MGC	Boeing 737-83N	Mavi Gok Airlines	
TC-MGK	Boeing 737-85F	Mavi Gok Airlines	
TC-MGL	Boeing 737-8S3	Mavi Gok Airlines	
TC-MGN	Boeing 737-8S3	Mavi Gok Airlines	
TC-MGO	Boeing 737-85F	Mavi Gok Airlines	
TC-MGP	Boeing 737-85F	Mavi Gok Airlines	
TC-MGR	Boeing 737-85F	Mavi Gok Airlines	
TC-MKB	Boeing 737-MAX8	Corendon Airlines	
TC-MKC	Boeing 737-MAX8	Corendon Airlines	
TC-MKD	Boeing 737-MAX8	Corendon Airlines	
TC-MKE	Boeing 737-MAX8	Corendon Airlines	
TC-MKG	Boeing 737-MAX8	Corendon Airlines	
TC-MKS	Boeing 737-MAX8	Corendon Airlines	
TC-MNV	Airbus A.300B4-605R	MNG Airlines	
TC-MYA	Airbus A.321-231P2F	MNG Airlines	
TC-MYB	Airbus A.321-231P2F	MNG Airlines	
TC-NBA	Airbus A.320-251N	Pegasus Airlines	
TC-NBB	Airbus A.320-251N	Pegasus Airlines	
TC-NBC	Airbus A.320-251N	Pegasus Airlines	
TC-NBD	Airbus A.320-251N	Pegasus Airlines	
TC-NBE	Airbus A.320-251N	Pegasus Airlines	
TC-NBF	Airbus A.320-251N	Pegasus Airlines	
TC-NBG	Airbus A.320-251N	Pegasus Airlines	
TC-NBH	Airbus A.320-251N	Pegasus Airlines	
TC-NBI	Airbus A.320-251N	Pegasus Airlines	
TC-NBJ	Airbus A.320-251N	Pegasus Airlines	
TC-NBK	Airbus A.320-251N	Pegasus Airlines	
TC-NBL	Airbus A.320-251N	Pegasus Airlines	
TC-NBM	Airbus A.320-251N	Pegasus Airlines	
TC-NBN	Airbus A.320-251N	Pegasus Airlines	
TC-NBO	Airbus A.320-251N	Pegasus Airlines	
TC-NBP	Airbus A.320-251N	Pegasus Airlines	
TC-NBR	Airbus A.320-251N	Pegasus Airlines	
TC-NBS	Airbus A.320-251N	Pegasus Airlines	
TC-NBT	Airbus A.320-251N	Pegasus Airlines	
TC-NBU	Airbus A.320-251N	Pegasus Airlines	
TC-NBV	Airbus A.320-251N	Pegasus Airlines	
TC-NBY	Airbus A.320-251N	Pegasus Airlines	
TC-NBZ	Airbus A.320-251N	Pegasus Airlines	
TC-NCA	Airbus A.320-251N	Pegasus Airlines	
TC-NCB	Airbus A.320-251N	Pegasus Airlines	
TC-NCC	Airbus A.320-251N	Pegasus Airlines	
TC-NCD	Airbus A.320-251N	Pegasus Airlines	
TC-NCE	Airbus A.320-251N	Pegasus Airlines	
TC-NCF	Airbus A.320-251N	Pegasus Airlines	
TC-NCG	Airbus A.320-251N	Pegasus Airlines	
TC-NCH	Airbus A.320-251N	Pegasus Airlines	
TC-NCI	Airbus A.320-251N	Pegasus Airlines	
TC-NCJ	Airbus A.320-251N	Pegasus Airlines	
TC-NCK	Airbus A.320-251N	Pegasus Airlines	
TC-NCL	Airbus A.320-251N	Pegasus Airlines	
TC-NCM	Airbus A.320-251N	Pegasus Airlines	
TC-NCN	Airbus A.320-251N	Pegasus Airlines	
TC-NCO	Airbus A.320-251N	Pegasus Airlines	
TC-NCP	Airbus A.320-251N	Pegasus Airlines	

Notes	Reg	Type	Owner or Operator
	TC-NCR	Airbus A.320-251N	Pegasus Airlines
	TC-NCS	Airbus A.320-251N	Pegasus Airlines
	TC-NCT	Airbus A.320-251N	Pegasus Airlines
	TC-NCU	Airbus A.320-251N	Pegasus Airlines
	TC-NCV	Airbus A.320-251N	Pegasus Airlines
	TC-NCY	Airbus A.320-251N	Pegasus Airlines
	TC-NCZ	Airbus A.320-251N	Pegasus Airlines
	TC-NDA	Airbus A.321-271NX	Ajet
	TC-NDB	Airbus A.321-271NX	Ajet
	TC-NDC	Airbus A.321-271NX	Ajet
	TC-NDD	Airbus A.321-271NX	Ajet
	TC-NDE	Airbus A.321-271NX	Ajet
	TC-NDF	Airbus A.321-271NX	Ajet
	TC-NDG	Airbus A.321-271NX	Ajet
	TC-NDH	Airbus A.321-271NX	Ajet
	TC-NDI	Airbus A.321-271NX	Ajet
	TC-NDJ	Airbus A.320-271N	Ajet
	TC-OHA	Boeing 737-MAX8	Ajet
	TC-OHB	Boeing 737-MAX8	Ajet
	TC-OHC	Boeing 737-MAX8	Ajet
	TC-OHD	Boeing 737-MAX8	Ajet
	TC-OHE	Boeing 737-MAX8	Ajet
	TC-OHF	Boeing 737-MAX8	Ajet
	TC-OHG	Boeing 737-MAX8	Ajet
	TC-OHH	Boeing 737-MAX8	Ajet
	TC-OHI	Boeing 737-MAX8	Ajet
	TC-OHJ	Boeing 737-MAX8	Ajet
	TC-OHM	Boeing 737-MAX8	Ajet
	TC-OHR	Boeing 737-MAX8	Ajet
	TC-OHS	Boeing 737-MAX8	Ajet
	TC-OHT	Boeing 737-MAX8	Ajet
	TC-OHU	Boeing 737-MAX8	Ajet
	TC-RBA	Airbus A.321-251NX	Pegasus Airlines
	TC-RBB	Airbus A.321-251NX	Pegasus Airlines
	TC-RBC	Airbus A.321-251NX	Pegasus Airlines
	TC-RBD	Airbus A.321-251NX	Pegasus Airlines
	TC-RBE	Airbus A.321-251NX	Pegasus Airlines
	TC-RBF	Airbus A.321-251NX	Pegasus Airlines
	TC-RBG	Airbus A.321-251NX	Pegasus Airlines
	TC-RBH	Airbus A.321-251NX	Pegasus Airlines
	TC-RBI	Airbus A.321-251NX	Pegasus Airlines
	TC-RBJ	Airbus A.321-251NX	Pegasus Airlines
	TC-RBK	Airbus A.321-251NX	Pegasus Airlines
	TC-RBL	Airbus A.321-251NX	Pegasus Airlines
	TC-RBM	Airbus A.321-251NX	Pegasus Airlines
	TC-RBN	Airbus A.321-251NX	Pegasus Airlines
	TC-RBO	Airbus A.321-251NX	Pegasus Airlines
	TC-RBP	Airbus A.321-251NX	Pegasus Airlines
	TC-RBR	Airbus A.321-251NX	Pegasus Airlines
	TC-RBS	Airbus A.321-251NX	Pegasus Airlines
	TC-RBT	Airbus A.321-251NX	Pegasus Airlines
	TC-RBU	Airbus A.321-251NX	Pegasus Airlines
	TC-RBV	Airbus A.321-251NX	Pegasus Airlines
	TC-RBY	Airbus A.321-251NX	Pegasus Airlines
	TC-RBZ	Airbus A.321-251NX	Pegasus Airlines
	TC-RDA	Airbus A.321-251NX	Pegasus Airlines
	TC-RDB	Airbus A.321-251NX	Pegasus Airlines
	TC-RDC	Airbus A.321-251NX	Pegasus Airlines
	TC-RDD	Airbus A.321-251NX	Pegasus Airlines
	TC-RDE	Airbus A.321-251NX	Pegasus Airlines
	TC-RDF	Airbus A.321-251NX	Pegasus Airlines
	TC-RDG	Airbus A.321-251NX	Pegasus Airlines
	TC-RDH	Airbus A.321-251NX	Pegasus Airlines
	TC-RDI	Airbus A.321-251NX	Pegasus Airlines
	TC-RDJ	Airbus A.321-251NX	Pegasus Airlines
	TC-RDK	Airbus A.321-251NX	Pegasus Airlines
	TC-RDL	Airbus A.321-251NX	Pegasus Airlines
	TC-RDM	Airbus A.321-251NX	Pegasus Airlines
	TC-RDN	Airbus A.321-251NX	Pegasus Airlines
	TC-RDO	Airbus A.321-251NX	Pegasus Airlines
	TC-RDP	Airbus A.321-251NX	Pegasus Airlines

Reg	Type	Owner or Operator	Notes
TC-RDR	Airbus A.321-251NX	Pegasus Airlines	
TC-RDS	Airbus A.321-251NX	Pegasus Airlines	
TC-RDT	Airbus A.321-251NX	Pegasus Airlines	
TC-RDU	Airbus A.321-251NX	Pegasus Airlines	
TC-RDV	Airbus A.321-251NX	Pegasus Airlines	
TC-RDY	Airbus A.321-251NX	Pegasus Airlines	
TC-RDZ	Airbus A.321-251NX	Pegasus Airlines	
TC-RFA	Airbus A.321-251NX	Pegasus Airlines	
TC-RFB	Airbus A.321-251NX	Pegasus Airlines	
TC-RFC	Airbus A.321-251NX	Pegasus Airlines	
TC-RFD	Airbus A.321-251NX	Pegasus Airlines	
TC-RFE	Airbus A.321-251NX	Pegasus Airlines	
TC-RFF	Airbus A.321-251NX	Pegasus Airlines	
TC-RFG	Airbus A.321-251NX	Pegasus Airlines	
TC-RFH	Airbus A.321-251NX	Pegasus Airlines	
TC-RFI	Airbus A.321-251NX	Pegasus Airlines	
TC-RFJ	Airbus A.321-251NX	Pegasus Airlines	
TC-RFK	Airbus A.321-251NX	Pegasus Airlines	
TC-RFL	Airbus A.321-251NX	Pegasus Airlines	
TC-RFM	Airbus A.321-251NX	Pegasus Airlines	
TC-RFN	Airbus A.321-251NX	Pegasus Airlines	
TC-RFO	Airbus A.321-251NX	Pegasus Airlines	
TC-RFP	Airbus A.321-251NX	Pegasus Airlines	
TC-RFR	Airbus A.321-251NX	Pegasus Airlines	
TC-RFS	Airbus A.321-251NX	Pegasus Airlines	
TC-RFT	Airbus A.321-251NX	Pegasus Airlines	
TC-RFU	Airbus A.321-251NX	Pegasus Airlines	
TC-RFV	Airbus A.321-251NX	Pegasus Airlines	
TC-RFY	Airbus A.321-251NX	Pegasus Airlines	
TC-RFZ	Airbus A.321-251NX	Pegasus Airlines	
TC-SEI	Boeing 737-8Q8	SunExpress	
TC-SEJ	Boeing 737-8HC	SunExpress	
TC-SEK	Boeing 737-8HC	SunExpress	
TC-SEM	Boeing 737-8HC	SunExpress	
TC-SEN	Boeing 737-8HC	SunExpress	
TC-SEO	Boeing 737-8HC	SunExpress	
TC-SEP	Boeing 737-8HC	SunExpress	
TC-SEU	Boeing 737-8HC	SunExpress	
TC-SEY	Boeing 737-8HC	SunExpress	
TC-SEZ	Boeing 737-8HC	SunExpress	
TC-SLA	Boeing 737-MAX8	SunExpress	
TC-SLB	Boeing 737-MAX8	SunExpress	
TC-SLC	Boeing 737-MAX8	SunExpress	
TC-SLD	Boeing 737-MAX8	SunExpress	
TC-SLE	Boeing 737-MAX8	SunExpress	
TC-SLF	Boeing 737-MAX8	SunExpress	
TC-SMA	Boeing 737-MAX8	SunExpress	
TC-SMB	Boeing 737-MAX8	SunExpress	
TC-SMD	Boeing 737-MAX8	SunExpress	
TC-SME	Boeing 737-MAX8	SunExpress	
TC-SMF	Boeing 737-MAX8	SunExpress	
TC-SMI	Boeing 737-MAX8	SunExpress	
TC-SMJ	Boeing 737-MAX8	SunExpress	
TC-SMK	Boeing 737-MAX8	SunExpress	
TC-SML	Boeing 737-MAX8	SunExpress	
TC-SMN	Boeing 737-MAX8	SunExpress	
TC-SMP	Boeing 737-MAX8	SunExpress	
TC-SMR	Boeing 737-MAX8	SunExpress	
TC-SMS	Boeing 737-MAX8	SunExpress	
TC-SMT	Boeing 737-MAX8	SunExpress	
TC-SMU	Boeing 737-MAX8	SunExpress	
TC-SMV	Boeing 737-MAX8	SunExpress	
TC-SMZ	Boeing 737-MAX8	SunExpress	
TC-SNN	Boeing 737-8HC	SunExpress	
TC-SNR	Boeing 737-8HC	SunExpress	
TC-SNT	Boeing 737-8HC	SunExpress	
TC-SNU	Boeing 737-8HC	SunExpress	
TC-SNV	Boeing 737-86J	SunExpress	
TC-SOA	Boeing 737-86N	SunExpress	
TC-SOB	Boeing 737-8HC	SunExpress	
TC-SOC	Boeing 737-8HC	SunExpress	

Notes	Reg	Type	Owner or Operator
	TC-SOD	Boeing 737-8HC	SunExpress
	TC-SOE	Boeing 737-8HC	SunExpress
	TC-SOF	Boeing 737-8HC	SunExpress
	TC-SOG	Boeing 737-8HC	SunExpress
	TC-SOH	Boeing 737-8HC	SunExpress
	TC-SOI	Boeing 737-MAX8	SunExpress
	TC-SOJ	Boeing 737-MAX8	SunExpress
	TC-SOK	Boeing 737-MAX8	SunExpress
	TC-SOL	Boeing 737-MAX8	SunExpress
	TC-SOM	Boeing 737-MAX8	SunExpress
	TC-SON	Boeing 737-86J	SunExpress
	TC-SOO	Boeing 737-8AS	SunExpress
	TC-SOP	Boeing 737-8AS	SunExpress
	TC-SOR	Boeing 737-8AS	SunExpress
	TC-SOV	Boeing 737-8HC	SunExpress
	TC-SOY	Boeing 737-8HC	SunExpress
	TC-SOZ	Boeing 737-8HX	SunExpress
	TC-SPA	Boeing 737-8HX	SunExpress
	TC-SPB	Boeing 737-86Q	SunExpress
	TC-SPC	Boeing 737-8AS	SunExpress
	TC-SPD	Boeing 737-8AS	SunExpress
	TC-SPE	Boeing 737-8HC	SunExpress
	TC-SPF	Boeing 737-8K5	SunExpress
	TC-SPH	Boeing 737-82R	SunExpress
	TC-SPI	Boeing 737-82R	SunExpress
	TC-SPJ	Boeing 737-82R	SunExpress
	TC-SPK	Boeing 737-86N	SunExpress
	TC-SPM	Boeing 737-8MA	SunExpress
	TC-SPN	Boeing 737-8KV	SunExpress
	TC-SPO	Boeing 737-8MA	SunExpress
	TC-SPP	Boeing 737-8MA	SunExpress
	TC-SPR	Boeing 737-8JP	SunExpress
	TC-SPS	Boeing 737-MAX8	SunExpress
	TC-SPT	Boeing 737-8U3	SunExpress
	TC-SPU	Boeing 737-8U3	SunExpress
	TC-SPV	Boeing 737-8JP	SunExpress
	TC-SPY	Boeing 737-8EH	SunExpress
	TC-SPZ	Boeing 737-8FZ	SunExpress
	TC-SRB	Boeing 737-8AL	SunExpress
	TC-SRC	Boeing 737-8JP	SunExpress
	TC-SRE	Boeing 737-8JP	SunExpress
	TC-SRF	Boeing 737-81M	SunExpress
	TC-SRG	Boeing 737-8JP	SunExpress
	TC-SUU	Boeing 737-86Q	SunExpress
	TC-TJO	Boeing 737-86N	Corendon Airlines
	TC-TJR	Boeing 737-82R	Corendon Airlines
	TC-TJU	Boeing 737-8HX	Corendon Airlines
	TC-TJV	Boeing 737-86J	Corendon Airlines
	TC-TJY	Boeing 737-8AS	Corendon Airlines
	TC-TLI	Boeing 737-8FZ	SunExpress
	TC-TLJ	Boeing 737-8Z9	SunExpress

TF (Iceland)

Notes	Reg	Type	Owner or Operator
	TF-FIA	Boeing 757-256	Icelandair
	TF-FIC	Boeing 757-23N	Icelandair
	TF-FIK	Boeing 757-256	Icelandair
	TF-FIN	Boeing 757-208	Icelandair
	TF-FIO	Boeing 757-208	Icelandair
	TF-FIP	Boeing 757-208	Icelandair
	TF-FIU	Boeing 757-256	Icelandair
	TF-FIV	Boeing 757-208	Icelandair
	TF-IAA	Airbus A.321-271NX	Icelandair
	TF-IAB	Airbus A.321-271NX	Icelandair
	TF-IAC	Airbus A.321-271NX	Icelandair
	TF-IAD	Airbus A.321-271NX	Icelandair
	TF-IAE	Airbus A.321-271NX	Icelandair
	TF-IAF	Airbus A.321-271NX	Icelandair
	TF-IAG	Airbus A.321-271NX	Icelandair
	TF-ICA	Boeing 737-MAX9	Icelandair
	TF-ICB	Boeing 737-MAX9	Icelandair

Reg	Type	Owner or Operator	Notes
TF-ICC	Boeing 737-MAX9	Icelandair	
TF-ICD	Boeing 737-MAX9	Icelandair	
TF-ICE	Boeing 737-MAX8	Icelandair	
TF-ICF	Boeing 737-MAX8	Icelandair	
TF-ICG	Boeing 737-MAX8	Icelandair	
TF-ICH	Boeing 737-MAX8	Icelandair	
TF-ICI	Boeing 737-MAX8	Icelandair	
TF-ICJ	Boeing 737-MAX8	Icelandair	
TF-ICL	Boeing 737-MAX8	Icelandair	
TF-ICM	Boeing 737-MAX8	Icelandair	
TF-ICN	Boeing 737-MAX8	Icelandair	
TF-ICO	Boeing 737-MAX8	Icelandair	
TF-ICP	Boeing 737-MAX8	Icelandair	
TF-ICR	Boeing 737-MAX8	Icelandair	
TF-ICS	Boeing 737-MAX8	Icelandair	
TF-ICT	Boeing 737-MAX8	Icelandair	
TF-ICU	Boeing 737-MAX8	Icelandair	
TF-ICV	Boeing 737-MAX8	Icelandair	
TF-ICY	Boeing 737-MAX8	Icelandair	
TF-ISN	Boeing 767-319ER	Icelandair	
TF-ISO	Boeing 767-319ER	Icelandair	
TF-ISP	Boeing 767-319ER	Icelandair Cargo	
TF-ISR	Boeing 757-256	Icelandair	
TF-ISW	Boeing 767-319ER	Icelandair	
TF-LLL	Boeing 757-256	Icelandair	

TS (Tunisia)

Reg	Type	Owner or Operator	Notes
TS-IFM	Airbus A.330-243	Tunis Air	
TS-IFN	Airbus A.330-243	Tunis Air	
TS-IMA	Airbus A.320-251N	Tunis Air	
TS-IMB	Airbus A.320-251N	Tunis Air	
TS-IMR	Airbus A.320-214	Tunis Air	
TS-IMS	Airbus A.320-214	Tunis Air	
TS-IMT	Airbus A.320-214	Tunis Air	
TS-IMU	Airbus A.320-214	Tunis Air	
TS-IMV	Airbus A.320-214	Tunis Air	
TS-IMW	Airbus A.320-214	Tunis Air	
TS-IMX	Airbus A.320-251N	Tunis Air	
TS-IMY	Airbus A.320-251N	Tunis Air	
TS-IMZ	Airbus A.320-251N	Tunis Air	
TS-INC	Airbus A.320-214	Nouvelair	
TS-IND	Airbus A.320-214	Nouvelair	
TS-INE	Airbus A.320-214	Nouvelair	
TS-INF	Airbus A.320-214	Nouvelair	
TS-ING	Airbus A.320-214	Nouvelair	
TS-INH	Airbus A.320-214	Nouvelair	
TS-INK	Airbus A.320-214	Nouvelair	
TS-INL	Airbus A.320-251N	Nouvelair	
TS-INM	Airbus A.320-251N	Nouvelair	
TS-INO	Airbus A.320-214	Nouvelair	
TS-INP	Airbus A.320-214	Nouvelair	
TS-INQ	Airbus A.320-214	Nouvelair	
TS-INR	Airbus A.320-214	Nouvelair	
TS-INT	Airbus A.320-214	Nouvelair	
TS-INU	Airbus A.320-214	Nouvelair	
TS-ITA	Airbus A.320-214	Tunis Air	
TS-ITB	Airbus A.320-214	Tunis Air	
TS-ITC	Airbus A.320-214	Tunis Air	
TS-ITD	Airbus A.320-214	Tunis Air	

UK (Uzbekistan)

Reg	Type	Owner or Operator	Notes
UK32021	Airbus A.320-251N	Uzbekistan Airways	
UK32022	Airbus A.320-251N	Uzbekistan Airways	
UK32023	Airbus A.320-251N	Uzbekistan Airways	
UK32024	Airbus A.320-251N	Uzbekistan Airways	
UK32025	Airbus A.320-251N	Uzbekistan Airways	
UK32026	Airbus A.320-251N	Uzbekistan Airways	
UK32027	Airbus A.320-251N	Uzbekistan Airways	

Notes	Reg	Type	Owner or Operator
	UK32028	Airbus A.320-251N	Uzbekistan Airways
	UK32029	Airbus A.320-251N	Uzbekistan Airways
	UK32040	Airbus A.320-251N	Uzbekistan Airways
	UK32101	Airbus A.321-253NX	Uzbekistan Airways
	UK32102	Airbus A.321-253NX	Uzbekistan Airways
	UK32103	Airbus A.321-253NX	Uzbekistan Airways
	UK32104	Airbus A.321-253NX	Uzbekistan Airways
	UK32105	Airbus A.321-253NX	Uzbekistan Airways
	UK32110	Airbus A.321-253NX	Qanot Sharq Airlines
	UK32111	Airbus A.321-253NX	Qanot Sharq Airlines
	UK78701	Boeing 787-8	Uzbekistan Airways
	UK78702	Boeing 787-8	Uzbekistan Airways
	UK78703	Boeing 787-8	Uzbekistan Airways
	UK78704	Boeing 787-8	Uzbekistan Airways
	UK78705	Boeing 787-8	Uzbekistan Airways
	UK78706	Boeing 787-8	Uzbekistan Airways

UN (Kazakhstan)

Note: Air Astana operates EI- registered Airbus A.321LRs.

UR (Ukraine)

	UR-SQB	Boeing 737-8H6	SkyUp Airlines
	UR-SQD	Boeing 737-73V	SkyUp Airlines
	UR-SQF	Boeing 737-8H6	SkyUp Airlines
	UR-SQG	Boeing 737-8Z0	SkyUp Airlines
	UR-SQN	Boeing 737-8FE	SkyUp Airlines
	UR-SQO	Boeing 737-82R	SkyUp Airlines

V8 (Brunei)

	V8-DLA	Boeing 787-8	Royal Brunei Airlines
	V8-DLB	Boeing 787-8	Royal Brunei Airlines
	V8-DLC	Boeing 787-8	Royal Brunei Airlines
	V8-DLD	Boeing 787-8	Royal Brunei Airlines
	V8-DLE	Boeing 787-8	Royal Brunei Airlines

VH (Australia)

	VH-OQA	Airbus A.380-841	QANTAS
	VH-OQB	Airbus A.380-841	QANTAS
	VH-OQC	Airbus A.380-841	QANTAS
	VH-OQD	Airbus A.380-841	QANTAS
	VH-OQG	Airbus A.380-841	QANTAS
	VH-OQH	Airbus A.380-841	QANTAS
	VH-OQI	Airbus A.380-841	QANTAS
	VH-OQJ	Airbus A.380-841	QANTAS
	VH-OQK	Airbus A.380-841	QANTAS
	VH-OQL	Airbus A.380-841	QANTAS
	VH-ZNA	Boeing 787-9	QANTAS
	VH-ZNB	Boeing 787-9	QANTAS
	VH-ZNC	Boeing 787-9	QANTAS
	VH-ZND	Boeing 787-9	QANTAS
	VH-ZNE	Boeing 787-9	QANTAS
	VH-ZNF	Boeing 787-9	QANTAS
	VH-ZNG	Boeing 787-9	QANTAS
	VH-ZNH	Boeing 787-9	QANTAS
	VH-ZNI	Boeing 787-9	QANTAS
	VH-ZNJ	Boeing 787-9	QANTAS
	VH-ZNK	Boeing 787-9	QANTAS
	VH-ZNL	Boeing 787-9	QANTAS
	VH-ZNM	Boeing 787-9	QANTAS
	VH-ZNN	Boeing 787-9	QANTAS

VN (Vietnam)

	VN-A861	Boeing 787-9	Vietnam Airlines
	VN-A862	Boeing 787-9	Vietnam Airlines

Reg	Type	Owner or Operator	Notes
VN-A863	Boeing 787-9	Vietnam Airlines	
VN-A864	Boeing 787-9	Vietnam Airlines	
VN-A865	Boeing 787-9	Vietnam Airlines	
VN-A866	Boeing 787-9	Vietnam Airlines	
VN-A867	Boeing 787-9	Vietnam Airlines	
VN-A868	Boeing 787-9	Vietnam Airlines	
VN-A869	Boeing 787-9	Vietnam Airlines	
VN-A870	Boeing 787-9	Vietnam Airlines	
VN-A871	Boeing 787-9	Vietnam Airlines	

VP-B/VP-Q (Bermuda)

Reg	Type	Owner or Operator	Notes
VP-BAA	Boeing 777F	Silk Way West Airlines	
VP-BAU	Boeing 777F	Silk Way West Airlines	
VP-BBR	Boeing 787-8	Azerbaijan Airlines	
VP-BBS	Boeing 787-8	Azerbaijan Airlines	
VP-BMG	Boeing 777F	Silk Way West Airlines	
VP-BMU	Boeing 777F	Silk Way West Airlines	
VQ-BBM	Boeing 747-83QF	Silk Way West Airlines	
VQ-BVB	Boeing 747-83QF	Silk Way West Airlines	
VQ-BVC	Boeing 747-83QF	Silk Way West Airlines	
VQ-BWY	Boeing 747-83QF	Silk Way West Airlines	

VT (India)

Reg	Type	Owner or Operator	Notes
VT-AEM	Boeing 777-3FXER	Air India	
VT-AEN	Boeing 777-3FXER	Air India	
VT-AEO	Boeing 777-3FXER	Air India	
VT-AEP	Boeing 777-3FXER	Air India	
VT-AEQ	Boeing 777-3FXER	Air India	
VT-AER	Boeing 777-3FXER	Air India	
VT-ALJ	Boeing 777-337ER	Air India	
VT-ALK	Boeing 777-337ER	Air India	
VT-ALL	Boeing 777-337ER	Air-India	
VT-ALM	Boeing 777-337ER	Air India	
VT-ALN	Boeing 777-337ER	Air India	
VT-ALO	Boeing 777-337ER	Air India	
VT-ALP	Boeing 777-337ER	Air India	
VT-ALQ	Boeing 777-337ER	Air India	
VT-ALR	Boeing 777-337ER	Air India	
VT-ALS	Boeing 777-337ER	Air India	
VT-ALT	Boeing 777-337ER	Air India	
VT-ALU	Boeing 777-337ER	Air India	
VT-ALX	Boeing 777-337ER	Air India	
VT-ANA	Boeing 787-8	Air India	
VT-ANC	Boeing 787-8	Air India	
VT-AND	Boeing 787-8	Air India	
VT-ANE	Boeing 787-8	Air India	
VT-ANG	Boeing 787-8	Air India	
VT-ANH	Boeing 787-8	Air India	
VT-ANI	Boeing 787-8	Air India	
VT-ANJ	Boeing 787-8	Air India	
VT-ANK	Boeing 787-8	Air India	
VT-ANL	Boeing 787-8	Air India	
VT-ANM	Boeing 787-8	Air India	
VT-ANN	Boeing 787-8	Air India	
VT-ANO	Boeing 787-8	Air India	
VT-ANP	Boeing 787-8	Air India	
VT-ANQ	Boeing 787-8	Air India	
VT-ANR	Boeing 787-8	Air India	
VT-ANS	Boeing 787-8	Air India	
VT-ANT	Boeing 787-8	Air India	
VT-ANU	Boeing 787-8	Air India	
VT-ANV	Boeing 787-8	Air India	
VT-ANW	Boeing 787-8	Air India	
VT-ANX	Boeing 787-8	Air India	
VT-ANY	Boeing 787-8	Air India	
VT-ANZ	Boeing 787-8	Air India	
VT-AWA	Boeing 787-9	Air India	
VT-JRA	Airbus A.350-941	Air India	

		Owner or Operator
	Airbus A.350-941	Air India
	Airbus A.350-941	Air India
VT-JRF	Airbus A.350-941	Air India
VT-JRH	Airbus A.350-941	Air India
VT-JRI	Airbus A.350-941	Air India
VT-JRO	Airbus A.350-941	Air India
VT-NAA	Boeing 787-8	Air India
VT-NAC	Boeing 787-8	Air India
VT-TSD	Boeing 787-9	Air India
VT-TSE	Boeing 787-9	Air India
VT-TSH	Boeing 787-9	Air India
VT-TSN	Boeing 787-9	Air India
VT-TSO	Boeing 787-9	Air India
VT-TSP	Boeing 787-9	Air India

XA (Mexico)

XA-ADC	Boeing 787-9	Aeromexico
XA-ADD	Boeing 787-9	Aeromexico
XA-ADG	Boeing 787-9	Aeromexico
XA-ADH	Boeing 787-9	Aeromexico
XA-ADL	Boeing 787-9	Aeromexico
XA-AMQ	Boeing 787-9	Aeromexico
XA-AMR	Boeing 787-8	Aeromexico
XA-AMX	Boeing 787-8	Aeromexico
XA-DHM	Boeing 787-9	Aeromexico
XA-DHN	Boeing 787-9	Aeromexico
XA-MFG	Boeing 787-9	Aeromexico

YL (Latvia)

YL-AAO	Airbus A.220-300	Air Baltic
YL-AAP	Airbus A.220-300	Air Baltic
YL-AAQ	Airbus A.220-300	Air Baltic
YL-AAR	Airbus A.220-300	Air Baltic
YL-AAS	Airbus A.220-300	Air Baltic
YL-AAT	Airbus A.220-300	Air Baltic
YL-AAU	Airbus A.220-300	Air Baltic
YL-AAV	Airbus A.220-300	Air Baltic
YL-AAW	Airbus A.220-300	Air Baltic
YL-AAX	Airbus A.220-300	Air Baltic
YL-AAY	Airbus A.220-300	Air Baltic
YL-AAZ	Airbus A.220-300	Air Baltic
YL-ABA	Airbus A.220-300	Air Baltic
YL-ABB	Airbus A.220-300	Air Baltic
YL-ABC	Airbus A.220-300	Air Baltic
YL-ABD	Airbus A.220-300	Air Baltic
YL-ABE	Airbus A.220-300	Air Baltic
YL-ABF	Airbus A.220-300	Air Baltic
YL-ABG	Airbus A.220-300	Air Baltic
YL-ABH	Airbus A.220-300	Air Baltic
YL-ABI	Airbus A.220-300	Air Baltic
YL-ABJ	Airbus A.220-300	Air Baltic
YL-ABK	Airbus A.220-300	Air Baltic
YL-ABL	Airbus A.220-300	Air Baltic
YL-ABM	Airbus A.220-300	Air Baltic
YL-ABN	Airbus A.220-300	Air Baltic
YL-ABO	Airbus A.220-300	Air Baltic
YL-ABP	Airbus A.220-300	Air Baltic
YL-ABQ	Airbus A.220-300	Air Baltic
YL-ABR	Airbus A.220-300	Air Baltic
YL-ABS	Airbus A.220-300	Air Baltic
YL-ABT	Airbus A.220-300	Air Baltic
YL-ABU	Airbus A.220-300	Air Baltic
YL-ABV	Airbus A.220-300	Air Baltic
YL-ABW	Airbus A.220-300	Air Baltic
YL-ABX	Airbus A.220-300	Air Baltic
YL-BTA	Airbus A.220-300	Air Baltic
YL-BTB	Airbus A.220-300	Air Baltic
YL-CSA	Airbus A.220-300	Air Baltic

Reg	Type	Owner or Operator	Notes
YL-CSB	Airbus A.220-300	Air Baltic	
YL-CSC	Airbus A.220.300	Air Baltic	
YL-CSD	Airbus A.220.300	Air Baltic	
YL-CSE	Airbus A.220.300	Air Baltic	
YL-CSF	Airbus A.220-300	Air Baltic	
YL-CSG	Airbus A.220.300	Air Baltic	
YL-CSH	Airbus A.220.300	Air Baltic	
YL-CSI	Airbus A.220.300	Air Baltic	
YL-CSJ	Airbus A.220.300	Air Baltic	
YL-CSK	Airbus A.220.300	Air Baltic	
YL-CSL	Airbus A.220.300	Air Baltic	
YL-CSM	Airbus A.220.300	Air Baltic	
YL-CSN	Airbus A.220.300	Air Baltic	

YR (Romania)

Reg	Type	Owner or Operator	Notes
YR-BEE	Airbus A.320-232	Hi Sky Europe	
YR-DSE	Airbus A.320-232	Dan Air	
YR-JOY	Airbus A.320-232	Hi Sky Europe	
YR-JUL	Airbus A.320-232	Dan Air	
YR-SKY	Airbus A.320-232	Hi Sky Europe	
YR-SUN	Airbus A.320-232	Hi Sky Europe	
YR-URS	Airbus A.319-132	Dan Air	
YR-WIN	Airbus A.321-271NX	Hi Sky Europe	
YR-WOW	Airbus A.321-271NX	Hi Sky Europe	

YU (Serbia and Montenegro)

Reg	Type	Owner or Operator	Notes
YU-AGC	Airbus A.320-232	Animawings	
YU-AGD	Airbus A.320-214	Animawings	
YU-APA	Airbus A.319-132	Air Serbia	
YU-APB	Airbus A.319-132	Air Serbia	
YU-APC	Airbus A.319-131	Air Serbia	
YU-APD	Airbus A.319-132	Air Serbia	
YU-APE	Airbus A.319-132	Air Serbia	
YU-APF	Airbus A.319-131	Air Serbia	
YU-APH	Airbus A.320-232	Air Serbia	
YU-APL	Airbus A.319-132	Air Serbia	
YU-APM	Airbus A.319-132	Air Serbia	
YU-APN	Airbus A.319-132	Air Serbia	
YU-APO	Airbus A.320-232	Air Serbia	
YU-APS	Airbus A.320-232	Air Serbia	
YU-APT	Airbus A.320-232	Air Serbia	
YR-CHR	Airbus A.220-300	Animawings	
YR-FUN	Airbus A.220-300	Animawings	
YR-GUN	Airbus A.220-300	Animawings	

3B (Mauritius)

Reg	Type	Owner or Operator	Notes
3B-NBP	Airbus A.350-941	Air Mauritius	
3B-NBQ	Airbus A.350-941	Air Mauritius	
3B-NBU	Airbus A.330-941N	Air Mauritius	
3B-NBV	Airbus A.330-941N	Air Mauritius	
3B-NCE	Airbus A.350-941	Air Mauritius	
3B-NCF	Airbus A.350-941	Air Mauritius	

4K (Azerbaijan)

Reg	Type	Owner or Operator	Notes
4K-AZ81	Boeing 767-32LER	Azerbaijan Airlines	
4K-AZ82	Boeing 767-32LER	Azerbaijan Airlines	
4K-BBH	Boeing 747-83QF	Silk Way West Airlines	
4K-BCH	Boeing 747-467F	Silk Way West Airlines	
4K-BCI	Boeing 747-467F	Silk Way West Airlines	
4K-SW008	Boeing 747-4R7F	Silk Way West Airlines	
4K-SW800	Boeing 747-4R7F	Silk Way West Airlines	
4K-SW888	Boeing 747-4R7F	Silk Way West Airlines	

Azerbaijan Airlines also operate VP- registered Boeing 787s

Notes	Reg	Type	Owner or Operator

4R (Sri Lanka)

	Reg	Type	Owner or Operator
	4R-ALL	Airbus A.330-343	SriLankan Airlines
	4R-ALM	Airbus A.330-343	SriLankan Airlines
	4R-ALN	Airbus A.330-343	SriLankan Airlines
	4R-ALO	Airbus A.330-343	SriLankan Airlines
	4R-ALP	Airbus A.330-343	SriLankan Airlines
	4R-ALQ	Airbus A.330-343	SriLankan Airlines
	4R-ALR	Airbus A.330-343	SriLankan Airlines
	4R-ALU	Airbus A.330-343	SriLankan Airlines

4X (Israel)

	Reg	Type	Owner or Operator
	4X-ABF	Airbus A.320-232	Israir
	4X-ABG	Airbus A.320-232	Israir
	4X-ABI	Airbus A.320-232	Israir
	4X-ABS	Airbus A.320-232	Israir
	4X-ABT	Airbus A.320-232	Israir
	4X-ABW	Airbus A.320-232	Israir
	4X-ABX	Airbus A.320-232	Israir
	4X-ABY	Airbus A.320-232	Israir
	4X-ECA	Boeing 777-258ER	El Al
	4X-ECB	Boeing 777-258ER	El Al
	4X-ECC	Boeing 777-258ER	El Al
	4X-ECD	Boeing 777-258ER	El Al
	4X-ECE	Boeing 777-258ER	El Al
	4X-ECF	Boeing 777-258ER	El Al
	4X-EDA	Boeing 787-9	El Al
	4X-EDB	Boeing 787-9	El Al
	4X-EDC	Boeing 787-9	El Al
	4X-EDD	Boeing 787-9	El Al
	4X-EDE	Boeing 787-9	El Al
	4X-EDF	Boeing 787-9	El Al
	4X-EDH	Boeing 787-9	El Al
	4X-EDI	Boeing 787-9	El Al
	4X-EDJ	Boeing 787-9	El Al
	4X-EDK	Boeing 787-9	El Al
	4X-EDL	Boeing 787-9	El Al
	4X-EDM	Boeing 787-9	El Al
	4X-EDN	Boeing 787-9	El Al
	4X-EHA	Boeing 737-958ER	El Al
	4X-EHB	Boeing 737-958ER	El Al
	4X-EHC	Boeing 737-958ER	El Al
	4X-EHD	Boeing 737-958ER	El Al
	4X-EHE	Boeing 737-958ER	El Al
	4X-EHF	Boeing 737-958ER	El Al
	4X-EHH	Boeing 737-958ER	El Al
	4X-EHI	Boeing 737-958ER	El Al
	4X-EKA	Boeing 737-858	El Al
	4X-EKB	Boeing 737-858	El Al
	4X-EKC	Boeing 737-858	El Al
	4X-EKF	Boeing 737-858	El Al
	4X-EKH	Boeing 737-85P	El Al
	4X-EKI	Boeing 737-86N	El Al
	4X-EKJ	Boeing 737-85P	El Al
	4X-EKK	Boeing 737-800	El Al
	4X-EKL	Boeing 737-85P	El Al
	4X-EKO	Boeing 737-86Q	El Al
	4X-EKP	Boeing 737-8Q8	El Al
	4X-EKS	Boeing 737-8Q8	El Al
	4X-EKT	Boeing 737-8BK	El Al
	4X-EKU	Boeing 737-8Z9	El Al
	4X-ERA	Boeing 787-8	El Al
	4X-ERB	Boeing 787-8	El Al
	4X-ERC	Boeing 787-8	El Al
	4X-ERD	Boeing 787-8	El Al

5N (Nigeria)

	Reg	Type	Owner or Operator
	5N-BVE	Boeing 777-21HER	Air Peace

Reg	Type	Owner or Operator	Notes
5N-BWI	Boeing 777-312	Air Peace	
5N-CEG	Boeing 777-246ER	Air Peace	

5X (Uganda)

Reg	Type	Owner or Operator	Notes
5X-CRN	Airbus A.330-841N	Uganda Airlines	
5X-NIL	Airbus A.330-841N	Uganda Airlines	

5Y (Kenya)

Reg	Type	Owner or Operator	Notes
5Y-KZA	Boeing 787-8	Kenya Airways	
5Y-KZB	Boeing 787-8	Kenya Airways	
5Y-KZC	Boeing 787-8	Kenya Airways	
5Y-KZD	Boeing 787-8	Kenya Airlines	
5Y-KZE	Boeing 787-8	Kenya Airways	
5Y-KZF	Boeing 787-8	Kenya Airways	
5Y-KZG	Boeing 787-8	Kenya Airways	
5Y-KZH	Boeing 787-8	Kenya Airways	
5Y-KZJ	Boeing 787-8	Kenya Airways	

7T (Algeria)

Reg	Type	Owner or Operator	Notes
7T-VJA	Airbus A.330-202	Air Algerie	
7T-VJB	Airbus A.330-202	Air Algerie	
7T-VJC	Airbus A.330-202	Air Algerie	
7T-VJD	Airbus A.330-941	Air Algerie	
7T-VJE	Airbus A.330-941	Air Algerie	
7T-VJF	Airbus A.330-941	Air Algerie	
7T-VJK	Boeing 737-8D6	Air Algerie	
7T-VJL	Boeing 737-8D6	Air Algerie	
7T-VJM	Boeing 737-8D6	Air Algerie	
7T-VJN	Boeing 737-8D6	Air Algerie	
7T-VJO	Boeing 737-8D6	Air Algerie	
7T-VJP	Boeing 737-8D6	Air Algerie	
7T-VJQ	Boeing 737-6D6	Air Algerie	
7T-VJR	Boeing 737-6D6	Air Algerie	
7T-VJS	Boeing 737-6D6	Air Algerie	
7T-VJT	Boeing 737-6D6	Air Algerie	
7T-VJU	Boeing 737-6D6	Air Algerie	
7T-VJV	Airbus A.330-202	Air Algerie	
7T-VJW	Airbus A.330-202	Air Algerie	
7T-VJX	Airbus A.330-202	Air Algerie	
7T-VJY	Airbus A.330-202	Air Algerie	
7T-VJZ	Airbus A.330-202	Air Algerie	
7T-VKA	Boeing 737-8D6	Air Algerie	
7T-VKB	Boeing 737-8D6	Air Algerie	
7T-VKC	Boeing 737-8D6	Air Algerie	
7T-VKD	Boeing 737-8D6	Air Algerie	
7T-VKE	Boeing 737-8D6	Air Algerie	
7T-VKF	Boeing 737-8D6	Air Algerie	
7T-VKG	Boeing 737-8D6	Air Algerie	
7T-VKH	Boeing 737-8D6	Air Algerie	
7T-VKI	Boeing 737-8D6	Air Algerie	
7T-VKJ	Boeing 737-8D6	Air Algerie	
7T-VKK	Boeing 737-8D6	Air Algerie	
7T-VKL	Boeing 737-8D6	Air Algerie	
7T-VKM	Boeing 737-8D6	Air Algerie	
7T-VKN	Boeing 737-8D6	Air Algerie	
7T-VKO	Boeing 737-8D6	Air Algerie	
7T-VKP	Boeing 737-8D6	Air Algerie	
7T-VKQ	Boeing 737-8D6	Air Algerie	
7T-VKR	Boeing 737-8D6	Air Algerie	
7T-VLA	Airbus A.330-941	Air Algerie	

9A (Croatia)

Reg	Type	Owner or Operator	Notes
9A-ABC	Boeing 737-8Q8	ETF Airways	
9A-BTH	Airbus A.320-214	Trade Air	
9A-BTI	Airbus A.320-214	Trade Air	
9A-BTK	Airbus A.320-214	Trade Air	

Notes	Reg	Type	Owner or Operator
	9A-BTL	Airbus A.320-214	Trade Air
	9A-BTM	Airbus A.320-216	Trade Air
	9A-CAE	Airbus A.220-371	Croatia Airlines
	9A-CAI	Airbus A.220-371	Croatia Airlines
	9A-CAL	Airbus A.220-371	Croatia Airlines
	9A-CAM	Airbus A.220-371	Croatia Airlines
	9A-CAN	Airbus A.220-371	Croatia Airlines
	9A-CAO	Airbus A.220-371	Croatia Airlines
	9A-CAP	Airbus A.220-371	Croatia Airlines
	9A-CTG	Airbus A.319-112	Croatia Airlines
	9A-CTH	Airbus A.319-112	Croatia Airlines
	9A-CTK	Airbus A.320-214	Croatia Airlines
	9A-CTL	Airbus A.319-112	Croatia Airlines
	9A-CTN	Airbus A.319-112	Croatia Airlines
	9A-CTO	Airbus A.320-214	Croatia Airlines
	9A-KOR	Boeing 737-8GJ	ETF Airways
	9A-LAB	Boeing 737-8K5	ETF Airways

9H (Malta)

Notes	Reg	Type	Owner or Operator
	9H-AKA	Boeing 747-4SE(BDSF)	Air Atlanta Europe/Saudia Cargo
	9H-AKB	DHC.8Q-402 Dash Eight	Luxwing
	9H-AKE	DHC.8Q-402 Dash Eight	Sky Alps
	9H-AKF	Boeing 747-4SE(BDSF)	Air Atlanta Europe/Saudia Cargo
	9H-AKJ	Boeing 747-412F	Air Atlanta Europe/Saudia Cargo
	9H-AKK	Boeing 747-467F	Air Atlanta Europe/Saudia Cargo
	9H-ALC	Airbus A.330-202	HiFly Malta
	9H-ALE	DHC.8Q-402 Dash Eight	Sky Alps
	9H-AMH	Airbus A.320-232	Avion Express Malta
	9H-AMJ	Airbus A.320-232	Avion Express Malta
	9H-AMK	Airbus A.320-232	Avion Express Malta
	9H-AML	Airbus A.320-232	Avion Express Malta
	9H-AMM	Airbus A.320-232	Avion Express Malta
	9H-BEL	DHC.8Q-402 Dash Eight	Sky Alps
	9H-CXA	Boeing 737-85R	Corendon Airlines Europe
	9H-CXB	Boeing 737-85R	Corendon Airlines Europe
	9H-CXD	Boeing 737-8GP	Corendon Airlines Europe
	9H-CXE	Boeing 737-8GP	Corendon Airlines Europe
	9H-CXF	Boeing 737-8KN	Corendon Airlines Europe
	9H-CXG	Boeing 737-8K5	Corendon Airlines Europe
	9H-CXH	Boeing 737-8ME	Corendon Airlines Europe
	9H-EUC	Airbus A.320-214	Eurowings Europe Malta
	9H-EUL	Airbus A.320-214	Eurowings Europe Malta
	9H-EUM	Airbus A.320-214	Eurowings Europe Malta
	9H-EUN	Airbus A.320-214	Eurowings Europe Malta
	9H-EUO	Airbus A.320-214	Eurowings Europe Malta
	9H-EUP	Airbus A.320-214	Eurowings Europe Malta
	9H-EUQ	Airbus A.320-214	Eurowings Europe Malta
	9H-EUR	Airbus A.320-214	Eurowings Europe Malta
	9H-EUS	Airbus A.320-214	Eurowings Europe Malta
	9H-EUT	Airbus A.320-214	Eurowings Europe Malta
	9H-EUU	Airbus A.320-214	Eurowings Europe Malta
	9H-EUV	Airbus A.320-214	Eurowings Europe Malta
	9H-EUW	Airbus A.320-214	Eurowings Europe Malta
	9H-EUX	Airbus A.320-214	Eurowings Europe Malta
	9H-EVA	DHC.8Q-402 Dash Eight	Sky Alps
	9H-EWA	Airbus A.320-214	Eurowings Europe Malta
	9H-EWB	Airbus A.320-214	Eurowings Europe Malta
	9H-EWC	Airbus A.320-214	Eurowings Europe Malta
	9H-EWD	Airbus A.320-214	Eurowings Europe Malta
	9H-EWE	Airbus A.320-214	Eurowings Europe Malta
	9H-EWF	Airbus A.320-214	Eurowings Europe Malta
	9H-EWG	Airbus A.320-214	Eurowings Europe Malta
	9H-EWH	Airbus A.320-214	Eurowings Europe Malta
	9H-EWI	Airbus A.320-214	Eurowings Europe Malta
	9H-EXQ	Airbus A.319-132	Eurowings Europe Malta
	9H-EXS	Airbus A.319-132	Eurowings Europe Malta
	9H-EXT	Airbus A.319-132	Eurowings Europe Malta
	9H-EXW	Airbus A.319-132	Eurowings Europe Malta
	9H-EXY	Airbus A.319-132	Eurowings Europe Malta
	9H-EXZ	Airbus A.319-132	Eurowings Europe Malta

Reg	Type	Owner or Operator	Notes
9H-FHA	Airbus A.320-214	Freebird Airlines Europe	
9H-FHB	Airbus A.320-214	Freebird Airlines Europe	
9H-FHY	Airbus A.320-214	Freebird Airlines Europe	
9H-HFA	Airbus A.330-343	HiFly Malta	
9H-HFH	Airbus A.330-202	HiFly Malta	
9H-HFI	Airbus A.330-302	HiFly Malta	
9H-HFK	Airbus A.330-223	HiFly Malta	
9H-HFL	Airbus A.330-223	HiFly Malta	
9H-IBJ	Airbus A.320-232	Lauda Europe	
9H-IHD	Airbus A.320-232	Lauda Europe	
9H-IHH	Airbus A.320-232	Lauda Europe	
9H-IHL	Airbus A.320-232	Lauda Europe	
9H-LAX	Airbus A.320-214	Lauda Europe	
9H-LMB	Airbus A.320-232	Lauda Europe	
9H-LMC	Airbus A.320-214	Lauda Europe	
9H-LMG	Airbus A.320-232	Lauda Europe	
9H-LMH	Airbus A.320-232	Lauda Europe	
9H-LMI	Airbus A.320-232	Lauda Europe	
9H-LMJ	Airbus A.320-232	Lauda Europe	
9H-LMP	Airbus A.320-214	Lauda Europe	
9H-LMT	Airbus A.320-214	Lauda Europe	
9H-LOA	Airbus A.320-214	Lauda Europe	
9H-LOB	Airbus A.320-232	Lauda Europe	
9H-LOI	Airbus A.320-214	Lauda Europe	
9H-LOM	Airbus A.320-232	Lauda Europe	
9H-LON	Airbus A.320-214	Lauda Europe	
9H-LOO	Airbus A.320-214	Lauda Europe	
9H-LOQ	Airbus A.320-232	Lauda Europe	
9H-LOR	Airbus A.320-214	Lauda Europe	
9H-LOS	Airbus A.320-214	Lauda Europe	
9H-LOT	Airbus A.320-232	Lauda Europe	
9H-LOU	Airbus A.320-214	Lauda Europe	
9H-LOW	Airbus A.320-214	Lauda Europe	
9H-LOZ	Airbus A.320-232	Lauda Europe	
9H-LWA	DHC.8Q-402 Dash Eight	Luxwing	
9H-LWB	DHC.8Q-402 Dash Eight	Luxwing	
9H-MATI	DHC.8Q-402 Dash Eight	Sky Alps	
9H-MAYA	DHC.8Q-402 Dash Eight	Sky Alps	
9H-MFS	Airbus A.330-203	HiFly Malta	
9H-MIM	DHC.8Q-402 Dash Eight	Universal Air	
9H-MLE	Airbus A.320-214	Avion Express Malta	
9H-MLP	Airbus A.320-232	Avion Express Malta	
9H-MLQ	Airbus A.320-232	Avion Express Malta	
9H-MLR	Airbus A.320-232	Avion Express Malta	
9H-MLS	Airbus A.320-232	Avion Express Malta	
9H-MLW	Airbus A.320-214	Avion Express Malta	
9H-MLY	Airbus A.320-232	Avion Express Malta	
9H-MMW	DHC.8Q-402 Dash Eight	Universal Air	
9H-NEB	Airbus A.320-251N	KM Malta Airlines	
9H-NEC	Airbus A.320-251N	KM Malta Airlines	
9H-NED	Airbus A.320-251N	KM Malta Airlines	
9H-NEE	Airbus A.320-251N	KM Malta Airlines	
9H-NEF	Airbus A.320-251N	KM Malta Airlines	
9H-NEG	Airbus A.320-251N	KM Malta Airlines	
9H-NEH	Airbus A.320-251N	KM Malta Airlines	
9H-NEO	Airbus A-320-251N	KM Malta Airlines	
9H-PAUL	DHC.8Q-402 Dash Eight	Sky Alps	
9H-PET	DHC.8Q-402 Dash Eight	Sky Alps	
9H-QAA	Boeing 737-8AS	Ryanair/Malta Air	
9H-QAB	Boeing 737-8AS	Ryanair/Malta Air	
9H-QAC	Boeing 737-8AS	Ryanair/Malta Air	
9H-QAD	Boeing 737-8AS	Ryanair/Malta Air	
9H-QAE	Boeing 737-8AS	Ryanair/Malta Air	
9H-QAF	Boeing 737-8AS	Ryanair/Malta Air	
9H-QAG	Boeing 737-8AS	Ryanair/Malta Air	
9H-QAH	Boeing 737-8AS	Ryanair/Malta Air	
9H-QAI	Boeing 737-8AS	Ryanair/Malta Air	
9H-QAJ	Boeing 737-8AS	Ryanair/Malta Air	
9H-QAK	Boeing 737-8AS	Ryanair/Malta Air	
9H-QAL	Boeing 737-8AS	Ryanair/Malta Air	
9H-QAM	Boeing 737-8AS	Ryanair/Malta Air	

Notes	Reg	Type	Owner or Operator
	9H-QAN	Boeing 737-8AS	Ryanair/Malta Air
	9H-QAO	Boeing 737-8AS	Ryanair/Malta Air
	9H-QAP	Boeing 737-8AS	Ryanair/Malta Air
	9H-QAQ	Boeing 737-8AS	Ryanair/Malta Air
	9H-QAR	Boeing 737-8AS	Ryanair/Malta Air
	9H-QAS	Boeing 737-8AS	Ryanair/Malta Air
	9H-QAT	Boeing 737-8AS	Ryanair/Malta Air
	9H-QAU	Boeing 737-8AS	Ryanair/Malta Air
	9H-QAV	Boeing 737-8AS	Ryanair/Malta Air
	9H-QAW	Boeing 737-8AS	Ryanair/Malta Air
	9H-QAX	Boeing 737-8AS	Ryanair/Malta Air
	9H-QAY	Boeing 737-8AS	Ryanair/Malta Air
	9H-QAZ	Boeing 737-8AS	Ryanair/Malta Air
	9H-QBA	Boeing 737-8AS	Ryanair/Malta Air
	9H-QBB	Boeing 737-8AS	Ryanair/Malta Air
	9H-QBC	Boeing 737-8AS	Ryanair/Malta Air
	9H-QBD	Boeing 737-8AS	Ryanair/Malta Air
	9H-QBE	Boeing 737-8AS	Ryanair/Malta Air
	9H-QBF	Boeing 737-8AS	Ryanair/Malta Air
	9H-QBG	Boeing 737-8AS	Ryanair/Malta Air
	9H-QBH	Boeing 737-8AS	Ryanair/Malta Air
	9H-QBI	Boeing 737-8AS	Ryanair/Malta Air
	9H-QBJ	Boeing 737-8AS	Ryanair/Malta Air
	9H-QBK	Boeing 737-8AS	Ryanair/Malta Air
	9H-QBL	Boeing 737-8AS	Ryanair/Malta Air
	9H-QBM	Boeing 737-8AS	Ryanair/Malta Air
	9H-QBN	Boeing 737-8AS	Ryanair/Malta Air
	9H-QBO	Boeing 737-8AS	Ryanair/Malta Air
	9H-QBP	Boeing 737-8AS	Ryanair/Malta Air
	9H-QBQ	Boeing 737-8AS	Ryanair/Malta Air
—	9H-QBR	Boeing 737-8AS	Ryanair/Malta Air
	9H-QBS	Boeing 737-8AS	Ryanair/Malta Air
	9H-QBT	Boeing 737-8AS	Ryanair/Malta Air
	9H-QBU	Boeing 737-8AS	Ryanair/Malta Air
	9H-QBV	Boeing 737-8AS	Ryanair/Malta Air
	9H-QBW	Boeing 737-8AS	Ryanair/Malta Air
	9H-QBX	Boeing 737-8AS	Ryanair/Malta Air
	9H-QBY	Boeing 737-8AS	Ryanair/Malta Air
	9H-QBZ	Boeing 737-8AS	Ryanair/Malta Air
	9H-QCA	Boeing 737-8AS	Ryanair/Malta Air
	9H-QCB	Boeing 737-8AS	Ryanair/Malta Air
	9H-QCC	Boeing 737-8AS	Ryanair/Malta Air
	9H-QCD	Boeing 737-8AS	Ryanair/Malta Air
	9H-QCE	Boeing 737-8AS	Ryanair/Malta Air
	9H-QCF	Boeing 737-8AS	Ryanair/Malta Air
	9H-QCG	Boeing 737-8AS	Ryanair/Malta Air
	9H-QCH	Boeing 737-8AS	Ryanair/Malta Air
	9H-QCI	Boeing 737-8AS	Ryanair/Malta Air
	9H-QCJ	Boeing 737-8AS	Ryanair/Malta Air
	9H-QCK	Boeing 737-8AS	Ryanair/Malta Air
	9H-QCL	Boeing 737-8AS	Ryanair/Malta Air
	9H-QCM	Boeing 737-8AS	Ryanair/Malta Air
	9H-QCN	Boeing 737-8AS	Ryanair/Malta Air
	9H-QCO	Boeing 737-8AS	Ryanair/Malta Air
	9H-QCP	Boeing 737-8AS	Ryanair/Malta Air
	9H-QCQ	Boeing 737-8AS	Ryanair/Malta Air
	9H-QCR	Boeing 737-8AS	Ryanair/Malta Air
	9H-QCS	Tyoeing 737-8AS	Owanair/Oalta Air
	9H-QCT	Boeing 737-8AS	Ryanair/Malta Air
	9H-QCU	Boeing 737-8AS	Ryanair/Malta Air
	9H-QCV	Boeing 737-8AS	Ryanair/Malta Air
	9H-QCW	Boeing 737-8AS	Ryanair/Malta Air
	9H-QCX	Boeing 737-8AS	Ryanair/Malta Air
	9H-QCY	Boeing 737-8AS	Ryanair/Malta Air
	9H-QCZ	Boeing 737-8AS	Ryanair/Malta Air
	9H-QDA	Boeing 737-8AS	Ryanair/Malta Air
	9H-QDB	Boeing 737-8AS	Ryanair/Malta Air
	9H-QDC	Boeing 737-8AS	Ryanair/Malta Air
	9H-QDD	Boeing 737-8AS	Ryanair/Malta Air
	9H-QDE	Boeing 737-8AS	Ryanair/Malta Air
	9H-QDF	Boeing 737-8AS	Ryanair/Malta Air

Reg	Type	Owner or Operator	Notes
9H-QDG	Boeing 737-8AS	Ryanair/Malta Air	
9H-QDH	Boeing 737-8AS	Ryanair/Malta Air	
9H-QDI	Boeing 737-8AS	Ryanair/Malta Air	
9H-QDJ	Boeing 737-8AS	Ryanair/Malta Air	
9H-QDK	Boeing 737-8AS	Ryanair/Malta Air	
9H-QDL	Boeing 737-8AS	Ryanair/Malta Air	
9H-QDM	Boeing 737-8AS	Ryanair/Malta Air	
9H-QDN	Boeing 737-8AS	Ryanair/Malta Air	
9H-QDO	Boeing 737-8AS	Ryanair/Malta Air	
9H-QDP	Boeing 737-8AS	Ryanair/Malta Air	
9H-QDQ	Boeing 737-8AS	Ryanair/Malta Air	
9H-QDR	Boeing 737-8AS	Ryanair/Malta Air	
9H-QDS	Boeing 737-8AS	Ryanair/Malta Air	
9H-QDT	Boeing 737-8AS	Ryanair/Malta Air	
9H-QDU	Boeing 737-8AS	Ryanair/Malta Air	
9H-QDV	Boeing 737-8AS	Ryanair/Malta Air	
9H-QDW	Boeing 737-8AS	Ryanair/Malta Air	
9H-QDX	Boeing 737-8AS	Ryanair/Malta Air	
9H-QDY	Boeing 737-8AS	Ryanair/Malta Air	
9H-QDZ	Boeing 737-8AS	Ryanair/Malta Air	
9H-QEA	Boeing 737-8AS	Ryanair/Malta Air	
9H-QEB	Boeing 737-8AS	Ryanair/Malta Air	
9H-QEC	Boeing 737-8AS	Ryanair/Malta Air	
9H-QED	Boeing 737-8AS	Ryanair/Malta Air	
9H-QEE	Boeing 737-8AS	Ryanair/Malta Air	
9H-QEF	Boeing 737-8AS	Ryanair/Malta Air	
9H-QEG	Boeing 737-8AS	Ryanair/Malta Air	
9H-QEH	Boeing 737-8AS	Ryanair/Malta Air	
9H-QEI	Boeing 737-8AS	Ryanair/Malta Air	
9H-QEJ	Boeing 737-8AS	Ryanair/Malta Air	
9H-QEK	Boeing 737-8AS	Ryanair/Malta Air	
9H-QEL	Boeing 737-8AS	Ryanair/Malta Air	
9H-QEM	Boeing 737-8AS	Ryanair/Malta Air	
9H-QEN	Boeing 737-8AS	Ryanair/Malta Air	
9H-QEO	Boeing 737-8AS	Ryanair/Malta Air	
9H-QEP	Boeing 737-8AS	Ryanair/Malta Air	
9H-QEQ	Boeing 737-8AS	Ryanair/Malta Air	
9H-QER	Boeing 737-8AS	Ryanair/Malta Air	
9H-QES	Boeing 737-8AS	Ryanair/Malta Air	
9H-QET	Boeing 737-8AS	Ryanair/Malta Air	
9H-QEU	Boeing 737-8AS	Ryanair/Malta Air	
9H-QEW	Boeing 737-8AS	Ryanair/Malta Air	
9H-QEY	Boeing 737-8AS	Ryanair/Malta Air	
9H-QFA	Boeing 737-8AS	Ryanair/Malta Air	
9H-QFB	Boeing 737-8AS	Ryanair/Malta Air	
9H-QFD	Boeing 737-8AS	Ryanair/Malta Air	
9H-QFE	Boeing 737-8AS	Ryanair/Malta Air	
9H-QFJ	Boeing 737-8AS	Ryanair/Malta Air	
9H-QFK	Boeing 737-8AS	Ryanair/Malta Air	
9H-QFM	Boeing 737-8AS	Ryanair/Malta Air	
9H-QFN	Boeing 737-8AS	Ryanair/Malta Air	
9H-QFO	Boeing 737-8AS	Ryanair/Malta Air	
9H-SOP	DHC.8Q-402 Dash Eight	Sky Alps	
9H-SUN	Airbus A.340-312	HiFly Malta	
9H-SWC	Airbus A.320-232	Avion Express Malta	
9H-SWF	Airbus A.320-232	Avion Express Malta	
9H-SWJ	Airbus A.320-232	Avion Express Malta	
9H-SWN	Airbus A.320-214	Avion Express Malta/Eurowings	
9H-SWW	DHC.8Q-402 Dash Eight	Universal Air	
9H-TJB	Boeing 737-8FH	Corendon Airlines Europe	
9H-TJC	Boeing 737-86N	Corendon Airlines Europe	
9H-TJD	Boeing 737-84P	Corendon Airlines Europe	
9H-TJE	Boeing 737-85R	Corendon Airlines Europe	
9H-TJF	Boeing 737-85R	Corendon Airlines Europe	
9H-VUA	Boeing 737-8200	Ryanair/Malta Air	
9H-VUB	Boeing 737-8200	Ryanair/Malta Air	
9H-VUC	Boeing 737-8200	Ryanair/Malta Air	
9H-VUD	Boeing 737-8200	Ryanair/Malta Air	
9H-VUE	Boeing 737-8200	Ryanair/Malta Air	
9H-VUF	Boeing 737-8200	Ryanair/Malta Air	
9H-VUG	Boeing 737-8200	Ryanair/Malta Air	

Notes	Reg	Type	Owner or Operator
	9H-VUH	Boeing 737-8200	Ryanair/Malta Air
	9H-VUI	Boeing 737-8200	Ryanair/Malta Air
	9H-VUJ	Boeing 737-8200	Ryanair/Malta Air
	9H-VUK	Boeing 737-8200	Ryanair/Malta Air
	9H-VUL	Boeing 737-8200	Ryanair/Malta Air
	9H-VUM	Boeing 737-8200	Ryanair/Malta Air
	9H-VUN	Boeing 737-8200	Ryanair/Malta Air
	9H-VUO	Boeing 737-8200	Ryanair/Malta Air
	9H-VUP	Boeing 737-8200	Ryanair/Malta Air
	9H-VUQ	Boeing 737-8200	Ryanair/Malta Air
	9H-VUR	Boeing 737-8200	Ryanair/Malta Air
	9H-VUS	Boeing 737-8200	Ryanair/Malta Air
	9H-VUT	Boeing 737-8200	Ryanair/Malta Air
	9H-VUU	Boeing 737-8200	Ryanair/Malta Air
	9H-VUV	Boeing 737-8200	Ryanair/Malta Air
	9H-VUW	Boeing 737-8200	Ryanair/Malta Air
	9H-VUX	Boeing 737-8200	Ryanair/Malta Air
	9H-VUY	Boeing 737-8200	Ryanair/Malta Air
	9H-VUZ	Boeing 737-8200	Ryanair/Malta Air
	9H-VVA	Boeing 737-8200	Ryanair/Malta Air
	9H-VVC	Boeing 737-8200	Ryanair/Malta Air
	9H-VVD	Boeing 737-8200	Ryanair/Malta Air
	9H-VVE	Boeing 737-8200	Ryanair/Malta Air
	9H-VVF	Boeing 737-8200	Ryanair/Malta Air
	9H-VVG	Boeing 737-8200	Ryanair/Malta Air
	9H-VVH	Boeing 737-8200	Ryanair/Malta Air
	9H-VVI	Boeing 737-8200	Ryanair/Malta Air
	9H-VVJ	Boeing 737-8200	Ryanair/Malta Air
	9H-VVK	Boeing 737-8200	Ryanair/Malta Air
	9H-VVL	Boeing 737-8200	Ryanair/Malta Air
	9H-VVM	Boeing 737-8200	Ryanair/Malta Air
	9H-VVN	Boeing 737-8200	Ryanair/Malta Air
	9H-VVO	Boeing 737-8200	Ryanair/Malta Air
	9H-VVQ	Boeing 737-8200	Ryanair/Malta Air
	9H-VVR	Boeing 737-8200	Ryanair/Malta Air
	9H-VVS	Boeing 737-8200	Ryanair/Malta Air
	9H-WAA	Airbus A.321-271NX	Wizz Air Malta
	9H-WAB	Airbus A.321-271NX	Wizz Air Malta
	9H-WAC	Airbus A.321-271NX	Wizz Air Malta
	9H-WAD	Airbus A.321-271NX	Wizz Air Malta
	9H-WAE	Airbus A.321-271NX	Wizz Air Malta
	9H-WAF	Airbus A.321-271NX	Wizz Air Malta
	9H-WAG	Airbus A.321-271NX	Wizz Air Malta
	9H-WAH	Airbus A.321-271NX	Wizz Air Malta
	9H-WAI	Airbus A.321-271NX	Wizz Air Malta
	9H-WAJ	Airbus A.321-271NX	Wizz Air Malta
	9H-WAK	Airbus A.321-271NX	Wizz Air Malta
	9H-WAL	Airbus A.321-271NX	Wizz Air Malta
	9H-WAM	Airbus A.321-271NX	Wizz Air Malta
	9H-WAN	Airbus A.320-271N	Wizz Air Malta
	9H-WAO	Airbus A.321-271NX	Wizz Air Malta
	9H-WAP	Airbus A.321-271NX	Wizz Air Malta
	9H-WAQ	Airbus A.321-271NX	Wizz Air Malta
	9H-WAS	Airbus A.321-271NX	Wizz Air Malta
	9H-WAT	Airbus A.321-271NX	Wizz Air Malta
	9H-WAU	Airbus A.320-232	Wizz Air Malta
	9H-WAV	Airbus A.321-271NX	Wizz Air Malta
	9H-WAW	Airbus A.321-271NX	Wizz Air Malta
	9H-WAX	Airbus A.321-271NX	Wizz Air Malta
	9H-WAY	Airbus A.321-271NX	Owizz Air Malta
	9H-WAZ	Airbus A.321-271NX	Wizz Air Malta
	9H-WBA	Airbus A.320-271N	Wizz Air Malta
	9H-WBB	Airbus A.320-271N	Wizz Air Malta
	9H-WBE	Airbus A.321-271NX	Wizz Air Malta
	9H-WBF	Airbus A.321-271NX	Wizz Air Malta
	9H-WBI	Airbus A.321-271NX	Wizz Air Malta
	9H-WBK	Airbus A.321-271NX	Wizz Air Malta
	9H-WBL	Airbus A.321-271NX	Wizz Air Malta
	9H-WBM	Airbus A.321-271NX	Wizz Air Malta
	9H-WBN	Airbus A.321-271NX	Wizz Air Malta
	9H-WBP	Airbus A.320-232	Wizz Air Malta
	9H-WBQ	Airbus A.320-232	Wizz Air Malta
	9H-WBR	Airbus A.321-271NX	Wizz Air Malta

Reg	Type	Owner or Operator	Notes
9H-WBS	Airbus A.321-271NX	Wizz Air Malta	
9H-WBU	Airbus A.321-271NX	Wizz Air Malta	
9H-WBW	Airbus A.321-271N	Wizz Air Malta	
9H-WBX	Airbus A.321-271NX	Wizz Air Malta	
9H-WBY	Airbus A.321-271NX	Wizz Air Malta	
9H-WBZ	Airbus A.321-271NX	Wizz Air Malta	
9H-WDA	Airbus A.320-232	Wizz Air Malta	
9H-WDD	Airbus A.320-232	Wizz Air Malta	
9H-WDE	Airbus A.321-271NX	Wizz Air Malta	
9H-WDF	Airbus A.321-271NX	Wizz Air Malta	
9H-WDG	Airbus A.321-271NX	Wizz Air Malta	
9H-WDH	Airbus A.321-271NX	Wizz Air Malta	
9H-WDI	Airbus A.321-271NX	Wizz Air Malta	
9H-WDJ	Airbus A.321-271NX	Wizz Air Malta	
9H-WDK	Airbus A.321-271NX	Wizz Air Malta	
9H-WDL	Airbus A.321-271NX	Wizz Air Malta	
9H-WDM	Airbus A.321-271NX	Wizz Air Malta	
9H-WDN	Airbus A.321-271NX	Wizz Air Malta	
9H-WDO	Airbus A.321-271NX	Wizz Air Malta	
9H-WDP	Airbus A.321-271NX	Wizz Air Malta	
9H-WDQ	Airbus A.321-271NX	Wizz Air Malta	
9H-WDR	Airbus A.321-271NX	Wizz Air Malta	
9H-WDS	Airbus A.321-271NX	Wizz Air Malta	
9H-WDT	Airbus A.321-271NX	Wizz Air Malta	
9H-WDU	Airbus A.321-271NX	Wizz Air Malta	
9H-WDV	Airbus A.321-271NX	Wizz Air Malta	
9H-WDW	Airbus A.321-271NX	Wizz Air Malta	
9H-WDX	Airbus A.321-271NX	Wizz Air Malta	
9H-WDY	Airbus A.321-271NX	Wizz Air Malta	
9H-WDZ	Airbus A.321-271NX	Wizz Air Malta	
9H-WMA	Airbus A.321-271NX	Wizz Air Malta	
9H-WMB	Airbus A.321-271NX	Wizz Air Malta	
9H-WMC	Airbus A.321-271NX	Wizz Air Malta	
9H-WMD	Airbus A.321-271NX	Wizz Air Malta	
9H-WME	Airbus A.321-271NX	Wizz Air Malta	
9H-WMF	Airbus A.321-271NX	Wizz Air Malta	
9H-WMG	Airbus A.321-271NX	Wizz Air Malta	
9H-WMH	Airbus A.321-271NX	Wizz Air Malta	
9H-WMI	Airbus A.321-271NX	Wizz Air Malta	
9H-WMJ	Airbus A.321-271NX	Wizz Air Malta	
9H-WMK	Airbus A.321-271NX	Wizz Air Malta	
9H-WML	Airbus A.321-271NX	Wizz Air Malta	
9H-WMM	Airbus A.321-271NX	Wizz Air Malta	
9H-WMN	Airbus A.321-271NX	Wizz Air Malta	
9H-WMP	Airbus A.321-271NX	Wizz Air Malta	
9H-WMQ	Airbus A.321-271NX	Wizz Air Malta	
9H-WMR	Airbus A.321-271NX	Wizz Air Malta	
9H-WMS	Airbus A.321-271NX	Wizz Air Malta	
9H-WMT	Airbus A.321-271NX	Wizz Air Malta	
9H-WNA	Airbus A.321-271NX	Wizz Air Malta	
9H-WNB	Airbus A.321-271NX	Wizz Air Malta	
9H-WNC	Airbus A.321-271NX	Wizz Air Malta	
9H-WND	Airbus A.321-271NX	Wizz Air Malta	
9H-WNE	Airbus A.321-271NX	Wizz Air Malta	
9H-WNF	Airbus A.321-271NX	Wizz Air Malta	
9H-WNG	Airbus A.321-271NX	Wizz Air Malta	
9H-WNH	Airbus A.321-271NX	Wizz Air Malta	
9H-WNI	Airbus A.321-271NX	Wizz Air Malta	
9H-WNJ	Airbus A.321-271NX	Wizz Air Malta	
9H-WNK	Airbus A.321-271NX	Wizz Air Malta	
9H-WNL	Airbus A.321-271NX	Wizz Air Malta	
9H-WNM	Airbus A.321-271NX	Wizz Air Malta	
9H-WNN	Airbus A.321-271NX	Wizz Air Malta	
9H-WNO	Airbus A.321-271NX	Wizz Air Malta	
9H-WNP	Airbus A.321-271NX	Wizz Air Malta	
9H-WNQ	Airbus A.321-271NX	Wizz Air Malta	
9H-WNR	Airbus A.321-271NX	Wizz Air Malta	
9H-WNS	Airbus A.321-271NX	Wizz Air Malta	
9H-WNT	Airbus A.321-271NX	Wizz Air Malta	
9H-WNU	Airbus A.321-271NX	Wizz Air Malta	
9H-WNV	Airbus A.321-271NX	Wizz Air Malta	
9H-WNW	Airbus A.321-271NX	Wizz Air Malta	
9H-WNX	Airbus A.321-271NX	Wizz Air Malta	

Notes	Reg	Type	Owner or Operator
	9H-WNY	Airbus A.321-271NX	Wizz Air Malta
	9H-WNZ	Airbus A.321-271NX	Wizz Air Malta
	9H-WZA	Airbus A.321-231	Wizz Air Malta
	9H-WZB	Airbus A.321-231	Wizz Air Malta
	9H-WZC	Airbus A.321-231	Wizz Air Malta
	9H-WZD	Airbus A.321-231	Wizz Air Malta
	9H-WZQ	Airbus A.320-232	Wizz Air Malta
	9H-WZR	Airbus A.320-232	Wizz Air Malta
	9H-WZW	Airbus A.320-232	Wizz Air Malta
	9H-WZX	Airbus A.320-232	Wizz Air Malta
	9H-XLA	Airbus A.321-271NY XLR	Wizz Air Malta
	9H-XLB	Airbus A.321-271NY XLR	Wizz Air Malta
	9H-XLC	Airbus A.321-271NY XLR	Wizz Air Malta
	9H-ZTB	Airbus A.321-211P2F	Titan Airways Malta
	9H-ZTC	Airbus A.321-211P2F	Titan Airways Malta
	9H-ZTD	Airbus A.321-211P2F	Titan Airways Malta

9K (Kuwait)

Notes	Reg	Type	Owner or Operator
	9K-AKL	Airbus A.320-251N	Kuwait Airways
	9K-AKM	Airbus A.320-251N	Kuwait Airways
	9K-AKN	Airbus A.320-251N	Kuwait Airways
	9K-AKO	Airbus A.320-251N	Kuwait Airways
	9K-AKP	Airbus A.320-251N	Kuwait Airways
	9K-AKQ	Airbus A.320-251N	Kuwait Airways
	9K-AKR	Airbus A.320-251N	Kuwait Airways
	9K-AKS	Airbus A.320-251N	Kuwait Airways
	9K-AKT	Airbus A.320-251N	Kuwait Airways
	9K-AOC	Boeing 777-369ER	Kuwait Airways
	9K-AOD	Boeing 777-369ER	Kuwait Airways
	9K-AOE	Boeing 777-369ER	Kuwait Airways
	9K-AOF	Boeing 777-369ER	Kuwait Airways
	9K-AOH	Boeing 777-369ER	Kuwait Airways
	9K-AOI	Boeing 777-369ER	Kuwait Airways
	9K-AOJ	Boeing 777-369ER	Kuwait Airways
	9K-AOK	Boeing 777-369ER	Kuwait Airways
	9K-AOL	Boeing 777-369ER	Kuwait Airways
	9K-AOM	Boeing 777-369ER	Kuwait Airways
	9K-APF	Airbus A.330-841N	Kuwait Airways
	9K-APG	Airbus A.330-841N	Kuwait Airways
	9K-APH	Airbus A.330-841N	Kuwait Airways
	9K-API	Airbus A.330-841N	Kuwait Airways
	9K-APJ	Airbus A.330-941	Kuwait Airways
	9K-APK	Airbus A.330-941	Kuwait Airways
	9K-APL	Airbus A.330-941	Kuwait Airways
	9K-APM	Airbus A.330-941	Kuwait Airways
	9K-APN	Airbus A.330-941	Kuwait Airways
	9K-APO	Airbus A.330-941	Kuwait Airways

9M (Malaysia)

Notes	Reg	Type	Owner or Operator
	9M-MAB	Airbus A.350-941	Malaysia Airlines
	9M-MAC	Airbus A.350-941	Malaysia Airlines
	9M-MAD	Airbus A.350-941	Malaysia Airlines
	9M-MAE	Airbus A.350-941	Malaysia Airlines
	9M-MAF	Airbus A.350-941	Malaysia Airlines
	9M-MAG	Airbus A.350-941	Malaysia Airlines
	9M-MAH	Airbus A.350-941	Malaysia Airlines

9V (Singapore)

Notes	Reg	Type	Owner or Operator
	9V-SFI	Boeing 747-412F	Singapore Airlines Cargo
	9V-SFK	Boeing 747-412F	Singapore Airlines Cargo
	9V-SFM	Boeing 747-412F	Singapore Airlines Cargo
	9V-SFN	Boeing 747-412F	Singapore Airlines Cargo
	9V-SFO	Boeing 747-412F	Singapore Airlines Cargo
	9V-SFP	Boeing 747-412F	Singapore Airlines Cargo
	9V-SFQ	Boeing 747-412F	Singapore Airlines Cargo
	9V-SJA	Airbus A.350-941	Singapore Airlines
	9V-SJB	Airbus A.350-941	Singapore Airlines
	9V-SJC	Airbus A.350-941	Singapore Airlines

Reg	Type	Owner or Operator	Notes
9V-SJD	Airbus A.350-941	Singapore Airlines	
9V-SJE	Airbus A.350-941	Singapore Airlines	
9V-SJF	Airbus A.350-941	Singapore Airlines	
9V-SJG	Airbus A.350-941	Singapore Airlines	
9V-SJH	Airbus A.350-941	Singapore Airlines	
9V-SJI	Airbus A.350-941	Singapore Airlines	
9V-SKM	Airbus A.380-841	Singapore Airlines	
9V-SKN	Airbus A.380-841	Singapore Airlines	
9V-SKP	Airbus A.380-841	Singapore Airlines	
9V-SKQ	Airbus A.380-841	Singapore Airlines	
9V-SKR	Airbus A.380-841	Singapore Airlines	
9V-SKS	Airbus A.380-841	Singapore Airlines	
9V-SKT	Airbus A.380-841	Singapore Airlines	
9V-SKU	Airbus A.380-841	Singapore Airlines	
9V-SKV	Airbus A.380-841	Singapore Airlines	
9V-SKW	Airbus A.380-841	Singapore Airlines	
9V-SKY	Airbus A.380-841	Singapore Airlines	
9V-SKZ	Airbus A.380-841	Singapore Airlines	
9V-SMA	Airbus A.350-941	Singapore Airlines	
9V-SMB	Airbus A.350-941	Singapore Airlines	
9V-SMC	Airbus A.350-941	Singapore Airlines	
9V-SMD	Airbus A.350-941	Singapore Airlines	
9V-SME	Airbus A.350-941	Singapore Airlines	
9V-SMF	Airbus A.350-941	Singapore Airlines	
9V-SMG	Airbus A.350-941	Singapore Airlines	
9V-SMH	Airbus A.350-941	Singapore Airlines	
9V-SMI	Airbus A.350-941	Singapore Airlines	
9V-SMJ	Airbus A.350-941	Singapore Airlines	
9V-SMK	Airbus A.350-941	Singapore Airlines	
9V-SML	Airbus A.350-941	Singapore Airlines	
9V-SMM	Airbus A.350-941	Singapore Airlines	
9V-SMN	Airbus A.350-941	Singapore Airlines	
9V-SMO	Airbus A.350-941	Singapore Airlines	
9V-SMP	Airbus A.350-941	Singapore Airlines	
9V-SMQ	Airbus A.350-941	Singapore Airlines	
9V-SMR	Airbus A.350-941	Singapore Airlines	
9V-SMS	Airbus A.350-941	Singapore Airlines	
9V-SMT	Airbus A.350-941	Singapore Airlines	
9V-SMU	Airbus A.350-941	Singapore Airlines	
9V-SMV	Airbus A.350-941	Singapore Airlines	
9V-SMW	Airbus A.350-941	Singapore Airlines	
9V-SMY	Airbus A.350-941	Singapore Airlines	
9V-SMZ	Airbus A.350-941	Singapore Airlines	
9V-SNA	Boeing 777-312ER	Singapore Airlines	
9V-SNB	Boeing 777-312ER	Singapore Airlines	
9V-SNC	Boeing 777-312ER	Singapore Airlines	
9V-SWB	Boeing 777-312ER	Singapore Airlines	
9V-SWG	Boeing 777-312ER	Singapore Airlines	
9V-SWH	Boeing 777-312ER	Singapore Airlines	
9V-SWI	Boeing 777-312ER	Singapore Airlines	
9V-SWJ	Boeing 777-312ER	Singapore Airlines	
9V-SWK	Boeing 777-312ER	Singapore Airlines	
9V-SWL	Boeing 777-312ER	Singapore Airlines	
9V-SWM	Boeing 777-312ER	Singapore Airlines	
9V-SWO	Boeing 777-312ER	Singapore Airlines	
9V-SWP	Boeing 777-312ER	Singapore Airlines	
9V-SWQ	Boeing 777-312ER	Singapore Airlines	
9V-SWR	Boeing 777-312ER	Singapore Airlines	
9V-SWS	Boeing 777-312ER	Singapore Airlines	
9V-SWT	Boeing 777-312ER	Singapore Airlines	
9V-SWU	Boeing 777-312ER	Singapore Airlines	
9V-SWV	Boeing 777-312ER	Singapore Airlines	
9V-SWW	Boeing 777-312ER	Singapore Airlines	
9V-SWY	Boeing 777-312ER	Singapore Airlines	
9V-SWZ	Boeing 777-312ER	Singapore Airlines	

9XR (Rwanda)

Reg	Type	Owner or Operator	Notes
9XR-WN	Airbus A.330-243	RwandAir	
9XR-WP	Airbus A.330-343	RwandAir	
9XR-WX	Airbus A.330-243	RwandAir	

Some of the key radio frequencies used by busier airports and airfields are listed below.

TWR = Tower   APP = Approach   A/G = Air Ground or Flight Information Service

Radio frequencies can and do change during the life of this publication; this information should not be used operationally.

	TWR	APP	A/G
Aberdeen	118.105	119.055	
Alderney	125.355	128.655	
Andrewsfield			130.555
Beccles			120.380
Belfast International	118.300	133.125	
Belfast City	122.830	130.850	
Bembridge			123.255
Biggin Hill	134.805	129.405	
Birmingham	118.305	123.980	
Blackbushe			122.305
Blackpool	118.405	119.955	
Bodmin			120.330
Bournemouth	125.605	119.480	
Breighton			129.805
Bristol	133.850	125.650	
Caernarfon			122.255
Cambridge	125.905	120.965	
Cardiff	133.105	119.155	
Carlisle			123.605
Clacton			118.155
Compton Abbas			122.710
Cosford	128.650	135.875	
Coventry			123.830
Cranfield	134.930	122.855	
Cumbernauld			120.605
Denham			130.730
Derby			118.355
Dundee	122.905	122.905	
Dunkeswell			123.480
Duxford			122.080
Earls Colne			122.430
East Midlands	124.005	134.180	
Edinburgh	118.705	121.205	
Elstree			122.405
Enniskillen			123.205
Enstone			129.880
Eshott			122.855
Exeter	119.805	128.980	
Fairoaks			123.430
Farnborough	122.780	134.355	
Fenland			122.930
Fife			130.455
Fowlmere			135.705
Glasgow	118.805	119.100	
Gloucester (Staverton)	122.905	128.555	
Goodwood (Chichester)			122.455
Guernsey	119.955	128.655	
Haverfordwest			123.605
Hawarden	124.955	120.055	
Henstridge			130.255
Humberside	124.905	119.130	
Inverness	118.405	122.605	
Isle of Man (Ronaldsway)	119.005	135.905	
Isle of Wight (Sandown)			119.280
Jersey	119.455	120.305	
Kemble			118.430
Kirkwall	118.305	118.305	
Land's End	120.255		
Lasham			131.030
Lashenden (Headcorn)			122.210
Lee On Solent			118.930
Leeds Bradford	120.305	134.580	
Leeds East			120.710
Leicester			122.130
Liverpool	126.355	119.855	
London City	118.080	132.700	
London Gatwick	124.230	126.825	
London Heathrow	118.505	119.730	
London Stansted	123.805	120.625	
Londonderry	134.155	123.625	
Luton	132.555	129.550	
Lydd	119.380	120.705	
Manchester	118.630	118.580	
Manchester Barton			120.255
Netherthorpe			123.280
Newcastle	119.705	124.380	
Newquay	134.380	133.405	
Newtownards			128.305
North Weald			123.530
Northampton (Sywell)			122.705
Northolt	120.675	126.450	
Norwich	124.255	119.355	
Old Warden			130.705
Oxford	133.430	125.090	
Perth			121.080
Peterborough/Conington			129.730
Peterborough/Sibson			120.330
Popham			129.805
Prestwick	118.150	129.450	
Redhill			119.605
Retford/Gamston			130.480
Rochester			122.255
Sandtoft			130.415
Scilly Isle	124.880	124.880	
Seething			118.435
Sherburn in Elmet			122.610
Shobdon			118.155
Shoreham	125.405	123.155	
Sleap			122.455
Southampton	118.205	120.230	
Southend	127.730	130.780	
Stapleford			122.805
Stornoway	119.480	119.480	
Sumburgh	118.255	131.300	
Swansea			119.705
Tatenhill			124.080
Teesside	119.805	118.805	
Thruxton			118.280
Turweston			122.180
Wellesbourne			124.030
Welshpool			128.005
White Waltham			122.605
Wick	119.705	119.705	
Wickenby			122.455
Wolverhampton			123.005
Woodvale	119.750	121.000	
Wycombe Air Park			126.555
Yeovil	125.405	130.805	

AIRLINE FLIGHT CODES

Those listed below identify many of the UK and overseas carriers appearing in the book

Code	Airline	Reg
AAL	American Airlines	N
AAR	Asiana Airlines	HL
ABR	ASL Airlines Ireland	EI
ABY	Air Arabia	A6
ACA	Air Canada	C
AEA	Air Europa	EC
AEE	Aegean Airlines	SX
AFL	Aeroflot	RA
AFR	Air France	F
AHY	Azerbaijan Airlines	4K
AIC	Air India	VT
AIH	AirZeta	HL
AJA	AJet	TC
ALK	SriLankan Airlines	4R
AMC	Air Malta	9H
AMX	Aeromexico	XA
ANA	All Nippon Airways	JA
ANE	Air Nostrum	EC
APK	Air Peace	5N
ASA	Alaska Airlines	N
ASL	Air Serbia	YU
ATV	Avanti Air	D
AUA	Austrian Airlines	OE
AUR	Aurigny A/S	G
AVA	AVIANCA	HK
AWC	Titan Airways	G
AWG	Animawings	YU
AXE	AirExplore	OM
AZG	Silk Way West Airlines.	4K
BAW	British Airways	G
BBC	Biman Bangladesh	S2
BCS	European A/T	OO
BEL	Brussels Airlines	OO
BGA	Airbus Tpt International	F
BGH	BH Air	LZ
BLX	TUIfly Nordic	SE
BOX	AeroLogic	D
BTI	Air Baltic	YL
CAI	Corendon Airlines	TC
CAL	China Airlines	B
CAO	Air China Cargo	B
CBJ	Beijing Capital Airlines.	B
CCA	Air China	B
CES	China Eastern Airlines	B
CFE	BA Cityflyer	G
CFG	Condor	D
CGF	Cargo Air	LZ
CHH	Hainan Airlines	B
CJT	Cargojet Airways	C
CKK	China Cargo Airlines.	B
CKS	Kalitta Air	N
CLH	Lufthansa CityLine	D
CLX	Cargolux	LX
CMA	CMA-CGM Air Cargo.	F
CPA	Cathay Pacific	B
CSG	China Southern Cargo	B
CSN	China Southern Airlines	B
CSZ	Shenzhen Airlines	B
CTN	Croatia Airlines	9A
CXI	Corendon Airlines Europe	9H
DAH	Air Algerie	7T
DAL	Delta Air Lines	N
DHK	DHL Air	D/G/OE
DKH	Juneyao Airlines	B
DLA	Air Dolomiti	I
DLH	Lufthansa	D
DNA	Dan Air	YR
DTR	Danish Air Transport	OY
EDW	Edelweiss Air	HB
EFW	BA Euroflyer	G
EIN	Aer Lingus	EI
EJU	EasyJet Europe	OE
ELY	El Al	4X
ENT	Enter Air	SP
ETD	Etihad Airways	A6
ETH	Ethiopian Airlines	ET
EUK	Aer Lingus UK	G
EVA	EVA Airways	B
EWG	Eurowings	D
EWL	Eurowings Europe	9H
EXS	Jet 2.com	G
EZS	easyJet Switzerland	HB
EZY	easyJet	G
FDX	Federal Express	N
FHY	Freebird Airlines	TC
FIA	FlyOne	ER
FIN	Finnair	OH
FLI	Atlantic Airways	OY
GCR	Tianjin Airlines	B
GEC	Lufthansa Cargo	D
GFA	Gulf Air	A9C
GTI	Atlas Air	N
HFY	HiFly	CS
HKC	Hong Kong Air Cargo	B
HYM	HiSky	ER
HVN	Vietnam Airlines	VN
IBE	Iberia	EC
IBS	Iberia Express	EC
ICE	Icelandair	TF
ICV	Cargolux Italia	I
IGO	IndiGo	VT
IMX	Zimex Aviation	HB
IOS	Isles of Scilly Skybus	G
IRA	Iran Air	EP
ISR	Israir	4X
ITY	ITA	I
JAF	TUI Airlines Belgium	OO
JAL	Japan Airlines	JA
JBU	Jet Blue	N
KAC	Kuwait Airways	9K
KAL	Korean Air	HL
KLC	KLM CityHopper	PH
KLM	KLM	PH
KQA	Kenya Airways	5Y
KZR	Air Astana	UN
LAN	LATAM Airlines Chile	CC
LAV	AlbaStar	EC
LBT	Nouvelair	TS
LDA	Lauda Europe	OE
LGL	Luxair	LX
LHX	Lufthansa City Airlines.	D
LOG	Loganair	G
LOT	LOT Polish Airlines	SP
LWG	Luxwing	9H
LYD	Lydd Air	G
LYX	Smart Lynx Airlines Malta	9H
LZB	Bulgaria Air	LZ
MAC	Air Arabia Maroc	CN
MAS	Malaysian Airlines	9M
MAU	Air Mauritius	3B
MAY	Malta Air	9H
MEA	Middle East Airlines	OD
MFX	Centrum Air	UK
MGH	Mavi Gok Airlines.	TC
MMZ	Euro Atlantic Airways	CS
MNG	MNG Airlines	TC
MPH	Martinair	PH
MSR	EgyptAir	SU
MUK	Maersk Air Cargo UK	G
NBT	Norse Atlantic Airways	LN
NCR	National Airlines	N
NOS	Neos	I
NOZ	Norwegian Air Shuttle	LN
NPT	West Atlantic Airlines	G
NSZ	Norwegian Air Sweden	SE
NVD	Avion Express	LY
NVR	Novair Airlines	SE
OAW	Helvetic Airways	HB
OMA	Oman Air	A4O
PAC	Polar Air Cargo	N
PAL	Philippine Airlines	RP
PGT	Pegasus Airlines	TC
PIA	Pakistan International	AP
PLM	Wamos Air	EC
PVG	Privilege Style	EC
QAC	Qatar Air Cargo	A7
QFA	QANTAS	VH
QNT	Qanot Sharq Airlines	UK
QTR	Qatar Airways	A7
RAM	Royal Air Maroc	CN
RBA	Royal Brunei Airlines	V8
RGN	Cygnus Air	EC
RJA	Royal Jordanian	JY
RUK	Ryanair UK	G
RWD	RwandAir	9XR
RXI	Riyadh Air	HZ
RYR	Ryanair	EI
RYS	Buzz	SP
SAS	SAS	SE/ OY/ LN
SEH	Sky Express	SX
SIA	Singapore Airlines	9V
SQC	Singapore Airlines Cargo	9V
SQP	SkyUp Airlines	UR
SRR	Maersk Air Cargo	OY
SVA	Saudi Arabian Airlines	HZ
SWN	West Atlantic Airlines	SE
SWR	Swiss International	HB
SXS	SunExpress	TC
TAM	LATAM Airlines Brazil	PT
TAP	TAP Air Portugal	CS
TAR	Tunis Air	TS
TAY	ASL Airlines Belgium	OO
TDR	Trade Air	9A
TFL	TUIfly Netherlands	PH
THA	Thai Airways International	HS
THY	Turkish Airlines	TC
TOM	TUIfly	G
TRA	Transavia	PH
TSC	Air Transat	C
TUA	Turkmenistan Airlines	EZ
TUI	TUIfly	D,G
TVF	Transavia France	F
TVS	Smart Wings	OK
UAE	Emirates Airlines	A6
UAL	United Airlines	N
UGD	Uganda Airlines	5X
UPS	United Parcel Service	N
URO	European Cargo	G
UVL	Universal Air	9H
UZB	Uzbekistan Airways	UK
VIR	Virgin Atlantic Airways	G
VKG	Sunclass Airlines	OY
VLG	Vueling Airlines	EC
VOE	Volotea Airlines	EC
WDL	German Airways	D
WIF	Wideroe's	LN
WJA	Westjet	C
WMT	Wizz Air Malta	9H
WUK	Wizz Air UK	G
WZZ	Wizz Air	HA

Notes	Registration	Type	Previous Operator	Current status
	G-CGMC	Embraer EMB-135ER	Eastern Airways	D-BJME Travelcoup
	G-CMEI	Avions Transport ATR-72-212	Eastern Airways	OY-NZR Nordic Aviation Capital
	G-CMFI	Avions Transport ATR-72-212	Eastern Airways	OY-NZS Nordic Aviation Capital
	G-CMLI	Embraer ERJ170-100STD	Eastern Airways	stored
	G-CMPI	Embraer ERJ170-100LR	Eastern Airways	N702SY SkyWest Airlines
	G-DHLL	Boeing 767-304ERF	DHL Air Ltd	OE-LYB DHL Air Austria
	G-EUOA	Airbus A.319-131	British Airways	to be scrapped
	G-EUPT	Airbus A.319-131	British Airways	scrapped
	G-EUPY	Airbus A.319-131	British Airways	to be scrapped
	G-EZDD	Airbus A.319-111	easyJet	to be scrapped
	G-EZDF	Airbus A.319-111	easyJet	to be scrapped
	G-EZDI	Airbus A.319-111	easyJet	to be scrapped
	G-GATJ	Airbus A.320-232	BA Euroflyer	to be scrapped
	G-HAGI	Boeing 737-MAX8	Ascend Airways	CN-RHG Royal Air Maroc
	G-IACY	Avions Transport ATR-72-212	Eastern Airways	OY-NZT Nordic Aviation Capital
	G-IACZ	Avions Transport ATR-72-212	Eastern Airways	OY-NZU Nordic Aviation Capital
	G-ISLO	Avions Transport ATR-72-212	Blue Islands	stored as 2-ISLO. Due to join Danish Air Transport as OY-stored as 2-JMCL
	G-JMCL	Boeing 737-322	West Atlantic UK	stored as 2-JMCL
	G-JMCV	Boeing 737-322	West Atlantic UK	N560XG due to become HK-5473
	G-MIDT	Airbus A.320-232	British Airways	to be scrapped
	G-NPTF	Avions Transport ATR-72-202F	West Atlantic UK	LZ-SWF
	G-NSEY	Embraer ERJ190-200LR	Aurigny Air Services	YU-ATC Air Serbia
	G-POWW	Airbus A.321-211F	Titan Airways	9H-ZTD Titan Airways Malta
	G-RUKL	Boeing 737-8AS	Ryanair UK	SP-RNL Buzz (Ryanair)
	G-SAJS	Embraer EMB -145EP	Loganair	stored
	G-TUKV	Boeing 737-8K5	TUI Airways	OO-TNB TUI Airlines Belgium
	G-VINE	Airbus A.330-343	Virgin Atlantic	HS-TEX Thai Airways
	G-VKSS	Airbus A.330-343	Virgin Atlantic	EC-OLG Wamos Air

Reg	Type	Owner or Operator

UK REGISTER Additions

Reg	Type	Owner or Operator
G-BDSE	Cameron O-77 balloon	A. A. Brown
G-BGON	GA-7 Cougar	Grade Digital Ltd
G-CHWY	Standard Cirrus G/81	M. J. Cook
G-CMZX	Schempp-Hirth Arcus M	P. J. Pengilly
G-DSCC	Leonardo AW169	Gama Aviation (UK) Ltd
G-EPIK	Glasair II-SRG	S. A. Bowkett (G-KSIR)
G-MILS	Pilatus PC-12/47G	Nigel Brunt Properties Ltd
G-OENE	Leonardo AW189	Bristow Helicopters Ltd
G-SAPR	Skyranger 912(2)	C. M. Wilkes (G-WAZP)
G-SOON	Cessna 182N	G. W. Shedden (G-AYWD)
G-TESK	Diamond DA.40D Star	Tesla Solutions Ltd
G-ULFD	Gulfstream GVIII	Executive Jet Charter Ltd
G-WSAS	Airbus Helicopters MBB-BK 117 D-3	Airbus Helicopters UK Ltd

GUERNSEY REGISTER Additions

Reg	Type	Owner or Operator
2-BASE	Boeing 737-8MC	BASE Aircraft Leasing & Management LLC
2-HFNU	Fokker 100	Airline Fleet Support B.V.
2-JOLF	Airbus A.320-214	International Lease Finance Corporation
2-LGGG	Airbus Helicopters AS.332 L1	Airbus Helicopters Deutschland GmbH
2-LYRA	Boeing 737-800	Safair Operations (Proprietary) Ltd
2-MACH	Cessna 750 Citation X	Viewdart Ltd
2-OSPR	PA-31 Navajo C	Osprey Aviation Ltd
2-RAJY	Boeing 737-48E	V78A-734 LLC
2-RAJZ	Boeing 737-48E	V79A-734 LLC
2-RANI	Bombardier CL600-2B16 Challenger	Leprechaun Leasing LLC

IRISH REGISTER Addition

Reg	Type	Owner or Operator
EI-JAD	Canadair CRJ900ER	Cityjet/SAS

OVERSEAS AIRLINES Additions

Reg	Type	Owner or Operator
A6-FWK	Boeing 777-F	Emirates SkyCargo
A6-EWL	Boeing 777-F	Emirates SkyCargo
A6-EXY	Airbus A.350-941	Emirates Airlines
A7-AOI	Airbus A.350-1041	Qatar Airways
A7-AOJ	Airbus A.350-1041	Qatar Airways
A7-BIA	Boeing 787-9	Qatar Airways
A7-BTD	Boeing 777-F	Qatar Airways Cargo
C-GWJJ	Boeing 737-MAX8	Westjet
C-GWJN	Boeing 737-MAX8	Westjet
C-GWJQ	Boeing 737-MAX8	Westjet
CS-TVR	Airbus A.320-251N	TAPAir Portugal
F-HOZD	Airbus A.220-300	Air France
F-HXIA	Airbus A.320-252N	Transavia France
F-HXIC	Airbus A.320-252N	Transavia France
F-HXIE	Airbus A.320-252N	Transavia France
F-HXIF	Airbus A.320-252N	Transavia France
F-HXSY	Airbus A.320-252N	Transavia France
HA-LDE	Airbus A.321-271NX	Wizz Air
HA-LDF	Airbus A.321-271NX	Wizz Air
HA-LDN	Airbus A.321-271NX	Wizz Air
HZ-RXAB	Boeing 787-9	Riyadh Air
HZ-RXAC	Boeing 787-9	Riyadh Air
JA11WJ	Airbus A.350-1041	Japan Airlines
JY-RBA	Boeing 787-9	Royal Jordanian

Reg	Type	Owner or Operator
N927UP	Boeing 767-300F	United Parcel Service
N929UP	Boeing 767-300F	United Parcel Service
OE-IUL	Airbus A.321-251NX	easyJet Europe
SX-NAV	Airbus A.321-271NX	Aegean Airlines
SX-NAW	Airbus A.321-271NX	Aegean Airlines
SX-NAX	Airbus A.321-271NX	Aegean Airlines
SX-NAZ	Airbus A.321-271NX	Aegean Airlines
TC-NDO	Airbus A.320-271N	Ajet
TC-OHK	Boeing 737-MAX8	Ajet
TC-OHL	Boeing 737-MAX8	AJet
TS-INJ	Airbus A.320-251N	Nouvelair
YL-BTC	Airbus A.220-300	Air Baltic
YL-BTD	Airbus A.220-300	Air Baltic
9H-WZT	Airbus A.320-232	Wizz Air Malta
9M-XBE	Airbus A.330-343	Air Asia X
9M-XBF	Airbus A.330-343	Air Asia X
9M-XBG	Airbus A.330-343	Air Asia X
9M-XBH	Airbus A.330-343	Air Asia X
9M-XBI	Airbus A.330-343	Air Asia X
9M-XXC	Airbus A.330-343	Air Asia X
9M-XXD	Airbus A.330-343	Air Asia X
9M-XXE	Airbus A.330-343	Air Asia X
9M-XXF	Airbus A.330-343	Air Asia X
9M-XXG	Airbus A.330-343	Air Asia X
9M-XXJ	Airbus A.330-343	Air Asia X
9M-XXK	Airbus A.330-343	Air Asia X
9M-XXQ	Airbus A.330-343	Air Asia X
9M-XXR	Airbus A.330-343	Air Asia X
9M-XXU	Airbus A.330-343	Air Asia X
9M-XXV	Airbus A.330-343	Air Asia X
9M-XXW	Airbus A.330-343	Air Asia X
9M-XXY	Airbus A.330-343	Air Asia X
9M-XXZ	Airbus A.330-343	Air Asia X

Reg	Type	Owner or Operator

Reg	Type	Owner or Operator

Reg	Type	Owner or Operator

Reg	Type	Owner or Operator

Reg	Type	Owner or Operator

Reg	Type	Owner or Operator

Reg	Type	Owner or Operator

Reg	Type	Owner or Operator
Reg	Type	Owner or Operator

Reg	Type	Owner or Operator

Reg	Type	Owner or Operator